Ireland

Footprint

Handbook

The travel guide

Pat Levy and Seán M Sheehan

O
Tell me all about
Anna Livia! I want to hear all
About Anna Livia. Well, you know Anna Livia? Yes, of course,
we all know Anna Livia. Tell me all. Tell me now.

James Joyce, *Finnegans Wake*

Ireland Handbook
Second edition
© Footprint Handbooks Ltd 2002

Published by Footprint Handbooks
6 Riverside Court
Lower Bristol Road
Bath BA2 3DZ. England
T +44 (0)1225 469141
F +44 (0)1225 469461
Email discover@footprintbooks.com
Web www.footprintbooks.com

ISBN 1 903471 25 7
CIP DATA: A catalogue record for this
book is available from the British Library

Distributed in the USA by
Publishers Group West

® Footprint Handbooks and the
Footprint mark are a registered
trademark of Footprint Handbooks Ltd.

The maps for the Republic of Ireland
are based on Ordnance Survey Ireland
and used by permission of the
Goverment Permit No 7476 ©
Government of Ireland.

The maps of Northern Ireland are based
on Ordnance Survey of Northern Ireland
material with permission of the
Controller of Her Majesty's Stationery
Office © Crown Copyright. Permit
number 1371 (2nd edition). Ordnance
Survey of Northern Ireland, Colby House,
Stranmillis Court, Belfast BT9 5BJ,
T028-90255755, F028-90255700, Email
osni@nics.gov.uk. OSNI have large and
small scale products available in both
digital and/or paper format.

Credits

Series editors
Patrick Dawson and Rachel Fielding

Editorial
Editor: Sarah Thorowgood
Maps: Sarah Sorensen

Production
Page layout: Davina Rungasamy
Maps: Robert Lunn, Claire Benison and
Leona Bailey
Colour maps: Kevin Feeney
Advertisements: Maxine Foster
Cover: Camilla Ford

Design
Mytton Williams

Photography
Front cover: gettyone Stone
Back cover: Image State
Inside colour section: Image State,
Pictures Colour Library, gettyone Stone,
Eye Ubiquitous

Print
Manufactured in Italy by LEGOPRINT

Every effort has been made to ensure
that the facts in this Handbook are
accurate. However, travellers should still
obtain advice from consulates, airlines
etc about current travel and visa
requirements before travelling. The
authors and publishers cannot accept
responsibility for any loss, injury or
inconvenience however caused.

A foot in the door

Highlights

Ireland is often portrayed as a charming laboratory time capsule of pre-industrial Europe and its people as either a beguiling race of quaint and gullible country folk, fondly imbued with an affectionate lack of logic, or as irrational individuals with a disingenuous blarney. The truth is more complicated but Ireland has leapfrogged over the industrial age into a high-tech, postmodern economy, and the country is far from being a social or cultural backwater. Indeed, the very vibrancy of the people and their society is what attracts so many visitors. But Ireland remains bewitchingly different from mainstream Europe and continues, with good reason, to fascinate travellers seeking an alternative to packaged holidays and predictable tourist attractions.

A celtic soul? The image of Ireland as the last home of the Celtic soul may be a fanciful one but nevertheless this small island perched on the fringe of Europe is felt to be home to an anarchical and poetic spirit, one profoundly at odds with the Anglo-Saxon temperament. And even though much of the unconscious beauty of Ireland's past has vanished – donkey carts loaded with turf belong more to postcards than real life – there are still cute thatched cottages to admire and the living and talking Irish people of today have created a lifestyle that will rub off on most visitors sooner or later.

Dublin: what's in a name? The Republic of Ireland's capital city is a cracking place. James Joyce called it Dubbyling, Dublovnik, Tumbin on the Leaf, and Dungbin. It's all these places and more. The city buzzes with a youthful modernity, best soaked up in a comedy or dance club or enjoying live music in a pub before the vodka 'n' Red Bull starts to slur the Dublin wit. Alongside the dot.com-ers in the sushi bars, the old Dublin is still there. The Georgian architecture, Dublin Castle, Trinity College, the Book of Kells and Christ Church Cathedral – all are steeped in centuries of history. Love it and leave it: the Wicklow countryside is a bus ride away to the south and Newgrange, the most remarkable prehistoric sight in Europe, can be visited on a day trip.

Wild west A wander around the west coast takes in spectacular coastal routes, remote offshore islands, Gaeltacht areas where Irish is spoken, village pubs, castles and fading country houses, traditional music, craic, unbelievable long-distance walks, and landscapes and seascapes that will astonish your senses and subdue your soul. Heady stuff, indeed, but not idle boasts. Mind you, the capricious weather can dampen your spirits as well as your gear and much depends on knowing where not to go. Driving around the Ring of Kerry is a waste of time, Killarney town is the pits, Doolin is overrated and Inishmór, the largest of the fabled Aran islands, must now have the playwright Synge spinning in his grave. But seek out a quiet backwater in west Cork, walk the western end of the Dingle Way, experience the sheer buzz of Galway City or explore the wilderness of west Mayo, and the best of what Ireland has to offer will open up before you.

Northern exposure Just for a minute forget the term Northern Ireland, it's a political and not a geographical concept, and remember that County Donegal is also part of Ulster. Seen in this way the northern counties offer the traveller an engrossing amalgam of landscape and culture. Donegal is so ruggedly beautiful, so visually stunning, that we are half tempted to play down its appeal in case too many visitors go there and spoil it. The neighbouring city of Derry, a cool place indeed, is remarkably charming and relaxed and also has one of the most enlightening museums anywhere in the country. The coastal route that passes the Giant's Causeway and runs down past the Antrim mountains is a succession of delightful surprises and the Mourne Mountains and south Armagh are just waiting to be discovered by a new generation of travellers.

Left The Glenmacnass waterfall in the heart of the Wicklow mountains now handily accessible, thanks to the Military Road built following the 1789 rebellion
Below Riding through the shallows in Connemara, Co. Galway. "Like breathing champagne," remarked one visitor, "silvery, level, water-striped and overflowing with light," said Limerick's Kate O'Brian

Above Dublin's, placid River Liffey, Joyce's Anna Livia, reflects a row of fine old houses on Bachelor's Walk
Left From Dún or Dur lios (strong fort), the site of Dunluce Castle, Co. Derry, was a home long before the days of castle building
Previous page The ultimate doorway into Ireland's tourist industry – a traditional thatched cottage in Clougher Head, Co. Louth
Next page The forbidding appearance of Dublin Castle, has deterred many would-be attackers since it was founded in 1204 – not, however, Michael Collins, see page 81

Room to roam

Surf & turf Uncrowded and unpolluted space is Ireland's great gift when looking for a beach to surf from or build sandcastles on, a river to fish, roads to cycle on, hills to climb or long-distance trails to tramp along. Throw in other watersports, birdwatching, mountain climbing, rock climbing or horse riding and you'll see how Ireland as a whole offers freely to all what has to be jealously pocketed when found in other parts of Europe. Travellers will find their own favourite haunts but walkers and climbers can happily wear out their footwear in Kerry and Cork, Connemara and Clare, anglers die for north Cork and Tipperary, surfing beaches are dotted around from Portrush in the north to Wexford in the southeast and Achill in the west.

Telling tales Forget the history books, heritage centres and the stately homes, and just take a wander through any village. Ireland's history is still a living, breathing part of the landscape. It is impossible to cover much ground at all in Ireland without bumping into an historic site of some kind. The big ones have been packaged just like everywhere else but all over the country, in fields, at the side of the road, even in people's gardens, ancient raths, stone circles, dolmens, beehive huts, old churches, castles and Iron-Age mines sit contentedly, largely ignored by the people who gladly share their space without much thought of their significance. On the Dingle Peninsula it is almost impossible to distinguish the thousand-year-old beehive huts from the modern ones since the design is still in use for storage sheds or animal shelters. Dig even deeper into the Irish countryside and you will find elderly people who still remember stories passed down through their families for generations – stories going back to the Famine and before. Travel through the northern counties and you'll see a new history chapter being written before your eyes as some communities reassert their long-repressed culture while others readjust to a new era.

Ways to walk Only when the car is abandoned and a townscape is what you see departing over your shoulder does Ireland's rich natural diversity come into its own. Waymarked long-distance walks cover nearly all the scenic locations: the Ulster Way in the north, the Wicklow Way south of Dublin, the Beara Way in the southwest, the Burren Way along the cliffs of Moher, the Bangor Trail in wild Mayo – these are just some of our favourites but there are many more. With a little planning it is possible to walk for a single day or cross the entire country on foot, rarely passing a vehicle. But the real beauty of Ireland is that it has what other European countries have lost – a variety of wildlife and habitats unspoiled by industrialization or even the heritage industry. The Burren is an amazing place, a limestone upland area with alpine plants uncommon in the British Isles, underground river systems and wild cliff edges supporting a diverse bird life. The desolate and unpopulated bogland of northwest Mayo is unique, despairing when the rain sets in but profound and strangely disturbing at other times. The offshore islands of the southwest are home to a mind-boggling number and variety of sea and migrant birds, as well as plants which are becoming increasingly rare in other places. Around Killarney, that nadir of tourist traps, a strange flora and fauna can be found nestling beside the tea shops and tour buses. A number of plants and insects, unknown in Britain, flourish here, while at Derrynane the near-extinct Kerry lily has its last ecological niche.

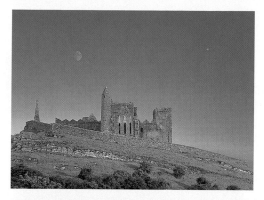

Left The Rock of Cashel, Co. Tipperary, once the seat of kings, now home to a beautiful 12-century chapel
Below Looking down on Doogort beach from Slievemore mountain on the north coast of Achill, Ireland's largest island

Left A view of the rock-bound Healy Pass on the Beara Peninsula in west Cork – if you're the sort of person who likes to work hard when you're on holiday, try cycling up it
Above You can check in on all manner of mountain and lake habitats in the 25,000-arcre Killarney National Park, Co. Kerry
Next page The dramatic and rather threatening basalt columns of the Giant's Causeway, Co. Antrim

Right An afternoon spent in one of Dublin's original Victorian era pubs may well have you seeing weird colours, as well as double
Below The 19th-century Jameson's whiskey distillery at Midleton, Co. Cork – one of Ireland's better heritage centres...the benefits speak for themselves

Right Halfpenny Bridge, Dublin, named after its toll, connects the north bank of the River Liffey with Temple Bar
Above Like it or not, you are never far away from the sound of traditional music in a pub during the summr months in Ireland
Next page Cows chew the cud in the morning mist of Co. Cork

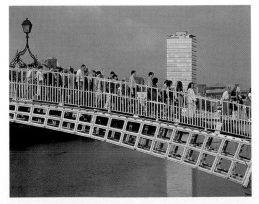

Rhythm and music

The music scene in Ireland is diverse, starting with an alarmingly unhealthy interest in awful Country and Western sounds but quickly ascending through ageing rock bands like U2, as well as the more modern The Frames, DC and The Divine Comedy, and hitting a high with pukka traditional music from The Pogues and the poetry of Shane MacGowan (when you can make out the words). Seek out traditional folk sessions in pubs where musicians who may be complete strangers to one another, and without a score sheet in sight, entertain themselves and anyone else who happens to be around – whether they like it or not! Doolin in County Clare is one of the places renowned for traditional music, but any town worth its tourist salt will have something on. **Melody makers**

Lovers of literature will find associations with their favourite writers all over Ireland. A Joycean walk through the streets of the Dublin would take in major sites, obscure byways and an excursion south to Sandycove. Echoes of Gerard Manley Hopkins, Oscar Wilde, Sean O'Casey, Brendan Behan and Flann O'Brien resound in the city's pubs, parks and houses. The counties of Sligo and Galway have essential associations with WB Yeats, Derry with Seamus Heaney, Carrickfergus with MacNeice, County Down with the Brontë family, Monaghan with Kavanagh, west Cork with Swift, the list goes on and on. **A way with words**

Literary festivals and summer schools are dotted around the country during the summer months, open to all and refreshingly non-academic. Totally free is the literary state of mind that finds expression in everyday talk. People choose their words with care, savouring the good turn of phrase and recycling the best ones. Irish English has its own rhythms and patterns, less harsh than British or American English with their sharply defined meanings and questions that require a yes or no answer. Best of all is the craic that you can hear in the pub when a few well oiled friends of 30 years start the slagging, a heartless form of teasing where anything goes. The trick is not to show you that are offended or the other person has won!

Anyone returning from a tour bus trip around Ireland could be forgiven for thinking that its chief cultural artefacts are stuffed leprechauns and tea towels with crass rhymes printed on them. But Ireland is an amazing source of small cottage industries, all producing attractive, individually designed artefacts that have found a market worldwide. While there are big factories like the famous one at Waterford making glass crystal, or the lesser known concern in Belleek creating Parian ware china, some of the best discoveries are in the tiny craft centres scattered around in places like Donegal or Enniskillen, or the larger workshops south of Kilkenny City. They are quite genuine places where craftspeople make their own designs on the premises. Some individuals have an international reputation, such as Louis Mulcahy, whose pottery, made at the end of the Dingle Peninsula, is shipped all over the world. **Small is beautiful**

Sure, internet cafés are popping up like mushrooms and cars get wheel-clamped in the capital, but at a deeper and more pleasurable level the pace of life and the instincts of many Irish people remain traditional and deeply appealing. There is a surface egalitarianism that works a disarming magic and helps make Ireland a country to explore in a quietly personal way. There is a quirkiness in the people and the landscape that is both enjoyable and fulfilling: a day of glorious sunshine is followed by a couple of days or more of misty rain; people have the time for aimless conversations but there are also countless opportunities to get away from the human and commercial world to appreciate a wild but benign nature. In the ambivalent dawn of the 21st century, a visit to Ireland must be compelling for travellers sensitive to the depressing march of an increasingly globalized world. **Easy life**

Ireland

See colour maps at back of book

Great Blasket Island	Natural feature
Rock of Cashel	Historical feature
Strangford Lough	Water feature

North Channel

Malin Head

Giant's
Causeway

Mount
Errigal

Derry

ANTRIM

Larne

Letterkenny

DERRY

Antrim

BELFAST

DONEGAL

NORTHERN
IRELAND

Donegal

Omagh

TYRONE

Lough
Neagh

Strangford
Lough

Glencolmcille

Lough
Erne

FERMANAGH

Armagh

DOWN

Downpatrick

Enniskillen

ARMAGH

Carrowmore
Megalithic
Cemetery

Sligo

Monaghan

MONAGHAN

Castleblayney

Ballina

SLIGO

LEITRIM

Cavan

Dundalk

MAYO

Castlebar

ROSCOMMON

Carrick-on-
Shannon

CAVAN

Carrickmacross

LOUTH

Irish Sea

Strokestown
Park House

Longford

Newgrange

Drogheda

Connemara
National Park

Roscommon

LONGFORD

Navan

MEATH

GALWAY

Athlone

WESTMEATH

Mullingar

DUBLIN

Galway

Ballinasloe

Tullamore

KILDARE

DUBLIN

Aran Islands

REPUBLIC OF IRELAND

OFFALY

Naas

Bray

Droichead
Nua

Greystones

Atlantic Ocean

The Burren

Portlaoise

Wicklow
Mountains

Wicklow

CLARE

LAOIS

Glendalough

WICKLOW

Ennis

Nenagh

Carlow

Saint
George's
Channel

Thurles

CARLOW

Limerick

TIPPERARY

Kilkenny

St Canice's
Cathedral

Tralee

LIMERICK

Rock of
Cashel

KILKENNY

WEXFORD

Tipperary

Clonmel

Wexford

KERRY

Killarney

Knockmealdown
Mountains

Waterford

Great Blasket
Island

CORK

Saltee Islands

MacGillycuddy's
Reeks &
The Kerry Way

Cork

WATERFORD

Skellig
Michael
Monastic
Settlement

Caha
Mountains &
Beara Way

Kinsale

Clonakilty

Drombeg
Stone Circle

Cape Clear
Island

Celtic Sea

N

0 miles   20
0 km   20

Contents

Inside front cover
Exchange rates, Hotel and restaurant price guide and dialling codes

Inside back cover
Map symbols

Essentials

2

18

Essentials

Planning your trip

Where to go

Ireland is a fairly small country, about 310 miles (500 km) north to south and a little over 186 miles (300 km) west to east, and although it is not difficult to get around (see 'Getting around', page 43) there is plenty to see, and some choices have to be made about where not to go, or at least where not to dawdle. Some of the decisive factors are how long you have for your trip, what your mode of transport will be, your interests and inclinations, and whether this is a first-time trip or not. The level of your budget is a factor, but not a critical one, because costs are fairly uniform, although accommodation is pricier in Dublin than anywhere else in the country, and the wider range of options for spending money in the capital should be borne in mind. The more you travel, the higher the transport costs, and with single tickets on buses and trains often costing almost as much as return tickets this factor may be worth considering.

Length of trip If your stay is from three to six days there is little point in tearing around the country, so think about which airport to arrive at. First-time travellers will probably want to see Dublin, and international travellers may have little choice but to land there, but Cork airport is well serviced from London, as is Belfast, and with an affordable service between London and Derry the northwest of the country is more accessible than it used to be. With a hired car waiting at Shannon airport, the west coast is half a day's drive away. With a short stay a choice probably has to be made between a city-based vacation or a short burst of rural bliss.

For a stay of a week or more it is quite feasible to take in Dublin, a few excursions such as Glendalough and Newgrange, and spend some time on the western seaboard visiting the Burren, Kerry or Galway City. With two weeks or more, depending on mode of transport, the visitor can pick and choose two, three or more locations and explore them in some depth. There would be time to skip from one end of the country to the other and briefly explore several places in between or, alternatively, focus on just one or two locations and have time for a leisurely walking or cycling trip. With a month or more it should be possible to visit most regions in the country that match your interests, and have time to slow down and get to know some places in real depth.

Modes of transport The 'Getting around' section (page 43) covers the transport options in detail, but bear in mind that internal flights are limited in choice and usefulness and that the use or non-use of a car or motorcycle is likely to be a determining factor in deciding where to go. With vehicular transport the length of stay will be the only major factor limiting your choices, but reliance on public transport will necessitate a fair degree of planning if you wish to get out of the cities and big towns and optimize your time. If you're planning a walking holiday or are focused on other particular activities, such as mountain climbing or wind surfing, public transport is generally adequate, and for walking trips the use of a car can be a hindrance because there is always the need to get back to the vehicle.

Scenery & beaches The obvious destination for visitors interested in getting away from urban life and appreciating wild scenery and beaches is the west coast and County Donegal. From the Inishowen peninsula, just north of Derry, to Roaringwater Bay in West Cork, the coastline follows an almost uninterrupted margin of stunning seascapes and glorious countryside. Patches worth skipping are the stretches between the towns of Donegal and Sligo, between Rossaveal and south of Galway city, and the coastline between Ennis and Tralee; just about everywhere other than those stretches covers the best of Donegal, Mayo, Connemara, the Burren, Clare, and the peninsulas of Kerry and West

Essentials

★ **Top 10 beaches**

Keem, *Achill Island, County Mayo (page 459)*
Keel, *Achill Island, County Mayo (page 458)*
Inch Beach, *Clonakility, County Cork (page 289)*
Dog's Bay, *Roundstone, Connemara, County Galway (page 427)*
Inishbofin, *Inishbofin Island, County Galway (page 432)*
Clogherhead, *County Louth (page 154)*
Portacloy, *County Mayo (page 462)*
Barley Cove, *County Cork (page 301)*
Stradbally and Castelgregory, *County Waterford (page 235)*
Portstewart Strand, *County Derry (page 540)*

Cork. This still leaves out some marvellous areas in the rest of the country, chief amongst which are the Antrim coastline, the Mourne Mountains in Down, and the Wicklow Mountains south of Dublin. The southern coastline, between Wexford and Cork, is tepid in comparison with the west coast.

Ireland's islands A favourite for devotees of **nature, wildlife and solitude** are the offshore islands that pepper Ireland's coasts. The most famous are the Aran Islands in County Galway, and although fame has turned the largest of the three islands into a tourist ghetto in July and August, the other two, Inishmaan and Inisheer, are always worth visiting, and the main island of Inishmór is still rewarding in off-season months. Achill Island off the west coast of Mayo is reached by a causeway and is large enough to accommodate its popularity, and Mayo also has the lesser known and far smaller Clare Island, which is ideal for getting away from it all. The main island of the Blaskets in Kerry is glorious in spring and autumn; no accommodation and no restaurants here so if you bring a tent you'll have the place to yourself once the last boat has departed. The Skelligs, also in Kerry, are justly famous for their bird life, but it is not possible to stay overnight. County Cork has Dursey Island, reached by a cable car, off the Beara Peninsula, and like the Blaskets there is no accommodation or restaurants. Further south, reached from Baltimore, are Clear Island and Sherkin Island; both popular in the summer but never overbearingly so. The Saltee Islands in County Wexford, like Clear Island, are noted for bird life. The islands of Rathlin and Tory, off the north coast of Ireland, are easily reached and bask in the glory of not being well known or spoiled by tourism.

Activity trips Destinations for activity trips vary but **walking** and **cycling** are the most readily available and easy to arrange activities across the length and breadth of the country, though opportunities for a diverse range of **sports** are well distributed across Ireland. For details of these and other special interests see the 'Sport and special interest travel' (page 52). This also covers where to go for **surfing** and **scuba diving**.

Museums, galleries & stately homes Museums, galleries and stately homes are dotted around Ireland and the trick is to know which ones to skip. Dublin has major museums and galleries which should not be missed, and Derry, Strokestown in Roscommon, Enniscorthy in County Wexford, and Limerick all have excellent museums which are worth special journeys, and Glebe House and Gallery in County Donegal can probably be added to the 'essential visit' list. As a general rule, beware of places proclaiming themselves to be heritage or interpretation centres. A few are awful and a waste of money, many are just plain mediocre and only suitable for a wet afternoon, some are well thought out and genuinely educational. The **Céide Fields Interpretative Centre** in north Mayo, the **Blasket Centre** on the Dingle Peninsula, and the **Cobh Heritage Centre** outside Cork are some of the better ones which should not disappoint.

Essentials

Top 10 places for kids ★

Dingle Harbour and Fungie the dolphin, Dingle, County Kerry *(page 358)*
Watersports at Portrush, Country Antrim *(page 543)*
Kerry the Kingdom, 40 English Street, Tralee, County Kerry *(page 352)*
St Patrick's Trian, Armagh, County Armagh, T521801 *(page 610)*
Carrick-a-rede Rope Bridge, Antrim, County Antrim, T20731159 *(page 547)*
Aillwee Caves, County Clare, T7077036 *(page 390)*
Downpatrick Steam Railway, Market Street, Downpatrick, County Down, T615779 *(page 598)*
Boat ride to Sherkin Island and cart ride to the beach, County Cork *(page 297)*
Dolphinwatch, The Square, Carrigaholt, County Clare, T9058156 *(page 392)*
Dingle Oceanworld, Dingle, County Kerry, T9152111 *(page 358)*

Essentials

The stately homes of the Anglo-Irish aristocracy that are open to the public are alluring places, but very often a disappointing anti-climax. Mount Stewart House in Down and Westport House in Mayo are notable failures, but **Strokestown House** in Roscommon is absolutely superb, and **Castle Coole** in Fermanagh is a wheeze.

Castles & sites of archaeological interest

You'll find castles and sites of archaeological interest everywhere; indeed it is hard to think of a town in Ireland that doesn't have something of interest in its vicinity. **Dublin Castle** in the capital and **Newgrange** in County Meath, the most famous of Ireland's passage graves, within striking distance of Dublin, should not be missed; **Kilkenny Castle** and the **Rock of Cashel** are equally compelling, while Cork and Kerry are choc-a-bloc with stone circles and other sites of prehistoric interest.

Cultural events

For mainstream cultural events such as theatre and classical music, Dublin has the famous **Abbey**, the **Gaiety**, **Olympia** and **Gate Theatres**, and the Dublin Theatre Festival which takes place in October. Theatres in the cities of **Cork**, **Galway** and **Sligo** usually feature an interesting programme, and **Tralee** is home to the National Folk Theatre. The **National Concert Hall** and events organized by the Royal Dublin Society feature performances of classical music in the capital. Some religious sites are of major cultural interest: these include **Clonmacnois** in County Offaly, **Glendalough** in County Wicklow, **Mellifont Abbey**, and the **High Crosses** at Monasterboice in County Louth.

Socializing & partying

In Ireland socializing and partying are art forms in their own right, with a tendency to be confined within pub culture. Dublin would seem the obvious destination, but there is a hopeless shortage of pubs for the actual population (see the box on page 49) and this makes them terribly overcrowded. There is also the small problem that licensing laws tend to be enforced in the city centre. For serious boozing and chatting into the early hours of the morning head for small village pubs or just about anywhere off the beaten track. At night and during the summer, some of the off-shore islands like **Clare Island** or **Achill**, **Sherkin** or **Inishbofin**, can have very flexible closing hours.

Festivals are great occasions for partying because licensing hours are sometimes officially extended; the summer festival in Galway city is enormously popular with young people, while Killorglin's Puck Fair in Kerry attracts an older crowd. There are countless other festivals taking place throughout the summer in most regions of Ireland, and not all of them are of the partying kind. Visit the Irish Tourist Board website for information on festivals and events: www.ireland.travel.ie

See also 'Festivals', page 52

When to go

There is no easy answer to this question. The weather is notoriously changeable and you can have a week of mild, dry days in February or a week of depressing drizzle in August. These are exceptions, however, and extremes of wind, rain or sunshine are rare; the climate is generally mild, thanks to the benign influence of the Gulf Stream. July and August are definitely the busiest months in terms of visitor numbers, so a trip in early spring or late autumn has a lot to recommend it. Dublin is busy throughout the year, and accommodation in the capital always needs advance planning.

Some important **festivals** take place at fixed times of the year, so this may be a factor determining when to visit Ireland. The Galway Arts Festival takes place in late July/early August, and this is a popular time for many summer festivals across the country. Cork's International Jazz Festival takes off in October, as does Wexford's two-week Opera Festival. See 'Festivals' section, page 52 for a list of important dates.

In Northern Ireland the 'marching season' reaches a climax in July and, while this used to be a time to avoid parts of Belfast and towns like Portadown and Kilkeel, the situation looks to improve. If you feel unsure, contact the Northern Ireland tourist board in Belfast and they will advise on the current situation. As a general rule, consider avoiding loyalist towns in July (in-your-face Union Jack flags clearly demarcate these areas) because, if nothing else, travel plans may be scuppered by having so many streets and roads blocked off to vehicular traffic.

Climate Ireland's climate (a quip with some truth is that Ireland doesn't have a climate, just weather) is equable, with fairly uniform temperatures across the country as a whole: summer temperatures average between 15°C to 20°C while winter temperatures average between 5°C and 10°C. The coldest months are January and February, but temperatures usually stay above 3°C, it rarely snows, and in the southwest heavy frost is unusual. July and August are the warmest months, with exceptional days at this time of the year climbing into the very high 20°Cs. Across a whole year about six hours of daylight is the average, but in July and August it is still light at 2300 while in winter it can start getting dark at 1600.

They say in Galway that if you can see the Aran Islands it's going to rain, and if you can't see them then it's already raining

Average rainfall in low-lying areas is between 800 and 1,200 mm, while in mountainous areas it may exceed 2,000 mm. The southeast is the driest part of the country, with less than 750 mm. But pay scant heed to the statistics, because rain is endemic to Ireland and only its unpredictability is certain. When people say it's a "soft day" this can mean anything from light drizzle to continuous rain. Winter on the western seaboard can be exhilarating, to put it mildly, when an Atlantic storm that has been brewing up for thousands of miles across the ocean finally hits land in the shape of western Ireland. Hurricane-force storms are not unknown, 15m-high waves lash the rocks, and cuts to the power supply are predictable.

Once you are in Ireland, detailed national and **sea area forecasts** are available on RTE Radio 1 (89FM) at 0602, 0755, 1253 and 2355. For area forecasts, call T1550-123 + 721 (Munster), 722 (Leinster), 723 (Connacht), 724 (Ulster), 725 (Dublin) or 726 (sea area).

Tours and tour operators

Popular regions of Ireland, such as Killarney, the Burren, the Aran Islands and Connemara, are well served by local tour companies, and from Dublin local tours run to Newgrange, the Wicklow mountains and further afield. *Iarnród Éireann,* the national railway, organizes a variety of guided one-day tours to Connemara, Cork, Kerry, Dingle, Burren, Leitrim, Wexford, Waterford, Kilkenny, and Antrim and Donegal. For full details contact *Railtours Ireland*, 58 Lower Gardiner Street, Dublin 1, T01-8560045.

The following companies offer a variety of tours and holidays, including all or some of accommodation, activity holidays including angling, city and rural breaks, cycling, golf, walking, car hire, air tickets, river cruising, horse-drawn gypsy caravans and self-catering.

Tour operators in mainland Britain offering holidays in Ireland *Aer Lingus Holidays*, T0845-9737747, www.aerlingus.com; *Cresta Holidays*, Tabley Court, Victoria St. Altrincham, Cheshire WA14 IEZ, T0870-1610910, www.crestaholidays.co.uk; *Enjoy Ireland Holidays*, Suite 425, Glenfield Park II, Blackburn, Lancashire BBI 5QH. T01254-692899, www.enjoy-ireland.co.uk; *Irish Ferries Holidays*, Reliance House, Water St, Liverpool, L2 8TP, T08705, wwwirishferries.com; *Leisure Breaks*, 33 Dovedale Rd, Liverpool LI8 5EP, T0151-7345200, www.irelandbreaks.co.uk; *Slattery's*, 162 Kentish Town Rd, London NW5 2AG, T0800-515900, F020-74821206, ireland@slattery.com; *Stena Line Holidays*, Charter House, Park St, Ashford, Kent TN24 8EX, T08705-747474, www.stenaline.co.uk; *Swansea Cork Ferries*, King's Dock, Swansea, West Glamorgan, Wales, T01792-456116, www.swansea-cork.ie; *Travelbag Adevntures*, 15 Turk St, Alton, GU34 1AG, T01420-541007, travelbag-adventures.com

Tour operators in the USA *Adventures Abroad*, T1-800-6653998, www.adventures-abroad.com; *CIE International Tours*, T1-800-2486832, www.cietours.com; *Collette Tours*, T1-800-2488986; *Destinations Ireland*, T1-800-8321848, info@ digbtravel.com, www.digbtravel.com/tours; *Distinctive Journeys*, T1-800-9222060; *Irish American International Tours*, T1-800-6330505; *Kenny Tours*, T1-800-6481492; *Saga Holidays*, T1-800-3430273.

Tour operators in Australia *Adventure World*, 73 Walker St, North Sydney, T02-99567766; *Eblana Travel*, 4th Level, 67 Castlereagh St, Sydney, T02-92328144.

Essentials

Tour operators in Ireland *Time Out Tours*, T074-73030, www.timeouttours.com Donegal-based company offering activity, educational and special interest holidays across Ireland. Examples include trips via old-style narrow-gauge railways, Highlands and Islands tour, organic farm stays.

Finding out more

A great deal of tourist information is available from the tourist boards and their websites. If contacting Bord Fáilte (The Irish Tourist Board) or the Northern Ireland Tourist Board, be as specific as possible, because they have far too much literature to send out everything to everybody. The two tourist boards are set to merge, but for the immediate future they will continue to operate separately.

Bord Fáilte *Bord Fáilte* is the official Irish tourist organization. Their main address in Ireland is PO Box 273, Dublin 8, T01-6024000, F01-6024100, user@irishtouristboard.ie www.ireland.travel.ie In other countries Bord Fáilte's offices are, in Britain: 150 New Bond St, London WIY OAQ, T0800-0397000, F020-74939065, info@irishtouristboard.co.uk There is also All-Ireland information at the Britain Visitor Centre, 1 Regent St, London SW1Y 4XT. T0870-1555250. In the USA: 345 Park Av, New York, NY 10154, T800-2236470, F0212-3719052. In Canada: 120 Eglinton Av, East Suite 500, Toronto M4P IE2, T416-9292777, F416-9296783. In Australia: 5th Level, 36 Carrington St, Sydney NSW 2000, T02-92996177, F02-92996323, ib@next.com.au In New Zealand: Dingwall Building, 87 Queen St, Auckland 1, T09-3798720. In Holland: Het Nationaal Bureau voor Toerisme, Spuistraat 104, 1012 VA Amsterdam, T020-6223101, F020-6208089, info@irishtouristboard.nl In Germany: Irische Fremdenverkehrszentrale, Untermainanlage 7, D60329 Frankfurt/Main, T069-92318550, F069-92318588, info@irishtouristboard.de In France: Office du Tourisme Irlandais, 33 Rue de Miromesnil, 75008 Paris, T01-53431212, F01-47420164, info@irlande-tourisme.fr

Northern Ireland Tourist Board The *Northern Ireland Tourist Board*'s head office is at 59 North Street, Belfast BT1 1NB, T028-90231221, F028-90240960. In Britain its address is 24 Haymarket, London SW1Y 4DG, T020-77669920, F020-77669929; there is also All-Ireland Information at the Britain Visitor Centre (see above); in the USA: 551 Fifth Avenue, Suite 701, New York, NY 10176, T800-3260036, F212-9220099; in Canada: 111 Avenue Road, Suite 450, Toronto, Ontario M5R 3J8, T0416-9256368, F0416-9612175; in Australia and New Zealand the NITB shares offices with Bord Fáilte (see above). In Germany the NITB is at Taunusstrasse 52-60, 60329 Frankfurt, T69-234504, F069-233480; and in France at 3 rue de Pontoise, 78100 St Germain-en-Laye, T01-39219380, F01-39219390.

Websites You will find a growing number of informative websites about Ireland on the World Wide Web. Among the most useful are *Bord Fáilte*'s site at www.ireland.travel.ie and the *Northern Ireland Tourist Board*'s at www.gb.ni-tourism.com For Irish cuisine, www.irishfood.com is a well designed site. Jobs in Ireland can be found at www.exp.ie and the Republic of Ireland government website is at www.irlgov.ie A site devoted to Irish goods is www.shopirish.com, while the *US Irish Network* has a site at www.usairish.net

Language

English is spoken by everyone in Ireland, and this is the only language you need to know. There are regional accents and if you travel around for any length of time you will begin to appreciate the distinct differences in sound between, say, the English spoken in Dublin and the English spoken in Cork and Kerry. Stay for long enough in the southwest and you might begin to detect the differences between English in Cork and

What's the story?

English spoken in Ireland has some delightful inflections and idioms and this list is a mere smattering. Keep your ears open and many more will be heard. See also the glossary on page 685.

Yoke *anything vaguely functional, from an ancient screwdriver to a satellite space station*

Craic *a good time, good conversation, 'that's the craic' means 'that's the news'; pronounced 'crack'*

Eejit *gentle (sometimes not-so-gentle)*

term of contempt for a complete fool

Good luck *idiomatic expression of farewell, heard in some parts of the west*

What's the story? *what's the news? A polite request for idle gossip*

Knacker *term of abuse for someone felt to be objectionable*

Culchie *a country yokel*

Sláinte *cheers*

Sambo *a sandwich*

Feck *a deletable expletive, mispronounced deliberately*

Essentials

the English spoken in Kerry. The accent in the north of Ireland is different again and it can take a few hours, or even days, to pick it up. There are colloquial and slang expressions peculiar to the English spoken in Ireland, as there are in all cultures that use English, but they are never a barrier to communication and simply add to the pleasure of everyday communication. It often does seem to be the case that the Irish use the English language in a particularly rich and idiosyncratic way and if you keep your ears tuned you will soon collect some creative (and scatological) expressions.

Gaeltacht

Gaeltacht is the name for areas where Irish is still spoken. When Ireland became independent in 1922 the Irish language was still the everyday language of communication in parts of Cork, Kerry, Waterford, Galway, Mayo and Donegal, and it is the more rural parts of these counties that constitute the Gaeltacht. This does not mean English is not understood or spoken as well, but in Gaeltacht areas you will have an opportunity to hear Irish being spoken and used on a daily basis.

The Irish language, and its offshoots of Scottish Gaelic and Manx, is the Irish branch of the Celtic languages that include Welsh, Cornish and Breton. The number of people speaking Irish in Ireland today is somewhere in the region of 80,000 but you are more likely to hear it spoken on *RTE* radio where occasional programmes and daily news bulletins are broadcast in Irish. There is also an Irish-language radio station broadcast from Connemara, *Radio na Gaeltachta*, and a national Irish-language television station, *TG4*.

Some everyday words commonly appear in Irish and it helps to be familiar with them:

'Mná'	*me-naw*	women
'Fir'	*fear*	men
'Gardai'	*gar-dee*	police
'Oifig an Phoist'	*ifig-on-pwist*	post office

See the glossary page 685 for Irish words that are commonly found in place names. If you want to impress or just show off you can occasionally use fairly common Irish words like 'slán agat' (*slawn-aguth*), meaning goodbye, or 'go raibh maith agat' (*go-rev-moh-aguth*), meaning thank you. 'Fáilte' (*fawl-cha*) means welcome.

Disabled travellers

Improvements continue to be made, but generally speaking Ireland is still lagging behind some countries in its provisions for disabled travellers. However, with advance planning and all the available information at your disposal, a visit can still be an enjoyable experience. Contact both Bord Fáilte and NITB for their specialist literature, and in the Republic the *National Disability Authority* is well worth contacting for their guides to accommodation, tourist facilities, restaurants and pubs. They also produce a detailed guide to Dublin which contains good general information and advice as well as listings which include a list of wheelchair accessible public toilets. Some of these toilets require a special key, available from the NRB. *The Restaurant Association of Ireland* will send you their free *Dining in Ireland* booklet which identifies wheelchair-accessible restaurants and *Iarnród Éireann* (Irish Rail) will send their free *Guide for Mobility Impaired Passengers*. Contact *Dublin Bus Customer Service* for their No 3 route through the city with wheelchair access and see page 66 for other information pertaining to Dublin. Travellers from Britain using a car should contact the *Disabled Drivers Association*. *Irish Ferries* and *Stena Line* have discounts for disabled travellers, but it is advisable to check their details *before* booking passage because the date of travel will make a difference. In the USA, *Directions Unlimited* specialize in vacations for disabled travellers. In Northern Ireland, information is available from *Disability Action*.

Contacts *Bord Fáilte*, see page 24. *Directions Unlimited*, 720 N Bedford Road, Bedford Hills, NY 10507, USA, T1-800-5355343. *Disability Action*, T028-909297880, hq@disabilityaction.org *Disabled Drivers Association*, Ashwellthorpe, Norwich, NR16 1EX, England, T01508-489449. *Disability Action*, 2 Annadale Avenue, Belfast BT7 3JH, T028-9049. *Dublin Bus Customer Service*, 59 Upper O'Connell Street, Dublin 1, T01-8734222. *Iarnród Éireann*, Travel Centre, Connolly Station, Amiens St, Dublin1, T01-7032369. *Irish Wheelchair Association*, Blackheath Drive, Clontarf, Dublin 3, T01-8338241/8335366. *National Disability Authority*, 25 Clyde Road, Dublin 4, T01-6080400, www.nda.ie *Northern Ireland Tourist Board*, see page 24. *Restaurants Association of Ireland*, 11 Bridge Court, Dublin 8, T01-6779901.

Gay and lesbian travellers

Contact information for gay and lesbian travellers is given below, but apart from in the main cities, there is little understanding of gay life, and society is generally blinkered if not intolerant. In rural areas especially, there is widespread ignorance, and overt gay behaviour is not advisable. Dublin (see page 116) has gay accommodation, pubs and clubs.

Contacts *Dublin Lesbian Line*, T01-8729911 (Thu, 1900-2100). *Gay Switchboard Dublin*, Carmichael House, North Great Brunswick St, Dublin 7, T01-8721055 (Sun-Fri, 2000 to 2200). *Lesbian Line Belfast*, T028-90238668 (Thu, 1930-2200) *Gay Lesbian Youth Northern Ireland (GLYNI)*, meets every Mon at Cara-friend, Cathedral Building, 64 Donegall St, Belfast, T028-90664111, glyni.org.uk *National Lesbian and Gay Federation*, 6 South William St, Dublin 2, T01-6706377.

Student and youth travellers

Some form of identity card confirming your student or youth status is required for any discounts available on travel to and within Ireland, entry charges to museums and sundry other benefits and discounts. As a general rule, before paying for any form of travel or for any entrance fee or ticket, ask whether a student or youth discount is available. Admission prices quoted in this book are for adults and do not take into account the discounts that are commonly available to students, families, and children. The most commonly recognized form of ID is an **International Student Identity Card** (ISIC), available to anyone in full-time education and obtainable from *STA*, *Council Travel* or *Travel Cuts* offices in your country; in Ireland the card is obtainable through USIT offices.

Consulates and embassies

Irish

United Kingdom *17 Grosvenor Pl, London SWIX 7HR, T207-2352171, F207-2352851*
USA (Washington) *2234 Massachusetts Av, N.W. Washington DC 20008-2849, T202-4623939, F202-2325993, embirlus@aol.com*
USA (New York) *Ireland House, 345 Park Av - 17th Floor, New York, NY 10154-0037, T212-3192555, F212-9809475, congenny@aol.com*
USA (Boston) *Chase Building 535 Boylston St Boston, MA 02116, T617-2679330, F617-2676375, irlcons@aol.com*
USA (Chicago) *400 North Michigan Av, Chicago, IL 60611. T312-3371868, F312-3371954, irishconchicago@aol.com*
USA (San Francisco) *44 Montgomery St, #3830, San Francisco, CA 94104, T415-3924214, F415-3920885, IrishCGSF@aol.com*

Australia *Embassy of Ireland, 20 Arkana St, Yarralumla A.C.T., 2600 Canberra, T02-62733022, 612-62733201, F02-62733741, irishemb@cyberone.com.au*
New Zealand *6th Floor, 18 Shortland St, 1001 Auckland, T09-3022867, F09-3022420*

British

Ireland, 29 Merrion Rd, Dublin 4. T01-2053700, F01-2053885. bembassy@internet-ireland.ie
USA, 3100 Massachusetts Av NW, Washington DC 20008. T202-5886500
Australia, Commonwealth Av, Yarralumla, Canberra, ACT 2600, T02 - 6270 6666 (2) 6273 3236, bhc.canberra@uk.emb.gov.au, www.uk.emb.gov.au
New Zealand, 44 Hill St, Wellington, T04-9242888, F04-9242822, ppa.mailbox@fco.gov.uk

The **Go-25 Card**, if you are 25 or under, performs much the same function as an ISIC card and is obtainable through *Council Travel* in the US or *STA* in Australia and New Zealand. Holders of ISIC cards, once in Ireland, can pay €10.15 and obtain a **Travelsave Stamp** from USIT offices. This allows for discounts on some bus fares and a 50% discount on rail fares.

Working in Ireland

Although Ireland's economy is presently tightening its belt and non-skilled work is not as readily available as it was a couple of years ago, employers in Dublin and other cities are still looking for experienced professionals in various fields. Part-time work in restaurants and hotels in the Republic, and the service industry generally, is not difficult to find between April and August. EU citizens can stay and work for as long as they like but non-EU citizens need to register with the local garda as an alien once they have obtained a work visa. Websites worth consulting include **www.gojobsite.ie** (employment agency) and the government-sponsored **www.jobsireland.com** site which has job opportunities as well as information on taxation, visas and relocation. It is also worth looking at the websites of newspapers to see the kind of employment being advertised: **www.examiner.ie**, **www.ireland.com** and **www.loadza.com** For information on work visas, contact the Department of Foreign Affairs **www.ir/gov.ie/iveagh** and click on the Travelling to Ireland tab.

Business travellers in the Republic can consult the *Chamber of Commerce of Ireland*, 22 Merrion Sq, Dublin 2, T01-661 2888, F01-661 2811, **www.chambersireland.ie** The *Irish Chamber of Commerce* in the US have its own web site: **www.iccusa.org** There is also a business information centre in the *ILAC Centre*, Henry St, Dublin 1, T01-873 3996.

Essentials

Before you travel

Getting in

Passports All visitors to either the Republic or Northern Ireland require a valid passport, except British nationals. Holders of UK passports not born in Great Britain or Northern Ireland should bring their passport, and even British nationals should consider bringing theirs because some form of valid ID is required for collecting air tickets booked online, changing travellers' cheques and perhaps also for cases of emergency medical treatment.

Visas EU nationals can stay in the Republic indefinitely without a visa; travellers from the USA, Canada, Australia and New Zealand can stay for three months without a visa, and this can usually be extended by making an application at the local main Garda Síochána (police) station. In Dublin, go to the *Aliens Registration Office*, Harcourt St, T01-4755555. Nationals of other countries should contact the Irish Embassy for details about visa regulations. Further information for the Republic available from the Department of Foreign Affairs in Dublin, T01-4780822.

EU nationals can stay in Northern Ireland without a visa; citizens of the USA, Canada, Australia and New Zealand can stay for up to six months without a visa, though evidence of a return ticket and sufficient funds may be required. For an extension of the six-month rule write in advance to the Undersecretary of State, Home Office, 40 Wellesley Rd, Croydon CR92BY England. Nationals of other countries should contact the British Consular office for details about visa regulations.

Customs There are no customs restrictions affecting travel within the EU, and there are no duty free allowances. Pets can be taken freely between Britain, Northern Ireland and the Republic, but strict quarantine regulations are in force for pets from any other part of the world (details from T01-6072000, www.irlgov.ie/daff for the Republic and T028-71319500, www.dardni.gov.uk for Northern Ireland). USA visitors can take home US$400 worth of goods per person (www.customs.ustreas.gov/travel for details), Canadians $500.

Vaccinations None are compulsory or even necessary unless arriving from an infected area. See also the 'Health' section (page 59).

What to take

The two essentials are a state of mind that won't get you down if it rains and wet weather gear for the times when it does rain. Health insurance is advisable for non-EU travellers (see 'Health', page 59) and a basic first aid kit should include pills for possible hangovers and/or stomach upsets. Walkers should be prepared for blisters and small cuts, and a compass, possibly a mobile phone as well, is advisable for walks in mountainous areas. A sleeping bag and/or a sheet with a pillow cover is a very good idea for stays in hostels. Other useful items, depending on circumstances, might include an adapter plug for electrical appliances, a small torch and sunglasses.

Money

Currency
See inside front cover for further details of exchange rates

In the Republic, European Monetary Union (EMU) currency came into use at the beginning of 2002. The new currency, the euro, consists of 100 cents. Notes are in 5, 10, 20, 50, 100, 200 and 500; coins are 1, 2, 5, 10, 20 and 50 cents, and 1 and 2 euro.

In Northern Ireland, British Sterling currency is used, with £5, £10, £20, £50 and £100 notes. Coins are £2, £1, 50p, 20p, 10p, 5p, 2p and 1p. However, notes are also issued by Northern Ireland banks and, while these are interchangeable with the standard British notes within Northern Ireland, they are *not* generally accepted in mainland Britain other than through banks.

Until the euro comes into circulation in Northern Ireland (a date still to be decided for Britain), the currencies of the Republic and Northern Ireland are not interchangeable, and at the current rate of exchange one pound sterling is worth around €1.62.

Credit cards

Visa and Mastercard credit cards are widely accepted in the Republic and Northern Ireland and, if you have a personal identification number (PIN), cash withdrawals can be made using them from automatic teller machines (ATMs) which are found in all towns. International money systems, like Cirrus and Plus, are linked to ATMs. Check with your bank or credit card company regarding which ATMs and banks you can use and what charges might be applicable.

UK travellers can use cashcards to withdraw money direct from accounts in the Republic and Northern Ireland, but check with your bank or building society regarding which banks or building societies to use and what charges may be applicable.

American Express and Diners' Club cards, especially the latter, are not as readily accepted as credit cards.

Travellers' cheques

Travellers' cheques are rarely directly accepted in lieu of cash

Using travellers' cheques is the safest way to carry money and all the main brands, Thomas Cook, Visa and American Express, are readily accepted at banks across the whole of Ireland. If travelling between the Republic and Northern Ireland it makes sense to have them issued in sterling, but US dollar cheques are just as also accepted. Keep a record of the cheque numbers separate from the cheques themselves as to facilitate a refund should they get lost or stolen. A commission charge is made when cashing traveller cheques, this may be avoided by cashing American Express or Thomas Cook cheques at their own offices in Dublin (see page 131) or Belfast (page 587). Eurocheques can also be cashed across Ireland with a Eurocheque card.

Changing money

The best exchange rates are available at banks; the worst are across the counter in hotels. Bureaux de change, found at airports and ferry terminals, city centres and some key tourist areas like Killarney, are useful when banks are closed, but the rate will not be as good. In the Republic banks generally open Mon-Fri 1000-1600, but in many towns they may close between 1230 and 1330. On Thu banks often stay open until 1700 or sometimes 1900. In Northern Ireland normal banking hours are 0930-1630 (0930-1700 on Thu), and often also Sat morning in cities.

Value Added Tax

Visitors from non-EU countries leaving the Republic within two months of a purchase (three months in Northern Ireland) can obtain a refund of the Value Added Tax (VAT) added to the price of most goods. The shop has to be a participant in the Retail Export Scheme, and there will usually be a display at the entrance or on the counter to this effect, but shops have different ways of operating the scheme so enquire before making a purchase. The scheme does not apply to hotel bills and other services.

Money transfers

If the need arises you can telephone, your home bank and arrange for money to be transferred to a local bank in Ireland where you can collect it after showing your passport. Before you leave home, ensure you have the necessary bank details. American Express cardholders can arrange for money to be sent to Ireland; check out the details before you leave home. Western Union arranges money transfers and there is also MoneyGram, a quick international money transfer service. For MoneyGram, T008-008-971-8971 (in the UK), T1-800-543-4080 (in USA) T01-6671577 (Bank of Ireland in Dublin).

Cost of living Ireland is not a cheap place to stay or travel in. As a bare minimum, if you stay in hostels and use their facilities to prepare your own lunches and most evening meals, but eat out occasionally at night, and spend about €7 a day on admission charges and/or entertainment, you will need a budget of over €200 a week, and this will exclude any transport costs or other expenses. If you stay in a decent B&B or guesthouse, enjoy a pub lunch and a mid-range evening meal each day, and spend about €15 a day on admission charges and/or entertainment, a budget of at least €500 a week is needed, excluding transport costs and any other expenses. To give you an idea here are some sample prices: pub lunch €7.50; petrol per litre €0.69; pint of beer €2.95; Dublin to Galway monthly return bus fare €15.24. And if you are planning to stay in Dublin for any length of time and have much fun, consider taking out a second mortgage.

Getting there

Air

From Britain The only consistently available and reasonably priced tickets are the so-called **Apex** (Advanced Purchase Excursion) tickets which have various conditions attached to them, the most important being that your return date is fixed and no refunds are available. Apex return fares between London and Dublin range from between €75 and €100, between London and Cork around €115, between London and Belfast around €100. In order to secure these prices it is advisable to book as far ahead as possible, especially at peak times like summer, Easter and Christmas. Supply and demand means there are often special offers that represent very good value like two return tickets for the price of one or especially low return fares, sometimes as low as E10. But beware: soemtimes *Ryanair* fares can prove more expensive than *Aer Lingus* fares when demand is high On-line booking is available with both *Aer Lingus* and *Ryanair*.

Bicycles are normally carried free of charge on *Aer Lingus* but *Ryanair* rake in €19 extra each way (same for surf boards). Always check before you purchase a ticket.

Student/Youth fares are always worth asking about, though different airlines have different rules and regulations. An International Student Identity Card (ISIC) is usually required. It is advisable to check through a specialist agency like *STA Travel*, 86 Old Brompton Rd, London SW7 3LH, T020-73616161, who also have offices in a number of other cities across Britain. Another company worth trying is Usit Campus, 52 Grovesnor Gardens, London SW1W OAG, T020-77303402, who also have regional offices in cities and at universities in Britain. *Usit Now* is the Irish youth and student travel organization. Its head office is 19 Aston Quay, Dublin 2, T01-6798833; other offices are listed in relevant directories.

Specialist travel agents Companies in London are *Pat Carroll Travel*, T020 -76259669; *Tara Travel*, T020-76258601 (London) T0161-2251133 (Manchester), T0121-7022929 (Birmingham), T020-85145141 (Essex). *Claddagh Travel*, T0121-2003320, and in Scotland *Sibbald Travel*, T0131-6679172 or *Going Places*, T0141-2215715.

From Britain to the Republic It takes about an hour to fly between London and Dublin; about 90 minutes to Cork or Shannon. The main destinations in the Republic are Dublin, Cork and Shannon, but it is also possible to fly to Knock, Kerry, Waterford and Galway.

From Britain to Northern Ireland It takes about an hour and a half to fly between London and Belfast, a bit longer to Derry. The airports are Belfast International, Belfast City and City of Derry and while most departures are from London (Heathrow, Stansted and Gatwick), Manchester and Birmingham.

Airlines operating between British airports and Ireland

From	To	Airline
Aberdeen	Belfast, City Dublin	British Airways
Birmingham	Belfast Int. and City, Cork, Dublin, Shannon	Aer Lingus/British European/Ryanair
Blackpool	Belfast City, Dublin	Platinum Air 2000
Bournemouth	Dublin	Ryanair
Bristol	Belfast Int. and City, Cork, Dublin	British European/Go/Aer Lingus/ British Airways/Ryanair
Cardiff	Belfast City, Cork, Dublin	Air Wales, British Airways/Ryanair
Coventry	Knock	Mayo Air+
East Midlands	Belfast City, Dublin	British European/BMI British Midland
Edinburgh	Belfast Int. and City, Cork, Dublin, Shannon	Aer Lingus/Go/Ryanair/British European/ British Airways/Easyjet
Exeter	Belfast City, Dublin	British European
Glasgow	Belfast City and Int., Derry, Cork, Dublin, Shannon	British Airways/British European/Aer Lingus/Go/Easyjet
Glasgow Prestwick	Dublin	Ryanair
Guernsey	Belfast City	British European
Isle of Man	Belfast City, Dublin	British European/Manx Airlines
Jersey	Belfast City, Cork, Dublin	Jersey European/British European
Leeds Brad.	Belfast City, Dublin	British European/British Airways/Ryanair
Liverpool	Belfast Int., Cork, Dublin	Easyjet/Keenair/Ryanair
London City	Belfast City, Dublin	British European/Aer Lingus
London Gatwick	Belfast City, Cork, Dublin, Shannon	British European/Aer Lingus/ British Airways/Ryanair
London Heathrow	Belfast City and Int., Cork, Dublin, Shannon	Aer Lingus/BMI British Midland
London Luton	Belfast Int., Dublin, Knock, Waterford	Easyjet/Ryanair/Mayo Air+/Euroceltic
London Stanstead	Belfast City and Int., Cork, Dublin, Kerry, Knock, Shannon	Go/Ryanair
Manchester	Belfast City, Derry, Cork, Dublin, Knock, Shannon	British Airways/Aer Lingus/Luxair/Ryanair
Newcastle	Belfast City, Cork, Dublin	British European/Aer Lingus/ British Airways
Plymouth	Cork, Dublin	British Airways
Southampton	Belfast City, Dublin	British Airways
Sheffield	Belfast City	British Airways
Swansea	Dublin	Air Wales
Teeside	Dublin	Ryanair

Airline details   *Aer Lingus*, T0845-9737747, www.aerlingus.com *Air Wales*, T0870-0133151, www.travel.com *British Airways*, T1800-626747, www.britishairways.com

☛ **Airlines operating between major European cities and Ireland**

Amsterdam	Aer Lingus
Barcelona	Iberia, AB Airlines
Berlin	AB Airlines
Brussels	Aer Lingus, Ryanair
Cologne	Lufthansa
Copenhagen	Aer Lingus
Dusseldorf	Aer Lingus
Frankfurt	Aer Lingus, Lufthansa
Lisbon	TAP
Madrid	Aer Lingus, Iberia
Milan	Aer Lingus, Alitalia
Moscow	Aeroflot
Nice	AB Airlines
Munich	Lufthansa
Paris	Aer Lingus, Air France, Cityjet, Ryanair
Rome	Aer Lingus, Alitalia
Zurich	Aer Lingus, Crossair

bmi British Midland, T0870-6070555, www.flybmi.com **British European**, T0870-5676676, www.british-european.com **Celtic Airways**, T01752-766111. **EasyJet**, T0870-6000000, www.easyjet.com **Euroceltic**, T0870-400100, www.euro celtic.com **Go**, T0870-6076543, www.go-fly.com **Keenair**, T0151-4480606, www.keen air.co.uk **Lukair**, T01293, www.luxai.lu **Mayoair**, T08702-417037, www.mayoair.ie **Platinum Air 2000**, T01253-400100. **Ryanair**, T0870-1569569, www.ryanair.com

From Europe There are numerous direct and indirect flights to Ireland from European cities. Students under the age of 30 with valid ID and travellers under the age of 26 with a European Youth Card (EYC) are eligible for discounted fares. The above box shows the airlines that offer flights to Ireland from European cities.

From North America There are direct *Aer Lingus* flights to Dublin and Shannon from New York, Boston, Chicago and Los Angeles. *Continental Airlines* and *Delta Airlines* also fly to Shannon and Dublin.

Flights from the West Coast cost considerably more and it may be a better deal to fly to London and take an Apex flight from there to Ireland. Airlines and some specialist travel agents are listed below and the weekend sections of papers like the *New York Times* and the *San Francisco Chronicle* are worth checking out. Student fares are available through agents like STA Travel in New York and Travel Cuts in Toronto.

There are no direct flights to Ireland from Canada, but *Air Canada* fly to Dublin, Shannon and Belfast via London from Montréal, Toronto and Vancouver. The cheapest flights from Montréal or Toronto to the Republic entail fixed dates that cannot be changed. Prices average around Can$1000, but can cost from Can$100 to Can$200 more or less depending on the season. As with flights from the US West Coast, it is worth checking out the cost of flying to London and having a separate Apex ticket from there to Ireland.

From Australia & New Zealand There are no direct flights from Australia or New Zealand, so the usual route is to fly to London and then on to Ireland. Various airlines offer indirect tickets to Ireland this way and ones to check out include not only *Aer Lingus* and *British Airways*, but also *KLM*, *Singapore Airlines* and *Malaysia Airlines*. The single most important factor determining the price of a ticket is the season and peak times. Between May and August is peak time.

Airlines operating between USA and Ireland

Aer Lingus
T800 IRISHAIR
www.aerlingus.com

From: Boston, Chicago, Los Angeles, New York
To: Shannon/Dublin

Continental Airlines
T800 231-0856
www.continental.com

From: Newark
To: Shannon/Dublin

Delta Air Lines
T800 241-4141
www.delta.com

From: Atlanta
To: Shannon/Dublin

Royal Jordanian Airlines
T800 223-0470
212 949-0050

From: Chicago, New York
To: Shannon

Before making a decision check out other major airlines that fly to London, because very often it does not cost a lot to have a London-Dublin ticket added to your Apex-type main fare.

Airlines and agents offering flights from Australia and New Zealand Aer Lingus, World Aviation Systems, 64 York St, Sydney, T02-93219123; 6th Floor, 229 Queen Street, Auckland, T09-3794455, www.aerlingus.com *Air New Zealand*, Queen Street, Auckland, T09-3662424; 5 Elizabeth St, Sydney, T02-92234666 *British Airways*, 64 Castlereagh St, Sydney, T02-92583300; 154 Queen Street, Auckland, T09-3568690 *KLM*, Level 6, 5 Elizabeth Street, Sydney, T02-92316333 *Malaysia Airlines*, 16 Spring Street, Sydney, T02-93643535; 12th Floor, The Swanson Centre, Swanson Street, Auckland, T09-3732741 *Qantas*, 70 Hunter Street, Sydney, T02-99514294; Qantas House, 154 Queen Street, Auckland, T0800-808767 *Singapore Airlines*, 17-19 Bridge Street, Sydney, T02-93500121; Lower Ground Floor, West Plaza Building, Customs & Albert Sts, Auckland, T0800-808909 *STA Travel*, 855 George Street, Sydney, T1-800-637444 *Traveller's Centre*, 10 High Street, Auckland, T09-3090458 (and branches throughout both countries) *Thomas Cook*, 175 Pitt Street, Sydney, T02-92296611; 159 Queen Street, Auckland, T09-3793924 *UTAG Travel Agents*, 122 Walker Street, North Sydney (and branches throughout the country) T02-99568399.

Ferry

From Britain The box on the next page covers the routes and sailing times of passage to Ireland by car and passenger ferries. Car hire in the Republic (see page 44) is more expensive than in Britain or the USA and so, if you are planning to use a car, a journey by ferry can be worthwhile. Bear in mind, too, that the cost of a ferry fare for a car and passengers may compare favourably with two, three or more individual air fares for the same journey. The Swansea-Cork ferry does not operate over the winter months.

Fares vary depending on the time of year, type of vessel and sometimes the time of sailing. But bear in mind that in the age of low-fares airlines like Ryanair, this is not a cheap way to travel. For example: it costs two people with a car approximately £220 to cross from Heysham to Belfast, £250 from Troon to Belfast, £180 from Liverpool to Dublin. Members of a Youth Hostel/Hostelling International organization (see page 42) receive a 20% discount on foot passenger fares on Irish Ferries and Stena Line.

Essentials

Essentials

Ferry crossings and operators between the British mainland and Ireland

From	To	Operator	Approx travel time
Cairnryan	Larne	P&O Irish Sea	Fastcraft, 1hr Superferry, 1¾ hrs
Fishguard	Rosslare	Stena Line	Stena Lynx Fastcraft, 99 mins Superferry, 3½ hrs
Fleetwood	Larne	P&O Irish Sea	8 hrs
Heysham	Belfast	Sea Cat	Fastcraft, 3 hr 55 min
Holyhead	Dublin port	Irish Ferries	Cruise Ferry, 3¼ hrs Dublin Swift, 109 min
Holyhead	Dublin port	Stena Line	Superferry, 3¼ hrs
Holyhead	Dun Loaghaire	Stena Line	Stena HSS Fastcraft, 99 mins
Isle of Man	Belfast	Sea Cat / Isle of Man Steam Packet Co	2¾ hrs
Isle of Man	Dublin	Sea Cat / Isle of Man Steam Packet Co	2¾ hrs
Liverpool	Belfast	Norse Merchant Ferries	8½ hrs
Liverpool	Dublin	Norse Merchant Ferries	7½ hrs
Liverpool	Dublin	Sea Cat	3¾ hrs
Mostyn (near Chester)	Dublin	P&O Irish Sea	6 hrs
Pembroke	Rosslare	Irish Ferries	3¾ hrs
Stanraer	Belfast	Stena Line	HSS Fastcraft , 1¾ hrs Superferry, 3¼ hrs
Swansea	Cork	Swansea Cork Ferries	10 hrs
Troon	Belfast	Sea Cat	2½ hrs

Bear in mind extra costs like the price of meals and drinks on board and a possible need for overnight stays in Britain and/or Ireland in order to make unhelpful departure or arrival times. On many of the routes, especially the 10-hour Swansea-Cork ferry, there are extra charges for cabin accommodation, although you can bring a sleeping bag and try to find a quiet corner for a night's sleep. Some companies, like *Irish Ferries*, insist on travel insurance, and unless you can quote an existing policy that covers you (an annual world or Europe travel policy for instance) there will be an extra charge for this as well.

Travelling as a foot passenger on a combined coach/ferry or train/ferry ticket can be good value although obviously it takes far longer than a flight. Holders of ISIC cards should ask about student reductions, whether travelling as a driver or foot passenger, although discounts are not available on all the routes. Cheapest travel of all for a foot passenger is to try and hitch a ride at the ferry terminal, because in a car with fewer than four passengers there would be no extra charge.

There are some big ships sailing to Ireland. The *Stena HSS* is the size of a football pitch, accommodates up to 1,500 passengers and, with four gas turbines producing 100,000 horsepower, belts along with a top speed of over 50 mph. *Ulysses*, an *Irish Ferries* ship doing the Holyhead-Dublin route, ranks as the world's largest car ferry (over 1,300 cars) and with 12 decks to play with there are plenty of amenities on board.

Ferry operators *Irish Ferries*, T08705-171717, www.irishferries.ie *Sea Cat/Isle of Man Steam Packet Co*, T08705-523523, www.steam-packet.com www.seacat.co.uk *Norse Merchant Ferries*, T0870-6004321, www.norsemerchant.com *P&O* T0870-2424777, www.poirishsea.com *Stena Line*, T08705-707070, www.stenaline.co.uk *Swansea/Cork Ferries*, T0800-7838004, T01792- 456116, www.swansea-cork.ie **Belfast to Troon:** *Seacat Scotland* run daily services (2½ hours; £250 for two adults and a car), T08705-523523, www.seacat.co.uk

Irish Ferries run three routes from northern France to Rosslare in Co Wexford, and two routes to Cork. The fastest, over 18 hours, is from Cherbourg to Rosslare; the route from Le Havre to Rosslare takes 22 hours. The fare for both routes with four passengers and a car in the summer months is around €508. Between May and September there is a ferry service between Le Havre and Cork, taking over 20 hours, and between May and August a Roscoff to Cork ferry also operates, taking 15 hours. **From Europe**

Essentials

Train/coach

The cost of combined train and ferry tickets depends on the time of year and departure times. Combined train and ferry tickets can be booked through a travel agent or from a mainline railway station. *Stena Line*, T08705-455455, also offer competitive rail/ferry packages, and their London to Dublin route, for example, ranges from £39, travelling off-peak times, to £65. Travellers under the age of 26 with a Young Person's Railcard can get one-third off standard rail fares. Contact the *National Rail Enquiry Service*, T0845-7484950 (information), T0845-7222333 (credit card bookings), www.co.uk/travel For details of **European rail passes** that can be used to get to and travel throughout Ireland, contact CIE T1-800-CIE-TOUR or 973-2923899 or Rail Europe T1-800-4387245 in the USA and T1-800-5552748 in Canada. **Train/ferry**

This is the least expensive but also the most time-consuming method of getting to Ireland. The largest operator of scheduled coach services to Ireland is *Slattery's*, with daily services to Dublin, Galway, Cork, Tralee, Waterford, Limerick and many other towns. Coaches depart from London, Bristol, Birmingham, Reading, Liverpool, Manchester and Leeds. An adult return from London to Dublin at peak times is £39 by day, £49 by night. **Coach/ferry**

National Express Eurolines run regular day and night services between London and Dublin, via Birmingham, taking an average of 12 hours, depending on the ferry crossing. Combined tickets from other cities across Britain are available. Tickets using other ferry crossings are also available, as are combined tickets to other parts of Ireland using the *Bus Éireann* network. Enquiries and ticket purchases may be made in person from any National Express station or their agents, or by phone (contact details are given below). Reductions are available to passengers under 26 and to senior citizens.

Ulsterbus operates a coach/ferry service between London and Belfast via Birmingham, from Birmingham via Manchester, and from Edinburgh via Glasgow using the Stranraer ferry. The return fare from London is around £50 and takes 12 hours; from Edinburgh the coast is €46 and takes 7 hours. Tickets can be purchased through *National Express*.

Contacts *Bus Éireann*, Busaras, Store Street, Dublin 1. T01-8366111 (Dublin), www.buseireann.ie *National Express Eurolines*, 52 Grosvenor Gardens, Victoria, London SW1W OAU, T0870-808080 (National Express call number), 0870-143219 (credit/debit card bookings), F020-77308721, www.eurolines.co.uk *Slattery's*, 162 Kentish Town Road, London NW5 2AG. T0800-515900/020-74851438, ireland@slatterys.com *Ulster Bus Enquiry Service*, Europa Buscentre, Belfast BT12 5AH. TT028-90337002.

Essentials

Touching down

Airport information
The main airports at Dublin, Shannon, Cork and Belfast all have money exchange facilities, car hire desks, taxis and public transport to and from the city. For detailed information on the airports see page 64 for Dublin, page 374 for Shannon, page 564 for Belfast and page 274 for Cork. Information about the smaller regional airports at Derry, Galway and Waterford is given under their relevant sections.

Airport tax
Airport taxes are added on to the price of your air or ferry ticket at the time of purchase.

Tourist information
Tourist Boards   The airports at Dublin, Shannon and Belfast all have tourist information offices which include an accommodation booking service. Local tourist information offices are found in cities and towns all across Ireland and, while they are nearly always staffed by helpful and considerate people, some are better organized and more orientated to the independent traveller than others. In the Republic, most tourist offices are run by the national tourist organisation, called *Bord Fáilte*, though you will also come across some that have been set up and funded on a local basis, and this includes *Dublin Tourism* as well as village-based offices. Non-Bord Fáilte offices will not usually arrange to book accommodation for you outside of their local area. The *Northern Ireland Tourist Board* (NITB) runs all the tourist offices in Northern Ireland; you will see the brown signs pointing to them in town centres.

Normal hours for most tourist offices are 0900-1700 Mon-Fri, 0900-1300 on Sat. In larger towns and major tourist areas, during high season, the closing hours are often extended and they may open all day Sat and Sun. But also be prepared to find a tourist office closed on a Sat, Sun or a public holiday anywhere and at any time of the year. Outside of the summer months, opening hours can be frustratingly idiosyncratic.

For guide books about Ireland see page 677
Maps & guides   There is no shortage of good quality maps of Ireland. For a single, large-scale road map of the whole country try the No 405 Michelin 1:400,000 or the AA 1:350,000 map. For more detail of a large area your best bet are the four maps that make up the *Ordnance Survey Holiday Maps* series (North, West, East and South), at a scale of 1:250,000. For more detail of a particular area, and essential for walking, it is impossible to beat the *Ordnance Survey Discovery Series* at a scale of 1:50,000 (2.5 in to 1 mile/2 cm to 1 km). Avoid the seriously out-of-date Ordnance Survey 1:25,000 (½ in to 1 mile) series of maps which are still being sold.

Contacts   *Stanfords*, 12-14 Long Acre, London WC2, T020-78361321, can supply all these maps by mail. In the USA, *Rand McNally*, T1-800-3330136, can do the same.

Concessionary cards
A *Heritage Card*, purchased in the Republic for €19, gives unlimited free admission to all the parks, monuments, gardens, inland waterways and cultural institutions under the management of *Dúchas*, the national heritage department of the Irish government. The card can be bought at the first site you visit or from their main office at 51 St Stephen's Green, Dublin 2, T01-6472461, www.heritageireland.ie Dúchas sites are indicated as such in this guide.

In Northern Ireland *The National Trust* is a similar kind of organization but their card costs £28, or £13 if you are under 25. It covers the whole of Britain and Northern Ireland, and does not represent value for money if you are only visiting Northern Ireland.

Rules, customs and etiquette

Conduct
By and large the Republic is a laid-back place with a healthy disregard for authority and nit-picking rules. Social customs and etiquette are much the same as the

Touching down

Business hours

Normal business hours are 0900 to 1700, Mon-Fri; shops open 0900-1730 or 1800, Mon-Sat; the large stores in Dublin stay open late on Thu and Fri. In small towns, shops and even businesses may close for an hour over lunchtime and for the whole of one afternoon each week. In popular tourist towns like Killarney shops usually stay open until 2100 in the high season.

Directory enquiries

T11811 in the Republic, T192 in Northern Ireland.

Electricity

230V AC in the Republic and 240V AC in Northern Ireland. Plugs are the 3-pin flat sort, and 2-pin round wall sockets are also found. British electrical appliances will work everywhere, North American ones will require a transformer and a plug adaptor, and Australian and New Zealand appliances just a plug adaptor.

Emergency services

T999 or T112

IDD codes

The international direct dialing code (IDD) code for the Republic is 353 and for Northern Ireland is 44.

Official time

Ireland is on Greenwich Mean Time (GMT), so when it is 1800 in Dublin or Belfast it's 1300 in New York, 1000 in San Francisco, and 0400 in Sydney. However, daylight saving time changes mean that clocks are advanced by one hour between mid-Mar and the end of Oct.

Weights & measures

Confusion reigns because metrication has been adopted but not enforced. Distances are measured in both miles and kilometres; drinks in pubs come in pints, in shops they come in litres; food is weighed and sold in both pounds and kilograms, petrol comes in litres.

***To convert**: miles to kilometres multiply by 1.61; kilometres to miles multiply by 0.62; pounds to kilograms multiply by 0.45; kilograms to pounds multiply by 2.20.*

average European, North American or Australasian visitor would expect, although, as noted above, attitudes to gay life need to be taken into account. A dress code in a restaurant is rare indeed and even in the most expensive establishments smart but casual attire is generally acceptable. Acute class divisions certainly exist in Ireland, and in Dublin, Belfast and certain other cities they are very obvious, but in the Republic it can often be more difficult to demarcate social class in terms of behaviour, dress or language than it is in Britain.

Northern Ireland is socially very conservative. Racist attitudes, especially as regards black travellers, are common across Ireland as a whole, and the best that can be said is that more often than not it is rooted in plain ignorance rather than deliberate malice. The recent arrival of refugees from eastern Europe has exposed a very ugly strain of virulent racism behind the very discreet charm of the Irish bourgeoisie.

There is nothing in Ireland that is unusually illegal, and the law is pretty much as one **Prohibitions** would expect it to be in a modern European country. Travellers caught importing illegal drugs will be prosecuted according to the law, up to and including imprisonment, but punishments do reflect the nature of the drug in question. In the Republic, possession of cannabis for personal use carries a fine of €381; for other drugs €1270 or 12 months in jail before a District Court and an unlimited fine and/or prison up to seven years if tried before a judge and jury, and the *garda* (police) can detain anyone for up to seven days without charge on suspicion of a drug offence. The legal age for drinking alcohol is 18, and in city pubs customers may be asked to prove their age. There are strict laws regarding driving while under the influence of alcohol and the traditional tolerance towards drink and driving in rural areas in the Republic is fast disappearing.

Religion	In theory the Republic is overwhelmingly Roman Catholic, but times are changing and in the cities church attendance is not as high as one might expect. In rural areas going to church is a social obligation for the majority of people and should not be mistaken for devotional piety, although that exists in large doses as well. In Northern Ireland religious affiliation is all too often a marker for political and social differences, and visitors are well advised to tread carefully in this area.
Tipping	When it comes to tipping there are no hard and fast rules. Upmarket hotels and restaurants will usually have a service charge (10-15%) added to the bill, but if paying by plastic a space will still be left on the receipt for a tip. As a general rule, a tip of 10% is the norm if you do decide to tip. In bars certainly, and even pub restaurants, tipping is not generally necessary or even expected. For porters in hotels or elsewhere think in terms of a 75¢/50p tip for each piece of large luggage; taxi drivers are usually tipped 10% of the fare.

Safety

Northern Ireland has some of the lowest crime statistics to be found anywhere in Europe and, generally speaking, Belfast is a far safer city for the visitor than Dublin

The general level of personal safety in Ireland is high for both male and female travellers, especially in the countryside, but do not be lulled into a false sense of security. Crimes, minor and major, do occur and common sense should always govern your behaviour. Parts of Dublin are highly prone to street crime, largely fuelled by drug addiction, and this includes the city centre. Northern Ireland is remarkably safe for the traveller, both in the cities and in the countryside, and there is no more need to take precautions about personal safety, or where to park your car, than you would anywhere else in Europe. As always, exercise your common sense. Women travellers tend to find Ireland an easier place in which to travel around, alone or in company, than other countries of Europe, and chauvinism is relatively easy to deal with. It is not uncommon to see women hitchhiking alone, but they usually live locally and expect a hitch from another local.

Where to stay

See inside front cover for hotel price codes

The choice of accommodation ranges from top-drawer luxury hotels and historic country houses to dormitory beds in a hostel or free camping in a farmer's field. In between there are medium-range hotels, one-star hotels, guest houses, farm houses, self-catering, the ubiquitous bed and breakfast (B&B) in a private home, and camping and caravan parks. Prices quoted in this book refer to the price of a double room in high season, so usually expect to pay less at other times of the year, though the more expensive establishments are less likely to have variable rates. Single person supplements are common and sometimes exorbitant. Rates for families with children vary depending on the number of children and their ages, and the rate is often negotiable. Most rooms in hotels and guesthouses, and in a growing number of B&Bs, have a tea and coffee making facility. In this guide, email addresses are not given when they can be accessed through the website address which is provided.

Breakfast is usually included in the price of accommodation, but some of the more expensive hotels and most hostels charge extra for this. Travellers who are vegetarian, or just diet conscious, often have good reason to feel aggrieved about the inadequate alternatives to the hearty fry-up that is served as the standard breakfast in most establishments. A recent development has been the growth of small hotels charging a flat rate for a room, usually up to three adults or two adults and two children, and not including breakfast. Usually called a travel lodge or an inn, they can be very good value if a cholesterol-laden breakfast is not something you want to feel obliged to eat. Guesthouses, (but not B&Bs), especially in tourist towns like Kinsale and Dingle, often have interesting breakfast menus that include delights like poached egg and smoked salmon.

Top 10 Hostels ★

Whitepark Bay Hostel, Ballycastle, County Antrim, T20731745 (page 548)
Killarney International Hostel, Aghadoe House, Killarney, County Kerry, T31240 (page 322)
Old Monastery Hostel, Letterfrack, County Galway, T41132, (page 433)
Ballintaggart Hostel, Dingle, County Kerry, T9151454 (page 359)
The Climbers Inn, Glencar, on the Kerry Way, T9760101 (page 350)
Dublin International Hostel, 61 Mountjoy St, Dublin, T8301766 (page 104)
Aghadoe House, Killarney, County Kerry, T31240 (page 322)
Glendalough Hostel, Glendalough, County Wicklow, T01-8301766 (page 171)
Wild Haven Hostel, Achill Island, County Mayo, T45392 (page 460)
Valentia Island Hostel, Kingston, T9476141 (page 336)

Essentials

Always confirm the price of your accommodation when making a reservation and, whenever possible, always try to make a reservation. In Dublin this is essential whatever the time of year, and in popular tourist areas the summer months and holiday weekends can sometimes see most of the reasonably priced accommodation fully booked. This is particularly true at the time of popular festivals (see page 121). A surprising amount of accommodation choices, including hotels, close down for varying periods over Christmas.

Online & telephone booking

Resireland is a computer data base system that includes a booking system for a wide range of accommodation (hotels, B&Bs, farmhouses, guesthouses, hostels, self catering) across the whole of Ireland through call-free numbers. The cost of a booking is €4, and €1.27 for each subsequent booking, and there is also a non-refundable deposit, 10% of the accommodation cost, taken on your credit card; with self-catering accommodation it is also possible to pay by cheque.

Telephone reservations can be made Monday-Friday, 0800-2000, and Saturday and Sunday, 0800-1900. Freephone + 800-66866866 (+ denotes the international access code in the country where the call is made), thus within Europe (including Northern Ireland) T00800-66866866, and within the USA T011-800-66866866. Within Ireland the final 66 is not used, so T1800-668668. The web address for Resireland is www.gulliver.ie or www.ireland.travel.ie/reservations/

General information on accommodation, including availability but without a booking facility, can also be obtained on T0800-0397000. Prices, availability and online booking for accommodation is also available on www.wannabeinireland.com

Country houses, castles & heritage houses

There is a tempting choice to choose from across Ireland, nearly all of which are to be found in the Republic. Many of the country houses belong to the *Blue Book Group*, while castles as well as some country houses belong to *The Green Book of Ireland* group. *The Hidden Ireland* is an interesting collection of buildings of character and architectural interest offering accommodation and sometimes meals. All three groups have glossy illustrated brochures, but bear in mind that places pay to be part of the group and their inclusion does not guarantee quality of accommodation.

Contacts *Blue Book Group*, Ardbraccan Glebe, Navan, Co Meath, T046-23416, www.ireland-blue-book.com *The Green Book of Ireland*, 12 Lower Hatch St, Dublin 2, T01-6762555, F01-6762995, ireland@greenbook.ie www.iol.ie/green-book-of-ireland *The Hidden Ireland*, 37 Lower Baggot St, Dublin2, T01-6627166, www.hidden-ireland.com

Hotels Hotels are graded from 5-star to 1-star, and for €4.45 Bord Fáilte retail the Irish Hotels Federation's *Be Our Guest* illustrated guide to many (but not all) of the hotels and guesthouses in the Republic registered with them. NITB have a similar, non-illustrated, *Where to Stay* guide for £4.99 that includes hotels. Some of the classier hotels in Ireland belong to the Manor House group (typically in the **XL-L** range) or the Coast & Country or Village Inn group (typically in the **AL** range).

Many traditional hotels have touches of character that are sadly missing in a new breed of hotels that are popping up with alarming frequency across Ireland. Often built by business consortiums as a tax avoidance strategy, the latter invariably have a leisure centre and their rooms are like the one Gloria Graham looked into in *The Big Sleep*: "Hey, I like this, early nothing."

Depending on supply and demand, room rates are a lot more negotiable than many people realize, and if you can think of a reason for asking for a discount – more than one night's stay, only one night's stay, booking a dinner, commercial traveller's rate, off-season rate, weekend rate, mid-week rate – it is often worth negotiating. You can also find discounted hotel rates through package deals with a ferry company or an air-line like *Aer Lingus* (see the B&B section below). *Irish Ferries*, for example, have a deal which allows travellers to choose their hotels from the Manor House Hotels group, at a basic rate (some supplements apply) of €164 for two nights, or €226 for two nights from the Irish Country Hotels group.

Contacts *Irish Hotels Federation*, T01-4976459, www.beourguest.ie *Manor House Hotels*, *Coast & Country* and *Village Inn*, Sandyford Office Park, Foxrock, Dublin 18, T01-2958900, www.cmvhotels.com

Guesthouses Guesthouses can provide better value than many hotels because they are invariably family-run, and can often offer a more satisfying degree of pampering by your host. The higher-grade ones will have direct dial telephones in the rooms, a private car park, a lounge and sometimes a bar, and often a more interesting choice for breakfast than many hotels and most B&Bs.

Contacts *Friendly Homes of Ireland*, Tourism Resources, 71 Waterloo Rd, Dublin 4, www.tourismresources.ie contains details of a fairly mixed group of guesthouses and small hotels. *Premier Guesthouses* 4 Whitefriars, Aungier St, Dublin 2, T01-4751813, www. premier-guesthouses.ie

B&Bs If you stay in bed and breakfast places more than just occasionally you will soon discover what a surprising variety of people, decors, gewgaws, and styles of welcome and service lay behind those innocuous B&B boards that pop up everywhere outside farms and houses. The most typical is an owner-occupied bungalow with two or three rooms set aside for guests, which are increasingly likely to have their own toilet and shower room. Prices average between €12 and €16 22 per person sharing, and the less expensive ones are likely to have shared bathroom facilities. Similar prices in sterling apply to the North.

The best B&Bs are professionally run, clean, friendly and helpful. Evening meals are sometimes available, though they tend to be expensive (around €19) considering the lack of choice and the milieu, while afternoon tea can be a delight if fresh breads and scones are served. The least satisfying B&Bs tend to be those where you are made too conscious of being in someone's home and where it is taken for granted you wanted a fried breakfast.

B&Bs can be booked through tourist offices on payment of a 10% booking deposit (which is what the tourist board charges the establishment) plus a small fee for a local booking. At the height of the season in popular tourist areas like Dublin, Killarney or Galway this can be well worth the money, because a number of calls may have to be made. There is a *Town & Country Homes* illustrated guide to B&Bs in Ireland, sold in tourist offices, and an *Irish Farmhouse* guide which at least allows you to see which ones are modern bungalows and which traditional buildings. The NITB's *Where to Stay* guide (£4.99) includes B&Bs. Aer Lingus, T0845-9737747 in Britain, www.aerlingus offer a *Go As You Please* package with vouchers for B&Bs from a list of thousands that you choose and book ahead when you are travelling. The B&B rate is fixed at €40.50 for a double, €26.65 a single. There is a similar deal for 3-star hotels, at €63.50/44.50 in the summer.

A number of B&Bs choose not to register with Bord Fáilte and opt instead for the Family Homes of Ireland group. They tend to be a little less expensive, being mostly in the bottom end of the **B** price category, and the group's illustrated booklet (€3.75) is available from their office.

Contacts *Family Homes of Ireland*, Fough West Park, Oughterard, County Galway, T091-552000, www.family-homes.ie *Town and Country Homes Association*, www.townandcountry.com *Bed & Breakfast Association of Northern Ireland*, T028-70823823. *Irish Farm Holidays*, T061-400700, www.irishfarmholidays.com *Northern Ireland Farm and Country Holidays*, T028-82841325, www.nifcha.com

Houses, and apartments to a far lesser extent, are usually rented on a weekly basis, though outside of the summer months it is also possible to book a place for shorter periods, like a long weekend or four or five days over Easter. **Self-catering**

Bord Fáilte retail a *Self Catering* guide which is packed with over 3,000 premises, and the NITB's *Where to Stay* guide includes self-catering. Tour operators like **Stena Line Holidays**, **Enjoy Ireland Holidays** or **Slatterys** (see page 24) also arrange self-catering deals and **Family Homes of Ireland**, (see above) have an illustrated booklet with some very good-value choices. Also worth contacting are **Irish Cottages and Holiday Homes Association**, 4 Whitefriars, Aungier Street, Dublin 2, T01-4757596, www.irishcottageholidays.com and **Home from Home**, T1850-665599 (Ireland), www.homefromhome.ie For Northern Ireland, contact **Northern Ireland Self-catering Holidays**, T028-70822779, www.nischa.com

Self-catering tends to be more economically viable if part of a small group because the rent is fixed and beds for six or more people are more common than one-room apartments. Prices range enormously depending on the location and time of year. A house in Cork or Kerry in August could cost from €400-€750 a week, less than half that outside of the peak season or in less popular regions like counties Monaghan or Roscommon.

Hostels in Ireland fall into three basic categories: independent ones but belonging to a hostel organization, more traditional ones that belong to *Hostelling International* (HI), though they are still called Youth Hostels despite the fact that people of any age can use them, and truly independent ones that don't belong to any organisation. The traditional hostels have a membership scheme; the independent ones do not. Hostels can represent the best value for money when it comes to accommodation in Ireland. They also provide great opportunities to meet fellow travellers, chat and exchange information in an informal atmosphere. **Hostels**

Independent hostels There are two hostel associations in Ireland which do not require membership. The largest is the **Independent Holiday Hostels** (IHH), approved by Bord Fáilte, and a list and map giving full details of all their 150 member hostels is available from their Dublin office. They operate a book ahead system, and for a nominal fee a bed at the next hostel will be guaranteed. The other association is the **Independent Hostel Owners** (IHO), the original independent hostel group and still outside Bord Fáilte's domain, and a map and list of their 130 member hostels is available from their Donegal office.

The overnight fee for a bed, outside of Dublin, in high season is around €10 and this gives you a bed in a dormitory, varying in size from two beds to well over a dozen, and use of the hostel's facilities which at their most basic include an equipped kitchen, a common room with usually a television, hot showers (a very few hostels make a small charge for a shower), and telephone. Some hostels will provide free pick-up from the nearest town or village, some include a free continental breakfast and provide evening meals at reasonable prices and some will have camping space with use of all or some hostel facilities. Better equipped ones have laundry facilities, bicycles for hire and other amenities. It helps to travel with a sleeping sheet or sleeping bag, though some hostels include fresh linen and all will rent you sheets; duvets or blankets are freely provided. There is usually no curfew at independent hostels and you can stay indoors all day if you wish.

Most hostels will also have private rooms, usually for two people (though singles are available in some) or for a family with young children. Outside of Dublin, the price averages about €15 per person and this represents a very viable alternative to B&Bs if you are going to make use of the kitchen and prepare your own meals. At peak times, when some hostels get overcrowded, a private room does provide some private space and also minimizes the problem of being kept awake by inebriated hostellers returning early in the morning.

The Backpackers Press publishes annually *The Independent Hostel Guide: Britain & Europe*. This includes descriptions of some 40 hostels in Ireland, nearly all IHH and IHO but some completely independent ones as well, and is available for £4.95 (including postage) from their England address. It is not worth the money just for the Ireland section; far better value is *Ireland – All the Hostels* (£4) which carries details of all the hostels in Ireland, including the totally independent ones, plus short reviews of 200 of what are considered the best hostels.

Traditional hostels Traditional hostels, now under the general umbrella of Hostelling International, are, in the Republic, part of *An Óige*, the official Irish Youth Hostel Association, and the equivalent organization in the North is the *Youth Hostel Association of Northern Ireland* (YHANI). You can become a member for €15.24 at any of their hostels in Ireland or join through a Youth Hostel/Hostelling International in your own country. An Óige members receive a 20% discount on ferry passenger rates on Irish Ferries, (and smaller discounts on most other ferries, including ones to the to the Aran Islands, and Inishbofin) and there are discounts on car hire, some tours, some shops and a host of historical and cultural attractions. Various touring holidays, including cycling, walking and historical ones, can also be booked through An Óige. For £75, YANI offer seven days unlimited travel on buses and trains in Northern Ireland, vouchers for six nights of accommodation in their hostels and timetables.

So while it helps to be a member, anyone can still usually book a bed for the night, and the rates are usually a pound or more cheaper than the independent hostels; under 18s receive an even better rate. Hostel facilities can match those of independent hostels but some tend to be a little spartan. Some hostels have private rooms and some have outstanding locations and/or fine and spacious buildings. A free booking-ahead service is available at the hostels and many provide breakfast, packed lunches and evening meal. A disadvantage is that some close for part of the day, usually the afternoon, and some will have a curfew hour before which time you have to return.

Contacts *An Óige*, 61 Mountjoy St, Dublin 7, T01-8304555, F01-8364700, mailbox@anoige.ie www.irelandyha.org *Hostelling International-American Youth Hostels*, 773 15th St NW, Suite 840, PO Box 37613, Washington DC 20005, T1-800-4446111 *IHH Office*, 57 Lower Gardiner St, Dublin 1, T01-8364700, F01-8364710, ihh@oil.ie www.hostels-ireland.com *IHO Information Office*, Dooey Hostel, Glencolmcille, Co Donegal, T073-30130, F073-30339, www.holidayhound.com/ihi/ *Ireland – All the Hostels*, Flat 2A, 72 Woodstock Rd, Moseley, Birmingham B13 9BN, England *The Backpackers Press*, 2 Rockview Cottages, Matlock

Bath, Derbyshire, DE4 3PG, England, T/F01629-580427 *Youth Hostel Association (YHA) England & Wales*, 8 St Stephen's Hill, St Albans, Herts AL1 2DY, England, T01727-845047, F01727-844126, yhacustomerservices@compuserve.com *Youth Hostel Association of Northern Ireland*, 22-32 Donegall Rd, Belfast BT12 5JN, T028-90324733, F028-90439699.

Camping for free is a lot easier in Ireland than many other countries, but you should always take the trouble of finding the landowner and asking their permission. If you camp in a field near the farmhouse you should be able to access an outdoor water supply. Some farmers, in touristy areas mainly, may charge a small amount for camping in their fields.

Camping & caravanning

A number of independent hostels have an area set aside for camping, and usually the charge includes the use of hostel facilities.

Organized camping and caravan parks vary a lot in the level of services they provide, and this is reflected in the rates they charge, from €6to €15 for a small tent. Most places will also have different rates for campers on foot, on a motorcycle, in a car or a motor home. *The Irish Caravan & Camping Council* publish an annual illustrated guide, *Caravan & Camping Ireland*, available from PO Box 4443, Dublin 2. F098-28237, www.camping-ireland.ie This does not include all the camping sites in Ireland, and in tourist areas there are quite a few independent operators. For Northern Ireland, NRIB's *Where to Stay* guide covers all the camping and caravan parks.

You won't find the Irish using them, but horse-drawn gypsy-style caravans can be hired through tour operators like *Slattery's* or *Enjoy Ireland Holidays* (see page 24).

Getting around

Air

Aer Arann, T01-8141058 (in Ireland), www.aerarannexpress flies from Dublin to Cork, Donegal, Galway, Kerry, Knock, and Sligo. From Galway, *Aer Arann* flies to the Aran Islands. *British Airways*, T0845-7733377 (in Britain), www.britishairways.com operate a Dublin to Derry service.

Bus

Bus Éireann operates most of the buses in the Republic, but in some areas, like Donegal, private bus companies are an important supplement and no more expensive. *Ulsterbus* run the buses in the North. Bus Éireann offer various deals that improve on the cost of standard single/return tickets: day return tickets (costing little more than single fares), monthly midweek returns (Tue-Thu), student discounts, and family tickets covering a monthly return. A single ticket from Dublin to Cork is €17, an open monthly return is €26, and a student single fare is €13.33. Similar tickets for other journeys from Dublin are €12.19/€18.41/10.79 for Ballina, €11.43/€15.24/€9.14 for Galway, €15.87/€24.12/€12 for Doolin, €8.89/€12.70/€8.89 for Waterford, €13.97/€19/11.43 for Belfast. Bicycles are €6.35 single, whatever the journey, but space is limited and cannot be taken for granted.

Fares & timetables

If you are going to be using buses a lot it is worth buying the inexpensive *Bus Éireann* national timetable (fare information is not provided). Missing a bus, and they do run on time, can mean a long wait or even an overnight stay. *Ulsterbus* provide a free booklet detailing the express services between the main towns as well as booklets covering local area bus and train timetables. In the Republic few towns have a bus station as such, so you need to find out where they stop because there are no prominent signs; the relevant timetable is usually, but not always, displayed nearby. Large towns in the North have bus stations near the centre of town.

| Discounts & passes | Students with a Travelsave stamp (see page 36) on their ID receive deductions on bus fares in the Republic, while in the North an ISIC card will suffice. A *Rambler Pass* covers 3/8/15 day's travel out of 8/15/30 consecutive days in the Republic for €40/92/133. A *Rover Bus Pass* is similar but includes Northern Ireland and costs €114 for 5 days out of 8 consecutive days. In the North a *Day Tracker Pass* gives unlimited travel on trains on Sun for £3. See the 'Rail' section above for combined bus and train passes. |

Contacts For general *Bus Éireann* information: *Busáras*, Store St, Dublin 1, T01-8366111/8302222, www.buseireann.ie For *Dublin Bus*, T01-8734222, www.dublinbus.ie For *Ulsterbus*, T028-90333000, www.translink.co.uk.

Car

Drivers should carry a current licence and non-UK drivers will also need an international driving permit which is readily purchasable through motoring organizations in your country. If you are bringing your own car, bring the registration/ownership documents and check with your insurance company that your policy covers driving in Ireland. If you belong to a motoring organization like the AA, RAC or AAC, check with them before you depart because there is usually a reciprocal agreement with the Irish AA in relation to their 24-hour emergency breakdown service.

| Driving in the Republic | Driving is **on the left** and the national speed limit on main roads is 60 mph/96 kmph, 70 mph/112 kmph on motorways. In towns and built-up areas the normal speed limit is 30 mph/50 kmph but on approach roads to urban areas the speed limit is usually 40 mph/64 kmph. Front seat occupants must wear seat belts, and motorcyclists and their passengers must wear helmets. Unleaded petrol is around 83¢ per litre. Disc parking, purchasable in newsagents and displayed inside your car, applies to an increasing number of towns. |

| Driving in Northern Ireland | Driving is **on the left** and the national speed limit on motorways/freeways is 70 mph/110 kmph and 60 mph/100 kmph on other main roads. In towns and built-up areas the normal speed limit is 30-40 mph/50-60 kmph, but be guided by posted signs. Front seat occupants must wear seat belts and motorcyclists and their passengers must wear helmets. Unleaded petrol is around 75p per litre. |

| Car rental | Major car hire companies have desks at airports, ferry terminals and cities across Ireland. Car rental in the Republic is expensive, around €254-380 a week, and it is worth checking out advanced car hire booking or combined fly/drive or ferry/drive tickets when working out your travel to Ireland. Tourist areas have their own local car hire companies and these can often be a little cheaper. If a car hire deal is quoted at a rate that is significantly less than others check that it includes a collision damage waiver, for if this is not included the hirer will be responsible for the first €600-1000 of damage to the car. Car hire to people under the age of 23 is unlikely; over 21 is sometimes possible. Car hire in Northern Ireland follows more or less the same rules as in the Republic but it will cost less. If you are planning to drive between the North and the Republic, starting in either direction, check that this is allowed for under the contract. |

Contacts *Europcar* (ISA), T1800-667788 (Republic), T0800-667788 (Northern Ireland or Britain), www.europcar.ie is a reliable company with offices throughout Ireland. *Thrifty*, T0800-7830405 (Britain), www.thrifty.ie and *Argus*, T1800-973490 (Britain), www.argusrentals.com are also competitively-priced car hire companies. *Avis*, www.avis.com, *Hertz*, www.hertz.com and *Budget*, www.budgetrentcar.com have desks at the main airports.

There is always a risk in hitching, whatever your gender, so it can never be recom- **Hitching** mended as a safe way to travel; this applies to Ireland as it does to anywhere else in the world. Having said that, hitching in the Republic is fairly common, and you will often see single people and couples outside towns and cities patiently waiting for an oblig- ing driver. It will often take some time, but sooner or later someone usually stops and it can often lead to interesting and informative conversations. Hitching in Northern Ire- land is a lot less common, especially for single males, but getting lifts from the Republic into Northern Ireland does not present any special problems.

Bicycle

The weather notwithstanding, cycling around Ireland is definitely one of the most enjoyable and meaningful ways to explore Ireland (see page 24). Cycling allows you to experience the countryside in a way that cannot be compared to seeing it through the window of a car. Country roads, compared to Britain certainly, are less crowded with traffic and the experience can easily become the highlight of any visit to Ireland. An alternative to relying on a bicycle for the whole duration of your trip is to hire one for a few days, or for a week or more; see page 54 for more information.

Cruising

If holidaying in inland Ireland, cruising the rivers and canals is an option for all or part of your stay. *Carrick Craft*, T028-38344993 (Northern Ireland), www.cruise-ireland.com is a com- pany specializing in cruising the Shannon and Erne waterways. *Locaboat*, T078-45300 (Ire- land), www.locaboat.ie is another company, based in Ballinamore in county Leitrim, handling trips on the Shannon and Erne waterways. See also the box on page 635.

Rail

Trains in the Republic are run by *Iarnród Éireann* (Irish Rail), and while there are a num- **Fares &** ber of routes the system is by no means comprehensive and is very much based **timetables** around routes in and out of Dublin. Many parts of the west and the north are without trains. Sample return fares (and single fares are often almost as much and never half the price) from Dublin are €40 to Belfast, €44.50 to Cork, €29 to Galway, €45 to Killarney. In Northern Ireland, standard return fares from Belfast are £30 to Dublin and £12.30 to Derry. In the North, free booklets contain train and bus information for differ- ent areas, and are available from stations.

Students (see page 36) can obtain substantial discounts and non-students should **Discounts &** consider the various train, and train and bus, passes available. A €91 *Explorer Rail* **passes** *Pass* allows five days travel out of 15 consecutive days in the Republic and includes DART (page 67); the *Rover Rail Pass* is similar but includes Northern Ireland trains. A €135 *Explorer Rail/Bus Pass* allows 8 days of travel out of 15 consecutive days, in the Republic; for €157/271 for 8/15 days out of 30, the *Emerald Bus/Rail Pass* is similar but includes Northern Ireland trains. A *Freedom of Northern Ireland Pass* allows for 7 days unlimited travel on all rail and bus services for £40, unlimited travel for one day is £11 and for any three days out of 8 consecutive days is £27.50. A *Sunday Rambler* gives unlimited bus travel on Sun for £5. These passes are available from main train and bus stations, online and in the USA from *CIE Tours International*, T800-2438687.

Essentials

Overseas passes Rail passes that cover Europe are worth considering if Ireland is part of your itinerary. *Eurail Youthpass* is for travellers under 26 and starts at US$376 for 15 consecutive days; 1-month and 2-month versions are also available. A version for over-26s costs US$538. Perhaps more useful is the *Eurail Flexipass* which covers 10 or 15 days of travel in a 2-month period: for under-26s for 10 days the cost is US$444, over 26 and it costs US$634. These can be purchased in North America, Australia and New Zealand, through some travel agents catering for students as well as some tour operators, or contact *Rail Europe*, T1-800-4387245 in the USA (T1-800-5552748 in Canada), or *CIT*, 263 Clarence Street, Sydney, T02-92671255, or one of their branches across Australia. Internal train and bus passes can also be purchased in advance in Australia and New Zealand.

Contacts Tickets and passes can be bought at *Iarnród Éireann* Travel Centres, 35 Lower Abbey Street, Dublin, T01-703182, as well as main railway stations. Credit card bookings on T01-7034070 or T021-504888. Iarnród Éireann head office is at Connolly Station, Dublin 1, T01-8363333. Timetable information on T8366222, www.irishrail.ie *Northern Ireland Railways* can be contacted at Central Station, Belfast, T028-90899400, but for general enquiries T028-90333000, www.translink.co.uk

Keeping in touch

Internet Internet cafés are to be found in all Irish cities and large towns, and in a growing number of small towns and even villages. They are listed under 'Communications' in the Directory sections of this guide but you can also expect to find wall-mounted internet access points in the lobbies of many hotels and bars. These are coin-operated and the usual charge is around €0.63 for six minutes.

Post Postal services across Ireland are efficient and reliable, with a range of services that include recorded or registered mail. From the Republic, a standard letter or postcard to Britain or Northern Ireland, is 38¢ (up to 20g), to other EU countries is 41¢, and to the USA and the rest of the world is 57¢. In Northern Ireland, a letter or postcard to an EU country costs 37p and to anywhere outside the EU is 45p.

Most post offices in the Republic and Northern Ireland are open 0900-1730, Mon- Fri, and 0900-1300 on Sat. In rural areas and small towns the post office may close for one afternoon during the week, often on a Wed. For enquiries in the North T0345-740740.

Telephone
See inside front cover for dialling codes for phoning out of and within Ireland

Republic Public payphones are easy to find and come in two versions: coin-operated or cardphone-operated. Sometimes the two types are found next to each other in separate booths and sometimes there will only be the one kind available (and, increasingly, this will be the card-operated version). Phonecards, bought at newsagents and post offices, are more convenient to use, especially for long-distance or international calls. Phone cards are sold in various denominations and all calls, whether local, long-distance or international, are cheapest after 1800 or on a Saturday or Sunday.

Making an international call from the Republic T00+country code+area code (without the 0)+number. So, to phone the UK number 020-71231234, T00-44-20-71231234. To call Northern Ireland, however, T80+ area code (without the 0)+number.

Northern Ireland Public payphones, as in the Republic, are either operated with coins or cards (called phonecards), and sometimes the same payphone will accept either. In towns, and rural areas especially, coin-operated payphones are less common than card-operated ones.

Making an international call from Northern Ireland The procedure is the same as in the Republic: T00+country code+area code (without the 0)+number. So, for example, to phone the US number 01-212-1231234, T00-1-212-1231234. The same applies to phoning the Republic, so to reach the Dublin number 01-6024000 you would dial T00-353-1-6024000.

Using mobile phones Only digital phones with GSM subscriptions and a roaming agreement will work in Ireland. Check with your supplier before you leave.

Operator services

In the Republic
Emergency services	T999 or T112
Operator	T10

In the Republic and Northern Ireland
Irish (Republic and NI) enquiries	T11811
International directory enquiries	T11818
International operator services	T114
Telegram	T196

In Northern Ireland
Emergency services	T999
Operator	T100
Directory enquiries	T192
International directory enquiries	T153
International operator services	T155
Telegrams	T0800-190190

Fax If you need to send or receive a fax the first place to try is your place of accommodation, as all hotels, nearly all hostels and some B&Bs will have a fax machine which you will often be able to use for the cost of the call. The next best place to try is the nearest post office or public library, and if they don't have one they might be able to suggest the nearest place that does. In Northern Ireland, if you have a credit card, faxes can be sent over the phone on T0800-190190 for £7.11.

Media

Newspapers **Republic** The quality daily newspaper is *The Irish Times* and Saturday's edition is the best value for money. Of the other dailies, the *Irish Independent* is lighter in tone while *The Examiner* makes for more interesting reading. The *Star* is a fairly useless tabloid, as is the Irish edition of *The Sun*. All the English daily and Sunday newspapers are readily available on the day of publication, and in Dublin city centre, foreign newspapers are also available. Irish Sunday newspapers don't amount to much; the *Sunday World* is sensationalist and the *Sunday Tribune* is probably the best read. Counties produce their own local papers, and Dublin and Cork have evening papers, mainly of local interest.

Northern Ireland Apart from the British dailies there is the *Irish News*, read mainly by the nationalist community and usually a good read, and the tabloid *News Letter* which presents a staunchly loyalist view of events. The *Belfast Telegraph* is a local interest evening paper. *An Phoblacht* (Republican News) is a Sinn Féin weekly paper.

Magazines   There is a host of Irish-produced magazines catering to special interests and hobbies. The *Phoenix* is a satirical magazine along the lines of Britain's *Private Eye* and there is never any shortage of political and business scandals fuelling its contents. *Magill* is also worth reading when it uncovers a juicy story of yet more political shenanigans. *Hot Press* carries listings of musical gigs and other cultural events and its features on music, politics and much else is often interesting.

Television   RTE (Radio Telefís Éireann) runs RTE 1 and Network 2, 2 national stations in the Republic. RTE 1 broadcasts the more interesting news programmes and shows of cultural and historical interest. Network 2 has the occasionally riveting programme but the usual diet is a mix of chat shows, cheap films and serials. There is also an Irish-language channel (see page 25). Most British channels can be picked up in Ireland through satellite or cable. In Northern Ireland there are the British television channels, and the Republic's channels can also be received. Cable or satellite television is usually found in hotels and guesthouses, but too often only the basic package is subscribed to and the film channels are not available.

Radio   In the **Republic** three radio stations are also run by RTE: Radio 1, a disappointing mix of news and cultural programmes; 2FM for pop music; and Radio na Gaeltachta, which is an Irish-language station. There is also Lyric FM, a classical music station. Today FM 100-104 provides some competition to RTE and is best listened to in the evening. There is also a host of independent local stations. In **Northern Ireland** there is the full gamut of British radio stations and some local station.

Food and drink

Food

Restaurants
See inside front cover for restaurant price grades

The much-heralded wave of new Irish cooking does indeed have a lot going for it, and anyone returning to Ireland after an absence of a few years will be in for gastronomic treats. The best restaurants use local produce to serve up an array of traditional and modern dishes, and when it is done well the results are truly terrific and often good value for money. Sometimes a restaurant tries too hard to be international: Parmesan shavings and goat's cheese on a menu does not guarantee an interesting meal. Hotel restaurants sometimes use rich sauces to disguise overcooked food.

Seafood is often the highlight of menus in coastal counties, but do not assume that because a restaurant is near the sea its fish is absolutely fresh. It is not unknown for fresh fish to be landed, hauled up to Dublin and sold through a national wholesaler before being delivered to a restaurant close to where it was first landed. It is always worth asking how fresh the fish is, and more times than not you will receive an honest answer. Locally sourced beef and lamb is another speciality to look out for, and a steak or leg of lamb from Kerry should not disappoint. Vegetarian restaurants are very scarce outside of Dublin and Cork, and we have drawn attention to every one we could find. Most menus include a 'vegetarian dish of the day', but if it turns out to be lasagne then forget it, for in our experience that is one sure sign of a restaurateur's indifference to non-meat cuisine.

County Cork is currently enjoying a well deserved reputation for some of the best food in the country, and other counties in the west are beginning to catch up. Northern Ireland, with a few individual exceptions, is generally awful as regards eating out, and while Dublin, Wicklow and Wexford have some excellent restaurants, the capital city has its fair share of trendy and expensive dross. For a combination of value for money and a sense of occasion, excellent meals can be enjoyed in some of the country houses dotted around the country, and most of them welcome non-residents (and vegetarians) as long as a reservation is made in advance.

Where to go for a drink – not Dublin!

Unbelievable but true: Dublin is short of pubs. The capital has 29% of the population but only 9% of its pubs, an anomaly due to an antiquated system that makes it well nigh impossible to open new licensed premises (pub licences in the capital change hands for half a million punts). A 1902 law, strenuously upheld by the Catholic Church and the Licensed Vintners Association, puts the brake on new licenses being created other than for exceptional circumstances. Unfortunately, exceptional circumstances do not include population shifts and the result is that an area like Tallaght in Dublin has the record for the fewest number of pubs per head in the whole of Ireland. In the 1960s, when Tallaght was a village of 400 souls, there were eight pubs; it is now a working class suburb of nearly 90,000 people and the number of pubs is 10. A tragedy for people living there, but visitors can leave the capital and head for just about anywhere else – where the situation is just a little different…

Essentials

Restaurants offering Chinese food, and Indian to a lesser extent, are fairly common in the cities and a number of towns but, apart from a few noted places in Dublin, Kilkenny and Belfast, the food is fairly hideous; most offer a take-away service that is slightly better value. Italian restaurants offer good value, and many towns will have places serving pasta and pizza dishes, while the cities have Italian restaurants in their own right. There are also some interesting Japanese restaurants dotted around Ireland; as described in the text.

The price range for a restaurant is given in the text, but remember that this is an indication of the average price for main dishes. Expect to pay around €32 for a three-course evening meal, excluding drinks, and around €15 for lunch in a fairly formal restaurant.

Pub food The quality of the food varies enormously, but pubs are nearly always your best bet when looking for an informal and affordable meal at lunch or dinner time. Many pubs serve food from 1200 to 2100 and some will have separate dining areas. The standard price for a pub lunch is around €7, and while there is a tendency to rely on the standard meat/fish with potatoes/chips and vegetables, pubs in tourist areas can be relied on to offer alternatives. Home-made soups may not be filling enough for everyone, but they are often tasty, and salads and open seafood sandwiches are worth considering. Unless you ask for brown, expect tasteless white bread.

Bars in hotels, especially at lunchtime, offer comfortable seating most of the time, and competition from pubs ensures that their prices are similar. There is no obligation to consume alcohol as other drinks are also available. Pub food in the North is generally disappointing: the idea of a meal without meat seems quite foreign, overcooked vegetables and unimaginative presentations the norm. Champ, potatoes mashed with spring onions, is a tasty speciality in the North, and there are some superb soda breads.

Picnic food When the weather is fine, a picnic lunch is a satisfying and economical way to enjoy a meal, and every town has a supermarket or two, the larger ones with a delicatessen section, and often a good bakery where fresh delicious breads and scones are usually available. Local cheeses are always worth seeking out, and such is their popularity that you will often find them far from their origins. If a town has a river there will usually be bankside benches or somewhere suitable to lay out your food, and while planned parks are not so common most towns are not far from the countryside.

Drink

Ireland is not in the top 10 list of alcohol-consuming countries of the world, but it ranks second, after the Czech Republic, in the list of beer-drinking countries, at 250 pints/142

👈 For peat's sake have a whiskey

There are many differences in the distilling process that account for the distinct taste of Irish whiskey as opposed to Scotch whisky (but they don't account for the spelling), and the peaty smokiness of Scotch is often contrasted with the smoothness of Irish. This seems odd to some tipplers who appreciate the spiky aromatics found in some Irish whiskeys and, besides, there is an Irish single malt called Connemara that is sweeter and

more peaty than most Scotches. Millar's and Inishowen are blended whiskeys distilled by the same company, and they also turn out an unpeated single malt called Tyrconnell. Bushmills whiskey, smooth and creamy indeed, is distilled in County Antrim (see page 545), while Jameson comes from Midleton near Cork (see page 279). Near-relations of Jameson's are Power's and Paddy, and Tullamore Dew.

---

litres per year per head of the population. (The UK ranks in seventh position at 180 pints/102 litres and the USA is ranked 13th.) **Guinness** is the world-renowned Irish drink, and it is no idle boast that the best pint of Guinness is served in Ireland, Dublin to be exact, and if you have tasted draught Guinness in an ordinary pub in Britain this will soon become apparent. Guinness with oysters is a classic lunchtime dish, and on some menus you will see the famous black stuff featured in dishes. There are alternative stouts, and both Beamish and Murphy's should be sampled; they are not only cheaper, but fine drinks in their own right. A variety of lagers, draught and bottled, is also readily available in all pubs. A pint of beer costs around €3 and unless you ask for "a glass (ie a half pint) of Guinness", or whatever your drink is, a pint will automatically be served.

Irish **whiskeys** taste quite different to Scotch and there are quite a few you can try in order to be convinced. A hot whiskey comes with cloves and lemon and is a heart-warming drink on a cold day. Any spirit served in a pub is a substantially larger measure than its counterpart in Britain or North America.

Wine in pubs is most likely to come in the form of a ¼-bottle, and costs around €3. It is not that usual to order a whole bottle of wine in a pub and while it is possible there is often not much of a choice. Some restaurants have a BYO (Bring Your Own) policy and a reasonable choice of wines is available in most supermarkets. Expect to pay at least €7 for the cheapest, and usually not very palatable, wine and from around €12 and upwards for a half-decent bottle.

Non-alcoholic drinks come in the form of a limited choice of bottled beers and outrageously priced soft and fizzy drinks. A cup or pot of tea is available in nearly all pubs and coffee is served with milk.

Shopping

What to buy Visitors from Britain or North America will not find any spectacular shopping bargains in Ireland, but that does not mean there aren't lots of interesting and well priced purchases to be considered. As a general rule, the best buys are in the form of Irish-produced craft and art products like clothing, pottery and jewellery, and tourist areas all have shops filled with a wide choice of possibilities. In these shops you will find everything from tacky leprechaun-shaped telephones to expensive hand-knitted garments, and if you are travelling around Ireland they are a good place to start in order to get some idea of prices, because you will usually come across similar stock in another tourist town.

Aran sweaters, named after the County Galway islands where the women traditionally knitted them, are world famous. If you prefer something less chunky and white, there is a choice of shawls, skirts, blouses, and jackets for both sexes, in a variety of materials from thick tweeds to fine linens.

Top 10 pubs

O'Connor's Pub, Fisherstreet, Doolin, County Clare (page 385)
Mansworth's, Midleton St, Cobh, County Cork, T811965 (page 278)
The Smugglers Creek, Rossnowlagh, County Donegal (page 493)
Fisherman's Bar, Valentia Island, County Kerry, T9477103 (page 337)
Crown Liquor Saloon, Great Victoria St, Belfast (page 572)
M Hughes, Chancery St, Dublin (page 113)
Henry Downes, 10 Thomas St, Waterford, County Waterford (page 233)
House of McDonnell, Ballycastle, County Antrim (page 549)
Neachtain's, Cross St, Galway (page 409)
Fitzpatricks, Kilcrohane, County Cork (page 302)

Irish pottery can be exquisitely beautiful, and is available to suit most budgets both in terms of quality and quantity. It mostly takes a practical form in the shape of plates, mugs, bowls, table lamps, clocks and candlesticks, but decorative items, like the Belleek pottery that comes as brooches and little pots of flowers, are also available, and some of the more expensive pottery is best reserved for display anyway. A similar mix of the practical and decorative is found in Irish crystal, of which the Waterford variety is famous around the world.

The craft shops that sell pottery often have small but enticing collections of Irish jewellery which are often fashioned around Celtic designs; look out also for the distinctive Claddagh rings that originated in Connaught and are composed of a crowned heart nestling between a pair of hands, or jewellery worked in the form of Ogham script. You can often have a necklace made with your own name on it in Ogham.

Irish memorabilia takes myriad forms if looking merely for souvenirs or small gifts, including penny whistles with sheet music, shillelagh walking sticks which are traditionally made of blackthorn or oak, carved pieces of Connemara marble and CDs of traditional music ranging from John McCormack to Shane McGowan.

Where to buy

Individual shops worth mentioning are found under the Shopping section for particular towns and cities. Many travellers to Ireland first arrive in Dublin, and if this is where you will also depart from then it makes sense for serious shoppers to conduct a reconnaissance trip around the major shops (see page 124), taking note of the merchandise and their prices, before returning to make purchases after having travelled elsewhere. Some of the best crafts and arts are found in small workshop premises outside of the capital.

For Aran sweaters and other garments, some of the best clothing stores are to be found in the counties of Galway and Donegal, and to a lesser extent Wicklow. The city of Limerick is associated with Irish lace products. Small and large pottery shops are dotted all around Ireland but for real quality head for Kerry, particularly the Dingle Peninsula, and West Cork. The village of Belleek in Fermanagh, easily reached from Donegal, is famous for its bone china. Wexford also has some good pottery shops also in and around Kilkenny there are noted workshops. Outside of Dublin, Kilkenny has a claim to be the single best shopping city in Ireland, and there are quality examples of most crafts and arts as well as jewellery and pottery workshops to the south of the city. For crystal there is the Waterford factory with its comprehensive display of items for sale, but in the city of Waterford itself it is possible to purchase less expensive crystal products and there are other areas in the country that produce their own modest examples of this craft.

Shopping on the Internet

A growing number of Irish shopping outlets are adding an Internet-based mail order service to their offerings. Among those worth a visit are www.iol.ie/gnorman-photography (a gallery with outlets in Dublin and Kinsale); www. houseofnames.ie (House of Names, with heraldic shops in Dublin and Killarney); www. celticrhythm.com (Soundz of Muzic in Kenmare); www. heritagecrystal.com (Heritage Crystal in Waterford); www.moriartys.ie (tourist shop at the Gap of Dunloe in Kerry); and www.kilkennydesign.com (Kilkenny Design Centre in Kilkenny).

Entertainment

For specific listings, see the Entertainment section for each individual town

Ireland is very much a pub-orientated country. There are pubs to suit all tastes, from a quiet drink in surroundings untouched since Edwardian times to theme bars and sports bars. In summer especially, pubs means music and you needn't go a night without listening to someone singing or playing. Festivals are another flourishing activity in Ireland. There are festivals (see below) for every imaginable reason from all the sports, to walking, poetry, music, theatre, film, ploughing, coming home, going away, flowers, fish. Bantry even celebrates small sea creatures with a Mussel Fair.

The cities have good theatres, with a strong tradition of local dramatics as well as major theatre companies. Watching a local theatre group doing a Beckett or a John B Keane play can be worth a week of London's West End theatre. The theatres also play host to music and comedy events with Irish and British big names doing sell out tours.

Variations on the Riverdance theme abound in every tourist destination, or you can try out a medieval banquet at one of the castles around Limerick and Clare.

Sports too (see below) are fully catered for, whether it be hang gliding in West Cork, surfing in Bundoran, deer hunting in Kerry, golfing practically everywhere. Horse racing is an especially Irish sport and the race meetings are always a source of great fun.

Holidays and festivals

See the Festivals section of individual towns for information on local festivals

A *Calendar of Events*, a useful joint publication by Bord Fáilte and the NITB, has an awesome list of festivals held up and down the country along with dates, contact names and telephone numbers. It also lists the Irish racing calendar. Don't be too taken in by this, however, because tourist boards always feel overly obliged to present their countries as festive places brimming with carnival spirit. St Patrick's Day has never been a particularly festive occasion; those events that are now held on in or around the 17 March are nearly all recent inventions, and publicans and other merchants have recently seen the value of manufacturing and hosting local festivals at sundry times of the year. There are some notable exceptions with venerable histories and/or real carnival spirit, as well as some excellent annual cultural events, and these, plus some of the more successful recent inventions, are listed above. The dates refer to 2001 and may change slightly from one year to the next, so always check in advance and enquire from the tourist boards about literature specific to individual events. See also the box above.

Sport and special interest travel

Walking
The Northern Ireland Tourist Board dispense a useful booklet detailing 14 walks on the Ulster Way, accompanied with maps and sources of information

Walking is the least expensive and most ecologically sound activity worth pursuing in Ireland, and there are now some 30 waymarked trails covering over 1,492 miles (2,300 km) as well as countless local walking routes in scenic areas. Worth consulting are some of the specialist walking guidebooks that cover the whole country but, unless walking is going to be your sole activity for a fair length of time, they are a less worthwhile investment than some of the smaller books that focus on popular walking areas and which are ideal for one-day walks if staying a while in a particular region (see 'Books', page 677, and on the web www.obrien.ie for one of the main publishers). Bord

Major festivals and events 2002

(2002 dates unless otherwise stated)

Strokestown Poetry Festival	*4-6 May (2001)*
www.strokestownpoetryprize.com	
Listowel Writers' Week	*29 May-4 Jun*
www.writersweek.ie	
Kilkenny's Cat Laughs Festival	*31 May-2 Jun*
www.thecatlaughs.com	
Bloomsday (Dublin)	*16 Jun*
T.01-878 8547	
Galway Arts Festival	*18-28 Jul*
www.galwayartsfestival.com	
Galway Races	*29 Jul-4 Aug, 9-11 Sep, 27-8 Oct*
www.iol.ie/galway-races	
Kilkenny Arts Festival	*9-18 Aug*
www.kilkennyarts.ie	
Puck Fair (Killorglin)	*10-12 Aug*
www.puckfair.ie	
Connemara Pony Show	*16 Aug*
T095-21863, enquiries@cpbs.ie	
All Ireland Galeic Football Finals	*fourth Sat in Sep*
Wexford Festival of Light Opera	*21-30 Sep*
T051-375437, maor@eircom.net	
Galway Oyster Festival	*26-29 Sep*
T091-527282 www.galwayosyerfest.com	
Dublin Theatre Festival	*2-14 Oct*
www.dublintheatrefestival.com	
Cork International Film Festival	*7-14 Oct (2001)*
T021-427 5945, info@corkfestival.org	
Kinsale Festival of Fine Food	*10-13 Oct*
T021-477 2382	
Cork Jazz Festival	*25-8 Oct*
www.corkfestival.com	
Belfast Festival at Queens	*25 Oct-10 Nov*
T028-9066 3733, info@belfastfestival.co.uk	
Dublin Marathon	*28 October*
www.dublinmarathon.ie	
Wexford Opera Festival	*Oct-Nov*
T.053-224000 info@wexfordopera.com	

Fáilte (the Irish Tourist Board) sells an inexpensive **Walking Ireland** booklet that describes each of the waymarked Ways and gives contact details for further information, accommodation, travel and maps.

Detailed information about some of the more popular long-distance walks, such as the Kerry Way, the Beara Way, the Dingle Way and the Sheep's Head Way, are included in this book, and shorter details are given of some of the others (see below). To complete all or part of the best waymarked trails all that is really needed are the relevant **Ordnance Survey Discovery Maps** at a scale of 1:50,000 (2.5 in to 1 mile/2 cm to 1 km); they show the routes of the Ways. **EastWest Mapping**, Ballyredmond, Enniscorthy, County Wexford (T&F054-77835) also publishes 1:50,000 scale maps of particular Ways. It is worth checking with the *Ordnance Survey Service*, Phoenix Park, Dublin 8 (T01-8206100; F01-8204156) or *Ordnance Survey of Northern Ireland*, Colby House, Stranmillis Court, Belfast BT9 5BJ (T028-90661244) to see which is the latest update available and whether the route of the Way is included. Tourist offices in Dublin, Belfast, Cork and Galway, as well as smaller local tourist offices in the relevant areas, also sell mostly inexpensive guides covering a particular Way, such as those published by EastWest Mapping, and these can be a useful supplement to the Ordnance Survey maps. The Ordnance Survey maps are available in the big bookshops in Dublin, as well as the *Government Publications Sales Office Bookshop*, Sun Alliance House, Molesworth St, Dublin 2 (T01-6613111), and are often available in local bookshops and tourist offices around the country. For walks requiring overnight stays it is essential to have accommodation booked in advance.

Organized walking holidays, usually including airport transfers and luggage transport between accommodation stops, are available through various companies, including *Irish Ways*, The Old Rectory, Ballycanew, Gorey, County Wexford, T055-27479, info@irishways.com and *Go Ireland*, Killorglin, County Kerry, T066-9762094; freephone 0800-371203 (from the UK), 800-7214672 (from the USA), www.goactivities.com

For specialist walking holidays in the Burren contact *Burren Walking Holidays*, Carrigann Hotel, Lisdoonvarna, County Clare, T065-74036, F065-74567; and *Fertile Rock Study Tours*, Station Road, Lahinch, County Clare, T&F065-81168. For hikes on the Iveragh Peninsula, including guided trips to Ireland's highest mountain, contact *Wilderness Tours*, Climber's Inn, Glencar, County Kerry, T066-60101, F066-60104, climbers@iol.ie For walks in the vicinity of Kells in county Meath, contact *Keltic Walking Holidays*, White Gables, Headfort Place, Kells, County Meath, T046-49672, keltic@tinet.ie As an example of prices, Keltic Walking Holidays do a weekend walking package for €177 which covers accommodation, meals, transport and 2 days guided walking. A 3-day trip is €266.

British tour operators who also cover walking holidays include *Enjoy Ireland Holidays*, suite 425, Glenfield Park 2, Blackburn BB1 5HQ. T01254-692899, www.enjoy-ireland.co.uk; *Overseas Travel and Tourism,* T0870-7567000, www.ot-t.com In the USA, *Backroads*, T1-800/GO-ACTIVE, 4622848, www.backroads.com specializes in walking and cycling holidays.

For walking holidays in Northern Ireland contact *Enjoy Holidays* above, *Dal Riada*, 68 Station Road, Portstewart, Northern Ireland, T028-832832, www.dal-riada.com

Walking World Ireland is a monthly magazine that carries detailed maps and commentary on walks all over the country; it is available from newsagents or on subscription from 288 Harold's Cross Road, Dublin 6 (T01-4923030; F01-4923089).

Cycling There are very few motorways in Ireland so nearly all the roads can be cycled. There is a vast network of quiet country roads, and distances between towns and villages are never prohibitively long. Bicycles can brought to Ireland by air or boat, but check with your airline or ferry company for their policy and prices. Within Ireland, north or south, it is possible to carry bicycles on buses, and on nearly all train routes (but not the DART system around Dublin); prices vary, so always check.

Bicycles can be hired on a daily or weekly basis in most towns across Ireland: the daily rate varies from €9 to €13; weekly rates are around €45, plus a returnable deposit. There are also countless independent operators who operate on a local basis and details are given under the particular town. *The Federation of Irish Cyclists* can be contacted at 619 North Circular road, Dublin 1. T01-8551522. *Shannon Development*, Shannon Town Centre, Shannon, County Clare, T061-361555, have useful free leaflets detailing cycling tours in the region. The Northern Ireland Tourist Board issue a very useful *Information Guide to Cycling* with maps for suggested routes, details of bike

A genealogical trip

If you are planning a genealogical fieldtrip, it helps enormously to carry out some preliminary research before reaching Ireland. Try to establish the county and townland from which your ancestors departed plus full names, maiden as well as married ones, and dates of birth, marriage and death. Sources worth exploring in your own country include birth, marriage and death records, immigration and naturalization papers, and ships' passenger lists. For general information and details of local centres within the Republic contact the **Genealogical Office**, *2 Kildare St, Dublin 2, T01-603-0200, www.nli.ie or the* **Office of the Register General**, *T01-6354000, www.groireland.ie For Northern Ireland, contact* **The General Register Office**, *Oxford House, 49 Chichester St, Belfast BT1 4HL, T028-90252000.*

Central records prior to 1922 are held in Dublin, but the Belfast General Register Office will arrange for searches to be made of births, marriages or deaths in Northern Ireland before 1922. **The Public Record Office of Northern Ireland**, *66 Balmoral Ave, Belfast BT9 6NY, T028-90251318, F028-90255999, www.proni.nics.gov.uk does not conduct research but visitors can make their own searches there. In Dublin, records are kept at the National Library, T01-6030200, and the National Archives, Bishop St, Dublin 8, T01-4072300, F01-4072333.*

Birth, death and marriage certificates are available from the Office of the Registrar General, Joyce House, Lombard St East, Dublin 2, T01-6711000.

Bord Fáilte have a booklet, **Tracing your Ancestors in Ireland**, *which is packed with useful contact addresses.*

Essentials

hire places and operators offering package holidays. Bord Fáilte have a Cycling Ireland map highlighting the best cycling routes and giving basic details.

Organized cycling holidays are operated by a number of companies who include all or some services like bike hire, airport transfers, luggage storage and transport, booked accommodation, tours for groups or individuals, plus maps and route descriptions. For an idea of prices, *Irish Cycling Safaris* cost €685 per person per week, €305 for a weekend trip, and cover 7 nights hotel/guesthouse accommodation, bicycle rental, tour guide and luggage van. *Irish Cycle Hire* offer a 7-day Dingle Peninsula tour for €830 for two people, including bike, accommodation and packed lunches.

Contacts *Go Ireland* in Britain and *Backroads* in the USA (see under 'Walking'). *Celtic Cycling* (specializing in the southeast), Lorum Old Rectory, Bagenalstown, County Carlow, T0503-75282, www.celticcycling.com *Celtic Trails*, 28 Upper Fitzwilliam Street, Dublin 2. T01-6619546, F01-6619547, celtictrails@compuserve. com, www.celtictrails.com *Classic Adventures*, in the USA, T1-800/7778090. *Irish Cycle Hire*, T041-6853772, irch@iol.ie *Irish Cycling Safaris*, Belfield House, UCD, Dublin 4. T01-2600749, www.cyclingsafaris.com *Kingfisher Cycle Trail*, Tourist Information Centre, Wellington Road, Enniskillen, County Fermanagh BT74 7EF. T028-66320121, F028-66325511 *McCycle Tours*, 2 Brookesborough Road, Maguiresbridge, County Fermanagh, BT94 4LR. T028-6621749. *Raleigh in Ireland*. T01-6261333, www.iol.ie/raleigh. Bikes can be reserved in advance €12.70 a day, €50.79 a week. *South East Cycle Tours* (specialising in the south-east), 1 Mary Street, Enniscorthy, County Wexford, T&F054-33255, seastcyc@iol.ie *Sheep's Head Cycling*, West Cork, T027-61606 *Wrightlines*, The Old Mill, Ballydown, Banbridge, County Down BT32 5JN. T028-40662126. See also: www.irelandrentalbike.com

Ireland has some magnificent beaches, and while most are safe for **swimming** there are some that can be dangerous. Most of these are mentioned in the text but it is always   **Water sports**

Walking the Way

To give some idea of the walking possibilities here are brief details of some of the best Ways:

Wicklow Way *Ireland's first long-distance trail is 82 miles (132 km) in length and starts in south Dublin and finishes in Clonegal in the east of County Carlow. The entire Way would take at least 10 days but it is easy to choose a shorter section and variety of terrain is a feature of the Way; longest one-day stage is 14 miles (22 km). Map guides are available (see page 169) and Ordnance Survey Maps Nos 50, 56 and 62 cover the entire route.*

Kerry Way *Through and around the Iveragh Peninsula and infinitely more enjoyable than driving around the Ring of Kerry. Total length is 134 miles (214 km) and the longest stage is 15 miles (24 km). Some sections are more enjoyable than others (see page 346); map guides are available in Killarney or Kenmare and Ordnance Survey Maps Nos 78, 83, 84 and 85 show the route.*

Beara Way *Spectacular in places (see page 310) as it weaves its way around the Beara Peninsula in Kerry connecting Kenmare, Glengarriff and Castletownbere, with Dursey Island thrown in for good measure. Total distance is 120 miles (196 km); longest stage is 14 miles (23 km). Ordnance Survey Maps Nos 78, 84 and 85.*

Dingle Way *Another circular route, this time around the Dingle Peninsula, with the western end of the Way far more fulfilling than the east (see page 368). Total length 95 miles (153 km) and longest stage is 15 miles (24 km). Ordnance Survey Maps Nos 70 and 71.*

Sheep's Head Way *Starts and ends in Bantry in West Cork with some spectacular views of Bantry Bay and Dunmanus Bay along the way (see page 303). Total length is 55 miles (88 km) and longest stage is 10 miles (16 km). Ordnance Survey Maps Nos 85 and 88, and a local map and guide is available.*

Burren Way *Only 22 miles (35 km) but covering the jagged terrain of this unique landscape noted for its geological features, archaeological remains, special flora and the magnificent Cliffs of Moher. Longest stage is 12.5 miles (20 km) and Ordnance Survey Maps No 51 covers the route.*

Western Way *Starts at Oughterard in County Galway, and follows the shore of Lough Corrib and then through mountain ranges and down into the narrow valley of Killary Harbour. This leg is 31 miles (50 km)*

worth checking, especially if no one else is in the water. **Windsurfing** is growing in popularity. A list of recognized windsurfing schools in the Republic is available from the *Irish Sailing Association*, 3 Park Road, Dun Laoghaire, Dublin, T01-2800239, www.sailing.ie

Surfing beaches in the west of Ireland include Achill Island, Easkey in county Sligo, and Spanish Point and Lahinch in Clare. Further south, there is Castlegregory on the north side of the Dingle Peninsula, Inch on the south side, Caherdaniel on the Iveragh Peninsula and Barley Cove on the Mizen Peninsula. In the southeast, Rosslare Strand in County Wexford, and Dunmore East, Tramore, Ballinacourty and Dungarvan in County Waterford are all noted for their surfing beaches. In the north, Portrush on the north Antrim coast is the main surfing centre and here, as in most of the other areas (but not Barley Cove), it is possible to hire equipment and garner local information. *The Irish Surfing Association* is based at Tirchonaill St, Donegal, T073-21053.

Scuba diving For information on all aspects of scuba diving in Ireland contact the *Irish Underwater Council*, 78A Patrick St, Dun Laoghaire, Co Dublin, T01-2844601, www.indigo.ie/scuba-irl Their website has links to other sites and details of all the diving centres around Ireland are listed. *Subsea*, Ireland's diving magazine, is also online here.

Sailing Contact the *Irish Sailing Association* (ISA), 3 Park Rd, Dun Laoghaire, Dublin, T01-2800239, F01-2807558, www.sailing.ie They provide literature on visitor

in total. The second leg runs from Killary Harbour across County Mayo to the Ox Mountains near the Sligo border. Superb variety of terrains, including the unique boglands of Mayo. Total length of this second leg is 110 miles (177 km) and Ordnance Survey Maps Nos 23, 24, 30, 37 and 38 are required to cover the whole route. Local map guides available.

Grand Canal Way Perfect for the beginner, being flat all the way as it follows the canal; the starting point is reached by bus from Dublin to Lucan or Milltown. Total distance is 71 miles (114 km) and the longest stage is 18 miles(29 km).

Royal Canal Way A walk along the towpath of the Royal Canal from Dublin for 48 miles (77 km), eventually linking up with the River Shannon at Clondra in County Longford. The longest stage is 15.5 miles (25.5 km) and Ordnance Survey Maps Nos 12, 13 and 16 are needed. Information on this Way and the Grand Canal Way from **Waterways Service**, Department of Arts, Heritage, Gaeltacht and the Islands, 51 St Stephens's Green, Dublin 2 (T01-6613111).

Ballyhoura Way A 50-mile (80 km) walk between Limerick Junction, just north of Tipperary town, and St John's Bridge (nearest town is Kanturk in north Cork). The longest stage is 15 miles (24 km) and although parts of the Way are through forestry plantations this is compensated for by the route over Castle Philip and through the Ballyhoura Country Park. Ordnance Survey Maps Nos 65, 66, 73 and 74.

Lough Derg Way Lough Derg is one of the main lakes on the River Shannon, and the best part of the walk is along the eastern shores of the lake. Total distance is only 32 miles (52 km) and the longest stage is 11 miles (18 km). Contact **Shannon Development**, Shannon Town Centre, Shannon, County Clare, T061-361555, who also have information on other walks in the region.

Ulster Way The total length is around 560 miles (900 km), so choices have to be made. Sections following the north Antrim coast, the Glens of Antrim, and the Mourne Mountains (called the Mourne Trail) are the best, plus the 69-mile (111 km) Donegal section. Advance planning is necessary: The Northern Ireland Tourist Board has information on sections and Paddy Dillon's book (see page 681) should be consulted.

---

moorings as well as information on ISA-approved sailing programmes in dinghies, keel boats, catamarans and powerboats. **West Cork Sailing Centre**, Adrigole, Beara, County Cork, T27-60132, www.westcorksailing.com, is a good example of the kind of regional sailing centre available in the west of Ireland, offering courses for children and adults.

Canoeing Contact the *Irish Canoe Union*, House of Sports, Long Mile Rd, Walkinstown, Dublin 12, T01-4509838. Canoeing trips are run by *Shannon Adventure Canoeing Holidays*, The Marina, Banagher, Co Offaly, T&F0509-51411, and *Tiglin Adventure Centre*, Ashford, Co Wicklow, T0404-40169.

Water skiing Contact the *Irish Water-Ski Federation*, 29 Hermitage Rd, Lucan, Co Dublin, T01-6240526.

Ireland's reputation as Europe's last unspoilt fishing location is built on its unpolluted **Fishing** waters, a plenitude of fish-bearing rivers, miles of coastline and hundreds of game fishing lakes. There are superb opportunities for game and coarse angling, as well as sea angling. In the Republic, salmon and trout fisheries are either privately owned or managed by the state or angling clubs and organizations. Permits are required, the cost of which varies from €7 to €65 per day depending on the location. A state national licence is also required for salmon and sea trout fishing: a 21-day licence costs around €13, a daily license is €4. These are obtainable at local tackle shops, from the **Western Regional Fisheries Board**, The Weir Lodge, Earl's Island, Galway, T091-563118, or from one of the other regional boards in Ballyshannon, T072-51435, Ballina, T096-22788, Limerick, T061-55171, Macroom, T026-41222, or Clonmel, T052-23624. Licences are not needed for brown trout, rainbow trout, coarse fishing or sea angling.

In Northern Ireland a rod licence is required. For the Foyle area this is obtainable from the **Foyle Fisheries Commission**, 8 Victoria Rd, Derry BT47 2AB, T01504-42100; for other regions from the **Fisheries Conservancy Board**, 1 Mahon Rd, Portadown, Craigavon, County Armagh, T01762-334666. The cost of a licence for outside the Foyle area is £4 for one day, £21.50 for the season. Wherever you fish, a permit is also required, costing £5 for one day or £15 for 8 days, obtainable from the **Department of Agriculture**, Dundonald House, Upper Newtownlands Rd, Belfast BT4 3SB, T028-90520100.

Bord Fáilte publish a useful *Angling in Ireland* booklet with practical information about accommodation and charter-boat operators, and separate booklets on sea angling and coarse angling. The regional Fisheries Boards are also worth contacting for information and literature on their areas: **Western Regional Fisheries Board**, The Weir Lodge, Earl's Island, Galway. T091-563118, info@wrfb.ie **The North-Western Regional Fisheries Board**, Ard na Rí House, Abbey St, Ballina, County Mayo. T096-22788, info@nwrfb.ie; **The Shannon Regional Fisheries Board**, Thomond Weir, Limerick. T061-455171, info@shannon-fishery-board.ie **Ireland West Tourism**, Áras Fáilte, Galway, T091-563081, F091-565201, dispense a useful brochure, *The Coarse Angler's Paradise*, covering Counties Galway, Mayo and Roscommon and including practical information on suitable accommodation. **Game Angling Ireland West** is a similar brochure available from the Fishery Boards. **The Great Fishing Houses of Ireland**, PO Box 6375, Dublin 4, www.irelandflyfishing.com, issues a booklet with details of hotels specializing in fishing holidays. These include the *Pontoon Bridge Hotel* (see page 469) which runs courses for beginners as well as catering to old hands.

Many of the general tour operators, see above, organize specialist fishing packages and in the USA there is also **Fishing International**, T1-800/9504242.

Golf There are more golf courses per head of population in Ireland than anywhere else in Europe, ranging from lush parkland courses in the east to rugged and challenging links courses on the western coastline. Contact Bord Fáilte and the Northern Ireland Tourist Board for general literature and information on specialist golfing packages. Dublin Tourism dispenses *Golfing Around Dublin*, listing all the courses, their services and green fees. www.golfing-ireland.com is worth looking at and South East Tourism in Waterford dispense a useful *Golfers' Guide* with practical information on local golf courses and accommodation. Green fees range enormously: at H*otel Carrigart* in County Donegal residents can play for free on a links course, at *The K Club* in Straffan, County Kildare (designed by Arnold Palmer) residents can expect to pay €165. Average fees are in the €13 to €25 range.

Equestrian The possibilities range from a small farm with horses to hire by the hour to top-notch riding establishments offering post-to-post trail riding, instruction in show jumping, dressage and polocrosse. Contact Bord Fáilte and the Northern Ireland Tourist Board for literature and information. **Equestrian Holidays Ireland** issue a booklet with details of riding establishments in Ireland; T021-831950, www.ehi.ie Other contacts are **The Association of Irish Riding Establishments**, 11 Moore Park, Newbridge, Co Kildare, T045-431584, F045-435103; **The Association of Irish Riding Clubs**, 8 Main Street, Bray, Co Wicklow, T01-2860196; **The Irish Pony Club**, Tinnascarty, Freshford, County Kilkenny, T056-82966, www.irishponyclub.ie The southeast is especially resourceful in this area and a guide to *Equestrian Activity in Ireland's South East* is available from tourist offices in that region.

At Colmcille in County Donegal there are Irish language courses for adults as well as cultural activity holidays with separate week-long programmes in bodhrán and flute playing, Donegal dances, marine painting, archaeology, Celtic pottery, tapestry weaving and some other pursuits. For a brochure write to *Oideas Gael*, Gleann Cholm Cille, Co Dhún na nGall, T073-30248, F073-30348, oideasgael@iol.ie oideas-gael.com

Culture & crafts

There are various summer schools that can provide a focus for cultural, and especially language and literary interests. For details of the *James Joyce Summer School* that lasts a week and takes place in Dublin each July write to Helen Gallagher, Newman House, St Stephen's Green, Dublin, T01-7068480. For the *Yeats International Summer School* in Sligo each July, another annual week-long event, write to Sheila McCabe, Hawk's Well Theatre, Sligo, T071-42693, F071-42780.

Details of short courses given by craftspeople across Ireland, with accommodation sometimes arranged, available from the *Crafts Council of Ireland*, Castle Yard, Kilkenny, T056-61804, www.ccoi.ie This is your chance to take up basketry, furniture making, hedge laying, silver smithing, stone work and much else besides.

Essentials

Health

There are no alarming facts or fears to take into account when travelling within Ireland. The water is safe to drink, no inoculations are required or necessary, and there is a generally excellent health service; to cap it all there are no snakes and little danger of sunburn.

See the Directory of individual towns for information on local hospitals

Make sure you are covered for emergency medical treatment in Ireland. Visitors from **EU countries** are entitled to free medical treatment, but to facilitate this bring with you a Form €111 from your country (available from post offices in Britain). British visitors can receive emergency treatment and medicines without ever having to show this form, but it is still advisable to bring it because in some circumstances it could make a difference. British visitors to the North require no documents and will receive treatment as they would in Britain. Visitors from **non-EU countries** are charged for all medical treatment except out-patient treatment at accident and emergency units of public hospitals. **Medical insurance** is therefore highly advisable for those citizens.

What to take

Travel insurance is essential for all visitors to Ireland from outside the EU. A good policy will cover loss or theft of luggage, including money, and it will also cover medical expenses including emergency expatriation.

A **first aid kit** is useful and should include pills for possible hangovers and/or stomach upsets as well as any an adequate supply of any prescribed or essential drugs or medicines. Walkers should be prepared for blisters and small cuts and a compass is advisable for walks in mountainous areas.

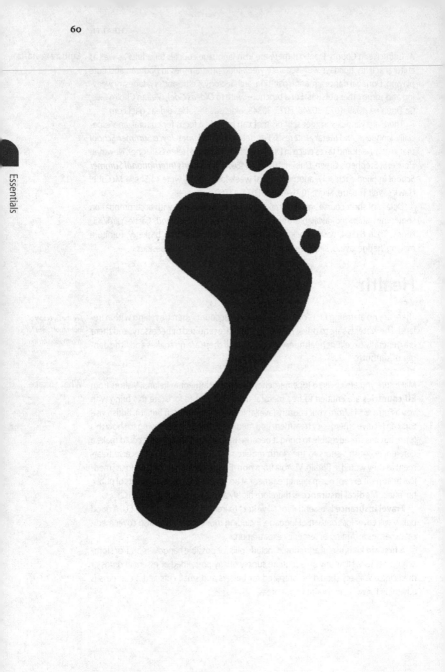

Dublin

3

Dublin

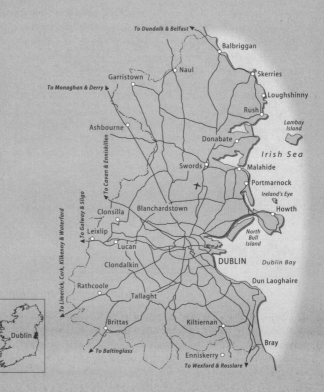

Dublin's marriage of modernity and tradition is an unsteady relationship, with neither side quite sure about accommodating the needs of their very different partner. The statue of the 19th-century nationalist Daniel O'Connell looks across the River Liffey to a grand old building that now retails an English soccer team's merchandise, and a gaudy sex shop has its premises opposite the General Post Office, symbolic heart of the unfinished business of the 1916 nationalist uprising. Harmony is attained when new wealth is used to celebrate the past, as with the National Gallery's new Millennium Wing, the Hugh Lane Gallery's acquisition of the London studio of Francis Bacon, or the new premises for the Chester Beatty Library. This is Dublin's fresh complexion, a city able to express pride in her culture and history, although modernity seems to have triumphed when young Dubliners adopt the dress sense and style of Eurokids. Don't, though, be deceived into thinking they are city folk born and bred. Many of them are from small Irish towns, villages or farms. They have come to Dublin for employment, or to study, but their childhood was spent in the countryside or in small agricultural towns surrounded by fields and farmland. In this way, traditional patterns of life and thought give a nuance to Dublin's city life. Dubliners love to talk, and they love talk with a deprecating pinch of banter and wit. They love to undermine highfalutin ideas with a touch of homespun irony and talking to Dubliners and listening to their line in chat is one of the highlights of any visit to Dublin.

Dublin

Ins and outs

Getting there

Dublin Airport
Dublin has one airport, T8444900, 12 km (8 miles) north of the city

The airport has **money exchange** facilities (there's a branch of the *Bank of Ireland* and a counter in the arrivals area), car hire desks, taxis and public transport to and from the city. In the main arrivals hall is a *Dublin Tourism* counter, open daily from 0800-2200 (2230 in Jul and Aug), which can book accommodation. Next to it is a *CIE* counter with information on bus transport. There are also left-luggage facilities as well as assorted shops, bars and cafés, and a post office at car park level. A **taxi** from the airport to town should cost around €23. For more details see page 129.

Bus
For more detailed information, see Transport page 128

There is no train service from the airport. *Dublin Bus* run 2 Airlink Express buses: the No 747 service to and from O'Connell St, the Central Bus Station and Connolly Rail Station, and the No 748 service to and from the Central Bus Station, Tara St DART station, Aston Quay and Heuston Rail Station. The fare is €4.57 single, €7.62 return; prepaid tickets are available at the CIE information desk in the arrivals hall; Rambler Tickets are valid on the Airlink service. The No 747 runs every 10-20 mins, from 0545 to 2330 from the

Dublin orientation

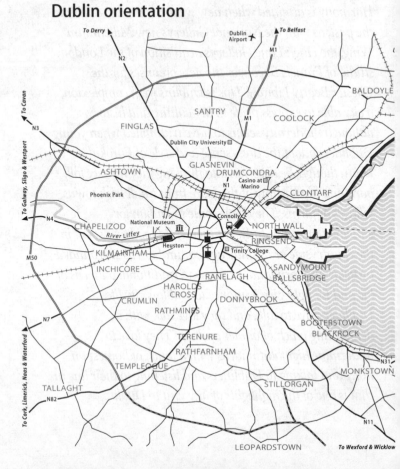

Things to do in Dublin

- Marvel at the hordes of gold in the **National Musuem**
- Take a healthy and historical walk around **Phoenix Park**
- Admire the floor tiles in **Christ Church Cathedral**
- Gawk at the **Book of Kells** in Trinity College
- Potter about in **Mother Redcap's market**
- Listen to the buskers in **Grafton Street**
- Enjoy dinner at **Ryans** in Parkgate Street
- Visit the dead famous in **Prospect Cemetery**, Glasnevin

airport (0715 to 2330 Sun), and from 0515 to 2250 from O'Connell St (0735 to 2315 Sun). The No 748 runs about every 30 mins, from 0625 to 2130 from the airport (0700 to 2205 Sun), and from 0710 to 2220 from Heuston Station (0750 to 2250 Sun).

Local buses Nos 41 and 41B travel between the airport and Eden Quay, cost €1.90 but take up to an hr. Their bus stop is outside the airport next to the Airlink Express bus stop. Bus Nos 16 and 16A travel between the airport and Aungier St, via O'Connell St and Drumcondra Rd. Bus No 58X is an express service that departs from the airport at 1710, Mon-Fri, to O'Connell St and Kildare St. There is also the No 746 service that runs between the airport and Dun Laoghaire, via Drumcondra Rd and Pembroke St, between 0915 and 2145 Mon-Fri, 0945 to 2145 on Sat and between 1000 and 1900 on Sun.

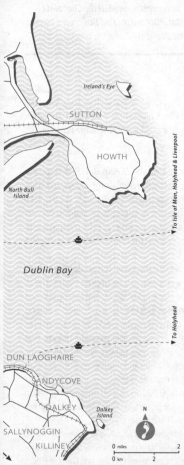

Ireland's Eye

SUTTON

HOWTH

North Bull Island

To Isle of Man, Holyhead & Liverpool

Dublin Bay

To Holyhead

DUN LAOGHAIRE

SANDYCOVE

DALKEY

Dalkey Island

N

SALLYNOGGIN

KILLINEY

0 miles   2
0 km   2

Another option is the privately run *Aircoach*, T8447118, www.aircoach.ie that operates every 15 mins from and to the airport between 0530 and 2330, €5.08 (children free); useful if staying south of the river because, unlike the Airlink Express, it runs to Merrion Sq, Pembroke Rd, Merrion Rd, Simmonscourt Rd and Donnybrook Rd before returning to the airport via Leeson St, St Stephen's Green, Dawson St and O'Connell St.

Dublin ferry ports Ferries from Britain dock at either **Dublin Port**, Alexandra Rd (3 km/2 miles east of the centre), T8722777, or **Dun Laoghaire** (for *Stena Line*), T2047700. From Dublin Port, Bus No 53 meets incoming ferries and takes passengers to the Central Bus Station. From Dun Laoghaire, there are DART trains and buses (see page 135) into the city centre. Some coach companies run their passengers into Dublin from the ferry port.

Dublin

Dublin

24 hours in Dublin

Try the **full Irish breakfast** (or, if available, Irish smoked salmon and scrambled eggs – particularly good in Ireland).

Spend the morning among the museums, wondering at the **gold at the National Museum**, admiring the **Picasso in the National Gallery** and shuddering at the things in alcohol in the **Natural History Museum**. If it's Saturday book yourself on to the amazing tour of the **government buildings**.

For lunch try **Chapter One** (Mondays excepted) for a really classy lunch or wander around Temple Bar and pick a café or a pub (try **Gallagher's Boxty House** for a traditional Irish potato pancake).

In the afternoon it's time for a bird's-eye view of the city. The **Guinness Storehouse** provides the view and a pint of Guinness as well, or try the **Chimney** at Smithfield for another panoramic view. If you want to fit in a spot of shopping, **Kildare Street** and **Nassau Street** have the best Irish crafts while there are more regular stores in Grafton Street.

For dinner it's back to Temple Bar and the charms of **Fitzer's** or **Eden**. For an ethnic dinner you can't beat **Rajdoot** in Clarendon Street. After dinner enjoy a drink in **Dohenny & Nesbitt** in Baggot Street or take a walk over to the **Brazen Head**, Dublin's oldest bar where, if you are lucky, there'll be some music on offer.

If all this hasn't exhausted you then your next port of call will probably be Harcourt Street where the clubbers get going around 2300. **Beaujangles** suits the thirtysomethings while the **Chocolate Bar**, **POD** and the **Red Box** are the hippest destinations in town.

Getting around

Central Dublin is such a tiny area that you can walk everywhere

If you are in Dublin for only a few days the chances are that you will get around mostly on foot, with the occasional bus ride to cross from one side of the river to the other. Buses, however, can be very useful for saving time and for reaching some noted places of interest that are not in the city centre.

Local bus
Dublin Bus, 59 Upper O'Connell St, T8734222, www.dublinbus.ie

The local buses, fairly frequent and cheap, are run by *Dublin Bus*. Bus stops are painted green, and carry a timetable. You pay the driver on entry and should have the correct fare if you know it; up to 3 stages costs €0.75, 4-7 stages €1.05, 8-13 stages €1.30, and 14 or more €1.45. Banknotes are not accepted and if you deposit more than the exact fare the driver issues a passenger ticket for the overpayment. Presenting this ticket and your original travel ticket at the O'Connell St office allows a cash refund.

A schedule covering all bus routes & timetables costs €1.90

See also colour street map of the city at the back of the book

If you plan to get about the city a lot by bus there are several **concessionary tickets** which will make travel easier and cheaper and which can be bought from some of the bigger newsagents as well as the tourist office in Suffolk St, and the Dublin Bus Head Office in O'Connell St, T8720000. **Rambler Tickets** allow unlimited travel on buses and cost €4.57 for 1 day, €8.89 for 3 consecutive days, €12.97 for 5 consecutive days and €16.51 for 7 consecutive days. There are also **prepaid tickets** that allow unlimited bus travel and the use of the DART light railway system. These cost €6.60 for one day, while the weekly one costs €21.59 and requires a photo ID ticket available from Dublin Bus. The monthly ticket costs €79.99.

A daily **Family Bus Travel Wide** ticket costs €7.20 and allows unlimited travel on buses. For €9.50 you can buy a family pass for bus and DART, and for €12.70 per adult a 4-day unlimited off-peak bus and DART travel pass.

There is a range of **student offers** for which you need an ISIC and Travelsave stamp (obtainable from Dublin Bus Head Office in O'Connell St). A student weekly ticket for unlimited bus travel is €13.30 and a monthly student ticket covering buses and DART is €60.

Dublin

The Easter Rising in Dublin

In 1916 a group of Republicans, led by James Connolly, Padraig Pearse, Joseph Mary Plunkett and Thomas McDonagh, seized the GPO and several other sites in Dubin in the vain hope that their stand would prompt other Republicans throughout the country to follow their lead and take up arms in the cause of Irish independence. In Dublin the Post Office was an unofficial focal point for the city and was the first place to be taken by Pearse and Connolly, with a complement of 1,200 supporters. The proclamation of the Irish Republic was read from the front steps of the building. Other contingents took St Stephen's Green and the College of Surgeons, and City Hall which was designated a field hospital.

The life of the city went on around the fighting with many non-combatants suffering. Those in the post office resisted for five days before withdrawing their troops. Countess Markievicz, not knowing about the surrender, held out for another day at the Royal College of Surgeons, but she too surrendered and, like the other leaders, was sentenced to death, reprieved only for fear of the international outcry sure to follow the execution of a woman. If the city wasn't roused to open rebellion by the sight of the republicans being shelled in the Post Office, both it and the world were outraged at the summary executions that took place afterwards, Connolly strapped to a chair since he was too badly injured to stand and face the firing squad.

Bus services stop at around 2330 but *Nitelink* buses run every Thu, Fri and Sat from the city centre to the various suburbs and cost €3.80.

Dublin's light railway system, DART (Dublin Area Rapid Transit), links the coastal suburbs with the city centre and is useful for short hops between the south and north of the city and for transport to some suburban areas where accommodation and the occasional place of interest are located. The system operates between Howth and Malahide to the north and Greystones in County Wicklow to the south. The trains are clean and fast but get very crowded at peak times. You cannot take bikes on the DART.

Rail
Pearse St Station, Dublin 2, T8363333, www.irishrail.ie

Dublin Tourism Centre, Suffolk St, T1850-230330. Jun-Sep, Mon-Sat 0900-2030, Sun 1100-1700; Oct-May, Mon-Sat 0930-1730. *Dublin Tourism*, Baggot St Bridge, 0930-1715.

Tourist information

History

Dublin's history has been a turbulent one. Celts gave way to Norsemen, who were driven out by Gaelic-speaking Irishmen, who in turn folded under the assault of the Normans. The English, in one form or another, held the city through many attempts to wrest it back into Irish hands, from the 1798 uprising to the 1916 Easter Rising. Finally Irish again in 1922, the city went into economic decline, from which it has recently been reborn, like a post-modern phoenix, all designer bars and on-line businesses.

Population: 900,000 Phone code: 01 Colour map 4, grid A2 & 3

The Viking town of Dyfflin, a corruption of the Irish name, *dubh linn*, probably established itself around 917 under Ivar the Boneless. Around 1000 the Vikings built a *thingmote*, a huge earth mound where they held meetings; College Green now stands there.

The Vikings

In 997 coins were being minted and in 1030 a wooden church was erected on the site of what is now Christ Church Cathedral. The settlement had around 5,000 citizens and was the first urban settlement in Ireland. The

Vikings gradually intermarried, learned Gaelic and converted to Christianity, and it is probable that the Battle of Clontarf in 1014, generally considered to be the moment when Viking power in Ireland was broken, had Vikings on both sides of the battlefield.

The Normans The Anglo-Norman invasion began in 1169 and Dublin was taken in 1170 by an army led by Richard FitzGilbert de Clare, Earl of Pembroke, better known to history as Strongbow. The Vikings still did not leave but shifted to Oxmantown on the north bank of the Liffey. By the 14th century they had become completely assimilated into the Anglo-Norman Gaelic society.

Reformation & restoration In the 16th century the Reformation freed the lands of the religious orders around the city and a wave of building began. Trinity College was built on land formerly owned by a religious order, and other monastic buildings were dismantled for use as building materials.

In the 18th century the first Georgian planned streets were constructed, to the northeast and southeast of the city. Grand public buildings were constructed as well as elaborate town houses, which expressed the confidence of the Anglo-Irish in their ownership of the city. Dublin became the second city of the British Empire, and each Anglo-Irish family kept a town house in one of the Georgian mansions, where they lived during the winter months. The city became the national centre for trade and commerce as well as the seat of government.

Dublin's decline The decline set in after the 1798 uprising: Britain saw Ireland as an unstable colony and passed the Act of Union, dissolving the Irish parliament. The effect on Dublin was enormous. With no parliament sitting, the landowners left for their country estates. Houses stood vacant and industries that had serviced their owners went into decline. Then, 46 years later, the Famine brought thousands of sick and homeless into the city. The great Georgian mansions became tenements.

The decline continued into the 19th century. Half the city's families lived in one-room slums in the old Georgian houses and the infant mortality rate soared. Most of the working classes were employed as casual labourers and experienced long periods of unemployment. By the turn of the century Belfast had replaced Dublin as the industrial heartland of Ireland and events such as the Great Lockout of 1913 (which started when Dublin employers compelled workers to withdraw from the Transport and General Workers Union or face dismissal, and climaxed with 20,000 workers on strike or locked out of their factories), and the 1916 Easter Rising burdened the city even further.

Modern times The Irish Free State began a series of planned housing developments, creating the suburbs of modern Dublin. Unobtrusively, in the 1990s Dublin began to revive, first with the development of the Temple Bar area, and then as businesses found cheap property and a well educated workforce desperate for employment. Now, the Celtic Tiger, as the economic boom in Ireland has been called, has finally put an end to two centuries of decline for Dublin. Today it is near impossible to walk down a city street without seeing planning application notices; and mobile-phone transmitters scar the skylines.

Sights in the centre

Grafton Street and around

With **Trinity College**, the **National Museum** and **National Gallery**, the **Bank of Ireland** and lots more places to see, this is the heart of tourist Dublin where restaurants, gift shops and pubs lie thick on the ground. Most of the big sights are well worth the visit and in between all the tourist stuff and places where Dubliners go about their everyday business are little gems of history, architecture, art and human nature. The main sights get very crowded during the summer months, with the biggest hordes around the **Book of Kells**, so if you need some time out, have a picnic by the waterfall in **Iveagh Gardens**, go for a stroll in **St Stephen's Green**, stop off for afternoon tea at the *Shelbourne Hotel*, or watch the Grafton Street buskers in the early evening. The area is bounded by Dame Street to the north, the canal to the south and Aungier and South Great George's Street to the west.

Pearse St & Tara St stations. For further transport information, see page 129

Founded in 1592 by Queen Elizabeth I, in the hope that it would prevent the young Protestant intellectuals of the Pale going to Europe and discovering Roman Catholicism, Trinity College opened its doors to Catholics in 1793, but few attended because of an edict against the college by the Catholic Church; women were admitted in 1903.

Entering Trinity College from the hurly-burly of College Green, you discover a little time capsule of smooth lawns, cobble stones, statuary and formal buildings, looking more like Oxford's dreaming spires than some of the Oxford colleges themselves do. Walking through the main gate, you see to your right and left two symmetrical buildings, the **chapel** and the **theatre**, both designed by the Scottish architect, Sir William Chambers, in the 1770s. The Chapel, originally Anglican, is now multi-denominational; its points of interest are original plasterwork, painted windows and Ionic columns. Over to your far right, behind the theatre is the **Provost's House**, built in 1759 from a copy of a mansion designed by Palladio. It has been lived in continually since that time by the various Provosts of the university.

The squares of Trinity College are dominated by the tower, or **campanile**. Beside the campanile is a Henry Moore statue, *Reclining Connected Form*. On the right side of the campanile is the finest building on the campus, the **Old Library**, built between 1712 and 1732. Trinity Library's collection began in 1601 and several famous libraries have been bequeathed to it. Since 1801 the Library has had the right to a copy of every book published in the UK, and its total collection now exceeds two million books. The library's most famous book is, of course, the *Book of Kells*.

Trinity College
Walking tours meet at the main gate; price includes entry to the Long Room where the Book of Kells *is kept*

Other examples of Chambers' work in Ireland are the Casino at Marino and Charlemont House (now the Hugh Lane Gallery) in Parnell Sq (see page 91)

The Book of Kells The crowds around the colonnades indicate the presence of the *Book of Kells*. This area has been transformed into an excellent display about the production of ancient manuscripts with two huge reproductions of pages from the *Book of Kells* explaining the religious symbolism and highlighting the work which went into its manufacture. Most fascinating are the unintentional signs of the craftsmen who made the book: holes in the vellum where the artist has worked around the damaged spot, the lines he drew to get his columns level, hair follicles still visible on the parchment and the unfinished final pages of folios 29v to 31r.

If you want a good browse without having to shuffle past in the crowd, plan your visit early in the day

Dublin

Besides the *Book of Kells*, the Library contains Trinity's collection of ancient books, including the 807 AD *Book of Armagh* and the late seventh-century *Book of Durrow* (an illustrated version of the Four

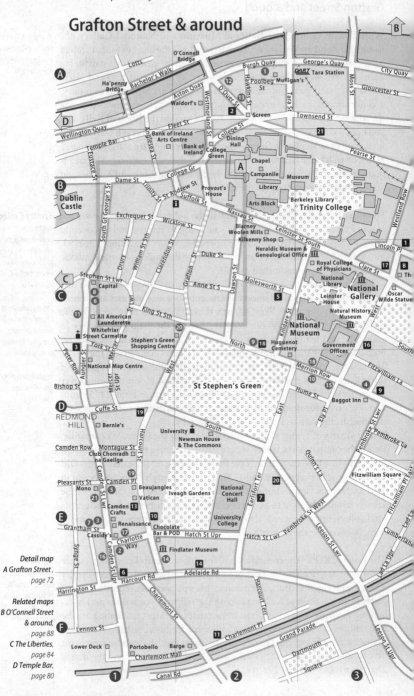

Grafton Street & around

Gospels, even older but less beautiful than the *Book of Kells*). After viewing the books on display you can go upstairs to see temporary exhibitions in the 65-m Long Room while admiring the barrel-vaulted ceiling and oak bookcases.

Dublin

■ Sleeping

1 Alexander *C3*
2 Ashfield House *A2*
3 Avalon House *C1*
4 Baggot Court *E4*
5 Buswell's *C2*
6 Camden Court, Court Restaurant & Pishogues *F1*
7 Conrad & Alexander Restaurant *E2*
8 Davenport *C3*
9 Georgian House *D3*
10 Harcourt *E1*
11 Hilton *F2*
12 Holiday Inn *B4*
13 Jackson Court & Copperface Jack's Nightclub *E1*
14 Kilronan Guesthouse *E2*
15 Latchfords Guesthouse & Restaurant *E4*
16 Merrion *C3*
17 Mont Clare *C3*
18 Shelbourne & Side Door *C2*
19 Stephen's Green *D1*
20 Stephen's Hall & Morel's Restaurant *E2*
21 Trinity Capital & Fireworks Club *B3*

● Eating & drinking

1 Beanery Café *A2*
2 Bleeding Horse *E1*
3 Devitt's Bar *E1*
4 Doheny & Nesbitt *D3*
5 Flannery's *E1*
6 Govinda's *C1*
7 Havana Tapas Bar *E1*
8 Hogan's *C1*
9 Il Posto *C2*
10 Kitty's Kaboodle *D3*
11 Long Hall *C1*
12 Messrs Maguire *A2*
13 Mona Lisa *A2*
14 Odeon *E1*
15 O'Donoghue's *D3*
16 One Pico *E1*
17 Pig & Heifer *E1*
18 Rubicon *D3*
19 Saagar *E1*
20 Wagamama *C2*
21 Whelan's *E1*

■ *Mon-Sat, 0930-1700; Sun, Jun-Sep, 0930-1630; Sun, Oct-May, 1200-1630. €5.71. Under-12s free. Closed for 10 days over Christmas and New Year. T6082320.*

The Arts Block Across Fellowes Square from the Old Library is the Arts Block, built in 1980 to a design by Paul Koralec. Inside is the **Douglas Hyde Gallery**, which shows collections of conceptual and avant garde art. ■ *Mon-Thu, 1100-1800, Fri, 1100-1645. Free.*

In the same building is the **Dublin Experience**, a 45-minute audio-visual description of Dublin from Viking times to the present. ■ *Late May-early Oct, 1000-1700, daily. €4.13. T6082320.*

Berkeley Library and Museum Building The east end of Fellowes Square is dominated by the Berkeley Library (1967, Paul Koralek) which is much admired by architects and considered to be the finest example of architecture of that period in Ireland. Beyond it is the Museum Building, now the Engineering Department. Built towards the end of the 19th century when the Victorian love affair with the Gothic form was at its height, the stonework was chosen for its decorative effect as well as its suitability as a building material. Inside, the columns and balustrades are made of

Grafton Street detail

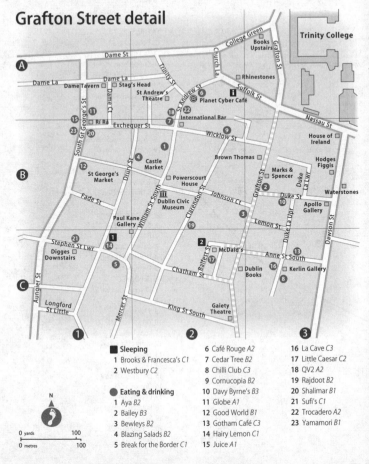

■ **Sleeping**
1 Brooks & Francesca's *C1*
2 Westbury *C2*

● **Eating & drinking**
1 Aya *B2*
2 Bailey *B3*
3 Bewleys *B2*
4 Blazing Salads *B2*
5 Break for the Border *C1*

6 Café Rouge *A2*
7 Cedar Tree *B2*
8 Chilli Club *C3*
9 Cornucopia *B2*
10 Davy Byrne's *B3*
11 Globe *A1*
12 Good World *B1*
13 Gotham Café *C3*
14 Hairy Lemon *C1*
15 Juice *A1*

16 La Cave *C3*
17 Little Caesar *C2*
18 QV2 *A2*
19 Rajdoot *B2*
20 Shalimar *B1*
21 Sufi's *C1*
22 Trocadero *A2*
23 Yamamori *B1*

The Book of Kells

Probably made around 800 AD, the Book of Kells is one of the oldest books in the world. It is thought to have been created by the monks of St Colmcille's monastery on the island of Iona, off the Scottish coast, and brought to the monastery at Kells in County Meath for safekeeping from the Viking raids on that island. Its beauty lies in the full-page illustrations, the minuscule creatures drawn on every page, and the wonderful illustrated capital letters that adorn this Latin version of the Four Gospels. In his Voices of Ireland, *P J Kavanagh quotes from a technical account explaining where the monks found their colours: "reds from red lead and kermes, made from the pregnant body of a Mediterranean insect (kermoccus vermilio) ... mauves and maroons from a Mediterranean plant (crozophora tinctoria) ... shades of blue from lapis lazuli ... brought via merchants of many nationalities from mines in the Badakshan district of Afghanistan in the foothills of the Himalayas!" It now consists of 680 pages, having lost 30 of the opening and ending folios during its turbulent history.*

It was stolen from Kells and buried, and then rediscovered in 1007; later the shrine it was kept in was taken by a particularly philistine Viking, who saw no value to the pages but just wanted the valuable metal casket. In 1653 the book was brought to Dublin through the efforts, there is good reason to suppose, of Henry Cromwell, the son of the infamous Oliver. In 1661 it came to Trinity College and in 1953 it was rebound into 4 volumes, two of which are usually on display; the pages are turned regularly. Ironic indeed, that such a national icon should have been saved by the efforts of the son of the most execrated man in Ireland.

different-coloured marbles, and the domed ceilings are covered in multi-coloured tiles. The exterior stonework is abundantly carved – the masons, the O'Shea brothers from Cork and Mr Rowe of Lambeth, London, were allowed to carve the stone at will in the manner of the medieval churches. Inside the main doors are the skeletons of two giant Irish elk, as well as some cabinets containing fossils and the like, while upstairs is a small geological museum. ■ *T6081477. Appointment to view necessary.*

The Bank of Ireland With its sweeping niched walls, Ionic porticos and piazza, enclosed by projecting pavilions, this building is altogether far too grand to house a humble bank. It is in fact the old Houses of Parliament, dissolved by the Act of Union in 1801.

The building was built between 1729 and 1739, at a time when Parliament represented the interests of the Protestant Anglo-Irish. Of 300 members, 234 were elected by a single patron, while the other 66 were elected on a narrow property-owning male franchise. Two houses, the Commons and the Lords, met at various times, every other year or every two years. For a time, during the period of 'Grattan's Parliament', it became fiercely independent of England, although never suggesting Catholics might be represented by its members. In 1801 it meekly voted itself out of existence, fearing independence and the Catholics far more than control from London.

In 1790, the original octagonal House of Commons was destroyed by fire and rebuilt as a circular chamber, and then in 1804 the building, no longer needed as a parliament house, was sold to the Bank of Ireland on the understanding that all signs of its former role would be destroyed. The bank's founders reneged on part of their promise, remodelling only the Commons as a boardroom and offices. But the Lords remains intact, complete with original

King Billy's usual mount, the white mare scrawled by loyalists on walls in Belfast, is here converted to a brow one

Dublin

☞ Bank Architecture

Some excellent examples of Victorian bank architecture are to be found in the vicinity of Trinity College and the Bank of Ireland.

The **Allied Irish Bank (AIB)**, at 3 Foster Place, off College Green, is a good place to start. A dozen highly decorated, cast-iron columns support the roof that looks down on a horseshoe-shaped counter. Across the road, at 27 College Green, **the National Irish Bank** has a fine set of carved heads linking the windows on the exterior. The

Venetian-style interior is replete with Byzantine columns and a dizzyingly ornate ceiling over the original mahogany counter. A few doors down, the **Bank of Ireland**, 34 College Green, has a fine central dome. But the most impressive bank of all was the **AIB** at 5 College Street with its stupendous Corinthian columns and frieze depicting capitalism as a benign force for the general good. The bank building is now the banqueting hall of the new Westin Hotel.

oak-panelled fireplaces, carved to an Inigo Jones design by Thomas Oldham, a carpenter who lived in Moore Street. Also kept in the room are 1730s tapestries depicting the Battle of the Boyne in 1690 and the Siege of Derry in 1689.
■ *Mon-Fri 1000-1600, (Thu 1700). Free admission and free tours of the Lords: Tue, 1030, 1130, 1345 (except bank holidays). T6776801.*

Story of Banking Museum
The safe depository still holds unopened trunks left there by victims of the Titanic

In the **Bank of Ireland Arts Centre** is the Story of Banking Museum, with self-congratulatory exhibitions on the wonderful things banks have done for the country over the centuries. The tour lasts about 40 minutes and includes a video aimed at the museum's many teenage visitors and potential future customers. There are often free lunchtime concerts in the main hall. Note the Trophy of Arms on top of the Arts Centre's exterior, echoing the time when the building functioned as an armoury for the militia who guarded the bank in the 19th century. ■ *Tue-Fri, 1000-1600. €1.90. Admission by tour only.*

Kildare Street to Merrion Square

Just south of Trinity College and tightly packed with museums and other places to visit, the area between Merrion Square, the Georgian heartland of Dublin, and the main gate of Trinity is Dublin's tourist centre. Starting from the corner of Leinster Street and Kildare Street, a whole day could be spent wandering around. First, though, look at the building on the corner of the two streets, the Kildare Street Club as was, now the **Heraldic Museum and Gene-alogical Office**, 2 Kildare Street. Designed in 1861 by Deane and Son, the same firm that built the museum in Trinity College, this red-brick and limestone edifice has fancy carved animals around its window-sills; one of them, a bunch of monkeys playing billiards, is said to be the stonemasons' comment on the wealthy men inside. If you like heraldry this is just the place for you, with exhibits of all kinds of examples of coats of arms, coins, seals and what not. ■ *Mon-Fri 1000-1630. Free. T6614877.*

Heading up Kildare Street to the next big stop, Leinster House, you pass on your left the **National Library**, which is open to the public, designed in 1884-90 by Deane and Son, as part of the complex of the National Library and Museum. The entrance to the library often holds exhibitions, and the reading room is certainly worth a look, especially for fans of the novel *Ulysses*. In December 2000 the library purchased a draft manuscript of the Circe chapter of *Ulysses*, handwritten by Joyce and given to one of his benefactors, John Quinn. It is quite unique in that it shows a stage where Joyce is choosing words

Kathleen Lynn, national hero

The Road to Independence exhibition traces one of many paths; but Kathleen Lynn (1874-1955) chose a very different road to freedom. Growing up in a respectable Protestant family in County Mayo, the daughter of the local vicar, her childhood years witnessed the struggle for land reform in Ireland. At an early age she decided to be a doctor – a radical step for a woman anywhere in Europe at the time. After graduation she was unemployed for some years since her male colleagues refused to allow a woman to work with them. She joined the suffragette movement as medical attendant during their hunger strikes and then joined the Citizen Army, a trade-union based nationalist organization run by James Connolly. She trained women as ambulance workers and nurses for the forthcoming armed struggle and began visiting the houses of the men involved in the great lockout strike of 1913, experiencing first hand the dire poverty in which thousands of Dublin families lived. At the same time she learned to drill and use a gun. When the uprising began in Dublin Kathleen Lynn was Chief Medical Officer and spent the week in City Hall
treating the many people who were brought in from the battle which raged around Dublin Castle. As senior officer there she surrendered her troops to the British and was imprisoned in Ship Street Barracks, Kilmainham and then Mountjoy. A massive petition was organized by the people of Dublin and, following her release from jail in 1918, she continued to take part in the yet-unresolved fight for Irish independence. She sat on the Sinn Fein National Council in 1917, making sure that equal rights for women were written into the constitution, campaigned to get political status for republican prisoners, campaigned for Constance Markeivicz, and was one of five women elected to the Dáil in 1923.

Outside politics she built and financed through fundraising a free children's hospital, and together with Dorothy Stopford Price, in 1936, undertook Ireland's first, groundbreaking BCG vaccination programme at a time when tuberculosis was decimating the population of Dublin, particularly its children. Her research was eventually taken up by Dublin Corporation, despite opposition by the Archbishop of Dublin John Charles McQuaid.

and elaborating on his ideas but not yet producing a final draft. It cost the library an arm and a leg at auction in New York and is now on display in the library. ■ *Kildare St. Mon-Wed, 1000-2100, Thu-Fri, 1000-1700, Sat, 1000-1300. Free. T6030200.*

Leinster House

When Parnell Square in north Dublin became a little too nouveau riche around 1745, James Fitzgerald, the Earl of Kildare, decided to move out to the country, and had a house built south of the river. The chattering classes said he was mad, but before long his peers were fighting each other to move south before all the space was taken. When Kildare became the Earl of Leinster he changed the name of his house to suit his title. His son, Edward, was a radical who fought in the American War of Independence and grew to admire the French Revolution. He would doubtless have become a leading figure in the United Irishmen's insurrection in 1798 if he had not been arrested and mortally wounded before the rebellion took place. Seventeen years later Edward's son sold the house to the Royal Dublin Society, which turned it into a museum and erected the two buildings on either side, as well as the School of Art and the National Gallery at the Merrion Square side of the estate. The building is now home to the Republic's two Houses of Parliament, *Oireachtas na hÉireann* in Irish.

Dublin

Tours only take place when the houses aren't sitting (Sep-Jan) & there's often a month's waiting list, so book well in advance

The Lower House, the *Dáil*, is in a converted Victorian lecture theatre. Visitors can watch the proceedings from a gallery above the floor of the house. The Upper House, the *Seanad*, meets in the very classy North-Wing Saloon which still has all the original plasterwork.

■ *Mon-Fri by prior arrangement only. You must show a passport to begin the tour. One way for Irish visitors to see the* Dáil *is to give the guards at the gate the name of your local TD who, if he or she is there, can vouch that you're not a terrorist. Kildare St, T6183066.*

The National Museum

Pearse St Station

The museum is full of the most wonderful things from Bronze Age gold hoards and a display of ancient Egyptian embalming techniques to an informative, though male-oriented, exhibition called *The Road to Independence*. Before entering the galleries, stop to admire the entrance lobby with its beautiful mosaic floor portraying the signs of the zodiac, and the domed roof which is 19 m (62 ft) high.

The **Prehistoric Ireland** exhibition, has displays on food gathering, burial customs and religion, and should be followed in an anticlockwise direction. Fortunately for Ireland's archaeologists, the many peat bogs around the country have a preserving effect on things which fall, or are pushed, into them. Many hoards of artefacts have been found, including remains of ritual burials and offerings, metal objects put into the bog for safekeeping, and things that just fell in. Curious among the many metal artefacts are musical horns looking strangely like those played by native Australians. The centrepiece of this collection is the **Ór – Ireland's Gold** display, full of gleaming gold hoards from the Bronze Age. Judging from the extent of it, our ancestors must have been a mistrustful (and forgetful) lot. Virtually none of these treasures was excavated by archaeologists – they have turned up in ploughed fields, in railway cuttings and peat bogs. Ranging from scrap gold to intricate brooches, torques and tiaras, the display fills the main hall and is the finest exhibition of prehistoric gold in Europe.

The **Treasury** contains gold and other items made by the Celts who arrived in Ireland around 300 BC, bringing their ironworking skills with them. There are also later artefacts produced during Ireland's Christian period, from the fifth century to the Middle Ages. Among the pieces on display look out for the Ardagh Chalice, the **Tara Brooch** and the Loughnashade Trumpet. Guarding the doorway to the treasury are two sheela-na-gigs (pagan fertility symbols).

Upstairs are exhibitions on Viking and medieval Dublin which follow on chronologically from the treasury but display a very different culture. From a society concerned with reliquaries and their contents, this later culture was more earthy and practical. Also upstairs are the museum's collections of ancient Egyptian artefacts.

In the exhibition called **The Road to Independence** the many Irish women who risked their lives as doctors, workers and fighters have been sadly ignored, with the exception of one big name (see box, page 67). The toys- for-the-boys exhibition charts the course of the early years of the 20th century in Ireland, and death masks and bullet-ridden uniforms figure largely, as well as banners and medals donated by those involved. A huge screen shows some interesting archive material.

■ *Kildare St. Tue-Sat, 1000-1700, Sun, 1400-1700. Closed Mon. Free. Café and shop. Daily tours. T6777444.*

Natural History Museum

Round the corner, in Merrion Street Upper, in another of the Victorian buildings established by the Royal Dublin Society, is the Natural History Museum. It is a very Victorian zoological collection, well kept up but dead just the same.

The Irish Collection

Occupying 3 X 5 m in the Shaw Room is the wacky 1854 **Marriage of Strongbow and Aoife** *by Daniel Maclise which was donated to the gallery in 1972. The wedding seems to be taking place amongst much gnashing of teeth and bewailing, but it is the attendant maidens' faces that really catch the eye. They seem deeply put off by the whole affair. Another exhibit not to be missed is* **The Opening of the Sixth Seal** *by Francis Danby. Painted in 1828, it depicts the vision of St John on the Day of Judgement. Again there seems to be much mortification but the skies are magnificent, as is the*

laser-beam effect as the seal is broken. The collection also includes works by John Lavery and William Orpen, both commissioned as official painters of the First World War. It is clear from Orpen's **The Holy Well** *that he was more profoundly affected by his war experiences than Lavery. The very modern style and use of colour contrast sharply with his earlier painting* **The Vere Foster Family** *, also on show. Here too are Paul Henry's* **Launching the Curragh** *and Augustus Nicholas Burke's* **A Connemara Girl** *, which may be recognized by anyone familiar with Irish hotel corridors and foyers.*

Dublin

There are stuffed things, skeletons (including three giant elk, extinct for 10,000 years), some exhibits that look as if Damien Hurst has practised on them, a butterfly collection, as well as cases of pinned insects and collections of African and Asian creatures, many of which met their fate at the hands of intrepid Victorian explorers. The museum is well worth a visit, if only to see the untouched Victorian fittings, the lovely glass cases, complete with cloths to cover the exhibits and the iron stairs. Opposite the museum, at No 24, is the house where the Duke of Wellington (who gave his name to the famous boot) was born, now the Merrion Hotel. ■ *Merrion St. Tue-Sat 1000-1700, Sun 1400-1700. Free. DART: Pearse St Station.*

While the National Gallery was being built, its collection had to be started from scratch and in 1856 the trustees acquired 16 paintings in Rome. With the purchase of a further 23 Italian works, the collection was under way. Although the gallery always functioned on a hand-to-mouth basis, depending on a meagre annual budget, loans and bequests, it still managed to acquire a remarkable collection. More prosperous times have seen the opening of a new Millennium Wing in 2002,

> **The National Gallery**
> *Pearse St Station is 5 mins walk away*

The Gallery, in Merrion Square West, has a worthy collection of art with the Italian school in the Milltown Rooms represented by Titian, Tintoretto, Mantegna, Fra Angelico and Caravaggio (*The Taking of Christ* was discovered in Leeson Street hanging on a wall in a dark corner of the Jesuits' study hall). There are sound collections of Flemish and Dutch paintings in the North Wing (including three works by Rembrandt and a Vermeer), a French collection (also in the Milltown Rooms), and a Spanish collection that includes El Greco, Velázquez and Picasso. There is also a British collection on the ground floor of the North Wing, and a fine Irish collection on the ground floor of the Milltown Rooms, with a room dedicated to Jack Yeats and his family.

■ *Mon-Sat 1000-1730 (Thu 2030), Sun 1400-1700. Closed 24-26 Dec and Good Fri. Free. T6615133, www.nationalgallery.ie*

Not usually a place that you might associate with a holiday in Dublin, the government offices in Merrion Street are open for tours on Saturdays. The tour goes through innumerable meeting rooms, one of which, the Beech

> **Government offices**

Room (they are all named for the wood which furnishes them), was used for some of the important negotiations attending the Northern Ireland Peace Process. When we last visited there were red stains in the middle of the carpet – wine I hope.

The furnishings put you in mind of a 1980s five-star hotel which has seen better days – all pale wood and arty objects lying about. Best of all is the Taioseach's Room with banks of ageing technology and a Blofeld-like lift to get him to the roof for a quick getaway by helicopter.

■ *Free tours on the hour on Sat only. Collect tickets from foyer of National Gallery. No pre-booking.*

Merrion Square Surrounding a central park, this near-perfect Georgian Square has doors, fanlights, door furniture, boot scrapers, door flaps and coal hole covers all intact.

Many plaques on the houses mark the homes of Dublin's well-to-do and downright famous. At **No 1** lived Oscar Wilde and his remarkable father who, as the plaque tells us, was an "aural and ophthalmic surgeon, archaeologist, ethnologist, antiquarian, biographer, statistician, naturalist, topographer, historian, folklorist"; a hard act to follow. ■ *Mon, Wed and Thu at 1015 and 1115, €2.54. T6620281.*

In the park opposite No 1 is a statue of **Oscar Wilde**, gloriously decorated with semi-precious stones – blue pearl granite trousers, jacket of jade, shoes of granite – reclining on a white quartz rock and holding a green carnation to his breast (and nicknamed by the populace "the quare in the square" or occasionally "the queer with the sneer" – look at his expression!). Daniel O'Connell lived for a time at No 58, WB Yeats lived at No 82 and scientist Erwin Schrödinger (winner of the Nobel Prize) lived at No 65. No 39 was the British Embassy until 1972, but was burnt down after Bloody Sunday.

At the south corner of the square, at **29 Fitzwilliam Street**, is a Georgian townhouse, owned by the Electricity Supply Board who demolished the rest of the row to build an office block. For all its grandeur, the 1794 house gives an idea of just how dark and cold and difficult to look after these tall narrow houses were. With only two rooms on each floor, mostly given over to display, the occupants actually lived huddled together in the basement and top floor. Only one of the servants lived in – in a little cubby hole with a window let into the pantry so that she could keep an eye on the food. Water was brought by a cart and carried around the house, lighting was by oil lamp, heating by coal and turf, and sewage was carted out and shipped away every few days. The front door has two brass rails beside it where the sedan chair poles were kept. Crockery, furniture and clothes are all originals and borrowed from the National Museum. The visit is preceded by a ten-minute video about the real and imaginary people who lived in and serviced the house. ■ *Tue-Sat 1000-1700, closed Sun and Mon and 2 weeks prior to Christmas. €3.17. Tea room and gift shop. Visit is by tour only. T7026165, www.esb.ie*

St Stephen's Green and around

St Stephen's Green is a pleasant enough little park, great for lunch on a sunny day with occasional music from the bandstand and lots of memorabilia. The main entrance at the corner of Grafton Street commemorates the Royal Dublin Fusiliers who died in the Boer War, and is modelled on the Arch of Titus in Rome. **Wolfe Tone** is commemorated at the northwest corner of the park, opposite Merrion Row. The statue was the subject of an attack by a unionist extremist group in the 1980s. Local wags have renamed the granite obelisks

Gay Byrne

Lingering on the landing between Room 9 and the Shaw Room, you will notice a strange installation plastered all over the wall and fronted by a garish yellow silhouette framed by an even more garish gilded frame. Gay Byrne, now an elderly gent, has occupied the nation's sitting rooms for decades, hosting the incomparable Late Late Show *forever, gossiping away on his own radio show and hosting the absurd Rose of Tralee Festival. He has retired so many times in the last decade that his house must be full of farewell gifts. But still he carries on and is currently doing the Irish version of* Who Wants to be a Millionaire. *Ireland owes much to this man who almost single-handedly dragged it, kicking and screaming, into the 20th century. In the old days, people would crowd into the house of the nearest telly owner every Friday night, and Saturday morning's talk was about the outrageous events of the previous night's* Late Late Show. *His catchphrase "and there's one for everybody in the audience" is known by Irish people everywhere, and it is a fitting tribute that the artist, John Kinaness, should have depicted Gay in this way, as wallpaper.*

Dublin

behind 'Tonehenge'. Both this statue and the one behind the obelisks, the **Famine Memorial**, are by Edward Delaney. There is a bust of Countess Markievicz who led the taking of the nearby Royal College of Surgeons in 1916.

Worth a quick look is the **Shelbourne Hotel**, famous for, among other things, employing Alois Hitler, half-brother to Adolf, as a wine waiter. Alois Hitler settled in Dublin, married Brigid Elizabeth Dowling, and was later tried for bigamy. Michael Collins and colleagues sat around the table in room 112 to draft the Constitution of the Irish Free State. Afternoon tea in the Lord Mayor's Lounge is a grand affair and worth considering for a splash.

A little way south of the green in Earlsfort Terrace is the 1978 National Concert Hall and behind it, the **Iveagh Gardens**, which is perhaps the most secret park in Dublin and makes an excellent quiet spot for a picnic lunch.

On the south side of St Stephen's Green are the two renovated Georgian houses known as Newman House. The buildings were bought in 1865 by the Catholic University of Ireland under John Henry Newman, a convert from the Anglican Church. Gerard Manley Hopkins spent a lonely five years in the attic at No 86, and his room has been restored to its original state. James Joyce, Padraig Pearse and Eamon De Valera studied here, and it was for their benefit, no doubt, that the naked female figures on the ceilings were clothed, giving them a more modest appearance. In the recent renovations, which began in 1989, one of the Jesuit alterations has been left for our edification.

Guided tours of the two buildings include visits to Hopkin's Room in the attic, the Apollo Room in No 85, with its stunning stucco work by the Lafranchini brothers, and the Saloon, where Georgian gentry would once have entertained beneath even more elaborate ceiling sculptures. In No 86 the saloon was turned into a chapel by the Jesuits (it is here that the beclothing of Juno and her nymphs took place).

■ *Jun, Jul and Aug only, Tue-Fri, 1200-1700, Sat, 1400-1700, Sun, 1000-1400. Closed Mon. €3.81. 85-86 St Stephen's Green, T7067422. Telephone in advance to confirm opening times.*

Newman House
If you have to choose one Georgian house to visit, make it this one rather than No 29 Fitzwilliam St: it has more history, and the Jesuit additions to the plasterwork are good fun

Five minutes from St Stephen's Green's northern corner with Grafton Street, at 58 William Street South, is this little museum, containing wa strange

Dublin Civic Museum

mishmash of artefacts to do with the city, including an original copy of the 1916 Proclamations of Independence, a series of 18th-century aquatints of the city, a giant pair of shoes and Nelson's head, blown off his shoulders in the IRA attack on Nelson's Pillar in 1966. During the War of Independence it was home to the outlawed Irish Supreme Court as well as lesser courts. One of the judges who sat here during the War of Independence was Kathleen Clarke, widow of one of the executed leaders of the 1916 Rebellion, Tom Clarke, and later senator and mayor of the city. Kathleen Clarke spent many years in prison in the name of Irish independence and was later a major thorn in the side of the De Valera government, which wrote out of the constitution all references to equality for all which the women of Sinn Féin had worked so hard to get. ■ *Tue-Sat, 1000-1800, Sun, 1100-1400. Closed Mon. Free.*

Whitefriar St Carmelite Church Whitefriar Street Carmelite Church, with its entrance at 56 Aungier Street, is famous because it apparently contains the remains of St Valentine which for some unaccountable reason were given to Father Spratt by Pope Gregory XVI on 14 February 1835. Up until then the remains had been resting peacefully in the cemetery of St Hippolytus in Rome. To see the bones (which a church in Scotland also claims to hold), which are in a casket inside the church, as well as a vial of the saint's blood, go down the right-hand aisle of the church, and into the alcove.
■ *Mon, Wed, Thu, Fri 0800-1830, Sat 0800-1900, Tue 0800-2130, bank holidays 0930-1300.*

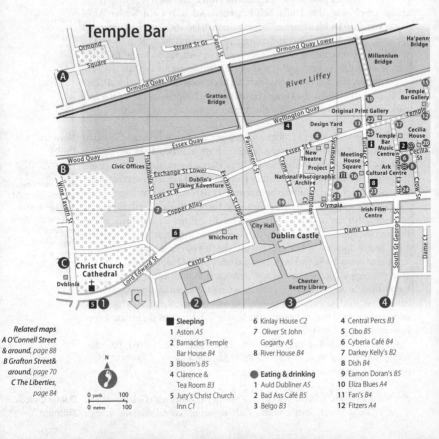

Temple Bar

0 yards 100
0 metres 100

■ **Sleeping**
1 Aston *A5*
2 Barnacles Temple Bar House *B4*
3 Bloom's *B5*
4 Clarence & Tea Room *B3*
5 Jury's Christ Church Inn *C1*
6 Kinlay House *C2*
7 Oliver St John Gogarty *A5*
8 River House *B4*

● **Eating & drinking**
1 Auld Dubliner *A5*
2 Bad Ass Café *B5*
3 Belgo *B3*
4 Central Percs *B3*
5 Cibo *B5*
6 Cyberia Café *B4*
7 Darkey Kelly's *B2*
8 Dish *B4*
9 Eamon Doran's *B5*
10 Eliza Blues *A4*
11 Fan's *B4*
12 Fitzers *A4*

Temple Bar

Nowadays a vibrant tourist ghetto, the network of narrow lanes that criss-cross between the river and Dame Street and from Fishamble Street to Fleet Street is known as Temple Bar, after its 17th-century developer, Sir William Temple. The landmark to head for is **Ha'penny Bridge** over the River Liffey. On the south side of the bridge is Merchant's Arch, which leads into the hub of streets and alleys that define Temple Bar.

Tara St Station is just east of Temple Bar, near Butt Bridge For further transport information, see page 130

Despite recent renovation and redevelopment, a few remnants of the old part of the city are still intact. Well worth noticing, on the corner of Parliament Street and Essex Quay, is **Sunlight Chambers**, built for Lever Brothers in 1901 and with multi-coloured terracotta reliefs displaying the benefits of soap, which seem mostly to be providing work for women to do. Another relic of a past age is Merchant's Arch, part of a Merchant's Hall built in 1822. It leads out to the Ha'penny Bridge, a cast-iron footbridge built in 1816 and named for the toll levied on it until 1919.

The **Irish Film Centre** (see page 119), in Eustace Street, shows art house films in a very post-modern conversion of an old Quaker Meeting House; the **Temple Bar Information Centre**, also in Eustace Street, provides fairly up-to-date maps of the area (places come and go here quite quickly) and information about what's on.

From O'Connell Bridge follow the quayside to Ha'penny Bridge; from Grafton St, follow Dame St & turn down any street towards the river

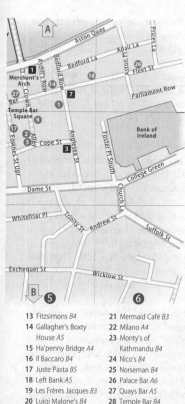

There are plenty of schlock attractions in Temple Bar, but the **Gallery of Photography**, Meeting House Square, is a major exception if the exhibition on show can match the present *Underexposed*, display of censored photographs. They also offer a range of photography courses. ■ *Mon-Sat 1100-1800. Free. T6714654, gallery@irish-photography.com*

The **National Photographic Archive**, also in Meeting House Square, has a collection of some 300,000 photographs from the National Library of Ireland and changing exhibitions display some idea of the intrinsic wealth of this material. There is a small shop with postcards, prints and publications. ■ *Mon-Fri, 1000-1700. Free. T6030200, www.heanet.ie/natlib/-photoarchive*

13 Fitzsimons *B4*
14 Gallagher's Boxty House *A5*
15 Ha'penny Bridge *A4*
16 Il Baccaro *B4*
17 Juste Pasta *B5*
18 Left Bank *A5*
19 Les Frères Jacques *B3*
20 Luigi Malone's *B4*

21 Mermaid Café *B3*
22 Milano *A4*
23 Monty's of Kathmandu *B4*
24 Nico's *B4*
25 Norseman *B4*
26 Palace Bar *A6*
27 Quays Bar *A5*
28 Temple Bar *B4*

Dublin Castle and around

It is difficult to surmise from the hand-tufted carpets and 18th-century plasterwork that this was once Dublin's biggest stronghold, built in 1204 to defend the city against the

From Temple Bar, a suicide dash across Dame St brings you to Dublin Castle

Dublin

native Irish. Constructed into the city walls and protected on two sides by the rivers Liffey and the now-defunct Poddle, the castle had a central circular keep surrounded by a curtain wall with massive towers, and a portcullis barring the entrance in Castle Street. It must have looked the part too, because apart from a Fitzgerald attack in 1534 and an aborted attempt at seizing it in 1641, the castle has seen very little action. The most exciting thing to take place here must have been the night during the Black and Tan War, at its height between 1920 and 1921, when Michael Collins infiltrated the records office to find out what information the British had on him. In 1922 the castle was officially handed over to him as Commander in Chief of the Irish Army. The moment is lovingly recalled in the film *Michael Collins* when the British dignitary tries to reprimand Collins for being late, only to be reminded that the Irish have been kept waiting for some 800 years.

In St Patrick's Hall it's worth getting a crick in your neck to admire the ceiling

The guided tour (the only way to get a look inside) explores the still used **State Apartments**. Notable is the inlaid table given to Queen Victoria, only to have her royal majesty leave it here because some of the inlaid designs were a bit saucy for her taste. The ceiling paintings in St Patrick's Hall are by Vincent Waldré and one depicts an allegory of George III receiving the homage of the Irish kings.

The tour gets more interesting as it passes out of the State Apartments and into the Upper Yard, where you can see the **Statue of Justice** over the gateway, unblindfolded and with her back to the city she should have been defending. Until she was mended in the 1980s, her scales of justice regularly tipped when it rained and they filled with water. A fitting comment, many noted, on British justice in Ireland.

From here you visit the **Undercroft**, the most interesting part of the tour because you can see the remains of Viking fortifications, part of the old medieval city wall, the moat, postern steps for deliveries, and a dribble of the River Poddle itself.

■ *Mon-Fri 1000-1700, Sat, Sun and bank holidays, 1400-1700. €4. Guided tours only, lasting approximately 40 mins. Last admission 1 hr before closing. Free admission to Castle Yard, Chapel Royal and Dubh Linn Garden. Coffee shop and restaurant, serving a set lunch for (€8.25. T6777129.*

Chester Beatty Library
Book lovers will adore this museum, winner of the all-Ireland Museum of the Year Award in 2000

A priceless collection of cultural and religious treasures, mostly Oriental but also Early Christian, this superb library, in Dublin Castle, was bequeathed by New York-born Chester Beatty who died in 1968. Only a fraction of his 35-ton collection is on display, including rare Japanese and Thai texts, Chinese jade books, Turkish miniatures, Samurai armour, Buddhas and some extremely rare Biblical papyri. There are over 250 copies of the Koran in the collection and one of the most beautiful on display is a 10th-century fragment written in gold on blue-dyed vellum, written in Kufic and originating from north Africa or Spain. ■ *Mon-Fri, 1000-1700 (closed Mon, Oct-Apr); Sat, 1100-1700, Sun, 1300-1700. Closed bank holidays. Free lectures every Sun at 1500 and 1600, every Wed at 1300. Café, shop and roof garden. T4070750, www.cbl.ie*

City Hall
The restructured vaults now accommodate a permanent exhibition on Dublin's history

Turning left out of the main gates of the castle into Dame Street, you come to City Hall – an outstanding piece of Georgian architecture, marking the introduction in Ireland of the neo-classical style, displaying proudly its Portland stone and elaborately carved capitals on the outside. Inside, a stupendous circular entrance hall, the **Rotunda**, greets visitors, and free leaflets explain in detail the frescos, the coat of arms and the imposing statues, including an 18-ft-high O'Connell with an inscription in four languages that decorate the commodious space.

The Waldorf in Dublin

Not a hotel, but a shave in style at **The Waldorf**, 13 Westmoreland St, below stairs next to Bewley's Café, T677 8608. Down the stairs and into the past with a 1946 steamer still producing the towels for their role in the 10-minute lathering session, as laid down in the Waldorf Manual. This is the real McCoy, a place that waited long enough to come back into style with its authentic 1940s décor and cut-throat razors. Not cheap mind, at around €25.

In the exhibition downstairs, look out for the Chain Book, a medieval *Yellow Pages* that also defined the rights of citizens. The *Queens of Tarts* restaurant, located across the road, has a café point near the ticket office and serves light meals and hot drinks.

■ *Mon-Sat, 1000-1715. €3.80. T6722204, www.dublincorp.ie/cityhall*

Christ Church Cathedral is a gratifying mixture of Victorian fantasy Gothic, Norman doorways, Romanesque arches and wonderful fake medieval floor tiles, all perfumed by that Church of Ireland polish and damp hymn book smell that never seems to find its way into Catholic churches.

Christ Church Cathedral
Leaflets, in a dozen European languages, give a useful guided tour of the building

Inside the church there is much to see. Walking anti clockwise around the building you come to the **Tomb of Strongbow**, the Norman conqueror of Ireland and the man who contributed so much to building the cathedral. On the floor are original medieval tiles, rediscovered during the Victorian renovations and copied throughout the building. There are 63 different patterns.

In the centre of the church is the Choir; the archbishop's throne rests alongside Victorian stalls where the choir and canons sit during services. From here you can see that the north wall of the nave is 50 cm out of kilter.

The **Crypt** is a long underground chamber, untouched by the Victorian renovations and supported by rough stone pillars which bear the entire weight of the building. It is the only crypt in Britain or Ireland that runs the length of a building, and it contains a collection of all the old bits and pieces left over after renovations or shifted here from other parts of the city, including statues of Charles I and II. Look out for the 17th-century stocks and the mummified cat and mouse discovered in the old organ pipes when the organ was replaced recently.

Outside are the remains of the 13th-century **Chapter House**, and set into the wall of the church, a 12th-century Romanesque doorway.

■ *Daily 0945-1730 except Christmas Day. €2.54 donation. Sat 1700 and Sun 1530 choral evensong. T6778099.*

The flying Gothic bridge over Winetavern Street links the cathedral with the 19th-century Synod Hall, now Dvblinia, an audio-visual attempt to recreate the sights and sounds of medieval Dublin, including finds from various excavations in the city and life-size recreations of local scenes: a merchant's kitchen, a cobbler's shop and the quayside, which was once a centre for medieval wine bars and keg makers; even the bars that found their way into the church. ■ *Apr-Sep, 1000-1700, daily; Oct-Mar, Mon-Sat, 1100-1600, Sun and bank holidays, 1000-1630. €5. Gift shop. T6794611.*

Dvblinia

Also lurking in Temple Bar, and a good outing for children, is Dublin's Viking Adventure, in the 1815 Franciscan church of St Michael and St John in Essex Street West. Nowadays it's a re-creation of Viking Dublin, complete with

Dublin's Viking Adventure

Dublin

people dressed up in Viking gear, reconstructions of huts and wall divisions, and original artefacts. Tours begin with a five-minute simulated Viking boat ride, followed by a 40-minute guided walkabout ending up in the museum. ■ *Tue-Sat 1000-1630. Closed Sun and Mon. €6.20, family tickets €17. Craft shop. Wheelchair access. T6796040.*

The Liberties

For transport information, see page 130

The Liberties is an area west of the city centre, between the High Street, next to Christ Church, south to the Coombe, with **St Patrick's Cathedral** at its eastern border. Beyond, heading west from Christ Church Cathedral, you can reach the **Guinness Brewery**, home of the famous brew, and Heuston Railway Station via Thomas Street. This is a working-class part of town where street traders set up shop and contribute to the workaday atmosphere of the area. To the south of St Patrick's Cathedral are the **Irish Jewish Museum** and the Grand Canal.

St Patrick's Cathedral

The largest church, the largest ringing peal of bells & the first university in Ireland

If Christ Church became the Norman cathedral, St Patrick's was the people's cathedral. It is reputed to stand on the site of a church founded by St Patrick himself who is said to have baptized converts from a well in the grounds. A stone church was built here in 1192, only 20 years after the other major expenditure on Christ Church, less than a mile away. The two cathedrals began to vie for glory and a major rebuilding programme began in the early 13th century. The pope stuck his oar in around 1300 and declared that Christ Church was the supreme church, but this didn't end the unholy rivalry between the two cathedrals. The Reformation saw St Patrick's demoted back to church status, while Christ Church flourished as the state representation of religious power.

The Liberties

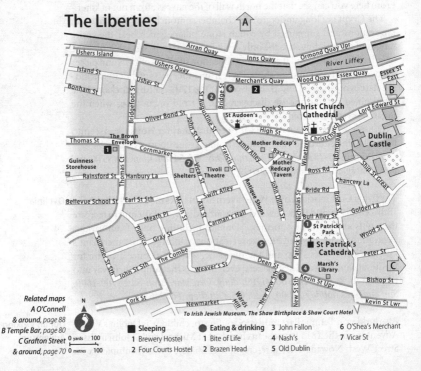

Related maps
A O'Connell & around, page 88
B Temple Bar, page 80
C Grafton Street & around, page 70

To Irish Jewish Museum, The Shaw Birthplace & Shaw Court Hotel

■ **Sleeping**
1 Brewery Hostel
2 Four Courts Hostel

● **Eating & drinking**
1 Bite of Life
2 Brazen Head

3 John Fallon
4 Nash's
5 Old Dublin

6 O'Shea's Merchant
7 Vicar St

Despite its ugly exterior, St Patrick's, the national cathedral of the Church of Ireland, is the more interesting of the two cathedrals, with much more of the medieval interior intact. For many years it was the workplace (and burial ground) of the 18th-century writer, satirist and dean Jonathan Swift, and memorabilia of his deanship is plentiful, including a death mask; not the cheeriest of mementoes. The steps down to the entrance indicate how far the street level has risen since medieval times.

Inside the baptistry by the main entrance is an enormous wooden monument to the Boyle family, the 17th-century earls of Cork. The monument once decorated the east end of the choir, where the entire congregation had to look at it, and seemingly bow before it, every time they prayed. The monument is indeed an exercise in pomposity, with several generations of the entire family depicted around the centrepiece of Richard Boyle and his wife. The carved small boy is said to be his son, Robert Boyle, who grew up to be the great physicist who gave us all the Charles/Boyle gas law to learn in school.

Leaving aside 17th-century aggrandizement, an anticlockwise stroll around the church brings you into the south aisle where Dean Swift and his friend Esther (also known as Stella) Johnson are interred.

There is a reasonable range of literature on sale and free introductory leaflets in an impressive range of foreign languages. Outside the church, the 19th-century changes are quite obvious with the obligatory Gothic flying buttresses, the entrance porch and a corresponding porch on the north side as well as the main doors and windows at the west end of the church.

■ *Daily, 0900-1800 (1700 on Sat and 1500 on Sun in Nov-Feb). €3.43. Choir sings at Matins (0940 during school terms only) and Evensong (1735 daily except Sat throughout the year and on Wed only in Jul and Aug). Shop. T4539472, www.stpatrickscathedral.ie*

German writer, Heinrich Böll wasn't impressed by his visit to St Patrick's: "At Swift's tomb my heart had caught a chill, so clean was St Patrick's Cathedral, so empty of people and so full of patriotic marble figures; so deep under the cold stone did the desperate Dean seem to lie, Stella beside him"

Dublin

"He lies where furious indignation can no longer rend his heart" (Swift's epitaph over the door of the robing room)

Outside the church, a short stroll down St Patrick's Close brings you to a Victorian iron gateway that leads up the original staircase to Ireland's earliest public library and the interior, all dark wood panelling and smelling of ancient leather, is little changed from when it was first built in 1701. The old oak shelves form stalls surmounted by a bishop's mitre, and books used to be put on chains that ran along the shelves. For the really valuable volumes, readers were locked in cages, still to be seen, to prevent them from walking away with the precious books. Swift used the library regularly, his fading death mask is on display, and the visitors' book shows that James Joyce also came here. The library, still open to scholars, holds exhibitions of ancient works which change every June. ■ *Mon and Wed-Fri, 1000-1245, 1400-1700, Sat, 1030-1245. Closed Tue and Sun. €1.27 donation. T4543511, www.kst.dit.ie/marsh*

Marsh's Library
The collection includes about 25,000 books from the 16th-18th centuries

The Guinness Brewery, St James's Gate, has always dispensed a 'free' pint of the black stuff in exchange for your entrance ticket. Now, in the new super-duper Guinness Storehouse, your 'ticket' is a blob of perspex with a drop of Guinness embalmed inside and the blob is scanned at the bar so you can retain it as a souvenir. President Clinton was one of the first visitors when he returned to Dublin at the end of 2000, but don't let that put you off. Begin the self-guided tour in the colossal entrance area where the original 9,000-year lease is encased in the floor. Escalators channel visitors up through the various levels and in the course of your walkabout you will learn that the famous drink doesn't use water from the Liffey after all (a popular misconception to account for the unique taste of the drink in Dublin). You'll also see a copper barrel holding 172,800 pints, and absorb masses of information from the

Guinness Storehouse

various displays. Not much about the Guinnesses, though, who were real patriarchal Victorian liberals and who deserve more credit for what they did for the people of Dublin. The fifth level has the Brewery Bar, in fact a bar and restaurant, and above that is the stylish Gravity Bar, offering a 360° view of the city with the Dublin mountains in the background. This is where you collect your pint. Back on ground level, *The Store* is a Guinness emporium selling socks, luggage, clothes, posters and more of that ilk.

■ €1140. 1 Apr-30 Sep, Mon-Sat, 0930 to 1900 (last admission). Sun and Bank Holidays 1030 to 1630 (last admission). 1 Oct-31 Mar, Mon-Sat 0930, last admission 1600. Sun and bank holidays 1200, last admission 1600. Shop, bar and restaurant (see below). T4084800 www.guinness.ie If walking from the city centre, you can follow the river along a series of quays but, apart from the view of the Four Courts across the Liffey, there is little to see in return. Instead, walk down Crane St from Thomas St and turn right at the end of the cobbled section of the street. The entrance to the brewery is down on the right, through the double gates.

Irish Jewish Museum

The fictional hero of Ulysses, Leopold Bloom, is Jewish and his 'birthplace' is not far away, marked with a plaque at 52 Upper Clanbrassil St

The Portobello area bordering the Grand Canal was home to a thriving Jewish community from around the 1880s onwards. The **Bretzel Bakery**, has been in its spot at the start of Lennox Street for a century (on the other side of the street, at No 1, is the birthplace of Barry Fitzgerald, he of *The Quiet Man* fame). One of the synagogues, at 3-4 Walworth Street, off Victoria Street, closed up in the early 1970s and the house remained empty for 10 years until a group worked to restore it. Today the museum occupies the two houses and the synagogue, upstairs, has been faithfully restored using the original colour scheme and prayer seats.

The two floors of the museum are packed with memorabilia that bring to life ordinary and extraordinary aspects of life for Jews in Ireland. There is a faithful restoration of the original Victorian kitchen of one of the houses as well as artefacts of everyday life. Look out for a photograph of the 1937 marriage of Ester Steinberg, an Irish woman, to her Dutch husband. Their baby was born in Paris two years later but they all ended up on a train to Auschwitz. The last letter sent to her from Ireland to her Paris address is marked "Gone Away."

The dispiriting story of the Irish government's indifference (to put it mildly) to the plight of Jewish refugees is told by a letter from the Irish Chief Rabbi to De Valera requesting permission to admit half a dozen Jewish doctors and dentists. This was October 1938 and the request was turned down. The insularity of the cultural nationalism that so repelled Joyce reveals itself in an anti-Semitic comment on a Sinn Féin advertisement displayed in the museum.

■ May-Sep, Sun, Tue and Thu, 1100-1530, Oct-Apr, Sun, 1030-1430. Free. T4901857/4531797.

The Shaw Birthplace

Combined tickets are available with the James Joyce Museum (see page 96)

"Author of many plays" reads the plaque outside the house at 33 Synge Street, where the playwright was born, and this more or less sums up most people's perception of George Bernard Shaw. A once legendary figure, and winner of the Nobel Prize for Literature, Shaw is currently suffering a dip in his reputation. An audio guide talks you through the rooms, which have been faithfully restored to reflect Victorian Dublin and visitors walk around with an audio guide. ■ May-Oct, Mon-Sat, 1000-1700. Sun, 1100-1700. €5. Bookshop. T4750854.

The day Lord Nelson lost his head

Outside the GPO stood Nelson's Pillar, erected in 1808 (several decades before the London version). The Doric column it stood on was hollow with an internal staircase allowing visitors to climb to the top and look out over the city. In 1966, to commemorate the 50th anniversary of the Easter Rising, Sean Treacy, an IRA activist, allegedly stole a key to the entrance, got inside and planted explosives. The resulting explosion quite neatly took the statue and the top of the column off with no damage to surrounding buildings. Someone, realizing the commercial value of such an act, appropriated the head and it went on the market soon after. Later, the Irish army was called in to demolish the rest of the column and did extensive damage to the surrounding buildings in doing so. For a time two heads of the statue were circulating, but the genuine one is now in the Dublin Civic Museum in South William St. Like the Berlin Wall, more ordinary remains of the pillar went on sale all over Ireland and England.

Sean Treacy allegedly went on to release colleagues out of prison twice, using on one occasion a helicopter and on another an earth mover with a reinforced steel frame. He retired from active service and returned to his profession as a steel erector. He was killed in July 1998 when an unsupported ditch he was working in collapsed on him.

The destruction of Nelson's Pillar was the last in a long Irish tradition of blowing up imperial monuments. William III on horseback was blown off his pediment in College Green in 1928, George II and his horse copped it in the 1940s and George I also bit the dust. Queen Victoria, who stood outside Leinster House till the 1940s, was dismantled for safe keeping and is now an asylum-seeker in Australia. William III was melted down and used to patch sewer pipes. Another Protestant, Wolfe Tone, was hit in 1989, this time by the Ulster Volunteer Force, who must have objected to his aligning himself with the cause of Irish freedom. He was collected up and rebuilt and still stands on St Stephen's Green. For some reason no one has taken exception to the statue of Prince Albert that lurks outside the Natural History Museum, or, come to that, the enormous memorial to Wellington in Phoenix Park.

***The Stiletto in the Ghetto** which will be appearing shortly in O'Connell Street, on the site where Nelson's Pillar once toppled, will be a 120-m (394-ft) stainless steel spire officially known as the Monument of Light. Dublin wits soon came up with alternative titles (including the unwieldy but funny Syringe to Make You Cringe) and more may well sprout when the structure is seen at night. Tapering from 3 m in diameter at its base to a mere 4 ins (0.1 m) in the sky, it will be lit internally at the very top and by projections of light from surrounding buildings for most of its height.*

O'Connell Street and around

Most of the hyped tourist spots are in the southern half of the city, but the north has lots to offer and fewer crowds; there is also a more genuine, earthy feel to it, being less geared up to the tourist market. The area has strong historical and literary associations and some of the earliest Georgian buildings in the city, many of which are far more accessible to the public than snooty Merrion Square. Here too are the excellent **Hugh Lane Gallery** with its fine collection of modern art, important James Joyce associations and the attractive **Writers' Museum**.

O'Connell Street itself is a broad boulevard in the centre of North Dublin that stretches for over half a kilometre in a straight line from the River Liffey to Parnell Square. Running parallel with O'Connell Street, to the east, is

Connolly Station For further transport information, see page 130

Dublin

Gardiner Street, full of guesthouses and hostels, and running off O'Connell Street on the west side is pedestrianized **Henry Street** where shops and department stores pay the highest ground rentals in the capital.

In 1916 large tracts of the street were destroyed by the British, as they shelled the republicans who were occupying the GPO. Most of the impressive buildings lining the street today were built during the 1920s, including Gresham's Hotel, the Carlton and Savoy cinemas and the façade of Clery's department store.

O'Connell Street & around

Before you begin the stroll up O'Connell Street from the river, a small diversion along Eden Quay and Custom House Quay brings you to the Custom House. Built on the river in order to collect duties on boats arriving in Dublin, the building underwent restoration work twice in the 20th century, last reopening in 1991. The style is neo-classical and the skyline sculptures by Edward Smyth are outstanding. Instead of using the traditional ox skulls seen on Roman temples, Gandon's frieze had heads of cattle, representing Ireland's beef trade. In its original form the building had chimneys.

Custom House

Dublin

The small entrance fee is good value for anyone interested in architecture or the history of Dublin. Touch-sensitive screens summarize relevant bits of history and detail the many personalities involved with the Custom House, like the novelist Flann O'Brien who worked here as a civil servant.

■ *Mid-Mar to Oct, Mon-Fri, 1000-1230, Sat and Sun, 1400-1700; Nov to mid-Mar, Wed-Fri, 1000-1230, Sun, 1400-1700. €1.27. T8787660.*

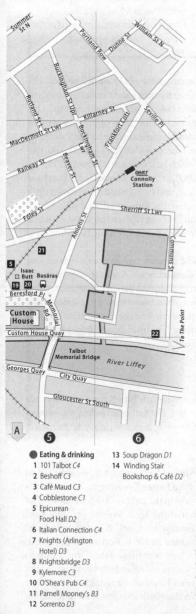

Opened in 1904, it was a radical place in its time, having been founded by the Gaelic Revival Movement, notably Lady Gregory and WB Yeats. Revolutionary plays were produced there, such as Synge's *Playboy of the Western World*, in which the protagonist murders his father and the use of the word 'shift' (referring to women's underwear) caused riots in the streets. In 1926 O'Casey's *The Plough and the Stars* ended in open fighting between the cast and the audience when the Irish flag was taken, dramatically speaking, into a public house where prostitutes were drinking. One of the actors in that 1926 production was Michael Scott who went on to design the new building that you see today.

Abbey Theatre

For booking, see page 119

The theatre went into a decline in the middle years of the 20th century, was burned to the ground in 1951, and for a time became the city morgue. The new theatre has two incarnations, the Peacock, where more experimental work is performed, and the Abbey itself, where newly commissioned works by Irish playwrights take turns with more conventional and better known productions.

One of the most famous theatres in the world, it is, architecturally, one of the city's least distinguished structures

Dublin

👉 **The Dublin Lockout**

The Irish Transport and General Workers' Union was founded by James Larkin in 1909. In August 1913 the Tramway Company sacked 100 men in the Union and this led to a strike and some brutal encounters between the workers and the state. The strike/lockout was prolonged and bitter, and two workers were killed in a police charge. In October, plans to send the starving children of workers to sympathizers in British towns were opposed by the Catholic Church, who said non-Catholics would be involved. By January 1914, workers' resources were at an end and the Great Dublin Lockout was over. A depressed Larkin went to America where he was imprisoned for "criminal anarchy", and when he returned to Ireland in 1923 he found himself in conflict with a less radical leader of the trade union he had formed.

O'Connell St statues & buildings

Back at the head of O'Connell Street stands a statue of **O'Connell** himself. The statue took 30 years to erect, 214 committee meetings and two design competitions, and offended innumerable architects whose designs were rejected. One rejected design had the Liberator entwined in the arms of a young woman (tasteless in the light of his known infidelities), while another had him sitting on a stove! The present one portrays the Liberator clutching a cloak and surrounded by winged victories, some of which bear bullet marks from 1916.

Close to the **General Post Office (GPO)**, at the junction of Henry Street and Earl Street North, stood Nelson's Column, and even before it was blown up in 1966 there had been suggestions to replace the famous admiral with John F Kennedy or the Virgin Mary! But Nelson has been replaced by a new, apolitical creature, **Anna Livia**, spirit of the River Liffey, better known to her admirers as 'the floosie in the jacuzzi'.

The GPO is O'Connell Street's most famous building, although all that remains of the original (1814-18) is the classical façade. Gutted by fire and shelling in 1916 it suffered further damage in 1922 during the Civil War before being rebuilt in 1929. It is still a functioning post office, useful too for its public phones during inclement weather, and inside there is a series of paintings on the walls depicting moments from the 1916 uprising. The front façade of the building is scarred with bullet holes from the two battles.

Parnell Square and around

Connolly Station is a 10-min walk away For further transport information, see page 130

Back on O'Connell Street, a short walk northwards brings you to the Rotunda and Parnell Square at the top of the street. ■ *If The Rotunda is locked, you will need to convince the staff that you are a bona fide visitor, alternatively turn up for mass at 0900 on Sun.*

Garden of Remembrance

At the heart of the square is the Garden of Remembrance, established in 1966 to mark the 50th anniversary of the Easter Uprising and commemorating all those who have given their lives in the cause of Irish freedom. The site was chosen because it was here that the Irish Volunteers were held overnight, before being taken to Kilmainham Gaol. A statue called *The Children of Lir*, by Oisín Kelly, was added in 1971. According to legend, they were the children of the sea god whose wife turned them into swans in a fit of jealousy, doomed to swim the shores of Ireland for 900 years. At the end of that time they staggered ashore and died of old age. The connection between this and the martyrs to Irish freedom isn't too clear since the children

Safe Houses

The men and women who fought the guerrilla campaign against the British in Dublin in the Anglo-Irish War between early 1919 and the truce in July 1921 were largely working-class and the streets around Parnell Square and North Dublin were their home turf. Most of the insurgents in the 1916 uprising were also from Inner North Dublin. Like all successful guerrilla forces, they had the support of the local population and this accounts for the numerous safe houses in the area. Many of the hotels around Parnell Square were apparently used, including The Castle (see page 103), Barry's in Great Denmark Street and Vaughan's Hotel, now a trade union headquarters (SIPTU). The escape of Michael Collins from the Gresham Hotel on Christmas Eve 1920 has been verified, while an equally daring escapade is supposed to have taken place on the corner of Dorset Street and North Frederick Street. Acting on a tip off, Black and Tans raided the area while Collins observed the scene disguised under shaving lather in the barber shop, now Dargan's Chemists.

Dublin

didn't seem to suffer in any particular cause; perhaps it's just the general sense of doom that appeals. Anyway, it's a remarkable piece of artistry.

Nos 18 and 19 of Parnell Square are occupied by the Dublin Writers' Museum, which includes memorabilia and rare copies of the works of famous Irish writers including Swift, Sheridan, Oscar Wilde, GB Shaw, Yeats, Beckett and Seamus Heaney. The exhibition rooms at the entrance level are packed with information and displays on writers, and items on show include the telephone used by Beckett in his Paris apartment and a classic photograph of Brendan Behan with his wife Beatrice taken in 1958. Upstairs are the splendidly decorated Adamesque ceilings of this Georgian townhouse, completed in 1769. The colonnade and the flamboyant frieze were added much later. Back downstairs there is a pleasant café and a bookshop with an excellent selection of Irish literature and literary souvenirs like posters, T-shirts and so on. ■ *Mon-Sat, 1000-1700 (until 1800, Mon-Fri, Jun-Aug), Sun and public holidays 1100-1700. €3.94. Bookshop and coffee shop open museum hrs. Restaurant (see page 109). Combined tickets available with James Joyce Museum (see page 96) and The Shaw Birthplace (see page 86). T8722077.*

Dublin Writers' Museum

The Hugh Lane Gallery, a collection of 20th-century Irish and international art, is housed in a fine building on the north side of Parnell Square. It includes works by Corot, Millet, Monet, Degas and Burne-Jones. In the Irish collection, as well as Jack Yeats, there are works by Walter Osborne, Sarah Purser (with a daft portrait of Maud Gonne), Frank O'Meara and Limerick-born Norman Garstin whose early work, *The Stranger*, is a good example of his atmospheric paintings. The stained-glass room contains *The Eve of St Agnes*, the best-known work of Harry Clarke, one of Ireland's foremost artists. His style is strange, almost surreal and slightly reminiscent of Beardsley. His works were commissioned all over the world and you can see more of them in the National Gallery (*The Song of the Mad Prince*) and, oddly enough, in Bewleys Café in Grafton Street.

The reconstructed London studio of Francis Bacon, whose Irishness is often passed over by English critics, has opened in the gallery.

■ *Tue-Thu 0930-1800, Fri-Sat 0930-1700, Sun 1100-1700. Closed Mon. Free. Wheelchair access. Shop and restaurant open during gallery hrs. Sun lunchtime concerts and public lectures during winter, T8741903, www.hughlane.ie*

Hugh Lane Gallery
It is the collection of Irish art that makes this such an outstanding gallery

James Joyce Centre

For the many Joycean associations in this area, see Joyce's Dublin, page 94

North Great George Street, where Shane McGowan and Sinead O'Connor once lived, is now home to the James Joyce Centre. The Centre is unmissable for anyone with any interest in Joyce, and be sure to catch the short video about the writer for it uses old photographs to tremendous effect. Upstairs there are collections of photographs of people and places associated with Joyce and his books. The coffee shop incorporates the door of No 7 Eccles Street, fictional home of Leopold and Molly Bloom. Lots happens at the Centre during the **Bloomsday Festival**, 9-17 June 2001 (see page 121).

■ *Mon-Sat 0930-1700, Sun 1230-1700. Closed 24-26 Dec. €3.81 Coffee shop, book and gift shop. 35 North Great George's St, T8788547, www.jamesjoyce.ie*

Smithfield

For transport information see page 130

Smithfield itself is a small area that lies to the west of the centre on the north side of the Liffey. It has long been known as the site of a horse fair, a fruit and vegetable market and the **Jameson Distillery** but was otherwise an undistinguished part of town. Recent developments have created **Smithfield Village**, a residential and tourist area with a smart new hotel, a traditional music centre, the old whiskey distillery and new apartments. It's still a diverse area because the quayside between Capel St and the **Four Courts** is just a bridge-walk away from trendy Temple Bar, while few visitors venture along Parkgate Street even though it has some good pubs and excellent restaurants. In spite of the obvious tourist attractions, Smithfield retains its lived-in character and walking through its streets opens a window on ordinary Dublin life that you won't see in the centre of the city.

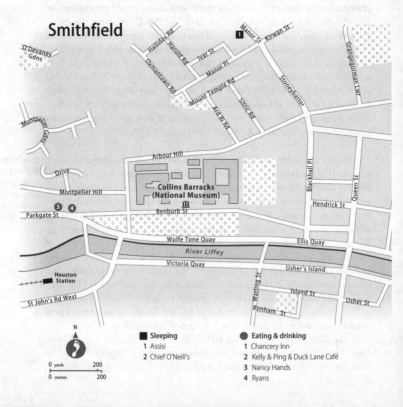

Smithfield

Sleeping
1 Assisi
2 Chief O'Neill's

Eating & drinking
1 Chancery Inn
2 Kelly & Ping & Duck Lane Café
3 Nancy Hands
4 Ryans

The Four Courts, completed in 1802, was occupied by the anti-Treaty forces in the civil war in the 1920's and eventually bombarded by government troops using field guns borrowed from the British. Renovation began soon after and the Four Courts reopened in 1931. ■ *The courts are currently open to the public when they are sitting, so take a seat in one of the public galleries (hearings start at 1100 and 1430 but not in Aug or Sep), especially the District Court that sits round the east side in Chancery Lane; it can provide a salutary antidote to the more cosmetic lifestyles characteristic of Dublin nowadays.*

The Four Courts

Just round the corner in Church Street is St Michan's Church (pronounced 'mickan'), founded in 1095 by the Vikings. None of the original building remains, although the distinctive grey limestone tower is 15th century. The church's chief claim to fame is the rather un-Christian display of some of the corpses in its vaults, hundreds of years old, preserved by the magnesium salts in the limestone absorbing the moisture in the air. Inside the church itself is an organ, one of the oldest still in use in Ireland, said to have been used by Handel for the first performance of his *Messiah*. ■ *31 Mar-31 Oct, Mon-Fri, 1000-1230, 1400-1630, Sat, 1000-1245; 1 Nov-30 Mar, Mon-Fri 1230-1500, Sat, 1000-1245. €2.50. Guided tours of the crypt are available. T8724154.*

St Michan's Church

Dublin Corporation invented the name of Smithfield Village to represent their efforts to create a new civic identity for this part of town. It includes the area's hotel and museums as well as the large cobbled and granite-paved plaza that is dominated by a sci-fi-looking structure that consists of 12 imposing gas-lighting masts, each with a 2-m flame flank. It all makes more visual sense on Friday and Saturday nights when the gas flames are lit.

Smithfield Village
The plaza area can hold up to 8,000 people and hosts major civic events

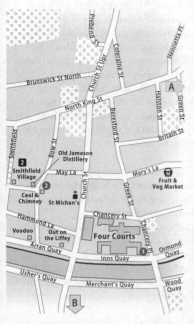

A few minutes away from St Michan's in Bow Street is the **Old Jameson Distillery**, now dedicated to the history of whiskey production. A trip to the old Jameson Distillery is by way of a guided tour with an opportunity to ask questions along the way. There is a bar and of course a complimentary tipple at the end of the tour. If you are keen to taste more than one, then hurl yourself forward when the guide looks for four volunteers for the whiskey-tasting session that concludes the tour. This involves comparing the tastes of four Irish whiskeys with a Scotch whisky and a Jim Breem before staggering away with a certificate to validate your connoisseurship. ■ *Daily, 0930-1800 (last tour 1700). €6.28. Tours last 45 mins. Self-service restaurant, bar and giftshop. T8072355.*

The comedian Ed Byrne explains in his show how he's been travelling the world apologizing for Riverdance: "the reason it tours the world is because it was asked to leave Ireland"

Part of the Chief O'Neill complex, all built in Smithfield Village on the site of the original Jameson Distillery, **Ceol** is a very interactive, modern exhibition about traditional music. ■ *Mon-Sat, 1000-1800. Sun, 1100-1800. €6.35. Café/bar, gift shop. T8173820, www.ceol.ie*

Outside the entrance to Ceol is **Jameson Chimney**, 175 ft (53 m) high with a glass-walled lift to take you to the top, from where the city spreads out beneath you. The chimney is the original Jameson Distillery Chimney, built in 1895. ■ Mon-Sat, 1000-1800. Sun, 1100-1900 (may be subject to seasonal change). *€3.81. T8173820. Same bus routes as for Ceol above.*

Collins Barracks

Close by the park in Benburb Street is the oldest and largest military barracks in Europe, designed by Thomas Burgh in 1701 to house 5,000 men. It was finally decommissioned in 1969.

The barracks now house the part of the **National Museum** dedicated to decorative arts, with some intriguing displays such as the curators' favourite pieces, a collection of fascinating rural furniture, displays on disappearing rural crafts, a new costume exhibition and lots more. There are interactive computer displays and some knowledgeable tours. The whole museum is distinguished by the quality of the displays. It lacks a history of the building itself and the events that have taken place there, but it is early days and that will hopefully come in phase two of the museum's development. ■ *Tue-Sat 1000-1700, Sun 1400-1700. Free. Café and bookshop open museum hrs; guided tours. T6777444.*

Joyce's Dublin

Generally agreed to be the greatest 20th-century novel in the English language, *Ulysses* is set in a single day, 16 June 1904, the day when Joyce first walked out with Nora Barnacle, the woman with whom he shared the rest of his life. The novel traces the wanderings around the city of Leopold Bloom, mirroring the wanderings of Odysseus on his journey home to Ithaca. Stephen Dedalus, Bloom's Telemachus or figurative son, joins him for part of the day. Joyce took the job of getting Bloom's journey technically correct very seriously, consulting timetables, getting relatives and friends to time journeys, check entrance-ways and so on. While many of the shops and pubs he lists have disappeared, several still stand and you can join in the annual fun on **Bloomsday** (details from the James Joyce Centre) and spend near enough 24 hours wandering in Bloom's footsteps around the city.

Eccles Street & onwards

No 7 Eccles Street, the home address of Leopold Bloom, no longer exists. It was knocked down in 1980 to make way for an extension to the Mater Hospital, but a plaque marks the spot where Bloom would have lived if he had existed and the real front door is on view in the James Joyce Centre (see page 92).

Turning right into Dorset Street, on his way to the butcher's, Bloom pauses at Larry O'Rourke's bar (now the *Snug*) to smell the odour of beer. After returning home and finishing breakfast, Bloom wanders into town down Hardwicke Place, past **St George's Church** (now the Temple Theatre). At the junction of Temple Street and Great Denmark Street you could detour from Bloom's journey to view **Belvedere House** (previously College), where Joyce attended school between 1893 and 1898.

Directly opposite Belvedere House is North Great George's Street, a row of what were very dilapidated Georgian terraces, but now a bijou area once again. At No 35 is the **James Joyce Centre** (see page 92).

To Leinster Street

Back on the *Ulysses* trail, Bloom heads into town along Gardiner Street. He passes under the railway bridge at the bottom of the street and crosses Butt Bridge, walks along St George's and City Quay and along Lombard Street and Westland Row. In Lombard Street Bloom notices Nichol's Undertakers, which is still there, its appearance barely changed since 1904. In Westland Row he stops at the Post Office, now part of the DART station, and collects a secret letter, which he takes round to the back of the railway arch in Cumberland Street – still much the same as Bloom would have seen it. His next port of call is **St Andrew's Church** in Westland Row, All Hallows in the novel, and watches the sleepy congregation

He travels along Westland Row past **Conway's Pub**, still doing the same trade but now called *Fitzsimon's*, and calls in at **Sweny's Chemist**, still there doing business, with the same shop front and sign 97 years later! Bloom buys lemon soap in the chemist, and it is still sold there: as Bloom says, "Chemists rarely move."

Joyce's Dublin

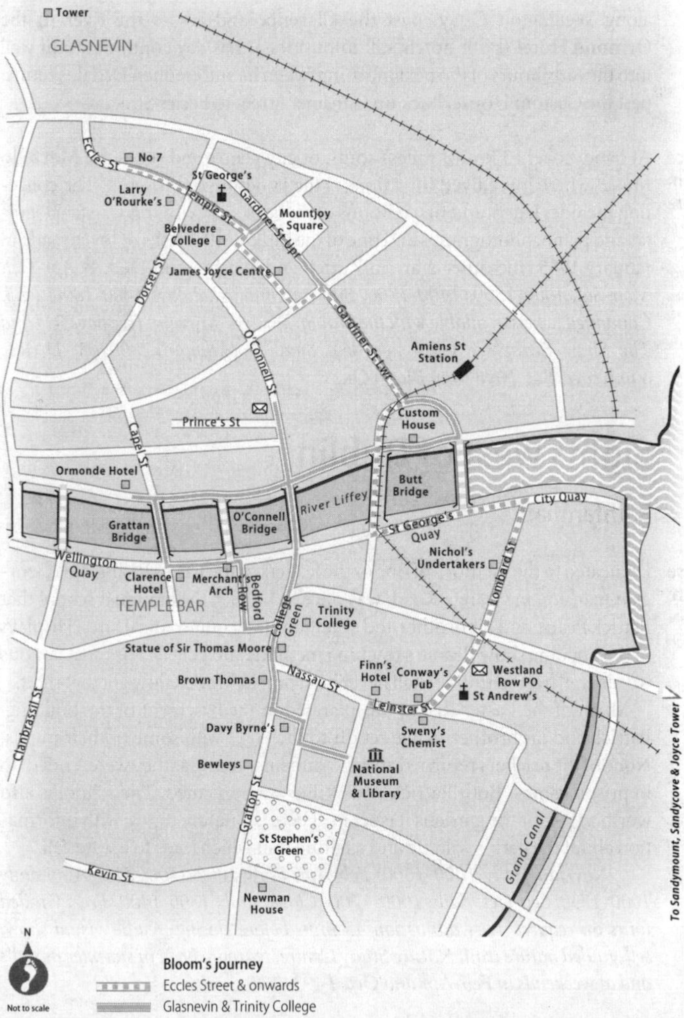
Tower
GLASNEVIN
Eccles St
No 7
Larry O'Rourke's
St George's
Temple St
Gardiner St Upr
Mountjoy Square
Belvedere College
Dorset St
James Joyce Centre
O'Connell St
Gardiner St Lwr
Amiens St Station
Prince's St
Custom House
Capel St
Ormonde Hotel
Butt Bridge
River Liffey
City Quay
O'Connell Bridge
Grattan Bridge
St George's Quay
Nichol's Undertakers
Lombard St
Wellington Quay
Clarence Hotel
Merchant's Arch
Bedford Row
TEMPLE BAR
College Green
Trinity College
Statue of Sir Thomas Moore
Finn's Hotel
Conway's Pub
Westland Row PO
St Andrew's
Brown Thomas
Nassau St
Leinster St
Sweny's Chemist
Davy Byrne's
Bewleys
National Museum & Library
Clanbrassil St
Grafton St
St Stephen's Green
Kevin St
Grand Canal
Newman House
To Sandymount, Sandycove & Joyce Tower
N
Not to scale
Bloom's journey
Eccles Street & onwards
Glasnevin & Trinity College

Grafton Street

On O'Connell Bridge he pauses to watch a Guinness Brewery barge go past, buys a bun from a stallholder and throws it to the seabirds over the river. In **College Green** Bloom passes the statue of Thomas Moore, the poet, famous for *The Meeting of the Waters*, and is amused that this man should stand in effigy above a public toilet. He passes down Grafton Street, then as now "gay with housed awnings". **Brown Thomas**, the department store, still in Grafton Street but now on the other side, is noted. Bloom turns into Duke Street and famously pops into **Davy Byrne's**, 'the moral pub', for a Gorgonzola sandwich and a glass of burgundy. Davy Byrne's is still in business and serves the Gorgonzola every 16 June.

National Library to Temple Bar

After this Bloom heads towards the National Library, turning right into Dawson Street. Bloom leaves the library and heads to **Temple Bar** for the second-hand bookshops – he wants to buy his wife a paperback novel to read. He walks along Bedford Row, passes through Merchant's Arch and on to Wellington Quay. By this time it is about half past three. From here he walks along Wellington Quay, past the **Clarence** and across the river to the **Ormond Hotel** (both hotels still in business). His day continues until well into the early hours of the next morning, when he and Stephen Dedalus return past the Custom House, back up Gardiner Street to Eccles Street.

James Joyce Museum

Joyce aficionados might also like to visit the house in Bray where Joyce lived as a toddler (see page 173)

At Sandycove, 13 km (8 miles) south of city centre and set in the **Martello tower**, where Joyce lived for a time, is the James Joyce Museum. The collection includes letters and first editions of his books as well as his waistcoat, guitar and piano, photographs and one of the three death masks of Joyce made in January 1945 (the other 2 are in Zurich and Washington DC). ■ *Apr-Oct, Mon-Sat, 1000-1300, 1400-1700, Sun and public holidays 1400-1800. (€5. Combined tickets available with the Dublin Writers' Museum (see page 91) and The Shaw Birthplace (see page 86). Small bookshop. T2809265. DART: Sandycove. Bus: No 8 from Burgh Quay.*

Sights west of Dublin

Rathfarnham

The Pearse Museum

Look out for the photo of Michael Collins standing on the steps of the school signing Dáil bonds. The block of wood he is leaning on is now in Kilmainham Gaol & is thought to be the execution block of Robert Emmet

Dedicated to the memory of one of the leaders of the Easter Rising, this Georgian mansion in Grange Road, was once St Edna's, the bilingual school that Patrick Pearse and his brother and sister ran along quite radical lines. Displays in the building show Pearse's teaching methods and beliefs. His most famous words are: 'Ireland unfree shall never be at peace'. He certainly got that right.

Much of the Easter Rising was planned in the basement of the building. Patrick and his brother Willie set off to the GPO with some of their pupils. None of the teachers returned and the students, young as they were, ended up in prison camps. Both Patrick and Willie were executed. The school is also worth a visit for the gardens it is set in. There is a nature centre with information about the park's wildlife and a nature trail which leads to a waterfall.

Nov-Jan, daily 1000-1600; Feb-Apr, daily 1000-1700; May-Aug, daily 1000-1730; Sep-Oct, daily 1000-1700. Closed daily 1300-1400. Free. Guided tours on request. Last admission 45 mins before closing. Audio-visual show, self-guided nature trail, Nature Study Centre, tearoom open in summer months and at weekends in Feb-Apr and Oct. T4934208.

The 16th-century building was originally a proper castle with battlements and **Rathfarnham** 18 fireplaces, making it the biggest building in the Dublin area. The battlements **Castle** were removed in the more settled times of the early 18th century. The castle is undergoing renovations and visitors are shown around the works as they progress, getting a different glimpse of structures and alterations at each visit.

■ *Jun-Sep, daily 1000-1800; May and Oct, daily, 1000-1700; Easter weekend, 1000-1700. € 2. Last admission 1 hr before closing. Access by guided tour only. Tearoom open all year. Rathfarnham Rd, Rathfarnham, Dublin 16. T4939462.*

The Royal Hospital at Kilmainham, now the **Irish Museum of Modern Art**, **Irish Museum** was built between 1680 and 1684 as a retirement home for old soldiers, in a rect- **of Modern Art** angle with an interior courtyard and a loggia with open arches on three sides. *Less than 10 mins on foot from Heuston Railway Station* The museum organizes a wide-ranging programme of exhibitions, and there are always brochures outlining the displays of the moment. The current programme includes exhibitions on Irish art from the second half of the 20th century, Mughal textiles, Dennis Oppenheim's installation art, and a number of smaller exhibits and projects. The bookshop in the gallery has an excellent collection of books on art and architecture.

■ *Tue-Sat, 1000-1730, Sun, bank holidays, 1200-1730, closed Mon. Free. Guided tours, Tue-Fri at 1000, 1145, 1430 and 1600; free, advance booking is required. Tours not requiring pre-booking take place on Wed and Fri at 1430 and Sun at 1215. Talks and lectures all year, and on Thu at 1130 there's an opportunity to meet artists at work in the museum's studios. Garden, coffee shop and bookshop open museum hrs. Military Rd, T6129900, www.modernart.ie*

Built in 1792, and open just in time to take in the survivors of the 30,000 rebels **Kilmainham** who died in the 1798 uprising, this building saw hundreds of men suffer and **Gaol** die for their belief in independence in the uprisings of 1798, 1803, 1848, 1867, *Give yourself an hour* 1916 and 1922. Most of the big names in Republican history spent time in here *for the tour and at* and some of them died here. The last man to walk out was De Valera, at the *least half an hour* end of the Civil War in 1923, whereupon the gaol was abandoned as it stood. *more for the museum* Forty years later a voluntary group of history buffs decided to restore it, the work was completed by the state and Kilmainham was opened to the public.

There is a museum of early 20th-century political history as well as prison memorabilia where you can wait for a guided tour. It takes you around the dungeons, tiny cells, the chapel where Joseph Plunkett was married three hours before his execution and the grim yard where Connolly, Plunkett and 15 other leaders of the 1916 uprising were executed.

■ *Apr-Sep, daily 0930-1645; Oct-Mar, Mon-Fri 0930-1600, Sun 1000-1645, closed Sat. €4.44. Visits include a guided tour. Last tour is 1 hr before closing. Inchicore Rd, Dublin 8. T4535984, www.heritageireland.ie*

Phoenix Park

It's easy to put on a good pair of walking shoes and take a whole day pottering *For transport* about the sights in the Phoenix Park. The 1,752 acres (710 ha) make it the largest *information,* enclosed public park in Europe and it includes **Dublin Zoo**, a police museum, a *see page 131* visitor centre, an early 17th-century fortified house, monuments to assorted public figures, the homes of the Irish president and American ambassador, several lakes, deer, a thriving wildlife community, a **neolithic cromlech** and the interesting ruins of a **magazine fort** to wander around. Dubliners use Phoenix Park for all sorts of activities, from practising their golf swings to flying model aeroplanes, hurling matches and just sitting about in the sunshine. The park lies about 2½ km (1½ miles) west of O'Connell Bridge in the city centre and can be reached on foot by walking along the north quays or by bus.

Dublin zoo

The MGM lion's roar is said to have been recorded from a lion bred in Dublin zoo

Dublin Zoo, set in 30 acres (12 ha), is the second oldest zoo in Europe and has a petting zoo and monkey islands. A new extension calls itself the African Plains and serves as home to animals like the rhino, giraffe and hippo. ■ *Mon-Sat 0930-1800, Sun 1030-1800 (closing at 1700 daily between Nov and Feb). €8.90, family ticket €25.40. Daily tours, restaurant, gift shop. T6771425, www.dublinzoo.ie*

Approaching the Wellington Testimonial, the sheer scale of the thing is what strikes the eye. It was begun in 1817, and the money for its construction was used up on the first 30 m (98 ft). Wellington fell from grace at around this time and the monument was not completed. In 1861 work on it began again, with the addition of the bronze plaques celebrating Waterloo, the defeat of the Indian Mutiny and, strangely with regard to someone who opposed Catholic emancipation, civil and religious liberty. But the project was never completed according to the original plan. The lions intended for the statue's feet were never made, and the plinths that had been set out to hold them were taken down.

Sights north of the city

Glasnevin and Clontarf

For transport information, see page 131

Spreading northwards from the city centre, beyond the Royal Canal which marks the outer edges of the city proper, are the twin suburbs of Glasnevin and Clontarf, mainly residential areas, and home to some impressive Edwardian estates full of much sought after terraced houses. Apart from the bed and breakfast accommodation, visitors are drawn by two major attractions, the **Botanic Gardens** and the **Prospect Cemetery** at Glasnevin. They are close enough to each other to be visited on the same day.

Prospect Cemetery

Prospect Cemetery opened in 1832 after a long campaign to make religious funerals for Catholics possible. Until the final repeal of the Penal Laws, Catholics had practised their religion in a sort of underhand way, tolerated as long as they kept a low profile. Most cemeteries were officially Protestant and, while Catholics were still buried in them, no Catholic prayers were allowed at the graveside. In the 19th century the great church-building spree began, and along with this came the opening of Prospect Cemetery, officially non-denominational, but sponsored by Daniel O'Connell's Catholic Association.

It's not often you see a cemetery on a list of sightseeing places, but this one is seriously worth a visit for many reasons. First, within its 120 acres (50 ha) are interred the bodies of probably hundreds of people who have played significant parts in the history, art, literature and religious life of Ireland and beyond, and standing beside their graves gives their stories an immediacy that a dull paragraph in a history book never does. Second, it is a stunning piece of social history, written in the architecture and design of the thousands of tombstones, revealing the pretensions, passions, wealth and poverty of the people who are buried there. Whoever said that death doesn't distinguish between rich and poor? Highly recommended is the free tour of the cemetery.

The gardens, close by the cemetery, comprise 500 acres (200 ha) of plants, both indigenous and exotic collections. Established in 1795, they are worth the visit just to admire the great 19th-century glasshouses. There are more than 20,000 species of plant here, including several that were developed at Glasnevin. It is one of Glasnevin's collectors that the British Isles has to thank for the stands of pampas grass that grace suburban gardens. The Botanic Gardens are undergoing a massive facelift with the curvilinear range almost completely replaced, a new alpine house and a visitor centre with a good café.

National Botanic Gardens

■ *Gardens: summer, Mon-Sat, 0900-1800, Sun, 1100-1800; winter, Mon-Sat, 1000-1630, Sun, 1100-1630. Free.* **Glasshouses:** *summer, Mon-Fri, 0900-1715, Sat, 0900-1745; winter, Mon-Sat, 1000-1615, Sun, 1400-1615. Closed Christmas Day. Guided tours by arrangement, €1.90. T8374388.*

Essentials

Sleeping

Grafton St, Temple Bar and around form Dublin's chief accommodation area, with prices either pretty high at the 3-star hotel and upwards end, or low at the couple of hostels, and with not much in between. Guesthouses tend to be at the expensive end of the market and there are simply no B&Bs in the area.

From the airport bus No 16A travels down Aungier and South Great George's St while No 746 travels along Kildare St and Leeson St. The Airlink bus, No 748, departs half hourly for Aston Quay, not in this area but close by. The bus follows the river west to Heuston railway station, but get off at Aston Quay and any street on the left will bring you to your Temple Bar accommodation, 5-10 mins away on foot.

From Dun Laoghaire the DART will bring you to Pearse St station or buses 7, 7A or 8 come into the city centre through Merrion Sq.

The **O'Connell St** area has a concentration of the more affordable guesthouses and hostels, but the central location, and the proximity of the bus and a railway station, means they tend to fill up the most quickly. **Gardiner St** is full of guesthouses and quite a few hostels are here or in the nearby streets. The top end of O'Connell St, around Parnell Sq, also has some interesting possibilities.

O'Connell St lies immediately north of the River Liffey and every bus from the airport, including the Aircoach service, travels down it so transport is straightforward. If your accommodation is on Gardiner St, parallel to O'Connell St, it takes 5-10 mins to walk through the couple of blocks separating the two streets. Airport bus No 747, however, stops at the central bus station and this is more convenient for the lower end of Gardiner St. Airport bus No 748 also stops at the bus station. For guesthouses along Upper Gardiner St, near Mountjoy Sq, bus No 41 is handy because it stops close by. If your accommodation is north of O'Connell St, in the Drumcondra area, ask the bus driver to drop you off along Drumcondra Rd.

The **Ballsbridge** area, southeast of the city centre, is a 15-20-min walk, or by buses Nos 5, 7, 7A and 8 from Burgh Quay or the No 45 from Eden Quay; use the Aircoach for public transport to and from the airport. The Lansdowne Rd DART station is also convenient for many of the hotels and guesthouses. Ballsbridge is one of the most expensive parts of the city, housing many of the major embassies, and not surprisingly the cost of accommodation is high. There are no economically priced rooms but an excellent range of top-notch hotels, quality guesthouses and a cluster of interesting restaurants. Nearby Herbert Park is good for jogging.

North of the city, **Glasnevin** is a pleasant residential area characterized by red-brick Edwardian housing estates. Most of the accommodation are B&B establishments in family homes. The Botanic Gardens are on your doorstep, as is Glasnevin Cemetery, and the city centre is about 10 mins away by bus. Glasnevin is manageable on foot from O'Connell St by heading up Dorset St, into Lower Drumcondra Rd and taking a left into Iona Rd or Botanic Av. To or from the airport requires a taxi or a walk to Drumcondra Rd for buses Nos 16, 16A, 41A-C and 46X. Public transport to and from the city centre is more direct with bus No 13 from Merrion Sq and O'Connell St, Nos 19 and 19A from Aungier St and O'Connell St and No 134 from Middle Abbey St.

Grafton Street & around
■ *on map, page 70*

XL *Merrion Hotel*, Upper Merrion St, T6030600, www.mrrionhotel.com The ultimate in understated luxury in the middle of the city. 4 converted Georgian houses, one of which was the birthplace of Wellington, plus a new block in the same style surround pretty formal gardens. Big comfortable rooms, 2 restaurants, pool and fitness centre plus a fairly astounding collection of artwork scattered around the beautiful Georgian interiors. **XL** *Stephen's Hall*, Earlsfort Centre, Lower Leeson St, Dublin 2, T6610585, www.premgroup.com This all-suite hotel is certainly the best value for money at this end of the market with large spacious rooms, open fireplaces, workstations with computers, fully equipped kitchens, dining and lounge areas, and a shopping service. Californian-style bistro restaurant (see *Morel's*, page 106). More orientated to long-stay business visitors, this is nevertheless centrally located and perfect for a holiday visit, especially for families. The penthouse suites have excellent rooftop balconies and views. Some non-smoking rooms.

LL *Brooks*, Drury St, Dublin 2, T6704000, www.sinnotthotels.com Stylish and located in the heart of Dublin, with a restful library and a pleasantly quiet restaurant. No car park, but a multi-storey one is opposite the hotel and special rates are available. **LL-L** *Camden Court Hotel*, Camden St, Dublin 2, T4759666, www.camdencourthotel.com Huge modern hotel with above average restaurant. Away from the street noise of late night clubbers but close enough to all the sights. Popular bar (*Pishogues*) nicely done out with illustrations of Irish myths, serves an excellent carvery lunch which gets very busy on weekdays. Leisure centre with a large pool, jacuzzi and steam room available to guests. Secure car parking. Best value in this price range and area. **LL-L** *Trinity Capital Hotel*, Pearse St, Dublin 2, T6481000, www.capital-hotels.com Newish, fashionable hotel in a quiet area of the city centre between Trinity College and the river. Outlandish décor, comfortable rooms, free entrance to and no bother from *Fireworks*, the nightclub on the corner. Key card gets you into 8 other pubs and clubs around the city for free. **LL-AL** *Harcourt Hotel*, 60 Harcourt St, T4783677, www.harcourthotel.ie Very busy hotel in the heart of the clubbing area. Great if you plan to have a late night out in Harcourt St, but if you want an early night ask for a room at the back. Lots of traditional music, good bar food.

L-AL *Georgian Hotel*, 18-22 Lower Baggot St, T6618832, hotel@georgianhouse.ie Small comfortable hotel in a quiet area right beside St Stephen's Green and close to the Grand Canal. Lots of space in the big open lobby, breakfast is in the trendily decorated bar next door. Secure parking. **L** *Holiday Inn*, 99-107 Pearse St, Dublin 2, T6703666, www.holidayinndublin.ie 10-min walk from the city, located at the working-class end of Pearse St. Nearly 100 rooms and the benefit of a gym and sauna. The bar, the *Esther Keogh*, is popular with locals and has live music at weekends, ranging from jazz to karaoke. **L** *Buswell's*, Molesworth St, Dublin 2, T6146500, www.quinnhotels.com Much of the original Georgian plasterwork is listed, and while the hotel has been extended it still retains all its originality and charm.

AL *Jackson Court Hotel*, 29-30 Harcourt St, Dublin 2, T4758777, info@jackson-court.ie Big rooms with spacious bathrooms and actual baths, carvery meals in the popular bar, and nightclub free to guests. Right in the centre of the non-Temple Bar nightclub area.

Guesthouses and B&Bs L-AL *Baggot Court*, 92 Lower Baggot St, Dublin 2, T6612819, baggot@indigo.ie. Close to the centre but in quiet area, pleasantly appointed albeit identically pine-furnished bedrooms with bath and shower, small guest lounge area, off street parking. **L-AL** *Kilronan Guesthouse*, 70 Adelaide Rd, Dublin 2, T4755266, www.dublinn.com An award-winning guesthouse that can rival most small hotels for its level of service and comfort, and a private car park.

Hostels A-B *Ashfield House*, 19-20 D'Olier St, Dublin 2, T6797734, F6790852, ashfield@indigo.ie Multi-bed, single and double rooms, lots of facilities. **B** *Avalon House*, 55 Aungier St, Dublin 2, T4750001, F4750303, www.avalon-house.ie Singles and doubles at reasonable rates as well as family rooms and mixed dormitory rooms. Some en suite, toilets also mixed. Problems with noisy guests and very overcrowded when full, as it is from Easter onwards. Price includes breakfast. No lounge area. Café/restaurant open unreliable hours.

Self-catering A-B *Trinity College*, Dublin 2, T6081177. 16 Jun-3 Oct. Single rooms, some en suite. Bar, kitchens, laundry, sports facilities, car park. Breakfast included. *Latchfords*, 99 Lower Baggot St, Dublin 2, T6760784, www.latchfords-accomm.com Studio apartments with up to 2 bedrooms costing from around €120 for a double for one night to over €500 a week.

Hotels XL *The Clarence*, 6-8 Wellington Quay, Dublin 2, T4070800, www.theclarence.ie Owned by U2, the original wood panelling has been preserved amidst modish embellishments like leather-clad lifts, Egyptian cotton on the kingsize beds, CD player (but no kettle) in the individually designed bedrooms enlivened by rich colours and Irish craftwork. Friendly staff, wearing designer outfits that look vaguely clerical and a bookless lounge called the *Study* with original art work contribute to the strange mix of the Spartan and the sybaritic that characterizes a hotel originally built in 1852.

Temple Bar
■ *on map, page 80*

LL-AL *Blooms*, 6 Anglesea St, Dublin 2, T6715622, www.blooms.ie Small hotel with 86 rooms all well designed, centrally located. Nightclub doesn't bother guests, popular bar for lunches. Restaurant and café.

AL *Jurys Christ Church Inn*, Christ Church Pl, Dublin 8, T4540000, www.jurysdoyle.com Based on a single-room rate for 3 adults, or 2 adults and 2 children, this is reasonable value for fair-sized, comfortable rooms, nice pub with traditional music, secure car park and informal restaurant (breakfast not included in room rate).

Hostels A-B *Kinlay House*, 2-12 Lord Edward St, Dublin 2, T6796644, F6797437, kinlay.dublin@usitworld.com IHH, mixed washrooms and toilets, breakfast included, internet access. One of the smartest kitchen and dining areas in any Dublin hostel. Very central, good security, but the usual noise problem at weekends. **A-B** *Barnacles Temple Bar House*, 19 Temple Lane, Dublin 2, T6716277, F6716591, tbh@barnacles.ie IHH, nice modern lounge area, big windows, all rooms en suite, good security, left-luggage facility and safes, breakfast included. **B** *The Oliver St John Gogarty*, 18-21 Anglesea St, Dublin 2, T6711822, www.olivergogartys.com IHH hostel, lift, safes, luggage storage, internet access, laundry, TV room.

Hostels A-C *Four Courts Hostel*, Usher's Quay, T672 5839. This is west of the Liberties area itself, directly opposite the Four Courts and close to the Guinness Storehouse. Now under new management, the hostel is better value than it used to be and a quiet non-smoking reading room has been added. Dorm beds and private doubles available. **A-C** *The Brewery Hostel*, 22-3 Thomas St, Dublin 8, T453 8600, www.irish-hostels.com

The Liberties
■ *on map, page 84*

Good to find a hostel in this part of town and this IHO and IHH establishment is open all year with over 50 dorm beds and 5 private doubles. Breakfast included, and a paved area out the back with picnic tables. Staying a night or 2 in Thomas St can be interesting because this is not tourist Dublin and there are some lively pubs and clubs along here.

Self-catering *Shaw Court*, Synge Pl, T4783677 (from USA, T1800 44UTELL; from UK T0990-300200), www.harecourthotel.ie Tucked away in the Portobello district of town, in the area of the Jewish Museum, these are new apartments with futon sleeping for up to 4 or 6 people in 1 and 2 bedrooms respectively.

O'Connell Street & around
■ *on map, page 88*
Most budgets are allowed for, but this area is rich in mid-range guesthouses, hotels and hostels

Hotels XL-LL *The Gresham*, O'Connell St, Dublin 1, T8746881, www.gresham-hotels.com The hotel claims to have the highest ratio of porters to rooms in Ireland. Close to the GPO, it was destroyed by the shelling of the British in 1916 and withstood the Beatles in the 1960s. A scene in Joyce's *Ulysses* is set in one of the hotel rooms. **LL-L** *Morrison*, 15 Ormond Quay, Dublin 1, T8872400, www.morrisonhotel.ie Part of the gentrification of north Dublin, this classy new building, Ireland's first designer hotel, sits unobtrusively on the bank of the river and vies with *The Clarence* as Dublin's most hip hotel. New-fashioned décor, themed in black and white, refreshingly un-Irish. CD players (but no kettles), mood lighting, quality fabrics and original art work in the chic, air-conditioned bedrooms. Lots of designer touches about the place waiting to be noticed. Breakfast not included in room rates; brilliant restaurant (see page 109).

L *Royal Dublin*, O'Connell St, Dublin 1, T8733666, www.royaldublin.com Popular with visitors, this is a friendly well run hotel at the top end of Parnell St. Gregarious bar alongside the decent *Café Royal* restaurant (see page 110). **L-AL** *Academy Hotel*, Findlater Pl, T8780666, www.academy-hotel.ie Modern centrally located hotel off O'Connell St, with *Fadó Fadó* bar and *Oscars* restaurant. Free private car park. **L-AL** *Hotel Isaacs*, Store St, Dublin 1, T8550067, www.isaacs.ie Adjacent to the bus station, an attractive lobby compensates for the dingy location; smart rooms, car parking around €7 a day, Italian-style restaurant, page 110. **L-AL** *Hotel St George*, 7 Parnell Sq, Dublin 1, T8745611, hotels@indigo.ie The bedroom décor may be a little twee but the marble fireplace and original plasterwork in the lounge of this Georgian building help distinguish it. Car park available. **L-AL** *Lynam's Hotel*, 63 O'Connell St, Dublin 1, T8880886, www.lynams-hotel.com Bang in the centre of O'Connell St, but not noisy in the 40 smart and modern bedrooms in 2 Georgian houses once owned by the inventor of the Tilly Lamp. A comfortable lounge area on the first floor overlooks the main drag, and breakfast is served downstairs in the *West Coast Café*.

AL *Castle Hotel*, 3/4 Great Denmark St, Dublin 1, T8746949, hotels@ indigo.ie Another lovingly restored Georgian building that offers so much more, and better value, than some of the faceless hotels around town. Car parking available, elegant lounge area and comfortable bedrooms (Michael Collins is said to have used room 201, originally room No 23, when sleeping in one of his familiar safe houses, see page 91). **AL** *Waltons*, 2-5 North Frederick St, Dublin 1, T8783131, F8783090, waltons@eircom.net What looks from the outside like just another small hotel turns out to be a carefully restored Georgian building. The lounge is a treat, with paintings of Michael Collins and other republicans on the wall. Comfortable bedrooms, including singles, a car park, and the friendly efficiency contribute to make Waltons a very decent hotel. **AL** *Jurys Custom House Inn*, Custom House Quay, Dublin 1, T6075000, www.jurysdoyle.com All the rooms have a flat rate of around €95, except during rugby weekends when the price almost doubles. Rooms at the front offer views of the river and the Wicklow hills in the distance; rooms at the back will be quieter. Breakfast not included in the room rate but there is a self-service cafeteria serving mediocre meals.

Guesthouses **L** *Comfort Inn*, 95 Talbot St, Dublin 1, T8749202, www.comfort-inn-dublin.com A refurbished, professionally run guesthouse with a pleasant lounge area and an outdoor patio area for picnic meals. All 48 bedrooms are smartly furnished and well maintained. Rates are on a room basis for up to 4 people, breakfast not included. **AL** *Georgian Court Guesthouse*, 77 Lower Gardiner St, Dublin 1, T8557872, georgiancourt@eircom.net Secure car parking, showers but no baths, a lounge area with a leather sofa, an airy dining room for above-average breakfast. Triple and family rooms. Popular in summer so advance booking required. **AL-A** *Glen Guesthouse*, 84 Lower Gardiner St, Dublin 1, T8551374, theglen@eircom.net Small, 12-room guesthouse, central, reasonable rates, well restored. **L-A** *Clifden Guesthouse*, 32 Gardiner Pl, T8746364, www.clifdenhouse.com A fair spread of rooms with singles, doubles, triples and family rooms. Rates don't include breakfast but parking is free. **AL-B** *Harvey's Guest House*, 11 Upper Gardiner St, Dublin 1, T8748384, www.harveysguesthouse.com Family-run, 14 bedrooms, free car parking; bus No 41 from the airport stops close by.

A *Othello Guesthouse*, 74 Lower Gardiner St, Dublin 1, T8554271/8555442, othello1@eircom.net Some rooms are larger than others but pot luck seems to determine which one you get. A small, boxy conservatory serves as a public guest area. Secure car parking available and all rooms are en suite, with a television and telephone; breakfast included. **A** *The Townhouse*, 47-8 Lower Gardiner St, Dublin 1, T8788808, gtrotter@indigo.ie Doubles and triple rooms at competitive prices, some with kitchenette, all have their own bathrooms, tea- and coffee-making facilities, satellite TV. Rates include continental breakfast. The house has a literary heritage which is proudly displayed around the lobby area and which complements the period details which help make this a rather elegant guesthouse. **A-B** *Marian Guesthouse*, 21 Upper Gardiner St, Dublin 1, T8744129. Family-run, standard guesthouse, B&B prices, fair value, close to Mountjoy Sq and bus No 41 from the airport stops close by.

Hostels **AL-B** *Globetrotters Tourist Hostel*, 46-8 Lower Gardiner St, T8735893, F878-8787, gtrotter@indigo.ie IHH hostel, one of the most expensive in Dublin if paying for a private room, breakfast included. **A-B** *Abbey Court*, 29 Bachelor's Walk, Dublin 1, T8780700, F8780719, info@abbey-court.com Newish, IHH hostel accommodation in central location by O'Connell Bridge. All rooms en suite, barbecue area, TV room, key card access, breakfast included. **A-B** *Abraham House*, 82-3 Lower Gardiner St, Dublin 1, T8550600, F8550598, stay@abraham.house.ie IHH, dorm beds and private rooms, though not a lot of comfort. Free car park, launderette, breakfast included in price. Fills up very quickly so book early. **A-B** *Jacob's Inn*, 21-8 Talbot Pl, Dublin 1, T8555660, jacobs @isaacs.ie IHH, café-style restaurant, internet, free left-luggage facility, TV lounge, safes.

Dublin

A-C *Litton Lane*, 2-4 Litton Lane, Dublin 2, T8728389, F8720039, litton@indigo.ie Only 3 private rooms in this new IHO and IHH hostel, breakfast included, laundry. **A-C** *Celts House*, 32 Blessington St, Dublin 7, T/F8300657, www.celtshouse.ie Small IHH hostel with some of the cheapest dorm beds in high season, private rooms, family and multi-bed rooms. Meals available. **B-C** *Mount Eccles Court* , 42 North Great George St, Dublin 1, T8730826, www.eccleshostel.com The Joyce Centre is a few doors down from this fairly new hostel with all the expected facilities for an IHH member. Dorm beds are more reasonably priced than many are during the high season; only 4 private rooms. **B-C** *Backpackers Ireland Citi Hostel*, 61-2 Lower Gardiner St, Dublin 1, T8550035, www.backpackersireland.com Dorm beds, double, triple and quad bedrooms, TV lounge, internet facility, pool table. Rates almost double for a Sat night. **A-B** *Isaac's Hostel*, 2-5 Frenchman's Lane, Dublin 1, T8556215, hostel@isaacs.ie IHH place with deli, cyber café, multi-bed dorms, singles and doubles, safes, free left-luggage facility. No access even to private rooms between 1100 and 1430 but still very popular place, helped by being so close to the bus station. **B-C** *Marlborough Hostel*, 81-2 Marlborough St, Dublin 1, T8747629, mail@marlborohostel.com IHH, good-value, relaxed small hostel. Twin rooms particularly reasonable value, TV room, rear garden with BBQ area, security lockers, breakfast included.

C *Dublin International Youth Hostel*, 61 Mountjoy St, Dublin 7, T8301766, dublin-international@anoige.ie *An Óige* (Hostelling International) hostel, multi-bed and a few double rooms, in a renovated old convent. Huge kitchen, secure parking, brilliant dining room in old chapel, TV room, supplement for non-members. **C-C** *Goin' My Way*, 15 Talbot St, Dublin 1, T8788484, goinmyway@esatclear.ie Open between 4 Jan and 22 Dec, vaguely Christian IHHhostel, tiny, ageist hostel, good-value twin rooms, breakfast included.

Self-catering *Jacobs Apartments*, 21-8 Talbot Pl, Dublin 1, T8555660, F8555664. Apartments sleeping 2 from around €450 or 3 from around €600.

Smithfield
■ *on map, page 92*

Hotels XL-L *Chief O'Neill's Hotel*, Smithfield Village, Dublin 7, T817 3838, www.chiefoneills.com Toll free USA & Canada 1800 44Utell. Modern hotel, all frosted green glass and modish lighting, and bedrooms (with CD players, kettles and nifty sinks) that successfully strive to be different. Café/bar downstairs, in the centre of the newly renovated Smithfield Village. Breakfast is extra. If you are fed up with anonymous, all-too-similar hotels, consider staying here.

Guesthouses and B&Bs **A-B** *Assisi*, 84 Manor St, Dublin 7, T6770897, shirley.stafford @oceanfree.net Tucked away behind Collins Barracks, this B&B has 2 rooms with their own bathroom facilities. Open all year but belonging to the Family Homes of Ireland group and not bookable through Bord Fáilte.

Ballsbridge & around

Still within walking distance of the centre, but more conveniently reached by bus, Ballsbridge is an expensive residential neighbourhood in the south of the city. Home to some of the plummiest Dublin 4 accents, upmarket cars, tasteful faux Victorian conservatories, and with the densest population of antimacassars, doilies and toilet roll covers in all Ireland, these streets of Edwardian and Victorian houses exude comfortable, middle-class values. What the area does possess, in addition to the UK and US embassies, is a cluster of quality **hotels** and **guesthouses**. And even if you're not staying in Ballsbridge, it's worth the effort to go there just for the excellent **restaurants**.

Hotels XL *Four Seasons*, Simmonscourt Rd, Dublin 4, T6654000, www.fourseasons.com Very luxurious hotel, huge public areas, neo-classical decor, attentive staff. Large bedrooms and suites large enough to live in. Silver service in a grand, roomy restaurant with windows looking out to garden courtyard. **XL-LL** *The Towers*, Lansdowne Rd, Dublin 4, T6670033, (T0870-9072222 from the UK; 1-800-4236953 from USA), www.jurysdoyle.com One of Dublin's best hotels without a doubt. 8 floors, 100 larger than average bedrooms with a/c, walk-in wardrobe, work area. Hospitality lounge with complimentary cocktails and hot drinks throughout the day, a residents' bar serving until 0130 (0030 on Sun), and all the facilities of the main Jurys Ballsbridge hotel which is reached through a walkway. **XL-L** *Jury's Ballbridge* , Pembroke Rd, Dublin 4, T6605000, (T0870-9072222 from the UK; 1-800-4236953 from USA), F6605540, ballsbridge_hotel@jurysdoyle.com Remarkably friendly for such a large hotel, over 300 spacious bedrooms, and well provided for in the food and beverage departments. As well as the top-notch *Raglans* restaurant (see page 111), there is a coffee shop serving meals nearly 24 hrs, and a carvery lunch in the Dubliner pub. Indoor/outdoor pool and gym, free parking, hair and beauty salon.

LL-L *School House Hotel*, 2-8 Northumberland Rd, Dublin 4, T6675014, F6675015, school@schoolhousehotel.iol.ie Beside the canal, this prettily renovated old schoolhouse offers a high standard of accommodation, restaurant in a classroom, and a blackboard in the lobby with lines to memorize. Small and friendly and closer to town than most of the Ballsbridge hotels.

L-AL *Lansdowne Hotel*, 27 Pembroke Rd, Dublin 4, T6682522, www.lansdownehotel.com Small hotel with 40 bedrooms, a little way out of the centre in a quiet location. Beer garden, good bargain at this price range. *Druids Restaurant*. **L-AL** *The Mespil Hotel*, Mespil Rd, Dublin 4, T6671222, www.leehotels.ie This quality 3-star hotel is not as far south as Ballsbridge and is easily walkable to and from the city centre. Bus No 10 from O'Connell St and Kildare St travels close by, down Baggot St, and the Aircoach is a 5-min walk away outside the *Burlington Hotel* in Upper Leeson St. Free car parking. The Mespil is a modern hotel with a pleasant cosmopolitan feel with a room rate for up to 3 people, excluding breakfast, in generously sized bedrooms.

AL *Bewley's Hotel*, Merrion Rd, Dublin 4, T6681111, www.bewleyshotels.com Bedrooms are around €90 for up to 3 adults or a family of 4 and this represents excellent value for smart, spacious and comfortable accommodation, especially in the Ballsbridge area. The red-brick Victorian building has been converted from a convent school and the original entrance way opens into a roomy public area with the quality *O'Connells* restaurant downstairs (see below) and a café.

Guesthouses **L-AL** *Aberdeen Lodge*, 53-55 Park Av, T2838155, www.halpinsprivatehotels.com Luxurious Edwardian guesthouse where you are welcomed in with tea and biscuits. Elegant lounge area, gardens, hotel-standard rooms. Close to Sydney parade DART station. Hot drinks on call all day. Exemplary breakfast. A nice alternative to noisy city hotels. **L-AL** *Ariel House*, 52 Lansdowne Rd, Ballsbridge, Dublin 4, T6685512, www.ariel-house.com Listed, red-brick Victorian house, all non-smoking, car park, 3 mins on foot from the Lansdowne Rd DART station. Built in the 1860s, this is a classy guesthouse with a choice of rooms, all with a bath and shower, and 3 with 4-poster beds. Americans, with good reason, adore the décor and antiques. **L-AL** *Merrion Hall*, 56 Merrion Rd, T6681426, www.halpinsprivatehotels.com Quiet welcoming place with ample lounge area, a library with lots of tourist information, lovely, sunny breakfast room serving an award-winning breakfast, gardens.

Self-catering *UCD Village*, Belfield, Dublin 4, T2697111, F2697704, ucd.village@ usitworld.com 11 Jun-9 Sep. Choice of 3- or 4-bedroomed apartments, 24 hr reception, campus bar, restaurants and coffee shop, nightly or weekly.

Dublin

Camping and caravanning 35-min drive from Central Dublin is **D** *Camac Valley Tourist Caravan and Camping Park*, Naas Rd, Clondalkin, Dublin 22, T4640644, www.irishcamping.com 163 pitches and a good range of facilities including a TV lounge, good for those rainy days. 2 people plus tents from around €15. No hire caravans. No dogs in Jul and Aug.

Eating

Grafton Street
● on maps, pages 69 & 72
Price codes: see inside front cover

While many of Temple Bar's restaurants (see page 108) are fun, fashionable and relatively inexpensive places to enjoy a meal, the area from St Stephen's Green to Merrion Square is where the real money tends to eat. Don't even look at the menus if you are on a tight budget, but for seriously fine dining and for splashing out on a treat, this is where many of the capital's best restaurants are to be found. Reservations are advisable at all times, often essential. Many more moderately priced places can be found in the streets around Grafton St, while South Great George's St and Aungier St have lots of affordable restaurants.

Expensive *The Commons*, Newman House, 85-86 St Stephen's Green, T4752597. Situated downstairs in the beautiful old Jesuit university building, it serves a sophisticated combination of classical and nouvelle Irish cuisine, surrounded by a collection of Joyce-inspired paintings. Open for a pricey lunch, Mon-Fri, when men in suits predominate; Mon-Sat for dinner, with the weekends noticeably less formal; when the summer days are long be sure to enjoy pre-dinner drinks outside on the terrace. *Rubicon*, 6 Merrion Row, T6765955 is furiously busy at lunchtime but is much quieter and more reflective in the evenings. A muted modern interior with bare floors, two floors with a very welcoming open fire in the basement in winter lends itself to a subtle, and sensible, fusion menu incorporating Irish cheeses, lots of seafood, and some good options for vegetarians. The more limited lunch menu (weekdays only) is available all week from 1730-1900 as an early-bird dinner.

Mid-range *Aya*, 48 Clarendon St, T6771544, is Dublin's only conveyor-belt sushi bar. Different menus for breakfast, lunch and dinner, all authentically Japanese and regular tables too. *Francesca's*, *Brooks Hotel*, 59-62 Drury St, T6704000, is in the basement of the hotel but is uplifted by soothing background music and a calm, sedate air. Modern Irish food, like salmon and spiced couscous for example, with lots of organic touches and a flair for tasty non-meat dishes like a tartlet of aubergine, orange marmalade, feta cheese and rocket pesto. Come here for good food and quiet dining. For a pre-dinner drink, see if the seats in the front window of the *Hairy Lemon Pub* are empty, a couple of doors down on the corner of Drury St and Stephen St. *Juice*, T4757856, at number 73-78 South Great George's St, is a rare commodity in Dublin, a vegetarian restaurant which serves interesting meals in a quiet atmosphere. Inexpensive set lunches and good-value early-bird menu. Open late at weekends. *Little Caesar*, 5 Chatham House, Balfe St, T 6718714, is a Dublin institution. It has operated out of Balfe St for 12 years, a very long time in the life of a Dublin restaurant and judging by the queues to get in, hasn't lost its touch. It serves pizzas and pastas and some old favourites such as pollo al fredo and bistecca alla griglia; none of the main course dishes cost more than €12. *Morel's*, in the basement of *Stephen's Hall Hotel*, 14-17 Lower Leeson St, T6622480, is another lively bistroish kind of place to eat. It has a relaxed atmosphere and buzzes pleasantly. Cuisine is definitely Californian with some superb combinations. Try the white chocolate with cherry and pepper sauce. It's wonderful. Eamonn O'Reilly's *One Pico Restaurant*, 1 Upper Camden St, T4780307, is 5 mins from the centre and well worth the walk. Set in an old convent, its cosy street-side dining room is often full, popularity due to excellent dishes in the modern Irish style. Expect clever turns with fish, like tuna sashimi for starters or salmon teriyaki, mildly curried scallops or cod tempura for a main course. *Rajdoot*, 26-28 Clarendon St, T6794274, is much more than an Indian meal. The restaurant is designed to be an evening out in itself, from the elaborate wall hangings and lamps to the unintrusive background Indian fusion music and spacious seating area where you can pick out your meal and discuss your choices with the staff. There is no hassle, no second sitting, calm and deliberate service, from the toasted chickpeas while you wait for your order to the careful coffee service at the end. The dishes are huge, tasty and subtle – no chilli blasts here. Vegetarian Indian food lovers are in seventh heaven – real dishes, not a frozen vegetable in sight. If you eat late you need have no fear of the traditional English lager lout making his appearance after the pubs shut – they are gently moved on. *Saagar*, 16 Harcourt St, T475060, is another restaurant serving Indian home cooking, set in the basement kitchen of a Georgian house once lived in by Bram Stoker in the trendy Harcourt St area. The décor is a strange mix of authentic Georgian and ethnic wall-hangings with a lovely barrel-vaulted ceiling. The restaurant is open weekdays for lunch when it is very busy and even in the evenings a reservation is advisable. There is a cartoon on the wall of some of the guests who have been here.

Cheap In Grafton St itself is *Bewleys*, open till 0530 on Fri and Sat nights and 0100 every other night. Long lost in the tearoom-with-cream-cakes market, they are moving into all-night food places, and are really getting better. *Cornucopia*, 19 Wicklow St, T6777583, is a wholefood, vegetarian place a cut above the traditional sandals and dreadlocks image of some wholefood places. Breakfast is served from 0800-1200 and ranges from boxty (a kind of potato pancake) to granola and yoghurt, French toast and vegetarian fry-ups, while lunch and dinner are posted up on blackboards daily. Expect quiche, lots of salads, rice and stews. Scary drinks list includes wheatgrass. Lunch comes into the seriously affordable category. Noticeboard with useful flyers. *Good World Restaurant*, 18 South Great George's St, T6775373, opens late and gets lots of its customers when the pubs turn out. During the day it is famous for its dim sum, and the fact that many of its customers are Chinese vouchsafes its authentic cuisine. *Havana Tapas Bar*, 3 Camden Market, T4780046, serves Spanish tapas – little dishes which you can eat while you enjoy the wine and beer. Try the gambas *con aioli* (prawns with garlic mayonnaise) or for a more substantial dish, paella. It also does a takeout service. Open till 2200 weekdays and till late Thu, Fri and Sat. *Kitty's Kaboodle*, 14 Merrion Row, T6623351, has an enormous menu ranging from sandwiches to 3-course meals, pizzas, pasta dishes and a whole burger section. The same menu operates all day, Mon-Fri, 0730-midnight, 1200-midnight at weekends; nice café-type atmosphere, very mellow in the afternoons. Lots of the owner's artwork around the walls. *Messrs Maguire*, in Burgh Quay, is a pub with a difference. Besides brewing its own beer (you can get a guided tour of the brewery while you wait for your food), it has an extensive bar menu and restaurant. A lively atmosphere, good food at very reasonable prices and big-screen TVs for sports fans. Traditional music some nights. *Blazing Salads*, 2nd floor, Powerscourt Townhouse, South William St, is a very popular sandwich bar, serving vegetarian and vegan salads and sandwiches. Its tables look out over the shopping centre and if you are lucky you can listen to a free lunchtime concert. Open till 1800 Mon-Sat. There is a takeout branch of this excellent vegetarian wholefood place at 42 Drury St selling sandwiches, soups, lots of interesting breads, and hot dishes such as pizza, samosas and spring rolls. *Govinda's*, at 4 Aungier St, T4750309, does very inexpensive vegetarian food with good lunch specials and breakfasts. Upstairs in the *Hodges Figgis Bookshop*, 56-58 Dawson St, and open bookshop hrs (0900-1900 daily, 1200-1800 Sun, 0900-2000 Thu), is a grand little café where you have lots of choices of filled sandwiches and hot things like quiche. A huge round window lights the place, tables are

Dublin

well spaced, no muzak, and no-one hassles you to go away when you've finished your coffee. Buy a book and settle down on a rainy day. The *Pig and Heifer*, opposite the *Camden Court Hotel* on Charlotte Way, is a useful café serving all-day breakfast, bacon bagels, ham and eggs, etc. *Whelan's*, 25 Wexford St, is a pub doing an inexpensive carvery lunch or 3 courses. *Wagamama*, South King St, T4782152, in the basement of the St Stephen's Green Shopping Centre is a Japanese noodle house serving meat and vegetarian noodle dishes plus lots more at very low prices in a unusually clinical atmosphere. Open Mon-Sat 1200-2300, Sun 1200-2200. Check in Dublin Tourism for a 5% discount voucher.

Temple Bar
● *on map page 80*

Temple Bar is a little mecca of eating places, some pretentiously overpriced, others good, basic value for money and some in between, but there's almost no end to the list of eateries in this area. For the money-conscious, check out the early-bird menus that some places do here.

Expensive The impishly named *Tea Room*, at the *Clarence Hotel*, 6-8 Wellington Quay, T670 7766, attracts the beau monde. Modern Irish cuisine amidst hushed elegance from 1830 nightly, last order 2245, lunch between 1230 and 1500 and a Sun brunch from 1100 to 1500. Simple table decorations, simple menus and subtle service belie exciting and imaginative dishes: artichoke soup with truffles is excellent; or try the cider-flavoured crème brûlée with an apple and raisin won ton for a pudding to remember. Smoking and non-smoking areas.

Mid-range *Darkey Kelly's*, Fishamble St, is a pub next to the *Harding Hotel* and across from the cathedral. Tables are laid out for meals: steak around €18 and seafood tagliatelle around €12. *Dish*, 2 Crow St, T6711248. Of the 3 restaurants in Crow St, this is many Dubliners' favourite. Polished floorboards, painted walls and a hip feel to this trend-conscious place complement a menu of salads, pasta, steak and fish; a typical main dish is chicken and almond with sherry sauce and aubergine.

Ethnic cuisines are also abundant in Temple Bar. The hustle and bustle of Temple Bar is left behind when you step down into *Il Baccaro*, T6714597, a mock-Italian wine tavern on a corner of Meeting House Sq. Traditional fare on the menu, like *coppa di parma* as a starter, and meat-filled tortelloni for a lunch under €7 or a grilled steak for €16.50. *Fan's*, 60 Dame St, T6794263. Open daily 0900-2330, offering Cantonese cuisine and an early-bird menu between 1730 and 1930. *Fitzers*, Temple Bar Sq, T6790440, has become a Dublin institution with very different branches around the city. This one is laid back; jazz accompanies the food, which is trendy European in style, and an enormous menu runs to steaks and burgers as well as more sophisticated fare. Open daily 1200-2330. *Gallagher's Boxty House*, 20-21 Temple Bar, T6772762, sells the eponymous filled potato pancakes. It has a nice old-fashioned country-kitchen feel to it, with newspapers for the clients to read and bookcases with real books in them.

Mermaid Café, 70 Dame St, T6708236, one of Dublin's better restaurants, has changing menus that show an American influence in the mussel and smoked fish chowder, the New England crab cakes, and the pecan pie with maple ice cream. The wine list is above average. Open daily for lunch and dinner. *Nico's*, 53 Dame St, T6773062, is a popular Italian restaurant, serving quite traditional dishes with a strong Irish influence and live music, open for lunch Mon-Fri and dinner Mon-Sat.

The Indian subcontinent is well represented in Temple Bar, primarily at *Monty's of Kathmandu*, 28 Eustace St, T6704911. Don't let the photos of Tarantino put you off – this is excellent Nepalese cooking. Set lunch is superb value and there is an early-bird menu.

Cheap *Belgo* 17 Sycamore St, T6727555. Opposite the stage door of the *Olympia Theatre*, Belgo crosses the mid-range/affordable divide in its prices, depending on what you eat. It's a big place but tables are small and suffer from bench seating. Meals vary from mussel dishes, wild boar sausages, cod with beer batter, all under €15, to surf 'n' turf lobster for around €25. Gravedlax is one of the starters and home-made ice creams complete the desserts. Belgo has the mother of all drinks list. Open Mon-Thu, 1230 to 1500 and 1730 to 2300, open till midnight on Fri and Sat and until 2230 on Sun. Very popular indeed is *Luigi Malone's* (Italian-Irish and a sense of humour) in Fownes St Lower, T6792723, which claims to have food and drink from the 4 corners of the globe. It has a vast menu, comes recommended by lots of Dubliners and has a fair-priced lunch offer, of any main course meal with a glass of wine or beer, that lasts until 1700. BBQ ribs are a house special and the stone-baked pizzas are popular at lunchtime when the large eating area is filled to capacity. Across the road, *Juste Pasta*, T6703110, has murals on its 2 small floors and is possibly cramped at night but fine for a lunch of 2 courses and a hot drink for €9.

There are plenty of other places doing food in Temple Bar and most of the pubs do Irish stew, carvery lunches or sandwiches. And there's no shortage of places to snack either, including the *Cyberia Café* in Temple Lane, where you can slurp coffee, nibble a sticky bun and surf the net all at the same time. *Central Percs*, 10 East Essex St, does filled baguettes and sandwiches, while *Quays Bar*, in Temple Bar Sq, does soup and sandwiches.

Mid-range *Brazen Head*, 20 Lower Bridge St, T6795186, famous as Dublin's oldest pub (see below), has a restaurant upstairs with an authentic period feel. A Victorian dresser and piano, low ceiling and decorative stucco complement the interesting menu which combines Californian and modern Irish cuisine, a decent vegetarian choice and hearty helpings. Downstairs they serve carvery lunch and hot specials. Reservations are usually essential and ask for the charming booth that seats two. *The Old Dublin Restaurant*, 91 Francis St, T4542028, is one of the best examples of a rare breed of restaurant which is not easy to pigeonhole. Using 3 rooms of what was a house of tenement apartments until 1981, the restaurant has a relaxed living-room style that has seasoned with age. The food is delightfully influenced by Scandinavian and Russian cuisine and the wine list is impressive. Check out the early-evening set dinner, ordered between 1830-1930.

The Liberties

Cheap *Nash's*, corner of Patrick St and Kevin St, close to St Patrick's Cathedral. This pub is a great budget place for a midday bite when visiting the cathedral. The tuna special, a giant sandwich with salad, plus a pot of tea is less around €4 and unlike so many Dublin pubs there is space to move around. No loud music, just locals sipping their black liquid lunches and a warm fire in winter.

The O'Connell St area seems to be woefully lacking when it comes to decent and half-decent places to eat at night but all is not lost. With one noble exception, the best restaurants are found in hotels and there are also some pleasant middle-of-the road places. To the west of O'Connell St, around Liffey St Lower and just across the river from Temple Bar, there is a good choice of cafés for an inexpensive lunch but they close up around 1800.

O'Connell Street & around

Expensive *Chapter One*, at 18-19 Parnell Square below the *Dublin Writers' Museum*, T8732266, serves the best food north of the Liffey – organic pork, spicy duck, roast venison – and in the basement of an elegant Georgian house to boot. *Halö*, *Morrison Hotel*, Ormond Quay Lower, T8872400. A huge black slab, large mirrors and lamp shades that resemble something the Wright brothers might have flown, form a monumental backdrop to this oh so chic restaurant, where no-one over the age of 30 seems to venture. Munchy Guinness and treacle bread for openers, while choosing from a menu of stylish fusion dishes. Eclectic starters include *tour de force* blinis of smoked tuna, scallops, caviar and wasabi crème fraîche. Main courses are split evenly between fish and meat dishes.

Dublin

Mid-range *Café Royal* is in the *Royal Dublin Hotel* at the top end of O'Connell St, T8733666. Popular, brasserie-style restaurant, usually busy but never frantic, adjoins the hotel bar. Dubliners flock here for meals at a decent price and the assurance of nothing scandalously minimalist appearing on a plate. Hearty main courses are meat-based – steak, Irish lamb with vegetable stew, duck, chicken kiev – plus a couple of fish dishes. The menu, with dependable starters like smoked salmon salad, is available throughout the day. To the young nouveau riche the *Café Royal* is unfashionable but no-one here hurries you out and the place is mercifully free of mobile phones. *Il Vignardo*, *Hotel Isaacs*, Store St, T8556215. Mostly pizzas here, in a cellar-like vault (a converted wine warehouse) enlivened, if that's the right word, by florally decorated columns. *101 Talbot*, at 100-102 Talbot St, T8745011, serves modern Irish food with a Mediterranean inflection; prices are reasonable and the reviews posted outside suggest there is good food within. Open 1800-2300, Tue-Sat.

Cheap There are a few places worth seeking out that are close to O'Connell St, like *The Italian Connection*, 95 Talbot St, T8787125. This is one of the best places for an inexpensive meal, if you can get an empty table in the tiny but pleasant restaurant where a set evening meal goes for around €12. Pizzas take pride of place on the menu, open from 0800 to 2200.

At first it seems there are not so many choices on this side of the river unless you like fast food. O'Connell St has most of them, plus shops selling sandwiches to take out *Beshoff*, at No 6, is one of a chain offering very reasonable fish and chips amidst pleasant but scruffy Edwardian décor, and at comfortable prices. Open from late morning to 2100 Mon-Wed, 2300 Thu-Sat. It is named after Ivan Iylanovich Beshoff, a Russian sailor who fled after mutinying on the battleship *Potemkin* in 1905; he came to Dublin en route to Canada but missed his boat and stayed put.

O'Shea's Pub, dominating one of the corners of Talbot St and Gardiner St, has a reputation for good food and prodigious amounts are served up for lunch. Pasta, omelettes, salads and vegetarian options are about €8; traditional Irish music most nights. *Isaac's Deli*, 2-5 Frenchman's Lane, is in the same building as the eponymous hostel. On a fine day, the paninis, crêpes and open sandwiches might be enjoyed more as a takeaway because space is at a premium here.

Liffey St Lower has a few eating places that fill with shoppers from Henry St and around. *The Epicurean Food Hall* lives up to its name with a cosmopolitan range of eateries tucked together under one roof. Turkish, Indian, Italian, sushi, taco, crêpe and seafood outlets compete for an informal lunch around €7, with most places closed up by 1830. *Soup Dragon*, 168 Capel St, is a tiny joint tucked in close to where the street meets Ormond Quay. Soups, mostly vegetarian but some meat and seafood, come in 3 sizes averaging (€6, plus bread and a piece of fruit. Takeaway service, and open 0800-1730 Mon-Fri, 1100-1700 on Sat).

Smithfield **Expensive** *Ryans of Parkgate*, 28 Parkgate St, T6719352. A pre-dinner drink in the eponymous Victorian pub (see below) will not prepare you for the cosy elegance of the restaurant upstairs. The carpeted restaurant, with a Victorian slate and marble fireplace at either end of what was once the pub proprietor's living room, exudes comfort and contentment. Food comes in hearty servings and with flair. The half dozen fish choices are matched by meat dishes and, with smoked chicken or trout and creamed cheese mousse for starters and rum soaked berries for desserts, this is an exceptional pub restaurant. Early-bird menu available, 1800-1900, Tue-Sat.

Cheap *Nancy Hands*, 30 Parkgate St, T6770177, is an Irish theme pub (yes, in Ireland), but one which does get favourable reviews. Large meat-based salads around €9 are popular and the place won a Pub of the Year award a few years back.

Voodoo, Arran Quay, T8736013, is a lively club at night and during the day it functions as a regular pub, serving food like goulash, lasagne, pork chops and burgers.

The *Duck Lane Café*, just by the side of *Kelly and Ping*, does a good self-service range of baguettes.

The main eating area in Ballsbridge is a cluster of small restaurants where the River Dodder cuts across the junction of Pembroke Rd, Merrion Rd and Anglesea Rd. There is another smaller gathering of restaurants and some comfortable old-fashioned pubs around the junction of Upper Baggot St and Mespil Rd.

Ballsbridge

Expensive *Raglan's*, *Jury's Ballsbridge Hotel*, Pembroke Rd, T660 5000. Style and amiability have no trouble mixing in this rather good, reassuringly Irish restaurant. Carpeted, white linen, pianist playing a Yeats song in the background, comforting, sedate atmosphere in Edwardian-Irish setting. The food is traditional Irish (lamb, Dover sole) with contemporary sauces and a spiky Thai curry that makes a welcome change from the usual vegetarian option. Parsimonious menu but generous wine list.

Ernie's, Mulberry Gardens, Donnybrook, T2693300. Off the tourist trail but well worth the bus ride. A miniaturist garden with a pear tree is the first distraction and then comes a veritable art gallery of original paintings adorning the dining room (check out John Doherty's Castletownbere and Connemara scenes). Impeccable service without servility from dinner-jacketed waiters and the set dinner menu is a treat. The à la carte menu has fish and choice meat dishes like venison with cranberry and chestnut stuffing with gin and juniper. Bus No 46 from Fleet St or Ballsbridge or No 10 from O'Connell St or Kildare St, ask to be dropped off at *Kieley's Pub* in Donnybrook and take the lane that runs down the side of the fish and chip shop at the end of the row of small shops.

Mid-range *O'Connells*, at *Bewley's Hotel*, Merrion Rd, T6473400. Situated alongside, but not managed by the hotel this is an excellent bistro-style restaurant where diners can view the giant wood oven and see Caesar salads being expertly prepared. Interesting meat dishes and the vegetarian choice puts many restaurants to shame. Open for lunch and dinner, with outdoor tables in the summer, and the main dining area lit by natural light during the day. Discerning wine list for the mainly Dublin 4 clientele. *Canaletto's*, 71 Mespil Rd, T6785084. Closer to the city centre than Ballsbridge proper, a few doors up from the *Mespil Hotel*. Small and intimate, walls painted in bordello red, subdued lighting, a suitable setting for the Mon-evening fortune teller who can be booked in advance. A menu of fish, like grilled sea bass, chicken dishes and hand-rolled cannelloni.

If the weather is good enough to consider a day out at Phoenix Park then it's probably suitable for a picnic lunch. The other option is a pub lunch. The *Hole in the Wall*, Blackhorse Av, is so named because of the hole broken into the park for soldiers to buy their beer through, in the days when the army was stationed in the park. The pub claims to be the longest in Ireland, and does pub food and live countryish music sessions.

Phoenix Park

Mid-range *Casa Pasta*, 55 Clontarf Rd, T8331402, is a casual café open from 1230 till late and serving pastas and pizzas. *The Yacht*, 73 Clontarf Rd, T8336364 serves bar food from 1200-1500 and with a more formal evening menu. It also does a good Irish breakfast.

Glasnevin & Clontarf

Cheap The *Garden Tea-rooms*, in the Botanic Gardens, is an airy self-service restaurant, fine for just a hot drink, light snacks or lunch.

Dublin

The Bleeding Horse

The present pub building is a 19th-century replacement of a timber-faced inn that functioned as a halting spot for coaches running to and from Rathmines, to the south of Dublin. One story goes that when coach horses suffered from 'head staggers' they were bled at the inn by a farrier. Another genealogy goes back to 1649 when Cromwellian forces, having defeated Royalists at the Battle of Rathmines, brought their wounded horses to the thatched, timber inn that stood here, surrounded by fields of corn. In Joyce's Ulysses, Corley says of Bloom, "I saw him a few times in the Bleeding Horse in Camden Street with Boylan the billsticker." All a far cry from the modern pub with its internet café and busy street traffic.

Pubs and bars

Grafton Street
This is the entertainment heart of the city

Go to next page for more music-based pubs, entertainment & nightlife

If it's a quiet drink you want this isn't the place to look. Grafton St has several music-free if not quiet pubs such as *Davy Byrne's*, just off Grafton St, with the *Bailey* opposite. Further east, *Dohenny and Nesbitt*, 5 Baggot St, is quiet in the afternoons and free of music at night. There are 2 famous pubs in the city centre that are always full without the lure of live music. *Davy Byrne's*, 21 Duke St, heaves by day and night. There are remnants of its famous and literary past with sketches by Cecil Ffrench Salkheld, an amazing old mirror, good pub food at lunchtime, but not the Gorgonzola sandwiches that Leopold Bloom ate here in *Ulysses* (except on Bloomsday, see page 121). *The Hairy Lemon*, 42 Lower Stephen St. Said to be named after one of those apocryphal Dublin characters, this one being a dog catcher in the 1950s who was distinguished by a lemon-shaped face and hairy stubble. The pub itself, of the type that Irish theme pubs try to imitate, featured in the film *The Commitments*.

Around Camden Street

The Bleeding Horse, 24 Camden St Upper, has a prime location at a major road junction. Big dark timbers and high ceilings, and all genuinely 19th century, although a pub has stood here since Cromwell's time.

Temple Bar

There are lots of pubs and if they are not jammed packed during the evening then someone died of the plague the previous day. They have atmosphere of a sort but few regulars and when you're struggling to the bar to place an order it can be difficult to differentiate the pub you're in from the one you just left. Nearly all the pubs have live music at some time or other and the ones most dedicated to music include *Fitzsimons*, *Eamon Doran's* and *Danger Doyle's*. For somewhere relatively quiet, try *The Palace Bar* in Fleet St. *Project*, 39 East Sussex St, is a theatre with a bar upstairs that doesn't fit the usual bill. Here is beer brewed the traditional way, minus the chemical additives, preservatives and head enhancers, and names to conjure with: Beckett's, Maeve's Crystal, Revolution Red and D'Arcy's Dublin Stout.

The Liberties

Two pubs for food, *Vicar St* (also a great music venue, see page 115) and *Nash's*, have been mentioned above. A third, the *Brazen Head*, 20 Lower Bridge St, deserves another plug too. This is Dublin's oldest inn, chartered in 1688 but in existence as an inn of one sort or another since the 12th century. The present building was erected in 1754. It's well worth a visit for its moody, low-beamed rooms reeking of history but the live traditional music every night helps keep the place overfull with revellers and space is often at a premium during the summer months. The leaders of the United Irishmen planned their rebellion here and one of them brought a new friend along, one Thomas Reynolds, who promptly informed on them to the government.

Finding bar space or a table in a pub in the centre of Dublin is not easy, whatever the time of the day, but the *Toddy Bar* in the *Gresham Hotel* at the top end of O'Connell St is always worth trying for comfortable seating and its selection of 63 different brands of whiskey.

O'Connell Street & around

The *Chancery Inn*, Inns Quay, and *M Hughes* Chancery St, are 2 excellent little pubs close to the city centre side of this area. At the other end, out at Parkgate beyond Collins Barracks, *Ryans* is another delightful pub. Full of old mirrors, a carved oak and mahogany central bar with a double-faced clock, and the fittings for brass lamps still on the counter, this is the real McCoy. All is original and dates back to 1896.

Smithfield

Entertainment and nightlife

Although most of Dublin's nightlife gravitates towards the area just south of the Liffey, other parts of the city shouldn't be ruled out. Dubliners tend to choose their club and hang out in a restaurant or pub until 2300 or so before making their way to the real night's entertainment. Harcourt Street is the centre of clubland. Most clubs serve drinks until 0200 and close at about 0300. Then it's off to an early-morning pub in one of the markets. Pubs are a major source of entertainment in themselves and many Dublin pubs are great for live music any night of the week. The rock and pop music scene is as vibrant as ever too, with a seemingly inexhaustible supply of fresh young talent raring to be heard and seen. A good variety of classical music seems harder to come by, though. There are several great venues for comedy and performing arts; the best times of year being spring, during the film festival, and in the autumn when there's an important theatre festival.

There are pubs for every taste, from real Victoriana to fake, from basic 1950s plywood to expensive fantasias high-tech, early-morning, musical, literary, sporty, the list is endless. The pubs of Dublin are not all wonderful places, the craic inside isn't necessarily better than anywhere else in the world, and drunks are drunks wherever they are but, that said, Dublin has some curious places where you can drink, eat, people-watch, listen to some good music, chat to strangers and eavesdrop on other people's lives. Closing time is 2330, Mon-Thu, and 2400 on Fri, Sat and Sun. If a pub has a food licence, drinks can be served until 2430. Pubs with a disco or nightclub stay open until 0230 and can serve drinks until 0130. Quieter pubs tolerate children at least to early evening.

Music in pubs
"Good puzzle would be to cross Dublin without passing a pub," thinks Leopold Bloom as he wanders about the city

The Baggot Inn, 143 Lower Baggot St, has lots of live rock music while *The Capital*, Aungier St, has DJs at work every night of the week and at weekends is heaving with folk. Regular RnB sounds from Wed to Sat but more interesting music on Mon and Tue nights. *Modern Green Bar*, Wexford St, T4780583, has a mixed bunch of DJs that usually come up with something worth listening to while choosing from one of the many foreign beers on offer. Music every night of the week.

The Harcourt, Harcourt Hotel, Harcourt St, is a well known music venue that draws in regular crowds of Irish revellers and a sprinkling of tourists. Traditional music on Mon nights, big bands on Wed, disco nights Thu to Sat. A quieter Fri night's entertainment can be enjoyed by winding your way through the heaving bar of drinkers to *Barneys*, a small bar adjoining the main one, where traditional musicians gather. The *Harcourt* also has a disco next door (see below).

At 15 Merrion Row is *O'Donoghue's*, famous because The Dubliners played and drank here, where there are lots of impromptu music sessions in the unreconstructed and pleasant old pub. A nice mix of real people and tourists.

Around Camden Street Not a million miles away is *The International* at 23 Wicklow St, where there is always something going on, whether it's the comedy club upstairs, live music or a play. Lovely old interior, quiet in the afternoons. *Whelan's*, 25 Wexford

Where to buy tickets

For most events you can book by telephone using a credit card or in person at the box office. The following outlets also sell tickets for various events, especially gigs in clubs.
Big Brother Records, 168 Fade St, T672 9355.

Freebird Records, 1 Eden Quay, T873 1250.
HMV, 65 Grafton St, T679 5334.
Road Records, 16B Fade St, T671 7340.
Sound Caller, 47, Nassau St, T677 1940.
Ticketmaster, T456 9569, or book online at www.ticketmaster.ie/

Useful sources of information

*The glossy **In Dublin** magazine costs €2.54, available from Easons and newsagents from every second Thursday, and carries day by day listings as well as reviews, interviews and features. Covers movies, music, gay, food, books, theatre and visual arts. The **Event Guide**, www.eventguide.ie is a free weekly magazine that carries a broad range of listings, including literary gigs, talks and children's events. Easily the best for information and acerbic commentary, **The Slate** is an irreverent free monthly listings guide to Dublin aimed at the youth market; especially good on the club scene. These free guides are available in clothes shops, music stores, cafés, internet cafés, universities and cinemas in the city centre, particularly in the Temple Bar area. Also check the **Irish Times** on a Saturday for its reviews and news on the entertainment front. Temple Bar has its own web site – **www.temple-bar.ie** and a telephone Culture Line, T671 5717. Other websites worth consulting for information include: **www.mcd.ie/** for music listings; **http:/entertainment.ie/** for cinema, music, clubbing, theatre and exhibitions; **www.clubie.com** clubbing information and useful links to other sites, plus discussion groups and a mailing list; **www.soundout.net** information on the independent music scene.*

St, T4780766, www.whelansalive.com Live music nightly and a Sun afternoon session at 1600. When you're at the stone bar, buy a drink for the sawdust man who is always propping up the counter.

Temple Bar At night in summer the heart of Temple Bar turns into a huge street party with people overflowing from the pubs on to the street, more people in sidewalk cafés, pavement artists, musicians busking, policemen chasing pickpockets and a general feeling of bonhomie. The overall feeling is young and inebriated, with a fair sprinkling of pubescent punks, but if you want a more sedate night in Temple Bar the periphery, especially the pubs in Dame St, are a little quieter. There has been a general agreement among the Temple Bar publicans to bar stag and hen nights, although whether this will actually work in the light of the vast profits to be made from these shindigs is another matter. If they do stick to the ban the street party will be a far more enjoyable experience. The following list is not comprehensive but it covers the best on offer.

The Auld Dubliner, 17 Anglesea St, recently spruced up a little, is one of the area's oldest residents and not too badly tuned into tourists. It has traditional music on Sun mornings and Tue nights and part of its lunchtime menu is coddle. *Bob's*, in East Essex St, is seriously dedicated to live music of various sorts and drinking, with a happy hour 1600-1930 when cocktails are half-price. *Danger Doyle's*, 24 Eustace St, is also young, very loud and very popular, with bar food until 1900 and a club taking over after hours. It has live traditional Irish music Wed evenings and Sat afternoons. *Fitzsimons*, Temple Bar, attracts a lot of tourists due to its sessions of traditional music Mon-Thu, Sat and Sun afternoons and the Ballroom Club in the basement (see page 117).

The Temple Bar, 44 Temple Bar, is an unmissable red on the outside, and heaving inside at all hours of the day. Live traditional music starts at 1530 from Mon to Thu, from 1300 the rest of the week and a singalong on Sun nights. *Eamon Doran's*, 3A Crown Alley, has live music of various sorts during the evening and turns into an indie and house disco after midnight. *The Ha'penny Bridge*, 42 Wellington Quay, is a lively traditional pub with lots of locals and comedy nights. For film buffs Close to the Temple Bar pub is *The Norseman*, 27 Essex St East, with a clientele of arty types and theatre-goers, many of whom end up on the street in the general crowd. No renovation for this place – its mahogany bar is the genuine Victorian article. Traditional music sessions upstairs on Fri and Sat nights and informal sessions downstairs on Sun nights.

The Liberties The *Brazen Head*, 20 Lower Bridge St, T6795186 (see page 109), is a famous old Dublin pub with traditional Irish music every night of the week in summer and on Wed to Sun in winter. Also in Lower Bridge St is *O'Shea's Merchant*, at No 12, T6793797, where live music can also be enjoyed every night of the week. For details of some other interesting pubs in this area, see page 112.

O'Connell St and around There are no pubs on O'Connell St itself, apart from bars in the *Gresham Hotel* and the *Royal Dublin Hotel*, but *Lanigan's Bar* comes close, being on the corner of Eden Quay and O'Connell St Bridge. Bare wood floor, old photographs on the wall and the smell of cigarette smoke provide the backdrop for sessions of traditional music every night from 2130 and Irish dancing during the weeknights.

On Talbot St, near the corner with Gardiner St, *The Celt* is a lively little joint with traditional live music between 2000 and 2100. It can become unbearably crowded, especially on Fri, with a mixture of locals and tourists. *Knightsbridge*, Arlington Hotel, Bachelor's Walk, T8049100, is tourist Dublin to a tee. If it's ballads, reel   s and jigs you want, step right in and spare time for the bouts of stiff Irish dancing after 2000 most nights plus 1700-2000 on Sat and from 1230 on Sun. For a more authentic blast of good Irish music, seek out *Cobblestone*, North King St, near the junction of Capel St and Bolton St. Different musicians turn up each night and this is the place to hear pipes and sean nos singing. The pub entertainment is free and while there is also a music joint upstairs that charges an entrance fee the word on the street in that the money is better spent extending your stay at the bar. *Lanigans*, *Clifden Court Hotel*, 11 Eden Quay, T8743535, has free music most nights but there is also a basement venue, T9741329, which has Fri night sessions costing around (€5) to get past the door. *Parnell Mooney's*, on Parnell St, also has comfortable seats and a music-rich late-night bar on Wed.

Smithfield *The Chancery Inn*, 1 Inns Quay, is only a short walk from Temple Bar across the river but Thu night's decent music and good atmosphere is in a class of its own. *M Hughes*, Chancery St, is a lovely pub for an evening's entertainment of traditional Irish music. It's the sort of place that doesn't feel the need for posters of Yeats and Joyce on the walls to remind you what country you're in. Fri nights are excellent, set dancing on Mon, Wed and Thu, and pipes on Fri.

Magazines like *In Dublin* and especially the *Event Guide* provide details of what's on while posters and flyers around Temple Bar are usually up-to-date. For big names you will need to book in advance, either over the telephone with a credit card or direct from the outlets listed on page 114. Expect to pay from €8 to €30.   **Larger music venues**

The largest venue for major non-classical concerts in Dublin is *The Point*, North Wall Quay, T8363633. *Vicar St*, 58-9 Thomas St, T4545533 (information), T6097788 (credit card bookings) www.aikenpromotions.ie, is another main venue for non-classical events. The *RDS Concert Hall*, Royal Dublin Show, Ballsbridge, Dublin 4, T6680866. The

Dublin

Gay venues

The George, South Great George's St near the junction with Dame St, is Dublin's longest-established gay bar. Theme nights include a 70s night on Thu and a bingo session on Sun at 1800. The George is busy, busy, busy and if you want somewhere quieter, more cosy and unassuming, head for **Out on the Liffey**, 27 Upper Ormond Quay, T872 2480. Lunchtime food and peaceful evening atmosphere; men's night is Sat from 2000 to 0200. **Dakota**, 8 South William St, is next to Outhouse and only a discreet brass plate announces its existence. Several clubs have gay and lesbian nights, which tend to vary, so check in the listings. Most popular are **Strictly Handbag** at Rí Rá, 1 Exchequer St, the basement of the Globe pub, T677 4835, on Mon nights. **Ham**, at the POD, Harcourt St, on Fri nights, T478 0225 for details. Ham is currently hosting the liveliest gay club night in the capital but admission is a hefty €10. Other spots include **Switch**, Eustace St, from 2300 on a Mon night; €5 admission before midnight. Also worth a gander on a Tue or Thu night is **Pegs**, Earl of Kildare Hotel, Kildare St. A mostly young crowd of thirsty males on Tue when pints are discounted. *Dedicated gay venues* are Incognito, 1-2 Bow Lane East (off Aungier St) T478 3504, a men-only sauna, Mon-Thu 1300-0500, Fri,

Sat 1300-0900, Sun 1400-0500; *Boilerhouse*, Crane Lane, off Dame St at the Oak pub, T679 5128. Sauna and café, open Mon-Thu, 1800-0500, Fri and Sat, 1800-0900 and Sun 1800-0400; **Vortex**, 1 Great Strand St, off Capel St near the bridge, T878 0898. A new sauna and leisure club that stays open 64 hours over the weekend and with breakfast served from 0600. *Stonewalz*, Molly's Bar, High St, next to Christ Church, a women-only club on Sat 2100-0300. Three floors with diverse music; €5 admission and doors close at 2230. **Outhouse**, 6 South William St, on the floor above the Jolt Café, T670 6377, is a community centre that provides a meeting place dedicated to gay and lesbian issues. **LOT** (Lesbians Organizing Together), 5 Capel St, Dublin 1, T872 7770, is a small resource centre and library open Tue-Thu 1000-1700. **LEA** (Lesbian Education and Awareness) is based at the same address, T872 0460. **Waterstones**, the **Winding Stair**, and **Books Upstairs** (36 College Green), all have gay and lesbian sections. **Basic Instincts**, 56 South William St, T671 2223, and **Condom Power**, at 8 Crow St in Temple Bar and 57 Dame St, T677 8963, sell magazines, sex toys and accessories. For fetish wear, there is **Miss Fantasia**, Ground Floor, 25 South William St, T671 3734.

huge hall, in what is the venue for the annual horse show-jumping competition, is also used for concerts and special exhibitions. Access for disabled. Bus: Nos 5, 7, 7A and 8 from Burgh Quay or the No 45 bus from Eden Quay.

Club scene Most clubs serve drinks until 0200 and don't close until 0300. Then it's off to an early-morning pub in one of the markets. Clubs usually charge an entrance fee, which varies from €6-16 according to the day of the week, the gig, or the visiting DJs. They sometimes have a dress code and on student nights ID is usually checked. Most venues host very different events on different nights, from the downright cheesey, with muted TVs in the corners and frayed boozers escaping a hard day at the photocopy machine, to genuine off-the-wall madness, so try to get a handle on what's on before heading off into the night. The listings in the free the *Event Guide*, *The Slate* or the purchasable *In Dublin* magazine can be of some help. One night draws in hordes of student types attracted by booze promotions promising instant oblivion, while the next night the same club has yuppies waving BMW keyrings in your face. Best of all, of course, are reasonable prices and excellent music and atmosphere to match. Clubs go in and out of fashion rapidly, and this week's wild spot is next week's bore of the week and the week after's half-empty dance space.

Harcourt St was *the* nightclub area of Dublin before Temple Bar clubs and their clones mushroomed elsewhere and it is still a favourite place for Dubliners and culchies to get blind drunk and enjoy themselves to excess in defiance of the truly awful music. Ravers from Britain occasionally turn up but Harcourt St's preferred drug comes in a glass not a pill.

Grafton St and around *Break for the Border*, in Lower Stephen St, Thu-Sun, T4780300, is a bit of a cattle market for young Dubliners, but a good place to drink yourself to oblivion. By day it's a country-music joint, while late on it is a popular hits and oldies disco. Over 23s. *Digges Downstairs*, in the basement of the *Drury Court Hotel*, 30 Lower Stephens St, is a late-night drinking club, Thu-Sun, with table service and fine wines. Free admission. *Eamon Doran's*, 3A Crown Alley (see also page 115), T6799114. Does assorted DJ-driven sessions nightly. More laid-back than some of the more famous clubs, playing mostly hip-hop, and with affordable prices for admission and alcohol. *Fireworks*, for late-night drinking, 3 levels and a dance floor in the old central fire station on Tara St, T6481099, is open until 0230 on Wed-Sat. *Gaiety Theatre*, South King St, T6771717, hosts a variety of activities on Fri and Sat from movies to cabaret, live jazz or soul and salsa discos. Lots of floor space and bars. Fri is always salsa night and attracts energetic 30-year-olds. *Hogan's*, South Great George's St, where the basement opens 2200 till late, while the bar becomes a quieter place to chat. No cover charge. *Howl at the Moon*, 8 Lower Mount St, T6761717, is open all week from 2300 till late. It features disco music, a bar and tarot readings. €6.35 weekends, cheaper weekdays. *Mono*, 26 Wexford St, T4758555, has a booze-fuelled student night on Wed and some fairly unchallenging music the rest of the week. International DJs make a difference, so check to see what's happening before parting with hard-earned money. *Renard's*, 35 South Frederick St, T6775876, has a well heeled appearance but it is basically an alcohol-fuelled pick-up joint with too-loud music. *Rí Rá*, 1 Exchequer St, the basement of *The Globe* pub, T6774835, is young, lively with techno, funky and dance music. Less expensive on Tue nights when it's €2.50 for a bottle of Grolsch and half that for a shot of rum. *Viva*, 52 South William St, has good jazz sessions on 3 floors every Wed from 2230. *Whelan's*, 25 Wexford St, T4780766, www.whelansalive.com There is always something happening in this well known pub, with late clubs every Wed-Sun.

Temple Bar *Ballroom*, in the basement of *Fitzsimon's* pub, Temple Bar, T6779387, is not a ballroom. It's a very run-of-the-mill club that has received some poor reviews but, who knows, it could improve. *Club M* is in *Bloom's Hotel* in Anglesea St, open Tue-Sun, T6715622. Laser lights, VIP room and busy at weekends. *Fleet Club*, Fleet St, Temple Bar is open Fri and Sat with disco music. *Kitchen*, *Clarence Hotel*, East Essex St, T6776635, www.the-kitchen.com, is owned by U2 who occasionally turn up, but don't let that put you off visiting a consistently good Dublin club. Even on a Tue night there are queues forming when pubs are closing up, and on a Sat night hard work and patience is needed just to get through the door. *Temple Bar Music Centre*, Curved St, T670 9202, www.tbmc.ie/ has a mix of vibes that vary nightly: Salsa Villa on Tue (salsa lessons followed by a night of dancing) and a wild indie dance rave on Thu nights. *Switch*, Eustace St, has a small subterranean venue with a reputation for good techno nights, and an excellent drum 'n' bass session on Fri, that often builds up an atmosphere.

Harecourt St *Beaujangles*, Harcourt St, is not a ravers' hangout, the piano makes that clear, and attracts people in their 30s. *Chocolate Bar*, *POD*, Wed-Sun, and *Redbox*, Thu-Sat, are at the top end of Harcourt St in what was an old railway station, T4780225, www.pod.ie *POD*, seriously well designed with rather self-consciously gorgeous clubbers, utilizes 2 stone vaults of the old railway station, and being one of the hippest joints in town can also be one of the most expensive. Celebrities hang out in the VIP bar while lesser mortals enthuse over the waterfall feature in the gents' washrooms. Wed is student night, women free admission before 2400, otherwise around €7. Thu has resident and guest DJs from Britain, opens at 2300 and admission is around €10; student reduction. Fri is a gay night, €10, while Sat nights have DJ luminaries and the yuppie-dominated clubbers fuel up with happy hour in the *Chocolate Bar* from 2130 to 2230. Sun is a quieter night, with DJs playing street soul and a hint of UK garage. Bouncers at the top of the steps have their excuses ready to bar anyone not looking beautiful. Thu night is a student night in Redbox while Fri and Sat nights attract big crowds for the homegrown and international DJs. Bear in mind that George Wilkinson, who designed the railway station in 1859, also designed lunatic asylums. ***Copperface Jacks***, *Jackson Court Hotel*, T4758777. Nurses and policemen love this off-the-wall club, but, unlike one postman who used to turn up every weekend, they are not in uniform. ***The HQ***, 57 Middle Abbey St, T8783345, www.imhf.com has some good DJs keeping the dance floor filled, but if you're picky about your music check in advance who's playing what. Fri nights, for instance, is nothing but soul, funk and hip-hop and Sat is currently for garage devotees. ***Vatican***, a few doors down from the *Jackson Court Hotel* in Harcourt St, attracts a young crowd of boppers in their late teens and early 20s. ***Velvet***, next to the *Harcourt Hotel*, T850-6644455 (24-hr gigline), plays clubby, dance music most nights with admission around €10. Thu night is student night with reduced admission charge and pints for a punt. Sun nights, mostly R'n'B, is a favourite with Dublin's black community, while Fri and Sat are crowded with booze-driven hordes with a high energy level. Good clean fun.

O'Connell St and around *Issac Butt*, Store St, opposite the bus station, gets the weekend going with resident DJs who know their audience. ***Parnell Mooney's***, Parnell St, is the pub opposite the Rotunda around the corner at the top of O'Connell St. A loyal gathering of music lovers every Wed night from 2300. Admission charge for a night of heavy reggae and rasta DJs. ***Temple Theatre***, Temple St, T8745088, www.templetheatre.ie/ This, Ireland's largest dance venue, is out of clubland and all the better for it. Guest DJs vary the vibes, Mon is currently R'n'B, and big shows draw in big crowds and high prices. ***Voodoo***, Arran Quay, T8736013, opened early in 2001 to general acclaim as a venue for black music – hip-hop, soul and reggae – Thu-Sat. Food also served (see page 111).

The Liberties *Vicar St*, 58-9 Thomas St, T4545533, www.aikenpromotions.ie One of the best venues in town, with a varied programme that ranges from straightforward live gigs to the ***Velure Club*** on Sat night that kicks in when the gig finishes. *Velure* uses the bar with DJs upping the pace as the night unfolds. Good lighting and non-stop bopping until 0300. Arrive before midnight. Food is available. Also check out the new club, ***Shelter***, an extension to *Vicar St*.

Classical &
opera
The International
Opera Festival
takes place in Jun,
see page 122

Opportunities for classical music are not so prolific, with the National Concert Hall being the most regular provider. Both Christ Church and St Patrick's Cathedral have regular organ recitals and student groups occasionally get together for choral recitals at either Trinity or UCD. Operas turn up now and again, a ballet troupe finds its way infrequently to the Point, the Bank of Ireland Arts Centre often has something on; check the classical listings in the *Event Guide* for current info.

Bank of Ireland Arts Centre, Foster Pl, T6711488, T6707555. ***The National Concert Hall***, Earlsfort Terr, Dublin 2, T4751572, info@nch.ie, www.nch.ie Box office open 1000-1900, Mon-Sat; tickets, usually €10.16 to €17.76 available 2-3 months in advance and bookable on-line. What was the Great Hall of University College Dublin

Those were the days

1930s Dublin had, proportional to its population, the largest number of cinema seats in Europe and four of the biggest cinemas graced O'Connell Street where every weekend saw long queues forming either side of the street. Two of the cinemas were demolished in the 1970s to make way for what is now Penny's department store but the Savoy (1929) and the Carlton (1937) kept going. In the 1980s the Carlton

closed down but you can still see its flamboyant façade with columns and Egyptian-style capitals. On the other side of the road, close to the Gresham Hotel, the Savoy could hold up to 3,000 people in the days there was only one auditorium. Ireland's first independent government, socially reactionary and under the influence of the Church, wasted no time in introducing a Censorship of Films Act in 1923.

(now shifted to Belfield, southeast of the city centre) is the main venue for classical orchestral performances and what it gains in historical and architectural interest is lost in the less-than-excellent acoustics. Access for disabled. Buses Nos 10, 11, 13, 14, 14A, 15, 15A, 15B, 44, 46A, 47, 47A, 47B, 48A and 86.

Cinemas

Dublin's cinemas are centrally located and the largest is the 9-screen complex at the Parnell Centre near the top end of O'Connell St. To escape the blockbusters and Hollywood generally, the *Irish Film Centre* is a place of refuge although the *Screen* in D'Olier St is also worth checking out. Daily newspapers carry details of what's on and when, while for reviews look in the *In Dublin* magazine, the *Event Guide*, *The Slate*, or Sat *Irish Times*. **Dublin's Film Festival** comes early in the year (see page 121). Cinema tickets cost at least €7 in the evenings, less before around 1800; student discounts are sometimes available.

Irish Film Centre, 6 Eustace St, T6793477, http://www.fii.ie Weekly membership €1.27 allows you to buy tickets for yourself and 3 guests. Tickets are €5. in the afternoon; €6 after 1800 (1600 at weekends). This is the best venue for catching an interesting film and tickets can be booked in advance from 1330 daily. *Sheridan IMAX*, Parnell Sq, Dublin 1, T8174222. Big-screen, stomach-churning movies of roller-coasters and people falling out of aeroplanes. *Savoy*, O'Connell St, T8746000. 5 screens, all the big releases. *Screen*, D'Olier St, T6725500. 3 screens show a mix of arty and commercial films. *UGC Cinemas*, Parnell Centre, Parnell St, T8728444. 9 screens.

Theatres

Dublin's big theatre festival is in Oct (see page 122), but most visitors should find something that appeals to them throughout the year. Performances usually start around 1930 or 2000, plus some matinées, and tickets cost around (€22 in the mainstream theatres and from around €11 elsewhere).

Cheap stand-by tickets and student rates are sometimes available during the week

The *Abbey Theatre*, 26 Lower Abbey St, Dublin 1, T8787222, www.abbeytheatre.ie One of the most famous theatres in the world, this was rebuilt in the 1960s in a fairly brutalist style that will disappoint anyone who knows the stirring role of the original National Theatre of Ireland founded by Yeats and Lady Gregory in 1902. *Andrew's Lane Studio and Theatre*, 9-13 Andrew's Lane, T6795720. Commercial productions from foreign touring companies and provincial companies. The *Ark Cultural Centre*, Eustace St, T6707788. A children's cultural centre with a programme of drama, music and dance. School parties often monopolize events during school months, but during the summer and at weekends throughout the year places can be booked in advance. The building was once a Presbyterian school where children were only allowed one toy on a Sun, a Noah's ark. The *Crypt Arts Centre*, Dublin Castle, Dame St, T6713387. Intimate place in the crypt of the church used

Dublin

Dublin in film

Ireland has always provided an excellent source of actors and locations for movies; although it hasn't always had the cash to play around with. It has attracted in the last decade. Educating Rita, a movie about an English Open University student and her tutor, was filmed in Trinity College. In recent years Dubliners have rarely had a day without a film crew blocking the streets, one of the latest being the filming of Rebel Heart in the Iveagh Gardens. In 1994 a piece of Irish mountainside outside Dublin in Wicklow became Scotland for a few weeks while Mel Gibson filmed Braveheart, and lots of Irish students as well as the territorial army filled in the crowd scenes. The biggest surprise hit movie made in Ireland has to be The Commitments, directed by Alan Parker in 1990, filmed with an entirely Irish cast around North Dublin and displaying the grim reality of North Dublin life as opposed to the quaint beauty of the Irish countryside in earlier big movies about Ireland. The

Commitments, and the previous year's My Left Foot, the story of a paralysed young boy's life directed by Jim Sheridan, set a high standard and created interest in the real Ireland which has spawned several good films since.

1996 saw Neil Jordan's blockbuster Michael Collins, which set the whole of Ireland arguing about the treatment of De Valera and displayed Julia Robert's feeble efforts at an Irish accent. One of the best recent movies to come out of Ireland, The General, directed by John Boorman in 1998, is about a comical Dublin thug who gets caught up with the UVF and suffers the consequences. New films set in Dublin include Gerald Stembridge's About Adam, the first Irish film with a bisexual hero (starring Howth's own Stuart Townsend) and one of a new batch of films reflecting the reinvented Dublin that has emerged in the last few years. Another such film is When Brendan Met Trudy, directed by Kieron J Walsh from a Roddy Doyle script.

by smaller, avant garde companies. The **Dublin Writers' Museum**, Parnell Sq, T8722077. Productions of classic Irish theatre. **Gaiety Theatre**, South King St, T6771717. Where every possible variety of theatre and musical production turns up sooner or later, including a late-night club at weekends (see page 117). **Gate Theatre**, 1 Cavendish Row, T8744045. Dublin's other famous theatre, workplace of Orson Welles (who, accused of being a godless communist subversive, had to face pickets here in 1951), and where James Mason put on Oscar Wilde's Salome when it was banned in Britain. A little more conservative and less avant garde now, less inclined to host 'progressive plays unfettered by theatrical convention', but a beautiful theatre with no balconies or pillars or boxes for the wealthy. The theatre was founded by Mícheál Mac Liammóir and Hilton Edwards in 1928, a theatrical gay couple whose defied sexual conventions, with Liammóir acting in over 300 roles. **Hall of Fame**, 57 Middle Abbey St, T8899499 (information), T4569569 (bookings), or buy online at www.imhf.com A variety of acts can turn up here; currently its the Nualas show to be followed by a John B Keane play. **The New Theatre**, 43 East Essex St, T670 3361. In the heart of Temple Bar and often the venue for excellent events from travelling theatre groups. **Olympia Theatre**, 72 Dame St, T6777744. Old music-hall theatre with lots of variety in its shows. **Peacock Theatre**, 26 Lower Abbey St, Dublin 1, T8787222. The experimental wing of the Abbey (see page 89). **Project**, 39 East Essex St, T1850-260027. One of the best places to catch something new and experimental on the stage (see page 112 for its interesting bar). **Samuel Beckett Centre**, Trinity College, T6082461. **Tivoli**, 135-8 Francis St, Dublin 1, T4544472. Theatre, musicals, and much more. **Tivoli Theatre**, Francis St, T4544472. A newish theatre with a variety of acts from Shakespeare to rock musicals.

Dublin has several venues for comedy clubs including one 400-seater, purpose-built **Comedy clubs** place, but as well as those listed here there are often one-offs in the clubs and pubs around town, so you should keep an eye out in the *Event Guide*, free in most hotels, hostels, etc, or watch for flyers around town. Standards vary enormously from one night to the next and from one performer to the next – a brilliant newcomer followed by the truly embarrassing is par for the course. All in all, though, you'll be a cold old fish if not entertained by some of the riffs.

The *Ha'penny Bridge*, Wellington Quay, has an open-mic comedy night on Tue, with the Lucky Duck award to whoever wins the audience's vote, and an improvisation night on Thu; both at 2100. The *International Bar*, 23 Wicklow St, has comedy shows Mon, Wed and Thu from around 2100. Entrance is around €7. *Milano*, in Dawson St, T670 7744, has a Sun-night effort, which involves a meal and comedy show with a cheap cover charge. plus your meal. Reservations advisable. *Murphy's Laughter Lounge*, T1800-266339, is a large venue at Eden Quay and has live shows every Thu, Fri and Sat night at 2100, bar opens at 2000. Tickets cost around €14 depending on who's on.

Cultúrlann na hÉireann, 32 Belgrave Sq, Monkstown, T2800295. Every Fri night from **Dance lessons** 2130, costing around €6, visitors are guided through country set-dances to the music of *céilí* bands. Apart from the salsa nights mentioned above under 'Club scene', *Mother Redcap's Tavern*, Back Lane, Christchurch, T4538306, has salsa classes for beginners and improvers from 1900. For details, T2276464. *Belly Dancing with Yasmina*, St Kevin's Community Centre, 46 Bloomfield Av, T4530680. Women only, bring a loose skirt and a scarf, Tue at 2030; around €7.

Holidays and festivals

Festival time is a good time to be in Dublin, although of course room rates and air fares can mysteriously rise to coincide with the festival dates. For the big ones it is important to book everything early because apart from prices rising as the event approaches, places to stay fill up alarmingly quickly, as do the big events at the film and theatre festivals.

St Patrick's Day is 17 Mar and anyone expecting green beer, etc, should try to be in **March** Dublin: it is altogether a pretty quiet affair everywhere else. The evening of 16 Mar sees a spectacle by the river between Capel Street and O'Connell Bridge. On the day itself there is a parade with floats, bands and costumes starting at midday and travelling from Christ Church to O'Connell Street; possibly also a fun-fair. A 2-day traditional music festival is held in Temple Bar at the weekend nearest Paddy's Day. There's free music all over Temple Bar, in the pubs and in Meeting House Square, and there is also a 2-day dog show at Cloghran, County Dublin. For information on the St Paddy extravaganza, T6763205, info@stpatricksday.ie www.stpatricksday.ie

The *Dublin Film Festival* usually spans the end of Mar and early Apr. Festival movies are shown at all the major city movie-houses as well as lots of suburban ones. Book early: T6792937, F6792939, dff@iol.ie, www.dublinfilmfestival.com

Diversions is the name given to the outdoor cultural programme of events in Temple **May to** Bar over the summer: dance, music, film, the visual arts and family events. T6772255, **September** info@temple-bar.ie, www.temple-bar.ie

After that not much happens until 16 Jun when, for several days, *Bloomsday* is cele- **June** brated. There are readings, lectures, performances and lots of dressing up and drinking. Book early for the big events: T8788547, joycecen@iol.ie www.jamesjoyce.ie Between 15-17 Jun also sees the *Dublin Docklands Festival* when people build flying machines in which they jump off a ramp and try to fly. It all happens at St George's Dock, T460 671. The *Anna Livia International Opera Festival* takes place at the Gaiety Theatre between 15 and 23 Jun, T6617544, operaannalivia@eircom.ie, www.operaannalivia.com

August Early in Aug (8-12 Aug in 2001) is the *Kerrygold Horse Show*, at the RDS in Ballsbridge, T6680866, deirdre.oreilly@rds.ie www.rds.ie Thu is Ladies' Day, when everyone puts on silly hats, and Fri is the Aga Khan Cup. It's a very big international event so again book early. At the National Concert Hall, between 16 and 19 Aug, *Beo 2001* is a series of concerts, workshops and talks featuring top Irish music artists. T4751572, info@nch.ie, www.nch.ie

September The *Dublin Fringe Festival*, T8729016/8729433, www.fringefest.com, is a lively mix of theatre, comedy and dance that lasts from late Sep into early Oct. Most tickets are around €12.70 or less.

October In the second week of Oct is the *Theatre Festival*, organized from 47 Nassau St, T677 8439 (information), T8748525 (booking), dubfest@iol.ie, www.iftn.ie/ dublinfestival The programme is available from Aug and bookings for the big events should be made as soon as possible (as well of course as accommodation arrangements). The last Mon in Oct is the *City Marathon*, T6263746, www.dublincitymarathon.ie which attracts thousands of competitors and even more spectators.

Sport

Dublin's parks are pleasant and safe for jogging Dublin can provide the sports-orientated with a full range of sporty things to do and watch, from Ireland's own 2 field sports – hurling, which dates back maybe 2,000 years, and Gaelic football, which has a slightly briefer pedigree – to the many golf courses that some might say blight the land. In between there's go-karting, ice skating, windsurfing and even skiing. Horse-racing is a national preoccupation and Dublin has plenty to offer there too. The public parks have lots of pitches marked out for hurling, football and rugby, as well as basketball courts, which are all free to the public; there are tennis courts too.

Bowling Ten-pin bowling is dominated by the Leisureplex group. There are alleys all around the suburbs: among others at Malahide Rd, Coolock, T8485722; Tallaght, T4599411; and Stillorgan, Co Dublin, T2881656. Bowling greens open to the public are at Moran Park in Dun Laoghaire and Herbert Park in Ballsbridge.

Soccer Increasingly popular in Ireland since Jackie Charlton recruited a national team and took them through to the quarter-final of the 1990 World Cup, football is played professionally by several teams in Dublin, the best being Shamrock Rovers at *Spawell Leisure Complex*, Dublin 6.

Gaelic football A kind of invention of the Gaelic Athletic Association, Gaelic football had existed in Ireland as a form of football played with the hands as well as the feet from about the 17th century, but no formalized set of rules existed until the GAA invented them in 1885. It evolved over the next 20 years to become the game that is so popular in Ireland today. There are 15 players in a team, who play with a ball similar to an English football, but can use their hands to pass it or score goals. The goal resembles that of rugby with a score over the bar being worth less than a score below the bar. You can watch amateur games in the Phoenix Park at weekends for free, or check out Croke Park.

Dublin for kids

Dublin Tourism issue a free booklet, Family Fun in Dublin, *with some interesting ideas.*

Bray *A day at the seaside in Bray and a climb of Bray Head. Amusement arcades, intranet gaming, sand and shingle.*

Dvblinia *History with a sense of fun; see page 83.*

Dublin's Viking Adventure *Temple Bar; see page 83.*

Dublin Zoo *Over 700 animals and tropical birds and train ride around the place; see page 98.*

Fry Model Railway *Children and anoraks love these models; see page 137. While you're there check out* **Tara's Palace***, paradise for lovers of dolls' houses.*

Kart City *Out of town at Santry.*

National History Museum *Stuffed animals, skeleton of the extinct giant Irish deer and ones of whales hanging from the roof; see page 76.*

National Print Museum *Loads of hands on bits and pieces to pore over, old computers and more.*

National Wax Museum *North of O'Connell St.*

St Michan's Church *North of the river in Smithfields. The mummified bodies in the vaults are the big draw; see page 93.*

Sherdian IMAX *Giant screen four times the height of a double decker bus; see page 119.*

The Ark *A children's cultural centre in the heart of Temple Bar.*

The Candy Shop *Corner of Gardiner Row and North Frederick St. It's not the candy that will have children glued to the window: coins, medals, stamps; historical bric-a-brac, curiosities.*

The Chimney *Original distillery chimney with panoramic 360-degree views of the city.*

Toft's Fun Fair, *Skerries; see page 139.*

Dublin

Horse racing

Somehow, when Ireland entered the motorized age, no one thought to tell Irish people that they should stop loving horses, and so they didn't. In Britain horses and horse-racing tend to be the pursuit of the monied classes. This is not the case in Ireland, where kids in the council estates keep horses tethered on grass verges and Smithfield Market heaves with horses and owners every month. There are 23 race meetings a year at *Leopardstown*, 10 km (6 miles) south of the city centre at Foxrock, Dublin 18 during the year, T2891000, www.iha.ie/iharace Admission €8.88-16.51. This is the most popular race-meeting spot with Dubliners, and has been since it opened in 1888 in what was then named Leperstown. Another good race course is *Fairyhouse*, 19 km (12 miles) northwest of Dublin, T8256167, admission €7.62-12.70. A special bus service from Dublin (Busáras) is operated on race days, T8734222.

Hurling

Europe's oldest field game, hurling is played with a curved ash stick and small hard ball in public parks from Aug-May. Big game watchers could try for the *All Ireland Football and Hurling Finals* in early Sep, held at Croke Park, T8363222; the big date in 2001 is 9 Sep.

Rugby

The season is from Aug to May and details of international matches, which take place at Lansdowne Road Stadium, T6689300, are available from the Irish Rugby Football Union, T6684601. There are 14 domestic rugby clubs, which compete over the course of the season for the Leinster Senior Cup. For domestic matches, you could try

Bective Rangers, Donnybrook, Dublin 4, T2838245; *Blackrock College RFC*, Stradbrook Rd, Co Dublin, T280151; *Old Belvedere*, Anglesea Rd, Dublin 4, T6603378.

Sailing

Sailing is a distinctly élitist affair in Ireland. There are schools that offer courses in sailing, but nowhere to hire boats. The *Irish National Sailing School*, T2844195, at Dun Laoghaire, offers intensive courses in sailing throughout the year at €140 for adults.

☞ Adventure in the city

Dublin Bat Group, Harriston Lane, St Margaret's, County Dublin, T834 7134. Spotting bats in and around the city. Hang-gliding and Para-gliding Centre, Kilmacanogue, County Wicklow, T830 3884. Wicklow is only a bus ride away. Surf Dock, The Grand Canal Dock, South Dock Road, Ringsend, Dublin 4, T668 3945. Including a wind simulator for expert surfers.

*For a range or adventure sports, like **rock-climbing** and **abseiling**, contact the following organizations: **An óige**, 61 Mountjoy Square, Dublin 1, T830 4555; **Adventure Activities Ltd**, 5 Trintonvill Avenue, Dublin 4, T668 8047; **Blessington Land and Water Sports Centre**, Blessington, County Wicklow, T045 865092.*

Skiing *Ski Club of Ireland*, Kilternan, T2955658, open Sep-Mar. Equipment hire.

Swimming As we all know since Michelle Smith hit the world's headlines, Ireland has no pool longer than 25m. Most public pools are in the suburbs and open Mon-Fri from 1130-1500, 1600-2000; Sat, 1000-1300 and 1400-1800; Sun, 1000-1400. One inner-city pool is in *Sean McDermott Street*, the continuation of Cathal Brugha St that runs off the east side of O'Connell St near the Parnell Monument, T8720752. Other locations include *Coolock Shopping Centre*, T8477743; *Finglas*, Mellowes Rd, T8348005; and *Rathmines*, T4961275. Also try *St Paul's College*, Raheny, Dublin 5, T8316283, or *St Vincent's CBS Swimming Pool*, Glasnevin, Dublin 9, T8306716.

Tennis The following parks have tennis courts that can be booked by the public: *Albert College Park*, Glasnevin, Dublin 9, T8373891; *Bushy Park*, Terenure, Dublin 6, T4900320; Eamonn Ceannt Park, Crumlin, Dublin 12, T4540799; *Herbert Park*, Ballsbridge, Dublin 4, T6684364; *St Anne's Park*, Raheny, Dublin 5, T8331859.

Windsurfing *Fingall Windsurfing*, Malahide, T8451979. *Surfdock Windsurfing*, South Docks, T6683945.

Shopping

Grafton Street The real shopping heart of Dublin is around Henry St, north of the river, but Grafton St and Nassau St and the streets leading off them have a bit to offer. Grafton St is home to lots of chain stores which will be very familiar to British visitors, most of the familiar shoe shops, as well as the home-grown *Dunnes Stores* and some upmarket department stores. At St Stephen's Green is the Stephen's Green Shopping Centre with more of the same. Along Nassau St and Dawson St are lots of arts and crafts and book shops. If you wander around the side streets between Grafton St and South Great George's St, lots of tiny fashion and furnishings places offer some pretty things. In the Market Arcade, South Great George's St, stalls sell good second-hand books, hippy fashions, posters and ethnic jewellery. Following South Great George's St southwards is the charity shop Mecca of Ireland where discerning shoppers can find all the retro stuff they ever wanted at prices much lower than the dedicated retro shops in the same street. Along this street are more interesting places such as a Chinese herbalist, an oriental grocer's, a futon shop and lots more.

Art In Powerscourt is *Giles Norman* selling black and white photographs of Irish scenes, including Dublin. If you want some original bargains try the railings of Merrion Sq at weekends. In between the pierrots, cute street children with rags, and painted velvet there are some good things and their painters are often standing by them to tell you all about them.

Antiques Powerscourt Townhouse has several classy antique shops on its 1st level although there are no great bargains. *Renaissance*, 41 Camden St, has mirrors, chandeliers, furniture and framed paintings for sale and runs more to the junk end of the market selling old pub fittings and bric a brac.

Bookshops *Waterstones*, Dawson St, has a fair range of books while, across the road, *Hodges Figgis* has a cultured atmosphere and a range of books to justify this as well as a neat café. *Tower Books*, Wicklow St, has a large selection of popular culture, music and gay literature. *Hughes and Hughes* in St Stephen's Green Shopping Centre has a fair range of books, especially children's and Irish interest. There is also a branch at the airport. *Dublin Books*, in Grafton St, is imaginatively stocked, independent and friendly. *Fred Hanna's* in Nassau St is academic and bigger than it looks from the outside, also with a second-hand and antiquarian section. *National Map Centre*, 34 Aungier St, T4760471, info@mapcentre.ie is the best map shop in Dublin, open Mon-Fri, 0900-1800, and does mail order. *Books Upstairs*, 36 College Green, looks small but is worth a browse. *Cathac Books*, 10 Duke St, is an antiquarian bookseller focusing on Irish interest and writers. It has signed first editions by all sorts of people as well as old maps and prints.

Crafts You can't go far in Ireland without bumping into a branch of *Blarney Woollen Mills* and Dublin is no exception. It's in Nassau St and sells the usual barrage of hand-knitted jumpers, hand-woven clothes and things with leprechauns on. There are some good bargains to be found if you poke around. *Cleo Ltd*, 18 Kildare St, sells 'wearable art', ie hand-made clothes, as well as ceramics, wooden bowls and lots of other things, all of Irish origin. *House of Ireland*, in Nassau St, sells fine china and crystal, woollens and hand-made cloth and leather goods, all of Irish origin *Viva*, 52 South William St, has good jazz sessions on 3 floors every Wed from 2230.

The *Kilkenny Shop* in Nassau St has another vast range of very classy woollens, hand-woven clothes, crafts and a great café upstairs for lunch. The *Crafts Council of Ireland*, in Powerscourt Townhouse Centre has a collection of the best of Irish crafts. In the same centre are several other jewellery, crafts and funny T-shirt shops, as well as antique shops, so give yourself time for a long browse.

Jewellery Powerscourt Townhouse is the trendy place for your jewellery needs with *Michael Perry*, *Arkland Studios*, *Emma Stewart*, *Equinox* and *Appleby*, all selling fashionable silver and gold jewellery. In the same shopping centre are some places selling cheaper silver jewellery. In Sussex St is the glorious *Rhinestones* which has a wonderful collection of very stylish antique jewellery, much nicer than the modern stuff. For more silver ethnic things you could look in St George's Market, off Aungier St.

Music *Waltons*, 70 South Great George's St, T4750661, is an old-established music business, with shops either side of the river, retailing CDs, cassettes and books on Irish music. A range of Irish instruments available, from harps, bodhráns and accordions to whistles and flutes. *Celtic Note*, 15 Nassau St, T670 4157, www.celticnote.ie, is a modern store opposite Trinity College with a reasonable collection mainstream of Irish music.

Shops in Temple Bar are squarely aimed at visitors, whether from abroad or other parts **Temple Bar** of Ireland, and every retail joint tries to look hip. *Cecilia House* has 4 floors of designer-type gear amidst dazzlingly white lighting and security men lurking near the exit. Crowne Alley has half a dozen small shops pretending to be boutiques, but for some quality Irish-designed crafts visit *Design Yard* in East Essex St. *Carbon* is an interesting new music store in Temple Bar Sq, while for knick-knacks of the Irish leprechaun variety there is an outlet of the ever-dependable *Carroll's* in Merchant Arch. At the other end of the shopping spectrum, in many senses of the term, there is a food market every Sat in Temple Bar Sq. Not a food market like Moore St or Camden St; oh no, this is food for the chattering classes who find balsamic vinegar rather passé and want something new to impress their friends.

Art *Temple Bar Gallery and Studios*, 5-9 Temple Bar, T6710073, has special exhibitions of work for sale. Currently on show is the work of Patrick McAllister with price tags starting at €1,079. The studio galleries, rented out to artists on 2 floors, retail their work for 100s rather than thousands of punts. There is also the Multiplies Gallery, changing content every 6 months, selling more portable art work by wannabe artists from €12 and up. Next door, the *Original Print Gallery* sells mostly unframed work from around €114.

Crafts At 5 Castlegate is *Whichcraft*, with really neat crafts from Ireland and around the world. See also the *Crown Alley* shops.

Fashion Temple Bar has its fair share of clothes shops and the largest selection is to be found in *Cecilia House* at the junction of Cecilia St and Crow St. 4 brightly lit levels of kitsch couture for the young with disposable income. Crown Alley is packed with small boutique shops retailing clothes, jewellery, gifts and anything else that seems to fit Temple Bar's outré image. Places include *Purple Haze*, *Christoper* and *Skate* for clothes, *Skate City* for rollerblades. For gear to get you where rollerblades can't reach, *Lowe Alpine*, Temple Lane, sells outdoor gear, boots and maps.

Jewellery *Celtic Gifts* and *Ad Hoc* for jewellery and gifts. *Design Yard*, 12 East Essex St, T6778453, www.designyard.ie, sells reasonably priced and very expensive Irish-designed jewellery and crafts on its ground floor. No claddagh rings here.

Markets On Sat, Meeting House Square in Temple Bar hosts an esoteric food market where sun-dried tomatoes, balsamic vinegar and olives nestle beside smoked fish, goat's cheese, strange Mexican health foods and snail-nibbled organic vegetables.

Music *Carbon*, Urban Outfitters, Temple Bar Sq. Specialist music store for electro/techno and deep house. *Future Sounds* for music.

O'Connell Street & around Forget Temple Bar and Grafton St, the place for down-to-earth shopping is in and around Henry St. This is where all the major department stores are based and weekends are a hectic affair. O'Connell St itself has few if any shops of distinction, although *Clery's* department store is a venerable Dublin institution.

The O'Connell St area is renowned for its bookshops **Bookshops** *Easons* in O'Connell St has a vast magazine section, stationery, art supplies and lots of Irish interest books. *Waterstones*, in the Jervis Centre, has a wider range of literature and special-interest books. Abbey St Middle, off O'Connell St, has a couple of shops, like *Chapters Bookshop*, selling discounted and remaindered titles of hardbacks and paperbacks, as well as second-hand books. On Ormond Quay is *The Winding Stair Bookshop and Café*, good second-hand Irish classics over 3 floors, plus a schmooze-friendly café overlooking the river. There are also books, videos, CDs, posters and postcards at the *James Joyce Centre*, and more literary texts and memorabilia at the *Writers' Museum*.

Crafts *Dublin Woollen Co*, in Lower Ormond Quay, is a cheaper clone of Blarney Woollen Mills. Around O'Connell St it is easy to find places selling T-shirts with leprechauns, videos of *Riverdance*, Celtic candles, Guinness-inspired tack, bodhráns, mugs and a plenitude of joke-Irish stuff. *Carroll's*, www.carrollsirishgifts.com have created a little industry out of this and their shops are located in O'Connell St, Westmoreland St, Moore St, Merchant's Arch in Temple Bar and in the Stephen's Green Centre. If you want to experience the strange phenomenon of post-tourism, pop into a Carroll's and find yourself thinking that you know someone who might actually enjoy one of the items as a gift.

Department stores *Arnott's*, 12 Henry St, specializes in clothing, lots of designer concessions but by no means exclusively so. It's a huge store, one of the largest in Europe, and there are road signs inside to help you exit onto the street you want. The restaurant upstairs gets very busy at lunchtime. *Clery's* dominates O'Connell St with its vast *Selfridges*-style window displays (the designer of *Selfridges*, in London, also designed *Clery's*) and enormous range of goods. Reasonable prices, lots of Irish gifts, and a café upstairs. *Debenhams* has 4 storeys in the Jervis Centre down Henry St. *Dunnes* has branches all over town, notably in Henry St. *Roches* in Henry St focuses on housewares but has clothing sections too. Competitive prices.

Markets *Moore St* is Dublin's famous market, used by one and all for their fresh fruit and vegetables and good for listening to Dublin accents, if not actually buying anything.

Music *Waltons*, 2-5 North Frederick St, T8747805. Branch of the established music business. CDs, cassettes, books on Irish music, harps, bodhráns, accordions, whistles and flutes.

Duck Lane, reached from the courtyard outside the Old Jameson Distillery in Smithfield, is a large tourist shop where Irish merchandise from clothes to crockery are handsomely displayed. It has a section devoted to women's jackets, coats and jerseys from Irish designers and also sells jewellery, homewear, gifts and craft items like Irish scented soaps. **Smithfield**

Smaller gift shops attach themselves to the Collins Barracks and the Old Jameson Distillery, while along Upper Ormond Quay, *The Bridge* is an interesting commercial art gallery.

Tours and tour operators

An excellent way to get an insight into the city that tourists often don't have access to is to join one of the many specialist tours doing the rounds of the familiar and not-so-familiar sites of historical and cultural interest. These usually run daily and can be joined at the starting point or booked ahead. Some of the more unusual ones should be booked, since they may not run if there isn't enough interest. They can be booked at the numbers given, or through Dublin Tourism, Suffolk St. **Tours of the city**

Bus tours *Hop on-Hop off*, Dublin Bus, 59 O'Connell St, Dublin 1, T8734222. Most of the city's major attractions can be reached on the tour and the green and cream open-top buses operate from 0930 to 1630 every 15 mins. The €8.89 tickets can be purchased on the bus or from the O'Connell St office. *Guide Friday*, 13 South Leinster St, T6057705, www.hoponhopoff.com, have their own black and gold buses, with guides, for a similar kind of service. Their tickets are €10.80 and are also available on the bus or from the tourist offices in Suffolk St and O'Connell St. *Irish City Tours*, Keatings Park, Rathcoole, T4011092, www.irishcitytours.com, is yet another hop on/off tour company. It runs daily through the city centre and out to Phoenix Park, every 10-20 mins depending on the time of year, and tickets are also valid on the Guide Friday buses and visa versa. *Mary Gibbons Tours*, T2839973, marygibbonstour@tinet.ie do a daily, morning tour of the city's main sites for €16.51, with various pick-up points around the city.

Bike tours *Dublin Bike Tours*, T6790899, www.connect.ie/dublinbiketours Apr-31 Oct, Mon-Fri, 1400; Sat-Sun, 1000, 1400. Also *Dublin at Dawn* at 0600, Sat only. Meet at the front gate of Christ Church Cathedral, opposite the *Lord Edward* pub; €19, including bike hire. Tour leader takes cyclists through quieter streets with frequent stops. Child seats available. Arrive 15 mins before the tour starts. Tickets are obtainable from Dublin Tourism in Suffolk St or call in to the *Harding Hotel* in Fishamble St next to Christ Church Cathedral.

Historical tours *Footsoldiers Revolutionary Dublin*, T6629976, focuses on the period between 1916 when the Easter Rising took place and 1923 when the Civil War ended. Run by Trinity graduates, it visits Stephen's Green, Trinity College, O'Connell St, Dublin Castle, Crow St and Ha'penny Bridge. €6.35. Daily at 1230. *Historical Walking Tours of Dublin*, T8780227, www.historicalinsights.ie, May-Sep, daily, 1100, 1500, and a 1200 tour as well on Sat and Sun; Oct-Apr, Fri-Sun, 1200. The tours are conducted by history graduates of Trinity College and visit most of the important sites around the old city. They conclude with a look at the current Peace Process. Meeting point is the front gate of Trinity College; €7.62. *The 1916 Rebellion Tour*, T6762493, 1916@indigo.ie, good fun and my favourite, meets at *The International Bar*, 2 Wicklow St, at 1130, Tue-Sat and 1230 on Sun. This is between late Apr and late Sep; in winter, Sat and Sun only. The tour lasts 2 hrs and travels to the relevant sites describing and analysing the events that took place. A free copy of the *Proclamation of the Republic* is included. €7.62, payable on the day or tickets from Dublin Tourism. Don't forget, too, the **free tours** of Glasnevin Cemetery every Wed and Fri, see page 98.

Literary tours *Literary Pub Crawl*, T6705602, www.dublinpubcrawl.com, starts upstairs in *The Duke* pub, 9 Duke St, and crawls its way around pubs associated with Dublin's famous writers. A team of actors perform from their works *in situ*. 2¼ hrs of Joyce, O'Casey, Behan, Yeats and the occasional drink. Easter-end of Oct, nightly at 1930, and Sun 1200 as well; winter, Thu-Sat 1930, Sun 1200, 1930. €8.25. A *Literary/Georgian walk*, T4960641, T4909341, lasting 2 hrs and costing €6.30 starts at the James Joyce Room in *Bewleys Café* in Grafton St at 1030 on Mon, Wed, Fri and Sat. *WildeTours*, Oscar Wilde walks and occasional dramatics, T4951380, are on Wed at 1900 and Sun at 1600.

Transport

Long distance
Bus Éireann, Busáras, Store St, Dublin 1, T8366111/8302222, www.buseireann.ie

Bus For excursions outside County Dublin, *Bus Éireann* operates an extensive system of express buses to all parts of Ireland from the Busáras (Central Bus Station) in Store St. Express buses go to **Cork** 4 times a day at an adult midweek return fare of €16.50. Journey time including a 30-min stop takes about 4½ hrs. There are hourly buses to **Galway**, 0800-2100, at a midweek return fare of €11.43 and a journey time of 3½ hrs. Up to 7 daily buses go to **Belfast**, 0800-1945, at a midweek return fare of €14, and with a journey time of about 3 hrs.

Express buses also travel daily to **Armagh**, **Athlone**, **Ballina**, **Derry**, **Donegal**, **Killarney**, **Letterkenny**, **Limerick**, **Portrush**, **Portumna**, **Rosslare**, **Shannon**, **Sligo**, **Waterford**, **West Clare**, **Westport** and **Wexford**, and many other towns. Express bus tickets must be bought before you get on the bus. If you intend to do much travelling by bus you might want to consider the **Rambler Ticket**, which allows you to travel throughout the *Bus Éireann* network for 3, 8 or 15 days of your choice over a limited period. The 15-day ticket costs €124.46 and is valid for a month, out of which you may choose any 15 days to make as many journeys as you choose, on local as well as express buses. Avoid seats at the back if you get at all travel-sick, and if you are travelling alone it is a good idea to get on towards the end of the queue, when you can choose who you sit next to, rather than have someone choose you. Buses fill up and there is not much room for baggage inside the bus; being squashed beside the window next to someone with several shopping bags or worse is no fun at all.

Train The national rail system, *Iarnród Éireann*, provides the swiftest means of getting out of the city for an excursion. Dublin has 2 intercity railway stations: **Connolly Station** in Amiens St, T8363333, www.irishrail.ie, north of the river and on the DART line, serves **Belfast**, **Derry**, **Sligo**, **Roslare**; **Heuston Station** in St John's Road West, T8365421, serves **Cork**, **Galway**, **Westport**, **Tralee**, **Killarney**, **Limerick**, **Wexford** and **Waterford** and places in the south and west. Both these stations have left-luggage offices and bus No 90 runs between the 2 stations. The other city stations are **Tara St** and **Pearse St**.

Suburban rail lines run out westwards and northwards, stopping at suburbs, towns and seaside villages like **Skerries** and **Drogheda**.

Taxis tend to congregate at cab ranks rather than cruise around looking for fares. Flagfall is €2.75 and then the meter goes up by €0.13 per ninth of a mile or 30 seconds. If you are out clubbing and want a cab at 0300, remember that so does everyone else, so make for a cab rank or carry a phone cab number. *Ballyman Cabs*, T8343333, charge €14 to the airport, €10 to the North Wall ferry and €7 to Heuston Railway Station. You won't get cheaper rates than this in Dublin. Their office is opposite the Gate Theatre, on Parnell Square East. Other phone cab companies include: *ABC Taxis*, T2855444; *Access* and *Metro Cabs*, T6683333; *Black Cab Company*, T8722222; *City Cabs*, T8722688; *Co-op Taxis*, T6766666; *Pony Cabs*, T6612233. For complaints or queries contact the *Irish Taxi Federation*, T8364166.

Taxi
There are 24-hour taxi ranks at Aston Quay, College Green, Eden Quay, O'Connell St Upper & Lower, Westland Row Station, St Stephen's Green & Lansdowne Rd

For a short stay in Dublin, a car is really not necessary. Even if you have a car with you for some reason, it would only be useful for trips out of the centre to places like Bray in the south or Skerries to the north. See page 138

Car

Being fairly flat and comparatively uncongested (as long as you don't try to cycle during the rush hour), Dublin is a pleasant city to cycle around in. There are no bike lanes and all over the city centre are signs warning that chained bicycles will be removed from railings, but cycling would be an excellent way to reach some of the out-of-the-way places and to see the rest of the country. Bike rental from *Dublin Bike Tours*, T6790899, F6796504, dublinbiketours@connect.ie, who also organize city bike tours, costs €12.70 a day or €50.80 a week. Rain gear, helmets, panniers and baby seats are also available. Or call in at the *Harding Hotel* on Fishamble St, beside Christ Church Cathedral. The only hostel with bikes for hire is Belgrave Hall in Monkstown (see page 134).

Bike
For more information on cycling, see page 128

Train DART Pearse St and **Tara St** stations link with Howth and places in the north of the city and with Dun Laoghaire and Bray in the south. **Bus** This area is a central point for buses travelling south of the city. O'Connell St in the north of the city, and **Busáras**, the central bus station, are reached via O'Connell Bridge. **Heuston Railway Station** is reached by bus No **79** from Aston Quay or the No **90** rail-link bus from Tara Street Station. The half-hourly **Airport Link** bus No **748** also travels close to the area, stopping at Aston Quay and Tara Street stations. For **Kildare St** and **Merrion Sq** (Leinster House, the National Museum, Natural History Museum, and National Gallery): Nos 7, 7A and 8 from Burgh Quay, and Nos 10, 11 and 13 from O'Connell St. For **Fitzwilliam Sq**: Nos 7, 8, 10 and 45 from the city centre. For **St Stephen's Green** (for Newman House and nearby Dublin Civic Museum): Nos 10, 11, 13, 14, 14A, 15A and 15B. For **Whitefriar St Carmelite Church**: Nos 16, 16A, 19, 19A, 22 and 22A from O'Connell St.

Grafton Street

Dublin

Temple Bar **Train** DART Tara St Station. **Bus** For **Christ Church Cathedral** and **Dvblinia**: Nos 78A from Aston Quay and No 50 from Eden Quay. For **Dublin Castle** and **City Hall**: Nos 50, 50A, 56A, 77, 77A and 77B from Eden Quay and No 54 from Burgh Quay. For **Dublin's Viking Adventure**: Nos 51, 51A, 51B, 79 and 90 from Aston Quay. From the **airport**, take No 748 which travels down O'Connell St and crosses the river before turning into Aston Quay. The bus follows the river west to Heuston Railway Station but get off at Aston Quay and take any street on the left to Temple Bar. (See also under Grafton St, page 128.)

The Liberties **Bus** For **St Patrick's Cathedral** and **Marsh's Library**: Nos 50, 54A and 56A from Eden Quay. For **Guinness Storehouse**: Nos 51B and 78A from Aston Quay, No 123 from O'Connell St, to Thomas St; ask to be dropped off near Crane St. For the **Irish Jewish Museum** and **Shaw's Birthplace**: Nos 16, 16A, 19 and 19A from O'Connell St and Aungier St to Victoria St, South Circular Rd; Nos 14, 14A, 15 and 15A-C, from Kildare St to South Richmond St.

O'Connell Street and around **Train** **Connolly Train Station** is within easy walking distance of O'Connell St. There is also a **DART** station at Connolly. **Bus** O'Connell St lies immediately north of the River Liffey and every bus from the **airport**, including the *Aircoach* service, travels down it, so transport is straightforward. **Busáras**, the main bus station, is just eat of O'Connell St. For **Parnell Sq** (Hugh Lane Gallery, Dublin Writers' Museum, James Joyce Centre and National Wax Museum): Nos 10, 11, 11A, 11B, 13, 16, 16A, 19, 19A, 22, 22A and 36 all pass Parnell Sq. For **Mountjoy Sq**: No 41. For the **Gaelic Athletic Association Museum**: Nos 3, 11, 11A, 16, 16A and 123 from O'Connell St.

Smithfield **Bus** For **St Michan's Church**: No 134 from Middle Abbey St. For the **Old Jameson Distillery**: Nos 67 and 67A from Abbey St Middle, Nos 68, 69 and 79 from Aston Quay, and No 90 from Connolly Station. For **Ceol, the Irish Traditional Music Centre**: Nos 25, 25A, 67 and 67A from Abbey St Middle. Nos 68, 69 and 79 from Aston Quay, No 90 from Connolly, Tara and Heuston stations. All the buses stop at Merchant's Quay, on the other side of the river, except the No 90 from Heuston which stops at Arran Quay. For **Collins Barracks**: No 90 from Aston Quay or Nos 25, 25A, 66 and 67 from Abbey St Middle. The **Museumlink shuttle bus** departs regularly from the National Museum in Kildare St and National Gallery in Merrion St. **Car** A one-way system operates along the south and north banks of the Liffey to the west of O'Connell Bridge, with traffic coming into the city along the north quays and heading out along Wellington, Essex, Wood, Merchant's, Usher's and Victoria quays on the southern side.

Ballsbridge **Train** DART: Lansdowne Rd Station. **Bus** Ballsbridge is less than 10 mins by buses Nos 5, 7, 7A and 8 from Burgh Quay, or the No 45 from Eden Quay. Any of these buses are good for the **National Print Museum**. **Car** Pembroke Rd, the main road through Ballsbridge, changes its name to Merrion Rd as it continues south towards Dun Laoghaire on the coast. The other main road that heads south out of Dublin passes through the suburb of Donnybrook before becoming Stillorgan Rd and the N11 to Wicklow.

Rathfarnham **Bus** For **Pearse Museum**: No 16 from city centre. For **Marlay House**: 47A and 47B from Hawkins St. For **Rathfarnham Castle**: No 16, 16A, 16C, 17 and 75 from city centre. For **Drimnagh Castle**: No 56A from Eden Quay.

Kilmainham **Bus** For the **Irish Museum of Modern Art**: Nos 68, 69, 78A and 79 from Aston Quay, No 90 from Heuston, Tara St and Connolly stations. For **Kilmainham Gaol**: Nos 51B, 78A and 79 from Aston Quay.

Bus For **Phoenix Park** (Ashtown Castle, Áras an Uachtaráin, the visitor centre and the zoo): No 10 from O'Connell St to **Park Gate** on Infirmary Rd; then the park **shuttle bus**. Nos 37 and 38 from Lower Abbey St and No 39 from Middle Abbey St go to the **Ashtown Gate**, from where there is a 20-min walk into the park.

Phoenix Park

Train DART: Clontarf Rd Station then, for **North Bull Island**, a very long walk or a bus ride (No 130). **Bus** For **Prospect Cemetery**, Glasnevin: Nos 40 and 40A, from Parnell St. For the **Casino at Marino**: Nos 20A, 20B, 27, 27A, 27B, 42 and 42C from the city centre near Busáras. For **Clontarf** and **North Bull Island**: Bus: No 130 from Lower Abbey St goes to the Bull Wall, the start of the area.

Glasnevin & Clontarf

Directory

There are branches of the *AIB* in Grafton St and Merrion Rd, *Bank of Ireland* in Baggot St Lower and *Ulster Bank* in College Green. *American Express Travel Service*, 41 Nassau St, T6775588 (travellers' cheques), T6799000 (foreign exchange), Mon-Sat, 0900-1700, until 2100 Thu. *First Rate Bureau de Change*, 1 Westmoreland St, T6713233. *Thomas Cook*, 118 Grafton St, T6771307. Irish Banks with cash dispensers are at the River Liffey end of O'Connell St and on Liffey St Upper. **Bureaux de Change**: GPO, O'Connell St. *Joe Walsh Tours*, 69 Upper O'Connell St, T8725536. Two department stores, *Arnott's* in Henry St and *Clery's* in O'Connell St, have currency exchange facilities and so too do *Connolly Station* and *Busáras*, the central bus station. North of the centre, *AIB*, Church St, Skerries, *Bank of Ireland*, Strand St, Skerries, *National Irish Bank*, Strand St. All have exchange facilities.

Banks & Bureaux de change

Post office St Andrew's St, Mon-Fri 0900-1730, Sat 0900-1300. *General Post Office*, O'Connell St, T7057000. Mon-Sat 0800-2000; Sun and bank holidays 1000-1830 (for stamps and bureau de change only). **Internet** Internet and email facilities are popping up everywhere in pubs, cafés and shops. The minimum rate is usually at least €1.27 for 15 minutes, with hourly rates starting around €5. Opening hours vary but the Global Internet Café is fairly typical and they're open Mon-Fri from 0800 to 2300, Sat 0900-2300 and Sun 1000-2300. **Grafton Street and around**: *Bleeding Horse* pub, Camden St. Above the pub (see page 112) and open until early hours of the morning. *Global Internet Café*, 6 Grafton St, T6778298. *Lazer Home Entertainment Video Library Internet Café*, 23 South Great George's St, opposite the tourist office, T6790583. *Internet Exchange*, Dublin Tourism Centre, Suffolk St, T6422553. *Planet Cyber Café*, 13 St Andrew St, T670 5183. Open Sun-Wed, 1000-2200, and Thu-Sat, 1000-2400. Situated opposite the tourist office. There is another branch at 23 South Great George's St, T6790583. **Temple Bar and around**: *Amnesty International Café*, almost opposite the Temple Bar Hotel on Fleet St. *Internet Exchange*, The Granary, Temple Lane South, T6797607. Internet Exchange also have outlets in Crow St, T6705601, and Cecilia St, T670 3000. *net house*, Wellington Quay, T4960261, www.nethousecafes.com/ tuition Hourly rate only, student discount, various learning courses. Their other inner city branch is at 9 Lord Edward St, T4960261. **O'Connell Street and around**: *Cafe Maud*, next to the *Savoy* cinema on O'Connell St. Tiny area above the café. *Global Internet Café*, 8 Lower O'Connell St, Dublin 1, T8780295, www.globalcafe.ie *Internet Exchange*, 146 Parnell St, T8740300. *Muse Café*, on the second floor of Easons bookshop on O'Connell St, but closes early, at 1730 Mon-Sat (1830 on Fri) and open from 1300-1715 on Sun. *Swiftcall*, The Basement, 7 Bachelors Walk, T8049991, www.swiftcall.com/shop *Isaacs Hostel*, 2 Frenchmans Lane, T8556215. **Dun Laoghaire**: *net house*, 28 Upper George's St, T4960261. Games nights, printing, computer courses.

Communications

Dublin

Dublin

Embassies **Australia** 6th floor, Fitzwilliam House, Wilton Terrace, Dublin 2, T6761517. **Canada** 65-8 St Stephen's Green, Dublin 2, T4781988. **Denmark** 121 St Stephen's Green, Dublin 2, T4756404. **France** 36 Ailesbury Rd, Dublin 4, T2601666. **Germany** 31 Trimleston Av, Bakerstown, Co Dublin, T2693011. **Italy** 63 Northumberland Rd, Dublin 4, T6601744. **Japan** Nutley Building, Merrion Centre, Nutley Lane, Dublin 4, T2694244. **Netherlands** 160 Merrion Rd, Dublin 4, T2693444. **Norway** 34 Molesworth St, Dublin 2, T6621800. **Portugal** Knocksinna House, Foxrock, Dublin 18, T2894416. **Spain** 17A Merlyn Park, Dublin 4, T2691640. **Sweden** Sun Alliance House, Dawson St, Dublin 4, T6715822. **Switzerland** 6 Ailesbury Rd, Dublin 4, T2692515. **UK** 31 Merrion Rd, Dublin 4, T2053700. **USA** 42 Elgin Rd, Dublin 4, T6688777.

Radio stations by wavelength *Energy*, 88FM Dance music. *Radio 1*, 88-94FM A national station with far too many phone-ins of mindlessly bland chat but good for the news and cultural evening programmes. *JazzFM*, 89.8FM White DJs playing mostly Black music. *2FM*, 90.2-92.4FM Commercial blather. *Phantom*, 91.6FM Lots of Indie. *Premier*, 92.6FM Chart music from the 70s and 80s. *Energy*, 97.2FM 94FM Currently the best pirate station for commercial club music. *Nova Dance*, 94.7FM Pirate station playing commercial club music. *Trinity*, 96.7FM College station. *Power FM*, 97.2FM Dance music: hip-hop, reggae, drum and bass, techno. *98FM*, 98FM More commercial blather. *KIC FM*, 97.2FM The acronym stands for Keep It Country. *Darc*, 99FM Alternative. *Lite 102*, 102.2FM Very light indeed. *Pulse*, 103FM Dance music. *Anna Livia*, 103.2 Community radio. *104FM*, 104.4FM Commercial. *Radio Na Liffe*, 106.4FM Irish-speaking station with good music.

Language schools & cultural centres *American College*, 2 Merrion Square, Dublin 2, T6768939. *Centre of English Studies*, 31 Dame St, Dublin 2, T674233. *Dublin School of English*, 11 Westmoreland St, Dublin 2, T6773322. *English Language Institute*, 99 St Stephen's Green, Dublin 2, T472965. *Gael-linn (Irish)*, 26 Merrion Square, Dublin 2, T676 7283. *Alliance Française*, I Kildare St, Dublin 2, T6761732. *British Council*, Newmount House, 22-4 Mount St Lower, Dublin 2, T6764088. *Goethe Institute*, 62 Fitzwilliam Square, Dublin 2, T6618506. *Instituto Cervantes*, 58 Northumberland Rd, Dublin 4, T6682024.

Medical services **Dentists** *Molesworth Clinic*, 2 Molesworth Place, Dublin 2, T6615544. **Emergency services** Dial 999 or 112. Accident and emergency departments at *Adelaide & Meath Hospital*, Tallaght, T4143500; *Beaumont Hospital*, Beaumont Rd, Dublin 9, T8092714. **Help lines** *Samaritans*, T1850-609090. *Alcoholics Anonymous*, T4538998/6795967/6796555. *Drug Advisory & Treatment Centre*, T6771122. *Astma Line*, T1850-445464. **Late-night pharmacies** *Corrigans*, 80 Malahide Rd, Dublin 3, T8338803. Open 0900-2200 Mon-Sat; 1030-1900 Sun. *O'Connell's Late-Night Pharmacies*, Grafton St, T6790467. Open 0830-2030 Mon-Sat; 1100-1800 Sun. Westmoreland St, T6778440. Open 0830-1900 Mon, Wed, Fri, Sat; until 2030 Thu. O'Connell St, T8730427. Open 0830-2200, Mon-Sat; 1000-2200, Sun. Henry St, T8731077. Open 0830-1800, Mon-Sat; 1300-1800 Sun. **Women's health** *Rotunda Hospital*, Parnell St, Dublin 1, T8730700. Maternity hospital. *Well Woman Clinic*, 73 Lower Leeson St, T6610083. The 'morning-after pill' can be prescribed here.

Useful information **Disabled travellers** *National Rehabilitation Board*, 25 Clyde Rd, Ballsbridge, Dublin 4. Also 44 North Gt George's St, T8747503. Wheelchair-accessible taxis can be booked in advance through *Eurocab/Dublin Black Cab*, T8445844, and *National Radio Cabs*, T8365555. *Vantastic*, T8304926, require a day's notice but can provide a door-to-door service in their adapted vans (also, see page 25). **Flight information** Dublin Airport, T8866705. **Help lines** *Samaritans*, T8727700. *Alcoholics Anonymous*, T4538998/6795967/6796555. *Drug Advisory & Treatment Centre*, T6771122. *Asthma Line*,

T1850-445464. **Libraries** *Central Library*, ILAC Centre, Henry St, Dublin 1. T8734333. *Dublin Corporation Library*, 138-142 Pearse St, Dublin 2, T6772764. **Motoring** *Automobile Association (AA)*, 23 Suffolk St, Dublin 2, T6779481. Breakdowns, T1800-677788. *RAC*, breakdowns, T1800-535005. *Alert Towing & Breakdown*, T8555220. *Auto Centre*, T4901600. **Police** Emergency telephone number for the garda (police), fire or ambulance is 999 or 112. Garda stations in the city centre are found at: Store St, Dublin 1, T8557761. Pearse St, Dublin 2, T6778141. Fitzgibbon St, Dublin 1, T8363113. Garda Síochána Dublin metropolitan HQ, Harcourt Sq, Dublin 2, T4755555. **Public toilets** St Stephen's Green, St Stephen's Green Shopping Centre, National Gallery, National Museum.

South of Dublin

Dun Laoghaire

If you feel jaded by too much street life you might consider an excursion to the seaside south of the city. Or you may just find yourself in Dun Laoghaire (pronounced Dunleary) waiting for a ferry departure. Nowadays Dun Laoghaire is both an important seaport and a seaside town, with huge Victorian villas lining the seafront and looking out at the great passenger ferries trawling their way in and out of the harbour.

Dun Laoghaire Station, 20 mins from Central Dublin. Go to page 135 for transport details

A fishing village until the middle years of the 18th century, Dun Laoghaire became a major resort and harbour when the two mile-long piers were built between 1817 and 1827. The first car ferry made the journey from Holyhead to Dun Laoghaire in 1966. Thirty years later the harbour got a new lease of life with the opening in 1996 of the new Stena Line ferry terminal. Nowadays the Stena high speed ship swishes in and out and there are warning signs along the shores, telling walkers to keep back for half an hour after the ferry has docked and departed.

History

The **tourist office** is at Old Court House, Main St, T2866796/2867128. Jun-Sep, Mon-Fri 0900-1700, Sat 1000-1600; Oct-Apr, Mon-Fri 0900-1630, Sat 1000-1600. Closed 1300-1400 throughout the year.

The National Maritime Museum is housed in the Mariner's Church (1837) in Haigh Terrace, Dun Laoghaire. Its interesting collection includes a captured ship's longboat, used for ferrying officers to and from shore, and taken during the aborted French invasion at Bantry in 1796. There are also models of ships and a very large optic which was once the light from the Bailey Lighthouse at Howth. ■ *May-Sep, daily 1300-1700. €1.90. T280 0969.*

National Maritime Museum

The two piers, each over a mile long, are grand for a stiff walk. The West Pier, nearest to Dublin, is the least used, while the East Pier is a Sunday constitutional kind of walk with a bandstand, often with some performance going on, a gadget for measuring wind speed, a memorial to a Captain Boyd and, at the end, an unmanned lighthouse. From the end of either pier you can see the shape of Dublin Bay with Killiney at the southern extent and Howth Head to the north.

Dun Laoghaire piers

A very short distance away from the Forty Foot, the James Joyce Museum occupies the **Martello tower** built on a rocky promontory. The first chapter of *Ulysses* is set in this tower, where Joyce lived for a week, and a collection of literary memorabilia and the open roof are the main attractions inside. See page 96 for details.

James Joyce Museum

Dublin

Sleeping

Dun Laoghaire **XL-L** *Gresham Royal Marine* , Marine Rd, T2801911, www.gresham-hotels.com By far the classiest hotel in Dun Laoghaire, open to the public since 1865, with a grand Victorian staircase and fine views of the incoming boats (supplement for sea views). Elegant restaurant, pretty landscaped garden, some of the rooms are Victorian in style but there is also a modern wing.

B *Avondale House*, 3 Northumberland Av, Dun Laoghaire, T2809628, F2805764, is a small and basic B&B in a quiet side street, with shared bathroom facilities. **B** *Phylilis Brady*, 81 Adelaide Rd, Glenageary, Dun Laoghaire, T2806781, info@family-homes.ie 3 twin rooms with shared facilities, it only just comes into this price category. Head down Dun Laoghaire's main street in the direction of Sandycove and on Glasthule Rd turn right at the corner with the *Eagle House* pub. The B&B is up here on the right side.

C *Marina House*, Old Dunleary Rd, Dun Laoghaire, T2841524, www.marinahouse.com This is Dun Laoghaire's only hostel, an IHH and IHO place with dorm beds and 6 private rooms. **B-C** *Belgrave Hall*, 34 Belgrave Sq, Monkstown, T2842106, www.dublinhostel.com This IHO hostel is situated between Blackrock and Dun Laoghaire in a rather splendid building. Dorm beds and private rooms. Breakfast included, laundry facility and bikes for hire.

Camping and caravanning **E** *Shankill Caravan and Camping Park*, Shankill, Co Dublin, 19 km (12 miles) south of the city, T2820011, F2820108, shankillcaravan@eircom.ie Smaller, close to the Shankill DART station, Bus No 45A from Dun Laoghaire ferry terminal, and Bray, with caravans to hire. Backpackers' rate from €7.62. No dogs in mobile homes.

Eating & drinking

Dalkey & Blackrock offer more fashionable eating places

Dun Laoghaire has lots of trendy café/bars & its fair share of fast-food outlets along George's St

Dun Laoghaire and Sandycove *Brasserie Na Mara*, T280 6767, close to the DART station and harbour where the innovative, fashionable, mostly seafood menu is good value and where dinner should be around €25. *Duzy's*, 18 Glasthule Rd, Sandycove, T230 0210, just fits into this price category but 3 courses could go higher. Casual dining here – beech tables, no table linen, chesterfields in the bar, and a health-conscious menu of meat and fish. *Gaviston's*, 59 Glasthule Rd, Sandycove, T280 6097, is an excellent small seafood restaurant, offering really fresh fish dishes. Open from 1200-1800 Tue-Sun. *The Haddington Bistro*, 12 Haddington Terr, T2801810, opens each evening at 1730 with starters like Thai fish cake and main courses of steaks, roast duckling and fish. Unexciting décor but a couple of tables are by the window facing the sea.

The *Powerscourt Room* in the *Royal Marine Hotel* is a very popular venue, set in a big old Victorian dining room with huge bay windows looking out to the harbour. Service is pleasant and the atmosphere is relaxed. Fairly traditional menu, but the food is well cooked. Try the hotel's afternoon tea on Sun, a dowager kind of affair in the Victorian drawing room. *The Red Onion*, George's St Upper, T230 0275, is a small bright place with a Continental atmosphere and menu to match. An interesting combination of Mediterranean – olive oil roasted vegetables, goat's cheese – and Irish figures in the menu. Good food at reasonable prices.

At the *The Haddington Bistro*, see above, there is an early-bird menu from 1730 until 1900, daily, around €18. If it's Indian food you have a hankering for there is a good restaurant, *Lal Qila*, in Convent Rd, off George's St Lower. Prices are very reasonable.

Pubs & bars *Scott's Café*, in George's St Upper, Dun Laoghaire, has *Scott's Pub* upstairs where there is live music most nights and a late bar. The *Purty Kitchen*, Old Dunleary Rd, is opposite Dun Laoghaire's only hostel and serves mighty good pub food. Open till mid-night daily. *Walter's*, at 68 George's St Upper, T280 7442, is another trendy café bar with wood panelling and a lively atmosphere. In Sallynoggin, a small village a little way out of Dun Laoghaire up Glenageary Rd, is *The Noggin Inn*, T2854602, a pub which regularly has traditional music.

Ferry At the ferry terminal, there is a tourist office with a bureau de change and a computerized video unit for booking accommodation when the tourist office is closed. **Transport**

Bus Nos 7, 7A and 8 go to Blackrock and Dun Laoghaire from Burgh Quay in Dublin, via Merrion Sq. No 8 goes on from Dun Laoghaire to Dalkey. No 45 goes to Blackrock and on to Bray from Eden Quay in Dublin, via Merrion Sq, while the 45A just runs between Bray and Dun Laoghaire.

No 46A travels to Dun Laoghaire from Fleet St in Dublin, via Kildare St. Bus No 59 runs between Dun Laoghaire, Sandycove and Killiney. No 746 operates between Dun Laoghaire and Dublin Airport (see page 64).

Bike *Mike's Bikes and Fitness Store*, 107 Patrick St, Dun Laoghaire, T280 0417. Mon, Tue, Wed, Fri, Sat 0900-1800. Thu 0900-2100. *Bike Rack, Hill's Hire Centre*, Johnstown Rd, Cabinteely, T2840609.

Train The **DART** runs at approximately 20-min intervals stopping at Blackrock, Seapoint, Salthill, Dun Laoghaire, Sandycove, Glenageary, Dalkey and Killiney and Bray. The last train out of Tara St is 2321. The last train leaves Bray for Dublin at 2320.

Internet access *The Braynet Café*, upstairs in the Star Leisure amusement arcade at the Bray Head end of Strand Rd, is open daily until 2330. Children pack the place out for the internet games. A quieter internet café is Main St, near the junction with Novara Av. **Directory**

North of Dublin

Howth

Howth is 15 km (9 miles) northeast of Dublin, a lumpy peninsula that forms the northern part of the lovely horseshoe curve of Dublin Bay and looks south towards Dun Laoghaire. There are also **beaches**, *starting with the small and stony Balscadden beach which is just past the harbour where the bus arrives. Sutton beach, to the west, is sandy but incredibly shallow. Howth doesn't have that dormitory-town feel of Portmarnock or Malahide, further north of the city, and retains a fishing-village atmosphere.*

DART trains run from Connolly Station in just over 20 mins (be sure to sit on the side looking out to sea). For transport information see page 137

A pleasant afternoon's walk can be spent walking around the peninsula and across the hill of Howth. From the DART station go directly across the road to a gap in the wall which used to be the entrance to the tram station. Follow the steps and then the footpath uphill and behind some houses to a subur-ban street, **Grace O'Malley Drive**. Turn right, follow the road a little way, still climbing the hill and then turn right between some houses into a street called **Balkil Park**, and through a fence into the open land of the hill. Head south and uphill across the open land, towards a mobile-phone transmitter aerial. From here there are excellent views of the peninsula.

Dublin

Beaches

The whole northern coast is awash with long sandy beaches, plenty of birdlife, opportunities for sailing and swimming and great places for a picnic. The sand dunes along the coast have sprouted vast numbers of golf courses, but there are still lots of unspoiled beaches to enjoy. The first beach out of Dublin in this area is Velvet Strand at Portmarnock which runs for miles from Portmarnock into Malahide. In summer the beach fills up and you might even get a donkey ride. Towards Malahide the beach gets rockier and emptier. At Donabate there are more miles of dunes (and about nine golf courses!). At Portrane, further north the beaches are shingly but at low tide there are caves to explore; keep a careful weather eye for the returning tide. Further north, again is Loughshinny, a pleasant scramble from Skerries with another smugglers' cave en route and not so many other people because there is no transport. There are some archaeological sites around the beach here which some people claim are Roman. All the way from Loughshinny to Skerries are more sandy beaches and in Skerries itself is a lifeguard station. The beach is dotted with car parks and toilets all the way along here, and again the beach fills up in summer. More beaches can be found at Balbriggan with little booths selling ice-creams along them. The coast road follows the shore from Skerries to Balbriggan and the beach is sandy from the Ladies' Stairs northwards. If you explore even further north in search of beaches, the entire coastline from Gormanstown to Bettystown is made up of pretty sandy strands.

Make your way downhill and west, following a line of white painted stones, to get a view of the golf course and then across heather-covered slopes, but always keeping to pathways, to **Carrickbrack Road**. Turn right and follow the road for a few hundred metres until a sign appears on the seaward side of the road indicating a dangerous cliff edge. Continue along the path towards the cliffs and you will find yourself on the **Howth Head cliff walk**. Follow the cliff round to the left and a two-hour walk brings you back past amazing views of beaches and seabirds to the village, passing on your way footpaths that lead to the summit, from where there are more magnificent views. It was in the area where this cliff walk starts, that Erskine Childers landed a shipment of machine guns to help the anti-Treaty party in their struggle against the new Irish Free State. He was captured and executed by his erstwhile friends. His boat, *The Asgard*, is at Kilmainham Gaol.

Eating & drinking
Howth has lots of good pubs, a few very good restaurants and a bustling nightlife

Expensive *King Sitric*, East Pier, T8325235, is a well established fish restaurant with lots of recommendations to its name. Now moved to the first floor, reserve a table with a sea view. Terrific choice of totally fresh fish, from poached turbot to lobster thermidor, and sirloin steak. Strong wine list, mostly French. Open Mon-Fri for a set lunch around €20, and dinner Mon-Sat.

Mid-range *The Bloody Stream*, Howth Railway Station, T8395076. Don't let the name or the trains put you off. Good seafood restaurant with open-air seating doing lots of things from open sandwiches to seafood platters. *Citrus*, 1 Island View House, Harbour Rd, T8320200. Café bar with live jazz. Seating outside and a more formal restaurant upstairs. Asian fusion menu with some more regular dishes such as surf and turf. Try the meatballs in coconut and mint sauce with noodles or the tiger prawn curry. *Porto Fino*, Harbour Rd, T8393054. Pastas, pizzas and grills. Affordable early-bird menu from 1700-1930.

Dublin

Cheap *Casa Pasta*, 12 Harbour Rd, T8393823, is very good value with lots of pasta dishes, but plenty more on offer as well as sea views. *Caffé Caira*, 1 East Pier, serves bags of fish and chips to a long queue of customers. Some seating inside. *Dee Gees*, Harbour Rd, is a busy coffee shop which serves pasta dishes, burgers, filled rolls and more. *Beshoff's*, the exemplary fish and chip shop chain has a takeout place in Harbour Rd and there is also the *Dragon Boat* Chinese takeaway.

Bus Nos 31 and 31B travel to Howth from Lower Abbey St via Connolly Station but they take a lot longer than the DART. The last bus back to Dublin leaves Howth at 2400 daily except for Sat when the last one departs at 2245.

Transport

Train DART trains run regularly from Connolly Station. Don't get off at Howth Junction, an interchange for trains north to **Skerries** and **Dundalk**, but stay on until the train reaches its terminal at Howth. Sutton, the station before Howth, is closer to some of the accommodation. The last train leaves Howth for Dublin at 2359 Mon-Sat; a few mins earlier on Sun.

Malahide

Malahide, Mullach Íde in Gaelic, is a coastal town north of Howth and is pretty much a suburb of the city. It has that feel of a sleeper town which buzzes with activity at rush hours and sleeps quietly in between. The main reason for visiting is the **castle**, set in its own demesne of 1,250 acres (506 ha) with the **Fry Model Railway** in the grounds, the **Talbot Botanic Gardens** beside it and a great children's playground.

DART trains from Connolly station See page 137 for Transport information

Malahide Castle is a three-storey fortified house open to the public and owned for almost 800 years by one family, the Talbots, with a brief interlude during Cromwell's invasion of Ireland. It was bought by Dublin County Council in 1975 and opened to the public. Nothing remains of the original building erected in the 12th century, but a tiny part of one tower (which you don't actually see on the tour) is 14th century.

Sights
You can hire the Great Hall at Malahide Castle for parties

■ *Apr-Oct, Mon-Sat, 1000-1700, Sun and public holidays, 1100-1800; Nov-Mar, Mon-Fri, 1000-1700, Sat, Sun and bank holidays 1400-1700. Closed for tours, 1245-1400, daily. Restaurant, craft courtyard. €5. Combined ticket with Fry Model Railway available. T8462184.*

Children will appreciate the Fry Model Railway, in an old corn store in the grounds of the castle. ■ *Apr-Sep, Mon-Fri, 1000-1800, Sat 1000-1700, Sun and public holidays, 1400-1800; Apr and May closed Fri; Oct-Mar, Sat 1400-1700, Sun and public holidays, 1400-1700. €3.80. T8463779.*

Fry Model Railway

There is an exhilarating walk along the foreshore from Malahide to the southern end of Portmarnock, full of fresh air and lovely sea views of Howth to the south and Ireland's Eye out to sea. Lots of seabirds pick their way through the shells on the beach; the entire stretch of shore has sandy beaches, although the southern end gets tangled up with Portmarnock Golf Links. Also at Malahide is **Broadmeadow**, a wildfowl reserve and inland lake and wetlands created where the estuary of Broadmeadow River has almost been enclosed by sand dunes.

Malahide to Portmarnock

Newbridge House, Donabate

Around Portrane there are excellent beaches & views over Lambay island. Further north is Rogerstown Wildlife Sanctuary, another river estuary full of wading birds

One stop on from Malahide on the Dundalk line is Donabate, worth the trip for Newbridge House, an 18th-century manor house built by Richard Castle for the Archbishop of Dublin, in 1737, and set in 350 acres (142 ha) of land. The family still live in and own the house and all the original furniture and paintings are still in place. The original plasterwork is by Robert West and the rooms are full of period furniture. The park is maintained in its 18th-century state and includes a deer park, walled garden and arboretum. In the courtyard of the house and the outbuildings is a museum of 19th-century farming, complete with pettable animals. ■ *Apr-Sep, Tue-Sat, 1000-1700, Sun and public holidays, 1400-1800, closed for tours, 1300-1400; Oct to Mar, Sat, Sun and public holidays, 1400-1700. Coffee shop, craft shop, organized tours. €5. T8436534, F8436534.*

Eating & drinking

Malahide is an expensive sleeper town with lots of restaurants aimed at the well-to-do commuters who live there.

Expensive *Bon Appetit*, 9 James Terr, Malahide, T8450314. Classy place specializing in seafood and game with a mixture of modern Irish and French.

Mid-range *Giovani's*, 3-4 Townyard Lane, Malahide, T8451733. Cosy steak, pizza and pasta place opposite the seafront. *Kingsford Smith Restaurant*, White Sands Hotel, Portmarnock, T8460420. Sound hotel fare, in a comfortable oak-panelled room. Lots of fish and vegetarian choices. *The Orangerie*, 15 Townyard Lane, T8451299. Californian cuisine with a good early-bird menu from 1700-1900 of 2 courses for around €17.

Cheap *Kupz Tapas Bar*, Main St. Licenced tapas bar serving little platefuls for around €5 a each. Basic but busy. *Café Provence*, 1 Church Rd, T8450719. Small scones and tea place for Malahide's shoppers. Unlicensed.

Pubs & bars

Duffy's Bar and Lounge, Main St, Malahide, T8450735, is a staid-looking Victorian pub, but well known for its traditional music sessions on Thu nights after 2100.

Transport

Bus For **Malahide**: No 42 from Beresford Pl, near Busáras, the central bus station. No 32A, a limited service, goes to Malahide via Portmarnock. For **Donabate**: No 33B from Eden Quay. For **Portmarnock**: Nos 32 and 32B from Lower Abbey St. Between Portmarnock and Malahide the No 102 follows the coast road, terminating at **Sutton**. No 230 connects both Portmarnock and Malahide with **Dublin Airport**, more or less every hr.

Train The **DART** runs out as far as Malahide, stopping at Portmarnock, although this station is a good way out of the village with no transport into town. A better route into Portmarnock is via Sutton or Malahide and catch the feeder bus No 102. Beyond Malahide the **suburban rail network** serves Donabate, Rush and Lusk (again a good way out of either village), Skerries.

Skerries

For Transport information, see page 140

Half an hour by suburban train from the city centre, Skerries makes an excellent out-of-town base for those who prefer the quiet of the countryside to the rush and bustle of the city. Skerries offers pleasant accommodation, good food and a whole slew of places to visit in the surrounding area. The harbour is pretty and there is an abundance of wildlife, including seals.

There is a **tourist information** office in Skerries Mills Complex, Miller's Lane, Skerries, T8495208. Apr-Sep daily, 1030-1800, Oct-Mar daily 1030-1630. Closed 20 Dec-2 Jan.

The major attraction in the village itself is the **Skerries Mills Complex**, Miller's Lane, a heritage centre set in the village park. Visitors can walk around the working water mill and watch it operate as well as see inside the two windmills and inspect the bakery which makes bread from the wholegrain flour ground in the mills. There's a café selling products made at the bakery. ■ *Apr-Sep, daily 1030-1800, Oct-Mar, daily, 1030-1630. Closed 20 Dec-2 Jan. €3.80. Café, tourist information point and craft shop. T8495208.*

Sights

A half-hour walk or brief bus ride out of town brings you to **Ardgillan House and Demesne**, which has one of the most spectacular views of any country estate in Ireland or Britain. Set on a hillside with panoramic views of the sea all the way north to the Mountains of Mourne this is a castellated 18th-century house. ■ *House: Apr-Sep, Tue-Sun and public holidays, 1100-1800 (Jul, Aug, daily), Oct-Mar, Tue-Sun and public holidays, 1000-1630. Closed 23 Dec-2 Jan. **Park**: Nov-Jan, 1000-1700, Feb-Mar, 1000-1800, Jun-Sep, 1000-2000, Oct, 1000-1900. €3.80. includes tour of the building. Coffee shops. Coast Rd, Balbriggan, T8492212.*

Within comfortable walking distance of both Skerries & Balbriggan

AL *Redbank Guesthouse*, Church St, Skerries, T8490439, redbank@eircom.net Luxurious, friendly place attached to the well known *Red Bank* restaurant. Big comfortable rooms, sitting room, courtyard garden. The proprietors regularly arrange golfing, fishing, walking and sailing trips in the area. Amazing breakfast. Try the scrambled eggs and locally smoked salmon. **AL-A** *Redbank Lodge*, 12 Convent Lane, Skerries, T8490439, redbank@eircom.net Comfortable guesthouse in quiet lane close to the *Red Bank* restaurant. Rooms are smaller than the Guesthouse but there is a huge lounge area. Breakfast is 2 mins away at the restaurant and excellent. Pretty garden.

Sleeping
Price codes: see inside front cover

B *Malting House Inn*, Holmpatrick, Skerries, T8491075. Pub accommodation in pretty old stone-built pub close to the Skerries Mills complex. Breakfast not included in the rate.

Expensive *The Redbank Restaurant*, 7 Church St, Skerries, T8491005. If it swims in Dublin Bay, it's on the menu in this top-drawer seafood-based restaurant set in an old bank building. The wine cellar is in the bank vault. The chef greets you at the door and you have lots of time to choose your dishes while enjoying the tasty pre-dinner snacks. Dublin Bay prawns are the specialty of the house, served in several different styles but for a starter you should try the sizzling garlicky shellfish which comes noisily to your table wafting heavenly smells behind it. Check out the dessert trolley, not just for the great desserts but for its wacky design.

Eating & drinking
There's an excellent restaurant in Skerries and lots of places for good pub/ café food

Mid-range *Cactus Charlie's*, 24 Strand St, Skerries, T8492091. Sunny Mexican wine bar and café, trendy menu from blackened chicken to warmed goat's cheese salad, salmon and mango salsa. Good early-bird choices from 1700-2000, Tue-Thu. *The Windmill*, New St, T8491215. Pub and restaurant serving steaks, fajitas and lasagne. Pubby kind of food with lots of chocolate on the dessert menu.

Cheap *Black Raven*, 3 Church St, Skerries, T8491242. Good restaurant serving all day breakfast and good pub food. *Café Jazz*, 88C Strand St, Skerries, T8029841. Small café with big menu of ciabattas, pizzas, pasta and hot meals. Breakfast till late.

There are several pubs offering music of one kind or another in Skerries. *Joe May's*, *Nealon's*, The *Black Raven*, *Coast Inn*, *Fingal's Cave*, and the *Yacht Bar*, a little south of town in Loughshinny, all have music, while *The Windmill* in New St traditional and folk music on Sun evenings. You could also check out *The Gladstone*, at the Square in Skerries where there is sometimes some good traditional music.

Pubs & bars
There's a funfair, slot-machine arcade and a small community theatre in Skerries

Dublin

Transport   **Bus** For **Skerries** and **Balbriggan** (Skerries Mills and Ardgillan House): No 33 from Eden Quay in Central Dublin travels via Swords, Donabate, Lusk and Rush. For Ardgillan House, ask for the Ladies' Steps and walk up to the house across the bridge.

Train Skerries is 30 mins by **suburban rail**, then a 5-min walk. The last suburban train to Skerries leaves Connolly at 2210.

Taxi For short journeys around Skerries the best bet is a cab. *Fingal Cabs*, T8492263, and *Abacus Cabs and Minibuses*, T8491111 are both based in Skerries.

Directory   **Banks** *AIB*, Church St, Skerries, *Bank of Ireland*, Strand St, Skerries, *National Irish Bank*, Strand St. All have exchange facilities. **Birdwatching** *Bird Watch Ireland*, bird@indigo.ie, Frank Prendergast, T8490787. **Funfair** *Toft's*, South Strand, T8490681. **Laundry** *Concept Laundry and Dry Cleaning*, 51A Thomas Hand St, T8493080.

Central North

4

Central North

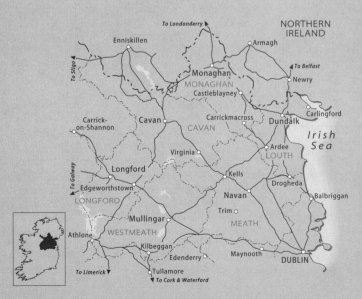

This mixed set of counties has little in common other than the dubious distinction of being either places that visitors tend to pass through on their way to somewhere else, or counties with particular attractions, such as Newgrange or the Cooley peninsula. While this elides their separate histories and identities, it also gives the visitor a valuable chance to discover a part of Ireland for themselves without the preconditioned images and clichés of touristland. The main route from Dublin to Donegal passes through the area and along the route there are lots of unspoiled villages such as Virginia in County Cavan where anyone tired of the shillelagh and pishogue syndrome of Irish tourism can spend a few days walking or fishing or just enjoying untouristified Ireland.

County Meath

*The rich soil of the Boyne valley that first attracted farmers in the Stone Age has now produced a fresh crop of prosperous farmers, who manage to make Meath's ancient past infinitely more interesting than anything the contemporary scene has to offer. **Newgrange** is unmissable and can be managed as a day trip from the capital or an excursion while travelling between Dublin and either Drogheda or Sligo. Both **Slane** and **Trim**, with modest but interesting sites in their vicinities, suggest themselves as possible bases for an overnight stay.*

Newgrange and Knowth

Phone code: 014
Colour map 4,
grid A2

The valley of the Boyne has a cluster of prehistoric tombs and two of them, Newgrange and Knowth, near to the village of Donore, constitute one of the major Stone Age sites in Europe. Along with the Pyramids and Mycenae, they are variations on the passage grave theme, but any profound cultural connection between these sites is nebulous, to say the least, given that the Boyne tombs have been dated centuries earlier than those in the Nile valley.

Getting there Donore is south of the River Boyne on the L21, and the Brú na Bóinne Centre is 1 mile to the west; signposted from Drogheda, off the N1, and from Slane, off the N2. *Bus Éireann* run a daily return service between Dublin and Donore, via Drogheda, leaving the capital, Mon-Sat, on the hour between 0900 and 1100 and then 1330, 1415 and 1500, and on Sun at 1045, 1215 and 1415. The last bus back to Dublin is 1605, and 1525 on Sun.

Newgrange Newgrange (see page 660) has mythological overtones – the home of the *Tuatha de Danainn*, a subterranean race of supernatural beings dedicated to the goddess Danu – though it was only in 1699 that the central tomb was accidentally discovered. The 62-ft (19-m) passageway from the entrance to the central cavern slopes upwards, so when light shines through it only reaches about half-way. The builders inserted a **roof box** in the roof above the entrance, so that when the sun rises on the shortest day of the year a pencil of light penetrates all the way to the central chamber. This only occurs around the winter solstice, and even then only for a maximum of 17 minutes in the morning: it is not possible for members of the public to experience this on the solstice itself, but the guided tour simulates the effect to give some idea of just how magical a moment this must have been. For the rest of the year, presumably, the massive carved stone that now rests outside blocked up the doorway.

The **geometric art motifs** that decorate the interior stones give credence to the idea that Newgrange was far more than just a burial place for some important ruling clan. Lozenge and zigzag designs, and especially the double and triple spiral patterns, have never been interpreted to everyone's satisfaction so your guess is as valid as most, but what remains undisputed is the sense of awe associated with finely executed stonecarving chiselled by craftspeople over 5,000 years ago.

Standing in the central chamber the most spectacular sight is **the roof**: it is not regular corbelling, but each stone rests on the twin halves of stones underneath, and the whole construction slopes downwards away from the centre. The effect is dizzyingly angular when viewed from below, and, as a feat of engineering that has kept the chamber bone dry for millennia, there is little to match it in the ancient world.

★

Things to do in the Central North

- Gaze up at the beam-walled roof of the **Newgrange passage grave**
- Take in the view of the **Mourne Mountains** from the Cooley peninsula
- See sixth-century **Monasterboice** in the early morning
- Visit the kitchens at **Tullynally Castle**, County Westmeath
- Have dinner at **Castle Leslie**, County Monaghan

Not as well known as Newgrange, Knowth continues to excite the archaeo- **Knowth**
logical world. The large central mound, which most unusually has two passage graves back to back, is surrounded by 18 smaller satellite tombs, each
with its own grave. The central mound has yielded a number of surprises,
the most remarkable being the twin chambers orientated to the east and
west. They are built in two different styles and the eastern one, which has a
cruciform chamber, is an astonishing 130 ft (40 m) long. A wealth of deco-
rated stones has been found in both chambers, almost as many as previously   *Passage graves are*
existed from all other passage graves in Ireland. Unlike Newgrange, the   *neolithic burial*
guided tour of Knowth does not bring visitors inside.   *chambers,*

Visits to Newgrange and Knowth must now begin at the **Brú na Bóinne**   *characterized by*
Visitor Centre at Donore, reached via Drogheda or Slane. A shuttle bus   *a circular mound*
takes visitors to Newgrange and Knowth for guided tours, and be warned   *reached via a*
that in summer there are long delays due to the limited number of people   *straight, long*
allowed to enter Newgrange at any one time. Try to arrive for opening time   *passageway, both*
and still be prepared for a wait. ■ *Donore. T041-9820300. Jun-mid Sep,*   *lined with stones*
daily, 0900-1900; May and mid-end of Sep, daily, 0900-1830; Mar-Apr and
Oct, daily, 0930-1730; Nov-Feb, daily, 0930-1700. €2.50 for Centre. €5 for
Centre and Newgrange; €8.80 for Centre, Newgrange and Knowth; €3.80 for
Centre and Knowth. Dúchas site. Guided tours. Tearoom.

Some 10 miles (15 km) west of Drogheda, the small town of Slane has a cer- **Slane**
tain Georgian charm, but as Slane Castle is still closed to the public since a   *Phone code: 041*
disastrous fire nearly a decade ago, there is little to do except admire the   *Colour map 4*
stone buildings and take a walk up the **Hill of Slane**. The hill is less than a   *grid A2*
mile above the village to the north and on a fine day, climbing the steps of the
always-open **tower** on the summit that was once part of a Franciscan friary,
provides a vantage point for taking in the Boyne valley.

Less than a mile east of the village is the **Francis Ledwidge Museum** in the
house where a poor peasant family brought up a family of eight children,
including the poet Francis Ledwidge. A republican and trade unionist, he
wrote feelingly in a Keatsian manner and yet went off to fight in France
where he died in 1917. ■ *Apr-Sep, daily, 0900-1300, 1400-1900; Oct-Mar,*
daily, closes 1630. €2.

AL *Conyngham Arms Hotel*, T9884444, www.conynghamarms.com Francis **Sleeping**
Ledwidge supped an occasional pint here; it's convenient for bar food and has a restaurant. For a B&B, it is hard to avoid the ubiquitous bungalow and one is **B** *Bondique*
House, Cullen, Beauparc, T/F9824823, bondique.iol.ie It is on the N2 road 4 km south
of Slane. Rooms with and without their own bathrooms. **B** *Boyne View* , Slane,
T9824121. Also on the N2. It is not a bungalow but a 2-storey house, open all year
except over Christmas.

County Meath

Around Navan

Phone code: 046
Colour map 4, grid A2

An ancient and modern crossroads, Navan town today has little to distinguish it, although it suggests itself as a watering hole. The **tourist office** is at hand with local information, and banks, post office and pubs serving food are conveniently located around the shopping centre on Kennedy Street.

Athlumney Castle makes a good destination for an easy stroll out of town: head south over the bridge and follow the signs. A 15th-century four-storeyed tower stands next to a Tudor edifice with its mullioned windows intact. Legend has it that the owner of the place set it alight, rather than see it fall into the hands of the English. Keys to the place can be picked up at the nearby Loreto convent.
■ *Tourist office: Railway St, T215181. Mon-Sat 1000-1700, Sun 1000-1300.*

The main attractions around Navan are outside of town on the Dublin road and the chief attraction is the hill of Tara.

Tara What you see is not what you get, and it requires an act of imagination to empathize with the tremendous historical and mythological significance of Tara. What is basically a mound in a meadow is traditionally regarded as the seat of the high kings of Ireland. Whether any one ruler could have had influence over the whole of Ireland before the ninth century is doubtful, but there is no mistaking the symbolic clout accorded to the notion of a kingship of Tara. The origins and functioning of Tara are lost in the prehistory of late neolithic and Bronze Age times, but so entwined is the place with mythology that what you see today was in some sense the capital of ancient Ireland. The god Lug, the Zeus of the Irish pantheon, is associated with Tara, as are the ancient female fertility figures of Eithne and Medb. A seventh-century history of St Patrick relates how he provocatively lit a bonfire on the hill of Slane and was called to account by the king of Tara, whom he managed to convert in the process. The significance of Tara was not lost in the 1641 uprising, it also played a part in the 1798 insurrection, and in 1843 a million supporters of Daniel O'Connell apparently turned up here to hear him speak.

The **Visitor Centre** brings some of all this to life with a 20-minute audio-visual show, *Tara, Meeting Place of Heroes*, and a useful guided tour of the site that includes a chance to peer in at a passage grave dated 2000BCE, which yielded a treasure trove of artefacts. There is also the Rath of the Synods, which was vandalized by British Israelites in 1899, putative excavators searching for the biblical Ark of the Covenant. A few days before their visit some Roman coins were buried for them to find by supporters hoping to encourage their belief that Tara was a biblical site, but excavations in the 1950s revealed genuine Roman finds, indicative of trade with the Roman world of the early centuries CE. ■ *Navan, T25903. May-Oct, daily, 1000-1800; Nov-Apr T9824488. €1.90. Dúchas site. Tara is 8 miles (12 km) south of Navan off the N3.*

Dunsany Castle From Tara it is a short hop to the village of Dunsany and its eponymous castle where the poet Francis Ledwidge found an honourable patron in Lord Dunsany (1878-1957), who introduced the poet's first collection of verse: "I hope that not too many will be attracted to this book on account of the author being a peasant, lest he come to be praised by the how-interesting school." Lord Dunsany later went on to become a most strange writer in his own right. Shot in the face while attempting to help the British in the Easter Rising, He also played a part in supporting another local writer, Mary Lavin. Tours of the house, taking in a noted collection of art and assorted artefacts, are conducted but telephone ahead to reserve a place. ■ *T25198. Jul and Aug Mon-Sat 0900-1300. €3.80.*

While in the area, it is worth the short journey west of Dunsany to admire **Bective Abbey**, one of the earliest Cistercian abbeys in Ireland. Founded in 1147, precious little remains from that era and most of what you see today, including a fine cloister, was constructed in the 15th century.

Trim

Trim wouldn't be Trim without its splendid castle in the centre of town, which waited until 1995 before film people discovered its potential as a film set and brought in Mel Gibson to re-enact the Scots' assault on the perfidious English at York for the film *Braveheart*. The castle was built by the Norman de Lacy family in the early 13th century and, with the main tower having walls some 11 ft (3 m) thick, was built to withstand anything the Irish might hurl at them. A great curtain wall with D-shaped towers was constructed as a secondary line of defence, but in the English Civil War the castle was twice captured and left in disuse after the Cromwellians departed. ■ *T38618. Mid Jun-mid Sep, daily 1000-1800. €3.10 for castle and keep; castle only €1.20. Guided tours every ½ hr.*

Trim Castle
Phone code: 046
Colour map 4, grid A2

On the opposite side of the river to the castle stands **Talbot Castle**, an impressive manor house built by the viceroy of Ireland, Sir John Talbot, in 1415. It was built using part of an earlier Augustinian abbey but all that now remains of this is the **Yellow Steeple**, a tall bell tower that was badly damaged by Cromwell's army. Also here is the **Sheep Gate**, a surviving remnant of the 14th-century town walls.

A mile-long walk along the Dublin road from Trim Castle, crossing the river once again, brings you to the signposted ruins of **St Patrick's Church** and its cemetery. Points of interest are the medieval grave stones and the 16th-century tomb of a couple known as the jealous man and woman; the sword that lies between them giving rise to a story of marital discord!

A visit to **Butterstream Gardens**, on the western outskirts of Trim, has been recommended by a reader. This highly imaginative garden was created in the early 1970s and there is certainly a lot to see and discuss. ■ *Open May-Sep, 1100-1800. €5 admission. Kildalkey Rd, T36017*

For tourist information, call in at the **Trim Visitor's Centre** where there is a modest exhibition on the town's medieval history. ■ *Mill St. T37227. Mon-Sat 1000-1700, Sun 1200-1730. €3. For tourist information, www. meathtourism.ie*

B *Brogan's Guesthouse*, High St, T31237, brogangh@iol.ie has 8 bedrooms which have been thoroughly modernized and 7 which retain their traditional character; this guesthouse goes back to 1915. **C-D** *Bridge House Holiday Hostel*, Bridge St, T31848, silversue@eircom.net An IHH place next to the Visitor's Centre, open all year and includes 3 private doubles for €31.75.

Sleeping & eating

Nothing to write home about when it comes to enjoying a good meal in Trim. *Kerr's Kitchen*, Haggard St, T37144, is ok for open sandwiches, quiche, shepherd's pie, chicken curry, especially on a fine day when the take-away service facilitates a picnic. Take your pick from the pubs or try the *Wellington Court Hotel* for a restaurant meal.

Kells and around

As it is situated on the N3 road between Dublin and Enniskillen, Kells only tends to be visited when travelling that route. Of course, if the famous Book of Kells was actually kept here then life would be very different; as it is, visitors need content themselves with a heritage centre, some fine high crosses and the local memorial to Jim Connell.

Phone code: 046
Colour map 4, grid C1

☛ **To Cover My Socialist Bones**

When in or around Kells, consider a short trip along the R163 before turning off for the village of Crossakeel and its memorial to Jim Connell, author of the socialist anthem "The Red Flag". Connell was born here in 1852 and wrote the song on a 20-minute train ride from Charing Cross to Lewisham in London in 1889.

His memorial carries his own epitaph:

Oh, grant me an ownerless corner of earth,
Or pick me a hillock of stones,
Or gather the wind-wafted leaves of trees,
To cover my socialist bones

Sights **Kells Heritage Centre and Tourist Office** has an audio-visual presentation and an exhibition on the culture of monastic Ireland; both best saved for a rainy day. ■ *T47840. May-Sep, 1000-1730 and Oct-Apr, Tue-Sat, 1000-1700. €4 for the exhibition and audio-visual show.*

The **Church of St Columba**, in the centre of town, is where the monastic settlement stood that received the Book of Kells when it arrived here in 807. Close to the neighbouring round tower there are three **high crosses** as well as the remains of a fourth.

Walking At Oldcastle, 12 miles from Kells, **Loughcrew Gardens** are on your left just before entering the town. Apart from the intrinsic appeal of these 17th-century gardens, redeveloped in the 19th century, there is a 15-minute walk to the Loughcrew megalithic cairns (the keys are obtainable in return for a €25 deposit). ■ *Oldcastle T049-8541922. Apr-Sep, daily, 1200-1800; Oct-mid-Mar, Sat and Sun, 1200-1600; mid Mar-end Mar, daily, 1200-1600. €4.45*

For something more organized, contact *Kelltic Walking Tours*, based in White Gables B&B just across from the tourist office. They do a weekend walking package for €177 which covers accommodation, meals, transport and two days' guided walking. A 3-day trip is €266.■ *Headford Pl, T49672, keltic@tinet.ie*

Sleeping
Price codes:
see inside front cover

A *Headford Arms Hotel*, T40063, F40587. A run-of-the-mill hotel in the centre of town; with food available daily until 2200 it makes a convenient resting place. **B** *White Gables*, Headfort Pl, T40322, kelltic@tinet.ie A pleasing B&B establishment with a garden at the back and a residents' sitting room. All the local information you could wish for and good breakfast too. **C- D** *Kells Hostel*, T49995, F40680, hostels@iol.ie An IHH hostel, part of the *Carrick House* pub on the Cavan road, a 5 min walk from town, and includes a few private rooms.

Eating *The Ground Floor Restaurant*, Bective Square, T49688, serves as an example of what is rare in Ireland – good food served in pleasant surroundings at prices that can't be complained at. Open nightly, the wide-ranging menu is full of surprises from eastern Mediterranean cuisine and a 3 course meal could be enjoyed for under €20. On weeknights there is an early-bird menu between 1800 and 1900 for €15.24. The *Round Tower* in Farrell St features Irish, Chinese and Thai food from 1500-2200 as well as lunch, and live music on Thu and Sat nights. Try the *Westway Bar* in Bective St for lunch.

County Louth

The name of Ireland's smallest county, Louth, doesn't quite trip off the tongue. But hold on a while, for the two main towns of Drogheda and Dundalk are intrinsically interesting and ideal bases for exploring the surrounding countryside. Drogheda, just north of Dublin, is perfect for taking in the Boyne valley and Dundalk is at last coming into its own as a jumping-off point for the Cooley Peninsula and the county of Armagh.

Drogheda

Scruffy and unpretentious, Drogheda is in the process of reinventing itself, but hopefully it will take a long time before Dublin yuppyland and its new money lowers the tone of this historic and ancient town. The town was founded by the Vikings, then was a medieval walled town of consequence, ethnically cleansed by Cromwell in the 17th century and ruled solidly thereafter by Protestants through prosperous times over the following two centuries. The **Drogheda Heritage Centre**, in the old Church of Ireland in Mary Street, is currently closed but should have reopened by the time you read this. A fine example of the town walls can be seen in the grounds of the Centre and it was here that Cromwell breached the walls to enter the town. The **tourist office** is at the bus station on Donore Road, T9837070. Open all year, Mon-Sat, 0900-1730. Sun, 1145-1700, Apr-Nov. There is also one at Millmount, T9845684, Mon-Fri, 1000-1300 and 1400-1700.

Phone code: 041 Colour map 4, grid A2

Starting from the tourist office and bus station head east towards town and before the bridge turn right up Barrack Street for the **Millmount Museum** housed in former barracks built for the British and occupied by anti-Treaty forces in the civil war. Drogheda was fiercely anti-Treaty and some of the artillery used to shell the Four Courts in Dublin was brought up here to shell the rebels. This is a lovely old museum, run by dedicated local people who on a quiet day will find time to explain the arcane iconography of the precious 18th-century guild banners on display. ■ *T9833097. Mon-Sat, 1000-1800; Sun, 1430-1700. €3. The Martello Tower at Millmount is now open to the public (same hrs as the Museum).*

A walking tour

Back down to the bridge and a pause to admire eastwards the elegant viaduct that carries the Dublin to Belfast trains (original journey time was 17 hours), a superb example of Victorian engineering, with an Irish-designed 1920s, single-track steel girder in the centre replacing the original wrought iron.

Cross the bridge and up Shop Street, turning left into West Street, where the Bank of Ireland utilizes the 1770 Tholsel with its clock tower that chimes every 15 minutes. The building has style, unlike the Gothic enormity of **St Peter's Roman Catholic Church** in West Street, in your face on the right. The church is famous as the final resting place of **St Oliver Plunkett** – well, his head at least – and you will also find the door of his cell from Newgate prison in London, where he was held for eight months before being hung, drawn and quartered on 1 July 1681. Oliver Plunkett (1625-81) was a Catholic Archbishop who was arrested on suspicion of planning a French invasion. The case against him collapsed when witnesses, mostly fellow priests he had managed to antagonize, withdrew, but Plunkett was shipped off to London for a second trial. He was canonized in 1975.

By the church corner, turn right into Duke Street and right again into Fair Street, which leads across Peter Street into William Street where **St Peter's Church of Ireland** stands. Citizens fleeing Cromwell and seeking refuge here were burned to death in its former wooden steeple. There are interesting memorial tablets inside the church and though it may not always be open the graveyard has a fascinating cadaver tombstone dated 1520. The father of Swift's Vanessa, Bartholomew Van Homrigh, who came to Ireland from Amsterdam with William of Orange before the Revolution of 1687, is buried here – Van Homrigh acquired the Freedom of Dublin by 1685, was a member of Dublin Corporation, and then Alderman (1688). Walk down William Street, turn right into Palace Street and go to the end to stand before the 13th-century **St Laurence's Gate**, an impressive reminder of the way most important Irish towns were walled and protected by barbican gates such as this.

Turning right into Laurence Street leads back to Shop Street and the Tholsel.

Sleeping
■ *on map*
Price codes:
see inside front cover

L *Boyne Valley Hotel*, T9837737, www.boyne-valley-hotel.ie Almost a 30-min walk from town on the Dublin Rd, but if arriving on bus from Dublin ask to be dropped off outside. It is a comfortable country house with good sports facilities. **L** *Westcourt Hotel*, Wall St, T9830965, www.westcourt.com Where Michael Collins and Harry Boland stayed in Sep 1921 (then the *White Horse*), this is in the centre of town. **L** *Neptune Beach Hotel*, Bettystown, T9827107, www.neptunebeach.ie A place to escape to, overlooking the beach, with good restaurant and leisure centre. **B** *Boyne Haven House*, T9836700, www.boynehaven.com On the Dublin Rd near Bettystown, this is a top-notch B&B with a breakfast menu to die for. **B** *River Boyne House*, Oldbridge, T9836180, is out of town at the Battle of the Boyne site: a quieter place to bed down for the night. **C-D** *The Green Door*, 47 John St, T9834422, www.greendoorhostel.com An IHH hostel, open all year with some 20 dorm beds and 3 private rooms. well equipped hostel, with bikes for hire and pick-up available from bus or train station.

Drogheda

■ **Sleeping**
1 Green Door Hostel
2 Westcourt

● **Eating & drinking**
1 Bensons Pub
2 Bridie Mac's Pub
3 Carberry's Pub
4 Humaa & Burke's Café
5 La Pizzeria
6 Le Boheme
7 Martello's
8 McPhails Pub
9 New Central
10 Weavers Pub

0 yards 200
0 metres 200

From Wolfe Tone to Samba

Wolfe Tone came to Drogheda in 1792 and described it as "a small town enclosing four broad streets, and a collection of miserable cottages within ancient walls".

Gaze down on the town from Millmount and you'll see his point, but come in July for the Samba Festival and the Latin rhythms tell you Drogheda has moved on.

Martello's, Millmount Sq, T9834759, has a spacious upstairs restaurant with window tables overlooking the town. Opens Tue-Sun from 1800. The next best place is *Le Boheme* on Shop St, T9845684, for lunch or dinner (closed Mon). Out of town at Bettystown, *Bacchus*, T982851, has been recommended for the quality of its cuisine. Tue-Sat for dinner, Sun lunch, and an early-bird menu from 1800 for good value. Another good-value meal, 10 mins away by car, is the early-bird menu at *The Triple House* in Termonfeckin (see page 154).

The *Terrace Café* in the *Westcourt Hotel* has a self-service system and choice of places to plonk down your tray of standard carbohydrate bulk for around €7. *Bridie Mac's* pub next door is a comfortable alternative for lunch, or cross the road to *Jalapenos*. *Weavers* next door is popular with locals, especially for Sunday lunch, serving beef, lamb and the like with chips. The cheapest pub lunches are available at *Sweeneys* pub and *The New Central*, 29 Peter St. Also on Peter St, *Burke's Restaurant* is a plain café open daily until 1800 (1600 on Sun) with a breakfast menu, grills, omelettes, salads and sandwiches. *Humaa*, T9844990, close by is an Indian/Pakistani restaurant with a good local reputation. Opposite, 38 Peter St, *La Pizzeria* has pizza and pasta dishes for around €8. *The Black Bull Inn*, T9837139, just outside of town on the road to Dublin, is open all day for a good choice of meals, and a delicatessen for picnic supplies.

Eating
● *on map*
*Price codes:
see inside front cover*

When night falls, from a window table at Martello's in Drogheda, the Dublin to Belfast train chugging across the Victorian viaduct east of town is a stirring sight

Carberry's on North Strand is the town's best known traditional Irish music venue, sessions every Tue night and Sun morning. *The New Central*, 29 Peter St, has music every night and an Irish night on Wed. Other good music venues are *McPhails* in Laurence St and *Bensons* in Trinity St. Check out, too, the Droichead Arts Centre in Stockwell St, T9833496,

Entertainment

Samba Festival, T9833946, www.solo.ie/samba Second week in Jul.

Festivals

Bicycle hire from €6-8 a day, from *Quay Cycles*, 11a North Quay, T9834526. **Bus** the station, T9835023, is on Donore Rd south of the river and there are a number of daily connections with **Dublin**, **Dundalk** and **Belfast** as well as services to **Athlone**, **Downpatrick**, **Galway**, **Kells**, **Mullingar**, **Navan**, **Newgrange**, **Newry**, and **Slane**. **Taxis** From T9838439, T9832211, T9837082, T9832244 and T9822666. **Train** The station is east of town, also south of the river, off the Dublin Rd, T988749. Drogheda is on the **Dublin-Belfast** line and there are at least 7 trains a day in either direction and 4 on Sun.

Transport

Banks, *AIB*, *Ulster Bank*, *TSB* and others are found in West St. **Walking tours** Mon-Fri at 1020 and 1420 departing from the Donore Rd tourist office; to book in advance, T9845684.

Directory

Around Drogheda

Drogheda makes a great base for visiting Boyne valley sights such as Newgrange and these are covered in the Meath chapter beginning on page 144. There are other nearby sights within the county of Louth, which can easily be taken in on day trips from Drogheda by bicycle or car.

County Louth

The Curse of Cromwell?

The 1640s was a particularly unstable decade in Ireland, beginning with the rising of 1641 and ending with the fall of Drogheda to Cromwell in 1649. Events were complicated by the outbreak of civil war in England, with royalists in Ireland on the defensive and the insurgents organizing themselves into the Confederate Catholics. A ceasefire was established, but this broke down in 1646 and Cromwell arrived in August 1649 with an army of 20,000 men, a navy and heavy artillery. On the 10th September his handwritten ultimatum was delivered to the governor of Drogheda, a royalist town, promising that an "effusion of blood may be prevented" if surrender was swift. There was to be no surrender, Cromwell's army breached a hole in the city's defensive walls and in the ensuing fighting some 3,000 people lost their lives. At Millmount, a converted Viking fort, the leaders were cornered and slain and the town's governor, Aston, was seized upon, for rumour had it that his wooden leg was packed with gold and angry soldiers, finding the leg empty, used it to beat him to death.

In his Cromwell, An Honourable Enemy (see page 677), Irish historian Tom Reilly argues that there is no primary evidence for the folk tradition of wholesale slaughter at Drogheda. He sees the siege as a military encounter between two English factions struggling for power where there was no more indiscriminate killing than the rules of war allowed for. The folk tradition of Cromwell's infamy arose later in accounts of the siege by people who never took part in it.

Mellifont Abbey The first Cistercian abbey in Ireland was founded five miles (8 km) north of Drogheda in 1142 at the behest of St Malachy of Armagh as part of his drive to reform the laid-back monastic life of Irish monks. Mellifont, with hundreds of resident monks, came to preside over dozens of other Cistercian abbeys across the country until they were all suppressed by Henry VIII in 1539. The place was converted into a private mansion and gave refuge to Hugh O'Neill, who surrendered here in 1603 after his defeat at Kinsale.

Like the ruins of a Greek temple, there is not a lot to see on the site but with the help of the free ground plan it is possible to trace out the buildings from the excavated foundations. The substantial remains of a 13th-century **lavabo**, an octagonal washing house for the monks, help evoke the architectural elegance that the French brought to monastic design.

It is easy to get misty-eyed imagining pacifist monks tending beehives and chanting dulcet tones about the place, but history presents a less flattering picture. Irish monks affiliated to Mellifont did not take kindly to spot checks by the order; not untypical was a monastery in County Limerick, which barred its doors, laid an ambush and attacked the visitors. It wasn't just the Cistercians who took to fisticuffs; in-fighting by Franciscan monks led to a pitched battle in 1291 with several fatalities. ■ *Tullyallen, T9826459. May-Oct, daily 1000-1800; Nov-Apr telephone for opening hrs. €1.90. Dúchas site. One mile (1.5 km) off the main Drogheda to Collon rd. No bus service; car, taxi or bicycle from Drogheda.*

Monasterboice
Colour map 1, grid C5

Monasterboice is an old Irish monastery founded by St Buite in the sixth century, the kind of place that the Cistercians of Mellifont were designed to eclipse. Nothing remains of the monastery, but there is an elegant **round tower** and one of the most elaborately decorated **high crosses** to be seen anywhere in Ireland.

Getting there Take the signposted slip road off the N1 at the *Monasterboice Inn* seven miles (10 km) north of Drogheda. If travelling by bus between Drogheda and Dundalk, it is usually possible to ask to be dropped off by the pub and still use the ticket to resume the journey by hailing down a later bus on the same route.

The not-the-12th July Battle of the Boyne

The Battle of the Boyne in July 1690, the one that loyalists in the North are so intent on celebrating, took place at Oldbridge three miles upstream from Drogheda. The battle itself, which saw the retreat of the Jacobites, was not as decisive as the later encounter at Aughrim, but its fame developed from the personal presence of both William and James. The Orange Order, celebrating the event from the 1790s onwards and misunderstanding the workings of the 1752

calendar reform, incorrectly dated it as the 12th July when it fact it took place on 1st July. To reach a point overlooking the site of the battle, take the N51 Slane Road for 1.8 miles (3 km), passing the Obelisk Bridge Information Centre, T9841644, at Oldbridge. This 1869 wrought-iron bridge had an obelisk beside it marking the battle which was blown up in 1921. A stroll can also be taken along the Towney Hall Nature Walk, just further along.

There are two crosses to admire and the best is the first one that you come to on entering the churchyard: **Muiredach's Cross**, dating from the 10th century. It is astonishing to find such priceless art plonked here in a quiet countryside setting. On the east side, there are two animals on the base, with the panel above showing Adam and Eve on the left and Cain and Abel on the right. Above this there are scenes from the life of David, a panel showing Moses striking a rock for water, and then a panel of the Adoration of the Magi. Below the central cross depicting Christ in Majesty there is a graphic scene of St Michael weighing a soul on scales with the devil pulling for all his worth from below. The scene at the very top is hard to decipher.

The west side has an inscription at the bottom with cats, then a panel showing the arrest of Christ, a panel above depicting the doubting Thomas and then a scene with the Apostles. The central cross, showing the Crucifixion, is surmounted by a biblical scene featuring Moses.

The other cross, the **West Cross**, has faded badly, but there is a notice board explaining the content of its panels. The round tower is a fine example of its type but is closed to the public.

Not-so-ancient tombstones fill the churchyard and one, on the east side of the crumbling old church near Muiredach's Cross, erected by Thomas Cregan to members of his family is, literally, monumental proof of the Irish diaspora.

The *Monasterboice Inn*, owned by a controversial ex-minister of defence in a 1970s government, serves the same lunch food in the lounge and bar (it costs less in the bar) and there is also an evening menu.

The main N1 road is the speediest way to travel between Drogheda and Dundalk, but apart from accessing Monasterboice along the way the journey it is purely functional. An inland route is possible via Collon and Mellifont Abbey and, midway to Dundalk, the rural town of **Ardee** offers itself as a tranquil backwater for anyone with a lazy itinerary wishing to take in this little-visited corner of Ireland. There are a couple of crumbling castles, nature walks in Ardee bog, fishing and other activity possibilities, and a smattering of places to eat and stay. There is no tourist office, but the town library has some local information. **B** *Setanta*, 7 Castle St, T6853319, setanta@destination-ireland.com offers B&B in a comfortable, centrally located Georgian town house. For a touch of Georgian luxury **AL** *Red House*, T/F6853523, is a fine country house with pool and tennis court. *The Railway Bar*, Main St, is an attractive, old-style pub with a restaurant at the back serving good food.

Drogheda to Dundalk

County Louth

If time allows, take the coastal road via Baltray, with its famous golf course, T9822329, and refreshments at the nearby *The 19th Hole* pub. There is also lovely **Termonfeckin** with its old castle (key available from neighbouring bungalow), and fine food at *The Triple House*, T9322616, a converted 200-year-old farmhouse, or, less expensively, the *Waterside Inn* pub. Follow the coastal road north to **Clogherhead** and a superb beach – one of Ireland's least known safe and sandy beaches – that stretches up to Port and looks across to the Sellafield nuclear plant in England. From Port the road travels inland rather scenically to reach the coast again at **Annagassan**, which also has a huge, safe beach, and then it is just a short hop to **Castlebellingham**, where pub and restaurant food and bedrooms await in **AL** *Bellingham Castle Hotel*, T9372176, F9372766.

Dundalk

*Phone code: 042
Colour map 1,
grid C5*

Dundalk is a lively, underestimated town, well worth considering as a base for exploring south Armagh and Monaghan. Once tagged as a border town of ill-repute, the town is justifiably fed up with tired clichés from the past, and for visitors who appreciate a town unsullied by mass tourism smart Dundalk is a place to see and savour.

Walking tour

Starting outside the **tourist office** on Jocelyn Street (T9335484, May-Sep, Mon-Sat, 0900-1800; Oct-Apr, Mon-Fri, 0930-1730), the **County Museum** is next door in a restored 18th-century warehouse and houses two new floors, one devoted to archaeology and early history and the other to Norman and medieval history. ■ *T9327056. Tue-Sat, 1030-1730, Sun 1400-1800. €2.54.*

Walk down Jocelyn Street, past the tourist office, to the road junction; don't turn directly right into Castle Street but take the right fork along Roden Place, pausing before you do so to admire the art nouveau *Century Pub* on the corner. Built to celebrate the beginning of the 20th century, original features of its design are retained externally and inside there are more features, such as the fireplace, to admire over a morning drink. Crowe Street leads past the Greek-style **Courthouse**, one of the finest examples of a 19th-century courthouse in Ireland, on the corner with Clanbrassil Street. Doric columns cut from white Portland stone and the granite ashlar blocks of the stern flanking walls of this still functioning courthouse proclaim a Spartan rather than Athenian sense of justice.

Go up Clanbrassil Street, passing the superb example of Victorian commercial architecture at No 70, to where **St Nicholas' Church** stands on the right just past Yorke Street. A mishmash of architectural styles, the churchyard has the grave of Agnes Galt, sister of the poet Robert Burns, who lived just outside of town for nearly 20 years. Continue along Yorke Street and turn right into Chapel Street to return to the *Century Bar*.

Sleeping
■ *on map
Price codes:
see inside front cover*

L *Ballymascanlon House Hotel*, T9371124, info@ballymascanlon.com Out of town on the road to the Cooley peninsula, this is a grand Victorian edifice modernised with top-class sports facilities but hardly able to forget the past with the Proleek Dolmen from around 3000BCE in its grounds; a good restaurant. **AL** *Derryhale House Hotel*, Carrickmacross Rd, T9335471, F9335471, info@minotel.iol.ie A listed Victorian building within walking distance of town. **B** *Fáilte House*, Dublin Rd, T9335152, reliable B&B, on the corner with Long Av. **B** *Rosemount*, Dublin Rd, T9335878. South of town, this is generally regarded as one of the best B&B establishments in the area.

Camping *Gyles Quay*, T9376262, is a well provided caravan and mobile home site but has space for 10 tent pitches between Apr and Sep. Situated 11 miles (16 km) west of town on the Cooley Peninsula. *Tain Holiday Village*, Ballyoonan, Omeath, T9375385

Both the bar food and the restaurant at the convivial *Derryhale Hotel* on Carrickmacross Rd are reasonably priced, and food from the bar menu can also be enjoyed sitting in the period reception area. Easy to find, opposite St Patrick's Cathedral, the cosy *Townhouse*, T9329898, in a Georgian building with original features, has a mixed menu of European and Asian tastes. The trendy *Café Metz*, Francis St, opens for breakfast, €10 lunch, and dinner around €25; drop in for a coffee and check out the menu. The retro-style *No 32*, 32 Chapel St, T933113, serves substantial lunches and a varied menu with dishes like leek sausages, pork and cider, and decent vegetarian choices. For an excellent carvery head for *The Jockeys*, 47 Anne St, or try pleasant *Courtney's* in Patrick St for light food.

Traditional Irish music every Fri at *The Jockeys*, 47 Anne St. *Moe's Bar*, close to Courtneys on Park St. Popular beer garden and music most nights. On a Thu, try *Corbetts*, Seatown, and on Mon and Fri nights music starts at 2100 in *McManus's*, Seatown. For a quieter atmosphere, *P McArdles*, Anne St, attracts a more purist crowd of performers and audience on the first and third Thu of each month. *Cavanaghs*, Park St, is a big modern pub with sessions every Tue night. On a Tue head out of town for a couple of miles on the Dublin Rd and enjoy traditional music at *Sextons's* pub. On the Quay, check out *The Spirit Store*, T9352697, www.spiritstore.ie Very atmospheric music venue; trad, jazz, rock, and world beer on draught. Music of a non-traditional kind comes alive in the *Terrace Bar* of the Ballymascalon Hotel on Sat night and there is also a live band in the ballroom. Weekend discos in the *Imperial Hotel* and *Mr Ridleys*, both in Park St.

Eating

● *on map*
Price codes:
see inside front cover

Pubs & music

County Louth

Dundalk

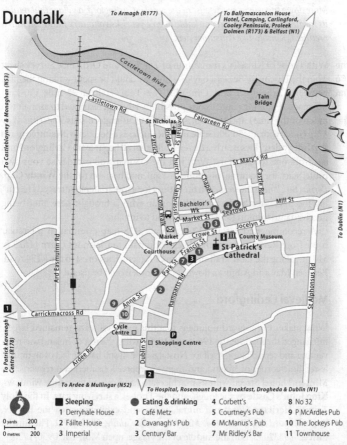

To Armagh (R177)

To Ballymascanion House
Hotel, Camping, Carlingford,
Cooley Peninsula, Proleek
Dolmen (R173) & Belfast (N1)

Castletown River

To Castleblayney & Monaghan (N53)

Castletown Rd

St Nicholas

Fairgreen Rd

Tain Bridge

To Dublin (N1)

St Mary's Rd

Castle Rd

Mill St

Seatown

Bachelor's Wk

Market St

Chapel St

Jocelyn St

County Museum

Crowe St

St Patrick's Cathedral

Market Sq

Courthouse

Francis St

Park St

Ramparts Rd

St Alphonsus Rd

Anne St

Carrickmacross Rd

Ard Easmuinn Rd

To Patrick Kavanagh Centre (R178)

Cycle Centre

Dublin St

Shopping Centre

Ardee Rd

To Ardee & Mullingar (N52)

To Hospital, Rosemount Bed & Breakfast, Drogheda & Dublin (N1)

N

0 yards   200
0 metres   200

■ **Sleeping**
1 Derryhale House
2 Fáilte House
3 Imperial

● **Eating & drinking**
1 Café Metz
2 Cavanagh's Pub
3 Century Bar

4 Corbett's
5 Courtney's Pub
6 McManus's Pub
7 Mr Ridley's Bar

8 No 32
9 P McArdles Pub
10 The Jockeys Pub
11 Townhouse

Transport **Bus Station**: Longwalk, T9334075. Services to Armagh, Belfast, Carlingford, Drogheda, Dublin, Enniskillen, Galway, Mullingar, Newry and Sligo. **Taxis** *Classic Cabs*, T9336000; *Top Rank*, T9326555; *Whiteline*, T9326999. **Train** Station: Carrick Rd, T9335521. Dundalk is on the Dublin to Belfast line; at least 7 trains a day in either direction, and 4 on Sun.

Directory **Banks** Clanbrassil St and Park St. **Bureaux de change**: there is a money exchange desk (pounds/euros/dollars only) in the Dundalk Shopping Centre near the bus station. **Communications** Post Office: Clanbrassil St. **Walking tours** History-based, conducted by Hugh Smyth, T9328061, once a week during the evening. Also, self-guided walking brochure from the tourist office.

Cooley Peninsula

Phone code: 042
Colour map 2,
grid B6

Nestled between Dundalk Bay and Carlingford Lough (a true fjord), the Cooley Peninsula and the view across to the Mourne Mountains never looks better than on a soft day when a gentle mist shrouds the land. The area's association with a rich vein of Irish mythology then seeps through the landscape evoking the tales of Cú Chulainn who, in just one of his adventures, had to cope with the magic of Morrígan in the triple guise of a red-eared heifer, a she-wolf and then a black eel. More down to earth in every sense of the word is Carlingford, a village that retains its medieval heritage to a remarkable degree yet risks voluntary mutation into a prettified, Kinsale-like consumer den.

Walking in the steps of Cú Chulainn

With a copy of Kinsella's translation of *The Táin* and Ordnance Survey sheet 29 in the Discovery Series a day or a holiday could be spent walking the hills between Carlingford and Omeath. The Táin Trail, a 25-mile (40-km) waymarked walking route, is one possibility (though restricted to asphalt too much of the time) and the tourist office in Carlingford sells *The Táin Way Map Guide* with a 1:50,000 scale map. *Rambles* is a booklet with simple maps that briefly describes nearly a dozen walks that all begin from Carlingford and last from one to six hours. With just the OS map you can devise your own route: start, for example, on the Táin Trail, and head off for the **Windy Gap**, *Bernas Bo Ulad* in the saga, and the setting for a much later love tragedy featuring the tragic death of a Spanish woman who is brought here after being deceived into thinking she has a rich land to inhabit.

A recommended 8-mile (12-km) walk (OS map essential) is a circular route from Ravensdale up the Black Mountain to Clermont Cairn (1675 ft; 510 m), along the Táin Trail and through Ravensdale Forest to the R174 road. Between May and August a flower guidebook would be useful.

Medieval Carlingford

What makes Carlingford unique is that this medieval town remained largely unchanged throughout the 1960s and 1970s, when the rest of Ireland was reinventing and repackaging itself for Nostalgia Inc. It still has the feel of an unmolested little corner of Ireland and there are marvellous medieval remains: the **Mint** in Tholsel Street, with its machicolated and carved limestone windows, **King John's Castle** by the lough, and the Tholsel, a surviving gate. In the **Holy Trinity Heritage Centre**, a mural, video and exhibitions tell the history. ■ *Churchyard Rd, T9373454. Mid-Mar to Sep, daily, 0930-1700.* The **tourist office**, T9337033, is in the middle of the village, open Mon-Sat, 0930-1730.

The Cattle Raid of Cooley

One of the most ancient tales in Europe's oral tradition, the Táin Bó Cuailnge (Cattle Raid of Cooley) received a written form in the eighth century. It tells of Medb, Queen of Connaught in the west, and her attempt to steal a great bull from the Ulstermen on the Cooley Peninsula to rival her husband's fine beast. Only the Homeric Cú Chulainn is free of a debilitating curse and able to mount resistance and the saga recounts in fantastic manner his superhuman exploits and the final duel between the two bulls. The best modern translation of this Celtic saga, complete with a map, is by Thomas Kinsella, The Táin (1969).

A *Beaufort House*, Ghan Rd, Carlingford, T9373879, www.beauforthouse.net By the water's edge, this guesthouse has rooms with views and runs a seaschool. **AL** *McKevitt's Village Hotel*, Market Sq, Carlingford, T9373116, www.mckevittshotel.com A welcoming place but busy in the summer. **B** *Murphy's*, 9 Dundalk St, Carlingford, T9373735. In the centre of the village. **C-D** *Carlingford Adventure Centre & Holiday Hostel*, Tholsel St, Carlingford, T9373100, cacentre@iol.ie An IHH place with over 30 dorm beds and 2 private rooms.

Sleeping
Carlingford can get very busy, but accommodation is also available at Omeath, which is up the main road

The Oystercatcher Bistro, T9373922, opposite *McKevitt's Hotel*, is keen on seafood. Oysters cooked half a dozen different ways or black pudding mousse for a startling change, with fish and meat dishes around €15. *Magee's Bistro*, Tholsel St, T9373751, has an affordable menu of pizzas and a more formal, middle-range restaurant area.

The long-standing *Jordans*, T9373223, had a reputation for culinary adventures but is changing hands so maybe worth checking out. Reservations are advisable at *Ghan House*, T9373682, which runs a cookery school and serves expensive country-house dinners. The *Kingfisher Bistro*, in the Heritage Centre, is open for affordable and middle-range dinners.

One place that should not be missed is *Georgina's*, a little walk up Castle Hill, T9373346, a modest little teashop dishing up superb open and regular sandwiches, perfect cakes such as cream gâteaux or cheesecake, and a takeaway service. *O'Hare's Pub* does oysters and Guinness.

There's also a **cookery school**, *Ghan House*, Carlingford, T/F9373862, www.ghanhouse.com, which includes accommodation if necessary.

Eating
Everywhere's a bistro in Carlingford and many of them only open for dinner and closed on Mon

The pubs are nothing to write home about but *P J O'Hare's*, aka *the Anchor Bar*, T9373106, has the old-style grocery/bar division and traditional music on Mon and Sat nights. For a quiet evening, head out to *Lily Finnegan's Pub* at Whitestown, a couple of miles outside Carlingford, on the Dundalk Rd. Go as far as *The Cooley Inn*, take a right, pass the church and go through the village. If you hit the beach, you've gone too far.

Tholsel Crafts, *Irish Secrets*, and *Memories* with a little café open daily from 1100 to 1800, are 3 little craft shops squeezed into Tholsel St. *Village Antiques* is next to McKevitt's Hotel. *Contemporary Crafts Gallery*, T9373005, houses the best in locally produced quality crafts.

Pubs & music

Adventure sports Land-and water-based activities, bookable through *East Coast Adventure*, T/F9373118. **Sailing** courses and yacht chartering through the *Carlingford Yacht Charter & Seaschool*, T9373878, and *Dundalk & Carlingford Sailing Club*, T9373238. *Deep Sea Angling*, Peader Elmore, T9373239.

Sport

Buses *Bus Éireann* runs a service, Mon to Sat, between Dundalk and Newry via Carlingford 5 times a day. On Sun, mid-Jun to Sep, a service runs once, one way, from Newry to Dundalk via Carlingford. **Taxi** *Gally Cabs*, T9373777.

Transport

County Monaghan

County Monaghan

Monaghan's characteristic drumlins, hills formed by the retreating Ice Age, stretch from Donegal to Strangford Lough and formed a natural barrier that helped define Ulster from prehistoric times onwards. The main town, bearing the same name as the county, is where most visitors pause and it makes an obvious base for sampling the surrounding countryside. The political border is best forgotten, for in terms of history, culture and geography the county should be explored and enjoyed along with its Ulster neighbours of Fermanagh and Armagh. Nine people were killed in Monaghan in 1974 when a car bomb exploded, planted by a loyalist group from Northern Ireland.

Ins and outs

Getting there & around

Five *Bus Éireann* buses run daily between Dublin and Monaghan via Slane. The routes to Letterkenny and Derry, 5 a day and 2 on Sun, also stop in Slane, Carrickmacross and Omagh. Three times a day, and twice on Sun, the Dublin – Dungannon – Coleraine – Portrush service stops in Slane and Monaghan.

The daily Belfast to Galway service connects Monaghan with these towns as well as Armagh, Athlone, Cavan, Clones, Enniskillen, Longford, Roscommon, and Sligo. The Sligo to Dundalk and Dundalk to Cavan routes both come through Monaghan. There is no bus link with Glaslough, but for Iniskeen a local service between Dundalk and Cavan, 4 times a day, Mon-Sat, stops here before going on to Carrickmacross.

Monaghan town

Phone code: 047
Colour map 1, grid C4

Monaghan is a town to walk around, admiring the Victorian civic edifices that range from an elaborate drinking fountain to a distinguished and very churchified bank building built on a curve in Church Square. Monaghan needs to be appreciated as a splinter of Ulster, divorced from its natural context. "Men not prone to emotion shed tears", relates a historian, when it was learnt that Monaghan, Cavan and Donegal would be severed from the six counties making up Northern Ireland.

The **Monaghan County Museum** has an excellent collection of finds and a visit here is worth the time. Look for the riveted Bronze Age cauldron, stone mounds for bronze spears, the Cross of Clogher, a Viking sword, 13th-century leather shoes with stitches intact, medieval combs, hairpins and a thumb-screw. ■ *Tue-Sat, 1100-1300 and 1400-1700. Free.*

The **tourist office** on Market St, T81122, www.monaghantourism.com, is open Jul and Aug, Mon-Sat, 0900-1800 and Sun 1000-1400; Mar-Jun and Sep-Dec, Mon-Fri, 0900-1300 and 1400-1700, Sat, 0900-1300.

Sleeping & eating

A *Fortsingleton*, Emyvale, T86054, is a period house about 5 miles outside of town but makes a nicer place to stay than the hotels in town. **B** *Ashleigh House*, 37 Dublin St, T81227. Centrally located, has 12 rooms and charges €25 per person. **B** *Hilldene House*, Canal St, T83297, charges €23 but the rooms share bathroom facilities.

After a short walk around the town centre you will find a few places to eat a cheap yet decent evening meal, around €20. Try *Andy's Bar and Restaurant*, T82277, opposite the tourist office in Market St, or *Paramount Restaurant*, Market St, T77333. *The Squealing Pig Bar* at the Diamond has a restaurant serving American-style food.

Hypocrites

*"Hypocrites, humbug", the priest went on,
"coming here Sunday after Sunday –
blindfolding the devil in the dark as the
saying goes. And the headquarters of all
this rascality is a townland called
Drumnay." The congregation smiled. Tarry
Flynn stooped his head and smiled too,*

*although he was a native of that terrible
townland. The calf-dealer at the door
cocked his ear more acutely; he too was
interested in his townland and pleased
when its evil deeds got the air.*

Patrick Kavanagh, Tarry Flynn *(1948).*

Around Monaghan town and county

Places of interest are scattered about the county like drumlins and your own transport is pretty essential. Glaslough is six miles (9 km) northeast of Monaghan town, Clones is 12 miles (19 km) to the southwest, while Carrickmacross and Iniskeen are tucked away in the east near Dundalk.

The pre-plantation ruling family in Monaghan were the MacMahons, and after the death of Ross MacMahon in 1589 the English partitioned the land amongst members of his family in a classic divide-and-rule ploy designed to extend England's control. Plantation properly got under way the following century and there is no better expression of Protestant hegemony, in what is now the Republic, than in the earnest, saturnine soberness of Glaslough's stone cottages.

Glaslough
*Colour map 1
grid B4*

Sleeping Whether staying or not, try to visit the baroque **LL** *Castle Leslie*, 3 miles out on the L46 road towards Ballyhaise, T88109, www.castle-leslie.ie Come here for a 2-night package, no television, no children, bedrooms worth photographing, and let the eccentricity of the place work its magic. Dean and satirist Jonathan Swift stayed here and wrote of the library with its "rows of books upon shelves, written by Leslies all about themselves". Excellent, candle-lit dinner at €43. Vegetarian menu also.

The railway station at Clones was the scene of a shoot-out between constables and republicans early in 1922, just after the Treaty was signed, and sparked sectarian attacks by loyalists in Belfast that saw 44 dead. Convivial Clones (pronounced *clo-nez*) today carries no trace of such discord and a rich Protestant legacy is to be seen in the centrally located **St Tiernach's Church**. What remains of St Tiernach's monastery can be seen in Abbey Street near a damaged round tower. More satisfaction may be gained by deciphering the fine **high cross**, which stands in the Diamond.

Clones
Colour map 1, grid C3

Some 3 miles (5 km) south of Clones on the Ballyhaise Road, **Hilton Park** has been replanted to reflect the original 18th-century formal garden. ■ *T56007. May-Sep, daily 1400-1800, €3.*

Sleeping and eating L *Hilton Park*, T56007, F56033. A country house with a reputation for hospitality and organic produce in the restaurant. **B** *Lennard Arms Hotel*, The Diamond, T51350. A modest hotel but proud to portray photographs of the town's most famous son, Barry McGuigan, world featherweight boxing champion. **B** *Creighton Arms*, Fermanagh St, T51055. A couple of pounds more. While both hotels serve food, it is worth first checking out *Cúil Darrach* at The Diamond or *The Round Tower Bar* on Cara St.

Transport Bicycles can be hired from *Ulster Canal Stores*, T52125, on Cara St.

County Monaghan

Carrickmacross
*Colour map 1,
grid C4*

A one-street town famous for its hand-made lace industry, established in the early 19th century, is still surviving and with items for sale in the town centre. The Catholic church has two Harry Clarke windows and for country walks the **Dún a Rí Forest Park** is a couple of miles away on the R179 Kingscourt Road.

Sleeping and eating **LL** *Nuremore Hotel & Country Club*, Carrickmacross, T9661438, www.nuremore-hotel.ie Outstanding hotel in terms of facilities, comfort and service. The restaurant is exceptionally good; expect to find beef, lamb, maybe duck, even plain old chicken is enlivened by foie gras tortellini, and vegetables cooked to perfection. With a set dinner for €38 and a vegetarian one for €25

Iniskeen
Colour map 1, grid C4

To the east, the village of Iniskeen celebrates being the birthplace of Patrick Kavanagh (1904-67), Ireland's best poet after Yeats and Heaney, and author of the great *Tarry Flynn*, but hardly known outside the country. The **Patrick Kavanagh Centre**, which has a set of paintings illustrating the poet's greatest epic, *The Great Hunger*, dispenses an inexpensive Kavanagh Trail Guide which usefully locates sites associated with the poet. ■ *T/F9378560, www.patrickkavanaghcountry.com Open all year, Mon-Fri, 1100-1700; mid-Mar-Nov also Sun, 1400-1800; Jun-Sep also Sat, 1400-1800. €2. Patrick Kavanagh Weekend, annually, last weekend in Nov.*

County Cavan

A sister county to Monaghan, historically and geographically, Cavan is more likely to be visited as it is on the main route between Dublin and Donegal. Until the plantations of the early 17th century the land belonged mostly to the O'Reilly clan and they took their revenge in the 1641 rebellion by releasing their prisoners "turned naked, without respect of age or sex, upon the wild, barren mountains, in the cold age, exposed to all the severity of the winter". Since partition, when Cavan was cut adrift from Ulster, like Donegal and Monaghan, life has proceeded fairly uneventfully and this is part of the county's appeal. Everything is low key, there are no major places of interest, and time spent here is best devoted to the wilder west Cavan around Ballyconnell.

Ins and outs

**Getting there
& around**

The Dublin to Donegal service, at least 4 times a day and 3 on Sun, stops at Cavan, and Ballyconnell on request. Ballyconnell can also be reached on a local bus, Mon- Sat, that travels between Cavan and Bawnboy. From Cavan itself buses connect with Armagh, Athlone, Belfast, Clones, Dundalk, Enniskillen, Galway, Kells, Killybegs, Longford, Monaghan, Portadown and Roscommon.

Cavan town and around

*Phone code: 049
Colour map 1, grid C3*

Cavan developed from a Franciscan friary of 1300 and, although nothing of this now remains, the **tourist office** has some information on a few places of minor interest, namely the **Lifeforce Mill**, T4362722, by the Kennypottle River. A tour begins with the making of soda bread and ends with collecting it hot from the oven. The **Cavan Crystal Factory** just outside town is also worth a visit. ■ *Tourist office: Farnham St, T4331942, www.cavantourism.com Mon-Fri, 0900-1700; Sat, 0900-1300. Crystal Factory: Dublin Rd, T4331800.*

For an excursion, try the **Killykeen Forest Park**, or the miscellany of folk artefacts at the **Pighouse Folk Museum**, T4337248. At Cornafean, bikes can be hired from *On Yer Bike*, Abbeyset Buildings, Farnham Street, T4331932.

Sleeping & eating

Price codes:
see inside front cover

B *Lisnamadra*, Killeshandra Rd, Crossdoney, T4337196, F4337111. Offers pleasant accommodation on a dairy farm 4 miles (7 km) southwest of Cavan, so why stay in town? For quick meals the pubs in town offer much of the sameness, while for something more memorable the *Annalee Restaurant*, Hotel Kilmore, Dublin Rd, T4332288, has a reputation for dishing up local fish and game. Open for lunch and dinner, closed Mon. *Lifeforce Mill* has a coffee shop, serves snacks and wholesome meals. Open between May and Sep, Tue-Sat 0900-1700, and dinner between Thu and Sun.

Virginia

Right on the main route from Dublin to Donegal this village is a regular retreat for Dubliners wanting a quiet weekend. This is drumlin country, low quiet hills with lots of lakes for fishing. It is also a great location to spend some time exploring the passage tombs of Lough crew. The village has some good pubs and a theatre, T049 8547074 with regular travelling theatre companies. The best place to stay and to eat is **L** *The Park Hotel*, T049-8546100, www.bichotels.com which is set in vast parklands where you can walk for hours without ever leaving the hotel grounds. Great restaurant with a good reputation. Alternatively there is **AL** *Sharkeys*, on the main street, T049 8547561, www.destination-Ireland.com/sharkeys busy with carvery lunches and popular bar.

West Cavan

If you're just speeding through between Dublin and Donegal you will miss the most interesting part of the county, though it is only a short detour off the N3 at Belturbet to access **Ballyconnell** on the R200. The **Cavan Way**, a 17-mile (26-km) waymarked walking trail, connects Blacklion with Dowra and could be completed in a day. Accommodation and food is better in Blacklion, so start from Dowra with the help of Ordnance Survey map No 26 and the *Cavan Way Mapguide* available from the tourist office in Cavan. From Blacklion the Way is mostly by road but it ends up as hill walking.

Phone code: 049

Sleeping & eating

Price codes:
see inside front cover

L *Slieve Russell Hotel*, Ballyconnel, T9526444, www.quinnhotels.com All the facilities expected from 4-star accommodation, plus a 18-hole golf course; worth popping in for the food. **A-B** *Macnean House and Bistro*, Main St, Blacklion, T072-530220. B&B on the Cavan Way and serving dinner. **B** *Hi Way Inn*, Dowra, T078- 43025. Another B&B handy for those walking the Cavan Way. **B** *Mount View House*, Ballyconnell, T9526456. A B&B departing from the vernacular on a grandiloquent scale **D** *Sandville House Hostel*, T9526297, sandville@eircom.net 2 miles west of Ballyconnell (telephone for a pick-up), this makes a comfortable base for walking or cycling through the local countryside. Bikes are available, there is no extra charge for double rooms, €9.50 per person, and camping is also possible.

County Cavan

Counties of Longford and Westmeath

*When visitors dismiss the midlands of Ireland as boring, it is the counties of Long-ford and Westmeath they usually have in mind. But speak to the anglers who fly in from Britain and head straight for **Lanesborough** and they wouldn't have it any other way, left alone to pursue their sport with not a tour coach or backpacker in sight. The waterways of Longford – the **River Shannon**, **Lough Ree**, the **Royal Canal** (see page 635) – have boating and other water-based activities that attract families on holidays, but there is precious little else to detain the traveller.*

*Westmeath is a county of some consequence, benefiting from some of the richest farming land in the country and within commutable distance of Dublin. The main N4 road from the capital to Sligo passes through Mullingar, and while this busy commercial town sums up what is unappealing about Westmeath ,other areas of the county are worth exploring: the **Fore Valley** in the northeast and **Athlone**, on the N6 road between Galway and Dublin.*

Mullingar

Phone code: 044
Colour map 2,
grid B6

The county town of Westmeath is not the kind of place to fall in love with but convenient nevertheless for breaking a journey, and with a couple of places of interest around town that might detain you longer than anticipated. Mullingar's one long street changes its name from Austin Friar Street at the Dublin end to Pearse Street and Oliver Plunkett Street in the centre, and finally to Dominick Street and Patrick Street heading out west to Athlone. The Royal Canal does a perimeter loop around town, and Mount Street heads south to Belvedere House and Kilbeggan from the junction of Pearse and Oliver Plunkett Streets. It's hard to get lost.

Ins & outs

Getting there *Bus Éireann's* Dublin to Ballina service goes via Mullingar at least 3 times a day, as does the Dublin to Sligo service. Twice a day, and once on Sun, the Galway to Newry bus stops in Mullingar and connects the town with Athlone, Navan and Dundalk. Trains from Dublin to Sligo stop in Mullingar, T48274, at least 4 times a day, 3 on Sun.

The **tourist office** is centrally located on Pearse St at Market House, T48650. Open daily 0930-1300 and 1400-1700.

Museums

Of the three museums in town, the least interesting is the **Ecclesiastical Museum**, in the aesthetically offensive Cathedral of Christ the King at the top of Mary Street. ■ *T48338. Key from the house on the right inside the gates.*

The **Market House Museum**, in the centre of town near the tourist office, is a worthy example of that endangered species, the unreconstructed heritage centre. Full of artefacts donated by local people, from ancient quernstones to rubber bullets, a visit here would comfortably while away a wet afternoon. Best of all, it may set you off on the trail of Adolphus Cooke (see page 163). ■ *Pearse St, T48152. Jul to Sep, Mon-Sat 1400-1730. €0.65.*

The **Military Museum**, was built as a barracks for the British and is now home to the Irish army. It has a weird and wonderful collection of uncatalogued items ranging from a weighing chair for recruits to weapons and uniforms. Telephone before your visit. ■ *Columb Barracks, T48391.*

L *Greville Arms Hotel*, Pearse St, Mullingar, T48563, www.grevillearms.com A busy and popular town centre hotel redeemed by its garden, conservatory and general air of hospitality. **B** *McCormacks*, Old Dublin Rd, Mullingar, T41483. A working farm well geared up to visitors and with various packages. **B** *Woodside*, Dublin Rd, Mullingar, T41636. B&B within walking distance of town, and there are plenty more B&Bs along the main roads going into and out of Mullingar. **Camping** *Lough Derravaragh Caravan & Camping Park*, Multyfarnham, T71500. The *Lough Ennell Caravan & Camping Park*, Tuddenham Carrick, T/F48101, Apr to Sep. Four miles (6 km) south of Mullingar, on the road to Kilbeggan, by the shore of Lough Ennell and popular with Irish holiday-makers.

Sleeping
If staying overnight, a short drive on the N4 to the less frantic village of Multyfarnham is where there are pubs with traditional music, good food and accommodation

Canton Casey & Fat Cats Brasserie in Market Square, more old-fashioned than the name suggests, is worth considering during the day, and for light meals try the *Gallery 29 Café* at 29 Oliver Plunkett St. Good food too at the *Greville Arms* and *Austins* at the *Austin Friar Hotel*, Austin Friars St, T45777. For something on a grander scale head for the late 18th-century rectory of *Crookedwood House*, Crookedwood, T72165 (with accommodation in the **L** category) a few miles north on the R394 road. Set dinners vary in price, with an early-bird menu around €22, plus à la carte, lunch also on Sun.

Eating
There is no problem finding places to eat in Mullingar, with a host of busy cafés, restaurants and pubs all easy to find in the town centre

Banks All located along the name-changing main street. **Communications Post office**: on the Dominick St stretch at the west end of town.

Directory

Around Mullingar

A visit to the Market House Museum will have introduced the eccentric Adolphus Cooke who served under Wellington before losing his mind to the notion that the family turkey was his grandfather reincarnated. When he later sentenced his dog to death for immoral behaviour, the executioner was attacked by his dog; this convinced him of another family connection and the dog was duly pardoned. To find his highly individual tomb, the shape of which makes sense when you know he was destined to be reincarnated as a bee, take the N52 to Delvin for 8 miles (12 km) and park outside the *Bee Hive Nite Club*. Inside the arched entrance, cross the field to the old churchyard and the beehive grave is easily found.

Adolphus Cooke

Belvedere House and Gardens, south of town on the N52 road to Tullamore, are noted for the Jealous Wall, an elaborate folly built by Lord Belvedere to block the sight of a neighbouring house belonging to his younger brother. If you think this was taking sibling rivalry too far, then pity the plight of his poor wife who was incarcerated in the house for 31 years because Lord Belfield suspected another brother of having an affair with her. She died protesting her innocence and the brother was jailed in London for the rest of his life. ■ *T49060, www.belvedere-house.ie Open daily 1030-1900 (earlier closing from Sep-Mar). €5.*

Belvedere House & gardens

Further south at Kilbeggan, Locke's Distillery has produced whiskey for 200 years and now dispenses a wee drop to visitors as well. ■ *T0506-32134. Open daily 0900-1800 (1000-1600 in winter). €4. Food all day, including a take-away service, and drink at the nearby* Black Kettle *pub.*

Locke's Distillery

Some 12 miles (20 km) north of Mullingar the R394 leads to Castlepollard, and then the road to Granard and Tullynally Castle and Gardens. Owned by the Pakenhams, later the Earls of Longford, since the 17th century, the exterior of this vast Gothic Revival 'castle' is not pleasing to the eye, but the guided tour

Tullynally Castle & gardens

reveals a wealth of features and includes an educational glimpse of working life for the army of servants who slaved away in the kitchen and laundry. ■ *T61159. Castle: mid-Jun to Jul, 1400-1800. Gardens: May to Sep, 1400-1800. Combined ticket, €6.35; Gardens only, €3.80. Coffee shop*

Fore To the east of Tullynally, reached via the R195 from Castlepollard, the village of Fore is the natural starting point for walks into the **Fore Valley**. The village has pubs, but a day out with a picnic from Mullingar is quite feasible. The valley is home to the **Seven Wonders**, a group of early Christian sites associated with St Fechin and illustrated in murals in the *Abbey* village pub. St Fechin's Church, with a Greek cross on the lintel, is easy to find and from here a path leads to the Anchorite's Cell (key available from *Seven Wonders* pub in the village).

Athlone

Phone code: 0902
Colour map 2, grid B5

The strong castle of Athlone, commanding a strategically important crossing point of the Shannon, sums up the town's troubled history as a place to be fought over down the centuries. The **tourist office** is next to **Athlone Castle and Museum**, with exhibits on the Shannon's flora and fauna and the life of the great tenor John McCormack, as well as the castle's history. The top floor of the museum is well worth a visit, a little gem of a folk collection which includes a working gramophone that John McCormack travelled with. Ask for a record to be played while sauntering around the miscellany of other exhibits. ■ *Market Sq, T92912. May-Sep, Mon-Sat, 1000-1600. €4.44. Tea rooms*

Sights The road north of Athlone, the N55, heads up the east side of Lough Ree to what numerous brown signs will tell you is **Goldsmith Country**. The poet, playwright and novelist. Oliver Goldsmith (1728-74) was born just north of Glasson in County Longford. The country is pleasantly flat for cyclists and mildly distracting and the village of Glasson is picturesque enough, but there is not a great deal to see or do other than pass through admiring the countryside.

Sleeping **L-AL** *Hudson Bay*, T80500, www.hodsonbayhotel.com On the shore of Lough Ree, 4
Price codes: miles from town. Great for water-based activities on the lough and good restaurant.
see inside front cover **A** *Dun Mhuire House*, Bonavalley, Dublin Rd, T75360. Typical of the countless B&Bs spread out along the approach roads (but at least it's not a bungalow).

Eating *Restaurant Le Château*, St Peter's Port, the Docks, T94517, is an old church on the banks of the river down from the castle. A romantic atmosphere at night, open daily at 1730 for an early-bird menu until 1900 at €20, a set dinner for €33 until 2000 plus à la carte. Another place with good food is the middle range *The Olive Grove*, Bridge St.
   Sean's Bar, T92358, on Main St close to the tourist office, claiming with some justification to be the oldest in the land, similar to many others but at least it does have some character, and a beer garden overlooking the Shannon.

Transport The **bus and train stations** (T73300) are on the other side of the river to the castle. Athlone is a major transport link and there are buses to just about every main town in Ireland. Trains connect the town with Westport, Galway and Dublin.
   Lough Ree cruises, lasting 90 mins with a commentary, are conducted daily through *Athlone Cruisers*, T72892, for €6.35. Self-drive cruises can also be arranged through the sae company on a weekly or weekend basis. Departures from the *Jolly Mariner* marina eside the Athlone bypass. *Rosana Cruises*, T73383, conduct river trips in a 'Viking Longboat' from the town centre.

Counties Wicklow & Wexford

5

Counties Wicklow & Wexford

*County Wicklow's sobriquet, 'The Garden of Ireland', gives some hint of the beauty that singles out this part of the country. The northern border of Wicklow is only 12 miles (19 km) from Dublin's city centre, which is astonishing to reflect on when walking alone in the heather-coloured **Wicklow Mountains**. As well as the grandeur of the mountains the county boasts stately homes, archaeological and historical sites, superb beaches and some of the best food in the Republic. The county divides neatly into three areas: the north including the picturesque village of **Enniskerry** and the seaside town of **Bray**; Glendalough and West Wicklow including **Blessington**; and south of Glendalough with the county town of **Wicklow**, nearby **Arklow** and the **Vale of Avoca**, better known to couch potatoes as Ballykissangel.*

*Dubbed the 'sunny southeast' because of slightly higher average temperatures and lower rainfall than the rest of Ireland, County Wexford, and especially the towns of **Wexford** and **Enniscorthy**, has strong historical connections with the 1798 rebellion. The south Wexford coast is most attractively represented by the fishing village of **Kilmore Quay** and the **Hook peninsula**, while the east coast has long stretches of sandy beach.*

County Wicklow

Ins and outs

Getting there & around

Bus The county of Wicklow is just a short bus ride away from Ireland's capital city. Daily Dublin buses serve Bray, Enniskerry and Blessington, details are shown in the Transport sections for these towns. Provincial buses serve Arklow, Avoca, Laragh, Jack White's Cross (for Brittas Bay), Rathdrum, Wicklow and Woodenbridge. *Bus Eireann* also have full and half-day tours from Dublin to Glendalough, Glenroe, Powerscourt and Avoca. For timetables and details, contact *Bus Eireann's Travel Centre* at T01-8366111, www.cie.ie There is a useful *Saint Kevin's* daily bus service to Glendalough; see details under Glendalough.

Rail The main Dublin-Wexford line runs through Bray, Wicklow town, Rathdrum and Arklow. *Railtours* offer a tour that departs from Dublin's Connolly station by train to Wicklow town, then a bus to Avoca, T01-8560045, www.railtours.ie

    DART The DART line from Dublin goes as far south as Bray and Greystones. Trains run between Bray and Dublin about every 15 mins during weekdays and up to every 30 mins at weekends.

Tours Private companies running tours into Wicklow from Dublin include *Wild Wicklow Tours*, T01-2801899, www.arantours.ie/wildwicklow *Grey Line Tours* have full and half-day tours to Glendalough, Enniskerry, Powerscourt and Avoca, T01-6057705. *Mary Gibbons Tours* have full and half-day tours to Avoca, Glendalough and Powerscourt Gardens, T01-4604464. Another company, *Over the Top and into the West Tours*, specialize in more wacky trips to Wicklow, T01-8386128, www.irishbustours.com

North Wicklow and the Wicklow Mountains

Phone code: 01
Colour map 4,
grid B2/3

Discerning Dubliners know well how blessed they are by having the granite hills and purple glens of the Wicklow Mountains almost in their backyard. The R115 road, better known as the **Military Road**, makes its way through Glencree and the Sally Gap before meandering south to Glendalough and it can be joined at Glencree from Enniskerry and Bray. The Military Road was made by the British in the years after the 1798 rebellion, in a determined effort to wipe out the remaining insurgents who were using the inaccessible mountains as their base.

    A **suggested tour** of the area starts with the seaside town of Bray before taking the road west to the postcard-pretty village of Enniskerry and – the reason for the village's existence – the Powerscourt Estate. From Enniskerry the road continues west to Glencree, where the Military Road can be picked up. Rather than stay on this road all the way south to Laragh, it is worth heading off to **Roundwood** at the Sally Gap and then going on to Laragh and Glendalough from there. The scenery between the Sally Gap and Roundwood is quite spectacular and the village of Roundwood itself makes a pleasant place to stop for a meal and a rest.

Things to do in Counties Wicklow and Wexford

- Visit the **1798 Centre** in Enniscorthy
- Go bird watching on the **Hook peninsula**
- Walk the **Wexford Coastal Path**
- Check out the fringe events at the **Wexford Opera Festival**
- Hike up **Maulin** in County Wicklow

The Wicklow Way

There are many well laid-out and exciting walks in the Wicklow Mountains, all eagerly walked by local people and visitors. The best way to see the mountains is by walking the five days of the Wicklow Way, Ireland's first and oldest waymarked walking route (81 miles/131 km). It is well signposted and you are unlikely to travel as much as a day without meeting anyone.

EastWest Mapping produces a strip map and booklet about accommodation along the Way, which you could just about get by with, but ideally you should bring with you the Ordnance Survey Discovery Series maps Nos 50, 56 and 62. You must have good walking boots, wet weather gear, food for each day you intend to walk, and, as a minimum for safety equipment, a whistle, compass and first aid kit.

Mapping & information

County Wicklow

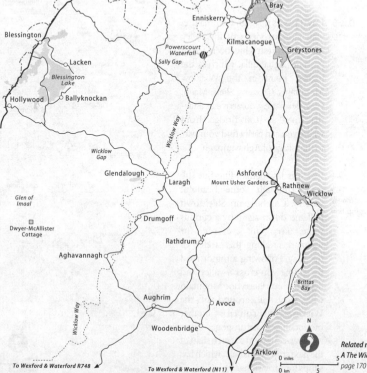

Related map
A The Wicklow Way,
page 170

County Wicklow

Day 1
Wicklow to Knockree
(13 miles/21 km)

Day 1 begins in Marlay Park to the south of the city. It quickly leaves suburbia behind as you head up Kilmashogue Lane to Kilmashogue Wood. As you make your way upwards, views open up of the coast and the city that have been left behind. Crossing **Two Rock Mountain**, high up at about 1,476 ft (450 m) you come to the R116 and Glencullen. Out of the village and on to open moorland again you come eventually to Knockree. There you can break for the evening and perhaps make a trip into Enniskerry for dinner and provisions. ■ *Marlay Park open 1000. Bus No 47B from city centre.*

Day 2
Knockree to
Glendalough
(18 miles/29 km)

Day 2 is a lovely walk along a river and then past the waterfall at Powerscourt; you are truly among the Wicklow Mountains, with the Sugarloaf behind you and Maulin stretching beautifully up to the north. Go down to the Dargle River and then along the shoulder of Djouce Mountain to Lough Tay. The day could end at Roundwood, which is a little way off the track. There are a few B&Bs there (see 'Sleeping'). Alternatively, you can walk on to Glendalough, which is an excellent place to rest for a day or so and explore the walks in the area.

Day 3
Glendalough to
Aghavannagh
(18 miles/29 km)

Day 3 passes through Glenmalure, with glorious views of the valley since the forestry has been felled, passing Lugnaquilla, which is the highest point in the Wicklow Mountains. Crossing Slieve Maan, Carrickashane, you arrive at a tarmac road at Iron Bridge, from where you can easily find your way to the village of Aghavannagh.

Day 4
Aghavannagh
to Tinahely
(14 miles/22 km)

Day 4 is less demanding but still passes through some beautiful scenery. Climbing up Shielstown Hill and down again by a curious route, keep an eye out for waymarkers along this stretch of the Way. Following a minor road for a time you cross a valley and begin to climb Garryhoe Mountain with views all around of the Wicklow Hills. You cross another mountain, Coolafunsgoge, along its lower slopes and to catch sight of the next stop – Tinahely, which has shops for provisions.

The Wicklow Way

Walking in Wicklow

If you can only afford one day on the Wicklow Way, the best in our opinion is Day 2 from Knockree to Glendalough past the Powerscourt Waterfall. Do not walk if it is misty. An alternative to walking the Wicklow Way comes by way of a useful Wicklow Walking Guide *booklet available in tourist offices. It contains details and useful maps for a number of short walks in the county.*

For an organized walk consider **Footfalls Walking Holidays**. *They conduct group walking tours of from 6-10 miles (10-15 km) each day, with luggage, food, accommodation and transport organized as part of the package. Self-guided tours are also available for independent walkers. For details contact: Trooperstown, Roundwood, T/F0404-45152, cstacey@iol.ie Also worth considering, if you want a tad more comfort, is a walking package through Ballyknocken House (see page 181). They offer 3- and 7-day packages which include transport and packed lunches.*

Day 5 involves quite a lot of road walking but it will be deserted most of the way. The highlight of the walk is Urelands Hill, where there are wonderful views of Mount Leinster.

Day 5
Tinahely to Clonegal (18 miles/29 km)

B *Ballincar House*, Mary Malone, Roundwood, T2818168. B&B with rooms from around €20 per person sharing. **B** *Park Lodge Farm*, Clonegal, T055-29149. B&B, evening meal by arrangement. **B** *Woodside*, Mrs Nancy O'Brien, Roundwood, T2818185. Rooms from around €20 per person sharing in this B&B. **D** *Glendalough Hostel*, Glendalough, T01-8301766 (Dublin hostel). *An Óige* hostel: advance booking advisable. **D** *Knockree Hostel*, Lacken House, Knockree, T2864036. Advance booking essential at this *An Óige* hostel.

Sleeping

Enniskerry

The pretty, busy little village owes its existence to the Powerscourt Family who had the nearby estate and the village was laid out during the 18th century, when they were lords of all they surveyed. Besides a few cafés and pubs and one of the first Gothic Revival Catholic Churches in Ireland (1843, Patrick Byrne), its chief claim to fame is as a stepping-off point for walks in the area, and of course the nearby Powerscourt Gardens.

*Phone code: 01
Colour map 4, grid B3*

The Powerscourt estate lies just 12 miles (19 km) south of Dublin, in the foothills of the Wicklow Mountains. It is a huge estate – the approach road to the house is a mile (nearly 2 km) long and it has the magnificent backdrop of the two Sugarloaf mountains. It also has the imposing presence of Powerscourt House, designed, like Russborough House on the other side of the mountains, by Richard Castle in the first half of the 18th century.

Powerscourt gardens & waterfall

The house is open to the public but don't expect a restored period house because only the ballroom and a garden room are on show, with other parts of the building housing the visitor centre and its amenities. The house burnt down in 1974 and photographs of its former glory can be seen as part of the exhibition at Powerscourt.

The **formal gardens** are the major highlight of any visit, if only to admire how the natural landscape helps moderate the ostentatiousness of the landscaping. The gardens were laid out in the 18th century but substantially modified in the 19th century; there is a free leaflet available with routes for a

County Wicklow

A Paddywood Tour

A tour of Paddywood begins just west of Bray, in the village of Enniskerry. Here, at the Powerscourt waterfall, scenes from John Boorman's Excalibur *were shot. One of Boorman's more recent films,* The General, *the tale of a noted Dublin gangster, has an amusing scene on a mountain road, the Sally Gap, when the gardai run out of petrol. The General drove back to Dublin, but stay on the road south to Laragh before turning left for the road through Wicklow Gap to Hollywood. The pulse of Ireland's film world is felt amongst the small towns and countryside of county Wicklow, including a village named Hollywood which was converted for Neil Jordan's memorable film* Michael Collins. *Remember the scene where Collins dashes with glee into his local West Cork pub? Dancing at* Lughnasa *also used the village and its two pubs, and Hollywood was also used in* Rebel Heart. *Before reaching Hollywood, a small road runs off to the right, the R758, along the eastern shore of Blessington Lake to Lacken. Scenes from* Dancing at Lughnasa, Braveheart *and* Widow's Peak *were filmed here.*

There are plenty more links with films in Wicklow. Angela's Ashes, Far And Away *and* The Commitments *all used locations in the county and maps and brochures are available from the Wicklow Film Commission, T404-20176, www.wicklow.ie and from the tourist office in Wickow town.*

one-hour walk and a 40-minute stroll around the various points of interest. Accounts of the Italian garden often tell the story of how it was designed by Daniel Robertson while he was being wheeled around in a barrow with a bottle of sherry to stimulate the flow of his imagination; it then took 12 years for over 100 labourers to transform his visions into reality. The Japanese gardens attract a lot of attention but numerous manifestations of European high art have also been imported into the landscape: the entrance gate comes from a Bavarian cathedral, classical statutory and urns copied from Versailles are dotted around and there is a fountain imitating that in the Piazza Babberini in Rome.

There is a signposted four-miles 6-km) walk through the estate to the lovely Powerscourt Waterfall. The walk is recommended for the opportunity to admire the landscape and wonder at the sheer size of this estate and the Anglo-Irish ebullience that led to its creation. ■ *Powerscourt Estate, Enniskerry. T2046000, www.powerscourt.ie Gardens and house open all year, daily 0930-1730 but check winter opening times as they are subject to alteration. Waterfall: summer, daily 0930-1900; winter, daily 1030-dusk. €7.62 for garden and house; €5 garden only; €3.20 waterfall. Restaurant, shops, picnic area.*

Sleeping **AL** *Powerscourt Arms Hotel*, Enniskerry, T2828903. Conveniently located in the centre
Price codes: of the village, with 12 bedrooms. **AL** *Coillte*, 4 Enniskerry Demesne, Enniskerry,
see inside front cover T2766614, smyt@eircom.net About 5-min walk from the village, en-suite rooms, but pricey. **B** *Corner House*, Enniskerry, T2860149. Also in the village , 3 bedrooms sharing bathroom facilities. **D** *Glencree Hostel*, Stone House, Glencree, T2864037. An Óige hostel as popular as that at Knockree, 4 miles (7 km) away, and requires advance booking in summer. **D** *Knockree Hostel*, Lacken House, Knockree, T2864036. *An Óige* hostel, 4 miles (7 km) southwest of Enniskerry and on the Wicklow Way, and reached by taking Bus No 185 from Bray to Shop River.

Camping *Roundwood Caravan & Camping Park*, Roundwood, T2818163. Opens 10th Apr until late Sep.

There are a number of little cafés and restaurants serving food in Enniskerry. Try *Poppies*, on the village square, offering snacks and light meals around €7. The *Glenwood Inn* serves pub food at lunchtime. The Powerscourt hotel has a restaurant and pub food. *Powerscourt Terrace Café*, T2046070, at Powerscourt House, is run by the same family that cooks the food at Avoca Handweavers and it is equally satisfying. Open daily until 1700, outdoor seats on the terrace.

Bus From **Dublin**: Bus No 44, T8734222, from Hawkins St. **Rail** DART electric trains, T8366222, run from **Howth** to **Bray** via Dublin city centre every 15 mins on weekdays and up to every 30 mins at weekends. Bray bus No 85 goes to Enniskerry and *Alpine Coaches*, T2862547, runs a summer service from Bray DART station to Powerscourt and Glencree. **Road** Enniskerry is just over 1 mile (1.6 km) away from the main N11 road that connects Dublin with Waterford.

Bray

Once a genteel Victorian resort town and now a rather run-down dormitory town that stirs to life in the summer when hordes of Dubliners and their families come and fill up the boarding houses, play on the stony beach and in the amusement arcades, and pack the pubs at night. On the plus side, there is plenty of accommodation, an excellent little town brochure that the tourist office dispenses and a delightful cliff walk, and with DART transport to Dublin the town could be considered as a place to stay for a day or two as a base for exploring parts of County Wicklow.

Phone code: 01
Colour map 4,
grid A3 & B2

"They halted,
looking towards
the blunt cape of
Bray Head that
lay on the water
like the snout of a
sleeping whale."
Ulysses, James Joyce

James Joyce came to live at 1 Martello Terrace, with his family, when he was six and remained there until 1891. The dining room of this house was the setting for the acrimonious Christmas dinner scene in *A Portrait of the Artist as a Young Man*. Martello Terrace is at the north end of the esplanade, easily reached by walking to the end of Strand Road or down Seapoint Road from the tourist office (see below). The pub on the corner, the *Harbour Bar*, marks the site where two United Irishmen were executed in 1798 for their part in the uprising.

The **tourist office** is in Old Court House on Main St, T2866796. It's open Jun-Sep, Mon-Fri, 0900-1700, Sat, 1000-1600; Oct-Apr, Mon-Fri, 0900-1630, Sat, 1000-1600. Closed 1300-1400 throughout the year.

For an **architectural tour** of the town and its fine examples of Georgian and Victoian dwellings, get the tourist office's booklet and set off to explore some of the streets and buildings it describes. An excellent 5-mile (8-km) **cliff walk** threads its way from the south end of the promenade to Greystones and you could return on the No 84 bus. It is easy to find a well worn path at the south end of the esplanade, near the beginning of the cliff walk, that brings you up to Bray Hill with its cracking views, as far as Wales on a fair day. This is an easier walk, taking from 30 minutes to an hour.

A big attraction in Bray is the **National Sea-Life Centre**, a hi-tech aquarium, on the seafront. ■ *T2866939, www.sealife.ie Open Easter-Sep daily 1000-1700, weekends only the rest of the year.* The tourist office also houses a **heritage centre** focusing on local history and personalities. Just south of town, near the roundabout on the Greystones road, **Kilruddery House and Gardens** has the largest surviving French-style garden in the country, dating back to the 1680s, with twin canals and a lovely avenue of lime trees. ■ *T2862777. Gardens, Apr-Sep daily 1300-1700. House, May, Jun and Sep daily 1300-1700. €5.70 for house and garden, €3.80 garden only.*

County Wicklow

Kilmacanogue The **Avoca Handweavers** have one of their large craft stores open daily in Kilmacanogue, just a couple of miles south of Bray, and there is also a terrace restaurant that serves excellent food. The store has its own **gardens**, created by a member of the Jameson whiskey family in the 1870s, which contain the only mature specimen of the rare Weeping Monterey Cypress in the world. ■ *Open daily. Bus No 145 runs between Bray's DART station and Kilmacanogue.*

National Garden Exhibition Centre Garden-lovers may wish to make another 4-mile (7 km) journey south to the National Garden Exhibition Centre, Kilquade. Stay on the N11 as far as Kilpedder and take the signposted left turning for Kilquade. There are 16 different gardens on three acres (1.2 ha), with names like the Seaside Garden, the Herb Knot, the Geometric Garden, Acid Garden, and Pythagoras at Play. A timbered pavilion houses a horticultural shop and a tea house serving lunch and snacks. ■ *T2819890. Mon-Sat 1000-1800, Sun 1300-1800. €3. Bray Bus Tours, T2828602, run a return trip on Tue at 1430 and Thu at 1000 for €6.30.*

Sleeping **L** *Esplanade*, Esplanade, T2862056, www.regencyhotels.com Victorian-era hotel on the seafront with reasonable restaurant and leisure facilities. **AL** *Westbourne Hotel*, Quinsboro Rd, T2862362. Minutes from the beach, a bar with live music from Wed to Sun, and a nightclub. **A** *Rosslyn House*, Killarney Rd, T2860993. Open from Mar-Oct, en-suite rooms, situated next to Bray town hall and close to everything.

Eating & drinking **Mid-range** Bray has no shortage of places providing quick meals but for something more interesting try the *Tree of Idleness*, on Strand Rd, T2863498. This Greek-Cypriot restaurant is famous for its roast, stuffed suckling pig, with plenty of mezze to nibble on and a dessert trolley laden with Middle Eastern temptations. Main dishes like roast monkfish or saddle of lamb are around €20, while moussaka is €14. *Cupels Bistro*, Upper Dargyle Rd, T2765803, is a smart diner reached by walking past the tourist office on Main Rd towards Dublin; it is visible on the left after 5 mins; a daily carvery and evening meals. The self-service restaurant at *Avoca Handweavers* produces above-average food that is well worth considering. Interesting soups and meals with a taste.

South of Bray, in Greystones, *The Hungry Monk*, T2875759, is in the centre of the village and specializes in fish in the summer and game in winter. For the good food and candlelit atmosphere expect to pay around €32. Open Tue-Sat, 1900-2100, and Sun, 1230-2000. Bus No 84 from Bray.

Cheap Bray has no shortage of places providing quick meals and such places can be found along Main St and Strand Rd. Typical of joints on the seafront is *The Porterhouse* between the DART station and the Esplanade hotel. Lunch is around €7 and nachos and baguettes with steak or chicken are popular at night.

Pubs *Clancy's Bar*, on Quinsborough Rd, the road linking Main St with the esplanade, offers refuge from families with noisy children. Dark wood, comfortable alcoves, and Sun night sessions of traditional folk music. *Katie Gallaghers*, by the DART station, has set dancing on Mon nights. A list of pubs and their musical nights is on the wall in the tourist office.

Transport **Bicycle** *Bray Sports*, 8 Main St, T2863046. Bike hire is a hefty €12.70 a day. **Bus** Bus No 45 from Eden Quay runs between **Dublin** and Bray regularly throughout the day from 0630 to 2300, travelling past Merrion Sq and Ballsbridge but not Dun Laoghaire. The 45A travels between Bray and Dun Laoghaire, also daily. The No 84 bus also runs between **Eden Quay** and Bray, Mon-Fri. *St Kevin's Bus Service*, T2818119, runs between Dublin and **Glendalough**, via the town hall in Bray. It is also possible to get off *Bus Éireann's* **Rosslare Harbour** to Dublin service at Bray, T8366111. **Train** DART trains run between Bray, T2363333, and **Dublin** about every 15 mins during weekdays and up to every 30 mins at weekends.

Directory

West Wicklow

*This area of Wicklow takes in the extremely scenic Glendalough and the equally
pretty area to the west including Blessington, where there is some excellent walking, the grand Russborough House and Baltinglass Abbey, a 12th-century ruin.*

*The major draw in west Wicklow is **Russborough House**, a Palladian mansion which, due to a quirk of history, has quite an exceptional collection of art. The
road there from **Glendalough** is a delightful one, rolling across the Wicklow
Mountains and through the Wicklow Gap down to Holywood on the N81.
Russborough House lies directly to the north while at Donard to the south there is
a turning for the sombre **Glen of Imaal**. Lugnaquilla (3,038 ft/926 m), the highest mountain in County Wicklow, is nearby.*

Glendalough

Glendalough has become enormously popular in recent years and if you
arrive on a busy day in summer and only visit the monastic sites, then the natural magic that attracted St Kevin and his cohorts may escape you. Up to 1,000
people can turn up on one day and the car parks at Glendalough may both
become overfull. At any time, the flavour of the place is best enjoyed by heading off for a walk in the area around the Upper Lakes.

*Phone code: 0404
Colour map 4, grid B3*

There is **a** tourist information **office** at the Glendalough Visitor Centre,
T45325, and there's also a smaller office, near the Upper Lake, T45425.

In the sixth century an early Christian monk, St Cóemgen (Kevin), a member
of the ruling clan of Leinster, established a monastery in a valley setting beside
two lakes (*Glean dá Loch*, glen of the two lakes) – at the time he was living in a
tree – and the wisdom of his choice is still apparent in the stark beauty of the
place. Perhaps the picturesque setting helped attract the growing number of

History

Glendalough

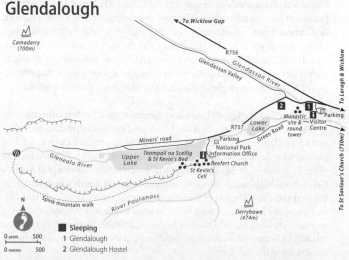

To Wicklow Gap

Camaderry
(700m)

R756

Glendassan Valley   Glendassan River

To Laragh & Wicklow

R757   Lower
Lake   Monastic
site &
round
tower

Miners' road   Parking   Green Road   Visitor
Centre

Glenealo River   Upper
Lake   Teampall na Scellig
& St Kevin's Bed   National Park
Information Office

Reefert Church

St Kevin's
Cell

Spink mountain walk   River Poulanass

To St Saviour's Church (750m)

Derrybawn
(474m)

N

0 yards   500
0 metres   500

■ **Sleeping**
1 Glendalough
2 Glendalough Hostel

County Wicklow

pilgrims and devotees who came after St Kevin, causing new monastic buildings to spring up as Glendalough's reputation as a place of learning spread across Europe in the Dark Ages. Monastic life was not finally extinguished until the early 17th century, having survived several Viking raids and, later, sacking by the English in 1398

Glendalough Visitor Centre

This is the logical place to begin a tour of the sites. There is an important cluster of buildings nearby at the Lower Lake, and from there you can take the 20-minute walk westwards along the designated green road to the sites around the Upper Lake. Guided tours of the site leave every half-hour and take an hour and there is a 17-minute audio-visual presentation on Irish monasticism. It is not necessary to purchase entry to the Centre in order to walk around the sites. ■ *T45325. Jun to Aug daily 0900-1830; Mid Mar-May and Sep-Mid Oct daily, 0930-1800; Mid Oct-Mid Mar daily, 0930-1700. €2.50. Dúchas site.*

Walking

The information centres at the Lower and Upper Lakes dispense a booklet, *Exploring Glendalough* (€1.90), with details of two short nature trails and a longer, 5-mile (8-km) route in the Upper Lake area. A half-hour stroll along the north side of the Upper Lake, parallel to the road, is pleasant enough and it leads to old zinc and lead mines. A more vigorous excursion would be to walk along the south side of the Upper Lake and this could be continued to complete a circuit of the entire lake. It takes about six hours to complete the 11-mile (17-km) circuit and it would be advisable to use a local walking guide, such as David Herman's *Hill Walkers Wicklow* (€4.76). This also includes a shorter and easier four-hour circuit of Spink Mountain to the south of the Upper Lake. ■ *Between May and Aug, on Tue at 1100 and 1400, there is a guided nature walk from the Upper Lake Information Office.*

Lower Lake monastic sites

The 10th-century **Round Tower**, with its doorway characteristically placed some 10 ft (3 m) above the ground, is not easy to miss. The nearest ruin to the Visitor Centre is the **cathedral**, begun perhaps as early as the ninth century but added to in the 11th-12th centuries, and with an ornamental east window worthy of appreciation. There are fine examples of 18th-century tombstones around the place. To the south, the **Priest's House** dates originally from the 12th century but a lot of what you see today was restored in 1875-80. The name derives from the practice of burying priests here. The most interesting site is **St Kevin's Church** or **Kitchen**, a fine two-storey oratory that may date back to St Kevin's own times although the belfry is 11th century and the sacristy at the other end was added later. The other main site involves walking eastwards to the other side of the Visitor Centre, but because the 12th-century **St Saviour's** has the finest examples of Irish Romanesque decoration in Glendalough it is worth the detour.

Upper Lake monastic sites

As you approach the Upper Lake along the green road, **Reefert church** is over to the left and overlooking the lake. It is a straightforward Romanesque structure of the 11th century and while in fairly good condition it cannot match St Saviour's for decorative details. There are steps from the churchyard leading to the Pollanass Waterfall and further to the west are the remains of **St Kevin's Cell**, a small beehive hut associated with the saint. **St Kevin's Bed**, further to the west and above the line of the water, is a cave on a rocky ledge where, legend has it, the holy Kevin dealt with the unwelcome solicitations of a young woman by hurling her into the lake below. Still further west are the very scant remains of **Teampull na Scellig** ('the church of the rock'), thought to be the earliest site in the valley.

County Wicklow

Dwyer and McAlister

Michael Dwyer (1771-1826), the 'Chief', was the leader of a guerrilla band that roamed the Wicklow Mountains in the aftermath of the 1798 insurrection. In the winter of 1799 he and his band took refuge in a cottage at Derrynamuck where they were surrounded and vastly outnumbered by English soldiers. One of the group, Sam McAlister, drew the fire of the English by running from the cottage, and his death allowed Dwyer to escape and flee barefoot in the snow pursued by a pack of hounds. On this occasion he escaped but finally surrendered at the end of 1803 and was transported to Australia where he spent some time on Norfolk Island and then Van Diemen's Land, both prison islands, before, ironically, ending up as High Constable of Liverpool, Australia in 1815. He was shortly afterwards sacked for drunkenness and became the owner of an inn.

In Derrynamuck, the cottage itself was later destroyed by fire but was finally restored in 1946 and renovated in 1992.

■ Mid-June to mid-September, 1400-1800. €4. To reach the cottage take the road from Knockanarrigan to Rathdangan in the Glen of Imaal and it is on the right about a mile from Knockanarrigan.

Sleeping
Price codes:
see inside
front cover

County Wicklow

AL *Glendalough Hotel*, T45135, info@glendaloughhotel.ie   Just beyond the Lower Lake car park, the only hotel in the vicinity and called the *Royal Hotel* when Yeats stayed there in 1932. **AL** *Glendalough River House*, Derrybawn, T45577. An old stone house, restored, with en-suite bedrooms overlooking the river. A walking trail leads past the house to Glendalough. **A** *Derrymore House*, Derrymore Lake Rd, Glendalough, T45493, has been recommended as a friendly and quiet B&B with pleasant en suite bedrooms, a garden to sit in and a guests' room. **C** *Glendalough Hostel*, T/F45342. *An Óige* hostel in a terrific location, being only a few hundred metres from the Lower Lake sites. Renovated to a high standard and the private rooms are a good way of minimizing the occasionally hectic atmosphere. **D** *Wicklow Way Hostel*, Laragh, T43545/45364. Next to *Lynham's Inn*. Completely independent hostel, which also has private rooms.

The *Glendalough Hotel* is the most convenient place for a meal after visiting the monastic sites. The evening fixed meal, available 1900-2130, is around €25 and usually has a choice of fish and meat dishes and the ubiquitous vegetarian lasagne – often a bad omen – may make an appearance. The lunch menu has €8 main courses like lamb stew and fried plaice and also offers open and toasted sandwiches and an identical menu serves for bar food.

Eating

Lynham's Inn, at the main junction in the village of Laragh, is a comfortable low-ceilinged hostelry with a bar food menu and specials on a blackboard. Tables and beer garden outside and in winter a warm inviting fire. Prices from €8 for fish and chips to €15 for a steak. Around the corner, on the road to Glendalough, the *Wicklow Heather*, T45157, has fairly standard meals of fish, chicken and meat for around €10.

Bicycle *J Kenny*, Laragh, T45236. Bike hire. **Bus** *Bus Éireann* offer a day tour of Glendalough and Wicklow Apr-Oct, T01-836111. Departs from Busáras in **Dublin** at 1030 and the tourist office at **Dun Laoghaire** at 1100, for €22.86, but only returns to Dublin. From Jan-Mar, and Nov-Dec, the tour runs on Wed, Sat and Sun for €19. *St Kevin's Bus Service*, T01-2818119, daily via **Bray** to Glendalough (outside the College of Surgeons) off St Stephen's Green in Dublin, 1130 and 1800. From Glendalough 0715 (0945 on Sat and Sun) and 1615 (1730 on Sun). One-way/return fare €7.60/12.65. *Wicklow Tours Ltd*, T0404-67671, operates a daily mini coach service from Wicklow Town to Glendalough via Rathdrum, Jun-Aug. **Car** The car park at the Glendalough Visitor Centre is free, but it costs €1.90 to park in the Upper Lake car park.

Transport

☞ The House for Heists

The selection of paintings at Russborough House was especially rich when Rose Dugdale burgled 16 of them for the IRA in 1974, all of which were subsequently recovered undamaged. There was no political motive to a 1986 larceny and the loot of that heist has still not been fully recovered. The mastermind behind that robbery was Martin Cahill, a Dublin criminal known as The General, and 18 paintings were stolen. In 2001 there was yet another robbery, netting two paintings worth nearly €4 million. It is thought that the house was cased by two men who visited as tourists and joined one of the guided tours. The robbery itself was in broad daylight, with the thieves arriving at the front door in a jeep and driving off three minutes later with the paintings.

Directory **Money exchange** at *McCoys* newsagents opposite the *Wicklow Heather* restaurant in Laragh. **Internet** facility at the *Laragh IT* Centre, T45600, in Laragh, also near the *Wicklow Heather* restaurant.

Blessington

Russborough House
Phone code: 045
Colour map 4, grid B2

A particularly fine expression of Anglo-Irish confidence from the first half of the 18th century, though only one of a flush of extravagantly elegant houses built around that time. Like Westport House and Powerscourt, it was designed by Richard Castle who was brought to Ireland for just this kind of job. He worked on Russborough House with Francis Blindon, an architect from the west of Ireland. They almost went over the top with the immensely horizontal exterior; it stretches out on both sides from the main granite-built house with colonnades, walls, pillars and pavilions that finally terminate with kitchen and stable quarters. This is the Palladian style at its grandest and paler imitations are dotted around the Irish countryside.

The interior is noted for the plasterwork by the famed Lafranchini brothers. The art collection of Russborough owes its richness to the profits of South African diamond mines, when the owner who purchased the house in 1952 inherited the prized paintings of his uncle Sir Alfred Beit, co-founder with Cecil Rhodes of the De Beer Diamond Mining Company. The collection includes Gainsborough, Goya, Rubens, Velázquez and others, and while some may be on loan to the National Gallery of Ireland, at any one time there is always a remarkable set of paintings on show. The house also has its fair share of fine furniture, tapestries, porcelain, silver and bronzes, every example of which is tirelessly itemised on the compulsory tour. ■ *Blessington. T865239. May-Sep daily 1030-1730; Apr (from Easter) and Oct Sun and public holidays, 1030-1730. €5 for 45-min tour of main rooms and paintings. Café and small craft shop. 19 miles/ 30 km from Dublin on the N81, 2 miles (3 km) south of Blessington on the N81.*

The **tourist office** in Blessington, T865850, is open from Jun-Aug, Mon-Sat, 1000-1800.

Sleeping
Price codes:
see inside front cover

LL-L *Rathsallagh House*, Dunlavin, T403112, www.rathsallagh.com Converted stables from the late 18th century provide the setting for a comfortable and friendly country house which has been recommended for the quality of the food served. Just the place to stay if *Russborough House* has scratched an itch for aristocratic country-house living. **L** *Downshire House*, Blessington, T865199, www.downshirehouse.com On the main street in Blessington, over 20 bedrooms and above-average food.

AL ***Beechwood House***, Manor Kilbride, T4582802, www.beechwoodhouse.ie A pleasant house in the countryside where vegetarian food is a speciality and not a condescension. **A** ***The Heathers***, Poulaphouca, Ballymore Eustace, T864554, www.celtricretreat.com A bungalow next to Poulaphouca Lakes, reached by the 65 bus from Blessington, evening meal an option. **D** ***Baltyboys Hostel***, Baltyboys, T867266. *An Óige* hostel in a converted old school house overlooking water.

Eating

Pubs in Blessington are a good bet for lunchtime food and the ***Courtyard Restaurant***, T865850, has affordable meals like hake with mustard cream for €8.20. ***O'Connors***, a pub in Main St, has been recommended for its homecooked bar lunches. For an evening dining experience, in the expensive bracket, ***Rathsallagh House***, Dunlavin, T403112, can be relied on for traditional hearty fare in Irish classical style.

Sport

Adventure centre *Blessington Lakes Adventure Centre*, T865092. A few hundred metres south of Blessington on the shores of the Blessington Lakes. Land- and water-based activities, including windsurfing and lake tours on the ***MV Blessington***.

Transport

Bicycle *Hillcrest Hire*, Main St, Blessington, T865066. Bike hire. **Bus** *Bus Éireann* Dublin to Waterford and Dublin to Rosslare Harbour services stop in Blessington. The suburban No 65 bus service from Eden Quay in **Dublin** runs to Blessington.

County Wicklow

Baltinglass Abbey

Phone code: 0508
Colour map 4, grid B2

Glendalough and the area around Blessington are the most frequently visited parts of west Wicklow, but the N81 continues south through to County Carlow and on the Wicklow side of the border lies the small town of Baltinglass. Its abbey is to the north of town on the east bank of the River Slaney. It was founded by Diarmit Mac Murchadha, the king of Leinster, in 1148 for the Cistercians and functioned as a working abbey until the middle of the 16th century. Only fragments of the church and parts of the cloister have survived, but points of interest include the Romanesque doorways, the sedilla in the presbytery and details of the decorative stonework. The neo-Gothic bell tower belongs to the early 19th century, as does the granite mausoleum of local landed gentry. ■ *24 hours. Half a mile (800 m) north of Baltinglass. Free.*

Transport

Bus Éireann runs a **Dublin** to **Waterford** service, which stops in Baltinglass, as does the Dublin to **Rosslare Harbour** bus.

South Wicklow

*If your trip so far has taken you around the beauties of Glendalough and Blessington, and the glorious views over Lough Tay and Dan on the Wicklow Way, then a couple more days' travel will introduce you to equally pretty views and perhaps your first sighting of a small Irish market town. The **Vale of Avoca**, especially seen out of season when the tour bus syndrome subsides, has a still kind of beauty; while modest and engaging **Wicklow** town is small, with narrow winding streets and traditional ornamental shopfronts that lend the place some character. Further south is **Arklow**, another ancient and very popular seaside town with a long history and some pretty sights. Throw in a couple of gardens and **Brittas Bay** and you have a couple of days pleasant sightseeing.*

Wicklow Town

Phone code: 0404
Colour map 4, grid B3

A settlement of sorts here goes back to CE400, and after the Vikings arrived in the 10th century the town's Norse name, Vikinglough, gradually gave way to Wicklow. Its Irish name is *Cill Mhantáin*, (the church of St Mantan). Wicklow saw most of the action during the 15th and 16th centuries when the English lords were at the mercy of the O'Byrnes, the local clan who raided the place regularly, demanding rents and finally razing the castle in 1580. Soon after, Wicklow became part of the Pale, a safe area dominated by the English gentry who settled all around here in their great houses. The 1798 rebellion passed the little town by although there were several trials of rebels, one of whom, Billy Byrne, possibly a descendant of the O'Byrnes who caused so much trouble in the 16th century, was the son of a wealthy Catholic family and led the south and central bands of the Wicklow rebels until he was caught and executed at Gallow's Hill in the town. A monument in the town stands in his memory.

The **tourist office** is on Fitzwilliam Sq, T69117, and is open May-Sep, Mon-Sat, 0900-1800; Oct-Apr, Mon-Fri, 0900-1800.

Gaol Wicklow's historic gaol was built in 1702, held insurgents from 1798 and other political prisoners awaiting transportation in the years that followed. Exhibitions on three floors focus on the terrible prison conditions that people endured, the 1798 Uprising, the tragedy of the Famine years and the trauma of transportation that carried some 50,000 Irish people to Australia. The gaol also houses a genealogy centre, a shop and a café, but the best reason for a visit lies with the gaoler who summons you inside and scares the life out of you. ■ *Kilmantin Hill, Wicklow Town, T61599, www.wicklow.ie/gaol Mid Mar-Oct daily 1000-1800. €5.30. Regular tours every 10 mins. At the southern end of town, beside the courthouse.*

Mount Usher Gardens Mount Usher is regarded as an exemplary garden of the romantic Robinsonian type, with cascades, suspension bridges, and trees and shrubs introduced from many parts of the world. It dates back to 1860 and is laid out along the River Vartry in a style of natural, relaxed informality. In spring the meadows are bursting with flowering bulbs and the autumn colours are sublime. ■ *Ashford, T40116, www.mount-usher-gardens.com Open 14 Mar-end of Oct, daily, 1030-1800. €5. Tea room and craft shops but no picnics allowed. On the N11 road, under four miles (7 km) from Wicklow Town.*

Beaches **Brittas Bay** is one of the best beaches on the east coast of Ireland and especially popular with daytripping Dubliners. The Blue Flag beach is midway between Wicklow town and Arklow and stretches for over two miles (3 km) with lovely powdery sand, and sand dunes where botanists search for plants. ■ *Bus Éireann's No 2 service from Dublin to Jack White's Cross, then a walk of over a mile (2 km).*

Silver Strand is nearer to Wicklow Town and also has a car-park, but it is far smaller and lacks the grandeur and appeal of Brittas Bay.

Wicklow Town & cliff walk This walk begins outside Wicklow's historic gaol, from where you walk down to Main Street and turn left and pass the monument to Billy Byrne. Continue along Main Street and past the post office until another monument, the **Halpin Memorial**, is reached. Captain Robert Halpin sailed Brunel's steamship *The Great Eastern* to America, laying the first transatlantic cable from Valentia to Newfoundland. He was born in the town and also died nearby, from a septic toe that was not properly treated.

Turn up Church Street and take the first turning on the right, which leads towards the river. Do not go as far as the bridge but turn to the right and walk along South Quay by the side of the River Vartry. Clovers rare to Ireland, brought from Scandinavia by 12th-century Vikings, are said still to grow along the river. South Quay leads to the shore where the bare ruins of Black Castle stand. It was built in the 12th century by the Norman Fitzgeralds who were granted the land around Wicklow by Strongbow (Richard fitz Gilbert, ex-Earl of Pembroke who fought for Diarmit Mac Murchadha in his efforts to regain the kingship of Leinster around 1170). The castle was destroyed by local clans in 1301. With the ruins behind you, walk along Travilahawk Strand for a cliff walk of two miles (3 km) to Wicklow Head's three lighthouses.

LL *Tinakilly Country House & Restaurant*, Rathnew, T69274, www.tinakilly.ie An impressive Victorian mansion built for Captain Halpin (see above) and now a comfortable hotel with modern extensions sympathetic to the character of the place. Nautical artefacts and Halpin memorabilia (of course), large bedrooms, an excellent restaurant and service to a high standard. Dickens and Tennyson stayed here, if that helps. **AL** *Ballyknocken House*, Ashford, T44627, www.ballyknocken.com A superb guesthouse with some fine rooms with brass beds and claw feet baths, and a pretty good restaurant. **B** *Bridge Tavern*, Bridge St, T67718, F61192. Captain Halpin was born here but it is a pub now. **B** *Rospark*, Dunbar, T69615. A B&B about 1 mile south of town. **B** *Thalassa*, Dunbar Park, T67135. A Greek-inspired B&B, 10 mins on foot from town. **CD** *Wicklow Bay Hostel*, Marine House, The Murrough, T69213/61174, wicklowbayhostel@eircom.net Recommended for its friendliness and spaciousness. Open from Apr-early Dec and there are 2 private rooms and bikes for hire.

Camping *Avonmore Riverside Caravan and Camping Park*, Rathdrum, T46080.

Sleeping
Price codes:
see inside front cover

There is an unusual number of excellent restaurants in this part of the county. For an evening meal of distinction, *Tinakilly House*, Rathnew, T69274, is worth a visit to experience sophisticated country-house cooking in the hotel's non-smoking dining room. Wicklow lamb on the menu is a clear favourite but the seafood, like monkfish with goat's cheese, is equally satisfying. A 4-course dinner is around €50. Not far away, inland, on the Rathnew to Greystones road, the restaurant in *Hunter's Hotel*, T40106, can also be recommended for the quality of the food, and a pre-dinner drink in the garden that overlooks the River Vartry makes the perfect start to an evening's fine dining. Expect to pay around €40. Another worthwhile journey for a good meal takes you to the village of Rathdrum and the *Stone Restaurant*, T46036. The restaurant, behind the Cartoon Inn in the centre of the village, has starters like fried brie with black cherry sauce, terrines of venison, and crab with seaweed. Prize main courses include gherkins atop steak, duck with orange sauce, hake Molly Malone (stuffed with cockles and mussels), and game dishes. A gourmet lunch will cost about €15 and at night main dishes average €19.

The *Bakery Café & Restaurant*, in Church St around the corner from the tourist office, is undoubtedly the best place in Wicklow town for a meal. There is an early-bird menu for €19 and a bistro menu with 2 courses for €24 and 3 courses for €28. The *Grand Hotel*, T67337, Abbey St, offers carvery lunches, and pubs doing food include *The Leitrim Lounge* on the N11 and *The Old Court Inn*, The Square, which serves delicious crab specials.

Eating

O'Connor's pub has thoroughly enjoyable sessions music, especially on Thu nights. *The Bay View Hotel*, has music Thu to Mon and the *Bridge Tavern* has music of some kind every night.

Pubs & music

County Wicklow

Sport **Adventure centre** *Tiglin Adventure Centre*, at the Devil's Glen near Ashford, T40169, F40701. Specializes in weekend and weekly courses in orienteering, caving, hang gliding, rock climbing and various water sports. **Fishing** *National Disabled Angling Facility*, Aughrim, T0402-36552. 5-acre (2ha) lake stocked with game fish. Equipment for hire. €19 per day, €11.50 for 4 hrs, €6.50 for 2 hours. Open all year; summer 0800-2000 (to 2200 Jul and Aug). **Horse-riding** *Ballinteskin Farm*, near Wicklow Town, T69441. *Bel Air Riding School*, Ashford, T40109. *Broom Lodge Stables*, Nun's Cross, Ashford, T40404. *Devil's Glen Equestrian Centre*, Ashford, T40637.

Transport **Bicycle** *Wicklow Hire Service*, Abbey St, T68149. Bike hire. **Bus** *Bus Éireann*, T0902-73300. Service No 133, Dublin to Arklow, calls at Wicklow 9 times daily in each direction, stopping outside the *Grand Hotel*. The Dublin to Rosslare Harbour service stops outside the *Grand Hotel* at 0830 and 0930. From Rosslare to Dublin there is a drop-off service only at Wicklow. **Train** Station, T67329, at the north end of town, just off the N11 road to Dublin. Trains running between Dublin and Rosslare Harbour stop in Wicklow Town.

Vale of Avoca

Phone code: 0402
Colour map 4,
grid B3

The Vale of Avoca is one of those places highlighted on maps as a 'scenic route' and in recent years it has been rendered even more popular thanks to the previously nondescript little village of Avoca being chosen as the location for the *Ballykissangel* television series. The scenic highlight is the **Meeting of the Waters**, where the confluence of the rivers Avonbeg and Avonmore form the River Avoca, immortalized by Thomas Moore in a poem and now marked by a pub, *The Meetings*.

Avoca Village The village of Avoca is reached by a narrow bridge from the main road and the place everyone heads for is the pub, in the hope of nosing themselves into the background of a *Ballykissangel* scene. Another attraction is *Avoca Handweavers*, located in the oldest working mill in Ireland and offering guided tours to see weavers at work. The shop is open daily and has an excellent range of crafts and clothing, and the café is worth visiting in its own right.

Avondale House & forest park Charles Stewart Parnell, one of the great Irish nationalist leaders of the 19th century, was born into a Protestant landlord family in Avondale. The house, although it was built in 1770 and designed most likely by James Wyatt, has an interior restored to a mid-Victorian setting. There is also the obligatory video about the life and times of Parnell, one that fails to make any mention of the Catholic Church's role in his downfall. The adjoining forest park has nature trails from an easy 1.75 km stroll to a 5-km riverside walk that requires sensible footwear. There are also picnic tables at the coffee shop ■ *Rathdrum. T0404-46111. Mid-Mar-Oct daily 1100-1800; House: €4; Park in grounds: €3.80 (but not staffed outside of summer months). Bus Éireann's 133 service stops a mile (1.6 km) from the house.*

Arklow Busy traffic on the N11 Dublin to Wexford road, which passes down the town's main street, is coming close to destroying the appeal of this once-famous port. During the 1798 Uprising a bloody battle for control of the town saw hundreds of rebels mowed down by the superior guns and artillery of the English. There is a small **maritime museum** in St Mary's Road that traces the eventful history of the town and its port. ■ *Open daily 1000-1300 and 1400-1700. €3.*

The Parnell Split

Born in 1852 at Avondale to an Irish American mother, Parnell learned radical politics at an early age. In the US the family supported the anti-slavery and women's rights movements and in 1881 Parnell was asked by Michael Davitt to return to Ireland, the family home, to organize the Land League while its former leader was serving time in Kilmainham Gaol. The Land League was a disparate group ranging from the very radical who were prepared to use any tactics they could, to the conservatives, who were willing to use parliamentary politics to get what they wanted. The Land League embraced a range of demands, from the appropriation of the land by the people to the more modest fair rents and security of tenure.

Parnell travelled widely across the country, encouraging people to refuse to pay rent to the landlords, organizing meetings, distributing the Land League newspaper, arranging shelter for dispossessed tenants, but above all encouraging women to join the front line in the resistance against evictions. The right wing of the Land League, most notably her brother Charles Stewart Parnell who was negotiating a deal on a watered-down form of land reform, grew alarmed The now time-honoured epithets emerged in the press - "harpy", "harridan", "fanatic" - and eventually Anna's Ladies Land League was dismantled by Charles Stewart Parnell himself who cut off their funds. Anna Parnell left Ireland and never spoke to her brother again. She drowned in 1911.

County Wicklow

Clogga Beach is about 4 miles (7 km) south of town and is safe for swimming. There is a seasonal **tourist office**, T32484, next to the Ormonde cinema and town hall.

LL *Brook Lodge Hotel*, T36444, www.brooklodge.com A short, signposted, way from Aughrim lies this modern new hotel complex with a relaxed country house atmosphere. There is a micro distillery, a pub and an exceptional restaurant. **AL** *Vale View Hotel*, Avoca, T35236, valeview@indigo.ie Terrific views from the bedrooms of the only hotel in Avoca. Bar and restaurant food. **A** *Ballykilty House*, Coolgreaney, T37111, is a dairy and sheep farm, 1 mile from the village of Coolgreney. A peaceful location, and a tennis court on the grounds, €30 per person sharing. **A** *Bridge Hotel*, Bridge St, Arklow, T31666. Next to the bridge beside the River Avoca. **A** *Vale View*, Coolgreaney Rd, Arklow, T32622. A large Edwardian house with panoramic views from the rooftop sun lounge. **D** *Avonmore House Hostel*, Ferrybank, Arklow, T32825, F33772, avonmorehouse@eircom.net 1 private room and 20 dorm beds. Bikes for hire. Open Apr-Sep. **C-D** *The Old Presbytery*, The Fairgreen, Rathdrum, T46930, thehostel@hotmail.com. Cleverly designed modern hostel. 6 private rooms and over 50 dorm beds. Bicycles for hire and open all year.

Camping *River Valley Caravan & Camping Park*, Redcross Village, T41647. Open from mid-Mar-late Sep. On the R754.

In Avoca, *Avoca Handweavers*, T35105. Wholesome affordable food, open daily until 1700. *The Avoca Inn*'s décor won't be winning any prizes but the bridge-side location is enviable and the downstairs restaurant, with fairly standard food, overlooks the river. For a quick bite to eat, there is a fish and chip shop opposite. A little south of Avoca, on the main road and virtually impossible to miss, a very old coaching inn and now *The Woodenbridge Hotel*, T35146, is such a stupendous establishment it almost obliges one to stop (as did Eamonn de Valera, Michael Collins and others in their time). Bar food all day and a restaurant.

Sleeping
Price codes: see inside front cover

Eating

In Arklow, *Christy's*, 38 Main St, T32145. A smart pub that serves an interesting variety of dishes, from fish and chips to Mexican beef wrap. *The Birthistle* pub is at the Wexford end of the long Main Street and has a good range of starters, and meals around €8. In the middle of the same street, *Murphy's* pub is popular with shoppers for its restaurant's large menu of standard dishes, including steaks. Alternatively, pop into *Joanne's* on Main St, which runs a bakery as well as a restaurant, and consider taking a picnic down by the river where there are benches. From the car-park opposite Joanne's there is direct access to the river. *The Ostán Beag*, 33044, is a faded-looking hotel on Main St with an old-fashioned bar and a wide range of food, including lunch specials listed on a pavement blackboard. .

The Strawberry Tree Restaurant, T36444, in the Brook Lodge Hotel, has a most unusual decor that is likely to provoke mixed reactions but the food is a resounding success. Organic produce is the order of the day and the menu is meticulous in this respect. Well worth the journey.

Pubs & music In Avoca, the film pilgrim's shrine is *Fitzgerald's*, T35108, impossible to miss as you enter the village across the bridge. *The Meetings*, T35226, a pub and restaurant on the Vale of Avoca road, has an open-air ceilidh every Sun afternoon between Apr and Oct and entertainment of one sort or another most days of the weeks in summer. In Arklow, *Christie's* has live entertainment in its garden during the summer and *The Mary B* has some enjoyable informal music sessions. *The Brook House* has music Thu to Sun and *The Nineteen Arches* is also worth checking out to see what musical entertainment might be on. Live music at weekends in *Christy's*.

Shopping At the seaward end of South Quay, *Arklow Pottery*, T39442, was established in 1934 and now specializes in earthenware dinnerware. Guided factory tours, Summer, Mon-Fri. *Noritake Arklow Pottery*, South Quay, Arklow, T31101, opens its factory shop daily. *Wicklow Vale Pottery*, The Old School House, Tinahask, Arklow, T39442, has showrooms and tea-room and a range of crystal and Avoca Blue and Wicklow Vale ceramics. Open daily. On Sat, 1030-1200, there is a *country market* in the Masonic Hall, Arklow. *Fitzgerald's Crafts* in Avoca sell *Ballykissangel* souvenirs and general gifts, but *Avoca Handweavers* is a far more interesting proposition.

Transport **Bicycle** Black Cycles, Upper Main St, Arklow, T31898. Bike hire. **Bus** *Bus Éireann*'s 133 service, T01-8366111, connects Dublin and Arklow via Avoca, The Meetings, Woodenbridge and Arklow. Of the 9 daily buses from Dublin, only 2 stop at Avoca and Arklow; the majority terminate at Wicklow Town. On Sun, only the 1400 departure from Dublin goes on to Avoca and Arklow. **Trains** Trains running between Dublin and Rosslare Harbour stop in Rathdrum, T46426, and Arklow, T32519.

County Wexford

Wexford

Phone code: 053
Colour map 4, grid C2

The compact little town of Wexford, with a fair range of accommodation and restaurants, is an obvious base for a tour of the county. Its closeness to Rosslare and the ferry routes makes it a busy place in the summer months but its soul has not been lost to tourism, helped by the fact that there are no major attractions within the town itself. Satirist Jonathan Swift liked Wexford, advising Stella in 1711 to pay a visit: "Go and drink your waters and make yourself well; and pray walk there." Sound advice.

County Wicklow

Getting there and around See the Rosslare section for details of the ferry routes Ins & outs
from Britain and France to Rosslare Harbour, 12 miles (20 km) south of Wexford.
The bus and train stations are together and link the town with Rosslare Harbour,
Dublin, and other cities. The town is small enough to walk around, but this also
means parking space is limited: a parking-disc system operates. There is a free car
park opposite the *Talbot Hotel*. Bicycles can be hired for day trips out of town (see
'Transport' on page 184).

The **tourist office** is on Crescent Quay, T23111. Open Apr-Jun and Sep-Oct,
Mon-Sat, 0900-1800; Jul and Aug, Mon-Sat, 0900-1800 and Sun, 1100-1700; Nov-Mar,
Mon-Fri 0930-1300 and 1400-1730.

Wexford

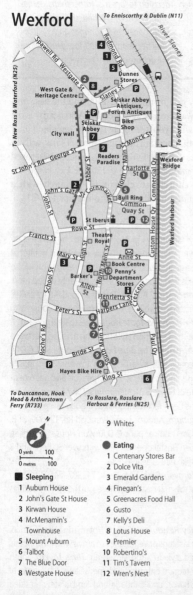

9 Whites

● **Eating**
1 Centenary Stores Bar
2 Dolce Vita
3 Emerald Gardens
4 Finegan's
5 Greenacres Food Hall
6 Gusto
7 Kelly's Deli
8 Lotus House
9 Premier
10 Robertino's
11 Tim's Tavern
12 Wren's Nest

■ **Sleeping**
1 Auburn House
2 John's Gate St House
3 Kirwan House
4 McMenamin's
  Townhouse
5 Mount Auburn
6 Talbot
7 The Blue Door
8 Westgate House

History

Wexford was a Viking settlement
until Dermot MacMurrough and
his Anglo-Norman chums took
over in 1169. The Normans built an
encircling wall in the 12th century
and the town was safe until 1649
when Cromwell (who stayed where
Penny's department store on North
Main Street now stands) left his
usual visiting card in the form of a
mass slaughter and the destruction
of the churches. In the momentous
1798 rising, Wexford was held by
the rebels and a commemorative
stone was laid in the town on the
200th anniversary of the event. Lady
Wilde, poet and mother of Oscar,
was born in a rectory in Main Street
in 1826 . A large historical map in
the George Street entrance of
White's hotel conveys a good
impression of the old walled town
and sites of historical interest.

Sights

In the centre of town where a number of streets meet, the **Bull Ring**
was where bull-baiting took place,
but the square also marks the place
where Cromwell's massacre
occurred. It was the obvious place
to erect the Lone Pikeman statue to
the insurgents of the 1798 rebellion,
and in 1998 a tree was also planted
to commemorate the revolutionary
event. A stone laid on the pavement
behind it is inscribed with the words
of the United Irishmen catechism,
about the tree of liberty growing in
the US (the American War of Independence), blooming in France
(the French Revolution) but falling
in Ireland (in 1798).

County Wexford

Radical mother to a radical son

Born in Wexford town, Jane Elgee (1826-96) was a champion for the romantic nationalists of the Young Ireland movement before she met and married William Wilde in 1851 and settled in what was to become the famous address of 1 Merrion Square, Dublin (see page 74). She became Lady Wilde after her husband was knighted, but this did little to dilute her strong republican sentiments and she continued to write nationalist pamphlets. Oscar Wilde was influenced by this political atmosphere and he went on to build and develop libertarian ideas that were probably first suggested by his mother. Lady Wilde shared with her husband a keen interest in folklore and after his death she moved to London where she published his collections of folktales and legends of the Irish countryside. She was fully behind her son's decision to face trial rather than flee the country, but by this time she herself had little money and managed on very little until her death in 1896, four years before the demise of Oscar himself.

The **West Gate** is a restored city gate from around 1300 and the best-preserved sections of the original **city walls** can be seen nearby. Also nearby is the 12th-century **Selskar Abbey**, but what you see today is what remained after Cromwell's troops paid a visit in 1649. There is a heritage centre of sorts, with an audio-visual film at scheduled times on the town's history, which is best saved for a rainy day. ■ *T46506. Summer only Mon-Fri 0900-1700.* €3.

On Main Street is **St Iberius church**, an elegant 1775 church with a 19th-century façade, offering a guided tour around the interior for €1.25. ■ *Daily 1000-1700.*

Sleeping
● on map
Price codes:
see inside front cover

L *Talbot Hotel*, Trinity St, T22566, www.talbothotel.ie Modern rooms, a good restaurant, and a leisure centre with pool, gym and sauna, in a family-orientated hotel that dates back to 1905. **L** *White's Hotel*, George St, T22311, F45000, info@whiteshotel. lol.ie There was an inn on the site in the 1790s and modernisation has recently added more rooms and improved facilities. **AL** *Auburn House*, 2 Auburn Terr, Redmond Rd, T/F23605, www.obriensaururnhouse.com Late Victorian dwelling, now a smart guesthouse with large bedrooms, some with views of the river. **A** *Westgate House*, Westgate, T/F22167. A guesthouse, close to Selskar Abbey, furnished in period style befitting a house that was a 19th-century hotel, and with its own car-park. **A** *The Blue Door*, 18 George St, T21047, www.thebluedoorwexford.com An elegant B&B in a Georgian townhouse opposite White's hotel. **A** *John's Gate Street House*, John's Gate St, T/F41124. This B&B has 6 bedrooms in a Georgian house in the centre of town. **B** *McMenamin's Townhouse*, Auburn Terr, Redmond Rd, T46442. This B&B has been recommended as a good place to stay if passing through the town. **B** *Mount Auburn*, Auburn Terr, Redmond Rd, T24609. B&B, next to Auburn House, en-suite bedrooms and car park. **C-D** *Kirwan House*, 3 Mary St, T21208, F2177, kirwanhostel@eircom.net Hostel open all year with over 30 beds and 2 private rooms. Breakfast included and bike hire available.

Camping *Ferrybank Camping & Caravan Park*, Ferrybank, T42987, F45947. Open Easter to Sep, and a 5-min walk from town across the bridge on the R741. Facilities include a heated indoor pool.

Eating
● on map
Price codes:
see inside front cover

Expensive and mid-range The *Slaney Restaurant*, Talbot Hotel, Trinity St, T22566, serves hearty and substantial food with lashings of vegetables so arrive with an appetite. Live classical guitar music and a relaxed style in a formal setting. *Tim's Tavern*, South Main St, T23861, has pub food and a restaurant entrance in Harper's Lane. A fair range of starters and traditional Irish food like bacon and cabbage and lamb's stew, entitled

Oliver Cromwell before the town of Wexford

For the Commander-in-Chief within the town of Wexford:

Before Wexford, 3rd October 1649
  Sir, Having brought the army belonging to the Parliament of England before this place, to reduce it to obedience, to the end effusion of blood may be prevented and the town and country about it preserved from ruin, I thought fit to summon you to deliver the same to me, in the use of the State of

England. By this offer, I hope it will clearly appear where the guilt will lie, if innocent persons should come to suffer with the nocent. I expect your speedy answer; and rest, Sir,
  Your Servant, O Cromwell.

Cromwell's Roundhead army took Wexford with force and 1,500 defenders were killed in the assault. The market place, now called the Bull Ring, is where a great deal of the killing took place.

United Irishmen Stew on the menu, alongside sweet and sour chicken. Such dishes are around €12. *La Dolce Vita*, Westgate, T23935, is an Italian restaurant with antipasti around €5 and main dishes, like duck with apricot and ginger, around €19, €16.50. *Lotus House*, 70 South Main St, T24273, and *Emerald Gardens*, 117 South Main St, T24836, are both Chinese restaurants with non-Oriental choices on the menu.

Cheap *Finegans* at the bottom end of South Main St is a cocktail bar and bistro, serving beef and Guinness casserole and chicken curry. Near the quayside, the *Wren's Nest* is a lovely old bar doing sandwiches, salads and takeaways. At 80 South Main St *Kelly's Deli* would suffice for a quick €5 meal or a coffee. *Gusto* is a little café serving breakfast and €5 lunches like chicken or vegetable curry displayed on a blackboard. *Robertino's*, 19 North Main St, has a bit of everything on the menu: pizza, pasta, burgers, steak, fish, starting around €7.60. *The Book Centre* on North Main St serves coffee. Further up North Main St, *Greenacres Food Hall* serves light meals and food to take away and *Premier* is fine for fish and chips.

Pubs & music The *Centenary Stores* on Charlotte St, worth a visit on Sun morning for its traditional Irish music, though every night is fairly lively and musical. *The Wren's Nest*, Custom House Quay, has traditional music on Wed during winter months. The *Trinity Bar* in the Talbot has music at weekends, attracting an older set of customers, and *Harper's* in *White's* hotel has entertainment most nights.

Entertainment The annual *Wexford Opera Festival* in late Oct/early Nov is internationally renowned for the opportunity it presents to see full stagings of lesser-known works, supported by a catholic programme of concerts, recitals and lectures. A healthy fringe programme of drama, art exhibitions, special tours and assorted events is now a regular part of the occasion. Devotees are advised to book as early as possible for the three main operas being performed. Contact *Theatre Royal*, High St, Wexford, T22144, F24289, info@wexfordopera.com, www.wexfordopera.com The theatre also plays host to visiting drama groups. The *Wexford Arts Centre*, Cornmarket, T23764, is open all year and with regular exhibitions.

Boat trips and seal spotting from Wexford Harbour, lasting 90 mins, €6.35, T40564.

Shopping Close to Selskar Abbey there are two antique shops: *Selskar Abbey Antiques*, Selskar Court, is on one corner while *Forum Antiques*, with a good selection of second-hand books as well as prints and bric-à-brac, is just across the road. *Barker's*, 36 North Main St, has an array of glass and crystal gifts plus pottery. *The Book Centre* on North Main St is a good bookshop for Irish-related literature and *Readers Paradise* on North Main St has lots of second-hand books. If you are in County Wexford for more than a day, pick up the *Design Workshops* brochure from the tourist office, describing craft shops in the area.

Sport **Fishing** Licenses and permits from *Murphy's Tackle Shop*, 92 North Main St, T24717. **Horse racing** at Wexford Racecourse, Battyville, Newtown, T421681. Admission €10.

Transport **Bicycle** Bike hire: *The Bike Shop*, 9 Selskar St, T22514. *Hayes Cycles*, 108 South Main St, T22462. **Bus** *Bus Éireann*, T33114/33162, arrive and depart from outside the bus station in Redmond Pl. Up to 6 buses a day run from Dublin to Rosslare Harbour stop in Wicklow via Wicklow and Enniscorthy. There is also a service from Rosslare Harbour to Tralee, which stops in Wexford as well as Waterford, and Cork. Other buses connect Wexford with Limerick, Kilmore Quay, Fethard-on-Sea and other parts of the county. **Taxis** *Jim's Cabs*, T47108, have a small office near *Dunne's* supermarket. Other taxi companies include *Abbey Cabs*, T41741; *Wexford Taxi Service*, T46666; *Whitty Cabs*, T22221. **Train** The railway station, T22522, is at the north end of town at Redmond Pl and up to 3 trains a day stop here on the Dublin to Rosslare Harbour route. Trains also run daily to Wicklow and Enniscorthy.

Directory **Banks** The *Bank of Ireland* is on Custom House Quay and money can also be changed at *Mulcahy's* newsagents on North Main St. **Communications** **Post office**: Ann St. **Laundry** *My Beautiful Laundrette*, Peter's St, T24317. Has complimentary hot drinks and ironing facilities. Mon-Sat 1000-2100. **Walking Club** The Wexford Hill Walkers Club meets on various Sun and visitors welcomed. Contact Senan O' Reilly, T44634, market@indigo.ie

Around Wexford

Irish National Heritage Park
Phone code: 053

Ambitious to say the least, this historical theme park sets out to encapsulate nearly 9,000 years in the country's development: starting with the earliest prehistoric settlements and finishing with the arrival of the Normans in the 12th century. Models of dolmens and other modes of burial, stone monasteries, a High Cross, and *raths* are just some of the displays making up a series of 14 replicated sites dotted around the park. There is, of course, the inevitable audio-visual show, and for young visitors or anyone with little or no acquaintance with pre-Norman Ireland the Park's guided tours do offer a bird's-eye view of what can be sought out for real in the rest of the country. ■ *T20911, www.wexford.ie Open daily 0930-1830. €6.35. Restaurant open throughout the day. Located at Ferrycarrig, 3 miles (5 km) from Wexford town just off the N11 road.*

North Sloblands

Not the most endearing of names but the white-fronted geese are not bothered because they arrive in their thousands every year from Greenland and stay for the winter. There are hides for bird watching, and a visitor's centre with exhibitions on the various birds that can be spotted here. See the box on page 189 for details of other bird-watching locations in Wexford. ■ *Wexford Wildfowl Reserve, North Slob, T23129. 16th Apr to end of Sep, daily, 0900-1800; Oct to 15 Apr, daily 1000-1700. Free. Reached from the R741 Gorey Rd. Leave Wexford over the River Slaney bridge and after 2.9 km (1.8 miles) turn right, beside Grannal's Mazda garage, into Ardcavan Lane.*

Rosslare Strand

Not to be confused with Rosslare Harbour, Rosslare is 5 miles (8 km) north of the ferry port and 9 miles (15 km) south of Wexford town. It is worth visiting for its long, safe, sandy beach, with a lifeguard, and opportunities for water sports.

Bird watching and the Saltee Islands

Apart from the North Sloblands (see page 188) there are other local locations suitable for bird watching. Viewing from the shore of Our Lady's Island, nesting terns may be observed in the summer alongside teals, redshanks and godwits. In nearby Tacumshin Lake waterfowl are present in the winter. Brent geese and herons can be seen at Fethard and at nearby Bannow Bay waterfowl also arrive in the winter. Hook Head is always a good place to visit with binoculars and migrant landbirds are the speciality here, but take care clambering over the rocks because there are unmarked

blowholes and a danger of freak waves. The last of the now extinct great auks to be found alive in the British Isles was brought past Hook Head in 1834 by local fisherman – so you're unlikely to spot any more of them.

The real draw for anyone with an ornithological interest are the uninhabited **Saltee Islands**. *From late spring to early summer the rocks are alive with puffins, kittiwakes, gannets, razorbills, shearwaters and other sea birds. Boat trips can be arranged in Kilmore Quay, and Declan Bates, T29900/29684, is one of the more established operators.*

Close to the beach is the *Oyster Restaurant*, T32439, open Thu-Mon from 1700 to 2130 between Easter and Nov, specializing in local seafood and costing about €19 for a three-course meal. ■ *The* Rosslare Sailboard and Watersports Centre, *T32566, opens from Jun-Aug, daily, 1000-1800.*

Two major ferry companies, *Irish Ferries* and *Stena Line*, operate out of Rosslare Harbour and so for many visitors this is their first or last port of call in Ireland. This is all Rosslare Harbour amounts to and there is no reason to stay any longer than it takes to board or disembark from one of the ferries. Depending on the weather, especially in the winter months, there can however be delays to the sailing schedules and sometimes an overnight stay may be necessary. If you are delayed for a long time at Rosslare harbour, there is a small sandy beach within walking distance.

At the harbour there is a **tourist office** (T33232, open Jun-Sep), open to meet scheduled sailings. There is a second tourist office north of the harbour on the main Wexford road at Kilrane, T33622, open May-Sep, daily, 1100-2000; Oct-Apr, Tue-Sun, 1400-2000.

Rosslare Harbour

LL *Great Southern Hotel*, T33233, F33543, www.greatsouthernhotels.com One of a number of plush hotels overlooking the harbour from a clifftop. A leisure centre with a swimming pool helps while away the hours waiting for a delayed ferry. **LL-L** *Kelly's Resort Hotel*, Rosslare, T32114, www.kellys.ie This is a real gem of a hotel, able to accommodate children without having them take over the place. Immaculate bedrooms, good restaurant, and delightful gardens that will interest amateur gardeners. All sorts of special interest packages, from gardening to art to feng shui. **L** *Hotel Rosslare*, T33110, www.hotelrosslare.ie Close by the *Great Southern* and offers diversions in the form of squash, snooker, sauna, and a comfortable maritime-inspired bar. **AL-A** *Ferryport House*, T33933, www.tuskarhousehotel.com Less than 500 m from the harbour, a very smart guesthouse with good facilities. **A** *Ailesbury*, 5 The Moorings, T/F33185. The closest B&B to the harbour, it is possible to get an early breakfast at this B&B, if catching an early ferry. **A** *Kilrane House*, T33135. B&B less than 5 mins from the harbour, with a pub and restaurant opposite. **A** *Carragh Lodge*, Station Rd, T33492. B&B off the N25, mins from the ferry. **A** *Clover Lawn*, Kilrane, T33413. It is possible to get an early breakfast at this B&B, if catching an early ferry. **A** *Marianella*, Kilrane, T33139, is a bungalow on the N25 and equally close to the harbour and early breakfast

Sleeping
*Price codes:
see inside front cover*

County Wexford

available. **D** *Rosslare Harbour Hostel*, T33399, F33624, rosslareyh@oceanfree.net *An Óige* hostel located on the hill overlooking the ferry port. There is one private double, the other beds are in 4- and 6-bed rooms. From the harbour, up the hill and left (right, coming from Wexford) by the church with the 10-m cross, then right at the supermarket into the car park and the hostel is over the green. If on foot, turn right at the top of the hill and immediate right after Hotel Rosslare.

Camping *Burrow Holiday Park*, Rosslare, T32190, F32256, burrowpk@iol.ie A 15-min drive from the ferry port and has 25 pitches for tents. *St Margarets Beach Caravan & Camping Park*, Our Lady's Island, T/F31169, stmarg@indigo.ie Open Easterend of Oct, follow the signs for Lady's Island/Carne from Tagoat on the N25. Six miles (9 km) from Rosslare Harbour.

Eating None of the B&Bs does an evening meal so if you are staying overnight there is little choice but to eat in one of the hotels. The average price for a dinner is €23, while the *Portholes Bar* in the *Hotel Rosslare* is the best bet for bar food and serves complete meals in comfortable surroundings. A good bistro at *Kelly's* hotel, at Rosslare not Rosslare Harbour, is excellent, and the formal dining room is especially recommended for quality meals, live music and dancing afterwards in the Ivy Room.

Transport **Bus** *Bus Éireann*, T33114, run up to 6 buses a day between **Dublin** and Rosslare Harbour, via **Bray**, **Wicklow**, **Enniscorthy** and **Wexford**. Up to 3 a day run from the harbour to **Tralee**, via **Wexford**, **Waterford**, **Cork** and **Killarney**. In the summer 1 bus a day runs to **Galway** via **Cahir**, **Limerick** and **Ennis**. **Car** Cars can be rented from a desk in the terminal at Rosslare Harbour. *Dan Dooley* T0800-282189 in UK; T1800-3319301 in USA **Ferry** *Irish Ferries*, T33158, sail daily to and from **Pembroke** and **Cherbourg**. *Stena Line*, T33115, sail daily to and from **Fishguard** on a 3½ hr voyage *Stena Line* also run a daily service to and from Fishguard. **Train** The railway station at Rosslare Harbour, T33114, now has the grand name of Rosslare Europort and trains depart at 0720 (0852 on Sun), 1445 and 1825 for **Dublin**, via **Wexford**, **Wicklow** and **Bray**. There is also a Mon-Sat service from the harbour to **Waterford**, which connects with a service to **Limerick**.

Enniscorthy

Phone code: 054
Colour map 4, grid C2

The town of Enniscorthy is worth visiting for its 1798 connections, but there is little else to recommend about the place. The **tourist office**, is in the centre of town. T34699, Jun-Sep, Mon-Fri, 1000-1800.

1798 Visitor Centre This is the highlight of any visit to Enniscorthy and should not be missed; a brilliant example of a visitor centre that achieves the opposite of dumbing down, and which places the 1798 rebellion within both its Irish context and the larger European and American dimensions that gave such it such force and meaning. Allow at least an hour's visit to immerse yourself in the revolutionary mood of late 18th-century Europe, listening to the debate between Edmund Burke and Thomas Paine, and visiting the Chess Room, which graphically depicts the struggle of the times. The Wexford Room focuses on the events in the county itself, a 15-minute film brings to life on a multi-screen the showdown at Vinegar Hill, and the aftermath of the event is chronicled in a look at the growth of democracy in Ireland. The shop includes a good selection of books on 1798, including two recently released CDs (see page 682), which help bring to life this defining moment in Irish history. ■ *T37596, www.1798centre.com Mon-Sat, 0930-1800, Sun, 1100-1800. Picnic area, café and gift shop.*

1798 and County Wexford

One of the four main centres of action during the insurrection of 1798 (see page 647) was County Wexford. On 27th May the rebels attacked the yeomanry at Oulart, before moving on to capture Enniscorthy. Within three days Wexford town was taken and for the next three weeks it remained the revolutionary capital of the insurgents. Unfortunately, after the failure to take New Ross and Arklow early in June, the rebels chose to encamp on Vinegar Hill and await a showdown with the English military. This decision was not unanimous, but calls for rural guerrilla tactics were not heeded and the decisive encounter duly took place on 21st June. The Irish survivors were lucky to

escape and on the following day Wexford itself was reclaimed by the English.

Some controversy surrounds the Wexford uprising because in the southeast, where there was a relatively large Protestant presence, a vein of sectarianism manifested itself in acts like the burning to death of 200 Protestants in a barn at Scullabogue and mass executions by the rebels in Wexford town. Notwithstanding this, recent research has confirmed that the Wexford uprising was a remarkably revolutionary act that involved some 20,000 men and women, many of whom were quite aware of the political significance of what they were attempting to achieve.

County Wexford

It was at Vinegar Hill that the rebels encamped in June 1798 to await developments in the tumultuous aftermath of the initial uprising. On the 21st June General Lake, with 400 coaches of ammunition and 20 pieces of artillery, stormed the hill with 10,000 men. However, reinforcements under General Needham arrived too late to complete the encirclement of Vinegar Hill and through a gap, known thereafter as Needham's Gap, the majority of the 20,000 insurgents managed to escape southwards to Wexford, leaving behind 500 dead and many injured. There are great views of the surrounding countryside from the top of the hill, which is reached from town by crossing the bridge, taking the first right turn after *Treacy's Hotel* and following the signs. The sight is 10 minutes away from town in a car.

Vinegar Hill
At Vinegar Hill, in the memorable words of Heaney (Requiem for the Croppies), the rebels faced the English 'shaking scythes at cannon'

L *Riverside Park Hotel*, The Promenade, T37800, www.riversideparkhotel.com A short walk from the town centre and overlooking the River Slaney but hardly merging with the landscape. Two bars and a restaurant, dreadful modern décor. **A** *Oakville Lodge*, Ballycarney, T88626. Six miles (9 km) north of town on the N80 road to Bunclody and Carlow, this B&B has seatrout fishing on private waters. **B** *Lemongrove House*, Blackstoops, T36115. A large B&B house with 5 rooms. Less than a mile (1.6 km) north of town at the roundabout on the Dublin/Rosslare N11 road. **C** *Platform 1*, Railway Sq, T37766, plat@indigo.ie A new IHH hostel, usefully situated next to the railway station (and a swimming pool and leisure complex), with a pool table and internet facility. There are nearly 60 beds and a number of private double rooms that can cost as much as €48.

Sleeping
Price codes:
see inside front cover

A difficult town to find a decent place to eat. For a light meal the most comfortable place is the small and snug *Antique Tavern* at the end of Slaney St that runs down to the river from near the monument in the centre of town. Some meals are available plus sandwiches, toasted or plain, with a large choice of fillings. The *Promenade Bar* in the *Riverside Park Hotel* has a spacious dining area for standard lunch meals around €8 and there is also a carvery at lunchtime in the hotel's *Mill House Bar*. For an evening meal the hotel's *Moorings* restaurant, T37800, is worth considering; main dishes range from €12 for chicken or spinach and ricotta tortellini to €18 for fish.

Eating

Along Rafter St, the main street that runs down to the central monument, there are a number of small restaurants and cafés serving inexpensive meals. *Paris Café* is a self-service cafeteria but *Karen's Kitchen* is next door and offers a better choice of meals. *The Baked Potato* serves lunch for around €8.

Festivals Late Jun and early Jul sees the *Strawberry Fair*, 9 days of music and craic, T056-21688. The **end of Aug** witnesses a lively *Music Festival*, T37950, fleadh@tinet.ie and in **early Sep** there is the *Blackstairs Blues Festival*, T053-42211 ext. 285/369.

Shopping Local potteries, dating back to the 17th century, can be visited and their produce purchased. *Carleys Bridge Potteries*, Carleys Bridge, T33512, is on the road to New Ross, while *Kiltrea Bridge Pottery*, T35107, is northwest of town and reached by taking the signposted right turn off the R890 road.

Sport **Greyhound racing** T33172, Mon and Thu at 2000, €4. **Horse-riding** *Boro Hill Equestrian Centre*, Clonroche, T44117.

Transport **Bicycle** *Kennys for Bikes*, Slaney St, T33255. Bikes hire. **Bus** *Bus Éireann's* **Dublin** to **Rosslare Harbour** and Dublin to **Waterford** services stop in Enniscorthy. On Wed only there is a bus to and from **New Ross** and on Wed and Fri there is a service to and from **Wexford**, T01-8366111. **Train** The **Dublin** to **Rosslare Harbour** train service stops in Enniscorthy and the station, T33488, is on the east bank of the river.

Directory **Guided walks** T36800. May-Sep. Depart from town at 1030 and 1430. €3.50.

Courtown harbour and east coast beaches

Phone code: 055
Colour map 4, grid B3

The R742 road follows the coast for most of the way from Courtown Harbour, near Gorey in the north of the county, south to Wexford town. Courtown and Curracloe have Blue Flag beaches and it was at Curracloe that scenes from Spielberg's *Saving Private Ryan* were filmed. The beach at Courtown is the most commercially developed and the best choice of accommodation is here. The Wexford Coastal Path (see page 194) runs close to the coastline for most of the way between Courtown and Wexford. There is a **tourist office** in Gorey. ■ *Main St, Gorey, T34699. Jun-Sep, Mon-Fri, 1000-1800.*

Sleeping **AL** *Bayview Hotel*, Courtown Harbour, T25307, www.bayview.ie Overlooks the marina and there is a squash and tennis centre for guests. **A** *Harbour House Guesthouse*, Courtown Harbour, T/F25117. A residents' lounge, garden, just 3 mins away from the beach.

Camping *Morriscastle Strand*, Kilmuckridge, T053-30124, camacmorriscastle@tinet.ie Large and popular with Irish families. *Parklands Holiday Park*, Ardamine, T25202, F25689. A large camping and caravan park.

Eating A reliable place for food is the *Bayview Hotel* in Courtown Harbour and there are also a couple of restaurants in Kilmuckridge as well as in Gorey itself.

New Ross

Phone code: 051
Colour map 4, grid C2

Given its prominent position by the River Barrow and on the N25 road between Wexford and Cork, the town of New Ross is frequently passed through by travellers and just as quickly dismissed for not looking sufficiently glamorous or twee. But there are fine views of the river from the top of the steep and narrow streets, which have their own unreconstructed character, and the ruins of the 13th-century **Church of St Mary** contain some interesting medieval tombs. The failure by the insurgents to capture New Ross in the 1798 uprising was decisive in halting the march of the revolutionaries and thousands died in the battle for the town.

Places of interest in the vicinity include the **John F Kennedy Arboretum**: the US president's grandfather was born in nearby Dunganstown. ■ *T388171. May-Aug, daily, 1000-2000; Apr and Sep, daily, 1000-1830; Oct-Mar, daily, 1000-1700. €2.50. Dúchas site. Eight miles (12 km) south of New Ross on the R733.*

Time could also be spent visiting a reconstructed 19th-century Famine ship, the **Dunbrody**. ■ *T5142539, www.dunbrody.com Apr-Sep daily 0930-1700. €4.*

AL *Creacon Lodge Hotel*, Creacon, T421897, www.creaconlodge.com A comfortable place outside of town, with pleasant garden, restaurant and bar. **A** *Milltown House*, Milltown, Glenmore, New Ross, T880294. A farmhouse B&B, just off the N25, with en-suite accommodation and farm tours for interested guests. **D** *MacMurrough Farm Hostel*, T421383, machostel@eircom.net A couple of miles northeast of town, off the N30, and includes 1 private room for €21. This is a working farm and produce is available for sale in season.

Sleeping
*Price codes:
see inside front cover*

The *Galley Cruising Restaurants*, T421723, operating from New Ross between Apr and Oct, cruise the River Barrow and include either lunch for €17.78, afternoon tea for €10 or an evening trip with dinner for €31.75. A foodless cruise is €8.89/€7.62/€13.97 at lunch/afternoon/evening time. In New Ross itself the pubs are the best bet for a meal, while for a special night out there is the *Old Rectory Restaurant*, Rosbercon, T421719, situated in a country house hotel.

Eating

County Wexford

South Wexford Coast

Most travellers head north from Rosslare Harbour to Wexford before going north to Dublin or west to Waterford – entirely forgetting the south coast – and on leaving Ireland there is the same tendency to speed by on one's way to the ferry port using the main roads. But the south coast of Wexford, and the Hook Head Peninsula in particular, has its modest charms and with the help of the 7-minute ferry journey across Waterford Harbour, you can enjoy a leisurely meandering journey between Rosslare Harbour and Waterford.

South Wexford Coast

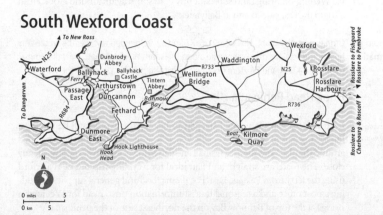

Kilmore Quay

Phone code: 053
Colour map 4, grid C2

This fishing-cum-tourist village, the departure point for trips to the Saltee Islands, has thatched cottages, craft shop, sandy beach, a marina, and probably too many visitors in summer months for its own good. Early to middle July is especially busy, when a **Seafood Festival** brings the place alive with food tastings and music and dance.

Sleeping

Price codes:
see inside front cover

AL-L *Hotel Saltees*, T29601, F29602. The only hotel in the village is a characterless-looking place although the restaurant is fine. **A** *Quay House*, T29988, www.quayhouseguesthouse.com A neat and tidy guesthouse that attracts divers and fishing folk because of its storage and freezing facilities. **C-D** *Kilturk Hostel*, T/F29883, opens all year and with over 20 dorm beds and seven private rooms, this might be the best place to stay if just passing through.

Eating

The *Coningbeg Seafood Restaurant* in the Hotel Saltees has fresh fish, as you would expect. *The Silver Fox Seafood Restaurant*, T29888, open for lunch and dinner, serves mostly seafood and dull vegetarian choices. There are a couple of pubs doing bar food, like the graceless *Kehoe's Pub*, T29830, with a dedicated maritime theme, a beer garden to the rear and an affordable bar menu of seafood and meat dishes.

Sport

Kilmore Quay has a few places catering to **fishing** and **diving** enthusiasts: *Kilmore Quay Angling & Diving Centre*, T29988; *Kilmore Quay Boat Charters*, T29704; *Sharkhunter*, T29967; *Wexford Boat Charters*, T45888.

Transport

Bus *Bus Éireann*, T01-8366111, runs a limited service, on Wed and Sat only, between **Wexford** and Kilmore Quay. The bus leaves Wexford at 1000 and 1530 on Wed, returning at 1035 and 1610. The corresponding times on Sat are 1100 and 1620, returning at 1135 and 1700.

The Wexford Coastal Path

The Wexford Coastal Path is a signposted long-distance walk of 125 miles (200 km) in total, starting at Courtown Harbour near Gorey on the east coast and making its way south to Carnsore Point. It then heads west to follow the south Wexford coast as far as Kilmore Quay, passing lagoons and fine views of the Saltee Islands. The Way then diverts inland to pass around Bannow Bay via Wellington Bridge and subsequently goes south again around Hook Head and up the east side to end at Ballyhack.

Mapping & information

Ordnance Survey maps, Nos 62, 69, 76, 77 and 82 are needed to cover the whole Way but shorter sections may be enjoyed along the south Wexford coast. Further information from T42211 and Wexford County Council also publish a guide to the Way.

Hook Head Peninsula

Phone code: 051
Colour map 4, grid C2

Even if the peninsula weren't steeped in history this would still be the most interesting part of the south Wexford coast to visit. Accommodation is dotted around the place and the area is small enough to make everywhere conveniently close. The roads are straight and flat, ideal for a cycling trip out of Waterford using the ferry from Passage East. For picnic food and general supplies, including a post office and a seasonal tourist information post, head for Wellington Bridge at the top of Bannow Bay on the northeast side of the peninsula.

County Wexford to County Waterford Ferry

The Passage East Car Ferry, T(051) 382480, runs a service between Ballyhack in county Wexford and Passage East in County Waterford. The service is a all-year one (except 25 and 26 December) between 0700 (0930 on Sunday) and 2200 (2000
between October and end of March). No reservations, just turn up and wait a few minutes for the 5-minute crossing.
€5.71/€8.25 for cars single/return;
€1.27/1.90 for pedestrians single/return;
€2.54/€3.20 for cyclists single/return

It was in **Bannow Bay** in May 1169 that a force of mercenaries landed and met up with Dermot MacMurrough (see page 643) before their combined forces captured Wexford. This brought Strongbow and then Henry II to Ireland, thus setting the stage for 800 years of conquest. In the 17th century when Oliver Cromwell was playing his part in that sorry drama, he noted that Waterford would be taken by "Hook or by Crooke", signifying the two places where an assault could be launched: the Hook peninsula or Crooke on the other side in county Waterford.

Tintern Abbey An austere but impressive and well preserved Cistercian abbey founded around 1200 and named after the famous Tintern Abbey in Wales, from where its first monks came. The founder, William the Earl Marshall, on a particularly rough voyage over to Ireland is said to have promised God he would found a church if he survived the journey (anyone who has made a stormy passage in winter will find this quite believable). Occupied as a private home from the 16th century until the 1960s, the nave, chancel, chapel, cloister and a tower remain. ■ *T562650. Mid-Jun-late Sep daily 0930-1830. €1.90. Near the village of Saltmills, off the R734 road. Dúchas site.*

Ballyhack Castle Strategically located on a slope overlooking Waterford estuary, this substantial tower house was built around the middle of the 15th century. Very little is definitely known about its history, and although the official line is that it was probably built by the Knights Hospitallers of St John this is just speculation based on the fact that the Knights Templar did have a presence at this inlet in the estuary. On another tack, the castle is a roosting site for a colony of whiskered bats. ■ *T389468. Jun-early Sep daily 0930-1830. €1.20. In Ballyhack village. Dúchas site. Café.*

Dunbrody Abbey The second of two Cistercian abbeys on the peninsula, Dunbrody was founded in the late 12th century by an uncle of Strongbow. It has the distinction of being one of the longest Cistercian churches in Ireland (195 ft/59 m) and the east window is architecturally the most interesting part to have survived the centuries. The adjoining Visitor Centre has a small museum, the ruins of an old castle, a hedge maze, and a craft gallery. ■ *T388603. May-Jun & Sep daily 1000-1800; Jul-Aug daily 1000-1900. €1.90. Admission to hedge maze is €2.54.*

Hook Head lighthouse The story goes that this is Europe's oldest lighthouse, monks having lit a beacon here from the fifth century onwards, and that marauding Vikings never visited their customary ransacking on the place because of this. A more permanent lighthouse structure was built by the Normans in the late 12th century and the circular keep that is still visible dates back to this time. If tempted to wander over the rocks take note of the sign warning of freak waves. ■ *T397055, www.thehook-wexford.com Mar-Oct daily 0930-1730. €4.45*

Sleeping
Price codes:
see inside front cover

LL *Dunbrody Country House Hotel & Restaurant*, Arthurstown, T389600, www.dunbrodyhouse.com A Georgian manor set in 200 acres of parkland, which boasts an award-winning restaurant. On the R733 and close to the Ballyhack ferry. Large bedrooms with pacific views and lavish breakfasts. **A** *Glendine Country House*, Arthurstown, T389258, www.glendinehouse.com A substantial 1830s building, but there are only 4 rooms for guests in this B&B so reservations are useful. **A** *Marsh Mere Lodge*, Arthurstown, T389186. Pink-coloured guesthouse at the Ballyhack end of town, with 4 rooms. **A-B** *Arthur's Rest*, Arthurstown, T389192, a large yellow-coloured house, is a B&B just past the ferry.**D** *Coastguard Station*, Arthurstown, T389411, anoige@iol.ie *An Óige* hostel, ½ km from the ferry, open from Jun-Sep, with about 30 beds and including two double rooms.

Camping *Ocean Island Caravan & Camping Park*, Fethard, T397148, F397148. Within walking distance of the sea. *Fethard Caravan & Camping Park*, Fethard, T397123/397230. At the north end of the village.

Self-catering Places to contact at Duncannon include *Clonsharra*, T389122, and *Eileen Roche*, T389188, F389346. At Fethard there is *Conna*, T397146, and at Hook Head itself there is the *Hookless Holiday Village & Leisure Centre*, T/F397329.

Eating
There are bars in Fethard serving the usual run of bar food. At the Ballyhack end of Arthurstown the *Waterfront Restaurant*, T389534 (closed Mon), does lunch and dinner at affordable prices but featuring unexciting dishes like roast beef and 'vegetarian dish of the day'. *Templers Inn*, T397162, on the road from Duncannon to Hook Head, at the junction for Templetown, is a large pub with outdoor tables, serving bar food as well as having a seafood restaurant.

Pubs & music
Fethard is the best place for evening entertainment, in pubs like *Molloy's*. *Neville's*, is more a place to go for a quiet drink and a chat. *Droopy's Inn* is very popular, often has music, and local fisherman frequent the place.

Transport
Bus *Bus Éireann*, T01-8366111, run a service between Waterford (T051-879000) and Wexford, which on Mon and Thu only travels via Duncannon, Templetown and Fethard. Buses depart Waterford at 0945 and Wexford at 1450. **Ferry** (see box above).

Central South

6

Central South

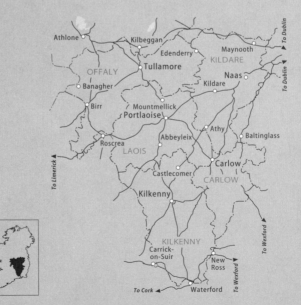

The city of **Kilkenny**, with its medieval history and flavour, has excellent transport links which make it an obvious destination as a base for exploring the lush and picturesque countryside to the south. Cycling is an ideal way to discover the quaint villages that lie dotted along the **Nore** and **Barrow Valleys**, and for walkers the undemanding **South Leinster Way** winds its way gently through the county.

Carlow is one of Ireland's least distinguished counties, covering a small area of land surrounding the rivers Barrow and Slaney. **Laois** (pronounced 'Leash') is another of Ireland's lesser-known counties, one of those places that travellers can pass through without ever registering the fact. A dull kind of prosperity characterises the towns, but the **Slieve Bloom Mountains** open up unspoilt Irish countryside.

County **Kildare** is close enough to the capital to turn parts of it into commuter land, but this also makes it handy for excursions out of Dublin. The north of **County Offaly** is marked by bogland, the northwest by the twisting **River Shannon** and the south by the rising hills of the Slieve Bloom range. Though visitors find this region relatively flat, it holds much of interest to those who appreciate places off the well trodden tourist tracks.

County Kilkenny

Kilkenny

Phone code: 056
Colour map 4, grid B1

Most of Ireland's more interesting cities are found close to the sea, a pattern first established by the Vikings, but Kilkenny is a rich exception to the rule and we have the Normans to thank for this. The town developed in importance under their influence, and the medieval legacy of their era is one of the chief delights of a visit to a humming city that integrates tasteful shops and restaurants into time-hallowed streets and preserves a tangible sense of olde-Ireland. The downside to the town's unique blend of the medieval and the cosmopolitan is that Kilkenny features on countless coach tours, and at the height of summer the major attractions and shopping venues are heaving with visitors. In summer, make sure you book your accommodation well in advance.

Ins and outs

Getting there & around
The bus and train stations are together. There are direct bus links to Dublin, Cork and Waterford and trains to Dublin (2 hrs away) and Waterford. See 'Transport', page 207 for further details.

Kilkenny is a small and compact town and the medieval attractions and the castle are within walking distance of the centre. Bicycles and cars can be hired. A disc system governs parking in the city centre, and you can get discs from newsagents and other shops.

The **tourist office** is in Shee Alms House, Rose Inn St, T51500. Open Apr-Jun and Sep, Mon-Sat, 0900-1800; Jul-Aug, Mon-Sat, 0900-2000, open Sun May-Sep, 1100-1700. Oct-Mar, Mon-Fri, 0900-1700.

History

Kilkenny's known history goes back to early Christian times but it was in the 13th century that the place grew to prominence under the Marshall family, the earls of Pembroke and lords of Leinster. William Marshall married the daughter of Strongbow and spent a lot of time in Ireland consolidating his position and putting Kilkenny on the political map. Wealth to some came from trading in wool, and in medieval times Kilkenny had its own Anglo-Norman parliament that at times made the town the effective capital of Ireland. The most famous legislation arising from its parliament was the notorious Statutes of Kilkenny of 1366, aimed at reversing the growing Gaelicization of the English colony. In the 16th and 17th centuries Kilkenny was the political capital for the great Ormond family, also known as the Butlers because an ancestor who came over with the Normans became chief butler to Prince John. After the rising of 1641, an important gathering of Catholic interests took place here, known as the Confederation of Kilkenny, under a lord related to the Ormonds and the Papal Nuncio Rinuccini. Papal power wanted the full restoration of Catholicism and excommunicated any party willing to do business with Cromwell. The Protector himself turned up in 1650 and battered the town walls for five days, but although economic power passed to Protestants in the last quarter of the 17th century the town never quite lost its Catholic flavour. Kilkenny prospered through to the 19th century, with an important road link to both Dublin and Cork, and never lost its cultural influence within

★

Things to do in the Central South

- Visit **St Canice's Cathedral** and its tombstones
- Go for a quiet drink in **Tynan's Bridge** pub
- Spend your money in the **craft shops** of Kilkenny and Bennettsbridge
- Come face-to-face with a 14th-century Norman knight in **Kilfane church**
- Get on your bike in the **Nore Valley**
- See the impressive 12th-century Cistercian **Jerpoint Abbey**

the country as a whole. In the last quarter of the 20th century this cultural significance has reasserted itself with Kilkenny emerging as a provincial centre for the arts and, in particular, for the promotion of native craft design.

Sights

Kilkenny Castle

The original castle was built in 1192 by William Marshall, Strongbow's son-in-law, but the strategic site commanding the river suggests that a defensive site of some kind existed before the Normans arrived. In the late 14th century ownership passed to the Ormonds and in 1967 the 24th Earl of Ormond sold the castle to the State for a nominal sum, after most of the contents had been auctioned. While the outer walls of the castle are original, substantial rebuilding and renovation work took place in the 1820s and 30s under the supervision of the London architect William Robertson. So what is seen today as you are led around on the guided tour is very much a 19th-century creation.

Much of the guided tour focuses, naturally enough, on the **Long Picture Gallery** on the first floor. The wooden hammer-beam roof is profusely decorated in Pre-Raphaelite style, undertaken by John Hungerford Pollen in 1861, and while the array of exotic beasts and birds is undeniably a surprise, the images are fading and what can be seen is not artistically brilliant by any means. The walls are lined with countless family portraits. In the basement there is an exhibition of contemporary art in the Butler Gallery and the original kitchen area is now a very good restaurant. ■ *T21450. Open Jun-Sep, daily, 1000-1900; Apr and May, daily, 1030-1700; Oct-Mar, Tue-Sun, 1030-1245 and 1400-1700. Compulsory 1-hr guided tour. €4.40. Café open during summer months. Dúchas site.*

St Canice's Cathedral

The largest medieval cathedral in Ireland after St Patrick's in Dublin was built in the 12th and 13th centuries, but suffered enormous damage after the usual bout of vandalism by Cromwell's army. The English took the roof off, stole the bells and the valuable glass, and left only the hinges on the doors "that Hogs might come, and root, and Dogs gnaw the bones of the dead". Restoration work means that none of this is now obvious and the architectural form of this Early Gothic church remains sufficiently unaltered to make it the finest example of its kind outside of Dublin. The actual site has an ecclesiastical history that goes as far back as perhaps the sixth century, and this itself suggests the ground may have a pre-Christian significance. The philosopher George Berkeley and satirist Jonathan Swift, at the end of the 17th century, were educated in a school that once stood in the cathedral grounds.

Do not be put off by the symmetrical dullness of the exterior; the inside of St Canice's Cathedral is a rich pot-pourri of funeral monuments and effigies, our favourite being the tombstone near the stall that sells postcards and the like. Its 10-line epitaph records the death of Mary Stoughton, who died in

County Kilkenny

☞ **The Statutes of Kilkenny**

Terms like 'apartheid' and 'ethnic cleansing' were not around in the 14th century, but clauses in the Statutes of Kilkenny seem to have been directed along those lines. Anglo-Normans residing in the colony of Ireland were required to use only the English language and to have recourse only to English law in settling disputes. Marriage to the native Irish was forbidden in an attempt to preserve the racial purity of the colonizers and non-martial games of Gaelic provenance were also punishable activities.

In order to prepare for the military quashing of any outbreaks of native Irish rebellion, the sale of horses or armour to the Irish was outlawed and regular reviews of the colonial forces were instituted. Many of these clauses had been promulgated before but the Statutes were a systematic attempt to reinforce colonial rule and preserve the ruling class from infiltration by the resurgent Irish. They were broadly enforced throughout the 15th century and were not repealed until the early 17th century.

childbirth in 1631. There is no end of fine carved effigies accompanying the tombs of more illustrious folk and while most of them are 16th-century, there are a couple dating back to the 13th century. The naturalistic style of the effigies of Margaret and Piers Butler in the south transept makes a dramatic contrast with the inept renderings of various Apostles liberally dotted around, but this is all part of the wonderful variety of sculptures in the church.

The **round tower** that abuts the south apse has the distinction of being accessible to visitors and offers good views from the top, but forego the experience if given to claustrophobia or fear of heights. ■ *T64971. Mon-Sat, 0900-1300 and 1400-1800, Sun, 1400-1800. Free admission but a donation is requested for Restoration Fund. €1.90 to climb the round tower.*

Rothe House This stone-built Tudor merchant's house is a superb and unique survival of Kilkenny's prosperous era. The Rothes came to Ireland from Yorkshire in the 14th century and by the late 16th century they were sufficiently wealthy to have built for themselves this substantial house in the centre of the town. It is made up of three buildings linked by courtyards and small rooms, and the Kilkenny Archaeological Society, which now owns the place, has used the rooms to display a fairly uninspiring collection of costumes and assorted artefacts. These are laboriously described in a 20-minute video, which is worth missing, but the building itself has been remarkably well restored and contains some fine features. The stonework is original and the Irish oak roof on the second floor has been sensitively restored using the methods and style of the medieval period. Features worth admiring include the octagonal chimneys, the mullioned windows, and the original escutcheon next to the restored oriel window that rests on the original corbel. The reception area, entered through an original arcade and where 400 years ago the merchant owner laid out his wares for prospective buyers, has a collection of new and second-hand books about Ireland for sale. ■ *Parliament St, T22893. Open Jul and Aug daily 0930-1800; Jan-Jun and Sep-Dec Mon-Sat 1030-1700, Sun 1500-1700. €2.54.*

Other historical sights **Black Abbey**, Abbey Street, is a Dominican church, founded in 1225 by William Marshall and dissolved in 1543. It earns the name because the Dominicans were called the Black Friars. Cromwell's army vandalized the place and it remained a ruin until it was again used as a church in the 18th century. Worth admiring are some of the original windows that date back to the 14th century.

County Kilkenny

The Tholsel, High Street, was built in 1761 by an amateur architect and perhaps this helps account for its aesthetic appeal. A *tholsel*, or *tolsel* or *tolzey* court, is an ancient name for a tollbooth or guildhall and here in Kilkenny it continues – uniquely – to fulfil its historical function as it is now the local office for the collection of rates. It has a projecting arcade and an octagonal clock tower, built on the spot where the unfortunate Petronilla was executed as a witch in 1324 (see over the page).

Just past the Tholsel, a little further up the High Street, there is a narrow medieval alley, **Butter Slip**, that takes its name from the custom of selling butter there. Nowadays you can purchase sushi rolls instead in a modern little restaurant housed in the lane, which leads down to *Dunne's* supermarket.

Continuing back up the High Street, which turns into Parliament Street, there is a **monument** marking the location of the Confederation Parliament of 1641

Kilkenny

To Brookfield Bed & Breakfast, Dunmore Cave, Castlecomer & Dublin (N77)

To Freshford (R693)

St Canice's Cathedral

St Francis's Abbey

Watergate Theatre

St Francis Abbey Brewery (Smithwick Brewery)

Green's Bridge

Dean St

Black Abbey

Rothe House

Old Jail & Courthouse

Confederation Hall Monument

Market Cross Shopping Centre

St Mary's Cathedral

Blarney Woollen Mills

Liam Costigan

Butter Slip

Tholsel (City Hall)

Book Centre

Buggy's Buses

Rudolf Helzel

Stoneware Jackson

Kilkenny College

Brett's Launderette

McDonagh Station

JJ Wall Bike Hire

Murphy

Kilkenny Castle

Kilkenny Design Centre

To Callan, Clonmel & Cork (N76)

To Kells (R697), Newlands Country House, Knocktopher & Waterford (N10)

To campsite, Bennettsbridge, Thomastown, Nore Valley, Wexford & Rosslare

To Carlow & Dublin (N10)

County Kilkenny

N

0 yards   100
0 metres   100

A riverside stroll with Thomas Moore

The grounds of Kilkenny Castle are open all year around and on a fine day they make a delightful place in which to wander and enjoy a picnic. The poet Thomas Moore (1779-1852), famed for his Irish melodies, while performing in an amateur theatrical in Kilkenny, found himself acting alongside a 14-year-old girl, Elizabeth Dyke, whom he married two years later in 1811. He was then 32. Two decades later they were still together and returned to Kilkenny to stroll along the river by the castle where they first flirted. He wrote in his diary how they "recollected the time when we used, in our love-making days, to stroll for hours there together. We did not love half so really then as we do now."

and just past this, opposite Rothe House, the **courthouse and former prison** is where insurgents from the 1798 rebellion were executed. The only way to see some of the cells is by joining Tynan's walking tour of the town (see page 207).

Shee Alms House, home to the tourist office in Rose Inn Street, dates back to the late 16th century, when it was built as an alms house by local bigwig Sir Richard Shee.

St Francis Abbey Brewery Now part of the Guinness empire and producing Smithwicks, Budweiser and Kilkenny Irish beer for home and abroad, the fact that the brewery occupies the site of a Franciscan monastery founded by William Marshall in 1232 has little to do with the enormous popularity of a visit here. ■ *T21014. Late Jun-Aug, Mon-Fri. A limited number of tickets available from 0900, free admission to a video of the brewing process at 1500. And yes, there is a free drink (but no guided tour).*

Essentials

Sleeping
■ *on map*
Price codes:
see inside front cover

Kilkenny is close enough to Dublin to attract weekenders and some unscrupulous B&Bs, guesthouses and even hotels in the centre of town have a habit of jacking up their room rates to milk the demand. None are listed here but they do exist.

LL-L *Butler House*, Patrick St, T65707, www.butler.ie Easily the best place to stay in Kilkenny, a Georgian residence restored in the early 1970s in a kind of Art Deco style featuring light colours and natural fabrics which blend remarkably well with the original features of the house. There is a lovely walled garden, which gives access to the Kilkenny Design Centre where Butler House breakfast is served. **LL-L** *Kilkenny Ormonde*, Ormonde St, T23900, www.kilkennyormonde.com The glitzy modernism of the Kilkenny Ormonde, with coaches regularly disgorging large groups of guests outside its doors, is a complete contrast to Butler House. Restaurants, bars, large bedrooms and leisure centre. **L** *Hibernian*, 33 Patrick St, T71888, www.thehibernian.com A 19th-century bank building converted to a spacious hotel but retaining original features, old paintings and a comfortable bar. **L** *Newpark Hotel*, Castlecomer Rd, T22122, www.newparkhotel.com Just outside of town, a smart modern hotel with a refreshing style of decor as well as a lively bistro and a more formal, non-smoking restaurant.

AL *Kilford Arms*, John St, T/F61018, kilfordarms@indigo.ie A pub guesthouse about 50m from the bus and rail stations. Traditional Irish restaurant, a night club and 3 bars. **AL** *Kilkenny River Court Hotel*, The Bridge, John St, T23388, www.kilrivercourt.com Tucked away beside the river, in a private courtyard, with all the mod cons and views of the castle.

County Kilkenny

Alice Kyteler and Petronella – the witches of Kilkenny

Ireland largely escaped the great witch hunts of the 16th and 17th centuries, but around the 1320s Alice Kyteler and her maid Petronella de Midia got a foretaste of what was to come. Alice was of Flemish descent and the first of her four husbands was a member of the influential Outlawe family. She was accused by a witch-obsessed English bishop of having sex with a demon spirit named Robin FitzArt and sacrificing cockerels to the devil. Family members of her subsequent husbands, who saw a chance to weaken the power of the Outlawes, accused her of sorcery in order to favour her first son. She was put on trial and, though she managed to escape to England, her unfortunate maid was put to death.

B *Carriglea*, Archers Av, Castle Rd, T61629. A family home up past the castle in a residential cul-de-sac offering B&B. There is a string of family homes offering B&B along Castlecomer Rd, past the Newbury Park hotel and just about within walking distance of town. They would be ok for a one night stay, and include **B** *Mena House*, T65362, **B** *Chaplins*, T52236, and **B** *Brookfield*, T65629. **B** *Newlands Country House*, Seven Houses, Danesfort, T29111, F29171, newlands@indigo.ie B&B in a very modern house, 4 miles (7 km) outside of town just off the N10. Plush décor, canopied beds and room facilities to rival most hotels. A place to feel pampered in, and €23 multi-course dinners to boot.

C-D *Kilkenny Tourist Hostel*, 35 Parliament St, T63541, kilkennyhostel@eircom.net An IHH place, open all year, with over 60 beds, including 2 private rooms at €33. **D** *Foulksrath Castle*, Jenkinstown, T67674. *An Óige* hostel, 8 miles (13 km) south of Kilkenny on the N76 road but *Buggy's Coaches*, T41264, run a Mon-Sat bus service (last bus 1730) that will stop nearby at Conahy Cross. The hostel building is superb, a 16th-century tower house with medieval features, spiral staircase and stupendous dining room with fireplaces big enough for bunk beds.

Camping *The Tree Grove Caravan & Camping Park*, Danville House, T70302, treecc@iol.ie Good facilities and well regarded, about a mile (2 km) from the city on the New Ross Rd (R700). Open Mar-mid-Nov. There is another camp site at Bennettsbridge, 7 miles (11 km) away (see page 208).

Eating
● *on map*
*Price codes:
see inside
front cover*

Expensive *Zuni*, 26 Patrick St, T23999. A trendy, currently popular restaurant serving modern Irish cuisine. The style of the dining room is very 'contemporary', open plan, minimalist, that kind of a place. Equally popular, and with food that is every bit as good, is *Pordylo's*, Butterslip Lane, T70660. Starters like oak-salmon blinis and a good choice of chicken, steak, duck, fish, pasta and vegetarian dishes. Chinese food at *The Emerald Gardens*, High St, T61812, is as good as it gets in Ireland in this sophisticated eatery (with a takeaway service). Try the *yuk sung* for starters, followed by dishes like monkfish with crabmeat and sweetcorn sauce or Thai beef curry.

Mid-range *Ristorante Rinuccini*, The Parade, T61575. A very decent 3-course meal for €25 makes Rinuccini good value, which explains why it is packed out with visitors and locals and why a reservation is necessary. Tasty dishes like tortelloni alla Gorgonzola are around €13, half as much again for sphagetti with lobster and truffle; unashamedly Italian wine list. On entering *Langton's*, 69 John St, T65133, you may be flummoxed by the greenery amidst the dark cavernous interior and mullioned windows. A popular restaurant with a large menu offering any two courses for €22, 3 courses for €25.

Main dishes at the *Bengal Tandoori*, Pudding Lane (behind the Book Centre), T64722, range from €8 to E15, lunch is under €8. *Parliament House Restaurant*, Parliament St, T63666, offers lunches ranging from sandwiches with salad for €4.50 to enchilada for €7. The evening menu includes lamb for €16 and sole or duckling for €20.

County Kilkenny

Cheap *Key Largo*, Canal Sq, T23922, facing the river and just up from the tourist office, is a tiny restaurant with an early-bird menu between 1500 and 1900 of two courses for €9, basically pasta or pizza with salad. The dinner menu includes fish and meat dishes and fajitas around €13 and there are a couple of outdoor tables. OK for lunch too, with vegetarian possibilities. *Italian Connection*, 38 Parliament St, T64225. Another pasta and pizza restaurant, cosier than *Key Largo*, with fish and curries on the menu as well and open daily from noon to 2300. *Pantry* is on pedestrianized St Kieran's St, opposite *Dunnes* supermarket, and serves its own breads and cakes and quick lunches; there are outdoor tables, and another tea-shop is next door. Open until 1800 on Thu and 2100 on Fri. The self-service café in the *Kilkenny Design Centre* in The Parade has good food but can become too full. The restaurant in *Kilkenny Castle* has a delightful setting and you don't have to have a ticket to visit the castle in order to eat there. *Café Sol*, William St, opens from 1000 to 1700, closed Sun, for sandwiches, panninis and various meals all around €7.

Bollard's, where Kiernan St meets Parliament St, T21353, is a pub and restaurant serving snacks, lunches and evening meals. *Kyteler's Inn*, Kiernan St, is where Alice Kyteler (see page 205) lived and although the food is not bewitching the place is very popular with locals. *Anna Conda*, Parliament St, is an old pub with tables for diners and an above-average choice of bar food.

A picnic by the river is always a possibility on a fine day and there are some benches along Bateman's Quay and, on the other side, eastwards past the swish *Kilkenny River Court* hotel. Takeaway hot drinks are available from a sandwich bar next to the riverside Key Largo restaurant.

Pubs & music *Anna Conda*, Parliament St, T71657, has a beer garden and regular sessions of traditional music that attract older folk. *John Cleere* is a couple of doors down, T62573, and has music as well as a tiny theatre bursting to the seams with a mixed crowd when something is on. *Langton's*, John St, T65133, is a very lively pub indeed with a disco and live music. *Matt the Millar*, at the bottom of John St, attracts a younger crowd. Other places worth checking out include the lovely old-fashioned *The Widow's* , Parliament St, T52520, which also has music on Sun mornings, and *The Pumphouse*, Parliament St, T63924, which is popular with students. *Bollard's* (see above) has traditional music every Tue from 2130.

Kilkenny's bustle can rush you off your feet but Tynan's by the river or The Hibernian in town are places of welcome repose

The antiquarian and wonderfully civilized *Tynan's Bridge House* at St John's Bridge is a sheer delight, the kind of place that Irish theme pubs try so dismally to imitate. Even better is *The Hibernian* in Patrick St, a modern bar with seats that compel you order another round and peruse the palatable menu of good food. *Lenehans*, Castlecomer Rd, an old-style pub with Victorian decor, offers quiet repose. *The Bróg Maker* further out on Castlecomer Rd, T52900, has an olde worlde atmosphere and a regular programme of music as well as a restaurant.

Entertainment The *Kilkenny People* is a weekly local newspaper that carries details of what's on and where. Every Wed and Thu, 2100 to 2330, there is a traditional family-orientated Irish music entertainment, song and dance, at the *Newpark* hotel, €6.35 admission.

Theatre *Watergate Theatre*, Parliament St, T61674, www.watergatekilkenny.com Regular programmes of theatre, dance and music.

Festivals **June** *The Cats Laugh Festival*, 50 John St, Kilkenny, T51254. Features comedy and theatre and is very popular. **August** *Kilkenny Arts Festival*, 92 High St, Kilkenny, T63663, www.kilkennyarts.ie The big event of the year, this is a multi-arts event with all kinds of music, sculpture, painting, literature, film and theatre. This is a very popular festival and tickets sell out quickly for many of the events. **October** *The Kilkenny Racing Festival*, T26225. Takes place at Gowran Park (see 'Sport', below).

The Kilkenny Design Centre, The Parade, is opposite the castle and has a comprehensive range of Irish craft goods for sale: ceramics, clothing, crystal, linens and assorted gifts. It is open every day from 0900 until 1800, except from Jan-Mar, when it closes on Sun and national holidays. This area was Kilkenny Castle's stables and a number of studio showrooms under the aegis of the Crafts Council of Ireland occupy the grounds.

There is also a number of upmarket studio workshops in the Nore valley and the tourist board has a brochure with a map highlighting 6 of them, as well as small display cases exhibiting some of their products. One of these studios, *Rudolf Heltzel*, 10 Patrick St, T21497, specializes in jewellery with contemporary designs. *Liam Costigan*, Collier's Lane, T62408, creates jewellery using gold, silver and platinum. Another, more traditional, jewellery store is *Murphy*, 85 High St, www.gemnet.co.uk/ptmurphy Next to the tourist office there is a *Kilkenny Crystal* shop, and *Katz*, selling craft items for the home. *The Book Centre* in High St has a good selection of books and an upstairs café.

Shopping

Birdwatching T62130, birdwatchkilkenny@aircom.net (Pat Durkin). Local outings on 1st Sun of each month. Meet at Castle Park, 1000. **Outdoor** *Countryside Leisure Activity Centre*, Bonnettsrath. One mile (2 km) outside of the city. Quad biking, archery and clay pigeon shooting. **Racing Greyhounds**: James Park, Freshford Rd, T21214. Wed and Fri, 2000. Reached from the R693 road out of town. **Horses**: *Gowran Park Racecourse*, Gowran, T26225. Admission around €9. Just east of town.

Sport

Coach: T4580054. Open-top coach tour of city, May-Sep, daily 1030, 1130, 12.30, 1400, 1500, 1600, 1700. Departs from Castle Gates area, €7.62. **Walking**: *Tynan Tours*, T2651745, www.tynantours.com Mar-Oct, up to 6 tours a day; winter, Tue-Sat 3 a day. 45 mins long, covering all the main sights except the castle, commencing from the tourist office. €4.44. *Kilkenny County Tours*, Hebron Rd, T61584, has tours departing from the coach parking area at Kilkenny Castle at 1000 and 1430. Bookings for this €1.43 trip through the local countryside can be made at the tourist office.

Tours

Bicycle *JJ Walls*, 86 Maudlin St, T21236. Bike hire for €9 a day. **Car hire** *Michael Lyng*, Hebron Rd, T70700; *Barry Pender Motors*, Dublin Rd, T65777. **Bus** *Bus Éireann*, T64933, operates from the railway station but also stops in Patrick St outside the useful little Tea Shop. Daily buses to **Dublin**, **Cork** and **Waterford**, and the Waterford to **Longford** via **Athlone** bus stops in Kilkenny. On Thu there is a local bus to and from **New Ross** and **Bennettsbridge**. *Buggy's Coaches*, T41264, run buses Mon-Sat from The Parade to the *An Óige* hostel at Jenkinstown, Ballyragget, Dunmore Cave and Castlecomer. **Taxis** *Kevin Barry*, T63017/088-574343. *Mick Howe*, T65874/ 088-574141. *David Nagle*, T63300/088-586060. *Mike O'Brien*, T61333/ 088-586085. **Train** Station: T22024, at the top end of John St. Daily trains to **Dublin** and **Waterford**.

Transport

Banks Junction of High St and Friary St, and Parliament St. Money exchange at the tourist office as well. **Communications** Post office: High St. **Internet**: access from next door to the tourist office, from the *Computer Centre* in James St and the *Paris Texas* pub in High St. **Medical services** Hospital: *St Luke's Hospital*, T51133. **Pharmacy**: *White's Pharmacy*, 5 High St, T21328. **Language school** *Kilkenny Language Centre*, Office 6, Cashel Cres, Waterford Rd, Kilkenny, T51441, F51449, klc@iol.ie Summer courses. **Local radio** *Radio Kilkenny* 96.6 FM. Daily 0700-0200.

Directory

County Kilkenny

Around Kilkenny

Historically, the city and the county of Kilkenny prospered because of the gently flowing rivers and their pasture-rich valleys and today a rewarding day or two could be enjoyed exploring the elegant countryside outside the city. The River Nore, which flows through Kilkenny city, is particularly attractive as it winds its tree-lined way through hill and vale in the south of the county, while further to the east the lush valley of the River Barrow competes for the traveller's attention.

From Kilkenny you could travel (by car or bicycle) south on the R700 following the River Nore to Bennettsbridge and Thomastown, and then pick up the N10 at Knocktopher after visiting Jerpoint Abbey. Then make a short detour to visit medieval Kells on the return journey to Kilkenny, although it is close enough to the city to make a pleasant excursion in its own right.

Kells

Phone code: 056
Colour map 4, grid C1

This little village nestles on the banks of a Nore tributary and is only 8 miles (12 km) south of Kilkenny. Not to be confused with its more famous namesake in county Meath, Kells is a showcase for the beauty of the Nore valley. Its lovely stone bridge and ancient watermill are a treat to behold on a summer's day and close by are some of the most captivating monastic ruins you are likely to come across in Ireland.

Kells Priory The priory was founded in 1193 by Augustinians brought over from Cornwall but what you see today dates mostly from the 14th and 15th centuries. The survival of the church, and especially the complete wall with towers enclosing a 2-ha site, creates a more tangible sense of what a medieval settlement was like than most other ruins of this period in the country (including, ironically, Kells in Meath). To the south of the church there are remains of what were the priory's domestic buildings. The entire site is freely open to the public and makes for a better investment of one's time than many a heritage centre that carries an admission charge.

Kilree Round Tower & High Cross The ruins of another monastic site lie just over a mile south of Kells and the way is signposted from Kells Priory. The church is in ruins and there is a well preserved 17th-century tomb in the chancel, but what dominates the site is a 95-ft-high (29 m) round tower, minus its top. In a field just to the west of the tower there stands a faded High Cross that is thought to date back to the ninth century. It is hard to make out any of the original pictorial representations, although various geometric patterns can be traced and on the east face a stag-hunting scene with a chariot has been discerned. The story that the cross commemorates Niall Caille, a king of Ireland who drowned while trying to save a squire, is apparently a piece of blarney.

Bennettsbridge

Phone code: 056
Colour map 4, grid C1

The main attraction in the village of Bennettsbridge is two of the country's finest pottery workshops. **Stoneware Jackson Pottery** is just north of the village and the workshop can be viewed from a relaxing garden setting before you are tempted to make a purchase in the showroom. There is also a modest selection of seconds on sale. ■ *T27175. Mon-Sat, 0930-1800.*

County Kilkenny

Nicholas Mosse Pottery is based around an old mill by the river and water from the Nore is used to generate the electricity for firing the pots, which are brightly coloured earthenware with traditional, floral-style motifs. Seconds are for sale. ■ *T27505, www.nicholasmosse.com Sep-Jun, Mon-Sat, 1000-1800; Jul-Aug, Mon-Sat, 1000-1800, Sun, 1330-1700.*

For snacks or light lunches there is a coffee shop in Nicholas Mosse, and in the village there is the *Café Nore*, opening from noon to 1700. Bennettsbridge is also home to the *Nore Valley Caravan & Camping Park*, T27229, F27748, open from Mar-Oct. Coming from Kilkenny turn right just before the bridge in Bennettsbridge.

Sleeping & eating

Thomastown

Situated on the busy Dublin to Waterford N9 road, but worth considering as a place to rest for a drink or meal either before or after visiting Jerpoint Abbey and nearby Kilfane. In town there are fragmentary ruins of the wall that enclosed this medieval settlement and the uninteresting ruins of a 13th-century church with only the north aisle and parts of the foundation still to be seen.

Phone code: 056
Colour map 4, grid C1

Getting there Dublin to Waterford buses, 5 a day, stop in Thomastown, outside O'Keefe's supermarket. As too do the twice daily Waterford to Longford buses, and this service also connects Thomastown with Kilkenny and Athlone. On Thu only the local 374 New Ross to Kilkenny service travels via Inistioge, Thomastown and Bennettsbridge. The town is also serviced by the Dublin to Waterford railway line.

Ins & outs

This impressive Cistercian abbey, one of the best monastic ruins in the country, was founded between 1163 and 1165. After the Dissolution of the Monasteries in 1540 it was leased to the earls of Ormond. The church retains Romanesque features, although the arches in the aisles are recognizably Gothic, and there are some excellently preserved sculptured tombs. These include a bishop who died in 1202 and two knights from the late 13th century. There is also a harper and his wife, one of only 2 civilian effigies from the 16th century remaining in Ireland. The real highlight, however, is the cloister that dates from the 15th century and delights the eye with a very lively array of sculptured knights, saints and other figures. ■ *T24623. Open daily Jun-13th Sep, 0930-1830; 14th Sep-Oct daily, 1000-1700; Mar-May, daily, 1000-1700; Nov, daily, 1000-1800. €2.50. Dúchas site. Guided tours available. 1½ miles (2.5 km) southwest of Thomastown on the N9.*

Jerpoint Abbey

Kilfane, a small village just north of Thomastown on the N9 road, is signposted to the right just before the Long Man pub. It is noteworthy for its ruined 14th-century church. Inside you will be surprised by the imposing, big-ger-than-life effigy of a medieval knight. With his legs crossed, wearing a fine suit of chain mail, spurs and accompanied by his trusty shield, this is Thomas de Cantwell, who died some time around 1320. History is suddenly brought to life by this animated Norman conqueror who displays in his figure and accoutre-ments the daunting new forces that came from across the water to subdue the native Irish. At one time the church was used as a school and the story goes that naughty scholars were chastised by being forced to kiss the forbidding lips of this conquering Norman.

Kilfane

Further along the road that leads to Kilfane church, less than two miles (3 km) from Thomastown, **Kilfane Glen and Waterfall** is a woodland garden dating from the late 18th century. There are paths to stroll along, a hermit's grotto, a waterfall and one of those little villas with an affectation of rusticity

County Kilkenny

known as a *cottage ornée*. These diversions add to the charms of the planted woods and invite a leisurely picnic on a good day. ■ *T24558. May-late Sep, Sun, 1400-1800; Jul and Aug, daily, 1100-1800. €5. Tea-shop.*

Sleeping
Price codes: see inside front cover

LL *Mount Juliet Estate*, Thomastown, T73000, www.mountjuliet.com Hotel and self-styled sporting estate beside the river, with rooms in the 18th-century house or adjoining lodges. Golfing, fishing, shooting, archery, tennis and an equestrian centre available. The Georgian, high-ceilinged Lady Helen dining room at the Mount Juliet Estate is justly renowned for classic dishes using home-grown vegetables, herbs, and Nore salmon. Dinner daily, lunch only on Sun. **B** *Abbey House*, Jerpoint Abbey, T24166, F24192. A delightful period house directly opposite the abbey, with a spacious lounge and a patio by the river, offering B&B. Closed at Christmas. **B** *Carrickmourne House*, New Ross Rd, T/F24124. B&B but no evening meals. Closed at Christmas.

Eating

Dinner at *Mount Juliet Estate* is definitely in the expensive price range. Coming into the village from Bennettsbridge, *The Watergarden* on your left is fine for coffee and snacks. You can also eat at the pubs in Thomastown and *Carrolls*, Logan St, T24273, is worth a visit because as well as serving doorstep sandwiches and Irish stew there is a beer garden and sessions of traditional music. Outside of town, on the N9 Dublin road, the *Long Man of Kilfane*, T24774, has a large bar area serving food until 2200.

Inistioge

Phone code: 056
Colour map 4, grid C1

This quaint little village, pronounced 'Inisteeg', is on the west bank of the Nore and the agreeable 18th-century, 10-arched bridge adds considerably to its charms. The photogenic quality is further enhanced by an ancient-looking church and neat lime trees in a village square from which spidery lanes radiate. Such an evocation of the past makes it not surprising that a number of films have used the location, including *Widow's Peak* in 1993. Inistioge derives its name from the Tighes, and their family seat was in a grand 18th-century house that was burned down in 1922. The Tighes left for England when the War of Independence broke out and later the Black and Tans used it as a local headquarters. The empty house was burned down during the civil war. What was the Tighe demesne, Woodstock Park, is now the state-owned **Woodtsock Gardens**, T52699, and open to the public all year round. There are various walking trails and picnic areas and an admission charge may have been introduced by the time of your visit.

Mount Brandon stands 1,693 ft (519 m) high and lies to the northeast of Inistioge and a road leads through the mountain to the village of Graiguenamanagh.

Sleeping
Price codes: see inside front cover

A *Cullintra House*, The Rower, Inistioge, T051-423614. An old farmhouse at the foot of Mount Brandon where dinner, €21, is announced with a bell at 2100. **B** *Ashville*, Kilmacshane, Inistioge, T58460. B&B but no evening meals. Open Mar-Oct. Situated on the Kilkenny to Rosslare road. **B** *Nore Valley Villa*, Inistioge, T/F58418. Modern house, in the village.

Eating

In addition to the above, *The School House Café* is by the river and serves snacks and standard light meals during the summer. For a culinary adventure try *The Motte*, Plas Newydd Lodge, Inistioge, T58655. Flowers on the table, intimate lighting and superb food. Dinner only, closed Mon, set dinner around €30.

Graiguenamanagh

The small town of Graiguenamanagh ('the granary of the monks'), is attractively situated on the banks of the River Barrow, and has another of those pleasing 18th-century arched bridges and with your own transport the town is easily reached from Inistioge. The attraction of Graiguenamanagh, apart from the beauty of the location and pleasant walks along the riverside using the South Leinster waymarked route (see below), is the Cistercian abbey in the town.

Phone code: 0503
Colour map 4, grid C2

Founded in 1207 by William Marshall, Earl of Pembroke, and well-preserved after a restoration project in the 1970s for parts of it to be still in use today. Inside the church, there is a fine doorway from the early 13th century that is considered to be one of the best examples of its type to have survived the Dissolution of the Monasteries. Equally eye-catching is an effigy of a knight from the same period and nearby a glass panel reveals some authentic fleur-de-lys tiling of the 13th century, the present floor of the church being over 6½ ft (2 m) above its original level. Outside the church there are two high crosses and the nearby **Abbey Centre** houses a modest exhibition on the abbey.

Duiske Abbey

AL *Waterside*, The Quay, T24246, www.watersideguesthouse.com All rooms overlook the river in this highly picturesque building; the midweek package for 2 nights B&B and 1 dinner is worth considering. **B** *Woodside*, Ballynakill, south of Graiguenamanagh, T24765. B&B between Mar and Oct. A modern house.

Sleeping
Price codes:
see inside
front cover

Waterside, T24246, is a restaurant in a restored 19th-century corn store overlooking the river. An evening meal here is over €25. The *Café Duiske*, T24986, opposite the abbey at the moment but may be moving inside. Quality light meals and dinner, closed Tue. Town bars such as the *Anchor*, Main St, T24207, serve pub food.

Eating

The South Leinster Way

The total length of this long-distance waymarked walk is 62 miles (100 km), starting at Kildavin on the slopes of Mount Leinster in County Carlow and finishing at Carrick-on-Suir in County Tipperary. It takes four to five days to complete the journey and the first day's walk ends in Borris on the border between Carlow and Kilkenny. The second day is a very manageable 8 miles (13 km), which mostly follows a towpath alongside the River Barrow as far as Graiguenamanagh. The distance on the third day is similar and skirts Brandon Hill before reaching the lovely village of Inistioge. The fourth day, 12 miles (20 km) in length, follows the river and uses forest roads before ending in the village of Mullinavat in southern Kilkenny. The last day's walking crosses into Tipperary over farmland a lot of the way but also using roads in places.

EastWest Mapping produce the *South Leinster Way Map Guide* and *Ordnance Survey* maps Nos 68, 75 and 76 are needed to cover the whole walk. Maps and information are available from the tourist office in Carlow (see page 212) or Kilkenny (see page 200).

Mapping &
information

North of Kilkenny

Castlecomer is the main town in the north of the county, but there are few places of interest either in the town or the surrounding area and most visitors to the county content themselves with a trip to Dunmore Cave, which is only a few kilometres north of Kilkenny. Castlecomer rose to local prominence after

Castlecomer
Colour map 4, grid B1

County Kilkenny

the discovery of anthracite in the 17th century and in the 1798 uprising (see page 647) the town was captured by insurgents led by Father John Murphy. All that remains of the Anglo-Norman castle that gave the town its name is a mound, so from a sightseeing point of view there is little point in making the journey here from Kilkenny.

Dunmore Cave This site consists of limestone caverns and impressive calcite formations. There is an exhibition centre and a compulsory guided tour that lasts about 45 minutes. Geology aside, there is a reference in Irish sources to a Viking massacre at the cave in the year 928 and excavations in the 1970s did reveal the skeletons of nearly 50 women and children. ■ *Ballyfoyle. T0503-67726. Mid Jun-mid Sep, daily, 1000-1900; mid Mar-mid-Jun and mid Sep-Oct, daily 1000-1700. €2.50. Dúchas site. Seven miles (10 km) from Kilkenny and signposted off the N78.*

County Carlow

Carlow and around

Phone code: 0503
Colour map 4,
grid B1 & 2

Carlow town is too easily dismissed as a one-street town, but the main drag, besides having plenty of affordable places to eat, boasts a buzzing nightlife with lots of pubs offering live music. There is also an absolutely superb restaurant – *Danette's Feast* (see next page) – just a couple of miles away. The town has a long history, being for centuries an Anglo-Norman base perched at the dangerous interface between Gaelic Ireland and the Pale, and it's regrettable there is so little to see beyond the crumbling remains of Carlow Castle in Castle Street.

There might be a little more to see here had it not been for the crazy Dr Middleton who blew up most of the castle in 1814, in order to make space for a lunatic asylum. Far more interesting to look at, and well worth seeking out, is the courthouse at the top end of Dublin Street. Most of Ireland's most impressive courthouses were built just before and after the 1798 insurrection – hardly a coincidence – and the Greek style of architecture was highly popular. Perhaps ancient Athens conjured up a suitable image of the rule of law because the Carlow courthouse, designed by William Morrison in 1830, is an unashamed copy of the Parthenon. There is a small **County Carlow Museum** in the town hall on Centaur Street. ■ *T40730. Year-round, Tue-Fri 1100-1700, Sat and Sun 1400-1700. €2.*

One way to enjoy what Carlow has to offer is by joining the new **guided town tours**, starting from the tourist office (see below). ■ *T30411. Mid-Apr to mid-Oct, Tue, Thu and Sat 1430. €3.50.*

The **tourist office** is on Bridewell Lane, T31554. Open from May-Sep, Mon-Sat 1000-1730; Jan-Apr and Oct-Dec, Mon-Fri 1000-1700.

Browneshill dolmen Weighing in at 100 tons as the heavyweight champion of Europe, the capstone of this dolmen is now stuck in the earth at one end while resting on three stones at the other. As the construction dates back to around 2500BCE, the individual who occasioned this feat of engineering and toil is now completely lost to time. The dolmen is beside a car-park, just two miles (3 km) from town on the R726 road to Hacketstown.

AL *Barrowville Town House*, Kilkenny Rd, T43324, www.barrowvillehouse.com
Within walking distance of town, this above-average guesthouse serves a good break-
fast from a conservatory overlooking gardens. **B** *Borlum House*, Kilkenny Rd, T41747.
Ivy-clad old coaching inn set amidst secluded gardens. **C-D** *Otterholt Riverside Lodge*,
Kilkenny Rd, T30404. Open all year, an IHH hostel with nearly 40 beds and a few private
rooms that push the room rates into the higher price category. **D** *Verona Hostel*,
Pembroke St, T31700/31846. An IHO place, also open all year. 10 beds including 2 private rooms. Camping is also possible, and meals can be arranged and bicycles hired.

Sleeping
*Price codes:
see inside
front cover*

You will quickly realize where *The Beams Restaurant*, 59 Dublin St, T31824, gets its
name from once inside the door, and the menu of decidedly French-style Irish cuisine
should not disappoint. Expect to pay around €35 for dinner, closed Sun. Tullow St has
a whole range of places to eat from good bar food at *Scragg's Alley* to a very exotic
range of dishes upstairs in the same place at *Fitzoraldo's*, T42233, where dinner is
around €23. In the arcade in Tullow St is *Brook's Café Bar* with a very modern themed
interior and lots of Californian options. Near the SuperValu supermarket, the *Plough
Bar* has its own restaurant and, across the road, *Reddy's*, 67 Tullow St, T42224, also provides meals. *Buzz's*, 7 Tullow St, T43307, serves food and alcohol on cast iron tables on
wooden floors and lives up to its name. In Dublin St the very down to earth *Pepper Pot*
does breakfasts and sensible lunches. For a memorable Epicurean experience book a
table at *Danette's Feast*, Urglin Glebe, T40817, where the quality of the food is
matched by what must be the best background music to be heard in any restaurant in
Ireland. The chef, who happens to be a musician, cooks imaginatively (especially Mexican food) with superb vegetarian options, organic vegetables and a margarita sorbet
to die for. Dinner is around €35, Wed-Sat, and lunch on Sun. Take the Hackettstown
road from Carlow for 2 miles and turn left at the Burma garage.

Eating

Carlow has a booming nightlife with lots of trendy places opening up and music everywhere. For traditional music you could try *Ewings*, Haymarket, T31138, next to the
town hall or *The Quays* in the same street. *The Castle*, 24 Governey Sq, T41200, has
music on Fri nights and *The Barge*, Castle Hill, also has music and bar food.

Pubs & music

Bicycle *Coleman Cycles* 19 Dublin St, T31273. Bike hire. **Bus** *Bus Éireann*, T31633,
has daily services to **Dublin**, **Kilkenny** and **Waterford**. **Taxi** *Tierney's* T33339.
Train **Station** at Railway Rd, T31633. A 20-min walk from the town centre. Carlow is
on the **Dublin** to **Waterford** line. **Train** Trains go to **Dublin** 9 times a day, 3 on Sun,
while trains leave for **Waterford** 6 times a day, 4 on Sun.

Transport

Banks Green Lane, Tullow St, Court Pl. **Communications** Post office: Bridewell Lane.

Directory

County Laois

Around Portlaoise

Travellers always used to pass through Portlaoise ('Portleash'), because it is
on the major Dublin to south and southwest of Ireland route, and dutifully
take note of the town's maximum security prison and its Ulster-style concrete
observation posts at the east end of the main road. With a modern bypass,
even that dubious claim to fame will pass unnoticed, but at least the town
should benefit from the decline in heavy traffic. There is a **tourist office** in the
centre of the town, T21178. Open May-Sep, Mon-Sat, 1000-1800.

*Phone code: 0502
Colour map 2,
grid C6 &
colour map 4,
grid B1*

Rock of Dunamase The Rock of Dunamase, a few miles outside of town, is the best reason for lingering around Portlaoise, for although not much remains of the castle that once stood there, the site is extraordinarily well situated and on a fine day there are superb views of the surrounding countryside from atop the mound. An Iron Age fort predates the castle, which was built some time around the end of the 12th century and changed hands between Irish and English lords more than once before Cromwellian forces took it apart in 1650. It was briefly restored as a residence but little now remains of what must have been a spectacularly sited fortress. ■ *Open access. 3 miles (5 km) east of Portlaoise on the N80 road to Stradbally.*

Stradbally The town of Stradbally will interest steam train buffs, being home to a Guinness Brewery steam locomotive of 1895 that runs to Dublin half a dozen times each year. The town is on the N80 road west of the Rock of Dunamase. Its **Steam Museum** has a collection of traction engines. ■ *Easter-Oct, Mon-Fri 1100-1300 and 1400-1600. €2.*

Emo Court An impressive example of neo-classical architecture, Emo Court was designed in 1790 by James Gandon for the first earl of Portarlington but not completed until 1874. It was run as a novitiate by the Jesuits until the 1960s and is now open to the public. Combine a visit with a walk through the extensive grounds. ■ *T26573. Mid Jun-mid Sep, daily, 1000-1800. Guided tours. €3, free admission to Garden. Dúchas site. 1½ miles (2½ km) from Emo, 7 miles (13 km) from Portlaoise, and signposted off the Kildare to Portlaoise N7 road.*

Mountmellick Six miles (10 km) north of Portlaoise, Mountmellick was founded by Quakers in the 17th century and a number of Georgian houses remain from its heyday in the late 18th century, when the famed Mountmellick linen was exported by canal to Dublin and beyond. There is a small heritage centre, T24525, on the Portlaoise road just outside of town.

About 8 miles (12 km) west of Portlaoise the picturesque little village of **Coolrain** is nestled in the foot of the Slieve Bloom Mountains and bicycles can be hired from *The Thatched Village Inn*, T35277, which will also suggest routes and provide maps for trips in the local uncrowded roads. **Accommodation** is available in a restored thatched cottage next to and belonging to the inn, T35216, and the pub serves meals throughout the day. Sessions of set dancing and traditional music also take place here.

The Slieve Bloom Way This 2-day energetic walk covers 51 km (32 miles) with sweeping views of the Slieve Bloom Mountains as the Way makes its way through moors, valleys and forests. However, it is a Way that requires planning because of the limited public transport in the area and the need to book accommodation in advance.

For a one-day excursion covering part of the Way consider parking on the R422 between Mountmellick and Clonaslee and heading off for a day's exhilarating walk with a picnic. On the south side of the mountains, **B** *Conlán House*, Killanure, Mountrath, on the R440 road, is a B&B with good information on the Way, and you can also enquire here about guided walks.

Mapping and information *Ordnance Survey* map No 54 in the Discovery series covers the Way, and *EastWest Mapping* publish *The Slieve Bloom Way Map Guide* using the same 1:50,000 scale. There is also a booklet published by the local council, *Slieve Bloom Environment Park*, available from the tourist office in Portlaoise, and see page 677 for walking guides that cover the Way.

B *O'Loughlin's Hotel*, Main St, Portlaoise, T21305. Small, well run hotel in the centre of town, musical entertainment many evenings. **D** *Traditional Farm Hostel*, Farren House, Ballacolla, Portlaoise, T34032, F34008. IHH. Open all year. 5 private rooms at €1.43 per person. Good amenities including bicycle hire and space for camping.

Sleeping
Price codes:
see inside
front cover

Portlaoise town centre is littered with pubs serving food and at *O'Loughlin's Hotel*, Main St, T21305, food is served from 0800 until 2100, including à la carte in the restaurant. Better, though, is *The Kitchen & Foodhall*, Hynds Sq, T62061, serving delicious home-cooked food for daily lunches and dinner from Thu to Sat.

The *Montague Hotel*, Emo, T26154, serves a carvery lunch and evening meals in the Maple Room restaurant. The *Gandon Inn*, Emo, T26622, has 2 bars, a restaurant and accommodation.

Eating

Bus Buses from most parts of the country pass through Portlaoise, especially routes between **Dublin** and the south and southwest of the country, T01-836611, **Trains** T21303. Services to and from **Dublin** and **Cork**, **Limerick**, **Tralee** and **Tipperary** stop in Portlaoise.

Transport

Abbeyleix and around

Abbeyleix, about 10 miles (16 km) south of Portlaoise, has an interesting story to tell. It grew up around a 12th-century Cistercian abbey, but 600 years later the local landlord, Viscount de Vesci, relocated the village to its present site and planned the layout that is such an attractive part of the modern town. The country house of de Vesci, **Abbeyleix House**, outside of town on the Rathdowney road, was built by James Wyatt and remodelled in the Victorian age, but it remains closed to the public apart from the occasional opening of the gardens. Worth admiring is the architecture of the town's **Bank of Ireland**, replete with mullioned windows, classical columns, a corner oriel and a copper-domed tower, all built at the beginning of the 20th century. *Morrissey's*, half-pub and half-shop on Main St, Abbeyleix, T31233, is well known to discerning travellers on the Cork-Dublin run who value a place to rest and relax without being forced to listen to the blather of radio phone-ins or crass music. It's been in the same family since 1775, and with ancient shelves packed with old biscuit tins and a pot belly stove there is little to suggest that much has changed since. The perfect place for a quiet pint or a cup of Morrissey's own special brand tea.

Phone code: 0502
Colour map 4,
grid B1

County Laois

Off Main St, this was one of the two schools that de Vesci had built, and its interesting and well presented displays are worth a look. With a coffee shop, tourist information and a craft shop, it's worth considering as a place to stop when travelling between Dublin and Cork. ■ *T31653, www.laois.local.ie/abbeyleix Mar-Oct, Mon-Sat, 1000-1800, Sun, 1300-1800; Nov-Feb, shorter hrs. €3*

Heritage House

Heywook House has a noted garden designed by Edwin Lutyens and thought to have been landscaped by Gertrude Jekyll, now well restored and open to the public. The house itself was destroyed by fire in 1960 and nothing of it remains. Picturesquely framed views of inland Ireland can be seen through the *oeil-de-boeuf* windows in Lutyens' sunken terrace. ■ *Ballinakill, T33563/ 056-21450. Open during daylight hrs. Tours can be arranged by telephoning in advance. Free. 4 miles (7 km) southeast of Abbeyleix off the R432 road to Ballinakill.*

Heywood House

Sleeping
*Price codes:
see inside
front cover*

A *Preston House*, Main St, Abbeyleix, T/F31432, has 4 large bedrooms handsomely furnished with antiques and makes canny use of the available space to incorporate modern facilities. **AL** *Castle Arms Hotel*, The Square, Durrow, T/F36117, has 10 bedrooms and this conventional, family-run hotel is one of the few places to stay in Durrow. The *Traditional Farm Hostel*, (see under Portlaoise) is only a couple of miles from Durrow on the R434.

Eating

It is well worth checking out creeper-covered *Preston House* restaurant in Main St. Tasty scones and home-made preserves in the morning, while the lunch menu includes appetizing chowder with brown bread and delicious vegetarian dishes. Dinner (not on Mon) is good value. In Durrow the choice is disappointing: standard hotel food at the *Castle Arms* or more interesting choices at the modest *Copper Kettle* in The Square.

Transport

Bus *Bus Éireann*'s Dublin to Cork service stops in Abbeyleix 3 times a day, twice on Sun.

County Kildare

Castletown House, Maynooth and around

*Phone code: 01
Colour map 4
grid A2*

Head due west from Dublin's city centre for about 12 miles (19 km) – though it will seem a lot longer if you get caught in rush-hour traffic – and a mixed landscape of rolling countryside and suburban dwellings awaits you. This is modern Ireland, depressingly modern at times, and the key sights can be comfortably taken in on a day trip.

**Castletown
House**

Ease of access from Dublin, and its reopening in 1999 after a long period of closure, increases the appeal of a visit to Ireland's largest and architecturally most important country house. Castletown House was built around 1722 for William Conolly, the Speaker of the Irish House of Commons. He spared no expense in employing the Italian architect Alessandro Galilei, although the work was completed by Edward Lovett Pearce, an Irish Italophile architect, and others. It is the finest expression of the Palladian style to be found in the country and this can first be appreciated by simply standing outside and admiring the symmetry of the façade. The philosopher Bishop Berkeley was more aware of the type of stone that went into its building, "fine wrought stone, harder and better coloured than the [English] Portland" stone, and like other Ascendancy figures rejoiced at what he saw as an expression of Irish culture.

Conolly died before the house was finished, but his wife lived for another 23 years and in 1740 she commissioned the building of a monumental **folly** in the grounds as a way of providing relief to the local poor. Before she died in 1752, she had a tent put up on the lawn so that she could admire her home for the last time. She died childless and the house ended up with Conolly's grand-nephew whose wife, the English Lady Louisa, daughter of the Duke of Richmond, was responsible for much of the interior decoration. Some of her ideas, like the Pompeii-style decorations on the walls, can be seen in the most distinctive room, the Long Gallery on the first floor. She also created the Print Room, the last surviving example of its kind in Ireland. ■ *Celbridge, T6288252. 15 Apr-Sep, Mon-Fri, 1000-1800, Sat-Sun, 1300-1800. Same times in Oct except the house closes at 1700. Nov, Sun, 1300-1700. Guided tours. €3.80. Dúchas site. 12 miles (20 km) from the centre of Dublin on the R403; Bus No 67/67A from Middle Abbey St, and No 66X.*

William Conolly

William Conolly (1662-1729), regarded in his time as the richest commoner in Ireland, is said to have made his money by dealing in land exchanges in the tumultuous years following the Battle of the Boyne; hence the snobbish contempt of men like Sir John St Leger who wrote in 1717, "our quality and old gentry are much offended at Mr Conolly's being one of them; this gentleman was lately an attorney, his father keeping an ale-house in the north of Ireland… but by making long wills and good bargains he is now reported to be worth eight thousand a year."

Only three miles (5 km) southwest of Celbridge, the village of Straffan has a **Steam Museum** with working steam engines and a small exhibition about the impact of steam power. The best time to visit is over the holiday weekend at the very beginning of August when an annual Steam Rally brings together a big display of steam engines and working models and an opportunity to ride on the longest established steam-powered narrow gauge railway in Ireland. ■ *Easter to Aug, Tue-Sun, 1400-1800. €4. Café. T25444, and best to telephone first.*

Straffan

Close by is the **Straffan Butterfly Farm**, with its array of colourful butterflies and scary-looking insects and spiders. ■ *Open May-Sep, daily 1200-1800. €4.* Also in Straffan, next to the Steam Museum, is **Lodge Park Walled Garden**, part of a late 18th-century house. ■ *Open Jun and Jul daily except Mon, 1430-1730; Aug, Tue-Fri, 1430-1730. €2.54.*

A famous place to the Irish, the town being home to the country's leading seminary for the training of priests. **Maynooth College** was founded in 1795, at a time when the government wanted the support of moderate Catholics, and Augustus Pugin was commissioned to design the college; building began in 1847. Architecturally, it is not a particularly interesting example of Victorian Gothic and there is little here to engage your attention. University colleges are now based here and they account for the majority of students seen about the place; young men actually studying for the priesthood are an endangered species. At the college entrance stand the ruins of Maynooth Castle, a stronghold of the Norman Fitzgerald family, the Earls of Kildare. It was treacherously taken in 1535 after a rebellion by its owner, 'Silken Thomas', the son of the ninth Earl of Kildare, against the English, and abandoned some time around 1656.

Maynooth
Christopher Paris, the constable of Maynooth Castle in 1535, was bribed into betraying it with a promise of leniency but, nevertheless, was executed afterwards. The pardon of Maynooth' became an ironic term for such breaches of trust

These are more interesting than Maynooth, and only 4 miles (6.5 km) away. Here you will find what is claimed to be the only surviving example in Ireland or England of the mid-18th century style of a *ferme ornée*. A circular walk links 10 follies, with gazebos along the way and a tiny island with a Greek-style temple. ■ *Kilcock, T6287354. Open May-Sep, daily, 1200-1800. €4.12. West of Maynooth on the N4. Bus No 66 from Middle Abbey St, Dublin.*

Larchill Arcadian Gardens

LL *Moyglare Manor*, Maynooth, T6286351, www.moyglaremanor.ie The nearest country house to Dublin airport, this is the place to make your first or very last stop in Ireland a memorable one. Antique furniture, portraits and gilt-framed mirrors everywhere, rooms with 4-poster beds and a very good restaurant. **B** *Rosturk House*, Old Rail Park Lane, Maynooth, T6285310, F6290021. One mile (1.6 km) from the college and close to the train station, this is one of the better-value B&Bs in this well heeled part of the country.

Sleeping
Price codes: see inside front cover

County Kildare

Eating *Moyglare Manor Restaurant*, Maynooth, T6286351. Enjoy pre-dinner drinks in an antique-laden room with a turf fire while perusing a non-nonsense, refreshingly direct menu devoid of poncy nomenclature. A 4-course dinner is around €46, live piano music in the background and a mostly French wine list that ranges from a €119 Merlot to a €1900 dessert wine.

The Castle Restaurant, T6288157, in the Barberstown Castle hotel in Straffan, wins hands down for character and atmosphere. Dining tables occupy whitewashed rooms in a basement setting with low lighting and the food includes sumptuous seafood and satisfying vegetarian dishes. Lunch is around €23 and dinner €42.

The Byerley Turk, T6017200, in the Kildare Hotel & Country Club in Straffan, specializes in French cuisine and does it with classical panache: crisp white linen tablecloths and enough fine china, crystal and silver around your table to make you feel rich enough to afford one of the racehorses painted and framed on the walls.

Back in Maynooth, the *Glenroyal Hotel* also has a decent restaurant and a carvery and a bar serving food. Pubs in Maynooth offer the usual pub food.

Transport **Bus** Bus No 67/67A from Middle Abbey St, and No 66X, connect Maynooth and **Dublin**. Many of the *Bus Éireann* services to **Galway** and **Sligo** also make a stop, T01-8366111. **Train** Suburban and main line trains stop at Maynooth station, T6285509.

Kildare Town and around

Phone code: 045
Colour map 4,
grid B2

Try to avoid a drive between Kildare Town and Dublin during the morning or evening rush hours. There is a motorway, the M7, for a stretch of the way, but traffic snarls are still very common. Another tip is not to bother stopping at Naas (pronounced 'nace') unless there is a desperate need to do some shopping or grab a bite to eat in one of the pubs. The county town has little else to recommend it, unlike the pretty and prosperous little town of Kildare.

Kildare This town is forever associated with the legendary St Brigid, who by the middle of the seventh century already had a church and shrine dedicated to her here. Very little is known about her life and there is reason to think that worship of St Brigid evolved from the cult of an earlier pagan goddess; by the ninth century she was the major saint in Ireland. She remains a very popular figure and St Brigid's Cross, easily crafted from reeds, is commonly found in souvenir shops.

The Protestant Cathedral of St Brigid The cathedral dates back to 1243. It was largely destroyed in the 17th century but rebuilt around 1875, following the original cruciform structure with a dose of Victorian romanticism thrown in for good measure. The adjoining **round tower** has an elaborate, Romanesque doorway and battlements added during the 19th-century rebuilding work on the cathedral. ■ *May-Sep, Mon-Sat, 1000-1300 and 1400-1700, Sun, 1400-1700. €2.54.*

The Curragh Some 2,000 ha of land, dedicated to dozens of studs and a famous racecourse, constitute the Curragh. The word itself means 'racecourse' though the origins of the area's association with horses is lost in time but may have something to do with its being flat and fertile or something to do with soil which builds strong bones in horses. Organized horseracing has been taking place uninterruptedly from at least the 18th century, and in the 19th century the British established a training camp here, which developed into a permanent military base. Visitors cannot just wander around the private studs– remember this is a multi-million pound business– but the government-owned **National Stud** is open to the public, includes a museum as well as tours of the stables and is within walking

Race meetings at the Curragh

Big flat races include the 2,000 and 1,000
Guineas towards the end of May, the Irish
Derby and the Pretty Polly Stakes towards
the end of June, the Irish Oaks in early July,
the Moyglare Stud Stakes in early
September, the Irish Leger and the Aga
Khan Studs National Stakes in

mid-September. Bord Fáilte issue more
information and their annual Calendar of
Events booklet includes a racing calendar.
For big meetings at the Curragh, T441205,
there are often special bus and train
services running to and from Dublin;
T01-8302222/8366111 for transport details.

distance of Kildare town. ■ *T521617. Mid-Feb to mid-Nov, daily 0930-1800.*
South of Kildare town. €6.35 joint ticket with Japanese Gardens.

It seems an unlikely mix but the eccentric Colonel William Hall Walker, who
established what is now the National Stud in 1900, also had an area of bog
drained and brought in two Japanese gardeners to landscape the place. The
resulting Japanese Gardens is an odd philosophical/garden tour based around
various stages of male life from birth to the hereafter. ■ *See the Curragh.*

Japanese Gardens

L *Martinstown House*, the Curragh, T441269. Part of a large farm, B&B is not exactly at
giveaway prices, but this is a welcoming house that has been recommended by visitors who stayed here. **B** *Mount Ruadhan*, Old Rd, Southgreen, T521637. Typical modern bungalow signposted at the traffic lights in Kildare.

Sleeping
Price codes:
see inside
front cover

Restaurant and bar food is available in the *Curragh Lodge Hotel* and in the town square
Silken Thomas, T521264, is a popular pub with decent food and a restaurant that
opens for lunch and dinner every day.

Eating

Bus Numerous *Bus Éireann* services between Kildare and **Dublin**, T01-8366111, taking about 1hr 20 mins. **Train** Kildare, T21224, is on the main route from **Dublin** to the
west and southwest, so there are good connections with **Ballina**, **Westport**, **Galway**,
Ennis, **Tralee**, **Cork** and **Waterford**.

Transport

South Kildare

Ballitore and around

The Quaker origins of the village of Ballitore are remembered in the **Ballitore**
Quaker Museum, in the centre of the village, and the walled Quaker cemetery
is also worth a visit. The most famous product of a Quaker education in Ireland is the political thinker Edmund Burke (1729-97), and he attended the
village school, which was run by an ancestor of Ernest Shackleton of Antarctic
fame. Just outside of Ballitore, within walking distance and signposted from
the centre, is the functioning **Crookstown Mill**. ■ *Museum: Mon-Sat*
1100-1800. Mill: All year, daily 1000-1800. €3.

Ballitore
Phone code: 0507
Colour map 4, grid B2

South of Ballitore, on the N9, this village would hardly merit attention were it
not for the **Moone High Cross** on the site of an Early Christian monastery just
to the west of the village. The highly attractive High Cross shows Daniel, the sacrifice of Isaac, Adam and Eve, and the Crucifixion on the east side, the Apostles on
the west side, various miracles on the south and two saints breaking bread in the

Moone
Phone code: 0507
Colour map 4, grid B2

County Kildare

Canals – Royal and Grand

*Linking Dublin with the River Shannon through 44 locks, and with a branch that heads south to Waterford, the Grand Canal was built between 1756 and 1804 and stayed in operation until 1960. It is now managed by Dúchas whose Waterways Visitor Centre in Dublin provides information on its history. Cruises are available through **Celtic Canal Cruises** (see page 224). Dúchas manages the Royal*

*Canal as well, which also links Dublin with the River Shannon and which is currently in the process of being cleaned up. Its towpaths are being restored for walkers at the same time. **Leisureways Holidays**, T01-8225034, have boats for hire.*

Now that the Shannon to Erne Waterway is running (see page 635), it is possible to travel from Belturbet in Fermanagh to Dublin.

---

desert on the north side. A few miles south, *Irish Pewter Mill* has a casting room open to the public and a factory shop. ■ *Shop: T24164. Mon-Fri, 1000-1630.*

Athy
Phone code: 0507
Colour map 4,
grid B1/2

The town of Athy (pronounced 'a-thigh'), west of Ballitore, has the potential to make itself far more interesting to visitors and the **heritage centre** in the 18th-century town hall gives a good idea of why this is so. This local museum highlights the past history of Athy in relation to major events such as the 1798 uprising and the explorer Ernest Shackleton. ■ *T33075. Mar-Oct, Mon-Sat, 1000-1800, Sun, 1400-1800. Shorter hrs in winter. €2.54.*

To find out more about the locality, including details of local walks along the Grand Canal (see box), visit the **tourist office** in the Town Hall. T31859.

Castledermot
Phone code: 0503
Colour map 4,
grid B2

South of Ballitore, on the N9, is Castledermot, where there is a surprisingly large amount to see. As you come into town down Main Street there are reminders of an ecclesiastical past that goes back to a monastery founded by St Dermot and raided by the Vikings in 841. What stands today is a remarkable Romanesque doorway, a round tower and two fine granite crosses. Nearby Kilkea Castle (see 'Sleeping' below), though originally built in 1180, has been substantially modified and restored between the 17th and 20th centuries. At the southern end of town stand the remains of a Franciscan friary founded in the early 14th century and suppressed in 1541. ■ *A caretaker lives next door and will open the gates on request.*

Sleeping
Price codes:
see inside
front cover

LL *Kilkea Castle*, Castledermot, T45156, www.kilkeacastle.ie The oldest inhabited castle in Ireland, this hotel has installed an indoor pool and gym and an 18-hole golf course around itself. **AL** *Tonlegee House & Restaurant*, Athy, T/F31473. Five mins outside of town and signposted off the Kilkenny Rd. **B** *The Rath House*, Moone, T24133. L-shaped bungalow with 4 bedrooms, including a single. **B** *Woodcourte House*, Moone, Athy, T24167. B&B in a large country house and with the option of an evening meal for €20.

Eating
Pubs in Athy
serve bar food

Dinner in Kilkea Castle's *D'Lacy's Restaurant*, T45156, is a grand affair and worth making a reservation for. Dinner is around €40 and diners can enjoy splendid views from the dining room and excellent food using local produce and fresh vegetables from the hotel's garden. The roast of the day rarely disappoints and there is a terrace for drinks before or after meals. *Tonlegee House & Restaurant*, T31473, is a fine restaurant for anyone wishing to tuck into local Kildare lamb. Quail and wild mushroom pie with Maderia sauce is a house speciality.

Transport

Bus *Bus Éireann* services on the **Dublin–Kilkenny–Clonmel–Cork** route stop in Athy, and Bus No 130 between Dublin and Kilkenny also stops daily in Athy as well as **Moone** and **Castledermot**, T01-8366111.

County Offaly

Clonmacnois

Phone code: 0905
Colour map 2, grid C5

Between the seventh and 12th centuries Clonmacnois was the largest and most important monastic centre in Ireland, developing around the nexus where the River Shannon meets the Eiscir Riada, a 'running ridge' formed at the end of the Ice Age and a legendary boundary dividing Ireland. Founded by St Ciarán in the mid-sixth century, the monastery attracted scholars from all over Europe as well as artists working with stone and metal, and such was its fame that high kings of Ireland were buried here. It also attracted marauders and between the ninth and 12th centuries was plundered some 35 times by Vikings and natives alike. The size and prosperity of Clonmacnois may be gathered from the fact that over 100 houses were destroyed when the Anglo-Normans attacked in 1179. When English forces from Athlone robbed the monastery of everything in 1552 the life of the centre was finally brought to an end.

There are three impressive **High Crosses**, which have been moved inside the Visitors' Centre for safe-keeping, including one that is very unusual due to its probable representation of a non-biblical scene. The **cathedral**, which is not as impressive a building as the name might suggest, was originally built in the early 10th century but sections have been added over the centuries. The other buildings dotted around are the remains of eight churches from the 10th to the 13th centuries but again with additions, some as recent as the 17th century. One of them, the Nun's Church, is to the east of the main centre and well worth seeking out for its Romanesque doorway and chancel arch. Of the two **round towers**, one, O'Rourkes, is named after a high king of Connaught and the other, overlooking the river, is next to one of the eight churches, Teampall (church) Finghin.

Architectural sights

The visitor's centre presents a not very engrossing audio-visual show. There is also a separate tourist information office, *T74134 ▪ Shannonbridge. T74195. Open mid May-mid Sep, daily, 0900-1900; mid Mar-mid May and mid Sep-Oct, daily, 1000-1800; Nov-mid Mar, daily, 1000-1700. €4.40. Dúchas site. Coffee shop. 13 miles (21 km) from Athlone and Ballinasloe, sign-posted from the N62 and the R357.*

Visitor's centre

The Clonmacnois and West Offaly Railway runs on a narrow-gauge line, which trundles a 5-mile (8-km) circular route around the Blackwater Bog. The journey is a surreal one with the forbidding towers of Bord na Móna's (Irish Peat Development Board) peat-fuelled power station reminding you that the bog is being exploited to extinction while it is Bord na Móna that runs the tour and shows a useful video on the flora and fauna that will one day disappear. ▪ *Shannonbridge, T74114. Apr-Oct, daily 1000-1700. Trains leave every hr, on the hr, but try to view the video first. €5. On the R357 Tullamore Rd.*

Clonmacnois & West Offaly Railway

B *Kajon House*, Creevagh, T74191. B&B with the option of an evening meal, about 1 mile from Clonmacnoise, 3 miles (5km) from Shannonbridge. **B-C** *Glenderham House*, Cloghan Rd, Shannonbridge, T/F74205. Modern bungalow family home offering B&B, within walking distance of Shannonbridge.

Sleeping
Price codes: see inside front cover

County Offaly

Eating In Shannonbridge, pub food is available, and while the *Shannonside Diner* serves light meals it is worth trying the food at the new *The Bog Oak*, T74224, for lunch and dinner.

Transport **Bus** There is no *Bus Éireann* service but taxis run from **Athlone** to **Clonmacnois** in the summer; enquire at the tourist office, or the Athlone tourist office, T0902-94630.

Banagher

Phone code: 0509
Colour map 2, grid C5

Banagher is the epicentre of Offaly's new-found identity as a leisure centre for the Midlands and the first place to visit is the **tourist office**, in Crank House, Main St, T51458, which has information on various local places of interest. Open Mar-Oct, Mon-Fri, 0930-2000, Sat-Sun, 0930-1700.

Sleeping
Price codes:
see inside
front cover

A *Brosna Lodge Hotel*, Main St, Banagher, T51350, www.brosnalodge.com Good restaurant and bar in this family-owned hotel. Close to the river. **B** *Lakyle*, Cross, T51566. Open May to Oct. About ½ mile (1 km) outside of town, a 2-storey Georgian-style modern house doing B&B. **D** *Crank House Hostel*, Main St, T/F51458, abguinan@eircom.net. IHH. Open all year. 40 beds and 2 private room for €21. Not as zany as the name suggests, the beds, bathrooms and kitchen are all tip-top.

Eating There is a coffee shop in Crank House, Main St, and a couple of pubs in the town centre worth checking out for their pub fare. Close to the river, *The Vine House*, T51463, has seafood and meat dishes for around €112 while *The Snipes Restaurant* in the *Brosna Lodge Hotel* is a tad more expensive and perhaps a little more interesting.

Transport **Bicycle** *K Donegan*, Main St, T51178. Bike hire. **Bus** *Bus Éireann*'s **Dublin** to **Birr** service stops daily in Banagher and also connects the town with **Tullamore**, T01-8366111. **Boat hire** *Carrick Craft*, T51189.

Birr

Phone code: 0509
Colour map 2, grid C5

If you are thinking of basing yourself in Offaly for a day or two then the pretty, Georgian town of Birr competes favourably with Banagher as the place to stay overnight.

Heritage centre John's Mall, one of the most picturesquely elegant streets in Birr, is where a heritage centre tells the story of the town's creation by Sir Laurence Parsons in the 18th century. ■ *May-Sep, Mon-Sat, 1430-1730, Sun, 1500-1700. €2.*

Birr Castle Demesne The Parsons climbed the social ladder, became earls of Rosse and settled into Birr Castle on their estate, where they still live. The house is not open to the public but Birr Castle Demesne is, a superb 18th-century park with a lake, river, waterfalls, box hedges that have to be seen to be believed, and an astonishing collection of 2,000 species of rare trees and shrubs. Also to be found here is the **Great Telescope**, built in 1845 as the largest in the world (which it remained for 75 years), and now fully operational once again. The 6-ft-diameter reflector is still in London's Science Museum, to where it was removed during the Troubles. The telescope, which in its time made many important astronomical observations, is just the most dramatic achievement of a remarkable family of Irish scientists and their story is told in the adjoining Science Centre. ■ *T20336. Demesne and Telescope: all year, daily 0900-1800. €5. Science Centre: Jul-Dec. Ticket with Demesne and Telescope €7. Guided tours, gift shop, tea-rooms, plants and flowers for sale.*

Outside of town, on the road between Kinnitty and Roscrea, a little way past **Leap Castle**
Clareen, are the spooky remains of Leap Castle. It was widely believed to be the
most haunted house in Ireland, if not the whole of Europe, with a renowned
'smelly ghost' manifesting itself to the senses. The house was destroyed by
Republican ghostbusters in 1922, but some say the smell still lingers...

LL *Kinnitty Castle*, T37318, www.kinnittycastle.com Gothic pile on a 8,000-ha **Sleeping**
estate on the slopes of the Slieve Bloom hills, stuffed with antiques and the benefits *Price codes:*
of a multi-million-pound refurbishment that do justice to the huge bedrooms. *see inside*
A *Dooley's Hotel*, Emmet Sq, T20032, www.doolyshotel.com Old coaching inn with *front cover*
a jolly atmosphere and modern bedrooms. **A** *Maltings Guesthouse*, Castle St,
T21345, themaltingsbirr@eircom.net A dozen or so rooms in an old malt storage
building with a riverside location close to Birr Castle.

Gourmet food, with dinner every evening in the expensive bracket and lunch also on **Eating**
a Sun, may be enjoyed in *Kinnitty Castle*'s *The Slí Dála*. *The Stables Townhouse Res-*
taurant, Oxmantown Mall, T20263, has bare brick walls and serves filling meals at
lunchtime and at night. For a quick bite try the *Castle Kitchen*, which is opposite the
entrance to Birr Castle in town.

Bus *Bus Éireann* have a daily service between **Dublin** and **Portumna**, via **Transport**
Maynooth and **Tullamore**, which stops in Birr. The **Cork** to **Athlone** service and the
Athlone to **Tralee** services also make daily stops in the town square, T01-8366111.

Tullamore

The Victorian-style town of Tullamore on the Grand Canal has three wor- *Phone code: 0506*
thy attractions, two in the town and one a few miles to the north. The **tourist** *Colour map 2,*
office, is on Bury Quay, T52617. Open May-Sep, Mon-Sat, 0900-1800, *grid C6*
Sun, 1200-1700; Oct-Apr, Mon-Sat, 100-1700, Sun, 1200-1700.

Tullamore is famous for its whiskey, and though it is no longer distilled here **Tullamore Dew**
the Tullamore Dew Heritage Centre recounts its history and looks at the **Heritage**
impact of the Grand Canal on the development of the town. The Centre is **Centre**
located in an 1897 warehouse on the banks of the Grand Canal and you can
try on clothes from the 1850s and see bees making honey for the Irish Mist
liqueur. The customary courtesy tipple rounds off a visit to the Centre, in an
old warehouse on the banks of the canal. ■ *Bury Quay, T25015. May-Sep,*
Mon-Sat, 0900-1800, Sun, 1200-1700; Oct-Apr, Mon-Sat, 1000-1700, Sun,
1200-1700. €4.45. Shop and café bar.

The Bury family founded Tullamore in 1750 and their family home was **Charleville**
Charleville Forest Castle, a superb Gothic-Georgian pile with everything **Forest Castle**
you might expect: turrets, spires, ivy on the walls, dark trees. In 1875 William Morris was commissioned to decorate the interiors but his socialist
sympathies led him to show more interest in the plight of the rural Irish and
he never publicized this work of his for the super-rich. Most of his contributions, including wallpapers, have disappeared but there is some painted
decoration and a frieze in the dining room. ■ *Charleville Rd, T21279.*
Jun-Sep, Wed-Sun, 1100-1600; Apr-May, Sat and Sun, 1400-1700. €4.45.
South of town on the road to Limerick.

Durrow Abbey Durrow Abbey, founded in the sixth century and birthplace of the famous illustrated gospel, the *Book of Durrow*, now in Trinity College Library, Dublin (see page 69), is long gone but a Georgian mansion and a deserted church stand near the site. The house was burnt down in 1922 but the owners rebuilt it, 'a rare example of a house improved as a result of its destruction in the Troubles' says Jeremy Williams in his excellent *Architecture in Ireland* (see page 677).

Sleeping
Price codes: see inside front cover

AL *Moorhill Country House*, Clara Rd, T21395, www.moorhill.ie Victorian retreat set amidst chestnut trees and manicured lawns. **A** *Sea Dew Guesthouse*, Clonminch Rd, T/F52054. Purpose-built edifice within walking distance of town centre. Benefits from a conservatory breakfast room. **B** *Ivy Lodge*, Daingean Rd, T41151. A mile (1.5 km) from the town centre. Really does justify its name. **B** *Littlewood*, Culleen, Durrow, T51364. One of those modern olde-worlde houses that has to be seen to be believed.

Eating *Anatolia*, Harbour St, T23669, is the best place for lunch (but not on Sat) or dinner (not Fri or Sat) in Tullamore. The food is a mixture of European and Turkish and main courses are in the €10 to €20 range. *The Bridge House*, Bridge St, T21704, is a pub restaurant serving familiar dishes throughout the day.

Transport **Bicycle** *Buckley Cycles*, Canal Pl, T52240. Bike hire. **Bus** The bus station is by the railway station and the **Dublin** to **Portumna** bus stops daily, as does the **Waterford** to **Longford** bus via **Kilkenny** and **Athlone**. **Train** The station, T21431, is south of town off Charleville Rd. **Dublin** to **Galway** trains stop at Tullamore throughout the day.

Directory **Banks** William St and Bridge St. **Tours** *Celtic Canal Cruises*, Tullamore, T21861, F51266. Boats for 2-9 people.

County Offaly

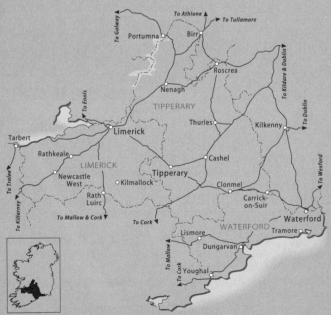

Waterford's coastline stretches for more than 50 miles (80 km), but it is only 27 miles (44 km) from the north of the county to the south. Despite these modest dimensions there is enormous variety in the cultural and physical landscape: **wood-clad hills** and **sheltered inlets** in the east, **sandy beaches** and resorts along the coast, a tiny Irish-speaking area around **Ring** to the west, and the **Comeragh/Monavullagh Mountains** in the north of the county, where historic river valleys frame castles and great houses bear testimony to the English invasions of the past.

Tipperary, Ireland's largest inland county, has some of the best farming land in the country in the aptly named **Golden Vale** that stretches westwards to Limerick. Most people who visit, though, are drawn instead to the historic towns of **Cashel** and **Clonmel**.

County Limerick has diverse attractions: the unbelievably cute **Adare** so beloved of gawking tour groups; **Lough Gur**, a major Stone Age site in Europe; and **Limerick city** booming with new money and home to the amazing **Hunt Collection** and the beautiful old Church of Ireland **cathedral**.

Ins and outs

Getting there   **Air**   Shannon Airport, with international flights to the USA and Europe, and internal flights to Dublin and Belfast, is a ½-hr journey by car from Limerick city.

Waterford Airport, a few miles south of Waterford city, has flights to some English cities but not London. **Train** There are railway stations at Waterford, Carrick-on-Suir, Clonmel, Cahir, Tipperary, Limerick Junction and Tipperary, which are on the same Ennis-Rosslare line. Dublin is served via Kilkenny, Limerick Junction or Rosslare. **Bus** There are buses between Dublin and many of the main towns: Waterford, Clonmel, Cashel, Limerick; and Shannon Airport.

Getting around   All the main towns are served by *Bus Éireann* and details are given under the town entries. Cars can be hired at the airports or in the main cities. The N25 road heading west to Cork from Waterford offers fine views approaching Dungarvan, but there is little of interest along the way. An alternative route west is by the coastal R675, which can also be picked up from Dunmore East to the south of the city. For general tourist information on County Waterford, see www.waterfordtourism.org

County Waterford

Waterford

Phone code: 051
Colour map 4,
grid C1

Waterford oozes a sense of the ancient, with modern shops squeezed into the narrow spaces of the medieval town centre, and no end of fine old buildings to admire. With good facilities, it warrants a short stay before you head off to the varied attractions south and west of the city.

Ins and outs

Getting there   Waterford has an airport, train and bus links, and easy access to the ferry ports of Rosslare and Cork. A 7-min car ferry across Waterford harbour saves times travelling between Waterford and County Wexford. From Rosslare it takes about 45 mins to drive to Ballyhack, where the ferry hops over to Passage East in Waterford. Dublin is 2½ hrs away from Waterford, Cork about an hr.

Getting around   The city centre is small and compact, and though the Waterford glass factory is on the outskirts of town there are bikes and taxis for hire (see 'Transport', page 233). The **tourist office** is at The Quay, T875823. Open Apr-Sep, Mon-Sat, 0900-1800, and on Sun in Jul and Aug, 1100-1700; Oct, Mon-Sat, 0900-1700; Nov-Mar, Mon-Sat, 0900-1700. There is also a tourist office at Waterford Crystal, T358397, Apr-Oct daily, 0830-1800; Nov-Mar daily, 0900-1700.

History

The town's history begins with the Vikings who established a settlement in the early 10th century close to where Reginald's Tower now stands. Vadrafjord, as they named it, prospered undisturbed until the King of Leinster, Dermot MacMurrough, called upon his Welsh Anglo-Norman allies to help him take

★

Things to do in Waterford, Tipperary and Limerick

- Go walkabout through Waterford city to admire its **18th-and 19th-century buildings**
- Spend half a day at the **Waterford Treasures** in Waterford city
- Walk the **Knockmealdown Mountains**
- Visit the incomparable **Hunt Museum** in Limerick city
- Enjoy the unreconstructed **Museum of Folk Life** in Cashel

the town. Led by Strongbow, Waterford fell in 1170 and the significance of this Norman-Irish alliance was cemented by Strongbow's marriage to MacMurrough's daughter. Henry II arrived the following year to claim the town for himself, putting his Welsh barons in their place, and then this English power was further reinforced by King John, who turned up in 1210. Between them, John and Henry had firmly established the city of Waterford as a Norman town; it became the unofficial capital of Ireland and flourished as a European port well into the 16th and 17th centuries.

Cromwell failed to take the city in 1649, but it fell to his son-in-law General Ireton the following year. Although this led to a Protestant elite, Catholic interests were not erased, and between 1750 and 1850 Catholic merchants rose to prominence as food exporters. Religious sectarianism seems not to have blighted the city and this helps explain why Waterford was one of the few places that did not register a victory for Sinn Féin in the 1918 general election. A recent resurgence in commercial life and trade with the continent has restored the port to the kind of importance it held in medieval times.

Waterford

Eating & drinking
1 Haricot's Wholefood
2 Henry Downes pub
3 Kazbar
4 Maxim House
5 Muldoon's Bar
6 Ulysses
7 Woodman

Sleeping
1 Brown's Town House
2 Ivory Lodge
3 Travelodge

County Waterford

Sights

This is a kosher museum, bringing to life the 1,000-year history of the city with exhibits that include, on the third floor, an 11th-century pestle, a 12th-century ring mould for manufacturing finger rings for the merchants and a 12th-century gaming board for the Viking game of *hnefataf*. The second floor covers Cromwell, the 19th century and Waterford crystal. There are also exhibits and information on T F Meagher (see over the page). ■ *The Granary, The Quay. T304500; www.waterford-treasures.com Jun-Aug, daily, 0930-2100; Apr, May and Sep, daily 0930-1800; Oct-Mar, daily, 1000-1700.* €*6 Multi-lingual handsets for self-guided tours, and*

Waterford Treasures at The Granary

Detail map A Waterford city centre, page 230

regular guided tours at 1030 and 1500. A City Pass ticket for €8.90 saves a few euros if visiting The Granary, Waterford Crystal and Reginald's Tower.

Reginald's Tower Possibly the oldest civic building in Ireland, this late 12th-, early 13th-century pepper-pot tower built by the Normans stands on the site of a Viking tower that was built in the early 11th century. The upper floors date from the 15th century. Despite the busy flow of city traffic past it, the tower remains as solid and unyielding as it did in 1495 when it was subjected to the first artillery siege in Ireland. It now houses a collection of artefacts and material relating to the history of the city. ■ *Parade Quay. T304220. Jun-Sep, daily 0930-1830; Easter-May, daily 0930-1830, Oct; daily 0900-1930. €1.90. Dúchas.*

The Mall buildings The Mall, a broad street built in the 18th century, contains a number of fine buildings, and pride of place goes to the 1783 **City Hall**, built as a meeting hall for merchants and reflecting their self-confidence in its stately proportions. A municipal collection of art is on view, including works by Jack Yeats, Paul Henry, Seán Keating and others (tours are available by prior arrangement, T873510), while the council chamber is famed for its superbly wrought Waterford crystal chandelier. Next door, the **Theatre Royal** has retained, uniquely, its original 19th-century features and the tiered horseshoe balconies add tremendously to the atmosphere of the annual opera festival held here (see 'Festivals' below). Also worth admiring is the nearby **Bishop's Palace**, built in the 1740s and designed by Richard Castle.

Waterford city centre

N

0 yards   50
0 metres   50

■ **Sleeping**
1 Granville
2 Tower

● **Eating & drinking**
1 California Café
2 Olde Stand pub
3 T & H Doolans bar

▪▪▪▪ City walls
▬▬▬ Existing walls

County Waterford

The Newfoundland Connection

It was around 1650 that fishermen from south-east Ireland first began crossing the Atlantic on a regular seasonal basis to take advantage of the lucrative fishing grounds off the coast of Newfoundland. This seasonal migration continued throughout the 18th century, and from around 1800 people and families from Waterford and its hinterland began to settle on a permanent basis in that part of North America. By 1830 an estimated 30,000 people, the vast majority from the county of Waterford, had emigrated and begun to make their cultural presence felt. Linguistic studies have shown that, until very recently at least, echoes of this unique wave of Irish immigration could literally be heard in the language of the communities where they settled.

Continue into Parnell Street, and a little way past the junction with John Street the road meets remnants of the **medieval city walls** and their towers. Turn right to follow a well preserved section of the line of the wall that formed the western side of the old city.

Churches

The Waterford designer John Roberts was responsible for both the Protestant and Catholic cathedrals here, but they are quite different in their style and mood. The Protestant **Christchurch Cathedral**, rebuilt in the 1770s, has the cool reticence of Georgian architecture, and the removal of furnishings in the 19th century created a sense of space that allows one to appreciate its elegant proportions. Look for the fine stucco ceiling and the gory *memento mori*: a tomb of a 15th-century mayor. A 45-minute audio-visual show relates the cathedral's history. ■ *Bailey's New St. T858958. Jun-Sep, Mon-Sat 1000-1300, 1400-1700; Sun 1130-1300, 1400-1700. Donation of €3 requested.*

The Catholic 1793 **Holy Trinity Cathedral**, modified in the 19th century, is by contrast a monument to ornateness, with a multitude of Corinthian columns, opulent Waterford glass chandeliers and a carved oak pulpit. Though the tourist literature describes the place as "warm, luscious and Mediterranean", this may not be everyone's response. ■ *Barronstrand St. No admission charge.*

Municipal Art Gallery, **Greyfriars** is a newly opened treasure house of Irish art including works by Jack Yeats, George Russell, Sarah Purser and Evie Hone in beautifully renovated buildings. ■ *T860856. Wed-Fri 1000-1630, Sat and Sun 100-1600. Free.*

St Patrick's, a small but interesting Catholic church off Great George's Street, was built in the mid-18th century with funds from Irish merchants in Spain and remains substantially unaltered. Revisionist historians would pounce on the fact that it remained in use throughout Penal times.

Waterford crystal

The city's most famous export is its crystal, dating back to 1783 when George and William Penrose opened their first glassmaking factory. The mix of silica sand, potash and litharge (a form of lead) is transformed into a glowing ball of molten crystal before being fashioned by craftsmen and then cut and engraved into intricate patterns. Tours of the factory are popular and there is also an audio-visual presentation, a restaurant, and a gallery with a comprehensive display of items for sale. ■ *The Visitor Centre is 2 miles out of town on the N25 road to Cork. Factory tours Mar-Oct, daily 0830-1600 (last tour); Jan-Feb, Mon-Fri 0900-1515. €5.70. T332500. Tickets available from the tourist office. Free admission to the shop, daily 0830-1800 (slightly shorter hrs in winter).*

County Waterford

Meagher of the Sword

Thomas Francis Meagher (1823-67) was born in what is now the Granville Hotel in Waterford. He became a member of the Young Ireland movement, a romantic nationalist movement of the 1840s, and his disagreement with the more cautious approach of Daniel O'Connell earned him the epithet, 'Meagher of the Sword'. He was transported to Tasmania for his involvement in the abortive 1848 rebellion but managed to escape in 1852 to New York where he became a journalist. During the American Civil War he commanded the pro-Union Irish Brigade in Fort Sumter and Fredricksburg. He became a temporary governor of Montana territory in 1866 but died the following year after falling overboard from a Missouri paddle steamer. Meagher is credited with having chosen the Irish national flag.

Essentials

Sleeping
■ on maps
Price codes:
see inside front cover

XL *Waterford Castle*, The Island, Ballinakill, T878203, waterfordcastle.com A short ride on the hotel's private ferry brings guests to this idyllic retreat with fairytale bedrooms and heart-stirring views. 3 miles from the city.

L *Granville Hotel*, Meagher Quay, T855111, www.granville-hotel.ie Former home to Thomas Meagher (see box), a centrally located, waterfront hotel. It was originally an 18th-century merchant's house and still has the original staircase from that period. No car park of its own but a public one directly opposite the hotel. **L** *Tower Hotel*, The Mall, T875801, www.towerhotelgroup.ie Comfortable but characterless, the sauna, gym and 20 m swimming pool is the main draw to this modern 4-storey hotel. **L** *Woodlands Hotel*, Dunmore Rd, 3 miles south of town on the road to Dunmore East, T304574, www.woodlandshotel.ie Pretty good sports centre and above-average food in the restaurant (see 'Eating' below) makes the package deals an attractive proposition.

A *Brown's Town House*, 29 South Pde, T870594, www.brownstownhouse.com Ten mins from the quayside, this brightly decorated Victorian house offers B&B with modern comforts and well equipped bedrooms. **AL-A** *Ivory's Hotel*, Tramore Rd, T358888 www.ivoryhotel@voyage.ie On the outskirts, near the crystal factory, with its own pub, big screen television for sporting events; various package deals are available.

B *Portree Guesthouse*, Mary St, T874574. Another centrally located B&B, in a Georgian building across the bridge from the rail and bus stations. **L-B** *Travelodge*, on the N25 road to Cork, T1800-709709 (T08700-850950 from the UK), www.travelodge.co.uk A motel with room rates for sleeping up to 3 adults and 1 child. Lots of other B&Bs along the Cork Rd.

Eating
● on maps
Price codes:
see inside front cover

Expensive and mid-range *Dwyer's*, 5 Mary St, T877478, has deservedly attracted the attention of food critics. Between 1800 and 1900 there is a set €22.20 dinner based around dishes such as monkfish with spices, or honey and mustard glazed bacon. The à la carte menu falls into the expensive price range; Mon-Sat 1800-2200. *O'Grady's Restaurant*, Cork Rd, T378851, can be relied on for well cooked food, with imaginative touches, for lunch or dinner. Set dinner, modern Irish, in the *Arbutus*, in the Woodlands Hotel out on Dunmore Rd, is a healthy €28.

Cheap *California Café*, 8 The Mall, T855525, has a fresh and modern look about it. Newspapers to read while you munch on paninis and other light meals. *Haricots Wholefood Restaurant*, 11 O'Connell St, T841299, has lots of vegetarian meals like Basque ratatouille, plus some meat dishes like chilli con carne. *Maxim House*, 8 O'Connell St, T875820, offers Cantonese and Szechuan food, including affordable lunch specials and a takeaway service. *O'Neills*, The Granary, is fine for a quick lunch of home-made soup and baked potato or bacon and cabbage; or an evening meal if one of their occasional jazz nights is scheduled. *The Olde Stand*, 45 Michael St, T879488, is a Victorian-style pub specializing in steak and seafood dishes, around €15 in its upstairs restaurants and with a lunchtime carvery and salad bar downstairs in the bar. *T&H Doolans*, Great George St, T841504, is a pub that serves up Irish stew and oysters with Guinness as well as traditional music.

T&H Doolans, Great George St, T841504, is famous for its traditional Irish music sessions, and proud of the fact that Sinéad O'Connor begun her career here. *Henry Downes*, is worth squirreling out at 10 Thomas St. It has been in the same family since the late 18th century, and the proprietors blend their own whiskey, Downes No 9.

John St has a number of pubs popular with the young, including *Muldoon's*, T873693, with live music, a night-club and a steak and seafood restaurant. Best of all are *The Kazbar*, T843729, *Ulysses* and *The Woodman*.

Pubs & music
Pick up a copy of Whazon? from the tourist office for the current music and entertainment scene. www.whazon.com

Entertainment The *Garter Lane Arts Centre*, 22a O'Connell St, T855038, www.iol.ie/~glac has a rich programme of music, theatre, film, exhibitions, workshops and talks. The Waterford Show takes place in the City Hall every Tue, Thu and Sat, May-Sep, at 2100. It lasts 90 mins and the cast in period costume bring to life the culture and history of the city. The €10 tickets, available from City Hall, T875788, the tourist office or from the Waterford Crystal Visitor Centre, include a pre-show drink and a glass of wine during the show. T358397 for details. The Waterford Viking Show, at the Granary, T304500, is something similar on Mon, Wed and Fri at 2000, €12.70.

Festivals From around **19 Sep until early Oct** there is the *Waterford International Festival of Light Opera*. Contact Theatre Royal, The Mall, T874422, www.waterfordfestival.com See Tramore section on page 235 for details of Waterford and Tramore Racecourse Festival in mid-Aug. A couple of days in **late Sep** witness the *Waterford Estuary Mussel Festival* at Passage East, T382677.

Shopping The Granary/Tourist office has a shop area selling gifts, jewellery, and the useful *Discover Waterford* by Eamon McEneaney (O'Brien Press) for €12.70. *Joseph Knox*, 3 Barronstrand St, T875307, is centrally located and stocks Waterford crystal, Donegal china, Belleek pottery and the like. The modern *City Square Shopping Centre* is packed with consumer outlets, 2 department stores and fast food places.

Sport **Golf** *Waterford Castle Golf and Country Club*, an 18-hole course, T871633. *Waterford Golf Club*, T876748, is an 18-hole parkland course in Ferrybank.

Tours A 1-hr **walking tour** covers the main sites and meets daily at the Granary/Tourist office at 1145 and 1345 between Mar and Oct, T873711, €5. **Cruises** operate Jun-Aug from Meagher Quay at 1500 for €10.16, T421723. *Ray McGrath*, T382629, F382689, runs walking holidays in the county of Waterford.

Transport **Airport** *Waterford Airport*, Killowen, T875589, 7 km (4 miles) south of the city, with flights to Luton (see page 31). **Bus** *Bus Éireann*, The Quay, T879000, has express services to Dublin, Rosslare, Galway, Cork, Killarney, Tralee and Athlone. *Rapid Express Buses*, Parnell Court, Parnell St, Waterford, T872149, is a private bus company running several buses daily between Waterford and Cork via Dungarvan, Youghal and Midleton. *Suirway*, T382209 (24-hr talking timetable T382422), is another private company operating from Waterford to Dunmore East and Passage East. **Ferry** *The Passage East Car*

County Waterford

Ferry, T382480, www.passageferry.com Provides a useful shortcut between Waterford and Wexford by crossing the harbour between Passage East and Ballyhack in County Wexford. A continuous service, with first sailing at 0700 (0930 Sun) all year and last sailing at 2000 Oct-Mar; 2200 Apr-Sep. €5.08 single, €7.62 return. **Taxi** *Metro cabs*, 24 hrs, should be metered and charge €5 for up to 3 miles/12 mins, T857857. **Train** *Iarnród Éireann*, T873401/873402 (24-hr talking timetable T876243), operates from Waterford's Plunkett Station, on the north side of the river, and serves Dublin via Kilkenny, Rosslare via Wexford and Limerick via Carrick-on-Suir.

Directory **Communications** Post Office: Keyser St, The Quay. Money exchange also at the tourist office and Waterford Crystal. **Internet**: *Voy@ger Internet Café*, Parnell Court, Parnell St, closed Sun, T843843. **Medical services** Doctor: *Dr Keogh & Partners*, 0900-1700, T855411, emergency T580935. Hospital: *Waterford Regional Hospital*, Dunmore Rd, T873321. Pharmacy: *Gallaghers Late Night Pharmacy*, Barronstrand St. **English language schools** *English Language Centre*, 31 Johns Hill, T877288, F854603, welc@ iol.ie Runs language courses for adult and young learners; individuals and groups. *Waterford Language Learning*, 9 Leoville, Dunmore Rd, T872227. **Launderette** *Boston Cleaners*, 6 Michael St.

The Waterford coast

The Waterford coast has a number of sandy beaches, and is perfect for water sports and exhilarating coastal walks. There are good bus connections to Waterford city in the summer season, but a bicycle is the best way to reach and explore lesser-known spots. Both Dunmore East and Tramore are possible day trips from Waterford.

Dunmore East

Phone code: 051
Colour map 4,
grid C1

Dumore East is not as picturesque as the tourist literature suggests. Thatched cottages and a winding main street give the appearance of a quaint old-fashioned village, but this is a fairly affluent area and the big old houses that were built for British merchants are now owned by well heeled Irish families, the herring boats of the 1960s replaced by ocean-going yachts.

There are two beaches: one is in the village itself while Counsellor's Strand, a Blue Flag beach, is near the golf course and has a car park above it. The large colony of seabirds nesting in the cliffs are kittiwakes.

Sleeping **AL** *Haven Hotel*, Harbour Rd, T383150, www.thehavenhotel.com Built as a family
Price codes: home for a shipping magnate, this family-friendly hotel has a decent restaurant and
see inside front cover attracts holidaymakers. **B** *Carraig Liath*, Harbour Rd, T383273, a large house in the centre of the village and overlooking the harbour, has 4 rooms open between Apr and Oct. **B** *Church Villa*, T383390, is a comfortable Victorian town house, close to the Protestant church, and open all year except Christmas.

Eating & *Power's*, is the local's local and is definitely worth a visit. *The Ship*, T383141, a bar and res-
drinking taurant overlooking the harbour, is the best place for a seafood meal. *The Strand Inn*, T383174, has a picturesque spot by the water's edge and there are a few outdoor tables.

Sports The *Dunmore East Adventure Centre*, T383783, F383786, offers water- and land-based sports and summer camps for children aged 10-17 in Jun-Aug. **Sea angling**: very popular and daily or weekly charters can be arranged. Contact *Sea Angling Charters*, Pelorus, Fairybush, Dunmore East, T/F383397; *South East Charters*, Dunmore East, T/F389242.

County Waterford

Suirway, T382209 (24-hr talking timetable T382422). Private bus company operating **Transport**
from Waterford to Dunmore East via Passage East.

Tramore

Tramore deserves its name (*Trá Mhór* meaning 'big strand') and the   *Phone code: 051*
three-mile (5-km) beach has turned the place into one of Ireland's most pop-   *Colour map 4, grid C1*
ular holiday resorts. This inevitably means amusement arcades, fast-food
joints and family-orientated attractions, but there is also the signposted
five-mile (8-km) Doneraile Walk, which starts at the tourist office, as well as
opportunities for water sports. There is a seasonal **tourist office** on Turbey
Road, T381572.

AL *Majestic Hotel*, T381761, F381766. Popular with Irish holiday-makers, with guests   **Sleeping**
having use of a nearby leisure centre. **AL** *O'Shea's*, T381246,   **& eating**
www.osheas-hotel.com Sociable hotel, bar and restaurant with nightly entertainment
throughout the summer. B&Bs line Cliff Rd and one of the better ones, to judge by holiday guides that recommend it, is **B** *Cliff House*, Cliff Rd, T/F381497, www.cliffhouse.ie
    The hotels all serve bar food and have their own restaurants but worth seeking out
is *Rockett's The Metal Man*, T381496, at the west side of the beach. A speciality here is
crubeens (pig's trotters), but don't let that put you off because the pub has a sociable
atmosphere and food is served until 2100.
    Camping *Newtown Cove Caravan & Camping Park*, T381121, opens from early
Apr to 27 Sep. Take the R675 coast road to Dungarvan and take the left turn opposite
the golf course less than a mile from the town. There is also *Fitzmaurice's Caravan
Park*, T381968, which has only a few pitches for tents.

Horseracing The *Waterford and Tramore Racecourse* at Tramore, T421861, has   **Sport &**
occasional fixtures in Jan, Mar and Nov, but the main 4-day event is in mid-Aug.   **entertainment**
Surfing The *Tramore Surf Club*, T386022, located at the end of the promenade, has
facilities for water sports and surfing lessons. Another surf school is at 3 Riverstown,
Tramore, T390944, oceanic@tinet.ie **Family attractions** For water-based fun there
is *Splashworld*, T390176.

Bus *Bus Éireann*, T879000, has plenty of buses running daily to **Waterford** and on   **Transport**
Wed and Fri a **Dungarvan** to Waterford service stops at Tramore. The No 4 **Dublin** to
Dungarvan service also makes a stop.

Tramore to Dungarvan

The R675 stays inland west of Tramore before dropping down to the village of   *Phone code: 051*
Annestown, where the beach is popular with surfers and is safe for swimming.
A short way before Bunmahon, **Waterford Woodcraft**, T396110, sells items
sculptured from Irish timbers and stays open until 2100. Bunmahon has its
own Blue Flag beach, which can be reached on foot from the village though it
also has its own car park.
    The beach at Stradbally is sandy and suitable for families. The village also
has a Protestant church with an interesting old churchyard which includes an
early 17th-century tombstone with an incised skull and crossbones.
    Clonea Strand is a Blue Flag beach that fits snugly into the coastline and fur-
ther west there is another surfing beach at Ballinacourty. It is 25 miles (41 km)
between Tramore and Dungarvan.

👉 The Women of Dungarvan

Two stories about Dungarvan bear testimony to the seductiveness of its womenfolk. In 1649 Cromwell was about to wreak his usual bout of wanton violence on the place when his eye was drawn to a woman apparently drinking his good health at the town walls. Charmed and disarmed, he desisted. Given Cromwell's penchant for slaughtering the Irish this seems remarkable, but there is another story that lends credence to the allure of the town's females. Before a bridge was built over the River Colligan there was a crossing point where the water was shallow and it was known as 'Dungarvan's Prospects' because men couldn't resist ogling when local women raised their skirts to negotiate the crossing.

Sleeping
Price codes:
see inside front cover

L *Clonea Strand Hotel*, Clonea, T42416, www.clonea.com is virtually on the sandy beach 4 miles east of Dungarvan. It has the usual leisure centre facilities and the distinction of being Ireland's only hotel to boast a tenpin bowling complex. **A** *Annestown House*, Annestown, T396160. **A** *Knockmahon Lodge*, Bunmahon, T384656. **B** *Park House*, Stradbally, T293185. 5 rooms, some of which share bathroom facilities.

Dungarvan

Phone code: 058
Colour map 3,
grid B6

The origins of the town go back to Anglo-Norman times, but it was in the early 19th century that the Duke of Devonshire established the grid design of streets around the generous space of Grattan Square. The town is a humdrum kind of place but it suggests itself as a possible base for trips to the Comeragh mountains, the Irish-speaking Ring Peninsula or the Ardmore beaches. The well resourced and helpful tourist office at The Courthouse, Meagher Street, T41741, dispenses a town map and inexpensive local walks sheets, with trails lasting from 45 minutes to three hours. **Open** May-Sep, 0930-1800, Mon-Sat; Oct-Apr, 0930-1730, Mon to Fri. **Tours** Walks arranged by prior arrangement with Mr David O'Connor, T44957. There is a small museum of local history: **Dungarvan Museum**. ■ *Augustine St, T45960. Mon to Fri, all year, 1000-1645. Free. St*

Sleeping

AL *Park Hotel*, T42899, www.co-waterford.com/park-hotel Overlooking the River Colligan at the Waterford end of town at the N25 roundabout, this is a congenial resting place with comfortable rooms and a leisure centre. **B** *Rose Bank House*, Coast Rd, T41561. Just over a mile outside town on the R675, this pleasant little B&B has a varied breakfast menu – the soda bread is delicious – and large gardens. **D** *Dungarvan Holiday Hostel*, Youghal Rd, T44340, F36294. Opposite the police station, open all year, dorms and private rooms; occasional coach-party groups.

Camping *Bayview Caravan & Camping Park*, Coast Rd, Ballinacourty, T45345. Open from Easter to Sep. *Casey's Caravan & Camping Park*, Clonea, T41919. Open from May to early Sep, and has direct access to the beach. No pre-booking between 9 Jul and 15 Aug.

Eating

If spending time in west Waterford, pick up the free food guide from the tourist office. The most interesting place to eat is undoubtedly *The Tannery*, 10 Quay St, T45420, with starters like roast red pepper soup with basil, innovative fish chowder, good-value lunches, formal dinners that finish with suitably indulgent desserts or, if you want a first-rate introduction to local produce, go for the cheese board. For hearty pub food head out to the *Seanchaí Bar* (see below).

Festivals

The **Féile na nDéise** is a traditional music festival that enlivens the town over the bank holiday weekend, early in May. The sessions of live music are spread around the various pubs and for further information contact the tourist office or T42998.

An Poc ar Buile, O'Connell St, has good sessions of music; also worth checking out are *Bean a'Leanna* at the weekends and the *Anchor* down by the quay. *Seanchaí Bar*, off the Cork road, T46285, is a lovely thatched pub far more spick and span than the traditional scene it evokes, but when the music gets going, especially at the popular Sat night session, there is a good atmosphere.

Bicycle Bikes can be hired from the hostel and from Murphy Cycles, Main St, T41376. **Bus** *Bus Éireann* No 4 service connects Dungarvan with **Cappoquin**, **Lismore**, **Waterford**, **Kilkenny** and **Dublin**. The No 40 Rosslare Harbour to **Tralee** bus goes via Waterford, Dungarvan and **Cork**. No 362 Waterford - Ring - Ardmore bus stops as well and No 364 goes along the coast road between Dungarvan and Waterford. No 366 Waterford to **Mallow** stops at Dungarvan and **Lismore** and there is also the 386 service between **Clonmel** and Dungarvan.

An Rinn (Ring)

An Rinn, eight miles (12 km) south of Dungarvan, is a little oasis of Gaelic culture and famous for its language school. Follow the Cork road out of Dungarvan, and take the signposted left turning on to the R674. Shortly afterwards there is another left turning, signposted for An Cuinigear, that leads to a sand and shingle beach and a three-mile (5-km) finger of land that stretches into Dungarvan Bay. It makes for a pleasant stroll and there are bird-spotting opportunities along the way. The Irish Language college, *Coláiste na Rinne*, T/F46128, is along this road and summer language courses are run for 10- to 18-year-olds. Back on the R674, the road leads to Ceann Heilbhic (Helvic Head) and along the way there is a sign for *Criostal na Rinne*, a workshop producing and selling crystal giftware, T46174, which is also on sale at 30 Parnell Street in Dungarvan.

Phone code: 058

The Marine Bar & Restaurant Pulla, Ring, T46520 is a traditional Irish pub with Irish music every night in the summer (Sat and Mon, Oct-Apr). Bar food served daily.

Transport   Bus *Bus Éireann's* 362 service links Ring with **Waterford**, **Dungarvan** and **Ardmore**. An inland road from Ring goes on to Ardmore, avoiding the N25 road.

Ardmore

A popular seaside resort with four very lovely beaches to choose from, Ardmore is surprisingly picturesque and with a history to boot which claims that St Declan established the first Christian settlement in Ireland here. The **tourist information** office has a free leaflet describing an undemanding 2½-mile (4-km) circular **cliff walk** that begins just beyond the Cliff House Hotel and close by St Declan's Well. ■ *Tourist information office, seafront carpark, T94444. May-Sep 1100-1600.*

Phone code: 024
Colour map 3, grid B6

Built on the site of the saint's original monastery, the church dates back to 1203, with parts of the walls and the east gable dating from the 14th century. The chancel, however, is formed from parts of an older church, probably from the ninth century. It is the west gable, however, that you should look out for – it carries Romanesque sculptures depicting biblical scenes that, though badly eroded in places, can still be discerned. Try to make out Michael the Archangel weighing souls, Adam and Eve, the Judgement of Solomon and the Adoration of the Magi.

Two Ogham stones have been placed inside the church, one of which carries the longest known Ogham inscription in Ireland. The 12th-century tower is in good condition and is just under 97 ft (29.5 m) in height. There is a small oratory said to contain the grave of the saint.

Sleeping
Price codes:
see inside front cover

AL-A *Round Tower Hotel*, T94494, rth@tinet.ie Only 10 bedrooms but with a bar and reasonably priced restaurant. **A** *Newtown View*, Grange, T/F94143. A guesthouse on a working farm some 4 miles (6 km) from Ardmore on the N25, with seaviews, well provided rooms, lounge, tennis court and good food. **B** *Byron Lodge*, T94157. A fine Georgian house at the end of town, overlooking the beach. Open from Apr to Oct. **D** *Ardmore Beach Hostel*, Main St, T94501. Has over 20 beds and some private rooms.

Eating

There are a couple of tourist-friendly restaurants and pubs along Main St serving standard meals but for something more interesting consider the *White Horses Restaurant* on the main street, T94040. Fine for snacks and lunches during the day while at night the menu offers imaginative dishes that include above-average vegetarian choices.

Transport

There are daily buses to and from **Cork**, via **Youghal** and **Midleton**, and a **Waterford** to Ardmore service, via **Dungarvan** and **Ring**, that does not operate on Sun. They all stop outside *O'Reilly's* pub on Main St.

St Declan's Way

This is a 58-mile (94-km) walk that is based upon an ancient pilgrim's route that connected the churches of Ardmore and Cashel. The tourist office in Ardmore sells a map guide covering the route in a series of strip maps, and while the Ordnance Survey 1:50,000 maps (the same scale as the strip map guide) would be a very useful addition, you would need four of them – Nos 66, 74, 81 and 82 – to cover the whole Way. Generally speaking, the walk is not especially difficult and the only part that is critically dependent on good weather is the way through the Bearna Cloch an Bhuidéal pass in the Knockmealdown mountains. *Crystal Walks*, T048-44957/41741, www.amireland.com/declan can arrange the walk based on daily journeys of 9-11 miles (16-18 km).

Lismore and around

Phone code: 058
Colour map 3, grid B6

Perhaps it was Lismore's charming location, on the River Blackwater with the Knockmealdown Mountains as a backdrop, that appealed to St Carthage in 636 when he chose the place for a monastic school. It developed into a major European seat of learning and despite being attacked by Vikings on a number of occasions it retained its importance until falling into decline towards the end of the 12th century after the arrival of the English. The rest of the town was laid out in the early 19th century and the tourist office dispenses a walking guide that takes one on a tour of the main streets and places of interest, chief amongst which is St Carthage's Cathedral. The long-distance St Declan's Way passes close to Lismore.

Lismore Castle & gardens

Henry II visited Lismore in 1171 to meet with the chiefs of Munster and chose a site for a castle overlooking the river, but it was left to Prince John to start building it in 1185. At the end of the 16th century the castle passed to Walter Raleigh, but he sold it to Richard Boyle, first Earl of Cork, who went on to become the richest man in Ireland. It was Richard Boyle who set about landscaping the countryside around Lismore in the style of an English

County Waterford

The sceptical chemist

Robert Boyle (1627-91), the son of Richard Boyle, the first Earl of Cork, was born in Lismore castle and educated at Eton. He returned to Ireland in 1652 for a couple of years but lived most of his life in Oxford and then London. He is famous for formulating the principle that the pressure of a gas varies with its volume at a constant temperature – Boyle's Law. Although a deeply religious man, he played an important part in debunking the pseudo-scientific, scholastic explanations for the physical world. His best-known work in this respect is The Sceptical Chymist, *published in 1661.*

estate. In 1753 the castle passed to the fouth Duke of Devonshire, though it was the sixth Duke in the 19th century who hired Joseph Paxton to fashion the imposing and dramatic edifice that now towers over the river, incorporating into the structure parts of the earlier castle and monastic remains. During this rebuilding work a 13th-century crozier was found hidden in the walls and this famous Lismore Crozier can be seen on display in the National Museum in Dublin. Also hidden, presumably during the Reformation years, was a 15th-century book recounting the lives of saints, along with an Irish translation of Marco Polo's travels.

Lismore Castle remains the private property of the Devonshires and is not open to the public. *Hoi polloi*, however, can enter the gardens and there are fine views of the castle from within these gardens as well as from the Ballyduff road.

The lower level of the gardens, planted with peat from the Knockmealdown Mountains, is rich with rhododendrons and magnolias, while the formal upper level still has an Elizabethan layout. ■ *T54424. 14 Apr-14 Oct, daily 1345-1645. €3.80.*

Lismore Heritage Centre In the old courthouse, along with the **tourist office**, the Lismore Heritage Centre offers an introduction to the history of the town through a multimedia presentation in the guise of Brother Declan, a follower of St Carthage. ■ *T54975. Tourist office and heritage centre open all year, daily 0930-1800, but closed on Sun between Nov and the end of Feb.*

Cappoquin This small town, to the west of Lismore, is a renowned centre for both course and game angling and *Tight Lines Tackle Shop*, Main Street, T54152, is the place to visit for information and tackle. But fishing aside, the countryside around Cappoquin is delightful and at the town the River Blackwater makes an audacious 90-degree turn to the south for its descent into Youghal Bay. In the centre of town, an 18th-century Georgian mansion was built on the site of an old castle that commanded the river at this point and Cappoquin House and gardens offer a superb view of the Blackwater. The gardens are mostly informal and boast a magnificent rhododendron arboretum, with some interesting architectural plants dotted around the place. ■ *T54004. Apr-Jul, Mon-Sat, 0900-1300. €3.*

Glenshelane Forest Tourist Park Close to Cappoquin is the Glenshelane Forest Tourist Park. There are some eight miles (12 km) of riverside walks. Accommodation is in three-bedroomed self-catering log cabins, and camping is also possible. The recommended walk is the one that brings you close to **Mount Melleray**, a Cistercian abbey about 4 miles (6 km) north of Cappoquin. The Cistercian order was finished off in Ireland during the Reformation but was

County Waterford

The Book of Lismore

In the course of some home decoration on the castle in 1814, a box of 15th-century manuscripts secretly recessed behind a wall came to light. Known as the Book of Lismore, *the texts contain both sacred and secular tales including one about three sinners who retreat into a vow of silence. After the first year one of them comments on the wisdom of their deed; after the second year another voices his agreement; after the third year the last one complains that he is sick and tired of their chatter and contemplates a return to the world.*

re-established in 1832 when a dozen or so monks came here and developed a community that numbered around 140 in the 1950s. Numbers are once again in serious decline, but visitors who wish to visit the abbey for peaceful contemplation can stay in the **guesthouse** on the grounds. ■ *Glenshelane Forest Tourist Park T52132. Mount Melleray, T54404, F52140.*

Walking the Knockmealdowns

Lismore is an excellent base for a one- or two-day walk across the wild and amazing scenery of the Knockmealdown Mountains. The route is fairly simple since it forms part of the waymarked Blackwater Way, but getting to and from the walk can pose some problems. From Lismore you need transport for about 8 miles (12 km) to the **Vee Gap**; there is no public transport but ask at your accommodation about a taxi there or consider hitching. The Vee Gap is a beauty spot on the R668 road to Clogheen and you could begin in Clogheen and follow the Blackwater Way from there to the Vee Gap. Once there, you are in the middle of the of the Knockmealdowns with the Blackwater Way stretching off to the west over Knockolugga, through some very rugged territory and with glorious views of the surrounding countryside. To the east, the waymarked route is less interesting; it goes through forest at quite a low level.

At the Vee there is a Bianconi hut, used in the last century for changing horses on the big carriages that once travelled across the mountain road (see page 246). From here you will see paths and waymarkers threading the way uphill to the west. The route is quite challenging to begin with, as it makes its way over rocky tumbled stones, but it then meets a forestry road for a while before climbing above the young trees. As you climb Knockolugga the path is merely a series of markers and sheep tracks, so choose a clear day or you could lose your way uphill. At the top spend a little time just taking in where you are and what you can see: on a windy, sunny day it is truly exhilarating.

A wide tumbled road takes you west and downhill past some strange objects – an abandoned car nowhere near where it could possibly have been driven to, pieces of corrugated iron roofing which must have been carried by the winds since there are no buildings for miles around. At the bottom of the hill you travel briefly along a tiny road and then head off west again up Crow Hill, with wide, worn footpaths that bring you down eventually to farmland and minor roads to **Carran Hill**. **Araglin** is a couple of miles to the south.

At Carran Hill or Araglin there are B&Bs that are very walker-friendly, or you can walk on and make a day of it to the road junction known as **Mountain Barracks**, mostly along country lanes but pleasant enough. Staying overnight at Carran Hill keeps you on the Way, but from Araglin you will need to walk a couple of miles to get back on the route. There is no accommodation at Mountain Barracks but there is a featureless pub (no food) from which you can ring for a taxi (T025-32816, 31718) to Fermoy.

From the Vee Gap to Araglin is about 9 miles (15 km) while to Mountain Barracks is a much stiffer 21 miles (35 km). Even though the walk is well provided with waymarkers, it would be useful to have the OS Discovery series map 74 or the Blackwater Way Map Guide published by EastWest Mapping. For organized walks contact Helen McGrath, T36359, or Verona Nugent, T36494, F36617. For organized walking trips in the **Comeragh Mountains** contact T36238, hiking@indigo.ie

Mapping & information

Essentials

AL *Ballyrafter House Hotel*, T54002, F53050. Built in the 1880s as part of the Devonshire estate, the hotel offers fine country-house accommodation, and game fishing enthusiasts are particularly well catered for. The atmosphere is genuinely laidback, nothing pretentious in the air of this welcoming house. **AL** *Lismore Hotel*, T54555, F53068. Built as a lodge for the Devonshires, this lovely old house in the centre of town has big, old-fashioned rooms. **AL-L** *Richmond House*, Cappoquin, T54278, www.richmondhouse.net An 18th-century country house full of charm offering accommodation and a very fine restaurant open to non-residents. **B** *Beechcroft*, Deerpark Rd, Lismore, T/F54273. A bungalow on the outskirts of town and also offers self-catering accommodation. **C** *Mrs Norah Fennessy*, Creamery View, near Araglin, T60007. A useful B&B if walking the Knockmealdowns. **D** *Barnahoun Farm Holiday Centre*, Carran Hill, T60077. A B&B that will provide packed lunches and has lots of advice on walks. **D** *Kilmona Farm Hostel*, T54315, kilmorna@ireland.com   A small IHO hostel but a few private rooms and being part of a functioning farm there is also space for camping; free pickup from Lismore.

Sleeping
Price codes:
see inside front cover

The restaurant at *Ballyrafter House Hotel*, T54002, has a menu that changes nightly, and fresh salmon from the Blackwater is one of the specialities. Sun lunch is very popular. Also recommended is dinner at the *Lismore Hotel* restaurant, T54555, where main courses are around €13. The bar in this hotel also does good food. *Richmond House* (see 'Sleeping', above) offers traditional country-house cooking with touches of more adventurous cuisines and pukka vegetarian options. A 4-course dinner is around €35, from 1900-2130 but may be closed on Sun and Mon to non-residents. *Madden's* pub, Main St, T54148, is worth considering for lunch but *Eamonn's Place* also in Main St, T54025, is better, serving generous portions of dishes like lamb's liver and bacon casserole and lovely puddings. Main courses in the restaurant at night are in the €8-15 range. *Buggy's Glencairn Inn*, Glencairn, T56232, is a couple of miles outside Lismore and has acquired a reputation for mighty good food. The bar itself is tiny and space is at a premium in the dining room too, so booking is essential. Open from 1930 to 2100, but closed on Tue except for guests in the 4 bedrooms. Lunch is usually available in the summer, but phone to make sure.

Eating
A quiet place for a pint is the delightful O'Brien's in Main St, T54816

Enquire at the tourist office about **guided walks** around town, which usually run twice daily during the summer months.

Tours

Buses *Bus Éireann* run a daily service between **Dublin** and Lismore via **Waterford**. On Fri and Sun there is a service from Lismore to Waterford and **Cork** via **Dungarvan** and **Cappoquin**. There is also a daily local bus to Dungarvan.

Transport

County Waterford

County Tipperary

Cashel and around

Phone code: 062
Colour map 3, grid A6

The ecclesiastical remains on the stupendous Rock of Cashel consist of a round tower, a 12th-century chapel, a 13th-century cathedral and 15th-century residential buildings. The rock is conveniently located just off the main Dublin to Cork road, making the market town of Cashel a major stopping-off point for travellers.

Rock of Cashel The Rock, a limestone outcrop that rises 200 ft (61 m) above the plain like the Acropolis of Athens, was the seat of Munster kings from the fourth to the early 12th century, and in 978 Brian Bóruma (Brian Boru) was crowned here. In 1101 the Rock was given to the Church, and Cormac's Chapel was consecrated in 1134 under the auspices of the king and Bishop Cormac McCarthy. The cathedral was built in the following century, on the site of an earlier one, but in 1495 it was set alight by the Earl of Kildare because, as he later humourously explained to the understandably irate Henry VII, he thought the archbishop was inside. The cathedral was plundered in 1647, and its lead roof was removed some time in the 18th century: a consequence of the fact that the archbishop of the time was said to be too lazy to climb the rock and so he took little interest in preserving the building.

P J Kavanagh in *Voices in Ireland* (see page 678) describes how the Rock of Cashel "jumps out of the Tipperary plains like an Edinburgh Castle in a sea of green". He tells how when St Patrick baptized a king here in 450, he accidentally thrust his crozier through the foot of the King, who kept mum in the belief that it was all part of the ritual.

The Rock of Cashel is extremely popular with coach tours, and during summer months it is advisable to arrive early in the morning to avoid the crowds; don't say you weren't warned. There is a **tourist office** in the town hall, Main St, T61333. Apr-Sep, Mon- Sat 0900-1800; Jul-Aug, also on Sun.

Hall of the Vicars Choral This 15th-century building is now the entrance to the Rock and home to the useful video that recounts the history of the site. There is a small museum, the chief exhibit of which is the famed **St Patrick's Cross**. It originally stood outside, where there is now a replica, and tradition states that the cross's plinth was the coronation stone for the inauguration of Irish kings, including Brian Bóru.

Found immediately to the south of the cathedral, this is the earliest and most elegant Romanesque church in Ireland. Its remarkable steep stone roof, unusual twin square towers instead of transepts, and carved arcading are all noted features of its exterior. Above the north door, which was the main entrance before the cathedral got in the way, there is a lively sculpture of a lion being shot at with a bow and arrow by a helmeted figure that looks like a centaur.

Cormac's Chapel

The ribbed, barrel-vaulted nave is wonderfully small, and recent restoration work on the chancel roof has revealed some of the frescos that once were probably a feature of the whole church ceiling (Cromwell's troops are said to have whitewashed over them), lending glorious colour to what is now a dark interior. There are many fine sculptures over the archway that leads to the east chancel, and there is also a superb **sarcophagus** that dates back to around the 12th century and is said to be the tomb of King Cormac. Its sophisticated decorative design of interlacing beasts is Ireland's best example of the Urnes style, chiefly recognizable by the intertwining of broad and narrower animals, which came to the country from Scandinavia at the end of the 11th century. Like the design of the square towers, which are thought to hail from Germany, this is another example of how remarkably open to European art Ireland was at this time.

What you see today is the shell of a cathedral that was first built in the 13th century but which was restored more than once over the centuries. The west side has the addition of a small castle, built as a secure residence for the archbishop early in the 15th century, the main hall of which was spread over the top of the nave, the corbels being still visible. It was also in the 15th century that the central tower of the cathedral was raised to its present position of dominance. The tower reduces the length of the nave, so that the choir is actually longer, and the main attractions inside the church are the high-set lancet windows, classic examples of 13th-century style, and a multitude of memorial tombs. The adjoining round tower is the earliest surviving structure on the Rock and was part of the early Christian enclosure. ■ *The Rock of Cashel (including Cormac's Chapel). T61437. Mid Mar-mid Jun daily 0900-1730; mid Jun-mid Sep daily 0900-1930; Mid Sep-mid Mar daily 0930-1630. €4.40. Dúchas site. Guided tours every hr on the half hr in summer (worth joining) and scheduled times for an audio-visual show.*

Cathedral

County Tipperary

Brú Ború ('Palace of Brian Boru') Heritage Centre This centre, with some very naff sculptures outside, stands at the foot of the Rock adjoining the car park. The centre offers a 15-minute audio-visual presentation on cultural history, a restaurant and gift shop. A theatrical show of music and dance takes place here, Tuesday to Saturday, at 2100. ■ *T61122 www.comhaltas.com Tue-Fri, 0900-1930; Sun and Mon, 1000-1700.*

Heritage Centre

Story of Cashel Next to the tourist office, the exhibition here includes a model of the 17th-century town. ■ *Town Hall, Main St, T62511, Jan-Mar and Sep, Mon-Fri, 0930-1730; Apr-Jun, daily, 0930-1800; Jul and Aug, daily 0930-2000. Free.*

This is a brilliant museum and more engaging than many of the heritage centres created off the back of government subsidies. To say it is a collection of house fronts, shops, farming implements, and memorabilia from the 18th-20th centuries fails to do justice to the sense of history that it evokes. Information on all of the exhibits in half a dozen European languages. ■ *T62525. Dominic St. Daily, 0930-1930. €2.54.*

Museum of Rural Life
Skip the Brú Ború centre and come here instead

Bolton library A specialist museum for connoisseurs of the printed word: the library has manuscripts and maps, some of which date back to the earliest days of printing. Check out the smallest book in the world (a photographic reduction), the ultra-tiny New Testament from the 1860s and 2 pages from a Caxton's Chaucer. ■ *T61944. Mar-Oct, Tue-Sun, 0930(1230 on Sun)-1730; Oct-Feb, Mon-Fri, 0930-1730.* €3.

Essentials

Sleeping
Price code: see inside front cover

LL-L *Cashel Palace Hotel*, Main St, T62707, reception@cashel-palace.ie Built in 1730 as an archbishop's palace and a distinctive hotel since 1962, with its own walled gardens and a private walk to the Rock. The entrance hall has its original wood panelling and grand staircase and the basement bar displays the names of famous guests, from the sublime to the ridiculous (George Best, Robert Mitchum, Charles Bronson…). Has to be the best place to stay in Cashel.

AL-A *Bailey's of Cashel*, Main St, T61937, www.baileys-ireland.com A fondly restored period piece, pre-Georgian, with parking area, restaurant and some rooms with Rock views. **A** *Ballyowen House*, Dulla, T61265, www.ballyowenhouse.com A few minutes drive from Cashel, off the N8 road to Dublin, this Georgian country house offers refuge from the coaches and tour groups jamming up the town. Huge, antique-filled rooms, lakeshore walks, tennis court, croquet, restaurant.

B *Georgesland*, T/F62788. B&B in a large modern bungalow less than a mile outside of town, on the Dualla Rd. Has a good reputation. **B** *Indaville*, T62075. Another Georgian house close to the town centre that provides largish rooms. It is on the left after the N8 turn south to Cork after Main St. **B** *Maryville*, Bank Pl, T61098. Guesthouse with its own parking area and views of the Rock. **B** *Thornbrook House*, Dualla Rd, T62388, F61480, a ponderosa-style dwelling. **C-D** *O'Brien's Holiday Lodge*, St Patrick's Rock, Dundrum Rd, T61003, obriensholidayhostel@eircom.net A short walk from the town centre, just far enough away to escape the traffic noise. A converted stone stable and excellent views of the Rock; 23 private rooms and camping is also possible.

D *Cashel Holiday Hostel*, John St, T62330, F62445, cashelho@iol.ie 6 John St is a turning off Main St and the hostel has over 40 beds and 4 private rooms.

Eating

Expensive *Ches Hans*, Dominick St, T61177, is an ex-Wesleyan chapel with a dinner-only, very French menu. Starters like paté of chicken liver with foie gras and main courses that include grilled lobster; closed Sun and Mon. An early-bird menu between 1800 and 1930 with 2 courses for €20 or 3 courses for €25. At the *The Bishop's Buttery*, in the Cashel Palace Hotel dishes come to your table, appropriately enough, on ecclesiastical-style silver plates. Perhaps, too, the bishops enjoyed the whiskey-cured smoked salmon and the vodka-fuelled sorbet. The restaurant has a cellar-like setting enlivened by light colours and, over weekends, the subdued piano playing of popular Irish parlour music. Main courses of lamb, guinea fowl, duck, steaks, and fish. Afternoon tea in the Cashel Palace is a grand affair.

Mid-range *The Spearman*, 97 Main St, T61143, a dozen doors down from the Cashel Palace Hotel. Tasty daily specials for lunch, including pasta usually. For dinner, a good choice of starters and main courses which are European with a faint touch of the orient. For €65, two people could wine and dine the night away; but not on Sun when it's lunch only, or anytime on Mon between Oct and May. *Legends*, The Kiln, T61292, is adjacent to the Brú Ború Heritage Centre and an evening meal of conventional dishes could be enjoyed here for under €25. Between Tue and Fri, there is an early-bird menu.

Cheap Along Main St there are a couple of modest restaurants offering fairly predictable meals under €12.70 and there are a number of cafés at the foot of the Rock and near the tourist office. *Dowling's*, at the bottom of the main street heading towards Cork, T62130, is a lovely unreconstructed pub serving homely food and good coffees. For picnics, plonk yourself on the Rock and watch the tour buses come and go.

Larkspur Park, The Green, T61626. Provides golf, tennis, badminton and snooker. **Sport**
Angling *Ryans Shop*, Friary St, T61106. Dispenses information and tackle.

Cashel Heritage Tram, T62511. Runs a circular tour of the main sites and includes **Tour operators**
entry to Cashel of the Kings Heritage Centre and Bolton Library. Hop on or off anywhere on the circuit. Jun-Sep, Tue-Sat, 1200-1800.

Bicycle Both hostels in the town rent bikes. **Buses** *Bus Éireann* run 3 buses a day, 2 **Transport**
on Sun, between Dublin and Cork via Cashel, Cahir and Fermoy. In the summer
months 4 extra buses run daily between Cashel and Cahir, and there is also a daily
service between Cork and Athlone that stops at Cashel. Contact *Rafferty's Travel*,
102 Main St, T62121, for schedules. *Bernard Kavanagh*, T056-31189, runs a Mon-Fri
service between Dublin and Cashel and another private bus company called
Kavanaghs, T51563, runs a Mon-Fri service between Clonmel and Thurles via Cashel.

Tipperary town

Is it just nostalgia that makes Tipperary a name that still evokes something *Phone code: 062*
imagined about a past Ireland? The town that actually carries the resonant
name is a dreary, workaday kind of place that will disappoint visitors seeking
something more than the prosaic. A statue to Charles Kickham (1828-82),
Fenian and author of *Knocknagow* (who came from the county, not the
town) is proudly plonked in Main Street. The father of the American playwright Eugene O'Neill came from a farm just outside of town. For information on anything that might be happening in the town, call into the new
tourist centre which is on the road that goes off Main St by the AIB and
Bank of Ireland. ■ *T33466, www.tipperary-excel.com Daily, 0900-1800.*

Cahir

Cahir (pronounced 'care') is home to a massive castle, originally built in **Cahir Castle**
1142 by Conor O'Brien, which later came into the possession of the *Phone code: 052*
Anglo-Norman Butler family in 1375. It was the Butlers who built most of
what you can see today. After a 10-day siege in 1599, during the Elizabethan
Wars, they lost it to the Earl of Essex but it stayed in the Butler family only to
be again attacked by English artillery in 1647; the castle was then surrendered to the Parliamentary commander, Lord Inchiquin. Three years later it
was surrendered again, this time without a shot being fired, after Cromwell
had delivered a terse statement that grimly concluded: "if I be necessitated
to bend my cannon upon you, you must expect the extremity usual in such
cases"; message understood.

There is an exhibition on the 1599 siege of the castle by the Earl of Essex,
display panels on Irish castles and on women in Tudor Ireland; all good stuff
for a rainy afternoon. You'll get most out of a visit by joining one of the
guided tours, available on request and there is a 17-minute video, a portcullis to admire and walls to walk along. ■ *Castle St, T41011. Mid Mar-mid Jun,
daily, 0930-1730; mid Jun-mid Sep, daily, 0900-1930; mid Sep-mid Oct,
daily, 0930-1730; mid Oct-mid Mar, 0930-1630. €2.50. Dúchas site.*

The tourist office is in the car park next to Cahir Castle. ■ *T41453. Open
Apr-Sep, Mon-Sat 0900-1800; Jul-Aug also Sun 1100-1700.*

County Tipperary

Finn McCools & Massey Dawsons

Charles Bianconi (1786-1875) came to Ireland from Lombardy in 1802 at the age of 16 as a pedlar of prints. He was sent to Ireland to avoid a scandal over his friendship with a local girl who was betrothed to a nobleman. His travels across the country convinced him of the need for a low-cost system of public transport, and in 1815 he started the first service between Clonmel and Cahir using one horse to pull a two-wheeled car with passengers, mail and small freight. Success was instant and, taking advantage of low prices for horses and cars following the end of the long war against Napoleon, he was soon able to upgrade the quality of the service. Stage coaches continued to make long-haul trips out of Dublin and other large cities, but Bianconi's open-topped cars were ideal for inexpensive and shorter journeys between small towns. By the 1840s Bians, as they came to be known, were operating across 3,000 miles of road every day and the largest coaches, called Finn McCools and Massey Dawsons, could carry up to 20 passengers. For countless thousands of ordinary people, Bians opened up the Irish countryside and made travel affordable in a way that was undreamt of before the Italian began his first service from outside what is now Hearn's Hotel on Parnell Street in Clonmel.

Swiss Cottage From the car park at the side of Cahir Castle there is a 3.2-mile (2-km) path running alongside the river and under horse chestnut trees that leads to Swiss Cottage, a delightful *cottage orné* built in the early 19th century by Richard Butler but designed by the Regency architect John Nash. An Alpine look is discernible from the outside, hence the nickname it acquired some decades after it was built, but the interior is unique. The elegant spiral staircase is worth admiring and the Dufour wallpaper in the salon that displays the Bosphorus was one of the first commercially produced Parisian wallpapers. ■ *Kilcommon, T41144. May-mid Oct, daily, 1000-1800; mid Mar-Apr and Oct-Nov, Tue-Sun, 1000-1300 and 1400-1700. €2.50. Dúchas site. To drive there, take the R670, the road to Ardfinnan, from by the side of the Cahir House Hotel in town.*

Sleeping
Price codes: see inside front cover

AL *Cahir House Hotel*, The Square, T/F42727, www.tipp.ie/cahir-house This fine Georgian building in the centre of town, home to Lord Cahir's family until 1961, has over 40 rooms and a pleasant old-fashioned feel. **A** *Castle Court Hotel*, Church St, T41210, F42333. A family-run hotel in the centre of town with a popular pub. **B** *Carrigeen Castle*, Cork Rd, T/F41370, less than a mile outside of town. Quite a remarkable sight and one of Ireland's more unusual B&Bs. **B** *Silver Acre*, Clonmel Rd, a bungalow in a cul-de-sac offering B&B that has been well spoken of. **D** *Lisakyle Hostel*, Church St, T41963, is opposite *The Craft Granary*, on your right, if entering town from Cashel. Dorm beds, 2 private rooms and bikes for hire.

Eating Knowing what the food was like in their Cork restaurant in years gone by, *Clifford's*, at the Bell pub in the centre of town in Pearce St, should easily be the best place for a meal. A set dinner is €30 while main courses are in the €21-28 range; closed Sun (except for lunch) and Mon. The cosy *Butler's Pantry* in the *Cahir House Hotel*, offers steaks, fish and poultry for lunch and dinner. Set dinner is €28.50. For a light meal try the *Galtee Inn* in the main square or enjoy a picnic by the side of the river walk to Swiss Cottage; there are benches, once you get past the golf course, overlooking the Suir. *The Mill*, next to *The Craft Granary*, closes at 1700 but the home-made quiche is fine for lunch.

The Craft Granary, which can be reached from the castle by crossing the road and following the river a short distance, sells woodwork, glass, textiles and the like; not a terrific choice of goods. **Angling** Contact Tom Butler, *Cahir Anglers Club*, Railway View, Cahir Abbey, T41167. **Horse-riding** *Lissava House Stables*, T41117.

Shopping & sport

Buses Both of *Bus Éireann's* Dublin to Cork services stop in Cahir, by the tourist office and castle. The No 7 connects Cahir with both cities as well as Clonmel, Carrick-on-Suir and Kilkenny, while the No 8 travels via Kildare, Cashel and Fermoy. The Galway to Rosslare Harbour service also stops in Cahir and connects with Ennis, Limerick, Clonmel, Carrick-on-Suir, Waterford and Wexford. Once a day the Cork to Athlone bus also stops and there are local services to Clonmel and Carrick-on-Suir. **Train** T41578. A service between Cork and Rosslare Europort stops twice, Mon-Sat, in Cahir.

Transport

Clonmel

The lively town of Clonmel has at least two claims to fame: it is the birthplace of both Laurence Sterne (1713-68), a novelist whose hilarious style predates post-modernism by a couple of centuries, and author of freewheeling *Tristram Shandy*; and of the Bianconi system of public transport. Another noted resident was the novelist Anthony Trollope, who left his homeland to set up house here in 1848, (the epitome of the style that Sterne so delightfully subverted). The many fine old buildings dotted around Clonmel are a chief attraction of the town and the **tourist office** (Sarsfield St, opposite the Clonmel Arms Hotel, T26500. Jul-Aug, Mon-Fri, 0930-1900, Sat, 0930-1400; Sep-Jun, Mon-Fri, 0930-1300, 1400-1700) dispenses a Heritage Trail booklet with a location map that is very useful for nosing them out.

Phone code: 052
Colour map 3, grid B6

County Tipperary

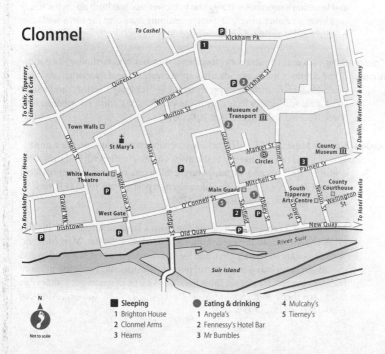

Clonmel

Sleeping
1 Brighton House
2 Clonmel Arms
3 Hearns

Eating & drinking
1 Angela's
2 Fennessy's Hotel Bar
3 Mr Bumbles
4 Mulcahy's
5 Tierney's

A buildings tour

If nothing else, find time to stand before the **Main Guard** at the eastern end of O'Connell Street. It was built in the 1670s as a courthouse, one of the oldest public buildings in Ireland, and recently restored to give some idea of its imposing structure. It was not here, however, that the leaders of the Young Ireland movement were prosecuted for their part in the abject failure of the 1848 rising; by that time the County Courthouse in Nelson Street had been standing for nearly 50 years. To get there from the Main Guard continue eastwards along Mitchell Street and turn right into Neilson Street after passing Dowd's Lane (and a statue to the '98 rebellion, erected in 1904), also on the right. It was at the County Courthouse that Thomas Francis Meagher and others were sentenced to transportation to Australia (see box on page 232). Dramatic re-creations of some trails form part of an evening entertainment's programme inside the courthouse (see below).

Retrace your steps back up Neilson Street to Parnell Street and **Hearns Hotel**, where Bianconi started his cart transport system in 1815. Return to the Main Guard and walk down to the western end of O'Connell Street where, facing the Main Guard from this end of the street, is the **West Gate**. It was built in 1831 on the site of an original gate in the medieval walls that once enclosed the town. The Tudor style was being popularly imitated at the time and this shows in the inclusion of machicolated battlements, hardly a necessary feature of town planning in the 1830s, even in Ireland. On the other, west, side of West Gate lies **Irishtown** This is a name commonly found in towns to designate the living area for the indigenous, non-Anglo-Normans who could work, but not live, inside the town walls. From the West Gate, walk north up Wolf Tone Street, passing **White Memorial Theatre** that was built in the Greek Revival style in 1843 as a Weslyan Methodist chapel. Continue up to **St Mary's Church**, dating back to 1204 but largely rebuilt in the 19th century and boasting a superb, 84-ft ziggurat belltower that was built up on the foundations of an earlier tower. The only remaining section of the **town walls** can be seen nearby, restored and renovated 20 years ago.

County Courthouse

Song, dance and theatre come together at the County Courthouse when some of the county's more famous trials are recreated where they originally took place. Each show includes a presentation of Tipperary's history, and a light snack meal and local cider feature in the festivities. ■ *County Courthouse, Nelson St, T22960. Jul-Aug, Fri-Sat, 2100. €12.*

Museums

County Museum This delightfully unreconstructed museum has a miscellany of items relating mostly to the town's history in the 19th and early 20th centuries, and occasional temporary exhibitions of a more sophisticated nature. Check out the anti-DeValera election poster from 1932. ■ *Parnell St, T25399. Tue-Sat, 1000-1300, 1400-1700.*

Museum of Transport Opposite the town's large supermarket, this has exhibits dating from the earliest motorized vehicles. Jaguar, Mercedes and Rolls Royce are all represented, and there is also a section on motorbikes and memorabilia such as period petrol pumps. Unfortunately, the few items of Bianconi interest are not on show because of a lack of space, but visitors can ask to see them. ■ *Richmond Mill, Market Pl, T29727. Jun-Sep, Mon-Sat 1000-1800, and Sun 1430-1800.*

Bicycle excursion from Clonmel or Cashel

The small town of **Fethard** is 10 miles (15 km) north of Clonmel and about the same distance east of Cashel, suggesting itself as an ideal destination for a cycle ride from either town. Fethard is not on the tourist trail, but there are a surprising number of medieval remnants to be found in the town. Main Street has a **15th-century church** and the **town walls**, which were not strong enough to withstand Cromwell in 1650, have been reconstructed in a number of places and can be reached from the church. At the end of Watergate Street, to the south of the church, there are some **17th-century tower houses** and at the east end of town an **Augustinian abbey**, founded in 1306, is now a functioning church but retains an ancient atmoshere. On Sunday mornings a **Folk, Farm & Transport Museum**, T31516, opens in Cashel Road.

LL *Knocklofty Country House*, Knocklofty, 4 miles (6.5 km) from Clonmel, T38222, F38300. Dating back to the 16th century, suitably oak panelled and beautifully Georgian, and set in extensive private grounds by the River Suir (fishing rights for a mile of the river), this hotel has weekend deals that reduce the cost somewhat. **L-AL** *Clonmel Arms Hotel*, Sarsfield St, T21233. Ideal for anyone wanting to be in the heart of town with a lively bar and a popular restaurant. **AL** *Hearns Hotel*, Parnell St, T21611, F21135. Has changed a bit since Bianconi's days in the 19th century – now has a nightclub, for starters – but history clings on to the place. **AL-L** *Hotel Minella*, Coleville Rd, T22388, www.hotelminella.ie A little way out of town and offers comfortable accommodation, a leisure centre and a good restaurant with views of the River Suir flowing along. **A** *Brighton House*, Brighton Pl, T23665, brighton@iol.ie A Georgian, family-run guesthouse with hotel-standard facilities.

Sleeping
■ on map
Price codes:
see inside front cover

Mr Bumbles, Richmond House, Kickham St, T29188, is a terrific all-purpose restaurant in the centre of town, open daily. Everything from tea and cakes to slabs of steak and Tipperary lamb, and some interesting starters and desserts. Expect to pay at least €30 for a good dinner, around €8 for something off the lunch menu. In Abbey St, *Angela's* has specials posted on a blackboard, lunches like chicken with Thai curry, gourmet sandwiches, some non-meat choices from this popular self-service restaurant that closes at 1730. Pubs are a good bet, especially *Tierney's* on O'Connell St with its truly vast menu; bar food and main courses in the restaurant from €7.62 to €16.51. *Mulcahy's* on Gladstone St is a pub with restaurant seating and a menu that ranges from €8 panninis to €19 steaks; popular with townspeople.

Eating
● on map

There are a few pubs with music. Try *Lonergan's* on O'Connell St or the *Sows Ears* or *Fennessy's Hotel*. *Sean Tierney*, 13 O'Connell St, T24467, serves food upstairs but the bar area on the ground floor is worth looking into. It has more exhibits than many a small museum.

Pubs & music

Swimming Borstal Sq, T21972. Swimming pool with 25 m lanes, also a sauna and gym. **Snooker** The internet café in Market St has an adjoining snooker hall.

Sport

Internet *Circles Internet Café*, 16 Market St, T23315, daily 1100-2300. **South Tipperary Arts Centre**, Nelson St, T27877, well worth checking out to see what's on because there is a lively arts scene in south Tipperary and art exhibitions, drama, literature readings, and a writers' festival in Oct all take place here.

Directory

County Tipperary

Carrick-on-Suir

Phone code: 051
Colour map 4, grid C1

As towns go Carrick-on-Suir is a dull, workaday kind of place and without the attractions of Ormond Castle and the neighbouring high crosses there would be little good reason to make a visit.

Heritage centre

Housed in a former Protestant church off Main Street, this is part of the **tourist office** and contains a collection of photographs, artefacts and documents relating to local history. ■ *T640200. Jun-Sep, Mon-Sat, 1000-1700, Sun 1400-1700; Oct-May, Mon-Fri, 1000-1700. €2.50.*

Ormond Castle

The fact that Ireland was far from being a settled country in the 1560s, when this castle was built, makes this imposing Elizabethan mansion all the more remarkable. Its tranquility, reflected in the steady repetition of mullioned windows, would not be out of place in Shakespeare's England, but this was a turbulent Ireland at a troubled time in her history. The first castle was built at the beginning of the 14th century, and then in the mid-15th century a larger fortified enclosure was built on this side of the River Suir. A century later Thomas, Earl of Ormond, added a mansion, and further sophisticated improvements were to follow. The original motive for the Earl's substantial tarting up of the place was an expected visit by the queen, Elizabeth I, and portraits of her are decorated in stucco around the Long Gallery, part of a highly elaborate use of decorative plasterwork. This is the highlight of the castle's interior and the guided tour draws attention to it. ■ *Castle Park, off Castle St, T640787. Mid Jun-early Sep daily 0930-1830. €2.54. Dúchas site. €2.50. Access by guided tour only.*

Ahenny high crosses

About three miles (5 km) north of Carrick-on-Suir, signposted off the R697 road to Windgap, there are two highly decorated and unusual high crosses. Instead of the usual pictorial panels, the main body of each cross is covered with geometric, reticulated patterns of spirals. There are human figures found along the base: on their north sides there is a strange scene of travelling figures, but easier to interpret is the other side that shows Christ and the apostles. The Ahenny crosses make an interesting contrast with those at Monasterboice (see page 152), representing what is probably an earlier and abstract kind of Celtic aesthetic before a more didactic strain of Christianity was imposed on it. By this reasoning, the Ahenny crosses are dated a century earlier than the ninth-century crosses at Monasterboice.

Tipperary crystal

Waterford crystal may have a more successful marketing history, but there are alternatives and one of them is Tipperary crystal, housed close to the River Suir at Ballynoran on the N24 road between Carrick and Clonmel. ■ *Free guided tours are available Mid Mar-Sep, Mon-Thu, 0900-1630, Fri, 0900-1530. There is also a restaurant.*

Sleeping & eating

There is no hotel or guesthouse in Carrick town that is worth singling out and it would make more sense to stay in Clonmel or Waterford. **AL** *Hollywell Country House*, T21124, hollywell@esat.biz.com is just outside of Carrick beside the Shannon River. Try to reserve one of the rooms overlooking the river for maximum atmosphere; no dinner.

B *The Grand Inn*, T647035, 11 km from Carrick on the N76 Clonmel to Kilkenny road, is a former coach house inn with antiques around the place to testify to its venerable past.

Ó Ceallacháin, the pub opposite the post office, does soup, salads, potato wedges, roast of the day, home-made burgers, steak and curries (including a vegetarian one) – all at affordable prices. For picnic supplies, try *Cheese Etc* on Bridge St.

Bike hire *OK Sports*, New St, T640626. **Buses** 3 buses a day travelling between **Dub-** **Transport**
lin and **Cork** stop in town as well as in **Kilkenny**. 4 buses a day also stop on the **Galway**
- **Limerick** - **Waterford** - **Rosslare Harbour** route. Local buses go to **Waterford**,
Clonmel and **Cahir**. T79000. **Train** T40044. Once a day, Mon-Sat, and twice daily in
the summer, it is possible to travel by train from Carrick-On-Suir to **Waterford** and
Rosslare Europort and to **Limerick**.

North Tipperary

Attractions in the north of the county are a scattered mix and it is very much a
case of catching places of interest as one is travelling through to somewhere
else, partly because there is no town or area that can be singled out and recom-
mended as a base for a longer stay and partly because the countryside is very
boring, unless you enjoy looking at large farms, their crops and their cattle.
Holy Cross Abbey is a good example because while the abbey is definitely
worth seeing there is not much to detain the traveller in the nearby town of
Thurles, (4 miles) 6 km, to the north.

Benefiting from a new roof 25 years ago, the Cistercian abbey of Holy Cross **Holy Cross**
exhibits itself proudly as both one of the most accomplished 15th-century **Abbey**
churches in the country and a functioning place of parish worship. The foundations go back to the 12th century though most of what stands today was
built around 1440-70, almost certainly a reflection of the increasing popularity of the place with pilgrims, based on the abbey's claim to hold a sacred relic
from Cavalry (hence the abbey's name). In medieval Ireland, Holy Cross sur-
passed all other places of pilgrimage and the relic was still there when
O'Donnell and O'Neill stopped over on their way to Kinsale in 1601, but it
hardly brought them much luck. Medieval pilgrims visiting the abbey
donated alms for the upkeep of the shrine, and this accumulated wealth was
used to finance the costly 15th-century re-building programme that used the
best craftsmen available.

Aesthetically, the most successful part of this rebuilding programme is the
chancel with its delicate ribbed vaulting and an exquisite window on the east
side. Here you will also find a superb sedilia, stone seats for the priests, with
graceful arches, delicate foliage patterns and finely sculpted with the royal
arms of England and the escutcheon of the Earls of Ormond. The transept to
the north, left of the nave, is of note because the west wall carries a rare example of medieval wall painting in Ireland. The fresco shows a hunting scene,
with the helpless deer seeking refuge on its knees behind a tree, with the three
original colours reasonably well preserved. The other walls of the church
make no such overt artistic claim and plain whitewash is used instead.

There is a visitor information centre within the abbey complex, a shop selling crafts, and snacks are available as well as drinks. Holy Cross Abbey, on the
R660, is signposted from Thurles and Cashel.

Roscrea

Roscrea is the most pleasant town in the north of the county, marred unfortu-   *Phone code: 0505*
nately by having the Dublin to Limerick main road running not just through   *Colour map 2, grid C6*
the town but also right by the side of the remains of the 12th-century **St**
Crónán's Church, with a truncated round tower on the other side of the busy
road. It is said that the British reduced the tower's height in 1798 after a gun

County Tipperary

shot at the castle was thought to have been fired from it. **Roscrea Heritage**, a Dúchas site, consists of a castle and the early 17th-century Damer House. The castle – made up of a gate tower, curtain walls and two corner towers – dates from the late 13th century while Damer House is a fair example of a prototype Palladian architecture. Despite being used as a military barracks at one stage, Damer House retains its original staircase gloriously intact and provides space for temporary exhibitions. ■ *Centre of town, T21850. Apr-Oct, daily, 1000-1800, €3.10. Guided tours available.*

Sleeping & eating For a meal or an overnight stay, **AL** *Grant's Hotel*, Castle St, T23300, F23209, is centrally located and serves a carvery lunch and evening meals in its bar. The hotel's restaurant, *The Lemon Tree*, is for a more formal meal.

County Limerick

Limerick

Phone code: 061
Colour map 3,
grid A3

If you ever wondered what Irish people do when they're not being engagingly disingenuous, playing traditional music or writing some major work of literature, you should spend some time in Limerick city. It's a busy working town with bus queues, crowds of kids coming out of school and bickering and fighting for the bus, loud country music in naff theme pubs, steak houses, hideous out-of-town three-star hotels with highly priced restaurants full of wedding parties, and muzak-ridden shopping malls. What is great about that is that you can disappear into this heaving mass of people getting on with their lives and enjoy the unrenovated Georgian buildings, sit in the park and be glad you're not at work, wander round the Custom House opening the drawers to find the small wonders inside, and visit John's Castle. In a country that is becoming filled to the brim with heritage, Limerick has a down-to-earth quality to it which can be refreshing after time spent in a more touristy spot.

Ins and outs

Getting there Shannon Airport, 15 miles (24km) west of Limerick city is approximately a 35-min drive away. It has both international and internal flights to Europe and the US, Dublin and Belfast. The bus and train stations are in Parnell St and have services to most cities and nearby towns. For further details, see 'Transport', page 258.

Tourist office Arthur's Quay, T317522. Jul-Aug, Mon-Fri, 0900-1830, Sat-Sun, 0930-1530; Sep-Jun, Mon-Fri, 0930-1730.

Getting around Limerick city centre is a compact area and there is no need to use local buses. Taxis can be found outside the bus and train stations, and off O'Connell St along Cecil St and Thomas St. Driving around the city can be confusing because of the plethora of one-way streets and for parking it is best to follow signs for the tourist office; the Arthur's Quay multi-storey carpark is opposite.

History

The very word 'Limerick' conjures up wars, treaties, betrayals, suffering, starvation. Even its most famous writer, Frank McCourt, wrote the most depressing account of the place in his novel, *Angela's Ashes*. But it is worth noting that when they came to make the movie of the book, they didn't film in Limerick: there weren't any locations that looked poor enough, so they went to Dublin and Cork instead.

The very first Limerick men were Vikings, who built a settlement in the middle of the river in 922. From here they raided far and wide until the Irish kings, King Mahon of Thomond and his brother Brian Boru, decided they'd had enough and took them on, in 967. The armies met at Solohead in County Tipperary and Mahon's troop went on to Limerick and sacked the place. The island became Inis Sibhton, the capital of the O'Briens for 200 years until the Anglo-Norman invasion, when the walled city came under Norman control and Gaelic families were moved out to the area now known as Irishtown. From the 12th to 17th centuries the town remained loyal to the English crown and flourished as a trading centre; there were 15 parish churches by the turn of the 17th century.

In 1642 the town was taken by Catholic forces but suffered little damage. Nine years later Cromwell's troops came through and took the town back again, but it was in 1691 that the real trouble started. As the Jacobite forces lost ground in the north they fell back to Limerick and a great 12-month siege began. A Williamite force of 22,000 attacked the town, but a daring raid led by Jacobite military commander. Patrick Sarsfield behind the Orange lines and the brave

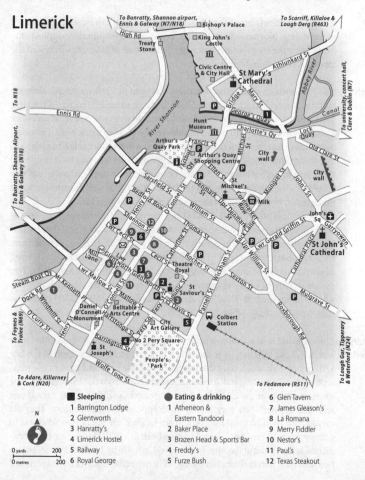

Limerick

Sleeping
1 Barrington Lodge
2 Glentworth
3 Hanratty's
4 Limerick Hostel
5 Railway
6 Royal George

Eating & drinking
1 Atheneon & Eastern Tandoori
2 Baker Place
3 Brazen Head & Sports Bar
4 Freddy's
5 Furze Bush

6 Glen Tavern
7 James Gleason's
8 La Romana
9 Merry Fiddler
10 Nestor's
11 Paul's
12 Texas Steakout

0 yards 200
0 metres 200

defence of the breach in the walls drove William back. The following year a second attempt was made to take the city, and this time the Jacobites surrendered. The Treaty of Limerick allowed the Jacobite leaders, almost all the ruling native Irish families, to leave for France and promised to protect Catholic rights. Two months later, ironically, a huge French fleet sailed into the estuary, too late to defend the Jacobites.

The Treaty of Limerick led to huge Protestant dismay: they wanted redress and punishment for the Catholic forces and within a few years they got it. Catholic rights were discounted, and by 1695 the Penal Laws gradually wore away at Catholic property, leading to great resentment on the part of the Catholics.

The town recovered from the siege and kept on growing till it had outgrown the city walls and a new area was developed – Newtown Pery, named after the developer – where most of the town's Georgian buildings stand today. After the Act of Union and due to lack of investment, the 19th century saw a period of decline for Limerick that continued well into the 20th century. Nowadays, Limerick is enjoying relative prosperity and this goes a long way to explaining the annoyance felt at the way the city is portrayed in *Angela's Ashes*.

English Town

This is the ancient part of the city whose early origins can be seen in the curve of the streets. Not actually in English Town but across the river opposite the cathedral is the treaty stone which Sarsfield is said to have actually rested the treaty on as he signed it in 1691.

King John's Castle The castle, which dominates the town, was built in 1210, an Anglo-Norman bastion. Now called King John's Castle it is best viewed from across the river since a daft-looking conservatory has been built over where its east wall once stood. It is five sided, with one of its sides reaching down to the river. The original entrance is at the north side with two round towers either side and a portcullis between them. In the 18th century a military barracks was built inside the castle and in 1935 a block of council houses went up inside. Conversion to a tourist destination has recovered the basic structure as well as exposing some much earlier buildings below the castle which can be seen inside.

The castle is great to walk around and the views off the ramparts are frightening. The interpretative element isn't too bad – the audio-visual show is a bit high on pathos and the dummies inside the towers are suffering a little from the damp, but the information panels are good. The courtyard has a nice smell of peat and is full of little tents with people demonstrating ancient crafts. You can also watch the ongoing excavations although it's not immediately obvious what is happening. ■ *T360788. Apr-Oct, daily, 0930-1730 (1800 in Jul and Aug, Nov-Dec, daily, 1030-1630. €6.35.*

St Mary's Cathedral The cathedral is in a constant state of repair, but even partly dismantled it's a wonderful old building. It is the oldest building in Limerick, built in the late 12th century, although only the west doorway, the nave and parts of the transepts and aisles are original. Most of the chapels are from the 15th century. The main attraction in the cathedral is the misericords, 15th-century carved oak seats that allowed their user to rest while appearing to be standing. They are carved with mythological figures and are labelled for the person who was to occupy them. In the Lady Chapel (dating back to 1997!) the reredos (the ornamental screen behind the altar) was carved in 1907 by Michael Pearse, whose two sons took part in the Easter Rising. When the chapel was being constructed an ancient vault was found with three decapitated skeletons inside, but there is no indication of how they arrived there in that state. In the Chapel of the Holy Spirit, the Leper's Squint (which was the original nave of the church) was where people suffering from leprosy could be given communion without infecting the righteous. ■ *Jun-Sep, Mon-Sat, 0900-1300, 1430-1700; Oct-May, Mon-Sat, 0900-1300. Visitors are asked to donate €1.27 to the upkeep of the cathedral.*

Limerick Museum

The museum has been recently housed in these purpose-built quarters in Nicholas Street, next to the cathedral. It is full of the usual bits and pieces that cities collect over the years, including a letter written during the Easter Rising from Padraig Pearse, one of the leaders of the 1916 Easter Rising and son of Michael who carved the cathedral reredos. There is a lot of information on the Lough Gur site, as well as some artefacts, so if you intend to visit the site this might be a good introduction. ■ *Tue-Sat, 1000-1300, 1430-1700. Free.*

Irish Town

This is the place where the Normans sent the native Irish when they adopted the walled city for their own. It developed as an important trading centre and it was given its own set of walls, some of which remain near to **St John's Catholic Cathedral**, not so old as the Church of Ireland one but still quite beautiful and without that sense of not quite knowing what it should look like that other Catholic cathedrals in Ireland have. It was built in the style of Pugin by a London architect, Hardwick, who used light very effectively to create the sense of spirituality that so many modern cathedrals lack. Outside is a statue of Sarsfield.

Hunt Museum

This has to be the main place of interest in Irish Town: its front is on the river side and is best viewed from the opposite bank. Built by a Sardinian, Davis Duckart, in 1765, it is Palladian with a three-bay pilaster frontispiece creating a sense of grandeur when approached from the river. Inside is the **Hunt Collection**, the most fascinating collection of artefacts in Ireland. It is only part of the private collection of the Hunts, antique dealers who ducked and dived around Europe until the Second World War, when they found themselves interned in England since Mrs Hunt was German. They offered, and were allowed, to leave for Ireland, which they made their home, first in Howth and then Limerick. They bought and sold antiques from all and sundry, and there were a lot of things going cheap in the 1930s, and out of the profits built up this amazing collection. In Ireland they took part in the Lough Gur excavations and eventually people just started to bring them things they had turned up while ploughing. In Howth they kept all their antiques lying about the place and there is a photo in the museum of the kitchen with a Picasso hanging next to the stove. It would be fruitless here to point out the most interesting items since the whole place is a wonder. Get on one of the guided tours or just wander about opening the drawers, but give yourself lots of time. ■ *Rutland St, T312833. Tue-Sat, 1000-1700, Sun 1400-1700. €5. Shop, restaurant. Telephone in advance for tours.*

Pery Square

Built in beautiful Georgian straight lines, these old buildings, like many of those in Dublin, survived because there was no money to redevelop the area in the 1960s. The men who planned this part of the city had great expectations of Limerick's potential and this can be seen in Pery Square, which was to be 49 houses built as a tontine, the last of the original builders to survive to inherit

County Limerick

the lot. Only six were built, Pery Square as you see it now, but they are an excellent example of Georgian architecture at its most confident, built in 1839 and symmetrically patterned, the two end houses having gable entrances. Number 2 has been restored to form an Ashes Exhibition, based on *Angela's Ashes*. ■ *T314130. Mon-Fri, 1000-1630.*

City Art Gallery Opposite the terrace in Pery Square is the People's Park, originally to have been the private park in the middle of the square and made into a public park in 1874. The gallery cum library is found at its corner; it was paid for by Andrew Carnegie and built in 1906 in an uneven mixture of Celtic Revival and Arts and Crafts styles. Inside there are paintings by Irish artists from the 18th century to the present, with Jack Yeats well represented as is Sean Keating. It also hosts temporary exhibitions. ■ *Pery Sq, T310633. Mon-Sat, 1000-1300, 1400-1800. Free.*

Essentials

Sleeping
■ *on map, page 253*
Price codes:
see inside front cover

Limerick is a busy commercial centre and en route to most tourist destinations in the south which is reflected in its accommodation. There is a whole string of 3- and 4-star hotels on the Ennis Rd, taking up great swathes of parking and garden space, but the best hotels are right in town. In addition, there are a number of B&Bs, and an enormous number of holiday hostels, most of which are student accommodation let out in the holidays. The hostels listed below are open all year.

LL-L *Jury's Hotel*, Ennis Rd, T327777, www.jurysdoyle.com All the comforts one would expect form a Jury's hotel – 2 restaurants, bar, leisure facilities and closer to town than the others on Ennis Rd. **L** *Limerick Inn Hotel*, Ennis Rd, T326666, www.limerick-inn.ie Vast 2-storey modern building with swimming pool and fitness centre. Very spacious comfortable rooms with all the technology you could hope for. 15-mins, drive from town but also on bus route. Close to Bunratty and on the road to Shannon Airport. **L-AL** *Limerick Ryan Hotel*, Ardhu House, Ennis Rd, T453922, www.ryan-hotels.com On the Shannon Airport road. A featureless modern block redeemed by the hotel's use of a house that dates back to 1780, plus a residents' bar that comes into its own when the public bar closes. The graciously styled *Ardhu* restaurant has a set dinner for €24 that is good value. **L-AL** *Royal George Hotel*, O'Connell St, T414566, www.royalgeorge.com They don't come any more central than this busy hotel with a very popular lunchtime trade and a good restaurant, as well as live music in the traditional bar. The spacious rooms are well away from the noise, though, and this place has lots of history behind it.

AL *Glentworth Hotel*, Glentworth St, T413822, F413073, modernized old hotel between the railway station and the centre of town. **A** *Hanratty's Hotel*, T410999, F411077, close to centre of town with a nightclub, restaurant and bar. **A** *Railway Hotel*, Parnell St, T423653, www.railwayhotel.ie Opposite the railway station, this is another busy city hotel and not the quietest place to stay but fine if you want to be in the centre.

B *Clifton House*, Ennis Rd, T451166, cliftonhouse@eircom.net Not far from the city centre, this is a huge B&B with 16 rooms and lots of facilities, set in landscaped gardens. **B** *Mount Gerard*, O'Connell Av, T411886. A B&B that is a little further out of town but in an attractive Victorian house. **B** *Rosmoy Town House*, O'Connell Av, T314556. Tastefully furnished, very central B&B with radios in rooms as well as the usual conveniences. Reasonable value.

C *Summerville Holiday Hostel*, Dock St, T302500, www.summerwest.com There are only 16 beds in 4-person rooms but nearly a hundred in private rooms. **C-D** *Summerville and Westbourne Holiday House*, Courtbrack Ave, T302500, F302539. Purpose-built hostel accommodation with some private doubles, tennis, pool table. **D** *Barrington's Lodge and Hostel*, George's Quay, T4152222, F416611. Nice location, in old nurses' lodgings.

County Limerick

D *Clyde House*, St Alphonsus St, T314357. Hostel with dorm beds and some private rooms. **D** *Finnegans Holiday Hostel*, 6 Perry Sq, T310308 An IHH hostel with no private rooms but 40 beds at €12.70 per person; fairly basic but with laundry facility. **D** *Limerick Youth Hostel*, 1 Pery Sq, T/F314672. At the other end of the tontine block, *An Oige*, closing between 1000-1700, apply. No private or family rooms.

Expensive The upmarket section of Limerick restaurants is a fairly traditional sort of place – steak, chicken served with accompanying vegetables and the occasional cheeky sauce. At *Freddy's*, Theatre Lane, T418749, the menu is Italian home cooking in a quiet, woody sort of place in a back lane. Main courses, like salmon in chablis sauce or chicken in whiskey sauce, in the €17-€22 range. Open Tue-Sat.

Mid-range *Paul's*, 59 O'Connell St, T316600, all beech wood and track lighting: a bright, spacious atmosphere inside a beautiful old exterior. The menu centres somewhere in the Mediterranean and if the pasta dishes don't appeal there are fine meat-based choices. Dinner only, and an early-bird menu, with any 2 courses for €14 or 3 for €18, from 1730 to 1900. Still in O'Connell St is *Nestor's*, T317333, where someone has spent a great deal of money creating a theme restaurant with a long bar downstairs looked over by a huge gallery restaurant above. Food is fun, spicy, pasta stuff. Right opposite Nestor's, is *Texas Steakout*, T410350, and there's no prize for guessing the theme or menu of this place: lots of steaks, from €18 to €22, speciality burgers for around €11, fish, chicken and vegetarian options, children's menu, lots of waiters dressed as cowboys. *Atheneon*, Steam Boat Quay, T411655, a Greek restaurant with traditional dishes like moussaka and lamb souvlaki, plus steaks and non-meat dishes. Next door, *Eastern Tandoori*, T311578, charges around €13 for most main dishes, and has a Sunday buffet for €15.

Another very young, theme sort of place is the *Brazen Head/Sportsbar* at 102-3 O'Connell St, T417412. Brazen Head is basically a modern bar with a million miniature spirit bottles in glass cases, and quite a large bar menu at lunchtime, ranging from filled baguettes to ragout of lamb. Sportsbar opens at 1800 and does food like cajun chicken, sambo, until 2100, Another good place for lunch is the *Furze Bush*, 12 Glentworth St, T411733. It is small but quaintly decorated, and does appetizers like prawn tempura for €9 and main dishes, that include vegetarian meals like ragout of aubergine and chick peas, between €14 and €20. Crepes are €12.70 and there is an early-bird menu, 1730-1900 except for Sun, that puts the bill into the affordable price bracket.

Cheap *La Romano*, opposite the Royal George Hotel, opens at 1700, but closed Mon, for pasta and pizza dishes and a reasonable wine list for a restaurant in this price range. A great place to eat and to stock up on excellent delicatessen fare for a picnic lunch is *Mortell's*, 49 Roches St, T415547. It's a cheery fresh food shop with an upmarket fish restaurant at the back. It closes at 1830, but is open from breakfast onwards and is well worth a visit for both lunch and its deli counter.

Pub food is everywhere. The *Glen Tavern* in Lower Glentworth St does food from 1200-1500 in a cheery olde worlde sort of pub. *Baker Place* in Dominick St is a nicely renovated old pub with a good lunch menu and dinner options. *James Gleeson's*, on the corner of Glentworth and O'Connell St's, is the most gloriously unreconstructed Victorian pub for many a mile and has a limited bar food menu but great atmosphere. The *Merry Fiddler* in Cecil St is vast, with old things everywhere and a menu of steaks, burgers and sandwiches.

An Sibin, in the *Royal George Hotel*, has music every night, often traditional stuff in the summer in a quite authentic shebeen atmosphere. The bar in *Hanratty's Hotel* has traditional music at weekends and the *Glen Tavern* gets musical on Wed, Thu and Sun nights. *Nestor's* often has various sorts of live music. Another place to check out is *Nancy Blake's* in Upper Denmark St. *Dolan's Warehouse*, T314483 for advance tickets, upstairs from the pub has seriously interesting modern Irish bands from Thu to Sat at varying prices for tickets depending on the fame or quality of the performer.

Eating
● *on map*
Price codes:
see inside front cover

County Limerick

Pubs & music

Theatre & The *Belltable Arts Centre*, 69 O'Connell St, T319709, www.com-
cinema merce.ie/belltable often has performances by travelling theatre companies, traditional music performances, dance shows as well as a gallery and a film club. The *Savoy
Centre*, T311900, is a cinema in Henry St with 8 screens. At Castletroy, east of town, is
the *University Concert Hall*, T331549 for details of events, where concerts of classical
music take place regularly. The *Theatre Royal* is in Upper Cecil St, T414224, and hosts
regular raves, jazz, dance, comedy and more.

Festivals In **February** is the *Kate O'Brien Literary Weekend*, T415799 for information, which
involves readings, lectures, musical evenings all centred around the work of this
important novelist. **March** (on the Sun closest to St Patrick's Day) sees the *Limerick
International Band Festival*, where there are competitions for drill and dance band
recitals, T410777 for information. The *Limerick Film Festival* also takes place in **March**,
focussing on Irish films and film-makers: T202986 (Fiona Fennell) for details. **May** sees
the *Paddy Music Expo*, on the May bank holiday, with concerts, street music and lots of
events in the pubs. The *Food Festival* in **August** is a big event with food tastings, competitions between the restaurants and special offers all over the city: T302035 for details.

Shopping Limerick has all the usual gamut of department stores as well as Arthur's Quay shopping mall with lots of little boutique-type places to browse around. **Books** The *Celtic
Bookshop*, Rutland St focuses on books of Irish interest and also has some nice maps
and craft items. They will search for out-of-print books. **Clothes** *Irish Handcrafts*, Patrick St and Arthur's Quay, sells expensive but lovely handknitted and handwoven
jumpers, tweeds, linens and mohair, while there is a branch of *Carraig Donn*, which
does some fashionable things with Aran jumpers, in O'Connell Mall. **Gifts** *Decorum*
sells Irish and foreign pottery, rugs, mirrors and lots of other goodies. *Pzzazz*, Foxes
Bow, Thomas St, sells very nice silver, bronze and pewter jewellery as well as amber.
Markets On Fri there is an arts and crafts market from 1100 to 1600 at the Milk market
on the corner of Ellen St and Wickham St. It is also good for a browse here on Fri or Sat,
when the regular market is open, or any weekday when the little shops around the
market are full of unusual food, second-hand clothes, ethnic clothes and craft items.

Sport **Bowling** *Funworld*, Ennis Rd, T325088. *Savoy Bowling Centre*, Bedford Row,
T419192. **Greyhound Racing** Market's Field, T417808. Meetings Mon, Thu, Sat 2000.
Karting *Jetland Raceway*, Ennis Rd, T454700. **Snooker** *Victoria Club Leisure Cen-
tre*, Hartsong St, T418822.

Transport **Air** *Shannon Airport*, T061-471444, in County Clare is 38.5 miles (24 km) from Limerick
and has international flights to Europe, the US and Britain as well as internal flights to Dublin, and Belfast (see page 43). **Bicycle** Bikes can be hired from *The Bike Shop*, O'Connell
Av, T315900; from *Emerald Cycles*, 1 Patrick St, T416983, www.irelandrentalbike.com and
from *Mahons Cycleworld*, 25 Roches St, T415202. The last two places have a delivery and
collection service for Shannon Airport. **Bus** T313333 between 0900 and 1930, and
T319911 for 24-hr talking timetable. The bus station is in Parnell St, next to the train sta-
tion, and there are buses to most parts of the country: **Athlone**, **Armagh** (Fri only),
Ballina, **Belfast**, **Castlebar**, **Clonmel**, **Cork**, **Derry**, **Dublin**, **Ennis**, **Galway**, **Killarney**,
Omagh, **Roscommon**, **Sligo**, **Tralee** and **Waterford**. There is also a bus to **London**, via
Dublin. The **Shannon Airport-Limerick Bus** The bus service takes 45 mins, €4.50,
and the first bus departs Limerick at 0630, last bus at 2315 (0710 and 2315 on Sun).
Train Limerick station in Parnell St, T315555, has services to **Dublin**, **Rosslare**, **Cahir**,
Tipperary, **Cork**. From Limerick Junction, southeast of Limerick, more connections are
possible. T315555. **Taxis** Along Thomas St and Bedford Row, off O'Connell St. A taxi to
or from the airport is €20 at least: T411422, T417777, T417417.

County Limerick

Ringforts

Ringforts are the most numerous ancient monument found in Ireland. There are some 45,000 of them, dating from the early Christian period around 600-900CE, but their distribution is unevenly spread. Donegal, Kildare and Dublin have the lowest density; Roscommon, Sligo and Limerick the highest. One likely explanation is that they were built as a defence against cattle raids and where an area couldn't support many farming communities they were not necessary. Excavations reveal them to be the homesteads of single farming families, although where one ringfort is found there are usually more in the vicinity. Ringforts were first mapped in the mid-19th century, but since then thousands – nearly 40 %, it has been estimated – have been destroyed, especially in recent decades when EU financing encouraged the creation of large fields. Afforestation programmes in upland areas are contributing to this process.

Our knowledge of ringfort culture is supported by contemporary sources, which reveal a hierarchical society based around territorial units, known as tuath, each with a population of around 3,000. At the head of each tuath was a king and filling the next rank down were lords, aire, of varying status. The lowest grade of non-nobles were the bóaire, independent farmers who leased land and paid for it in the form of cattle. There is good reason to believe that the different sizes of ringforts reflected these social and economic ranks.

Directory **Banks** *AIB*, Arthur's Quay, 63, O'Connell St, 109 O'Connell St. *Bank of Ireland* 94 and 105 O'Connell St. **Car hire** *Dan Dooley*, Shannon Airport; *Budget Rent-a-Car*, T471361/471098. **Communications** Post office: Lower Cecil St. **Emergencies** Garda (police), T414222; *St John's Hospital*, T415822. **Laundrette** *Speediwash*, 11 Gerard St, T319380. **Walking Tours** It had to happen: *Angela's Ashes* tours, daily, 1430 from the tourist office, lasting 2 hrs for €5.

County Limerick

Lough Gur

One of the most productive and informative Neolithic sites in Europe, Lough Gur doesn't have the grandeur of Newgrange but it is an atmospheric place none the less, and anyone prepared to scramble about a bit and use their imagination can get a good sense of the life of this place 4,000 or more years ago. The lough is shaped like a large horseshoe, and scattered all around it are ring forts, burial chambers, houses, stone circles and middens. You can stop at the interpretative centre and have a look at Grange stone circle or spend the whole day with a map looking for sites. The best compromise is perhaps a walk around the lough, looking at the big sites.

Colour map 3, grid A5

The first site of importance as you approach the lough from Limerick is the huge **Grange Stone Circle**, the most impressive of the remains here. It consists of 113 contiguous orthostats, which basically means a lot of big stones. They are bedded into a perfect circle with other stones pegging them into the ground. In the centre, the post hole that men used thousands of years ago to draw the circle with a piece of string was found when the site was excavated. Soil is drawn up around the outside of the stones. An entrance passage way lined with more stones is at the northeast of the circle.

One kilometre further along the road after the stone circle take the left turn marked Lough Gur, then past a 15th-century church ruin to find a wedge tomb. Another 2 km brings you to the car park and interpretative centre which is, for once, a useful addition to the site. From the interpretative centre the next place to head for is **Knockadoon** where there are an enormous number of barely visible remains, including a circular dwelling, and a rectangular stone-age house. ■ *Lough Gur, T360788. May-Sep, daily, 1000-1800. €3.80. Car parking. Sites 24-hr access and free. South of Limerick on N24 and then the Kilmallock road. Look for sign to Lough Gur. Enquire in advance about walking tours.*

Adare

To the south of Limerick is Adare, created in the 19th century by the third Earl of Dunraven, to house his tenants prettily. Pretty is about the right word too – a row of quaint thatched cottages, only a couple of which are actually lived in by anyone. The rest are kitsch antique shops and restaurants catering to the busloads of tourists who are brought in here to be separated from their money. Add on a **heritage centre,** and a manor house converted into an extremely exclusive hotel that you have to pay to get into, and you have a perfect recipe for a naff day out. What is good about the village is the **Augustinian Priory** at the edge of the village on the road to Limerick. It was built in 1325 and is Ireland's most unaltered intact church of that date. It still functions as the Church of Ireland parish church. There is also Ireland's only **Trinitarian Abbey** in the main street, founded in 1230, greatly enlarged in the 19th century and now the Catholic parish church. Surrounded by the golf course is the 15th-century **Franciscan Friary** and an early 13th-century castle, which has been in ruins since the end of the 14th century. It's nice to look at but you can't explore because it's bricked up with warning notices around it. If you don't want to brave the flying golf balls you can just look from the bridge with the tour groups. There is **tourist information** in the heritage centre, Main St, T396255. Jun-Sep, daily, 0900-1900; Oct-Dec and Feb-May, Mon-Sat, 0900-1700.

Sleeping **XL-LL** *Adare Manor*, T396566, www.adaremanor.ie A 19th-century manor house in a neo-Gothic style, elaborate gardens, 900 acres to walk around, a pool, golf course, a river to fish, and horses. **LL-L** *Dunraven Arms Hotel*, Main St, T396633, www.dunravenhotel.com In the middle of the village, this Georgian hotel has individually furnished rooms, lots of antiques and a leisure centre. **AL** *Fitzgerald's Woodlands House Hotel*, Knockanes, T396118, www.woodlands-hotel.ie 1 mile (1.6 km) from Adare, this is a busy place with a leisure centre and pool, big spacious modern rooms and a good bar with traditional music. **B** *Ivy House B&B*, Craigue, T/F396270. 1 mile (1.6 km) outside Adare, this is a lovely old Georgian house full of antiques and set in a well established garden.

Eating The *Maigue* restaurant in the *Dunraven Arms* has a good reputation and serves local dishes with a Californian twist, in the expensive price range. In the same price category, the *Wild Geese*, T396451, is in one of the thatched cottages and also has a high reputation. French cuisine, each course at a set price with supplements for expensive items, classic desserts. The *Woodlands House Hotel* has a popular restaurant where dinner falls in the middle range bracket, also serves affordable food in the bar/bistro. If it's a light meal you're after, try the café in the visitor centre, *Lena's Bar*, or *O'Coleáin* in the main street.

Back in the expensive bracket, in nearby Ballingarry, is *The Mustard Seed*, T069-68508, which has an enormous reputation and very stylish food. The garden is the nicest part of the place. Book well in advance and order a table for later in the evening: if you book for 1900 you may feel the service is a little hurried.

Transport **Buses** There are 5 buses a day between Dublin, Limerick and Killarney, a summer only service from Limerick to Liskard via Adare, and 1 daily service connecting Limerick and Ballingarry via Adare. For times T061-313333.

County Cork

8

County Cork

To Limerick

Rath Luirc

To Dublin

Kanturk

To Dingle

Killarney

Fermoy · Lismore

Mallow

CORK

To Waterford & Rosslare

Kenmare

Macroom

Youghal

Cork

Dunmanway

Bandon

Kinsale

Bere
Island

Bantry

Clonakilty

Skibbereen

Baltimore

Clear
Island

Sherkin
Island

Cork city and the coastal route through West Cork remain highly popular with visitors, but the county's magic is that it rarely feels overcrowded. Easy accessibility by air and sea makes the city a contender with Dublin as a first point of arrival in Ireland, especially if you want to head off for a rural idyll in one of the most beautiful corners of the country. From Cork city it is a short hop to **Kinsale**, Ireland's self-proclaimed food capital, before meandering along the south-west coast, where the landscape plays second fiddle to the mesmerizing **seascapes** and where reminders of the Anglo-Irish legacy are dotted between the **history-laden small towns** that keep their dignity and character in spite of tourism.

None of this quite prepares the unsuspecting traveller for the three narrow peninsulas that jut out into the Atlantic, justifying the description by one addicted visitor as a **"geographic narcotic"** where "it is hopeless to resist the pressure of non-pressure". The pleasures of West Cork are no longer a secret, but little has been spoilt by tourism.

Ins and outs

Getting there   Cork city has an international airport, ferry connections to Britain and France, and a railway and bus stations with good links to other towns and cities across Ireland. There is also ferry service across Cork harbour that can save driving time if wishing to avoid the city altogether. Main roads to Cork city include the N8 from Dublin, the N25 from Waterford, the N20 from Limerick, the N22 from Killarney and the N71 from West Cork.

Getting around   Driving around the county of Cork is easy as the roads are good, petrol stations plentiful, and the nearest thing to a traffic jam is when a few cars wait for a farmer to guide his cows along a stretch of road. Out of the city, parking is not generally a problem although some of the towns (Bantry in particular) have limited space at the height of summer.

All year, *Bus Éireann* run daily services between Cork, Bantry and Glengarriff, and between Cork, Clonakility, Rosscarbery, Skibbereen, Ballydehob, Schull and Goleen. There are also services between Cork, Cork airport and Kinsale and a Mon-Fri service between Skibbereen and Baltimore. A Saturday-only bus runs between Macroom and Kilcrohane via Bantry. For details contact Bus Éireann in Cork, T021-4508188.

Between 24th May and 19th Sep, *Bus Éireann* also run a daily service between Cork, Clonakility, Owenahincha, Rosscarbery, Leap, Skibbereen, Bantry and Glengarriff, with the bus continuing on to Kenmare, Killarney and Tralee. There is also a daily service between Schull, Ballydehob, Skibbereen, Bantry and Glengarriff and a Mon-Sat bus between Skibbereen and Baltimore. The all-year service between Cork and Glengarriff continues in the summer to Castletownbere.

Tourist information   For general tourist information on County Cork, www.cork-guide.ie

Cork

Phone code: 021
Colour map 3, grid B5

Mildly cosmopolitan and yet engagingly Irish, Cork is pleasantly spread out amongst the hills that rise up on both sides of the Lee Valley where the river meanders its way to the open water of Cork harbour. The city centre is actually a small island between two channels of the River Lee and the plethora of bridges can disorientate the visitor. Though Cork is a major port, there is little maritime activity in the city centre and the river is usually free of traffic. At night, the pubs fuel a mood of ebullience that never becomes rowdy, and while it is not a conventionally beautiful city its urban identity is worn lightly and the feel of the place is distinctively different from Dublin. Cork is an easy city to like and if the traffic could be taken out it would reclaim its homely beauty. It makes a good base for day trips to nearby sights including the famous Blarney Castle and the historical towns of Cobh and Youghal.

Ins and outs

Getting there   From the airport a ½-hourly bus service takes you into the city where the bus station is in Parnell Pl near Merchant's Quay. Taxis from the airport cost about €11.50. Taxis are usually metered; otherwise ask for a price first. The rail station is a 20-min walk away from the centre, east of the city, but a frequent bus service brings passengers into the bus station and St Patrick St, and taxis are about €3.80.

Getting around   City buses go out from St Patrick St to all areas of the city. There is a taxi rank in the centre of St Patrick St and another beside the bus station. Most of the city's interesting sights are walkable, but the No 8 bus route is useful for the hostels and sights at the west of the city.

★

Things to do in County Cork

- Search for the Viking boat in St Mary's church, Youghal
- Explore the coast between Timoleague and Clonakilty
- Explore Clear Island on foot
- Swim at Barley Cove, Mizen Peninsula
- Walk the Beara Way
- Appreciate Irish art at the Crawford Art Gallery, Cork city
- Stay overnight at Lettercollum House, Timoleague

Tourist office Grand Parade, T4273251. Sep-Jun, Mon-Sat, 0930-1730; Jul-Aug, Mon-Sat, 0900-1900, Sun, 0900-1500. *Usit Now* (student travel), 10 Market Pde, St Patrick St.

History

The Gaelic for Cork, *Corcaigh*, meaning marshy, evokes the city's origins in broad marshland formed by two channels of the River Lee. St Finbarr founded a monastic settlement here, some two centuries before marauding Vikings arrived in the ninth century. The Danes eventually established a permanent trading post and, after the Anglo-Norman invasion in the 1170s, this evolved into a walled city under Norman control. It wasn't until after a successful five-day siege by the armies of William of Orange at the end of the 17th century that the walls were torn down. By 1800 Cork was a prosperous city built upon trade, increasingly with the English who valued the city's harbour both for its imperial navy and for shipping home the county's agriculture, especially butter. Shandon, to the north of the city centre, was the centre of commercial life at this time and the city's harbour became the major transatlantic port in Europe, with ships calling in for provisions and butter being exported to Australia and South America. In the aftermath of Easter 1916, Cork began to develop a reputation for political opposition to Britain and in 1920 the mayor, Thomas MacCurtain, was murdered by the British who also burnt down the city centre. Today, Cork is a thriving city with light industry providing much of the employment.

Early Irish literary and historical texts often reveal an obsession with topographical exactitude but this is not always the case with contemporary sources. Cork city's main street is St Patrick St but you may come across it as St Patrick's St. Similarly, Western Rd and Lancaster Quay often elide into just Western Rd.

County Cork

Sights

St Finbarr's Cathedral Not necessarily an essential place to visit, but this is the site traditionally associated with the birth of the city when St Finbarr in the seventh century came here from his hermitage in Gougane Barra and founded a monastery on the site of the present late 19th-century cathedral. The interior is as richly embellished as the splendour of the exterior suggests it will be, and no doubt the wealthy merchants who paid for its construction were pleased with the way the English architect, William Burges, combined his love of medievalism with a conspicuous display of Protestant affluence. Highlights include the statuary of the ornate west door, the 1930s roof of the sanctuary, and a memorial stone near the pulpit to Elizabeth Aldworthy, the only woman ever initiated into the Masons. ■ *Bishop St. Mon-Sat 1000-1700. €2.50 donation suggested.*

St Anne's Church, Shandon As the salmon-inspired weathervane on the famous steeple might suggest, this church is an altogether different kettle of fish. Built in the early 18th century to replace a church destroyed by the Williamite besiegers, the curious-looking steeple has limestone sides looking down on the city and red sandstone on its other two faces. Climb up the steps for an opportunity to ring the bells that a Cork priest, Francis O'Mahony (1804-66, pen-name Father Prout; he later left the priesthood and took up journalism in Paris), rendered famous in some forgettable doggerel. Further steep steps lead up to the very top for aerial views of the city. The Shandon clock, known as the 'four-faced liar' because the east and west faces tell slightly different time, has an inscription which wisely reads "Passenger, measure your time, for time is the measure of your being." The modest Georgian-style church interior could be skipped. ■ *Church St and Eason Hill. Mon-Sat, 1000-1700. €4.45 (church, tower and bell ringing).*

Other Shandon sites

St Anne's notwithstanding, the Shandon area is characterized by 19th-century vernacular architecture and two distinctive buildings that bear witness to Cork's butter market being the largest in the 19th-century world. Butter from all corners of the county found its way to Shandon, where it was weighed, traded and packed in casks (firkins) before being hauled down to the river for export to England. A self-important Doric façade fronts the **Cork Butter Market**, built in 1730 and now a craft centre (see page 273), while the pleasing rotunda of the **Firkin Crane Centre**, T5074817, is open to the public for cultural events such as plays and dance performances: check with the tourist office to see what is on. In O'Connell Square, the **Cork Butter Museum** tells the story of Shandon and the butter trade but there is not a lot to see for the €3 entrance charge. ■ *T300600. May-Sep, Sun-Fri, 1000-1300 and 1400-1700.*

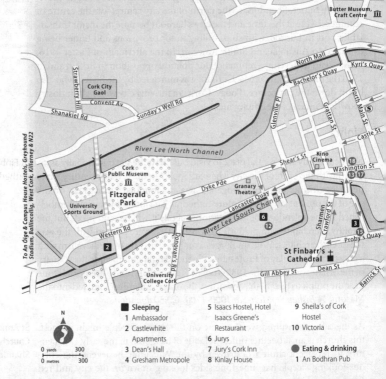

Cork city centre

■ **Sleeping**
1 Ambassador
2 Castlewhite Apartments
3 Dean's Hall
4 Gresham Metropole
5 Isaacs Hostel, Hotel Isaacs Greene's Restaurant
6 Jurys
7 Jury's Cork Inn
8 Kinlay House
9 Sheila's of Cork Hostel
10 Victoria

● **Eating & drinking**
1 An Bodhran Pub

A pleasant stroll up through the grounds of University College leads to its Victorian quadrangle, opposite the late 20th-century Boole Library named after the radical mathematician who died in 1864 while a professor at the college. With your back to the library entrance walk directly across the square to enter the quadrangle building. Along both sides of the corridor stands a collection of Ogham stones with a plaque explaining this ancient form of writing. To the east of the library it is worth seeking out the resplendent, Celtic-inspired interior of the Honan Chapel. Built in 1916, the eye-catching mosaic floor is matched for beauty by the Harry Clarke stained glass windows. ■ *Bus No 8 from the city centre.*

University College & Honan Chapel

This late 18th-century neo-classical residence was built for a wealthy Cork merchant and *aficionados* of interior design will appreciate the bifurcated staircase of Bath stone and the Adam fireplaces. There is also a collection of water-colours by one of the five Gubbins sisters who lived here in the early 20th century. ■ *T4821014. Situated at the east side of Cork, off the N25 road to Rosslare, 750m after the roundabout. May to mid-Oct, Wed-Sun, 1400-1800. €2.50 (guided tour).*

Dunkathel House

Museums and art galleries

The museum, situated in a Georgian building in Fitzgerald Park opposite University College, is good on Cork's eventful and significant role in the war

Cork Public Museum

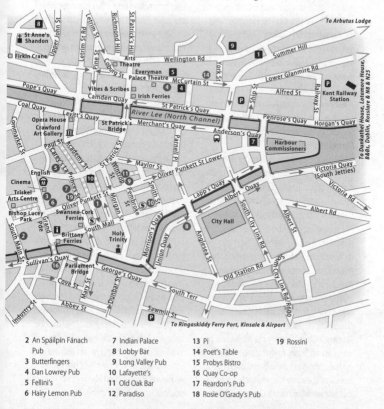

County Cork

2 An Spáilpín Fánach Pub	7 Indian Palace	13 Pi	19 Rossini
3 Butterfingers	8 Lobby Bar	14 Poet's Table	
4 Dan Lowrey Pub	9 Long Valley Pub	15 Probys Bistro	
5 Fellini's	10 Lafayette's	16 Quay Co-op	
6 Hairy Lemon Pub	11 Old Oak Bar	17 Reardon's Pub	
	12 Paradiso	18 Rosie O'Grady's Pub	

A city tour

This lengthy stroll, starting outside the tourist office, goes across the city, past many of the places of interest described in this chapter. There is too much to see in one day, so either curtail your walking and sightseeing drastically or consider it as two one-day walks.

Day 1 From outside the tourist office turn to the right and look for the first entrance to the **English Market** on the right, before the cinema but after the junction with Oliver Plunkett Street. Pass straight through this interesting arcade of shops, noting On the Pig's Back, a shop selling excellent breads and cheeses, and exit on the other side past the fountain on to the pedestrianized Princes Street. Turn left and walk up to the main thoroughfare of **St Patrick Street**. Cross to the other side and take the first left down Carey's Lane. This area around **Paul Street** has a number of restaurants and shops well worth checking out. Turn right into Emmet Place, passing the **Crawford Art Gallery** on the left; the gallery's café is a smart place for mid-morning tea and cakes. Carry on to the river, cross the bridge and continue straight ahead to the junction with the **Cork Arts Theatre** on the right. Turn to the left here, crossing over Upper John Street and taking the left up John Redmond Street to the **Shandon sites**.

Retrace your steps to the Cork Arts Theatre and go down Coburg Street and straight across to **MacCurtain Street**. A formerly shabby thoroughfare leading to the railway station and roads to Dublin and the southeast, MacCurtain Street is gradually sprucing itself up. The ex-temperance Metropole Hotel has been refurbished, but the exterior still evokes a bygone age, while across the road Isaacs Hostel has a good restaurant and there are also some interesting small shops (see 'Shopping' on page 273).

Day 2 After passing the Metropole on MacCurtain Street, take the second turning on the right, Brian Boru Street, and cross the bridge of the same name that leads to the bus station. **Merchant's Quay** shopping centre is close by, but this route carries on down the street you are on, until you reach the south branch of the river and cross Clontarf Bridge to Albert Quay. Turn right and pass the stately **City Hall**, the last large-scale edifice to be built in Ireland in the classical style. The original building was burnt down by the British in 1920, but it was reopened in 1936 by De Valera, and in 1963 when President John F Kennedy spoke from its steps, the largest crowd ever to be seen in Cork filled every space hereabouts. Continue along the riverside on Union Quay and when this turns into George's Quay notice the 18th-century houses and their very high roofs. On the other side of the river the distinctive exterior of the neo-Gothic Holy Trinity Church, designed by GR Pain in 1832, is difficult to miss. Cross over to this side by the next bridge, Parliament Bridge, which leads up to South Mall, characterized by solicitors' offices and other commercial premises. Turn to the left and walk to the end of the street where the baroque Maid of Erin monument commemorates nationalist heroes of the past. From the nearby footbridge there is a fine view of **St Finbarr's Cathedral**. Stay on the monument side, opposite the tourist office, and walk up Grand Parade. Before reaching the junction opposite the cinema look for the entrance gate to the Bishop Lucey Park on the left; inside the gate there is a fragment of the medieval city walls. Walk through the park and exit in the right corner that comes out by the side of an old church, now the Cork Archive Centre; attached to it is the **Triskel Arts Centre**, which has a small café. Turn right and go up to join Washington Street, where a left turn will lead on to Western Road. After passing Jury's Hotel on the left it is a short way to the main entrance of **University College**, while across the street there is a short road that leads to Mardyke Walk, a mile-long (two-kilometre) avenue that was laid out in the early 18th century. Walk along here past a cricket ground and into Fitzgerald Park and the **Cork Public Museum**. Bus No 8 on Western Road brings you back to the city centre.

Ogham

Ogham, or ogam, is the earliest Irish form of writing, preserved on stone and dating from the period between the fourth and seventh centuries. Its alphabet has 20-25 letters and takes the form of a series of slashes of different lengths inscribed down the edges of stone pillars. Although *the writing is thought to have its origins in a Celtic class of pagan priests, the examples that have been preserved on the 300 or so ogham stones, found mostly in Cork and Kerry, translate into perfunctory statements of descent: x is the son of y and y is the son of z.*

for independence; the unstylish archaeological displays on the first floor are less appealing. The adjoining green is a quiet retreat for a picnic lunch and, unlike the Bishop Lucey Park on Grand Parade, is rarely crowded. ■ *T4270679. Mon-Fri, 1100-1300, 1415-1700 (1800 in summer), Sun, 1500-1700. Free. Bus No 8 from city centre.*

Cork City Gaol

The city gaol, remarkably well preserved in its essentials, functioned from the 1820s for just under a century. A guided tour by tape comes with the admission charge, followed by a melodramatic audio-visual display. Also housed in the prison is a radio museum. From the city centre either take a taxi or bus No 8 as far as University College and then walk through Fitzgerald Park, over the delightful suspension footbridge bridge and up the hill to the right before turning left into Convent Avenue. From here a sign points the way to the gaol. ■ *Sunday's Well Rd, T4305022. Mar-Oct, daily, 0930-1800. Nov-Feb, daily, 1000-1700. € 4.83.*

Crawford Art Gallery

Even if time short, spare some for a visit to Ireland's most important art gallery outside of Dublin. The building served as the city's Custom House in the 18th century. Jack B Yeats, Sean Keating, Harry Clarke, William Gerard Barry and Edith Somerville are some of those represented, as well as work by contemporary artists working in Cork. British artists include George Romney, Frank Bramley and Jacob Epstein and there is a new gallery open for temporary exhibitions. ■ *Emmet Pl, T4273377. Mon-Sat 0930-1700. Free. Restaurant.*

County Cork

Essentials

There is a reasonable spread of accommodation, covering most budgets, but in Jul and Aug it is advisable to have a room booked in advance or leave it to the tourist office to find somewhere for you. Along Glanmire Rd heading out east of town near the railway station there is a string of similarly-priced B&Bs (see **B** category, below), and the main cluster of hostels is at the bus station end of town.

Sleeping
■ *on map*
Price codes:
see inside front cover

L *Arbutus Lodge*, Montenotte, T4501237, F4502893, www.arbutuslodge.net At the west side of the city, this Victorian townhouse offers country-house style in a city. Individually decorated rooms and original paintings by the likes of Anne Yeats and Patrick Scott around the place. Bar and superb restaurant. **L** *Jury's Hotel*, Lancaster Quay (though the address is often given as Western Rd), T4276622, F4274477, www.jurysdoyle.com is Cork's best known hotel. A pool, 2 restaurants and a popular bar serving food with a few tables in niches overlooking the river. **L** *Great Southern Hotel*, Cork Airport, T4947500, F4947501, www.gsh.ie Worth checking out for special rates which make can reduce the price of a room considerably.

Walking on water – St Patrick Street

The curving shape of Cork city's main thoroughfare is due to the fact that it was built over a tributary of the River Lee, and up until the beginning of the 19th century small boats made their way up and down the waterway. At the junction of Tuckey Street and Grand Parade one can still see a bollard where boats moored, and in St Patrick Street itself, outside the Château Bar *not far up from* Waterstone's

bookshop, the tall steps bear witness to the days when boats moored beneath them. When the Black and Tans set the city aflame at the end of 1920, it was the north side of the street that was burnt down and if one walks along this side – between the two bookshops of Waterstone's *and* Eason's – *you can look across to the other side and spot some of the original 18th-century bow windows.*

L-AL *Hotel Isaac's*, 48 MacCurtain St, T4500011, F4506355, www.isaacs.ie Free car parking nearby. City centre hotel with a courtyard garden. Restaurant. **L-AL** *Ambassador Hotel*, Military Hill, T4551996, F4551997, www.ambassadorhotel.ie A former military hospital, built in the 1870s, with views over the city. Bar and restaurant. **AL** *The Gresham Metropole*, MacCurtain St, T4508122, F4506450, www.ryan-hotels.com This was once the largest temperance hotel in Ireland. Refurbishment has retained some feel for the past and the rooms are comfortably large. Leisure centre includes a pool. Streetside rooms can be noisy at weekends so ask for a river view. Bar and Restaurant. **L-AL** *Victoria Hotel*, St Patrick St, T4278788, F4278790, www.victoriahotel.com No car-park, better value outside of summer, the hotel is entered from Cook St. This was where Joyce once stayed, as recounted in *A Portrait of the Artist as a Young Man*.

A-B *Forte Travelodge*, Kinsale Rd roundabout, South Ring Rd, Blackash, T4310722, F4310707 www.travelodge.co.uk Room rate charged, handy for the airport and for families, but special offers may make the *Great Southern* better value. Little Chef restaurant next door. **A** *Jury's Inn Cork*, Anderson's Quay, T4276444, F4276144, www.jurysdoyle.com Reasonable value for money with a room rate rather than price per person, this hotel offers modern comfortable accommodation. Restaurant **A** *Lotamore House*, Tivoli, T4822344, F4822219, lotamore@iol.ie Just off the dual carriageway to the Dublin/Waterford roundabout. Georgian guesthouse set in very agreeable grounds and with a period feel but no bar or restaurant.

The following guesthouses are all large 3-storey Victorian houses alongside one another on Western Rd between Jury's Hotel and the entrance to University College Cork. They all have hotel-level room facilities and are within walking distance of the city centre. **AL-A** *Killarney Guesthouse*, T4270290, F4271010, www.killarneyhouse.com Large and comfortable guesthouse opposite University College Cork, car-park to the rear. Closed for 2 days over Christmas. **AL-B** *Garnish House*, Western Rd, T4275111, F4273872, www.garnish.ie Has 24-hr reception and above-average breakfast menu. **A-B** *Redclyffe Guest House*, Western Rd, T4273220, F278382, redclyffe@eircom.net Stands out with its red brick colour and there is car parking at the front and rear. **A-B** *Antoine House*, T4273494, F4273092, antoinehouse@eircom.net Private car-park at the rear and open all year. **A-B** *Saint Kilda's Guesthouse*, T4273095, F4275015, gerald@stkildas.com 20 rooms and closed between 10 Dec and 10 Jan.

Less expensive accommodation tends to be clustered along Lower Glenmire Rd, heading east out of town and close to the railway station. They do not have car-parks and to avoid having to pay for parking on the street, even where this is possible, cars need to be left up the hill behind Glenmire Rd. **B** *Kent House*, 48 Lower Glenmire Rd,

T4504260, kenthouse47@hotmail.com. B&B with some rooms en suite. **B** *Number Forty Eight*, 48 Lower Glanmire Rd, T/F4505790. B&B adjacent to the train station. **B** *Oakland*, 51, Lower Glanmire Rd, T4500578. B&B. **B** *Aaran House*, 49 Lower Glanmire Rd, T4551501, aarankev@hotmail.com.

Two B&Bs at the western end of Cork are **B** *Lisadell House*, Western Rd, T4546172, matt@indigo.ie and **B** *55 Wilton Gardens*, off Wilton Rd, T4541705. Both can be reached by bus No 8 from the city centre and the last one can be reached by bus No 5.

Other B&Bs in the same price range are found a little way outside Cork in the Douglas area and reached by bus No 7 from the city centre. Douglas has its own shops and restaurants and is convenient for the airport or ferry port. **B** *River View*, Douglas, T4893762, edwardsc@tinet.ie is in Douglas village near *Barrys Pub*. **B** *Coolfadda House*, Douglas Rd, T4363489, is near *St Finbarrs Hospital*.

C-D An Óige *Cork International Youth Hostel*, 1&2 Redclyff, Western Rd, T4543289, F4343715 www.irelandyha.org/anoige/cork3.html A smart establishment at the western side of town, with 2-bed rooms in the **C** category. **C-D** *Isaacs*, 48 MacCurtain St, T4508388, F4506355. IHH hostel, nearest to town, money exchange and email facility. **C-D** *Kinlay House*, Shandon, T4508966, F4506927,kinlay.cork@usitworld.com Bob and Joan Walk. Lots of private rooms, IHH, laundry facilities available, breakfast included, bike hire. **C-D** *Sheila's of Cork*, Belgrave Pl, Wellington St, T4505562, F4500940, info@sheilashostel.ie Provides meals, laundry facilities, private and family rooms, sauna, money exchange and bicycle hire.

D *Aaran House Tourist Hostel*, Lower Glenmire Rd, T4551566, is directly opposite the railway station and not to be confused with the B&B of the same name on the other side of the street. An IHO hostel, includes 3 private rooms for €24, open all year, bikes for hire and breakfast included. **D** *Campus House*, 3 Woodland View, Western Rd, T4343531, F4343531. Has 20 beds and some family rooms. **D** *Cork City Independent Hostel*, 100 Lower Glanmire Rd. T4509089. A short way past the railway station, on the opposite side of the road. There are 25 beds and these include 7 private rooms. **D** *Kelly's*, 25 Summerhill South, T4315612, kellyshostel@hotmail.com IHO hostel, a little way south of the city centre, 2 private rooms in the **C** category, bike hire.

Camping *Bienvenue Ferry Caravan & Camping Park*, T4312711. Opposite the airport, this is handy if heading out to West Cork. *Cork City Caravan & Camping Park*, Togher Rd, T4961866. This is the nearest to the centre, reached by the No 14 bus.

Self-catering *Deans Hall*, Crosses Green, T4312623, www.deanshall.com Apartments for 4 or 6 persons from €95a night or €495 a week. *Castlewhite Apartments*, University College, T4902793, F4344099. Rents apartments between mid-Jun and mid-Sep. *Isaac's Apartments*, MacCurtain St, T4500011, F4506355. Has 2- and 3-bedroomed apartments.

The narrow lanes between St Patrick St and Paul St are home to quite a few reasonably priced restaurants, varying in quality but usually worth a visit for a mid-morning break, a quick lunch or a look at their dinner menus. Better restaurants are found at the Western Rd and MacCurtain St ends of town. The price ranges below refer to dinner only; lunch is usually around €6.50 - €9 wherever you go. 'Expensive' is around €38; 'Middle range'' around €25; and 'Affordable'' around €12.

Eating
● *on map*
Price codes:
see inside front cover

Expensive For seriously good food the *Arbutus Lodge* restaurant, T4501237, is hard to beat. Fresh seasonal produce, especially fish, and a very impressive wine list.

County Cork

☞ Live events

To find out what's on at the moment and what is coming up within the week, check out the flyers on the noticeboards, windows and doorways of the following places: for theatre, film, dance and other cultural events check the Triskel Arts Centre and the Granary Theatre. For live music, concerts and gigs in general the pubs in Washington St and Union Quay will have all the latest information.

Mid-range *Amicus*, French Church St, T4276455. Value-for-money meals means Amicus is rarely empty and there are separate breakfast, lunch and dinner menus. Lots of vegetarian choices and evening dishes range from a Thai-style curry for €10 to steaks and salmon around €17. *Probys Bistro*, Probys Quay, T4316531, across from St Finbarr's Cathedral, is smart and modern and serves dishes like chicken with pineapple and chilli pepper salsa for €12. Tasty choice of daily specials, speciality seafood nights on Wed, an early dinner menu for €12.63 on weeknights, and good service. *Isaacs Restaurant*, 48 MacCurtain St, T4503805, remains very popular due to dependably good food – prawns and chilli, Thai chicken curry for example – at reasonable prices. It is not related to *Greene's Restaurant* in *Hotel Isaacs* at the same address. Greene's is a little more expensive but it is worth comparing their menus. *Paradiso*, T4277939, on Lancaster Quay opposite *Jury's* hotel, is Cork's quality vegetarian restaurant. *Pi*, T4222860, opposite the courthouse on Washington St, is a modern, arty kind of place with 26 pizzas on the menu and all sorts of trendy coffees and teas. Open until 2300; later at weekends. If an Art Nouveau setting seems more appealing, eat at the *Lafayette's* in the *Hotel Imperial* on South Mall.

Cheap *Fellini's*, 4 Carey's Lane, T4276083, is good for coffee, snacks and meals, open daily until 1900. *Indian Palace*, 31 Princes St, has an affordable lunch in arty surroundings; main dishes for dinner are under €11. Next door, the roomy *Ristorante Rossini*, T4275818, has lunch specials, mostly pasta, with pizzas at night around €13. The *Quay Co-op* on Sullivan's Quay, T4317026, serves vegetarian dishes, including breakfast, in a spartan setting quite unlike the stylish layout of the more expensive *Crawford Gallery Café*, Emmett Pl, T4274415. *Poet's Table*, in MacCurtain St T4509274, is a vegetarian café open weekdays until 1630 for meals like salmon and potato cake, spiced corn burgers, cauliflower and leek bake for around €4.50. Lovely cakes, tea and coffee at a modest price, plus occasional poetry readings on Thu lunchtimes. *Butterfingers*, near the tourist office, has a variety of inexpensive dishes and light meals.

Dan Lowrey's Tavern in MacCurtain St (see Pubs below) serves pub food in a characterful setting and *The Long Valley* at the top of Winthrop St dispenses doorstep-sized sandwiches.

For picnic provisions, visit the English Market (see page 268).

Pubs & music Cork city had a lively pub and music scene and most of the pubs mentioned below have notice boards carrying flyers that advertise what is coming up as regards live music around the town. The tourist board also dispenses a free listings magazine and events may also be checked out at www.whazon.com

The *Lobby Bar*, Union Quay, T4311113, www.lobby.ie Free musical sessions downstairs on Mon to Wed and Fri at 2130. About €7 for regular appearances by Irish and international singers and groups. *Rosie O'Grady's*, 27 South Main St, T4278253. Traditional Irish music on Mon, Wed and Sun nights. *An Spáilpín Fánach*, T4277949, is a wonderfully old-looking establishment on South Main St with regular musical evenings (usually a cover charge). *Reardon's* on Washington St is a cavernous place, with live music on Wed and Fri. The *Old Oak*, 113 Oliver Plunkett St, T4276165, www.oldoakbars.com, has a nondescript exterior but plenty of *craic* inside. *An Bodhran*, on the same street, had traditional music on Mon night. Also on the same street, *Hairy Lemon* attracts drinkers for its cheap pints between 1600 and 2000, Sun to Thu. *Dan Lowrey's Tavern*, 13 MacCurtain St, has no music but beautiful old furnishings and a sense of character.

The Comedy Club at *City Limits*, Coburg St, T4501206, www.thecomedyclub.ie has live comedy on Fri and Sat nights. The pubs in Washington St have live music, mostly weekends, and attract students.

Theatre The Everyman Palace, MacCurtain St, T4501673, www.everymanpalace.com often has Irish drama on its programme. *Triskel Arts Centre*, Tobin St, T4272022. Tucked behind Washington St, this is usually worth checking out for visiting theatre groups. The *Cork Opera House*, Emmet Pl, T4270022, hosts plays and classical concerts, rarely operas, and tends to be conservative in its choice of productions. The *Granary Theatre*, Mardyke, T4904275, is on the one-way road coming into Cork from the west, parallel to Western Rd, and is run by University College Cork. **Cinema** *Capital cineplex*, Grand Parade, T4278777. The main cinema in town. *Kino* Washington St, T4271571, is more of an art house cinema. **Greyhound Racing** *Curraheen Park*, T1850-525575, www.igb.ie has racing every Wed, Thu and Sat at 2000.

Entertainment
Cork Booking Office, facing Washington Street near the tourist office, T4543210, handles tickets for most theatres and other entertainment events

Literary Walking Tour Meets outside the Imperial Hotel on South Mall at 1930 on Tue and Thu, Jun to Sep, €6.35. T4291649. **Open Top Bus Tour** Departs from the bus station at 1030 and 1445, lasts 3 hrs and takes in Blarney with time for a visit to the castle. €7.60.

Tours

16-19th Mar *Celtic Flame Festival*, including a St Patrick's Day parade in the city centre. **Late Apr/early May** *Cork International Choral Festival*. Events taking place in the City Hall, cathedrals, churches and arts centres. T4308308, www,corkchoral.ie **Late Jun/ Midsummer** *Cork Arts Festival*. Music, theatre, literature and visual arts. **Jul** The weekend around the 10th launches *Seisiún Cois Cuan* in Cobh, featuring sessions of traditional ballads, folk and celtic rock. **Early Oct** *Cork International Film Festival*. World renowned film festival. T4271711 www.corkfilmfest.org **Late Oct** *Cork Jazz Festival*, with the Metropole Hotel hosting many events. T4278979. www.corkjazzfestival.com **Nov** *Cork Arts Festival*, expect something worthwhile given that Seamus Heaney and dance troupes from Africa have graced previous events. T4326567,

Festivals

St Patrick St may be the main street but most of the shops are disappointingly familiar; more rewarding is the nearby pedestrianized area around Paul St and Emmet Pl. There are a couple of antique shops appropriately located on Fenn's Quay. This street was laid out in the 1720s and 2 antique shops occupy part of a row of the old houses, which were recently reconstructed, preserving the original internal panelling and staircases. For straightforward purchases of consumer items and clothes there are 2 department stores on St Patrick St – *Roches* and *Cash's* – while the modern *Merchant's Quay* shopping centre near St Patrick's Bridge has a supermarket and decent clothes shops.

MacCurtain St has an appealingly eclectic range of shops, including *The Living Tradition* at No 40 that specializes in Irish music. The old *Cork Butter Market* in Shandon is now a craft centre with shops, most of which close on Sat afternoon and Sun, selling Irish crystal, Celtic-inspired jewellery and stained glass.

Shopping

County Cork

Cork has a good number of bookshops, all boasting a generous stock on subjects relating to Irish literature, history and the like. *Waterstone's* and *Eason's* are both on St Patrick St while *Connolly's* on Paul St deals in second-hand books, mostly 19th- and 20th-century literature. On the same street, *Mainly Murder* specializes in thrillers, while *Mercier Press* have a shop in nearby French Church St. *Vibes & Scribes*, just over St Patrick's Bridge before reaching MacCurtain St, has a large selection of discounted books on Ireland and most other subjects, and a café upstairs.

For camping and walking equipment try *Tent & Leisure*, on York St but visible from the corner on McCurtain St, T500702, or *The Tent Shop*, 7 Parnell Pl, T278833. For fishing gear and tackle *Murray & Co* are centrally located in St Patrick St, T272842.

Transport

Air **Cork Airport**: T1800-626747/4313131, for flight information T4327100. 5 miles (8 km) south of the city, reached by the south city link road. Direct flights to Dublin, both London airports, Amsterdam, Paris and Rennes. Exeter, Jersey, Manchester and Newcastle are also directly served. *Aer Lingus*, Academy St, T4327155; Cork Airport, T4327100.

Bicycles **Bike hire**: *Cycle Scene*, 396 Blarney St, T4301183. *Irish Cycle Hire*, railway station T4551430. *Kilgrew's Cycles*, 6 Kyle St. *Rothar*, 2 Barrack St, T4313133.

Bus **Bus station**: Parnell Pl (opposite Merchant's Quay), T4508188. Regular services to all parts of Ireland including Dublin (4½ hrs, €17 single, €26 return), Killarney (2 hrs) Bantry (2¼ hrs), and Wexford (3¾ hrs).

Car Cars can be hired at Cork Airport or the Cork tourist office. Apart from the car-park at *Merchant's Quay* shopping centre and one next to the tourist office, hourly parking vouchers are needed for the limited street space. They're available from newsagents.

Car hire Familiar names have desks at the airport, including *Eurocar*,T4917300, *Budget*, T4314000. *Avis*, T4281111. *National*, T4320755. Better rates available outside the airport: *Malone*, T4506744. *Grandons*, T4866217. *Top Car*, T4343366. *Budget* have a desk in the tourist office.

Sea **Ferry terminal**: Ringaskiddy, about 16 km southeast of the city. *Brittany Ferries*, 42 Grand Pde, T4277801; at the terminal, T4277801. Provides a service to Roscoff between Mar and Oct. *Irish Ferries*, 9 Patrick's Bridge,T4551995. Handles routes to Le Havre, Cherbourg and Roscoff. *Swansea Cork Ferries*, 52 South Mall, T1800-620397; ferry terminal, T4378036. Services to the UK; closed between early Jan and early Mar.

Cork city and around

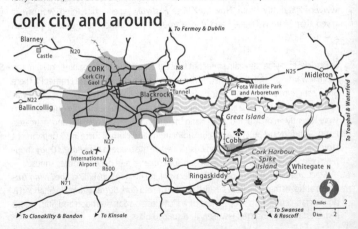

Taxis Taxis are often parked in the middle of St Patrick St at the bridge end, while 24-hr companies are based in MacCurtain St T4272222, T4505522.

Train Kent railway station: T4504777. Tickets and information also from *The Travel Centre*, 65 St Patrick St, T4504888. Services to Dublin and other cities. A local service to Cobh also stops at Fota Wildlife Park.

Banks and bureaux de change Banks are located on South Mall and St Patrick St, and money can also be changed at the tourist office, where there is also a Western Union outlet. **Communications** Post office: Main post office in Oliver Plunkett St, smaller offices in Mac Curtain St and Washington St. **Internet**: 8 Winthrop St, T4273090, opens daily from 0900 until 0300. **Medical services** *Cork University Hospital*, Wilton Rd, T4546400. **Laundry** 14 Mac Curtain St, Mon-Sat 0900-2000. **Pharmacy** *Phelans*, 9 St Patrick St, T4272511, open daily until 2200. **Tour operators** *USIT*, 10-11 Market Pde, T4270900.

Directory

Around Cork

There are a number of places of interest that can be easily reached by bus, car or bicycle from Cork. An interesting day out could combine Blarney with the Royal Gunpowder Mills at Ballincollig, and along the way, it is difficult to miss the spectacular 330-m-long Victorian façade of a former hospital on the other side of the river, while on the left side Cork's only high-rise building, County Hall, is notable for its tongue-in-cheek bronze statue, 'Men Watching' (1975) by Oisín Kelly.

Another day out, by car or train, could take in the Fota Wildlife Park and the historic town of Cobh to the east of the city. Either of these places could also be visited as part of a longer excursion taking in the distillery at Midleton and the historical sights at seaside Youghal, although there is a fair bit to see in both Cobh and Youghal and an overnight stay in either town is worth considering.

Blarney

Getting there Follow the N22 to Killarney (ignore the less interesting road signposted for Blarney that keeps on the north side of the River Lee), signposted as a right turn off the Western Rd that heads out to West Cork. The road to Blarney (the R579) crosses the Lee after a long, straight stretch of road, and there is another right turn on to the R617 before the village and castle are reached. Buses 224 and 234 run to Blarney Mon-Fri, from the Parnell Pl bus station in Cork.

Ins & outs
Phone code: 021
Colour map 3, grid B4

Tradition has it that the garrulous Cormac MacCarthy, the Gaelic lord of Blarney, was so successful at inventing excuses for not complying with the demands of the English that Queen Elizabeth I dismissed his blather as so much blarney. Kissing the stone of his 15th-century castle in order to gain the gift of the gab is itself a mighty piece of blarney played out on a daily basis to countless visitors, but this is all part of the fun and as long as you turn up early enough to miss the queues an enjoyable time can be had. It does help to have a head for heights and care should be taken with children because, although only the one machicolated tower survives, the stairs are steep and accidents have occurred. ■ *T4385252. May-Sep, Mon-Sat, 0900-1830, Sun 0930-1730; Jun-Aug, 0900-1900. €4.50.*

Blarney Castle

County Cork

Blarney Castle House Next door to the castle, this is a turreted mansion from the late 19th century. Descendants of the original Jeffreys family are still in residence, while the rooms open to the public are handsomely furnished and decorated in period style. ■ *Mon-Sat 1200-1800. €3.80.*

Blarney village The neat green that defines Blarney village (*An Bhlarna*) is very un-Irish, being laid out by General Sir James Jeffreys in the early 18th century: the MacCarthys' blarney had run dry and they had left in the Flight of the Earls after the defeat at the Battle of the Boyne. Everything is compactly together around the village green, including a small tourist information office, in the old woollen-mill buildings, the bus stop, a large *Blarney Woollen Mills* store that opens daily, pubs and restaurants. **Tourist information office**: T4381624.

Eating Hotels like *Blarney Castle*, T4385116, the Blarney Park, T4385281, and *Christy's*, T4385011, are all reliable sources for competitively priced lunches in their bars and all have more expensive restaurants. However, like everywhere in Blarney at the height of summer, it only takes the disgorging of one mammoth coach to suddenly overwhelm a place. This can also happen at *Blair's Inn*, Cloghroe, T4381470, about 5 mins by car from Blarney on the R579. Bar menu until 2130, daily, and also a restaurant open for lunch and dinner. Food is served between 1230 and 1530 and from 1830 and there is also a beer garden and traditional music on Sun nights; also on Mon in the summer.

Ballincollig

The **Royal Gunpowder Mills**, established in the garrison village of Ballincollig, were, in the 18th century, Britain's most important gunpowder manufacturing plant, and the largest of its kind in Europe. It closed in 1903 and reopened as a visitor attraction in the 1990s. Food is available every day until 2200 in the five bars that make up *Darbys Bar & Restaurant*, T4870584, in the centre of the village. ■ *Apr-Sep, Mon-Sat, 1000-1800. €3.80. Situated on the N22 road west of Cork: there is also a bus service to the village from Cork, T4874430.*

Fota Wildlife Park

More than an open-air zoo, Fota was successfully established with the intention of breeding endangered animals. Situated 10 miles (16 km) outside of the city, its 70 acres of open land will appeal especially to families, given the roaming cheetahs, giraffes, kangaroos, monkeys, oryxes, ostriches and penguins. Children will enjoy a visit to the café where a troop of lemurs descend for freebies. Visitors walk around at will or take one of the small trains that regularly chug around the park. ■ *T4812678. 17 Mar-4 Nov, Mon to Sat 1000-1800, Sun 1100-1800. Winter, Sat 1000-1600, Sun 1100-1600. €6. €1.27 car park fee. Café. From Cork take the N25 to Rosslare and take the signposted road to Cobh. The park is signposted off this road. Or take the Cork to Cobh train, T4506766, which stops at the park.*

Cobh

Ins & outs
Colour map 3, grid B5

Getting there There is a regular train service between Cork and Cobh. Car and passenger ferries cross Cork harbour from outside of Cobh, on the road to Cork, but they only save time if heading for the main ferry terminal at Ringaskiddy or skipping Cork and travelling west to Kinsale and beyond.

County Cork

Pronounced 'cove', and named Queenstown between 1849 (when Queen **History** Victoria dropped by) and 1922, the picturesque town houses rising up the slope of a hill were the last sight of Ireland for the millions of emigrants who left here for America in the 19th and 20th centuries. The scene is graphically described in an 1842 travel book: "Mothers hung upon the necks of their athletic sons; young girls clung to elder sisters; fathers – old white-headed men – fell on their knees, with arms uplifted to heaven, imploring the protecting care of the Almighty on their departing children."

The offshore Spike Island was a holding prison for political offenders prior to their enforced departure for Botany Bay. Cobh itself is on an island, Great Island, though it is easy to forget this when one looks out from the town's promenade. To add to the town's unfortunate associations, the *Titanic* paid its last call here in 1912, and three years later the *Lusitania* was torpedoed not far away by a German submarine, an event that brought the US into the First World War. Hundreds of the drowned passengers are buried in an old graveyard to the north of town.

Today, Cobh is a bustling little place with a lively holiday air that attracts as **Sights** many Irish tourists as overseas ones, and a hugely ugly church that dominates the skyline. Back in 1720 the **Royal Cork Yacht Club**, possibly the oldest yacht club in the world, established a home here. The building they commissioned for their headquarters in 1854, in the very centre of the town, now houses temporary art exhibitions and a well run **tourist office**. Cobh Tourist Information Centre, T4813301 is open in summer, Mon-Fri, 0900-1800, Sat-Sun, 1000-1800; winter, Mon-Sat, 0930-1730. They publish a *Titanic Trail* guide, €6.28, and can provide details of cruise liners about to arrive in the harbour.

The town's heritage centre, **Cobh, The Queenstown Story**, located in the old **Heritage** railway station, is devoted to the town's poignant associations and there are **centre** interesting and touching displays covering the tragedy of mass emigration and the disasters at sea. ■ *T4813591. www.cobhheritage.com Mar-Dec, Mon-Sat 1000-1800. €5*

County Cork

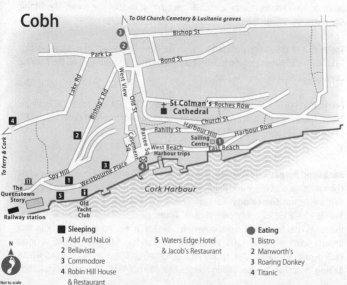

Cobh

To Old Church Cemetery & Lusitania graves

Bishop St

Park La

Bond St

West View

Lake Rd

Bishop's Rd

Old St

St Colman's Roches Row
Cathedral

Church St

Rahilly St

Harbour Hill

Harbour Row

Parsee St

Casement Sq

Sailing Centre

West Beach
Harbour trips

East Beach

To ferry & Cork

Spy Hill

Westbourne Place

The Queenstown Story

Old Yacht Club

Cork Harbour

Railway station

N
Not to scale

■ Sleeping		● Eating
1 Add Ard NaLoi	5 Waters Edge Hotel	1 Bistro
2 Bellavista	& Jacob's Restaurant	2 Manworth's
3 Commodore		3 Roaring Donkey
4 Robin Hill House		4 Titanic
& Restaurant		

Cobh Museum There is also a small museum in a defunct Presbyterian church, on the right side as you walk into town from the railway station. The exhibits relate to local, especially maritime, history. ■ *T4814240. Summer, Mon-Sat 1100-1300, 1400-1800, Sun 1500-1800. €1.*

A town walk From opposite the museum, walk up Spy Hill to enjoy a fine view of the harbour. The nearest island is Haulbowline Island, while Spike Island is closer to the mouth of the harbour. Carry on up Bishop's Road as a right turn at the top provides a startling view of just how steeply the houses stand on the hillside. From here it is a short walk across to **St Colman's Cathedral**, designed by EW Pugin and GC Ashlin. Building began in the 1860s but wasn't completed until 1915. If arriving in Cork by ferry, the commanding presence of the church is hard to miss and the granite and limestone exterior is equally impressive when close up. The spire boasts the country's biggest carillon, with 47 bells covering a range of four octaves, the largest bell weighing in at 7,584 pounds (3,440 kg).

Sleeping
■ *on map*
Price codes:
see inside front cover

Accommodation needs booking in advance during the **regatta** in the middle of Aug. **L-AL** *Waters Edge Hotel*, next to the Heritage Centre, T4815566, www.watersedgehotel.ie Attractive new hotel; 2-night packages. **AL** *Robin Hill House*, Lake Rd, T4811395, www.robinhillhouse.com An old rectory with 6 delightfully modern, uncluttered bedrooms (ask for one overlooking the harbour) and a superb restaurant. Easily the smartest place to stay in town. **A** *Bellavista*, Bishop's Rd, T4812450. This B&B is a good example of Cobh's Victorian houses. **B** *Ard Na Laoi*, 15 Westbourne Pl, T4812742. B&B, with fine views of the harbour.

Eating The €35 dinner at the *Robin Hill Restaurant*, Lake Rd, T4811395, is worth every euro. Starters like gravadlax from wild salmon or avocado and boilie cheese, main courses of meat and fresh fish and a serious wine list. Reserve a harbour-view table if possible. The characterful *Titanic Restaurant*, T4855200, does expensive dinners nightly except Mon. *Jacob's Ladder*, in the *Waters Edge* hotel, has lunch specials and main courses for dinner range from €11 to €24. The *Commodore Hotel*, T4811277, serves conventional hot meals at lunch and evening time. The *Bistro*, T4811237, serves dishes like bacon and mushroom quiche and chilli con carne at inexpensive prices. The *Titanic Bar*, has outdoor seats over the harbour for regular pub meals.

Pubs The best 2 of the many pubs with music are close to one another: *Mansworth's*, T811965, on Midleton St, which dates back to the late 19th century, and the *Roaring Donkey*, T811739, on Oreleia Terr.

Transport **Ferry** T4811485. Daily service from 0700 to 2415. €4.45 return, €3 single. **Train** There is a regular train service (no bicycles carried) between **Cork**, T4504777/ T4506766, and Cobh, T4811655.

Directory **Banks and Bureaux de change** Banks: Westborne Pl and West Beach. **Bureaux de change**: at the post office and *Blarney Woollen Mills* shop at the entrance to the Cobh Heritage Centre. **Genealogy** For family research contact the *Cobh Heritage Centre*, T4813591; F4813595; cobhher@indigo.ie **Tours** Guided Titanic Trail walks through the town,1100 from the *Commodore Hotel*, T4813878, €6. An hr-long harbour tour departs from the pier at 1200, 1400, 1500; 1600 on Sun, T4815211, €3.80. A Ghost Walk departs from *Pillars Bar*, opposite tourist office, at 2030, Tue, Thu and Sat, €6.35. **Sailing** Dinghy and cruiser sailing courses, East Beach, T4811237, www.sailcork.com

County Cork

Midleton

You will find Ireland's chief distillery in Midleton, 15 miles (24 km) east of Cork. When a new distillery was opened here, the original 19th-century works were preserved and opened to the public as the **Jameson Heritage Centre**. The conducted tour starts with a film show, but the interesting part is the walkabout that takes you through the whole process, from the yard where local farmers arrived with their barley through to the massive machinery, including a powerful waterwheel and a steam engine, and the obligatory free taster in the bar. Further drinks can be purchased and there are some vintage whiskeys for sale. There is also a café serving light meals, but for something more substantial try the pub lunches at the Victorian-style O'Donovans, 58 Main Street, T4613594. ■ *Guided tours, Mar-Oct, daily,1000-1800, last tour at 1400; Nov-Feb, tours at 1130, 1430, 1600. €5. There is a frequent Bus Éireann service between Cork and Middleton.*

Colour map 3, grid B5

Youghal

Pronounced 'yawl' (from *Eochaill* a 'yew wood'), the town is at the mouth of the Blackwater and was founded in the 13th century by Anglo-Normans, probably on the site of an earlier Danish settlement. During the Elizabethan age the town and surrounding land became the property of Sir Walter Raleigh and during his years as mayor in 1588 he is credited with having smoked the first pipe of tobacco in Ireland. In 1602 Raleigh sold out to Richard Boyle, later the Earl of Cork, and he spent far longer in residence here than Raleigh ever did. Nowadays, it is the summer season that attracts most visitors and the Blue Flag beach makes Youghal popular with Irish families, while the places of interest within the town justify at least a half day's visit.

Phone code: 024
Colour map 3, grid B6

Youghal

To Aherne's Seafood Restaurant & Waterford (N25)
Myrtle Grove
Church St
Almshouses 1
Red House
Tynte's Castle
Emmet Pl
De Valera St
O'Neill Crowley St
Cross La
North Main St
Bow St
St Mary's +
Chapel La
Meat Shambles La
Ashe St
O'Rahilly St
2
Clock Gate
3
i
Market Place

To Avonmore House, Evergreen House, Ballmakeigh House & Brown's Restaurant & Cork (N25)

● **Eating & drinking**
1 Nook Pub
2 Perfect Blend
3 Tower

Not to scale

The main road between Cork and Waterford (N25) passes through Youghal. Bus Éireann's Cork-Youghal-Ardmore service, No 260, runs daily with 6 express buses taking 90 mins. The first bus leaves Cork at 0840 and the last bus departs from Youghal at 2225. The main Expressway bus, No 40, travelling a number of times daily between Tralee and Rosslare stops at Youghal and also connects the town with Killarney, Macroom, Ballincollig, Cork, Dungarvan, Waterford and Wexford.

Ins & outs

Tourist office T20170, near Market Sq at the harbour side of town. Apr-Sep, Mon-Sun 1000-1730; Jul-Aug longer hrs; Oct-Mar, Mon-Fri 1000-1730. **Tours** *Walking tour*, Jun-Aug, Mon-Sat 1100. €4.45. Depart from tourist office.

County Cork

A walking tour A good place to begin a walking tour is outside the **Clock Gate**, the quaint but striking structure that divides the town's long thoroughfare into South and North Main Streets. A gate of the original 13th-century town walls stood on this spot, but in the late 18th century the present structure was built as a gaol and the story goes that political prisoners were tortured here and publicly hanged from the windows. Make your way up North Main Street for about 500 yds, passing on your left the post office and then the **Red House** on the same side of the road. This Dutch-inspired house was built in the early 18th century and a few doors up there is a different and older type of architecture, a set of restored **Alms Houses** built in 1610 by Richard Boyle a few years after Raleigh sold his land to him. On the opposite side of the street stands **Tynte's Castle**, a 15th-century structure.

St Mary's Church The real highlight, however, is the Protestant St Mary's Collegiate Church, reached by turning left a little way further up North Main Street. The church has had a chequered history; originally built in the early 11th century, and restored in the 1850s; some of the Victorian excess, such as the plastering that covered the stone walls, has now been removed. Check out the flamboyant tomb of Richard Boyle and his family. Designed by a London sculptor and brought over to Youghal, this is one of the best 17th-century tombs in Ireland. Boyle's two wives are either side of him, the reclining figure at the top his mother-in-law, and his children are below.

The explanation of the 'leper's squint', at the entrance to the north transept is worth reading and the north-facing wall of this transept, which is thought to date from an original 11th-century church built by Christianized Vikings, carries an etching of a Viking boat inscribed on a lower stone. Interesting old tombstones may also be found outside in the churchyard and there is a stepped path that leads up a handsome stretch of the medieval town wall. ■ *T91076. Donation requested.*

Myrtle Grove Next to the church gates is a rare example of a 16th-century unfortified house. The home of Walter Raleigh, where it is said that under a yew tree in the garden, Edmund Spenser read parts of his *Faerie Queene* to him; far more probable than another old wives' tale that Raleigh also planted the first potatoes from the New World here. It is not possible to visit the house, but by peeping over the church wall, on the right after passing through the church gate, the Elizabethan chimneys can be seen.

Fox's Lane Folk Museum At the other end of town, in North Cross Lane near the tourist office, Fox's Lane Folk Museum is filled with an miscellany of domestic artefacts from the late 19th century to the 1950s: moustache cups, hat irons, sausage makers and so on. ■ *Summer, Tue-Sat, 1000-1300 and 1400-1800. €2.50.*

Sleeping **AL** *Ballymakeigh House*, at Killeagh 6 miles west of Youghal, T95184, is part of a working farm and has won plaudits for its accommodation and above-average breakfasts. **A-B** *Avonmore House*, South Abbey, T92617. A centrally located B&B; if coming from Cork it is just before the road splits into a one-way system. **B-C** *Evergreen House*, The Strand, T92877, www.evergreenireland.ie, is a new hostel with dorm beds and private rooms.

Camping *Clonvilla*, Clonpriest, T98288. Only 10 pitches available for tents.

Eating *Aherne's Seafood Restaurant*, T92424, at the Waterford end of town, has a bar serving seafood pizza, chowder and open chicken sandwiches in the €7-12 range. The

County Cork

restaurant comes under the expensive bracket. At the other end of town, on Main St near the clock tower, *The Perfect Blend*, T91127, is good for lunch and a mid-range evening menu. *Tower Restaurant*, South Main St, T91869, serves quick lunches and middle-range evening meals between Thu and Sat. Out on the road to Cork at Killeagh, *Browne's Restaurant*, T91373, serves hearty Irish cooking, from breakfast to dinner.

The Nook, Main St, has traditional Irish music on Wed nights, as does the aforementioned *Browne's Restaurant* on Thu.

Pubs & music

Macroom

From Cork the N22 road can be taken direct to Killarney by car or bus, missing out West Cork entirely. Macroom would be the best place to stop for a meal and the town could also serve as a base for forays into West Cork or the Killarney area itself.

Phone code: 026
Colour map 3, grid B4

In **Macroom** the **AL** *Castle Hotel*, Main St, 41074, www.castlehotel.ie has a decent restaurant, a pool and gym. The **A** *Victoria Hotel*, Main St, 41082, www.thevictoria-hotel.com, where William Penn once stayed, is a friendly place with affordable bar food and a modest restaurant. *Café Museli*, South Sq, T42455, serves affordable vegetarian and Italian-style dishes.

Sleeping & eating

Bandon and Dunmanway

The above route will also take you from Cork to Bantry via Gougane Barra (see page 306), but a more direct, though far less scenic, route to Bantry is by way of the N71 to Bandon and then the R586 through Dunmanway. Bandon was once a famous old Protestant town, ("even the pigs are Protestant" goes the old saying). Someone painted on the walls of 17th-century Brandon "Jew, Turk or atheist may enter here, but not a papist." A reply appears afterwards "whoever wrote this wrote it well, for the same is written in the gates of Hell." It was also a military barracks during the War of Independence that came under fire from rebels and was the scene of an attempted assassination on Major Percival (see page 290) as described in Tom Barry's *Guerrilla Days in Ireland*. The West Cork Heritage Centre, in an old church on North Main St, T023-44193, explains just how important the potato once was to Irish life.

Phone code: 023
Colour map 3, grid C3/4

County Cork

The best place to stay or stop for a meal is the **AL-A** *Munster Arms Hotel*, Oliver Plunkett St, 41562 (see The 'last day in the life of Michael Collins' box on page 290). Dunmanway has the highly recommended **D** *Shiplake Mountain Hostel*, T/F45750, a converted 19th-century farmhouse with woodburning stove, dorm beds and 4 private rooms for €23 to €38 each, depending on the time of year. There is space for camping, bikes can be hired and meals can be arranged.

Sleeping & eating

North Cork

North Cork is heaven to fishing folk who flock here annually to cast on the River Blackwater, and **Fermoy** has a fishing shop, *Brian Toomey Sports*, 18 McCurtain St, T025-31101, who can advise and sell tackle. However, finding an edible meal in Fermoy is not an easy task. Try the creperie, *La Bigoudenne*, T025-32832, 28 McCurtain St, which opens every evening except Monday.

The prosperous market town of **Mallow** has a far better choice of places to stay and eat and is another major base for anglers.

Sleeping & eating

To the west of Mallow at **Kanturk**, *Assolas Country House*, T029-50015, F50795, is a gracious country house (dinner for residents only) with elegant rooms, blazing log fires and an admirable policy statement: "We do not apply a service charge and gratuities are not expected." *The Vintage* in O'Brien St, T029-50549, is a pleasing traditional pub with food.

Kinsale and further west

For details of festivals in west Cork, see page 292

West Cork begins in Kinsale with stage-managed brouhaha of the culinary kind and ends with the desolate beauty of the remote Beara peninsula where restaurants of any kind are thin on the ground and picnic provisions are the order of the day. In between there are towns, villages and places that will feed and nourish the soul, for West Cork is rich with a natural and cultural diversity that takes in ancient stone circles and medieval castles, villages and houses still resonant with dwindling evocations of Anglo-Irish colonialism and seascapes and landscapes to die for, best appreciated by dipping into the long-distance walks that encircle two of the peninsulas. The latest cultural layer comes in the form of a small wave of immigrants from northern Europe ranging from impoverished New Age folk (still called 'hippies' or, even after living here for decades, 'blow-ins') to well heeled retirees who arrive in spring and only stay if they become reconciled to the quite different lifestyle imposed by West Cork winters.

Kinsale

Phone code: 021
Colour map 3, grid C5

This harbour town, some 20 miles (32 km) south of Cork city, offers a hedonistic introduction to this corner of Ireland and the town may lure you back like an English captain who arrived here in a storm in the early 18th century and observed, there is "very good French claret in the taverns and we did not a little indulge ourselves". The town is pretty but 'historical Kinsale' has been marginalized, and the virtual takeover of the town by non-locals, never mind tourists, has helped dilute its West Irish identity.

West Cork

History

Kinsale was settled by the Anglo-Normans as early as the 12th century, but it was in 1601 that the town became the scene of one of the most decisive battles between Irish and English forces. Under O'Neill, the Earl of Tyrone, the Irish forces marched south and cut off the supply lines from Cork of the English army that was besieging some 4,000 Spanish soldiers inside Kinsale. The English had control of the sea, however, and supplies were brought in by ship. The Spanish were made to surrender and O'Neill was forced back to Ulster and eventual exile in Europe. Kinsale's fate – it became an English town and Irish people were not allowed to live inside its walls – was the model for what happened to the rest of the country, because O'Neill's defeat precipitated the end of the old Gaelic civilization in Ireland.

In 1689 James II of England landed in Kinsale in his doomed attempt to regain the throne. He was proclaimed king in the church of St Multose, and returned here finally to sail away after defeat at the Battle of the Boyne. In the 18th century the small winding streets that characterize contemporary Kinsale developed, and in the last 20 years or so they have gradually been converted to restaurants, galleries and gift shops.

Sights

The bare ruins of early 17th-century James Fort are hardly worth a visit, but on the opposite bank of the estuary stand the more extensive remains of **Charles Fort** built in 1670. Although substantial damage was incurred during the Civil War of 1922-23, the impressive size is still very apparent and the guided tour explains the significance of what was one of the largest military forts in the country. ■ *T4772263. Mid Mar-Oct, daily, 1000-1800; rest of the year, weekends only. €3.17. Dúchas site.*

Built as a customs house around 1500, the Spanish used Desmond Castle as an arsenal during the 1601 siege. American sailors captured during the War of Independence were imprisoned here; their cells later being used to hold French sailors captured during the war against Napoleon. During the Famine it was a workhouse, but less deprived times have seen its rebirth as the

County Cork

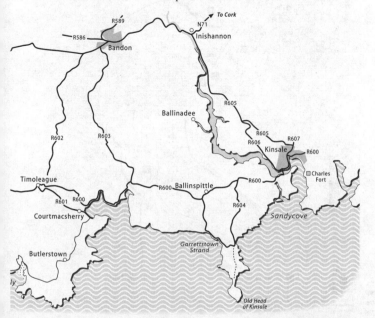

International Museum of Wine. Unless you are particularly interested in the history of Ireland's wine link with mainland Europe, there is not a lot to see. ■ *Cork St. T4774855. Mid-Apr-Oct, daily (closed Mon until mid-Jun). 1000-1715. €2.53. Dúchas site.*

In the centre of town, the early 17th-century courthouse with an 18th-century façade is a local **museum** full of craft tools and artefacts on the ground floor, and maritime memorabilia upstairs. ■ *Market Sq. T4777930. Summer, Mon-Sat 1030-1730, Sun 1400-1730. Irregular opening times during winter. €2.54.*

Tourist office Emmet Pl, T4772234. Jul and Aug, Mon-Sat, 0900-1845, Sun, 1000-1255, 1415-1745; Nov-Mar closed. Rest of year, daily, 0930-1730, closing for lunch.

Sleeping
■ on maps
Price codes:
see inside front cover

LL-L *Perryville House*, Pearse St, T4772731, www.perryvillehouse.com Has a lovely wrought-iron exterior and plush bedrooms. The fact that **L** *Old Bank House*, Pearse St, T4774075, was an old bank explains its prime location in the centre of town. It's a tasteful guesthouse with antiques and the original 200-year-old walls exposed in the sitting room and breakfast room. **L** *Blue Haven*, Pearse St, T4772209, F4774268. This hotel has elegantly decorated rooms named after French-Irish wine families. **L** *Trident*, World's End, T4772301, F4774268. More relaxing than the exterior suggests, and with a variety of packages worth enquiring about. **L** *Harbour Lodge*, T772376,

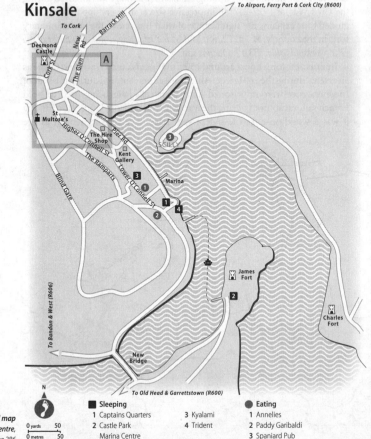

Kinsale

To Airport, Ferry Port & Cork City (R600)

To Cork
To Cork
Barrack Hill
New Rd
The Glen
Cork St
Desmond Castle
A
St Multose's
Higher O'Connell St
The Hire Shop
Pier Rd
Kent Gallery
The Ramparts
Lower O'Connell St
Marina
1
3
2
1
4
Blind Gate
S SILLY
3
James Fort
2
Charles Fort
To Bandon & West (R606)
New Bridge
To Old Head & Garrettstown (R600)

N

0 yards 50
0 metres 50

■ **Sleeping**
1 Captains Quarters
2 Castle Park Marina Centre
3 Kyalami
4 Trident

● **Eating**
1 Annelies
2 Paddy Garibaldi
3 Spaniard Pub

*Related map
A Kinsale centre,
page 286*

County Cork

Kinsale's International Gourmet Festival

The four-day International Gourmet Festival usually takes place in the first or second week of October, and has been doing so for over 25 years. A membership fee costing €254 covers the champagne opening, the cocktail-fuelled farewell plus the daily special events that take place during the day and at night and a €95 voucher redeemable in any of the Good Food Circle restaurants. Accommodation and restaurant reservations need to be made independently. Details from The Good Food Circle, c/o Peter Barry, Sicily, Kinsale, Co Cork, T4774026, F4774438.

www.harbourlodge.com, is out at Scilly and it makes the perfect place to escape the hustle and bustle of town, with sea-facing rooms with kingsize beds and a huge conservatory to while away time.

AL *Kieran's Folkhouse Inn*, Guardwell, T4772382, folkhse@indigo.ie B&B and an evening meal in the seafood bistro downstairs available as a package.

A *Old Presbytery*, Cork St, T/F772027. This guesthouse has a reputation as one of the best B&Bs in town. **A** *Pier House*, Pier Rd, T/F4774475. A smart, centrally located and relatively quiet B&B. **A-B** *Captain's Quarters*, Dennis Quay, T4774549, www.captains-kinsale.webjump.com is situated away from the traffic but very central. Rooms are refreshingly uncluttered and the maritime theme is inoffensive.

B *Amarach*, The Glen, T4774633. Townhouse B&B with 3 en-suite rooms; closed in winter. **B** *Rock View*, The Glen, T4773162. B&B with car park behind the house. **B** *Kyalami*, 16 Lower O'Connell St, T/F4772074. One of the less expensive B&Bs in town.

D *Castlepark Marina Centre*, Castlepark, T4774959, maritime@indigo.ie. Modern hostel, about 2 miles (3 km) from town and reachable by ferry from outside the *Trident Hotel* during the summer. Only one private room; bike hire. **D** *Dempsey's*, Eastern Rd, T4772124. Next to a garage, this is a fairly basic hostel with €8.90 dorm beds, but private rooms also, and handy if coming from Cork as the bus will stop outside.

The plethora of restaurants here is a distinguishing feature of the town that calls itself the gourmet capital of Ireland. Cynics say that the whole gourmet scene in the town has more to do with successful promotions and advertising notions of Kinsale as a 'product' than with good food at competitive prices. But there is a certainly a generous choice of dishes to consider, from black pudding poached in pink champagne and Thai fish cakes to home-made burgers and chips.

Expensive The *Blue Haven*, T4772209, on Pearse St has a nautical theme to the décor, modern Irish cuisine, and worth trying to reserve a table by the waterfall. The wine list is based around Irish families who established vineyards around the world, especially in France, between the 17th and early 19th centuries. The *Vintage*, T4772502, on Main St serves classical dishes with innovative touches in a comfortable atmosphere. Lots of seafood, a surprise 5-course menu and a cosy little snug for pre-dinner drinks. *Restaurant D'Antibes*, at the top end of Pearse St, does lobster, as well as main dishes around €20. *Annelies*, Lower O'Connell St, T4773074, is a smart steak and seafood place opening at 1815 and last orders at 2215. *Jim Edwards*, T4772541, can be relied on for meat and fish dishes and starters like kidneys spiked with madiera and garlic. Out at Scilly, *Man Fridays*, T4772260, maintains standards while packing in diners for oysters, steaks and seafood.

Eating
● on maps
Price codes:
see inside front cover

County Cork

Mid-range The best deals for 3-course meals under €25 come in the form of early-bird menus and other set dinners. *Crackpots*, T4772847, has a 3-course dinner for €18.50 between 1800 and 1930. The *Cottage Loft*, T4772803, on Main St has a €17.80 menu for early evening dining and a set dinner for around €23.50; vegetarians have a choice of dishes here. Almost next door, *Hoby's*, T4772200, has a €19 set dinner and à la carte. The *Little Skillet*, T4774202, almost next door, has a cosy, home cooking atmosphere, is open from 1800, and main dishes are around €15. Coming in at the bottom end of the mid-range category is *Paddy Garibaldi* on Lower O'Connell St: starters like smoked salmon and asparagus wraps and main courses like scallops or Thai prawn curry.

Cheap Mad Monk, Main St, T4774602 is a brash pub with a kinky monastic theme but serves good pub grub like chilli bean burrito, and chicken curry for around €9 until about 2130 when the music takes over. One of the reliably best places of all for a decent meal at lunch or dinnertime is the bar food at the *Blue Haven* on Pearse St. Main courses like Thai chicken curry or catch of the day are around €10. Tasty open sandwiches are about €7.50. *The Greyhound*, usefully situated in a pedestrianized area near the museum, has outdoor tables and pub food in the €5-€10 range: home-made burgers, baked potatoes, salmon platter, sandwiches. *Pisces Bistro*, on the corner of Market St and Guardwell, is open 7 days and has reasonable prices for interesting food served from lunch 'till late. Lots of filled things as well as simple hot food for lunch, and a more sophisticated dinner menu. Out at Scilly *The Spaniard* is worth the journey for top drawer pub grub and traditional Irish music many nights of the week. *Max's Wine Bar*, T4772443, Main St, has an affordable early-bird menu; otherwise a meal here comes under the middle-range bracket. Some vegetarian choices. *Patsy's Corner* is a tiny tea-shop, chairs outside, doing sandwiches and snacks. *Mango Café* in Short Quay is also tiny and with a few tables out on the street. Lots of sandwiches, filled paninis and a tempting dessert menu. *Dino's*, Pier Rd, serves traditional fish and chips.

Pubs & music
For festivals information, see page 292

Throughout the summer, most of the pubs in Kinsale are packed with groups of revellers intent on having a good time, occasionally enlivened even more by weekend merrymakers from Cork. Old-time favourites include the *1601* on Pearse St, and the nearby *Shanakee*. *The Blue Haven* bar has music at weekends and *An Seanachai* has live music or a DJ every night. Quiet pubs in town are difficult to find but *Sam's Pub*, The Glen, and the *Tap Tavern*, near St Multose Church, are both local pubs where conversation is more important than loud music; though the Tap Tavern has traditional music on Thu nights.

Shopping

There are 2 shops stocked with souvenirs and Irish crafts – *J Cronin*, a beautifully designed place made to look like an old fashioned hardware store, and *Bolands* – facing each other opposite the post office. The galleries and shops along Main

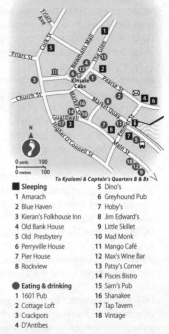

Kinsale centre

0 yards 100
0 metres 100

To Kyalami & Captain's Quarters B & Bs

■ Sleeping
1 Amarach
2 Blue Haven
3 Kieran's Folkhouse Inn
4 Old Bank House
5 Old Presbytery
6 Perryville House
7 Pier House
8 Rockview

● Eating & drinking
1 1601 Pub
2 Cottage Loft
3 Crackpots
4 D'Antibes
5 Dino's
6 Greyhound Pub
7 Hoby's
8 Jim Edward's
9 Little Skillet
10 Mad Monk
11 Mango Café
12 Max's Wine Bar
13 Patsy's Corner
14 Pisces Bistro
15 Sam's Pub
16 Shanakee
17 Tap Tavern
18 Vintage

West Cork Gardens

The influence of the Gulf Stream and mild winters that rarely bring frost make West Cork a gardener's dream and there are plenty of gardens to show what can be achieved. For two weeks in June every year the West Cork Garden Trail sees the opening of many small private gardens to the public and a brochure listing is available from Bord Fáilte.

St are worth a browse. The *Giles Norman Photography Gallery* is a large place stacked with evocative black and white images of Irish life from around €20. Small craft shops can be found in the pedestrianized area past the *Greyhound* pub near the museum. For antiques there is *Linda's Antiques* and *Victoria Murphy* in Market Sq with lots of antique jewellery. In Market St *Kinsale Crystal* offers an alternative to Waterford glass and *Molly's* has antique and modern jewellery. The *Kent Gallery*, Quayside, has paintings, prints and sculptures by its resident artist.

Sport **Fishing** Deep sea angling: T4778969 and T4774946. **Golf** *Old Head Golf Links*, T4778444. 18 holes. **Hillwalking** *Hike Those Heights*, 3 Short Quay, T4773669. Provides transport from and back to Kinsale. **Horse Riding** *Balinadee Stables*, T4778152. 10 mins from town off the road to Bandon. Pony-trekking available. **Sailing** T4772898, www.oec.ie/kinsale and T4770738, www.oysterhaven.com

Transport **Bicycles** *The Hire Shop*, 18 Main St, T4774884. €10.16 a day for a mountain bike; tandems available. **Bus** Bus Éireann run a number of daily buses, No 249, throughout the year (and extra ones in summer) between Cork and Garrettstown that stop at Cork Airport, Kinsale and Ballinspittle. The first bus departs Cork at 0645; last one from Kinsale at 2220 (1945 on Sat). Timetables are posted in the window of the tourist office and the bus stop is across the road on Pier Rd. **Taxis** *Kinsale Cabs* T4772642; or try T4773600.

Directory **Communications** Post office: Pearse St. Internet: 71 Main St, opposite the *Mad Monk* pub, T4773571. **Tours** Cruises: T4773188. 1-hr cruise of harbour and River Bandon. 1100-1700. €6.35. **Walking Tour**: T4772873. Starts outside tourist office at 1115, daily, €4.45. **Ghost Tour**: T4772240. Starts outside *Tap Tavern* in Guardwell, Mon, Wed and Fri at 2100. €6.35.

Kinsale to Clonakilty

Garrettstown & Old Head of Kinsale

The quickest route west is to follow the road out of Kinsale past the *Trident Hotel* to Ballinspittle and Timoleague (R600) and then join up with the with the N71 road that continues west to Clonakilty and Skibbereen. A slower but more interesting route is to head south for **Garrettstown**, where there are two superb beaches, with a short excursion on to the **Old Head of Kinsale**. The entire headland has been shamelessly turned into a golf course and there is a €1.90 charge to pass through it to the ruins of an ancient lighthouse and a modern lighthouse at the extremity. The headland looks out to where the *Lusitania* was sunk in 1915 by a German submarine.

Timoleague
Phone code: 023
Colour map 3, grid C4

From here to Clonakilty the balmy scenery begins to intrude gently and the appeal of West Cork to north European immigrants seeking a new home starts to assert itself.

Approaching the small town of Timoleague the road hugs the coast and there are good opportunities to spot wading birds. **Timoleague Friary**, founded by Franciscans in the 14th century, is open to the public. The

County Cork

Spanish came here to trade wine and when English forces vandalized the abbey in the 17th century they discovered a thousand barrels of wine stored here. **Timoleague Castle Gardens**, T46116, is testimony to the benign West Cork climate that barely brings a frost. ■ *Jun-end Aug, Mon-Sat 1100-1730, Sun 1400-1730. €3.80.* Worth seeing, and it's free, is the astonishing interior of the Church of Ireland next to the Castle Gardens. The story behind the mosaic work and the role of the Maharajah of Gwalior is explained inside. If shut, ask for the keys from Dolly in the salmon-coloured cottage opposite the nearby Catholic church.

Sleeping & eating For accommodation and/or food **A** *Lettercollum House*, T46251, F46270, info@letterco.ie is a real delight. A former convent, the chapel is now a restaurant serving multi-ethnic cuisine with a French inflection and a penchant for vegetarian dishes. Evening meals are €30.50 and lunch, Sun only, is €17. The large bedrooms, mixing traditional forms with contemporary art, are good value at €61 for a double and there is a hostel-style kitchen for use by guests. *Gráine's*, in Timoleague has an affordable menu of meals like shepherd's pie and vegetarian pizza.

Courtmacsherry to Clonakilty
Phone code: 023

West Cork at its purest opens up on the small coastal road to Clonakilty via Courtmacsherry. The village of Courtmacsherry has a couple of pubs, tearooms, a small but safe sandy beach, and a gem of a hotel. From Courtmacsherry the road continues on to a superb beach at Donworly, only useable at low tide. After Donworly the coastal scenery is quietly stunning as the road unfolds its way alongside Clonakilty Bay.

Sleeping & eating The **AL** *Courtmacsherry Hotel*, T46198, F46137, has a pleasing air of gentility and offers a mollifying escape from money-spinning Kinsale. The house lost its pitched roof in the War of Independence, was burnt by the IRA, but there is still an enticing Anglo-Irish nuance to the place. Its *Cork Tree* restaurant has a set meal for €28 or a menu of fresh, local seafood and beef. Or one could picnic instead at the wooden tables that look out across the estuary from the side of the road approaching the village. Failing that have an open sandwich at the *Travara Lodge*, or pub food at *The Lifeboat Inn* or *Pier House Bar*, all 3 places on the waterfront.

Clonakilty

Phone code: 023
Colour map 3, grid C4

Etched into Irish folk memory as a synonym for deprivation – "Clonakilty, God help us" was a familiar expression dating back to post-Famine times – the town of today has not reneged on its history as Kinsale has. In the 18th century it developed around a prosperous linen industry and reminders of the past have been preserved. The reconstructed shop fronts in a traditional style, and an air of indifference to modernity, help give the place some character.

Sights
Dedicated to local social, economic and political history, the **West Cork Regional Museum** can prove fascinating. There is material on Michael Collins and the area's contribution to the War of Independence, a display cabinet on Castlefreke, and artefacts from the past. ■ *May-Oct, Mon-Sat, 1030-1730, Sun, 1430-1730. €2.50.*

Michael Collins (see page 652 and box page 290) was born in a farm outside Clonakilty at Sam's Cross in 1890, and although burnt down by the Black and Tans in 1921, the place has been partly restored as a memory to the man who led the war against the British. Take the N71 west of Clonakilty and look for the sign pointing right after 3 miles (5 km). ■ *Open 24 hrs, free.*

T46107, www.reachireland.com signposted off the R600 road to Timoleague, has slide and talk shows about Collins and related coach tours in the summer.

The value of a visit to restored **Lisnagum Ring Fort**, complete with a *souterrain* and thatched dwelling, partly depends on how knowledgeable the tour guide turns out to be; without a good guide the artefacts on show will seem scant reward for the entrance charge. ■ *Mon-Sun 0900-1700. €3. To reach it, take the N71 road to Bandon and look for the signposting.*

Inchydoney Beach is a superb beach some 3 miles (5 km) south of town, but beware of the riptide and check with the lifeguard. It is signposted from the roundabout at the east end of Clonakilty.

Lisselan Gardens is the most satisfying Robinsonian garden in West Cork, not least because it has the Argideen River flowing through it. There is the usual horrible extravaganza of rhododendrons, but this can be forgiven as you stroll along the flagstone pathways to admire the rockery and the unusual plants flourishing here. ■ *€3.80, T33249. 17 Mar-Oct, 0800-dusk. 3 km east of Clonakilty on the N71 road.*

Tourist office Rossa St, T33226, late Feb-12 Nov, daily 1000-1800, sometimes closed 1300-1400.

Sleeping
■ *on map*
Price codes, see inside front cover

AL *O'Donovan's Hotel*, Pearse St, T/F33250, www.odonovanshotel.com has been in the same family for 5 generations. **A-B** *Wytchwood*, off Emmet Sq, T33525, wytchost@iol.ie. A pleasant town house in a quiet location. **B** *The Well*, T35249, and **B** *Chez Nous*, T34582, are out on the R600 road to Timoleague; reasonable room rates at the bottom end of this price category, but too far to walk from town. **B** *The Glendine*, Tawnies Upper, T34824, www.glendine.com is at the top end of this price range and a 10-min walk from town. **D** *Old Brewery Hostel*, T/F33525, wytchost@iol.ie Directly opposite the Wytchwood, and run by the same owners, with 8 dorm beds and 3 double rooms. **Campsite** *Desert House*, Coast Rd, T33331, within walking distance of town, overlooks the muddy end of Clonakilty Bay and is signposted from the roundabout at the eastern end of town.

Eating

Nearly all the eating places are on the long main street that changes its name a few times; the tourist office dispenses a useful food and entertainment guide giving full details. The *An Súgán Pub*, 41 Wolfe Tone St, T33498, at the east end, serves local seafood though the specials advertised in the window may be better value. Opposite *O'Donovan's Hotel*, *Macehiter's Restaurant*, T34863, has ostrich fillet on the menu but otherwise predictable chicken and pork dishes at affordable prices;

County Cork

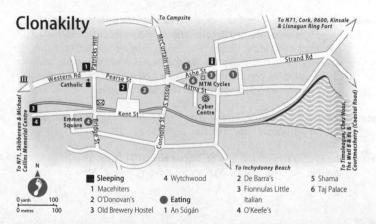

Clonakilty

To Campsite
To N71, Cork, R600, Kinsale & Lisnagun Ring Fort
Strand Rd
Patricks Hill
McCurtain Hill
Ashe St
Pearse St
Western Rd
Catholic
MTM Cycles
Astna St
Rossa St
Kent St
Cyber Centre
Emmet Square
Bridge St
Connolly St
To N71, Skibbereen & Michael Collins Memorial Centre
To Inchydoney Beach
To Timoleague, Chez Nous, The Well B & B & Courtmacsherry (Coastal Road)

0 yards 100
0 metres 100
N

■ **Sleeping**
1 Macehiters
2 O'Donovan's
3 Old Brewery Hostel

4 Wytchwood

● **Eating**
1 An Súgán

2 De Barra's
3 Fionnulas Little Italian
4 O'Keefe's

5 Shama
6 Taj Palace

☞ The last day in the life of Michael Collins

At 0600 in a bedroom in the Imperial Hotel in Cork City, Michael Collins arose to unknowingly meet his last day. He had planned a tour around West Cork, dangerous to a degree because this was militant Republican territory and anti-Treaty men were active in the area. He arrived in Macroom at 0730 outside what is now the Castle Hotel and collected a local driver from the hotel before setting off for Bandon. The road to Bandon was blocked in places and taking side roads led at one stage to uncertainty over what direction to take (still a hazard in this area). A local man outside a pub helped them but they were not to know he was a Republican scout who recognized Collins and alerted anti-Treaty men, secretly meeting in the area. They guessed correctly that Collins would return along the same road because they knew the main Bandon to Cork road was impassable due to anti-Treaty sabotage.

Collins and his armed escort made a quick stop in Bandon before heading off for Clonakilty, where they stopped at O'Donovans Hotel before leaving for Rosscarbery and then Skibbereen. They stopped in Skibbereen at the Eldon Hotel until about 1630.

The return journey to Bandon was taken via Sam's Cross in order to visit the ruins of Collins' family home burnt out by Major AE Percival (who years later would blunder into surrendering Singapore to the Japanese). He had a drink in the Five Alls pub before setting off for Bandon and what is now the Munster Arms Hotel. A final photograph (now hanging in the lobby of the hotel) was taken of Collins as he sat in his car for the journey back to Cork. On the way back, in the area of Béal na mBláth, Collins and his convoy were ambushed and the Commander-in-Chief of the Army of the Provisional Government was shot dead. Each year, on the anniversary of his death, a commemorative service takes place at the stone memorial at the site of the ambush.

To reach the site of the ambush from Bandon, take the road to Macroom and follow the signs to Béal na mBláth. His family home at Sam's Cross may also be visited (see page 288).

closed Sun. The appealing *Fionnuala's Little Italian Restaurant*, 30 Ashe St, T34355, with bare stone walls, candles in bottles, serves pasta and pizzas for between €9 and €14. Similar prices for Indian food, a couple of doors down, at *Taj Palace*, T35957, and at *Shama*, T36945, across the road. The self-service restaurant in *O'Donovan's Hotel* is busy but OK for a quick meal; on a fine day, Emmet Sq would be fine for a picnic. Facing the square, *O'Keefe's* serves meals in the middle range bracket.

Pubs & music Along the main thoroughfare, pubs like *An Súgán* and *De Barra's*, www.debarra.ie in Pearse St, as well as nearby *O'Donovan's Hotel*, can be relied on for lively musical sessions most nights in the summer. Down the lane by the side of O'Donovan's, the whitewashed and tin-roofed *An Teach Beas* has traditional music while the glossy-looking *The Venue* next door has jazz and blues bands. Details of other musical pubs available from the tourist office's entertainment guide.

Festivals The week-long *Clonakilty Festival*, at the end of Aug, is a musically rumbustious affair with bands playing in many of the bars. (See also page 292)

Directory **Banks** On Pearse St and Ashe St. **Bicycle hire** *MTM Cycles*, 33 Ashe St, T33584. **Internet** Access at O'Donovan's hotel and at *Cyber Centre*, 10 Astna St.

West Cork's Anglo-Irish

West Cork has fascinating reminders of colonial days in the 19th and early 20th centuries when Anglo-Irish families lived in a grand style in their stately Big House. One of the best examples of the ambitious scale of some of these country houses can be seen outside of Castletownbere on the Beara Peninsula, while in Castletownshend it is possible to stay a night in one. Though Castlefreake is one of the most delapidated remains, it can prove remarkably evocative if Mary Carbery's published journals (see page 681) are on your holiday reading list. Mary was the mother of the last Lord Carbery, a flamboyant figure who showed off at local fairs by looping the loop in his airplane, and later suddenly left his mansion for ever (giving rise to the story of how he shot out the eyes of the portrait of the first earl of Carbery before he left), and her account of living on her own in the house as a widow provides a tantalising glimpse of the Anglo-Irish fin de siècle as well as a tale of a remarkable woman who grew to love West Cork and its people.

Clonakilty to Skibbereen (coastal route)

It is a short run on the main N71 road from Clonakilty to Skibbereen but the coastal road from Rosscarbery via Glandore and Castletownshend offers interesting diversions as well as outstanding coastal scenery, for this is where West Cork comes into its own. Small houses splashed with Mediterranean blue and burnt umber, quaint-looking pubs, yachts moored in small harbour and off-shore retreats like Sherkin and Clear Island. At times the picture is very continental but always with an unmistakably Irish idiom that sets an ancient stone circle in a local farmer's field or has remnants of the old Anglo-Irish ascendancy happily co-existing in communities which, in the War of Independence, saw fit to burn down some of their big houses.

A right turn off the N71, at the end of the causeway, leads up to the town square of Rosscarbery. During the War of Independence the capture of the Rosscarbery barracks, under Tom Barry's Flying Column, led to the rebels controlling over 270 square miles in West Cork. There is little to see today apart from the Romanesque church off the town square, a craft shop, a bookshop, places to eat and pubs of course. The town is named after the Carbery family, and an imposing statue of a Lord Carbery rests inside the church. The lagoon and sand flats by the Rosscarbery causeway are good for bird-watching: over 60 resident species and half more again as winter visitors and migrants.

Rosscarbery
Phone code: 023
Colour map 3,
grid C4

Sleeping and eating The startling **L-AL** *Celtic Ross Hotel*, T48722, www.celticrosshotel.com, on the N71 has another surprise inside in the form of an unusual bogwood sculpture. Its *Druid Restaurant* is fine if you stick with the traditional dishes. *O'Callaghan Walshe*, T48125, is a seafood restaurant in the town square in the mid-range - expensive price bracket; closed Mon. Less expensive fare at *Pilgrim's* T48063, across the road and a bookshop to browse in as well. Open until 2000 weeknights but 1800 on Mon. Pub grub at the *Celtic Ross Hotel* bar that looks like an Irish theme pub. Nearby holiday homes draw the Irish to Rosscarbery, and the place is busier at night than one might imagine.

The ruins of the Carbery home, Castlefreke, are buried in the remains of a nearby oak wood like some long-forgotten Mayan shrine. The last Lord

Castlefreke

West Cork festivals

April
Rosscarbery Oyster Guinness Festival	T023-48117
Ballydehob Road Trotting Races	T028-37191

May
Caha Mountain Walking Festival, Glengarriff	T027-63555
Rosscarbery Art and Literature Weekend	T023-48063
Seafood Festival, Baltimore	T028-20159

June
The Humours of Bandon - Traditional Music Festival	T023-41785
West Cork Chamber Music Festival, Bantry House, Bantry	T027-52789
Rosscarbery Annual Regatta	T023-48444
Schull Family Arts Festival	T028-28201
Glengarriff Village Festival	T027-63072

July
West Cork Family Festival, Clonakilty	T1850-230730
Union Hall's 30th Annual Festival	T028-33722
Glandore Classic Boat Regatta & Summer School	cormac@euro.apple.com
Courtmacsherry Harvest Festival	T023-46170
Sherkin Island Regatta	T028-20347

August
Castletownbere Heineken Festival of the Sea	T027-70386
Calves Week – Schull Regatta	T028-28523
Ballydehob Gala Festival	T028-37191
Allihies Festival, Allihies	T027-73004

September
Courtmacsherry Storytelling Weekend	T023-46170
Rosscarbery Autumn School (William Thompson, Socialist)	T028-33223

October
International Gourmet Festival, Kinsale	T021-4774026
West Cork Walking Festival	T028-22812
Kinsale Fringe Jazz Festival	T021-4772382
Ballydehob Vintage and Old Time Threshing	T028-37191

County Cork

Carbery dramatically walked out of his castle in the early 20th century, never to return, leaving everything as it was, including tiger skins on the walls and valuable furniture. To get there, take the N71 east from Rosscarbery and take right turn on the R598 to Ownahincha beach; take the left fork at the end of the caravan site, signposted to Rathbarry, and go left into the woods after 0.7 miles. The crumbling ruins of the castle are tucked away in the trees. The house was occupied by the Irish army during the 'Emergency' (as the Second World War was called in Ireland), dances were held there from time to time in the 1950s before the leaded roof was taken off.

A well preserved circle of 17 stones dating back to around 150BCE and known today to pockets of discerning New Age folk, who come here to watch the sun's rays falling between the flat stone and the tall portal stones around the time of the winter solstice. Nearby there is a *fulacht fiadh*, an ancient cooking site that used hot stones to boil water in a pit before meat wrapped in straw was added. Take the coastal road for Glandore from Rosscarbery and look for the sign pointing left after a couple of miles.

Drombeg stone circle

In 1830, Glandore, a highly picturesque fishing village, was the first to organize a regatta, part of its claim to be the oldest holiday resort in Cork, and it still attracts a yachting fraternity. The village of Leap (pronounced 'Lep'), a little way north of Glandore, gets its name from a gorge that is now hardly noticed if whizzing past on the N71 which forms its Main St.

Glandore & Leap
Phone code: 028

Sleeping and eating AL *Marine Hotel*, in Glandore, T33366, is the place for a rest, though bar food is also available at the *Glandore Inn*, T33468, as you come into the village.

The original name of this town, *Bréan Trá*, meant 'foul beach' but then it was changed – presumably in the spirit of improvement – to commemorate the Act of Union in 1801, which abolished the Irish Parliament. Either way there is little to see in this odd little village.

Union Hall
Phone code: 028

Sleeping and eating Worth considering for an overnight stay is **D** *Maria's Schoolhouse*, T33002, a National School converted to a hostel with dorm beds and private en-suite rooms available. **B** *Ardagh House*, T33571, www.ardaghhouse.com, is a B&B and restaurant, facing the water, open for food all day: steaks, seafood and open sandwiches, nothing special, but outdoor tables. **D** *Curraheen Lodge*, Rosscarbery, T48498, is a useful hostel with 8 beds, 1 private room and camping space. 2 pubs: *Caey's*, with a beer garden, and *Dinny Collins* do food.

This unique village was developed by English settlers in the late 17th century, and in 1859 one of these families, the Somervilles, returned here from a military posting in Corfu. Edith Somerville was a young girl at the time and she spent the rest of her life here. She met her cousin from Galway, Violet Martin (whose pen-name was Martin Ross), and together they embarked on an unusual literary partnership (see page 679). The entrance to Drishane House, where Edith lived, is on your right as you approach Castletownshend, just before the road takes a sharp left turn down into the village and immediately after signs point to the right to B&Bs and Tragumna. Both women were buried in the graveyard of St Barrahane's Church, reached by turning left at the bottom of the village, and while Violet's name is written on her tombstone Edith's is a simple slab of granite next to it. They are both behind the altar end of the church. The church interior is well worth a visit, littered with memorial stones to members of the Townshend and Somerville families, who all seemed to die in far-flung corners fighting for the Empire. The mosaic floor in the chancel was designed by Edith Somerville and she also commissioned the Harry Clarke stained glass window behind the main altar, though my favourite is the one depicting the unlikely pairing of St Patrick with St George.

Castletownshend
Phone code: 028
Colour map 3, grid C3

County Cork

Sleeping and eating AL *Bow Hall*, T36114. Family-friendly, has 3 rooms and dinner for around €31 at a communal table. B&B is available in **A** *Castle Guesthouse*, T36100, F36166, the castellated seat of the Townshend family (it is said that George Bernard Shaw's mother-in-law changed her name from Townsend to Townshend hoping that society would assume she was related) and self-catering apartments are also available. *Mary Ann's* is an olde-worlde pub serving bar food throughout the day in the €7-25 bracket, while dinner can be enjoyed in the upstairs restaurant or in the vine-covered room for around €32.

Skibbereen

Phone code: 028
Colour map 3, grid C3

www.skibbereen.ie
information and
town map

In the not-too-distant past Skibbereen, like Clonakilty, was associated with some of the worst horrors of the Famine, and it is only during the last 20 years that the town has shrugged off its negative image. A traditional song speaks of "the reasons why I left auld Skibbereen" but nowadays this lively market town suggests itself as a base for deeper excursions into West Cork. There are good transport links, supermarkets, places of interest in the vicinity and a refreshing sense that the town is going about its working life while accommodating visitors with a relaxed friendliness.

The **tourist office** is on North St, T21766. At the Cork end of town and open 0900-1900, daily in Jul and Aug; shorter hrs but open the rest of the year. The West Cork Arts Centre has regular exhibitions, and the noticeboard carries details of any theatrical or other arts events in the vicinity. ■ *North St, opposite the modern library, T22090*

History

The town's history is unique because it was founded when English families who survived the Algerian raid on Baltimore in 1631 (see page 296) moved inland for security. In the 17th century more English colonials moved in and they were still there when the Famine brought death and despair to the region. Three miles west of town, on the road to Ballydehob, the Abbeystrowery graveyard contains a mass grave that was kept open so that Famine victims could be added each day, and recently established memorial stones lend a grim grandeur to the tragedy of the Famine era. *Roycroft's* bicycle shop, on Ilen St, was used as a soup house. The tourist office sells a useful Skibbereen Trail walking trail booklet for €1.27 covering such sites. *The Maid of Erin* statue at the tourist office end of town is a tribute to those who struggled for Irish independence. Tom Barry, leader of the famous Flying Column guerrilla force during the War of Independence, comments in his autobiography *Guerrilla Days in Ireland* that Skibbereen was never a safe town for the rebels because of the forelock-tugging mentality of its townsfolk.

Great Famine Exhibition & Lough Hyne Interpretative Centre

An audio-visual show, lasting 15 minutes, covers Lough Hyne, and the Famine exhibition amounts to a few display boards, touch screens and an original soup pot. Worth a visit, perhaps, on a rainy day. ■ *Upper Bridge St, T40900. Mid May-mid Sep, daily, 1000-1800; Mid-Mar-mid May and mid-Sep-end of Oct, Tue-Sat. €3.*

Sleeping
Price codes:
See inside front cover

In the middle of town on Bridge St the **AL-B** *Eldon Hotel,* Bridge St, T22000, www.eldon-hotel.com A comfortable old hotel in the middle of town with small rooms and a miscellany of prints, pictures and photographs that includes one of Michael Collins leaving the hotel on his last day (see page 290). **B** *Bridge House,*, Bridge St, T21273. A 19th-century house, across the road from the Eldon, which offers B&B in a veritable shrine to Victoriana. **C** *Riverview House*, Newbridge, T21516, is a farmhouse dwelling within walking distance of town and some rooms have their own bathrooms. **C-D** *Russagh Mill Hostel & Adventure Centre*, T22451, F22988. On the Castletownshend road 1 mile (2 km) from town with dorm beds and private rooms. The owner has climbed Everest, and various hyper-activities such as rock climbing may be available through the hostel.

Eating

Expensive *Ty Ar Mor*, 48 Bridge St, T22100, is a seafood restaurant, with a minor nautical theme to the decor and an appealing menu that features dishes like monkfish and cognac, wild salmon and John Dory, plus a couple of meat items. Opens daily at 1830. €28.50 for set dinner, à là carte includes lobster as a speciality.

Mid-range *Kalbo's Bistro*, 48 North Rd, T21515, serves chicken tortillas and home-made burgers for lunch and dinner courses of steak, lamb, crab and chilli.

Cheap The food at the *Potters*, in the Eldon hotel, might disappoint a gourmet but will satisfy a hungry stomach; starters like goat's cheese salad, pasta dishes and lunch specials posted outside. A few doors down from the hotel, *Annie May's* pub/restaurant, T22930, has a large menu, subtitled in Irish (though this is not Gaeltacht area), of meat, fish and salad dishes as well as cheaper bar food and a special evening menu.

Pubs & entertainment

Baby Hannah's, 42 Bridge St, T22783, with sawdust on the floor of one bar, is the favourite venue for music on Thu and Sat nights. The *Corner Bar*, 37 Bridge St, T21522, has sessions of traditional music on Mon, Tue and Wed. The *Little Fox Tavern* in the *Eldon Hotel* has music at weekends but the quality varies. *Sean Óg's*, T21573, in Market St near the post office is the haunt of hippies and has some excellent music and *Annie May's*, T22930, in Bridge St is also worth checking out for its weekend sessions which attract locals as well as visitors. The *Cellar Bar*, T21329, Main St, is the town's sports bar.

The *West Cork Arts Centre*, North St, T22090, has temporary art exhibitions and the noticeboard at the entrance is a good source of information on current cultural events taking place in the area.

Directory

Banks On Bridge St and on Main St. **Bicycle** *Roycroft's*, Ilen St, T21235. For bike hire. **Communications** Internet: in the *Eldon Hotel*, in the public library on North St and at *coffee.com* out on the Castletownshend road. *J Connolly's*, jconn@tinet.ie on the corner opposite the post office charges €1.90 for 15 mins. **Post office** on the corner of Main St and Market St. **Fishing** Gear and information on salmon and sea trout fishing on the River Ilen from *Fallons*, North St, T22246. **Hospital** T21677. **Sports** Skibbereen Sports Centre, Gortnaclohy, T22624. **Taxi** T21258 and 086-8346396.

Lough Hyne

Signposted off the road to Baltimore, Lough Hyne was once a freshwater lake that sank below sea level, became flooded with sea water and is now a tidal seawater lake with Mediterranean marine life.

Colour map 3, grid C3

This is a pretty walk through pleasant woodland to the top of Knockomagh, beside Lough Hyne. There are great views on the route up the hill, taking about half an hour, and an amazing panorama at the top.

From the car-park beside Lough Hyne go back to the Skibbereen road and turn left. Walk about 500 yards to where a boreen branches off to the left. Opposite is a track going up into the woods: follow this until it comes to a ruin and bear sharp left in front of the ruin. From here your path to the top is quite clear.

The trees you are walking through are an interesting mixture. This is largely an oak wood, possibly even an aboriginal one; the ancestors of these oak trees may have stood here just after the ice sheets departed. In the 18th century, beech were planted and the children of those trees are still very much alive in the woods. Below the canopy of the oak and beech, holly, honeysuckle and ivy thrive. On the forest floor are great stands of wood rush while in spring more woodland plants make use of the period before the oak and beech leaves emerge to flower: bluebells, wood sorrel, and primroses. All summer long herb Robert and its pungent perfume flowers in the shade.

The forest is protected as a nature reserve and as you continue up the well made stepped path look out for Irish yew trees, another aboriginal plant, and spindle trees, a low deciduous shrub rather than a tree, with inconspicuous flowers in May but glorious coral pink berries in autumn.

The panoramic view at the top of the hill is breathtaking. Before you lies a whole stretch of West Cork's coastline laid out like a section of an Ordnance Survey map. Immediately below is the lough and it is possible to see the nature of its unusual geography. It lies below the sea level beyond and is almost blocked at its seaward end by a wall of rock allowing only a small channel of water out of the lough. As fresh water feeds into the lough from feeder streams, the water flows out of the creek. But at high tide the sea level rises above the level of the water flowing out, and suddenly the water turns and starts to flow back into the lough raising its level considerably. As a result, it is a salt-water lough, and because it is only exposed to the open sea for part of the day its water is much warmer than the open ocean. Consequently, a very unusual ecosystem has evolved here with plants and animals more like those of the Mediterranean than northern Europe. It is possible also to see how over the millennia the sea has risen and flooded the once-dry land valleys of this area. Out to sea is Cape Clear Island, once part of the mainland chains of mountains thrown up 300 million years ago by massive tectonic movements originating in southern Europe. Return to the road, going left past the ruin and down through modern conifer plantations.

Baltimore

Situated 13 km (8 miles) down the River Ilen from Skibbereen, Baltimore's resident population of around 200 souls swells to an almost unmanageable number of visitors in the summer as the harbour area overfills with people flocking to Cork's two most popular off-shore islands. But Baltimore is nothing if not laid-back and welcomes all and sundry, even in winter when the Mediterranean-style harbour, where the guesthouses, restaurants and pubs rub shoulders, is transformed into a wild and windy shelter from fierce Atlantic winds.

In 1631 an Algerian raiding party sailed in to Baltimore and kidnapped 100 people for the white slave trade. Apparently some of their descendants can still be traced in Algeria through their family names. Before the 17th century, the land and islands around Baltimore were in the hands of the O'Driscoll family, who collected dues from Spanish and French boats fishing for mackerel and pilchards and using the safe harbour, and the ruined castle in the village harks back to that era. In the 18th century a profitable small industry developed along this part of the coast sending salted mackerel to the US, and as late as the early 20th century some 16 trains were leaving Baltimore packed with fish. Today, it is boats that are leaving on a daily basis, ferrying passengers to and from Cape Clear and Sherkin Island. The first lighthouse on the rock here was swept away by gales in 1865 but replaced in 1906.

Tourist information *The Islands Crafts & Information Centre*, T20347, is at the pier and open from May to Sep. They provide scheduled, day-long, guided cultural and archaeological tours of West Cork, including Sherkin, from *The White House*, Lough Hyne, Baltimore, T/F20566.

Sleeping
Price codes:
see inside front cover

L-AL *Casey's of Baltimore*, T20197, www.baltimore-ireland.com/caseys A family-run hotel with lovely views over the bay. B&Bs in the town itself include **AL-A** *Baltimore Bay Guest House*, T20600, www.youenjacob.com has 5 of its 8 rooms overlooking the harbour but all share a modern, clean style with touches of old furniture alongside contemporary wall hangings. Breakfast, including smoked salmon, is downstairs in the *La Jolie Brise* restaurant, and **B** *Corner House,* T20143, a B&B overlooking the harbour. **B** *Algiers Inn*, T/F20145. The rooms here are pleasant, but remember that the pub can get a little raucous at weekends. **B** *The Stone House*, Lifeboat Rd, T/F20511, www.aquaventures.ie has views of the bay, homely atmosphere and home-made bread every morning. **C-D** *Rolf's Holiday Hostel*, T/F20289, has dorm beds and 8 private doubles. The place has a good reputation and bikes can be hired here. **Camping** It is pleasant at the spacious *Hideaway*, T22254, on the road to Castletownbere from Skibbereen.

Chez Youen, T20136, specializes in locally caught fresh fish brought to your white-linen table in a cosy restaurant with art work by Dali, Sokolov and James Dixon around the walls. Duck and game also available on the menu with dinner prices starting around €24 and a *tarte tatin* that just might be the best in the world. *The Custom House*, T20200, has a plain but elegant style and fresh seafood is a choice on the 2 set meals of €19 and €27; closed Mon. *La Jolie Brise*, T20600, has great value pizzas, using fresh dough, from around €8.50 for a delicious one using goat's cheese to €16 for a rich creamy smoked salmon version. 2 people could share one for lunch, the house wine is superb, and food is available from 0830 to 2300. For affordable but catholic food try *Café Art*, T20289, next to Rolf's hostel, or any of the pubs.

Eating

Diving The *Aquaventures*, T/F20511, www.aquaventures.ie, serves beginners and experienced divers and has been recommended by a reader. **Fishing** Trips can be organized through the *Algiers Inn*, T20352. **Horse riding** *Limbo Riding Centre*, T21683. **Sailing** *Baltimore Sailing Club*, T20426. *Sailing schools*: T20141 and T20154. **Sea angling and shark fishing** through *Michael Walsh*, T20352.

Sport

McCarthy's, T20159, on one side the *La Jolie Brise* restaurant, has music most nights and attracts well known bands; see the programme in the window. *Bushe's Bar*, on the other side, does not have music but is equally popular; at quiet times the display of nautical memorabilia can be appreciated. The *Algiers Inn*, T20145, with occasional sessions of music and a beer garden. *Casey's*, T20197, by the road coming into the village, has music on Sat all year, on Sun between May and Sep, plus Wed in Jul and Aug.

Pubs & entertainment

County Cork

Sherkin Island

Sea As well as buses (see page 264) there is a boat service between Baltimore and Schull, Jun to mid-Sep, T39153. Departures from Baltimore at 1030 and 1400, and from Schull at 1130 and 1500 ; bicycles are carried free.

Transport

Boat hire *Atlantic Boating Service*, T22145, absboat@indigo.ie **Lifeboat** T20101/20143.

Directory

Sherkin Island

Boats leave from Baltimore, T20218, regularly through the summer, €6.35 return. There is also a service from Schull, T28138.

Ins & outs
Phone code: 028

Sherkin Island, 3 miles by 1 (5 km by 2 km) has safe sandy beaches by day

Sights

(with a tractor, T20218, waiting at the pier to tow you to them in the morning and back again in the evening) and opportunities for quiet walks spotting birds and flowers, while at night the island's two pubs are alive with sociable buzz and mercifully within staggering distance of the harbour for the last boat back to Baltimore.

Sleeping & eating
Price codes:
See inside front cover

If you decide to stay overnight B&B and an evening meal for €10.16 is available at **B** *Cúinne House*, T20384, with ocean views from the bedrooms and evening meals an option. Other places offering B&B are **B** *Island House*, T20314, **B** *Horseshoe Cottage*, T20598, and, including self-catering cottages, **B** *Windhoek*, T20275. **D** *Sherkin Hostel & Campsite*, T20572, is basic.

Murphy's Bar, T20116, does bar food all day as well as serving meals in its *Islander Restaurant*. Across the road, the *Jolly Roger Tavern*, T20379, also does food and encourages musicians to play so there is often some live music. Food can be obtained from the *Abbey Stores Shop* (also the post office).

Cape Clear Island

Phone code: 028
Colour map 3, grid C3

Cape Clear International Storytelling Festival First weekend in Sep, T39116 Island web site: www.oilean -chleire.ie

It takes 45 minutes to reach this, Ireland's southernmost island, from Baltimore with the boat weaving its way out of the harbour on the same route as the Algerian pirates of 1631. Unlike Sherkin, there are no sandy beaches but for exhilarating country walks, inspiring seascapes, bird-watching and heather-clad hillsides Cape Clear Island, three miles by one mile (5 km by 2), is a very accessible and enjoyable destination. There is a small **Heritage Centre**, open daily in summer from 1400 to 1730, focusing on the island's history and culture. Before your visit, try to collect the useful map brochure from the tourist office in Baltimore or from the small tourist information post at the harbour when you arrive. About one-third of the 931 different plants in Ireland can be found on the island, so a flower identification book may be helpful. Guided walks of an ecological, T39193, or historical, T39157, nature can be arranged.

A country walk

After disembarking, turn left at the end of the pier and head up the path to the café and pub and continue uphill to the shop. Turn left here and follow the road to the hostel, but just before reaching it turn left and follow the road that passes a lane to the post office. Continue past the windmills on your right and turn right at the T-junction to head out to the eastern edge of the island. Alternatively, turn left and head back to the pier, passing the Heritage Centre on the way.

Sleeping

It is advisable to book accommodation before departing from Baltimore (see page 296). B&Bs include **B** *Ard Na Gaoithe*, T39160, and **B** *Cluain Mara*, T39153. There is an **D** *An Oigé* hostel, T39198, ("your last Irish stop before the South Pole") complete with an adventure centre, as well as a basic campsite, T39119.

Eating

There are a couple of pubs on the island, and one of them, *Ciarán Danny Mike's*, T39172, has a restaurant in the evening, and *Cotters*, T39102, serves food. There is also a chip van by the harbour serving food, but a stopover in Skibbereen for picnic food is a good idea if you are staying for the whole day.

Transport

From Baltimore, T39135, boats, €5.08 single, depart at 1100 (1200 on Sun), 1415 and 1900 in Jul and Aug, returning at 0900 (1100 on Sun), 1200 (1300 Sun) and 1800. There is a reduced service other times of the year. Another company, T39153, departs from Baltimore to Cape Clear via Schull, mid-Jun to mid-Sep, at 1030 and 1400, and returns at 0900, 1215 and 1700, taking 90 mins.

Bird-watching on Cape Clear Island

In the summer months thousands of manx shearwaters (a large bird, black on top and white underneath), kittiwakes and fulmars sweep past the southern end of the island on their way to fishing grounds south of Ireland from their rocky abodes off the Kerry coast to the north. In the evening they return along the same route and it is a spectacular sight at any time of the day. Ornithologists should write in advance to the Bird Observatory, Cape Clear Island, Co Cork, T028-39181, for information on organized trips and accommodation. However, all interested visitors arriving on the island are welcome to call in at the Observatory, the white two-storey building near the harbour, or just head off for Blananarragaun at the southwest tip of the island. To get to Blananarragaun follow the path from the harbour up to the café and uphill to the shop. Turn right here, signposted for the camping site, carry on to the end of the road and keep going to the end of the spur of land. Also look out for guillemots (black plumage with a large white area that makes them look like black and white ducks in the water), which breed on the island.

From Schull, T28278, the *Karycraft* departs daily in Jul and Aug at 1030, 1430 and 1630, returning at 1130, 1530 and 1730. Single fare is €7.62, return €11.43. In Jun and Sep there is one departure at 1430, returning at 1730, and in May and Sep it depends on the level of demand.

Ballydehob and the Mizen Peninsula

From Skibbereen the N71 main road continues west, turning northwards just before the small town of Ballydehob to head towards Bantry. The R592 road leads west from Ballydehob to Schull and out to Goleen near the end of the Mizen peninsula. From near Goleen you can take a smaller road back along the north side of the peninsula to the village of Durrus, from where the Sheep's Head peninsula or Bantry can be reached.

The bulky Mizen peninsula lacks the splendid isolation of the Beara peninsula and the quiet beauty of the Sheep's Head, but it strives to assert its own identity once you travel west beyond Goleen and the open Atlantic beckons.

Ballydehob

Situated at the head of an inlet of Roaring Water Bay, Ballydehob was the market village for islanders from the Bay until it declined after the islands gradually depopulated in the 1930s. Tourism has revived its spirits, and when in the 1980s a small number of well known writers and the like bought up holiday homes in the area, Ballydehob became a small retreat for the London chattering classes. In the summer there is still a middle-class bohemian touch to the place, but in winter Ballydehob drifts back to being a sleepy Irish village. When entering the town from Skibbereen, look out on the left for the disued 12-arched tramway bridge. There is a café, a bookshop and a craft shop along the main street.

Phone code: 028
Colour map 3, grid C3

B-C *The Old Crossing*, Shanavagh, T37148, a former railway crossing cottage within walking distance of the village. **C-D** *Twelve Arch Hostel*, Palm grove, Church Rd, T/F37232, info@12archhostel.ie Has 30 beds and 3 private rooms; bikes for hire.

Sleeping
Price codes:
see inside front cover

County Cork

👉 Fastnet Lighthouse

Standing at the top of the Goat's Path on the Sheep's Head peninsula the blinking light that periodically sweeps the night sky emanates from the automated lighthouse on Fastnet Rock. The first cast-iron 1854 lighthouse, replaced by a granite one in 1906, was the last bit of Ireland that thousands of hapless emigrants glimpsed on their journey from Cobh to the New World. Trips to Fastnet, T028-28278, depart from Schull on Tuesday and Thursday at 1900 in July and August, and there is usually a weekly morning departure in June and September; €12.70 return.

Eating *Annie's Restaurant*, T37292, on the main street, has pricey dishes like roast duck with port and orange from 1900, closed Sun and Mon. *Duggan's*, opposite the Shell garage, serves affordable lunch and dinner of the steak and chicken curry kind. Near the Texaco garage, *Hudson's Wholefoods* has a vegetarian café doing cakes, pizzas, samosas and lunch specials. *Clara*, in the centre of the village, serves toasted pitta bread with various fillings and open crab sandwiches. The quaint little pub across the road, *Levis*, is popular with patrons of Annie's restaurant while the otherwise-featureless *Irish Whip* bar at the Schull end of town has a faded display on the Ballydehob wrestling champion, Dan O'Mahony, who invented the wrestling throw known as the Irish whip, and to whom a commemorative statue now stands in the village. For music (and internet access), try *The Mines* pub on Wed nights or *The Sandboat* on Sat.

Schull

Phone code: 028
Colour map 3, grid C3

Lying beneath the slopes of Mount Gabriel, with aircraft tracking dishes on the summit, Schull bursts into life every summer with Irish and non-Irish visitors. Good restaurants, a decent bookshop, pubs with music, and boats to Sherkin, Cape Clear Island, Fastnet lighthouse and Baltimore all draw in the crowds. The Republic's only **Planetarium** is also here. ■ *T28552. Star show Mar-Sep, 45 mins. €4.45.*

The busiest time of all is during Calves Week, at the beginning of August, when various sailing events take place. Boats to Cape Clear, T39153, depart at 1130 and 1500, and for Baltimore at 1730, mid-Jun to mid-Sep. Another boat, the *Karycraft*, departs for Cape Clear island at 1430 and 1815 in Jun and Sep, and at 1030, 1430 and 1630 in Jul and Aug.

Sleeping **AL** *Grove House*, Colla Rd, T28067, billyoshea@yahoo.com once accommodated the
Price codes: likes of George Bernard Shaw and Edith Sommerville and its 5 bedrooms are individu-
see inside front cover ally decorated, with lots of quaint and quirky features. **AL-A** *East End Hotel*, Main St, T28101, F28012. Family-friendly and family-run small hotel. **AL-A** *Corthna Lodge Country House*, Schull, T28517, F28032, a short distance west of the village, enjoys views of Roaring Water Bay from its hill-top position. **B** *Glencairn*,T28007, Ardmanagh Drive, is an archetypal bungalow B&B; a 3-min walk from town. **B** *Adele's*, Adele's Bakery, T28459, www.adelesrestaurant.com has 4 rooms, sharing bathroom facilities, on the top floor. **C-D** *Schull Backpackers Lodge*, Colla Rd, T/F28681, www.schullbackpackers.com Dormitory beds, double and single rooms, en-suite double, limited camping space, and bikes for hire. At the Goleen end of town, and looks quite different inside from what the woody exterior might suggest.

Eating Locally sourced ingredients at the expensive *The Restaurant in Blue*, Crookhaven Rd, T28305, a couple of km outside the village but our favourite is *Adéle's*, Main St, T28459, with a deservedly popular coffee shop for light meals and a middle-range dinner menu with delicious fish dishes. The *Bunratty Inn* serves tasty mussels and bar food is also available at *The Waterside Inn* and the old-style *Hackett's Bar*. For fresh fish and take-away cooked fish, *The Fish Shop* at the pier is reliable and the *The Courtyard* pub in Main St sells a good variety of local cheeses and fresh bread; ideal for a picnic.

Many of the pubs along Main St have musical evenings. Check to see what is on at *The Courtyard* pub or *Arundel's Bar*. *TJ Newman's*, up the hill from the harbour, is a lovely old-fashioned pub for a quiet drink and a chat with locals.

Pubs & music

Books *Fuschia Books* has a wide range of second-hand books on Irish subjects from paperbacks to first editions. **Clothes** *Irish Knitwear*, Main St. **Gifts** *Celtic Crafts*, Main St. Sells gifts such as jewellery and pottery. *The Courtyard* pub in Main St has a craft shop attached, selling pottery, jewellery and hand-knit garments.

Shopping

Mizen Head, Barley Cove, Goleen and Crookhaven

After passing the brightly painted villages of Ballydehob and Schull, well known retreats for well heeled North Europeans, the social and physical landscape changes as you approach Goleen. The local TD once memorably described his constituency as in danger of becoming a land of "briars, bullocks and bachelors", and indeed the land does become barren with small farms struggling to cope with the centralizing farming policies of the EU and young people not always keen to grow up as farmers and farmers' wives. Outside of winter you will be struck by the flora and fauna with teeming birdlife off Mizen Head, wild thyme growing by the roadside and the hills turning yellow and purple with autumn gorse and heather.

Phone code: 027
Colour map 3, grid C2

The most unforgettable sight on this peninsula is the view of the crazy rock formations from the small bridge that takes one out to the **Mizen Vision**, the Mizen Head signal station, at the end of the peninsula. One has to pay the €4.45 entrance charge to reach the bridge which is unfortunate because a visit to the signal station, T35115, may prove a disappointing experience. To make matters worse, what used to be a spectacular clifftop walk from here to **Three Castles Head** has been closed off. Notwithstanding, a visit to the 13th-century O'Mahoney castle near the edge of sheer cliffs at Three Castles Head, with a lake in front is recommended. Do not be deterred by the sign at the farm entrance which gives access to the castle; the owners were dismayed at coaches disgorging groups who trooped across their land. Individual visitors are entitled to visit the castle: to get there from the car-park at the *Barleycove Beach Hotel* turn right on leaving the car-park, then left at the first T-junction and right at the next junction where a sign points left to the *Ocean View* B&B. Follow the road to the end where a gate leads up to a farmhouse; the castle is a 10-minute walk beyond. An exciting walk with astonishing views of the Atlantic can be enjoyed by following the road that leads to the *Ocean View* B&B and heading south along the clifftop to Mizen Head, when the road comes to an end

The sandy expanse of surfable Barley Cove comes as a terrific surprise near the end of the Mizen Peninsula and, although there can be a dangerous undercurrent in places, lifeguards are on duty in the summer and flags indicate where it is safe to swim. If you leave Goleen by heading straight out of the village, instead of turning right for Mizen Head, you will see Crookhaven on your left. Once an important harbour, Crookhaven is still patronized by sailing folk and there are a couple of undistinguished pubs serving food. The nearby village of Goleen has a **tourist office**, T35255.

County Cork

Sleeping
Price codes:
see inside front cover

The **AL-A** *Fortview House*, Gurtyowen, Toormore, T35324, is on the Durrus to Goleen R591 road. Guests have recommended this B&B for the quality of the breakfast and evening meal, around €25. A self-catering house is also available. **AL** *Barleycove Beach Hotel*, T35234; F35100, was closed at the time of research but may have reopened. The only other local place for a room – **B** *Ocean View B&B*, T35217 – is a farmhouse and rooms share bathroom facilities. **Camping** *Barleycove Holiday Park*, Crookhaven, T35302, accepts campers, if they like the look of you, but you could follow the example of others and camp for free at the Crookhaven end of the beach.

Eating

There are a couple of restaurants in and around Goleen, but not everyone finds them good value. *The Green Kettle*, Main St, Goleen, T35033, might be your best bet with an day menu of affordable sandwiches and seafood and a mid-range evening menu featuring local steak, a fish platter, chicken and lasagne. Open from late Jul to mid-Sep. Crookhaven, impressing many visitors as a rather cliquey village, has *O'Sullivans* pub, T35319, serving home-made soups, chowder and open sandwiches.

The Sheep's Head Peninsula

Phone code: 027

Bikes for cycling the peninsula available: call T61606

This is a modest peninsula of green beauty washed by the wide water of Bantry Bay to the north and the more placid Dunmanus Bay to the south. Returning from Goleen on the Mizen peninsula, take a left turn at the Toormore junction and enjoy the scenic coastal road along the north side of the Mizen peninsula to the village of **Durrus** at the head of Dunmanus Bay. A loop road runs west from here to the small village of **Kilcrohane** (stop in Eileen's friendly pub, Fitzpatrick's, at the start of the Goat's Path in Kilcrohane for exposed, original beams and low-ceilinged character) on the Sheep's Head and then north up the Goat's Path to head back to Bantry along the north side of this peninsula. The best reason for coming to the Sheep's Head peninsula is to walk the **Sheep's Head Way**, whole sections of which are truly spectacular.

Sleeping

A worthy B&B west of Durrus is **B** *Durrus Court*, T61169; the ruins of a Jacobean mansion sit proudly in the garden with its Elizabethan chimneys intact. In Durrus itself, **B** *Avoca House is a friendly B&B* , T61511.

Eating

Durrus has a number of pubs serving good bar food throughout the day, including the *Long Boat Bar* and *Ivo's*. In Kilcrohane tea and cakes can be enjoyed in the olde-world post office. For that special meal to write home about, consider *Blairs Cove House*, T61127, for dinner at €40 in a Georgian country house that is outside Durrus on the R591, just on the Mizen peninsula; mid-Mar to Oct, closed on Sun, and Mon in Jul and

Sheep's Head Way

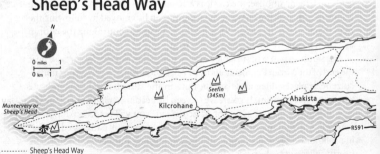

Sheep's Head Way

Aug. A little further along the R591, and open all year, is **Three Gables**, T61534. This lovely restaurant practises the art of slow food and dinner is a leisurely 3-hr affair. Bougainvillaea flourishing near the entrance, sea views, and home-cooking using fresh local produce with a tincture of Italian to the cuisine; set dinner is €36.50.

The Sheep's Head Way

The Sheep's Head Way is a four-day, 55-mile (88-km) walk which begins firstly along the mountain spine that dominates the centre of the peninsula, and then continues out to the western extremity. The final day of the walk, from Durrus, is less exciting and can be skipped but the first three days are spectacular. Arrange accommodation in Bantry before setting off.

Phone code: 027

The *Ordnance Survey* map No 88 in the 1:50,000 series covers most of the Way, which is plotted on the map. To cover the whole Way you would also need map 85 for short stretches near Bantry, but it would be possible to get by just using the waymarked signs along the route. There is also the locally produced *Guide to the Sheep's Head Way* (€6.35), which has its own 1:50,000 map and a booklet that describes the route and gives some local history. These maps are available at the tourist office in Bantry (see page 304). The *Bantry Independent Hostel* (see 'Sleeping' on page 304) also has information on the Way.

Mapping & information

This is a 17-mile (28-km) walk along the central spine of the peninsula to Kilcrohane just below Seefin Mountain. The walk begins in Bantry but some time would be saved by staying west of town on the Way at **B** *Dromcloc House*, T027-50030, at Cappanaloha, which is open from March-October.

From the car-park of Bantry House follow the waymarkers that direct you around the grounds and past the *West Lodge Hotel*. The way crosses the main road to Cork and heads off down a minor road lined with wild iris and meadowsweet. A little further on is a turn to the left and then the Way leaves the tarmac and starts to climb. After a time, the fields are left behind again and its route goes along some pleasant country roads for a time before striding out on to the central mountain ridge, where the views over Bantry Bay to the north and Dunmanus to the south are amazing. From Seefin, head down to Kilcrohane Village where there is some accommodation at the **B** *Bay View Inn*, T027-67068, or at the IHH **D** *Carbery View Hostel*, T027-67035.

Day one

This circular 20-mile (33-km) walk starts at Kilcrohane village and goes to the western end of the peninsula. From the village, retrace your steps to the top of the Goat's Path and follow the signs. At one stage, the route follows the cliff edge then heads inland to Tooreen, where it meets the road back to Kilcrohane. But your route is uphill past the ruins of a signal tower before it descends to the shore and follows a lowland route through farms and then along a road back to Kilcrohane.

Day two

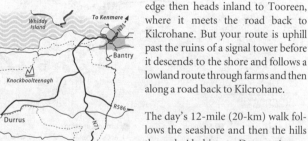

The day's 12-mile (20-km) walk follows the seashore and then the hills through Ahakista to Durrus, As you head east of the village on the road to Durrus, the markers send you down a

Day three

County Cork

boreen, past a few bungalows to the shore and a lake. There are usually swans on the lake which breed here every year. The area is called Farranamanagh, "the fields of the monks", and it is thought that one of the sets of ruins above the lake is an ancient bardic school where it said that a medieval king of Spain sent his son to study, only to have him drown on the journey there. From the lake the route follows an abandoned road to Ahakista, an apology for a village with two bars but a very pretty garden to peer into and some deciduous woodland. En route, the trail passes a tumbledown stone circle discovered only a few years ago. The old road heads across farmland and uses old roads and boreens.

Day four This is a 12-mile (20-km) walk through minor roads and forestry and does-n't come up to the standard of the first three days. A lift back to Bantry might be in order here. The Way leaves Durrus going east and where the road forks at the east end of the village takes the right fork, past a few shops and then some bungalows and, finally, along the minor road through fields. After a couple of miles it turns right on to another minor road through fields. It enters forestry and then joins another road, which meets the N71. The route then goes uphill and along a series of minor roads, descending through Vaughn's Pass to rejoin the outward leg of the route in Bantry.

Bantry

Phone code: 027
Colour map 3, grid C3

"God gave us Bantry Bay and we gave it to Gulf Oil"; So said the wise folk who objected to the oil company building a major oil depot on the island of Whiddy. In 1979, after a fire broke out at the depot and 51 people died, Gulf Oil departed and left behind the statue to St Brendan the Navigator as their gift. The sweeping entry into Bantry from the Cork road, with Whiddy visible across the harbour, suggests something rather special, but there is surprisingly little of interest in the town itself. What was a vast town square, Wolfe Tone Square, has been turned into a concrete garden and parking space is consequently at a premium. The town is at its best on the first Friday of each month when the traditional market fair still takes place. The main attraction is a visit to Bantry House while the town itself is a useful base for organizing visits to the peninsulas.

The **Tourist office** is on Wolfe Tone Sq, T50229. It is open from Mar-Oct, Mon-Sat 0900-1800; Jul-Aug, Mon-Sat 0900-1900, Sun 1000-1800.

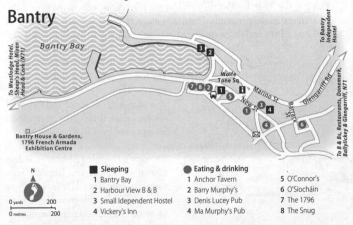

Bantry

Bantry Bay

To Westlodge Hotel, Sheep's Head, Mizen Head & Cork (N71)

To Bantry Independent Hostel

Wolfe Tone Sq

Marino St

New St

Glengarriff Rd

Barrack St

To B & Bs, Restaurants, Donemark, Ballylickey & Glengarriff, N71

Bantry House & Gardens, 1796 French Armada Exhibition Centre

N

0 yards   200
0 metres   200

■ Sleeping
1 Bantry Bay
2 Harbour View B & B
3 Small Idependent Hostel
4 Vickery's Inn

● Eating & drinking
1 Anchor Tavern
2 Barry Murphy's
3 Denis Lucey Pub
4 Ma Murphy's Pub

5 O'Connor's
6 O'Siocháin
7 The 1796
8 The Snug

History is a funny old thing

In December 1796 Wolfe Tone (see page 647), arrived in Bantry Bay as part of a French invasion force of 50 ships, some 15,000 soldiers and a military band whose instructions were to teach the Irish the revolutionary 'Marseillaise'. The aim was to drive the British out of Ireland, but it was not to be. The weather was against them: fewer than a score of ships reached Bantry Bay and after six days struggling with winter gales they reluctantly returned to France. Richard White, the local English landlord, alerted the authorities when he heard the French had arrived and was later rewarded with a peerage. In 1801 he was made Viscount Bantry and became the first Earl of Bantry in 1816.

The irony is that part of Bantry House, still in the same family, now enjoys a tidy little earner from an exhibition devoted to the failed invasion that would have removed that family, as part of the English ruling class, from Ireland. The French Armada Exhibition Centre is in the grounds of Bantry House (see below). ■ Open daily, same hours as Bantry House. €3.80.

In the 1820s and 1830s Viscount Berehaven, later the second Earl of Bantry, went on a European Grand Tour, periodically sending back art and artefacts to his family home in Bantry. Visitors walk over them – literally – when entering the porch tiled with panels taken from Pompeii. The rooms are an eclectic blend of the functional and the exotic: tapestries, fireplaces and Spanish chandeliers alongside items such as a 16th-century mosque lamp and a Tibetan water ewer.

The interior architecture is remarkably successful, especially the dramatic entrance to the library, and all part of a mastery of style that allows the building and the bow-fronted garden to complement their location. The backdrop is provided by Bantry Bay, with the Caha Mountains of the Beara Peninsula overlooking Whiddy Island. Inside the house there are tantalizing views from the drawing rooms but the baroque dining room cannot match the airy and graceful library. ■ *T50047, Mar-Oct, daily, 0900-1800. House and garden €7.62; Garden only €2.54 (combined ticket for the French Armada Exhibition available).*

Bantry House

L-AL *Sea View House Hotel*, Ballylickey, T50462, www.cmvhotel.com The best place to stay is a couple of miles out of Bantry on the road to Glengarriff; a 19th-century building with attractive rooms, a library of good books to read and an excellent restaurant. **A** *Vickery's Inn*, New St, T50006, www.westcork.com/vickerys-inn is right in the centre of town, has a sense of history (and an internet service) and charges around €62 for a double room.

B *Atlantic Shore*, T/F51310. One of the very best B&Bs on the road out to Glengarriff, which is plastered with them, and has been recommended for comfort and friendliness. **C** *Harbour View*, T51140, is part of the independent hostel, see below, and is three doors away. **D** *Bantry Independent Hostel*, Bishop Lucey Pl, T51050. Dorm beds and doubles in this IHH hostel. There is also the small and completely independent **D** *Small Independent Hostel*, T51140, tucked away on the road on the far side of the harbour. A new IHO hostel is **D** *Par Four*, T50205, out of town at Donemark (buses from Glengarriff could drop you off); open all year, bike hire, and includes 2 private rooms.

Sleeping
■ *on map*
Price codes:
see inside front cover

A spacious dining room, a bar, and first-rate traditional Irish food at *Sea View House Restaurant*, T50073, 3 miles (5 km) outside town on the road to Glengarriff. Dinner

Eating

County Cork

around €35; Sunday lunch is especially popular. *Larchwood House Restaurant*, Pearsons Bridge, Bantry, T66181. Take the road out of Bantry to Glengarriff and look for the sign pointing right after a couple of miles. Intelligently cooked Irish dishes and good value, around €28 per person, considering the quantity and quality. *O'Connor's Seafood Restaurant*, The Square, T50221, makes a speciality out of mussels; dinner dishes are around €18 and bar food, variations on the sandwich theme, is available from 1215 to 1700.

O'Siocháin is an affordable "Irish breakfast served all day" kind of place but open until 2200. Pubs like the *Barry Murphy's*, *1796* and *The Snug*, and the *Bantry Bay Hotel* all serve affordable bar food, while *Vickery's Inn*, opposite the supermarket, serves unexciting but filling and affordable meals in the attractive context of what was the lounge of this old hotel.

Pubs & music

In the summer, finding a pub with music is not difficult. Try the *1796* or *Barry Murphy's* or the *Bantry Bay Hotel*, all facing the main square. The ugly-looking *Westlodge Hotel* on the Cork road has music nightly in its bar and the *Anchor Tavern*, New St, is always worth a visit for its crazy décor. For a quiet pint, try old-fashioned *Ma Murphy's* or the friendly *Denis Lucey*.

Entertainment

A *Mussel Fair* enlivens Bantry in early May and classical musical entertainment takes place in Bantry House in Jul.

Transport

Bus Bus Éireann buses stop near *Barry Murphy's* pub and there are regular daily services to Cork, Glengarriff and Castletownbere. Single/return to Dublin is €21/32. **Bicycle** *Kramer's*, Glengarriff Rd, T50278. Bike hire.

Directory

Medical services Hospital: T50133.

Gougane Barra

Some time around the seventh century, St Finbarr established a hermitage on a tiny island in a beautiful lake, the source of the River Lee, in a glacial valley surrounded by hills and trees. The church that stands today on its ruin is of little interest, but the scene retains its natural charm and on a fine day is worth a visit. Gougane Barra is signposted off the main Bantry to Macroom road.

Sean O'Faolain set a short story, 'The Silence of the Valley' in the *Gougane Barra* hotel, but the more infamous literary association comes from a local tailor and his wife whose memories of local folklore were recorded by an Irish writer and published as *The Tailor and Ansty* (short for Anastais, his wife) in 1942. The following year the book was banned by the Censorship Board as indecent, but anyone reading it today will be hard put to find what offended them. The ban was revoked in 1964, but not before the poor tailor and his wife had suffered so much local hostility that police protection was necessary. (When the tailor was dying his police guard was cycling to his house with a bottle of whiskey for him.) The tailor and his wife are buried in the graveyard by the lake opposite Finbar's Island.

Sleeping & eating

The solitary hotel, the comfortably old-fashioned **AL** *Gougane Barra*, T026-47069, has a useful €1.27 booklet detailing walks around the lake and recounting local history. Bar food is available as well as lunch, and evening dinner around €25. Ask for a table overlooking the lake.

Glengarriff

Visit Glengarriff when the sun is out and it is easy to concur with Thackery's rhetorical conclusion after his 1842 visit that tourists need not bother travelling to the Rhine and Switzerland when places like this exist. But come here on a wet day and the place seems depressingly dank, the tourist shops seem tackier than ever.

Phone code: 027
Colour map 3, grid C3

The **Tourist office** is on the right, after the *Eccles Hotel*, coming into Glengarriff from Bantry. Open from end of May to mid-Sep, Mon to Sat, 0930-1730 but closed between 1300-1400.

There are a few attractions: an island, a noted hotel, and walks along the shore line. **Garinish Island** has a beautiful Italian garden, Illnacullin, designed by Harold Peto, and using sub-tropical plants that only thrive in this corner of Ireland warmed by the Gulf Stream. Look for a larch tree in an ancient Roman pot and a rare and beautiful hanging tree from Tasmania ■ *T63040. Mar-Oct, daily 0930-1830 (shorter hrs in winter). €3.10. Dúchas site. Boats depart regularly, T63116, from the pier opposite the Eccles Hotel for €6.35 return.*

The boats to Garinish include a viewing of seals on the rocks, but you can see them for free by walking along the shoreline, in the direction of town, from where the boats depart. A free leaflet outlining different walks around Glengarriff is available from the tourist office.

The **Eccles Hotel**, where Shaw wrote part of *St Joan*, exudes charm with its wrought-iron balconies and period lobby. Enjoy a drink or meal, inside or out, but watch out for the coach parties that can destroy the atmosphere.

Glengarriff Bamboo Park is not yet a mature garden, so the bamboo, tree ferns and palms may disappoint some, but there are some interesting plants, like the *trachycarpus takil* from India. ■ *T63570. Apr-Oct, daily, 0900-1900. €3.80.*

L-A *The Eccles*, T63003, www.eccleshotel.com Ancient lineage and the rooms have been modernized without losing all their old charm. Beware of disco nights. **AL** *Golf Links Hotel*, T63500, F63500. 4 km outside the village on the road to Bantry, offers some peace, a nice bar, good evening meals and comfortable rooms. **B** *Island View House*, T63081. Near to the *Eccles*, this B&B has only doubles for €45.

Sleeping
*Price codes:
See inside
front cover*

C-D *Murphy's Village Hostel*, T63555, is an IHH hostel in the village with over 30 beds and 5 private rooms. **D** *Cottage Bar Hostel*, T63226, is an IHO place with 12 beds, 4 private rooms; bikes for hire. **Camping** is also available at *Dowlings Caravan & Camping Park*, Castletownbere Rd, T63154.

Tourist places to eat dot the village and *Casey's Hotel* in the village, T63010, does bar food and fresh fish in the €12-20 range. The busy *Eccles* bar serves food from 1100 to 2100, while the hotel's *Garinish Restaurant*, T63003, has a superb old dining room serving dinner in the middle-range bracket; reserve a table by the window for views of the sea.

Eating

Music nightly at *Johnny Barry's*, and the *Blue Loo* has occasional blues or jazz sessions. *Harrington's* and *Casey's* also have music, though like the others they can get crowded. Consider a short trip out to the public bar at *Dowling's Camping Park* on the road to Castletownbere. Entertaining, traditional Irish music sessions nightly. At the *Eccles* on Thu nights there is an Irish dance night with audience participation.

Pubs & music

Forget the shops with names like *Shamrock*. The large *Quills* shop has a good range of woollen cardigans and Aran knitwear.

Shopping

Bike hire from *Jem Creations*, round the corner from *O'Shea's* supermarket, T63113.

Directory

County Cork

Beara Peninsula

Beara Peninsula has its own website: www.beara tourism.com

Without exaggeration, the Beara Peninsula can be described as one of the bleakest and stoniest corners of Ireland yet despite this – or because of it – the land possesses a haunting beauty that finds expression whatever the season. Stretching for 30 miles (48 km) and accessible from Glengarriff or Kenmare, the peninsula is unspoiled and boasts a long-distance walk, **The Beara Way,** *which is the ideal way to experience the beauty of the landscape.* **Hungry Hill** *is the highest point, at 2,247 ft (685 m) – easily climbed until the last gruelling stage to the summit that helps make this a whole day's climbing – and four miles (7 km) off Adrigole a sign points a route to the top.*

The **Healy Pass** *is a spectacular stretch of road that cuts across the backbone of the Caha Mountains and links the south side of the peninsula with the county of Kerry at its 360-ft (330-m) summit. The stretch of the Beara Peninsula that is part of the county of Kerry is covered in the Kenmare section of that chapter, see page 343.*

Castletownbere

Phone code: 027 Colour map 3, grid C2

The largest white-fishing port in the country is the largest town (officially named Castletown Bearhaven) on the peninsula and the departure point for a short ferry ride to Bere Island. There is a seasonal tourist information office in the square, a good supermarket that also rents bicycles – *Murphy's Supervalue* T70020, and a choice of restaurants and pubs. Between around the 25th July and 8th August some of the events in the Beara Arts and Allihies Theatre Festival take place in Castletownbere. ■ *Tourist office: T70054. Easter and Jun-Sep, Mon-Fri 1000-1700. Arts events information: T70765.*

Puxley Mansion & Dunboy Castle

The ruins of both these sites are close to one another though they have nothing in common. Puxley Mansion was the 19th-century home of the family whose wealth came from copper mines further west (see page 309). Commissioned in 1866, it was burnt down by the IRA in 1921 but the ghostly shell of this gothic extravaganza is still very impressive. It was built by Henry Puxley, supposedly as a gesture for his wife who was becoming ill through constant pregnancies, but she died giving birth before able to live here. Puxley then left for England and never returned. The interior ambitiously imitated a Gothic cathedral with vaulting arches and arcades, and the remains that can be seen are sufficient to give some idea of just how outlandish and colonial Puxley Mansion aspired to be.

Walk on to the end of the land belonging to Puxley Mansion and the very meagre but historically highly significant ruins of Dunboy Castle lie crumbling away. It was here in 1602 that O'Sullivan Beare mounted the last great act of tragic defiance at the English after the defeat of the mighty O'Neill at Kinsale. O'Sullivan refused to accept the authority of the Crown and dug in his forces at Dunboy under MacGeoghegan. The English came across from the Sheep's Head Peninsula under George Carew and captured the castle before MacGeoghegan, knowing the end was nigh, tried to blow everything and everyone up. The Irish were slaughtered and O'Sullivan Beare set off for Ulster in winter time with a thousand followers; only a handful survived and O'Sullivan fled to Spain.

Sleeping

Price codes: see inside front cover

B *Sea Breeze*, Derrymihan, T70508, is a couple of mins on foot from the town centre, follow the Beara Way signs. **B** *Island View*, T70415, signposted off the main street has good views over the harbour. **C** *Harbour Lodge Hostel*, North Rd, T60228, bearalodge@eircom.net is a new hostel that caters for group bookings so check availability.

County Cork

Seafood chowder, crab sandwiches and the like are served at *MacCarthy's* in the main
square. The *Mariner*, T71111, is open for dinner and Sunday lunch, serving a Mediterranean-style cuisine of seafood, meat and pasta dishes. Main courses around €15. At the
west end of town the *Old Bank Seafood Restaurant*, T778564, serves tourist fare.

The best reason for visiting Bere Island would be to walk around it as part of
the Beara Way (see page 310). The ferries, T75014, www.murphysferry.com,
run from Castletownbere's harbour. Daily from 0730 (0915 on Sunday) until
2000 from June to August. A Monday to Friday service operates the rest of the
year. There is also a service from *The Pontoon*, a couple of miles east of
Castletownbere on the main road, with boats departing half an hour later.

B-C *The Admirals House Hostel*, T75213, www.bereislandhostel.com calls itself a
"luxury hostel", hence the above-average prices for an IHH place, but maybe you're just
paying for the peaceful beauty of the place. At Rerrin village there is a shop, post office
and a pub and this is also where *Kitty's Café*, T75996, serves lunch and evening meals.

Allihies

Situated in the far west of the peninsula this small village of brightly painted Phone code: 027
houses overlooks Ballydonegan Bay and a white quartz strand, safe for swim- Colour map 3, grid C2
ming, that lends considerably to the astonishing beauty of the locality. There
is a small, seasonal **tourist information** post in the village and between
around the 25th July to 8th August some of the events in the **Beara Arts and
Allihies Theatre Festival** take place here.

The unhappy story of the copper mines begins in the early 19th century, when the
Anglo-Irish Puxley family opened the first mine. At one time well over a thousand
people were employed here, including a whole community of Cornish miners
brought in for their specialist skills. These English workers were boycotted by the
locals who felt their chances of employment were threatened, and the ships that
carried away the ore to Swansea brought in essential supplies for the Cornish families. The mines finally closed in 1930, but only after producing tremendous
wealth for the Puxleys, as the ruins of Puxley Mansion (see page 308) make clear.
   To walk around the mines, leave Allihies at the top, northern end, go right
at the first fork and look for a dump area on the left of the road. This is the
entrance to the mines, and a pathway leads up past the ruins and the chimney
stack of one of the pumping stations. The mineshafts are fenced in, but be
careful and stick to the pathway.

A *Sea View House*, T73004; F73211. In the village with en-suite doubles/singles but no
evening meals. B *Veronica's*, T73072. Does B&B as well as food (see 'Eating', below).
C-D *Village Hostel*, T73107, has some 50 beds and 10 private rooms. D *An Óige's Allihies
Hostel*, Cahermeelabo, T73014, is 2 km from the village and opens from Jun-Sep.

Touristy pub food and à la carte meals at the bright-red-painted *O'Neill's*, in the village,
T73008. Both the *Lighthouse Bar* opposite the playground and the *Oak Bar*, next door to
O'Neill's, have pub grub. *Veronica's* at the Dursey end of the village does soup and salads.

The *Lighthouse Bar* has music (Wed and Sun nights) and attracts a younger set than
the *Oak Bar*, which has good sessions of traditional music on Sun and Thu nights.
O'Neill's next door has music on Wed nights, while *O'Sullivan's* has a comfortably
quiet atmosphere, which is sometimes enlivened by impromptu singing.

Dursey Island

Phone code: 027

At the end of the peninsula the apparatus of a cable car awaits to carry you over to Dursey Island. The cable car, which has operated since 1969, was designed to carry six people or one person and a cow across the 722-ft-wide (220-m) Dursey Sound. Only a few people still live on the island and the only road ends in a pathway that continues out to a Martello tower on the highest point. Tracks also lead out to Dursey Head where the three rocks off the tip of the island – the Bull, the Cow and the Calf – can be admired for their stark beauty. Folk legend has it that the Bull was where one of the original invaders of Ireland, the so-called Milesians, wrecked a boat and was buried. The rock became one of the entrances to the isles of enchantment in the Gaelic afterlife.
■ *Cable car, Mon-Sat 0900-1100, 1430-1700 and 1900-2000. €3 return. T73017 for Sun service.*

The opportunity to spot bird life is one of the joys of a walk on Dursey. Gannets and choughs are often seen, as are skuas and terns in spring and autumn, and the island is home to a huge colony of fulmars. Windswept migrants, such as an albatross, are occasionally seen. Dolphins, harbour porpoises and minkie whales may also be spotted close to the shore.

The island's history is well told in *Discover Dursey* by Penelope Durrell, and the book is available in the supermarket in Castletownbere and a few other places. It tells the story of Dursey from the time of the Vikings, through the 1602 massacre by the English and up to modern times.

Sleeping & eating
There is no accommodation on the island, but **B** *Windy Point House*, T/F73017, within walking distance of the cable car does B&B for €47, and evening meals are available for guests only. During the day it functions as a café, closing at 1800. **C** *Skellig View*, T73129. This B&B is also close by and has rooms with shared bathroom facilities, and evening meals for residents only.

The Beara Way

Phone code: 027

This is a well established 122-mile (197-km) walk around what is certainly the wildest countryside in Ireland with coastal views, two island walks, a cable-car ride, old mineworkings, and a sandy beach. It takes upwards of nine days, depending on how much you choose to do, and most of it is well worth the effort, though the last two days are probably better completed on a bicycle. The Way begins in Glengarriff in County Cork, travels westwards to Allihies at the end of the peninsula via Castletownbere and Bere Island and then returns along the northern shore, entering County Kerry but ending back in Glengarriff. If you have only one or two days the tour given for day five (a circular tour based on Allihies and taking in Dursey Island) has the best views.

Mapping & information
The best maps to use are 84 and 85 in the *Ordnance Survey* (OS) 1:50,000 series. They have the Beara Way plotted accurately, apart from the change noted below for day 2. There is also a tourist board map of the Way, but it is not needed if you have the OS maps. The maps and information about accommodation should be available at the tourist offices in Glengarriff, T027-63201 and Castletownbere, T027-70054. See also the bibliography on page 681 for specialist walking guides to Ireland.

Day one
Glengarriff to Adrigole
This is a 10.1-mile (16.8-km) walk through wild, open land. The walk begins in Glengarriff and heads west on the main road to Castletownbere. Beyond

two caravan parks the route turns to the right along a narrow, easily missed boreen, signposted to the Magannagan Walk. At the end of the boreen the route crosses a gate and heads across sheep territory with the stark hillside of Shrone Hill to the right and open land to the left. It meets forestry and skirts its edge, heading uphill towards the next stage of the walk, a narrow valley between Sugarloaf Mountain and Gowlbeg Hill. If you look back at this stage, you will see views over Bantry Bay. The walk passes the steep and forbidding sides of Sugarloaf Mountain to the sound of the nearby waterfall and climbs to meet an old road that runs parallel with the coast and the main road far below. The whole route to Adrigole is a series of panoramas over first Bantry Bay and then Adrigole Bay. The route follows the old road where occasional stone bridges testify to a period when this was the main road to Glengarriff. Descending through a sheep pen, the route joins a tarmac road through still more wild countryside, littered with standing stones, mass rocks and other signs of ancient habitation. The road gradually descends into Adrigole where there are several B&Bs, a hostel, pub and a grocery store where you can get supplies for the next day. You could try **B** *Beachmount*, T60075, or **B** *Ocean View*, T60069, though best value is **C-D** *Hungry Hill Lodge*, T60228, which has dorm beds and private double rooms, including one which is en-suite for €32.

This is 13.1 miles (21.7 km) and is a challenging but manageable and very satisfying day's walk. From Adrigole head west along the main road before leaving it at Reen Bridge and heading uphill. It turns on to a green road but departs from the route marked out on the OS map at a point just west of Dereeny and goes south to avoid a very damp part of the walk. Rejoining the main road, it follows this for a few 100 yds (or m) before heading very steeply uphill for about ¾ of a mile (just over 1 km) to meet an old turf road way up at 820 ft (250 m) on a spur of Hungry Hill. From here the route curves around the flanks of Hungry Hill with its stark, blasted hillsides looming above. It continues along this line, joining and leaving old turf roads and climbing the flanks of Maulin Mountain at about 980 ft (300 m) until it joins an old road down to Castletownbere where food and accommodation are available.

Day two
*Adrigole to
Castletownbere*

Boats from Castletownbere travel at regular intervals daily to the island where you will experience a scenic pretty walk, mostly around the island's roads but with one outstanding stretch over the island's highest point. The total distance is 13 miles (21 km).

  From the pier, follow the road until it meets a T-junction where you should turn left. This road has very little traffic on it and meanders around the northern shore of the island with pleasant views of Castletownbere and Hungry Hill. It climbs over the ridge at the centre of the island, passing a Martello tower on the left. At Rerrin, the island's main village, there are some shops and cafés. Here you take a left fork at Rerrin harbour and approach the eastern end of the island past an army training ground and increasingly rugged land where wild flowers fill the roadsides and the fields are full of iris and gorse. The road ends at a locked gate and the route returns to Rerrin by a gravelled road. At the southern shore of the island you have views of the Sheep's Head Peninsula and Bantry Bay. The coast is littered with the remains of the island's days as a British naval base. Returning to Rerrin you retrace your steps for a while over the saddle between the island's two hills and then your next route is clear as you can see a path snaking its way up to the island's highest point, Knockanallig. It is a glorious walk up a clear path through well-nibbled grass and amazing views behind. At the top you can rest for a time by a tumbled

Day three
Bear Island

signal tower and take in the glory of the coastline and open sea. The route returns through sometimes boggy land along the southern cliffs to meet the lighthouse and then return to the pier via an excellent old military road.

Day four
Castletownbere to Allihies

This is 8 miles (13.6 km) of hillwalking with views of both shores of the peninsula, numerous megalithic sites and a pretty walk through lanes into Allihies. Leaving Castletownbere and heading west on the main road, the route quickly heads right along a minor road, past a very well preserved stone circle. Further on it heads uphill along an old turf road, and then heads west across the bog with fine views back to Castletownbere. It joins a tarmac road for a short distance and then climbs quite rapidly for fine views to the north of the peninsula. Descending through forestry it follows tarmac for a while and then climbs steeply through more forestry to find a long pleasant green road, which eventually meets a narrow boreen. This descends through ever prettier country lanes into Allihies where there is accommodation and a lovely beach.

Day five
Allihies to Allihies via Dursey Island

This is a lot of walking – over 20 miles (32 km) – and an occasional bit of hitch-hiking might suggest itself. The first few miles are on the main road to Castletownbere, which can be quite busy in summer. Then the route heads rapidly uphill, first over a boreen and then open, heather-covered moorland with the most glorious views of the whole of the southwest opening up behind you all the way to the Iveragh and beyond. The path crosses the northern coastline high up and descends to meet the road to Dursey Island. It then heads out to Crow Head across more wild moors and descends to meet the cable car. You must be here before 1045 because the cable car stops operating at 1100, before working again in the afternoon. The cable car ride is good fun if you like swinging in a small box over a chasm, and the trip around Dursey Island is quite excellent, passing the island's village and heading out to the

Beara Peninsula and Beara Way

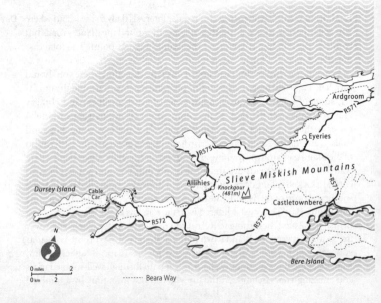

westernmost point where the sea views defy description. Back on the mainland you might want to ignore the rest of the Way around the northern shores of Garinish Bay, although it is quite pleasant, and head back to Allihies.

This is about 15 miles (24 km) along old roads, open moor and the shores of Coulagh Bay.

Day six
Allihies to Ardgroom

    The Way heads out of Allihies on the roads built when the copper mines were working. It passes the old office building, now converted to a home, several mineshafts surrounded by wired and a still-standing pumping station which kept the seawater out of the mines. Heading uphill on a wide track it crosses a little spur of Knockoura and follows a tarmac road along the flanks of the mountain. At Coulagh it meets the main road for a time and then arrives at Eyeries. From here the route follows the shores of Coulagh Bay before heading over moorland and then steeply downhill into Ardgroom. Here there are a few B&Bs. You could try **C** *Canfie House*, T74105, or **C** *Sea Villa*, T74369. At Eyeries the **D** *Ard Na Mara Hostel*, T74271, has 9 beds with 6 of them in private rooms, from €22.85 each, and space for camping.

This is 12 miles (19 km), chiefly along boreens but with two good hill walks. From Ardgroom, turn left at the *Holly Bar*, where the road starts to climb for a time and before it meets the main road again. After two miles (3 km) it leaves the road and heads over wild moorland to Lauragh. Another spell on a minor road brings you to Tuosist, where there is accommodation at **B** *The Lake House*, T84205.

Day seven
Ardgroom to Tuosist

Rejoining the waymarked walk, the Way crosses the flanks of Knocknagarrane Mountain and meets a track passing between the two loughs Inchiquin and Cloonee. The track peters out and the Way continues

Day eight
Tuosist to Kenmare

County Cork

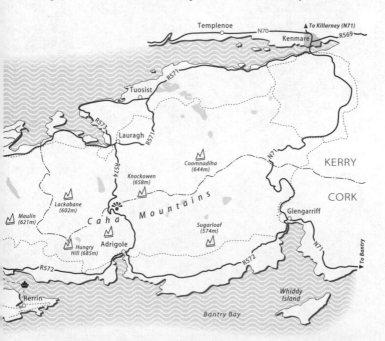

eastwards overland through a high saddle between two unnamed hills. There are fine views of the loughs behind you as you descend to meet a minor road beside a stone circle near Lough Dromoghty. This road meets another minor road where the Way turns left to Kenmare following more minor roads. At this junction it is possible instead to go to the right and follow another minor road through wild rocky territory, where you might expect an ambush at any moment, back down to Glengarriff and end the walk there. The distance to Kenmare is 11 miles (18 km).

Day nine
Kenmare to Glengarriff

There is a choice of walks here, both around 15 miles (24 km) along minor roads but through very wild and beautiful scenery. The first route retraces the steps of day eight to the shores of Lough Dromoghty. There it keeps on past the lough and heads towards Kenmare on the walk outlined in day eight's first route. The other route leaves Kenmare and turns left to follow a long minor road through the valley of the Sheen River. Its finest point is the crossing between the Esk and Barraboy Mountains at 1,200 ft (369 m) before descending through a wood to join the N71 back to Glengarriff.

County Kerry

9

County Kerry

Atlantic Ocean

Tarbert

To Limerick

Listowel

Tralee

To Dublin

Dingle

KERRY

Killarney

Cahersiveen   *Macgillycuddy's Reeks*

Kenmare

To Cork

To Bantry

Superlatives attach to Kerry: the highest mountain in Ireland, **Carrauntoohill***; the most spectacular island,* **Skellig Michael***; two of the grandest long-distance walks; and the* **Gallarus Oratory***, one of the country's most precious ancient buildings. Kerry is also home to* **Killarney***, Ireland's premier tourist town, and the* **Ring of Kerry** *is the most travelled scenic route in Ireland. Kerry's enormous popularity with visitors, however, need not deter the traveller, because although masses of tourists crowd into the main towns and cars clog the coastal roads, it is very easy to escape the crowds.*

There are four main towns, three of them on the coast: **Kenmare** *in the south,* **Dingle** *on the famed Dingle Peninsula and* **Tralee** *at the northern head of it.*

Kerry's more rugged beauty is to be found on the **Iveragh peninsula***, though to appreciate its wildness it is well nigh essential to make detours off the main Ring of Kerry road. Only then can you appreciate the brooding mountains and dark valleys, the glorious long-distance walks across the dazzlingly scenic peninsulas and the semi-deserted islands. Then there are the grand old houses and gardens such as* **Derrynane***. Add this to the tourist kitsch of fake thatched cottages, hordes of camera-toting tour bus riders and olde-worlde village pubs, and Kerry becomes a series of wild contradictions.*

Ins and outs

Kerry Airport, T066-9764644, is about 10 miles (15 km) north of Killarney at Farranfore, off the N22. *Aer Arann* flies to Dublin and *Ryanair* flies to London's Stanstead airport. Farranfore has a train link with both Killarney and Tralee. There are railway stations at Killarney, T064-31067, and Tralee, T066-7123566, connecting with Dublin, Cork and other towns. All the main towns are served by *Bus Éireann* and details are given under the town's 'Transport' entries.

Getting around

In the summer months both the Iveragh and Dingle peninsulas, unlike the Beara, are reasonably well serviced by **buses** (see pages 332 and 351). There is also a summer only service between Killarney and Castletownbere via Kenmare, Lauragh and Ardgroom. **Cars** can be hired at the airport, where companies like *Hertz*, T066-9764733, have outlets, or in Killarney. A host of companies are based in Killarney, Dingle and Kenmare: see those sections for details. For general tourist information on Kerry County see www.travelireland.org/kerry

Killarney

*Phone code: 064
Colour map 3, grid B3*

Victorian tourists were the first to come to Killarney; they waxed lyrical over the natural beauty of its lakes and, with well over a century to build up and consolidate the hype, it should come as no surprise to learn that this is Ireland's premier tourist town. Indeed, considering the sheer multitude of visitors who come and go every summer, the ordinary citizens of the town deserve a prize for the way in which they go about their business seemingly oblivious to the tourist tumult around them. Ironically, the town itself is of very minor interest, and as all the attractions lie outside Killarney there is little good reason to stay here for long. But while you are here there are countless restaurants, shops and pubs with music dedicated to providing creature comforts.

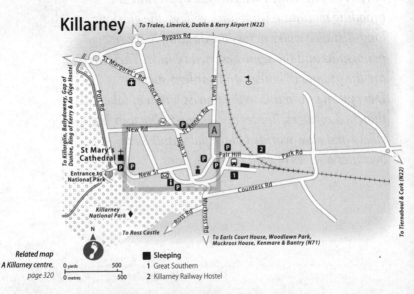

Killarney

To Tralee, Limerick, Dublin & Kerry Airport (N22)

*Related map
A Killarney centre,
page 320*

■ **Sleeping**
1 Great Southern
2 Killarney Railway Hostel

County Kerry

Things to do in County Kerry

- Spot the birdlife on a boat trip to the monastic dwellings of **Skellig Michael**
- Exhaust yourself by walking the **Kerry Way** from Waterville to Cahersiveen
- Drive a **quad-car** across the **Kenmare** countryside
- Explore the **cliffs at Inch** for their multitude of fossils
- Pay homage to the King of the Fair at **Puck Fair**
- Enjoy a meal and a bed at An Bóthar after walking from Dunquin on the **Dingle Way**
- Enjoy fresh seafood at **The Point**, where the ferry leaves for Valentia Island

Ins and outs

Getting there
See the 'Getting there' section for Kerry, above. *Bus Éireann's* No 286 service departs daily from the airport to Killarney at 1218 and then every 2 hours until 2218; from Killarney at 0615 (Mon only), 0900, 1000 and every 2 hours until 1800; journey time 20 mins. A taxi costs about €20.

Getting around
Most of the sights in Killarney are accessible on foot, or, if you can take the embarrassment, there are horse-drawn jaunting cars willing to drive you around the place. The **tourist office** is off High St, T31633. Open all year, daily at the height of the season. This is the place to gather information for the whole Kerry region and there is also a bureau de change as well as an extensive range of gifts and literature.

History and sights

English landlords in the 18th century developed copper and iron mines in the area, smelting the iron using the rich supply of oakwoods, and when word spread of the natural beauty of the surrounding mountains and lakes early tourists arrived in Bianconi cars (see page 246). Later in the 19th century the introduction of a railway line transformed the tourist scene and Queen Victoria's visit in 1861 really put the place on the map. Before the English ever arrived there were two chief Gaelic clans, the McCarthys and the O'Donoghues, and while the O'Donoghues' territory was confiscated by Cromwell, the McCarthys managed to hold on to land, some of which passed by inheritance to the Herbert family, the people responsible for building Muckross House and creating the estate.

Muckross House, gardens & traditional farms
Some 4 miles (6 km) south on the N71 road and with a scheduled bus service from the town centre, the Muckross House complex is a major attraction. The house itself is a fine Victorian mansion (see page 327) replete with the gentry's elegant rooms full of period furniture, while the servants' working quarters in the basement now house various craft workshops. The gardens boast an attractive water garden, a rock garden and more rhododendrons than you may care to see. The traditional farms, brought to life with real animals, pay tourist homage to Eamon de Valera's idyll of rural life in the 1930s, though surely he would have disapproved of the splendid decadence of the 'vintage coach' that shuttles visitors around. Near the house there are maps showing a number of local scenic walks; the most popular route, also suitable for bicycles, heads around the north side of Middle Lake towards the Meeting of the Waters where the Upper Lake – the most beautiful of the three lakes – comes into view. ■ *T31440. House: Mid-Mar-Oct, 0900-1800 (1900 in Jul and Aug);*

Nov-mid Mar, 0900-1730). €5. Farms: Jun-Sep, 1000-1900 (shorter hours in other months). €4. Dúchas site: joint ticket for house and farms €7.60. Gardens: 24 hours. Free.

Muckross Friary
The remarkably well-preserved Muckross Friary dates back to 1440, although General Ludlow arrived in 1652 and trashed the place after expelling the monks. The solid square tower is the most distinctive feature though the cloisters, surrounding an ancient yew tree, and a vaulted quadrangle are also in good condition. ■ *Mid-Jun-early Sep, 1000-1700. Free.*

St Mary's Cathedral
The finest example of AWN Pugin's work in Ireland was begun in 1842 and restored in the 1970s. Opinions of the exterior range from celebration of its mastery of Early English Gothic to denigration of its repressive presence, but the interior is a minor masterpiece of Irish-inspired architecture. Despite some terrible gaffes in the restoration of the cathedral, Pugin's inspiring vision of an Irish medieval cathedral endures in the delicate use of lancet and rose windows set against the solid interior buttresses. During the Famine, building work on the church was still in progress, and it was used as a shelter for the distressed; the large tree on the lawn marks a mass famine grave.

Ross Castle
The 15th-century Ross Castle, just outside of town off the N71 road to Kenmare, has gone down in popular history as one of the last strongholds in Ireland to hold out valiantly against Cromwellian forces. In 1652 General Ludlow received its surrender from Muskerry after bringing ships up to Killarney by land and river, thus fulfilling a prophecy that the castle "could not be taken until a ship should swim upon the lake". The truth is that Muskerry,

Killarney centre

Sleeping
1 Arbutus *B3*
2 International *B3*
3 Killarney Avenue *B3*
4 Killarney Park *B3*
5 Linden House *A2*
6 Neptune's Hostel *B2*
7 Súgán Hostel *A3*

● **Eating & drinking**
1 Blue Door *A2*
2 Bricin *A2*
3 Carragh *B2*
4 Celtic Cauldron *B3*
5 Danny Man Inn *B2*
6 Dingles *B1*
7 Eastern Tandoori *A2*
8 Eviston House *B2*
9 Foley's *A2*
10 Gaby's *A2*
11 Laurels *B3*
12 Mac's *B2*
13 Macudda's *A2*
14 Mustang Sally's *B3*
15 O'Connor's *B2*
16 Robertino's *A2*
17 Scott's Gardens *B3*
18 Sheehan's *B3*
19 Sheila's *B2*
20 Stella *B3*
21 Stone Chat *A2*
22 Swiss Barn *A2*
23 Taste of India *B3*
24 Teo's *B2*

knowing full well that defeat was imminent, had already decided to surrender and the appearance of the boats provided a suitable excuse. The castle has now been completely restored, perhaps a little too clinically, but the lakeside location has its charms – Shelley briefly lived nearby in 1813 – and boats can be hired to row out to Inisfallen Island. ■ *T35851. Jun-Aug, 0900-1830 (shorter hours at other times). €3.80. Dúchas site.*

Nothing remains of the seventh-century monastery founded by St Fenian the Leper, although the ruins of a 12th-century oratory with a fine Romanesque doorway can be appreciated. You will have to travel to the Bodleian Library in Oxford to see the famed *Annals of Inishfallen*, a chronicle of Irish history from the 11th to the 13th centuries, completed on Inisfallen by monks. Rowing boats can be hired from near Ross Castle, €6.35 per person. The 21-acre island is about a mile (1.6 km) from the shore.

Inisfallen Island

A worthwhile place to visit on a wet day, the museum has a varied display of veteran, vintage and classic vehicles of the road. My favourite is the 1910 Wolseley that belonged to the Gore Booth family in Sligo and carried Yeats around with Countess Markievicz at the wheel. ■ *T32638. Apr-Oct, 1000-1800; Jul-Aug, 1000-2000. €3.80.*

Museum of Irish Transport

And on another wet day there is an excuse to come here and watch scores of trains running on over a mile of track across familiar European landmarks. ■ *T34000. Next to the tourist office. Mid-Mar-Oct, daily, 1030-1800.*

Model Railway Museum

Built in 1870, replacing an earlier church of 1812 (and another before that), this is a pretty, musty little church, full of Anglo-Irish names and memorials to long forgotten figures. It has pre-Raphaelite-style stained glass windows and beautiful patterned floor tiles. Right in the middle of the tourist frenzy it is a great place to spend a few minutes contemplation before buying that arran sweater/printed teatowel/cuddly toy in the gift shops outside. ■ *Open all year. €3.80.*

St Mary's Church

County Kerry

Essentials

There is a good range of accommodation in and around Killarney. A vast number of B&Bs, nearly all those registered with the Bord Fáilte, charge a standard rate of around €44.44 for a double and €31.74 for a single so you may as well take pot luck with the tourist office. Very few are located within the town and without your own transport it is better to consider a private room in one of the hostels. A number of B&Bs close over the winter, so be sure to check. The less expensive B&Bs mostly belong to the Family Homes of Ireland group (see page 41).

Sleeping
■ *on maps, pages 318 & 320*
Price codes: see inside front cover

XL *Aghadoe Heights Hotel*, T31766, www.aghadoeheights.com Lakeside hotel a few miles out of town at Aghadoe – all dark wood, chesterfields and antiques – plus a pool. **LL** *Great Southern*, T31262, www.gsh.ie Centrally located, recently refurbished hotel, dating from 1854 and is the place to stay for old-fashioned style plus modern amenities such as a heated pool. The uninspiring neo-Georgian exterior hides a lush extravagance of style and a sumptuous foyer, which, along with the stately dining room and its Greek columns, makes a visit here worthwhile if only for a drink. **LL** *Hotel Europe*, T31900, www.iol.ie/khl Also out of town, at Fossa on the N72. Has one of the most scenic locations of Killarney's many hotels, the lakeside rooms have balconies to boot, and the 82-ft (25-m) pool is complemented by a seaweed bath for the hyper health-conscious. **LL** *Killarney Park*, T35555, www.killarneyparkhotel.ie In the town centre, next to the cinema complex, a modern 4-star hotel with bourgeois charm and a good restaurant.

Accommodation in Killarney

Throughout July and August there is a long queue every morning at the accommodation desk in the Killarney tourist office. Hotels and guesthouses, and especially B&Bs and hostels, can all be oversubscribed and without an advance booking you may end up being forced into a higher accommodation bracket than you anticipated. Hotels are uniformly expensive and rooms under €75 are as rare as leprechauns. Guesthouses usually offer the comfort of a small hotel, but for good value consider also the private rooms in the hostels, charging around €32. Some of the hostels have their transport waiting outside the bus and train station and if you don't have a bed booked it may be worth arranging something on the spot.

L *Killarney Av*, Kenmare Pl, T32522, www.odonoghue-ring-hotels.com Centrally located, conspicuous exterior and swanky lobby, olde-Irish restaurant and Irish theme pub. **L** *Killarney Ryan Hotel*, Cork Rd, T31555, www.ryan-hotels.com Ideal for families with its crèche, a young teenagers' club and kids' menus. **L** *Randles Court Hotel*, Muckross Rd, T35333, www.randleshotels.com Good-sized rooms built in 1894, with some period features retained and within walking distance of town. **L-AL** *Arbutus*, College St, T31037, F34033. A friendly family-run hotel in the heart of town, but not the quietest location. **L-AL** *Gleneagle Hotel*, Muckross Rd, T31870, www.gleneagle-hotel.com A short way out of town, this hotel is geared up for fun-loving families who want leisure facilities and late-night musical entertainment. **L-AL** *International Hotel*, Kenmare Pl, T31816, F31837. Often busy with coach parties, a comfortable and conveniently located hotel opposite the cinema complex.

AL *Earls Court House*,Woodlawn Rd, T34009, homepage.tinet.ie/~earls Decorated entirely in 19th-century antique furnishings, with individually-styled bedrooms some of which have balconies looking out on countryside, this top-drawer guesthouse invites a stay of more than one night. **AL** *Fuschia House*, Muckross Rd, T33743, www.fuchsiahouse.com In this no-smoking guesthouse, tea and cakes are served on arrival; good breakfast, utility room with fridge and kettle, and the firm beds are a treat in the 10 large bedrooms. **AL** *Killarney Lodge*, Countess Rd, T36499, kylodge@aol.ie Superior, large guesthouse set in modern walled gardens.

A *Old Weir Lodge*, Muckross Rd, T35593, www.oldweirlodge.com Modern, Tudor-style guesthouse, short walk from town, good facilities. **A** *Linden House* New Rd, T31379, F31196. Hotel in a reasonably quiet part of town, restaurant and 3-night packages.

B *Fallow Lodge*, Tralee Rd, T/F33891. This B&B is 5 mins by car from the centre, open all year. **B** *Larkfield House*, Ballycasheen, T34438, jki@eircom.net B&B off the N22 Cork Rd at the Whitebridge sign. Has a good reputation. **B** *Tamara*, 9 Lewis Rd, T33357. B&B in town with own parking space.

C *Eagle View*, 21 Woodlawn Pk, T32779. B&B in a family home, within walking distance of town. **C** *Ashbury House*, Tieraboul, T36707. Within walking distance of town centre, off the N22 Park Rd roundabout; take the exit for the industrial estate. **C** *Killarney International Hostel*, Aghadoe House, T31240, anoige@killarney.iol.ie. This An Óige hostel is a superb old mansion, 3 miles (5 km) west of town on the road to Killorglin. Free transport from train and bus stations; private rooms, bike hire. **C-D** *Killarney Railway Hostel*, T35299. Opposite the railway station, well equipped and lots of private rooms. **C-D** *Neptune's*, off New St, T35255, F36399, neptune@tinet.ie IHH hostel, possibly the best organized one in town but only 5 private rooms.

D *Fossa Holiday Hostel*, Fossa, T31497. Out of town but worth considering if everywhere else is full. **D** *Park*, Park Rd, T32119. Hostel with 50 beds and 2 private rooms, and an admirable policy of charging the same rate, €10.16, per person. **D** *Peacock Farm Hostel*, Gortdromakiery, Muckross, T33557. Although there is a twice-daily pick-up service it helps to have your own transport; take Lough Guitane Rd, first left after Muckross House coming from Killarney. **D Súgan**, Lewis Rd, T33104. Good location in town, 2 private rooms, a little hip and a little squashed.

Self-catering *Accommodation Killarney*, 52 High St, T31787, F35238. Handles quality town houses and plush 3-bedroomed suites.

Camping There are a few 4-star sites near town: the *Flesk Muckross Caravan & Camping Park*, Muckross Rd, T31704, F34681, killarneylakes@tinet.ie *Fossa Caravan & Camping Park*, Fossa, T31497, F34459, on the road to Killorglin; and *Fleming's White Bridge Caravan & Camping Park*, T31590, F37474, just off the N22 Cork road. Camping is possible at *Killarney Railway* hostel.

Expensive *Foley's Restaurant*, High St, T31217, is fairly typical of the town's expensive seafood and steakhouse restaurants, as is *Dingles Restaurant*, New St, T31079. Dingles closes on Sun and between Nov and Mar and serves only dinner, while Foley's is open all year around for lunch and dinner. *Gaby's*, High St, T32519, has a reputation, not accepted by everyone, as the best seafood restaurant in town and prices to match; open for dinner except on Sun and for lunch Tue-Sat. Apart from the fresh seafood like lobster, Gaby's also serves steaks and Kerry lamb, and the salmon pâté is a house speciality when it comes to starters. The *Celtic Cauldron*, Plunkett St, T36821, specializing in traditional dishes from Scotland and Wales as well as Ireland, serves a tasty Irish stew flavoured with Guinness for lunch, and starters in the evening such as cockles and mussels. From Wales comes a vegetarian sausage dish and Scotland produces pheasant on the menu. The décor is a bit of a hoot, perhaps a tad too close to an Irish theme pub for comfort, but the food is grand. Also worth considering is the Italian-style *Chequers* restaurant in the Randles Court Hotel. Right at the borderline with the next category down is *Blue Door Bistro*, 57, High St, T33755, with a very trendy décor and menu to match. Open 7 days for lunch and dinner.

Mid-range *Peppers*, at the Great Southern hotel, T31262, offers modern Irish cuisine – scallops and prawns with couscous, monkfish and asparagus, veal with lemon-scented spinach – in a room that successfully blends period details with self-conscious modern art on the walls. Some dishes could push your bill into the expensive category. *Bricín*, High St, T34902, has been around for a while and is still a reliable place for a decent innovative lunch or dinner, closed Sun; speciality is *boxty*, a traditional Irish dish. Good value early-bird set menu and several vegetarian options. *Teo's*, New St, T36344, has a range of Mediterranean-style dishes served in a modern setting, a good children's menu, lots of pizzas, pasta and salads and tables outside for warm weather. *Swiss Barn* 17 High St, T36044, specializes in dishes such as fondue and veal Zurichoise, but standard meat and fish dishes are available. Open from 1730 and there is an early-bird menu before 1900. *Robertino's*, High St, T34966, has arty Italian décor and serves lunches of pizza, pasta and open sandwiches and an early-bird set dinner.

Cheap *Stella's* on Main St is a well established restaurant serving quick meals of fish and chips, pizzas, lamb and stew. *Mac's*, also on Main St, does similar fare and boasts an ice cream parlour. The *Stone Chat*, down Flemings Lane off High St, T34295, is an excellent little joint for café meals. Also on High St both the *Caragh Restaurant* and *Sheila's* are equally adept at catering to a busy crowd of hungry diners at lunch and dinnertime. The *Taste of India*, down the lane opposite the cinema and Killarney Park hotel, T37770, is a balti and tandoori restaurant, also with a take-out menu, open from 1700 until midnight at least. In High St *Eastern Tandoori* has a good early-bird dinner menu at €12.50. Another good place for an inexpensive early-bird menu is *Macudda's*, High St, where if you hang around after your meal you can listen to live music of one sort or another. Opposite the tourist office in the Innisfallen Centre there are inexpensive cafés suitable for a quick meal. Also here is a large supermarket, ideal for stocking up on picnic meals and other provisions.

Eating
● *on maps*
Price codes:
see inside front cover

County Kerry

Pubs & music   At the height of the season it seems as if every pub in the town has music of one sort or another. The hugely popular and undeniably touristy *Laurels*, Main St, T31149, and *Scott's Gardens*, College St, T31060, are both in the centre of town and while not to everyone's taste or musical ear, they can be good fun. *Charlie Foley's* on New St, T33920, might seem sophisticated by comparison and *O'Connor's* on High St has regular sessions of traditional music. So too does *Tatler Jack* on Plunkett St, T32361 and *McSorley's Pub*, in College St, T37278. The *Danny Man Inn* in the *Eviston House Hotel* on New St, T31640, has music every night from 2100, but coach parties can take over the place. The *Arbutus* hotel in College St has traditional music every night, and in the same street the bar in the *Fáilte* hotel has traditional music on weeknights. *Hannigan's* in the International hotel has Irish music every night except Sun. The *Great Southern Hotel* has live piano music in the lobby at night.

The best pub for young people is *Yer Man's* in Plunkett St and the *Fáilte* hotel has a disco on Fri, Sat and Sun nights. In Main St *Mustang Sally's* is a music bar with bar food and music 7 nights, while next door *Sheehan's* has traditional music and set dancing nightly. The *Gleneagle Hotel* on Muckross Rd has discos for all ages every night of the week.

Many of the hotels within town and out along the road to Kenmare have musical entertainment. The *Gleneagle Hotel*, T36000, has live musicians or singers every night of the week. The *Killarney Manor*, T31551, offers an Irish theme night conjured out of an imaginary social gathering in a 19th-century stately manor, and *Kate Kearney's Cottage* at the Gap of Dunloe has traditional music on Wed, Fri and Sun nights.

The *Lake Hotel* has traditional music on Mon, Wed and Sat, while *Hotel Europe* goes for Wed and Fri nights and confines itself to piano music on Sat and Sun.

Shopping   **Art and craft** *Earthstone Gallery*, 3 Plunkett St, T30166, www.earthstonegallery.com,
Shops stay open until   sells designer jewellery, sculptures, ceramics and decorative art. *Fred's Art Studio* is
2200 in the summer   devoted to miniature art and is open from Apr-Oct on the Mangerton Rd. Head towards Muckross, turn left immediately after *Molly D'Arcy's* pub. **Books** *Frameworks*, 37 New St, T35791. Has antique prints and books and a good selection of Irish maps. Shipping arranged. *The Killarney Bookshop*, 32 Main St. **Gifts** *Blarney Woollen Mills*, 10 Main St, has two floors devoted to Irish crafts – especially pottery and crystal – and Aran knitwear, open daily until 2300. *House of Names* in Kenmare Pl retails quality heraldic products for Irish and other European names. *Carraig Don* in Main St has lots of jumpers, crafts and gifts while *Lennon's* in High St has lots of embroidery and lace things.

Sport   **Fishing** Tackle, permits and information at *O'Neill's*, 6 Plunkett St, T31970. River Flesk gets spring salmon and peel (grilse), River Laune has salmon and trout while Barfinnihy Lake is stocked with trout. Permits required for rivers and Barfinnihy Lake but not for Killarney lakes. **Horse riding** *Killarney Riding Stables*, Ballydowney, T31686, www.killarney-reeks-trail.com 1 mile (1.6 km) west of Killarney off the R562 road to Killorglin. Trips from 1hr to 6 days. *Muckross Riding Stables*, Mangerton Rd, T32238, 1-3 hr rides.

Tours   **Lake Tours** Lake cruises on Lough Leane with a commentary on the local ecology and history. The boat departs from Ross Castle and there is a shuttle service from the Destination Killarney Information Kiosk, Scott's Garden, T32638. Sailings at 1100, 1230, 1430, 1600 and 1715, €7.62, subject to the weather. *Killarney Watercoach Cruises*, T31068 (also bookable through *Dero's*; see coach tours, or the tourist office). Sail from Ross Castle on the *Lily of Killarney* at 1030, 1200, 1345, 1515 and 1630 and with a commentary covering the folklore and history of the lakes. **Coach tours** *Dero's*, Main St, T31251. Offer the standard Ring of Kerry coach tour and a Gap of Dunloe tour, both departing at 1030. *O'Connors*, the pub in High St, T30200, www.

castlelough-tours-com, offers similar tours plus a bike and boat trip departing from Ross Castle at 1100. *O'Donoghue Brothers*, Old Weir Lodge Guesthouse, Muckross Rd, T31068. Trips through the Gap of Dunloe. **Jaunting cars** Gather on East Avenue Rd opposite the cineplex, opposite the entrance to Muckross House and around Kate Kearney's Cottage at the Gap of Dunloe. The price of a trip, including the services of the jarvey, varies from €21 to €57 for up to 4 people. **Walking** *Walking Tours*, T087-2919366. Daily from *Shell* petrol station in Lower New St, opposite the cathedral, 1100 for a 2-hr stroll around the National Park. €5. *Wilderness Tours*, T7160101. Have various trips, starting at €19.05 for a guided boat-and-walking tour around the lakes of Killarney or a guided climb of Carrauntoohill.

Transport
Iarnród Éireann
T01-8366222
Bus Éireann
T01-8366111

Bus Bus links to all the main cities, and Kerry Airport, from the bus station, T30011 (T34777 outside office hours), alongside the train station. Between Jun and Sep a twice-daily Ring of Kerry bus service runs around the peninsula on the N70, with the option to stop off and complete travel by a later bus or the next day. All year, there is a regular bus service from Killarney to Waterville via Cahirsiveen, and to Dingle via Tralee. **Train** The station is centrally located, T31067, with routes to Dublin and other main cities. **Bicycle** *O'Sullivan's Cycles*, Bishop's Lane off New St, also at the car park opposite the tourist office and in Brewery Lane, T31282. *O'Neill Cycle Store*, 6 Plunkett St, T31970. Bike hire: can be delivered to your accommodation place complete with pannier and lock. *Killarney Rent-A-Bike*, T32578. Bike hire with outlets at Market Cross in the town centre, *Súgán Hostel* and the *Flesk Shop* opposite the National Park. Have daily and weekly rates and children's bikes. Most of the other hostels also rent bikes. **Car** Car parking can be a problem in Jul and Aug. Use one of the designated pay and display car parks or park for free in the parking area next to St Mary's Cathedral. **Car hire**: *Budget Rent a Car*, International Hotel, Kenmare Pl, T/F34341. *Hertz*, Plunkett St, T34126, also have an office at the airport. *Randle's Car Hire*, Muckross Rd, T31237, F37635. A local firm; better rates. **Taxi** *Vincent Counihan*, 15a High St, T35025. *O'Callaghan Cabs* T37555.

Directory

Banks & bureaux de change All the main banks are centrally located and there is a money exchange office in the tourist office and also at the American Express office in East Avenue Rd and in the old town hall at 11 Main St. **Communications** Post office: New St. **Internet**: *Café Internet*, 49 Lower New St, T36741, cafeinternet@eircom.net Internet access also at *Web Talk*, 53 High St, and the *Great Southern* and *Killarney Av* hotels. **Local radio**: *Radio Kerry*, 97FM. **Medical services** Hospital: *Killarney District Hospital*, T31076. **Pharmacy**: *Donie Sheehan*, 34 Main St, T31113. Jul-Aug, Mon-Sat, 0900-1830 and 1930-2200, Sun, 1100-1300. **Launderette** *James Gleeson*, Brewery Lane, T33877. Mon-Sat, 0900-1800, Thu-Fri, 0900-2000. Another launderette is adjacent to *Atlas House* hostel off Park Rd. **Useful addresses and telephone numbers** Garda (Police): New Rd, T31222 and Victim Support T1800-661771.

Around Killarney

Gap of Dunloe

Ins & outs

Take the road out of town towards Killorglin and a short way after the village of Fossa the Gap is signposted on the left. No public transport.

Arrive at the head of this glaciated valley mid-morning in July or August and the scene resembles rush hour in a city, as coaches, buses and cars jostle for space, let alone the importuning jarveys and camera-toting crowds around Kate Kearney's Cottage. The Gap of Dunloe, however, is some 8 miles (12 km) in length and as many visitors walk or pony ride only a couple of miles it is not difficult to leave the crowds behind, either on foot or on a bicycle. A whole-day tour – bookable from any tour company in Killarney (see 'Tours' on page 318) or on the spot outside Kate Kearney's Cottage – is to ride through the Gap on a pony trap and lunch at Lord Brandon's Cottage before returning to Killarney by boat.

The name of *Kate Kearney's Cottage*, T064-44146, may conjure up an image of a cute, stone-washed, thatched dwelling with a big black kettle on a turf fire, and it probably was when Charlotte Brontë passed this way on her honeymoon, but it is now a hectically busy bar, restaurant, souvenir and gift store where the staff deserve a medal for their patience. Nearby, *Moriarty's*, T064-44144, is a clothing and craft shop with a range of Aran handknits, sports jackets, cashmeres, linens, jewellery, Waterford crystal and Belleek china.

Walks and cycling around Killarney

Killarney may be a busy town, but it is very easy to find beautiful and quite empty countryside in the immediate area. *Mac Publications* in Killarney produces a small pamphlet, available from the tourist office, showing maps of several walks and cycles in the area. It includes two excellent expeditions to the east of the lakes, one at Tomies Wood and one along the Gap of Dunloe. The monthly, free *Where Killarney* also has walk suggestions with maps.

Tomies Wood   The **Tomies Wood walk** can be reached by taking the first signposted road to the Gap of Dunloe, just after passing Fossa, a few miles out of town, on the N72. Go down here to a bridge over the road at the River Laune: a left turn here brings you to a wooden gate where it is possible to park a vehicle or leave a bicycle. From here a circular walk of about 4 miles (6.4 km) is possible. Through the gate the walk passes through a farm and enters forestry. The path

County Kery

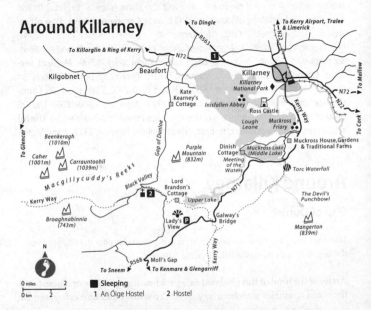

Around Killarney

History of the Muckross Demesne

The Muckross Estate belonged to the McCarthy clan, whose leader was known as McCarthy Mór, until the 18th century, despite various attempts at confiscation. It finally passed to a family called Herbert in 1770 and they had Muckross House built between 1840 and 1843. In the process they overspent on their budget and in 1899 the house and estate were sold to Lord Ardilaun, a member of the famous Guinness family. In 1910 the whole property was bought by an American, WB Bourne, as a wedding gift for his daughter, whose family later donated all 11,000 acres of it to the Irish nation.

forks and makes a circuit of the hillside far up above Lough Leane with wonderful views over the water. Red deer are very common in these woods. The forestry is not overbearing, with a great deal of larch and spruce, and much of the walk is over bare rock with the underlying old red sandstone very conspicuous. The walk passes O'Sullivan's Cascade, down by the lakeside and a short detour off the path.

Gap of Dunloe

The Gap of Dunloe is a much more strenuous walk and makes a much better cycle. The journey through the gap is 6 miles (9.5 km) and, although a steady climb, it is full of reasons to stop and admire the view. At the top of the gap you are in the Black Valley and a left turn brings you to the *Black Valley Hostel* (see page 350). From here the route takes you to Lord Brandon's Cottage and a spell over quite rough ground, cycling along the shores of the Upper Lake, following the route of the Kerry Way.

The path finally meets the main N71 road at Derricunnihy and where a left turn takes you back into Killarney (but this is not suitable for walkers). The first part of the route also makes a pleasant walk but both cyclists and walkers should be prepared for a very busy scene at the start of the gap where tour buses, tourist and jarveys jostle for places. The crowds soon fall away once you begin the journey into the gap.

Muckross

There are a number of walks around Muckross demesne, following the shores of Muckross Lake and around the house and gardens. One walk begins at the first entrance to the park where the jaunting car drivers wait. The walk goes along the main drive and then cuts over to the lake following its shores. This is a particularly interesting walk since it crosses intercut sections of limestone and sandstone rock where the flora change radically from one section to another. The walk goes around the shores of the lake finishing back at the gate you entered by.

Other walks that have been laid out in the demesne with markers and a description of the sights are **Arthur Young's Nature Trail**, which makes a loop around the little Doo Lough, and the **Mossy Woods Nature Trail** which is close by Muckross House. The house has leaflets describing both walks. Cyclists are welcome in the demesne and there are any number of possible cycle routes around the grounds.

The **Blue Pool** is another short, circular walk, taking about an hour. Its entrance is on the left a few 100 yards beyond the entrance to Muckross along the road to Kenmare. A left turn at the sign for Mangerton brings you to a signposted nature trail, complete with guide ropes for the visually impaired. The walk follows the shores of the Blue Pool, an old mill pond with a strange blue colour due to the large amounts of limestone dissolved in the water. The area around the pool has been planted at various times with beech, alder, and

County Kerry

pine, but the oak, holly and willow are naturally occurring. This is a good place to notice the devastating effects of the rhododendron that grows invasively here and has to be culled regularly. Its evergreen nature prevents seedlings of native trees from germinating and threatens the life of all the woods around Killarney.

Ross Castle To the southwest of Killarney is Ross Castle, and a pleasant 5-mile (8-km) walk around the castle and the shores of the lower lake starts in town at the Cathedral. From the cathedral the walk goes into Ross Road, then goes to Ross Island and passes Ross Castle. A circuit can be made of the island, taking in the viewing point at Governor's Rock. Another path goes north along the shores of the lake making a loop back to Ross Road. The walk is through woodland with views of the lake and Innisfallen Island. There are several possible routes for this walk, another taking you over the Deenagh River and back to your starting point via Knockreer House. This route is also suitable for cycling.

Crohane Mountain Travelling on the Kenmare Road out of Killarney (N71) a quite strenuous walk is possible to the summit of Crohane Mountain (2,152 ft/656 m). About two miles out of the town centre a left turn is signposted to Lough Guitane. Just after this a right turn sets off up the mountain, at first a wide tarmac road but gradually giving way to green road and then open hillside. The goal of the walk is the hilltop and, while there is no path, a route to the top is quite clear. The return journey is about 4 miles (6½ km) and takes about 4 hours to complete. A clear day is essential for this walk.

Cycling to Tralee Take the N22 out of town and take the road on the left at Cleeny for a more interesting route that avoids the traffic of the N22. A stiff cycle in places.

Ring of Kerry

The Ring of Kerry is a 112-mile (180-km) road route around the Iveragh Peninsula and throughout the summer months it becomes periodically clogged with traffic as a line of vehicles follows in the wake of a slow-moving coach, caravan or car. The mornings are particularly gruesome because this is when massive tour coaches trundle around, but at any time of the day it is difficult to understand the point of setting out to complete the circuit in one or even two days. At times though, the Ring of Kerry is unavoidable simply because it reaches the far west of the peninsula, where some of the most interesting sites in Kerry are to be found.

Ins and outs

Getting around The best way to see and enjoy the Iveragh peninsula is by walking part or all of the Kerry Way, a long-distance walk that is described in its relevant sections, beginning on page 346. It takes well over a week to complete the entire Way but with the help of the summer-only *Bus Éireann* service (see timetable) it is quite feasible to walk parts of the Way and return by bus to one's base. Another alternative to driving is to cycle and, while the Ring of Kerry itself is best avoided whenever possible – the roads are narrow and impatient drivers pose a threat to life and limb – there is a little-used route across the middle of the peninsula from Killorglin to Waterville via the Ballaghbeama Pass that is worth taking (see page 339). And to the west of Waterville and Cahersiveen there is a looped route along minor roads, called the Skellig Ring, that accesses Valentia and the Skelligs.

Puck Fair

The oldest festival still being celebrated in Ireland, Puck Fair has an unmistakable pagan heritage that dates back to the Celtic celebration of the god Lug and the beginning of the harvest. The Gaelic word for August is Lughnasa, the festival of Lug, and Puck Fair takes place around the middle of the month, from the 10th to the 12th August in Killorglin. The bacchanalian celebrations begin on Gathering Day when a white male goat is escorted into the market square, lifted on to a makeshift three-tiered platform and crowned with garlands as the King of the Fair. The goat remains perched there, 40 ft above the street, to preside over the alcohol-fuelled revelry that occupies the next couple of days. All the pubs have a special licence to extend their opening hours and the influx of visitors, musicians and assorted entertainers ensures a heady atmosphere. On the evening of 12th August, Scattering Day, the goat is ceremoniously brought down from its perch and led away. Further details available at www.puckfair.ie or from the tourist office in Killarney or Killorglin.

All year around, a bus runs Mon-Sat between Killarney and Waterville via Killorglin, Glenbeigh and Cahersiveen. In summer buses depart Killarney at 0830, 0950, 1345 and 1500 (outside of summer, only one bus departing at 1500, Mon-Fri); from Waterville, one bus only for the service back to Killarney, departing at 0735; but a second bus departs from Cahersiveen at 1215 in summer only.

Summer only, a Sneem-Kenmare- Killarney-Tralee service operates daily. For full details, contact Tralee bus station, T066- 712 3566, or Killarney T064-30011

Killorglin

The inland 13-mile (21-km) stretch west of Killarney along the R582 is fairly unremarkable until reaching the small messy-looking market town of Killorglin above the River Laune. During the time of the annual Puck Fair a visit is highly recommended (see box on page 329), but at other times of the year, apart from the angling, there is little to do or see. A short distance north of the town, at Ballykissane Pier, a monument commemorating the death of revolutionary nationalists whose car plunged into the sea in 1916 on their way to meet Roger Casement near Tralee (see box on page 356). The odd-shaped building, close to the roundabout where the road heads out to Glenbeigh is the **tourist office**, T9761451, open Apr-Oct, daily, 0930-1900.

Phone code: 066 Colour map 3, grid B2

County Kerry

AL-L *Caragh Lodge*, Caragh, T9769115, www.caraghlodge.com A laid-back atmosphere prevails in this elegant Victorian country house on the shores of Lake Caragh a few miles outside Killorglin. **AL-A** *Bianconi*, Lower Bridge Rd, Killorglin, T9761146. Family-run guesthouse, with access to Caragh Lake. **B** *Riverside House*, Killorglin, T9761184. B&B with rooms, not all en suite, overlooking the river. **C-D** *Laune Valley Farm Hostel*, T9761488, launehostel@ireland.com Just over a mile from town and has 5 private rooms.

Sleeping
Price codes:
See inside front cover

At *Caragh Lodge*, fresh seafood, Kerry lamb, home-grown vegetables and home-baking make up an excellent menu in the graceful restaurant overlooking the lake. A reservation for dinner at €41.90) is fairly essential for non-residents. In Killorglin itself, two well established restaurants are next to each other on Lower Bridge St. The *Bianconi*, T9761146, has bar food all day and, in the restaurant from 1830-2030, seafood and pasta dishes around €12. The steak, lamb and seafood in the neighbouring *Nick's Restaurant*, T9761219, has some uumph, and should not disappoint; dinner is €35.50.

Eating

Pubs & music *The Fishery*, The Bridge, Killorglin, T9761670, has traditional music some nights. *O'Grady's*, Upper Bridge St, favours a slow pint and a long chat.

Transport **Bicycle hire** *O'Shea's*, T9761919. Near the bridge at the Killarney end of town.

Glenbeigh

Phone code: 066
Colour map 3, grid B2

In Smith's 1786 *History of Kerry* the author recalls how he "accidentally arrived at a little house in a very obscure part of the parish [of Glenbeigh] where I saw poor lads reading Homer, their master having been a mendicant scholar at an English Grammar School at Tralee". Modern visitors are unlikely to hear any ancient Greek, but the small seaside resort of Glenbeigh, 6 miles (10 km) west of Killorglin, is still a surprisingly pleasant place to stay. Before entering the town from the direction of Killorglin it is difficult to miss the large *Red Fox* pub and adjacent **Kerry Bog Village Museum** by the side of the main road. The pub food is so-so ; regular musical evenings at weekends, but coach groups make regular stops here; the museum, T9769184 is open all year until 1830 but hardly worth a special trip, €3 admission. There is no **tourist office**, but local information is available at *Brennans* craft shop, T9768252, or the post office, T9768201, both on Main St.

Ring of Kerry & Kerry Way

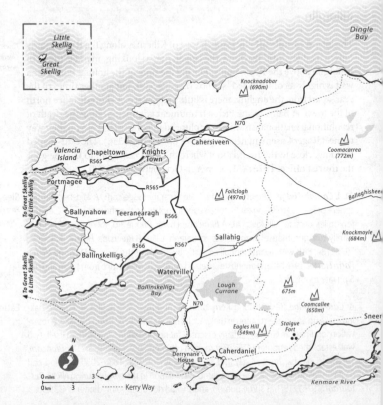

Glenbeigh itself has a lively pub scene; but on a fine day the real attraction lies outside the village where 3 miles of uninterrupted beach make up Rossbeigh Strand, a spit of land pointing out into Dingle Bay with sand on either side and no shelving. The area is safe for swimming, challenging for surfers, ideal for horseback-riding, and there is a pub nearby. To reach the beach area, bear right at the Y-junction at the Cahersiveen end of town.

The Kerry Way passes through Glenbeigh and a recommended local walk can be enjoyed by following the Way west up through Glenbeigh Woods, at the Cahersiveen end of town. The Way makes it way up to high ground from where there is a dramatic view of Rossbeigh Strand and the Dingle peninsula to the north. With a bicycle or car an excursion can be made to the southwest and the glen of the River Behy along any of the minor roads that branch off south of the N70 west of Glenbeigh. These minor roads peter out in a glorious Kerry landscape where three loughs are surrounded by an amphitheatre of forbidding mountains. If you spend time in the Glenbeigh area it is worth having a copy of map 78 in the Ordnance Survey Discovery Series.

AL *Towers Hotel*, T9768212, towershotel@eircom.net. Comfortable, old hotel with palm trees, a cosy bar and good restaurant. **A** *Sleeper's Nest*, T9769666, F9769667. Just outside Glenbeigh on the N70 at the Killorglin end, does B&B for €32 per person and also has a small kitchen where guests can prepare their own meals, plus a laundry.

Rossbeigh Strand

Local walk

Sleeping
*Price codes:
see inside front cover*

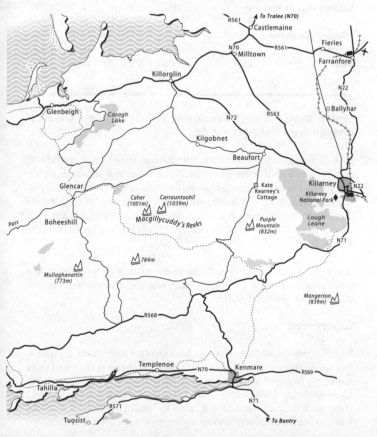

★ **Ring of Kerry bus services (service number 280)**

		Mon-Sat		Sun	
Tralee (Bus station)	dep	0750	1235	0900	1200
Farranfore	↓	0810	1255	0920	1220
Killarney (Bus station)	arr	0825	1310	0935	1235
Killarney (Bus station)	dep	0830	1345	0940	1245
Killorglin	↓	0900	1415	1010	1315
Glenbeigh		0915	1430	1025	1330
Kells		0935	1450	1045	1350
Cahersiveen		0950	1505	1100	1405
Waterville	arr	1015	1530	1125	1430
Waterville	dep	1105	1530	1215	1430
Caherdaniel	↓	1125	1550	1235	1450
Sneem	arr	1200	1620	1305	1520
Sneem	dep	1200	1710	1305	1605
Moll's Gap	↓	1225	1735	1330	1630
Killarney (Bus station)	arr	1310	1810	1405	1705
Killarney (Bus station)	dep	1425*	1815	1420	1710
Farranfore	↓	1440	1830	1435	1725
Tralee	arr	1500	1850	1455	1745

*Change coach

Camping *Glenross Caravan & Camping Park*, T9768451, F9737474, is next to the *Glenbeigh Hotel* at the Killarney end of town.

Eating If you do not plan to picnic for the day, the pubs offer the best bet at lunchtime. At night the *Towers Hotel Restaurant*, T9768212, offers good food and an elegant setting. There is a separate bar for cocktails and the warm dark colours of the décor provide a suitable backdrop for a lazy meal to the accompaniment of live classical piano music. Starters include oysters in a Guinness sauce, while lamb, veal, duck and steaks make up the main courses alongside fish freshly caught in Dingle Bay. Expect to pay about €33.

Pubs & music Glenbeigh has the usual quota of pubs: *Sweeney's* only opens in the summer and is usually as packed as the bar in the *Towers Hotel*, which attracts a younger crowd. The *Village Pub* has music most nights.

Cahersiveen

Phone code: 066
Colour map 3, grid B1

Both the location and the easy-going character of the place make Cahersiveen (also spelt Cahirciveen or Cahirciveen) worth considering as a base for a short stay on the Iveragh Peninsula. The town itself is agreeably unprepossessing, accommodating visitors with a sufficient number of amenities – and with 52 pubs, more than sufficient in one respect – while conveniently accessing Valencia Island, as well as providing some enjoyable local walks. Cahersiveen

Rhododendrons: the death of the woodlands

As you drive around the peninsulas of the southwest, especially in May, you will notice the beauty of the deep purple flowering rhododendron with its dark evergreen leaves. The plants make an excellent windbreak and, being evergreen, keep the gardens looking alive in winter. There are many different species of rhododendron but the only one to have naturalized here is the purple variety, Rhododendron ponticum. It can grow to over 19½ ft (six metres) in height, loves the acid soil of Kerry and West Cork and produces about 5,000 seeds for each flower head. It was introduced some time in the 18th century from its native habitat around the Black Sea, and it became very popular with the local landlords who planted it as cover for game birds to give their winter sporting activities an extra edge.

What they did not plan for was the ferocity with which the plant colonized the area. Its evergreen leaves, so good for pheasants and windbreaks, are wide and permanent and quickly cover all the ground available. Where they grow in open land this is no problem to other wildlife,

except that after several years they will have formed a dense thicket, which will need cutting back, but in Kerry's native woodlands the plant is a disaster. It takes the niche of holly in the oak and beech woods, resulting in a loss of all the wildlife that depends on those trees. Worse still, it provides a permanent shade on the forest floor, wiping out the woodland flowers such as wood sorrel, bluebells, rush, primroses and the many other ground layer plants as well as the insects that depend on them. Worst of all, it prevents the germination of seedling deciduous trees, such as beech and oak, which make the woodlands of Killarney so special. Unchecked it would wipe out the oak forests in a few generations, leaving great tracts of purple flowering woodland with little animal or plant diversity within it. Around Muckross, Torc Mountain, Tomies Woods and Glengarriff eradication programmes take place with people wandering the forests looking for the plants with herbicidal sprays. The pest is hardly likely to be eradicated around these important woodlands, but for the moment it is under control.

is also on the Kerry Way, with Glenbeigh easily reached in a day and Waterville an invigorating 8-hour walk away. From either town, public transport could return you to Cahersiveen. The **tourist office** is on Church St, T9472589. May-Sep, Mon-Sat, 0915-1300, 1415-1730.

An unexpected sight is the fearsome white-painted building that now houses a heritage centre. It was built by the British in the 1870s as a Royal Irish Constabulary barracks in response to the Fenian uprising of 1867, which it was feared might lead to a future attack on the new telegraph cable station on Valentia. Is it just pure local blarney or did the British really mix up two sets of building plans and construct in Kerry an edifice intended for the northwest frontier of India? When you see the Barracks you may well wonder. **The Barracks**

The **Heritage Centre** occupies two floors of the Barracks, costs €3.80 and includes, on the half hour, the obligatory 15-minute audio/visual show on local history. ■ *T9472777. May-Sep, daily, 1000-1700. Oct-Apr, same hours Mon-Fri but closed 1300-1400.*

The Kerry countryside around Cahersiveen lets you enjoy a lazy day's walk to a beach and a hill-top picnic and take in along the way excellent examples of stone forts. A useful walking booklet is available for €2 from the heritage centre, but if you are planning to spend more than a day or two in the area then Ordnance Survey Map 83 is ideal. A popular walk takes you across the River **Local walks**

Valentia, then taking the first turn to the left leads you past the Cahergal stone fort. Just before the fort there is a road on the left that heads south to the remains of Ballycarberry Castle. To continue, return to the road that leads to the fort and just after it turn to the right along a road that passes Leacanabuaile, another stone fort, before going to Kimego Wood via a small beach at Cooncrome harbour.

Heading out along the main road towards Glenbeigh brings you to the birthplace of Daniel O'Connell. Today it is just an ivy-clad ruin, but just opposite it there is the landscaped **O'Connell Memorial Park** and a bust of the man who led the highly successful campaign for the right of Catholics to sit in the British parliament.

Sleeping
Price codes:
see inside front cover

AL *Cahersiveen Park*, T9472543, F9472893. The only hotel in town, at the Valentia end, but perfectly adequate and has a pleasant bar and decent restaurant. **B-C** *Castleview*, T9472252. At the Valentia end of town with 1 en-suite room and 2 sharing facilities. **B** *Fransal House*, Foilmore, T/F9472997. Very convenient for walkers, being 4 miles (6 km) out of town on the Kerry Way. **B** *Iveragh Heights*, Carhan Rd, T9472545. Handy if walking into town on the Kerry Way. **B** *O'Shea's*, Church St, T9472402. A central B&B in a large town house next to the post office; open all year. **D** *Sive Hostel*, T9472717, sivehostel@oceanfree.net Sociable place in the centre of town, open all year and includes 2 private rooms.

Camping The *Mannix Point Camping and Caravan Park*, T9472806, F9472988. A good 10-min walk from town. Has a good reputation.

Eating

Mid-range Modish *Brennan's Restaurant*, 12 Main St, T9472021, Mon-Sat for daily evening meals with the option of an early-bird menu between 1800 and 1900. Expect to pay around €26 for an à la carte dinner of locally caught seafood or Kerry lamb. *QC's*, 3 Main St, T9472244, www.qcbar.com, has some style – original old fireplace, stone walls, oak bar counter – and tasty chargrills are a speciality. Lots of Spanish wines.

Cheap Opposite the post office *Frank's Corner* has meals of the 'with chips' variety for under €12.70, while opposite the massive cathedral-like church *Grudles*, T9473709, does take-away lunches and an evening menu. There are a couple of other cafés along the street and some of the pubs, like the *Fertha Bar*, serve food. The *Old Oratory* (see 'Shopping' below) has a little coffee shop.

Pubs & music

There is a good choice of pubs and some of the best serve more than drinks. The ancient-looking *Anchor Bar*, Main St, T9472049, with fishing tackle sold alongside pints, is always worth a visit and especially on Thu night, when the Kerry orchestra plays here. The *Shebeen Bar*, T9472361, at the Glenbeigh end has Irish dancing some nights while close by *Mike Murt's* is a real old farmer's pub with some character and a hardware section. *O'Donaghue's* also pulls a pint or two for customers not interested in its range of shoes, thermal underwear and other assorted items.

Festivals

Cahersiveen's *Celtic Festival of Music and the Arts* takes place at the beginning of Aug.

Shopping

On Main St at the Valentia end of town *Nautical Antiques*, T9473279, has an interesting collection of lamps, portholes, nameplates, bulkhead lamps and the like. *Biggs*, Old Rd, T9472580, is a more conventional antique shop while *The Old Oratory* is an art gallery and craft shop set up in a disused Protestant church at the Valentia end and selling batik, ceramics, glass, jewellery and knitwear.

Sport

Fishing *Hugh Maguire*, T9472049, for deep-sea angling.

County Kerry

Subterranean blues

The first attempt to lay a cable under the Atlantic Ocean took place in 1857 but ended in failure. A small fleet of ships set off slowly from Valentia lowering cables as they went, but after only 280 miles the cable snapped and the enterprise was put on hold. The following year, a second attempt was made, this time using an American ship leaving Halifax and laying cable on its route east while a British ship did the same in its route west from Valentia. The two boats met successfully in the middle and the first transatlantic radio link between the new and old worlds was made. The underwater cable was to snap more than once in those pioneering days but a permanent station was established on the island and Morse code was transmitted at the rate of 17 words a minute.

The cable operators on Valentia were a highly paid, non-Irish elite with their own cricket pitch and tennis courts, but one or two locals were also employed and one cable message did slip out to the US in 1916 with news of the Easter Rising. New technology, ironically developed on Valentia, saw the demise of the cable station and it finally closed down in 1965. Today the wind blows across the crumbling asphalt of the tennis courts and the empty houses of the operators are turning into ruins.

Bus In the summer, buses for Killarney depart at 0805 and 1215, and the Ring of Kerry bus comes through at 0950. **Bicycles** Bike hire from *Caseys Cycles*, T9472474, at the Valentia end of town. **Transport**

Communications Internet access from *Cyber Café* in New St. **Directory**

Valentia Island

In a mad rush simply to 'do' the Ring of Kerry travellers often skip Valentia Island and thereby pass up an ideal opportunity to slow down the pace and explore at leisure one of the modest gems of the area.

*Phone code: 066
Colour map 3,
grid B1*

There is a land bridge from Portmagee and a passenger and car ferry that operates a shuttle service throughout Apr-Sep, T9476141, from Reenard just west of Cahersiveen. €6.35/5return/single. **Ins & outs**

Even though the land bridge was only completed in 1971 Valentia had a distinguished role in the history of communication. Late-night listeners of the BBC will be familiar with the name of Valentia, the island being the former site of an important meteorological station (now moved to Cahersiveen). It was also the site for the first transatlantic cable station (see box), and a railway line was built so that travellers from Europe could make their way here for the shortest possible transatlantic sea crossing. The transatlantic sea link never happened and the railway closed down in the 1950s. Go back a hundred years, though, to when the first transatlantic cable was being laid, and Valentia was the Silicon Valley and Cape Canaveral of Victorian Britain. Today the appeal of a visit to Valentia is simply its off-the-beaten-track location, the remains and reminders of its past history and the opportunity to linger aimlessly around a sub-tropical corner of Kerry. The effect of the Gulf Stream ensures frost-free temperatures all year round and plants that would perish in other parts of Ireland manage to thrive on Valentia. The Irish poet Aubrey de Vere (1814-1902) advised his friend Tennyson to visit Valentia (which he did) and listen to the sound of the waves, assuring him that those at Beachy Head in England would pale into insignificance. **History**

County Kerry

The Skellig Experience This interpretative centre is on the left side immediately after reaching Valentia from Portmagee. Exhibits deal with the lives of the monks and the story of the lighthouse that was built on Skelligs in 1826 and operated until 1986, manned by a team of three who were relieved by helicopter from Castletownbere. A 15-minute audio-visual show focuses on the Skellig Michael monastery and there is also a section on the wildlife, very useful for brushing up on bird identification before actually visiting the Skelligs. Also useful is the retail area with books on local history and wildlife and a café serving snacks and light meals. ■ *T9476306. Daily 1100-1700. €3.80.*

Slate quarry Another ambitious Victorian enterprise that focused on Valentia was a slate quarry that opened in 1816 and operated until 1911, employing up to 400 men at its height. Huge sheets of slate 14 ft (4 m) long were lifted out of the mine and cut to size on site by a steam-powered saw, the remains of which can be seen at the mouth of the quarry. Valentia slate, possessing what experts call a good cleavage, could be easily split into thin slabs of exceptional length; it was highly valued and used to grace the roofs of noted London buildings (like the Houses of Parliament) as well as being exported to South America (San Salvador railway station). Although there is little to see nowadays, apart from a tasteless shrine constructed in one of the tunnels, the location and the vast piles of broken slate lying about help create a strong sense of place. ■ *Open 24 hrs. Signposted at the T-junction when approaching Knightstown from the west.*

Heritage centre The ex-National School setting for this little museum suits the educational content of what was the schoolroom, now devoted to the history of the cable station. There are also sections on local craft industries. Interesting any time and a godsend on a wet afternoon. ■ *T9476353. Apr-Sep, Mon-Sat, 1100-1700. €2. On the right-hand side of the road just outside Knightstown on the road to the slate quarry.*

Glanleam House subtropical gardens Despite strong winter winds, which occasionally wreak havoc on the gardens, the balmy influence of the Gulf Stream makes Valentia a subtropical greenhouse when it comes to cultivating plants that would not survive outside the southwest of the country. Glanleam House was the seat of the local 19th-century bigwigs, the Knights of Kerry, and its collection of exotic plants in the gardens can still be seen, although some visitors find it a disappointing experience. ■ *T9476176. May-Oct, daily 1100-1700. €2.50*

Sleeping
Price codes: see inside front cover

A *Moorings Guesthouse*, Portmagee, T9477108, www.moorings.ie Guesthouse overlooking the port with modern, comfortable rooms. B *Glenreen Heights*, Knightstown Rd, T9476241, glenreen@eircom.net On the road to Chapeltown, seaviews and an affordable evening meal can be arranged. B *The Islander*, Knightstown, T9476171. Convenient location in Knightstown and with its own restaurant.

B-D *Royal Pier Bar & Hostel*, Knightstown, T9476144. Overlooking the harbour, private rooms as well as dorms, camping space, and B & B. Despite its very faded elegance this is a lively and sociable place to meet people (and big enough to while away a wet afternoon in the bar). D *The Ring Lyne Hostel*, Chapeltown, T9476103. Has lots of facilities, including private rooms, B&B and bike hire. D *Valentia Island Hostel*, Knightstown, T9476154. *An Óige* hostel that uses the old coastguard cottages. It's a nice idea, with a tangible sense of history about the place, but the creature comforts are at a premium.

In Portmagee The *Moorings* has a small restaurant for evening meals and Sun lunch, serving run-of-the-mill seafood dishes like chowder and poached salmon, and steaks as well; mid-range prices. The *Fisherman's Bar*, T9477103, has outside tables when the weather is not inclement: the bar menu includes a tasty chowder and appetizing crab claws for starters or snacks, and meals of seafood and an Irish stew. *Bridge Bar*, belonging to the Moorings restaurant and guesthouse, does pub food during the day.

In Knightstown *The Gallery*, T9476105, is an interesting place to visit and not just for a meal; it combines its dashing restaurant with a gallery of ethnic art and opens daily for lunch and dinner. *Boston's* bar also has a restaurant, T9476140, serving tasty and affordable meals. *The Islander*, T9476171, has an agreeably affordable restaurant below its B&B and though the style of the place may be a little plain the speciality is fresh fish brought in at the local harbour. The *Lighthouse Café* has been recommended by a reader for its outsanding views and charming décor; lunch and supper menus with fresh fish, or just drop in for ice-cream or pancakes.

In Chapeltown The *Ring Lyne Bar*, T9476103, serves food all day along the lines of seafood specials, steaks and Irish stew.

At Reenard Point The ferry runs continuously, so linger as long as you like at *The Point Bar*, T9472165. It's been here since the middle of the 19th century and now serves delicious seafood, salads and sandwiches as well as hot meals around €15. All the fish is taken ashore from trawlers docking a stone throw's away for your table.

Diving *Des Lavelle*, T9476124. Well established. *Dive Centre*, T9476204. *Valentia Hyperbaric Diving Centre*, T9476225. **Fishing** Deep-sea fishing: *Michael O'Sullivan*, Royal Pier, T9476144.

The Skelligs

"Whoever has not stood in the graveyard on the summit of that cliff among the beehive dwellings and their beehive oratory does not know Ireland through and through." Hyperbole indeed from George Bernard Shaw, but it is difficult not to agree with him. When a sea mist swirls above the Skelligs they seem to float on the ocean like eerie volcanoes in an imaginary scene from Celtic mythology. The only problem with this magic is that so many people are now heeding Shaw's advice that attempts are being made to limit the number of visitors who can stand on the 44 acres of Skellig Michael, the largest of a group of three rocky islets that make up the Skelligs.

Skellig Michael (also called Great Skellig), with its twin peaks 715 ft (217 m) and 650 ft (198 m) rising above the Atlantic, is the only one of the rocks that can be landed on and, while a visit here is justifiably the main point of the boat trip, the journey there and back also affords a priceless opportunity to view and admire the sea birds that inhabit these rocky outposts of Europe.

"Moving about the coasts of Kerry afterwards, I understood what a symbol Skellig Michael must have been to those who were neither monks nor clergy, seeing it on the horizon, a single or a double peak, but always blue, always or often, with its nimbus of white cloud, its trailing coif of holiness." Geoffrey Grigson (1905-85), 'Country Writings'

County Kerry

Skellig Michael is home to some of the few surviving examples of domestic monastic buildings in the early Christian era. After disembarking, visitors follow a path, created in the days when a lighthouse was operating on Skellig Michael, along the southeast cliffs to a series of enclosures perched on steep terraces. The monastic settlement, dedicated to St Michael, the saint of high places, is made up of six beehive cells, and two oratories. The guides will explain their characteristic features, but the sense of wonder comes from being here and wondering why – and in the winter months how – anyone even thought of living here. The dry masonry structures are truly remarkable, and not least because they have survived for so long in such an exposed location.

Hermits and hedonists on the Skelligs

The desert sands of Egypt provide the unlikely backdrop to the Skelligs, because it was here that the Coptic Church based itself as a splinter Christian group in the sixth century, practising a strict monastic tradition. In the seventh century a group of eremetical Irish monks first established a settlement on Skellig Michael and their anchorite community remained there until the 12th century. They survived a Viking raid in 823 but eventually moved to Ballinskelligs on the mainland.

Although Pope Gregory decreed a 10-day change in the calendar in 1582, it was never applied to the Skelligs and out of this developed the scurrilous Skellig Lists. They arose from the tradition of marrying just before the onset of Lent, during which no marriage could take place, and the riling of those who remained eligible but unwed. The Skellig Lists paired off in comic and unkind verse suitable bachelors and spinsters. In fact the Skelligs, where Lent had still not started, did become popular for late marriages and occasionally they became infamous for all-night drinking binges, so much so that one occasion the police were called and they had to row out to Skellig Michael.

Bird life It helps to have some basic ornithological knowledge, and a visit to the Skellig Heritage Centre on Valentia will help in this respect (see page 336), but it is usually easy to recognize the yellow-headed gannet because of its size – a wing span of around 6 ft (1.8 m) – the elegant angle of its wings in flight and its dramatic vertical dive into the water. Some 20,000 pairs inhabit Little Skellig and these may be seen at close quarters if your boat goes in close to the rock for a view of basking seals, which are also a common sight. The guillemot, seen and heard particularly around the landing stage area, is a seagull with a black tip to its wings. They spend the winter out at sea but come to Skellig Michael to breed between March and August. The razorbill is similar to but smaller than the guillemot and is sometimes recognized by its habit of flying in line in small flocks. Both these birds nest in crevices and ledges of the cliff face. Up until around the first week of August it is difficult to avoid seeing the puffin, unmistakable due to its multicoloured beak, dutifully standing at the head of its burrowed nest and occasionally waddling away with as much dignity as it can muster.

Sleeping & eating If you want to spend a night on Skellig Michael you will have to become a tour guide for the summer months. Otherwise it is strictly a day trip, bring your own picnic and sensible footwear and be extremely careful with children or elderly folk when disembarking and making your way to the monastic buildings.

Tours There is a bewildering number of operators running boat trips to the Skelligs but their prices are constant and it is more a matter of choosing one that departs from somewhere you find convenient. Departure time is usually mid-morning and journey time is 45 mins. **From Ballinskelligs** *Sean Feehan*, T9479182; *Joe Roddy*, T9474268. **From Portmagee** *Brendan Casey*, T9472437; *Murphy's*, T9477156; *Brendan O'Keefe*, T9477103. **From Valentia** *Dermot Walsh*, T9476120; *Das Lavelle*, T9476124; *Seanie Murphy*, T9476214 (calling at Renard and Portmagee); *Dan McCrohan*, T9476142. **From Waterville** *Michael O'Sullivan*, T9474255.

Waterville

Phone code: 066
Colour map 3, grid B1

Another landmark town on the Ring of Kerry, Waterville is pleasantly low-key and consists of the usual range of pubs, hotels and restaurants; like Cahersiveen to the north it suggests itself as a base for exploring the western end of the

County Kerry (side tab)

peninsula. From Waterville there is also the very useful cross-peninsula road to Killarney via the Ballaghisheen Pass which accesses the frequently ignored interior and also allows one to escape the traffic on the main N70 road. There is little of note in the town itself, but all the attractions of the Iveragh peninsula are conveniently accessible. In addition, Waterville does have an attractive beach, which is safe for swimming, and at times it is possible to spot a porpoise or dolphin close to shore and terns may often be seen doing their acrobatic searches for a meal in the water. Shopping possibilities at the *Waterville Craft Market*, T9474212, five minutes, walk from town. The **tourist office** is open Jun-Sep, Mon-Sat, 0900-1800 but closed between 1300 and 1400. T9474646.

LL-AL *Butler Arms Hotel*, T9474144, www.butlerarms.com Facing the sea, this hotel has a wonderful air of faded elegance (though some bedrooms are in a new wing) as if reluctant to forget the era when star guests like Charlie Chaplin and Virginia Woolf came here to stay; deals available when staying more than 1 night. **AL** *Bay View Hotel*, T9474122, www.bayviewwaterville.com In the centre of town, dating back to the late 19th century, comfortable rooms with some nice sea views. **A** *Lakelands Farm Guesthouse*, Lake Rd, T9474303, out of town, lakeshore location, good for fishing enthusiasts. **C-D** *Bru Na Dromoda*, T9474782, caituichonaill@eircom.net An IHH hostel with dorm beds and 1 private room. It is signposted at the grotto on exiting Waterville on the Waterville Cahersiveen road and later 2 miles up the road at St. Finians Church. From here it is 5 miles along the road; so you need transport. **C** *Charlie's Hostel*, Spunkane, T9474272, swagman@esatclear.ie A new hostel with 11 private rooms and free pickup from Waterville.

Sleeping
Price codes:
see inside front cover

The bistro-style *Shéilin Seafood Restaurant*, T9474231, at the Butler Arms end of town, is recommended for its affordable and well prepared meals. Specials are on the blackboard outside and between 1800 and 1930 there is an affordable set dinner; also open for lunch. Just past the *Butler Arms* hotel at the *Huntsman*, T9472124, Kerry lamb and veal are available but this expensive restaurant focuses on fish, especially shellfish, and specials such as shark or black bream may be available depending on local catches. A new restaurant has opened at the *Old Cable House*, Cable Station, T9474233, with evening meals in the €20-55 range.

Eating

Perhaps it is a legacy from the Victorian and Edwardian times when genteel folk came to Waterville, but the music scene here is comparatively subdued. The *Lobster Bar* has a variety of non-traditional music some evenings during the week. The *Fisherman's Bar* in the *Butler Arms* hotel has no music but it is a comfortable place to relax and have a chat.

Pubs & music

Fishing Waterville has long been famous as an angling centre. *Tadhg O'Sullivan's* T9474433. Shop dispensing information and retailing tackle. **Bike hire** *Quinlands*, T9474307, in Lower Main St.

Sport & cycling

See bus information on pages 332 and 328.

Transport

Ballinskelligs and the Skellig Ring

The Skellig Ring is the name given to a scenic route that links Waterville and Cahersiveen via Ballinskelligs and Portmagee. Characterized by narrow roads and unmarked junctions it is ideal for cycling, and with map No 83 in the Ordnance Survey Discovery series, one could explore the landscape as well as fitting in a trip to the Skelligs from Ballinskelligs. There is no public transport, however.

Phone code: 066
Colour map 3, grid B1

County Kerry

From Waterville take the main road to Cahersiveen and after 3 miles (5 km) take the left turn signposted the Skellig Ring (R567). After 1.8 miles (2.8 km) from the beginning of this Skellig Ring road there is an unmarked road going south down to a lovely little inlet of Ballinskelligs Bay; a perfect spot for anyone wishing to enjoy Kerry in complete isolation. Back on the R567 road, carry on for another 2 miles (3.2 km) and turn left at the T-junction. This road leads to Ballinskelligs, passing the *Sigerson Arms* pub and reaching an unmarked cross-roads. The left turn goes down to a lovely expanse of sandy beach overlooking Ballinskelligs Bay and the sea-worn ruins of Ballinskelligs Abbey, where the monks from Skellig Michael are said to have moved to when they left their rocky sea-girt abode. The ruins at the western end of the beach are those of a McCarthy castle. Straight ahead at the crossroads leads to the departure point for boats to the Skelligs while a right turn passes the *An Óige* hostel before weaving its way to Portmagee and a route back (on the R565) to the main N70 road south of Cahersiveen. After passing the *An Óige* hostel the first left turn takes one along a bumpy road out to Bolus Head, passing the pre-Famine village of Kildreelig.

Cycle ride An exhilarating cycle, or a drive if you must, from Cahersiveen to Killarney via Ballaghasheen is a journey of 40 miles (64 km), with the option of an overnight stay at Glencar. Leave Cahersiveen on the road to Kells and after almost 2 miles (3 km) turn right on the 11-mile (17-km) road to Lissatinnig Bridge. At the bridge the spectacular route through the Pass rises to about 1,000 ft (300 m). Turn left at the Bealalaw Bridge junction, where the route meets the Kerry Way, which shortly bends to the right for Glencar and the *Climbers' Inn* (see page 350).

From Glencar, travel for 3½ miles (6 km), passing Lake Acoose, ignoring the turn-offs for Glenbeigh and then Killorglin. Follow the signs for Killarney and Beaufort.

Sleeping & **A-B** *Rascals The Old School House*, Barrys Cross,T9479340. Family-run home, close to
eating the beach, and a €16 evening meal is also available. **D** *Ballinskelligs Hostel*, T9479229, mailbox@anoige.ie An Óige hostel, 1 private double. Bring your own food for lunch. On the R566, before reaching Ballinskelligs from Waterville, *Siopa Chill Rialaig*, T9479277, displaying and selling some beautiful Irish crafts, has a café doing home-made soups and sandwiches.

Entertainment Set dancing takes place every Wed and Sat night at the *Sigerson Arms*. The *Ballinskelligs Inn*, T9479106, has live music most nights but telephone to make sure.

Caherdaniel to Sneem

Phone code: 066 Along the southwest coast of the Iveragh peninsula, between the small towns of Caherdaniel and Sneem, there are two major attractions – Derrynane House and Staigue Fort – as well as a fine stretch of beach. Two diving schools in the vicinity complement the cultural attractions, while the very touristy town of Sneem only serves to highlight the relative worth of towns like Cahersiveen that manage to avoid selling out completely to the summer tourist trade

Derrynane Derrynane House is the ancestral home of **Daniel O'Connell**, who earned his
House & park place on the old Irish £20 banknote as one of the most important figures in 19th-century Irish history. It was built in 1702 and Daniel O'Connell, the adopted heir of a childless uncle who had inherited the house, took up residence in 1825 and made substantial alterations. The O'Connell family lived in

The Great Liberator

Daniel O'Connell (1775-1847) was born just outside Cahersiveen, the nephew and future heir of a Catholic landowner. As a barrister he rose to fame for his opposition to legislation that prevented Catholics from sitting in Parliament and from holding senior positions such as that of a judge. The demand for Catholic Emancipation became a highly successful mass movement across the country and O'Connell's skill as an organizer and an orator played no small part in the eventual success of the campaign, with O'Connell himself becoming the first Irish Catholic to sit in the British House of Commons. He went on to campaign for the repeal of the Act of Union, although he was not a separatist and envisaged Ireland as a self-governing unit within the British state. The repeal movement reached a crisis in 1843 when a series of huge open-air demonstrations led to the British government banning such a 'monster meeting' due to be held at Clontarf in 1843. O'Connell backed down and a week later he was arrested and imprisoned. Although released soon after, the whole experience seems to have weakened his resolve and he died in 1847 worn out by a lifetime of struggle. He remained a potent figurehead for moderate nationalists and when the foundation stone for his statue was laid in what is now O'Connell Street in Dublin some half a million people gathered to pay tribute; it was the largest single political event in the history of Ireland in the 19th century.

Derrynane until 1958, but the house had begun to decay long before that and what you see today are largely the restored parts that O'Connell himself built. Some of his original furniture is still in place and there are various portraits of him, the most outlandish being an allegorical painting of the hero as Hercules breaking the chains of slavery. His library contains various gifts presented to him as well as personal items such as his duelling pistols, and many of the knick-knacks around the House are highly ornate and artistic but typically Victorian in their ugliness. ■ *T9475113. May-Sep, Mon-Sat, 0900-1800, Sun, 1100-1900; Apr and Oct, Tue-Sun, 1300-1700; Nov-Mar, Sat and Sun, 1300-1700. €2.53. Dúchas site; guided tours available, café. Signposted on the N70 at Caherdaniel.*

The 300-acre grounds are now part of the **Derrynane National Park** and contain pleasant gardens exhibiting many of the delicate sub-tropical plants that flourish in this corner of Ireland. The monstrous-looking palms that grow near the water as you approach the house are gunnera. From the house a path leads south to an excellent beach with an ogham stone and sand dunes; at low tide it is possible to walk out to Abbey Island, which has a footpath around it offering splendid views of the coastline and the Skelligs.

Staigue Fort

Staigue Fort is a superb stone ringfort, one of the finest to be seen anywhere in Ireland, complete with a finely constructed system of stairways that lead up to the 13-ft-thick (4 m) ramparts. Its walls stand up to 18 ft (5.5 m) high and while its age is uncertain it is likely to have been constructed in the Iron Age, roughly contemporary with the fortress of Dún Aengus on the Aran Island of Inishmore. Considering that Staigue Fort is around 2,000 years old, the intact state of its dry-stone walls is literally a monumental testimony to the skill of its builders and designers. In the *Staigue Fort Hotel*, where the road up to the site begins, the **Staigue Fort Exhibition Centre** has the obligatory video. ■ *Easter to end Sep, daily, 24 hrs. Honesty box requesting €1. Situated west of Caherdaniel, before Castlecove, and signposted up a narrow road off the N70.*

County Kerry

Sleeping
Price codes: see inside front cover

AL *Derrynane Hotel*, T9475136, www.derrynane.com Facilities include an outdoor pool, steam room, sauna, gym and tennis courts. Walking weekends are organized regularly. **AL** *Iskeroon*, Bunavalla, T9475119, www.iskeroon.com Not your usual B&B, distinguished by both location, at the bottom of a steep hill by the side of a pebbly beach, and individuality of style. To find it, turn left off the N70 at the Scarriff Inn, signposted to Bunavalla Pier, and just keep turning left. Regular B&Bs in Caherdaniel include: **B** *The Olde Forge*, T9475140, family-run B&B with access to the sea; **B** *Harbour View*, Farraniaragh, T/F9475292, rooms have views of Derrynane harbour and the sea, on the Kerry Way walking route; **D** *The Traveller's Rest*, T/F9475175, is a small IHO hostel in the village with 8 beds and 2 private rooms; **D** *Carrigbeg Country Hostel*, T9475229, a short distance to the west of town, this hostel includes 1 private room and laundry facilities. **D** *Kerry Way Hostel*, Derrynane Beg, T9475148, kerrywayhostel@ireland.com has 2 private rooms, at €15.24 per person.

Camping *Wave Crest Caravan Park*, T/F9475188. Overlooking Kenmare Bay, accepts tents and is a mile (1.6 km) from town in the direction of Sneem.

Eating

There are a couple of places to eat in Caherdaniel but nowhere to write home about. The restaurant in the *Derrynane Hotel* serves a decent dinner in the middle-range price bracket and you are well advised to book. There is always the *Scarriff Inn*, T9475132, out on the main road but this place can be overrun with coach parties. *The Stepping Stone*, T9475444, a short walk from the harbour and open nightly for dinner only, is a tiny place serving modern-style, affordable dishes like duck with roast pear. *The Blind Piper*, T9475126, opens between May and Sep, for affordable lunches and dinners around €32 in a traditional-style restaurant with exposed beams and stone walls. Seafood and local lamb are the specialities; closed Mon. The café in Derrynane House is not bad and the adjoining beach suggests itself for a picnic.

Sport

Diving *Skellig Aquatics Dive Centre*, T9475277, skelliga@iol.ie Handles scuba diving for experienced divers as well as complete beginners and also organizes sea angling and boat trips. **Walking** *Derrynane Walks*, T9475136. Based at the *Derrynane Hotel*, organizes walking weekends that cover the history and ecology of the area. Average price for a package €114.28 per person. **Water sports** *Derrynane Harbour Water Sports Centre*, T9475266. Open daily for windsurfing, sailing, canoeing and water skiing.

Sneem

Phone code: 064
Colour map 3, grid B2

This figure-of-eight town, joined in its centre by a picturesque little bridge, is pronounced 'shneem' (Gaelic *snaidhm*, meaning 'knot', describing the twisting course of the river that bisects the village). Tourist literature describes it as "a cornucopia of colour" and the small houses painted brightly and cheerfully suggest an organized and determined effort to woo the visitors into thinking that this is what a quaint Irish village should look like. An unusual attraction is the **Sculpture Park**, which consists of a strange series of sculptures from assorted exotic locations in Asia and elsewhere. The park includes a 1983 monument to an Irish president, Cearbhaill Ó Dálaigh (1974-76), who has been completely forgotten about by most people, but whom Sneem remembers because he retired here. In the old courthouse in the centre of the village the tiny **Sneem Museum** has a motley collection of items of local interest, best reserved for a wet afternoon, but no mention of the poet Alfred Percival Graves (1846-1931), father of the writer Robert Graves, who grew up in the area.

LL *Parknasilla*, T7145122, F7145323. Top-notch accommodation in a massive Victorian mansion set in acres of semi-tropical gardens. A luxury hotel, crammed with original artwork and quiet places to relax. **AL** *Tahilla Cove Country House*, T7145204, tahillacove@eircom.net Only a country house in the literal sense, 5 miles (8 km) east of Sneem and set in a beautiful shoreline garden with original pre-war décor. **B** *Arch House*, North Sq, T7145127. B&B. **B** *Bank House*, North Sq, T7145226. B&B in the centre of town, the blue house with window boxes galore. **B** *Old Convent House*, T7145181. Old stone-built house in private grounds, Kerry Way walkers are welcome.

Sleeping
Price codes
see inside front cover

The *Blue Bull*, T7145382, is a pub in South Sq that serves food for lunch and dinner. Seafood a speciality as well as traditional Irish fare like bacon and cabbage and Irish Stew. The *Sacre Coeur*, T7145186, is a well established restaurant at the other end of town, also open for lunch and dinner; mid-range prices. The *Riverain Restaurant*, T7145245, in North Sq does light snacks as well as lunch and candle-lit dinner, and the nearby *Village Kitchen* serves inexpensive, decent home-cooked food. The *Pygmalion*, T7145122, in the Great Southern Hotel is the place to go for a special night out, and it is worth arriving early enough to enjoy a stroll around the gardens and woods.

Eating

The *Blue Bull* usually has music some nights, as does the *Fisherman's Knot*. O'Shea's bar in North Sq is also worth checking out to see what might be playing. For a quiet drink, seek out *Sneem House* by the river and its bar at the back of the shop. Also has outside tables.

Pubs & music

Kenmare

This market town, along with Killarney and Sneem, completes Iveragh's tourist triumvirate. It used to offer itself as a sedate alternative to Killarney's summer mayhem, but in terms of restaurants and hullabaloo Kenmare is fast catching up. Given its location, however, it is difficult to avoid Kenmare and the amenities are useful, especially if en route to or from the Beara Peninsula or the Kerry Way. The town was founded by Sir William Petty in 1670 and laid out in the late 18th century by the first Marquess of Lansdowne. The English influence is apparent in the X-shaped design of the town, which is not at all typical of Irish settlements. **Fair day** of the year is 15 August, when farmers trade cattle and horses in hard cash and a slap of the palm, and a general air of roguery enlivens the place. The **tourist office** is on the right as one enters the town from the Sneem direction. ■ *T41233, mid-Jun-late Sep, Mon-Sat, 0915-1900. Rest of the year Mon-Sat, 0915-1730.*

Phone code: 064
Colour map 3, grid B3

County Kerry

The Heritage Centre displays a great deal of information on the history of the town and has separate sections on the town's association with lacemaking through the Kenmare Poor Clare Convent and with the radical nun, Margaret Anna Cusack (1829-99) who was forced to leave Kenmare because of her politics. The British politician, Margaret Thatcher, is descended from an O'Sullivan family who emigrated from Kenmare in 1811 to work in London as a washerwoman. ■ *T41491. Mid-Jun-late Sep, Mon-Sat, 0915-1900. Rest of the year Mon-Sat, 0915 to 1730.*

**Kenmare
Heritage
Centre**

The official full title for this park is the Glen Inchaquin Waterfall Amenity Area and there is a free leaflet available from the tourist office that includes a map. There is a set walk that takes one past the waterfall, streams, a bathing spot, lakes and woodland and the whole place is very suitable for families or

**Glen Inchaquin
Park**

anyone wanting a gentle stroll. Bring a picnic or make do with the shop selling hot drinks and home-baked snacks. For a more serious day's walking consider completing a day or two of the Kerry Way. ■ *Open daily. €2.54. Situated 8 miles (12 km) from Kenmare on the road to Castletownbere and then signposted on the left.*

Stone circle Kenmare's stone circle, easily reached from the tourist office along Market Street and across the bridge over the River Finnehy, is one of the largest in Ireland. There are 15 stones making up the circle and in the centre is a fine dolmen. ■ *In the summer there is a €1.27 admission charge which is hard to justify; anyway, the stone circle is clearly visible from the road.*

Derreen garden Derreen is a woodland garden planted by the fifth Marquess of Lansdowne in the 1870s. Visitors can collect a useful little map that describes and identifies some of the numbered plants, and there is plenty to see. The 140-ft (42-m) giant conifers seen here today were introduced from North America, and the exotic tree ferns came from New Zealand. One tree, the 60-ft-high (18 m) *Cryptomeria Japonica Elegans* with a girth of 10 ft (3 m), grows directly across the path in the rock garden and requires an artificial support. The Caha Mountains and Kilakilloge Harbour, which afford such stunning views from Derreen Garden, help shelter and protect the grounds and facilitate the healthy array of plants and trees that are rarely found outside of the southwest. ■ *Apr-Oct 1100-1800. €3.81. Tea room and picnic area. Situated at Lauragh, 15 miles (24 km) west of Kenmare on the R571 road.*

Sleeping
Price codes:
see inside front cover

Two of the country's most exclusive 5-star hotels are in Kenmare, as well as a number of regular 3-star places, but there are also many B&Bs, all charging around €45 for doubles/singles.

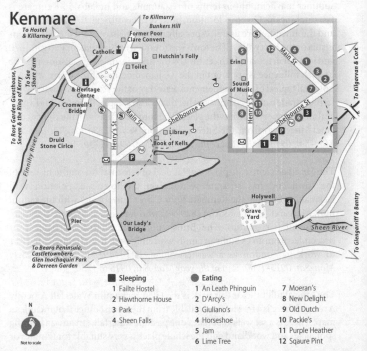

Kenmare

Sleeping
1 Failte Hostel
2 Hawthorne House
3 Park
4 Sheen Falls

Eating
1 An Leath Phinguin
2 D'Arcy's
3 Giuliano's
4 Horseshoe
5 Jam
6 Lime Tree
7 Moeran's
8 New Delight
9 Old Dutch
10 Packie's
11 Purple Heather
12 Sqaure Pint

County Kerry

XL *Park Hotel*, T41200, www.parkkenmare.com For sheer aristocratic class it is hard to beat this place, where each room is furnished with wonderful antique furniture. The Great Southern and Western Railway Company built the Park Hotel in 1897 for the idle rich from England who spent a night here, after reaching Kenmare by train, before being taken by horse and carriage to the sister hotel at Parknasilla (see page 343). **XL** *Sheen Falls Lodge*, T41600, www.sheenfallslodge.ie Equally classy hotel, all rooms have views of the bay or the Falls and, like the Park, boasts a top-notch restaurant. **L-AL** *Riversdale House Hotel*, T41299, www.kenmare.com/riversdale Just over the double-arched bridge at the Glengarriff end of town. Ask for a room with a view of the estuary and hills to take full advantage of the hotel's riverside location.

AL-A *Sea Shore Farm*, T41270, www.seashorefarm.com Well nigh perfect: peaceful, homely and friendly, with spacious rooms, a pleasant walk through the fields down to the shore and terrific views of the Caha Mountains. Look for the sign, past the *Esso* station on the left side of the road out of town to Killarney. **A** *Hawthorne House*, Shelbourne St, T41035, hawthorn@eircom.net Recommended for its comfort and professional service. **A** *The Rose Garden*, Gortamullen, T42288, /www.euroka. com/rosegarden A smart, meticulously run guesthouse just outside of town on the Ring of Kerry road. The Dutch owners provide exemplary service, and there is a decent restaurant.

C-D *Failte* Hostel , T42333, is an IHO place with over 30 beds and 2 private rooms. **D** *Hostel*, no telephone but the 5th bungalow on the left, after the petrol station on the right side of the main road from town to Killarney. Nora Burke welcomes hostellers and campers; a small charge for showers and the tumble dryer.

Camping *Ring of Kerry Caravan & Camping Park*, Reen, T41648, F41631. 3 miles (5 km) west of town on the road to Sneem.

Expensive The *Park Hotel Restaurant*, T41200, offers the best of Irish modern cuisine. Style is everything and at the *Park* it comes in the form of a grand high-ceilinged dining room with huge bay windows looking across water, well spaced tables with crisp white linen serviced by a bevy of attendants, and a wine list of 600 wines. Expect to pay around €50 for a superb meal. *La Cascade*, T41600, at the *Sheen Falls Lodge*, is on 2 levels; reserve a window table for views of the Falls. Set dinner is €54 and features starters like scallops with foie gras and oyster cream, vegetarian menu is €37; impeccable service, vast wine list. Both restaurants open for dinner only. *The Lime Tree*, 15 Shelbourne St, T41225, is named after the 100-year-old lime tree in its garden. The restaurant stretches over 2 floors and it is obvious from the atmosphere that many of the customers are regulars. Munch on the excellent breads and tapenade as you make your choices from traditional and modern dishes. Vegetarians have some good choices, the wine list is carefully designed and there are some excellent desserts. Apr-Nov dinner only, and reservations are essential.

Mid-range *Oscar's* at the Sheen Falls opens nightly for bistro-style dining and a good choice of seafood, meat and pasta dishes. Henry St is fairly littered with food places but some of the pubs serving food may prove disappointing and it might be better trying a smaller place like the *Old Dutch Restaurant*, T41449, where the Dutch chef has crab claws for starters, steak, lamb, duck and some fish for main courses. *Packie's*, T41508, in Henry St has been around for some time and earned a reputation for good seafood and Mediterranean-style dishes. Main St has its own sprinkling of restaurants like *D'Arcy's*, T41589, which has pretty table settings, an international menu and opens only for dinner at 1800, or the Italian-style *An Leath Phingin*, T41559, at No 35 which has been recommended for its pasta dishes. At 3 Main St, *The Horseshoe*, T41553, is a relaxed pub doing bar food with a restaurant to the rear that serves nourishing chowders and burgers and evening meals of steaks and other standard but well cooked dishes.

Eating

County Kerry

Cheap Henry St boasts one of Ireland's very few vegetarian restaurants, the *New Delight*, T42350. It lives up to its name, with open sandwiches and hot meals like quorn tikka masala pita. For economically priced daytime meals try nearby *The Purple Heather*, T41016, for soups, seafood salads, omelettes and the like, or *The Jam* café, popular with locals. *The Coachman* has an early-bird menu, 1730 to 1900, for €18 and affordable lunch specials. At the top of Main St, *Giuliano's*, T41952, specializes in Italian pasta and pizza, good for vegetarians; lunch and dinner, daily, between Mar and Nov.

On a wet afternoon, consider afternoon tea at the Sheen Falls Lodge for €15.80: home-made brown sandwiches, fruitcake, frangipani tartlets and lashings of tea.

Pubs & music One of the oldest buildings in town is now *Moerans Pub*, which as well serving food has some lively evenings of music and song. The *Square Pint*, near the tourist office, is usually packed with revellers but lacks any identity of its own. Try, instead, *Crowley's* in Henry St, or *O'Donnabháin's* that looks authentic despite the wooden beams going in different directions.

Shopping For its size, Kenmare is reasonably well endowed with shops catering to visitors' credit cards. There is a largish *Quills* store in the very centre of town, open daily until 2200, that sells designer handknits, woollen and cashmere garments and assorted merchandise. On Henry St there are a couple of antique shops and other stores dedicated to arts, crafts and souvenirs, including: *Sound of Music*, with a range of bodhrans, tin whistles, flutes, Irish music and dance videos; and *Erin* which is strong on Aran garments. On Main St *De Barra* is a small but enticing Irish jewellery shop. *Black Abbey* in Main St has some lovely pieces of craftwork while next door the *Blue Stone Gallery* has more in the same vein. Upstairs in the *Lime Tree* is an art gallery which is open while the restaurant is and has some excellent work by local artists. There is a good second-hand bookshop at 3 Bridge St, near the tourist office, and a regular bookshop on Shelbourne St.

Tours **Boat** *Seafari*, T83171. Departs regularly from the Pier for a 2-hr, 10-mile (15 km) cruise of Kenmare Bay (€15.88) with an ecological emphasis. Colonies of grey seals and sea otters are usually spotted and occasionally minke and killer whales are seen chasing shoals of mackerel. There is also a sunset cruise featuring a barbecue and live Irish music. To reach the pier walk out of town towards Killarney and turn right just before the double-arched bridge. This is a pleasant destination in its own right, especially when the tide is in and the Kerry Mountains look down on the graceful flow of the river. **Quad biking** *Forgotten Island*, T42900, forgottenireland@unison.ie, has been warmly recommended by a reader who thoroughly enjoyed his 4-hr beano in the countryside around Kenmare. You need to be over 25 and possess a driving licence.

Directory **Communications** Internet access at the post office at the top of Henry St.

The Kerry Way

See map page 330

This is nine or 10 days of glorious walking around some of the most beautiful scenery in Ireland. The walk is well established and several organizations will be glad to plan your entire trip, including luggage transfer and pickups where the route meets roads into towns. However, it is perfectly possible to do the trip without this and at your leisure, taking days off to enjoy the villages and make side trips to places such as Valentia and the Skelligs along the way. Car drivers can plan the walks in sections, basing themselves at Glenbeigh, Killarney or Waterville, doing one or two days and then moving on.

Climbing Carrauntuohill – and a warning

Carrauntuohill, at 3,414 ft (1,039 m), is Ireland's highest peak and reaching the top requires organization, lots of stamina, and a full awareness of the dangers involved on some of the routes to the top. The challenging Howling Ridge ascent claimed another fatality in December 2001 and since 1966 there have been 10 deaths on the mountain. The following route is relatively safe and requires no special skills.

Ordnance Survey Map 78 covers the area and the common starting point is signposted off the road that connects the Gap of Dunloe with Glencar. The signposted road ends near a farmhouse, with parking space and a coffee machine. Be sure to let someone know where you are going and/or leave a note on your vehicle. The walk has a terrific start, up between Lough Gooragh and Lough Callee, but pace yourself because the ascent of the steep Devil's Ladder requires stamina. From the top, it is less than 1000ft to the summit and, after celebrating, descend by the same route and take especial care coming back down the Devil's Ladder.

The walk is about 135 miles (215 km) and consists of the following:

Day 1: Killarney to the Black Valley 14 miles (22 km)
Day 2: Black Valley to Glencar 12 miles (20 km)
Day 3: Glencar to Glenbeigh 11 miles (17.5 km)
Day 4: Glenbeigh to Cahersiveen 17 miles (28 km)
Day 5: Cahirsiveen to Waterville 19 miles (30 km)
Day 6a: Waterville to Caherdaniel 17 miles (28 km)
Day 6b: Waterville to Caherdaniel 8 miles (12 km)
Day 7: Caherdaniel to Tahilla 16 miles (26 km)
Day 8: Tahilla to Kenmare 13 miles (21 km)
Day 9: Kenmare to Killarney 15 miles (24 km)

The first 6 days are the best for views and terrain while Day 8, Tahilla to Kenmare, is seriously not worth doing as it involves walking about 4 miles on the main Ring of Kerry Rd, a very dangerous activity. The Kerry Way is generally well signposted but the Ordnance Survey (OS) Discovery Series maps sheets 78, 83 and 84 are essential. *Cork-Kerry Tourism* produces a strip map of the walk which is less useful and not essential if using the OS map.

Mapping & information

County Kerry

Day 1: Killarney to the Black Valley

The walk starts just outside the town centre of Killarney at the River Flesk. The first section is along the pavement and then the walk enters Muckross Park with views of Killarney's lakes. It passes by Muckross Friary and Muckross House (see page 319) and emerges from the park at the foot of the Torc waterfall. Above the waterfall the route heads off along the Old Kenmare Road, quite boggy in places, across deer country with Mangerton Mountain looming ahead and McGillycuddy's Reeks in the distance. Passing a deserted church, the route crosses the Killarney to Kenmare road and heads downhill, following the course of the Derricunnihy River and then the Upper Lake. At a little landing stage and café, the route meets a minor road and follows it to the *Black Valley Hostel*, which is quite small and should be booked well in advance if you intend to stay there. Close by is *Hillcrest Farmhouse* B&B. This is simply the only accommodation at this stage (for details see 'Sleeping' on page 350).

14 miles (22 km); 7 hrs; total ascent 1,230 ft (375 m)

Day 2: Black Valley to Glencar

12 miles (20 km); 8 hrs; total ascent 1,640 ft (500 m)

This is the most stunning day's walk between Killarney and Glenbeigh. It passes through the Black Valley and even on a sunny day you can see why the place has earned the name. The walk climbs gradually up through rugged jagged peaks, leaving all idea of roads and civilization behind. It meets an old butter road and descends into a farmyard and valley and then climbs again over a pass on a spur of Curraghmore Mountain, finally meeting Lough Acoose and a road to Glencar. There are several B&Bs and guest houses around Glencar, including the walker-friendly *The Climbers' Inn*, (for details, see 'Sleeping' on page 350).

Day 3: Glencar to Glenbeigh

11 miles (17½ km); 6 hrs; total ascent 984 ft (300 m)

This day's walk goes through the Caragh River valley, along some road and forestry roads and culminates in a scenic climb up Seefin Mountain. From here there is a choice of routes skirting Seefin to the east and west, both equally beautiful and both descending into Glenbeigh. For accommodation in Glenbeigh see the Glenbeigh section on page 331.

The first three days of the Kerry Way are worth considering as a walking excursion from Killarney with a return by bus after spending the third night in Glenbeigh. With your own transport, the beginning of the first day could be shortened by leaving your car at the Torc Waterfall carpark.

Day 4: Glenbeigh to Cahersiveen

17 miles (28 km); 9 hrs; total ascent 2,100 ft (650 m)

This day and the next day's walk could be shortened by 4 miles by staying at Foilmore rather than going on into Cahersiveen. The first section of the route heads southwest out of Glenbeigh and follows the coast, first ascending Glenbeigh Hill with spectacular views of the coastline. There is a short spell along roads and then another climb up Drung Hill and more wonderful views. There follows a turn inland along the flanks of Been Hill to Foilmore where there is *Fransal House* B&B. Staying here means you can avoid the long trek into Cahersiveen and back out again if you intend to continue the walk another day. On the other hand, going on means you have a greater choice of where to stay, and if you intend to break your walk for a few days you are better placed for trips to Valentia or the Skelligs. For accommodation and food see the Cahersiveen section on page 334.

Day 5: Cahersiveen to Waterville

19 miles (30 km); 8 hrs minimum; total ascent 2,400 ft (730 m)

This distance includes the spur from Cahersiveen back to the main route at Foilmore and another at the end of the day into Waterville. Foilmore to Waterville is 15 miles (24 km). The day's walk climbs on to high ground and for much of the first half of it you are climbing and descending hills with 360° scenery. The walk eventually descends into Mastergeehy, a small village with a tiny post office selling very basic supplies, and then follows an old mass path up Coomaduff Hill and along another series of ridges with fine views into Waterville. On Coomaduff Hill the Way divides, one route going on to Caherdaniel and the other into Waterville. You should take the Waterville route as the final ridge walk to Waterville is well worth the effort. For accommodation see the Waterville section on page 339.

Day 6a: Waterville to Caherdaniel

This distance includes walking back to Coomaduff Hill from Waterville and then, at the end of the day's walk, walking away from the main route towards Caherdaniel. It is an excellent walk despite the length and detour, and if you wanted to make the route shorter you might try hitching from Waterville to Dromod, making the walk to Caherdaniel about 13 miles (21 km).

17 miles (28 km); total ascent 1,750ft (535 m)

The Way begins by retracing the ridge walk back from Waterville to Coomaduff Hill and then halfway down it meets the fork in the route to Caherdaniel. It skirts around the north side of Lough Currane, crosses some rough land where markers are not clear and meets a boreen, which it follows for a while close to the eastern shore of Lough Currane. The Way then turns east along another minor road past Lough Isnagahiny. Just beyond an old school, now a heritage centre, the route leaves the minor road and sets off southwards climbing Mount Eagle, crossing to the right of the summit at Windy Gap. The route down is a wide green road, easy to walk until it meets another branch of the Kerry Way travelling from Caherdaniel to Sneem. Your route is westwards to Caherdaniel and a signpost points the way along quite marshy ground but with some excellent views down into Derrynane Bay and the Kenmare River. For accommodation see the Caherdaniel section on page 342.

Day 6b: Waterville to Caherdaniel (alternative route)

This route is shown on the OS Discovery series sheet 83 and even without the markers is quite easy to follow. It heads east out of Waterville and takes the first minor road right, beside a mini golf course. It follows the minor road for about 1½ miles and then sets off across a field at a place called the Pound. This is an obvious looking, fenced-off area for collecting sheep on the left of the road. It climbs a little to find the Old Kenmare Road, just below the main Ring of Kerry Road, and runs along parallel to it for some miles, eventually crossing it to climb a small spur and then heading downhill at the *Scarriff Inn*. It follows the coast for some miles, giving very pleasant views of the coastline, passes through the outskirts of Derrynane National Park and emerges at Caherdaniel. For accommodation see the Caherdaniel section on page 342.

8 miles (12 km); 6 hrs; total ascent 984 ft (300 m)

Day 7: Caherdaniel to Tahilla

The route sets off backtracking yesterday's walk to the junction at the bottom of Eagle Mountain, takes the right fork and for most of the day follows the Old Kenmare Road in its modern incarnations of green road, boggy pasture and minor tarmac road. The walk is pleasant enough but has no spectacular sections like the previous day's walk. There are views south over the Kenmare River for most of the day and a pleasant stop can be had at Sneem. You might want to break your walk at that point and move on to Kenmare via one of the daily buses, cutting out the next day's section which really isn't worth the trouble of the long walk along the Ring of Kerry road with absolutely no footpaths and completely mad drivers travelling way too fast for such a narrow road. Accommodation at Tahilla is at *Hillside Haven*.

16 miles (26 km); 7 hrs; total ascent 1,300 ft (400 m)

County Kerry

Insectivores of Kerry and Cork

Bog land is nutritionally poor, but the plant world responds with species that trap and digest insects. The most conspicuous is the large-flowered butterwort, often encountered in wet patches along the Beara, Iveragh or Dingle Way. Commonly growing in clumps, the butterwort is a low-lying perennial with violet flowers in a starfish-like rosette and fleshy sticky leaves, which attract and trap their victims before they are consumed by digestive enzymes.

The leaves of the small reddish sundew family also trap insects, an estimated 2,000 annually, with their long, sticky, inward-curving hairs. Look closely and you will see the fine hairs tipped with a sticky globule.

The rootless bladderworts live underwater, but their yellow flowers may be seen above the surface of pools. Their leaves have tiny bladders with supersensitive bristles and when a water flea unwittingly brushes past, the bladder opens, expelling water and sucking in the victim aided by the vacuum effect.

In a bog near Listowel a species of pitcher plant from North America has been successfully introduced.

Day 8: Tahilla to Kenmare

13 miles (21 km); 7 hrs; total ascent 1,150 ft (350 m)

This is a fairly pleasant walk as far as Templenoe, where a long stretch on the Ring of Kerry road is not worth walking. From Tahilla the route rejoins the Old Kenmare Road as far as Blackwater Bridge where it enters woodland beside the Kenmare River, emerging west of Templenoe. From here a bus will take you into Kenmare, or you can follow the rest of the route along the main road to Reen where the route leaves the main Ring of Kerry road and heads uphill over Gortamullin Hill and then down into Kenmare.

Day 9: Kenmare to Killarney

15 miles (24 km); 8 hrs; total ascent 1,970 ft (600 m)

A thoroughly pleasant walk still following old roads, starts along minor roads and then continues through a saddle high up between Knockanaguish and Peakeen mountains with fine views over Killarney's lakes. Descending, the route follows the Derrycunnihy River, finally meeting up with the Kerry Way out of Killarney.

Essentials

Sleeping & eating
Price codes: see inside front cover

D *Black Valley Hostel*, Black Valley, T064-34712, mailbox@anoige.com An Óige hostel, which is quite small and should be booked well in advance if you intend to stay there. It opens at 1700, has a small shop next door and good cooking facilities, but gets crowded and noisy; no private rooms. **A-D** *The Climbers' Inn*, Glencar, T066-9760101, climbers@iol.ie Hostel accommodation and B&B at this walker-orientated inn established in 1875 as the first of its kind in Ireland. Kitchen, drying rooms, pub food and restaurant, information about other walks in the area; closed Nov-Mar. In the same area are several B&Bs and guest houses. **B** *Fransal House*, Glencar, T066-9472997. B&B open all year with a laundry, drying room, evening meals and packed lunches, and luggage transfer. **B** *Hillcrest Farmhouse*, Black Valley, T064-34702. B&B, close to the Black Valley hostel, which does evening meals and luggage transfer and has a drying room – essential if you hit bad weather. **B** *Hillside Haven*, Tahilla, T064-82065. **B** *Rocklands* , Cappantanvalley, Glencar, T066-9760177. B&B between Lake Caragh and Lake Acoose; evening meals, packed lunches, laundry facilities.

County Kerry

Dingle Peninsula

Stretching for 30 glorious miles (48 km) from the town of Tralee, the Dingle peninsula is characterized geographically by high central ridges running up to Mount Brandon at 3,127 yd (952 m) and the scenery as a whole, etched by the glaciers of the last Ice Age, reveals itself in an epiphany of natural beauty that is stunningly unique and unforgettable. Less rugged and wild than the Beara or the Iveragh, there is a distinct quality to the light and the colours that on a fine day transforms the Dingle into Ireland's most wonderful and magical peninsula. Nowadays more and more visitors are being drawn to the Dingle Peninsula and in July and August it is advisable to have accommodation booked in advance; come here outside of the high season and you will feel especially privileged to be here.

See map next page

Ins and outs

Getting there

There are two approaches to the peninsula: coming from the south on the N22 or the N70 it is possible to branch off at Farranfore or Castlemaine and head directly west to the town of Dingle along the road that skirts the south coast. Coming from the east or the north one first reaches Tralee at the head of the peninsula's north coast before heading west to the village of Camp. From here one road continues along the north coast before descending to Dingle via the phenomenal Connor Pass, while another road heads south west across the peninsula to Annascaul where the south coast road is picked up.

Getting around

Anyone spending much time on the Dingle peninsula, especially if planning to cycle or walk, should consider purchasing the Ordnance Survey Map No 70 in the Discovery series. There are so many minor roads and so few main ones – and, on top of that, the practice of signposting places in Irish (see box on page 361) – means that it is easy to get confused.

All year, *Bus Éireann* run up to 5 buses, Mon-Sat, between Dingle and Tralee via Annascaul and Camp. There is also a Mon-Sat service between Dingle and Dunquin, via Ventry, Slea Head and Ballyferriter. There is also a daily service between Killarney and Dingle via Tralee. There is a summer-only, Mon-Sat service, from Tralee travelling to Inch, Dingle, Ventry, Slea Head, Dunquin, Ballyferriter, then back to Dingle and on to Annascaul, Camp and returning to Tralee. Another summer-only service departs from Dingle at 1530 for Killarney, via Annascaul, and Inch, and passing the *An Óige* hostel at Aghadoe before reaching Killarney. For full details, contact Tralee bus station, T066-712 3566, or Killarney T064-30011

History

Ancient constructs litter the peninsula – megalithic tombs, cup and circle stones, oratories, beehive huts, high crosses –testimony perhaps to the sense of awe that the landscape inspired in the region's earliest inhabitants. Later groups of visitors – Norsemen in the 10th century, Anglo-Normans in the 13th century followed by traders from Spain – may have felt the same, but the Dingle Peninsula also bears the scars of England's colonialism. People around Ballyferriter still recount the story of the Dún an Óir massacre (near Smerwick, see page 364) and how workmen collecting stones at a nearby beach once refused to go on working when they discovered that this was the infamous "beach of the heads": the heads of those massacred, cut off by English troops, washed up on shore and buried by local people.

County Kerry

Tralee

Phone code: 066
Colour map 3, grid B2

Not the cutest of Irish towns, the county capital is metamorphosing into a thriving centre of local employment that seasonally tunes into the tourist market whilst otherwise busying itself with the new-found wealth of 21st-century Ireland. Tralee makes a useful base for a day or two before heading west and there are a few attractions to while away the time while planning an itinerary or plotting a route along the Dingle Way, a superb long-distance walk around the peninsula that provides an ideal introduction to Dingle's charms (see page 368).

The **tourist office** is in Ashe Memorial Hall, Denny St, T7121288. September-June, Monday-Saturday, 0900-1800; July-August, Monday-Sunday, 0900-1900. Rose of Tralee festival office also here, T7121322 and has a café and craft shop on the premises. The WALK-IN-formation Centre, T7128733, stocks OS maps and walking guide books: useful if planning or considering the Dingle Way or other walks in the region.

Kerry the Kingdom The history of Kerry is told through an audio-visual display, a museum and a 'time car' that ferries visitors through a reconstructed set of medieval Tralee. Families will appreciate the trolley ride and the museum is dense with information, though the admission charge is a bit steep. ■ *Mar-Oct, daily, 1000-1800 (1900 in Aug); Nov and Dec, 1400-1700. €7.*

Blennerville windmill & Jeanie Johnson shipyard The largest working mill in the British Isles is the centrepiece of this visitor attraction just outside of town on the N86 road to Dingle. The exhibition focuses on the history of 19th-century Blennerville, an emigrant port from where thousands departed for the long and painful journey to North America. ■ *T7129999. Apr-Oct, daily 1000-1800. €3.80*

Steam railway The first 1.8 miles (3 km) of the narrow-gauge Tralee and Dingle Steam Railway, which ran from 1891 to 1953, has been restored and every hour a train chugs from Ballyard Station in town to the Blennerville Windmill. The journey lasts 20 minutes and makes for a pleasant journey to the windmill (plus a

Dingle Peninsula & Dingle Way

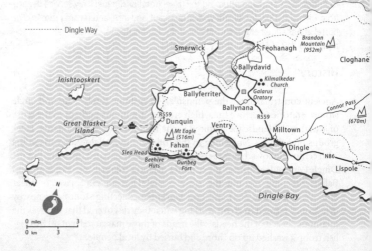

10 per cent discount on the windmill admission) and railway memorabilia is sold on the train. ■ *T7121064. May-4 Oct, daily, 1100-1700; closed on certain days in Jun and Jul.* €4.

Sleeping
■ *on map next page*
Price codes:
see inside front cover

L-AL *Meadowlands*, Oakpark, T7180444. Modern hotel, out on the road to Listowel, with stylish and well equipped rooms, and above-average restaurant. **AL** *Castlemorris House*, Ballymullen, T7180060, castlemorris@eircom.net A lovely house on the outskirts of the city where guests are greeted with afternoon tea, and an evening meal can be booked in advance. Take the N21 to Dingle and turn right at the T-junction after less than a mile. **AL** *Tralee Court*, Castle St, T7121877, F7122273. Modern, comfortable and convenient, being in the very centre of town. **B** *Denton B&B*, Listowel Rd, Oakpark, T7127637. Near the Meadowlands hotel on the N69, rooms en suite and open all year. **C** *Upton House*, 7 Clash Rd, T7125219. Near the bus and train station and charges from €31 to €38 for a double, sharing bathroom facilities. **C** *Westward Court*, Mary St, T7180081, westward@iol.ie Offers "superior budget accommodation", meaning a private double/single room with a continental breakfast for up to €51, or a bed in a 4-bed/6-bed room for €14 per person. There is also the use of a kitchen, launderette, security lockers and TV lounge. **C-D** *Collis-Sandes House*, Oakpark, T7128658, colsands@indigo.ie A pickup service from train or bus station, though a walkable journey out along Oakpark Rd (N69), on the left after a *Shell* garage. A lovely old Anglo-Irish house, with the full range of hostel amenities. **C-D** *Finnegans Holiday Hostel*, Denny St, T7127610. Limited facilities for the price, some private rooms and an atmospheric restaurant in the basement. **C-D** *Court House Lodge*, 5 Church St, T7127199. An IHH hostel with 3 private rooms, bikes for hire. **D** *Lisnagree Hostel*, Ballinorig Rd, T7127133. Situated off the N21 road, has private rooms but otherwise is fairly basic.

Camping *The Bayview Caravan & Camping Park*, Kileen, T7126140. A mile (1.6 km) out of Tralee on the R558 road to Ballybunion. *Woodlands Park*, South Circular Rd, Tralee, T7121235. A modern camping and caravan park. *The Seaside Camping & Caravan Park*, Camp, T7130116, F7130331. Has only 10 pitches for tents. Camping space, too, at *Collis-Sandes House* hostel.

County Kerry

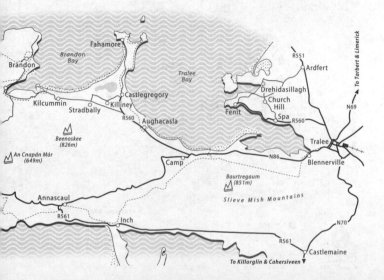

Eating
● *on map*

At the *An Pota Stóir*, T7180444, in the *Meadowlands Hotel*, a cheerfully informal restaurant with a Mediterranean-style character, go for the locally caught seafood: oysters, lobster, turbot, John Dory and sole feature regularly. While an à la carte dinner is around €40 there is also a mid-range set dinner. A good wine list and the usual wicked desserts. *McDades*, a pub and restaurant on Castle St, is recommended for anyone wishing to get away from the usual fish and meat dishes. The interesting menu includes delicious potato skins for a starter, fajitas and pasta dishes. *Kirby's Brogue Inn*, T7123221, in Rock St, might look like a contrived tourist trap but the food is surprisingly good. *Brat's* in Milk Market Lane opens at 1230 for vegetarian lunches with a small but authentic menu of tasty ideas.

Pubs & music

There is no shortage of pubs and many of them have live music during the summer. Kirby's *Brogue Inn* can usually be relied on for an entertaining night out and the cavernous *Seán Óg's* in Bridge St has music every night except Wed and Sat. *The Abbey Inn*, also in Bridge St, has music every night of the week until late.

Entertainment

Festivals *Samhlaíocht Chiarraí*, Main St, T7129934, F7120934. Contact for details of the Tralee Easter Arts Festival. **Theatre** *Síamsa Tíre*, T7123055, www.siamsatire.com The *National Folk Theatre of Ireland*, founded in 1974 to present theatrical entertainment based around Irish folklore music and dance. Summer season shows usually start at 2030, and advance booking is recommended in Jul and Aug.

Sport

Racing *Greyhound Stadium*, Oakview, T7180008. There is a grandstand restaurant and a bar and the first race starts at 2000 every Tue, Fri and Sat. Admission and dinner is around €17 and pre-booking is required. **Swimming** *Aqua Dome*, T7128899. A fun waterworld with slides and raging rapids open daily from 1000 to 2200.

Tours

Jackie Power Tours, 2 Lower Rock St, T7129444. Coach tours of the Ring of Kerry and Dingle peninsula and Killarney.

Tralee

County Kerry

Sleeping			Eating & drinking	
1 Finnegans Holiday Hostel	4 Tralee Court		1 Abbey Inn	5 McDade's
2 Lisnagree Hostel	5 Westwood Court		2 An Pota Stóir	6 Seán Óg's
3 Meadowlands	6 Woodlands Park Camping		3 Brat's Café	
			4 Kirby's Brogue Inn	

The secret of the rose

The annual week-long Rose of Tralee festival at the end of August begins with street bands welcoming the would-be Roses – woman of Irish descent from every corner of the world – for a revival of the traditional welcome, in which they were led through the streets with an escort of riders bearing burning sods of turf. While tickets to the contest are sold out well in advance there is still plenty of entertainment around town – street theatre, pub extensions, concerts, fireworks – and big names like Van Morrison appear on the stage. The actual contest to choose the Rose takes up two nights, and not a bikini in sight, for the women compete by way of interviews on stage followed by a display of some expertise, anything from an Irish jig to a belly dance. The stage event is laudably low-octane but goes on for a couple of hours too long, and while the winner is not hurled into an international limelight all the contestants enjoy a week-long freebie and publicans laugh all the way to the bank. The secret of the festival's success is hard to fathom, but it is growing increasingly popular. Information and bookings at T7121322, www.roseoftralee.ie

Air *Kerry Airport*, Farranfore, 10 miles (16 km) southeast of Tralee, T9764644. **Bicycle** *Dunworth Cycles*, 97 Rock St, T7120666. Bike hire. *Tralee Gas & Bicycle Supplies*, Strand St, T7122018. Bike hire. **Bus** *Bus Éireann*, T7123566. Buses to **Dublin**, **Rosslare** and other towns as well as scenic tours of the peninsula, **Cliffs of Moher** and **West Cork** in the summer months. All year, buses connect Tralee with **Killarney**, **Dublin**, **Cork** and other main cities. **Car** *Duggan's Garage*, Ashe St, T7121124. Car hire; will also deliver to the airport. **Taxis** Taxi rank in Denny St, T7123159. **Train** Train station: T7123522/7126555. Daily service to **Dublin** and connections to other towns around the country like **Cork** and **Ennis** from Limerick Junction and the west of Ireland from Portarlington. **Transport**

North of Tralee

Apart from the sights mentioned below, the flat rolling farmland of North Kerry has little to detain the traveller and if you're heading on to Clare, stay on the N69 and cross the Shannon by way of the very regular car ferry from Tarbert.

On the way to Tarbert, the small town of Listowel is worth noting because of its literary fame as the home of the playwright, John B Keane, who also runs *John B Keane's* pub, an authentic Irish bar. There is a seasonal tourist office, T22590, in St John's Church and if you plan a visit to the annual Listowel Writer's Week in May it is advisable to have accommodation booked in advance. Details of the festival are available from PO Box 147, Listowel, Kerry. T21074. Throughout the year, something is usually on at St John's Theatre and Arts Centre, The Square, T22566, and information is available at www.listowel.com Decent food and accommodation is available at **AL** *Allo's Bar & Bistro* at 41 Church St, T22880, and **AL** *Listowel Arms Hotel*, T21500. **Listowel** *Phone code: 068*

Depending on your interests and time, it could well be worth skipping the attractions in Tralee and journeying 5 miles (8 km) to the northwest to visit the cathedral in Ardfert. St Brendan founded a monastery here in the sixth century, but what you see today is a medieval cathedral with a superb Romanesque doorway on the west side, and a dramatic triple-lancet window typical of the Gothic style that had been introduced to Ireland by the Cistercians. The 13th-century east window, framed by two ecclesiastical effigies, is also worthy **Ardfert Cathedral**

County Kerry

Sir Roger Casement

Casement was a British diplomat, born in 1864 in Sandycove (County Dublin), who first became famous for his denunciations of the exploitation of native workers in the Congo and South America. He was knighted in 1911, but ill-health caused his early retirement, and he settled in Ireland in 1912. His commitment to the cause of Irish nationalism led him to Germany in 1914. The government there agreed to send a shipload of arms, but this was far less than he had anticipated and he returned to

Ireland in 1916 in order to try and postpone the planned rising. A German submarine brought him into Tralee Bay, but he was arrested after landing on Banna Strand. Put on trial for treason and sentenced to death, he attracted a lot of support and there were many appeals on his behalf. To discredit him, the government released extracts from his 'Black Diaries' that revealed his homosexuality. He was hanged in London in August 1916. In 1965 his body was returned to Ireland for a state funeral.

of attention. On the site there are also two other smaller 15th-century churches. ■ *May-late Sep, daily 0930-1830. €1.90. Dúchas site; guided tour available. Situated on the R551 Tralee to Ballyheigue road at Ardfert.*

Banna Strand The 5-mile (8-km) stretch of safe and sandy beach at Banna is popular with Irish families, and camping and caravan sites are dotted along the coast up to and including Ballyheigue. On the beach there are panoramic views over Tralee Bay, and Banna Strand has a particular significance in Irish history because it was here that Roger Casement landed and was arrested in 1916 (see box above). To reach the memorial look for a sign pointing to the left as you approach the beach; from here it is a 10-minute walk past the caravans.

Crag Cave A limestone cave discovered by accident in 1983 and now open to the public by way of a guided tour. As caves go this one is quite impressive and the lighting system underground is used to good effect to highlight some of the more dramatic formations. Above ground there is a restaurant and a minimarket of souvenirs. ■ *T068-7141244. Mid-Mar-Nov, daily 1000-1800 (1830 in Jul and Aug). €5.50. Situated on the N21 road at the Limerick end of Castleisland, T066-7141244, www.cragcave.com*

Inch and Annascaul

Phone code: 066
Colour map 3, grid B2

Coming from Killarney and the south the route west from Castlemaine follows the coast to Dingle, and the two main villages along the way are Inch and Annascaul. They are places to stay, but finding somewhere for a meal is not so straightforward, and this should be borne in mind. See page 367 for the other route out to Dingle via Camp and Castlegregory.

Inch The main attraction at Inch is the gorgeous 4-mile (6-km) beach that provided a location for the filming of *The Playboy of the Western World*. The strand and the two opposite on the Iveragh peninsula – Rossbeigh and Cromane – are gradually building up, and one day Castlemaine Bay will be enclosed. The beach is vast and you can walk a mile out to sea at low tide and the water is only about an inch deep, which is one explanation for the village's name. Ringed plovers and turnstones, distinctively small black and white birds with white legs, are non-breeding visitors to the beach where they are seen turning stones and weeds with their bills searching for food.

Nuala Ní Dhomhnaill

So many figures from the famed Irish literary tradition, or at least the version marketed by Bord Fáilte, are dead white males that it comes as a refreshing change to know that the Dingle area nurtured the poet Nuala Ní Dhomhnaill. She was born in England in 1952, but her Irish parents sent her back to the Gaeltacht Dingle Peninsula at the age of five. Her first collection of poetry arrived in 1981, announcing a new voice able to blend Irish mythology and folklore with an acute political and social awareness. Marrying feminism with the Gaelic tradition, her work has been translated by Seamus Heaney and other contemporary poets (see page 679).

Sleeping There are no restaurants in the area so staying in a hostel makes a lot of sense. The nearest is the IHH **D** *Inch Farm Hostel*, T9158181, at Ballinagrown and there are 2 private rooms. More amenities, including meals, laundry, bike hire and private rooms, are to be found in **D** *Bog View Hostel*, T9158125, at Lougher, half way between Inch and Annascaul.

Annascaul

In the one-street village of Annascaul visitors often wonder why a pub should be named the South Pole Inn. A villager, Tom Crean, accompanied Scott and Shackleton to the South Pole and he set up this pub afterwards. There is a small **tourist office** in the main street, T9157419. When facing **Annascaul Lake**, you are standing at the bottom of a glacier-carved valley, the lough itself having been carved out by the base of the glacier. The scree slopes on the other side have been broken off the top of the sandstone mountain by centuries of weathering. The green road leading away from the lough leads up to the valley following the course of the River Garrivagh, and it is a pleasant stroll in dry weather.

Even though the lake is signposted, it is not much visited, and you can usually have the place to yourself. About 4 miles (6 km) from Inch on the road to Dingle you will reach a T-junction: take the right turn for Annascaul and after just under a mile (1.2 km) the road for Annascaul turns to the right, while the left turn is signposted for Annascaul Lake.

Sleeping The hostel, *Fuchsia Lodge*, T9157150, fuchsia@eircom.net, has all the amenities, including bike hire, and it is a friendly and comfortable place to stay for a night or two; open all year and private rooms available. Half way between Annascaul and Dingle there is the *Seacrest Hostel*, T9151390, at Kinard West, Lispole, also open all year and with private rooms.

Dingle

The small town of Dingle, with barely half a dozen streets, has changed almost beyond recognition in the last few years, tourism being the catalyst. Such is the growing popularity of a visit to the peninsula, that Dingle has been forced to build car-parks and introduce one-way systems to cope with the traffic. Out of season, the town reclaims its identity as a market town and fishing port, but in July and August it becomes the main base for visits to the sights and sites west of Dingle. There are places to stay west of town but they are limited in number and, because this end of the peninsula is small enough to make most places accessible as day excursions, Dingle heaves with people and vehicles in the summer months. The **tourist office** is on Strand Street, Close to the pier and bus stop. ■ *T9151188. Open Mid-Mar-May, Mon-Sat 0915-1730; until 1900 in Jul and Aug and until 1800 in Jun and Sep.*

Phone code: 066
Colour map 3, grid B1

County Kerry

History   The Irish form of Dingle, *An Daingean* (fortress), suggests its early involvement in defensive wars, although it has a long history of friendly trade with Spain, and Spanish blood is said to still be noticeable in the dark hair and eyes of the inhabitants. In Green Street just past the library there are plaques, still visible, which were set above some of the doors to indicate that Spanish families lived within and, walking up this street from the pier, part of the original town wall can be seen in the old wall on the left.

Fungie the dolphin   When a bottlenose dolphin first appeared in the harbour in 1983 the chirpy little chap flirted and frolicked and made a lot of friends with the humans who doggie-paddled in the water hoping for a meaningful relationship. Over 15 years later and he is still there (or have the locals replaced him with an inflatable version?) and he surely deserves an award from Bord Fáilte for promoting tourism. Weather permitting, boats depart between 0800 and 1000 from the pier, T9152626, and the €8.90 charge is returned in the unlikely event of his non-appearance. There is also an early morning boat for people who want to swim with him and a wet suit can be hired from Flannery's, T9151967.

It is also possible to get reasonably close to where he usually appears without leaving dry land. Take the road out of town towards Tralee and take the right turn about a mile (1.6 km) after the *Esso* garage. It is a narrow lane with gateposts but no gate and there is a small parking area at the bottom; from here it is a short walk in the direction of the old tower.

Dingle Oceanworld   This Fungie-inspired aquarium is a cut above the average and presents a good opportunity to view at close quarters the local sealife, from cuttlefish to small sharks, including examples of most of the fish that appear on restaurant menus in Ireland. Children will enjoy the touch pool and there is also a café and a shop. ■ *T9152111, Jul-Aug, daily, 0900-2000; May, Jun and Sep, daily, 0900-1800; Oct-Apr, daily 0930-1700. €7.*

County Kerry

Dingle

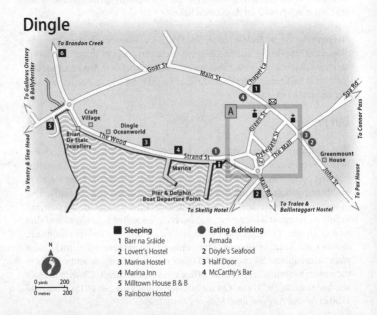

■ Sleeping
1 Barr na Sráide
2 Lovett's Hostel
3 Marina Hostel
4 Marina Inn
5 Milltown House B & B
6 Rainbow Hostel

● Eating & drinking
1 Armada
2 Doyle's Seafood
3 Half Door
4 McCarthy's Bar

There are quite a few B&Bs in and around Dingle, but most have only a few beds and fill up quickly. Join the queue at the tourist office or try to book up before arriving.

Sleeping
■ *on map*
Price codes:
see inside front cover

LL *Dingle Skellig Hotel*, T9151144, F9151501. Sea views from this 1960s hotel, with leisure centre and child-friendly attitude. **AL** *Milltown House*, T9151372, milltown@indigo.ie A superior guest house serving an above-average breakfast and providing fine views of the harbour from the garden; reached by crossing the bridge heading for Ventry and turning left immediately. Robert Mitchum lived here in the 1960s when *Ryan's Daughter* was being filmed. **AL** *Pax House*, Upper St John St, T9151518, paxhouse@iol.ie This really friendly and relaxing guesthouse is good value, with views of the water from the balcony where guests can linger over a drink as the sun goes down. A superb breakfast menu with homemade breads, jam and marmalade and lots of healthy alternatives to the heart-stopping Irish fry. **AL** *Heaton's*, The Wood, T9152288, heatons@iol.ie Just far enough from the town centre to avoid the noise, this top-notch guesthouse has spacious non-smoking rooms, modern facilities and a breakfast that includes Drambuie-topped porridge. **AL-A** *Greenmount House*, Gortonora, T9151414, www.greenmounthouse.-com Includes some rooms with their own fridge and balcony, the conservatory overlooks the harbour, a residents' room, terrific breakfasts.

B *Barr na Sráide*, Upper Main St, T9151331,barrnasraide@eircom.net Comfortable rooms above a pub in the centre of town. **B** *Captain's House*, The Mall, T9151079. A picturesque setting by a running stream and with a delightfully higgledy-piggledy interior that makes this one of the most enjoyable guesthouses in town. **B** *Quayside*, The Tracks, T9151068. Overlooks the harbour above a row of shops. **B** *Russell's*, The Mall, T9151747, maryr@iol.ie A detached house in the town centre with 6 bedrooms with their own bathroom facilities.

C-D *Ballintaggart House*, Racecourse Rd, T9151454. One of the better hostels in Ireland, a 20-min walk out of town on the Tralee road, with private rooms, a restaurant and shop, laundry, bike and wet-suit hire, pony trekking, riding lessons and lovely cobbled courtyard adjoining the self-catering kitchen. **C-D** *The Sleeping Giant*, Green St, T9152666. A new, independent hostel with private rooms and open all year.

Dingle centre

Foxy John's Bike Hire
Green St
Main St
An Liteártha
Lisbeth Mulcahy Shop
Dingleweb
Grey's La
Dykegate St
Mountain Man Shop
The Mall
Pol

N
0 yards   100
0 metres   100

Sleeping
1 Captain's House B & B
2 Grapevine Hostel
3 Mall House B & B
4 Quayside B & B
5 Russell's B & B

● Eating
1 An Droichead Beag
2 Bun Appetit
3 El Toro
4 Global Village
5 Greany's
6 Lord Baker's
7 O'Flaherty's Pub

D *Grapevine Hostel*, Dykegate, T9151434. A smallish house with 24 beds. No private rooms, but the atmosphere is convivial. **D** *Lovett's Hostel*, An Cuilin (Cooleen Rd), T9151903. On the road opposite the *Esso* garage, entering town from Tralee;12 beds in a friendly family house. **D** *Marina Hostel*, Strand St, T9151065. Camping space and private rooms at this independent hostel. **D** *Rainbow Hostel*, Milltown, T9151044. Hip place a short way out of town, with private rooms and camping space.

Camping *Ballintaggart House Caravan & Camping Site*, T9151454, F9152207. Has a 2-star rating and is next to the hostel outside of town on the Tralee road.

Expensive Under new management but keeping the old name, *Doyle's*, John St, T9151174, continues to attract American tourists who have heard of the original legendary seafood restaurant. Traditional

Eating
● *on map*
Price codes:
see inside front cover

County Kerry

Irish-inn decor, with tables too close together, not the place for a romantic dinner; dinner only, closed Sun. *Lord Baker's*, Main St, T9151277, is an old pub and restaurant that only comes into the expensive bracket when dining at night. Seafood is always the main draw, of course, but plenty of meat-based alternatives; Sun lunch always requires a reservation.

Mid-range At *The Half Door*, Mail Rd, T9151600, tuck into the seafood platter as either a starter or main course; early-bird menu available, closed Sun. Some of the more pleasant places are along Main St away from the harbour area. *The Global Village*, T9152325, deserves its name with a menu featuring Thai curries, stir-fried Chinese, German bratwurst sausage, Indian tikka masala, Italian pasta, and UK fish and chips. Open for lunch and dinner. *The Armada*, T9151505, opens 1800-2100, closed Mon, and has a decent 4-course dinner menu consisting of traditional Irish meat dishes and local seafood. *Bun Appetit*, The Mall, T9152323, is also in one of the quieter streets and offers a reasonably priced set meal as well as à la carte dishes such as lemon sole for €11.43. Given Dingle's historical links with Spain, a Spanish restaurant is not out of place and at *El Toro*, Green St, T9151820, Spanish and Mediterranean cuisine might make a change from the usual fare.

Cheap *Greany's*, Holyground, T9150924, is deservedly busy because of the location, the prices and the quality of the food. Go late in the evening for a quieter atmosphere. The pubs opposite the pier, like *Tigh Maire De Barras* and the *Marina Inn*, are the best bet for cheap eats and *Paudie's Bar* along here has bar food and its own *Longs Restaurant*, T9151231, serving food all day. With your own transport, consider too a short trip to Ventry for a meal at *The Skipper* (see next section).

Pubs & music On The Mall *O'Flaherty*, T9151983, is the kind of authentic pub that Irish theme pubs (and you will find one or two of them even in Ireland) use as a model: flagstoned floor, high ceiling, music sessions. The harbourside *Tigh Maire De Barras*, next to the Armada pub, has music every night in the summer and nearby *Paudie's Bar* has traditional music from Thu-Sun, starting at 2130. *An Droichead Beag*, T9151723, on Main St has nightly sessions of traditional music and is popular with tourists, while *McCarthys Bar*, T9151205, is further east on Upper Main St and also has regular sessions of music. There is a popular night club at the *Hillgrove Hotel* on Mon, Wed and Fri nights that attracts young revellers. Nothing happens until at least 2230 and there is a cover charge. On Thu nights there is a traditional Irish dancing session that attracts people of all ages. At the *Skellig Hotel*, the *Dingle Bay Cabaret* plays traditional Irish music with song and dance thrown in.

Festivals A blues, jazz and folk festival takes off in early **Sep** and in the past has attracted names like Mary Black, Albie Donnelly and Don Baker, T/F9152427.

Shopping **Antiques** *Antique Corner* in Main St has lace, jewellery as well as small antique pieces. *Fadó Antiques*, Main St, has a selection of curios, prints, clocks, and jewellery. **Books** *An Liteártha* on Dykegate St has a terrific selection of books on most aspects of Irish history and culture. *Léigh Linn*, the Dingle Bookshop, situated in Green St is also worth a browse. **Fashion** *Banshee* in Strand St has designer knitwear and handmade Irish lace as well as jewellery. *Lisbeth Mulcahy*, Green St. Perhaps the classiest shop in Dingle, specializing in quality fashion accessories, like scarves made from Irish linen, cotton, wool, alpaca and silk. **Gifts** *Celtic Fragments* is at Kilvicadomhnasigh, Ventry, and sells stone carvings and related items. *The Craft Village*, on The Wood a short way west of the pier, has a cluster of arts and crafts shops. *Dick Mack's Yard* is a small shop selling Celtic-inspired jewellery, off Green St. *Brian de Staic*, across the road, has a good selection of handmade Celtic-inspired jewellery on which names can be engraved in the Ogham script. **Music** *The Dingle Record Store* in the Green St Arcade stocks cassettes, CDs and bodhrans.

Gaelic place names on the Dingle Peninsula

Annascaul	Abhainn an Scáil	Cloghane	An Clochán
Ballydavid	Baile na nGall	Dingle	An Daingean
Ballyferriter	Baile an Fheirtéaraigh	Dunquin	Dún Chaoin
Blasket Islands	Na Blascaodaí	Inch	Inse
Brandon	Bréanainn	Lispole	Lios Póil
Brandon Creek	Cuas a Bhodaigh	Ventry	Paróiste Fionn Trá

Diving *Dingle Marina Diving Centre*, The Marina, T9152422, **Sport**
divedingle@eircom.net **Fishing** *Nicholas O'Connor*, Anglers Rest, Ventry, T9159947.
Golf *Ceann Sibéal Golf Club*, Ballyoughterach, Ballyferriter,T9156255. **Horse rid-
ing** *Ballintaggart House*, T9151454. *Dingle Horse Riding*, Ballinaboula,
T9152018. *Horseriding and Trekking Centre*, Mountain View, Ventry, T9159723.
Sailing *Dingle Sailing Club*, The Marina, T9151984. *Dingle Sea Ventures*, Holyground,
T9152244, jgreany@iol.ie *The Kimberly Laura*, a 41-ft (12.5 m) sailing yacht, departs
from the marina at 1030 for a day's sailing around Dingle Bay and trips ashore, T9159882.
Windsurfing *Focus Windsurfing*, T7139411, jamieknox@tinet.ie Based at Ventry
beach, hires gear and conducts training sessions for children.

Boat *Bá Draíochta*, The Pier, T87-2461591. *Dingle Boatmen's Association*, The Pier, **Tours**
T9151163. *Dingle Marine Eco Tours*, The Pier, T2858802. 2-hr trips cover archaeology,
geology, history, birdlife, sealife and local folklore. Tours go either east or west along
the southern part of the peninsula. **Coach** *Moran's Tours*, T9151155. 2-hr trip departing from the Pier daily at 1000 and 1400 and taking in most of the major sites on the
peninsula; €12.70. **Walking** *Sciuird Archaeological Adventures*, T9151937. Daily
2½-hr tours departing at 1000 and 1400 from the pier. Tour numbers are kept below 10
so booking is advisable.

Bicycle *Fios Feasta*, Holy Ground, T9151937. Rents bikes. *Foxy John's*, Main St, **Transport**
T9151316. Offers the Raleigh Rent-a-Bike scheme. *Tadgh Ó Coileáin*, Holyground,
T9151606. Bike hire **Bus** There is a regular bus service between **Tralee** and Dingle, 4
times Mon-Sat, 3 on Sun, and timetables are available from the tourist office. All year
around, on Mon and Thu, 3 buses run daily between Dingle and **Dunquin**, and on Tue
and Fri 3 buses between Dingle and **Ballydavid**. There are 5 buses a day between Dingle and **Killarney**, 3 on Sun.

Communications Internet: Access available at *Dingleweb*, Lower Main St, **Directory**
T9152477, info@dingleweb.com **Post office**: Main St, T9151661.

Dingle to Dunquin

Along the coast between Dingle and Dunquin (*Dún Chaoin*) there are a *Phone code: 066*
number of ancient beehive huts and forts and these are signposted along the
road. Following the Dingle Way to Dunquin is a fascinating and enjoyable
walk (see page 368) and one could skip the first few miles by taking a bus to
Ventry and then begin the walk on Ventry beach. There would be time to
visit the Blasket Heritage Centre at Dunquin before catching the bus back to
Dingle or one could walk back by taking the inland road across
Coumaleagua Hill. With fine weather, there is no better way of enjoying this
corner of the Dingle Peninsula.

County Kerry

Ins & outs The R559 road is the route most visitors take when heading west from Dingle, passing through Ventry (*Fionn Trá*) and following the coast around the majestically scenic Slea Head before turning north for Dunquin, the departure point for Great Blasket Island. An alternative and swifter route to Dunquin is by way of Coumaleagua Hill; take the signposted turning on the right, less than a mile (1.6 km) after the Ventry post office. Walkers will need a copy of Map 70 in the ***Ordnance Survey*** Discovery series. Bus 1555 runs a service between Dingle and Dunquin.

Dunbeg Fort This is a particularly well preserved promontory fort with two souterrains, underground tunnels used for storing food or perhaps as an escape route in times of trouble. The clifftop location is the most impressive aspect of the eighth- or ninth-century fort, although the remains of a dwelling can be discerned inside four earthen defensive rings. ■ *T9159070. €2. Signposted, about 4 miles (6.4 km) west of Ventry.*

Beehive huts Above the road and stretching for some distance is a group of ancient stone huts, known as the **Fahan group**. Very little is known about them for sure, though a plausible explanation is that they represent a late pagan or early Christian settlement that stretched out along some long-lost highway, with Eagle Mountain rearing up behind as a natural form of defence. The fact that they have survived for so long is eloquent testimony to the masonry skills of whoever built them. ■ *€2. Signposted, between Dún Beg Fort and Slea Head.*

Slea Head Slea Head, where the coastal road turns north towards Dunquin, offers spectacular views, and vehicles accumulate here. The Iveragh Peninsula and the Skelligs can be seen to the south, while to the west the Blasket Islands impose themselves on the view. To escape the crowds carry on for a short distance and descend to Coumeenoole Strand, a tiny beach with fine white sand. On a fine day it is tempting to go for a swim, but bear in mind that Robert Mitchum almost drowned in the strong undertow here while filming a scene from *Ryan's Daughter*.

Kruger's The fame of this pub derives from the eponymous Kruger Kavanagh (Kruger was his nickname). Amongst other achievements, he served in the US army in The First World War, became a bodyguard to Eamon de Valera and a Hollywood agent. The pub itself – "the most westerly pub in Europe" – is remarkably unprepossessing, but anywhere that Robert Mitchum drank regularly has got to be worth a visit. The black and white photographs adorning the walls are fascinating and the pub also hosts sessions of Irish set dancing. Film buffs should enquire here for directions to the remains of the partly fibreglass schoolhouse that was built for *Ryan's Daughter*. ■ *T9156127. Just off the R559 at Dunquin on a road that leads down to the departure point for the Great Blasket Island.*

The Blasket Heritage Centre The exterior of this heritage centre at Dunquin makes some people feel the architect and planning authority should be sacked from their jobs – it is unquestionably a blot on the landscape – but the interior is a masterpiece, and a visit here should not be missed, preferably before making a trip out to the island itself. The 20-minute audio-visual presentation, with archive material of interviews with Blasket islanders, is excellent, and there is also a wealth of material and photographs, including an amusing photograph that accompanies an islander's quote: "I looked west at the edge of the sky where America should be…" from Maurice O'Suillivan's *Twenty Years a Growing*. Scholars came to the Great Blasket and encouraged the islanders, to whom storytelling

County Kerry

DINGLE TO DUNQUIN **363**

and poetry was a part of everyday life, to write down their stories and record their memories. Their books are all on sale in the Centre and the Dingle book-shops and there is some consensus that O'Sullivan's book is one of the more enjoyable texts. ■ *T9156444. Easter-Jun, and Sep-Oct, daily 1000-1800; Jul and Aug, daily, 1000-1900. €3.10. Dúchas site. Self-service restaurant.*

B *An Portán*, T9156212. At the junction on the main road where one turns off for *Kruger's*. B&B. **B** *Caitlín Firtéar*, Coumeenoole, T9156120. Farmhouse charging around €45.71/31.11 for en-suite rooms and €40.63/28.57 sharing a bathroom. **B** *Kruger's*, Dunquin, T9156127. This famous pub has 7 beds charging €20.32 per person but they are not worth writing home about and bathroom facilities are shared. **D** *Dún Chaoin*, T9156145/9156121, F9156355. An Óige hostel on the main road near *Kruger's* and enjoying a wonderful view of the sea.

Sleeping
*Price codes:
see inside front cover*

At Ventry, west of Dingle on the Slea Head route, *The Skipper* restaurant, T9159900, offers a rare deal in Ireland – good food at affordable prices. Genuine French-style cui-sine for lunch and dinner, and an early-bird dinner between 1800 and 1930. Bar food is available at *Kruger's* and just up the road *An Portán*, T9156212, has a menu of fish and meat dishes in Gaelic, subtitled in English, but only opens for dinner between 1900 and 2200; expect to pay around €26 for a meal. They also provide the lunches that are available at the self-service restaurant in the *Great Blasket Centre*. The *Dunquin Pot-tery and Café* serves soups, savouries and home-baked goodies.

Eating

On the main road just past *Dunquin Louis Mulcahy Pottery*, T9156229, has 2 floors devoted to ceramic items for the home, ranging from egg cups to huge lamps. The designs are very attractive and distinctive and overseas delivery is regularly arranged for the larger items.

Shopping

Great Blasket Island

This whale-shaped and marooned-looking island is the largest of a group of islands off the coast near Dunquin A trip across Blasket Sounds to view the remains of the island's village and to walk to its western end is a highlight of any visit to Kerry. It also has one of the best beaches anywhere in the county, *An Trágh Bhán*, outstanding for its cleanliness and the sheltered location, which makes it safe for swimming.

*Colour map 3,
grid B1*

The island is now uninhabited, though in summer there is a small café and a craft shop. Boats, departing from Dunquin every half-hour, can only make the crossing in fine weather. Visitors are free to camp any-where on the island; but choose a shel-tered spot. ■ *Boats to the island: T9156422. From 1000 onwards, €18 return. Moran's in Dingle, T2753333, run a daily bus to the Dunquin pier at 0915, returning at 1700.*

Great Blasket Island

Pier

(231m)

Slievedonagh
(281m)

Croaghmore
(292m)

N

0 miles   1
0 km   1

Inishvickillane and Tearaght Islands

These two islands also belong to the Blasket group and, though neither can be visited by the public, they still have a remarkable presence for anyone

☞ An anarchist society – with a king!

Life on the Blasket Islands consisted of a self-sufficient community of farming families who lived peacefully without a government, a priesthood or a police force, but at some time or other the notion of a monarchy crept in and the islanders took up the practice of electing a notional king from amongst themselves.

The earliest records document families living on the island around 1700, and they were very healthy indeed, only falling sick if they left to go to the mainland. In 1821 there were 128 islanders, rising to 153 before the Famine, which seems not to have been as catastrophic as elsewhere, probably because their diet was not so dependent on the potato. Fishing had always been an important source of food, supplemented by rabbits, seabirds and their eggs.

The difficulty of landing on the island – readily apparent even today – helped preserve their independent way of life, and stories have been told of how the women of the island bombarded landing bailiffs with rocks from the cliffs above as they tried to get ashore. In the early 20th century a school was established, and a post office in the 1930s, but by 1953 there were only 22 inhabitants. The death in 1952 of a young man simply because the weather prevented him reaching hospital in time, helped the government decide the following year to offer mainland homes to the remaining islanders.

walking west on the Great Blasket. Inishvickillane is the one furthest to the southwest; it is partly visible from the mainland, but a clear view of it opens up from the western end of Great Blasket. The whole island was purchased by Charles Haughey, a one-time taoiseach of Ireland who 'forgot' being given a huge sum of money (€279,000) by a businessman in 1972, and he still occasionally visits his island by helicopter. The smaller island to the north of Inishvickillane is Inishnabro.

Tearaght Island is the small westernmost craggy island to the northwest of Great Blasket, distinguished from Inishtooskert, which is closer to Great Blasket, by its lighthouse on the southern side. Tearaght supports large colonies of storm petrels and Manx shearwaters.

Ballyferriter

Phone code: 066
Colour map 3, grid B1

The road from Dunquin continues on to Ballyferriter (*Baile an Fheirtearaigh*), a small village that would be well worth considering as an alternative accommodation base to Dingle if only there were more choice of places to stay. The serene beauty of the surrounding landscape, the closeness of the Gallarus Oratory and other sites, plus the nearby lovely Wine Strand beach are all good reasons to linger in the area. The beach, a few 100 yds north of Ballyferriter, is safe for swimming and is usually well sheltered from the wind. The village is named after Pierce Ferriter (c.1600-53), a love poet and soldier whose Norman ancestors had settled the Dingle Peninsula, and whose participation in the 1641 rebellion led to his hanging in Killarney. JM Synge, the playwright, came to Ballyferriter in 1905 to polish up his Irish.

Ballyferriter Museum A modest little museum devoted to local history and culture and covering topics like the Ogham alphabet, cross slabs and promontory forts. *T9156333. Easter and Jun to Sep, daily 1000-1700. €2.*

Dún An Óir Fort In 1580, in support of the Desmond rebellion, a party of Italians and Spaniards landed in the bay just north of Ballyferriter and established themselves

County Kerry

in a fort that had been built earlier by Irish rebels. While waiting for reinforcements they were besieged by the English under Lord Grey. After three days the fort surrendered and some 700 soldiers and a score or so of Irish were cold-bloodedly and systematically butchered by groups of executioners. Edmund Spenser, the English poet who wrote *The Faerie Queene*, was secretary to Grey at the time and was almost certainly present at the massacre. Grey was later recalled to England, but Spenser, who stayed to live on in Ireland, remained a hearty supporter of the methods used to suppress the rebellion. The stone sculpture near the remains of the fort commemorates those who died. The beauty of the location is rendered melancholy by the haunting memory of what occurred here. ■ *Going west from Ballyferriter, after less than a mile turn right at the brown sign pointing to Smerwick harbour. At the Y-junction bear right and right again at the T-junction; after 300 yds/m the fort is signposted left on a poorly surfaced road.*

C-D *Tigh An Phoist Hostel*, T9155109. IHH hostel outside of Ballyferriter, on the road to Ballydavid. Nearly 30 beds and 4 private rooms, and bicycles for hire. **D** *BlackCat Hostel*, in the village, T9156286. Has camping space with use of hostel facilities but no private rooms.

Sleeping
Price codes: see inside front cover

    Self-catering *Wine Strand Holiday Cottages*, T061-325125, F061-326450. Consists of modern self-catering cottages. Ideal for a long stay on the peninsula.

The café in the Ballyferriter Museum, open daily from 1000 to 1700, serves affordable hot meals like pork and chicken pie. Next to the post office, the *Tigh Pheig* pub (which under previous management astonished everyone by hosting topless dancers) serves food all day – lunch specials are posted on a blackboard – and at night main dishes are around €16 range. The pub opposite, *Tigh Uí Mhurchú*, is a quieter place, also serving lunch and dinner meals, and prices are reasonable. Next door, *Tis an Tobair*, T9156404, is a restaurant with dishes like courgette and coriander fritters with a red pepper tapenade.

Eating

Ancient and medieval sites

The first of these sites, Riasc, is just east of Ballyferriter on the road to Ballydavid and it is also the least engrossing, so if time is limited this is the one to skip. Excavations of the Riasc monastic site in the 1950s revealed that the ruins were built over an earlier site dating back to 400CE. The main attraction for visitors is a pillar stone inscribed with a cross and curling patterns typical of La Tène art; though this is an early Christian site, and La Tène decoration is mainly pre-Christian Celtic. ■ *24 hours. Free admission.*

Riasc

Of all the sites on the Dingle Peninsula, the Gallarus Oratory is the one you must not miss. Probably built between the ninth and 12th centuries as a place of prayer for monks, this beautifully crafted little hut, has stood intact without the aid of mortar for maybe 12 centuries. The seamless dry stone wall turns into a roof, and it is impossible to tell where the wall ends or the roof begins. The building method, known as corbelling, has each stone supporting another above it, which juts in beyond the perpendicular of the wall. As each stone also slopes slightly downwards, rain is kept out of the building by just running off. ■ *There is no admission charge to this Dúchas site, so feel free to ignore the nearby heritage centre which charges €2.54 for the predictable 15-minute audio-visual presentation. Signposted on the R599 road going east from Ballyferriter. Coming from Dingle, cross the bridge for the road west to*

Gallarus Oratory

County Kerry

St Brendan and Brandon Creek

Legend has it that St Brendan set out from here on the first transatlantic crossing in the sixth century. Brendan was born in 484, and as a young man travelled around Ireland, founding a monastery at Ardfert and building an oratory on Mount Brandon. His wanderlust went into a higher gear when he heard about a wonderful island far to the west of Ireland, and taking 14 monks with him, he set out in a curragh to find the place. An early port of call was an island that turned out to be the back of a whale but after seven years – with stops at what might have been Greenland, Iceland and Newfoundland – he finally reached

America. He returned safely to Ireland and died in 578. Improbable as this voyage sounds, Tim Severin showed in 1976 that it could be done. With a group of friends he built a similar boat and reached Newfoundland after a 13-month, 3,000-mile journey.

Coming from Dingle, cross the bridge for the road west to Ventry and Dunquin and take the first right that heads north to Murreagh (An Mhuiríoch). Just before Murreagh turn right for the village of An Bóthar Bui, carry on north to Dooneen Pier and follow the road until it ends at Brandon Creek (Cuas an Bhodaigh).

Ventry and Dunquin and take the first right for 3 miles (5 km) before bearing left at the Y-junction for the Oratory and Ballyferriter.

Kilmalkedar Church This Romanesque church is thought to date from the 12th century and seems to represent a transitional stage in architecture between the corbelling of the Gallarus Oratory and a tiled roof, as part of the roof remains is similar in style to the oratory. An interesting feature of the church is the design over the doorway: the tympanum has a head on one side and an imaginary animal on the other. The remains of other monastic buildings are in the vicinity including **Brendan's House**, a two-storey medieval building, and there is an Ogham stone in the church graveyard. The road between the church and Brendan's House is the beginning of the Pilgrim's Way, the traditional route to the summit of Mount Brandon. ■ *From Ballyferriter: take the R559 road eastward at Murreagh (heading south back to Dingle); the church is on the left side of the road about a mile (1.6 km) east of Murreagh. Coming from Dingle: cross the bridge for the road west to Ventry and Dunquin and take the first right for 3 miles (5 km) before bearing right at the Y-junction for Kilmalkedar Church.*

Cloghane and Mount Brandon

Phone code: 066
Colour map 3,
grid B1 & B2

Cloghane might make a pleasant alternative to staying at *An Bóthar* in Brandon Creek. It is a good base for the many walks around Mount Brandon and Brandon Ridge.

Sleeping & eating
Price codes:
see inside front cover

B *O'Connor's*, T7138113, is a pub and B&B, open Mar-Oct. Pub food and evening meals for guests are available. Further along the street is **C-D** *Mount Brandon House*, T7138299, www.mountbrandonhostel An IHO hostel with en-suite dormitory rooms and some family rooms. Next door is *Tigh Tomsi*, a pub owned by the same people with pub food and live music in summer. A local B&B that caters for walkers is **B** *Abhain Mhor*, T7138211. Both O'Connor's and Abhain Mhor have details of walks in the area. There is a small shop opposite Tigh Tomsi's.

County Kery

Climbing Mount Brandon

It takes about six hours to climb of Mount Brandon (952 m) and the place to start from is outside the local information office in Cloghane, T7138277/7138137. Mount Brandon has been appropriated by Christianity, but the pilgrim trail known as the saint's road, which goes from Cloghane to Faha, at the foot of the mountain, has pagan Celtic origins. Anyway, after reaching the grotto at Faha there is a walking trail marked by red and white poles that leads you gently on your journey. Gradually, after passing a series of small lakes, the route becomes rockier and after crossing a river it starts to zig-zag in a steep ascent. The views at the top should provide ample compensation for the sore muscles that might make themselves felt the next day.

Camp, Castlegregory and the Connor Pass

As you travel to the Dingle Peninsula from Tralee, the road heads west to the village of Camp – which is strung out along the road and characterized only by a couple of pubs – where a fork in the road leads either southwest to Annascaul or straight on along the northern coast of the peninsula to Cloghane and the Connor Pass. Before reaching Cloghane, a right turn off the road leads to the Castlegregory Peninsula and the village of Castlegregory (*Caisleán Ghriare*) itself. The village offers little else than a place to stay and eat, but the peninsula and its beaches attract holiday-makers and there are a number of caravan and camping sites. Far better to stay on the road to Cloghane where Fermoyle Beach is a lovely stretch of sand, safe for swimming and safe for cars, which can be driven onto it.

Phone code: 066
Colour map 3, grid B3

The Connor Pass connects Cloghane with Dingle and at 1,496 ft (456 m) the pass offers spectacular views of both Mount Brandon and Dingle to the south. The car-park at the summit is clogged with cars during the summer months.

AL *Crutch's Country House*, T7138116, macshome@iol.ie Tucked away off the main road and conveniently close to Fermoyle Beach, this hotel has good-sized bedrooms with sea views and a laid-back atmosphere. **A** *Barnagh Bridge*, Camp, T7130145, bbguest@eircom.net A guesthouse, which avoids looking like the standard bungalow B&B. Floral-patterned bedrooms, a breakfast room with glorious views of Tralee Bay and a morning menu of smoked salmon, home-baked breads and other alternatives to fried food. Coming from Tralee, it is 1 mile on the left after taking the Connor Pass/Castlegregory road. **B** *The Fuschia House*, West Main St, Castlegregory, T7139508. Stone-fronted B&B with a reputation for good food at the breakfast table; dinner can be arranged for under €20. **B** *Strand View House*, Connor Pass Rd, Kilcummin, T7138131, strandview@eircom.net A quality B&B, hard to miss on the main road, overlooking the bay. **D** *Connor Pass Hostel*, Stradbally, T7139179. On the main road, a very basic hostel but including 3 private rooms.

Sleeping
*Price codes:
see inside
front cover*

Camping At Castlegregory both *Green Acres Caravan Park*, T7139158, and *Sandybay Caravan Park*, T7139338, accept campers.

At Camp *The Junction Bar* serves light snacks throughout the day and there is a pool room and dart board for rainy afternoons, while *The Railway Tavern*, T7130188, may have music sessions on Sun evenings. The best food is at *Ashes Restaurant & Bar*, either the pub food or the dinner menu.

Eating, pubs & music

In Castlegregory, *O'Riordan's Cafe*, T7139379, has more to offer than the name suggests. As well as tasty home-cooked snacks and light meals there is an enlightened menu that offers non-meat eaters something other than a revolting lasagne made from frozen vegetables, as well as local seafood, Kerry lamb and beef in Guinness. Open

County Kerry

daily, Jun–Sep, from 1200 to 2100; around €8 for lunch and around €15 for dinner. **Ned Natterjack's**, T7139491,West End, Castlegregory, is a family-friendly pub with garden seating that serves good food throughout the day and livens up on a Sat night with live music. **Ferriter's Loft**, T7139494, is a pub serving steaks, seafood and burgers and evening sessions of traditional music.

The Dingle Way

The Kerry Way is scenically stunning and the Beara Way is wild and empty, but the Dingle Way has touches of both and the largest variety of walks and the most fun things to do when not walking. From miles of empty sandy beaches to fossil-clad cliffs to long mountainside paths and a stiff climb up Mount Brandon this Way has so much to offer it seems a waste that anyone should leave the area not having walked for at least a couple of days.

To complete the Dingle Way requires about seven or eight days:
Day 1: Tralee to Camp 12 miles (19 km)
Day 2: Camp to Annascaul 10½ miles (17 km)
Day 3: Annascaul to Dingle 14 miles (22 km)
Day 4: Dingle to Dunquin 14 miles (22 km)
Day 5: Dunquin to Ballydavid 15 miles (24 km)
Day 6: Ballydavid to Cloghane 14 miles (22 km)
Day 7: Cloghane to Castlegregory 14 miles (22 km)
Day 8: Castlegregory to Tralee 14 miles (22 km)

Mapping   The Dingle Way is covered by the **Ordnance Survey** (OS) Discovery series sheets 70 and 71 and these are essential for the walks. *Cork-Kerry Tourism* produces a strip map for the Dingle Way, which is not essential but could be used in conjunction with the OS maps.

Day 1: Tralee to Camp

12 miles (19 km); 6 hrs; total ascent 410 ft (125m)

The walk begins on a road but does have the advantage of bringing you along the canal to Blennerville Windmill. Otherwise, catch a bus about two miles out of town to where the route leaves the main road and heads uphill. Be careful here, as the waymarker is skilfully disguised. The left turn off the main road is followed by a sharp right almost immediately. The route quickly finds the open hillside and rolls gaily along past boulder fields, over streams, by ancient waterworks, with the beauty of the hills to the left and the panoramic scene of the coastline below you. An added bonus is looking down at the vehicular traffic that looks like little Dinky toys scuttling about. The route follows the ditch between the fields and the upland pasture. Camp, the day's destination, is strung out along two or three miles of road, so if you are booking accommodation in advance – for example at *Daly's Bar* or the *Railway Tavern* (see 'Sleeping' on page 370) – enquire where exactly it is, since there are several places where you can leave the route.

Day 2: Camp to Annascaul

10½ miles (17 km); 6 hrs; total ascent 1,475 ft (450m)

The walk is largely along tarmac but the scenery more than makes up for the sore feet. The route crosses the peninsula, travelling through a low central valley inhabited only by sheep. Emerging on the southern coast it brings stunning views of the beach and sand dunes at Inch. Turning back inland, the

County Kerry

route goes uphill and crosses Ardroe and Maum, a saddle between two mountains. From here there are excellent views down into Annascaul Glen. At Annascaul, besides the two hostels mentioned in the Annascaul section below, there are some B&Bs, which include *Four Winds* and *Anchor House* (see 'Sleeping' on page 370 for details).

Day 3: Annascaul to Dingle

Another day largely on tarmac but with some good views, lots of antiquities to poke around in and a brilliant storm beach with huge boulders. Leaving Annascaul, the route travels via a minor road to the coast. For most of the day the route keeps close to, and high above, the southern coast, passing by the ruins of Minard castle, destroyed by Cromwell's armies, and an interesting old graveyard at Aglish where bodies are interred in stone mausoleums rather than buried in the ground. Lispole, a few miles east of Dingle, has the IHH *Seacrest Hostel* (see 'Sleeping on page 370). See also the Dingle section for accommodation in the town itself (page 359).

14 miles (22 km); 7 hrs; total ascent 1,312 ft (400m)

Day 4: Dingle to Dunquin

After a long, rather dull section of the walk on tarmac to Ventry the route takes off with a glorious walk around Ventry Harbour and then a cliff walk around the coast, with Mount Eagle looming to the landward across a landscape littered with clocháns and other ancient remains. The views are amazing along the last section and more than make up for the little bit of walking that is necessary along the main road. For accommodation and restaurants, see the Dunquin section on page 363.

This day's walk could be accomplished as a day trip from Dingle by catching the afternoon bus (1555, July and August only; 1825 Monday and Thursday only, all year) from Dunquin back to Dingle. Alternatively, with your own transport you could park at Ventry and have time to reach Dunquin and then walk back to Ventry by taking the short inland road across Coumaleagua Hill.

14 miles (22 km); 7 hrs; total ascent 1,150 ft (350m)

Day 5: Dunquin to Ballydavid

A long wonderful day's walk around Slea Head, first climbing the lower slopes of Croaghmartin and then dropping down to Clogher Beach where there are huge (and dangerous) waves and ancient fossils of ferns and shelled creatures in the rocks at the northern end of the beach. Beyond Clogher the route travels for a time along tarmac roads to Smerwick Harbour, where it follows the line of the shore as far as Ballydavid. From there, another spell on tarmac along a desolate windswept road brings you to Brandon Creek where there are some B&Bs. The best place to stay, the *An Bóthar* pub and restaurant, is very comfortable and has live music most nights in summer (for details, see 'Sleeping' on page 370).

15 miles (24 km); 8 hrs; total ascent 656 ft (200m)

Day 6: Ballydavid to Cloghane

Of the many amazing walks that this peninsula has to offer, this has to be the best. The walk starts with a long, challenging walk up to a saddle of Mount Brandon with the most amazing views behind, growing more panoramic the higher you climb. Over the saddle the descent is rapid and the path runs past more stunning views, but to the north this time. On a fine day the coastline

14 miles (22 km); 8 hrs; total ascent 2,640 ft (750m)

County Kerry

Natterjack toads

Visitors flock daily to Dingle to catch sight of one socially maladjusted dolphin (naturally gregarious creatures living in large communities) when Kerry's real zoological treat lies croaking very loudly on the north side of the peninsula near Castlegregory. The natterjack is Ireland's only toad, looking like a frog but darker and with a yellow stripe along its spine. If you lurk around Lough Gill at night with a torchlight you should be able to see one during the mating season between April and June. Their blaring croaks attract females, but the male will launch itself on the first fellow natterjack spotted until a female catch has been confirmed and mating can proceed. The male is possessive, and determined to prevent anyone else from mating with his betrothed, and the poor female remains encumbered by the male clutching her around the abdomen until she is ready to spawn. This encourages her to spawn as soon as she can, up to 4,000 eggs at a time.

around Sauce Creek looks as if it has been painted on. The Way carries on through a country park area on wide stony tracks and then through Brandon village before following the coast around to Cloghane. For accommodation, see the Cloghane section on page 366.

Day 7: Cloghane to Castlegregory

14 miles (22 km); 6 hrs

After a few miles of tarmac the route meets the beach and spends the rest of the day following the coastline around Fahamore and into the village of Castlegregory. The beach is usually quite empty with occasional anglers fishing for plaice in the surf. The beach is wide and firm and makes a great walk, even at high tide when there is always some sand still exposed. It passes Stradbally where the church ruins and the wildlife sanctuary at Lough Gill can be explored. There are more ruins at Kilshannig at the end of the peninsula. Castlegregory has B&Bs as well as the hostel listed in the Castlegregory section on page 367.

Day 8: Castlegregory to Tralee

14 miles (22 km), 6 hrs; total ascent 900 ft (275m)

After walking along the shoreline, the route meets the main road and then the outward leg of Day 1, which you follow in reverse back to Tralee. The first part of the walk is well worth the effort and the hillwalk back to Tralee is just as pretty as it was on the way out but, if you don't like backtracking, the Annascaul to Tralee bus can be hailed. There is a daily bus from Dingle, and two buses from Castlegregory to Tralee on Fridays only. Check in Castlegregory for times. For accommodation, see the Tralee section on page 352.

Sleeping
Price codes: see inside front cover

Daly's Bar, Camp, T7130125. In the village, with en-suite rooms at €19.05 per person sharing. *The Railway Tavern*, Camp, T7130188. On the main road to Tralee a little out of the village, and has en-suite rooms. **C-D** *An Bóthar*, Brandon Creek, T9155342. Pub and restaurant, also offering accommodation. About half a mile inland, this pub caters to walkers and can organize packed lunches and walks in the area.

County Clare

10

County Clare

*From the sublime to the absurd, Clare has much to offer
the visitor. Sublime is the majestic, almost frightening
beauty of the **Burren**, with its sulky grey limestone hills
and abundance of wild flowers; the absurd is the tourist
ghetto of **Bunratty Castle** with students dressed up in
daft clothes to pay for next year's college and coachloads of
the gullible disgorging at a rate that almost comes close to
Killarney in August. In between are **ancient tower
houses** lurking in fields, mighty **dolmens** and **ring forts**,
medieval **church ruins**, the terrifying **Cliffs of Moher**, a
hippy musical centre at Doolin, the seasoned tourist
villages of **Lisdoonvarna** and **Ballyvaughan**, and the
long caravan-dotted western coast from Lahinch, where
the Atlantic surf crashes ashore to **Loop Head**.*

County Clare

Ins and outs

Getting there   **Shannon Airport** is in eastern Clare, 17 miles (27 km) from Ennis, and is a major entry point for many travellers. It's a transatlantic airport with direct flights from a number of US cities, some of which continue on to Dublin. There are also direct flights to London as well as other cities in England and the rest of Europe. During the summer there is an extensive charter programme from many European destinations, Most visitors will move on to Limerick, 15 miles (24 km) away, from where there are connections by bus and rail to other parts of Ireland but Ennis (also 15 miles/24 km away) and the rest of County Clare are an equally good route to take from Shannon. Flights to other parts of Ireland are run by *Aer Lingus*, T061-471666. There are frequent buses from the airport to Ennis, Bunratty and Limerick, T061-474311 for times. *Bus Eireann* also has services from Shannon to Galway and Dublin. There is a café and a restaurant at the airport as well as a **tourist information** desk, T061-471664, which will make bookings. Opening hours match arrival times. A *Bank of Ireland* counter operates similar times. For flight information, T061-715494.

Getting around   There are **buses** to Ennis several times a day from Shannon Airport, Galway, Dublin, Cork and Limerick. **Trains** link Ennis with Limerick, from where there are connections to Cork, Waterford and Dublin. If you are travelling between Clare and Kerry there is the Killimer-Tarbert **ferry**, a useful way of saving a long drive round the coast to Limerick. The ferry crosses at half-hourly intervals, takes about 20 mins, and costs €11 per vehicle (details under Transport below). **Car hire** is available at the airport from *Avis*, T061-471094; *Budget*, T061-471361; *Dooley*, T061-471098; *Hertz*, T061-471369; *Johnson & Perrot*, T061-471094; *Murrays*, T061-701200; *National*, T061-472633.

Ennis

Phone code: 065
Colour map 3,
grid A4

Bursting at the seams, this 11th-century market town is the major shopping area for the villages around it as well as a major summer tourist destination. Its narrow streets groan under the weight of modern traffic and O'Connell, towering over the lot of it in the centre of town, must be wondering whatever happened. But it's a pleasant little town with an amazing amount of really good traditional music in the summer months and a few places to keep you busy. Better still, use Ennis as a base for visiting east Clare before moving on to the real highlight of the county – The Burren.

Ins & outs   Getting there and around Ennis is easily walkable. *Bus Éireann* runs limited summer services to towns in west and north Clare. From Lisdoonvarna a connection can be made with the Galway to Tralee bus which goes via the Killimer-Tarbert ferry.

     The **tourist office** is on Arthur's Row, T6828366. Open Jul-Aug, Mon-Sat 0900-1800; Sep-Jun, Mon-Sat 0930-1730.

Sights   Ennis is a compact little town bisected by the river Fergus. It has expanded south of the original heart of the city, which is around the **Friary** in Abbey Street. Established in the 13th century by the O'Briens, kings of Thomond, the Friary now stands in a state of beautiful ruin. What you see is largely 14th-century, with the beautiful east window with its fine thin mullions between the lancet windows dating back to the original building. In the 14th century there was a large school here with 600 pupils and about 350 friars. The west end of the church is probably 15th century. On the southwest face

★

Things to do in County Clare

- Take a tour of **Ailwee Cave** to see the giant bear prints
- Admire **Maire Rua's house** on the road from Ennis to Ballyvaughan
- Enjoy the **music** in Ennis and Doolin
- Take part in the **matchmaking festival** at Lisdoonvarna
- Relax in a hot sulphur bath at the **Spa Wells** in Lisdoonvarna
- Walk in the karst scenery of **The Burren**
- Eat chocolate pudding and take in the skyscapes at **Ballinalacken Castle Hotel**

of the tower is a carving of St Francis showing the stigmata. Inside the tower is a carving of the Virgin and child and at the east end of the south wall is the ornately carved McMahon tomb, which depicts a bishop giving benediction, and scenes of the arrest and crucifixion of Christ, all dating to around 1475. On the east side is the figure of a woman, thought to be More Ni Brien, the woman who founded the tomb.

The Friary was the last school of Catholic study to survive the Reformation. Franciscans came and went through the 17th century, as the buildings gradually decayed and the school dissolved. It was deserted by the end of the 17th century. ■ *Abbey St, T29100. Apr-May, Tue-Sun, 1000-1700; Jun-mid Sep, daily, 1000-1800; Mid Sep-Oct, Tue-Sat, 1000-1700. €1.20. Duchas. Guided tours available on request.*

The *Riches of Clare* exhibition at the **Clare Museum** adjoins the tourist office. From stone axes to Clare-born JPHooland's contribution to the development of the submarine. ■ *Arthur's Row, T6823382. Jan-Feb, Mon-Fri, 0930-1300 and 1400-1730; Mar-May, Mon-Sat, 0930-1300 and 1400-1730; Jun-Sep, daily, 0930-1730; Oct-Dec, Mon-Sat, 0930-1300 and 1400-1730. Last admission 1630. €5.*

Sleeping
■ *on map*
Price codes:
see inside
front cover

LL-L *Woodstock Hotel*, Shanaway Rd, T6846600, www.woodstockhotel.com A golf course with a hotel, 1 mile (1.6 km) out of town on the Lahinch Rd, with all the expected amenities. **L-AL** *Auburn Lodge Hotel*, Galway Rd, T6821247, www.irishcourthotels.com Another big, golf-orientated, conference type of place redeemed by its garden, 1 mile (1.6 km) out of town on the Galway Rd. Live traditional music nightly in the bar. **L-AL** *Old Ground Hotel*, O'Connell St, T6828127, www.flynnhotels.com In the centre of Ennis, this lovely ivy-clad building has been receiving travellers since the 18th century and modern improvements have not diminished the appeal of this graceful establishment. **AL** *Magowna House Hotel*, Inch, Kilmaley, T6839009, www.magowna.com A small hotel set in large grounds, 4 miles (6.4 km) west of Ennis but good value. Bar, restaurant, drying facilities for walkers.

A *Fountain Court*, Lahinch Rd, T6829845, www.fountain-court.com A 5-min drive from the town centre, this is a spruce guesthouse with kingsize beds, strong showers and a good choice of breakfast. **A** *Glencar Guesthouse*, Galway Rd, T6822348, www.glencar.ennis.ie This 12-bedroomed house is fine for a short stay and, with the *Auburn Lodge Hotel* next door, food, drink and music is a short walk away. **A** *Clonrush*, Lahinch Rd, T6829692, clonrushennis@eircom.net B&B with 4 en-suite rooms, on the N85, restaurant and bar nearby. **A** *Moyville*, Lahinch Rd, T6828278, moyville.ennis@ircom.net Dormer bungalow B&B with 4 en-suite rooms and the option of dinner for €17. **D** *Abbey Tourist Hostel*, Harmony Row, T6822620. Has a great location overlooking the river and single and double rooms.

County Clare

Eating

● on map
Price codes:
see inside
front cover

There are a few restaurants in town with an attitude so your nights here should be filled with good things to eat. In Abbey St, beside the Queen's Hotel is the old style *Cruises Pub & Restaurant*, T6841800, which serves interestingly cooked fish and meat in a traditional Irish style. *Brannagan's* at Mill Rd, T6820211, serves modern Irish steak and seafood at around €25 for dinner. The *O'Brien Room* at the grand *Old Ground Hotel* serves a mixture of traditional and innovative dishes, served largely to lunchtime eaters but doing dinner also. *Domaine Wine Bar*, River Lane Wood Quay, T68448844, is a tidy little wine bar serving Mediterranean-style food, wine by the glass and bottle, and a warehouse upstairs. Open until 2400 but closed on Sun.

In Parnell St is *Sicilian*, T6843873, serving pizzas and pasta dishes from 1700 to 2300. On the opposite side of the road is *Punjab*, T6844655, serving Indian food.

Several of the pubs do good lunchtime food at very reasonable prices, around €7. Further along Abbey St is *Cloisters* bar and restaurant, T6840011, where there is bar food till late, but the restaurant needs a reservation and can set you back €35. Along O'Connell St are 2 pubs doing very good bar food, *Brogan's* , at number 24, T6829859, has menu of chicken curry, Irish stew, and fish, in pleasant environment. Just along the road at number 70 is *Brandon's Bar*, T6828133, with a similar menu.

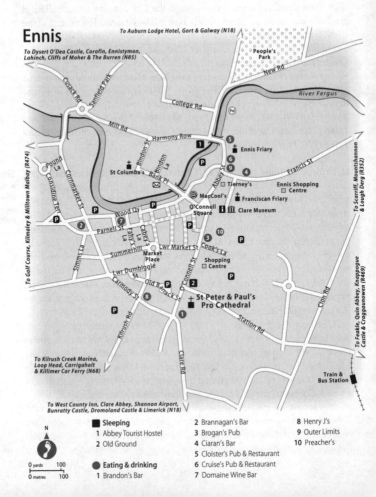

County Clare

Ennis

To Auburn Lodge Hotel, Gort & Galway (N18)

To Dysert O'Dea Castle, Corofin, Ennistymon,
Lahinch, Cliffs of Moher & The Burren (N85)

People's
Park

River Fergus

New Rd

College Rd

Mill Rd

Harmony Row

Ennis Friary

St Columba's

Bank Pl.

Francis St

Tierney's

Ennis Shopping
Centre

MacCool's

Franciscan Friary

O'Connell
Square

Clare Museum

Wood Qy

Parnell St

Summerhill

Lwr Market St

Cook's La

Market
Place

Shopping
Centre

Lwr Dumbiggle
St

Old B. rack St

St Peter & Paul's
Pro Cathedral

Station Rd

To Scariff, Mountshannon
& Lough Derg (R352)

To Feakle, Quin Abbey, Knappogue
Castle & Craggaunowen (R469)

To Golf Course, Kilmaley & Milltown Malbay (R474)

To Kilrush Creek Marina,
Loop Head, Carrigaholt
& Killimer Car Ferry (N68)

To West County Inn, Clare Abbey, Shannon Airport,
Bunratty Castle, Dromoland Castle & Limerick (N18)

Train &
Bus Station

N

0 yards   100
0 metres   100

■ Sleeping
1 Abbey Tourist Hostel
2 Old Ground

● Eating & drinking
1 Brandon's Bar

2 Brannagan's Bar
3 Brogan's Pub
4 Ciaran's Bar
5 Cloister's Pub & Restaurant
6 Cruise's Pub & Restaurant
7 Domaine Wine Bar

8 Henry J's
9 Outer Limits
10 Preacher's

This is where Ennis shines as a place to visit. Most pubs and the hotels have some kind of live music, usually traditional Irish. *Cruises* has live traditional music every night all year round, *Ciarán's*, 1 Francis St, T6840181, has live traditional music Thu-Sun from Jun-Oct, while *Paddy Quinn's*, 7 Market St, T6828148, has music every Sat night. Other pubs with at least 1 night of Irish music are *P.J. Kelly's*, Carmody St, T6828155 (Sat and Sun), *Preacher's* in the *Temple Gate Hotel*, T6823300 (Sat), Sessions start late so if you can't find any music on, take a cruise around town and listen, or just wait where you are. At *Cois na hAhna* in Galway Rd, T6822347, on Tue throughout the year at 2030 there are ceili dancing sessions. *Maoin Cheoil an Chláir*, T6841774, is a school of traditional music, which often puts on concerts.

Pubs, clubs & music

Other pubs have country and western music or tribute bands. For these you could try *Brannagan's*, *Darcy's Corner* in Upper O'Connell St, the *Porter Stall* in Market St or *Henry J's Cocktail Bar* in Upper Market St. Ennis also has nightclubs: *The Sanctuary* and the *Outer Limits* are in the *Queen's Hotel*, while *Central Park* in Brannagan's and *The Boardwalk* at *Brandon's* in O'Connell St are also worth a look.

Among the many festivals and events that take place in Ennis each year, 2 are worth looking out for – the *Fleadh Nua*, a traditional music festival usually held around the last week in **May** (T6828366 for details) and the *Ennis Arts Festival*, held in **Oct** (T6820166 for information). There is another, less well known traditional music festival around the middle of **Nov** (T6828366 for information).

Festivals

Fishing *ME Tierney Cycles and Fishing*, 17 Abbey St, T6829433.

Sport

Bus Bus Eireann station is by the train station in Station Rd, T6824177. First bus to Shannon Airport leaves at 0835 and they continue to depart regularly until 2305. Daily buses also to **Adare**, **Athlone** via **Galway**, **Ballina**, **Belfast**, **Castlebar**, **Cork**, **Derry**, **Donegal**, **Dublin**, **Galway**, **Killarney**, **Limerick**, **Tralee** and **Waterford**. A daily bus for **London**, via **Rosslare** and **Dublin**, departs Ennis at 1520. **Car** Car hire: *TMT Rentals*, 70 O'Connell St, T6824212. **Car parks**: in Abbey St, Parnell St, Temple gate and The Friary. **Ferry** The Killimer-Tarbert ferry daily, from Killimer on the hr, 0700-2100 (0900 Sun) Apr-Sep; Oct-Mar, 0700-1900 (1000 Sun). From Tarbert on the ½ hr, Apr-Sep, 0730-2130 (0930 Sun); Oct-Mar, 0730-1930 (1030 Sun) T9053124. **Taxi** *Abbey Taxis*, T6822646. *Banner Taxis*, T6821021. **Train** Trains to **Dublin** and other main cities from Ennis Railway Station, Station Rd, T6840444

Transport

Banks and bureaux de change Most of the banks are around O'Connell Sq. The tourist office and post office can also change money. **Communications** Post office: Bank Pl, T6821054. Mon-Fri 0900-1730, Sat 0930-1300. Internet: *MacCools Internet Café*, Brewery Lane, T6821988. , O'Connell St.

Directory

Around Ennis

Using Ennis as a base there are several sites of interest to the north and south of the town. The N18 south to Limerick is worth avoiding if you are cycling the suggested route east to Quin and Craggaunowen and Knappogue avoids the worst of it, although if you want to see Bunratty, part of it is unavoidable. Dysert O'Dea to the north can be done in a day from Ennis or taken in en route to the Burren.

Phone code: 061

A building of some kind has stood on this site since the 13th century when a church here was burned and replaced with a De Clare castle, part of the towers of which still survive here. In 1236 the castle was sacked by warring Irish clans and the castle replaced by another church, the restored version of which you

Quin Abbey
Colour map 3, grid A4

County Clare

see before you. If you think about it, quite a lot of murdering must have taken place on this site over the centuries. Hopefully, the Franciscans brought a bit of peace to the place. The ruins are very beautiful and well preserved and you can climb the tower and look down over the cloisters, which are some of the best preserved in Ireland. Inside the church are some 15th and 16th century tombstones. The little church on the other side of the river is 13th century. The nearby village of Quin is famous for the discovery of a huge hoard of gold, some of which found its way to the National Museum in Dublin. ■ *Jun-Sep, daily. Free. From near the train and bus station, take the R469 road from Ennis*

Knappogue Castle From Quin Abbey travel 2 miles (3.2 km) south on the L31 and you come to Knappogue Castle, a medieval castle built by Sean McNamara in 1467, which somehow never fell into ruin. It has a long history and probably owes its intactness to the fact that Cromwell used it as a headquarters rather than blow it up, which is what he did to any other place that could be fortified. The ground floor additions are 19th-century. If you like that sort of thing you can attend a medieval banquet there and listen to stories about women in Irish myth and history. ■ *Banquets, €40+. Apr-early Oct, daily, 1730 and 2045. Freephone, T1800-269811 to book. Castle: Apr-Oct, daily, 1000-1800. Last admission 1700. €3.81*

Craggaunowen This, another medieval tower house built by the family that built Bunratty Castle, is the basis for another heritage project. The castle itself is home to a series of 16th-century European woodcarvings, part of the Hunt Collection, most of which is in Limerick. The grounds of the castle hold reproductions of a *crannog* (a house built on to an artificial island in a lake), a ring fort and an outdoor cooking place. Young people, dressed in Celtic outfits practise making objects using ancient tools. There is also a genuine Iron Age road-way brought from a bog in County Longford. The most interesting exhibit there, in a glasshouse designed by Liam McCormack who has had a hand in so many Irish cathedrals, is the *Brendan*, a boat built and sailed across the Atlantic by Tim Severin in 1976. The boat is based on descriptions of the kind used by St Brendan to cross the Atlantic and was built and successfully sailed in an effort to prove that St Brendan's journey was possible (see box on page 366). Its hull is made from tanned oxhides stretched over an ash frame. ■ *Open Apr-Oct, daily, 1000-1800. Last admission 1700. €6.35. Tea-shop, guided tours, picnic area.*

Bunratty Castle From Cratloe you can head back towards Ennis on the N18 to come to Bunratty Castle. This is the leprechaun and shillelagh version of the Ulster American Folk Park in Northern Ireland, which is surprising since the castle is quite genuine and so are several of the buildings in the Folk Park. The cas-tle was built in 1460 (1425 in some versions of the story) by MacNamaras and later came into the possession of the O'Briens who held it until 1712. During the English civil war and Cromwell's invasion of Ireland it was held by the republican forces. What you see is the keep, the main building of the castle, which would have been well inside a curtain wall. Some time after 1712 the keep fell into ruins, which were then bought by Lord Gort in 1954 and restored. Very little of the renovations are invention or guesswork and the furnishing inside are quite genuine. The same for the village street and different styles of houses and their contents in the park, yet somehow it all has that air of Disneyland about it. Perhaps it's the gift shop, or the girls in period dress. Anyway, ignore the tour bus groups, dodge the group photos,

County Clare

squeeze through the crowd buying totally unrelated tea towels in the gift shop and have a good look round the old houses. They are a fascinating insight into a bygone, but still almost tangible, age. ■ *T061-360788. Open Sep-May, daily 0930-1730, last entry 1645; Jun-Aug, daily 0900-1830, last entry 1745. Last entry to castle 1600 all year. Closed Good Fri and 24-16 Dec. €5. Banquets daily 1730 and 2045, €40+.*

A *Bunratty Grove*, Bunratty, T369579. A large purpose-built guesthouse, a short drive from the castle. There are 2 good places to enjoy good food. One is *Durty Nelly's*, T364861, near the castle, a famous old pub with 2 restaurants to suit different budgets, and bar food, and managing to retain some dignity amidst the tourist clamour; live music on Mon and Tue in summer, and Thu all year round. *Muses Restaurant*, Bunratty, T364082, a short walk from the village green and, though unprepossessing outside, the food is above average.

Sleeping, eating, pubs & music

North to the Burren

Travelling north of Ennis on the R476 brings you to Dysert O'Dea, on the way to Corofin. This is a whole collection of ancient remains, the chief interest being the 1487 O'Dea Castle, which is now a museum. Cromwell's forces ruined the castle in 1651, but it was renovated in 1986 and has won a number of awards for its exhibitions on archaeology.

The actual dysert or anchorite church was founded some time in the eighth century by St Tola, after whom it was first named. What you see is a Romanesque ruin that has been reassembled, incorrectly in places. Particularly beautiful is the Romanesque doorway with carved geometric patterns and series of carved heads, human and animal. In the northwest of the site are the remains of a round tower built as a defence for the church property some time around the turn of the last millennium. The church and tower suffered the same fate as the castle in 1651. There is also a 12th-century high cross depicting the crucifixion and a bishop, and with geometric patterns and human and animal figures decorating the sides. The museum has a suggested walk around these sights and several other historic places in the area. ■ *Castle: open 1st May-30th Sep, daily, 1000-1800. T6837401. Café, shop. €4.*

Dysert O'Dea
Phone code: 065
Colour map 2, grid C1

This heritage centre is to be found in the village of **Corofin**, in a converted church. Inside are exhibitions on the Famine, emigration and living conditions in the 19th century as well as a room focusing on the 1798 uprising. It's a pleasant little place: no high-tech audio-visuals but lots of source materials. In the same building is a genealogical research centre where people with roots in Clare can search out their ancestors. ■ *Heritage centre, T6837955. Apr-Oct, daily 0930-1730. €3. Research centre:. Mon-Fri, 0900-1730; May-Sep, daily 0900-1730. www.clare.irishroots.net/*

Clare Heritage Centre

County Clare

Corofin has a good hostel, the **D** *Corofin Village Hostel*, Main St, T68537683. There are some family rooms as well as doubles. Camping in the grounds. B&Bs line the road to Kilfenora and Lisdoonvarna. The *Inchiquin Kitchen* serves bar food all day and has a beer garden, while the *Corofin Arms*, Main St serves food until 1900. You can hear traditional music there on Tue and Thu to Sun from around 2130. *Bofey Quins*, Main St, has one huge menu served in the bar and in the seafood restaurant. Main courses around €8. The really posh place to eat here is the *Le Catelinias*, Market St, T6837425 . Open Tue-Sat 1900-2130, Sun 1230-1430.

Sleeping, eating, drinking & music

The Burren

Phone code: 065
Colour map 2, grid C3

Leaving Corofin and heading north you enter the Burren (Boireann – 'a rocky place'), a strange, at times unearthly, looking place where it is difficult to imagine anyone could ever have eked out a living amongst the bare limestone rock. But eke they did since earliest times, as the hundreds of prehistoric sites in the area demonstrate. The 100 square miles of it is a little paradise for geologists, archaeologists, botanists and people with flashy cameras. It's also a great place for the inexpert traveller, with miles and miles of walking, brilliant views and some cute little villages where there is music, good food and good company.

Ins and outs

Getting there & around   From Ennis the best route into the Burren is via Corofin. From there a good way to proceed is towards Lisdoonvarna: it's a good place for a base and the journey is shockingly beautiful. If you are using public transport, **buses** (some of which are summer-only routes) travel from Limerick to Ennis and then through Inagh, Ennistymon, Lahinch, Doolin, Liscannor, the Cliffs of Moher to Lisdoonvarna and then on to Doolin, so this might make a better route around the Burren. The buses depart, Mon-Sat, at 1025, 1425 (25 Jun-Sep) and 1825; Sun at 1225 and 1955. There is also a 1500 and 2125 Mon-Sat bus to Ennistymon.

If you are heading straight to the Burren from outside Clare there are buses from Galway into various villages in the Burren, one of which connects with Tralee via the Killimer Tarbert ferry.

See transport under Doolin, page 386 for the **ferry** service between the Aran Islands and Doolin.

History

Since limestone is very high in nutrients plants flourished here, and after the last Ice Age these hills would have been covered in hazel scrub, pine and yew trees. Later, oak ash, and elm replaced them. It wasn't erosion that removed the trees but humans, arriving around 5,000 years ago and clearing the tops of the hills for farms, defence and places of worship. The earliest signs of humans are the huge dolmens dating back to 3000BCE. Later graves are smaller, the wedge tombs of around 1500BCE. By the Iron Age ring forts had started to be built, still on the tops of the hills, lived in by important men and surrounded by defensive stone walls. There are around 500 of these on the Burren. The 12th century gave us the church ruins and high crosses such as the one at Dysert O'Dea. The 15th century saw the building of the fortified houses such as Lemenagh Castle, where Maire Rua lived. Towns such as Lisdoonvarna or Doolin arrived much later some time in the 18th century. At that time the Burren was crowded with wood cabins thatched with mud, later replaced by stone buildings. Most of these are on the lower slopes of the hills, near to old butter roads or routes into the villages. The 19th century saw a vast reduction in the numbers of people living on the Burren. Death and emigration saw many people off and the trend has continued into the present day when finally as you walk around the hillsides, which are now bare of grazing animals, you can see, in the cracks in the limestone, blackthorn and hazel scrub building up again, creating a new forest until farming here becomes viable again.

County Clare

Máire Rua

Some women just get a bad press and Máire Rua is one of them. Máire O'Brien, neé Neylan from Ballynagowan was the wife of Conor O'Brien, the owner of Leamanagh Castle. Legend has it that she often accompanied her husband in his attacks on English settlers in the area. In 1651 Conor met Cromwell's forces in battle and was mortally wounded. Seeing his prostrate form being carried home Maire is said to have called out, rather callously, "We need no dead men here!" She nursed him all night until he died than promptly rode into Limerick and offered herself to any one of General Ireton's Cromwellian forces who would marry her. Her offer was taken up by a man called John Cooper, who lived to

regret it because she bumped him off along with 24 other unfortunate husbands. Her offer to Ireton was intended to secure her son's inheritance because she would have been driven out of her house otherwise. Other legends of her unladylike ways include hanging her servants out of the windows. She died the death she deserved: being entombed alive in a hollow tree.

In reality the house was occupied by Cromwell's troops until 1660, whether Máire was married to one of them or not. Her son, Donal, reclaimed the house in that year and found it ruined. He became the MP for Clare and served in that position for 20 years, to be followed centuries later by de Valera and Daniel O'Connell, who also held the job.

Geology

This area was the bed of a great sea 350 million years ago; its waters filled with tiny, shelled creatures and coral which, as they died, sank to the bottom. Aeons later mud and shale was dumped on top of the layer of shell, crushing it and forming limestone rock. Then the great upheaval that made the Swiss Alps and shook Ireland like a great rug into the huge folds of west Cork and Kerry threw up these lower hills. The erosion that rounded the tops of the Kerry mountains and removed the limestone from their tops removed the shale from the Burren, leaving great sheets of almost horizontal limestone bare to the elements. But limestone is highly soluble and the rain and ice filled cracks in the stone wearing them away and widening them so that what you see today looks like huge pieces of crazy paving with deep fissures. The Ice Ages further rounded and eroded the hills and left great lumps of granite rock abandoned as the meltwaters departed. You can see these huge incongruous boulders as you walk around the hills. Below the surface, underground cave systems were created by the water, which formed underground streams where it met harder, less soluble rock. In places caves collapsed, forming deep depressions in the rock above, called *turloughs*, which can fill with water when it rains and the land below becomes soaked.

Corofin to Lisdoonvarna

Continuing on the road to Lisdoonvarna brings you first to **Killinaboy Church**, a ruined 16th-century church up on the left-hand side of the road in a field. Not much to look at but worth the stop for the **Sheela-na-gig** over the south doorway. Next stop is **Leamanagh Castle**, rudely bursting out of a field beside the road to Ballyvaughan. The eastern side is a 14th-century fortified tower with a stone vault on the roof with gun emplacements. The rest of the building was a house added in the 1640s and lived in by various people, among them **Máire Rua**, one of Ireland's very wicked women. The castle is not accessible, being in a privately owned field whose owner has had to deal with visitors knocking his walls down, but there is a good view from the road.

Phone code: 065
Colour map 2,
grid C3

County Clare

Sleeping & eating
Price codes:
see inside front cover

AL *Clifden House*, Corofin, T/F6837692. Bed and breakfast at Clifden House has been recommended by a traveller praising the individuality of this mid-18th-century house. There are only 4 bedrooms, and dinner is served communally at 2000 (€32).

Kilfenora

Phone code: 065
Colour map 2, grid C3

This is a major part of the tour bus route around Clare. The **Cathedral** is probably one of the smallest you'll ever see, and it is still used for worship. The church was founded by St Fachtnan in the sixth century, replaced by a stone building, which was burned down in 1055 by an unfriendly O'Brien, rebuilt, destroyed in an accidental fire in 1100, rebuilt again and made into a bishopric in 1152, an event that you can see pictured on the Doorty High Cross (west of the church; the 12th-century equivalent of the Polaroid snap). It was never a popular place with bishops; Dr Richard Betts, offered the job by Charles I, said he had no wish to become bishop of the poorest see in Ireland.

The current building is a 13th-century site restructured in the 19th century. The chancel (the east end of the church where the altar was sited) has 13th- and 14th-century badly carved bishops on it and the north wall has a quite beautiful sedilia (a seat set into the wall) with delicate stone traceries on the three-arched design. Around the church and in a field to the west are the famous stone crosses.

The Burren

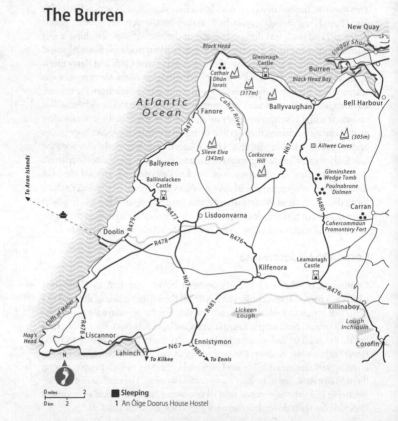

County Clare

Sleeping
1 An Óige Doorus House Hostel

Beside the church is the **Burren Centre**. It has information about the Burren, audio-visual displays and lots of people milling about. You'd be better off taking a walk around the Burren. ■ *Mar-May and Oct, daily, 1000-1700; Jun-Sep, daily, 0930-1800. €3. Café, shop.*

There's not much in the way of accommodation here. **A** *Carraig Liath*, on the R476 just outside of town, T7088075. This is a pleasant place that does an evening meal on request. **B** *Mrs Murphy*, Main St, T7088040. B&B in the village itself. **D** *Kilfenora Boghill Centre Hostel*, T7074644. A must for traditional music-loving vegans who don't mind dormitory accommodation. Great, big drawing room.

Sleeping & eating *Price codes: see inside front cover*

Entertainment is supplied by *Linane's*, which has traditional music every night in summer and *Nagle's*, which has music at weekends all year. *Vaughan's* T7088004, has traditional music, set dancing in the barn on Thu and Sun and pub food.

Entertainment

Lisdoonvarna

From Kilfenora a road leads to Lisdoonvarna, home of the famous song and the even more famous matchmakers. Until quite recently families would bring their daughters here in September, after the hay was in, to meet gentlemen, or, so they hoped, farmers. Nowadays the matchmaking festival is a good excuse for a party, with the various pubs in town, and around, each putting on events such as ballroom dancing, ceilidhs and live music. The month-long festival has a host of regular visitors, who come every year to see friends and enjoy the ballroom dancing. Midweek the party is good fun, at weekends it gets inevitably more inebriated and loud.

Phone code: 065 Colour map 2, grid C3

The town is a quiet and pleasant holiday destination for the rest of the year, another good place to consider as a base for your walks around the Burren, especially since the *Carrigan Hotel* organizes walking holidays and also has self-guided walks all over the Burren for its guests.

Lisdoonvarna's chief place of interest is the Spa Wells, Ireland's oldest and only working spa where the waters are drunk and bathed in. The water contains sulphur, iron, magnesium and iodine. The spa offers a sulphur bath, massage, wax treatments aroma therapy and reflexology: rates range from €15 for a massage or sulphur bath to €30 for an aromatherapy treatment. ■ *T7074023. Sulphur Hill, Lisdoonvarna.*

Spa Wells

Also in town is the Burren Smokehouse, on the Doolin Road where you can learn all about the traditional

Burren Smokehouse

County Clare

way of smoking salmon, try a bit and perhaps buy some. There is a shop and a pub, the *Roadside Tavern* where you can try locally smoked trout, salmon, mackerel and eel. ■ T7074303. Daily 0900-1900.

Sleeping
Price codes:
see inside
front cover

Lisdoonvarna has an inordinate number of hotels, most of which close down in the winter reducing the town to an empty shell. In summer they compete for custom and evening meals are competitively priced and really quite good. For all of the places listed here it is a good idea to book in advance if you intend to come in Sep.

L-A *Ballinalacken Castle Hotel*, Ballyvaughan Rd (if your budget stretches here!), T7074025, www.ballinlackencastle.com The views are stupendous and the rooms quaintly old fashioned and huge. Lovely big library, Victorian lobby with a Connemara marble fireplace, stunning views from the dining room of the Cliffs of Moher. **L-AL** *Sheedy's Restaurant and Country Inn*, T7074026, www.sheedyscountry-house.com Small but very popular place, very stylish with a lobby that wouldn't be out of place in a London warehouse conversion. Nice minimalist décor downstairs while the rooms are more traditionally furnished. Great service. **Al-A** *Carrigan Hotel*, Doolin Rd, T7074036, www.gateway-to-the-buren.com A modern, busy hotel, which caters to an interesting crowd of sporty types and walkers as well as the passing trade. The hotel organizes walking weekends and can arrange individual excursions as well as offering self-guided walks. Lots of information on walking in the area. Drying rooms are a blessing in this rainy country. **A** *Kincora House*, T7074300, is a guesthouse in the centre of town. Small, with popular pub and hostel attached. **A** *Hilltop*, Doolin Rd, T7074134. B&B within walking distance of village, 1 family room, 3 en-suite doubles. **A** *St Judes*, Coast Rd, T7074108. Bungalow B&B on the N67 Doolin Rd, 4 en-suite rooms. **D** *The Burren Hostel*, T7074300. On road to Ennistymon. Dormitory rooms and doubles. Bike hire, and music at the pub next door.

Eating

The most fun eating in Lisdoonvarna is at Sheedy's *Orchid Restaurant* where there is an excellent balance between stylish cooking and adequate portions. Menu is nouvelle Irish and the chef has lots of awards. Good wine list and lots of attention for the guests. Dinner is under €30. The restaurant at the *Ballinalacken Castle Hotel* has just expanded to take bookings as well as guests and is another rare treat of a place. More nouvelle Irish in admirable portions and without the pretentious vocabulary of more well known places. The best dark and white chocolate mousse cake on the planet, eaten while studying the stunning skyscapes of the Cliffs of Moher and the Atlantic Ocean. Ask for a window table when making a reservation, or get there early. Similar prices to the Orchid restaurant.

Back in the less rarefied atmosphere of town there is the *Dolmen Inn*, open till 2130, in the centre of the village where there are quick meals with main courses around €10. The *Royal Spa* and the *Rathbaun* are opposite each other in the main street. Both with a fairly wide and conventional menu of fish and meat dishes for around €9 for a main course.

Pubs & music

Any pub that doesn't put on traditional music in Jul and Aug is on to a loser. Most pubs will have some music, some nights, so look around town for notices. The *Roadside Tavern* is good fo music every night except Sun in summer, or the bar in the *Royal Spa* has a good reputation locally. The *Kincora Bar* on the Doolin Rd has music at weekends in summer, and *Meg Maguire's* in Main St has music nightly in summer.

County Clare

Bicycle *Burke's*, The Square, T7074022. Bike hire.

Banks and bureaux de change *Bank of Ireland*, the Square. *Mace's Minimarket*,
Church St, will also change money. **Communications** Post office: Main St.

West of Lisdoonvarna

To the southwest of Lisdoonvarna is the little village of Doolin, famous for its
traditional music; the frighteningly high Cliffs of Moher and beyond them,
Liscannor, quieter but with pleasant pubs and a good hostel; Lahinch, on the
very outskirts of the Burren, a popular family resort; and Ennistymon, quietly
mouldering inland but with some good music pubs and a stunning waterfall.
Part of the Burren Way follows the coast a little way inland, coming close to
the cliffs at Doolin and following them closely round to Hag's Head.

This is a long, drawn-out strip of a village, one that you couldn't imagine could
be a mecca for anyone. But every summer it heaves with budget travellers and   *Phone code: 065*
musicians from as far away as Canada, Australia, Sweden, Germany (not Ire-   *Colour map 2,*
land, note) and you're more likely to hear a foreign language here than English.   *grid C3*
The draw is its reputation as a centre for traditional music but what you hear -
chord sequences repeated ad nauseam - is not always what you might hope for.
     The north end of the village is called Doolin, while the next block of houses,
pubs and the post office is called Roadford and the southern end of the village
is known as Fisherstreet. Here are a couple of the hostels and *O'Connor's Pub*.

Sleeping Doolin gets very crowded in the summer, especially at the budget end of   *Price codes:*
the range. It is a good idea to book your accommodation well in advance of a visit here.   *see inside*
     AL *Aran View House Hotel and Restaurant*, Coast Rd, at the north end of the village,   *front cover*
T7074061, www.aranview.com Comfortable and friendly small hotel in a Georgian
house and one of the best places in Doolin to bed down for a night or so.
A *Churchfield*, Fisherstreet, T707429. B&B with 6 rooms, close to pubs and handy for
public transport as buses stop outside. **A** *Cullinan's Restaurant and Guesthouse*,
T7074183, www.cullinansdoolin.com In the centre of the village this is a small comfortable and reasonably priced place with a good restaurant. **A** *Toomullin House*,
T7074723. This B&B is a min's walk from the pubs and handy for the Aran ferry. **A** *Sancta Maria*, Fisherstreet, T7074124. B&B with 4 rooms and very central for the music.
     B-C *Westwinds*, Roadford, T704227. In the centre of the village, but tucked away,
this B&B caters to vegetarians. Good value. **B** *Castle View Farmhouse*, T7074289, an
old farmhouse, short walk from the village, reasonable value.
     C-D *Doolin Holiday Hostel (Paddy's)*, Fisherstreet, T7074006, F7074421. Very mod-
ern, lots of facilities good rate for double rooms. Book in advance. **D** *Aille River Hostel*,
Roadford, T70744260. Converted old farmhouse between Roadford and Fisherstreet.
Scenic location beside old stone bridge. Some private double rooms in this friendly,
closed-over-winter hostel. **D** *Fisherstreet House*. Hostel owned by same people as
Paddy's, but this one is usually reserved for group bookings. **D** *Flanagan's Village Hos-
tel*, T7074564. Open all year, mostly dorm beds available. **D** *Rainbow Hostel*, Roadford,
T7074415, rainbowhostel@eircom.net Small hostel in a typical cottage of the area.
Very laid back, some double rooms, turf fires.
     Camping *Nagle's Doolin Caravan & Camping Park*, T7074458. By the harbour,
€5 per tent plus €2 per person. May-Sep. *O'Connor's Riverside Camping & Caravan
Park*, T7074314. Rates depend on size of tent. Apr-Sep. Best of all, camp at the Aille
River Hostel and enjoy the hostel facilities, €5 per person.

County Clare

👉 ## Cornelius O'Brien

One of Ireland's many eccentric landlords, Cornelius O'Brien, a lesser scion of the O'Brien clan, was MP for Clare from the 1830s until he died in 1857. He helped select Daniel O'Connell for the job before he took it over and supported the repeal of the Act of Union. In the 1847 election he came close to a duel with the agent of his opponent. Lord Palmerston said about him: "He was the best Irish MP we ever had. He didn't open his mouth in 20 years." He was never an absentee landlord and history tells that he improved the conditions of his tenants, a rare enough activity. There were no evictions on his land during the Famine or at any other time. One slightly sour note, however, is the fact that the contributions towards the column erected to his memory by grateful tenants were actually written into their tenancy agreements! Besides his efforts at building cottages for the tenants he restored and improved St Brigid's Well and built O'Brien's tower. His house, Birchfield, is now a ruin in Liscannor. His mausoleum is difficult to miss in the cemetery above St Brigid's Well in Liscannor.

Eating *Bruach na hAille*, Roadford, T7074120, is the big name in the village, serves seafood and vegetarian dishes in an elegant old house. Open 7 days in summer, closed Nov to mid-Mar. It has an early-bird menu served 1800-1930. *Cullinan's* specializes in Irish and continental-style seafood using locally caught fish, but also has meat dishes. *The Lazy Lobster*, Roadford, T7074390, is a seafood restaurant, serves dinner between 1800-2130 at slightly lower prices than those above.

Pub food abounds. *McGann's*, Roadford, does typical pub food at good prices – Irish stew, garlic mussels, baked salmon, at around €8 for a main course. Food is served till 2130 in a dark, candle-lit interior. *Doolin Café* Roadford, has vegetarian food, and *O'Connor's*, Fisherstreet, T7074168, is also good for pub food.

More good food is available at the excellent *Doolin Crafts Gallery*, Ballyvoe, T7074511. Open for morning coffee, lunch and tea, it has home-cooked and baked delights. Even better, it has an excellent collection of art and craft work, particularly batik.

Pubs and music Considering the number of people in town in the summer it is surprising that they all fit into the 3 pubs, and during the summer expect live music every night of the week. *O'Connor's* in Fisherstreet is the most renowned of them. *McGann's* at the Roadford end is just as packed, and *McDermott's*, which used to be the place where the locals go to get away from the tourists, is no different. If you want a rest from the noise, try the bar in *Aranview House Hotel*.

Transport **Bicycle**: *Burren Bike Tours* Roadford, T7074429, and some of the hostels have bikes for hire. **Bus**: 3 buses on weekdays and 2 on Sun to and from **Ennis**. Mon-Sat buses for **Galway** depart at 0845, 1410, 1710, 1925 (the last 2 on Sun as well); for **Tralee** and **Cork** at 1010, 1235, 1535, 1935 (the first 2 on Sun as well). T6824177 for local bus details **Boat**: From Doolin, between Apr and Sep, it is possible to get ferries to each of the **Aran islands**, T7074455 (T7071710, after hours). Ferries run up to 5 times a day to Inisheer, and once a day to Inishmór. It is possible to get singles and travel on to **Galway** from the islands. Return fares average around €25, journey times are between 30 and 50 mins, and departure times are mostly in the morning but vary with the month; see the Galway chapter for details about the islands.

The Cliffs of Moher From Lisdoonvarna the cliffs are signposted on the R478. They're impossible to miss –a gigantic car and coach park, free to enter, €2.54 to leave, marks the spot. Pass beyond the visitor centre, which explains that these are cliffs, leave behind the tour groups who walk to the edge and take a photo and follow the path a little way to the south. The cliffs face due west and the best time to go is at sunset on a clear day. In front of you are the Aran islands, and beyond to the north are the hills of Connemara. A little to the north of the visitors' centre is the O'Brien Tower built by Cornelius O'Brien.

The cliffs soar five miles (8 km) all the way south to Hag's Head, and the Burren Way footpath follows them. The wall along the edge of the cliff was erected by Cornelius O'Brien. You can join the waymarked route, which isn't signposted from the car-park, at the O'Brien tower. Hop over the wall and head southwest. From Hag's Head the best way back is to retrace your steps.

Liscannor
Phone code: 065
Colour map 2,
grid C3

Prettier and quieter than Doolin and not so towny as Lahinch further down the coast, Liscannor might make a good place to stop over in the area. It has two sights to visit, one very old and the other very new. Nice pubs, a good hostel some B&Bs and a hotel – what more could you ask for?

On the road into Liscannor from the Cliffs of Moher is **St Brigid's Well**, noticeable by the enormous great pillar erected by tenants to Cornelius O'Brien at his suggestion. O'Brien improved the well, which is one of the most revered holy wells in Ireland, dedicated to the sixth-century Kildare nun. The grotto is filled with pictures and discarded crutches of the sick who have been healed here. The Aran Islanders traditionally came her to worship in October, but in modern times it is July when the crowds arrive to seek healing and attend services here. It is almost certain that the site is pre-Christian in origin, adapted by the Christian missionaries to suit their own needs and adopted into the Christian religion.

Continuing on into Liscannor you pass the ruins of Birchwood House, O'Brien's pile on the left, and then arrive at Liscannor's newest contribution to the culture of Ireland – **Liscannor Stone**, a heritage centre-cum-shop with displays about the area's wavy patterned slate, which you can see all over Ireland as street paving, stone cladding on houses and even roof tiles. At the western end of the village is a sandy beach. ■ *Liscannor Stone: summer only, daily.*

Sleeping L *Liscannor Bay Hotel*, T7081186, www.liscannorbayhotel.com Excellent views across the bay from some of its rooms and altogether a very comfortable place to stay. **B** *Seahaven* T7081385. B&B just out of the village on the way to Lahinch. It's a big house with 6 rooms, open Jan-Nov with good sea views. **D** *Village Hostel*, T7081385. Open from Mar-Nov, has private rooms at reasonable rates, and is well run.

Camping *Liscannor Caravan & Camping Park*, Clahane Beach, T7081714. A vast trailer park, which takes tents.

Eating and entertainment At the west end of town, up the boreen beside O'Brien's monument is the *Cottage Restaurant*, a single-storey, low white building with tables outside, again serving mostly seafood, with lots of paupiettes and daunes in the menu. Main courses around €15. Open for lunch and dinner.

The village's pubs all do good pub food with extensive menus, dominated by seafood. *Vaughan's Anchor Inn* has an attached restaurant serving lots of seafood at around €12 for a main course and does pub food and B&B as well, although since it also has music during the summer this might be a noisy experience. Next door is *Joseph McHugh*, a totally unreconstructed Irish pub with grocery section and all. It serves some food and has music on Tue nights. The *Captain's Deck*, T7081666, is at the west end of the village next to the hostel and serves food 1000-2200. It offers a set dinner at around €17 and à la carte main courses for about the same. At the east end of town is the glaringly painted *Mermaid Café*.

County Clare

Lahinch
Phone code: 065
Colour map 2, grid C3

A typical seaside town, Lahinch is full of places to eat and lots of places to stay, some good music pubs, a mile-long beach with crashing breakers and surf boards for rent (T7081543), and **Seaworld**, T7081900, a leisure centre and aquarium with a swimming pool, and sharks plus other sea creatures. ■ *Aquarium: €5.39. Pool and jacuzzi: €5.39.*

The **tourist office**, *Lahinch Faílte* is in The Dell, T7082088. Open summer, daily 0900-2200; winter, daily 0900-1700.

Sleeping **AL** *Atlantic Hotel*, Main St, T7081049, atlantichotel@eircom.net Family-run small refurbished traditional hotel. **A** *Dough Mor Lodge*, T7082063. Partly stone-fronted guesthouse with 6 en-suite rooms but no tea/coffee facility in them. **C-D** *Lahinch Hostel*, Church St, T7081040, F81704. Nice modern hostel with family and double rooms. Downstairs is a very popular restaurant.

Eating Lots of cafés and pub food here. Top of the posh list is *Mr Eamon's* in Kettle St, T7081050, serving modern Irish seafood. Open mid-Mar to mid-Jan, 1900-2200. Just outside Lahinch on the way to Milltown Malbay is *Barrtrá*, T7081280, set in a pleasant garden overlooking Liscannor Bay. It is a modern seafood restaurant, focusing on locally available sources but including oddities such as rollmops, duck, and several good vegetarian options. It has an early evening set menu 1700-1900, around €20. Later than that dinner will work out around €32. Mon except in Jul and Aug. Back in town the hotels all have restaurants doing good potato-based set lunches. Below the *Lahinch Hostel* is the *Bay View Restaurant*, serving basic dishes with main courses at lunch time around €10. The pubs also focus on seafood menus, *Kenny's* in Main St is a very touristy place, which closes for the winter but has music as well as a good seafood menu in summer. The *Village Inn* Main St, has a similar menu and does music.

Pubs and music All the pubs in town offer some nights of music in summer. The best of them are *The 19th*, Main St, with music every night in summer and Sat in winter, *Galvin's*, at the top of Main St with music Mon, Wed, Fri and Sat in summer and the aptly named *O'Looney's* with pub food and music Mon, Wed and Fri.

Transport **Bus**: The Limerick to Doolin bus passes through Lahinch 3 times a day in summer, and twice on Sun and the rest of the year. So too does the **Cork-Galway** service. T061-313333 or enquire at tourist office.

Ennistymonm
Phone code: 065
Colour map 2, grid C3

To complete this circuit of the area west of Lisdoonvarna head east out of Lahinch to Ennistymon, a backwater on the tourist trail, which probably looks very much like it did in 1950 or thereabouts. The chief point of interest here is waterfall known as the **Cascades**, especially if it has been raining. They are signposted in the village through a laneway beside the *Archway Bar*. The town has a couple of interesting old shops whose window displays can't have been changed in years, an interesting antique shop, *Hasset's*, T71964, and *Daly's Pub*, Main St, which has live music nightly.

North of Lisdoonvarna

The area around Ballyvaughan is really the most beautiful part of the Burren, with its wild coastline and cornucopia of wild flowers. To the west the coast road skirts around to Fanore, a little strip of a village, and to the east is Carron where there are a couple of interesting places to visit. There are lots of good walks in the area, including a section of the Burren Way. The route from Lisdoonvarna to Ballyvaughan passes through Corkscrew Hill, a famine relief road which twists its way down to the village through some outstanding views of Galway Bay.

Ballyvaughan is a tourist-centred village where one of the first holiday villages in Ireland was built. Basically a group of houses, post office, mobile bank and hotel built around a T-junction it isn't as busy as Lisdoonvarna or Doolin but might make a pleasant night's stay with its quiet pubs and a couple of good places to eat.

Ballyvaughan
Colour map 2, grid C3
See 'Sleeping' below

The **Burren Exposure** centre is east of the village on the coast road, and is a good idea for a rainy day or as an introduction to the Burren early on in your visit. It uses giant screens with videos and slide shows to explain the history and mythology and flora of the Burren as well as the nature of the rocks themselves. There is a good restaurant with amazing sea views and a shop selling knitwear and crafts. ■ *T707727. Mar-May, daily, 1000-1700; Jun-Sep, daily, 1000-1800. €4.45. On N67 ¼ mile outside Ballyvaughan on route to Galway.*

A little way beyond the Burren Exposure is **Bishop's Quarter Beach**, excellent for swimming, with a sandy beach and dunes. At Belharbour are the ruins of **Corcomroe Abbey**, founded by the O'Briens in the late 12th century. Cistercians ran this place, probably well into the 17th century. In a county where Romanesque carvings are ten a penny, these are well worth the visit with carved heads, opium poppies, and lilies of the valley. ■ *Half a mile (1 km) inland from Bellharbour.*

The little peninsula along this stretch of coast is called Finnvarra. Here is **Mount Vernon Lodge**, one-time home to Lady Gregory and temporary home to such luminaries as Yeats. West of the little village of New Quay is the **Flaggy Shore**, a place where the Burren limestone flags go right down to the sea.

Beyond Belharbour is a fascinating and undemanding walk around Abbey Hill, especially if you are interested in wild flowers. At Belharbour, instead of turning left for Burrin take the right turn, which brings you out to the road from Corofin to Galway. Around 2½ miles along this road look for a green road on the left as you pass Abbey Hill (also on your left). Park the car or bikes here and head along the green road to a gate into a field. The green road continues around Abbey Hill but your walk takes you higher and around the brow of the hill to the south. The glory of this walk are the wild flowers in this field though it is difficult to walk without crushing orchids or burnett roses underfoot. At the top of the hill there are excellent views of Corcomroe Abbey and the green valley that gave it its original name Sancta Maria de Petra Fertili – Saint Mary of the Fertile Rock. Following the contour of the hill round to the west there are stunning views over the long inlet from Ballyvaughan Bay and Bell Harbour, with a Martello tower visible way over to the west at Finavarra Point. Due west at the other side of Poulnaclough Bay is the site of a battle fought in 1267 where Conor O'Brien, whose tomb can be seen in the abbey, died. Follow the contour of the hill around until you can see the green road again below you and return to your vehicle.

Abbey Hill walk

County Clare

Heading west out of Ballyvaughan begins a scenic drive through Gleninagh and Fanore around the Gleninagh Mountains. About four miles (6 km) west of the village is **Gleninagh Castle**, a 16th-century edifice built by the O'Loughlans and inhabited by them until the 1840s. Continuing on, the road hugs close to

Ballyvaughan to Fanore

the coast. Just before a pier a green road sets off around the mountain and makes a pleasant walk above the road. You can climb anywhere here to the stone ring fort at the top of the hill and on a clear day see what an excellent defensive position it made for a fortified farmhouse. The hillside will be covered in a botanist's daydream of wild flowers depending on what month you are walking. Continuing round Black Head to Fanore brings you to a strung out-little village of a few houses, a shop and a pub. There is a good sandy beach with sand dunes and it is fairly safe for swimming with a lifeguard there for part of the year. The Atlantic breakers are often good for surfing.

Aillwee Cave On the road to Lisdoonvarna is the much-hyped Aillwee Cave, another good rainy-day activity. The cave system is typical of the caves that run throughout the Burren, usually where the limestone rock meets the shale or sandstone at the border between the two areas. The huge cave was discovered in 1944 and is about 600 yds/m long with side caves, a waterfall, and stalactite and stalagmite formations. There are also the remains of bear pits where the claw marks of giant brown bears which once inhabited the caves can still be seen. Outside the caves is a nature walk and you can also scramble up the hill above the cave to look at the views over Galway Bay. In the entrance there are cheese-making demonstrations of the local Burren Gold cheese. ■ *T7077036. Mar-Jun and Sep-Nov, daily, 1000-1800; Jul and Aug, daily, 1000-1900. Admission by tour only. Last tour 1830 Jul and Aug, 1730 Mar-Jun and Sep-Nov. €5. Café, shops. Best time to visit is early morning before the tour groups build up.*

Gleninsheen wedge tombs A little way south of the cave on the N480 are the Gleninsheen wedge tombs, a series of tombs constructed of slabs in a box formation, facing west and tapering to the east. They are Bronze Age burial places and nearby, indicated on the *Rambler's Guide & Map, Ballyvaughan*, is the spot where in the 1930s a small boy found a gold gorget, or neck collar, one of the most beautiful and undamaged in existence and now in the National Museum.

Poulnabrone Portal Dolmen Continuing along the N480 brings you to the 5000-year-old Poulnabrone Portal Dolmen, swathed in summer in tour buses but beautiful none the less. It rears up out of the bare limestone, not quite horizontal, aspiring to something . When excavated it revealed urns containing the cremated remains of 16 Late Stone Age people, and some polished flint implements.

Burren Perfumery East of the N480, just beyond the dolmen along a minor road, is Carron, a tiny village worth visiting for the Burren Perfumery, which has audio-visual displays on the making of perfume and you can walk around the still and extracting machinery to watch the process in action. Another good rainy-day activity. ■ *T7089102, www.burren-perfumery.com Mar-May, Oct-Nov, daily 0900-1700; Jun-Sep, daily 0900-1900; Dec-Feb, phone in advance. Free. Shop. From Ballyvaughan take the first left after the Poulnabrone Dolmen, and at Carron turn right at the church and then left to find the perfumery.*

Sleeping
Price codes: see inside front cover

There are lots of B&Bs all around the coast east of Ballyvaughan and all of them can get booked up in summer, so book your trip in advance.

LL-L *Gregan's Castle Hotel*, Corkscrew Hill, T707705, www.gregans.ie Lovely old country house with lots of room to relax and imagine you are the landed gentry. Big library, lounge, bar. Country-house-style bedrooms, no TV, excellent restaurant. **AL** *Hyland's Hotel*, Ballyvaughan, T7077037, F7077131. Attractive, old-fashioned hotel run by the same family for generations. **AL-A** *Rusheen Lodge*, Corkscrew Hill Rd, T7077092, www.rusheenlodge.com A very pleasant and welcoming guest house on road to Cork-screw Hill, good bedrooms and great breakfast, run by the son of the man who discov-ered the Aillwee Cave. **B** *Micko's Place*, Ballyvaughan, T7077060. Small B&B in village, pleasant atmosphere. **D** *The Bridge Hostel*, Fanore, T7076134, F7076134. Small 200-yr-old house in beautiful location between the hills and the sea. One private room, camping possible in the garden, bike hire. **C-D** *Clare's Rock Hostel*, Carron, T7089129, www.claresrock.com Dormitory and family rooms, laundry, kennels. Open May-Oct.

The grandest place to eat is *Gregan's Castle Hotel* but you should book well in advance since they expect guests to eat there, and book tables for them. Lovely views out the win-dows, especially at dusk as the Burren hills turn a dull Mars red. Food is well cooked, and comes stacked in little mountains. In Ballyvaughan *Hylands Hotel* has a restaurant serv-ing traditional fare at around €25 for dinner. The *Whitethorn Restaurant* at the Burren Exposure serves self-service lunches at around €8 and snacks during the day and is open for dinner on Fri and Sat in Jul and Aug. Beautiful views from the huge windows, main courses around €16, unusually good wine list. The *Aillwee Cave* café is not half bad, try the Burren Gold cheese with baked potatoes. **Eating**

In the village *Monk's*, T7077059, a pub and restaurant just beside the pier on the Fanore Rd has a big seafood menu and is very popular, but pricey. *An Fear Gorta*, right by the harbour, serves delicious light meals in a lovely garden or conservatory. Open from Jun-Sep, 1200-1730, this is one of the best value-for-money places in the Burren. On the Fanore Rd, *O'Donoghue's* pub does barfood while ½ mile (1 km) beyond it is *Admiral's Restaurant*, T7076105, again focusing on seafood.

Monk's and *O'Brien's*, T7077003, have traditional music in the summer, *Monk's* on Wed and *O'Brien's* at weekends. *O'Brien's* often gets Country and Western bands on Sun if you like that kind of thing. *Greene's*, also in the village, has traditional music on Wed while O'Lochlain's also has occasional music sessions but is more a pub for the locals. **Pubs & music**

Horseriding *Burren Riding Centre*, Fanore, T7076140. Daily 5hr trails at 0930; beach trails 0930 and 1100; 3hr Burren trails 1100, 1500. **Watersports** *River Ocean Kayak*, 2, Muckinish West, T7077043. Sea kayaking trips in Galway Bay. **Sport**

Bicycle *Monk's Bar*, T7077059. Bike hire. **Transport**

Banks and bureaux de change A bank comes to Ballyvaughan on Mon, Wed and Fri. *Burren Exposure* (see page 389) will also change money. **Directory**

West Clare

The west coast of Clare from Lahinch down through the seaside towns of Miltown Malbay, Quilty, Kilkee and Loop Head is a pleasant day's drive. Kilkee is an Irish family holiday destination, while Kilrush offers a heritage centre, trips to Scattery Island, and dolphins in the estuary of the Shannon.

Lahinch to Kilkee

Through fairly uneventful countryside, the road south from Lahinch finds its way along the coast down to Miltown Malbay, a Victorian resort close to Spanish Point: an excellent sandy beach with good surfing when the waves are high. Legend tells that in 1588 sailors from the shipwrecked Spanish **Miltown Malbay**
Colour map 3, grid A3

County Clare

Armada swam ashore here to be arrested on the orders of Richard Bingham, the governor of Connaught, and later executed.

From Miltown Malbay the road continues past occasional caravan sites to **Quilty** where there is a sandy beach. The next town along the route is **Doonbeg**, a tiny village with a white sandy beach and dunes beyond. Another Armada ship ran aground here in 1588, and its survivors were also carted away to execution.

Kilkee, Loop Head and Carrigaholt

Kilkee
Phone code: 065
Colour map 3, grid A2

A seaside resort since Victorian times, Kilkee is bucket-and-spade and amusement-arcade territory. The beach here explains the popularity of the place – long, golden and sheltered, with beautiful cliffs at its western end. At the same end of the beach are 'pollock holes', so called because pollock lurk about in them, as do lots of other interesting varieties of marine life. There is also a golf club, some excellent walks along the cliffs, and **Waterworld**, a leisure centre with water slides, a wave machine and kiddies' pools ■ *Jun 1200-2000; Jul, Aug 1100-2100. T9056855.*

Loop Head
Colour map 3, grid A2

Loop Head makes an interesting drive or an exciting cycle or walk. The coastline is full of sea stacks and bird life and a coastal path follows the cliffs all 15 miles (24 km) down to Loop Head. At **Intrinsic Bay**, named for the emigrant ship that sank here in 1836, is a sea stack with a medieval oratory on it. In Kilbaha in the church at Moneen is the **Little Ark** dating back to penal times when Catholics were prohibited from saying mass on land: this moveable altar was carried down to the shore and mass said there. The church stained glass window holds a portrayal of such a mass.

Carrigaholt
Colour map 3, grid A2

Carrigaholt has some nice pubs, a tiny beach and **Dolphinwatch**, which does trips out into the estuary to see one of only five known groups of bottlenose dolphins in the waters of Europe. There are about 80 of them and trippers are rarely disappointed, often spotting nursery groups of young dolphins. There is an information centre and booking office in the village with audio visual displays about the dolphins, and of course t-shirts. ■ *The Square, Carrigaholt, T9058156, www.dolphinwatch.ie Apr-Oct, weather permitting. Bookings begin at 0800 on day of trip. 2-hr trips. €14. Look for information about individual trips/weather on the pier.* The **tourist office** is on O'Connell St. Open Jun-Sep, Mon-Sat, 1000-1800.

Carrigaholt also has a 15th-century, five-storey tower house very strategically placed overlooking the Shannon. Over the doorway is a murder hole, placed there so that heavy objects could be dropped on to unsuspecting invading heads. The trick didn't work, though, in 1598, when Daniel O'Brien took the castle from the MacMahons. The O'Briens held it till Cromwell turned up in 1651 but got it back for a while at the Restoration in 1666. William of Orange reallocated it in 1691 to the Earl of Albemarle, who sold it to a family called the Burtons. They managed to hold on to it until the late 19th century.

Sleeping
Price codes:
see inside front cover

Kilkee makes a down-to-earth alternative if you've got tired of the ethnic rusticity of the rest of Clare, while Miltown Malbay and Carrigaholt are quieter and might make a good base if you want to do some walking in the area. Unless you book in advance the chances are you'll get whatever is still available when you turn up at the tourist office. Most of the B&Bs in Miltown Malbay charge the standard rate of around €23 per person sharing, but a few out of the village itself are a little cheaper.

County Clare

AL-A *Halpin's Hotel*, Erin St, Kilkee, T9056032, www.halpinsprivatehotels.com Very central, small renovated townhouse hotel and restaurant. Open fires, old-fashioned bar. **AL-A** *Bellbridge House Hotel*, Spanish Point, Miltown Malbay, T7084038, www.westireland.com/bellbridge Close to the golf course and beach. Open all year. **AL-A** *Kilkee Bay Hotel*, Kilkee, T9060060, www.kilkee-bay.com On the road to Kilrush, this huge complex of hotel and apartments is geared to longer-stay family groups. Restaurant, nightclub, pub, creche, cinema, tennis court. **A** *Stella Maris Hotel*, Kilkee, T9056455. Small, better value than the bigger hotels, in the centre of town, open fires, nice views over the bay. **A** *Strand Guest House*, The Strand Line, Kilkee, T/F9056177, www.clareguesthouse.com On the seafront, seafood restaurant. **A** *Bayview*, O'Connell St, Miltown Malbay, T9056058. Big, bright yellow B&B, good views of the bay. **A** *Purtill's*, O'Curry St, Kilkee, T/F9056771. B&B in nicely restored townhouse in the main street in town. Bar and restaurant, traditional music in summer. **C-B** *Barkers*, Spanish Point, Miltown Malbay, T7084408. Small home run by musical family close to the beach. Good value B&B. **C-B** *San Antone*, Drummin, Miltown Malbay, T7084511. B&B 2 miles (3 km) out of town, quiet location, good views. **D** *Kilkee Hostel*, O'Curry St, Miltown Malbay, T9056209, kilkeehostel@eircom.net Well run but no double rooms, just dormitory or family rooms. Café. Bike hire.

Camping *Cunningham's Holiday Park*, Miltown Malbay, T9056430. Camping site and mobile homes to hire. *Green Acres*, Doonaha, Kilkee, T9057011. Smaller place, signposted off the N67 Kilkee to Kilrush road.

Kilkee abounds with fast food of one sort or another. The big hotels all have reliable restaurants. In Carrigaholt the *Long Dock*, T9058106, is a pub/restaurant where you might want to eat and listen to some good music. **Eating**

In Kilkee is *Myles Creek* in O'Curry St, which has traditional music on Mon. In the same street is *O'Mara's*, which has traditional music 3 days a week (Mon, Wed and Fri). Miltown Malbay is home to the Willy Clancy Summer School in the first week or so of Jul, when everyone in traditional music turns up there. Outside of the festival, *Clancy's* is the place to find good music. In Doonbeg, between Miltown Malbay and Kilkee, is the *Ocean View Bar* with music on Tue, Sat and Sun. **Pubs & music**

Watersports *Kilkee Diving & Watersports Centre*, Harbour, T9056707. **Ponytrekking** Centre, Tarmon West, 2 miles outside Kilkee, T9060071. **Sport**

Banks *AIB* and *Bank of Ireland*, O'Curry St. **Directory**

Kilrush and Scattery Island

Unless you are a boating aficionado there doesn't seem much reason to spend any time in Kilrush. The old gaol is now a *Supervalu* supermarket and the new self-flushing toilets are a treat, but is that it? At the mouth of the creek is the marina. The renovated walled gardens of the local landlord family, the Vandeleurs, are open from 1000 to 1800 in summer (1600 in winter), T9051760, €3. The town also has a **Heritage Centre** telling the story of Kilrush in landlord times. ■ *The Square, T9051596. Jun-Aug, Mon-Sat 1000-1300, 1400-1600. €3*. There are also dolphin-watching trips from Kilrush harbour, T9051327, €12.70 for a 2-hr trip. The **tourist office** is in the Town Hall, Market Sq, T9051577. Open Jul-Aug only, Mon-Sat, 1000-1300, 1400-1800; Sun, 1200-1600.

Kilrush
Phone code: 065
Colour map 3, grid A3

County Clare

Scattery Island
Colour map 3, grid A3

The best reason to come to Kilrush is to make the trip to Scattery Island, inhabited until quite recently and worth visiting for the remains of the monastic settlement that was established there in the sixth century by St Senan, who first fought a monster called Cata on the island. There is a 120ft (36.5m) high tower, and the remains of the cathedral and several other churches. The settlements were attacked by Vikings, who settled there for a time before Brian Boru took it back. Then the churches were desecrated by an Englishman called William Hoel in 1179. The site became a place of pilgrimage and sailors sailed new boats sunwards round it and collected pebbles from the beach for luck. On the mainland, in Merchant's Quay, is an interpretive centre that tells the story of the island. ■ *Interpretive centre: Merchant's Quay, T9052114. mid-Jun to mid-Sep, daily 0930-1830. Last admission 30 mins before closing. Free. Ferry to island: Scattery Island Ferries, Kilrush Marina Building, T9051327. Phone for times. €7.62. Journey time 20 mins.*

Sleeping & eating

There are no hotels or guesthouses in Kilrush. Accommodation is either in B&Bs (around €24 per person sharing) or hostels.

A *Bruach na Coille*, Killimer Rd, T9052250, www.clarkekilrush.com B&B ½ mile (1 km) out of town on the N67 road to Killimer, set in pretty gardens opposite those of the Vandeleurs, breakfast menu. **A-B** *Crotty's*, Market Sq, T9052470. Very central B&B and above the pub/restaurant with live music many nights in summer. **B** *Fortfield Farm*, Donail, T9051457, fortfield@eircom.net B&B about 2½ miles (4 km) outside town on the road to Killimer, children might enjoy staying here and adults will appreciate the tea and scones on arrival. **D** *Bels House Hostel*, Moanmore South, T9052801. Some private doubles. **D** *Katie O'Connor's*, Frances St, T9051133, cwglynn@eicom.net Hostel with private and family rooms. **D** *Kilrush Creek Lodge*, Kilrush marina, T9052595. Independent hostel with single and family rooms.

Food is mostly found in cafés or pubs. *Crotty's* has a good reputation, while the *Haven Arms*, *Kelly's*, and the *Island House*, all close together in Henry St, all do good bar food. In the square are the *Central Restaurant*, T9052477, and *Coffey's Café Pizzeria*, T9051170 both doing inexpensive café-type food.

Pubs & music

Crotty's, T9052470, is the place to go for good music sessions midweek and Sat in summer, but you could also check out several other pubs in town – *The Haven Arms*, Henry St, which has music every Thu and Fri. Mid-Aug sees a festival celebrating Mrs Crotty, the one-time owner of Crotty's bar who was a renowned concertina player. In Jun, based in Kilbaha, Cross and Carrigaholt is the annual West Clare Jazz School, with classes in Kilbaha and free performances in the bars in those 3 villages. T9058229 for details.

Sport

Watersports *Kilrush Creek Lodge & Adventure Centre*, Kilrush marina, T9052855.

Transport

Bicycle *Gleeson's Cycles*, Henry St, T9051127. Bike hire. **Ferry** A car ferry operates between **Killimer**, 5 miles from Kilrush, and **Tarbert** in County Kerry. The ferry, T9053124, operates on the hr from Killimer Apr-Sep 0700-2100 (0900 on Sun); Oct-Mar 0700-1900 (1000 on Sun). €11 per car, €3.81 for bikes and foot passengers. Journey time is 20 mins.

Directory

Banks and bureaux de change *Tourist office*, Market Sq, will change money. **Communications** **Post office**: Frances St.

County Clare

Lough Derg and around

The area around Lough Derg is green pastureland set in a landscape of mountain and lake. The major town is Killaloe with its ancient cathedral, said to be the home of Brian Boru, the ancient Irish king. The East Clare Way, a signposted walking route, crosses the area, boats can be hired and there are lots of riding centres and golf courses. This is an area for activity holidays rather than a touring holiday.

Killaloe

Killaloe and Ballina in County Tipperary are joined by a beautiful old arched bridge over the river Shannon. The main point of interest in Killaloe is **St Flannan's Cathedral**, named after an abbot who led the monastery that stood here before the cathedral. The building you now see is late 12th century, built by an O'Brien, and it encloses the doorway of an earlier church in its southwest corner. Inside is one of the only stones in existence to have both Ogham and runic writing on it – probably erected by the man whose name it bears: Thorgrim – asking for prayer. The cross once stood at Kilfenora but was moved here in 1821. Beside the cathedral is **St Flannan's Oratory**, 12th century also and with a stone roof. Also in Killaloe, in the grounds of the Catholic church is **St Molua's church**, which is older than both of these buildings. It stood originally on Friar's Island in the Shannon estuary but was moved here in 1929 when the island was flooded in the Shannon hydroelectric scheme. Also in town is the **Heritage Centre**, with material on local history and the history of the abbey. ■ *Open Jun-Sep, €2.*

Phone code: 061
Colour map 3, grid A5

Long-distance walks

Starting off in Killaloe the **East Clare Way** covers 112 miles (180 km) of very untouristy east Clare, travelling through Broadford, O'Callaghan's Mills, Tulla, Feakle, Flagmount, Whitegate, Mountshannon, and Ogonnelloe. Half of the journey is along tarmac road, albeit very quiet tarmac. The best of it is the section between Tulla and Mountshannon: three days walking through open land, forestry and some road walking. There is accommodation at Mountshannon, Feakle and Tulla.

The **Lough Derg Way** passes through Killaloe on its route from Limerick and follows the eastern shore of Lough Derg to Dromineer in County Tipperary. This is a finer walk than the other, keeping close to the shores of the lake for most of its route but accommodation is a little harder to come by. For more information about the walk you can pick up the *Lough Derg Way Information Sheet* at Ennis Tourist office or the Clare section of the walk is mapped out on the *Ordnance Survey* Discovery series sheets 65 and 58.

North to Mountshannon & Holy Island

Heading northwards along the shores of Lough Derg brings you to Tuamgraney where the **10th century church** is now another heritage centre. It is the oldest Irish church still used for services and is said to have been repaired in 1000 by Brian Boru himself. Continuing north you come to Mountshannon, a quiet little town popular with fishing enthusiasts but where you can get a ferry to **Holy Island** (*Inis Cealtra*). A monastery was founded here by St Caiman in the seventh century, but was burned down by Vikings in 836 and again in 922. The Abbot of the monastery around 1000 was the brother of Brian Boru, who is said to have built one of the churches on the island. A church remained here into the 16th century but by the 17th this had

County Clare

become a place of pilgrimage rather than a working church. There are around 10 sites of interest on the island, including three churches, all predating the 13th century: a round tower, a tiny tomb known as the 'anchorite's cell', and the holy well that makes this place the centre for pilgrims. *T061-921351 to arrange trips. May to Sep.* €6.

Sleeping
Price codes: see inside front cover

In Killaloe there is a variety of accommodation, which can be supplemented by walking over the bridge into Ballina, and accommodation is also available along the lough at Mountshannon.

L *Kincora Hall Hotel*, Killaloe, T376665, kincora@iol.ie Just outside Killaloe, with its own marina, grand old fireplaces, small enough to make the guest feel welcome. **L-AL** *Lakeside Hotel and Leisure Centre*, Killaloe, T376122, www.lakesidekillaloe.com Lots of facilities including a pool, water slide, Jacuzzi and snooker room. Overlooks Lough Derg. **A** *Carranmore Lodge*, Killaloe, T376704. B&B in the village itself with big gardens and pleasant views over the river. **B** *Whitethorn Lodge*, T375257. Large modern house within walking distance of amenities; 1 double, 1 single and 1 family room; Apr-Oct. **B** *Ballyheefy Lodge*, Ballyheefy, T376016. Farmhouse B&B 2½ miles (4 km) outside Killaloe, good views of the lough.

Camping *Lakeside Caravan & Camping Park*, Mountshannon, T927225, F927336. On the shores of the lough with lots of facilities, mobile homes to hire, boat hire, café, bike hire, pony riding and much more. 2 adults in a small tent works out at around €10. *Lough Derg Holiday Park*, Scarrif Rd, Killaloe, T3786329. A big place with lots of facilities – including takeaway and shop, games room, laundry – but with prices to match. There are mobile homes to hire.

Eating

In Killaloe the 2 hotels both have restaurants, while the *Piper's Inn*, T376885, has a good restaurant and traditional music every day in summer and at weekends in winter. There is also the *Anchor Inn*, which does pub food and has music on Wed in summer, and on the Ballina side of the river *Molly's Bar and Restaurant*, T376632, has food and music (Thu, all year). In Mountshannon the hotel does good basic food with set dinner at under €20 while the *Bridge* does pub food and *Cois na Abhna* in the main street has music.

Sport

Fishing *TJ O'Brien*, Main St, Ballina/Killaloe, T376009. Tackle for game, sea, sport and coarse fishing. **Golf** *East Clare Golf Club*, Bodyke, T921322. 18 holes. *Liam O'Flannery*, Woodpark, Scarriff Rd, T921460.18-hole pitch and putt, 9-hole golf. **Horseriding** *Carrowbaun Farm Trekking Centre*, Killaloe, T376754. *East Clare Equestrian Centre*, Tuamgraney, T921157. **Walking** *East Clare Walking Club*, ECDA, Feakle, T924303. Organize regular walks every other Sun. *Green Boreen Holidays*, ECDA, Feakle, T924303, F924289. Packaged walking and cycling holidays. **Watersports** *Thomas Bottcher*, Mountshannon, T927225. Sailing, canoeing, windsurfing.

Directory

Banks *AIB*, Main St, Killaloe, T376115. *Bank of Ireland*, Scarriff, T921015. **Boats** *PJ Mason*, Broadford, T473194. Boat hire on Doon Lake. *Whelan's*, Church St, Killaloe, T376159. 19ft (5.7m) lake boats with outboard motors.

Counties Galway & Roscommon

11

Counties Galway & Roscommon

To Sligo
Drumshanbo
Boyle
Carrick-on-Shannon
Ballaghaderreen
ROSCOMMON
Claremorris
Castlerea
Longford
To Westport
To Dublin
Ballinrobe
Roscommon
Clifden
Tuam
Oughterard
Athlone
GALWAY
To Dublin
Ballinasloe
Atlantic
Ocean
Galway
Athenry
Banagher
Loughrea
Aran Islands
Portumna
Birr
Gort
To Limerick
To Limerick

Galway is a large county, but **Lough Corrib** splits it into two quite different regions. For the majority of travellers it is the land to the west, **Connemara**, that stirs the imagination. Here, a wilderness of bog and mountains rivals Cork and Kerry for splendid scenery and the wild beauty of nature. East Galway is dull by comparison, and it may be hard to find the time to include anywhere in east Galway when the famed Aran Islands and the exuberantly lively city of **Galway** are added to an itinerary that includes Connemara.

The inland county of **Roscommon** is Irish country life without the tourist trimmings: no spectacular sights but a relaxed pace of life and, as ever, history lurking in unexpected places. Few visitors make it their holiday destination, but anyone passing through should definitely take some time to visit **Strokestown**, Roscommon town and **Boyle**.

County Galway

Galway

Phone code: 091
Colour map 2, grid C3

If any one place in Ireland can sum up what the country is all about it has to be this ancient, prosperous and culturally dynamic little city. Easily walked from one end to another in half an hour, it is a tourist paradise of culture, shopping, friendliness, good accommodation, and even better eating. In summer the whole city centre teems with people out having fun, bars and restaurants spill out on to the streets, and with major festivals in July, August and September there is rarely no excuse for some craic.

Ins and outs

Getting there
See 'Transport', page 412, for further details

Air Galway airport, T755569, is 7 miles (10 km) east of the city at Carnmore. There are 2 daily *Aer Lingus* flights to and from Dublin and services to Manchester and Teeside in Britain. **Bus** Galway city's station services main towns throughout Ireland and there are some private companies also running useful routes: Dublin and Dublin Airport to Galway; Belmullet, Newport and Westport to Galway city; see the Inishbofin Island section on page 431 for services between Galway city and Cleggan. **Taxis** From the airport to the centre costs around €12. **Train** From the railway station in Galway city, T564222, daily trains service Dublin, stopping at Athlone for connections to other parts of the country.

Getting around
Galway's city centre is tiny. The bulk of the city is on the northwest side of the river Corrib, the main route across town being made up of Eyre Sq, a kind of hotchpotch of statuary, grass, bus queues and phone boxes, and then Williamsgate, William's St, Shop St, High St and Quay St, all busy shopping streets, although you would hardly notice that you are passing from one of these streets to the next. On the southwest side of the river is the ancient settlement of the Claddagh, which is mostly rebuilt with boring bungalows. From the airport there is a daily bus service or taxi, but most travellers without their own transport arrive close by Eyre Sq in the very centre of Galway either by bus or train. From your arrival point in the city most places are easily walkable. Taxi ranks are in Eyre Sq and by the railway station. Buses leave Eyre Sq for Salthill every 20 mins, but the distance is easily walked. For bicycle hire see page 412.

Tourist information
Ireland West Tourism (the main tourist office for the county) is in Galway city on Forster St, T537700. Main office open Jul-Aug, daily, 0830-1945; Jun, daily, 0900-1845; May, Mon-Sat, 0900-1745; Sep-Apr, Mon-Fri, 0900-1745, Sat, 0900-1200. There is another office in Salthill, at the junction of Seapoint Promenade and Upper Salthill Rd. The Aran Islands, Aughrim, Ballinasloe, Clifden, Oughterard and Salthill also have offices (see relevant sections).

History

The *Annals of the Four Masters*, a 17th-century compilation history of Ireland (see box on page 496) records the presence of a fort at the mouth of the River Corrib in 1124. This would have been the crossing place for traders and travellers moving from Dublin to the west, the route to the north being blocked by Lough Corrib. In 1232 Richard de Burgh, a powerful Anglo-Norman baron, took the area from the dominant Gaelic clan, the O'Flahertys. By 1247 there

TRAVELBAG
Adventures

Off the beaten track...

Jordan
Kyrgyzstan
Lebanon
Lombok
Libya
Madagascar
Mali
Malawi
Malaysia
Mexico
Morocco
Mozambique
Namibia
Nepal
New Zealand
N. Cyprus
Peru
South Africa
Spain
Sri Lanka
Syria
Tanzania
Thailand
Tibet
Turkey
Uganda
USA
Venezuela
Vietnam
Zambia
Zimbabwe

Discovery

If you're looking for adventure without too much physical exertion you're not alone. Thousands of people a year travel with us on escorted trips where culture, places and landscapes are the main focus and accommodation is in small, comfortable hotels. You could join a trip which explores the lively markets and historic Inca sites of Peru. Or a journey by boat, bus, rickshaw and train through Vietnam. There are ornately carved temples just waiting to be discovered in places like India or Mexico, ancient wonders in Egypt and Jordan, and ways of life that seem lost in time in Cuba, Bolivia, Libya, Mali, Japan…

Wildlife

Follow in the footsteps of Darwin on a cruise through the enchanted Galapagos Islands of Ecuador, a tiger safari in India, a gorilla search in Uganda, or on a journey into the rainforests of Costa Rica. Our safaris in Africa visit some of the world's finest reserves; like the Serengeti, the Ngorongoro Crater, Kruger, Etosha and the Okavango Delta. Our group leaders are assisted by local guides to bring out the best of nature's exuberance, as well as allowing time to explore local villages and perhaps walk local trails.

Walks & Treks

Easy day-walks, moderate hikes, challenging treks… Walk to remote villages in Andalucia or the Canary Islands, hike through stunning mountains in the Pyrenees or Corsica or snowshoe through pristine wilderness in Finland or Quebec. Join a classic trek in Nepal, hike through the Andes, visit tribal villages in Thailand or stay with the Berbers in Morocco's Atlas Mountains. All walks graded. No backpacking.

Tel: 01420 541007
travelbag-adventures.com

★

Things to do in Galway and Roscommon

- Enjoy a **day at the races** in Galway City
- Experience the fun of the **Galway festival**
- Walk on **Inis Meáin (Inishmaan)** and take in the views from Dún Chonchúir
- Try cocktails and dinner at **Currareveagh House**, Oughterard
- Spend a night in **Day's Bar** on Inishbofin
- Absorb the Yeats associations at **Coole Park** and **Thoor Ballylee**
- A Wednesday night's traditional music at **Kate Lavin**'s in Boyle

was a walled town of about 35 acres here. In the 15th century, the town was given a royal charter and control of the parish church of St Nicholas (built in 1320), enhancing Galway's power. For 150 years the townsmen grew wealthy on trade with Spain and France, and even with the Caribbean: animal pelts and fish in exchange for wine and fine cloth. The evidence of the wealth is still there in the fine old stone buildings in the town and the many tower houses of the surrounding countryside.

But the 17th-century English wars brought an end to Galway's prosperity. The cityfolk supported the losing side in both the English civil war – suffering the attacks of Cromwell's troops as a result – and the war between James II and William of Orange, surrendering to William's forces in 1691. After that things declined for about 200 years. There was a brief economic boom in Victorian times and then things began to look up again around the 1960s due to deliberate state policies and the inevitable move from the country to the cities. Now Galway booms with hotels and new developments and the outskirts have roundabouts popping up like mushrooms.

There was a brief economic boom in Victorian times and then things began to look up again around the 1960s when government funds were put into developing the west of Ireland and following the inevitable move from the country to the cities.

Sights

Eyre Square, with Kennedy Park in the middle, has become a kind of dumping ground for memorabilia that doesn't fit in too well anywhere else. The **Browne Doorway** was in the way of some redevelopment and got moved here – it's a piece of a 17th-century building consisting of a bay window and the eponymous doorway with the date and coat of arms carved into it. Two statues adorn the park: one of **Padraic O'Conaire** (1882-1928), local author of *M'asal Beag Dubh* (*My Little Black Donkey*), and another of **Liam Mellows** (1892-1922), a republican and socialist who fought in the 1916 Easter Rising and later in the civil war on the side of the anti-Treaty party. He was executed in 1922 as a reprisal against the murder of two Daíl deputies. When this area of the square was being excavated in 1955, human remains were found and this spot is thought to have been the town's place of execution where the bodies of those hanged would have been thrown down and buried beneath the gallows.

There is also a **plaque** in the square dedicated to John F Kennedy, who addressed the people of Galway from this spot in 1963, after which the park was renamed in his honour. Two ancient iron canons, formerly the property of the Connaught Rangers (see page 405), are also in the square, while the fountain erected in 1984 to commemorate Galway's 500 years as a town is in the shape of a Galway Hooker, the traditional sailing ship of the area.

Eyre Square
In summer the square is often a venue for concerts and other events

County Galway

Galway city

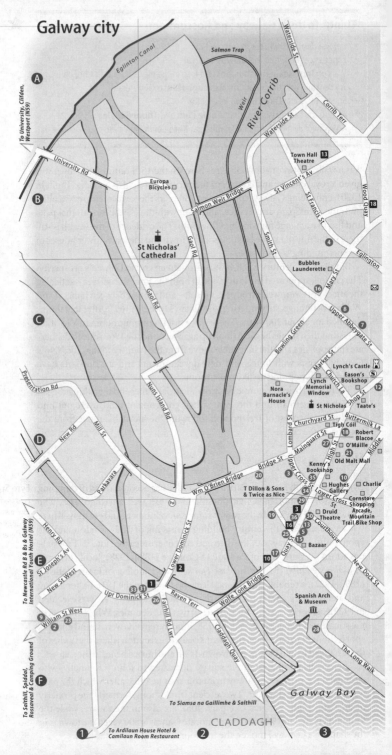

Eglinton Canal

Salmon Trap

River Corrib

Weir

Waterside St

Corrib Terr.

To University, Clifden, Westport (N59)

University Rd

Europa Bicycles

Salmon Weir Bridge

St Vincent's Av

St Francis St

Wood Quay

Town Hall Theatre **13**

18

St Nicholas' Cathedral

Gaol Rd

Smith St

4

Eglinton

Bubbles Launderette

Gaol Rd

Nuns Island Rd

16

Mary St

Upper Abbeygate St

8

7

Bowling Green

Market St

Lynch's Castle

Eason's Bookshop

12

Presentation Rd

New Rd

Mill St

Parkavara

Nora Barnacle's House

Lynch Memorial Window

St Nicholas'

Church La

Shop St

Taate's

Churchyard St

Buttermilk La.

Church St

Tigh Cóil

Robert Blacoe **18**

O'Máille

Old Malt Mall

21

Lombard St

Mainguard St

High St

Middle

27

Kenny's Bookshop

Bridge St

Wm O'Brien Bridge

20

Upper Cross St

3

35

Hughes Gallery

Charlie

10

Cornstore Shopping Arcade, Mountain Trail Bike Shop

T Dillon & Sons & Twice as Nice

34

Lower Cross St

29

Druid Theatre

Courthouse

19

36

30

16

3

13

25

5

15

Bazaar

Lower Dominick St

To Newcastle Rd B & Bs & Galway International Youth Hostel (N59)

Henry Rd

St Joseph's Av

New St West

10

17

Quay St

11

New Dock St

Upr Dominick St

33 **31**

1

26

2

Raven Terr.

Fairhill Rd Lwr

Wolfe Tone Bridge

Spanish Arch & Museum

William St West

9

2 **23**

To Salthill, Spiddal, Rossaveel & Camping Ground

Claddagh Quay

28

The Long Walk

Galway Bay

County Galway

To Siamsa na Gaillimhe & Salthill

CLADDAGH

1

To Ardilaun House Hotel & Camilaun Room Restaurant

2

3

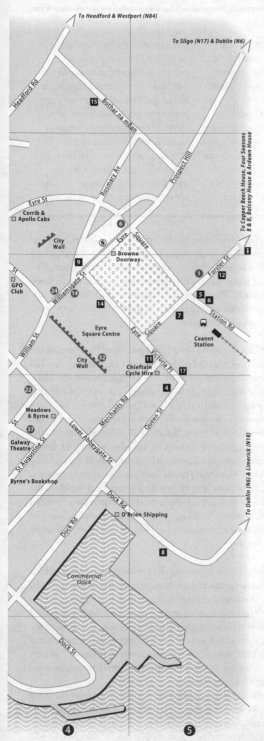

To Headford & Westport (N84)

To Sligo (N17) & Dublin (N6)

N

| 0 yards | 100 |
| 0 metres | 100 |

To Copper Beech House, Four Seasons
B & B, Balcony House & Ardawn House

Headford Rd

Bothar na mBan

Rosemary Av

Prospect Hill

Eyre St

Corrib &
Apollo Cabs

City
Wall

Eyre Square

Forster St

Browne
Doorway

GPO
Club

Williamgate St

William St

Eyre Square Centre

Eyre Square

Station Rd

Ceannt
Station

City
Wall

Victoria Pl

Chieftain
Cycle Hire

Meadows
& Byrne

Galway
Theatre

St Augustine St

Byrne's Bookshop

Merchants Rd

Lower Abbeygate St

Queen St

Dock Rd

O'Brien Shipping

To Dublin (N6) & Limerick (N18)

Dock Rd

Commercial
Dock

Dock St

■ Sleeping
1 Arch View *E2*
2 Atlanta *E2*
3 Barnacles Quay St Hostel *E3*
4 Celtic Tourist Hostel *D5*
5 Eyre Square & Red Square *C5*
6 Galway Hostel *C5*
7 Great Southern *C5*
8 Harbour & Krusoe's *E5*
9 Imperial *C4*
10 Jury's Galway Inn *E3*
11 Kinlay House *C5*
12 Park House *C5*
13 Salmon Weir *B3*
14 Skeffington Arms *C4*
15 Sleepzone *A4*
16 Spanish Arch *E3*
17 Victoria *C5*
18 Woodquay Hostel *B3*

● Eating & drinking
1 An Púcan Pub *C5*
2 Blue Note *F1*
3 Busker Browne's & Kirby's *D3*
4 Cactus Jack's Café Bar *B3*
5 Café du Journal *E3*
6 Club Cuba *B4*
7 Conlon's *C3*
8 Couch Potatoes *C3*
9 Crane Bar *E1*
10 Da Tang Noodle House *D3*
11 Eastern Tandoori *E3*
12 Elle's *D4*
13 Fat Freddie's *E3*
14 GBC Coffee Shop *C4*
15 Gemelles *E3*
16 Home Plate *C3*
17 K.C. Blakes *E3*
18 King's Head *D3*
19 Kirwan Lane Creative Cuisine *E3*
20 Lisheen Bar *D2*
21 Malt House *D3*
22 Mama's *D4*
23 Massimo's *E1*
24 Maxwell McNamara's *C4*
25 McDonagh's *E3*
26 Monroe's Tavern *E2*
27 Murphy's Pub *D3*
28 Nimmo's *F3*
29 Pierre's *E3*
30 Quays & Teach Na Céibhe Bar *E3*
31 Roisin Dubh Pub *E2*
32 Sails *C4*
33 Taylor's Bar *E1*
34 Tigh Neachtain's Bar & River
   God Café *D3*
35 Tomás O'Riada *D3*
36 Trattoria *E3*
37 Tulsi *D4*

County Galway

Lynch law

The Lynches were an important Galway family, 84 of whom became mayors of the city between the 15th and 17th centuries. One of them is said to have given the English language the word 'lynch'.

In 1493, James Lynch Fitz Stephens' son Walter and his girlfriend Ann were at a dance with their Spanish friend Gomez who, being a polite sort of chap, was very attentive to Ann. Walter became fiercely jealous and secretly followed Gomez home and murdered him. When the body was found Walter's hat and

knife were beside it. Walter, an otherwise saintly young man, was accused of the murder and confessed, whereupon his father James Lynch Fitz Stephens dragged him to the town jail. Walter was such a nice young man that the whole town begged James for mercy on his son and even the hangman refused to do the dirty deed. James, in a fury of righteousness and finding his way to the scaffold blocked by angry townspeople, threw his son out of the window, first tying him by the neck to a stake inside the room.

At the southwest corner of the square is the **Eyre Square Centre** in whose basement can be seen part of the original medieval walls of the city, although it's difficult to distinguish ancient remains from modern reconstruction. The square is a busy sort of place, what with the statuary, parked cars, phone boxes, bus queues and traffic. The recent pedestrianization of the roads leading down to the harbour has shifted the balance of the town a little away from here to the cafés and shops of Quay Street.

Lynch's Castle On the corner of Abbeygate Street and Shop Street the Allied Irish Bank occupies what was once Lynch's Castle, a building thought to date back to 1320 and occupying the centre of the medieval city. It is a single, four-storey block decorated on the outside with gargoyle water spouts. The original building would probably have been thatched but much of it burned down in 1473 and was rebuilt by 1503. Cromwell's troops did it considerable damage and it sank into mediocrity for a few hundred years. Before 1820, when the street to the west was rebuilt, the building was much larger, extending westwards. Inside the lobby of the bank are a number of panels telling the story of the building and its owners, as well as a 17th-century bridal fireplace, common to this area, celebrating the marriage of members of two important local families, the Blakes and the ffrenches. It does not belong in this building but was brought here in 1927 from another nearby building which was being remodelled. The entrance doors to the bank were constructed in 1933. ■ *Open during banking hrs, 1000-1600, Mon-Sat. Free.*

St Nicholas of Myra
Legend has it that Christopher Columbus worshipped here in 1477

Further south, along Shop Street, is the church of St Nicholas of Myra, which has been the city's church since the 14th century. St Nicholas is the man we all revere as Santa Claus, the fourth-century bishop of Myra in Lycia and the patron saint of sailors. The nave, chancel and transepts were built at this time and it is the largest medieval parish church in Ireland. In the 16th century, the north and south aisles were added, as well as the chapel of the Blessed Sacrament and the belfry. In 1652, the church was desecrated by Cromwell's forces who used the building as stables. It is a pretty little church and its various ornaments make it well worth a wander round.

From the entrance, the room above you in the porchway was once the living quarters of the sexton: legend has it that the last sexton who lived in this tiny room had a family of eight children. In front of you is the **baptismal font**, perhaps 16th century in origin, carved with a figure of a dog, a fleur-de-lys and a three-leafed clover. In front of the Chapel of the Blessed sacrament are **banners of the Connaught Rangers**, whose cannon decorate Eyre Square and who mutinied in India in support of the Irish War of Independence in 1920. In the north aisle are some ancient gravestones, some of which carry the trade symbols of the men buried beneath them including a goldsmith's, stonemason's and a wool merchant's. In this area is a mass grave with several hundred skeletons.

In the Chapel of Christ is a 13th-century tomb of a crusader, the oldest tomb in the church. Under the Lynch window is the tomb of Stephen Lynch with the figures of two angels, damaged by Cromwell's forces. Some of the original paintwork of the tomb can still be made out. Further along the south transept is another Lynch tomb, with the figure of Christ displaying the five wounds, also damaged by 17th-century soldiers. Here too is the tomb of the infamous James Lynch who hung his own son, Walter (see box). Of particular interest is the apprentice's column in the southeast nave of the church, bearing particularly fancy carvings and thought to be the apprentice's master piece, the work he had to do to pass his apprenticeship. All around the church are stone fragments found during various renovations and set into the walls of the church to preserve them.

Outside the church in the wall of the churchyard is the **Lynch Memorial**, a completely modern collection of fragments all said to be connected with James Lynch. ■ *Shop St. Apr-Sep, daily 0900-1745; Oct-Mar, daily, 0930-1430. Free.*

At No 8 Bowling Green is the erstwhile **home of Nora Barnacle**, now dedicated to the memory of the woman who captured James Joyce's heart. Joyce visited the house in 1909 and 1912 and wrote the powerful short story *The Dead*, based on the story of the young man, Michael Bodkin, who died after making his way in the rain to sing to Nora. ■ *Apr-Sep, Mon-Sat, irregularly. On request during winter months. Variable phone number in the window of the house. €1.50.*

Other sights

In Flood Street is the **Spanish Arch**, one of the remaining sections of the city walls of Galway. It is thought that this was a place where ships could unload their goods in the town's harbour. Its age or function is not really known nor is the origin of its name. Behind the arch, the walls of the city and the ditch that lay outside it can be seen.

Close by is the town's **museum**, a collection of trivia and flotsam representing the hundreds of years of the city's existence, all cluttered together rather haphazardly. It includes straw rattles, feeding bottles, an assortment of broken yokes, neolithic axe heads and bits of masonry with little tags suggesting their origins. ■ *Flood St. Mon-Sun, 1000-1715. €1.50.*

Beyond the Wolfe Tone Bridge is the **Claddagh**, one-time independent state with its own king, laws, language and dress code and later a fishing village where the Galway Hookers were built and used. It once had a population of about 8,000 Irish speakers living in tiny thatched cottages (see box page 406).

Over to the northwest of town is **St Nicholas' Cathedral**, dedicated in 1965. In an epiphany of 1960s bad taste, it is built of limestone blocks with copper streaks from the roof cutting crazy patterns down its walls and an excess of Connemara marble inside. The size of the interior makes it feel more like a hypermarket rather than inspiring any sense of the spiritual.

West of the city is **Salthill**, a rapidly developing seaside resort. It has a leisure centre, some interesting night life and a pebbly beach. After September, when the schools reopen, Salthill is a perfect place for lovers of deserted seaside towns. In summer there's not much to keep you there except lots of family entertainment such as **Leisureland**, with several pools and rides, **Atlantaquaria,** with big tanks full of fish and a touchy-feely pool, and

County Galway

☞ ## The Claddagh

When the Anglo-Normans took the settlement and began the development of Galway City, the native population settled to the south in the area known as Claddagh or beach. Like other Gaelic settlements all over Ireland it had its own laws and a ruler who functioned as law maker and judge. Long after other Gaelic settlements assimilated and learned English the Claddagh survived, a little pocket of Gaelic Ireland right up to the early 20th century, with its own customs,

dress, and economy based on fishing using the Galway Hookers. The little township of thatched cottages was demolished in 1937 when the area was needed for modern housing and the Gaelic-speaking residents dispersed. The only thing that remains now is the name, which has been given to a style of ring common to Connaught: the Claddagh ring. This shows a pair of hands, the symbol of friendship, holding a heart, the symbol of love, with a crown, a symbol, to some at least, of loyalty.

Seapoint, with a casino, video games snooker and daily bingo. The promenade is the longest in Ireland and at the western end is Blackrock diving area, once a men-only swimming spot. When you get to the end of the promenade, kick the wall – it's a tradition. ■ *Leisureland: The Promenade, T521455. Mon-Fri, 0930-1400, 2000-2200; Sat, 1400-1715; Sun, 1100-1800. €3.50. Seapoint: Seapoint Promenade, T521716. Daily, 1000-0100. Variable rates. Atlantaquaria, T585100, atlantaquaria@eircom.net Open daily 1000-1800.*

Essentials

Sleeping
■ *on map*
Price codes:
see inside front cover

During festival time, in Jul, Aug and Sep, accommodation becomes very scarce indeed and should be booked well in advance

The city abounds with hotels, both in the city and on the feeder roads into town, good inexpensive hostels, and lots of B&Bs. There are very few B&Bs or guesthouses within the city centre: most are in suburbs or Salthill. B&Bs tend to cost around €36 per person sharing a double room. Some do 25-50% reductions for children. If you turn up in the city with no accommodation try the Ireland West Tourism Office (see page 400), but there can be long delays queuing for attention there at the peak of the season. A possibility worth considering is Salthill, which is a brisk but stimulating walk from town, has lots of accommodation at all price ranges and another Ireland West Tourism office where the queues may be shorter. Galway is crowded with hostels, most of which offer single and double rooms as well as the usual kitchens, lounge area and laundry. The dormitory accommodation attracts a very young crowd whose habits tend to be late and noisy: do not expect a quiet, restful time in any of the Galway hostels during the summer months. Room rates in the bigger hotels expand during festival times but by the same token can be negotiated downwards in the off season.

Galway centre LL-L *Ardilaun House Hotel*, Taylor's Hill, T521433, www.ardilaunhousehotel.ie Extensive facilities including leisure centre with pool. Very smart, individually furnished rooms with fine views. Privately owned, friendly hotel sitting in its own manicured grounds; originally a mansion owned by one of the Galway tribes, the Pearses. Well out of the noise of the city. **LL-L** *Great Southern Hotel*, Eyre Sq, T564041, res@galway.gsh.ie Rates vary according to season, and whether weekends or weekdays; some good special offers. Spacious rooms, award-winning restaurant, roof-top pool. **LL-AL** *Eyre Square Hotel*, Forster St, T569633, www.byrne-hotelsireland.com All the facilities, centrally located, lively pub. **LL-AL** *Skeffington Arms Hotel*, Eyre Sq, T563173, F561679. Newly refurbished rooms, lively bar, carvery restaurant. This small place has been here for a hundred years so it must be doing something right. **L** *Victoria Hotel*, Victoria Pl, T567433, F565880. In a quiet part of the city centre, big spacious rooms individually furnished, pleasant guest areas. **LL-AL** *Hotel Spanish Arch*, Quay St, T569600, www.irisholidays.com/sp-index.html Boutique hotel with individually decorated rooms, nice Victorian bar, and bits of 16th-century walls.

AL-A *Atlanta Hotel*, Dominick St, T562241, F563895. Out of the main city centre, small family run hotel, guests' car-park. **L-A** *Harbour Hotel*, The Harbour, T569466 www.galwayharbourhotel.com Modern, stylish hotel with excellent room rates. Secure parking, quiet location, good views, lots of comfort and a restaurant, *Krusoe's*, with an excellent reputation. **L-A** *Imperial Hotel*, Eyre Sq, T563033, imperialhtl@hotmail.com Very centrally located, restaurant popular with locals. **AL-A** *Jury's Galway Inn*, Quay St, T566444, info@jurys.com Charging per room, not per person, this has to be the best value hotel in town for more than 2 people sharing. Pleasant, close to river. **AL-A** *Ardawn House*, College Rd, T568833, ardawn@iol.ie Big roomy guest house close to town and right next door to the greyhound track so fans can watch from their bedroom windows! Luxury breakfast, comfortable sitting room, lots of good tourist advice and fresh tea, coffee and cakes served all day.

A *Balcony House*, 27 College Rd, T/F563438. Small, comfortable, close to town. **A** *Four Seasons* 23 College Rd, T564078. Close to town and comfortable, a B&B with off street parking. **A** *Villa Nova*, 40 Newcastle Rd, T524849. Guesthouse west city centre. **A** *Bernie Kelly*, 3 Ash Grove, Newcastle Rd, T524285, info@familyhomes.ie Small friendly place, walking distance from town. **A-B** *Copper Beech House*, 26 College Rd, T569544, info@family-homes.ie Small B&B close to the city centre with views of Lough Atalia Bay.

B *Neesha*, 4 Ashgrove, Newcastle Rd, T524250, info@familyhomes.ie B&B close to the city centre, French spoken. **B-C** *Sleepzone*, Bothar na Mban Wood Quay, T566999, www.sleepzone.ie Very central, brand new, purpose built hostel and internet café. Dorm beds, doubles, singles. **D** *Arch View Hostel*, 1 Upper Dominick St, T586661. No private rooms. **B-C** *Barnacles Quay Street House*, 10 Quay St, T/F568644, qshl@arnacles.ie 6 private rooms, family rooms, a laundry. Near the harbour. **B-C** *Kinlay House*, Merchant's Rd, T565244, F565245. Just off Eyre Sq, with private rooms. Washrooms and toilets are not gender specific. Price includes continental breakfast. **C-D** *Celtic Tourist Hostel*, Queen St, Victoria Pl, T/F566606. Some private rooms. **C-D** *The Galway Hostel*, Eyre Sq, T566959. In an elegant old stone building, has several private double rooms. Open 24 hrs with no curfew. **C-D** *Woodquay Hostel*, Woodquay, T/F562618, www.indigo.ie/celticnet/woodquay/ Newly opened hostel, fairly central. Some private rooms.

D *Galway International Youth Hostel*, St Mary's College, St Mary's Rd, T527411, www.irelandyha.org.anoige/galway4.html *An Óige* hostel, half-way between Salthill and the city centre; has a cafeteria, laundry, double rooms and family rooms. Price includes breakfast. Open summer only. **D** *Mary Ryan Apartments*, 4 Beechmount Ave, Highfield Park, T523303. Open from Jun-Sep inclusive. No dormitory accommodation, only twin and family rooms. Price includes breakfast, evening meals are available. **D** *The Salmon Weir Hostel*, St Vincent's Av, T561133. Has private doubles, family rooms, and does evening meals. In the northwest of the city.

Furbo **LL-L** *Connemara Coast Hotel*, Furbo, T592108, F592065. This smart new hotel is 10 mins by car from Galway on the coast road west of Salthill. Stirring views over Galway Bay and a small library to help pass the time on a rainy day.

Salthill **LL-L** *Galway Bay Hotel*, The Promenade, T520520, www.galwybayhotel. net Vast, yellow, spacious but fairly bland place with leisure centre, pool, library and sea views. **L-AL** *Hotel Salthill*, T522711, F521855, infosh@indigo.ie Previously known as *Murrays*, a friendly hotel with refurbished, pleasant rooms; family-owned and run. The bar has live music every night in summer, very popular restaurant; sea views.

County Galway

AL-A *Anno Santo Hotel*, Threadneedle Rd, T523011, www.annosantosalthill.com Small, family run, on main bus route into city. Away from the sea front. **AL** *Rockbarton Park Hotel*, T522286, F527692. Family-run hotel in residential area. **AL-B** *Knockrea Guest House*, 55 Lower Salthill, T520145, F529985, knockrea@eircom.net On bus route, 300yds from seafront, walkable distance from city. Friendly atmosphere, car park. **AL-A** *Bayberry House*, 9 Cuan Glas, Bishop Donnell Rd, Taylor's Hill, T525171 www.galway.net/pages/bayberry Modern purpose built B&B. Child reductions.

B *Atlantic View House*, 4 Ocean Wave, Seapoint, T582109, F528566. Guesthouse close to the city, sea views.

Camping There are several campsites to the east and west of Galway along the coast. The best of them is *Ballyloughane Caravan and Camping Park*, Ballyloughane Beach, Renmore, T755338, F752029. About 5 mins, drive outside the city centre along the Dublin road. Shop, laundry, TV room. Tent, 2 people and a car around €9. At Barna, west of Salthill on the R337 to Spiddal is *Hunters Silver Strand Caravan Park*, Barna, T592040. Small shop and laundry. 2 people, tent and car €10 Both open Easter to 30th Sep.

Eating
● *on map*
Price codes:
see inside front cover

Expensive Best of the restaurants in Galway is the *Camilaun Room*, in *Ardilaun House Hotel* (see 'Sleeping' above). Its line-up of awards is quite stunning and its style is modern Irish with the emphasis on fresh local produce. Reservations necessary. At the bottom of Quay St is *K.C. Blakes*, T561826, a very fashionable-looking place with lots of beech and steel. The menu is extensive and runs to pizzas, pasta and fajitas. Open 1200-1500 weekdays and 1700-2230, 7 days a week in summer. *Gemelles*, 23 Quay St T568821, is relatively new in town but comes highly recommended. Italian cooking dominates.

Mid-range A city-centre, family-run place with a relaxed atmosphere and fine menu is *The Malt House*, T563993, in the Old Malt Shopping Mall. Its stone walls are ancient and it is the right size for comfort – not too many tables but not so small that everything you say is heard by the other customers. A small, traditional Irish menu, extensive wine list and reasonable prices ensure a great meal. There is an early evening menu. Attached to Busker Browne's in Cross St is *Kirby's*, T569404, a place that is visually very pleasing, with Munch-like oil paintings on the walls and a nice extensive menu including boxtys (Irish potato pancakes), parsnip soup, lots of fish and vegetarian choices. Open for lunch and dinner daily. Nearby in Kirwan Lane is *Kirwan Lane Creative Cuisine*, T568266, a classy looking place with a reputation for interesting dishes. In Long Walk, Spanish Arch, is *Nimmo's*, T563565, a tiny place with a very good reputation. Minimalist menu but the dishes are a surprise when they reach you. Dinner €26 plus. Nouvelle Irish. The restaurant in the *Harbour Hotel* (see above), *Krusoe's*, has acquired an excellent reputation in the few months that it has been open. Modern Irish cuisine with the emphasis on traditional dishes such as champ and Irish stew, it is very popular especially at lunchtime.

Cheap Along Quay St are a series of restaurants worth browsing through if you're after some good food. The *River God Café*, T565811, at No 2 above the *Tigh Neachtain* pub serves snacks and pastries as well as lunchtime and evening meals. Delights on the menu include fish in coral sauce and Creole turkey stir-fry. The off-season evening menu is excellent value. You can also bring your own wine. Vegetarians have lots of choices. Reservations necessary at weekends. Further along is *Pierre's*, T566066, open 7 days till 2300 in summer, with a similar good winter offers and French cuisine. The *Quays* restaurant at the back of the *Teach Na Céibhe* pub, T568347, is another themed place but nicely done. The restaurant has an extensive menu both for lunch and dinner. The *Trattoria*, still in Quay St at No 12, T563910, a pasta and pizza place is open 7 days. The setting is very Italian, dimly lit with lots of Chianti bottles. Dinner could work out at around €24. At the bottom of Quay St *Donagh's Seafood* does excellent fish and chips with a wide range of fish on the menu at café prices.

In Abbeygate street is *Conlon's Fish Restaurant*, a very popular place with an enormous menu and great fish and chips. In nearby St Francis St is brightly decorated *Cactus Jack's* with everything on a Mexican theme – burgers, steaks, fajitas, Cajun dishes – all at reasonable prices, a cocktail happy hr 1700-2000 which is very popular indeed. Close by in Main St, T501475, is *The Home Plate*, selling more Mexican stuff and some Thai dishes too. Midday-2130 daily. *Mama's*, easily missed in Middle St open for lunch weekdays and dinner 7 days has good lunch offers and a menu which runs to Thai, Singaporean and Philippino dishes. Nicely decorated and sells Tiger beer. Children's menu. Karaoke Fri and Sat nights.

If you have a sudden hankering after Asian cuisine there are a few more good places to try. *Da Tang Noodle House*, Middle St, T561443, has authentic noodle based Chinese cuisine with lots of vegetarian options. At 3, Buttermarket Walk, Middle St, T564831, is *Tulsi*, an Indian restaurant with lots of vegetable dishes, enough for a vegetarian to have a banquet. For more meaty kind of Indian food try *Eastern Tandoori*, 21, Spanish Pde, T564819, with lots of naans and nut-based sauces.

In the Eyre Square Shopping Centre are several places to consider. There is a *Kylemore* bakery on the ground floor, where you can get filled rolls and pastries while upstairs is their restaurant serving hot meals at reasonable prices. Upstairs there is also an open-plan eating area called *Sails*, which does soup and sandwiches and more substantial dishes for lunch if you don't mind the taped muzak of the shopping centre. Next door to it is *La Croissanterie*, which serves soup and all kinds of filled croissants. The Eyre Square Centre links up with Corbett Ct where there is an excellent sandwich bar, one of a chain in Ireland, *O'Brien's*. Both these shopping centres close at 1800.

Along the main Eyre Sq to Shop St route are lots of snackeries and theme pubs. In Williamsgate St is the homely *GBC Coffeeshop*, which does lunchtime food and has a restaurant upstairs for more substantial dishes, while opposite is the big and busy *Maxwell McNamara's* doing snacks and sandwiches, with a menu full of fish, steak and chicken options as well as a tiny box describing what vegetarians can have. Still in Shop St, at No 12 *Elle's* café serves soups and sandwiches, filled potatoes and pittas and a nice array of desserts, open until 1830, Mon-Sat, 1800 Sun. The *King's Head* at the junction of Shop St and High St is a vast, recently themed old pub, which seems to go on for ever, with some good pub food that ceases by early evening. *Tomás O'Riada* in Quay St is another genuinely old pub that has been themed and now forms a warren of little bars and a connected café called *The Front Door*. You can order the food in any part of the bars or eat in the café itself. Slightly more choices than the typical bar food menu with good vegetarian options and sandwiches. Food finishes about 1600. Relatively new in town is *Fat Freddie's* doing pizzas and quesilladas and more. Not a lot of room inside but put in your order and retire to the pub next door and they'll give you a shout when it's ready.

In Abbeygate St Lower is *Couch Potatoes*, a very busy place nicely decorated with potatoes dominating the menu from filled baked potatoes to potato pizza. A good, value-for-money place, with lots of vegetarian choices.

In Cross St is *Busker Browne's* pub, serving soups and more substantial choices till 2000, daily in summer. Rather more than a coffee shop *Café du Journal*, The Halls, Quay St, T568426, is a bookish sort of place where many different coffees are served with newspapers to read; it also offers stylish soups and main courses with lots of seafood dishes and delicious sauces. Open till 2230.

Town centre In summer there is music all around – in the street and in almost every **Pubs & music** pub – just wander down the street and follow the noise. *List Galway* is a free fortnightly publication listing what's on in town available from the tourist office, newsagents, pubs and the station. *Neachtain's*, Cross St is the most famous of the Galway pubs with little booths to sit in, turf fires in the winter and spontaneous traditional music sessions Mon, Fri, Sat.

County Galway

There is live music most nights in **Busker Browne's** in Upper Cross St with jazz on Sun mornings. **The King's Head** in High St has music ranging from jazz to traditional Irish every night and a good atmosphere to match, while **Taafe's**, next door is a more traditional bar also with traditional music nightly as well as sports on TV.

Similar in style, and with the same probability of live music as the King's Head, is the **Quays** in Quay St. But the most authentic, and the least brought-in-for-the-tourists, music is to be found in the **Lisheen Bar**, in Bridge St. Other places to check out are the **Drum Bar**, in Eglinton St, with disco music rather than live bands; **Red Square** in Eyre Sq with live music every night ranging from jazz to traditional music as well as rock, and **An Púcán** in Forster St, just off Eyre Sq. In Mainguard St is **Tigh Coil** which has traditional music sessions on most days at 1730 and 2100. Newly opened, close to the river, is **Bazaar** with a very young clientele and lots of chart music.

West of the river On the other side of the river **The Crane Bar** in Sea Rd oozes tradition with music every night. Close by are **The Róisín Dubh** in Upper Dominick St, where the music is definitely not traditional, **Monroe's** also in Dominick St where there is a wide variety of activities each night including set dancing 1 or 2 nights a week, **Taylor's** Bar, again in Dominick St with traditional Irish music most afternoons and evenings, and the **Blue Note**, in West William St, which features largely DJ-driven sounds with live music in between. Next door is **Massimo**, a designer bar with lots of open spaces, cool music and big sofas.

A quiet drink Bars to look out for if you enjoy genuine, unreconstructed spit and sawdust, or just calm in the eye of the Galway hurricane, are **Murphy's** in the High St, run by the same family for 3 generations and with special reductions on beer for pensioners, and **The Bal**, in Salthill, offering a quiet pint in the midst of bingo, karaoke, drum and bass and British stag parties.

Entertainment

Nightclubs When the bars close the nightclubs open. **ClubCuba** in Eyre Sq is open 7 nights a week till the early hours with chart music and special events in the **CubaLive** section. **Central Park** is in Abbeygate St and is the very trendiest place to be. Opens at 2300 and gets very crowded. The **GPO** nightclub in Eglinton St has a wide range of events starting at 2300. All have entry charges that vary according to what's on. Check the listings for details. There are also nightclubs at the *Skeffington Hotel* and the *Warwick Hotel* in Salthill which are very popular with local people.

Theatre and cultural centres *Town Hall Theatre* in Courthouse Sq, T569777, puts on more established material and travelling theatre groups. There is also an Irish-language theatre in Middle St called **An Taibhdhearc na Gaillimhe**, T562024. Look out for notices of events, especially in **List Galway** and on the noticeboards in the **Galway Arts Centre**. If it's *Riverdance* you're looking for, there is **Siamsa**, an Irish dance and music show at the Claddagh Hall, Nimmo's Pier, T755479. Shows are nightly at 2045.

Galleries There are several art galleries, including the **Bridge Mills Gallery** at O'Brien's Bridge and the **Kenny Gallery** in Middle St, selling local artists' work. The **Galway Arts Centre** Lower Dominick St, T65886, www.galwayartscentre.ie, exhibits local and national artists' work. It is sometimes also used as a performance space.

Festivals

Salthill has an air display in early Jul with aeronautical displays and live music, but there are 3 big festivals that are special to Galway city

The *Galway Races* are in the last week in **Jul** and the racing takes place in Ballybrit track, just over a mile outside the city on the road to the airport. The race track can accommodate 30,000 people, and usually does, and restaurants, bars and hotels stay open 24 hrs a day for the duration. T753870, galway@iol.ie, book early. There is another 2-day event in Sep and again in late Oct.

The 22-year-old *Arts Festival*, T566577, www.galwayartsfestival.ie, in the 2nd and 3rd week of **Jul** is the country's biggest and best cultural bash with theatre companies from all over the world and customary 24-hr opening for everything. Music, art exhibitions, and lots more. Book even earlier, especially for the events. Part of the Arts Festival is a week-long *film festival*.

The last week in **Sep** sees the *Oyster Festival*, T527282, oysters@iol.ie (see page 438); lots of free oysters and Guinness, street concerts, general craic and of course lots of licence extensions. The highlight of the event is the oyster opening competition.

Antiques For connoisseurs of old clothes there is *Twice as Nice*, at 5 Quay St, which sells vintage clothing and jewellery, while antique afficionados could have a look in *Tempo Antiques* in Cross St which is full of lovely things. There is an antiques market on level one of Eyre Sq shopping centre.

Art At *Hughes Gallery*, the owner sells his own works and will do commissions from photographs, frame your own works of art and offers painting lessons. The tiny gallery is in the High St, T25963.

Books Galway has a huge number of bookshops as you would expect in a university city. *Easons*, 33 Shop St, has lots of local interest stuff including maps and guides as well as international newspapers. In the High St is *Kenny's*, which seems to go on forever, with the largest stock of second-hand books in Ireland and lots of rare and wonderful tomes such as first editions of Seamus Heaney, Beckett, Yeats and many others. The same company have a bookstore on Merchant's Rd, with out-of-print books where you can spend many hours looking for just the right book. In Eglinton St is *Keohanes*, which has a wide range of subject areas but is particularly good on books of Irish interest. It has a children's bookstore in the next building. At 23 Abbeygate St Lower is *Book Exchange* with lots of second-hand paperbacks and comics, while in Middle St in the Cornstore Shopping Centre is *Charlie Byrne's*, with remaindered, second-hand and discounted books.

Clothes Jumper and woollens shops abound. Try *Ó'Máille* in the High St, which has the full range of chunky sweaters, tweeds, and jackets. It is open daily in summer. *Tribes* in William St is another gorgeous place but there are so many of them, it is impossible to list them all. Just start at the top of Eyre Sq and work your way down to Quay St.

Crafts As well as the locally made clothes, there are a number of places selling little wooden and ceramic things around Eyre Sq and Quay St. Other good craft shops are *Kelly's* in High St, and *Meadows and Byrne* in Castle St, which is more of a designer furniture and household goods place but has some attractive and functional pottery. A place which is part-shop and part-visitor centre is the *Galway Irish Crystal* heritage centre, Merlin Park, Dublin Rd, T757311, www.galwaycrystal.ie, which does factory tours then sells you stuff from the shop.

Jewellery A good local purchase is, of course, a claddagh design in a piece of jewellery. Start off in *T Dillon and Sons*, on the corner of Quay St and Cross St. They have a little museum (1000-1700) at the back of the shop dedicated to the history of the claddagh design (see page 406), lots of rings, brooches and necklaces to choose from, and a very famous clientele. Using their prices as a starting point, you could compare prices with any of the other jewellers in town who also sell the Claddagh designs, notably *Robert Blacoe* in Shop St, who also does other interesting Irish/Galway designs. In the Eyre Sq centre is *Claddagh Jewellers* with lots more of the same and in Dominick St is *Richard Quinn* with more still.

Shopping
Galway heaves with places where tourists can part with their money, often for quite pretty things totally unconnected with Galway

Fishing Information from the *Western Region Fisheries Board*, T563118. For the last few years sea trout have been a protected species in this area. The Corrib System allows trout and salmon fishing, and the season opens on Lough Corrib in Feb. A boatman can be hired for about €57 per day. *Feeney's Sports*, 19-23 High St, T568794, can arrange guides on Lough Corrib, and sea angling trips from Jul onwards.

Golf *Galway Bay Golf and Country Club*, Salthill to the southwest of the city, T790500, was designed by Christy O'Connor. Surrounded on 3 sides by the sea, 18 holes. *Don Wallace Pro Shop*, T523038, is in the club.

Horse-riding *Feeney's Equestrian Centre*, Toonabrockey, Bushypark, T526553. Organizes trekking and hacking around Galway, beach rides, hourly rates, unaccompanied

Sport

County Galway

children welcome. *Rusheen Riding Centre*, Salthill, T521285. Beach riding, trekking, lessons. *Rockmount Riding Centre*, Claregalway, 5 miles (8 km) from the city on main Galway to Sligo road, T798147. Indoor arena, trekking and hacking, lessons.

Tour companies & travel agents   Several tour companies have offices in the tourist office in Galway. *Lally Tours*, T553555, www.lallytours.com, do tours of Connemara, Westport and the Burren daily as well as a sightseeing tour of Galway. *O'Neachtain Day Tours*, T553188, www.wombat.ie/pages/oneachtain-tours, have tours to Connemara, the Burren and the Cliffs of Moher as well as a daily coach service to the Aran islands. **Boat trips** *Corrib Tours*, Furbo Hill, Furbo, T592447, organize 1½hr cruises daily cruises on Lough Corrib from Woodquay, Galway. **Air trips** *Executive Helicopters*, T792111, will take you on costly flights around Galway (€254), Connemara (€760) and Clare (€635).

Transport   **Bicycle**   Not really necessary for getting about Galway City, but bikes can be hired for longer journeys. Most of the hostels do bike hire as do *Flaherty's Cycles* in West William St and *Europa Bicycles*, Hunter's Building, Earl's Island,T563355. Mountain bikes can be hired from *Mountain Trail Bike Shop*, Cornstore, Middle St, T569888. **Bus**   Ceannt Bus Station, T563555/562000, is next to the railway station, off Eyre Sq and behind the *Great Southern Hotel*. There are hourly buses to **Dublin** as well as frequent buses to other cities in the Republic and the North. Several private companies also operate out of Galway. *Citylink*, T564163, do 8 buses a day to Dublin and **Dublin Airport**, departing from Forster St coach park. *Bus Nestor*, T797144, busnestor@eircom.net provide 4 buses daily, more on Fri. Departs Foster Pl in Galway, George's Quay and the airport in Dublin. Other companies do regular services to some of the smaller towns in the area. *McNulty Coaches*, T097-81016, do a service on Fri to **Belmullet** via **Westport** and **Newport**, leaving Eyre Sq at 1600, 1730 and 1800. *Nestor Travel*, T091-797144, run a service from Dublin and Dublin Airport to Galway. A once-daily bus service goes to **Galway Airport** from the bus station, price €3.50.   **Car**   *Windsor Rent-A-Car*, Monivea Rd, Ballybrit, T770707. On the way to the airport. **Taxis**   There are several taxi companies operating in the city. *Galway Taxi* T561111 is on Mainguard St while *Corrib and Apollo*, T564444, is on Eyre St, to the north of Eyre Sq. There is a taxi rank by the railway station. **Train**   T563555/562000. Trains for **Athlone**, **Tullamore**, **Portarlington**, **Kildare**, **Newbridge** and **Dublin** leave Galway 6 times a day (4 on Sun). Connections can be made at Kildare for towns in the south.

Directory   **Banks & bureaux de change**   There are 2 *Bank of Ireland* branches in Eyre Sq, an *Allied Irish Bank* in Lynch's Castle, Shop St. There are ATM machines outside all the branches. There is a bureau de change in the tourist office in Forster St. **Communications** Post office: the main post office is in Eglinton St, open Mon-Sat, 0900-1800. **Telephone**: there are card and coin telephone boxes in the post office and at key points around the city. **Hospitals & medical services**   Hospital: *University College Hospital*, Newcastle Rd, T563081. Pharmacy: *The Crescent Pharmacy*, 18 Fr Griffin Rd, T583956, Mon-Sat, 0900-1800, Sun, 1100-1300. **Language schools**   *Atlantic Language School*, Abbeygate St, T566051; *English in Galway*, Spanish Arch, T569896; *Galway Language Centre*, The Bridge Mills, T566468; *Westlingua*, Cathedral Buildings, Middle St, T568188. **Laundry** *Bubbles Laundrette*, Mary St, T563434. **Library**   *Galway County Library*, Hynes Building, St Augustine St, T561666.

County Galway

Aran Islands

Three small islands lying 28 miles (45 km) southwest of Galway across the mouth of Galway Bay – Inishmore, Inishmaan, and Inisheer – plus another three very small uninhabited islands make up the famous Aran Islands that continue to act as a magnet for travellers in search of the 'real' Ireland. The course of history helped preserve the islands' traditional way of life, but beginning in the early decades of the 20th century, writers and film makers celebrated and broadcast the pre-industrial culture of the Aran Islands, which turned the spotlight on them. The rest is history, of a very different kind, and in 1998 the authorities even talked of a 'tourist tax' to help cover the cost incurred by the annual invasion of visitors arriving by boats and planes from the mainland. The tax has not materialized but it gives you some idea of the numbers of people visiting the islands.

Phone code: 099
Colour map 2, grid C2

The good news is that two of the Aran Islands have not been destroyed by fame; the bad news is that Inishmore, at least in Jul and Aug, is best avoided. The two smaller islands, especially Inisheer, are rarely inundated with visitors and in many respects they retain much of the charm that first drew artists to Inishmore. However, the largest island is home to major archaeological sites and the tourist infrastructure has its advantages in terms of creature comforts.

Ins and outs

Air *Aer Arann*, T091-593034, F593238, aerarann@iol.ie, fly to all 3 islands, using 8-seater Islander aircraft, from Connemara Regional Airport at Inverin, off the main coastal road 17 miles (28 km) west of Galway. With flights every hr in peak months, the return fare is €44.50 and the connecting bus from the tourist office in Galway and Salthill costs €5 but takes longer to reach the airport from the city than the 10-min actual flying time. A package deal with 1 night's B&B and return fare is €63.

Getting there

 Boat *Island Ferries*, T091-568903/, travels to all 3 islands from Rossaveal, 26 miles (37 km) west of Galway. The journey takes about 40 mins and in Jul and Aug there are up to 6 boats a day to Inishmore. The boat to the other 2 islands departs at 1030 and 1830 daily; return fare is €19 and, if travelling from Galway, another €5 for the bus to Rossaveal that leaves from the office at Foster's Court beside the tourist office, 90 mins before departure. Tickets may also be purchased from the *Island Ferries* office at Rossaveal, T572050. Between Jun and Sep *Island Ferries* have a ferry direct from Galway to Inishmore; €23 return for the 90-min journey. Another company *Inis Mór Ferries*, T566535, 534553, 595036, does 4 sailings a day in summer from Rossaveal to Inishmore. Fares for their bus and ferry are the same. *O'Brien Shipping*, T091-567283/567676, with a desk in the Galway tourist office, run a ferry from Galway to all 3 islands daily between Jun and Sep, and Tue, Thu and Sat the rest of the year. The boat departs from Galway Dock at 1030, returning at 1700, taking 95 mins and €16 return. *Doolin Ferries*, T065-74455, run a service from Doolin to Inishere and Inishmore between Easter and Sep. The return fare is €19 and the journey takes about half an hour.

 Boat services between the islands are operated by *Sunda Teo*, T091-561767, a branch of *Island Ferries*, and in the summer there are daily links between the 3 islands. Outside of the summer the service is much reduced.

Only Inishmore is large enough to justify an alternative to walking and upon disembarkation a fleet of bicycles are waiting to be hired. Tour vans are now increasingly common on the island for set tours of the main sites of interest at around €6 per person, and pony traps with a driver may also be hired for around €12 per person.

Getting around

County Galway

Background

Ecology   Geologically, the islands are a continuation of the limestone karsts that are so prominent a feature of the nearby Burren in County Clare. Countless generations of Aran Islanders spent winter months collecting sand and seaweed with which to layer the thin surfaces of bare limestone rock. Although no longer practised, this method produced a soil capable of being planted by farmers and many of the small fields one sees today with their rows of potatoes and vegetables were built up from bare rock in this way. It is difficult not to notice the characteristic arrangement of 'lazy-beds' in the fields (the practice of using the soil dug for a trench as a bed to build up the adjoining ridge in which potatoes were planted) so minimizing the risk of waterlogged fields. Equally characteristic are the numberless, small, dry-stone walls that fence off one small field from another and create a maze-like filigree around the islands.

Well over 400 varieties of wildflower testify to the rich flora, seals are not too difficult to spot when they swim into shallow coves – Port Chorrúch is one of their haunts (see page 417) – and the occasional dolphin may be seen off shore. A bird book will be just as useful as a guide to wild flowers, with the increasingly uncommon chough seen around the coast and cuckoos galore heard in May.

History   The pre-historic stone forts found on the islands are testimony to an occupation by Iron Age and possibly late Bronze-Age people, though next to nothing is known about their history. The first records of island life relate to the lives of early Christian saints like St Enda, who around the sixth century founded a monastery that attracted like-minded ascetics from across Europe. In the Middle Ages the islands were fought over by the rival clans of the O'Flahertys and the O'Briens, but the squabbling of Gaelic chiefs was eclipsed by the English, who first took control in 1587. In the following century Cromwell established a garrison on the islands but, as the west of Ireland gradually lost its importance to the colonial power, the Aran islanders were left to themselves.

The outside world rediscovered the islands when their archaeological sites and the remarkable preservation of their Gaelic culture attracted notice. The playwright JM Synge made visits to listen to the Irish language and collect stories, and in 1932 the documentary film-maker Robert Flaherty made his now famously contrived film *Man of Aran*. In the last two decades of the 20th century, tourism has played a pivotal role not only in regenerating the islands' economy but also in their mythologization as the heartbeat of Celtic culture.

Local culture   Take with you JM Synge's *The Aran Islands* (1907), though you're unlikely to encounter the fellow passengers he shared passage with: "a couple of men going out with young pigs tied loosely in sacking, three or four young girls who sat in the cabin with their heads completely twisted in their shawls, and a builder, on his way to repair the pier at Kilronan". WB Yeats urged Synge to head for the Aran Islands, and one result of Synge's sojourn was this book which proved to be extremely influential in highlighting the islanders' traditional culture. Synge preferred Inishmaan because of the Irish spoken there but nowadays you will hear Gaelic spoken on all three islands and students of Irish arrive annually to practise their language. Flaherty's documentary made famous the islanders' involvement in fishing, and the traditional canvas-covered curragh is still used as a boat. Gone are the heel-less rawhide shoes that were so well adapted to clambering over rock but there is no shortage of the hand-knitted white sweaters with various patterns that the islands have given their name to. The novelist Liam O'Flaherty (1896-1984), who in 1921 ran up the red flag over the Rotunda in Dublin and occupied it for three days as "Chairman of the Council of the Unemployed", was born on Inishmore. A contemporary writer, Tim Robinson, has found inspiration on the Aran Islands and, while his *The Aran Islands: A Map & Guide* can be recommended, some may find his *Stones of Aran* books a bit heavy. Two anthologies of essays are worth dipping into: *The Book of Aran*, brought out by Tír Eolas, a local publisher, and available in Galway bookshops, and *An Aran Reader*, edited by Breandán & Ruairí Ó hEithir (Lilliput Press, Dublin).

Inishmore (Inis Mór)

Getting around The largest of the three islands, Inishmore is about 9 miles (14 km) long and over 2 miles (4 km) at its widest. Boats arrive at **Kilronan** (Cill Rónáin), the main village, and from there the island's chief road travels both west to Kilmurvey, close to the major archaeological site and an alternative base for accommodation, and east to Killeany where St Enda's monastery once stood.

Ins & outs

The **tourist office**, T61263, is in Kilronan, on the road up from the harbour, past the *American Bar*. Easter-mid-Sep, 1000-1845, closed 1230-1330; Nov-Mar, 1000-1600, Mar-May 1000-1700.

Ionad Árann (Aran Heritage Centre), in Kilronan, T61355 www.visitaranislands.com, introduces the history, geology and lifestyle of the islanders. The *Man of Aran* film is shown at 1200, 1345 and 1500, and there is a small café, gift shop and a bureau de change. Open Apr-Oct, 1000-1900. €3. Combined entrance and film €5.

Heritage centre

Dún Aengus (or Dún Aonghasa) is the most spectacular site on Inishmore, not least because of its location on the edge of a 300-ft (91-m) cliff. Islanders tell stories of the days when men used to climb down these cliffs to collect bird eggs. This stone fort, one of the finest examples of Iron Age building in Europe and approximately 2,000 years old, is made up of three concentric enclosures, each with walls of dry masonry. The middle wall is defended by a remarkable *chevaux-de-frise* – vertical, jagged, sharp stones set at various angles to entrap an enemy force – while the main, innermost fort is 148 ft (45 m) in diameter, with walls nearly 13 ft (4 m) thick. The parapet and stairways

Stone forts
Tours of the island in a van will get you around the main sites quickly but they have little else to recommend them. Hiring a bike and cycling the Inis Mór Way is a lot more fun

County Galway

Inishmore

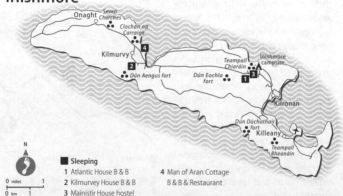

Sleeping
1 Atlantic House B & B
2 Kilmurvey House B & B
3 Mainistir House hostel
4 Man of Aran Cottage B & B & Restaurant

0 miles 1
0 km 1

of the inner walls were put in place when restoration work of questionable authority was carried out in 1881, but supporting evidence for this feature comes from the stone fort at Staigue in Cork. Be careful – extremely so with children – when approaching the edge because it is a sheer drop and the erosion that cut off the missing wall of the fort continues to eat away the land.

There are a number of other stone forts and ancient sites dotted around, and a copy of Tim Robinson's map is essential for anyone wishing to locate and really explore these pre-historic sites. One of the more important is **Dún Eoghanachta**, an impressive circular fort northwest of Kilronan and best reached by taking the main road west of Kilronan (then look for the sign pointing south). There is also **Dún Eochla** inland, less than halfway from Kilronan and Dún Aengus. However, for another dramatically situated fort it is worth seeking out **Dún Dúchathair**, to the south of Kilronan and surrounded by cliffs on three sides.

Monastic sights Continuing along the road west of Kilronan brings one to **Clochán na Carraige** on the north side of the road. This 19-ft-long (8-m), dry stone *clochán*, with the corbelled roof characteristic of early Christian buildings, is very well preserved. Travelling a little further west along the road accesses the **Seven Churches**, though you will only find two actual churches plus the ruins of monastic houses, assorted portions of cross-slabs and fragments of high crosses. One stone is inscribed with *VII Romans*, a fact that has given rise to various interpretations, including the unlikely one that Christian Romans are buried here. It is more probable that the graves are of pilgrims who made a journey to Rome.

An interesting ecclesiastical site is **Teampall Chiaráin** (Church of St Kieran), reached by taking the road south at Mainistir, complete with a high cross in the churchyard and an ancient holy well that probably marks a pagan site that early Christians expropriated. Just to the south of Killeany, **Teampall Bheanáin** (Church of St Benignus) is built on the rock orientated north to south and dates back to around the sixth century.

The Inis Mór Way **Mapping and information** To enjoy walking or cycling on the island it is essential to get off the main road, and the 21-mile (34-km) Inis Mór Way is fairly well signposted. The drawback is that too much of the Way uses surfaced roads that are hard on your feet, but compensation comes in the form of the sweeping views with the sea nearly always in view, enough stone-walled fields to last a lifetime and numerous opportunities to wander off and poke around archaeological and historical sites. The least expensive guide is the *Inis Mór Way* leaflet (€2), which includes a map and some brief descriptions. *Ordnance Survey* map No 51 in the Discovery series covers the island, and there is also Tim Robinson's map (see page 415) as well as specialist walking guides that cover the Way (see page 681).

Kilronan

Ionad Árann (Aran Heritage Centre)

0 yards 100
0 metres 100

■ Sleeping
1 Aharla Hostel
2 Aran Islands Hostel
3 Bayview Guesthouse
4 St Kevin's Hostel

● Eating
1 American Bar
2 Dun Aoghansa & Aran Fisherman
3 Joe Watty's Bar

County Galway

The Way begins at **Kilronan** and heads north past the shingle and sand **Trá na bhFrancach** (Frenchman's Beach) before turning west and staying fairly close to the coastline, passing **Port Chorrúch** and meeting the white, sandy beach at **Port Mhuirbhigh** where the width of the islands shrinks to only ½ mile (1 km). On the other side of the beach, the Way heads uphill and inland, close by **Clochán na Carraige**, **Dún Eoghanachta** and the **Seven Churches**. It descends to the coast once more and then inland to a T-junction near the western end of the island. From here the Way returns inland again and eventually rejoins the outward route as far as Port Mhuirbhigh, where there is a spur to **Dún Aengus**, before heading southwards to the village of **Gort na bPéist**, where Liam O'Flaherty (see page 415) was born. It continues eastwards to **Dún Dúchathair** before heading north back to Kilronan.

Sleeping

Price codes:
see inside front cover

There are no hotels to choose from on the island, although there is a range of other accommodation. The average B&B rate is €26 per person and while there is a lot to choose from, it is advisable to have somewhere booked before arrival. The Kilronan, Mainistir and Aharla hostels are open all year.

A *Ard Einne*, T61126, F61388. To the west of Kilronan village this B&B enjoys sweeping views of the mainland coast and Galway Bay. **A** *Man of Aran Cottage*, Kilmurvey Bay, T61301. This B&B, where part of the famous film was shot, charges a little above the average. **A** *Pier House*, Kilronan, T61416, F61122. Smartish guesthouse. **B** *Atlantic House*, Mainistir, T61185. Has cheaper rooms sharing bathroom facilities. **B** *Bayview Guesthouse*, Kilronan, T61260. Overlooks the harbour. **C** *Ti Eithne*, Kilronan, T61303. A short walk away from the harbour.

D *Aharla Hostel*, Kilronan, T61305. Near the pier, no private rooms. **D** *Killeany Lodge Hostel*, T61393. IHH hostel to the southeast of Kilronan, lacking private rooms and charging €0.50 for a shower, but a relatively quiet place. **B-D** *Kilronan Hostel*, Kilronan, T61255. Being in Kilronan, near to the pier and above a pub combine to make it both convenient and noisy. No private rooms. **B-D** *Mainistir House Hostel*, Kilronan, T61169, F61351. Within walking distance of the pier. It has a family room, doubles, twin and small dormitories and package deals with *Island Ferries* use this accommodation. **D** *St Kevin's Hostel*, Kilronan, T61125. Between the *Tí Joe Mac's* pub and the supermarket. No private rooms.

Camping Near the beach at Mainistir, the *Inishmór Camp Site*, T61185, is very basic, while the one attached to the *Killeany Lodge Hostel* has the use of its kitchen and showers.

Eating

In Kilronan the pubs serve food and *Joe Watty's Bar* comes recommended. The *Dún Aonghasa & Aran Fisherman* specializes in seafood and there is a choice of meat, pasta, pizza, and vegetarian dishes. *Pier House* and *Man of Aran Cottage* (see above) do evening meals till 2130 but a reservation is essential. Dinner for €10 at *Mainistir House Hostel* is self-described as a "vaguely vegetarian buffet" and diners are welcome to bring their own drinks. On the road up to Dun Aengus the *An Sunda Caoch* café opens daily 1100-1700 for sandwiches and cakes.

Pubs & music

Nearly all the pubs on the islands have some form of entertainment at night during the summer months. *Tigh Fitz* at Killeany involves a journey if not staying at the east side of the island but the musical sessions are very good. The *American Bar* in Kilronan itself is a popular place that caters to every type of visitor. Here you'll rub shoulders with an amazing mix of people – from salty fisherman to clueless tourists – enlivened by occasional outbursts of song. *Ragus* Halla Ronain, T572525, is a traditional Irish dance and music show lasting an hr. Shows are 3 times daily. €10.

County Galway

Shopping Inishmore is *the* place to purchase a genuine hand-knitted Aran sweater and there are a few places selling them. *Carraig Donn* in Kilronan has a selection as well as factory knitwear, tweed and wax jackets. A nearby shop, *An Teach Ceoil*, is crammed with CDs and cassettes of traditional Irish music.

Directory **Banks & bureaux de change** Banks: There are no ATMs on the island. *Bank of Ireland* in Kilronan. Jun-Aug, Wed-Thu; Sep-May, Wed. **Bureaux de change**: money can be changed at the post office, or the *Carraig Donn* shop. **Bike Hire**: *Burke Bike Hire*, T61402, €7.50 per day. **Communications** Post office: past the tourist office on the road up from the harbour.

Inishmaan (Inis Meáin)

Colour map 2, grid C2 Inishmaan is the second largest of the Aran Islands, with a population of less than 200 as compared to the 800 or so who live in Inishmore. Figures like Synge and Pearse came here because of its reputation as the least culturally spoilt of the three islands and even today, probably because it attracts fewer visitors, this still holds true.

Ins & outs **Getting there** Boats land at **An Córa** on the east side of the island and the main route leads across the island with *boreens* leading off to the north and south. The airstrip is in the northeast of the island.

Getting around Inishmaan is only about 3 miles (5 km) long by about 2 miles (3 km) wide, and with little high ground it is not difficult to explore on foot.

Tourist information The *Inis Meáin Island Co-operative*, T73010, in the middle of the island just north of the post office, is the place to make enquiries.

The Inis Meáin Way By walking the undemanding 5-mile (8-km) Inis Meáin Way from An Córa, mostly along surfaced roads and quiet boreens, it is still possible to experience the appeal of an island that drew Synge back for five summers in succession at the turn of the 19th century.

From the pier keep the rocky shore on your left and head inland to the remains of **Cill Cheannanach**, a small oratory that dates from the eighth or ninth century, and what was the island graveyard until 1940. Follow the boreen uphill to **Dún na Fearbhaí**, a stone fort from around the same time, which provides good views of Connemara and Clare on a clear day. The Way continues westwards to the village of **Baile an Mhothair** and the island's only pub before passing the island's church, with its startling stained-glass windows by Harry Clarke. On the other side of the boreen, the ruined **Synge's Cottage** comes into view; the playwright spent his summers here between 1898 and 1902 and his *Riders to the Sea* is set on the island.

Inishmaan

Sleeping
1 Angela Faherty
2 Máirin Concannon
3 Máirin Faherty
4 Máirin Mulkerrin

Eating
1 Conneely's

You will have already noticed the commanding presence of **Dún Chonchúir**, the island's most impressive sight, but now it comes clearly into view. Oval in shape and with an outer bailey, this theatrically situated stone fort has walls 18 ft (5.5 m) high and 16 ft (5 m) wide in places. This is almost the highest point on Inis Meáin and the views on a fine day are stunning: from the peak of Mount Brandon on the Dingle peninsula away to the south with the fantastic patches of surrounding tiny fields etched and defined by their stone walls.

Dún Chonchúir, the most eye-catching hill fort anywhere in Ireland, can be enjoyed in relative peace while hordes of visitors are tramping across Inishmore

The Way continues, uphill along a road for a while and then across bare rock, to the western coastline and **Synge's Chair**. This dry-stone shelter was built by Synge because he liked to come here on a daily basis to contemplate the view and compose his thoughts.

The Way then returns eastwards, a little to the north and at a lower level. It gradually turns into a tarmac road and turns to the left along a road, before the Way then turns right for the route back to the pier. Just before the Way turns to the right, a boreen on the left leads down to the beach, **Trácht Each**.

AL-A Ostan Inis Meain, T73020, www.aranislands.com Very small hotel with sea views, sound food and lots of music. **C** *Creig Mór*, about 500yds from the pier, T73012, F73111, info@familyhomes.ie This B&B has been recommended as a place for a comfortable night's stay on the island and an evening meal can be arranged. Open Mar-Oct. **C** *Máirin Concannon*, T73019. Welcoming B&B near the pub in the middle of the island. **C** *Máire Faherty*, Ard Alainn, at the end of the road that leads to Dún Chonchúir, T73027. B&B open from the end of Apr-Sep. **C** *Máire Mulkerrin*, welcoming B&B in the middle of the island, near the pub, T73016.

Sleeping
*Price codes:
see inside front cover*

Self-catering For the 'get away from it all' self-catering option contact *Pádraig o Fatharta* at the pub, T73047, or *Nora Concannon*, T55893.

There are limited opportunities for eating out on Inishmaan, especially outside the summer months, and you might want to bring a picnic for lunch. The island's only pub, T73003, serves light meals in the summer until around 1900 but most of the B&Bs will provide an evening meal if you arrange this in advance. There is a restaurant, *An Dun*, T73068, near the junction where you turn left for Dún Chonchúir, which opens in the summer for lunch and dinner. Closer to the pier, *Connely's*, T73085, is the only other restaurant.

Eating

Bank *Bank of Ireland* operates on the second Tue of each month.

Directory

Inisheer (Inis Óirr)

The smallest of the Aran Islands, with a population of around 300, is 6 miles (9 km) off the coast of Clare and receives a steady flow of travellers from Doolin as well as from Galway. The absence of any major archaeological attractions or other sights, however, helps ensure that the place is rarely overcrowded.

Colour map 2, grid C2

Getting there and around The pier where boats arrive is on the north side of the island and the airstrip is to the east. The best way to explore this small island is on foot.

Ins & outs

Tourist information is available from a small post near where the boats arrive. Open Jun-Sep, 1000-1900. Also available from the *Inis Óirr Island Co-operative*, T75008.

Dominating the harbour side of the island, O'Brien's Castle (Caisleán Uí Bhriain) was built by the O'Briens at the very end of the 14th century in the centre of an ancient stone ringfort, Dún Formna, and on a clear day there are panoramic views from the walls. Close by stand the ruins of a signal tower from the days when the British feared an invasion by Napoleonic forces.

O'Brien's Castle

County Galway

Churches On the beach stands – or rather, sinks – **Church of St Keevaun (Teampall Chaoimháin**), a little 11th-century church with a graveyard that was still being used even when sand had begun to submerge the church. To the west of the pier Cill Ghobnait is a small church dating from around the ninth century and dedicated to the female St Gobnait.

Heritage House At the West Village, Heritage House, T75021, is a stone-built thatched cottage with a collection of old photographs relating to life on the island, a craft shop and a tea-room. ■ *Open Jul and Aug, daily 1400-1600. €1*

The Inis Óirr Way

Mapping and information As on Inishmaan, the best way to visit these sights and at the same time enjoy the strange and desolate beauty of the landscape is to follow the waymarked Inis Óirr Way. The 6½ miles (10.5 km) that make up the Inis Óirr Way is well marked with Way signs but contents itself with tracing a route around the northern part of the island and sticking to surfaced roads, when you are just itching to break out across the tiny fields and explore parts of the limestone landscape for yourself. With a copy of map No 51 in the *Ordnance Survey* Discovery series this is very feasible indeed.

The Way starts from the pier where you disembark and heads east along the road, with the beach, **An Trá**, on your left. It then turns inland, passing **Teampall Chaoimháin** and the airstrip, before heading southwards to circle its way around **An Loch Mór** (the Big Lake). The wrecked ship that you see was the *Plassy*, driven aground and tossed onto the rocks in 1960. The Way heads north up the west side of the lake, with high walls (10 ft/3 m) to either side, to the tiny village of **Formna**. It then turns south for a brief while before going west, with **O'Brien's Castle** close by to the north. Turning south again, the route passes the signal tower, and makes its way delightfully alongside stone walls that stretch maze-like in every direction.

When the Way meets the shore on the western side of the island, it turns northwards and follows the coast. You meet the remains of **Cill Ghobnait** before moving inland a little, passing one of the island's pubs and returning to the pier.

A walk to the lighthouse

The road that leads to O'Brien's Castle continues on in the direction of a lighthouse at a southern tip of the island. It makes for an enjoyable walk and along the way there are superb views across to the Cliffs of Moher on the Clare coastline to the east. The road peters out at the shore a little way to the west of the lighthouse but it is easy to make your way across the slabs of limestone to the black-and-white strips of the 19th-century lighthouse. It was built in 1857 and though abandoned after being automated in 1978, the sturdily built and photogenic stone cottages built for the lighthousemen remain alongside the cylindrical tower. Either return via the same road or scramble past the lighthouse a little way to the east and find the road that heads north, parallel to the one you travelled south along. With a good map it is more enjoyable to leave the

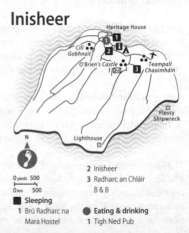

Inisheer

Heritage House

Cill Gobhnait

O'Brien's Castle

Teampall Chaoimháin

Plessy Shipwreck

Lighthouse

N

0 yards 500
0 km 500

■ **Sleeping**
1 Brú Radharc na Mara Hostel
2 Inisheer
3 Radharc an Chláir B & B

● **Eating & drinking**
1 Tigh Ned Pub

road, shortly after passing through a gate, and head down to the eastern shore to find a grassy path that heads inland for a little while to a junction where a right turn touches the shoreline again – the *Plessy* shipwreck is clearly visible – before heading northwards past the lake to meet the road near the airstrip.

A *Inisheer Hotel*, near the pier, T75020. A 1-star hotel but with doubles/singles at €63/33 the B&Bs might seem better value. **C** *Radharc An Chláir*, within walking distance of the pier, near O'Brien's Castle, T/F75019. Opens from Feb-Oct. There are rooms with and without their own bathrooms and doubles/singles are from €33/19 to €41/22. An evening meal is €15. These rates are more or less the same for the other B&Bs but not all do an evening meal. **C** *Strand House*, T75002. B&B. **C** *Suzanne O'Donnell*, T75064. B&B. **C** *Una McDonagh*, T75005. B&B. **C** *Mairead O'Reilly*, T75094. B&B. **C** *Maura Sharry*, T/F75024. B&B. **D** *Bru Radharc Na Mara Hostel*, T75024/75087, F75024. IHH hostel, close to the pier, has nearly 40 beds and 2 private rooms. **D** *Rory's Hostel*, T75077. A small private house behind the post office, has 8 beds for €9 each.

Camping The *Inisheer Camp Site*, T75008, functions from May to Sep and is situated by the beach.

Sleeping
Price codes:
see inside front cover

The *Rory Conneely* pub is less than a 5-min walk from the pier and pub food is served daily. Another possibility is the restaurant at the *Inisheer Hotel*, open for lunch and dinner. Anita Paul in *Mermaid's Cottage* T75062, Castle Village, is 5 mins from the hotel and does snacks and salads. The *Tigh Ned* pub, 200 yds from the pier, has sessions of traditional music.

Eating

Banks and bureaux de change *Bank of Ireland* operates on the 4th Tue of each month. Bureau de change at the *Inisheer Hotel*.

Directory

Connemara and Lough Corrib

Connemara is the land to the northwest of Galway – a geographical region and a mythologized one – framed by the sea on three sides. It is famous for its desolate landscape of bogs and mountains and extensive veins of green marble, which were traded in Neolithic times certainly as far away as Lough Gur in Limerick and possibly as far as the Boyne Valley as well. In Connemara geology, landscape and shifting weather patterns (one way of saying it rains a lot) translate into a singular and inspiring natural beauty: mist-covered mountains, transitory gradations of light and colour, craggy glens and poetic contours of land and sea.

Lough Corrib, to the east is the largest lake in the Republic and stretches for some 30 miles (48 km) from Galway city to the border with Mayo. Inchagoill, the largest of the 300 or so islands studded across its surface, is worth visiting for its unique Latin inscription on an obelisk and the photogenic remains of early Christian places of worship. Ask an angler about Lough Corrib, however, and Pavlovian glee will accompany any thought of the mayfly dapping season in early summer – it brings in anglers from all over Europe and beyond, lured by the chance of catching brown trout and salmon.

"Westward ho! Let us rise with the sun and be off to the land of the West". William Wilde, father of Oscar, warmed to the west of Ireland as the spiritual home of Gaelic culture in his 'Lough Corrib: its shores and Islands' (1867)

County Galway

Ins and outs

There is a daily non-stop bus service between Galway and Clifden and, between the end of Jun and the end of Aug, a daily service that also stops at Oughterard, Cashel, Roundstone and other smaller towns. The early morning bus on this route continues on from Clifden to Letterfrack, Kylemore, Leenane and Westport. Check with the bus station in Galway, T562000, for the schedule.

Getting there

If you are travelling by car or bike, there is a choice of routes west from Galway: the N59 road through the middle of Connemara via Oughterard and straight on to Clifden, or the R336 road that follows the coast via Spiddal, Rossaveel (departure point for the Aran Islands) and north to Maam Cross where it meets the N59. A mountain road cuts a scenic route through a hill pass and a beautifully brooding landscape to link Oughterard with Rossaveal.

Getting around Organized coach tours from Galway City are available. *Lally Coaches*, T091-562905, www.lallytours.com, has an €13 tour that departs from the city at 0945 and takes in most of the main sights before returning at 1645. *O'Neachtain*, T091-553188, www.wombat.ie/pages/oneachtain-tours, run a similar tour that departs from the Galway tourist office at 0945 and the Salthill tourist office at 0955 (see page 400).

Cruise boats operate between Oughterard and Cong on either side of Lough Corrib, and a cruise is also available from Galway with *Corrib Tours*, T592447. Daily sailings from Woodquay in Galway city at 1430 and 1630 in May, Jun and Sep, and with an extra sailing at 1230 in Jul and Aug.

Angling information *Thomas Tuck*, T552335, at the Clifden end of Main Street in Oughterard (see page 423), sells tackle and licences. Some of the hotels advise and facilitate angling guests.

Connemara

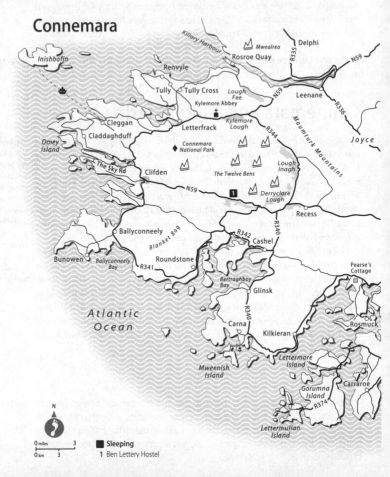

County Galway

0 miles   3
0 km   3

■ Sleeping
1 Ben Lettery Hostel

Background

Central Connemara is dominated by the Twelve Bens (see page 426) and the **Geology**
Maumturk mountain ranges, with their peaks composed of quartzite, while
the lowland to the west is more schist and gneiss.

  The southern part of Connemara, covered by the Spiddal to Clifden section (see page 427), has a different geographic complexion. The land is
equally boggy but low-lying and characterized by small lakes of assorted
shapes, a heavily indented coastline with tiny islands, and granite rock that
imparts a geology different from the central and northern areas. This is also
where the traveller is most likely to hear Gaelic being spoken.

At one time Connemara was a byword for cultural backwardness, and even **Prehistory**
prehistoric communities were thought to have shunned its terrain. In the
last 20 years a wealth of Neolithic and Bronze Age sites have been discovered, complementing the rediscovery of Connemara as a place of escape
from the metropolitan world.

Oughterard

The village of Oughterard, where the *Phone code: 091*
main Galway to Clifden road crosses *Colour map 2, grid B3*
the little Owenriff river, is renowned as
an angling centre, but it also serves as a
comfortable introduction to the wilder
Connemara that lies just west of here.
There is a good choice of accommodation and places to eat, a castle and a
mine worth visiting and the chance of
an excursion to Inchagoill Island.

  Tourist information available
from the Non-*Bord Fáilte* tourist
office on Main St, T552808, in the
centre of village. It also acts as an
agents for *Corrib Cruises*, air or boat
passage to the Aran Islands and the
boat to Inishbofin. Open in summer daily, 0900-1900, winter Mon-Fri, 0930-1700.

A trip to Aughnanure Castle, a well **Aughnanure**
preserved tower house built on an **Castle**
island of rock, is well worth the short
detour off the N59 road. This is one of
the best examples of how Gaelic chiefs
lived in the pre-Plantation era. There
is little to see inside, but this is an ideal
opportunity to view the elemental
architecture of a fortified home. The
castle is basically a tower house, built
in the 16th century as a stronghold for

County Galway

the O'Flaherty clan, and its excellent state of preservation is what singles it out. The approach along a footpath by the River Dimneen and across a natural bridge is picturesque, but this sturdy structure was not built for the fine view. Bartizans are still in place half-way up the walls and on all sides there are superb examples of machicolated galleries (galleries with openings between the corbels for dropping stones on to attackers).

To the south stand the remains of the east wall of a banqueting hall, which is said to have contained a trap door for dropping unwanted guests into the subterranean river that flows under the hall. The elaborately carved decorations on the windows of the remaining wall are worthy of appreciation, although the watch tower in the southeast corner is more eye-catching. ■ *T552214. Open mid-Jun-Sep, daily, 0930-1830. €2.50. Dúchas site. Under 2 miles (3 km) east of Oughterard, off the main N59 road.*

Glengowla Mines The mines dates back to the 19th century and have now being opened by the family who live on the land above them. A 25-minute guided tour takes you through the mineral-studded chambers with their lead, pyrite and veins of calcite and quartz, and there is a small exhibition area above ground which includes some minerals for sale. ■ *T552360. Open Mar-Nov, daily 0930-1830. €4. Outside of Oughterard and signposted off the main N59 road to Maam Cross.*

Inchagoill Island Inchagoill is the largest of the islands in Lough Corrib and the most intriguing of its ancient remains is the **Lia Luguaedon Mac Menueh** ('stone of Luguaedon, son of Menueh') burial stone. Less than 3 ft (75 cm) high, it is possibly the oldest Latin inscription of Christian origin in Europe (apart from the catacombs). It stands near the **Church of the Saints** (Teampall na Naoimh), a worthy example of Irish Romanesque from the ninth or 10th century, while the **Church of St Patrick** (Teampall Phádraig) is another small oratory of lesser architectural interest on the island. ■ *Corrib Cruises, T552808, www.corribcruises.com, has a daily sailing between Oughterard and Cong, which stops off at Inchagoill for ½ hr. Tickets are €13, obtainable from the tourist office, and departures are at 1100, 1445 and 1700 between May and Oct.*

The Owenriff Way

To enjoy a gentle 45-minute riverside stroll walk westwards out of Oughterard as far as the bridge next to the Catholic church. Cross the bridge and turn immediately to the right to walk along the footpath that follows the river downstream. Continue for about 400 yds to a green metal bridge and walk out along the road – the Glan road – taking the first right turn signposted to the *Camillaun & Corrib Country* B&Bs. After about 200 yds cross the river at the footbridge and after another 100 yds walk onto Camp Street and take the first turning on the left (the Owenriff Way is signposted on the corner behind greenery) to return to the riverside. Carry on downstream, past the sheds and across a stile. The path leads onto the Pier Road where a right turn returns you to the village.

Sleeping
Price codes: see inside front cover

LL-L *Currarevagh House*, T552312, currarevagh@Ireland.com Built as a wedding present in 1840, this guesthouse has a tranquil location on the shore of Lough Corrib and a 2-night stay here should prove terribly relaxing. Old-fashioned in the best sense of the word, and with an air of dignity: Irish hospitality with comforting rituals. No televisions, afternoon tea at 1600, dinner announced promptly at 2000 to the ring of a gong and, rather more worryingly, a tiger skin over the stairway. **L** *River Run Lodge*, Glan Rd, T552697, F552669, rivrun@indigo.ie Higher-quality B&B within walking distance of town. It has its own restaurant and the rooms are spacious and well equipped. Dinner at around €25. **AL-A** *The Lake Hotel*, T552275, F552794. Family run hotel in the centre of the village. **A** *Boat Inn*, T552196, www.theboatinn.com Guesthouse in the very centre of the village with pretty terrace and gardens and live music in the evenings. **A** *Corrib Wave*, Portacarron, T552147, F552736. A guesthouse with warm hospitality and a pleasing waterside location that guarantees serenity, plus reliable home-cooked evening meals. Fishing folk are particularly well taken care of here. **A** *The Western Way*, Camp St, T552475, westernwatbb@hotmail.com B&B within walking distance of the village. **C-D** *Canrawer House*, Station Rd, T552388, canrawer@indigo.ie While it only has 1 private room, the overall standard is very high in this new purpose-built, spacious IHH hostel with stone tile floors and smart bedrooms. Just before the Catholic church at the Clifden end of town.

Eating Both the *Boat Inn* and the *Lake Hotel* in the centre of the village do bar food throughout the day and have restaurants for more formal meals. *O Fatharta's*, on Main St, T552692, has a pretty exterior while the quiet, plain inside is still a pleasant place for a casual meal. Irish stew is €11 while the price of main courses in the evening is €13. The *Corrib Hotel*, on Bridge St, T552329, does a reasonable evening meal for €20. Another option is *Keogh's* a bar/restaurant/craft shop/delicatessen and supermarket. Something for everyone.

Shopping *Fuschia Craft*, in the centre of the village and open daily until 2200 in the summer, has Galway crystal, porcelain from Donegal, claddagh rings, tweeds, designer knitwear, prints, bodhrans, jewellery … and a bureau de change. At the Clifden end of the village *Galway Woollen Market* has the usual range of garments, souvenirs and gifts.

Sport **Fishing** *Keogh's*, The Square, T552583. Tackle and information. *Tuck's*, Main St, T552335. Tackle and information.

Transport **Taxi** *Sean Conneely*, Main St, T552299.

Directory **Banks & bureaux de change** Banks: Main St. **Bureau de change**: available at the 2 craft shops. **Communications** Post office: Main St. **Local radio** *Raidió na Gaeltachta*, 556m MW, 0800-1930, in Gaelic but music also broadcast.

Walking in the West

Oughterard, the self-proclaimed "gateway to Connemara", is indeed a good place to plan and organize a walking trip in the 'real' Connemara that lies just a short distance to the west. The tourist office (see page 423) has a good selection of maps, guides and general information: for local walks and cycle rides there is a €2.50 booklet that outlines a number of undemanding routes. Another useful publication is the €2 *Walking in the West* booklet that outlines the main long-distance walks such as the Aran Way and the Western Way and gives details of companies that specialize in organizing walks in Connemara.

Mapping & information The tourist office sells a map and guide to the Western Way by McDermott and Chapman for €7.50, but many walkers prefer the similarly priced *Mountains of Connemara* booklet by Joss Lynam that comes complete with a 1:50,000 map.

The Western Way, which begins outside of Oughterard and amounts to over 135 miles (217 km) on its journey across Connemara and Mayo, is the main long-distance walk, and while the whole Way could take not far short of 2 weeks to complete, most people choose a 1-, 2- or 3-day section. With the help of the *Bus Éireann* timetable it would be possible, for example, to leave one's transport at Oughterard and walk for 3 days to Leenane before catching a bus back to base. Public transport will help with a 2-day walk to Kylemore or even a one-day walk to Maam Cross.

County Galway

Oughterard to Clifden

Shortly after leaving Oughterard on the N59 the landscape opens up and the appeal of Connemara begins to make itself felt. Lakes and mountains majestically proclaim themselves, and as the bogland spreads out on either side of the road, mounds of turf set out to dry become a common site. The junction at **Maam Cross** is overshadowed by a huge craft and souvenir shop by the side of the road, and while the adjoining bar and teashop serve a purpose the place as a whole is a bit of an eyesore.

From Oughterard the N59 road carries on due west all the way to Clifden but there are several alternative routes you might consider. At the Maam Cross junction, the R336 road heads north to Leenane, skipping out west Connemara altogether and accessing Mayo. The R336 road also heads south to Screeb where a turning westwards takes the R340 through south Connemara hugging the coast nearly all the way to Clifden (and briefly rejoining the N59 west of Recess).

Then again, you could to stay on the N59 until shortly after Recess before heading north on the very scenic R344 road through the Lough Inagh Valley. You could also do this as a roundabout route to Clifden via Letterfrack.

Recess
Phone code: 095
Colour map 2, grid B2

Recess is just a couple of houses, a bar and a shop on the N59 between Maam Cross and Clifden but the area around here is interesting and a couple of diversions suggest themselves. **Ballynahinch Castle** is now a hotel (see 'Sleeping' below), but it was once the home of Humanity Dick (1754-1834), a member of the Martin family who acquired a fearsome reputation for his defence of animal rights. He is reputed to have fought duels on behalf of animals and imprisoned miscreants on his estate in the old tower by the lake for mistreating animals. Humanity Dick also played a pivotal role in establishing the RSPCA. Expensive to stay here but a passing visit to the public bar at Ballynahinch Castle Hotel is a great way to savour the mood of a fine Victorian mansion that was once reputed to have the longest drive of any country house in the land.

Twelve Bens &
Inagh Valley

West of Recess the scenery becomes breathtaking as the Twelve Bens mountain range comes into view. Legend has it that St Patrick came to the Twelve Bens but turned back on the assumption that no sane Christian would want to live there. Look for the turning for the R344 road north to Letterfrack and consider this route around to Clifden through the Inagh Valley. This wide valley has stirring views of the forbidding Twelve Bens to the west/left and the Maumturks to the east/right. After just over a mile (2.2 km) on the road there is the Lough Inagh Lodge (see 'Sleeping' below), and a few hundreds yards past the hotel there is a forestry track that leads to a bridge over the strait dividing Lough Inagh from Lough Derryclare. This is the starting point for a demanding climb to the summits of Derryclare and Bencorr, which should not be undertaken without the *Ordnance Survey* map No 37 and a specialist walking guide (see page 681).

Sleeping
Price codes:
see inside front cover

XL-L *Ballynahinch Castle Hotel*, T31006, F31085 bhinch@iol.ie Set in woodlands on the banks of the river of the same name this place is very comfortable and relaxed, with all the qualities of a swanky hotel. **LL-L** *Cashel House Hotel*, Cashel, T095 31001, www.cashel-house-hotel.com A hotel set in some of the most beautiful gardens in Ireland. Private beach, and award winning breakfast. If you don't stay here come just to wander round the gardens which are open to the public Tue-Sat, 1400-1630. **LL** *Lough Inagh Lodge*, T34706, F34708. Rates similar to *Ballynahinch Castle*. Makes a suitable place to stop for a rest while admiring the natural spectacle all around you. Some 4-poster beds, and a down-to-earth bar where anglers compare catches.

County Galway

Spiddal to Clifden

The alternative route through Connemara from Galway is by way of the R336 coastal road that follows the northern coastline of Galway Bay through Spiddal to Ballynahown. Then it turns north for Maam Cross but takes the R340 off to the west at Screeb that branches beforehand. The R340 stays close to the coast for most of the way around Kilkieran Bay and then Bertraghboy Bay before finally approaching Clifden from the south.

The Screeb to Clifden route is definitely for travellers who find journeying at least as interesting as the actual destination. Conventional places of interest are few and far between, but there are numerous small roads that weave their way into coastal crevices, and interesting opportunities to encounter a delightful spot while in the process of getting lost. Sommerville and Ross travelled through here in the 1890s, equipped with a spirit-lamp, Bovril and a revolver, and noted in *Through Connemara in a Governers-cart* (1893) how "every road we have seen in Connemara makes for water like an otter and finds it with seeming ease, sometimes even succeeding in getting into it". At Costello, the headquarters of Radio na Gaeltachta, a road heads south to **Carraroe** where there are splendid coral and shell beaches, which are rarely crowded, while at **Carna** there is an easy walk out to Mweenish Island and sandy beaches.

Pearse's Cottage, where Padraig Pearse (1879-1916) spent summers and used the cottage as a summer school for the students of his bilingual St Enda's School in Dublin, may prove disappointing because there is precious little inside. But a path runs past the front door and down to a bench by a lake where one imagines Pearse enjoyed the view. ■ *T091-574292. €1.50. Mid-Jun to mid-Sep, daily 0930-1830. Dúchas site.*

Roundstone

The village of Roundstone, quaint and quietly popular, is worth considering as a place to stop over for a night. One of the attractions is a climb to the summit of **Mount Errisbeg** (977ft/298m), because it only takes a couple of hours and the going is not difficult. Take the path that goes along the side of *O'Dowd's* pub and turns into a track up the mountain. From the top there are remarkable views of bog land, mountain peaks and coastline: the essence of Connemara.

Phone code: 095
Colour map 2, grid B2

Another attraction is the cluster of art and craft workshops that are open to the public, including the much-visited *Roundstone Musical Instruments*. Tin whistles, harps and flutes are all here, though pride of place goes to the *bodhrán*, the goatskin hand-held drum without which no group of traditional Irish musicians is complete. There is also a branch, the *Music Shop*, in the centre of Clifden. ■ *T35875, www.bodhran.com Workshop: Mar-Oct daily 0900-1900.*

Workshops

Some of the most wonderful beaches in Ireland are to be found around Roundstone and if the climate were more friendly to the tourist industry it would not be difficult to imagine the odd Club Med-type development mushrooming here. To reach them stay on the road west to Ballyconneely and turn south for **Gurteen Bay** and **Dog's Bay**; the incredible whiteness of the sand is produced by millions of microscopic foraminiferous seashells. It is only another 8 miles (12 km) to **Ballyconneely** where there is another splendid beach and the ruins of Bunowen Castle.

Beaches

Sleeping

Price codes:
see inside front cover

L-A *Eldons*, T35933, F35722. Views of the harbour and Twelve Bens. Most rooms at around €35 per person sharing but there are also more expensive ones. **AL** *Roundstone House*, T35864, F35944. Small family run hotel. **B** *St Joseph's*, T35865, F35930. A friendly B&B charging €20/29 for doubles/singles. **A** *The Angler's Return*, Toombeola, 4 miles outside Roundstone and overlooking the Ballynahinch River, T31091. Pretty rambling gardens and lots of fishing nearby. Nice for those who like the peace and quiet.

Camping The *Gurteen Beach Caravan & Camping Park*, T35882, is just west of town near the beach.

Eating

O'Dowd's, Main St, T35809, has bar food and a seafood restaurant that is very good and open for lunch and dinner. There is also the *Beola Restaurant* , T35871, not far away that serves lunch for around €7 and main courses for dinner around €15. If shopping at the art and craft workshops, there is a pleasant little teashop.

Clifden

Phone code: 095
Colour map 2, grid B2

Its size and location – the largest town west of Galway, 48 miles (78 km) away – makes Clifden the capital of Connemara. The town, laid out by a 19th-century English landlord, is characterized by its geometry, broad streets and the twin spires of 19th-century churches, with the Twelve Bens providing a dramatic backdrop. Travellers' attitudes to Clifden vary and some feel that its forced birth into tourism – the shops and restaurants have all sprung up comparatively recently – has left it strangely bereft of an identity; others revel in its creature comforts, especially welcome after a day or two spent walking in the surrounding countryside. The **tourist office** is on Market St, T21163. Open mid-Apr-Sep. The *Clifden Walking Centre* (see 'Tours', below) is also a good source of local information.

Museum

There is little to see in the town itself and the **Station House Museum**, sited in what was the engine shed of the Clifden railway station, is of limited interest. There is an exhibition on the Connemara pony alongside assorted memorabilia. ■ *Free*.

In Lettershea is **Connemara Heritage and History Centre**, complete with 5000-year-old dolmen, crannog, 19th-century farmhouse, ringfort, coach park and audio-visual show. ■ *T21246. Open Apr-Oct, 7 days, 1000-1800. €4.50. Café, giftshop.*

County Galway

Walks & cycle rides around Clifden

Maps Map No 31 in the *Ordnance Survey* Discovery Series covers these walks and makes the journeying a lot more interesting.

The views are magnificent on the **Sky Road**, heading directly west out of town and around a small peninsula. It is fine for cycling and could be enjoyable as an easy walk depending on the amount of cars – do everyone a favour and avoid driving along this road. The total distance is about 8 miles (13 km); take a picnic because there are no pubs or restaurants until the Sky Road meets up with the main N59.

You can enjoy an undemanding 1½-hour walk along an **old bog road** if you leave your car at the *Ardagh Hotel* on the Ballyconneely road and walk south for a short distance, until the road crosses Ballinaboy Bridge. Take the left fork there, signposted for Cashel and Recess, and keep the Ballinaboy River on your left after crossing it by another bridge. Turn round after reaching the next small bridge, Beaghcauneen Bridge, and on the way back turn left about 500 yds before Ballinaboy Bridge, signposted for Lough Fadda. Walking south to Lough Fadda, passing the much smaller Lough Enask on the way, adds less than an hour to the walk.

In 1919 the first aeroplane to cross the Atlantic, a Vickers Vimy, landed to the south of Clifden and John Alcock and Arthur Whitten Brown stepped on to land for the first time in over 16 hours. To reach the **Alcock and Brown monument**, walk or cycle to the Ballinaboy Bridge on the Ballyconneely road, as for the old bog road walk (see above), but then bear to the right, staying on the R341 for 500 yds until you reach a crossroads. Take the left turn, signposted for the landing site, and walk south, passing a small lake and heading for the white monument when it comes into view. This stretch of road follows the line of a narrow-gauge railway and it also passes the place where Marconi operated the first transatlantic wireless, now marked by a plaque.

Retrace your steps from the monument or continue westwards on the green road, passing a lake and then a quarry on your left, until you get to a small road. You will then pass the larger Lake Emlanabehy before rejoining the R341; after that you will have to walk back to Clifden along the main road. The entire walk takes about 1½ hours.

The **Omey Island** walk starts from the village of Claddaghduff, which is eight miles (13 km) northwest of Clifden near Cleggan, and easily reached by car or bicycle by heading out on the N59 to Letterfrack and then taking the signposted road to the left. You get to the island by following the markers across the sand from the beach at Claddaghduff, but you should avoid high tide; you can check the times either at the Walking Centre in Clifden (see page 430) or the pub in Claddaghduff.

Sleeping
Price codes: see inside front cover

There are a number of hotels in Clifden but for what you pay a more satisfying level of personal service can be enjoyed in some of the town's guesthouses. There is also a range of B&Bs – while most are hideous bungalows some at least have locations that provide superb views – and hostels. The average price for doubles/singles in B&Bs is €60/43.

L *Abbeyglen Castle*, Sky Rd, T21201, F21797, http://www.abbeyglen.ie Built in 1832 and looking just like you might imagine a castle hotel to look, this is a wonderfully laid-back place with an elegant drawing room and views over Clifden and the sea. **L** *Ardagh Hotel & Restaurant*, nearly 2 miles (3 km) outside of town on the road to Ballyconneely, T21384, F21314, ardaghhotel@eircom.net A more relaxing hotel than those in the town. Some of the rooms have enchanting views of Ardbear Bay, and the hotel has an excellent restaurant. **AL** *The Quay House*, Beach Rd, T21369, www.thequayhouse.com Prettily located by the harbour, this guesthouse, the oldest building in Clifden, dates back to 1820 when it was a harbourmaster's residence, and breakfast is a leisurely affair in the conservatory. There are also self-catering studio rooms for rent. **AL** *Station House Hotel*, T21699, F21667,www.stationhousehotel.com In town, on the left when approaching on the Galway road, a modern 4-star hotel with a leisure centre and pool and contemporary-styled bedrooms. **AL** *Sunnybank House*, Church Hill, T21437, www.sunnybankhouse.com This guesthouse enjoys fine views from a garden setting and has a heated pool, sauna and tennis court.

A *Ardmore House*, Sky Rd, T21221, info@ardmore-house.com B&B 3 miles (5 km) out from town, in a location that provides superb views. **A** *Dan O'Hara's Farmhouse*, Lettershea, 5 miles (8 km) from town on the N59 Galway Rd, T/F21246. A B&B that is also a working farm, but the rooms are smart and well equipped. **B** *Ben View House*, Bridge St, T21256, F21226. A guesthouse in a smart town house with an air of antique grace about the place.

County Galway

D *Ard Ri Bayview Hostel*, T21886. Tucked away on a pier behind King's Garage off Main St, has over 30 beds, which include some private rooms, bicycles can be rented, and has a warm and welcoming atmosphere. **D** *Blue Hostel*, Sky Rd, T21835. Independent hostel. **D** *Brookside Hostel*, Hulk St, T21812 brooksidehostel@eircom.net IHH hostel. Includes 2 private rooms. **C-D** *Clifden Town Hostel*, Market St, T21076. Has 2 private rooms , rents bikes, and has a hotel-style sitting room area and good facilities.

Eating

In summer, book ahead for one of the window tables at the excellent Ardagh Restaurant away from the bustle of Clifden town

There is no shortage of restaurants around the town, but the quality varies at the height of the tourist season. Dinner at the **Ardagh Hotel and Restaurant**, Ballyconneely Rd, T21384, is around €35 but worth splashing out for the quality cuisine and therapeutic view of Ardbear Bay. Signposted off the same road, the **High Moors Restaurant**, Dooneen, T21342, opens for dinner Wed-Sun and should cost below €25.

On Market St **Mitchell's Restaurant** opens in the evening with a reputation for good seafood. *Cullen's Bistro*, Market St, T21983, is a cosy little restaurant serving dishes from Irish stew for the punters to interesting salads and home-made pies and cakes. Open for lunch and dinner. *O'Grady's Seafood Restaurant*, Market St, T21450, charges around €20 for a main dish, but there are surprisingly few seafood choices. A better bet might be *Fogerty's*, T21427, on the other side of the road where lobster is around €25 and a set dinner €24. *Vaughan's*, at the tourist office end of Market St, has lunch specials and evening dishes like Irish stew for €9.

Most of the pubs serve bar food and both *Mitchell's*, Market St, T21867, specializing in seafood, and *EJ Kings*, T21085, have their own restaurants.

Pubs & music The bar at the back of *Foyle's Hotel* on Main St, T21801, has authentic sessions of local music and singing on a Thu night and a visit is recommended. *Lowry's* and *Mannion's Bar*, both in Market St, provide enjoyable evenings of traditional music while *EJ Kings* is more pop and rock.

Festivals Towards the end of **Sep** the *Clifden Community Arts Week*, T21164/21295, www.clifden-artsweek.com, takes off with a packed week of musical and theatrical events, lectures, walks, book events, story-telling and more. The *Connemara Walking Festival,* T21379, F21845, walkwest@indigo.ie http://indigo.ie/~walkwest/, is usually a 4-day event, organized by the *Connemara Walking Centre*, T095-21379, with walks varying in difficulty. The cost including B&B is around €165 and there is usually one towards the end of **May** and another one towards the end of **Sep** so as to overlap with the Arts Week.

Shopping The site of the old Clifden railway station is now a modern little complex with shops like the *House of Mag Aoide* that sells prints and pictures of nostalgic bygone times. *Clifden Bookshop* is on Main St and next door is a small jewellery shop and then the *Music Shop*, the place to go for a *bodhrán* and other musical gear if unable to visit Roundstone. On the other side of the bookshop *Wooden Treasures* sells expensive wooden crafts. *Millar's Connemara Tweeds*, T21038, sells products from its own mill using wool from local mountain sheep.

Tours *Clifden Walking Centre*, T21379. Walks from the Centre are regularly organized May-Aug, €13-31 per person.

Transport **Bicycle** Bicycles may be hired from some hostels and from *Mannions* Bridge St, T21160.

Directory **Banks** There are banks near the Square. **Communications** Post office: Main St.

Cleggan

This small fishing village, 12 miles (16 km) northwest of Clifden, is primarily   *Phone code: 095*
of interest for visitors heading for the island of Inishbofin. Boats also depart
from here for the island of Inishturk in County Mayo (see page 455). The
Cleggan Riding Centre, T/F44746, provides riding lessons and treks along
the beach, to Omey Island. The Sky Road will take you to the tiny village of
Claddaghaduff and when the tide is out it is easy to walk over to Omey Island
where there are good beaches.

Food is available from *Oliver's Bar* or in the pink-coloured *Pier Bar* at the harbour   **Sleeping**
which has a reputation far beyond the borders of County Galway. At night there is   **& eating**
music in *Joyce's Bar* and B&B is available from **A** *Harbour House*, T44702.

Inishbofin Island

Inishbofin can be as whimsical as its name suggests: a magical silence during   *Phone code: 095*
Colour map 2, grid B1
the day and gregarious pub life at night. This little island – only 4 miles (6
km) long by less than 2 miles (3 km) wide – is easily reached from Cleggan
(you can do it as a day's excursion or stay the night). Inishbofin has not been
spoiled by tourism – yet – because the majority of the few hundred inhabitants do not depend on the highly seasonal flow of visitors to sustain their
way of life. Come here for fresh-air walks and a sense of calm and enjoy the
feeling that not everywhere in the west of Ireland is being packaged and marketed by *Bord Fáilte*.

Getting there Inishbofin is 6 miles (10 km) west of Cleggan from where it takes 45   **Ins & outs**
mins to reach the island. *Kings Ferries*, T44642/21520, F44327, conamara@indigo.ie
www.faite.con/cleggan/, have departures from Cleggan more or less on demand in
Jul and Aug (scheduled for 1000, 1130, 1400, 1745 and 1915) and at 1130 and 1845,
Apr-Jun and Sep-Oct. Departures from Inishbofin at 0900, 1045, 1300, 1700 and 1815
in Jul and Aug, and at 0900 and 1700 the other months. Tickets, €15.20 return, from
the signposted shop on the main street in Cleggan and there is also a ticket office in
Clifden. Bikes are carried free.
    Michael Nee Coaches, T51082, runs buses from the Square in Clifden and from
Forster St in Galway to Cleggan between Jun and mid-Sep for €9/6.50 return/single.
The 0915 and 1200 buses from Clifden connect with the ferry and buses from Clifden
depart at 1100, 1335 and 1745.
    There is no official **tourist office**, but try either hotel for general tourist information.

St Colman came to Inishbofin from Iona in the seventh century to found a   **History**
monastery after quarrelling with Rome over a new calendar that changed
the date of Easter. Nothing remains of his original settlement, but the ruins
of a 13th-century church are supposedly standing on the original site.
Grace O'Malley, the pirate queen, used Inishbofin, and the ruins of the
castle that can be seen when approaching the harbour date from the 16th
century when she was active. Cromwell captured the castle in 1652 and
fortified it for the purpose of incarcerating prisoners. A variation on the
haunting theme of Cromwell's perfidy, the story goes that he chained a
bishop to a large rock in the harbour and left him there until the tide came
in and drowned him.

County Galway

Island walk/cycle Head west (left) after disembarking at the harbour and follow the road as it turns into a green road and passes, after about 20 minutes of walking, a sparkling little sandy beach. Carry on westwards until the green road fades away and then head for the most westerly point, clearly visible and quite safe to reach on foot or cycling because the ground is flat and there are no cliffs. Sheep, rabbits, seabirds and the occasional seal may be your only company on a quiet day. On reaching the western extremity walk over to the northern side of the island and pick up the path near the metal cross and head back as far as the lake and then south to rejoin the road you started on.

The road going eastwards from the harbour passes the church ruins and accesses a second beach. By following the round around to the north side a third beach is encountered.

There is a small **heritage centre** near *Day's Hotel*, ■ *Open summer, daily 1200-1700.€2.50.*

Sleeping & eating **A** *Day's Hotel*, T45809, F45803. Open from Apr-Sep, a convivial place at the east side of the island: walk to the right after disembarking. **A** *Doonmore Hotel*, T/F45804. Also a 10-min eastwards walk from the harbour, has similar rates and seasonal opening as *Day's*, but no service charge. **C** *Hy Brazil*, T45817, F45804. Open from Easter to end of Oct. Named after an enchanted island (*Tír na nÓg*) that appears every 7 years and is supposedly visible from islands off the west coast, this much more down-to-earth non-smoking B&B is reached by walking west/left from the pier until the sign points inland. **D** *Inishbofin Island Hostel*, T45855, F45803. Open from Apr-Oct. Has nearly 40 beds, including 4 private rooms. Camping is also possible.

Both hotels have small restaurants serving lunch, and evening meals for around €20.50, and *Day's Bar* has good pub food.

Pubs & music *Day's Bar* has music on Wed to Sun nights and the bar in the *Doonmore Hotel* has traditional music on Wed and Sat nights.

Directory **Bicycle** Bikes for hire are usually waiting at the harbour. **Trekking** *Trekking Centre*, T45853. Behind *Day's Hotel*. Treks on horseback for beginners or experienced riders.

From Clifden to Leenane

Letterfrack
Phone code: 095
Colour map 2, grid B2

Not so much a town as a roadside collection made up of shops, pubs and assorted houses on the N59 between Clifden and Leenane, Letterfrack lends itself to use as a possible base for a day or two because Connemara National Park and Kylemore Abbey are close by. Cleggan lies to the west and there is an interesting coastal region to the north.

Connemara National Park Managed by Dúchas, much of the Park area once formed part of the Kylemore Abbey estate but the expanses of bog, heath and mountains are now open to the public. At the Visitors' Centre there is a 15-minute audio-visual presentation every half-hour and guide books and maps are for sale. The 1-mile (1.4-km) **Sruffaunboy Nature Trail** is an undemanding self-guided stroll, and a useful €0.50 booklet is available that points out ecological features along the way, including Connemara ponies, 'lazy bed' cultivation ridges, bogland flora and fauna and types of Connemara rock. A more vigorous walk may be enjoyed by walking to the summit of **Diamond Hill** (1,460 ft/445 m), the unmistakable knob of rock overlooking the Centre. For serious walkers, some of the Twelve Bens are within the Park. ■ *T41054. Easter-May and Sep, daily 1000-1730; Jun, daily 1000-1830; Jul and Aug, daily 1930-1830. Closed Oct-Easter. Guided* *nature walks (2-3 hrs) in Jul and Augt on Mon, Wed and Fri mornings. Evening talks every Wed at 2030. €2.50. Outdoor and indoor picnic tables, café.*

Built as a gift for his wife in the 1860s by Mitchell Henry, an English industrial magnate and MP who was charmed by Connemara, the appeal of Kylemore Abbey is inseparable from its location. The buildings are stepped on terraces overlooking the lake and there are two buildings to admire: the neo-Gothic castle built as a family home and a small chapel a short distance away. Benedictine nuns acquired Kylemore in 1920 and is now run as a private boarding school for girls. This means that many of the rooms are off-limits to visitors and, combined with the fact that a fire destroyed many of the interiors anyway, the result is that there is not much really that much to see inside. The chapel, designed by James Fuller in 1868, is an imitation of an English 14th-century church and the stone vaulting has recently been restored to its former glory.

Kylemore Abbey gardens have recently opened to the public, restoring the late Victorian walled garden that was an integral part of Henry's plan to transform the wilderness of Connemara into a country estate. Alas, it was not to be. His wife's health was seriously impaired by the winter climate, Henry himself became bankrupt trying to maintain Kylemore and he died a few years after being forced to sell the property. ■ *T41146. Open Mar-Oct, daily, 0900-1800. €4. Self-service restaurant.*

Kylemore Abbey & gardens

Some of the best self-service food in Ireland, including black-eye bean casserole for vegetarians, is available at Kylemore Abbey

Look out for the wholesome home-made jams too

LL-L *Rosleague Manor*, Letterfrack, T41101, www.rosleague.com A Georgian country house overlooking Ballinakill Bay set in 30 acres of landscaped gardens and complete with a billiard table and tennis court. **B** *Diamond Lodge*, T41380, F41205. Standard B&B. **B** *Gearbi House*, T41023. B&B at the post office. **C-D** *Old Monastery Hostel*, T41132, F41680, oldmon@indigo.ie A solid 19th-century house with some character, this is one of Ireland's best hostels. It has been a favourite with travellers for some years now and with good reason. The room rates, whether sharing (€9-11) or in a private room (€15 per person), include a tasty, non-fried breakfast and an evening meal is available at a very reasonable rate. **Camping** is also possible and bikes can be hired.

Sleeping
Price codes: see inside front cover

Rosleague Manor, Letterfrack, T41101, F41168, welcomes non-residents if a booking is made in advance for its €38 dinner. The seafood is locally caught and always fresh and Connemara lamb is another speciality that can be relied on, along with fresh vegetables and herbs straight from their garden. The best place for a good and economically priced meal is the self-service restaurant in *Kylemore Abbey*, where meals are under €7; the café at the visitor's centre in *Connemara National Park* with its picnic tables (indoors and out) is also worth considering if entering the Park. There is a good food shop in Letterfrack near the main junction.

Eating

Outside of Letterfrack on the road to Clifden, *Avoca Handweavers*, T41058, is one of the better craft shops in Connemara with a large collection of clothes and crafts plus a bookshop and a café. The *Kylemore Craft Shop*, at Kylemore Abbey, is run by the Benedictine nuns and has a selection of Irish knitwear and accessories as well as pottery, which is thrown and glazed on the premises, china, crystal and jewellery. The shop can be freely visited, as can its above-average self-service restaurant.

Shopping

County Galway

Renvyle Peninsula and around

Another literary corner of Ireland (though not one of the better-known ones). Its fame is thanks to Oliver St John Gogarty (1878-1957) having a home here and inviting Yeats, Shaw and others to share his "faery land of Connemara at the

Phone code: 095
Colour map 2, grid 2B

extreme end of Europe, [where] the incongruous flowed together at last, and the sweet and bitter blended". The good news is that life is not quite so terminal around Renvyle and there are a number of modest diversions.

At **Lettergesh**, a mile east from Tully Cross, there is a lovely little beach and another one, the spectacular white-sand **Glassillaun Beach**, is just past Lettergesh. From the small golfing green at Renvyle House, you can go for a pleasant walk past the lake and along the pebbly beach to the ruins of an old O'Flaherty Castle.

Ocean's Alive This aquarium and maritime museum, scenically located on Derryinver Bay, is devoted to Connemara's marine life. It offers a useful introduction to the ecological richness of the local area. ■ *T43473. Open May-Sep, daily 0930-1900; Oct-Apr, daily 1000-1630. Closed for 3 weeks over the Christmas period. €5. Boats leave on the hr. Signposted on the road from Letterfrack to Tully. Picnic area and café.*

Under the management of *Ocean's Alive*, four sailings a day cruise around Ballinakill Harbour, Letter, Derryinver and Fahy bays and there is a good chance of seeing a few sociable dolphins and porpoises, perhaps a basking seal or two and certainly seabirds. ■ *T43473. €16 (cruise), €20 (fishing). Sailings at 1000, 1200, 1600 and 1800. Sunset cruises at 2030 (see 'Pubs & music' below).*

Sleeping **L-AL** *Renvyle House*, T43511, renvyle@iol.ie www.renvyle.com This is Gogarty's
"Nothing left but a charred oak beam quenched in the well beneath the house. And ten tall square towers, chimneys, stand here on Europe's extreme edge".
Gogarty's description of his ruined house

original house, where Yeats sat for his first portrait by Augustus John and where he held a séance in the belief that the place was haunted, and which was burned down in the Civil War but rebuilt. Country mansion with log fires, fishing, golf, pool, croquet. The hotel organizes a variety of special interest weekends; contact Renvyle House for details. **B** *Olde Castle House*, Renvyle, T43460. Near to the castle ruins, with a movie history – the house was in the film *Purple Taxi*. Evening meal at €17. **B** *Diamond's Bar*, Tully, T43431, castlehouse@eircom.net Modernised pub in the village of Tully. Sea views and dinner at €17. Child reductions. Bicycles may also be hired from here. **B** *The Little Killary Adventure Centre*, T43411. Dinner also available.

Camping The *Connemara Caravan & Camping Park*, T43406, open May-Sep, is at Gowlaun near Lettergesh. The *Renvyle Beach Caravan & Camping Park*, T43462, just west of Tully, is smaller and has fewer facilities but enjoys a glorious view of Mweelrea, the highest peak in Mayo.

Eating Dinner at *Renvyle House*, T43511, is €30 (book ahead in summer). For cheaper meals the best bet is Tully. *Diamond's Bar* has pub food throughout the day, as does the *Renvyle Inn*, T43954, it also has a restaurant with fairly unexciting but inexpensive main courses.

Pubs & music From Jun-Aug, *Ocean's Alive*'s evening cruise at 1800 often includes a session of traditional music and on particularly fine summer evenings there is a Sunset Cruise at 2030. On Sun afternoons in the café at the *Ocean's Alive* visitor centre there is a session of traditional Irish music from 1515 to 1700. Non-residents are welcome at *Renvyle House* and the music evenings in the bar often continue late into the night.

Sport **Cycling** Bicycles may be hired at *Diamond's Bar*, T43431, in Tully. **Diving** *Scubadive West*, Renvyle, T43922, F43923, scuba@anu.ie Conduct half-day sessions every day at 1000 and 1400 for €38 and this covers tuition and a supervised dive in sheltered water. **Horse-riding** At *Diamond's Bar*, T43431, in Tully enquires may be made regarding horse-riding. **Outdoor pursuits** *Little Killary Adventure Centre*, Salruck, T43411, F43591. Runs a variety of outdoor activities: rock climbing, sailing, canoeing and the like.

County Galway

Leenane and Killary Harbour

Whether coming from Clifden to the southwest or from Mayo in the north the approach into Leenane along Killary Harbour is unforgettably beautiful. Regarded as Ireland's only fjord, it is sublime or sinister, depending on the play of light. The philosopher Wittgenstein (1889-1951) found it inspiring, living for six months in 1948 near the mouth of the harbour at Rosroe while working on *Philosophical Investigations*. The house where he lived is now the *Killary Harbour Hostel*, and facing the hostel on the north side of the harbour is Mount Mweelrea (2,687 ft/819 m).

Phone code: 095
Colour map 2, grid B2

Getting around If travelling north into Mayo from Leenane be sure to take the R335 road via Delphi and not the main N59, especially if travelling by bicycle. The R335 route offers up a landscape of such serenity and melancholy that is hard to find anything to compare with it in the whole of Ireland. Praise indeed.

Ins & outs

Leenane is picturesquely situated at the head of the harbour and such is the grandeur of the scene that many travellers feel compelled to make a stop. The village makes the most of the fact that scenes from John B Keane's *The Field* were filmed here, and an enjoyable walk leads to the **Asaleagh Waterfall** where the church scene was filmed.

At **Leenane Cultural Centre**, the focus of interest is on the local wool industry and several breeds of sheep are, as it were, open to the public. Visitors can mingle with the flock and its collie dog in order to identify the different breeds. The **Wool Museum** demonstrates the arts of carding, spinning and weaving and a 13-minute video covers the woollen industry and local places of interest. ■ *T42323. Open Apr-Oct, daily 1000-1900. €3. Café.*

B *Portfinn Lodge and Restaurant*, Leenane, T42265. Comfortable purpose-built rooms. B *Killary House*, T42254. Short distance outside of town. Pretty house with lovely views. B *Glen Valley House*, Glencroff, T42269, gvhouse@yahoo.com Working farmhouse on the route of the Western Way walking route. Connemara ponies to pet.

Sleeping
Price codes:
see inside front cover

Portfinn Lodge Restaurant, T42265, hits the jackpot twice with magnificent views over Killary harbour and superb fresh seafood on the menu. Meat dishes, like local lamb, are also available, but the lobster, prawn and turbot are hard to beat. Expect to pay around €22 for the set menu, more for alcohol. Closed from Oct-Apr. For a casual meal that doesn't involve visiting a pub, the *Leenane Cultural Centre* has a café with a decent range of meals and snacks and wines. In the village itself there is a healthy smattering of cafés and pubs offering food, including the affordable *Field Restaurant* with seafood, stews, chowder and the like and *Gaynor's Bar*, which also milks the *Field* theme.

Eating

County Galway

South Galway

In 'Coole Park, 1929' Yeats imagined a time:
> *When all those rooms and passages are gone,*
> *When nettles wave upon a shapeless mound*
> *And saplings root among the broken stone.*

Coole Park
Phone code: 091

The rooms have indeed gone but saplings have a problem because the house where Lady Gregory lived and where Yeats spent summers writing poetry was demolished for no good reason in 1941 and the site cemented over. Frank

☛ **Lady Gregory**

Lady Gregory (1852-1932) first met Yeats in 1893 and he first stayed at her home, Coole Park, four years later. It was during this visit that they dreamed up the idea of a national theatre. They remained friends for the rest of her life and shared an interest in Irish folklore. Lady Gregory wrote her own plays as well as editing and publishing various books on Gaelic culture. Her collections of Irish legends and myth were praised by Yeats as "the chief part of Ireland's gift to the imagination of the world." There is an

Annual Autumn Gathering at Coole Park with lectures, plays and local excursions to places associated with Lady Gregory. Contact Shelia O'Donnellan, Kingston Rd, Taylor's Hill, Galway, T091-521836, F091-567421. At Kilartan Cross, 2 miles (3 km) north of Gort on the N128, Kiltartan Gregory Museum contains memorabilia and manuscripts associated with Lady Gregory and the Irish Literary Revival.

■ *T632346. Jun-Sep, daily, 1000-1830 and Sep-May on Sun, 1330-1700.*

O'Connor sardonically commented, "sold by Mr de Valera's Government to a Galway builder for £500 and torn down for scrap. Merely as a literary museum its value to the nation was almost incalculable; one feels they should have held out for at least £600." Coole Park is now a nature reserve with an audio-visual show and while the trails, from half an hour to 90 minutes, are self-guided the €2 guide booklet is still good value. The booklet also explains the signatures on the **Autograph Tree**, a beech tree on which Lady Gregory invited her literary guests (Shaw, Synge, Yeats, O'Casey and others) to carve their initials. ■ *T631804. Mid Jun-Sep, daily 0930-1630. €2.50. Dúchas site. 3 miles (5 km) north of Gort.*

Thoor Ballylee Thoor Ballylee, a Norman tower purchased by the poet in 1916 for £35, is the other Yeats attraction in the area. The poet called his tower "a powerful emblem" and some of his best poems were written with the place in mind. An audio-visual presentation tells the story and there is a bookshop of Anglo-Irish literature, a pleasant tea-room, bureau de change and riverside walks. ■ *T563081. May-Sep, daily 1000-1800. €3.80. Dúchas site. Less than a mile off the N18 Galway to Limerick road.*

Kilmacduagh In the vicinity of Gort, Kilmacduagh has an almost embarrassing richness of ecclesiastical ruins that owe their existence to a monastery founded here in the seventh century. The best preserved building is a slightly leaning but very elegant 115-ft (35-m) round tower, while the roofless cathedral dates mostly from the 15th century though its blocked-up doorway on its west side is possibly 10th-century. The ruins of two small churches, St John's and O'Heyne's, lay to the north and O'Heyne's is worth a visit for its decorated chancel pillars and carved windows. The ruins of St Mary's Church are on the east side of the cathedral but are not as interesting.

Eating In Gort there is the usual run of pubs serving food and *The Blackthorn*, Crowe St, T632127, on the left coming in from Coole Park, is a comfortable bar with tables for eating and a more formal restaurant area upstairs. Vegetarians could eat here. Lunch is around €7.50, evening dinner €19, and there is live music on a Sat night.

Kinvara

The natural prettiness of this coastal village on the main route between Galway and the Burren invites a stop, not least because of the surprising number of good places to eat. So far, the charm of the place has not been diluted by its popularity and as a village that has the potential to become another Kinsale, it is well worth visiting before it does so.

Phone code: 091
Colour map 2, grid C4

This 16th-century castle, perched on a promontory, has been well restored and the contents of each floor are devoted to a different period in its history. It was once owned by Oliver St John Gogarty but the last proprietor has also left her mark and one of the rooms is decorated in the style that the owner employed when living here in the 1960s. ■ *Open mid-Apr-Sep, daily 0930-1730. €4.*

Dunguaire Castle

A medieval-style banquet at Dunguaire Castle kicks off nightly with harp music, salted bread and mead, and chicken eaten with a dagger, followed by just under an hour of singing and story-telling from assorted sources in Irish culture. Coach parties can make up the bulk of the audience but it is all good fun and individuals are welcomed. ■ *T061-360788. Open May-mid-Oct, daily 1730 and 2045. €38.*

AL *Merriman Inn*, Main St, T638222, www.merrimanhotel.com For not much more than the price of a B&B this is good value. A comfortable, modern and relaxed hotel in the village close to the Castle, with a huge thatched roof. **B** *Burren View Farm*, Doorus, T637142, F6381381. B&B with a pleasant, away from it all location, nice views and some en suite rooms. **D** *An Óige Doorus House*, T637512. A hostel with literary associations, being the house where Yeats and Lady Gregory first discussed setting up a national theatre. "On the sea-coast at Duras, a few miles from Coole, an old French Count, Florimond de Basterot, lived for certain months in every year. Lady Gregory and I talked over my project of an Irish Theatre, looking out upon the lawn of his house, watching a large flock of ducks." WB Yeats. No private rooms. Some 4 miles (6 km) away to the northwest and signposted off the road to Ballyvaughan. **D** *Johnston's Independent Hostel*, T637164. Next door to the *Merriman Inn*, this hostel has 24 beds but no private rooms.

Sleeping
Price codes:
see inside front cover

The smart *Quilty Room* restaurant in the *Merriman Inn* has appetizing starters, such as local clams with grilled courgettes, and a decent wine list. The hotel bar serves pub grub from 1200 until 2200. The *Pier Head* bar and restaurant, off the road at the harbourside, has good pub food as well as steaks, and seafood. The brightly painted *Café on the Quay*, T637654, where it is worth getting the single window table overlooking the harbour, opens from 0900 for breakfast and the €7 lunches are posted on a blackboard outside. At night, main dishes are around €7.5 and there is a good selection of salads. Or, on a fine day, enjoy a picnic on the grass near the castle.

Eating

The *Winkles* pub has nightly traditional music between Thu and Sun and *Conoles*, popular with locals, has music on a Sun night. The bar in the *Merriman* hotel has music on Sat and Sun nights, but for somewhere genuinely old and flavoursome you can't beat *Tully's*, T637146, with its stone-floor, attached grocery store and traditional music on assorted days of the week.

Pubs & music

Clarinbridge is passed on the main N18 road, 10 miles (16 km) south of Galway City, and apart from the second weekend in September there is little reason to make a stop other than for a shopping trip to **Clarenbridge Antiques**,

Clarinbridge
Colour map 2, grid C4

County Galway

T796522, or **Clarenbridge Crystal & Fashion Shop**, T796178. When the **Oyster Festival** arrives, however, the place is bursting with visitors and *Paddy Burkes Inn*, T796226, in the village and *Moran's* pub and restaurant, T796113, a little further south near Kilcolgan, are two of the most popular venues associated with the festival. *Paddy Burkes* is a pub of character and while most famous for its seafood, its bar food menu includes steaks and curries. Check out its visitors' book to get an idea of how the Oyster Festival attracts celebrities from all over the world. ■ *For festival information, T76359.*

East Galway

Ballinasloe

Phone code: 0905
Colour map 2, grid C5

On the main N6 Dublin to Galway road, Ballinasloe and its surrounding places of interest may not be worth a special journey from Galway or Connemara for those that are not historically minded. For those with a fascination for Irish history, however, the area is important as the site of the Battle of Aughrim.

The Battle of Aughrim Interpretative Centre

In 1691 Aughrim was the site of the final battle, of momentous significance for European history, between the Protestant William of Orange and the Catholic James II. The Jacobite army was under General St Ruth and his reluctance to work with Sarsfield, his second-in-command, was one factor in their defeat by the numerically inferior Williamite army. The Centre has models and displays, and explains the European dimension to the battle. ■ *T73939. €43. Jun-Aug, 1000-1800. Tea-room. Tourist information centre. Four miles (6 km) southwest of Ballinasloe on the N6.*

Clonfert Cathedral

Also in the vicinity, this 12th-century cathedral, remarkable for its exemplary Irish Romanesque doorway, is baroquely Celtic in its love of ornamentation. Well worth viewing, the cathedral is 10 miles (15 km) southeast of Ballinasloe at Clonfert.

Sleeping
Price codes:
see inside
front cover

AL *Haydens Gateway*, Ballinasloe, T42347 cro@lynchotels.com one of the Lynch chain of hotels. All mod cons and restaurant in summer bar food in winter. **D** *Hynes Hostel*, T73704. Very close to the *Aughrim Interpretative Centre*, and has 2 private rooms.

Portumna

Phone code: 0509
Colour map 2,
grid C5
There is a
seasonal tourist
office, in town
T42131

The attraction of a visit to this small market town is **Portumna Castle and Gardens**, a semi-fortified house built in the early 17th century and the best example of Irish Jacobean architecture in the country. Restoration work is ongoing but the ground floor and the highly formal garden is open and there is an exhibition giving the background story. ■ *T41658. Mid-Jun to mid-Sep, daily 0930-1830. €2.*

Sleeping
Price codes:
see inside
front cover

L-AL *Shannon Oaks Hotel & Country Club*, T41777, www.shannonoaks.ie This very modern hotel, located by the shore of Lough Derg, with a gym, swimming pool and a comfortable bar serving food as well as a restaurant, makes for a comfortable stopover for accommodation and/or food.

County Roscommon

Strokestown

Strokestown is a quaint little place laid out in the 18th century to the usual cruciform design by a planter Maurice Mahon, his big house at one end of the village and the church at the other so every Sun he could drive through his domain with the lower classes watching admiringly. It has blossomed each year since 1999 with its tremendously powerful poetry festival (see box next page) and is home to one of the best museums in Ireland.

Phone code: 078
Colour map 2, grid B5

Of all the big houses of the Anglo-Irish open to the public, Strokestown Park House must rate as one of the most enjoyable and educational to visit anywhere in the country. Its history goes back to the 17th century, when an ancestor of Maurice's, Nicholas Mahon, was granted a vast estate of nearly 30,000 acres (12,141 ha) in the county as a reward for being on the winning side in his country's civil war. The house you see today is largely 18th century, designed by the prolific Richard Castle, while many of the contents are 19th century. The house stayed in the same family until 1981, when it was sold to a local business family, and its interior was never denuded like so many of these houses, so there is a wealth of well preserved furnishings to admire. The most infamous owner was Denis Mahon who, at the time of the Famine, shipped off his evicted tenants to America in the overcrowded and unsafe ships, which were suitably dubbed 'coffin ships', until he got his come-uppance in 1847 from an assassin's bullet.

Strokestown Park House

Tours of the house are well worth it, because there is so much to see, and take in the dining and living rooms, library and schoolroom. The kitchen also is a must-see, opening up some sociology with its out-of-reach gallery designed for the mistress to drop down messages without having to converse with the servants. Along the same lines, and like many Anglo-Irish houses, there was a brick tunnel running between the kitchen and the yard so that the beastly menials were not encountered in person.

The four-acre (9.9-ha) **walled garden** is another attraction of the place, having been carefully restored to some of its original beauty. The highlight for many visitors is the herbaceous border (listed in the *Guinness Book of Records* as the longest in the Britain and Ireland).

A visit to the **Famine Museum** complements the glimpse into the Anglo-Irish lifestyle afforded by Strokestown Park House. While the lady of the manor was dropping down her menus from the gallery of the kitchen the peasants were dying of starvation in their homes and in the fields. Much of the material in the museum consists of primary source material from the House but the portrayal of famine extends to the contemporary world and the exhibition as a whole, an exemplary showcase of how history could be presented, puts to shame many of the lacklustre heritage centres around Ireland that claim to offer an insight into past and present times. ■ *Strokestown Park House, Garden, and Famine Museum, Strokestown. T33013. Apr-Oct, daily, 1100-1730. House, €4; Garden, €4; Famine Museum €4; joint admission for any 2, €7.50; joint admission to all 3 €11.*

A-B *Lakeshore Lodge*, T33966 www.lakeshorelodgeireland.com 4.5 miles (7 km) outside of Strokestown, this is the best place for B&B. A modern bungalow on the shores of Kilglass Lake. *Strokestown Park House* has a restaurant, keeping the same

Sleeping & eating

County Roscommon

Strokestown Poetry Festival

If you've spent any time at all in Ireland you'll know that every tiny village with an eye to their profit margins has a festival – in honour of ancient rituals, music, returning emigrants, fishing, sailing, even vegetables and molluscs. In 1999 casting about for their own reason for a festival Strokestown came up with a little gem - poetry. Anyone who has spent the long winter months in Ireland knows also that if you wait long enough in any little bar someone, usually after several pints, will remember a piece of poetry. Not Yeats or Heaney but some inelegant, rumpty-tumpty piece of wickedness written years ago about a local boozer or womanizer or some local scandal. Those moments make the rain and the afternoon darkness and the terrible roads and the inability to ever get someone in to fix the plumbing/ electricity/TV totally worthwhile. The Strokestown festival has grown so that even the big names submit poems to the competition for the Strokestown Poetry Prize. Its 3 days in early May are accompanied by walks, music, drinking, Gaelic speakers and, best of all, older people who remember some of the satirical local poetry which is probably not written down anywhere. The Strokestown Poetry festival gets top marks for good craic, economic success and preserving a vital aspect of Irish culture. Anyone can submit a poem of up to 70 lines.

■ *For entry forms and details 078-33759 www.strokestownpoetryprize.com*

hours as the House, and serving light meals like tuna salad , tandoori chicken , home-made jam tarts and sherry trifle. There are lots of pubs in town for bar food.

Transport Strokestown can be reached by bus on the Dublin to Ballina service, which runs 3 times a day (2½ hrs from Strokestown). The Ballina to Athlone bus also stops once a day and there is also a daily service between Sligo and Athlone that makes a stop in Strokestown. The bus stop is outside Corcoran's on Main St.

West of Strokestown

Elphin About six miles (10 km) northwest of Strokestown, the neat little village of Elphin can claim Oliver Goldsmith and William Wilde, the father of Oscar, as famous products of its school and there is a thatched working windmill nearby on the road to Carrick-on-Shannon; but that's about it.

Douglas Hyde Interpretive Centre On the N5 road at Frenchpark is this centre, commemorating the academic who was hugely influential in the cultural revival at the turn of the 19th century as well as being a collaborator with Yeats and Lady Gregory on various theatrical productions. The Centre is in an old church, where Hyde is buried.
■ *T0907-70016. May-Sep, Tue-Fri 1400-1700, Sat and Sun 1400-1800. Free; donation requested.*

Clonalis House Just west of Castlereagh, reached from Strokestown via Tulsk though the usual route by the N60 Castlebar to Roscommon road, is Clonalis House. The house is the ancestral home of the O'Conor clan, the only chiefdom to be recognized by the Anglo-Normans as Celtic kings, and the present building is an Italianate mansion built in 1878. It was the first of its kind to be built of concrete in Ireland. The archives contain documents, some written on calf skin, that go back over 60 generations, including a copy of the last Brehon Law judgement and a 16th-century prayerbook. Also here is the harp of Turlough O'Carolan (see page 669), Sheraton and Louis Quinze furniture, portraits and assorted jumble.
■ *T0907-20014. Jun-mid Sep, Mon-Sat 1100-1700. €5.*

Roscommon Town

Harrison Hall, in Market Square, in the centre of town is a good place to start. Here you will find the County Museum, one of those wonderful unreconstructed museums where you while away some time and find something unexpectedly absorbing (our favourite here is the sheela-na-gig). The same building houses the **tourist office** (T26342. May-Sep, open daily 1000-1800). ■ *Mid-Jun to mid-Aug, daily 1000-1730. Free.*

County Museum
Phone code: 0903
Colour map 2, grid B5

The substantial remains of Roscommon Castle, on the road out to Boyle, are worth admiring. Built as a Norman castle in 1269, it passed through many hands and was captured by the O'Conors more than once. The mullioned windows that look so out of place were added in the late 16th century. ■ *Open access. Free.*

Roscommon Castle

At the other end of town, off Circular Road, are the ruins of a Dominican Priory founded in 1253 and deserving a visit for the effigy of its founder, Felim O'Conor. The effigy stands upon a later 15th-century tomb in the north wall and surrounding the figure are eight mail-clad gallowglasses (see box on page 501) with angels above them. ■ *Open access. Free.*

Dominican Priory

L *Abbey Hotel*, Galway Rd, T26240, cmv@indigo.ie Ask for a room in the old wing to savour the feeling of staying in this 18th-century manor house. Big gardens. **AL-A** *O'Garas Royal Hotel*, Castle St, T26317, F26225. In the centre of town and buzzing with local social life. Private car park. **A** *Regans*, Market Sq, T25339, www.regansbar.com Guesthouse that also has 2 self-catering apartments. **A-B** *Gleesons*, Market Sq, T26954, www.gleesonstownhouse.com A fine 19th-century manse with excellent guesthouse accommodation. **B** *Cav Ros*, Racecourse Rd, T25881. A B&B within walking distance of town. **B** *Hillcrest House*, Racecourse Rd, T/F25201. Modern country house, nice gardens. Good child reductions.

Sleeping
Price codes:
see inside front cover

The best place for a meal, light or substantial, indoors or outdoors, is *Glessons*, Market Sq, next to the tourist office. Its coffee shop opens from 0800. *Regans* is next door and offers economically priced meals. *O'Garas Royal Hotel*, Castle St, has reliable hotel fare, including a carvery lunch and a filling set dinner for around €22.

Eating

Buses T071-60066, arrive and depart outside *Regans* in Market Sq. The **Dublin** to **Westport** bus passes through 3 times a day, Mon-Sat, and once on Sun. The **Belfast** to **Galway** bus stops daily and the **Athlone** to **Sligo** bus stops twice daily and once on Sun. **Train** The **Dublin** to **Westport** train service, T26201, stops 3 times a day, T26201, and takes 2 hrs to reach the capital and 1½ hrs to reach Westport.

Transport

Banks Castle St, Church St. **Communications** Post office: Market Sq. **Hospital** *Roscommon County Hospital*, T26200. **Taxi** *Kilduff Thos Taxi Service*, 5 Circular Rd, T25299.

Directory

Boyle

A tranquil little country town, quite at peace with its slow pace of life, Boyle is worth a visit for its beautiful ruined abbey, interesting interpretive centre and a giant dolmen just outside the town.

Phone code: 079
Colour map 1, grid C1
& map 2, grid A5

Bus Éireann's Sligo to Dublin service, T071-60066, stops in Boyle 3 times a day and Sligo to Athlone buses also make daily trips through the town. The bus stop is opposite

Ins & outs

County Roscommon

👉 The Great Famine

After the introduction of the potato to Irish agriculture in the late 16th century it became the staple crop of the mass of Irish peasantry who lived almost entirely off potatoes and buttermilk, a diet just capable of sustaining life. Only the larger farmers or the better off included bread, grain or meat in their diet. Over the centuries there were periodic spells of crop failure caused by the fungal disease phytophthora infestans. Before the 1840s these crop failures had caused deaths and emigration, but on a local scale. Starting in 1845 the crop failure was national and lasted until 1849 in varying degrees. In 1846 only one-quarter of the national yield was produced, and while in 1847 there was no blight, there were few seed potatoes planted. In 1848 the blight came again and the yield was around two-thirds of normal.

To the Irish peasantry this was disaster on a national scale. More people died during this period from disease than starvation. Potatoes had provided iron and vitamins and suddenly the loss of these made thousands of people susceptible to disease. People flocked to the cities and towns in desperation hoping for relief from the Poor Houses, which became impossibly overcrowded. Typhus and cholera spread like wildfire and the young and the old were particularly vulnerable. Recent research suggests that over one million people died, while untold hundreds of thousands escaped to the coffin ships, many of whom, already weakened by starvation and disease, died on the journey. The country's population declined by one-fifth and the trauma of the Famine was so haunting and searing that a collective act of denial set in, which is only now in the process of being acknowledged.

A widespread fungal disease that attacks a staple crop is often thought of as a purely natural disaster, so it is difficult for many English people to understand why a term like 'genocide' is sometimes levelled against their country, or why Tony Blair felt he had to apologize on behalf of Britain in

Daly's pub on Bridge St. Trains on the Sligo to Dublin line stop in Boyle, T62027, 3 times a day in each direction. Journey time to Dublin is 3 hrs and to Sligo is 40 mins. The railway station is just south of town.

Boyle Abbey The abbey was founded in the 12th century by Cistercian monks settling here from the great abbey at Mellifont in County Louth, itself a scion of the abbey at Clairvaux in France. The ruins are well kept and it is possible to get some idea of the details of the monks' lives as you wander round the remains. During the period in which the monastery was built, the then-dominant Romanesque style of architecture was giving way to a Gothic style, and the church has gothic arches on one side and Romanesque arches on the other. If the ruins are closed you can ask at *Abbey House*, the B&B next door to the ruins, for the key. ■*T62604. Jun-Sep, daily 0930-1830. €1.20. Guided tours. Dúchas site. In Boyle, off the N4 Dublin to Sligo Rd.*

King House This building, which now houses the **tourist office** (T62145. May-mid-Sep, Mon-Fri, 1000-1700), was lived in by the local landed gentry, the Kings, who built it around 1730 and then moved on 45 years later to the even bigger Rockingham estate, now the Lough Key Forest Park. Serious social climbers, the Kings did everything they could to force their way into the ruling classes, including putting down any local opposition to English rule, for which they were given the land that King's House now stands on. By 1768 the head of the family had obtained an earlship. By the time of the Famine they were absentee landlords, having crawled their way up the social ladder by forcing the Irish off the land and into coffin ships to America. After their complete departure from

1997. The Famine was not genocide in the way that the Holocaust was, and historians disagree about the level of responsibility that can be laid at Britain's door, but there are certain facts about Britain's handling of the disaster which must be recognized. At the time there was general approval of the concept of laissez-faire, which dictated that any tampering with market forces, such as supporting the starving Irish, would destroy the economy and not solve the problem. In the first year of the Famine Peel's Tory government imported Indian meal to Ireland to be sold as replacement for the lost crop, but no one could afford to buy it. While this and the following Whig government introduced public work schemes in exchange for food (which generally made the situation worse because the work was so hard and the food so poor), neither interfered with the export, from Ireland, of grain which might have been used to feed people. In 1847, two years into the famine, soup kitchens were finally introduced without the imposition of public work in payment. This lasted only six months and then the workhouses were expected to support the starving, which they were hopelessly unable to do.

The same belief in laissez-faire saw the potato failure as an opportunity to reorganize the Irish economy, removing thousands of tiny smallholders and creating larger, more economic farms. Absentee landlords took the opportunity to evict tenants who could not pay their rents, and knock down their houses to prevent reoccupation. Some landlords bankrupted themselves keeping their tenants alive, but others paid their tenants' fares on the emigrant ships to get rid of them: the majority of English landlords saw the opportunity to rid themselves of unwanted people.

Ultimately, responsibility for the deaths of so many people surely rests on the shoulders of the colonial power that created the subsistence economy in the first place.

Boyle in 1775, the house became a garrison for the Connaught (or Connacht) Rangers (see page 405). The interpretive centre is a very hands-on place with lots of activities to try, including a set of building blocks that, when correctly assembled, make a vaulted ceiling of the type that can be admired for real in the house. There are displays on the Rangers, the construction and renovation of the house, the King family and early Connacht as well as some local art. ■ *T63242, kinghouseboylehotmail.com. May-Sep, daily 1000-1800; Apr and Oct, Sat and Sun 1000-1800. €4.*

Back in the middle of town beside the river is Frybrook House, built in 1750 and more modest in conception than King House. It was built by Henry Fry, an English Quaker, brought over by the Kings, the local landlords, who wanted to establish a weaving community in the town. It changed hands in 1986 and has been massively renovated although it retains its original Georgian plasterwork and an Adam fireplace. It is furnished with items from the same period and has some good paintings. ■ *T63513. May-mid Oct, daily 1000-1800. €4.* **Frybrook House**

Less than two miles (3 km) east of Boyle, a part of the Kings' Rockingham Estate is now a picturesque forest park with nature walks, boat hire, a camping park, and the ruins of an old castle on a small island. Rockingham House is gone but the tunnels that the servants used, so as not to disturb the equanimity of their masters, can be seen near the lake. If you hire a boat go to Trinity Island where WB Yeats had plans to set up a mystical-political cult. ■ *T62363. Open all year, 24 hrs. €4 car parking. Access via the N4, east of Boyle.* **Lough Key Forest Park**

County Roscommon

Woodbrook

One of the best books about the Anglo-Irish is Woodbrook, written by David Thomson (see page 681) who, as an 18-year-old Oxford student in the 1930s, took a summer school post as tutor to Phoebe Kirkwood of Woodbrook House. The lyrical style of the prose lures the reader into thinking it will be just a doomed love story and a nostalgic evocation of the past, but there is a sting in the tail that brings one back to social and political realities. Woodbrook, set in the countryside around Lough Key, has a strong sense of place and the house still stands on the N4 road, a little way past Lough Key Forest Park, on the way to Carrick-on- Shannon.

Sleeping

For a special country house near Boyle see page 483

AL *Royal Hotel*, Bridge St, T62016, F62505. In the centre of town and next to the river, this small, 250-year-old, owner-run hotel has a very popular restaurant. **AL** *Forest Park Hotel*, Dublin Rd, T62229. A small, modern family-run place with a good reputation for its food. **B** *Abbey House*, T62385. Next door to the ruins of the abbey, a Victorian house with 6 rooms offering B&B; most rooms have their own bathroom. Nice gardens, reductions for children. **B** *Avonlea*, Dublin Rd, T62538. Opposite the *Forest Park Hotel* is this modern house B&B within walking distance of the *Lough Key Forest Park*. Good child reductions.

Camping Camping is possible at the *Lough Key Caravan & Camping Park*, T62212. Open May-29th Aug.

Eating Near the clocktower is *An Craoibhín*, which does good pub food, while next door is *The Blue Moon*, T64586, serving dishes like Mexican chicken for €6. The *Royal* is very popular with locals at lunchtime, with meat and gravy dinners, while a few doors further down is *Chinese delight*, serving Chinese food, 1730-2300. The *Forest Park Hotel* is also popular with locals at lunchtime and does a set dinner at around €25. In St Patrick St, *Feighans* does pub food. *King House* also has a very pleasant coffee shop/restaurant. *Soul and Heal* by the bridge does lunch dishes and mends your shoes too.

Pubs & music In St Patrick St, *Kate Lavin's* has traditional music on Wed while the *Abbey Bar* entertains on Thu and Sat. *Kate Lavin's* first opened its door to customers in 1889 and shut them for 20 years before reopening around its centenary. Mercifully, very little has changed and the pub exudes authenticity. Back in the Crescent by the clocktower, *Moylburg Inn* has live music while further out of town, *O'Dowd's Railway Bar* is a lively place for a drink and some good music.

Festivals For a small town Boyle has a surprising number of festivals. In **mid-Jul** there is a *country and western carnival* with live music, line dancing, a beanfeast and late bars. The following week there is the *Gala Festival* with talent competitions, buskers, a firework display and lots of other activities. The *Arts Festival* takes place in **late Jul** and includes art exhibitions, theatre, poetry readings, and traditional music and jazz. There is also a *walking festival*, T62083/62624, in **Sep** and a *pike-angling festival*, T63659, at Easter.

Transport **Bicycle** *Brendan Sheerin*, Main St, T62010. Bike hire. **Taxis** *McKenna's Taxis*, Cootehall St, T63344.

Directory **Banks** Corner of Bridge St and St Patrick St, and Main St. Money can also be exchanged at the tourist office.

County Roscommon

12

Counties Mayo, Sligo & Leitrim

Counties Mayo, Sligo & Leitrim

There may come a time when Mayo is as successfully marketed as places like Killarney but until then, the county blissfully remains a connoisseur's corner of Ireland. Inland Mayo, characterized by limestone lowlands, is dull compared to the splendour that lies to the west. The bustling town of **Westport** plays the tourist tune but retains its dignity, while further westwards the easily accessible islands of **Achill** and **Clare** offer superb scenery in an unspoilt setting. North and northwest Mayo is a rarely visited, desolate paradise of lonely bogland, calm mountains and haunting beauty, in utter contrast to the village of Cong in the south where the John Wayne connection has been milked for all it is worth. But Cong is easily forgiven in a county that offers more in the way of isolation and remote beauty than anywhere else in Ireland. County Mayo is also one of Europe's top angling destinations with four great **lakes** – Conn, Cullins, Carra and Mask – all famous for their wild brown trout.

It is hard to travel very far around Sligo and Leitrim without noticing the name **Yeats** cropping up here and there. But even if you aren't a lover of WB Yeats' poetry or Jack Yeats' art, there is much to admire in the countryside of Sligo and Leitrim, from the surreal protrusion of **Benbulbin** to the long scenic coastline and the quiet tranquillity of **Lough Gill**. In the south of Leitrim are gentler, rolling hills, and the new tourist route of the **Shannon to Erne waterway**. There are some fine ancient sites to visit, one of which, **Carrowmore**, holds the only known evidence of a settled Palaeolithic culture anywhere in Europe, and the more modern settlement of **Sligo** with its pubs, fast food chains, malls and cybercafés.

County Mayo

Westport

Phone code: 098
Colour map 2,
grid B2 & B3

Westport may ring the tourist bell but it remains a town of some elegance. It acts as a magnet for young folk who fill the many pubs from early evening onwards, whilst also attracting a well heeled set of travellers drawn by the location, the good hotels and restaurants and the air of Georgian refinement that comes from a town designed by James Wyatt in 1780.

Ins and outs

Getting there   Knock Airport is about 25 miles (40 km) away and has scheduled flights to Dublin and England and charter flights to parts of Europe. *Iarnrod Éireann* operates several trains daily between Dublin and Westport. *Bus Éireann* connects Westport with most other large towns in Ireland and a number of the smaller towns in Mayo.

Getting around   Westport is a fairly compact town and has no bus service of its own. Places of interest are on the outskirts of town but within walking distance of the centre. Bicycles can be hired in town. The **tourist office** on James St, T25711, www.visitmayo.com, is open all year round.

Sights

Westport House   Built in 1730 and superbly designed by the master of Irish country-house building, Richard Castle, Westport House is still in the hands of the Browne family. Highlights include Chinese hand-painted wallpaper in one of the

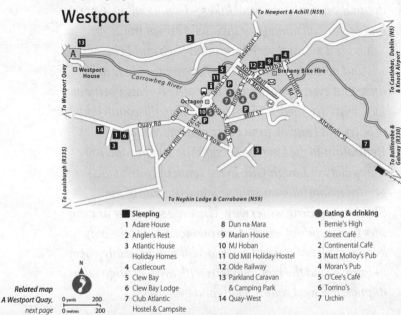

Westport

Sleeping
1 Adare House
2 Angler's Rest
3 Atlantic House
  Holiday Homes
4 Castlecourt
5 Clew Bay
6 Clew Bay Lodge
7 Club Atlantic
  Hostel & Campsite
8 Dun na Mara
9 Marian House
10 MJ Hoban
11 Old Mill Holiday Hostel
12 Olde Railway
13 Parkland Caravan
  & Camping Park
14 Quay-West

Eating & drinking
1 Bernie's High
  Street Café
2 Continental Café
3 Matt Molloy's Pub
4 Moran's Pub
5 O'Cee's Café
6 Torrino's
7 Urchin

Related map
A Westport Quay,
next page

0 yards   200
0 metres   200

★

Things to do in Mayo, Sligo & Leitrim

- Be on **Achill Island** on a fine day
- Seek solitude on the remote beach at **Portacloy**
- Climb **Croagh Patrick** for views of Clew Bay
- Admire the Jack Yeats collection at the **Niland Gallery** in Sligo
- Enjoy a boat trip out to **Inishmurray** and its monastic ruins
- Have a butchers at **Michael Quirke's shop** in Wine Street in Sligo
- Consider a **canal boat journey up the Shannon** all the way to Enniskillen
- Recite some **Yeats** looking out over the Lake Isle of Innisfree

bedrooms, a painting attributed to Rubens and doors of Caribbean mahogany (from the family's estates in the West Indies), but whether a visit is worth the hefty admission price is dubious. However, there is a host of other activities designed to attract families, from a model railway and hill slide to a children's zoo, pedaloes and boating. ■ *T25430. Easter weekend, 1400-1700; May, Sun, 1400-1700; Jun, daily, 1330-1730; Jul 26-Aug, Mon-Fri, 1130-1730, Sat and Sun, 1330-1730; 27 Aug-2 Sep, daily, 1300-1730; 3-23 Sep, daily, 1400-1700. €7.62 (€15.24 including the children's zoo). By bicycle or car, take Quay Rd out of town towards Louisburg and the entry is on the right.*

Crammed with local historical documents and artefacts and with none of the usual gimmicky presentations that pass for substance in heritage centres, this collection is most interesting when showing the role of Westport in the land and nationalist struggles of the 19th and early 20th centuries. **John MacBride** (1865-1916), a revolutionary who was executed for his part in the 1916 rebellion and who was married to **Maud Gonne,** came from Westport (a bust of him is opposite St Mary's church on the South Mall), and the museum has the gift of a spinning wheel that Mayo people gave Maud Gonne in recognition of her leadership. ■ *T26852. Open May-Oct, Mon-Fri, 1000-1700, Sun, 1430-1700. €2.50. The Centre is on Westport Quay, reached by turning right off Quay Road after passing the turn-off for Westport House.*

Westport Heritage Centre

Westport Quay

Heritage Centre □

Carrowbeg River

N

Not to scale

To Westport House & Westport

Quay Road

■ **Sleeping**
1 Granary Hostel
2 Harbour Mill self-catering

● **Eating**
1 Ardmore House
2 Asgard Tavern & Restaurant
3 Quay Cottage
4 Sheebeen Pub
5 Towers Seafood

Essentials

LL-AL *Castlecourt Hotel,* Castlebar St, T25444, www.castlecourthotel.ie Comfortable rooms (140 of them), indoor pool and health centre in this popular, modern hotel. **L-AL** *The Olde Railway Hotel,* The Mall, T25166, www.anu.ie/- railwayhotel Built in 1780 as a coaching inn for guests of Lord Sligo, William Thackeray stayed here, and a Victorian charm still characterizes Westport's most elegant hotel. **AL** *Clew Bay Hotel,* James St, T28088, www.clewbay- hotel.com Cerise-painted hotel, with a lively bar and restaurant.

Sleeping
■ *on maps*
Price codes:
see inside
front cover

Beware the Reek Weekend at the end of July when pilgrims climb Croagh Patrick (see box on page 452) and unbooked accommodation is hard to find

County Mayo

☞ **Grand Tour rip-offs**

Not a few of the treasures that adorn the interiors of Irish country-houses were 'collected' by their 19th-century big-wig owners whilst on their 'Grand Tour' around Europe. Classical antiquities of Greece and Rome were sometimes blatantly robbed by fobbing off the local officials with bribes, and loot ranged from Pompeii tile panels to entire architectural pieces of masonry. The owner of Westport House in the early 19th century, Howe Peter Browne, was particularly struck by a pair of columns from Mycenae dating back to the era of Agamemnon and the Trojan War and fancied they would look good back in Mayo. Until early in the 20th century, they adorned an entrance to Westport House, where replicas now stand; the originals are in the British Museum.

B *Adare House* Quay Rd, T26102, adarehouse@eircom.net Firm mattresses and fine views from this B&B just outside the centre of town. **B** *Angler's Rest*, Castlebar St, T25461. The least expensive guesthouse listed here, with doubles/singles for €43/23. **B** *Clew Bay Lodge*, Quay Rd, T28699. B&B. **B** *Dun Na Mara*, Castlebar St, T25205. Bedrooms with their own bathroom facilities, €53 for a double. **B** *Marian House*, Castlebar St, T25636. One of half a dozen B&Bs in this road. **B** *Quay-West*, Quay Rd, T27863. **C-D** *Club Atlantic*, Altamount St, T26644, F26241. Near the railway station, a large IHH hostel with a variety of rooms, including private ones, and good facilities. **D** *The Granary Hostel*, The Quay, T/F25903. An IHO hostel, Apr to Oct, no private rooms but meals available and laundry facilities. **D** *Old Mill Holiday Hostel*, Barrack Yard, off James St, T27045, F28640, oldmill@iol.ie IHH, open all year except Christmas, 1 private room. Bicycle hire is also available at this well run hostel.

Camping The best facilities are available at the *Club Atlantic Hostel*, Altamount Rd, T27045. The *Parkland Caravan & Camping Park* is in the grounds of Westport House, T27766. But this place is relatively expensive and makes the *Old Head Forest Caravan & Camping Park*, Louisburg, T66021, worth considering.

Eating
● *on maps*
Price codes:
see inside front cover

In town *The Olde Railway Hotel Restaurant*, The Mall, T25166. A good dinner for around €30 in a conservatory dining room, and the Victorian-style bar area is also worth considering for a more informal meal in comfortable surroundings. *The Urchin*, Bridge St, T27532. Opens from 1000 to 2200 and has a varied menu with main dishes around €14. *Torrino's*, Market Lane off Bridge St, T28338, has been recommended for its Italian-style offerings of pizza and pasta dishes around €12. *O'Cees*, Shop St, is fine for just something to snaffle while waiting for a bus at the Octagon. Near to the High St is *Continental Café*, which serves wholefood and vegetarian dishes, is worth seeking out for its fresh salads, baked potatoes, quiche, and even *gado-gado*. Two restaurants that have been recommended by readers are: *Kirwan's on the Mall*, South Mall, and *The Lemon Peel*, The Octagon.

Quay Road Out near the entrance to Westport House there are a number of expensive and mid-range restaurants specializing in local seafood and mostly open only for dinner; reservations are usually necessary. *Quay Cottage Restaurant*, Quay Rd, T26412. Overlooking the harbour, dinner amidst nautical gewgaws; check the daily specials for fresh fish. *The Asgard Tavern & Restaurant*, Quay Rd, T25319. Serves barfood 1200-1500 and 1800-2100, while the restaurant upstairs opens at 1800 for oysters, lobster and meat dishes. On the other side of the road is *The Towers Seafood Restaurant*, Quay Rd, T26534. Opens only for dinner at 1730. The *Ardmore House Restaurant*, on Ardmore Rd, which meets Quay Rd a little further down, T25994. Opens in the summer months at 1800 for a grand dinner with views of Clew Bay. The *Sheebeen Pub*, also on Quay Rd and past the Ardmore Rd turning, serves a more informal and less expensive lunch or dinner.

Maud Gonne

Maud Gonne was born in Surrey in 1866 into an army family which moved to Ireland the following year. She never went to school, so avoiding its gender indoctrination, and gave up an upper-class life of hunt balls and dinner parties for revolutionary politics. She went to Paris to campaign for Irish nationalism, where she had two children by a lover, returning to Ireland where she married John McBride, a disastrous marriage in view of his alcoholism, but divorced him after the birth of their son.

William Butler Yeats and Gonne formed a deep friendship, but the poet was driven mad with unreciprocated love, though whether they ever had sex (and even then only once) remains uncertain. Some of Yeats' greatest poetry had its inspiration in their relationship, and when he complained she comforted him with the fact that "you are making beautiful poetry out of what you call your unhappiness and you are happy in that." Their friendship haunted Yeats throughout his life, and twenty years after meeting her he could still feel blessed for having known her, even though "While up from my heart's root/So great a sweetness flows/I shake from head to foot."

Pubs & music

The town's most famous pub is *Matt Molloy's* in Bridge St, owned by the eponymous musician from the Chieftains who hails from Westport. It is also one of the most frequented, however, and finding the elbow space to lift a pint can be difficult. Across the road, *Moran's* has a small grocery store at the front and a tiny bar to the rear, and is patronized by locals seeking to escape the better known pubs. At the Octagon, *M.J. Hoban* is a popular bar with regular musical entertainment, and the bars out along Quay St have live music, especially at weekends. Other pubs that have been recommended include *P McCarthy's* on Quay St and *Tommie Nolan's* on Mill St.

Festivals

The *Westport Arts Festival*, T25078, takes place at the end of **Aug** and there is usually a caravan in Shop St with programmes and ticket sales. An *International Sea Angling Festival*, T27297, takes to the water in the third week of **Jun**.

Shopping

Along Quay St near the harbour, once dilapidated warehouses have been restored to house shops. The *Waterfront Gallery* offers the usual ceramics, glass and jewellery, and *Westport Crystal Glass*, a short way before the Asgard restaurant, has a range of stemware and gifts. *Carraig Donn*, Bridge St, opposite *Matt Molloy's* pub, has wide range of crafts and their own knitwear.

Sport

Horse-riding *Carrowholly Stables*, T27057. Guided scenic and coastal treks.

Tour operators

Adventure Centre, T64806. Covers canoeing, windsurfing, sailing, rock climbing, abseiling and hill walking. *Coagh Patrick Walking Tours*, T26090, www.walkingguideireland.com Handles some day trips as well as longer treks with accommodation and transport arranged. *Geotreks*, T/F28702, geotracks@anu.ie www.anu.ie/geotreks/ Conducts tours into gold-panning areas of south Mayo. *Gerry Greensmyth*, T26090. Offers guided walking tours, including Croagh Patrick. *Island Otterwatch*, T41048. Walking trips to spot otters.

Transport

Air Knock International Airport T094-67222, www.knockinternationalairport.ie Has connections with **Dublin** on *Aer Arann*, **London Stanstead** with *Ryanair*, and **Manchester** with *British Airways*. In the summer there are chartered flights from **Germany** with *Lufthansa*, from **Zurich** with *Crossair* and from **Amsterdam** with *Transavia*. **Bicycles** Bike hire from *Breheny's*, Castlebar St, T25020. *Sean Sammon*, James St, T25471. **Bus** *Bus Éireann* buses depart from the Octagon. Scheduled daily services run to **Achill**,

County Mayo

👉 The Pagan Way

The aninual Reek Sunday, the last Sunday in July, sees more than 30,000 devout Catholics setting off to climb Croagh Patrick, many of them unaware they are following in the footsteps of pagan pilgrims. As far back as 3000BCE, people climbed to the summit to mark Lughnasa (the festival of Lug, a god whose name occurs throughout the Celtic world), a pagan celebration of autumn; St Patrick's association with the mountain probably reflects his victory over paganism. The night before they ascend Croagh Patrick, the most devout of modern pilgrims begin their journey by walking 22 miles (35 km) from Ballintubber Abbey along an ancient pilgrim trail, then they attend one of the 15 masses celebrated on the mountain's summit from 0800. Archaeological research shows that a massive rampart enclosed the summit long before the foundations of an oratory were laid some time between 430 and 890CE. Glass beads excavated near part of the rampart date to the thrd century BCE.

Ballina, Belfast, Cork, Galway, Limerick and Sligo, and there are 4 buses a day to **Dublin**. *Walsh Coaches*, T35165, run a weekend service to **Galway**. **Car hire** at Knock Airport with *National*, T094-67252. **Taxis** Taxis *Christy Cawley*, T28282; *Conor Dever*, T27220; *Dever*, T27220/087-413722. *Hoban*, T25247/087-423107. *Brenda McGing*, T26319. *Road Runner*, T27050/087-428338. *Valley Cabs*, T26015/ 098-428338. **Train** The train station is on Altamount Rd, T25253, and within walking distance of town.

Directory **Banks** Branches of the main banks may be found in Shop St and on the North Mall. **Communications** Post office: North Mall.

Around Westport

Croagh Patrick
Phone code: 098
Colour map 2, grid B2

The pyramidal Croagh Patrick (2,500 ft/762 m), home to St Patrick in 441CE for a period of 40 days, and the site for his miraculous banishment of snakes (there are no snakes in Ireland), is Ireland's most popular mountain. It is not particularly difficult to climb and there is a well trodden path to the top, but the scree-laden slope that leads to the summit is steep and when there is a wind about some climbers are reduced to crawling up on their hands and knees in order to avoid the risk of a tumble. Forget the tradition of climbing Croagh Patrick in bare feet, use suitable footwear and consider bringing a staff-like stick for the final ascent. Allow two hours to reach the top and one for the descent.

The trail begins at the side of *Campbell*'s pub in Murrisk to the west of Westport on the road to Louisburg. There is a car-park alongside the **National Famine Monument**, a sculptured coffin-ship with skeleton bodies by John Behan, that was unveiled in 1997 on the 150th anniversary of the Famine. It's a 5-minute walk from here to the **Croagh Patrick Information Centre**, Murrisk, T64114, which has a self-service restaurant, gifts and books for sale, as well as raingear and walking sticks and shower facilities for walkers. ■ *Mar 17-Oct, daily, from 1000 to 1600 (1900 in Jul and Aug).*

Louisburg Possibly the most laid-back town in Ireland owes its name to Louisburg in Nova Scotia, Canada, where an uncle of the first Marquess of Sligo was part of a besieging force in 1758. Despite its proximity to Westport, Louisburg is contentedly indifferent to tourism although there is the interesting **Granuaile Visitor Centre**, dedicated to the 'pirate queen' Grace O'Malley. ■ *Church Street*, T66341. €3.20. *Jun-mid-Sep, Mon-Sat, 1000-1800. Coming from Westport, turn right at the main junction in town and the centre is a short way down on the left.*

County Mayo

Granuaile – pirate queen and feminist icon

Grace O'Malley (c.1530-c.1603), 'Granuaile' being a corruption of her Gaelic name Gráinne Ni Mháille, was the daughter of a Connacht chief who achieved fame in her own lifetime as a fiercely independent woman. In 1577 her piratical activities led the Lord Deputy of Ireland to mark her down as "a notorious woman in all the coasts of Ireland". She married twice, first Donal O'Flaherty and then Richard 'Iron Dick' Burke, with whom she had an agreement that either party could dissolve the relationship after one year (which she duly did, see page 456). She maintained

her own maritime power base from Clare Island and cunningly appeased the English without sacrificing her own independence. At one stage she was attacked by the English but never decisively beaten and in 1593 she came to London with other Connacht chiefs to complain about the heavy-handedness of English rule. Insisting upon regal status as an Irish queen, she petitioned Queen Elizabeth (in Latin, as she had little English and Elizabeth no Irish) for her own lands, because under Gaelic law a widow had no right to her husband's property.

There are two local beaches, **Silver Strand** and **Old Head**, which are gloriously sandy, safe for swimming and suitable for surfing. Bicycles may be hired from *Stauntons*, the chemist shop on the corner of the crossroads in the centre of town.

Sleeping Accommodation can be arranged through the Westport tourist office. Possibilities include **B** *Springfield House*, Westport Rd, T66289, and **B** *Whitethorns*, Bunowen Rd, T66062, which is 5 mins from town.

Price codes: see inside front cover

Self-catering houses in the area are available through *Old Head Holiday Villages*, Esplanade Properties, 36 Lower Clanbrassil St, Dublin 8, T01-4731315, F4731321. The *Old Head Forest Caravan & Camping Park*, T66021, opens from 22 May to 13 Sep, and is near the beach to the east of Louisburg.

Eating Home-made food is available at the *River Café* on Bridge St opens from 1000-1700 for well crafted salads, smoked salmon and fresh bread. *Durkan's Weir House and Restaurant*, Chapel St, T66140, serves delicious local seafood and steaks. Lighter meals in the bar are equally appealing.

The best way to travel between Connemara and Mayo is via the Doo Lough valley on the R335 road, because this part of Mayo is stunningly beautiful and rarely explored. The road skirts the shore of Doo Lough itself, which is sandwiched between the Mweelrea Mountains that overlook Killary harbour to the south, and the wild Sheeffry Hills to the east. The effect of light on the landscape – the massive mountain sides and the fast-slowing silvery stream – changes constantly with the elements. The long-distance walk, the **Western Way**, works its way up from Leenane in Galway to the south side of Croagh Patrick before turning east towards Westport.

Doo Lough Valley

Along the R335 by Doo Lough there is a monument by the side of the road to the hundreds of victims who, during the Famine, set out from Louisburg in winter to walk through the valley to their landlord to beg for assistance. It was a wasted journey and on the return leg of the journey some 400 died from hypothermia and lack of food.

A Famine Walk takes place every May, T4785100.

County Mayo

Sleeping and eating The best base for accommodation in the area is at **Killadoon**, a village on the coast with a small beach, about halfway between Louisburg and Killary harbour. The **B** *Killadoon Beach Hotel*, T/F68605, is a modest little hotel with a restaurant.

Clare Island

At the mouth of Clew Bay, Clare Island has a population nowadays of about 150, but in pre-Famine days it was over 1,500. The remains of a 15th-century castle, from where Grace O'Malley set off on her piratical excursions, are close to the harbour and further to the west is a 13th-century Cistercian abbey where legend has it she is buried. On a fine day, a visit to Clare Island is highly recommended because the place is blessed with an absence of heritage centres, there are superb walks to be enjoyed in all directions, bicycles may be hired from the harbour, T26250, and the beach is safe for swimming.

Ins & outs

Getting there Both *Clare Island Ferries*, T26307/28288, and *O'Malleys Ferries*, T25045, run services from Roonagh Quay, 5 miles (8 km) west of Louisburg; €12.70 return. Check their schedule, but the first boat from Roonagh usually departs at 1015 and the last one back from the island is at 1900; bicycles carried for free.

Walking

Mapping and information The highest point, **Mount Knockmore**, is a manageable 1512 ft (461 m), and for a longer day's exploration of the island map No 30 in the *Ordnance Survey* Discovery series would be useful but not essential. The *Bay View* hotel has a simple but useful little walking guide with sketches that outlines 5 walks on the island, lasting from 1 to over 5 hrs.

If you are staying overnight, a whole day's walk could begin by walking from your accommodation to the **lighthouse** at the most northerly point of the island and then setting off across hillocks along the north side en route to **Mount Knockmore**. You will cross several small hills and, although there are high cliffs with sheer drops, by keeping on the safe side of the sheep fencing there is no danger. There is a trigonometry point at the summit and from here it is simply a matter of heading down to the signal tower near the sea at the western end of the island, zig-zagging at times to avoid an inlet. From the tower at the western end a path leads across to the road on the south side of the island, which returns to the harbour. To complete this circuit of Clare Island takes about six hours.

On a day trip, there would be plenty of time for a walk out to the west end of the island by following the road along the southern side of the island from the pier. This road (which you come back along if completing a circuit of the island) passes the abbey where Grace O'Malley is buried, and the O'Malley plaque is clearly visible on the left side after entering the church.

Sleeping & eating

It is best to bring a picnic but food is available at the Bay View Hotel

L *Clare Island Lighthouse*, T/F45120, clareislandlighthouse@eircom.net At the top end of the island, this was originally 2 lighthouses built between 1804 and 1812, which operated until 1965. It has been restored and renovated and offers the unique opportunity of spending a comfortable night or two in one of its 5 rooms. Open all year, transport can be arranged from Westport, and an evening meal is €25.40. **A-C** *Bay View Hotel* T/F26307. The only hotel on the island, a short walk from the pier, and also

Clare Island

operating as a simple hostel with dorm beds . **B** *Sea Breeze*, T26746; F25649. This B&B is only 300 yds from the harbour and is signposted. A double is €51, a single €32 and there is the option of an evening meal. **B** *O'Malley B&B*, T26216. A couple of miles (4 km) from the harbour, rooms with and without their own bathroom facilities and an optional evening meal for €16.50.

Inishturk Island

Between May and Sep, the *Caher Star* ferry, T45541, departs daily from Roonagh at 1100, returning at 1700, €19. On Tue and Thu, there is a mail boat departing from Cleggan at 1100. Bikes, dogs and children under 6 are carried free.

Ins & outs
Colour map 2, grid B2

Inishturk is smaller than Clare Island and lies to the south, 7 miles (11 km) off the coast. It is one of Ireland's least visited destinations, which is a little surprising because it makes a delightful getaway, offering modest accommodation, a pub, restaurant, post office, two sandy beaches, and undemanding walks with terrific seascapes. To the east of Inishturk the tiny **Caher Island** has some strange pre-Christian stones and while there is no scheduled boat service, it is easy to arrange a boat trip from Inishturk, just ask around the harbour.

B *The Harbour House*, T45610, is right by the harbour and is the most convenient place to stay on a quick visit. There is also a restaurant here. **B** *Ocean View House*, T45520, F45655. Has rooms with bathrooms and an evening meal can be arranged. **B** *Teach Abhainn*, T45510, has a lovely quiet location, less than 2 miles from the main harbour, with terrific views and an evening meal can be arranged. The accordion-playing owner has been known to enliven an evening with live music. *The Community Club* functions as the village pub and also does light food like sandwiches.

Sleeping & eating

Newport and around

Near the northeast corner of Clew Bay, and 8 miles (12 km) north of Westport, the small town of Newport is often just hurried through on the way to Achill Island. There is a **tourist information office** at the western end of Main Street, and they sell inexpensive sheets detailing walks around **Rockfleet Castle** and **Lough Furnace**, which are useful if used with the OS Discovery Series map. ■ *Main St, T41895. Open May-Aug.*

Colour map 2, grid B2

This walk begins by turning left after leaving the tourist office and heading up to the corner to view the colourful **mural** depicting the trial and public execution of a rebel priest, Father Manus Sweeney, for his part in the 1798 rebellion. Facing the mural, turn left and walk up the hill to **St Patrick's church** where the stained glass east window of the Last Judgement was designed by Harry Clarke and painted under his supervision in 1900, the year he died. From the church, go down the steps and turn right for access to the **Old Viaduct**. Walk across the red sandstone viaduct, built as a railway bridge in 1892 and functioning up until 1937, and down the embankment on the other side. Cross back over the River Black Oak by the road bridge and up Main Street to the tourist office.

Town walk

County Mayo

The ruins of this late 15th-century Dominican abbey include the central tower, the vault supported by Romanesque arches and some of the windows. It is hardly worth a special trip, but if travelling on the N59 Newport to Achill road it is signposted on the left less than 2 miles (1.5 km) outside Newport.

Burrishoole Abbey

The Western Way The Western Way long-distance walk starts in County Galway and crosses into Mayo just north of Leenane. Skirting the shoulder of Croagh Patrick, it continues north through Westport and Newport and up to the north coast before swinging eastwards to reach Ballina via Ballycastle and Killala. The ideal way to experience North Mayo would be to take four days and walk the Western Way from Newport to Ballina. A problem with the first day's 21-mile (33-km) walk, from Newport to Bellacorick, is a lack of accommodation in the village of Bellacorick. Unless a pick-up could be arranged there, the only alternatives are either an extra 5-mile (8-km) walk to Bangor, or to catch the *Bus Éireann* 446 service from Ballina to Bangor that passes through Bellacorick at 1855. The day's journey could be reduced by starting from the *An Óige* hostel (see below) which is 5 miles (8 km) north of Newport. The second day's walk, from Bellacorick to Ballycastle, is another 21 miles (33 km) but the next day's journey, from Ballycastle to Killala, is a more manageable 14 miles (23 km). The last day's walk is a mere 9 miles (15 km) to Ballina, and while it is interesting, the surface is tarmac nearly all the way.

Rockfleet Castle Also known as Carrigahowley Castle, Rockfleet has an undisputed association with Grace O'Malley because it was a Burke stronghold before her second marriage to Richard Burke. The story goes that she dissolved this marriage (see box on page 453) by having the castle gates shut in his face and in 1553, after he died, this became her main residence. In a sheltered inlet of Clew Bay that gave safe anchorage to ships, the castle was an ideal base for a sea-faring character such as O'Malley, and she beat off an English attack here in 1574. ■ *The castle is signposted on the N59, after passing the turn-off for Burrishoole Abbey. The Newport tourist office has a sheet describing a 2-hr walk of 31 miles (6 km).*

Sleeping & eating
Price codes:
see inside front cover

LL *Newport House*, T41222, F41613. Well heeled anglers enjoy the period feel of this country house and the fine food that graces the dining table. **B** *Black Oak Inn*, T41249, F41984. On the Westport side of the river. **B** *Debille House*, in the centre of Main St, T41145, F41777. This Georgian building does B&B during the summer, €50 for a double, sharing bathroom facilities. *Traenlaur Lodge*, Lough Feeagh, T41358. This *An Óige* hostel is a few miles north of Newport and taxi transport, T087-2202123, costs €5.

Meals are available at both the **Black Oak Inn** and **The Village Bakery**, which is below Debille House, while dinner at **Newport House** is a cool €45. *Kelly's Kitchen*, Main St, opens daily between 1000 and 2100 for home-cooked food.

Mullaranny and the Curraun Peninsula

Colour map 2, grid B2

This village is on the N59 road west of Newport, where the R319 heads west to Achill and the main road continues north to Bangor. There is a garage, and a good-sized supermarket if stocking up on provisions for Achill. *Cowley's Restaurant*, T36287, a thatched cottage next to the supermarket, serves very reasonably priced lobster and other seafood meals.

From Mullaranny the R319 follows the route of a disused railway line to Achill Sound, where a bridge connects the Corraun Peninsula with Achill Island. A more leisurely route, signposted the **Atlantic Drive**, goes around the southern end of the peninsula and on fine days offers tremendous views. Food is available en route at the *George Pub*, where B&B accommodation is also available, T45228.

Achill Island

Ireland's largest island has a population of 1,800 people, and its five Blue Flag beaches give some indication of just how singularly unspoilt it remains. "The naturalist, the antiquary, the artist, the poet, will find much in Achill that harmonizes with their tastes", is as true today as when a visitor made this remark in 1884. When first-time visitors to Achill hit a spell of bad weather they leave wondering what was so special about the place, but when there is blue in the sky and the light weaves its magic on the landscape a stay on Achill is a memorable experience. The German writer, Heinrich Böll (1917-85), certainly found it so while living at Dugort in the 1950s. His house is now used as a retreat for writers, as specified in his will, and his Irish Journal (1957) would make suitable reading while on Achill.

Phone code: 098
Colour map 2,
grid A1, A2 & B2

Ins and outs

Achill is separated from the mainland by a channel of sea, Achill Sound, but the Michael Davitt Bridge spans the water at a narrow point, so there is no need for a ferry service. The nearest large town on the mainland is Westport, and from here and Ballina buses run to the island.

Getting there

A bicycle is the ideal way to get around the island, and if based near Dooagh or Dugort many places can be reached on foot. The main road crosses the island from Achill Sound to Keem Bay. Also starting at Achill Sound a loop road runs south through Dooega, and at Bunacurry a northern loop accesses Dugort and Slievemore and returns to the main road at Keel.

Getting around

Achill Tourism is in Cashel, T47353, open all year around, and in Jul and Aug there is also a *Bord Fáilte* tourist office at Cashel, T45384. Information available on the web at www.achill-island.com

Tourist information

Achill Island

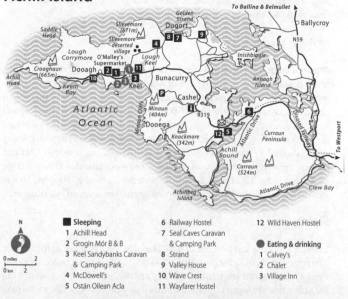

County Mayo

■ Sleeping
1 Achill Head
2 Grogin Mór B & B
3 Keel Sandybanks Caravan & Camping Park
4 McDowell's
5 Ostán Oileán Acla
6 Railway Hostel
7 Seal Caves Caravan & Camping Park
8 Strand
9 Valley House
10 Wave Crest
11 Wayfarer Hostel
12 Wild Haven Hostel

● Eating & drinking
1 Calvey's
2 Chalet
3 Village Inn

0 miles   2
0 km   2

☞ ## The Colony

In 1831 Edward Nangle, a young Church of Ireland minister, came to Achill and established the Achill Mission soon afterwards. Learning and using the Irish language, they leased 130 acres of land and established a school and a church on the southeast slopes of Slievemore. The Colony, as the Achill Mission became known, proved highly successful, and a printing press turned out regular publications, to the chagrin of the local Catholic authorities whose previous indifference to the islanders now proved an embarrassment. In the 1840s the Mission had its own hotel and various enterprises, which were able to survive the years of the Famine. By the 1850s, by which time the Mission owned about two-thirds of the island, the Catholic hierarchy fought back by

strengthening its presence on Achill and taking an interest in the welfare of its parishioners. A National School was established in 1852 and its success saw the eventual closure of the Mission schools. Emigration in the 1880s, combined with financial difficulties for the Mission, saw a gradual decline in its influence, and the Mission was wound up in 1886.

The now-closed Slievemore Hotel, the original Mission Hotel, stands in the middle of the Mission complex of buildings. The Mission church, a stone's throw from the hotel, has a photograph of the remarkable Edward Nangle. He died in 1883 and his recorded last words were, "Achill may well be called the Happy Valley. In spite of all our trials, I know of no place like it."

Geography

At 14 miles (22 km) long and 12 miles (19 km) wide but with an indented coastline of some 80 miles (129 km), Achill is Ireland's largest island. The western side is dominated by Mount Slievemore (2,201 ft/671 m) and Mount Croaghaun (2,182 ft/665 m), and the northwest face of Croaghaun has been eroded to form some of the highest seacliffs anywhere in Europe. Much of the island is heathland and bog, and the scarcity of good farming land goes some way to explaining the poignant history of emigration from Achill. But there is land, and archaeological evidence shows that people have been living here since about 4000BCE.

History

A period in the 19th century when proselytizing Protestants chose Achill for a mission, is a well documented piece of recent history that shares some intriguing similarities with a much more recent controversy. From the mid-1990s onwards coaches were bringing 15,000 pilgrims a year to visit the House of Prayer, a disused convent bought by Christina Gallagher following a vision she had received telling her to open a place of worship surrounded by water. Many people claimed to have experienced or witnessed miracles here, and Christina Gallagher was being invested with too saintly and supernatural an aura to suit the church hierarchy. There are different interpretations as to why it happened but in 1998 the closure of the House of Prayer was tearfully announced by Gallagher.

Sights

Beaches   Even on a fine day it is possible to have one of Achill's beaches all to yourself. The largest, stretching for over 2 miles (4 km) is at **Keel** and it is safe for swimming apart from one stretch, indicated by a notice, where a riptide occurs. On the north side at **Dugort** there are more sandy beaches, with fine views over

Captain Boycott

Charles Cunningham Boycott (1832-97) came to Achill in 1857 after selling his army commission. He became a tenant farmer for a landlord who leased Keel West from the Achill Mission, and lived in Corrymore Lodge, which may still be seen west of Keel. He acquired a reputation for brutality, running down geese on his horse if they strayed on to his roadway. He left after 20 years to become the land agent for Lord Erne's estates in Ballinrobe, County

Mayo and came into conflict with Michael Davitt's Land Leaguers. When Boycott refused to reduce tenants' rents he was ostracized: labourers on the estate refused to work for him; local suppliers refused to sell him food. Orangemen were recruited from Ulster to replace the farmhands but it took 1,000 troops to protect them. The word 'boycott' quickly entered English and other European languages as a synonym for social ostracism.

Blacksod Bay to north Mayo; the beaches are safe but **Golden Strand** has one section marked as dangerous. The most spectacular-looking beach is at **Keem Bay**, when it is first seen from the road above at a height of 600 ft (182 m).

The deserted village of Slievemore consists of about 75 houses, built in the 1820s of unmortared stone and mostly parallel to one another with south-facing gables, east-facing doorways and a window to the northeast. Research suggests that the origins of the village lay in the early medieval period, 500-1200CE. In the 19th century, cattle were tethered to the southern end of the houses and tethering rings can still be seen in the walls. Poor management by the landlords, who later sold their land to the Mission, and the effects of the Famine saw villagers move south to Dooagh. It is possible that the Mission ownership of the land in 1851 accelerated the process of abandonment. Up until the 1940s the houses were used as 'booley' dwellings, summer residences for cattle grazers, but they are now in ruins.

Slievemore Deserted Village

This is one of the most easily managed and enjoyable climbs on the island; it takes about 1 hour to reach the summit from the Deserted Village car-park. Head first for the white stone that is clearly visible on the slope up behind the ruins and from there head for the ridge and along it eastwards to the summit. There are magnificent views of Blacksod Bay and the Mullet. Descend by the same route.

Mount Slievemore

Almost as high as Slievemore but a decidedly more difficult climb and best undertaken with the help of *Ordnance Survey* map No. 30. From Keem Bay take the turning on the main road that heads north to Corrymore Lough and begin the climb from there. Precipitous cliffs drop down to the sea from close to the summit, so only climb when the sky is clear and likely to remain so for the rest of the day. Allow five hours for the return journey.

Mount Croaghaun

Essentials

The main accommodation centres are Keel and Dooagh in the south and Dugort in the north of the island though the new **AL** *Ostan Oilean Acla*, Achill Sound, T45138, www.achillislandhotel.com, is an exception. Situated at the island's gateway, perhaps it is too close to the mainland to provide that island experience.

A *Achill Head*, Keel, T/F43108. Close to the beach, pub food in the bar and sociable evenings. **A** *Gray's Guesthouse*, Dugort, T43244. Preferable in some respects to the island's hotels, especially if you don't want late nights, this is an engagingly cool place that invites relaxation. Child- and pet-friendly, and with a croquet lawn to boot.

Sleeping
■ *on map*
Price codes:
see inside front cover

County Mayo

A *McDowells*, Slievemore Rd, Dugort, T43148, F94801. A pretty, cottage-like exterior to a small 10-room hotel at the foot of Slievemore. **A** *Strand Hotel*, Dugort, T43241. Close to a Blue Flag beach. **B** *Groigin Mor*, Pollagh, Keel, T43385. B&B in a small house, not a bungalow, on the main road between Keel and Dooagh. No evening meals available. **B** *Joyces Maian Villa*, Keel, T43134. B&B overlooking the beach, open Easter-Nov. **B** *Wave Crest*, Dooagh, T43115. Rooms with and without their own bathrooms.

D *Railway Hostel*, Achill Sound, T45187. On the mainland just before the Michael Davitt Bridge and looking rather drab, this is nevertheless a roomy hostel with 2 kitchens, 1 private room, and open all year. **D** *Valley House Hostel*, The Valley, Dugort, T47334, www.valleyhouse.com A fine, spacious old residence converted into a hostel and with its own bar; camping space available and meters on the showers for everyone. **D** *The Wayfarer Hostel*, Keel, T/F43266. Open from early Mar-early Oct, an IHH & IHO hostel with 4 private rooms and over 30 dorm beds. **D** *Wild Haven Hostel*, Achill Sound, T45392. The first hostel on the island itself, just over the bridge. Enhanced by a comfortable old-fashioned living room and a conservatory for meals; also open all year and with private rooms. **D** *Rich View Hostel*, Newtown, Keel, T43462, is a new IHO hostel, open all year with 10 dorm beds and 4 private rooms.

Camping Camping is possible at the *Railway Hostel*, the *Wayfarer Hostel* and the *Valley House Hostel*. The *Seal Caves Caravan Park*, Dugort, T43262, is open from Apr to Sep and accepts tents. The *Keel Sandybanks Caravan & Camping Park*, Keel, T094-32054, F094-32351, is on the beach.

Self-catering *Achill Island Luxury Holiday Homes*, Keel, T43259, F43210, www.failte-reland.com/achillholidayhomes There are various individual houses and cottages for rent: *Minaun Cliff Cottages*, T43341; *Teach Cruachan*, T43301; *The Green*, Keel, T43246; *Riverside Cottage*, at Dooagh, T43181; and *Links Cottages*, also at Keel, T094-58152, F094-58377. Fully serviced mobile homes and 2- and 3-bedroomed cottages can be rented through the company that runs the *Keel Sandybanks Caravan & Camping Park*, Belcarra, Castlebar, Co Mayo, T094-32054, F094-32351.

Eating
● *on map*
Price codes:
see inside front cover

Keel has a few places to eat and one of the easiest to find is *Calvey's*, T43158, next to the police station on the main road by a junction. A lunch menu runs from 1200-1730 with dishes such as salmon and chips for €10, as well as salads and sandwiches. A candlelight dinner features starters such as crab claws or oysters and main dishes such as lamb or baked cod with Pernod. The *Chalet Seafood Restaurant*, T43157, also at Keel, opens from Apr-Oct, and has an attached gift shop selling knitwear and pottery. At Keel, the *Village Inn* does bar food, and the *Beehive*, T43134, is a pleasing restaurant and craft shop, using local produce to serve up quality home-made soups, chowder, breads and cakes. On a fine day, the food can be enjoyed from outdoor tables overlooking the beach. *Gray's Guest House*, Dugort, is always worth dropping into for coffee

Pubs & music Hotels are always a good bet on Achill for late-night drinking. At Golden Strand, *Mastersons* pub is worth checking out for live music. At Keel the *Achill Head* hotel has live entertainment and nearly all the pubs in the vicinity will have some form of musical entertainment. The bar at the *Valley House* hostel is a good place to meet fellow hostellers. At Achill Sound, *Patten's Lounge Bar* has music during the holiday season.

Sport **Diving** *Achill Island Scuba Dive Centre*, T087-2349884. Based at Purteen Harbour at Keel. *Dol-Fin Divers*, Achill Sound, T45473. Supplies gear and runs PADI courses. **Outdoor activities** *Achill Outdoor Education Centre*, T47253; *McDowell's Hotel*, T43148. Adventure and leisure centres, which offer activities, canoeing, coastal walks, sailing, surfing and windsurfing. **Sea angling** *John Johnston*, Dooega East, T45743. Conducts fishing trips to Clare Island from Kildavnait Pier, Cloughmore. *Tony Burke*, Cashel, T47257, departs daily from Purten Harbour at Keel.

County Mayo

The *Achill Archaeological Field School* takes places between **late Jun and late-Aug** at   **Festivals**
the Folklife Centre, Dooagh. Details available from T. McDonald, T43564. The cultural
programme of *Scoil Acla* (Summer/Winter School), in early Aug, is available from J.
McHugh, T47306. The summer school, which claims to be the oldest in the EU, takes
place in the first half of Aug. There is also an *Irish Dancing Festival* in **mid-Aug**, details
from D. Cafferkey, T45073.

At Keel, the *Beehive Craft & Coffee Shop* has pottery, knitwear, jewellery and the like   **Shopping**
and the *Shell Craft Shop* has a selection of semi-precious stones such as amethyst,
agate and onyx, as well as shell jewellery and other shell crafts. *Achill Island Pottery*
shop is also at Keel, as is the *Western Light Art Gallery*, T43325, and the *Chalet Craft
Shop*. At Dooega there is the *Yawl Art Gallery & Painting School*, T36137.

Bicycles Bicycles can be hired from some of the hostels and hotels and from *O'Mal-*   **Transport**
ley's Supermarket, T43125, at Keel. **Bus** A *Bus Éireann* service runs daily between
Dooagh and **Westport**, via **Keel**, **Dugort** and **Cashel** on the island and **Newport** on
the mainland, taking 2 hrs. The first bus departs Westport at 1500 (2205 on Sun), earliest departure from Dooagh is at 0825 (1600 on Sun). **Taxis** *M.T. Taxi*, T45491.

Banks No bank on the island; travelling banks visit. *Bank of Ireland*, T087-2375138.   **Directory**
Visits on Mon, Tue and Thu. *AIB Bank*, T098-25466, visits on Mon and Wed. **Communi-
cations Post office**: The main post office is in Keel at *O'Malley's Supermarket*,
T43125, and money can also be changed here. There is also a post office at Dooagh,
T43107. **Bureaux de change**: Beehive Craft & Coffee Shop at Keel. **Hospitals and
medical services Doctors**: Dr King, Achill Sound, T43105. Dr Lineen, Achill Sound,
T45284. Dr O'Leary, Pollagh, T43476. **Pharmacies**: *Achill Pharmacy*, Achill Sound,
T45248. **Useful addresses** Car repairs at *Sweeny's Garage*, T45243/45102.

Northwest Mayo

*The desolate northwest of Mayo is as far off the tourist trail as one can get in Ire-
land. There are only two towns of any size – Bangor Erris (usually just called Bangor) and Belmullet – and everything in between is bogland, heather, bare hills
and the occasional farmhouse or weather-beaten bungalow. Travel here for wildlife, walking, fishing, angling – you won't feel crowded whatever you do.*

Belmullet and the Mullet Peninsula

One of the least populated corners of Europe, the Mullet peninsula has its own   *Phone code: 097*
charms, although you won't be thinking this if you arrive on a wet day. At its   *Colour map 2,*
best it offers splendid wild beauty of an unconventional kind, and in mythology   *grid A2*
it was the final resting place of the four Children of Lir. Under a spell, they spent
their last 300 years here as swans until they heard the bell of a monk, a disciple of
St Patrick, who was searching for them. The monk cared for them but when a
local chief wanted the swans as a present for his wife they were turned back into
humans. But Irish mythology has a hard edge, for when the swans returned to
human form they were 900 years old and quickly withered away and died.

Belmullet was founded in the early 19th century by an English landlord, and
little has happened since to change the basic layout of the place. There is precious little to see, but travellers pass through on their way south to the Mullet
peninsula on the R313. The road goes to **Blacksod Point** at the southern tip of
the peninsula and passes two good beaches at **Elly Bay** and then **Mullaghroe**.

County Mayo

Blacksod Point looks out to where, in 1588, the *La Rata Santa Maria Encoronada*, the flagship of the Spanish Armada, was stranded. The Spanish commander, Don Alfonso de Leyva, was rescued but later lost his life off County Antrim.

There are a number of promontory forts in the area and the one worth seeing is at **Doonamo**, reached by taking a road northwest from Belmullet. Dating back to the Iron Age, it is strategically positioned for defensive purposes and inside it stands a ring fort. Off the west coast of the peninsula lie the islands of **Inishglora**, **Inishkea North** and **Inishkea South**. The Inishkea islands, where inscribed pillar-stones of uncertain provenance stand, can be visited by boat (see 'Directory' below).

Iorras Domhnann Rural Tourism Co-operative, have a seasonal **tourist office** on the left side of the R313 as one enters Belmullet, T81500.

Portacloy & Benwee Head
Colour map 2, grid A2

If you like the beach all to yourself then take the turning for Portacloy off the R314 road between Belmullet and Ballycastle. After a journey of 8 miles (13 km) across an incredibly flat landscape populated mostly by sheep, you reach a delightful beach, hemmed in by cliffs, at the northwest extremity of Ireland. There are no shops or pubs so bring everything you need. To the west of Portacloy, at Benwee Head, towering cliffs look out to a group of rock-stacks standing some 100 yds (90 m) high. From the quayside at the west end of the beach, you can head off up the hills and walk towards Benwee Head; stay clear of the cliff edges at all times as Benwee Head has cliffs of metamorphic schist that drop a sheer 800 ft into the sea.

Bangor Erris & the Bangor Trail

The Bangor Trail is a long-distance walk between Newport and Bangor, but for the first few miles north of Newport it shares a route with the Western Way. A short way beyond the *An Óige* Traenlaur Lodge hostel, T098-41358, which is 5 miles (8 km) north of Newport, it turns northwestwards towards Bangor and leaves the Western Way behind. Maps (€6.60) and a guidebook, *County Mayo: The Bangor Trail* by McDermott and Chapman (€7.60), are available in Westport or Ballina.

Mullet Peninsula

B *Drom Caoin*, Belmullet, T81195. B&B within walking distance of town, views of the sea, choice of breakfast, rooms en suite, includes a couple of self-catering apartments that can be rented for any number of nights. **B** *Coe na Mara*, Clogher, Blacksod, T/F85685. On the Belmullet peninsula and the proprietor is happy to cook what you bring her from the natural mussel beds in nearby Cartron Bay. **B** *Western Strands*, Main St, Belmullet, T/F81096. The only hotel in Belmullet. 10 rooms. **C** *Barnagh House*, Barnagh, Clogher, Belmullet, T81187. Open from Apr-Oct, a modern house with 2 doubles and one family room.

Self-catering possibilities include *The Old School House*, Bangor, T83583, and cottage apartments at Barnagh, Clogher, on the Belmullet peninsula, which can be booked through Mary Edwards, T81187.

Sleeping
Price codes:
see inside front cover

In Belmullet, the restaurant in the *Western Strands* hotel does an evening meal for €19. There is also *Paddy's Family Fare Restaurant* at the top of Main St, serving fairly predictable meals, and pub grub at the *Anchor Bar*. On Main St, *Lavelles Bar* has a coffee shop and serves seafood, plus a large-screen TV and a pool table for those inevitable wet days. In Bangor the food scene is even more dismal but there is a pub next to the *Hillcrest House* B&B on Main St that serves pub food throughout the day. There is also *Sizzlers* coffee shop and a supermarket.

Eating

Fishing Possible on Cross Lake, stocked by the fishery board and suitable for boat and shore angling. Boat hire and permits available from George Geraghty in Belmullet, T81492. In Bangor, day permits for local fishing are available in the *West End Bar*. **Boat hire** for angling is available through Vincent Sweeney, T85774.

Sport

Bus A daily bus service, Mon-Sat, departs from **Ballina**, T71800, for **Belmullet**, via **Bangor**, and continuing south to **Blacksod Point**, at 1810, and 2145 on a Fri; A daily 1300 departure from Ballina terminates at Belmullet. *McNulty Coaches*, Chapel St, Belmullet, T81086, run a daily service to **Castlebar**, 2 buses on Fri and 1 on Sun to **Limerick** via **Westport**, **Galway** and **Ennis**.

Transport

Banks The *Bank of Ireland* and the *Ulster Bank* have branches in Belmullet. **Communications** Post Office: at the western end of Main St in Belmullet. **Tour companies** Boat trips to the small island of Inishkea North through Josephine Geraghty, T85741.

Directory

Ballina and around

For many visitors the major attractions in Ballina is the **River Moy** itself, rich in salmon and trout, which passes through the town, and the river's bridges are regularly used by anglers for their sport. The town originally developed on the east side of the river, close to where the Victorian cathedral of St Muredach now stands, but from the 18th century onwards it was the west side that developed into the modest commercial centre one sees today. The **tourist office** on Cathedral Rd, on the east side of the river, T70848, has a good range of information, including free maps of local walks and full details of where to fish and obtain permits. Open Mon-Sat 1000-1300, 1400-1745; longer hrs in Jul and Aug. **Belleek Forest**, just over a mile (2 km) from the town centre, and about a mile (1.6 km) southwest of town, past the railway station, is a popular place for walks. There is the neolithic Dolmen of the Four Maols, associated with a legend of four foster-brothers of the early Christian era who murdered their master and were buried here after being executed.

There are two abbeys in the vicinity of Ballina, both reached by taking the R314 north to Killala, and while not especially spectacular they are worth a visit if travelling in that direction.

*Phone code 09:
Colour map 2,
grid A3*

County Mayo

Rosserk Abbey The 15th century was a good time for ecclesiastical architecture, not least because of the Franciscans who proceeded to build some of their finest monasteries around Ireland: Rosserk Abbey is a particularly good example of what they achieved. Highlights include a double piscina, which is rare due to the inscribed relief of a round tower, and very well preserved windows and substantial remains of the domestic wing. ■ *24 hrs. Free. After 4 miles (6 km) on the R314 north of Ballina take the signposted road to the right, left at the next junction and then a right at the next signpost.*

Moyne Abbey This is also a Franciscan abbey, contemporary with Rosserk, though apart from the cloisters it is not as well preserved. An adjoining tower with stairs still stands; however, it is none too easy for the untrained eye to make out the various domestic buildings that surround the church. The English governor of Connaught burned the abbey down in 1590 but the friars remained living there until the end of the 18th century. ■ *Open 24 hrs. Free Admission. Continue for over a mile (3 km) on the R314 after the turn-off for Rosserk until the abbey comes into view on the right near a farm.*

Enniscoe Gardens The original garden of Enniscoe House, an 18th-century country house, is gone but it has been sensitively restored and there is an adjoining little heritage centre housing domestic artefacts. Also home to the Mayo North Family Heritage Centre, www.mayo.irish-roots.net/ ■ *Castlehill, 4 km from Crosssmolina on the R315. Mid-Apr-mid-Sep, Tue-Sun, 1400-1800. €5 garden, €3.81 heritage centre, €7.62 for both.*

Sleeping
Price codes: see inside front cover

L *Enniscoe House*, Castlehill, near Crossmolina, Balina, T31112, mail@enniscoe.com Handsome Georgian house on the shore of Lough Conn, in the same family since the 1660s, with good food, great atmosphere and reasonable rates. L *Downhill Hotel*, Sligo Rd, T21033, www.downhillhotel.ie Its leisure centre, with pool, saunas, squash court, gym, all-weather tennis courts, and snooker table, is an inducement to stay here. A short way outside of town on the N59. A *Deanwood Hotel*, Bury St, T21655, F21028, deanhotel@tinet.ie, http://web.idirect.com/~amazing/deanwood.htm A small but pleasant establishment in the centre of town with 12 rooms and a Chinese restaurant in the hotel grounds. A *Downhill Inn*, Sligo Rd, T73444, www.downhillinn.com Sister-hotel to the *Downhill Hotel*, with 2- and 3-night deals. B *Errigal*, Killala Rd, T22563, F70968. This B&B is handy if heading north on the R314. B *Green Hill*, Cathedral Close, T22767. B&B in a quiet location near the cathedral.

Camping *Belleek Caravan & Camping Park*, north of town off the R314 road to Killala, T71533, lenahan@indigo.ie Nearly 60 pitches of which 20 are for tents. Open from mid-Mar to mid-Oct.

Eating *The Broken Jug*, in O'Rahilly St next to the post office, T72379, does pub food nightly until 2100, plus an affordable carvery lunch, and evening meals in its *Gallery* restaurant. You will find more pubs serving meals along Pearse St and in O'Rahilly St, the continuation of this street; *Gaughan's* serves its crab salads and home cooked ham salads in a laid-back, homely pub atmosphere. *Cafolla's Restaurant*, Tolan St, is a straightforward café serving quick and inexpensive meals. For a special night out make a reservation at *Enniscoe House* for the €42 dinner and the hint of a Sommerville & Ross setting thrown in.

Pubs & music There is the usual plethora of pubs in Ballina, and during the summer months many of them are alive with the sound of traditional Irish music. *Murphy Brothers* on Clare St and *Brogan's* on Green St have both been recommended, and *The Broken Jug* has its own nightclub, which attracts a fairly young crowd.

The *Ballina Street Festival* takes place before **mid-Jul** and lasts for a week. The highlight **Festivals** of the festival is National Heritage Day when shop fronts take on a Victorian character, proprietors dress accordingly, and music and theatre enliven the atmosphere. T70905.

Bookshop *Keohane's* bookshop in Tone St complements the tourist office in its stock **Shopping** of maps and local guides.

Bus Bus station on Kevin Barry St in the southwest of town, T71800, close to the train sta- **Transport** tion. Daily buses to **Achill**, **Athlone**, **Ballycastle** (not on Sun), **Belmullet**, **Castlebar**, **Cork**, **Crossmolina**, **Derry**, **Donegal**, **Dublin**, **Enniskillen**, **Foxford**, **Galway**, **Killala** (not on Sun), **Letterkenny**, **Limerick**, **Louisberg** (not on Sun), **Pontoon**, **Sligo** and **Westport**. There are 2 private companies: *Barton Transport*, T01-6286026. Runs a daily service between Dublin and Ballina; *Treacy's*, T70968. Runs to Sligo. **Trains** Train station: on Kevin Barry St, near to the bus station. The **Dublin** to **Westport** train service stops at Ballina 2 to 3 times a day, and connections to most other parts of the rail network are made at **Athlone**.

Banks The banks are located along Pearse St. **Communications** Post Office: at the **Directory** top of O'Rahilly St.

Killala and the north coast

On 22nd August 1798, three French frigates dropped anchor at Kilcummin *Phone code: 096* Strand in Killala Bay and put this quiet corner of North Mayo on the map. Gen- *Colour map 2, grid A3* eral Humbert had over 1,000 men and when they charged the 80 yeomanry outside of Killala with fixed bayonets the English forces quickly surrendered. Killala became the first place in Ireland to be occupied by French revolutionary soldiers, and peasants armed with pikes soon joined them.

Although Killala also boasts a Church of Ireland cathedral with a fine steeple, and a wonky round tower, it is the merging of the insurrectionary United Irishmen movement with Napoleon's revolutionary army that gives this area its powerful sense of history. To reach the beach at Kilcummin, 4 miles (6 km) west of town, take the R314 road north and take the signposted turning right. Along the road there is a stirring monument depicting a French soldier in solidarity with an Irish peasant. The **tourist office** (on Ballina Rd just before entering town, T32166) sells a short *Historical Guide to Killala and District*, €2, that covers the rich history of the area: "a miniature of the history of our land" indeed.

Accommodation is limited to B&Bs. **B** *Beach View House*, T32023, and **B** *Chez Nous*, **Sleeping** T32056. Both at Ross, which is reached by taking the road out to Ballycastle and turning *Price codes:* right at the sign pointing to Ross Strand. **B** *Rathoma House*, Rathoma, T32035. A couple *see inside* of miles outside of town. **B** *Avondale House*, Pier Rd, Killala, T32229. Has 4 rooms with *front cover* shared facilities. *The Old Deanery*, T32221, offers smart self-catering cottages at €155 for 3 nights in high season, or €500 a week.

B&Bs tend to do an evening meal for around €16. The *Golden Acres* pub, Market St, **Eating** serves home-cooked food at the bar and the food at the unprepossessing-looking *Anchor Bar* includes tasty open sandwiches of crab and scampi. The *Golden Acres* is also a good bet for live music between Wed and Sun nights. Other pubs doing food are *The Village Inn* in Church St, *Tower Bar* in Market St and the *Spinning Wheel* in George St.

Bus *Bus Éireann* service 445 runs Mon-Sat between **Ballina** and **Ballycastle** via Killala. **Transport** The first bus leaves Ballina at 0725 (0905 on Sat), then 1000 on a Fri, 1615 Mon-Fri and an 1800 bus on Sat only.

County Mayo

Ballycastle and Céide Fields

Phone code: 096
Colour map 1, grid A5

On a fine day, if coming from Killala, take the R314 to Ballycastle but after a short while take the signposted turning to the right for Kilcummin and Lackan Bay. The beach at Lackan is sandy and safe, and further along the coastal road there are superb views at Downpatrick Head.

Céide Fields

The small town of Ballycastle on the north coast would be a fairly forgettable place on the road between Killala and Belmullet were it not for the nearby phenomenon of Céide (pronounced 'cage-a') Fields, the largest known neolithic farm settlement in the world. A schoolteacher in the area had long suspected there was something worth exploring under the blanket bog but it was not until his son became an archaeologist that a proper examination became possible. The result was astonishing, for sealed under the layers of bog was a sophisticated 5,000-year old network of stone-walled fields. Picks and shovels and resinous pine chips have been found, suggesting the existence of early copper mining, but no signs of defensive walls: the pioneering farmers who worked these fields had little to fear from their neighbours because they didn't have any.

The story of Céide Fields is told at the Visitor Centre by way of a 20-minute audio-visual show, one of the best to be seen anywhere in Ireland, that sets the geological and historical context. Guided tours take visitors around the site and, because the place is not immediately dramatic, a lot depends on getting a knowledgeable and helpful guide who can interpret the scene for you. The centre has a restaurant, or a picnic can be enjoyed outside overlooking a spectacular vista of sea and land. ■ *T43325. Mid-Mar-May, daily, 1000-1700; Jun-Sep, daily, 1000-1800; Oct-Nov, daily, 1000-1700. €3.10. 5 miles (8 km) west of Ballycastle on the R314. Look for a pyramidal roof innocuously situated on the bare bog. Tearooms.*

Sleeping
Price codes:
see inside front cover
L *Stella Maris Hotel*, Ballycastle, T43322, www.stellamaris.com Overlooking Bunatrahir Bay and Downpatrick Head, a former coast guard station has been converted into a boutique hotel. Great sea views, and a restaurant. B *Céide House*, Main St, Ballycastle, T43105. This pub does B&B but it might not be the quietest place to stay. B *The Hawthorns*, Belderrig, T43148. This B&B in Belderrig, a village on the road west of Ceide Fields, is open all year and an evening meal is €17. B *Suantrai*, T43040. Outside of Ballycastle, on the road to Downpatrick Head, Mr & Mrs Chambers do B&B here from mid-Jun to mid-Aug, but no meals are available. A double room, en suite, is €48, a single is €32, and there is 1 family room. C *The Yellow Rose*, Belderrig, T43125. Some 4 miles (6 km) west of Céide Fields and is open all year. The house overlooks the sea, serves an evening meal and the excavated remains of a smaller Stone Age farm site are nearby.

Eating

In Ballycastle, *Céide House* has a restaurant serving café-style meals from 0900 to 2100. *Mary's Bakery*, a stone-built house at the other end of the street, does scones, salads and soups and more tempting dishes like wild Atlantic salmon with mayonnaise and soda bread. The evening menu always features a vegetarian dish, alongside a fish and meat choice. Meals in a restaurant setting, as well as bar food, is available *Doonferry House*, an odd red-coloured pub outside of town on the road to Céide Fields. The *Céide Fields Visitor Centre* has a decent tearoom serving meals.

Pubs & music

Céide House has sessions of traditional music at weekends and just next door at *Katie Macs* pub there is more of the same. *Polke's* is a traditional grocery and pub combined, a place to sit and while away some time.

Transport

Bus *Bus Éireann's* 445 service runs Mon-Sat between Ballina and Ballycastle.

Castlebar and around

With a population approaching 8,000, Castlebar is a thriving and commercially successfully town, and while there is a distinct lack of charm about the place there are places of interest nearby. Castlebar makes a suitable base for excursions north to Pontoon and Lough Conn, primarily of interest to fishing folk; east to Turlough, Strade and Foxford where there is a round tower, museums and shopping opportunities; or south to Ballintober Abbey, one of the most evocative old churches in Ireland. To the southeast there is also Knock, putative site of visions, apparitions and miracles but also home to an interesting folk museum. There's a **tourist office** on Linehall St in Castlebar, T26727. Open mid-Apr-early Sep, Mon-Sat 0930-1300, 1400-1730.

Phone code: 094
Colour map 2, grid B3

A monastery was founded at Ballintober in 1216, though parts of the church were rebuilt after a fire in the late 13th century. Pilgrims stopped here at a guesthouse on their way to climb Croagh Patrick. Sensitive restoration work has done wonders for the church, which, notwithstanding the aesthetically doubtful Stations of the Cross outside, manages to evoke a sense of ancient spirituality fairly unique for Irish churches. The cold grey limestone interior is startlingly non-Roman Catholic in its lack of adornment. The Early Gothic details in the transepts and nave are interesting and the west door, ascribed by experts to both the 13th and 15th centuries, was removed from the church in the 19th century and only returned in 1964. The nave itself is mostly 19th century. The **Celtic Furow** exhibition traces Celtic festivals. ■ *T30934. Open daily, 0900-2000. Free to enter abbey, €3.80 for the Celtic Furrow. Tours sometimes available from 1000. Take the N84 south from Castlebar: signposted (for Ballintubber) on the left after 8 miles (13 km).*

Ballintober Abbey

Knock's claim to fame goes back to 1879, when two local women claimed to have seen Mary, Joseph and St John appear at the south end of the church, and 13 other people confirmed the apparition. The place quickly became a place of pilgrimage, fuelled by alleged miraculous cures and the blessing of official Church investigations. Thousands turn up every day, and in the summer there is an amazing number of stalls selling religious bric-à-brac. The **Knock Folk Museum** is surprisingly interesting, with graphic details of the apparition (and photographs of the crutches donated by cured pilgrims) and well presented displays on local farming life. ■ *Museum: South of the church in the centre of the village, T88100. Open May-Oct, daily, 1000-1800. €3.81. From Castlebar take the N60 south to Claremorris and turn left on to the N17 for Knock.*

Knock
Colour map 2, grid B4

This is a well preserved round tower, perhaps a little stouter and shorter (70 ft/21 m) than most, built between the 10th and 12th centuries next to a church founded by St Patrick. The ruined church that stands here today is 18th century, though it incorporates a 16th-century mullioned window. ■ *Open 24 hrs. Free. About 4 miles (6 km) northeast of Castlebar on the N5 road to Ballina.*

Turlough round tower

Turlough Park, a few miles east of Castlebar, is home to the National Museum of Ireland's folklife collection. Turlough House, built in 1865, has been restored to grace along with the thousands of artefacts in the collection. The range is enormous, covering fishing, agriculture, clothing, furniture, crafts, transport and leisure. ■ *Open Tue-Sat, 1000-1700; Sun 1400-1700. Free. From Castlebar take the N5 road for Swinford and turn off for Turlough after 3 miles.*

Tulough Park

County Mayo

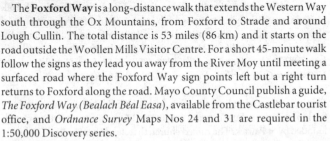

Wanted – dead or alive?

Castlebar is the birthplace of notable characters such as Louis Brennan, inventor of the monorail and the torpedo; Margaret Burke Sheridan, the soprano; and Charles Haughey, the former Taoiseach infamous for his financial shenanigans. But the most notorious individual associated with Castlebar is Richard John Bingham Lucan (1934-?), the alleged murderer of his nanny in London in 1974, and Ireland's best-known absentee landlord. A coroner's jury charged him with the murder, the nanny being apparently mistaken for his estranged wife. Some tenants around Castlebar still pay rents to the Lucan estate, which is now officially in the hands of his son, and around the corner from the tourist office there is a Lucan Street. The town park, known as the Mall, was once the cricket pitch of the Lucan family and it now contains a monument to the 1798 rising. In 1999 Lord Lucan was officially pronounced dead, but a body has never been found.

Michael Davitt Memorial Museum Michael Davitt (1846-1906) was a founding member of the Irish National Land League in 1879 (in Daly's hotel in Castlebar), but his socialist ideas for land reform later brought him into conflict with Parnell. Davitt, himself the son of an evicted tenant farmer from Strade, was jailed for his Fenian activities in the 1870s and his *Leaves from a Prison Diary* (1885) is still worth reading. This small museum in Strade, 10 miles (16 km) northeast of Castlebar, has material relating to his life and times. ■ *Strade, T31022. Daily 1000-1800. Take the N5 road to Dublin and turn left on to the N58 to Strade.*

Foxford If visiting the Michael Davitt Museum in Strade it is only a few miles further along the N58 to Foxford and the **Foxford Woollen Mills Visitor Centre**. The original woollen mill was founded in 1892 by a nun, and today Foxford is a big producer of quality tweed, rugs and blankets. Tours last 35 minutes and as well as the Centre's excellent shop, which sells a wide range of woollen products, there is a jewellery workshop and a woodcraft shop. There is also a self-service restaurant. ■ *Swinford Rd, Foxford, T56756. Open Mon-Sat 1000-1800, Sun 1400-1800. €4.76.*

The **Foxford Way** is a long-distance walk that extends the Western Way south through the Ox Mountains, from Foxford to Strade and around Lough Cullin. The total distance is 53 miles (86 km) and it starts on the road outside the Woollen Mills Visitor Centre. For a short 45-minute walk follow the signs as they lead you away from the River Moy until meeting a surfaced road where the Foxford Way sign points left but a right turn returns to Foxford along the road. Mayo County Council publish a guide, *The Foxford Way (Bealach Béal Easa)*, available from the Castlebar tourist office, and *Ordnance Survey* Maps Nos 24 and 31 are required in the 1:50,000 Discovery series.

Pontoon & Lough Conn
Colour map 2, grid A3 Life in Pontoon, a premier angling centre not only for Mayo but the whole of Ireland, revolves around two hotels on the narrow strip that divides Lough Conn and Lough Cullin. Pontoon's reputation has taken some flack in recent years because of a decline in the quality of the water due to pollution, and the effects this has had on the fish. But Lough Conn stretches for some nine miles (14 km), has an estimated stock of half a million brown trout and also enjoys runs of spring salmon and grilse, so all is not lost. One of the hotels runs a School of Fly Fishing (see 'Sport', next page).

County Mayo

L *Breaffy House*, Breaffy Rd, Castlebar, T22033, www.breaffyhouse.ie An imposing and spacious hotel, recently refurbished and now boasting a leisure centre, 2 miles south of Castlebar on the N60 road to Claremorris. **L-AL** *Pontoon Bridge Hotel*, T56120, www.pontoonbridge.com On the narrow peninsula between Lough Conn and Lough Cullin and geared up for the angler, cooking enthusiast or budding landscape painter (see 'Directory' below). **AL** *Knock House Hotel*, Ballyhaunis Rd, T88088, F88044. Large modern hotel. **AL-A** *Healys*, Pontoon, T56443, www.irelandmayohotel.com Close to the *Pontoon Bridge Hotel* and offering more modest accommodation but an appealing proposition for a couple of days of relaxation. **A** *Daly's Hotel*, The Mall, Castlebar, T21961, F22783. Formerly the *Imperial Hotel*, a Georgian coaching-inn, Daly's has retained the wonderfully old-fashioned dining room where the Anglo-Irish regaled themselves until Michael Davitt hired the place for the founding of the National Land League in 1879. **A** *Kennys Guesthouse*, Lucan St, Castlebar, T23091, kennys@castlebar.ie All rooms have en suite bathroom, a residents' lounge, reasonable room rates. **C-D** *Gannon's*, Providence Rd, Foxford, T56101. Hostel open all year, with a dozen beds and 3 private rooms. **D** *Hughes House Holiday Hostel*, Thomas St, Castlebar, T/F23877. Conveniently located in the centre of town near the tourist office, has 1 private room. Open May-Sep. **D** *Lonely Planet Hostel*, Moneen Roundabout, Castlebar, T21030/24822. Some way outside the town centre but includes 3 private rooms, bike hire and open all year.

Camping *Camp Carrowkeel*, Ballyvary, Castlebar, T31264. Open from Easter to the end of Sep. *Carra Caravan & Camping Park*, Belcarra, Castlebar, T32054, F32351. Open from early Jun-26 Sep. *Knock Caravan & Camping Park*, Claremorris Rd, Knock, T88100, F88295. Open from Mar to the end of Oct. Camping is also possible at the *Lonely Planet* hostel (see above).

Sleeping
Price codes:
see inside front cover

The best places for a meal in the mid-range price bracket are at the *Pontoon Bridge Hotel*, Pontoon, T56688, or *Breaffy House*, Breaffy Rd, Castlebar, T22033. Also in Castlebar, *Daly's Hotel*, The Mall, T21961, has a comfortable Victorian atmosphere and serves brasserie-style food in the restaurant, lunch specials, and a good bar food menu from 1500-2100. *McGoldricks*, Rush St, Castlebar, is near the tourist office and serves bar lunch daily and bar food until 1900. If visiting Foxford or Strade the *Foxford Woollen Mills Visitor Centre* has a pleasant restaurant serving cheap meals until closing time at 1800.

Eating

Johnny McHale's pub, opposite the *Welcome Inn* at the Pontoon end of Castlebar, serves a good pint in a congenial environment. The bar at *Healy's Hotel* in Pontoon is a pleasant place to while away some time and there is a beer garden for those odd days when the sun shines. The *Blues Festival* takes place in Castlebar over the holiday weekend at the beginning of **Jun**, T23111, and most gigs have free admission. Through **Jun** and **Jul**, there are cabaret evenings at Breaffy House outside of Castlebar on Wed.

Pubs, music & Festivals

Angling *Game Angling Ireland West*, Spencer St, Castlebar, T25006, F27279. Dispenses a free brochure on game angling in the west of Ireland as well as stocking all the necessary gear. *Northwestern Regional Fisheries Board*, Ardnaree House, Abbey St, Ballina, T096-22788, F70543, nwrfb@iol.ie General information, guides and maps available. *School of Fly Fishing*, Pontoon Bridge Hotel, T56120, www.pontoonbridge.com Runs 1- and 2-day courses for complete novices or those with some experience. **Horseriding** *Turlough Equitation Centre*, T26646.

Sport

Bus *Bus Éireann*, T096-71800, have an express service between Castlebar and **Dublin** as well as services to **Ballina**, **Cork**, **Derry**, **Shannon** and **Sligo**. There is a bus on Fri to Pontoon that departs at 0900, otherwise it is 1215 and 1630 Mon-Sat, and 1705 on Sun. Buses arrive and depart from *Flannelly's* pub in Market St, Castlebar. **Car hire** *Casey*

Transport

County Mayo

Auto Rental, Castlebar, T21411, F23823. **Train** The **Dublin** to **Westport** train stops at Castlebar, T094-21222; the station is outside of town on the N84 Ballinrobe road.

Directory Banks In the Castlebar on Market St and around. **Communications** Post office: the central post office is at the west end of the main street running through town, in the direction of the N5 road to Westport. **Courses** *Pontoon Bridge Hotel* (see 'Sleeping' above) runs 4-day courses for the *School of Cooking*, and 2- and 4-day non-residential courses between Apr and Oct for the *School of Landscape Painting*.

Cong

Phone code: 092
Colour map 2, grid B3

The Cong phenomenon, a tourist extravaganza that is a bit of an anomaly in Mayo, shares with Knock a doggedly fixed identity, this time in the form of John Wayne, who came here in 1951 to star with Maureen O'Hara in John Ford's *The Quiet Man*. The event has not been forgotten, as visitors quickly realize, and movie fans should buy the excellent *Complete Tour Guide to The Quiet Man Locations* from the tourist office before heading off for the day hunting down all the links to the film that the area still has to offer. My favourite is the sweet shop, used in the film as The Pat Cohan Bar (the one that the horse automatically pulls up outside), owned by a man who was an extra in the movie.

Hollywood apart, Cong would still be worth visiting for Cong Abbey and the archaeological remains in the vicinity, and the **tourist office** (Abbey St, T46542, open May-Sep, daily, 1000-1800) sells a useful archaeological guide. There is a series of nearby caves but more interesting is the **Ballymacgibbon Cairn** at Cross and the nearby stone circles at **Moytura**.

Ashford Castle is a noted nearby Victorian edifice, built for the Guinness family and now such an exclusive hotel that they charge just to enter the grounds between June and September.

Quiet Man Heritage Cottage

An exercise in ironic post-modernism? A replica of a Hollywood set of an Irish cottage interior but located in a real Irish cottage interior, with items such as a replica of Wayne's jacket made by the person who made the original, and an infinite number of video copies of the film for sale; a video about the film is shown upstairs. The blurred line between film and reality is thankfully brought into focus with the cottage's modest exhibition on local archaeology and history. ■ *Circular Rd, Cong, T46089. Open daily 1000-1800. €2.54.*

Cong Abbey

In the ultra-secular grounds of Ashford Castle, this Augustinian abbey was rebuilt in the very early 13th century, though the site has religious associations going back another 500 years and, like the neighbouring island monastery of Inchagoill (see page 424), probably usurped a place of Celtic worship. Not too much of the church itself remains but the

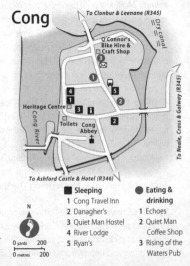

Cong

To Clonbur & Leenane (R345)
Dry canal
O'Connor's Bike Hire & Craft Shop
To Neale, Cross & Galway (R345)
Heritage Centre
Cong River
Toilets
Cong Abbey
To Ashford Castle & Hotel (R346)

N
0 yards 200
0 metres 200

■ **Sleeping**
1 Cong Travel Inn
2 Danagher's
3 Quiet Man Hostel
4 River Lodge
5 Ryan's

● **Eating & drinking**
1 Echoes
2 Quiet Man Coffee Shop
3 Rising of the Waters Pub

County Mayo

The John Wayne Connection

Wayne devotees who flock to Cong will tell you that The Quiet Man *is better than* Gone with the Wind *(true). There is an annual John Wayne lookalike contest and plans are apace to find a Maureen O'Hara double. The irony is that the film was always expected to flop and was only bankrolled on the understanding that the entire cast shot a western afterwards to recoup the anticipated losses. The film now seems to finance half the village and the story goes that the five-star Ashford Castle Hotel had to stop playing the video in the evenings because no one came to dinner until it had finished. Apart from the eponymous hostel and the coffee shop there is the Quiet Man Heritage Cottage and The Quiet Man Festival in June, with a midsummer ball. Dress code for men is cap, breeches and waistcoat and for women it's bonnets and pretty pinafores. T46155.*

most outstanding feature – the Romanesque doorway on the north wall, which was actually inserted later – is notable for its sculptured capitals, which represent the last flowering of Romanesque architecture in Ireland. The adjoining Chapter House also boasts fine examples of windows and decorated stonework. ■ *Open 24 hrs. Free. In the centre of Cong village, opposite the tourist office.*

Sleeping
■ *on map*
Price codes:
see inside front cover

LL *Ashford Castle*, T46003, www.ashford.ie With a rack rate approaching €500 for a double it seems only proportionate charging €5 to enter the grounds. It is about a mile south of the village. **AL** *Ryan's Hotel*, T46243, F466634. In the centre of the village. **A** *Danagher's*, T46028, F46495. A hotel with a *Quiet Man* connection (Maureen O'Hara played the headstrong Mary Kate Danagher in the film) in the centre of Cong. **A** *Dolmen House*, Drumsheel, T/F46466. B&B in a large modern bungalow just north of Cong, with a sauna available. **B** *Inishfree Farmhouse*, Ashford, T46082. B&B. **B** *River Lodge*, T/F46057. Another B&B that is often booked up in summer. **C** *Cong Travel Inn*, Circular Rd, Cong, T/F46310. Next to the heritage cottage and equipped with a self-catering kitchen and a flat rate per person like a hostel, but with no shared rooms. **D** *Cong Hostel*, Lisloughrey, Quay Rd, T46098, www.quietman-cong.com Next to the camping site, off the R346 road to Galway and about a mile (1.6 km) out of Cong. Private rooms and dorm beds in a friendly hostel; bike hire too. **D** *Courtyard Hostel*, Garracloon Lodge, Dowagh Estate, Cross, T/F46203. Out beyond *Cong Hostel* and belongs to an interesting organic farm, which oddly includes its own golf course. Includes a couple of private rooms and bike hire. **D** *Quiet Man Hostel*, Abbey St, Cong, T46089, F46448. In the village itself, has some private rooms.

Camping *Cong Caravan & Camping Park*, Lisloughrey, Quay Rd, Cong, T46089, F46448. Only 40 pitches for tents and caravans. Camping is also possible at the *Courtyard Hostel*, Cross, T/F46203.

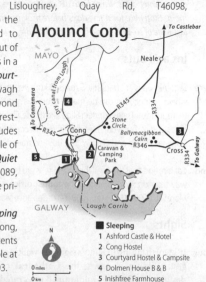

Around Cong

▲ To Castlebar

MAYO

Neale

To Connemara

DIY canal from Lough

R345

R334

R345 Cong

Stone Circle

Ballymacgibbon Cairn

R346

Cross R334

To Galway

Caravan & Camping Park

GALWAY Lough Corrib

N

0 miles 1
0 km 1

■ **Sleeping**
1 Ashford Castle & Hotel
2 Cong Hostel
3 Courtyard Hostel & Campsite
4 Dolmen House B & B
5 Inishfree Farmhouse

County Mayo

Eating
● *on map*
Price codes:
see inside front cover

The hotels offer the most comfortable setting for a leisurely meal, ranging from the decidedly expensive at *Ashford Castle* to under €30 at the other 2 hotels. *Echoes*, Main St, T46059, has a reputation for above-average food, approaching the expensive category. For a more straightforward repast, the *Rising of the Waters* pub, the bars in the village hotels, and the *Quiet Man Coffee Shop* all serve a reasonable range of meals.

Sport
Fishing Contact the *Courtyard Hostel*, T46203, for boat hire. Boat hire also from Gerry Collins, T46089; Frank Costello, T46348 and Marty Holian, T46403.

Tour operators
Lough Corrib Cruises, T46029, run a daily sailing between Ashford Castle and Oughterard with a stop-off and guided tour of the ruins on the island of Inchagoill (see page 424). Apr-Oct, 1000, 1100, 1445 and 1700. Tickets from the tourist office, T46029/46542.

Transport
Bicycle A day's cycling in the Cong area, with the local archaeological guide, is recommended and bikes can be hired from some of the hostels and from *O'Connor's*, Main St, Cong, T46008. **Bus** *Bus Éireann*'s summer-only, daily 420 **Galway** to **Clifden** service stops at Cong in the morning for Galway and in the evening for Clifden.

Directory
Banks No banks in Cong but money can be changed at the hostels or *O'Connors* craft shop on Main St. **Communications** Post office: on Main St.

County Sligo

Sligo

Phone code: 071
Colour map 1, grid B1

A rewarding mixture of Irish boom town and rural market town, Sligo is growing by the minute but still has that laid-back Irish charm that you came here looking for. It's just small enough to make walking to sights and places to eat comfortable, but still has the amenities of the county town – leisure centres, a cinema, loads of good places to eat, internet cafés, three festivals and lots of good lively music and other entertainment. Stop here for a few days before moving on into the north and experience your last taste of so-laid-back-it's-horizontal life.

Ins and outs

Getting there
See 'Transport',
page 472, for
further details

Sligo Airport is at Strandhill, 5 miles (8 km) west of town. It has daily flights to Dublin from where connections can be made to other airports. Car hire is available at the airport, or there are taxis. Trains connect Sligo with Boyle, Carrick-on-Shannon, Dublin and Mullingar 3 times a day, but your best bet is *Bus Éireann*, which connects the town with Derry, Donegal, Dublin and Galway. The bus and train stations are in Lord Edward St.

Getting around
Car hire and taxis are available in town, as are bikes for hire. The easiest and most pleasant way around town is on foot. The **tourist office** is on Temple St, T61201. Open Jul-Aug, Mon-Sat, 0900-2000, Sun, 1000-1400; Sep-Jun, Mon-Fri, 0900-1700.

Sights

Walking tour
It's worth taking in Sligo's sights by walking around the town. Begin at the biggest building in town, the **Cathedral of the Immaculate Conception**, designed by George Goldie and consecrated in 1874. Built to hold the masses,

The Yeats family

Sligo is forever associated with the Yeats family; not only the really famous ones, Jack and William, but also the sisters, Susan and Elizabeth, the father, portrait artist John, and the mother Susan Pollexfen. The connection with Sligo is through the Pollexfen family who owned a small shipping company in the town. John, a trained lawyer turned portrait painter, spent little time in Sligo, but the family lived in a kind of genteel poverty for most of their lives and the children often spent months at a time in Sligo with their

grandparents. Jack grew up to become a writer and painter, and many of his best paintings are based around the life that he knew in Sligo as a child. William wrote a great deal and many of his poems are also about the Sligo of his childhood; he and Jack also spent periods of their adult lives there. The sisters became leading members of the Arts and Crafts movement in Ireland. John ended his years in New York, Jack lived to a ripe old age in Dublin, a successful painter, while William became an occultist and admirer of Fascism.

it can seat 4,000 people, despite its relatively small size. It is built in a Germanic Romanesque style and has huge stained glass windows by the French stained-glass artist Lobin. No sign of the Celtic revival here. From the Cathedral continue along John Street to the other cathedral, St John's, designed in 1730 by Richard Castle, the man who created so much of Georgian Dublin. The cathedal was seriously altered in the early 19th century. The church contains a memorial to Susan Yeats (née Pollixfen) the mother of the famous Yeats', as well as the tomb of Sir Roger Jones (d. 1637), the first governor of Sligo.

Continuing on along John Street, turn right into to Market Street and the High Street, you come to the **Friary**. This is a 1973 building, which partly replaces a Victorian Gothic creation, retaining the apse of the older building. Turn left into Old Market Street and Teeling Street and head towards the river. You pass the beautifully renovated Gormenghast-like **Courthouse**, still in use and basically unaltered inside since it was built in 1878. It is built in sections, the octagonal tower with dormer windows and a chimney stack popping up through it. The entranceway is a great gabled arcade with twin towers at either side. On a working day it is possible to go into the public gallery and view the courtrooms themselves, as well as the top-lit entrance hall.

Opposite the court are solicitors' offices whose windows still bear the name Argue & Phibbs

Past the courthouse, turn right into Abbey Street, where you can view the remains of **Sligo Abbey**, a 13th-century Dominican Friary, established by Maurice Fitzgerald, the Baron of Offaly. In 1416 it was rebuilt after an accidental fire two years earlier. In the 1641 rebellion the whole town came under attack and the Friary was burned again, deliberately this time. The ruins are elegant with an intact 15th-century east window and carvings of various figures in the iconography of Christianity on a tomb of 1506: you can see St Katherine's wheel, St Peter's keys and the shield and sword of St Michael.
■ *Abbey Street, T46406. Open mid-Jun to mid-Sep, daily 0930-1830. €2.*

From the abbey go along Kennedy Parade, named after the President, and cross the river Garavogue at Bridge Street to Stephen Street, where a right turn brings you to the **Model Arts Centre and Niland Gallery**, housed in the 1859 Model School, designed by James Owen for the Board of Works. It was a non-denominational school and was the best chance of an education anyone in Sligo had during the 19th century. It now houses the Niland Arts Collection, put together by Nora Niland a former Sligo county librarian. The collection is a reputable one including works by Evie Hone who was a pioneer of abstract painting in Ireland and who later became famous after she became a

County Sligo

nun for her work in stained glass. Also on permanent display are paintings by Jack Yeats including *The Funeral of Harry Boland*, *The Island Funeral* and *Communicating with Prisoners* and a portrait of Yeats by George Russell. There are also works by Paul Henry, Estella Solomons, Linda Howards and John Yeats. Look out for a pencil drawing by Whistler showing an Irish shop owner serving her customers. The galleries are beautifully lit by low lying windows and have some fascinating temporary exhibitions by local and international artists. ■ *The Mall, T41405. Free. Café.*

Back along Stephen Street towards the river you come to the **County Museum** in an old Congregational Chapel of 1851. The museum has lots of old pictures of Sligo, objects belonging to WB Yeats, including his Nobel medal, and other artefacts discovered in and around the town over the years.

From the museum cross Douglas Hyde Bridge – pausing as you do to reflect on the fact that Jack Yeats once claimed to have learned his craft of

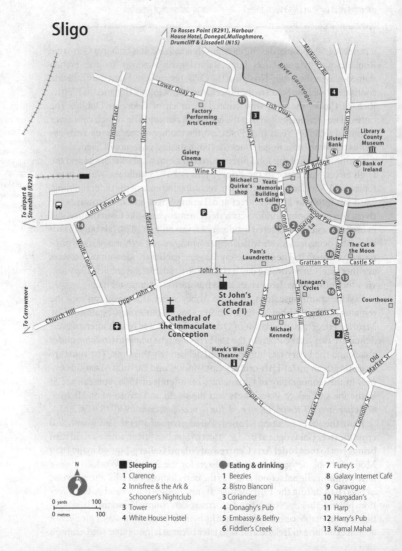

Sligo

To Rosses Point (R291), Harbour House Hotel, Donegal, Mullaghmore, Drumcliff & Lissadell (N15)

River Garavogue

Markievicz Rd

Sleeping
1 Clarence
2 Innisfree & the Ark & Schooner's Nightclub
3 Tower
4 White House Hostel

Eating & drinking
1 Beezies
2 Bistro Bianconi
3 Coriander
4 Donaghy's Pub
5 Embassy & Belfry
6 Fiddler's Creek

7 Furey's
8 Galaxy Internet Café
9 Garavogue
10 Hargadan's
11 Harp
12 Harry's Pub
13 Kamal Mahal

County Sligo

painting by looking over this bridge into the waters of the Garavogue River – to find the **Yeats Memorial Building**. Another version of the story has it that he learned his craft by spitting over the bridge into the Garavogue – doesn't sound quite so arty though. The Yeats Memorial Building has an exhibition relating the lives of all the Yeats' family to Sligo and hosts the annual Yeats Summer School. Its art gallery hosts travelling art exhibitions. It was originally built by the *Belfast Banking Company*, became the *Royal Bank of Ireland* in 1899 and was designed by Vincent Craig, the brother of Lord Craigavon, prime minister of Northern Ireland. The building was donated to the Yeats society in 1973. The exhibition includes photographs of the Le macha, the Irish navy corvette whose first official job was to bring Yeats' body back to Ireland via Galway. The old safe from the bank is still in place and the downstairs exhibit includes a 10-minute video about the Yeats'. ■ *Winter Mon-Fri, 1000-1700, Summer Mon-Sat, 1000-1700. €2.50.*

Essentials

To Lough Gill (R286),
Parkes Castle, Inishfree,
Manorhamilton & Enniskillen (N16)

Connaughton Rd

Model
Arts Centre
& Niland
Gallery

The Mall

Stephen St

Bridge St

Kennedy Parade

Riverside

To Doorly Park &
Lough Gill cruises

Sligo
Abbey

Thomas St

Teeling St

Abbey St

St Annes Terr

Chapel St

Cranmore Rd

Pearse Rd

Chapel Hill

Burton St

To Doorly Park, Lough Gill
cruises & Waterbus

To Sligo Park Hotel, Eden Hill Hostel,
Treetops, St Annes, St Theresa's B&Bs,
Lough Gill, Inishfree, Ballina & Dublin (N4)

14 Loft & MJ Carr's
15 McGarrigle's
16 Montmartre
17 Pepper Alley
18 Shoot the Crows
19 Tea House
20 Winding Stair

There are a number of hotels in town, and most of the B&Bs seem to be strung out along Pearse Rd, easily accessible by car and even walkable.

L *Sligo Park Hotel*, Pearse Rd, T60291, www.leehotels.ie Big, busy hotel, 1 mile (1.6 km) outside town with all the facilities you could want – pool, jacuzzi, fitness centre, nice big restaurant, music, open fires, big sofas, pub food. Rooms are spacious and those on the ground floor open into a little courtyard. Checking-in time is 1500. At the very top end of this price range. **L** *Tower Hotel*, Quay St, T44000, www.towerhotelgroup.ie Built beside the town hall and mirroring it architecturally, this is a small, quiet hotel, with modern, well laid out rooms, and lots of comfort. **AL-L** *Clarence Hotel*, Wine St, T42211, clarencehotel@eircom.net A small hotel in a beautiful old stone building. Music 4 nights a week and busy lunchtime bar trade. **AL** *Innisfree Hotel*, High St, T42014, innisfreehotelsligo @eircom.net Busy small hotel catering to both commercial and tourist trades. Nightclub and music in the bar at weekends. **A** *Treetops*, Cleveragh Rd, off Pearse Rd, 60160, www.sligoband-b.com Close to town, pretty rooms, lovely garden. Lots of tourist advice and an amazing art collection on the walls. **A** *Renate House*, Upper John St, T62014. A little more expensive than the other B&Bs further out of town, but very central. **A** *St Anne's*, Pearse Rd, T43188. This B&B is

Sleeping
■ *on map*
Price codes:
see inside front cover

There are several hostels in town, all of them getting very full at the peak of summer and around the Yeats festival so book in advance

County Sligo

next door to *St Theresa's*, but slightly larger with an outdoor pool. **A** *St Theresa's*, Pearse Rd, T62230. Small B&B with 3 en-suite rooms. **D** *Eden Hill Hostel*, Marymount, Pearse Rd, T/F43204, edenhill@iol.ie About a mile (1.6 km) out of town but well signposted. It is open all year, has family and double rooms and has bikes for hire. **D-C** *Harbour House Hostel*, Finisklin Rd, T71547, harbourhouse@eircom.net Has double rooms and also hires bikes. It's a good walk out of town but very new and well run. **D** *White House Hostel* Markievicz Rd, T45160, dorm beds only, some family rooms in this very basic place.

Eating

on map
Price codes:
see inside front cover

Nouvelle Irish hasn't really found its way to Sligo yet, although fajitas and tacos have arrived, and vol-au-vents and prawn cocktails never left

Expensive The big hotels all have sound restaurants with traditional potato-based evening meals. The poshest place to eat in Sligo is *Montmartre*, Market Yard, T69901 but make a reservation because it's quite small and very popular. Run by French staff and serving unstuffy French dishes it has a spacious, calm feel to it.

Mid-range The restaurant at the *Sligo Park Hotel* is very popular, set in a conservatory area. The set lunch is €16 and there is pub food in the bars. Similarly in the *Tower*, which has a darker atmosphere with lots of deep brown panelled wood. Set dinner is fairly traditional and works out at €25. Some interesting sauces. In town is *The Loft*, in Lord Edward St, T46770. Open 1200-1430 for a carvery lunch, 1800-2300 for dinner. It has an interesting menu, which includes Mexican dishes, a railway theme with seating in compartments, live music most nights and a good atmosphere. Worth making a reservation. Dinner around €20. In O'Connell St is *Bistro Bianconi*, T41744, open 7 days from 1730 till the customers stop, a cheery tiled place with the chefs making the pizzas in the window. Lots of vegetarian options and other Italian dishes. *The Embassy*, Kennedy Parade, T61250, looks like a big old hotel, which is what it used to be, but now it's a restaurant and snooker hall. Traditional potato-orientated food, set lunch €12, dinner around €20. Try the early-bird menu from 1800-1930 for €17. Next door the *Belfry*, its bar serves pub lunches and bar snacks in the evening. In Rockwood Parade, the little pedestrianized alley beside the river, there are a whole range of places. *Pepper Alley*, serves Mexican food till late, closed Mon evenings. At lunchtime it's a sandwich bar. Also along here is another pub, *Fiddler's Creek*, T418666, which serves lunch till 1600 and evening meals till 2200. Its menu is vaguely ethnic with Portuguese, Moroccan and Mexican dishes. Vegetarians will be impressed by the 4 choices. It has live music on special occasions. On the opposite side of the river are several pretty cool places to eat, all with tables outside for summer dining. *Garavogue*, 15-16 Stephen's St, T40100, names after the river is the coolest place in Sligo with clever lighting, raised balconies and a long bar. Downstairs is bar food redolent with grilled parmesan and guacamole and upstairs are more substantial meals in the same vein. It shuts however by 2000 at weekends and earlier during the week. Kid's menu. Close by is *Coriander*, Stephen St, T44134, open 7 days for lunch and dinner till 2200. It serves challenging good quality food in a an atmosphere of white linen and posh table settings, although a little cramped. Early-bird menu till 1930 of 4 courses for €20. Vegetarians will be safe here. No vegetable lasagnes on this menu!

Cheap For lunch there are too many places to choose from. The entire fast-food world is represented around O'Connell St, while a very trendy place to eat is *Beezie's*, T45030, in Tobergal Lane, the alley leading from O'Connell St to Rockwood Parade, which serves pub food. For internet freaks there is the *Galaxy Internet Café*, Riverside, T40441, open 0800-midnight, serving food all day, chiefly filled jacket potatoes, salads, breakfast, all at less than €5. The *Winding Stair*, Hyde Bridge House, T41244, might appeal to all those of us who still get pleasure from handling our printed material. It's a bookshop café, doing coffee, sandwiches and cakes. Its windows are a great place to find notices of upcoming events. For basic potato based meals you might try *The Tea House*, O'Connell St, or the *Roof Top Restaurant*, Wine St Car Park, T44421, which closes at 1800.

Pubs that do reasonable food include the *Ark*, High St; *The Harp Tavern*, Lower Quay St; *McGarrigles*, O'Connell St; *Donaghy's*, Lord Edward St; and *Murray's*, Connolly St.

Places to look out for music in are manifold. *The Ark* bar and, above it, *Schooner's* **Pubs & music**
Nightclub, T42014, at the Innisfree Hotel have karaoke and nightclub music, while the
Embassy *Toffs Nite Club* has disco music most nights of the week. *The Harp*, Quay St has
traditional sessions on Mon and jazz at lunchtime on Sun, while there are traditional sessions at *Foleys*, Castle St, on Sat, *McGarrigles* on Wed and Sun, and *Fureys* which you will
easily spot because of the gigantic and rather tasteless Sheela-na-gig over the door, in
Bridge St on Mon, Tue, Thu and Sun. *MJ Carr's*, downstairs from the Loft, has traditional
sessions on Sat and other forms of live music on Mon. *Shoot the Crows* in Market St is a
very trendy scruffy sort of place with unusual ladies' toilets and music most nights.
Donaghy's has traditional sessions on Sun nights. *Hargadan's* in O'Connell St doesn't
have music, but it's a genuinely traditional Irish pub, still with he groceries on the
shelves from the days when it was a grocer's-cum-bar. Quiet during the day but can
get crowded at weekends. Nice snugs and pub lunches.

Cinema The *Gaiety* cinema complex, Wine St, T74004, has 7 screens. **Theatre** The **Entertainment**
Hawk's Well Theatre, Temple St, T61526, hosts travelling theatre groups as well as
local efforts. *The Factory Theatre*, Lower Quay St, T70431, is home to the Blue Raincoat
Theatre company, who perform there and at the *Hawk's Well*.

The *WB Yeats Summer School* happens in **late Jul to early Aug** and is worth attend- **Festivals**
ing, even if you don't approve of Yeats, for the music and dancing sessions, T42693. At
Ballintogher, 8 miles south of Sligo the annual *Ballintogher Traditional Music Festival*
is held, usually in early **Nov**. There is a feis, concerts, ceili dancing and master classes as
well as lots of spontaneous sessions in the pubs at night.

Sligo has the usual slew of outlets, but there are 3 places worth seeking out. *The Cat &* **Shopping**
the Moon, 4 Castle St, Mon-Sat 0930-1800. Sells exclusive designer jewellery by
Martina Gillan as well as lots of other really great, functional stuff by other Irish designers. *Michael Kennedy Ceramics*, Church St. Sells pottery, and very attractive and useful
it is too. *Michael Quirke's*, Wine St. A butcher-turned-sculptor who carves figures from
pieces of wood that he finds.

Discover Sligo Minibus Tours, 47488, All manner of tours in the area which pick up at **Tours**
the major hotels. They also do a traditional music evening at the *Coleman Heritage Centre* and boat cruises.

Air *Sligo Airport* (68280) is 5 miles (8 km) west of town at **Strandhill**. There are daily **Transport**
flights to **Dublin** with connections to **Europe**. Taxis can be hired at the airport and
there is a car hire service at the terminal, *Avis*, T68396. A bus service connects the airport with Sligo town. **Bus** There are 4 *Bus Eireann* buses a day connecting Sligo with
Derry via **Bundoran**, **Donegal**, **Ballybofey** and **Letterkenny**. Sligo to Dublin buses
leave Sligo 3 times a day calling at **Ballysadare**, **Boyle**, **Carrick-on-Shannon** and
Longford. To **Belfast**, buses leave 3 times a day calling at **Enniskillen**. For **Athlone**
there are 2 buses a day. Five buses a day connect Sligo with **Galway**. To **Rosses Point**
there are 4 buses a day (none on Sun), and for **Strandhill** there are 4 buses a day (none
on Sun). A bus to **Ballina** leaves 5 times a day (once on Sun), connecting from Ballina
with **Castlebar**, **Westport** and **Newport**. The bus station is in Lord Edward St,
T60066. A private bus company, *Feda O'Donnell Coaches*, T075-48114, 091-761656,
runs a twice-daily service between Donegal and Galway calling at Sligo and lots of
smaller towns en route. There are 3 buses on Fri and Sun. At Sligo the bus stops outside *Matt Lyon*'s shop in Stephen St. *Innisfree Coaches*, T68138, another private company does coaches to Dublin. Pick up is at Quay St car park. **Train** There are 4 trains
a day to **Dublin** calling at **Collooney**, **Ballymote**, **Boyle**, **Carrick-on-Shannon**,

County Sligo

Dromod, Longford, Edgeworthstown, Mullingar, Enfield and Maynooth, T69888. **Car hire** Cars can be hired from *Hertz*, T44068 and from *Murrays Europcar*, Sligo Airport, T42091. **Taxi** *Joe's Cabs*, T68900. **Bike** *Flanagan's Cycles*, T44477, Market Yard, Sligo.

Directory **Banks** *Ulster Bank*, Stephen St; *Bank of Ireland*, Stephen St. **Laundrette** *Pam's* Johnstone Court, Mon-Sat 0930-1900. *Wash and Dry*, 4 Connolly St T41777. **Communications** Post office: Wine St.

North County Sligo

Ins & outs **Getting around** Drumcliff, Grange and Cliffony, all the places along the N15, are well served by **buses** since they are on the Sligo to Donegal route, with about 10 buses a day in summer in either direction. A day trip by public transport is feasible, with the last bus back to Sligo passing through Cliffony some time after 1800. **Boat** Inishmurray is accessible by boat from Murraghmore (Rodney Lomax, T66124) or Rosses Point (Tommy McCallion, T42391). There is no landing stage on the island and any poor weather will prevent boats going out.

Rosses Point
Colour map 2, grid A4

Immediately north of Sligo town is Rosses Point, where the north shore of Sligo Bay juts out into the sea. It's a seriously quaint little seaside resort with a long sandy beach. Jack Yeats painted it, his brother wrote about it, and in 1257 Maurice Fitzgerald, the man who gave us Sligo Friary, was cut down here in hand-to-hand battle with Godfrey O'Donnell, the chieftain of another local clan. The reason for the battle no longer matters to the golfers, who now carry irons rather than swords around the ancient battlefield. A bus from Sligo travels out to Rosses Point six times a day.

Sleeping & eating
This might make a quiet weekend alternative to Sligo, where the population tends to stagger a little after 2300

In Rosses Point the place to stay is the **A-L** *Yeats Country House Hotel*, T77211, F77203. It has everything you could want from swimming pool to concessions at the nearby golf club and is a cheery, family-orientated sort of place with a supervised crèche in the high season. There are B&Bs strung out all along the road to Rosses Point and there is a camp site, *Greenlands Caravan and Camping Park*, T77113, at Hughes Bridge. Two people and a small tent costs €22.

For food, there is the *Yeats* or the *Moorings*, T77112, serving mainly seafood. An excellent place to eat here is the *Waterfront*, T77122, a pub which overlooks the sea with outside seating and a pretty interior. It does pub lunches but rather superior Irish continental dinners till 2200 at around €25.

Drumcliff
Colour map 2, grid A4

From Rosses Point you can follow the northern coast road back towards the N15 and on to Drumcliff, where WB Yeats is buried. The main road cuts across the site of a sixth-century monastic settlement founded by St Colmcille, the left-hand side of the road revealing the remains of a round tower, struck by lightning in 1396, and the right-hand side a 10th-century high cross bearing the figures of Adam and Eve, David and Goliath, Daniel and the lions' den, and the Crucifixion, as well as mythical animals. Beside the high cross is the Protestant graveyard with the **grave of William Butler Yeats** and his wife George, with his famous epitaph "Cast a cold eye/On life, on death/Horseman, pass by". Yeats died in 1939 and was buried in France, but in 1948, in accordance with his wishes, his remains were dug up and brought here. There is a visitor centre beside the church where a rather incongruous 'interactive suite' tells of some local history. ■ *T44956, www.drumcliffe.ie All year Mon-Fri, 0830-1800, Sat, 1000-1800, Sun, 1300-1800. Craft and coffee shop. Free.*

The death of Diarmid

Benbulbin is the mountain where, according to legend, the mythical warrior Diarmid died. He had been chased all over Ireland by his best friend Fionn MacCumhaill – angry at Diarmid for, having run off with his woman, Grainne – but the two heroes had reconciled and were out hunting boar. Diarmid was invulnerable except for his ankle, but a boar's bristle caught Diarmid in the foot and he lay dying. Fionn had the power of healing and could have saved Diarmid, but every time he brought water to his dying friend he imagined Diarmid and Grainne together and let the water fall, until eventually Diarmid died. There's a moral there somewhere.

To the east rears Benbulbin, a massive dollop of carboniferous limestone that popped up in relatively recent times, geologically speaking. It appeared during the last ice age as a nunatak: an inland, cliffed, flat-topped peak standing out above the ice. David Marshall in *Best Walks in Ireland* describes an excellent, strenuous 5-mile (8.5-km) walk from close by Drumcliff. Wild plant spotters will be pleased to know that the mountain is a niche for some arctic alpine plants rare in Ireland – mountain avens, mountain sorrel and purple saxifrage.

Benbulbin

Three miles (5 km) east of Drumcliff is **Glencar Lake**, good for fishing and a walk to the waterfall that feeds the lough.

Famous for being rhymed with 'gazelle' by Yeats and as the home of the Gore Booth women (see box page 480), Lissadell House is open to the public for part of the summer. The house is an essay in early Victorian austerity, its straight lines undecorated as if to strengthen it in its exposure to Atlantic gales. It is a single block, the usual outhouses being all shoved down into the basement and a tunnel leads to the stable blocks. Inside is a family house, full of paraphernalia from over the years. It still belongs to the Gore Booth family, to whose ancestors the people of Sligo owe much: the house was mortgaged to feed the tenants during the Famine and the next generation gladly entered into selling the land to the tenants. Visit is by guided tour and it's well worth the detour. ■ *T63150. Jun-Sep, Mon-Sat 1030-1215, 1400-1615. €4. Tour lasts 40 mins. Teashop and craft shop. N15 to Drumcliff. Turn west following signs to Carney and Lissadell.*

Lissadell House
Colour map 2, grid A4

It's worth driving on to the end of the peninsula to **Raghly**, where there are views of the bay and coastline.

From Drumcliff the N15 heads on towards Cliffony where a left turn brings you to **Streedagh Point**: a stretch of sandy beach, with caves at the far end. North of Cliffony is the **Creevykeel Court Cairn**, probably dating back to 2500BCE, standing on high ground overlooking the sea. It is called a court tomb because of the open courtyard made from stones at its entrance, perhaps used for worship or for mourners. Inside, the tomb itself tapers down and narrows towards the rear and is divided into two chambers; other chambers have been added at a later stage. Four cremation burials were discovered when the tomb was opened in 1935, as well as neolithic pottery. These types of tomb are largely centred around Sligo and Mayo and this one is considered the best.

North to Mullaghmore

As the road approaches Mullaghmore, **Classiebawn Castle** appears, built in 1875 for the Hon. Cowper Temple, son of Lord Palmerston, whose family owned a large estate here. The austere baronial castle is built from local sandstone with a square tower and conical turret. The estate eventually passed into the hands of Countess Mountbatten, whose husband was murdered by the IRA in 1979 while boating from Mullaghmore harbour.

County Sligo

Constance Markievicz

Lissadell's most famous scion is of course Constance Gore Booth, later Countess Markievicz, who was a revolutionary, condemned to death after the Easter Rising and the first woman elected to the British Parliament (while she was in gaol in Reading). She never took her seat, although she went to the House of Commons after her release to have a look at her name on her coat hook. She was nominated the Minister for Labour in the first, illegal, Irish Dáil and became the first woman cabinet minister in Europe, albeit one constantly on the run from the British. In the civil war she found herself on the anti-Treaty side, taking part in some of the fighting in Dublin. She was elected to the Dáil again in 1927 but would not take her seat. She was a staunch socialist and spent her large fortune on helping the poor of Dublin, bringing turf into the city in her car for her constituents' fires. She died of appendicitis aged 59, having lost most of her possessions in various government searches of her Dublin house, and her body lay in the Rotunda Hospital, mourned by thousands, having been refused a state funeral by the Free State government.

In 1913, in the great lockout strike, she had manned soup kitchens; in the Easter Rising she commanded the rebels at St Stephen's Green; she fought in the civil war; worked in St Ultan's children's hospital in the great TB epidemics of the 1920s; and spent all her money training young men and women in the republican cause. Yet she is remembered chiefly as the friend of a man whose ideals came dangerously close to Fascism towards the end of his life, and as the subject of one of his lesser poems.

Mullaghmore is a quiet little fishing village, with another long sandy beach, and is great for fishing enthusiasts. The area also has lots of stables and both this beach and Streedagh are good for riding.

Difficult to get to, but well worth it, is **Inishmurray**, an uninhabited island 4 miles (6.5km) off the coast. Its last inhabitants sailed away in 1948, leaving behind a monastic site that had been in use since its foundation by St Molaise in the sixth century, despite being sacked by Vikings in the eighth century. The monastic settlement is enclosed by thick dry-stone walls: much of this was reconstructed in the late 19th century, but the rooms built into the wall are probably original. Inside, the enclosure is divided into three areas, one containing what has come to be known as the men's church, where the later islanders buried their male dead, and a much older, smaller church known as Teach Molaise. In this here are the famous 'cursing stones', *'bullauns'*, with smooth stones fitting into their depressions. Originally prayer stones, they came to be used for cursing one's enemies by turning them anticlockwise. In another section of the enclosure is a corbelled, roofed *clochain* used by the islanders as a schoolroom but probably originally an oratory. The island contains many more remains, including inscribed stones around the island marking the Stations of the Cross, as well as another church known as the women's church, where the women were laid to rest. North of the enclosure is a sweathouse.

Sleeping Mullaghmore is a good place to stop if you intend to spend more than a day in this area.
Price codes: **A-L** *Beach Hotel and Leisure Club*, The Harbour, Mullaghmore, T66171,
see inside www.beachhotelmullaghmore.com Very well endowed hotel looking out over the har-
front cover bour, with a swimming pool, sauna and gym. Definitely a family holiday sort of place with a crèche in the summer. Restaurant. Nightly entertainment in the summer. Murder mystery weekends. **AL** *Pier Head Hotel*, Mullaghmore, T66171, www.pierheadhotel.com Smaller hotel, but with equally panoramic views. Restaurant. Nightly entertainment in the summer. **A** *Armada Lodge*, Donegal Rd, Grange, T/F63250.

www.armadalodge.com B&B off the N15 looking out over the beach. Reductions for children. **A** *Mount Edward Lodge*, Ballinfull, T63263, mounted wardlodge@ircom.net B&B in lovely setting, with Benbulbin looming up behind. Child reductions. **D** *Karuna Flame Hostel*, Celtic Farm, near Grange, T63337. Includes 1 double room for €25, bikes for hire, non-smoking and unsuitable for children under 12.

Both the *Beach Hotel* and *Pier Head House* have good restaurants serving seafood, and bars with food. There is also *Eithna's Seafood restaurant*, T66407, at the harbour at Mullaghmore, serving locally caught seafood to an enthusiastic clientele some of whom drive a long way to eat there. Closed Tue weekends only in winter. Dinner could cost as much as €50. On the main road at Cliffoney is *La Vecchia Posta*, T071-76777, about the strangest place you'll ever find Italians serving Tuscan food! Dinner could cost €44. At Drumcliff is *Yeats Tavern Restaurant*, T 63117, serving a fairly standard Irish menu in an olde worlde setting and also *Davis's Pub*, T63117, near to the cemetery, does food, has music at weekends and traditional sessions in summer.

Eating

Horse riding *Horse Holiday Farm*, Grange, T66152, hhf@eircom.net. Easter-Nov. For experienced riders.

Sport

West of Sligo

The little chink of land to the south and west of Sligo is home to the seaside town of Strandhill, with 21 miles (4 km) of sand dunes, and waves good enough to bring surfers from all over Ireland. Behind the village, Mount Knocknaree dominates the skyline with the cairn of Queen Maeve at its summit and the Carrowmore megalithic complex on its western slopes. Coney Island can be reached on foot at low tide, there is a golf course, riding centre and good fishing. While you are in Salthill you might want to try out the Celtic Seaweed Baths, T68686, www.celticseaweedbaths.com, where you pay for the privilege of sitting in a tub of hot seawater and seaweed for their many apparently therapeutic qualities. At €14 a go, it had better be!

Miosgán Meadbha sits on the summit of Mount Knocknaree, a steep 1-hour walk from the car-park. At 33 ft (10 m) high and 180 ft (55 m) in diameter, it is visible from the surrounding countryside. The cairn has never been opened but is thought to cover a passage tomb built perhaps 5,000 years ago. There are lots of other sites around the cairn, with huge north and south markers, and little huts that may have been lived in by the men who built the cairn during construction: when these were excavated, lots of building implements were found. The connection with Maeve, the Iron Age queen of Connaught, is traditional, rather than based on fact. ■ *Open 24 hrs. Free. From Strandhill follow the R292, southern coastal road, till you see the car-park opposite the Sligo Riding Centre.*

Maeve's tomb

Continuing on towards Sligo on the R292 brings you to this enormous site full of standing stones, stone circles, and dolmens. It was in use for a vast period in time, its oldest constructions dating back to the fifth century BCE, making it older than Newgrange (see page 660), and all the tombs were reused many times. There were once 84 monuments here, but quarrying and land use cleared a great number of them. Thirty monuments are now contained here in a preserved Dúchas site, excavated each summer by a Swedish team of archaeologists. There is an interpretive centre and you can watch the archaeologists at work. ■ *Open May-Sep, daily 0930-1830. €1.90. Audio-visual presentation, guided tours, toilets.*

Carrowmore megalithic cemetery
In 1999 the Swedes identified the oldest tomb in Western Europe here, 7,400 years old

County Sligo

Sleeping
Price codes:
see inside frotn cover

AL *Ocean View*, Strandhill, T68641, www.ovhotel.com The only hotel in town, small and comfortable, with a respected restaurant. **A** *Knocknaree House*, Shore Rd, Strandhill, T68313, connollyma@eircom.net A B&B close to the beach. 50% reduction for children. **A** *Mardell*, Seafront, Strandhill, T68295. Small B&B with good views, very central. **A** *Shalom*, Seafront, Strandhill, T68314. An attractive modern B&B beside the sea. **C** *Strandhill Lodge and Hostel*, Strandhill, T68313, www.strandhill-accommodation.com Hostel with mostly doubles. Try out the aromatherapy class while you're there.

Eating

The *Strand*, T68641, serves bar food in the pub and more substantial food in the restaurant. *Rollers* n the *Ocean View* and the *Galley*, T68167, in *The Venue* are also good options. *Shell's cafe* is right on the beach and has good home cooked cakes and snacks.

Pubs & music

The Venue has folk and traditional music several nights a week and the *Strand* has music of some sort every night.

South and southwest of Sligo

Aughris
Colour map 2, grid A4

Aughris is a tiny fishing village, almost but not quite unspoiled by tourism and worth a visit for its sandy beach, good bar and, if you're into that type of thing, the promontory fort at Aughris Head. Just before Aughris, the road passes a tiny place called **Skreen**, where the present 14th-century church building has a much longer history, dating back to its foundation by St Adaman in 704CE. The graveyard contains box tombs, including a beautifully carved 19th-century tomb, and east of the church is a holy well. ■ *North of the N59, west of Sligo.*

Dromore West
Colour map 2, grid A4

Heritage centre lovers will enjoy Dromore West for **Culkin's Emigration Museum**, where the original shipping agent's shop is preserved inside a larger building dealing with the Famine and emigration. ■ *Cannaghanally, Dromore West, T096-47152. May-Sep, Mon-Sat, 1100-1700, Sun, 1300-1700. €3.50*

The coast
Colour map 2,
grid A3/4

Surfers will want to go to **Easky**, 5 miles (8 km) northwest of Dromore, where assorted surfing championships are held. There is also a 15th-century castle. A little further along the coast is **Inishcrone**, with an excellent Blue Flag beach 3 miles (4.8 km) long, caravan parks in the sand dunes, a golf course, and **Kilcullen's Seaweed Baths**, a beautiful Edwardian bath house where you can experience a steam bath followed by a high iodine salt water, seaweed bath in the original 1912 equipment. ■ *T096-36238. Open May-Jun and Sep-Oct, daily, 1000-2100; Jul and Aug, daily, 1000-2200; Nov-May, Sat, Sun, bank holidays 1000-2000. Tearoom. €12.50 per bath.*

Collooney
Colour map 2,
grid A4

If instead of taking the N59 west you head south, the first port of call is Collooney, nondescript except for the **Teeling Monument**, which commemorates the Battle of Carricknaget in 1798 and Bartholemew Teeling's part in it. He was in the French invading force that landed at Killala and was marching on its way to join the United Irishmen in Ballinamuck in County Longford. They had met and defeated English forces that day at Tobercurry, and were met in battle again by 600 English troops strategically holding a hill on their route: Teeling single-handedly shot the gunner in the English force. The French then moved on to Ballinamuck, where they were defeated and Teeling, being an Irishman, was executed. The other claim to fame of Collooney is **Markree Castle**, where you can stay if you can afford it: a 17th century pile with Victorian additions.

Pressing on southwards on the N17 brings you to Tobercurry, a working market town, which, as its advertising says, is probably as close as you'll come to the real Ireland. Its traditional Irish music scene is strong and in summer there is the South Sligo Summer School in the second week in July, when traditional Irish music students come from all over Ireland and America to study under the masters. For the unmusical, there is lots of craic to be had with ceili dancing, formal concerts each night and spontaneous outpourings of talent in every one of the pubs. If you plan to go you might want to book accommodation in advance. ■ *Contact Rita Flannery T071-85010.*

Tobercurry
Colour map 2, grid A4

XL *Cromleach Lodge*, Castlebaldwin, T071-65155, info@cromleach.com On the banks of Lough Arrow, accessed via Riverstown after Collooney. Modern with panoramic views over surrounding countryside, for those who like to get away from it all. It draws more people to its nouvelle Irish restaurant (see 'Eating') than to its accommodation. Closed Nov-Jan. **XL-LL** *Markree Castle*, Collooney, T071-67800, www.markreecastle.ie A seriously grand, oak-panelled, 17th-century castle with a 3-star rating from the tourist board and lots of family heirlooms lying about the place. Horse riding on the estate, lots of walks and a good restaurant where a reservation is a good idea and dinner in very grand surroundings will cost around €31. **L** *Coopershill House*, T071-65108, ohara-@coopershill.com Signposted off the N4 halfway between Sligo and Boyle, is an utterly authentic and very graceful Georgian house where a couple of days will comfortably slide by in understated luxury. **A** *Glebe House*, Collooney, T071-67787, www.glebe-house.com More a restaurant with accommodation than a guesthouse (see also 'Eating'). It is set in an old rectory and has only 6 rooms so it has a homely atmosphere. **A** *Castle Arms Hotel*, Enniscrone, T/F096-36516, www.castlearmshotel.com A reasonably priced 2-star hotel with a family atmosphere. **A-AL** *Cawley's*, Emmet St, Tobercurry, T071-85025, F85963. 10 rooms in a restaurant/guesthouse in the centre of the village. Nice gardens and comfortable rooms.

Camping The *Atlantic 'n' Riverside Caravan and Camping Park*, Easky, T096-490001. Lots of facilities including TV room, laundry and shop. *Atlantic Caravan Park*, Enniscrone, T096-36980. Despite its name, takes tents also, but is very small with few facilities.

Sleeping
Price codes:
see inside front cover

Nouvelle Irish cuisine can be found at *Cromleach Lodge*, Castlebaldwin (see 'Sleeping'), where seating is in a series of small rooms, best suited to small groups than couples, with a 5-course gourmet tasting menu at €32 plus, as well as à la carte and others. There is also *Glebe House*, Collooney, with good vegetarian options and fresh local produce. Easky's pubs are good for music in summer and there is food in several of them, and at Enniscrone your best bet for food is the *Castle Arms Hotel*, although you could also try *The Gable End*, T096-36110, new and flourishing. Open daily in summer but ring in advance in winter for the evening meal. Seafood menu. Pub food all year. In Tobercurry, there is the restaurant at *Cawley's* (see 'Sleeping'), but there is also *Killoran's*, T071-85111, a pub with a great reputation for both traditional music and dancing and traditional Irish cooking and where you can try boxty, colcannon, and stampy. They also do a good line in tourist information about the area.

Eating

Lough Gill

There are lots of good things to do around Lough Gill, the laziest of them being to take the 50-minute cruise on the Wild Rose Waterbus, T64266, from beside the sports complex at Doorly Park. The tour goes to Parke's Castle in County Leitrim, passing the Isle of Innisfree – immortalized, or at least included, in a poem by Yeats – pauses at Parke's Castle for an hour, and then makes its way back along the northern shore of the lough.

Colour map 1, grid C1

County Sligo

Cycling or driving, the best thing to do is go clockwise round the lough, following its northern shore. Take the N16 out of town until you meet the R286. Turn right and right again following the signs for Hazlewood. It's a 30-mile (48-km drive), the first stop on the drive being Hazlewood Forest Park Sculpture Trail, which is a park set on the shores of the lake full of carved wooden figures. Continuing on round the lough the next stop is the Deerpark Court Tomb, on a limestone ridge overlooking the lough. It is sign-posted from the R286, just after the road divides and you take the Lough Gill Loop sign. The site is a 10-minute walk to the top of the ridge.

Parke's Castle, County Leitrim, is the next stop on the trip round the lough, back on the R286. It is almost entirely a reconstruction of the original 17th-century building, which in turn was a reconstruction from the stones of an earlier castle. The original owner was hanged at Tyburn for sheltering a survivor from a wrecked Spanish armada vessel. It is now home to a heritage centre. n *Fivemile Bourne, T64149. Apr-May, Tue-Sun, 1000-1700; Jun-Sep, daily, 0930-1700; Oct, daily 1000-1700. E2.50. Guided tours available, audio-visual show, exhibition. Coffee shop.*

Creevelea Abbey is well worth a stop on the circuit of the lough, on the R288 now. It has to be unluckiest of all the early friaries in Ireland: it was the last to be built in 1508, was accidentally burned in 1536, and before it could be fully repaired was sacked by 1590, when Bingham, the Governor of Connaught, turned it into a stables. After his departure the friars were allowed back in, but then, at the end of his Irish campaign in 1650, Cromwell turned up and it was ruined once more. Still, it's a very picturesque ruin, with two well preserved windows and some good carvings. There are lots of outbuildings and it is possible to get a sense of the life that went on here within refectories, dormitories, the kitchen and other less easily identified buildings. ■ *Dromahair village. Open 24 hrs. Free.*

Re-entering County Sligo the road (the R287) rises and stays some distance from the lough until you see a sign for the **Isle of Innisfree**. The road then takes you down to the shore where you can gaze at the island and wonder that one person with a few words can change a place so much. There's a second opportunity to look at the lake in more touristy surroundings from **Dooney's Rock**, where the tour buses tend to congregate, just to make the place as much like Yeats' poem *The Lake Isle of Inisfree* as possible. From Dooney's Rock it is a short stretch back to Sligo.

County Leitrim

Here you are definitely off the main tourist circuit, and probably for quite good reasons. Leitrim is tiny, 50 miles wide with only two miles of coastline, but it has some mountain scenery to nod at and the large Lough Allen with its water sports and fishing. It shares its biggest attractions with County Sligo around Lough Gill and these have been covered as part of the tour of Lough Gill on page 483.

Carrick-on-Shannon

A good place to base yourself for any length of time in Leitrim, Carrick-on-Shannon sits prettily on the shores of the Shannon, with lots of very expensive motor launches bobbing about as they do the long trip from Belleek in County Fermanagh to the Shannon, or even travel further on to Dublin. Carrick's one sight is **Costello Chapel**, an 1877 tomb to the wife of one Edward Costello, a local shopkeeper. He bought a Methodist chapel and knocked it down to build this place, where he joined her in 1891. This wacky little oratory is stuck incongruously between two high-street shops. Their coffins lie either side of the tiny aisle, right in the middle of town, a little essay in self-importance. The **tourist office** is at the Old Barrel Store, The Marina, T20170, www.leitrimtourism.com It's open May-Oct, Mon-Fri, 0900-1300.

LL-AL *Landmark Hotel*, T22222, www.thelandmarkhotel.com A new hotel that deserves its name, plush bedrooms, leisure centre, and an above-average restaurant. **AL** *Bush Hotel*, T078-200014, www.bushhotel.com Recently renovated, an old-town hotel where some of the old-world charm has survived the construction of theme bars and cafés. **AL** *Hollywell*, Liberty Hill, T/F21124. Guesthouse beyond the bridge in town, with river frontage and fishing in the garden. Comfortable lounge area with open fire, good breakfast, no evening meals. **A** *Aisleigh Guest House*, Dublin Rd, T/F20313. Small, amenable guesthouse with games room, sauna, nice big rooms. **D** *The Town Clock Hostel*, Main St, T/F20068. Small hostel built around a courtyard in the centre of town. Two private double rooms and 4 dorm beds. Open Jun-late Sep. **D** *An Oiche Hostel*, The Bridge, T21848, is the second IHO hostel in town, with more dorm beds but only 1 private room, limited resources.

Sleeping
Price codes:
see inside front cover

The place to over-excite the palate has to be *La Gondola* at the *Landmark Hotel*. Italian tastes largely conjured out of local produce. Decent food on offer at the *Oarsman* pub in the evenings with the seafood and pizza menu making dinner around €20. The *Mariner's Reach* also has food in the evening till about 2130, and very delicious and good value it is too. *Cryan's* is another pub where the food fills the stomach. *The Pyramids*, T20333, is indeed an Egyptian restaurant, right in the town centre, and the food has been recommended by a reader. Carrick-on-Shannon is awash with pubs, the best of which do good music sessions – try *Cryan's* or *Burke's*, both on Bridge St.

Eating & pubs

Fishing *Tooman*, Bridge St, T21872; *Carrick-on-Shannon Angling Association*, T20489. **Horseriding** *Lisnagat Riding Centre*, T20598. Hacking and trekking.

Sport

Bicycle *Geraghty's*, Main St, T21316. Bike hire. **Boat** River trips set off daily from the Marina, organized by *Moon River*, T21777. Companies that hire out cabin cruisers in town include *Emerald Star*, T20234, www.emeraldstar.ie **Bus** The **Dublin** to **Sligo** bus passes through 3 times a day in both directions (stopping outside *Coffey's Pastry Case* close to the tourist office). Two buses a day connect with **Athlone** and Sligo in both directions, T071-60066 for information. **Taxi** *Joe Brock*, T20707; *Colm Spellman*, T086-8232424. **Train** The train station, T20036, is on the Roscommon side of the river. Trains link the town with **Dublin** and **Sligo** 3 times a day in both directions.

Transport

Banks *AIB*, Main St. **Communications** Post office: Bridge St.

Directory

South of Carrick

If you are travelling through this part of Leitrim, **Jamestown** is a good place to pause for a while. It was named after James I by Sir Charles Coote, who organized the plantation of the area in 1625. The old town gate is all that remains of the original planter town. You will go through it as you pass by on the Dublin to Sligo road. The arch of the gate was removed in the 1970s. It is a peaceful Georgian village full of people swapping fish stories and a couple of good pubs, especially the *Arch Bar*.

Jamestown
Colour map 1, grid C2

Water, water everywhere

Leitrim, like Cavan, is a watery country, but Cavan collects the water into a thousand little lakes and Leitrim, being hilly, indeed a maze of mountains and hills, pours it all over the place. It is a boggy, soggy rushy *land, full of burrowing streams, tiniest crevices of water everywhere and this I found very affecting like a tearful woman.* *Sean O'Faolain,* An Irish Journey, *(Longman/Green, 1940)*

Mohill
Colour map1, grid C2

Mohill is serious fisherman territory, with five loughs in the immediate area, and its chief claim to fame is its association with Turlough O'Carolan, the last of the travelling bards. He was born in 1670, the son of a blacksmith who worked in an iron foundry in County Roscommon. The wife of the foundry-owner took a fancy to the child, had him educated, and when he went blind at age 18 had him taught the harp. He travelled the countryside playing at the big houses, with a guide and horse supplied by his benefactress Mrs MacDermott Roe. He met and married May Maguire and settled in Mohill. After her death he took to the road again. He was welcome in the wealthiest of houses, and played to Jonathan Swift, and his music has been revived in modern times by the Chieftains. His portrait hangs in the National Gallery. Close by Mohill is another literary association: Anthony Trollope worked for the post office in Ireland for some years, and on a walk in Drumsna discovered the ruin of a house that inspired him to plan the novel *The Macdermots of Ballycloran*. If you stop in Mohill, look out for the art nouveau *Bank of Ireland* building.

Other sites

Close to Mohill is the **Lough Rynn Estate**, owned by the Clements family, better known as the Earls of Leitrim. The third earl, a notoriously bad landlord, erected most of the 19th-century buildings on the estate, before he was assassinated in Donegal in 1878. The house and grounds are open to the public – the walled garden is huge – and there is a craft shop and restaurant. ■ *T078-31427. Open Mid-May to mid-Sep, daily 1000-1900. €4.45 per car, plus €2 per person.*

At the southeastern and southwestern extremes of the county are two small places good for fishermen: **Carrigallen** and **Roosky**.

North of Carrick

Colour map 1, grid C2

Travelling north from Carrick, you come to the place that gave the county its name, but drive slowly or you'll miss it. Beyond it is **Drumshanbo**, another fishing centre on the southern shore of Lough Allen. For many years this was a small-scale coal-mining area, and the *Sliabh an Iarrain Visitor Centre* gives lots of information about the traditions of the area, from the methods of coal and iron extraction to the unusual tradition in this area of the sweat house: a kind of Celtic sauna. ■ *Apr-Sep, Mon-Sat, 1000-1800, Sun, 1400-1800. €2.*

Another good reason to come to Drumshanbo is the **Joe Mooney Summer School**, held in one week in July, where there are classes in traditional music for serious learners but also lots of sessions in the bars at night and lots of set dancing to join in with.

County Donegal

13

County Donegal

*All the superlatives that Bord Fáilte spreads out like jam
for Ireland would still apply if the rest of the country
floated off and sank in the Atlantic and all that was left
was the county of Donegal. It's a big county: a place for
hiking boots and binoculars during the day and cosy
corners in pubs at night. It stretches further north than
anywhere in Northern Ireland and by any reasoning,
other than those of sectarian politics, it belongs
historically and culturally with neighbouring Tyrone,
Fermanagh and Derry.*

   *In **Donegal town** you can enjoy the castle and the
craft village or go for a river trip but it is well worth
leaving the crowds behind and adventuring beyond
these safe confines. Try the surf at **Rossnowlagh** or the
melancholy of the seaside town of **Bundoran** in the off
season; drive along **Fintra Bay** with the coast on one
side and the mountains inland on the other. Walk
along the coast from **Kilcar to Teelin** or enjoy the real
Gaelic Ireland of **Glencolmcille**. Even in July and
August the county is never overcrowded, unless you are
stuck in Donegal town or Buncrana, and out of season
you will have the place to yourself.*

Ins and outs

Getting there   There are daily flights between Dublin and Donegal airport, T075-48284, F075-48483. The airport is not near Donegal town but in the Rosses between Dungloe and Crolly. Most travellers in cars arrive via Sligo on the N15 of from Enniskillen in County Fermanagh, but if your heart is set on wild Donegal, only when you get to Killybegs or Glenties does the adventure really begin. Alternatively, hit the Inishowen peninsula directly by entering the county from Derry.

Getting around   *Bus Éireann* does not provide comprehensive travel to all corners of Donegal but there are private bus companies that fill most of the gaps as well as competing with *Bus Éireann* in places. *McGeehan's*, T075-46150, is one of the biggest companies: their daily Dublin to Glencolmcille bus serving Donegal, Ardara, Killybegs, Kilcar and Carrick is very useful. Other companies worth using are *Feda O'Donnell Coaches*, T075-48114, 091-761656, *O'Donnell Buses*, T075-48356, *John McGinley*, T074-35201, and *North West Busways*, T077-82619, which links Derry, Letterkenny and the Inishowen peninsula. As an example of fares, *Feda O'Donnell* charges €12/16.50 for a single/return between Donegal and Galway, *McGinley* charges €18/36 for a single/return between Dublin and its furthest pickup point Annagry.

   Walking books and maps for Donegal don't come any better than *Hill Walkers' Donegal* by David Herman: over 30 walks with maps and directions and usually available in bookshops around Donegal. Other books worth considering include Alan Warner's *Walking the Ulster Way* and Patrick Campbell's *Rambles around Donegal*, both available in paperback. The **Ordnance Survey** Discovery series maps are essential for any long walks in the county.

Southern Donegal

Bundoran

Phone code: 072
Colour map 1, grid B1

Bundoran has two superb stretches of beach, but this has helped turn the place into a fairly conventional seaside resort packed with families in the months of July and August. It is a favourite destination for Catholic families from across the border seeking a respite from the marching season and there are some lively pubs at night, like the *Allingham Arms* on Main St. A big draw is **Waterworld**, an indoor complex with exciting-sounding gimmicks like a tidal wave, aqua volcano and tornado slide. It is host to the **World Surfing Championships** in 2003 and out of season it is a real gem for deserted seaside town lovers. At holiday weekends, there are often big names in Irish big bands and country music and the many hotels fill up. The **tourist office** is at Bundoran bridge, T41350. Open daily 0900-1800.

   A few miles further along the N15, before reaching Ballyshannon, the **Donegal Parian China Centre** is easy to spot on the right side of the road. There are free guided tours of the factory, purchases can be mailed home from the shop and there is an adjoining tearoom. ■ *T51826. All year Mon-Fri, 0900-1800, May-Sep, Mon-Sat, 0900-1800, Sun, 1300-1800. Bureau de change, Free.*

Sleeping
Price codes:
see inside front cover

LL *Great Northern Hotel*, T41204, greatnorthernhotel.com The most stylish place around, with huge rooms and amazing views over the beaches and is well away from the gadding about that goes on in the town at weekends. Pool and leisure centre, nice

★

Things to do in County Donegal

- Climb **Mount Errigal** and walk **Horn Head**
- See **Glebe House and Gallery**
- Eat chowder and home-baked bread at **Smugglers Creek Inn** at Rossnowlagh
- Visit the workhouse in **Dunfanaghy**
- Spend a few days out of season in **Bundoran**
- Go **sea fishing** from one of the coastal villages (ideal on a rainy day)

old dining room, and a golf course in the garden. **L-AL** *Grand Central Hotel*, T42722, grandcentral@eircom.net. More in the thick of things in the main street of town but offers good value modern rooms, family rooms and a good restaurant. **AL-B** *Gillaroo Lodge*, T42357, www.gillaroo.net At the west end of the village, near to all the facilities. It has lots of information on fishing in the area and hires tackle and boats. Drying room. *Surfer's Cove*, T42286, www.surferscove.com Rents out seaside bungalows on a weekly basis in summer but are open to negotiation in the off season. Rates are €139 for a 2-bedroom, 4-sleeper house over the weekend in the off season, higher during bank holidays. **D** *Homefield House*, Bayview Av, T41288, F41049. Hostel.

The really posh place to eat in Bundoran is *Chateaubrianne*, Sligo Rd, T42160. French **Eating** and nouvelle Irish in a seaside setting. Lots of seafood, as you would expect, but meat-eaters and vegetarians do well here too. Expect to pay €31 and more for dinner. Open Tue-Sat and Sun lunch (about €20). The restaurant in the *Great Northern Hotel* has lots of nostalgic charm about it. It is huge with enormous bay windows shrouded in 1990s over-the-top curtaining. Good quality, down-to-earth food, €26 for 3 courses. Out in the wild streets of Bundoran there are lots of places to dabble in a while. *Blazing Saddles* has a vaguely Mexican menu with vegetarian options for around €13 for a main course. *Fitzgerald's Bistro* in the hotel of the same name has a good reputation for steady food while *Tamarindo Blue* and *La Sabbia* are both good Italian-style places.

Bundoran has a *country music festival* in Oct when megabands turn up and perform **Pubs & music** that curiously Irish version of American country music – not so much "my wife has left me and my dog is dead" but "how sad I am to be leaving Ireland" type stuff. The festival also brings in 1960s-style showbands and thousands of party people from Dublin and further afield. In the summer there are nightclubs – *Planet Earth*, *Pepés*, *Jumping Jack's*, and more. Just stroll along and pick one. The *Astoria Wharf* has a late bar and live music on Thu. For traditional Irish music try *The Ould Bridge Bar* on Thu, Sat or Sun. *Brennan's* and *The Railway Bar* are good places for a quiet drink in traditional surroundings.

Angling There is game fishing in Drowes River and Lough Melvin, contact Paddy **Sport** Donagher, in Ballyshannon, T42357. Sea angling can be arranged with Michael Goodwin, T41256. **Horse riding** *Stracomer Silver Strand*, T41288. Tuition and trail riding. **Surfing** *Donegal Adventure Centre*, T42418, teaches surfing at all levels. Book in advance. They also hire out equipment. To purchase equipment try *Fitzgerald's Surfworld*, T41223. **Walking** There are lots of good cliff top walks around the town. Try the Roguey walk which goes from Bundoran Bridge to Tullan strand along the cliffs, passing fairy bridges and the wishing chair. The West End walk starts at Sheen Av and goes along the coast to Tullaghan, County Leitrim. *Donegal Adventure Centre* organizes guided hill walks.

Bus *Bus Éireann* run daily buses connecting Bundoran with **Sligo**, **Derry**, **Transport** **Letterkenny**, **Glenveagh National Park**, **Ballyshannon** (for connections to Dublin), and **Galway**. Call Ballyshannon Bus Station, T21101, for times. **Taxis** *Mulherns*,

County Donegal

☞ Tennyson ...

> **Tennyson**: *Couldn't they blow up that horrible island with dynamite and carry it off in pieces – a long way off?*
> **Allingham**: *Why did the English go there?*
> **Tennyson**: *Why did the Normans come to England? The Normans came over here and seized the country, and in a hundred years the English had forgotten all about it,*
>
> *and they were living together on good terms ... The Irish with damned unreasonableness are raging and foaming to this hour.*
>
> *From a conversation between Tennyson and William Allingham, as recorded by Allingham*

T42222, *Daly's*, T41111, *Carters*, T52111. **Bike Hire** *Hire and Sell Centre*, East Bundoran, T41526. Will deliver. *Donegal Adventure Centre*, hire mountain bikes.

Directory **Banks** *AIB* and *Bank of Ireland* are both in Main St. AIB has an ATM. **Cinema** *Bundoran Cineplex*, Main St, T29999. 6 screens. **Communications** Post office: Main ST, Mon-Fri, 0900-1230,1330-1730, Sat, 0900-1300.

Ballyshannon

Phone code: 072
Colour map 1, grid B2

The scruffy but rather charming town of Ballyshannon bursts into life over the holiday weekend at the beginning of August. This is the time of the **Folk and Traditional Music Festival**, which has been going for over 20 years, with a programme of street entertainment, workshops and a busking competition through the day, and pubs and a marquee overflowing with revellers at night. Big names like Christy Moore, Mary Black, Dervish and Sean Keane have appeared in past years so expect a full line-up of talented performers and book accommodation in advance. ■ *For advance information, T51088, F52832.*

Tony Blair, the British prime minister, has a family connection with Ballyshannon, and the poet William Allingham (1824-89) was born and educated in the town. Known to the Brownings and Pre-Raphaelites, he became a good friend of Tennyson (see box) and worked in London before moving to Surrey near where Tennyson was living. His ashes are buried in the Church of Ireland, easily reached by walking up Main St and taking the left turning after passing *Dorrian's Imperial Hotel* on the other side of the road. Go to the left after entering the churchyard and look for the word 'poet' on a tombstone.

Continue walking further up Main Street and take the left on to Bridge Street, which leads to the R231 road signposted for Rossnowlagh. A short way along, a sign points left for **Abbey Assaroe Mills and Waterwheels**. Only one wall by the graveyard stands as testimony to a Cistercian abbey founded here in the 12th century, but their water-powered mill inspired the interpretive centre and its displays on the legacy of the medieval monks in Ireland. There is a small coffee shop, and a signpost nearby points the way to **St Patrick's Well** overlooking the bay, where the saint himself is said to have once trod. ■ *T51580.*

Rossnowlagh

Phone code: 072
Colour map 1, grid B2

If time allows, the R231 road is a more attractive way of reaching Donegal town than the main N15, not least because it accesses the splendid 2½-mile (4-km) sweep of sandy beach at Rossnowlagh. This is Robinson Crusoe land compared to the beach at Bundoran, surfers often have it all to themselves and walks can be enjoyed across the hinterland of dunes and fields. Overlooking

County Donegal

the beach from the road is a Franciscan Friary, open to the public for walks in the garden or taking tea in the tearoom. It houses a small museum run by the Donegal Historical Society. ■ *T51342. Daily 1000-1800.*

Sleeping
Price codes: see inside front cover

LL-L *Sand House Hotel*, Rossnowlagh, T51777, www.sandhouse-hotel.ie This has transformed itself from a 19th-century fishing lodge into a superb hotel perched on the edge of a beach. Great views from the conservatory. **L-AL-** *Dorrians Imperial Hotel*, Main St, Ballyshannon, T51147, www.doriansimperialhotel.com Right in the town centre and dating back to 1781, this nicely modernized place has a small leisure centre with a gym and steam room. **B** *Rockville House*, Belleek Rd, Ballyshannon, T51106. Overlooks the river. **B** *Ceol na Mara*, Creevy, T52715. Overlooks the sea outside of town. **D** *Duffy's*, Donegal Rd, Ballyshannon, T51535. A useful hostel with camping space, bikes for hire, and 1 private room.

Camping *Lakeside Centre Caravan and Camping Park*, Belleek Rd, Ballyshannon, T52822. Overlooks Assaroe Lake and charges €12 for a tent.

Eating

The Sand House Hotel Restaurant at Rossnowlagh, T51777, has a 5-course dinner menu that changes nightly, but stick with the more traditional dishes. The pub food at *Smugglers Creek*, Rossnowlagh, T52366, is excellent and the clifftop location is hard to beat. Stone-flagged floors and open fires characterize the place. For quick lunches or coffee and cakes there are a couple of decent places in Ballyshannon, such as *Shannon's Corner*, Bishop St, and *Grimes Kitchen Bake*, on Main St, not forgetting the coffee shop at *Abbey Assaroe Mills and Waterwheels* just outside of town.

Pubs & music

Live music, traditional and modern, can be enjoyed in some of Ballyshannon's pubs throughout the summer and one of the best is *Sean Ógs*, Market St, T58964. On the other side of the road, *Dicey Reilly's* is worth checking out and on Bishop St the tiny *Thatch Pub* has character as well as live music most nights. Out at Rossnowlagh *The Smugglers Creek*, with timber beams everywhere, has traditional music every Sat and Sun and has been recommended by travellers.

Sport

Golf *Bundoran*, T41302. **Horse-riding** *Stracomer Riding Centre*, T41787.

Transport

Bus *Bus Éireann* run daily buses connecting Bundoran and Ballyshannon with Donegal, Derry, Sligo, Galway and Dublin, T074-21309. *Feda O'Donnell*, T075-48114, runs its private buses connecting Ballyshannon with Crolly, Donegal, Dunfanaghy, Gweedore and Letterkenny as well as another service heading west for Galway and Sligo.

Directory

Banks Main St, Ballyshannon. **Communications** Post office: Market St, Ballyshannon. **English Language Summer School** *Homefield House* (and hostel), T41288.

Donegal Town

Phone code: 073
Colour map 1, grid B2

A harmless little place, Donegal attracts far more visitors each year than the town warrants, possibly attracting them with its name, which makes it seem like the hub of the county. It's good for a couple of days' stay – with its lively bars, one or two places to visit, and a lovely walk along the river – but longer than that and the traffic will start to irritate. The **tourist office** is at The Quay, T21148. Open Mon-Fri 0900-1600.

The name, Donegal (*Dún na nGall*) means 'fort of the foreigners', and it was probably originally established by Vikings. Later, the O'Donnell clan built a tower here overlooking the river Eske. They held it for a 100 years or more before burning it to prevent it falling into English hands, when the town itself fell to Sir Basil Brooke after the flight of the Earls in 1607. Brooke planted the town with English settlers and laid out the modern streets, including the Diamond. The town passed into modern times little changed from the days when Brooke planned it.

O'Donnell's Castle O'Donnell's Castle, in the centre of town, is a largely Jacobean building, erected by Brooke with the 15th-century tower rebuilt and extended and a 17th-century three storey house added. It was abandoned in the 18th century and adopted by the Office of Public works in the late 19th century. The tower has been restored and holds displays about the history of the castle and the O'Donnell's, one of whom was St Colmcille (see page 504). The grand fireplace in the main room in the tower shows Brooke's coat of arms and that of his wife's family. It's a grand place to visit, at once a cosy house and a defensive tower, and the exhibitions inside are well worth studying. Visit before this place gets turned over to banquets as Bunratty has. ■ *Open May-Oct and St Patrick's Day, daily 0930-1830. Open at weekends Nov-Jan. €3.80.*

Franciscan friary Another O'Donnell construction is the very ruined but picturesque Franciscan friary, on the town side of the river Eske. It was built in1474 by Red Hugh O'Donnell and his wife Nuala O'Brien and, like most other defensible buildings in Ireland, was taken and taken again in the assorted wars between the clans and the English. At one stage there were gunpowder stores in the friary which exploded and destroyed most of the buildings. In 1607 under Sir Basil Brooke the building became the Protestant church, and it serves as a graveyard now. On

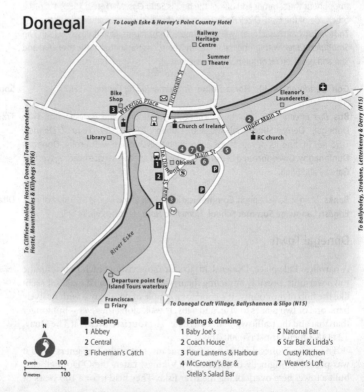

Donegal

To Lough Eske & Harvey's Point Country Hotel

Railway Heritage Centre

Summer Theatre

Bike Shop

Waterloo Place

Tirchonaill St

Eleanor's Launderette

Church of Ireland

Upper Main St

Library

RC church

Main St

The Diamond

Obelisk

Quay St

River Eske

Departure point for Island Tours waterbus

Franciscan Friary

To Donegal Craft Village, Ballyshannon & Sligo (N15)

To Cliffview Holiday Hostel, Donegal Town Independent Hostel, Mountcharles & Killybegs (N56)

To Ballybofey, Strabane, Letterkenny & Derry (N15)

N

0 yards 100
0 metres 100

■ **Sleeping**
1 Abbey
2 Central
3 Fisherman's Catch

● **Eating & drinking**
1 Baby Joe's
2 Coach House
3 Four Lanterns & Harbour
4 McGroarty's Bar & Stella's Salad Bar
5 National Bar
6 Star Bar & Linda's Crusty Kitchen
7 Weaver's Loft

County Donegal

the opposite bank a quiet pathway leads behind bungalows along the river bank in a 1½-hour walk to **Revlin Point**, a route that has been popular since the turn of the century. There is an accompanying leaflet that tells you about the plant life you can see, which can be picked up at the tourist office.

Donegal town has a collection of steam-train fanatics who are renovating old carriages, and the hope is that they will eventually resurrect a bit of the line and run trains. For now, however, you can visit the Donegal Railway Heritage Centre with lots of information, old posters and restored carriages and engines. Good for a wet afternoon. ■ *Old Station House, Tirconaill St, T22655. Jun-Sep, Mon-Sat, 1000-1730; Oct-May, Mon-Fri, 1000-1600. €1.*

Railway Heritage Centre

Part shopping centre, part tourist attraction this is a purpose-built village where craftworkers have their workshops and sell their produce. You can watch uilleann pipes being made, observe a jeweller making traditional designs, admire the stonemasonry of Brendan McGloin and the blacksmithing of Jack Voss, or see potters hand-throwing their work, and of course you can buy what you like best. A good activity for a rainy day. ■ *Ballyshannon to Sligo Rd. Open all year, Mon-Sat 0900-1800; Summer Mon-Sat 0900-1800, Sun 1100-1800. Coffee shop, picnic area. Half a mile (800 m) south of the tourist office.*

Donegal Craft Village

L *Central Hotel*, The Diamond, T21027, www.whites-hotels.com Very busy but comfortable hotel in the heart of the town. Big rooms, nice views of the river from the back, leisure centre with a big swimming pool available to guests, 2 restaurants. **L** *Harvey's Point Country Hotel*, Lough Eske, T22208, www.harveyspoint.com Only 3½ miles (6 km) from town but its alpine location on the lonely shores of Lough Eske takes you a million miles away from the bustle of Donegal. Famous restaurant and inspiring opportunities for country walking (see 'Tour operators', page 496). **AL** *Abbey Hotel*, The Diamond, T21014, F23660. A very busy place with lots of night-time entertainment. Restaurant and bar food. **A** *Ardeevin*, Lough Eske, Barnesmore, T073 21790, seanmcginty@eircom.net Out of town on the shores of Lough Eske but very scenic. **B** *Island View House*, T22411, wwweirbyte.com/islandview 10 minutes out of town at Tullacullion, modern B&B overlooking the bay. **B** *Meadowlane B&B*, T23300, Big country house 4 km outside of town on N15. **C-D** *Cliff View Holiday Hostel*, Killybegs Rd, T21684, F22667. This is budget motel accommodation rather than a hosteller's hostel. Very comfortable with 6-8 beds per room, which have their own keys, and access to kitchen and lounge area. Private rooms. **D** *Donegal Town Independent Hostel*, Killybegs Rd, T22805. €38 for a double room in this regular hostel with attractive murals on the walls and garden space for tents.

Sleeping
■ *on map*
Price codes:
see inside front cover

Harvey's Point Country Hotel Restaurant, Lough Eske, T22208, is noted for its French and Swiss gourmet cooking and opens daily for lunch and dinner. Weekends only Nov –Mar. Evening set dinner starts at around €35 and the calming views are thrown in for free. Opposite the tourist office in Quay St is the *Harbour Restaurant*, T21702, with stone walls, pine beams and bric à brac. Nice food too – seafood and steaks. Very popular, not much standing room, open all day till 2230. Next door is the *Four Lanterns*, one of a fast-food chain doing burgers and fish things. The two hotels have busy lunchtime and evening restaurants. The set dinner at the *Hyland* is priced in the mid-range and has a wide range of choices in a 3-course menu. It's an old-fashioned kind of setting with lots of food. If it's less formal eating you are after there's *Just William's*, downstairs in the hotel, where you serve yourself from the counter and lunch costs around €7. Lots of space. Next door at the *Abbey Restaurant* there are basic potato dinners.

Eating
● *on map*
Price codes:
see inside front cover

County Donegal

The Annals of the Four Masters

Annála Ríoghachta Eireann, *The Annals of the Kingdom of Ireland, are a compilation of all the ancient histories of Ireland put together by Míchéal Ó Cléirigh and three colleagues in the years following the English conquest of the area in 1607. These four friars left the church in Donegal town after it was granted to Sir Basil Brooke: as Franciscans they were not considered Catholic priests and were able to move freely. They travelled post-Reformation Ireland gathering older manuscripts and making copies, in an attempt to collect all the history and culture of Ireland in the face of the encroaching Anglicization. There are two memorials to the Four Masters in Donegal town – the obelisk in the Diamond and the new Catholic Church – but in fact the annals weren't written in the Friary here, but in Drowes, County Donegal between 1632 and 1636. They cover Irish history from the years before the flood to 1616 and several of their sources, older manuscripts held in other monasteries, are now lost, making the Annals an important source for early Irish history. Early copies of the Annals are in the National Library in Dublin.*

For lunch or a very early evening meal the *Weaver's Loft*, T22660, in the Diamond, serving inexpensive soups and fish-and-chip type meals is quiet and presentable, while *McGroarty's Bar* in the Diamond not only does good pub food but caters for vegetarians.

Pubs & music The *National* bar has Irish music at weekends all year round in an unreconstructed fifties sort of place while the *Star Bar* has live music but a younger, Irish crowd and trendier music. Inside is *Linda's Crusty Kitchen* which does good cheap breakfasts and sandwiches and some hot meals. The *Abbey Hotel* has a disco on Sun aimed at the over-21s, and at weekends and when a tour bus calls in, as they regularly do, there is an organized Irish session, featuring the Londonderry Air and suchlike. In Main St is *Baby Joe's*, a very trendy young spot where there is some interesting music.

Sport **Fishing** permits and licences for salmon and trout from *Doherty's*, Main St, T21119. **Golf** *The Park Golf Centre*, Ballyshannon Rd, T22779.

Tours operators **Hiking and biking tours in Donegal** If you prefer organized walking or cycling trips with food and accommodation sorted out in advance, try the following companies: *SOS Walking*, An Bhealtaine, Gortahork, Co Donegal, T/F074-35206, info@sosdonegal.com, www.sosdonegal.com; *Go Ireland*, Old Orchard House, Killorglin, Co Kerry, T066-9762094, F066-9762098, goireland@fexco.ie http://www.goireland.fexco.ie; *Irish Cycling Safaris*, Belfield House, Dublin 1, T01-2600749, F01-7061168, ics@kerna.ie www.cyclingsafaris.com; *Holyrood Hotels Walking Holidays*, Bundoran, T072 41232, holyroodhotel.com

Transport **Bicycle** *The Bike Shop*, Waterloo Pl, T22515. **Boat** *Island Tours Waterbus*, T23666. Organize twice daily tours of Donegal Bay during the summer months. Departure times are determined by the tide. The guided tour includes a sighting of Seal Island, where 200 harbour and Atlantic seals breed. **Bus** *Bus Éireann* has services to **Dublin**, **Cork** and **Limerick** in the south, **Galway** and **Sligo** to the west and **Belfast**, **Derry** and **Enniskillen** in Northern Ireland. *McGeehan Coaches*, T075-46150, have a daily service between **Dungloe** and **Dublin**, which calls at Donegal, and a **Glencolmcille** to Dublin service, calling at Donegal twice daily. Another private company is *Busana Feda*, T075-48114 for a timetable and list of towns served, which has a twice-daily service between Donegal and Galway and less regular services between Donegal and **Glasgow** and Donegal and Belfast airport. *O'Donnell Buses*, T075-48356, has a daily

A pilgrim's progress

In 1397 a courtier of King John of Aragon set off from France for Lough Derg in the hope that he could redeem the soul of his master, who had died too suddenly to confess his sins. When he reached Dublin from England he was warned of the dangers of "savage, ungoverned people" but an armed escort took him as far as Ulster from where he continued alone.

The courtier met King O'Neill who took him to Lough Derg where monks rowed him across to the island where he meditated and suffered visions of lost souls. On his return he spent Christmas with the O'Neills where "his table was of rushes spread out on the ground while nearby they placed delicate grass for him to wipe his mouth".

Donegal to Belfast via Derry service leaving Donegal at 0715. **Taxi** Taxi rank opposite the *Abbey Hotel*. Most taxis in town are individually operated, and their mobile number is lit up on the top of the cab.

Banks *AIB*, The Diamond, T21016. *Bank of Ireland*, The Diamond, T21079. **Communications** **Post office**: Tirconaill St. **Launderette** *Eleanor's*, Upper Main St.

Directory

Lough Derg

Special buses run to Lough Derg during the pilgrim season, and bookings and transport information are available from *The Prior*, T61518 or T61550. The shore of Lough Derg can be reached on the remote R233 road from Pettigo.

Ins & outs
Phone code: 072
Colour map 1, grid B2

Ireland's most historic penitential pilgrimage site lies to the west of Donegal town, and its lineage is indeed impressive. An 1184 text, the *Tractatus de Purgatorio Sancti Patricii*, referred to an island where St Patrick fasted to expel demons, and the earliest maps of Europe marked Lough Derg as the destination for medieval pilgrims in search of Patrick's island. A pope tried to forbid the practice in 1497, and Cromwell vandalized the place, but all to no effect, and an increasing popularity in the 19th century established the practice that is still followed every year between June and August, when thousands visit the small Station Island in the lough. They take part in retreats which last three days, walking barefoot and living off black tea and toast (plus smuggled supplies of chocolate bars) without proper sleep.

The **Lough Derg Centre** in **Pettigo** has background information on the history of the pilgrimage site, and some of Seamus Heaney's poems in his Station Island collection may inspire you to visit and experience the place. ■ *Main St, Pettigo, T61546. Apr-Sep, Mon-Sat 1000-1800, Sun 1200-1700.* €3

Lough Eske and the **Blue Stack Mountains** that lie to the north make for a superb day trip by bicycle or car from Donegal town. Take the N56 heading north out of Donegal town, and look for the sign pointing to a road on the right for the Lough Eske Drive. A small road loops around the lough and it is possible to join up with the N15 road on the east side of the lough and return to Donegal that way. Walks in the Blue Stack Mountains begin at the northern end of the lough but a map is essential, and David Herman's book usefully covers this area (see 'Getting around' on page 490).

Food is served all day at the *Pettigo Inn & Milers Restaurant*, Main St, Pettigo, T61720.

Sleeping & eating

County Donegal

Southwest Donegal

Donegal to Killybegs

Phone code: 073
Colour map 1, grid B2

The N56 road leaves Donegal for the route west to Killybegs and Glencolmcille and it is not long before Donegal Bay comes into view with Benbulben and the mountains of Sligo providing an impressive backdrop. The first village, **Mountcharles**, is strung out along the road and the attractive water pump that might catch your eye is dedicated to Seamus MacManus, a local storyteller and author. A sign points left down to the sea where a boat can be hired for sea fishing trips. ■ *T35257*.

The N56 speeds on through the village of **Inver**, where there is a small beach and the *Rising Tide* pub. At the next village, **Dunkineely**, there is a detour worth taking to **St John's Point** if a quiet picnic spot or scenic views seem in order. The signposted road goes south for 5 miles (8 km) and ends in a limestone enclave, where there is a splendid, little-visited sandy beach and a lighthouse.

Back on the main road at Dunkineely the **Killaghtee Heritage Centre** charges €3 for a fairly superfluous set of models of local archaeological sites, but ask about a proposed Heritage Trail that may allow you to see the sites for real. The neighbouring gallery has paintings of Donegal scenes for sale, and a framed watercolour of your own place can be commissioned for between €315 and €825. ■ *T37453. Daily 1000-1800.*

The last village before Killybegs is **Bruckless**, home to a holy well that has some early Christian cross-slabs near by. There is a good B&B and a hostel here, so the village makes a possible stopping point if somewhere quieter than Killybegs beckons.

Sleeping
Price codes:
see inside front cover

A *Bruckless House*, Bruckless, T37071, F37070, bruc@iol.ie An 18th-century house overlooking the bay, furnished with artefacts and art from the orient. You can practise your French or Chinese here. There are 4 rooms, one of which has its own bathroom. **B** *Grove House*, Brenter, Dunkineely, T37297, info@family-homes.ie A large house in a rural setting with sea and mountain views. **D** *Blue Moon Hostel*, Main St, Dunkineely, T37264. Pleasant hostel with private rooms and camping space. **D** *Gallagher's Farm Hostel & Camping Park*, Darney, Bruckless, T37057. An attractively converted stone-built barn with 2 kitchens, maps for walking, but no private rooms. Campers have their own facilities in a converted hay barn.

Eating

Not a lot of choice, and it is better to bring a picnic or eat in either Donegal or Killybegs. At night, though, the *Castlemurray House Hotel Restaurant*, St John's Point, Dunkineely, T37022, is noted for its French-style cuisine, with dinner at around €33. On the main road at Dunkineely the *Killaghtee Tearoom*, part of the gallery and heritage centre, does simple snacks and cake, and fairly basic pub grub may be available in the summer from a couple of pubs in Mountcharles and Dunkineely. The *Old Stone restaurant*, T35622, in the *Village Tavern*, Mountcharles has a good reputation.

Transport

Bus Éireann, T21101, runs a Mon-Sat service between Killybegs and Donegal, stopping at Mountcharles, Inver and Dunkineely.

Killybegs

Phone code: 073
Colour map 1, grid B1

Killybegs, as your nostrils will soon inform you, is a major fishing port, and the large fish processing plant is what blocks the view of the bay when arriving

Gaelic place names

The Irish language is alive and well in parts of southwest Donegal and place names on signs often appear in Irish as well as, or instead of, English.

		Cill Chartha	Kilcar
		Dún Chionn Fhaola	Dunkineely
		Gleann Cholm Cille	Glencolmcille
		Gleann Locha	Glenlough
		Málainn Mhóir	Malinmore
An Charraig	Carrick	Málainn Bhig	Malinbeg
An Caiseal	Cashel	Na Gleanntaí	Glenties
An Port	Port	Na Cealla Beaga	Killybegs
Ard a'Ratha	Ardara	Tamhnach an Salainn	Mountcharles
An Bhroclais	Bruckless	Port Nua	Portnoo
An Tráigh Bhán	Silver Strand	Ros Beag	Rosbeg

from the east. The piscine theme is hard to escape in Killybegs; it accounts for the best dishes on restaurant menus, and there are various sea-angling events during the summer that culminate in a major festival in late July. Fresh fish can be purchased from the quayside each evening after the boats come in and it is easy to arrange angling trips. ■ *For example: the* Persistance, *T31288 or the* Susanne, *T32444. Enquire at the large Harbour Store, T31569, down by the quayside, or look for the flyers in the window for details of other boat operators.*

The *Harbour Store* has a good selection of fishing and nautical gear as well as wet gear, camping equipment and a selection of gifts. There is no **tourist office**, but there is a town map and noticeboard in front of the Harbour Store and there are a couple of banks and a post office along the main street formed by the N56 running through the town.

For something non-fishy in nature, take a stroll up the hill from the main road to St Catherine's church to admire the Celtic-inspired carvings of gallowglasses on the tomb of Niall Mór MacSweeney (see box on page 501).

Without being facetious, you get the best of Killybegs when you leave the place, for as the road swings west out of town the seascape begins to take on some of the characteristics that make Donegal so special. **Fintragh Bay** comes into view, with the expanse of sea beyond it, while the mountains of **Crownarad** and **Mulnanaff** loom up inland. Look for the sign pointing left for a spectacularly scenic coastal route to Kilcar, and consider following the signs that appear along the route to **White Strand** or **Muckros Head** for a picnic spot and viewing point.

There is only 1 hotel, but B&Bs line the roads going in and out of Killybegs, especially the road to Kilcar, and it is difficult to differentiate them, for they are all variations on the bungalow theme, and most charge a fixed rate of €24 per person.

Sleeping
Price codes: see inside front cover

L-AL *Bay View Hotel*, Main St, T31950, F31856. Benefits from a smart leisure centre and indoor pool. **B** *Bannagh House*, Fintra Rd, T31108,bannaghhouse@eircom.net The archetypal bungalow, but with an elevated site overlooking the harbour. **B** *Oilean Roe House*, Fintra Rd, T31192, walsh01@eircom.net This B&B differentiates itself by having 2 storeys.

The Fleet Inn, Main St, T31518, has a restaurant with a small menu featuring dishes like steamed brill, as well as shellfish and steaks. Dinner only daily in summer. Closed Mon and Tue in winter. *Cope House*, Main St, T31834, has a nautical theme pub serving bar food and a restaurant serving Chinese-style dishes. *The Sail Inn*, Main St, T31130, serves toasties, open sandwiches and burgers and has a seafood restaurant

Eating

County Donegal

☞ Festivals and events in southwest Donegal

Southwest Donegal has a variety of events and festivals throughout the summer but the exact dates, and occasionally the theme, may change from one year to the next.

Mid-March	*Hillwalking Festival, Ardara*	T075-41518
April	*Hillwalking, Glencolmcille*	T073-30248
May	*Killybegs Sea Angling, Killybegs*	T073-31137
June	*Seafood Festival: Narin & Portnoo*	T075-45302
	Mick and Michael Carr	
	Traditional Music Weekend, Carrick	T073- 39009
July	*International Sea Angling Festival, Killybegs*	T073-31137
	Painting Summer School, Glencolmcille	T073-30248
	Irish Language & Culture School, Glencolmcille	T073-30248
	Traditional Music weekend, Tory Island	T073-31137
August	*Sailing Regatta, Killybegs*	T073-31950
	Downings Bay Shark festival	T074-55386
	Donegal Dances Summer School, Glencolmcille	T073-30248
	Archaeology Summer School, Glencolmcille	T073-30248
	Hill walking week Glencolmcille	T073-30248
	Ballyshannon Folk and Traditional Music Festival	T072-51088
	Patrick McGill Summer School, Glenties	T075-51103
	Agricultural Show, Ardara	T073-41103
September	*Glenties Harvest Fair*	T075-51124
October	*Traditional Music Festival, Carrick*	T073-39333

upstairs with an early-bird menu. A little way outside Killybegs on the road to Kilcar, *Kitty Kelly's*, Largy, T31925, has a mixed menu of seafood, pizzas and pastas and last orders at 2130.

Pubs & music In the summer there will usually be musical entertainment in at least one of the pubs at night. In Main St the *Harbour Bar* is a good place to try and the Fleet Inn usually has music at weekends and midweek. *The Sail Inn* is always worth checking out for informal sessions of Irish music at weekends, and the *Bay View Hotel* has nightly entertainment.

Transport *Bus Éireann*, T21101, runs Mon-Sat services between Killybegs and **Glencolmcille**, between Killybegs and **Portnoo** via **Ardara** and **Glenties**, and between Killybegs and **Donegal**. *McGeehan's* private buses, T075-46150, also stops in the village on its daily services between Glencolmcille and **Dublin**, and between **Letterkenny** and Glencolmcille.

Kilcar to Glencolmcille

Colour map 1, grid B1 As the road from Killybegs approaches Kilcar the N56 bears to the right and goes over the mountains to Carrick, while a smaller road bears left into Kilcar and continues to Carrick along the coast. **Kilcar**, a small village and a centre for the Donegal hand-woven tweed industry, is pleasantly low-key compared to Killybegs, or at least it is outside of the sea-angling festival and accompanying street festival that raises the jollity level in the five pubs. Good food, pubs with music and accommodation are all available and *Studio Donegal* is one of the community's small spinning and handweaving factory shops that you can visit. ■ *The Glebe Mill*, T38194. There is a **tourist office** in the Aislann Building in Kilcar on the road out to Carrick.

County Donegal

The Gallóglaigh

Gallóglaigh (a gall-óglach is a 'foreign warrior'), Anglicized to 'gallowglasses', came from the Hebrides in Scotland and were a mixture of Norse and Gaelic. When the Norwegian connection with Scotland had been severed in the late 13th century they were happy to hire themselves out as quality mercenaries to feuding Ulster chieftains. A gallowglass had two men of his own to look after his coat of mail, battle-axes, spears and swords. His prowess was vital to the task of holding

back a cavalry charge, supporting and supplementing the native kern who had no fancy weapons but fought "bare nakyd, saving their shurtes to hyde their prevyties, and those have dartes and shortes bowes".

In time, leading gallowglasses were given land as a reward and eventually became part of the medieval aristocratic nobility of Ireland. The MacSweeneys were one such clan and another were the even more successful MacDonnells.

There are also opportunities to arrange guided walks and fishing trips or attendance at a weekend writing workshop. The new tourist office can supply a map and brochure of the local **Kilcar Way** walk. They are also planning a computerized display on local history and the tweed industry.

Further along the main road at **Carrick**, a road is signposted to the left for Bunglas and Slieve League and walking along this stretch of coast is one of the highlights of a trip to Donegal. From the main road it is a few miles to the tiny Irish-speaking village of **Teelin** and its pub, and just beyond it the road divides: left for Bunglas and right for a signposted Slieve League walking trail.

Walking trails

Going left, vehicles can be taken up the steep and winding road around the southern slopes of Slieve League to a rough car-parking area and from here, Bunglas, there are awesome views of the cliffs and their shifting colours, while hundreds of feet below the silent sea churns up foam against coloured rocks (bunglas means 'green bottom').

Walkers have a choice of routes. From the first signpost for the Slieve League Walk the lengthier but less precipitous route leads on to **One Man's Pass** and the summit of **Slieve League** (1,952 ft/595 m). Alternatively, walking can start at the parking area up a well trodden route to **Scregeighter** (1,010 ft/308 m) and **Eagle's Nest** (1,060 ft/323 m; see box page 502) and then a very precipitous 5-ft-wide (1.5 m) path to One Man's Path (this section is not as scary as the 5-ft-wide steep stretch). While due warning needs to be given about proper footwear and avoiding windy or misty days (there have been fatal accidents), reaching the summit of Slieve League is more than ample reward. On a clear day it should be possible to make out the distinctive shapes of Croagh Patrick in County Mayo and Ben Bulbin in County Sligo.

From the summit, you can continue to Malinbeg along the edge of the cliff (from Teelin this walk takes about six hours). It will take another hour or more to reach accommodation at Malinmore, or on a little further still to Glencolmcille and a choice of places to stay and eat.

B *Cairnsmore*, Glen Rd, Carrick, T39137, info@family-homes.ie B&B in a quiet little bungalow with Slieve League in the background. Single and double rooms, evening meal available for €11.50. **D** *Derrylahan Independent Hostel*, Derrylahan, Kilcar, T38079, F38447. Popular IHH hostel with terrific views of the bay and good facilities. Includes 3 private rooms, and camping space is also available. Telephone for pick-up from Kilcar or Carrick. Closer to the village, **D** *Dun Ulun Hostel*, Kilbeg, Kilcar, T38137, is

Sleeping
Price codes: see inside front cover

Eagle's Nest

David Marshall in his excellent Best Walks in Ireland *retells a story first recorded in 1867 about the point on the walk from Bunglas known as Eagle's Nest. An 80-year-old woman, Nanny O'Byrne of Malinbeg, remembered her great-grandmother who, when only nine months old, was carried off by an eagle from the nest on the cliff. The bird was pursued and the child was dropped near Carrigan Head; although seriously injured she survived to a ripe old age bearing the scars from her abduction. The nest was apparently destroyed in the early 19th century after 'human limbs' (more probably sheep bones) were discovered inside it. Eagles from Scotland have been spotted between Slieve League and Glencolmcille, and there is a chance they will nest here again.*

more of a guesthouse with hostel accommodation and camping space included. The 8-room **D** *Cara's Hostel*, Kilbeg, Kilcar, T38368, is a thatched cottage with lovely traditional features. No private rooms.

Eating Two of Kilcar's pubs, *John Joe Byrne* (known to everyone as *John Joe's*) and *Kilcar House*, serve basic pub grub while a third one, *The Piper's Rest*, T38205, has a well deserved reputation for its seafood chowder, and a plate of oysters with a Guinness is a favourite combination here. On the other side of the road *Restaurant Teach Barnaí*, T38160, specializes in mid-range seafood and international dishes.

A mile from Carrick on the road to Glencolmcille, the stone-built *Gate House* tearoom, T39366, has indoor and outdoor seating for home-baked goodies, open 1000-1800, May-Sep. There is an attached craft shop selling handloomed knitwear. The *An Sliabh a'Liag*, T39041, does pub food.

Before reaching Kilcar on the road from Killybegs, the *Blue Haven*, T38090, is open for lunch and dinner, has amazing views, serves modern Irish food at very reasonable prices.

Pubs & music Kilcar's 5 pubs are all within staggering distance of each other on the same side of the street and between them there will be music most nights of the week in the summer. The *Piper's Rest* is thatched and has loads of atmosphere and really traditional music. In Carrick, between *Enright's*, T39070, the *An Sliabh a'Liag*, T39041, *Tigh Mhic Fhionnlaoich*, T39120, and the *Cellar Bar (Doc's)*, T39067, there should be a session most nights of the week.

Sport **Fishing** *Mc Breaty's*, Main St, Kilcar, T38492. Supplies tackle and information on where to fish. *SWD Angling Service*, T38211. **Horse riding** *Little Acorn Farm*, Carrick, T39386.

Transport **Bus** *Bus Éireann*'s **Killybeg** to **Glencolmcille** service, Mon-Sat, stops in Kilcar and Carrick, T21101. *McGeehan*'s private buses, T075-46150, also stop in both villages on their daily services between Glencolmcille and **Dublin**, and between **Letterkenny** and Glencolmcille. **Bicycle** *Boyle's*, Main St, Carrick, T39195. *Derrylahan* hostel (see 'Sleeping' above). **Taxis** *Curran*, Bogagh Rd, Carrick, T39141.

Tours **Walking** *Walkabout*, T38211. Walking through Donegal. **Writing workshops/literary weekends** T38448.

Glencolmcille

Phone code: 073
Colour map 1, grid B1

After leaving Carrick, instead of staying on the main road all the way, a more leisurely approach to Glencolmcille can be enjoyed by taking the signposted road to the left for Malinbeg. Along the way you will see a signpost for **portal tombs**, a line of six that make up the largest group of portal stones in Ireland. After passing them take another signposted left turn which ends in Malinbeg and its secluded, little-visited sandy beach of Silver Strand. The island you can see from here, **Rathlin O'Birne Island**, marks the northern entrance to Donegal Bay, and ruins of an early Christian hermitage are crumbling away on the island. Retrace your route to the junction, where a left turn leads to the *Glencolmcille Hotel*, and carry on to Glencolmcille this way. There is another sandy beach at Glencolmcille but, unlike Silver Strand, it is not safe for swimming.

Glencolmcille is a culturally vibrant, Irish-speaking area – the village itself is called Cashel and is basically one main street – well tuned to tourism but thankfully on its own terms. There is a spirit of independence here that was nurtured by that most rare breed in Ireland, a priest with a socialist conscience, who came here in 1951 to a community impoverished by emigration and government indifference. Father James McDyer spent 30 years encouraging community-based industries and a video about him can be seen in the Folk Village Museum that he established in the village. Informative displays on history and geology make this a useful first call when visiting the area and there are guided tours around a series of cottages devoted to aspects of local cultural life, including a shebeen and a schoolhouse. A shop sells local wines and some crafts, and there is a tearoom. Local guidebooks and brochures are available from the museum shop and from the combined **tourist office** (T30116, open Jun-Aug, daily 1000-1800) and **craft shop** in the main street; look for the lovely *Gleann Cholm Cille* guide (€7.50), illustrated in colour and including some of Rockwell Kent's paintings inspired by his stay here. ■ *T30017. Open Easter-Sep, Mon-Sat, 1000-1800, Sun, 1200-1800. €4.*

Folk Village Museum

An enjoyable walk, which is highly recommended, leads out of the village, past the Church of Ireland church and across a bridge, to the cliff top at **Glen Head** (769 ft/234 m) and an old watch tower built in the early 19th century when a French invasion was expected (another one can be seen at Malinbeg). There are superb views from here of the jagged **Sturral promontory**, and the walk can be continued by following the coastline to **Port** and then over Port Hill to the deserted and hauntingly lonely **valley of Glenlough**. This is where the American landscape painter Rockwell Kent (1882-1971) stayed, and where he was prevented from returning to live in the early 1950s because his government refused him a passport, on account of his left-wing sympathies and a visit to the Soviet Union. Some years later Dylan Thomas stayed in the same house in Glenlough, but he was not enamoured of the place and took off, leaving unpaid bills for food and accommodation. The walk from Glencolmcille to Glenlough will take about four hours, but you could also cycle or drive to Port and walk from there to Glenlough. *Ordnance Survey* Map No 10 in the Discovery series covers the walk.

Local walk

AL *Glencolmcille Hotel*, Malinmore, T30003, www.glenhotel.com The only hotel in the area. Family-run with great views over the Atlantic. **B** *Corner House*, Cashel, T30021. On the road to Ardara, 5 mins from the Folk Museum. Open Apr-Sep. **B** *Ros Mór*, Malinmore, T30083. A short way from Cashel, and overlooks Rathlin O'Birne Island. **C** *Atlantic Scene*, Dooey, T30186. Outside the village. Close to the hostel and shares with it breathtaking views of the Atlantic. **D** *Dooey Hostel*, T30130,

Sleeping
*Price codes:
see inside
front cover*

County Donegal

The Valley of Colm Cille

Glencolmcille is the anglicized form of Gleann Cholm Cille, the 'valley of Colm Cille', an important Irish saint (see page 518) up there with St Patrick and St Brigid. Colmcille (521-97), St Columba, achieved most fame after he left Ireland in 565 and established a church at Iona, but the ruins of more than one early church associated with him are to be found in southwest Donegal. Every 9th June there is a three-mile (five-km) pilgrimage walk, known as a turas, around a set of inscribed stones in Glencolmcille that is undertaken in bare feet and lasts up to four hours. On the 23rd June there is another turas in Teelin.

www.holidayhound.com/dooeyhostel/htm This honourable establishment was a founding member of the IHO, and is a mile (1.6 km) from the village. Superb location overlooking the bay and with part of the building built on to the rockface. Includes 6 private rooms and camping space.

Eating The *An Chistin Restaurant*, T30213, above *Foras Cultúir Uladh* (Ulster Cultural Institute) on the same road as the Folk Museum, is appropriately devoted to traditional Irish cooking and has fresh seafood on a daily basis, open 0930-2130. *Teach an Lása*, T30116/30363, is a restaurant and teashop above the Lace House in the main street, and seafood is also the speciality here at night. The Folk Museum has a tearoom serving home-made scones and light meals from 1000-1800, and the *Óstán Ghleann Cholm Cille* in the main street, T30003, has bar food and a small restaurant. Out at Malinbeg overlooking Donegal Bay, *Silver Strand House*, T30220, is a seafood restaurant worth checking out.

Pubs & music Glencolmcille is not Killarney, which means traditional music is not on tap, but when it is played in the pubs or at the fiddle festival in early Aug you can be sure you are hearing the real thing. *Roarty's Bar*, T30273, and *Glen Head Tavern*, T30008, both in Cashel, have fairly regular sessions.

Shopping A little south of the village on the R263 in Malin More Valley there is the *Glencolmcille Woollen Mill* shop, T30069, open daily during the summer, Mon-Fri 0930-2100, and at weekends 1000-1900. Quality knitwear is produced here in a small factory open to the public for demonstrations of knitting, hand-loomed spinning and hand-weaving of Donegal tweeds. As well as clothes, the shop stocks Donegal china, ceramics and jewellery. *Taipeis Gael*, T30325, taipeisgael@eircom.net, make art tapestries and hold tapestry-making courses. Mon-Fri all year. Handmade garments are also on sale at *Lace House*, and the craft shop in the Folk Museum has a range of knitwear, pottery and other handicrafts. Original paintings by Kenneth Ring are on sale in the *Marine Art Gallery*, Straide, T30126.

Sport **Outdoor activities** *Malinmore Outdoor Pursuits Centre*, T30123. Diving, canoeing, hill walking, boat trips and archaeological trails, among other activities.

Transport **Bicycle** *An Phríomhrsráid*, T39195. Bike hire. **Boat hire** T39117. **Bus** *McGeehan's* private buses, T075-46150/46101, connect Glencolmcille with Dublin, daily, via Carrick, Kilca, Killybegs, Ardara, Donegal and Cavan on one route and with Killybegs, Fintown and Letterkenny on their second route.

Directory **Irish language and culture courses** Between Apr and Oct a rich variety of courses is held around Glencolmcille and Glenfin. Irish language courses cater for complete novices as well as those wishing to improve their fluency, and the bilingual cultural activity programmes are open to all. For details of all the courses – Irish, hill-walking, archaeology, landscape and culture, marine painting, Donegal dances, celtic pottery, flute playing, bodhrán playing and tapestry weaving – contact *Oideas Gael*, Gleann Cholm Cille, Co. Dhún na nGall, Éire (Oideas Gael, Glencolmcille, Co. Donegal), T30248, F30348, oidsgael@iol.ie, www.oideas-gael.com Accommodation can be arranged. **Hospitals and medical services** Doctor: T30234.

Northern Donegal

North to Gweebara Bay

The road to Ardara from Glencolmcille travels through the Glengash Pass with its intoxicating views of Loughros Beg Bay, framed by mountains and luring one to take the road that is signposted on the left for Maghera and its caves. This road cuts its way through the rock, as does the magnificent Assarancagh Waterfall, passed on the route. A signposted way takes you to the beach in 15 minutes but don't explore the caves without checking the state of the tide. From Ardara there is an equally scenic five-mile (8-km) route leading out along the north side of the bay to the sparkling white stones at Loughros Point.

Phone code: 075
Colour map 1, grid B2
If you have a bike then cycle the minor road from Maghera to Port (11 miles/ 17 km) through lonely, unspoilt scenery

Ardara is a centre for the manufacture of handwoven tweed and handknit garments, and the **Heritage Centre** in the centre of town has an interesting exhibition on the history of the industry, with a weaver busy at work on the premises. ■ *T41704. Open Easter-Sep, Mon-Sat 1000-1800, Sun 1400-1800. €2.50. Café.* **Tourist information** is available at the entrance to the Heritage Centre, T41262.

Ardara

The Romanesque-style Catholic **church** in town has a startling wheel window at the west end: *Christ Among the Doctors*, designed by the Irish artist Evie Hone in 1953.

Dawros Head to the north of Ardara might look suitably remote on a map, but a vast sandy and safe beach at Narin and Portnoo and nearby camp and caravan sites combine to make this corner of Donegal very popular with families on holiday from other parts of Ulster. Come here outside of summer, however, and it's another proposition altogether. A picnic spot worth seeking out whatever the season is **Doon Fort**, situated on a tiny island in the middle of Lough Doon. To reach it, take the road signposted to Rosbeg on the road for Ardara outside of Narin, and then a right turn just past a school on to a narrow lane. Look for a sign advertising boats for hire on Doon Lake, and here a rowing boat can be rented for €5 to reach the fort.

Dawros Head

AL *Nesbitt Arms Hotel*, T41103, nesbitta@indigo.ie Small 19th-century hotel in the centre of town with restaurant. **AL** *Woodhill House*, T41112, yates@iol.ie Under 2 miles (3 km) from town taking Woodhill Rd from the Diamond. A 17th century country house this offers the best accommodation, and restaurant, in the area. **B** *Greenhaven*, Portnoo Rd, Ardara, T/F41129. Named after a shipwreck the ship's wheel and mast-head lamp of which now decorate the breakfast room. A comfortable place within walking distance of town. **C** *Brae House*, Front St, Ardara, T/F41296. In the centre of town, but with its own parking area. **C** *Whinecrest*, Loughros Point, T41254. Away from it all with miles of beach, a turf fire, and a piano in the guest room. Open Jun-Sep. **D** *Drumbaron Hostel*, the Diamond, Ardara, T41200. IHO hostel with over a dozen beds and 1 private room.

Sleeping
Price codes: see inside front cover

County Donegal

Camping *Dunmore Caravan and Camping Park*, Dawros Head, T45121. and *Tramore Beach Caravan & Camping Park*, Dawros Head, T51491.

Eating *Woodhill House Restaurant*, T41112, with a licensed bar and occasional music, has a well deserved reputation for good food; expect to pay around €32. The *Nesbitt Arms* does good basic meals with lots of fresh seafood. *L'Atlantique*, in Main St, T41707 does French cuisine, evenings only. There is a tearoom in the Heritage Centre serving sandwiches and cakes. There are 13 pubs in Ardara and some of them serve food in between their efforts at slaking the mighty thirst of the town. From the Diamond, cross the bridge for the road to Glenties and *Nancy's Bar*, T41187, serving toasties and meals, is on the right. *Charlie's West End Bar*, Main St, serves standard pub grub. Look out especially for The Beehive Bar.

Shopping There are many factory shops in Ardara and they are all worth sampling for their share of shirts, hats, caps, ties, socks, grandfather shirts, table linen, scarves, rugs and throws. Their tweeds and knitwear, which find their way into *Bloomingdales* and Liberty's, include items that are sold only in their own stores. In Front St you will find *Bonner*, T41303, and *Kennedy*, T41106, while *McGills*, T41262, is at the west end of Main St. Outside of town on the Killybegs Rd you can buy tweeds and knitwear from *John Molloy*, T41133, and in the summer there are free tours of the factory. In Cronkineen *Catherine Gallagher*, T41399, is a ceramic artist who hand paints and throws her own pieces, all individual.

Sport **Horse-riding** *Castle View Ranch*, T41212. Rides on the beach at Loughros Point.

Transport **Bicycle** *Don Byrne Bikes*, West End, Ardara, T41658. *Drumbaron Hostel* (see 'Sleeping' above). **Bus** *Bus Éireann*'s **Dublin** to **Donegal** service is extended to **Ardara** on a Fri. A local, Mon-Sat, service also runs between **Killybegs** and **Portnoo** via Ardara in Jul and Aug, and the rest of the year between Killybegs and Glenties via Ardara on Tue and Thu only, T074-21309. *McGeehan's Coaches*, T075-46150, also run through Ardara on routes to **Dublin**, **Glencolmcille** and **Letterkenny**.

Directory **Bank** Diamond, Ardara. **Communications** Post office: opposite the Ulster bank on the Diamond, Ardara.

Glenties and around

Phone code: 075
Colour map 1, grid B1
Brian Friel's play,
'Dancing at
Lughnasa', is set in
a house in Glenties

Glenties is as neat and pristine as you would expect for a four-times winner of the national Tidy Towns Award, and the town is a comfortable place to stop off for refreshments or even a night's stay to enjoy a night of traditional music in the many pubs. For quiet walks or cycle trips away from tourist attractions, there are scenic diversions to Dooey Point to the north and Fintown inland to the east, and the latter also provides an interesting route to Letterkenny and Derry, if there is not enough time to take in the northern coastline.

St Conal's
Museum &
Heritage
Centre

There is no tourist office in Glenties, but information is available from the hostel or **St Conal's Museum and Heritage Centre**, at the Ardara end of town which houses a miscellany of local memorabilia relating to the Famine era, a railway line which once serviced the town and other assorted bits and pieces. ■ *Jun-Sep, Mon-Fri, 1100-1300 and 1430-1700, Sat and Sun, 1430-1800.*

Dooey Point From Glenties the N56 goes north to Maas before crossing a bridge on the River Gweebarra and then, at Lettermacaward, a coast road is signposted to the left for Dooey Point at the end of the peninsula. The scenic road, with picnic

The Navvy Poet

Patrick MacGill (1889-1963) was 12 when he became a bonded servant at Strabane's hiring fair, a slave market by any other name, and two years later he was in Scotland as a 'tatie-hoker' (potato digger). Later a labourer on the railways, hence the 'navvy poet', MacGill wrote two novels – Children of the Dead End and The Rat-Pit – that shock the reader with their desolate tales of poverty and emigration. However,

they only came back into print in the 1980s. Perhaps no other writer has so successfully captured the Third World lifestyle of Ulster's poor and their stoical resistance, but his Glenmornan is also worth reading for its anti-clerical blast. Glenties, where the writer grew up as the eldest of 11 children, is home to an annual MacGill summer school, run by his niece Mary Clare O'Donnell. T51103.

tables along the way, ends in a cul-de-sac, but walking over the dunes from here leads to a long beach with fine views of the two bays.

The R250 from Glenties heads inland through bleak moorland and valley to Fintown, with poetic glimpses of the River Finn rushing into a lake surrounded by heather-coloured hills. A little way past the lake the R252 can be picked up for Ballybofey, where there is a very interesting hostel with horse-riding facilities and information on local walks in the hills (see 'Sleeping' below). Bikes can also be hired here, and if you want a couple of days away from Bord Fáilte land this is the place to stay.

Inland to Ballybofey

A *Highlands Hotel*, Main St, Glenties, T51111, highlandshotel@Ireland.com The only hotel in the area. Smallish, family run, good restaurant. **B** *Avalon*, Glen Rd, Glenties, T/F51292. B&B in a bungalow. **B** *Marguerite's*, Lower Main St, Glenties, T51699. Town house B&B. **C** *Aileach*, Station Rd, Glenties, T51326. Bungalow B&B. **D** *Campbell's Holiday Hostel*, Glenties, T51491, F51492. A welcoming place, on the left side of the road as you enter Glenties from Ardara. **D** *Finn Farm Hostel*, Cappry, Ballybofey, T074-32261. No need to book in advance at this hostel, where there is also camping space.

Sleeping
Price codes: see inside front cover

Not a great deal of choice, but the *Highlands Hotel* in the middle of Glenties is a comfortable hostelry with a comfortable and spacious eating area for bar food and meals, as well as a separate restaurant. A pasta dish or a vegetarian salad with brown bread and tea is €7 in the bar and in the hotel's *Owenea Restaurant*, T51111, grills, chicken, duck and fish dishes.

Eating

Glenties has some good pubs and *Keavney's*, Main St, T51333, is always worth a visit when sessions of traditional music are on. *Paddy's Bar*, Main St, T51158, usually has sessions on a Wed. *The Limelight & Molloy's Bar*, Main St, T51118, has a popular disco at weekends. *The Glen Tavern*, halfway between Glenties and Fintown, is famous for its musical entertainment on a Sat night.

Pubs & music

Bus *McGeehan's* buses, T46150, stop in Glenties and Fintown and so do *Bus Éireann's* Dublin – Donegal – Killybegs bus and the local Killybegs to Glenties service.

Transport

The Rosses

The Rosses is a rocky stretch of land, a stalwart Gaeltacht area, that takes in Dungloe in the south, Burtonport on the coast from where boats leave for Arranmore Island, and Crolly in the north.

Phone code: 075
Colour map 1, grid A1

County Donegal

Ins & outs **Getting there** *McGeehan's Coaches*, T46150, have a daily service in the summer between Dublin and Burtonport via Dungloe, Donegal and Enniskillen. *Feda O'Donnell* buses, T48114, run a limited service between Annagry to Killybegs, which stops in Dungloe, but check which days the bus operates. *O'Donnell Buses*, T48356, run a daily service that leaves Donegal early in the morning to reach Belfast at noon via Derry and stopping at Dungloe, Burtonport, Dunfanaghy, Cresslough and Letterkenny. *Bus Éireann* does not serve the Rosses.

Dungloe & Dungloe (An Clochán Liath) is not a particularly attractive place and, apart
Burtonport from having a meal here, there is little reason to stay. There is a small **tourist office** in Main Street. ■ *T21297. Jun-Sep, Mon-Sat 1000-1300 and 1400-1800.*

At the end of July and beginning of August the annual **Mary from Dungloe Festival** livens up the town, but the festival itself is an utterly synthetic event dating from the 1960s, which serves mainly as an excuse for late-night drinking.

Burtonport (Ailt an Chorráin) is the departure point for Arranmore Island, which is the main attraction of the Rosses. The small town is also a centre for sea angling and fishing trips can be organized with the Burtonport Sea Angling and Boating Centre on their 36-ft (11-m) boat. ■ *T/F42077.*

Sleeping A *Atlantic House*, Main St, Dungloe, T21061. Guest house in centre of town. B *Campbells Pier House*, Burtonport, T42017. Close to the pier and convenient for trips to and from Arranmore. B *Park House*, Burtonport, T21351. Caters especially for fishing folk. B *Sea View*, Mill Rd, Dungloe, T21353. B&B, which overlooks Dungloe Bay and is walkable from the town. D *Greene's Hostel*, Cornmare Rd, Dungloe, T21943. Has over 20 beds. Bike hire, family rooms and doubles, open all year.

Eating The *Riverside Bistro*, Main St, T21062, does basic potato meals in large servings. *Ostan n Rossan*, is a hotel with a pleasant dining room doing fairly traditional food. In Burtonport, the affordable *Lobster Pot Restaurant* in the main street, T42012, serves seafood and meat and has *Kelly's Bar* alongside.

Arranmore Island

Ins & outs **Getting there and around** *Arranmore Island Ferries Service*, T20532, runs an
Colour map 1, grid A1 all-year service from Burtonport. In Jul and Aug there are 8 boats departing daily (7 on Sun) from 0830 to 2000 and returning between 0900 and 2030. Between Apr and Jun, and in Sep, there are 6 to 7 journeys a day, and around 5 a day the rest of the year. €9 return for passengers, €26 return for a car and driver.

Arranmore Island

The boat trip to Arranmore, 5½ miles by 3 miles (9 km by 5 km), takes 25 mins; while there are places to stay overnight, a day trip with picnic provisions is feasible because the island can be walked around in a day if you catch the first and last ferries.

Most of the 900 inhabitants live on the eastern side of the island, around where the ferry lands at **Leabgarrow**, and to the south around **Aphort**, but to enjoy a spot of ornithology and

The Gaeltacht

The Gaeltacht means areas where Irish is still spoken: despite sustained government encouragement and vigorous support from concerned groups, some people claim that the term is becoming more and more notional because spoken Irish is in terminal decline. Supporters, however, can point to the burgeoning applications for places on language summer schools, the Irish-language television and radio stations, and places such as Glencolmcille and the Rosses where spoken Irish seems alive and well. Donegal has the largest Gaeltacht areas in the country but pockets can also be found in Connemara, Dingle, the Ring area west of Waterford, Ballingeary in Cork, west Mayo near Belmullet and a vigorous community in County Meath where Gaeltacht families were resettled in the 1930s.

views from high ground, head inland from Leabgarrow on the road that ends at the lighthouse in the northwest. Another enjoyable walk goes to **Torries** in the southwest, looking across to uninhabited **Green Island**. It is also to possible to follow the little known **Arranmore Way**, which is signposted on the island with colour-coded routes, but unfortunately the Way is not regularly waymarked and is not indicated on the relevant *Ordnance Survey* map, No 1. Call in at the shop next to *Phil Bans Bar* for an island map that does show the route.

B *Glen Hotel*, T20505. One-star establishment to the west of the ferry, with 10 rooms. **Sleeping**
C *Bonners Bed and Breakfast*, T20532. Conveniently situated close to where the ferry **& eating** lands. By the pier, *Bonners* also manage the *Ferryboat Restaurant*, T20532, which serves standard meals, or there is the small restaurant at the hotel. Some of the 6 pubs on the island serve light meals, including *Phil Ban's Bar* near the pier in Leabgarrow and *O'Donnell's* at Aphort.

Upper Rosses

If not visiting Arranmore, the chances are you will skip the Upper Rosses by *Colour map 1, grid A1* travelling directly between Dungloe and Crolly, but the road via Burtonport and Annagry has mixed diversions along the way, including a signposted road that leads to **Cruit Island** across a small bridge. There are beaches and scenic views of the bay that on a sunny day make a quiet destination for a picnic.

Back on the road to Annagry the village of **Kincasslagh** has local fame for its hotel, the *Viking House* owned by the inordinately popular Irish singer, Daniel O'Donnell, who hails from here. Beyond the village are the reedy waters of **Mullaghderg Lough**, near where a sign points to tiny **Donegal airport**. The road continues on to a T-junction, where it meets the N56 just outside the village of Crolly (Croithlí), which marks the boundary with the Gweedore area. Just before the village a sign points the way to *Leo's Tavern*, Menalck, home to both the group Clannad and the singer Enya, with gold and platinum discs lining the pub's walls and regular singsongs in the evening

A *Viking House*, T43295. Hotel owned by Daniel O'Donnell. A couple of miles outside **Sleeping** of Crolly the **D** *Screag An Iolair Mountain Centre*, Tor, T48593, is a hostel that receives **& eating** rave reviews from travellers who enjoy the physical and metaphysical comfort of a laid-back retreat some 800 ft (250 m) up in the mountains. Open Mar-late Oct, with 15 beds, 3 private rooms, and a free pick-up from Crolly or Gweedore if you arrange this in advance. This is the place to stay if you desire rural bliss with sociable evenings thrown in as a bonus.

County Donegal

Gweedore to Dunfanaghy

Phone code: 075
(Tory Island and
Gortahork to
Dunfanaghy: 074)
Colour map 1, grid A2

There are two routes between Gweedore and Gortahork: the coastal R257 road that runs west of Gweedore to Bunbeg, Derrybeg and Magheroarty before rejoining the N56 just before Gortahork, and the main N56 itself that travels inland.

Coastal route

This accesses the departure point for ferries to Tory Island from Bunbeg and Magheroarty, but as it passes on through Bunbeg and neighbouring Derrybeg there is little reason to stop until reaching a viewing point off the road at **Bloody Foreland**. The name suggests the site of another ungodly massacre from a chapter of Ireland's relations with the English, so it comes as a pleasant surprise to discover that the term refers to the startling red hue that the setting sun casts on the rocks. As the R257 continues eastwards the unmistakable outline of Tory Island stays in view and Horn Head rears up in the east.

Inland route

The N56 has its own unforgettable charisma as it takes you through empty countryside so shockingly beautiful that you will wonder what everyone is doing in Killarney when places like this exist. About 9 miles (15 km) south of Falcarragh look for a sign pointing down a road off the N56, the R251, to the Errigal youth hostel and the **Dunlewy Lakeside Centre** (*Ionad Cois Locha*) 2 miles (3 km) away by the side of Lough Dunlewy (also spelt Dunlewey). Here, in the shadow of the distinctively shaped Errigal, there is a tiny village where a famed weaver, Manus Ferry, lived and worked until his death in the mid-1970s. His home is now the centre for weaving and spinning displays and a craft shop selling Donegal tweeds, paintings, pottery and other crafts. There are story-telling trips on a 50-seater boat on the lough, activities for children, a reasonably priced restaurant and tearoom, and traditional music on a Tuesday night in July and August. ■ *T31699. Easter-Oct, Mon-Sat, 1030-1800, Sun 1100-1900. €4.50 for house and grounds. €4.50 boat trips. €8 combined ticket.*

From Dunlewy, signs point the way to the **Poisoned Glen**, which most probably got its name from local spurges with a distinctive milky sap (*Euphorbia peplus* and *Euphorbia amygdaloides*), a perfectly benign and beautiful place that is wonderful for walking.

Mt Errigal

A climb up the quartzite cone of Mt Errigal (2,467 ft/752 m) is highly recommended because there are unsurpassed views of the county from the summit and, as long as you choose a suitable day when winds or visibility are not a problem, it is a reasonably manageable hike that takes less than four hours. There are various well trod paths up the mountain, and a good place to start is from the R251, a little way past the Errigal youth hostel: it may be worth calling in here or at the Lakeside Centre (see above) for suggested routes. Whatever route is taken, the walk begins by walking across boggy grass and up the slope to the ridge of the summit, where a series of cairns mark the way. From here you should be able to see from Malin Head on the Inishowen Peninsula to Slieve League in the south. Map No 1 in the *Ordnance Survey* Discovery series covers the walk.

Sleeping

Price codes:
see inside front cover

L-AL *Ostán Gweedore Hotel*, Bunbeg, T31177, www.ostangweedore.com Good views and its own pool and leisure centre, which attracts families during school holidays. **AL** *Ostán Radharc Na Mara* (Sea View Hotel), Bunbeg, T31159, ostanradharcnamara@eircom.net Has rooms just a little less costly than the Gweedore. **B** *Bunbeg House*, T31305. By the harbour in Bunbeg. **C** *Ocean Lodge*, Bloody Foreland,

County Donegal

Brinlack, T32084. A quieter place where you can sleep with views of Bloody Foreland from the window. Double rooms for €19 per person and a €2.50 supplement for a single. **D** *An Óige Errigal Hostel*, Dunlewy, T31180. In a perfect position if you're going to climb Mt Errigal: 3 km to the northwest of the village and stays open all year. **D** *Backpacker's Ireland Lakeside Hostel*, Dunlewy, T32133. IHO hostel, ideally placed for climbing Donegal's highest mountain, Errigal. Opens from 17 Mar to end of Oct, has 30 beds including 8 private rooms and bikes for hire.

There is a good restaurant at the *Ostán Gweedore Hotel*, overlooking the Atlantic from where the seafood on the menu has been caught, with an evening meal around €32. The restaurant at the *Ostán Radharc Na Mara* (Sea View Hotel) is less expensive, and bar food is available at both hotels. The *Lakeside Centre Restaurant* is good value for lunch but closes early in the evening. There are a few pubs, cafés and fast-food-type places scattered along the road between Dunbeg and Derrybeg and while none are worth singling out, they will suffice for a quick bite.

Eating

Tory Island

Donegal Coastal Cruises, T31991/31340, from Bunbeg, Jun-Sep at 0900, returning at 1800, or from Magheraroarty at 1130, 1330 and 1700, returning at 1030, 1230 and 1600. There is usually 1 sailing a day from Bunbeg between Oct and May. Always check departure times as the schedule varies according to the season, the tides and the weather. €20 return. Bike hire is available on the island from T65614.

Getting there
Colour map 1, grid A2

Wind-swept Tory Island, under 4 miles long and only a mile wide (6 km by 2km), was infamously difficult to reach or leave, until a new 40-minute ferry-boat service was introduced a few years back. It lies 7 miles (11 km) off the mainland and the boat ride there is an excursion in itself as it churns its way along the rocky northwest coast and then out to sea to the island. St Colmcille founded a monastery on Tory in the sixth century, and there are scanty monastic remains and the ruins of a round tower made, uniquely, from rounded beach stones. A day trip allows time for invigorating walks around the island and some bird-watching, but there are a couple of places to stay and two pubs to while away an evening. The island's hotel has one of these pubs, *The People's Bar*, and any entertainment, like evening sessions of music, will be advertised here. What might inspire a longer stay is a visit beforehand to *Glebe Gallery* (see page 518), where there are some excellent examples of paintings by Tory Island painters who were inspired to paint by Derek Hill when he visited Tory.

Tales of life on Tory, from childbirth to wakes and a bit of poitín-making along the way, are collected in 'Stories from Tory Island' (see page 678)

AL *Ostán Thóraigh*, Oileán Thóraigh, T/F35920. A fairly new hotel with 14 beds, but it closes between Jan and Mar. **B** *Ms Grace Duffy*, East Town, T35136. Opens all year for B&B. **D** *Tory Hostel*, Seaview, T65145. Open from Apr to Oct, and camping is also possible, though there are no private rooms. The *Ostán Thóraigh* is the best place for a meal; expect to pay around €31 for a seafood dinner. *Ms Grace Duffy*'s B&B can do an evening meal for around €15. There is also *Creggan Restaurant*, T35856. *Tory Social Club*, T65121 has regular sessions of traditional music and ceili dancing.

Sleeping & eating

Gortahork to Dunfanaghy

Gortahork and Falcarragh are two small villages strung out along the coastal N56 road that leads to Dunfanaghy. During the day nothing much happens, but at night the pubs are lively enough and sessions of traditional music occur

Colour map 1, grid A2

County Donegal

on an irregular and impromptu basis. From Falcarragh there are small roads at both ends of the long main street that lead down to a stupendous stretch of wild and lonely beach; beware of swimming here, an unpredictable undercurrent has caused accidents.

Sleeping
Price codes:
see inside front cover

B *Ferndale*, Main St, Falcarragh, T65506. At the Gortahork end of the village, a large bungalow with 4 bedrooms, open Apr-Sep for B&B. **D** *Baile Conaille*, Falcarragh, T35363. Huge hostel with beds for 140 guests and private and family rooms. Take the coast road from the village and the entrance is signposted on the right. **D** *Shamrock Lodge Hostel*, Main St, Falcarragh, T35859. Above a busy pub and, depending on your tastes, this will be either a bonus or a blight. Private rooms.

Eating

In Falcarragh, *Mighty Mac's Café* is right in the centre of the village with a menu of chicken, lasagne, curry, baguettes. The nearby *Gweedore* pub has a restaurant upstairs serving standard meals in the evening. Inexpensive meat and vegetarian meals are available at *Baile Conaill*.

Dunfanaghy

Phoen code: 074
Colour map 1, grid A2

Dunfanaghy, tucked on the edge of a long inlet of Sheephaven Bay with majestic Horn Head to the north and flat-topped Muckish Mountain to the south, has a more rounded appeal than Falcarragh. There are better amenities and Horn Head offers irresistible clifftop walks or a scenic tour by bicycle or car, *tour de force* scenery and a safe beach for swimming. In the village itself there is an interesting museum devoted to local history.

The workhouse

The workhouse was built in 1844 for 300 'paupers', but that figure swelled to over 5,000 during the Famine; it evolved into a hospital and home, which closed in 1922. The place reopened recently as a museum and study centre with sensitively presented material. A nine-minute audio-visual show sets the scene for the exhibition area that tells its tale through the true story of a workhouse resident who died in 1926. A study room has books on the Famine to consult and an audio-visual on the local ecology; a craft shop and a coffee shop complete an admirable centre for visitors. On your visit, ask about the occasional sessions of traditional music and storytelling that take place in the evening. ■ *Main St, T36540. Easter-Oct, Mon-Fri 1000-1700, Sat and Sun 1200-1700. €4.50. No charge for art exhibition, shop, café or study room.*

Sleeping
Price codes:
see inside
front cover

LL *Shandon Hotel & Leisure Centre*, Marble Hill Strand, T36137, shandonhotel@eircom.net Enhanced by a seaside location, with its own grounds sliding down to the beach, a leisure centre, bar and restaurant and bedrooms that mostly face south for the unbeatable views. **L-AL** *Arnold's Hotel*, T36208, arnoldshotel@eircom.net Has been in the same family for 3 generations and travellers have recommended it for comfort and friendliness. **AL** *Carrig-Rua Hotel*, T36133, carrigruahotel@eircom.net Formerly the *Stewart Arms Hotel*, named after the Scottish landlord who created the village. Very accommodating. **B** *Carrigan House*, Kill, T/F36276. B&B 5 mins from the village on foot. **B** *Rosman House*, T/F36273, rossman@eircom.net B&B in a large bungalow with above-average room amenities and evening meals for around €19. **C** *Rockhaven*, Kill, T36159. A good-value B&B overlooking Sheephaven Bay. **D** *Corcreggan Mill*, T36409. Hostel on the N56 2 miles (3 km) west of Dunfanaghy, has some character with beds in the main house and adjoining wheel-less railway carriage, and a small camping space outside.

Both hotels do pub food and the *Carrig-Rua Hotel* has the *Copper Grill* for informal **Eating**
meals and the more elegant *Sheephaven Restaurant* with fresh seafood the highlight of
the menu. The restaurant in *Arnold's Hotel* benefits from seaviews. *Danny Collins*,
T36205, is a pub and affordable restaurant in the centre of the village. The Workhouse's
modern, airy café with flagged floor, open fire and art-work for sale, is fine for cakes.

On the main road to the southeast of Dunfanaghy, at Port Na Blagh, *The Cove Restaurant*, T074-36300, open daily 1000-2200, has a local reputation for quality seafood
and meat dishes.

Next door to the workhouse, *The Gallery*, T36224, has a vast collection of pottery, **Shopping**
clothes, handbags, prints and jewellery, besides its main gallery of paintings for sale. In
the coffee shop at the Workhouse, shifting art exhibitions of work are also for sale. In
the village centre is also *McAuliffe's* craft shop, T36135, with knitwear and handcrafts
and a overseas mailing service.

Golf *Dunfanaghy*, T36335. 18-hole. **Horse-riding** *Dunfanaghy Stables, Arnold's* **Sport**
Hotel, Dunfanaghy, T36208. **Sea angling** *Dunfanaghy Angling Association*, T36208.
Pat Robinson, Kill, Dunfanaghy, T36290, F36505, Dessie McGilloway, T074 66197,
Port-na-Blagh.

Bus *O'Donnell Buses*, T48356, run a daily service that leaves Donegal early in the **Transport**
morning to reach Belfast at noon via Derry, stopping at Dungloe, Burtonport,
Dunfanaghy, Cresslough and Letterkenny.

Around Dunfanaghy

In his book *The Way That I Went* (see page 681) RL Preger was not exaggerat- **Horn Head**
ing when he labelled Horn Head the "finest headland on the Irish coastline". *Phone code: 074*
The signposted Horn Head Drive circles its eastern side and, if only cars were *Colour map 1, grid A2*
banned from driving around it, a trip around the headland on a bicycle would
be a highlight of any visit to Ireland. Modern farming methods have destroyed
the haunts of the now-endangered corncrake, but the area around
Dunfanaghy is one of the few places where it can still, occasionally, be heard.
Horn Head is alive with birds: gannets dive-bombing vertically into the
ocean, puffed-up puffins, the not-so-common chough (like a blackbird but
with red legs), guillemots, storm petrels. It takes a good six hours to walk the
11 miles (18 km) around the perimeter of Horn Head, and in places there are
mildly scary stretches along the clifftop. A lot of walkers prefer to stick to the
west and north sides by walking across the Horn Head bridge for an
easy-going jaunt across the dunes and along Tramore Strand and, further
north, Pollaguill Bay and its smaller beach. From here follow a ruined stone
wall to **Marble Arch**, a tremendous arch in the rock formed by nature over the
millennia. If you are driving, go clockwise; the road is very narrow.

The N56 road passes through the village of Cresslough, and here what will **Cresslough**
surely catch your eye is the flowing white curvature of **St Michael's Church**, **& beaches**
designed to reflect the formidably solid outline of Muckish (*An Mhucais*
being 'the pig's back'). The church, built in 1970 and influenced by Le
Corbusier's ecclesiastical work at Ronchamp, adds a delightful touch of modernism perfectly at ease with rugged north Donegal. Inside, etched in glass, are
the names of the architects, builders and artists who brought this elegant
building into existence.

County Donegal

For a scenic detour follow the signposted road on the left, coming into the village from Port Na Blagh, for a Capuchin friary established here in the 1960s. A half-mile walk (800 m) from the friary leads down to tiny **Monk's Beach**, usually only visited by locals, while another half-hour walk leads on to the lovely **Silver Strand**. One quarter of all Ireland's beaches are in Donegal, and these are two of the lesser-known ones. **Marble Hill Strand**, a more populous beach safe for swimming and windsurfing, is reached by turning off at Port Na Blagh, and there are canoes and boogie boats for hire. The beach you can see on the other side of Sheephaven Bay is Rosapenna. **Ards Forest Park**, signposted off the N56 and free to enter, offers a quieter and more rural destination, with nature trails winding their way through the former estate of the Scottish landlord who once owned this land and Horn Head.

Doe Castle The sturdy, romantically sited fortress of Doe – built in the early 16th century by the MacSweeneys, and said to have provided refuge to some shipwrecked Spanish Armada sailors in 1588 – was constantly fought over throughout the 17th century. An English assault on the castle early in the century, headed by Sir Oliver Lambert, led him to exclaim that it was "the strongest hold in all the province which endured 100 blows of the demi-cannon before it yielded". A Captain George Vaughan Hart, his initials are over the door, converted the castle into a home in the early 1800s and the last occupant by one account was a Victorian rector from Cresslough who had nowhere else to live. ■ *3 miles (5 km) from Cresslough, signposted off the road, N56, to Carrigart. Free.*

Carrigart and the Rosguill peninsula

Phone code: 074
Colour map 1, grid A2

Carrigart is a little village between Sheephaven Bay and the Fanad Peninsula: it opens the door for the gratifying Rosguill Peninsula with its signposted seven-mile (12-km) **Atlantic Drive** that takes you past the resort of **Downings**, known for its popular caravan ground. During summer weekends, and particularly the August bank holiday period, the Atlantic Drive has its share of vehicles but at otherwise the road provides an enjoyable route for cycling and walking, with photogenic views of Horn Head and Tory Island. A recommended destination is the extremity at **Melmore Head** (Meall Mor), passing a hostel occupying a hunting lodge designed by Lutyens and a signpost pointing the way to the ruined Meagh Church with its ancient Latin cross and Ogham stone.

Sleeping A *Hotel Carrigart*, Carrigart, T55114, carrigarthotel@eircom.net Built in 1882, with its
Price codes: mansard-style façade, plus one of Ireland's first hotel swimming pools and a challenging
see inside front cover links golf course, this hotel is in the middle of the village and the friendly owner is a mine of local information. **B** *Beach Hotel*, Downings, T55303. Can get busy, but it's the only hotel on the Rosguill Peninsula. **B** *Shorewinds*, T55790. B&B with 4 bedrooms at €19-€21.50 per person in doubles and €6.35 extra for a single, unless the room is unbooked by 2100. **C** *Mevagh House*, Carrigart, T55693. Just outside the village and close to beaches. Opens all year **D** *Trá na Rosann*, Downings, T55374. *An Óige*'s most northerly hostel in Ireland, open Easter-Sep, is 3½ miles (6 km) from Downings.

Eating The old-fashioned and spacious dining room of the *Hotel Carrigart* has dinner for under €32. The *Weavers Restaurant* across the road serves inexpensive meals for under €13 and the bars do pub grub. *McNutts*, Downings, T53314, is a coffee shop where a good seafood lunch and homebaked goodies are always available. *McNutts* run a tweed shop next door, which also sells pottery and mails worldwide. In Magherabeg is *Ocean View*, T54970,. Nice location and views, good reputation locally.

In Downings, the *Fleet Inn* attracts youngsters off the caravan site, and they set the tone **Pubs & music** at the discos that take place here during the summer. The *Harbour Bar* is quiet during the day but a younger crowd livens it up at night.

If the Downings pubs don't appeal to you then take the road from Carrigart to the minuscule village of Glen and the *Old Glen Bar*, where locals and knowledgeable visitors escape for a quiet drink. The television over the bar comes only on for a sports fixture (though Manchester United fans will find no comrades here) and there is the occasional burst of live music. Another heartwarming, traditional bar is *The Singing Pub* on the Atlantic Drive road, which has good music and good food.

Angling 3-hour trips for mackerel off a boat, T55386, depart from Downings at 1300 **Sport** and 1800, Mon to Fri, gear provided and cost depends on number of people. **Horse-riding** *Carrigart Riding Course*, T53583.

Banks There is one bank in the centre of Carrigart. **Directory**

The Fanad Peninsula

Travelling south from Carrigart and reaching nondescript Milford, the R246 *Phone code: 074* can be taken for an approach up the west side of the Fanad Peninsula but it's *Colour map 1, grid A2* hard to think of a good reason for making this journey because the scenery is unspectacular and there is nothing that compels a stop. The west coast has far more to recommend it, but if time is limited and a choice has to be made, the Inishowen Peninsula further east wins hands down in terms of stirring scenery.

Rathmelton is the first town on the west coast and though its slightly rickety **Rathmelton** appearance is not instantly endearing, the place can grow on you and a picnic could be enjoyed on the quayside overlooking the River Leannan (also spelled Lennon), as it flows past towards Lough Swilly. Behind you stand some ramshackle but attractively gaunt warehouses that date back to the second half of the 19th century when Ramelton prospered from corn mills, linen works and a brewery. The Meeting House in the village, now restored as a genealogical centre, dates back to the 17th century when Rathmelton was laid out by William Stewart, a Scottish planter. ■ *T51266*.

You'll see signs to **Killydonnell Friary**, 4 miles (6 km) away, and though only the ruins remain, the tranquil setting is another inviting picnic spot. The River Leannan is a favourite cast for salmon and, though the nearest place for gear and tackle is Letterkenny (see page 516), fishing packages can be arranged through the *Bridge Bar*, T51119.

Sleeping B *Crammond House*, Market Sq, T51055. B&B in an 18th-century house *Price codes:* near the old grain miller's building. **C** *Lough View House*, Glenleary, T51550. A com- *see inside* fortable 2-storey house overlooking the lough and village, which stays open all year. *front cover* **C-D** *Lennon Lodge*, T51227/8. Round the corner from Crammond House, with some private rooms with bathroom. A good modern kitchen and a lounge for guests.

Eating The *Mirabeau Restaurant*, The Mall, T51138, does steaks and seafood, with a set dinner at €21.60. *The Bridge Bar*, signposted after crossing the bridge coming into town from the south, T51119, has a fish restaurant upstairs with reasonably priced dishes. *Lennon Lodge Cultural Centre*, T51055, is basically a pub that has bar food all day, with traditional music on a Thu night from 2130 and live music of some kind at weekends. (Around the time of opening a passing wag quipped that 'Agri'(cultural) was missing from the large sign above the place.)

Rathmullan
Phone code: 074
Colour map 1, grid A3

There are satisfying views of Lough Swilly from Rathmelton to Rathmullan, and as you approach the village the ruins of **Rathmullan Priory** are on your right. From just outside this Carmelite friary, founded in the 15th century, an event took place in September 1607, when "leaving their horses on the shore with no one to hold their bridles, they went aboard a ship". The "they" in question included the earls of Tyrone and Tyrconnell, and their departure, with other members of the cream of Irish aristocracy, signalled the end of a millennium of Gaelic rule in Ireland, and the *Annals of the Four Masters* (see box on page 496) recorded the significance of the event known to history as the Flight of the Earls: "Woe to the heart that meditated, woe to the mind that conceived, woe to the council that decided on, the project of their setting out on this voyage."

In the centre of Rathmullan village the **Heritage Centre** unfolds the historical background and consequences of the event through a series of text-based displays. If the lovely safe beach at Rathmullan tempts you to stay in the area the Heritage Centre also doubles as an unofficial tourist information office. ■ *T58178, Easter to mid-Sep, Mon-Sat, 1000-1800, Sun, 1200-1800.* €2.

Sleeping **LL** *Fort Royal Hotel*, T58100, fortroyal@eircom.net Good reputation for comfort and for food, set in private grounds with its own beach and tennis courts. **LL** *Rathmullan House*, Lough Swilly, T58188, rathhse@iol.ie 19th-century hotel with award-winning gardens, indoor pool and top-notch breakfasts. **B** *Pier Hotel*, T58178. Gregarious place in the centre of the village. **C** *Eileen Gallagher*, Pier Rd, T58177. Modern town house 100m from the beach offering B&B.

Eating For good food in the €38 bracket, the *Fort Royal Hotel* and *Rathmullan House* are contenders, and our vote goes to the country-house style of Rathmullan House. More affordable meals can be enjoyed at the *Ferrygate Restaurant*, T58131, just around the corner from the *Pier Hotel* as you head north.

The pleasant *Beachcomber Bar*, the first pub you see when coming into the village from Ramelton, does not do food, but a quiet drink can be enjoyed here with views of the water and outdoor tables by the beach. Try *The Water's Edge*, 58182, new olde-worlde restaurant with huge windows and views over Lough Swilly. Bar food served all day and dinner should come into the mid-range. If you like the place they also do B&B.

Fanad Head

The journey to the northern tip of the peninsula is signposted as the Fanad Drive and includes, a little way before the village of Portsalon, a viewing point that looks down on Ballymastocker Bay and its triple array of beaches. A left turn in the village of Portsalon, where there really is nothing to detain you, leads on along the coast to Fanad Head and a lighthouse. The nearby *Lighthouse Tavern*, T59212, serves light meals like garlic mussels with brown bread and chicken sandwiches until around 2100.

Letterkenny

Phone code: 074
Colour map 1, grid A2

Letterkenny is County Donegal's largest town, a thriving commercial centre with good transport links and supermarkets but with little of intrinsic interest. A number of main roads converge on the town, from Donegal in the west and Derry in the east, while the N56 heads up to the northern coast accessing Glenveagh National Park and the must-see Glebe House (see page 518) along the way. Letterkenny is a good place to stop over for a meal or collect provisions for a picnic on the Fanad or Inishowen Peninsula. The town also has some indoor activities, including the local history **Donegal County Museum**. ■ *High St, T24613. Tue-Fri, 1100-1230 and 1300-1630, Sat, 1300-1630. Free.*

On the R250 Churchill Rd the **Newmills Corn and Flax Mills** is a complex of machinery powered by one of the largest watermills in Ireland, using the power of the River Swilly. ■ *T25115. Mid-Jun to mid-Sep, daily 1000-1830. Dúchas site. 3 miles (5 km) from Letterkenny. €2.50.*

The **tourist office** is a couple of kilometres out of town on the Derry road, T21160. Open Jul-Aug, Mon-Fri, 0900-2000, Sat, 1000-1400, Sun 0900-1700.

L-AL *Holiday Inn*, T24369. This is a shiny new branch of the chain hotel. **L-AL** *Castle Grove Country House Hotel*, Ballymaleel, T51118, www.castlegrove.com 17th-century country house turned hotel. Overlooks Lough Swilly with lots of grounds, drawing room, library, classy dining room. **L-AL** *Mount Errigal Hotel*, T22700, F25805. This busy hotel rests about a mile east of town with leisure centre including pool, nightly entertainment.

B *Glencairn*, T24393. A large house with television and tea in the bedrooms, fairly typical of the B&Bs in town. **B** *Hill Crest House*, Lurgyback, Sligo Rd, T22300. On the N13 road to Ballybofey, just over a mile (2 km) from town, has good beds and facilities in the rooms. **C** *Killerein House*, Ballaghderg, T24563. On the N56 road to Glenveagh National Park and there is a pub a few minutes away serving meals. **D** *The Manse Hostel*, High Rd, T25238. A well organized Victorian detached house open all year and includes 8 private rooms for €20.50 each. Bikes for hire. **D** *Port Hostel*, 24 Port Rd, T26288. This hostel, near the cinema, which doesn't belong to any of the hostel organizations, is the least satisfying of the 2. If no one answers the door, enquire at the small shop next door.

Sleeping
Price codes:
see inside front cover

Eating places are competitively priced, and while there is nowhere really special, *The Mews*, 25 Lower Main St, T26867, is one of the better places to eat inexpensively in the town centre. At weekends the set dinner comes with a bottle of wine and is very good value for money. A carvery is available Mon to Sat between 1200 and 1500. The *Yellow Pepper*, 36 Lower Main St, T24133, is a bistro-style café with a wine bar open for breakfast, lunch and dinner 1030-2200 Mon to Sat, and 1600-2000 on Sun. A catholic menu of inexpensive chicken, fish, pasta and vegetarian meals.

The *Beanery*, Market Sq, T28883, at the entrance to the pedestrianized Market Centre shopping area in the middle of Main St, is justly popular for its range of decent coffees and light meals; it is on 2 floors, open daily. Student specials are highlighted in the front window. *The Quiet Moment* is a new tea-shop and sandwich bar that has opened on Upper Main St next to Gallagher's hotel. Across the road, *Galfee's* advertises itself as a gourmet takeaway, and light meals are available inside.

Eating

Quite a few pubs in the town centre have music, but the nights vary, and it is not always of the traditional kind. *McGinleys*, 25 Lower Main St, T21106, can be relied for traditional sessions on Mon nights and other places worth checking out include *Downtown*, 19 Lower Main St, T25291, and *Brewery Bar*, Market St, T27330.

The *An Grianan Theatre*, Port Rd. T24950, is host to both local and international music, theatre and dance performances.

Pubs & music

Bowling *Letterkenny Bowling Centre*, Ballyraine, T26000; Cinema Port Rd, T21976. **Fishing** *McCormick's*, 56 Upper Main St, T27833. Fishing gear. West Donegal Sea Angling Charters, Annagry east, T075 48403, mosh@indigo.ie **Squash** *Squash Club*, Lower Main St, T26706.

Sport

Bus From *Bus Éireann's* large bus station, T21309, daily buses run to and from **Dublin**, **Galway**, **Westport**, **Sligo**, **Derry**, **Enniskillen** and **Belfast**. Private bus companies also stop near here, including *John McGinley's* daily service, T35201, between **Cresslough** and **Dublin** via Letterkenny, *McGeehan's*, T075-46150, daily route between **Glencolmcille** and Letterkenny. *Busway's*, T077-82619, daily services to **Inishowen**,

Transport

Derry and Dublin leave from opposite *Bus Éireann's* station and from *Charlie's Café* on Pearse St. **Taxis** *Letterkenny Cabs*, T1800-272000. *Swilly Cabs*, T1800-216666.

Directory Banks On Main St and Port Rd. **Bookshop** *Browse-A-While*, Upper Main St. **Communications** Post office: Upper Main St. **Hospitals and medical services** Hospital: *St Conals*, T21022. **Supermarket** *Dunnes Stores* at the end of Main St.

Around Letterkenny

Colmcille Heritage Centre The life story of St Colmcille (see box on page 504) is told through illustrated panels and a wax model and there are other displays on the era that gave rise to Ireland's epithet as the "land of saints and scholars". Perhaps the most engrossing displays are those that cover the craft of ancient manuscript-making. ■ *Gartan, Churchill, T37306. Easter week and from first Sun in May to last Sun in Sep, Mon-Sat 1030-1830, Sun 1300-1830. €3.*

Glebe House & Gallery
The best value €3 spent anywhere in Ireland is the cost of admission to Glebe House & Gallery

Everything about this house is a wonderful surprise. Inside you will find paintings by Picasso, Kokoschka, Jack Yeats, Passmore and Bonnard, not to mention some work by the Tory Island painters that Derek Hill, the man who made Glebe House so special, inspired to take up a brush and easel. Hill decorated his Regency house with William Morris textiles alongside superb touches of Islamic and other oriental art. To cap it all there are beautiful gardens that sweep down to the lake shore. ■ *T37071. Easter week and mid-May to 27th Sep, Sat-Thu 1100-1830. €3. Coffee shop. Situated 11 miles (18 km) from Letterkenny on R251.*

Glenveagh Castle John George Adair was a 19th-century landlord who lorded it over 25,000 acres of land and was regarded as a tyrant even by his own class. When his steward was murdered in 1860 he felt sure that his tenants were behind the deed and so, over a period of three days in winter, he had all 244 of them

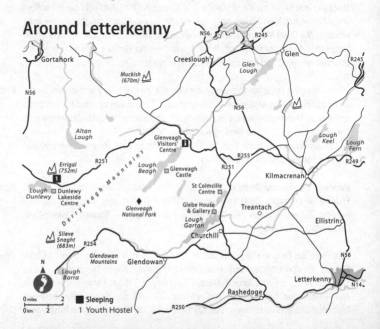

Around Letterkenny

County Donegal

evicted and their homes unroofed, so that "the police officers themselves could not refrain from weeping" it was said. A fund raised money for the former tenants to emigrate to Australia and many of the families left as a group to start a new life. Adair went on to build Glenveagh Castle in 1870. The property passed into the hands of the American Henry McIlhenny, who later donated the house and gardens to the state and it is now part of Glenveagh National Park. Self-guided walking trails meander through the park.

A visit to the park begins at the Visitors' Centre, where there are informative displays on the local ecology and the perfidious Adair. Glenveagh Castle is well worth a visit, for it is a particularly successful example of a mock castle, partly due to its setting on a promontory with the battlements set against a backdrop of mountains, and partly because this is a castle really built to defend its occupants against attack. Glenveagh Castle was built, as Williams in his definitive *Architecture in Ireland* puts it, "to ensure a sybaritic existence to inmates holding out against the vagaries of Irish politics or climate". Everything worth admiring inside, the fireplace and the wall-hangings for example, was put there by McIlhenny, while the lovely garden outside was a combined effort of McIlhenny and his wife Cornelia. ■ *Churchill, T37088. 14th-17th Mar and early Apr-Nov, daily 1000-1830. Closed Fri in Oct. €4 Tearoom and restaurant. 14½ miles (24 km) north of Letterkenny.*

The Inishowen Peninsula

The terminal attraction to the Inishowen Peninsula is Malin Head, Ireland's most northerly point, and even though north Donegal has scenically more exciting headlands, there is something enticing and irresistible about simply reaching this extremity of land. The bonus along the way comes in the form of unheralded scenic delights and, once you are away from Buncrana, the exhilarating absence of mass tourism. The area is often visited on speedy four-wheeled trips but as a place where people linger it is probably one of Ireland's least-known peninsulas and to do it justice a stay of a few nights is necessary.

Phone code: 077
Colour map 1, grid A3

Ins and outs

The route that follows works its way up the Lough Swilly west side, through Fahan and Buncrana and along to Cardonagh then north to Malin Head. The route then returns down the east side to Inishowen Head before moving down the coast along Lough Foyle and into Derry. Much of the way is signposted as the Inishowen 100 (*Inis Eoghain 100*), from the approximate distance in miles it takes to complete a circuit of the peninsula.

Getting there

Busways, T077-82619, run a daily service between Letterkenny and Moville stopping at Burt, Fahan, Buncrana, Clonmany, Ballyliffin, Cardonagh (with a connection to Malin Head) and Culdaff. There is also a Mon-Sat service between Carndonagh and Derry via Buncrana and a daily service between Carndonagh and Dublin via Buncrana, Derry and Monaghan. *John McGinley*, T074-35201, has a daily Inishowen to Dublin service.

Getting around

County Donegal

Grianán of Aileach

Grianán of Aileach is a stone fort strategically placed overlooking the flat land that separates the Inishowen peninsula from the rest of the county. Built during the early Christian period, it was the headquarters of the O'Neill clan who ruled from here for centuries until a revengeful king of

Colour map 1, grid A3

☞ **Self-catering on Inishowen**

Ballyliffin: Ballyliffen Self-Catering, T76498. Sleeps 6-8 from €412 to €632 per week in modern houses with good facilities.

Carpenters, T76457. Sleeps up to 6, from €273 to €489, depending on the season in cottage on private site.

Clonmany: Mamore Cottages, T76710. Sleeps 2 to 5 from €254 to €449 in 1- and 2-bedroomed cottages with open fire and turf supplied.

Greencastle: Drumaweir, T077-81178 Sleeps 4-6 from €254 to €445 in converted house close to beaches with views over Lough Foyle.

Malin: Goorey Lodge, T077-70612. Sleeps 2-8 from €178 to €345 in small cottage and purpose built self-catering house close to Trawbreaga Bay. Off season nightly rates on request.

Moville: River House, T077-82052, hknorris@hotmail.com Sleeps from 7 to 10 from €350 to €900 in 3 houses set in private woodlands.

Dunfanaghy: Lafferty's Holiday Homes, T074-36247, jameslafferty@eircomnet 3 bedroom cottages Sleep 6 from €152 to €355 in pretty countryside.

Munster attacked in 1101 and, so the story goes, ordered his men each to take away a stone from the walls. What you see today is largely a 19th-century reconstruction but managed more sensitively than what you might imagine a contemporary focus group from Dublin might come up with if given a free rein on the site.

Visitor Centre There is no charge to visit the stone fort, unlike the nearby Grianán of Aileach Visitor Centre, on the main road where you turn off for the fort, which is basically a restaurant with a fairly uninspiring exhibition on the top floor devoted to the fort's history. The *Grianán of Aileach Restaurant* is below the Visitor Centre and occupies the main space of a 19th-century church. Notwithstanding the rather crass advertising (a "holy different experience" proclaims a sign), the menu is imaginative, with starters like turbot and apricot salsa or lobster and prawn bisque. A carvery lunch operates during the week, and on Sunday there is a grander lunch. ■ *T68000. Mon-Sun 1100-2200. €2.*

Burt Church Burt Church, the modern functioning church that stands on the corner before turning uphill for the stone fort, was designed in the mid-1960s by the same team of architects that produced the church at Cresslough (see page 513). The same philosophy applies, and this time the church is designed to harmonize with the fort.

Fahan and Buncrana

Colour map 1, grid A3 There are three reasons to stop in the village of Fahan: a modest but good beach, superb food for an evening meal that outclasses anything Buncrana can offer and a cross-slab near the modern church that dates from around the eighth century, decorated with elegant Latin crosses and carrying a barely decipherable but unique Greek inscription from early Christian Ireland.

There is very little reason to stop in Buncrana, even though this is the main town and resort on the peninsula. The beach (3 miles/5 km long) attracts crowds of Irish holidaymakers during the summer, but you can escape the hustle and bustle by seeking out the small beach that is reached by a path from the pier at the north end of the long main street. There is a seasonal tourist office on the seafront, and a **Vintage Car and Carriage Museum** at the north end of town that will help occupy a wet afternoon. ■ *Tourist office: T62600/20020. Apr-Sep. Museum: T61130.*

St John's Country House Restaurant, T60289, at the Buncrana end of Fahan, has an established reputation for Donegal lamb and seafood served in a restored Georgian house with a lough-side setting. Expect to pay around €38 for an evening meal but make a reservation. In Fahan itself, the *Railway Tavern* bar and restaurant, T60137, cooks food on an open wood-burning firebox and opens for dinner Tue-Sun 1800-2200 and for lunch on Sun. *The Ubiquitous Chip*, 47 Main St, Buncrana, T62530, serves vegetarian balti or spicy vegetables with fajita, chicken enchiladas or trout. *The Town Clock Restaurant*, 6 Main St, Buncrana, T63279, is more of a café and opens for breakfast, lunch and dinner.

Eating

Buncrana to Ballyliffin

An alternative to the direct inland route to Cardonagh from Buncrana involves taking the R238 road north and following signs for **Dunree Fort** where there is a small military museum with displays on the fort's history, assorted weaponry and a tea-room. It is not very interesting, but the small sheltered beach has its charm and there are fabulous views of Lough Swilly across to Fanad Head. ■ *T61817. Jun-Sep, Mon-Sat 1000-1800, Sun 1300-1800. €3.*

Back on the main road the journey continues north up through the dramatic Mamore Gap before descending 800 ft (243 m) and bringing **Dunaff Head** and the bay into view. *The Rusty Nail*, T76116, is a fine old country pub passed on the road that serves food in the evenings during the summer and a popular Sunday lunch. Shortly after the pub a signposted turning off to the left leads to sandy Tullagh Bay, while the R238 continues on to the village of Clonmany where an angling festival takes place annually in August. A little way before entering the next village of Ballyliffin, on the main road, bicycles can be hired from *McEleney's Cycles*, T76541, and day trips to nearby **Pollan Bay**, sandy but not safe for swimming, could take in a picnic near the ruins of Carrickabraghy Castle at the beach.

For **self-catering** accommodation in Ballyliffin and Clonmany, see box.

Carndonagh

Carndonagh is an undistinguished small town but a useful watering hole and home to the last supermarket south before Malin Head. There is a helpful **tourist office**. ■ *Chapel St, T74933, F74935, info@inishowen.com http://www.inishowen.com Jun to Aug, Mon-Fri 0930-1900, Sat 1000-1800, Sun 1200-1800.*

Colour map 1, grid A3

If you are staying hereabouts for a night or two the tourist office can provide details of a surprising number of early Christian sites in the vicinity. Entering the village from Ballyliffin you will have already have passed **Donagh Church**, where there is a group of early Christian monuments made up of a cross and two carved stones from around the ninth century, while to the east of town there are the **Carrowmore high crosses** and the **Clonca Church cross**. They are not visually arresting and will prove disappointing if you are expecting something along the lines of Clonmacnoise; some archaeologists think they may be the result of some independent missionary movement from Scotland.

Local sites

County Donegal

☞ **Éire**

The word 'Éire', Irish for Ireland, that is marked out below the tower at Malin Head was put there during the Second World War to demarcate neutral Republic of Ireland from Britain's Northern Ireland. A high-ranking American officer flew around Ireland with a representative of the Irish government, and selected spots were agreed upon as suitable places to place the signs. Another one can be seen, but only from the sea, at the extremity of the Sheep's Head Peninsula in west Cork and they were partly there to help American pilots find their way back to bases in Northern Ireland. Occasionally, when pilots landed in southern Ireland by accident, they were semi-secretly whisked back to British territory.

Sleeping **B** *Ashdale Farmhouse*, Malin Rd, T74017, ashdalehouse@eircom.net A homely 2-storey house on the road to Malin **C** *Radharc na Coille*, Tiernaleague, T74471. A dormer house a few miles from town via Church St.

For **self-catering** accommodation, see the box on page 520.

Eating The best place for a good meal is the *Corncrake Restaurant*, Malin St, T74534, on your right leaving the village for Malin. The speciality is Donegal lamb and wild salmon with starters like mussels in cream sauce, but seafood addicts might be attracted to the seafood thermidor, a rich combination of monkfish, scallops, prawns, cod and mussels in a mustard and cream sauce! Several vegetarian choices. Open nightly Jun to Sep, but only weekends at other times. *Tul Na Rí* (Simpson's Bar), outside town on the Culdaff road, T74499, is an olde-worlde pub serving good food 1230-2200, booking ahead is often necessary to secure an evening table. For pub food try the *Sportsman Inn*, T74817, or *Trawbreaga Bay House*, T74352, both in the *Diamond*, T74352, or the nearby *Quiet Lady* on Malin Rd, T74777. *The Arch Inn Bar*, T73029, also in the *Diamond*, serves good bar food and has live music at weekends. While the *Boston Burger*, in Bridge St, does what its says over the door – burgers. *Bridge Street Café*, has soups and sandwiches and a take-away menu. For picnic provisions the *Centra* supermarket in Malin St opens daily from 0900 (1130 on Sun) until 2330.

For pub music try *The Persian Bar*, T74823, or the *Sportsman Inn*, T74817, both on the Diamond, or *Bradly's* on Bridge St, T74526.

Entertainment In the middle of July each year the Inishowen Agricultural Show has competitions with judging of sheep, cattle and horse in the morning and family activities during the afternoon. A street festival that takes place later in the month is not as much fun.

Transport **Bicycles** Bikes can be rented from *McCallions Bikes & Toys*, T74084, 3 miles (5 km) from Carndonagh on the Ballyliffin Rd, usefully with delivery and collection anywhere on the peninsula.

Malin and Malin Head

Colour map 1, grid A3

The R238 presses on to the village of Malin, situated where a charming 10-arch stone bridge crosses Trawbreaga Bay. The neat triangular village green bears testimony to its origins as a 17th-century planter's creation and the sparse tidiness of the place evokes a suitable sense of the terminal. North of the village a signposted detour leads to **Five Fingers Strand** and the oldest church (1784) still functioning on the peninsula. The beach is exhilarating to walk along but swimming is dangerous here.

County Donegal

Malin Head, marked by the remains of a 19th-century signal tower, lacks visual drama, so your imagination must get to work on the flat vista of surrounding grass that faces out to uninhabited Inishtrahull Island. You are standing on the most northerly piece of Irish mainland and the next stop north is Greenland. Weather reports, first recorded here in 1870, still feature in radio broadcasts and the buildings of the meteorological station can be seen at the head. Just east of the head, *The Cottage* has some photographs of historical interest and a path leads east past the *Seaview Tavern* to the Wee House of Malin, a hermit's rock cell in the cliff. Bird-watchers can listen for the elusive corncrake and in autumn time migrating gannets, shearwater and skuas pass overhead.

AL *Malin Hotel*, Malin Village, T70645, malinhotel@eircom.net faces the green and has a pleasant old-fashioned appeal. Look out for the good weekend offers. **B** *Barraicín*, Malin Head, T70184, overlooks the Atlantic. **C** *McLaughlin's*, T74491, is a hostel-style place with small double rooms with bathroom facilities and a self-catering kitchen. From Malin village cross the bridge on the R238 towards Cardonagh, turn left at the B&B sign and *McLaughlin's* is just up this road. **D** *Malin Head Hostel*, Malin Head, T70309. 2 miles (3 km) from the headland, beside the post office, and open from mid-Mar to Oct. A private room and camping space available. **D** *Sandrock Holiday Hostel*, Port Ronan Pier, Malin Head, T70289. Open all year, has a laundry, bikes for hire and suggested walking routes. No private rooms.

For self-catering accommodation, see box on page 520.

Sleeping
Price codes: see inside front cover

The *Malin Hotel* does bar food until 2115 and there is a comfortable restaurant in the evening that has a €19 set dinner as well as a choice of fish, chicken and grills around €9. At Malin Head *The Cottage*, T70257, does soup and sandwiches and light meals and opens Jun to Sep 1100-1830 (from 1330 on Sun), and Mar to May Sun only. The *Seaview Tavern*, Malin Head, T70117, is Ireland's most northerly pub and is open daily 0900-2100 for meals. *Bree Inn*, T70161, opens all year with a welcoming turf fire in winter. Meals available daily and their Sun lunch a speciality. Live music can be heard every Sat night, but if you prefer a quiet pint try *Farren's Bar*, near the weather station and Portmore Pier.

Eating

Culdaff

The route south that avoids going back through Malin takes you through the small village of Culdaff before carrying on through fairly deserted countryside as far as Moville or by way of a narrow winding road to Stroove. There is more to Culdaff than meets the eye. In late June every year the **Culdaff Sea Angling Festival** attracts anglers from all over the country and overseas for cash prizes, cups and trophies. ■ *T79141*.

In early October the **Charles Macklin Autumn School** is a festival of the arts based around the life of the actor and playwright Charles Macklin (1697-1797). ■ *T79104*.

While both these occasions bring seasonal life and laughter to Culdaff, there is entertainment most of the time at the remarkable *McGrory's pub*: it is worth checking to see what is lined up, for some big time entertainers appear here on a regular basis. ■ *T79104, www.mcgrorys.ie*

Bocan stone circle lies to the south of Culdaff near Bocan church, but many of the stones have collapsed. The Carrowmore high crosses and the Clonca Church cross (see page 521) could also be visited from here, but, as with the stone circle, there is not a lot to see.

Colour map 1, grid A3

County Donegal

Sleeping	*McGrory's*, T79104, 10 bedrooms with their own bathroom facilities. Restaurant serves
& eating	seafood as well as meat dishes, open Tue-Sun from 1800. **B** *Ceecliff House*, T79159,
	does B&B in a modern house for around €21.60 per person. **B** *Culdaff House*, T79103,
	is an established B&B in a 300-year-old Georgian farmhouse with views over a beach.

Stroove to Muff

The lough-facing east side of the Inishowen Peninsula stretches from Stroove and Inishowen Head to the blink-and-it's-gone village of Muff barely inside the border with Northern Ireland. At Stroove there is a signposted walk, with fine views of Inishowen Head along the way, to picnic tables near a lighthouse, and you could walk from here to Kinnagoe Bay and return by the same route.

Greencastle   Greencastle is a fishing port at the mouth of Lough Foyle with the ruins of an ancient castle; an early 19th-century fort, which is now a bar and restaurant; and the ruins of an ancient castle that are crumbling away on the coast. There is a fair choice of places to enjoy a meal, and infinitely better than what is available further down the coast in listless Moville.

Muff   The R238 hugs the coast all the way from Moville to the tiny village of Muff, where there is more going on than meets the eye. The place comes alive when the annual festival is unleashed over the holiday weekend at the end of July. ■ *T84024*.

The Flough is a traditional Irish cottage with sessions of song and dance but telephone ahead to check what might be on. ■ *T84024*.

Lenamore Stables is between Muff and Bridgend, offering horse-riding over quiet country roads or on a beach, and catering for novices as well as experienced riders. ■ *T84022*.

Sleeping   **A** *Castle Inn*, Greencastle, T81426. A sociable place running a public bar as well as
Price codes: doing B&B, situated next to the fort and the ruins of the castle. **B** *Brooklyn Cottage*,
see inside front cover   Greencastle, T81087. By the water's edge at the harbour and views of Lough Foyle can be enjoyed over breakfast in a conservatory. Free fishing trips if staying 3 nights. €22.25 per person. **B** *Tardrum Country House*, Greencastle, T81051, tardrum@iol.ie An early Victorian house and a 5-minute walk from the village. **D** *Moville Holiday Hostel*, Moville, T82378. A refurbished stone building 5 minutes by foot from the village and including private rooms.

For self-catering accommodation, see the box on page 520.

Eating   Greencastle has a few places close to each other along the seafront. *Kealy's Seafood Bar*, T81010, is a trendy-looking place doing dinner and bar food includes chowder, salads. Closed Mon. A little further on, *Greencastle Fort*, T81044, has an atmospheric interior in the old fort and does seafood as well as steaks and duck, and the menu is chalked up on blackboards in the spacious bar area. Next door, *Castle Inn*, T81426, specializes in steaks.

Northern Ireland

Northern Ireland

Counties Derry & Antrim

14

Counties Derry & Antrim

*Derry – energetic, creative and confident – is one of Ireland's most dynamic cities and a visit here will be a highlight of any trip to Ulster. You can either travel to Derry from Belfast through the gentle, purple-clad **Sperrin Mountains** that dominate the south of the county or, by way of contrast, along the spectacular, windswept and raw coastline of County Antrim. Traditional resort towns like **Portrush** dot the northern coast, while the famed **Glens of Antrim** make their way gracefully from inland moor to quiet rural villages clustered along the shore, completely unspoiled either by tourism or the ugly sectarianism of inland towns. These are communities connected by the stunning **Antrim coast road** that hugs the sea from just north of Belfast all the way to elegant **Portstewart**, a short way east of Derry. There are miles of good walks around the northern shores of Antrim and, of course, the busy **Giant's Causeway** with its car parks, tourist shops, audio visual presentations and behind it all, stunning rock formations.*

County Derry

Derry

Colour map 1, grid A3 *Source of the most fun to be had anywhere in Northern Ireland, Derry is a lovely, compact, vibrant little city, full of business and bustle, where life has moved on so far from the Troubles that it is hard to recognize the old ruins, and except for the red, white and blue in-your-face kerbstones of the Fountains area, there is little sign of sectarian divisions.*

Ins and outs

Getting there Derry is a very accessible city. The airport is 7 miles (11 km) northeast of the city on the A2, and access to the city is by *Ulsterbus* service 143 or cab. The railway station is in Duke St, and there is a free bus service to the *Ulsterbus* Depot in Foyle St. *Express Ulsterbus* buses, T71262261, connect Derry with Belfast and all major towns in Northern Ireland, while *Bus Éireann* has services to most major towns in the Republic.

Getting around Local buses begin their journeys at the *Ulsterbus* depot: they are indicated by the letter 'D' in front of the service number. Black taxis wait at Foyle St and collect a full load of passengers before setting off. Regular cabs (see page 539) operate around the city in the usual manner; ask the price before you set off, since few have meters.

Tourist information The tourist office is on 44 Foyle St, T71267284. It's open Jul-Sep, Mon-Fri, 0900-1900, Sat, 1000-1800, Sun, 1000-1700; Oct-Jun, Mon-Thu, 0900-1715, Fri, 0900-1700 (Easter-Jun also Sat, 1000-1700).

History

Early history The earliest settlement here was in an oak grove on an island in the River Foyle. Archaeological sites reveal that people lived hereabouts and revered the wooded hill long before St Colmcille (Columba) built a monastery on it in the sixth century. During medieval times, it expanded into a flourishing town with prestigious buildings, a school and the patronage of the Mac Lochlains, a local clan who claimed the kingship of all Ireland.

English settlement In 1566, an unsuccessful English garrison was established in the town. Then, at the turn of the 17th century, a more concerted attempt at settlement was made when another garrison was established and the town was given the status of city, but the settlement lasted only until 1608, when the O'Dohertys attacked it and erased the English presence.

Under James I a new settlement was established in 1613 using Protestant settlers from Scotland and England, who were more likely to be loyal to the crown. The project was financed by the wealthy London guilds, which is why the city spent the next 380 years under the name Londonderry. Great walls were erected around the city, while within the walls stone buildings were constructed, including St Columb's Cathedral. Despite this, the population grew slowly in numbers, perhaps deterred by the continuing unrest in the province. In 1649 England's internal divisions came to Derry when the city fathers declared themselves in support of the English Republic. The Catholic Irish and the Scottish

★

Things to do in County Derry and County Antrim

- Visit the excellent **Tower Museum** in Derry where you'll learn more about the Troubles than you will anywhere else in Ireland
- Walk the **city walls of Derry**
- Tread in the steps of Finn McCool at the **Giant's Causeway**
- Enjoy the pleasant olde-worlde charms and fine lunches at the **Londonderry Arms Hotel** in Carnlough
- Walk the **North Antrim Coast Path** between Portballintrae and Ballintoy
- Scare the life out of yourself on the **Carrick-a-rede rope bridge**

Presbyterian settlers, all of whom were condemned to live outside the city walls, besieged the town in support of King Charles I. Strangely, this is one act of loyalty to the crown that the Apprenticeboys don't celebrate each year!

The big event in Derry's history started on the day in 1688 when some apprentices shut the city gates against Catholic troops loyal to James II because the town had declared now its allegiance to William of Orange. As a result, Protestants fled to the city, increasing its population from around 2,000 to 30,000. A siege began later that same year and lasted 105 days. After a third of the people inside had died, of mortar attack or starvation, the siege was finally broken by a fleet of ships that broke through the barriers across the river. The siege held up the Catholic forces long enough for William of Orange to gather strength and win the Battle of the Boyne and the event is celebrated every year with bonfires and the ritual burning of an effigy of Protestant Governor Robert Lundy, who escaped from the siege, went to London and was forever known in the city as a traitor.

The seige of Derry
See also page 645

Over the next few centuries Derry developed as a major textile centre and more sadly a major emigration point for the poor, both Catholic and Protestant, who left Ireland for America. In the 20th century Derry suddenly found itself a border town when six of the counties of Ulster became 'Northern Ireland'. Like the other cities of Northern Ireland, sectarianism had become a major problem in Derry with streetfighting between Catholics and Protestants in 1920 and the withdrawal of the police force, the Royal Ulster Constabulary, from rural areas. Organizations like the IRA and UVF operated within their own communities and the struggle was, like in Belfast, over scarce jobs, housing and land.

The 20th century

    The Second World War brought prosperity and activity to Derry, as it became a base for refuelling and rearming destroyers and other escort ships for the transatlantic convoys. In early 1941 technicians from the US arrived in Derry and began building a new quay, a ship repair base, a radio station and personnel camps. By May 1942 there were 149 vessels and 20,000 American sailors based in Derry. A massive underground bunker and the most important radio station in the Western Approaches made Derry a vital link in the war in the Atlantic.

    After the war Derry found itself a manufacturing city on the extreme west of the United Kingdom. It attracted few big businesses, and unemployment rose to about 10 times that of the rest of Northern Ireland. Housing became a big issue, as the Unionist-run city council was afraid to extend the city's boundaries with housing estates since it might affect their electoral chances. Moderate organizations such as the Derry Housing Associations raised money to build houses while the protests against Unionist policy grew ever more vocal and physical.

County Derry

☞ Derry's part in the Troubles

In October 1968 civil rights marchers in Derry including John Hume, Gerry Fitt (both leaders of the moderate SDLP) and three Westminster Labour MPs were trapped by police and bludgeoned till they fled. Fitt was taken to hospital with head injuries. The event was filmed by an Irish film crew and broadcast worldwide – Ulster policemen were seen randomly hitting out at demonstrators and bystanders alike. This event was the trigger that sent Northern Ireland spiralling into the Troubles. Prior to this, the RUC had commanded the respect of the minority communities in Northern Ireland; after this they lost it.

By 1969 the civil rights movement had grown, become largely Catholic and contained socialist and republican elements, who had their own goals – a socialist Republic of Ireland. A march planned from Belfast to Derry turned into utter chaos as Loyalists attacked the participants, who got no protection from the police – on the contrary, they were seen and filmed joining in the attacks on the marchers. In Derry, policemen smashed their way into a supermarket and attacked shoppers; in the Bogside policemen rioted in the streets smashing windows and attacking anyone foolish enough to be out. All of this fuelled the Free Derry movement:

its slogan appeared on the gable end of a block of houses; moderates left the movement and it became dominated by Republicans. Support for the IRA, which had been practically defunct, increased.

Battle of the Bogside began in August 1969, when fighting broke out between the Loyalist Apprenticeboy marchers and Catholics from the Bogside. The battle raged for two days, and CS gas was fired into the Bogside. The Taoiseach, Jack Lynch, called for the UN to enter what was effectively an anarchic situation. Finally British troops entered the city, replacing the RUC. But three years later worse was to come: in January 1972 a civil rights march was fired on by paratroopers, killing 13, mostly by wounds to the back. Another person died later of his wounds. The event came to be known as Bloody Sunday.

During this time parts of the city had become no-go areas for the army. After a series of horrific IRA bombs in Belfast and Derry the British Prime Minister, James Callaghan, gave the order to clear the no-go areas, and Operation Motorman began. Tanks and armoured cars were brought into the city as the biggest British military operation since Suez began in the Bogside and in Protestant no-go areas.

To the present day Over the years new housing developments went up on the east bank and were allocated to Protestants, while Catholics moved into the untenanted houses they left behind. The river became a peace line with only the Fountains area on the west bank remaining Protestant. Gradually, the old slums of the Bogside were cleared and wide boulevards were created. In the early 1990s a major programme of investment began, clearing bombed-out buildings within the city walls, rebuilding the courthouse, creating the craft village, the museum and the genealogy centre. Since 1973 the Derry Council has been dominated by SDLP majorities, but they have regularly elected Unionist mayors as a gesture of goodwill. For many years there has been genuine power-sharing in this city which could teach some of the big names in Belfast quite a lot about compromise.

Sights

The city walls The city centre of Derry can easily be experienced in a day's wander around the walls, dropping down into the city to visit the various sights. Considering Derry's history, it is amazing the walls are intact: two-storey ramparts of earth and stone a mile long with a wide protected walkway along their top. Starting the walk at Shipquay Gate, one can imagine the 17th-century walled town. The gate had a drawbridge that could be closed against attackers and the river lapped against the walls themselves.

Inside the gate there are steps up on to the wall, which you can follow in a clockwise direction. At regular intervals bastions project out beyond the walls; they were used as defensive positions when the city was under attack. Beyond the third gate, **New Gate**, the Church of Ireland cathedral comes into view with its tower projecting above the walls. During the siege of Derry the tower was given wooden platforms for the defenders to use. The walls around the church are built higher than usual, again as a defensive measure

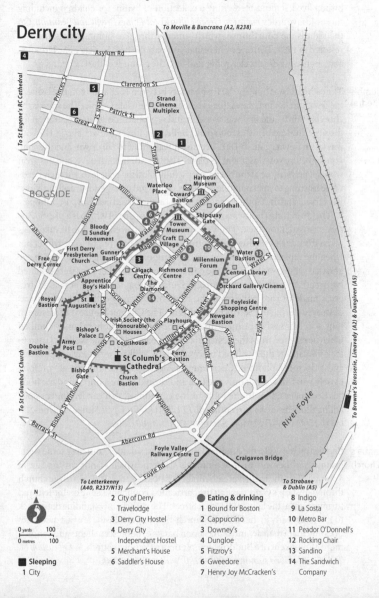

Derry city

County Derry

during the siege. Beyond the church and outside the walls is the Fountains area, distinguished by its red, white and blue decorations.

"The rich man in his castle, The poor man at his gate, God made them high or lowly And ordered their estate."
Cecil Frances Alexander (1818-1895), from her hymn 'All Things Bright and Beautiful'

Approaching **Bishop's Gate** you can see the one remaining tower of the old Derry jail which has a long list of famous inmates including Wolf Tone, the leader of the United Irishmen, and Eamon de Valera, later president of Ireland. Descending by the Bishop's Gate, notice the carved ornamentation on the gate, which is built like a triumphal arch, rebuilt in 1789 to honour William of Orange. After its construction a united procession of church leaders passed through the gate (in those days William of Orange represented order, not sectarianism). Passing along Bishop's Gate Within you pass the pink, columned **Bishop's Palace** on the left where Cecil Frances Alexander, the wife of a later bishop lived, famous for writing a collection of hymns for children including those old favourites *There is a Green Hill* and *All Things Bright and Beautiful*. On the right is the **courthouse**, which suffered three car bomb attacks and was restored in 1994. Turning right brings you past the Irish Society (The Honourable) houses where the clergy live and into the grounds of the Cathedral.

St Columb's Cathedral
This is the first post-Reformation church to have been built in the British Isles

The cathedral was built by the Irish Society between 1628 and 1633 and is one of the few churches in Ireland that is in a single style – late Gothic. The spire is the church's third – the first was wooden and was pulled down in preparation for the siege, the lead being used to make bullets; another spire went up in 1778 but was taken down again in 1801 because it was about to fall down, and the spire you see before you was put in its place. The interior is impressive, and has great wooden pews, those at the back very usefully allowing people to rest their heads while listening to interminable sermons. The regular pew ends are all individually carved, and the Gothic roof arches rest on the carved heads of past bishops.

The church also houses some crumbling flags, one of which is a pre-St Patrick's cross Union Jack. The yellow flags are replacements for Bastille flags taken from the besieging French troops of 1689; they ought to be white, but when the replacements were made, the originals had turned yellow with age and that yellow was taken for the correct colour. The other flags were donated by American battalions stationed in Derry during the war. There is a silver cross made of roof nails from the ruins of Coventry cathedral, which was destroyed during the Second World War. The Chapter House is a treasure of junk – a chair said to be made from the pear tree that Robert Lundy climbed when he escaped from the besieged city (see page 646), huge padlocks used to lock the gates of the city, gold pieces given by William to his loyal supporters and a doctored photo of Cecil Francis Alexander (see above) – if you look closely you will see that only the face and shoulders are a photo and the body has been painted in. In the lobby is the cannonball that carried the message telling those inside to surrender. ■ *T71267313. £1. Open Mar-Oct, Mon-Sat, 0900-1700; Nov-Feb, Mon-Sat, 0900-1300, 1400-1600.*

St Columba's Church

Back up on the walls, the double-bastioned west side looks out over some waste ground and beyond to St Columba's Church, which stands on the site of Tempull Mor (the medieval cathedral). It is possible to walk down to the church through Bishop's Gate, passing the barricaded Fountains Estate on the left, and turning right at the lights at Barrack Street. The church now standing dates back to 1784, very early in the Catholic church-building era. Inside are vast quantities of Connemara marble, and banks upon banks of fluorescent lights and candles, more reminiscent of a Buddhist temple than a Catholic church. ■ *Off Bishop St, T71262301. Open summer, 0900-2100; winter, 0900-2030.*

As the walls go on, past **'Roaring Meg'**, the cannon dedicated by the London **Bogside**
Fishmongers, the view becomes the Bogside, and beyond it the Creggan estate.
Below, out of sight, tucked in behind the wall, is the monument to those who
died on Bloody Sunday. To the right is the **Free Derry mural** and beyond all the
newly erected and already crumbling council houses is **St Eugene's Roman
Catholic Cathedral**, designed by several hands, the last of which was Liam
McCormack, creator of the altar in Armagh. ■ *T71262894. 0700-2100.*

Behind you, inside the city walls, is the **Apprenticeboys Hall**, built in 1937.
On the walls overlooking the Bogside once stood a 27-m-tall monument to
George Walker, successor to Lundy and governor of Derry at the time of the
siege. It was blown up in 1973, and the head changed hands several times. It
was beside this statue that the effigy of Lundy was traditionally burned in
December, but in recent times, out of respect for their Bogside neighbours,
the Apprentice boys now burn it outside the walls on the south side in the
Fountains area (see page 531).

Continuing along the city wall, you pass the **First Derry Presbyterian
Church**, originally built in 1690, rebuilt during the Georgian period and
added to in 1863. What you see is almost entirely of Victorian construction
with sandstone Corinthian pillars. This was one of the first places of worship
not affiliated to the Church of Ireland that was allowed within the city walls.

Next, you pass over Butcher's gate and, looking inside the walls, can see much **Calgach**
of the new investment in the city. At the corner of Butcher Street and Maga- **Centre**
zine Street is the Calgach Centre, where you can watch *The Fifth Province*, an
audio-visual experience about Celtic life based around the ancient warrior
Calgach, one of the Tuatha de Danaan – the legendary warrior-kings of Ireland: interesting information; good fun for kids. ■ *Butcher St, T71373177.
Open Mon-Fri, 1000 and 1430. Check times before arriving as these may change
with the seasons. £3. Café.*

At Magazine Gate in the north corner of the walled city, this is a modern recre- **Tower
Museum**
ation of an ancient tower house that once stood here. The museum has won
One exhibit you
many awards, and deservedly so: it's the only museum in Ireland that makes
won't see here is
any effort at all to confront the events of the last 30 years with anything near
the AK47 machine
objectivity. What's more, it's interesting, relaxing and provides an excellent
gun contributed
balance between information and artefacts. Towards the end of the trip
by the IRA, which
around the museum you enter a mocked-up street with orange, white and
was confiscated
green kerbstones on one side, and red, white and blue stripes on the other.
by the police
Above the kerbstones, display cases give two versions of the events of the last
century. ■ *Union Hall Pl, T71372411. Sep-Jun, Tue-Sat and Bank Holiday
Mon, 1000-1700, last admission 1630; Jul-Aug, Mon-Sat, 1000-1700, last
admission 1630. £4. Shop.*

The exit from the museum brings you into the Craft Village. Out of the sum- **Craft**
mer months this really doesn't shine as a place to visit, but in summer the **Village**
cafés, shops and open areas, where there is often live music and set dancing,
are well worth a visit.

Leaving the walled city by Magazine Gate brings you to this Gothic extrava- **Guildhall**
ganza built in 1887 and burned down three times, once in 1908 by accident
when only the main outer walls were left standing and the second and third
times in 1972 by design, when the entire interior was wrecked. One of those
convicted of the bombings in 1972 later sat as a council member in the same

The Irish workhouse

In 1838 the Irish Poor Law Act allowed for poor relief to take place within the confines of poor houses, which were to be built at the taxpayer's expense. In Derry, land was bought from a Major Bond and the poor house opened its doors in 1840, just in time for the Famine. Those who walked up to the house had to be truly desperate, because conditions inside were deliberately harsh so as to deter everyone but those at death's door from starvation from going inside. Once inside, the family was separated into women, girls, boys and men, who were not permitted to have any contact. Their clothes were taken and they were given a workhouse uniform. Daily life was organized around slave labour – women cleaned and sewed, men kept animals and broke rocks – and in this way the workhouse met some of its own costs. Rations were just enough to keep people alive, and punishment for indiscipline was harsh – usually deprivation of food.

Ironically, it was the Famine eight years later that temporarily did away with the poor houses since the buildings couldn't cope with the vast numbers of destitute and dying people who turned up there, and outdoor relief was allowed. The Poor Laws and the workhouses did not finally go out of operation until the creation of the Welfare State in 1948.

building. While the Bloody Sunday tribunal is taking place access to the inside is very restricted, but if the tribunal is finished or has moved to London then visitors can go inside. Inside is Victorian bombast, with vast stained glass windows representing the London liveries and the stories associated with Derry. Upstairs in the little kitchen alongside the great hall, look at the feet of George V in the stained-glass window portraying his coronation: he has his shoes on the wrong feet. In the Great Hall most of Brian Friel's plays were premiered. In the lobby is a stained-glass panel representing those who lost their lives on Bloody Sunday with, for some unaccountable reason, a sled with 'Rosebud' written on it. The statue of Queen Victoria has several fingers missing from the time when she was toppled over in one of the 1972 blasts. ■ *T377577 for tours, Jul and Aug only. No tours are available while the Bloody Sunday Tribunal is taking place.*

Harbour Museum Close to the Guildhall this museum contains some relics from when the harbour was an active commercial port, shipping linen and people to America. Vaguely interesting for a wet afternoon. ■ *Guildhall St/Harbour Sq, T71377331. Mon-Fri, 1000-1300, 1400-1600. Free.*

Foyle Valley Railway Centre Beside Craigavon Bridge is this museum representing Derry's years as a rail destination: old rolling stock, exhibitions about the railway and possibly a 20-minute diesel ride if they manage to fix the engine. Good for children. ■ *Foyle Rd, T71265234. Open Tue-Sat, 1000-1630. Free. Train ride £2.50.*

Amelia Earhart Centre Five kilometres north west of Derry is the Amelia Earhart Centre, commemorating the spot where she accidentally landed in 1932 having just made the first female solo crossing of the Atlantic. She mistook the village of Ballyarnett for Paris and landed there instead. Includes photos and memorabilia. ■ *Ballyarnett, T354040. Open Mon-Thu, 0900-1700, Fri 0900-1300. Free. Bus number D17 from the bus station.*

Workhouse Museum & Library This museum is on the other side of the river from the walled city and represents an excellent piece of reconstruction and renovation. Downstairs in the old workhouse building is a public library, while the upper floors are the unaltered sleeping quarters of the women's section of the poor house. Not much to look at here, but a fascinating insight into the conditions that these poor women must have lived in. There is also a permanent exhibition about Derry's part in the Battle of the Atlantic during the Second World War. There are often other temporary exhibitions and performances here. Those who died in the Workhouse during the Famine were buried in the yard, now a housing estate. When the estate was built hundreds of remains were exhumed and reburied in local graveyards. ■ *23 Glendermott Rd, Waterside, T71318328. Open Oct-Jun, Mon-Thu, 1000-1630, Sat, 1000-1630; Jul-Sep, Mon-Sat, 1000-1630. Free.*

Essentials

While hotels are not burgeoning here at the same rate as in Belfast, there is a good range of accommodation, but in the cases of hotels and hostels it would be well to book in advance. The tourist office will book accommodation for you if you arrive in town with none organized.

Sleeping
■ *on map, page 533*
Price codes: see inside front cover

XL-L *City Hotel*, Queen's Quay, T2144800, www.greatsouthernhotels.com Opening May 2002 this will be in the Great Southern style, offering quite reasonably priced accommodation as well as the luxury end. **L** *Beech Hill Country House Hotel*, 32 Ardmore Rd, T71349279, www.beech-hill.com Small country-house hotel, well away from the city, a pleasant place if you have transport. Reputable restaurant. **L** *Everglades Hotel*, 41-53 Prehen Rd, T71346722, www.hastingshotels.com Set in a pleasant location on the route into Derry on the banks of the River Foyle, this is Derry's only 4-star hotel. Big luxurious rooms, lots of lounge area, good restaurant. **L-AL** *Tower Hotel*, The Diamond, T71371000 www.towerhotelgroup.ie Opened Feb 2002. Right in the heart of the old city this brand new place might not have the charm of the older buildings but should bring lots of life into the city centre **AL** *Waterfoot Hotel and Country Club*, 14 Clooney Rd, T71345500, F71311006. Big, anonymous place well out of the centre of town. Pool and leisure centre. Breakfast is continental. **A-B** *Beechwood House*, 45 Letterkenny Rd, T71261696, beec.derry@amserve.net Small guesthouse, close to town with lots of facilities including gym, sauna, games room. Same place also does self-catering chalets. **A** *The Inn at the Cross*, 171 Glenshane Rd, T71301480, innatthecross@virgin.net.uk Out-of-town guest house with popular restaurant and bar, more of a hotel in style. **A** *City of Derry Travelodge*, Strand Rd, T71271271, F71271277. Best value in town this place charges per room not per person. In a rather noisy spot where several discos turn out late at night and the punters wait for taxis. Ask for a room at the back.

B *The Merchant's House*, 16, Queen St, T71269691 www.thesaddlershouse.com Lovingly restored Georgian house. Great breakfasts, lots of good information, sitting area and library. 1 en-suite room. The most central B&B in town. **B** *The Saddler's House*, 36, Great James St, T71269691, www.thesaddlershouse.com Equally lovingly restored Victorian townhouse. All rooms en suite, lots of info, nice informal breakfasts. The other most centrally located B&B in town.

B *Arkle House*, 2, Coshquin Rd, T71271156, arklehse@tinyonline.uk A Victorian house offering B&B, 1½ miles northwest of the centre of Derry. **B** *Number 10*, 10 Crawford Sq, T71265000, b-bno10@1C24.net. A B&B 5 mins from the city centre near the technical college. **C** *Aberfoyle*, 33 Aberfoyle Terr, Strand Rd, T71283333, aberfoyle@ntlworld.com A B&B 5 mins from the city centre. Good tourist advice. Extra charge for credit cards. **C** *Acorn House*,17 Aberfoyle Terr, Strand Rd, T71271156. 5 minutes from the city centre in the student area of town. Free pick up. **B-D** *Derry City Hostel*, 6 Magazine St, T71284100, F71284101. Purpose-built hostel. Dorm beds in dormitories, family rooms and private en suite doubles. Right in the heart of the city, bike hire, games room, restaurant, self-catering. *Derry City Independent Hostel*, 4, Asylum Rd, T71377989, derryhostel@hotmail.com all dormitory accommodation, internet and laundry.

Eating

● *on map*
Price codes:
see inside front cover

While Derry isn't overrun with exciting restaurants, there are enough places to keep you out of McDonald's during your stay

Expensive The *Ardmore* is at *Beech Hill Country House* (see 'Sleeping' above) and serves haute cuisine. Reservations in order at weekends.

Mid-range *Brown's Brasserie*, 1 Bond's Hill, T71345180. Excellent, small menu of innovative dishes in a little converted shop opposite the train station. Popular at lunch time when less than £7 will buy you something you'll remember for days. The restaurant at the *Everglades* is the *Satchmo*, where the food is very traditional – dishes of vegetables, with 2 kinds of potato – but it's nicely cooked and reasonably priced. A way out of town at the *Inn at the Cross* (see 'Sleeping' above) is *Companion's*, where there is a set menu as well as à la carte. The bar also does bar food. *Indigo*, 27, Shipquay St, T71271011. This place comes well recommended by locals. Modern Irish menu, dinner only. *Fitzroy's*, 2-4 Bridge St, T71266211, is big, popular, does inexpensive lunches and very modern dinner menu – lots of drizzles and pestos. Early dinner menu as well as post-theatre one. Open till late daily. *La Sosta*, 45a Carlisle Rd T71374817. Well established authentically Italian place, just outside the city walls. *Oysters*, 162 Spencer Rd, T71344875, is a little way out of town but worth the trip. Open for lunch and dinner.

Cheap At lunchtime the range of options is much wider with most of the pubs in town doing food of some kind. The café in the Calgach Centre, *Danini's*, 0900-1700 Mon-Sat, has some great lunch offers. Close by, in the Diamond is *The Diamond*, a new pub, part of some huge chain but which does good value all day meals of burgers, wraps, salads. Even vegetarians could find something to eat here. Along Waterloo St the *Rocking Chair*, T71265200, *Bound for Boston*, *Henry Joy McCracken's*, T71360177, the *Dungloe*, T71267716, the *Gweedore* T71263513, and *Peadar O'Donnell's*, T71372318, all do pub food and in summer you might catch some live traditional music. The *Metro*, T71267401, in Bank Pl does food from 1200-1500 weekdays, longer at weekends, is seriously touristy but has decent meals at around £5. At 61 Strand Rd is *The Sandwich Company*, T71266771, popular with lunchtime eaters. There is another branch of this popular shop, which closes early, between 1630 and 1730, 6 days, at the Diamond, T71372500.

Opposite the bus station *Cappucino's*, T71370059, I in Foyle St, does things and chips, filled rolls, jacket potatoes and has a high turnover of fresh food. On the other side of the road is Round the corner in Water St is *Sandino's*, T71309297, hideously yellow outside with lots of items on the menu for lunch all at around £5 plus.

Pubs & music

For traditional Irish music the bars in Waterloo St are the best bet. *Peadar O'Donnell's* and the *Gweedore*, close by, have music. The other pubs along Waterloo St will have notices up advertising their music nights. *Club Q*, has a local singer/songwriter night on Thu. Inside the walls the *River Inn*, *Downey's* and *Metro* have live music. *Sandino's* has traditional music on Sun at 1600. For the young and studenty there is *Café Roc*, T71309372, on the corner of Rock Rd and Strand Rd. The café does pub food, while upstairs *Earth* nightclub has a disco on Tue, Fri and Sat. At the *Delacroix*, on Buncrana Rd, T71262990, there is a comedy club while *Da Vinci's*, T71372074, in Conmore Rd has a disco at weekends and ballroom dancing in the restaurant late on Sat evenings. In Waterside, *The Gallery*, 14 Dungiven Rd, is a popular pub and restaurant.

Entertainment

Art galleries In addition to the *Playhouse* and the *Foyle Arts Centre* (see 'Theatre' below), there are several other art galleries. *The Orchard Gallery* in Orchard St is very innovative, while the *Context Gallery*, at 5-7 Artillery St, T71373538, has changing exhibitions of contemporary art, is open 1000-1530, charges no entry fee. The *Mc Gilloway Gallery*, 6, Shipquay St, T71360011, sells modern Irish paintings, which one can view free from 1000 until 1730. Evening viewing is available by appointment.

Cinema *The Orchard Cinema*, T71262845, is the town's film club and is housed in *St Columb's Theatre* (see below). The *Strand Multiplex* , Strand Rd, T71373939, has 7 screens and the Millennium complex will house a cinema.

Theatre *Millenium Forum*, Newmarket St, T72160516 www.milleniumforum.co.uk Gorgeously new and has a regular schedule of local productions and touring theatre groups. *Nerve centre*, 7-8 Magazine St, T71266946, www.nerve-centre.org.uk A performance venue, café and cinema as well as lots of very arty stuff. *Verbal Arts Centre*, Mall wall and Stables Lane, T71266946, www.verbart.demon.co.uk Worth a visit just to see the beautifully renovated former Blue Coat School (1894) and the glass sculpture by Killian Schuman which contains manuscripts donated by Ireland's many writers. The place is an archive of stories and poetry collected from storytellers and poets around Ireland. Mon-Thu 0900-1700, Fri 0900-1600. *Playhouse*, 5-7 Artillery St, T71268027. Another multimedia venue, where at various times you can catch art exhibitions, theatre, dance and concerts. *Foyle Arts Centre*, Lawrence Hill, T71266657. Home to a studio theatre and larger auditorium and holds lots of amateur productions as well as art exhibitions. *St Columb's Theatre*, Orchard St, T71267789, was Derry's major theatre and hosts *árd fheis* and visiting theatre companies.

Festivals There is a *Celtic Spring Festival* in Derry celebrated at varying dates in **March** and involving theatre, music and Gaelic events. The *Foyle Film Festival* takes place in **late April** and the *Southern Comfort Jazz and Blues festival* is in **late May**. The largest and noisiest festivals in Derry take place in **October** with the *Two Cathedrals* festival followed by a week or so of fireworks and fun at Hallowe'en. Look out for the Hallowe'en tours –great fun!

Sport **Bowling** *Brunswick Superbowl*, Brunswick Lane, T71371999. 0900-late. 10-pin bowling. **Fishing** *Enagh Trout Lake*, 12, Judges Rd, T71860916. *The Loughs Agency*, 8 Victoria Rd, T71342100. Information and licences. *Glenowen Fisheries Co-operative*, Creggan reservoir, T71371544. Licences, accommodation, equipment. **Gaelic** *Gaelic Athletic Association*, Gaelic football, hurling, camogie, T71342561. **Golf** *Foyle International Golf Centre*, 12, Alder Rd, T71352222, 18 holes. £9 weekdays, £11 weekends. Discounts for accompanying member. *The City of Derry Golf Club*, Victoria Rd, Waterside, T71311610. 18 holes. Mon-Sat 0800-2330. Weekdays £20, weekends £25. Discounts with member. **Greyhound racing** *Brandywell Greyhound Racing Co*, Brandywell Football ground T71265461. **Leisure centres** *Brandywell Sports Centre*, Lone Moor Rd, T71263902. Indoor football arena and handball arena. *Brooke Park Leisure Centre*, Rosemont Av, T71262637. Squash, fitness training, sauna, tennis, bowls. *Lisnagelvin Leisure Centre*, Richill Park, T71347695. Pool, wave-making machine. *Templemore Sports Complex*, Buncrana Rd, T71265521. Pools, sauna, squash, major sporting events in the main sports hall. **Riding** *Culmore Riding School*, 130 Culmore Rd, T71359248.

Transport **Air** From Derry Airport, Longfield Rd, Eglinton, T71810784, there are flights to **Dublin**, **Glasgow** in Scotland, **Stansted** and **Manchester** in England. From Dublin and Stansted there are connections to most British and European cities. The airport is 11 km from the city centre on the A2. At the airport, facilities include a free car-park, information desk, bureau de change, ATMs, shop, bar and café. **Bike hire** *Happy Days Rent-a-bike and Cycle Tours*, 245 Lone Moor Rd, T71287128: Raleigh Rent-a-bike scheme. **Bus** All buses depart from the *Ulsterbus* Depot in Foyle St, T71262261. Express services go to **Belfast** via **Dungiven**, **Coleraine**, **Dublin**, Belfast via **Omagh**. Local buses connect with most of the towns in the north. A private bus company, the *Lough Swilly Company* T71262017, connects with **Buncrana**, **Moville**, **Carndonagh**, **Letterkenny**, **Dungloe** and **Fanad**. *North West Busways*, T00353-77-82619 offers similar services operating out of the Republic. An *Airporter* bus, T71269996, operates between Clarendon St and the 2 Belfast airports. **Car** *Ford Rent-a-car*, Desmond Motors Ltd, 173 Strand Rd, T71360420. City of Derry Airport, T71812220. **Taxis** *A1 Taxis*, 7 Chapel Rd, T71342626. *Auto Cabs*, 85 Spencer Rd,

County Derry

T71343030. *Black Taxis*, Foyle St, T71260247. **Train** From the rail station in Waterside, T71342228, trains go to **Belfast** via **Coleraine**, **Portrush**, **Ballymena**, **Antrim** and **Lisburn**. There are around 7 trains a day. From Belfast there are connections to **Dublin** and other towns in the Republic.

Directory **Banks** *Bank of Ireland*, Strand Rd, T71264141, Shipquay St, T71264992. *First Trust*, Shipquay St, T71363921. Racecourse Rd, T71267722. Spencer Rd, T71348442. Waterloo Pl, T71262446. *Northern Bank*, Guildhall Sq, T71265333. **Bureaux de Change** *NW Money Exchange*, Foyleside, 68 Strand Rd, Richmond Centre, Wed-Fri, 0900-2100. **Communications** Post Office: Custom House St, T71223344. Mon 0830-1730, Tue-Fri 0900-1730, Sat 0900-1230. **Laundry** *Wringers*, 141 Strand Rd, T71312297, 0800-2000. **Library** Foyle St, T71266888, Mon, Thu 0915-2000, Tue, Wed, Fri 0915-1730, Sat 0915-1700. **Places of worship** Baptist: Fountain St, services Sun 1130, 1830. **Church of Ireland**: St Columb's Cathedral, services Sun 0800, 1600 (Evensong). **Methodist**: Clooney Hall, services Sun 1145, 1830. **Quaker**, 23 Bishop St, Sun 1100. **Roman Catholic**: St Eugene's Cathedral, Gt James St, services weekdays 0800, 0900, 1000, 1930; Sat 0900,1000, 1815, 1930; Sun 0700, 0830, 1000, 1100, 1215.

Derry to Coleraine

To Downhill
Colour map 1, grid A4

The A2 follows the south side of Lough Foyle, moves inland a wee bit to Limavady, then heads north to Magilligan where the B202 is a spur off to **Magilligan Point** and the incredible 7-mile (11-km) stretch of sandy **Benone Strand**. The A2 continues to Downhill where, on top of a 180-ft (55-m) cliff, a Bishop of Derry in the 1780s commissioned the building of an extravagant palace and a Greek-style temple. The whole project was manifestly absurd, cost a small fortune to build and decorate with paintings by Rubens, Dürer and Tintoretto, and the whole lot burnt to the ground in 1851. The bishop had taken off in the 1790s for a tour of the continent where, thought to be a spy, he was arrested by Napoleon and found in possession of more valuable works of art. "Oh, what a lovely thing it is to be an Anglican bishop or minister," exclaimed a French visitor to Ireland at the time. The ruins of **Downhill Palace** and the intact **Mussenden Temple** are National Trust properties and can be visited. ■ *Mussenden Rd, Castlerock, on the A2, T70848728. Grounds always open. Temple: Jul and Aug, daily 1200-1800; Apr-Jun and Sep, Sat and Sun, 1200-1800. Free.*

Hezlett House

Also on the A2, 4 miles (6.5 km) northwest of Coleraine, Hezlett House is another National Trust property, a thatched 17th-century former rectory noted for its cruck truss roof. ■ *T70848567. Open Jun-Aug, Wed-Mon 1200-1700; Apr-May and Sep, weekends only. £2*

Portstewart
Colour map 1, grid A4

The A2 takes one through **Coleraine** but there is little good reason to stop in this depressing urban centre when the seaside towns of the north coast are so close at hand. The main town on the coast is Portstewart, a bustling place popular with families and surfers, and a good stopping off point (either for a meal or a fresh-air walk along the seafront) between Derry and Portrush. Start at the Crescent area in the west end of town where the Dominican convent, now a school, is perched on the hilltop and follow the surfaced path along the cliff until the glorious vista of the **Portstewart Strand** opens up. Descend to the beach here: access by car costs £3. In places, signs warn of dangerous currents but this is a prime surfing beach. The **tourist office** is in the Town Hall, on The Crescent, T70832286. Open Jul and Aug, Mon-Sat, 1000-1630, closed 1300-1400.

Sleeping B *Craigmore House*, 26 The Promenade, Portstewart, T70832120. Facing the ocean and in the thick of the seaside scene. **D** *Causeway Coast Hostel*, 4 Victoria Terr, Atlantic Circle, T70833789. Open all year, its 30 beds include 3 private rooms at £19 each.

Price codes:
see inside front cover

Eating *Skippers*, in the **Anchorage Inn** at 87 The Promenade, Portstewart, T70834401, is open for lunch with the same menu of meat and chicken dishes for £4 available in the bar. From 1700 there is a fair choice of pasta, half of which are vegetarian dishes as well as meat and fish dishes and all for £9-£11. In the dark and cavernous interior of the *Montague Arms*, 68 The Promenade, Portstewart, T70834146, food is served in the evening until 2130 and mains work out at about £10. *Shenanigans*, 78 The Promenade, Portstewart has a varied menu and specialises in chicken till 2130.

Diving Scuba-diving and PADI courses through *Aquaholics*, T70836909. **Surfing** gear and information in Portstewart from *Ocean Warriors*, opposite the *Anchorage Inn*, on The Promenade.

Inland Derry

The appeal of inland Derry is limited, but there are some interesting alternatives if seaside resorts such as Portstewart and Portrush are not to your liking.

The Roe Valley Country Park stretches for 3 miles (5 km) along both sides of the Roe River near Limavady, the best of the walks pass industrial relics from the time when clattering water wheels powered machinery here for the manufacture of linen (see page 560). Head south, upstream, to see the bleaching greens where the cloth was spread out and guarded from the watch towers that still stand (stealing linen was a capital offence), cross by the first or second footbridge and return on the other side for a hour's walk. A second walk, downstream, passes a greater variety of industrial buildings, and returning via the second footbridge this way is also an hour's return walk. The Centre provides an slide-show on the linen industry and there is a separate Weaving Shed Museum. If industrial machinery really hooks you, request a visit to the Power House, Ulster's first domestic hydro-electric power station that opened in 1896. ■ *Open Mon-Fri. Once in the park, a sheet outlining short walks is available. The park is located off the B192, 1 mile (1.6 km) south of Limavady, from where the Bus No 146 runs.*

Roe Valley Country Park

There is a café serving burgers, but picnic tables near the Centre make a more attractive proposition. Come dusk on a summer's day otters can be spotted in the river and buzzards occasionally fly overhead, while in springtime the woodland floor is dotted with wood anemones and lesser celandine. ■ *T77722074. Open Jun-Aug, daily, 1000-1800. Shorter hours the rest of the year. Free.*

South Derry detains few travellers, but you could make a pit stop at one of the Plantation towns whilst journeying between Derry and Belfast on the A6. **Draperstown** is a short detour off the A6 but has the benefit of the **Plantation of Ulster Visitor Centre** and museum technology to bring alive the story of the plantations by London companies starting in 1595. There is a café and small shop. ■ *50 High St T79627800. Open Easter-Sep, Mon-Sat, 1000-1700, Sun 1300-1700. Oct-Easter Mon-Fri 1000-1700. £3.*

Plantation towns
Colour map 1, grid B4

The town of **Moneymore**, further south and close to the border with Cookstown and County Tyrone, is a veritable museum in itself, so well preserved and decorous are the Georgian houses. Close by, **Springhill**, on the B18 1 mile (1.6 km) southeast of Moneymore, is a 17th-century manor house

County Derry

characteristic of the type built by the planters and, true to its spirit, saw the UVF training in the grounds in 1913 in preparation for armed resistance to Home Rule. ■ *T86748210. Open Easter and Jul-Aug, Fri-Wed, 1400-1800; Apr-Jun and Sep, weekends only. £3.*

Sleeping
Price codes:
see inside front cover

L-AL *Radisson Roe Park Hotel*, Roe Park, Limavady. T77722222, F77722313. Has big bedrooms, indoor pool and gym and its own 18-hole parkland golf course. **B** *Alexander Arms*, 34 Main St, Limavady, T77763443, F77722327, is a town-centre pub with rooms and serves inexpensive food. **B** *Keady View Farm*, 47 Seacoast Rd, Limavady, T77764518, has only 2 rooms, but there are quite a few more B&Bs along this road.

Eating

The *Brasserie* at the *Radisson Roe Park Hotel* has dishes such as Singapore chicken, lamb kebab for £7, and more expensive steaks. The hotel's octagonal *Green's Restaurant* has à la carte only, serving imaginatively presented food. In Limavady town *The Lime Tree*, 60, Catherine St, T64300, is a little gem of a place in one of the main streets in the town. Menus are innovative and there are often special menus where regulars try out new dishes. This is one of those menus where you feel that the words 'balsamic', 'peppercorn', 'terrine' and 'goujons' are used purposefully rather than as dressing. Dinner at the top end of the mid-range category, but look for the early evening and lunch menus which are good value. If it's a quick fix you're after try *Crumpet*, in Market St, serving potato dinners till 1730 or *Shanvey* bar and restaurant in Aghanloo Rd.

County Antrim

Travelling the coastline of County Antrim is a memorable experience, and coming up the coast from Belfast the departure from cityscapes to sudden vistas of rock and sea is an instant therapy for any lingering urban blues. This chapter's route starts from the other end, in seaside Portrush just across the Derry border, and works its way along the northern coast to the Giant's Causeway and delightful Ballycastle before heading south past the Glens of Antrim and a string of settlements that dot the highly scenic journey down to Belfast.

Portrush

Colour map 1, grid A4

Portrush, is a busy seaside resort packed with activities for families, and while the downside may be the usual tackiness and the excess of buckets and spades dangling from shop doorways, there are upbeat surprises in store as well. It is a superb centre for surfing and in town you will also discover one of the best restaurants in Ireland. The **tourist office** is in the Dunluce Centre, Sandhill Rd, T70823333. Open Apr-mid-Jun, Mon-Fri 0900-1700, Sat and Sun 1200-1700; Mid-Jun-Sep, daily, 0900-1900; Mar and Oct, Sat and Sun, 1200-1700.

Sights

Curran Strand is the sandy beach, that stretches eastwards for over a mile, past the famous golf course, to the **White Rocks**, perfect for picnics, where erosion has weathered and sculptured arches and caves into weird shapes. Surfing is good here: try the East Strand, which can be reached by car, although the West Strand is just as good. For gear and advice see 'Sport' on page 542.

The **Ulster Way** path, rising up to clifftop level, follows the coast from Portrush to Portstewart. From Portrush Harbour, **boat trips** head out to tour The Skerries, a chain of small islands off the coast. Horse-riding is also available: see 'Sport', below.

The **Dunluce Centre** has three particular sensations: *Turbo Tours*, a film theatre with thrill rides, *Earth Quest*, with hands-on exhibitions of local wildlife, and *Myths & Legends*, a top-of-the-bill multimedia show based on local folklore. ■ *Sandhill Drive, T70824444. Separate admission charges or all 3 for £5, and family tickets as well. Closed mid-Sep-Apr, weekends only in Apr, daily in Jun Jul and Aug.*

Waterworld, by the harbour, is a water playground with all the works as well as a bowling alley. ■ *T70822001. Admission £4.25 but a variety of family tickets is available. Open daily Jul and Aug, weekends only Sep. Bowling alley £12 per lane.*

Behind the seafront, **Barry's** is the largest amusement park in Ireland, with indoor and outdoor entertainment. **Fantasy Island**, on the promenade, is an indoor adventure playground with a café and supervisory staff. ■ *Fantasy Island: T70823595.*

Portrush Countryside Centre is an exhibition centre covering local natural history. Raining or not, go hunting for fossil impressions on the seashore next to the Centre beside the car park. ■ *Lansdowne Cres, T70823600. Jul and Aug, daily, 1000-1800, Sep, days and times vary.*

Sleeping

*Price codes:
See inside front cover*

B&B rates peak in Jul and Aug to £18-£25 per person, dropping to around £15 at other times for rooms sharing bathroom facilities. Most of the caravan parks will take only a token number of tents, but a couple are listed that will take more.

AL-A *Magherabuoy House Hotel*, 41 Magherabuoy Rd, T70823507, www.magherabuoy.co.uk Outside of town with unrivalled views over the Atlantic Ocean. **A** *Maddybenny Farm*, 18 Maddybenny Park, T70823394, www.maddybenny. freeserve.co.uk This may be out of town, but a more gregarious guesthouse would be hard to find and your enjoyment of a visit will be proportional to your appetite for a gargantuan breakfast (porridge with Drambuie and cream as an appetizer) that makes the usual B&B offering seem like child's play. **AL** *Peninsula Hotel*, 15 Eglinton St, T70822293, reservations@peninsulahotel.co.uk A new hotel in the town centre with 25 double rooms. **B** *Atlantis*, 10 Ramore Av, T70824583. A B&B not in a quiet part of town, but with the advantage of a kitchen available for snacks. **B** *Windsor Guest House*, 67 Main St, T70823793. A family-run period town house in the heart of town. **D** *Macools*, 5 Causeway View Terr, T70824845. An independent hostel with a good name and 18 beds, including a private room.

Camping *Hilltop Holiday Park*, 60 Loguestown Rd, T70823537, off the A29. Caravan park, will take up to 50 tents. *Skerries Holiday Park*, 126 Dunluce Rd, T70822531. This caravan park will take up to 50 tents.

Eating

D'Arcy's, 92-4 Main St, T70822063, is big with a great bar to wait in upstairs while your food is cooked. Modern Irish menu – Clonakility black pudding and Irish cheeses sit happily beside harrissa and teryaki. Very reasonable prices, good lunches and a roast on Sun. Live music in the bar upstairs afterwards.

The *Snapper Restaurant*, Ballyreagh Rd, on the road between Portrush and Portstewart, T70824945, has main dishes like chicken kebabs and seafood paella and pizzas. Consider a trip to nearby Coleraine where the *Water Margin*, Hanover Pl, T70342222, overlooking the river, has been recommended for its Chinese food. A set meal for 2 is £18.

There are some truly dreadful places in the centre of town serving fish-and-chips-type meals; don't be misled by nautical themes and reasonable prices. *Donovan's*, 92 Main St, T70822063, is one of the better pubs, serving food daily at lunchtime for around £5, and in the evening offering a variety of grills, salads and the like. *Don Giovanni's*, 9 Causeway St, T70825516, is fine for pizzas and pasta and also does some veal and fish dishes.

County Antrim

Public transport along the North Antrim coast

Between 4th June and 22nd September (between 1st July and 23rd September for Sunday services) the **Ulsterbus 252 Antrim Coaster** service runs twice daily between Belfast and Coleraine and stops at all the main towns of interest around the coast. Buses leave **Coleraine** at 0940 and 1540, (departing from **Belfast** at 0900 and 1400) and stop at **Portrush**, **Portballintrae**, **Bushmills**, **Giant's Causeway**, **Ballintoy**, **Ballycastle**, **Cushendon**, **Cushendall**, **Carnlough**, **Glenarm**, **Larne**, **Carrickfergus** (morning service only), and Belfast.

In July and August there is an open-topped bus, service number 177, the **Bushmills Open Topper** running 5 times a day between **Coleraine** and the Causeway, via **Portstewart**, **Portrush**, **Portballintrae** and **Bushmills**, but flaggable anywhere along its route. For details of public transport, T70325400.

The **Ulsterbus 152** service runs throughout the year between **Ballycastle** and **Portrush** on the B146, via **Carrick-a-rede**, **Ballintoy** and the **Giant's Causeway**.

The **Causeway Rambler**, service number 376, operates daily, 7 times a day from **Bushmills Distillery** to **Carrick-a-rede** between June and early September, calling at the **Giant's Causeway**, **Dunseverick Castle**, **Ballintoy** and **Carrick-a-rede**.

Entertainment On summer nights pubs and hotels are blasting out music, but not of the traditional Irish kind. *Lush!*, Bushmills Rd, T70823539, is a disco of local renown and the *Magherabuoy House Hotel*, T70823507, has better musical entertainment than most of the hotels. For a pub with some character try the *Harbour Inn*, behind *Ramore's* wine bar at the harbour.

Sport **Golf** *Royal Portrush*, T70382231. Less expensive 18-hole courses are *Moyola Park*, T79668468, and *Masserene*, T94428096. **Horseriding** *Maddybenny Riding Centre*, 18 Maddybenny Park, T70823394. **Microflights and flying school** *Microflight Ireland*, 67 Main St, T70823793, F70824625. **Surfing** *Rock Bottom Surf Shack*, 18 Main St, T70825665.

Tour operators *Lynchpin (Ireland) Ltd* creates customized tours for individuals, T70823232, www.lynchpin-ireland.co.uk

Transport **Bus** See box above for details of the Antrim Coaster service. *Ulsterbus* services also connect Portrush with **Antrim**, **Armagh**, **Ballymena**, and **Cookstown**. **Train** From Portrush station, T70822395, there are 8 trains a day to **Coleraine** from where connections to **Derry**, **Belfast** and **Dublin** can be made.

Portrush to the Giant's Causeway

Colour map 1, grid A4 Between Portrush and the Giant's Causeway there are two points of interest. Dunluce Castle, beside the A2 and not-to-be-missed on a fine day, is just west of the small harbour at **Portballintrae**, while Bushmills and its famous distillery are just off the A2 a little further to the east. Bushmills makes a convenient watering hole for lunch, before or after a visit to the Causeway.

Dunluce Castle The castle at Dunluce, one of the most enjoyable to visit anywhere in Ireland, is not one of those brutal Norman impositions, for there is something whimsical as well as dramatic about its spectacular location on a rock-stack. A fortification of some kind here goes back two millennia perhaps, but the earliest of the castle walls were built for the MacQuillans, Scottish mercenaries originally, in the 14th century and completed later by the MacDonnells. The English under Sir John Perrott, determined to clear the Scots from Antrim, took the castle with artillery in 1584, but the following year Sorley Boy MacDonnell (see box on page 555) and his men scaled the cliffs on ropes and hung the constable (his Scots mistress is said to have played an invaluable part in this). Perrott was philosophical: "I do not weigh the loss but can hardly endure the discredit". The MacDonnells made a deal and remained the residents and their subsequent repair work lasted 60 years until the kitchen and servants' quarters collapsed into the sea and ruined a perfectly good night's dinner. There is plenty of the castle left standing and a visit is recommended. ■ *T20731938. Open Apr-May and Sep, Mon-Sat, 1000-1800, Sun, 1400-1800; Jun-Aug, Mon-Sat, 1000-1730, Sun, 1400-1600; Oct-Mar, Mon-Sat, 1000-1600, Sun, 1400-1600. £1.50. Visitor Centre, guided tours.*

Bushmills

Bushmills developed with the rise of water-powered industry in the early 17th century – the first hydro-electric tramway in the world came through here on its way from Portrush to the Causeway – and whiskey was first legitimately distilled here in 1608. A guided tour of **The Old Bushmills Distillery** covers history and technology and finishes with the customary taster of the famous single malt, triple distilled, whiskey. ■ *T20731521. Open Apr-Oct, Mon-Sat 0930-1730, Sun 1200-1730, last tour at 1600; Nov-Mar, Mon-Fri, tours on the hour between 1030 and 1530 (but not 1230). http://irish-whiskey-trail.com £3.95.* The nearest **tourist information** is at the Visitor's Centre, Giant's Causeway, T20731855.

Sleeping
Price codes:
see inside front cover

L *Bushmills Inn*, 25 Main St, Bushmills, T20732339. A hotel as well as a restaurant. **A** *Craig Park*, 24, Carnbore Rd, T20732496, www.craigpark.co.uk Big country house set in 20 acres with lovely views over the mountains of Donegal and the hills of Antrim. **B** *Ahimsa*, 243 Whitepark Rd, T20731383, a traditional cottage specializing in vegetarian meals and using produce from its organic garden.

Camping *Portballintrae Caravan Park*, Portballintrae, on the B145 towards Bushmills, T20731478. Has 16 tent pitches for £6.

Eating
If Bushmills Distillery has whetted your appetite, Bushmills Inn serves beef fillet strips in a sauce of cream mixed with more of the hard stuff

Bushmills Inn, 25 Main St, Bushmills, T20732339, has a comfortable and very inviting bar, an inexpensive brasserie open at weekends and a restaurant open daily and serving the best food in the area at around £22 for a meal. A few doors up the *New Mill Restaurant* is a new place doing bar snacks and meals like chicken and bacon for £5.50 and 10 oz steak for £10. In the summer *Sallie's* craft shop in Portballintrae, Beach Rd, T20731328, serves up pizzas and light meals until 1800. *Sweeney's*, Seaport Av, Portballintrae, T20732405, is a pleasant stone-built pub with a conservatory, and popular sessions of live and loud music; decent food is served daily.

Directory

Banks *Northern Bank*, 62 Main St, Bushmills. Money can also be changed at the Visitor's Centre at Giant's Causeway. **Communications** Post office: 67 Main St, *Bushmills*, by the roundabout in the centre of town. Will also change money.

Giant's Causeway

Colour map 1, grid A5

Formed by the cooking and cooling of vast quantities of basalt, the giant crystals of the Giant's Causeway have been attracting countless visitors since they were first 'discovered' by the Victorians. The novelist Walter Scott selected four of the basalt columns to take home with him but changed his mind, the poet Keats set out to walk here from Donaghadee but found it too long a journey, while

Thackeray in his 1842 tour was led to exclaim that when God fashioned the world out of chaos "this must have been *the bit over* – a remnant of chaos".

One version has it that the polygonal columns were spewed forth as the result of a cataclysmic convulsion in the crust of oceanic tectonic plates, but the Causeway Centre is not bound by modern dogma and the exhibition allows visitors to choose between this prosaic account and the rather more fanciful story about lusty Finn McCool (Fionn Mac Cumhaill), who wanted a passageway across the water to reach a giantess on the island of Staffa, off the coast of Scotland. (This is backed up by science, for similar rock formations are indeed to be found there as well.)

Once you leave behind the rather tasteless interpretive centre and actually see the rocks you can understand what has been bringing so many people here over the years to see them. It really does seems as though some bad tempered giant hand set the rocks down here in an ugly fit of pique.

From the Causeway Centre it is a short walk to the shore and Finn's stepping stones, but in summer you will have to dodge minibuses and hordes of visitors. Follow instead the path up behind the Centre and take the **North Antrim Cliff Path**, a few hundred steps bring you down to the shore.

■ *Giant's Causeway Centre. T20731159. Open Jul-Aug, daily 1000-1800. Shorter hours rest of the year. Audio-visual show £1. Car-park £3. Tea-room open Mar-Nov. There is no charge to visit the Giant's Causeway unless arriving by car or wishing to hop in the minibus, £1 return, from the Causeway Centre to the shore.*

The **Causeway School Museum**, an original 1920s classroom next to the Centre, is worth a visit with children, or on a wet day. ■ *T20731777. Open Jul-Aug, daily 1100-1700. 75p.*

Walking the Causeway coast

Having ticked off the Giant's Causeway on the 'been there, done that' list, it seems a pity to leave the majestic North Antrim coast too quickly, and luckily the **North Antrim Cliff Path** provides an exhilarating way of extending one's stay. It takes about five hours to walk the 17 km (10 miles) between Portballintrae and Ballintoy, and with the aid of a bus timetable it should be possible to catch a bus (see page 544) back to your vehicle or accommodation. While the path (marked on the *Ordnance Survey* sheet 5 in the Discovery series) can be walked in either direction, the best fun can be had if you start from Ballintoy and cross White Park Beach to the little harbour of Portbraddan, where St Gobhan's claims to be the smallest church in Ireland, and on to Dunserverick and up to the clifftop for a spectacular couple of miles to the Giant's Causeway. Walking in Northern Ireland doesn't come much better than this.

The tourist office in Portrush has a leaflet describing a walk following the tracks of the Causeway Tram that ran between Portrush and the Causeway between 1883 and 1949. There is talk of relaying part of the line.

Causeway coast

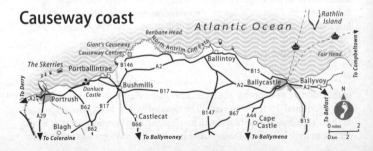

For sleeping and eating at the Portballintrae end see the 'Portrush to Giant's Causeway' section on page 544 and for the other end of the walk see the 'Giant's Causeway to Ballycastle' section below.

A stay at the **A** *Causeway Hotel*, Causeway Rd, T20731226, F20732552, should prove more satisfying than it did to Thackeray in 1842: "It was impossible to feel comfortable in the place, and when the car wheels were heard, I jumped up with joy to take my departure and forget this awful shore, that wild, dismal, genteel inn." **A** *Whitepark House*, Whitepark Rd, T20731482, www.whiteparkhouse.com With 3 rooms sharing bathroom facilities, this has been warmly recommended. B&B is £50 for a double and the odd-looking place is hard to miss on the road between the Causeway and Ballintoy.

For organized walks contact *Dal Riada*, 68 Station Road, Portstewart, T70832832, info@dal-riada.com http://www.dal-riada.com For organized cycling trips: *Ardclinis Outdoor Adventure*, T/F00-44-12667-71340, ardclinis@aol.com

Sleeping
Price codes:
see inside front cover

Tours

Giant's Causeway to Ballycastle

As well as the main A2 coast road there is also the B146 road, running parallel to it but closer to the coast, and this leads past the fragmentary ruins of **Dunserverick Castle**, and by the harbour, the small **Dunserverick Museum**. There is a meagre collection related to disasters at sea – parts from the doomed Spanish Armada and coal from the *Titanic* – but the location makes an attractive spot for a picnic. Emigrants used to be rowed out from here to hitch a ride on a passing schooner for Derry or Glasgow, thence to America or Australia, never to return. ■ *Open Jun-Aug, Mon-Sat 1000-1600.*

Dunserverick
Colour map 1, grid A5

From the village of Ballintoy a winding road leads down to the shore, passing the white-towered Ballintoy church: if you're thinking the tower looks a little incongruous you're quite right, for there used to be a steeple before a hurricane demolished it in 1894. The rocky but quaint limestone harbour, sheltered by basalt rocks like Sheep Island, was built to ship out sett stones from a nearby quarry that employed over 100 men in the 19th century. Now there are a few fishing boats, in summer a £1 boat service to Carrick-a-rede, and a satisfying teashop. From here from it takes half an hour to walk around the headland leads to the mile-long sandy **White Park Bay**, and if you want to continue walking follow the North Antrim Cliff Path signs (see page 546) for a most dramatic approach to the Giant's Causeway. Plans to open a clifftop walk eastwards to Carrick-a-rede may have been completed.

Ballintoy
Colour map 1, grid A5

Every year some 100,000 visitors cross the rope bridge at Carrick-a-rede but that may prove scant comfort when you are half-way across and you realize that turning back means going as far as carrying on to the other side. It's only 80 ft (24 m) above the sea, but when the rope bridge starts to sway and your nerves wither, try to remember you're really just on holiday – having fun. The bridge is erected annually by fishermen throwing a string across with a lead weight to access a salmon fishery on the small island. The centre by the car-park has information panels on the geology and the quarrying in the 1930s-50s that removed the entirety of Larrybane Head and the remains of a promontory fort. ■ *T20731159. Open May-mid-Sep, daily. Car-park £2. Centre and tea-room: Jun-Aug and weekends in May, daily 1200-1800.*

Carrick-a-rede

A couple of miles before Ballycastle the remaining walls and main tower of the 16th-century Kinbane Castle are worth visiting just for the location, perched

Kinbane Castle

on a limestone headland amidst basalt cliffs with Rathlin Island directly across the water and the towering majesty of Fair Head in the distance. Primroses and orchids in Spring and perfect for a picnic any time.

Sleeping
Price codes:
see inside front cover

B-C *Ballintoy House*, Main St, Ballintoy, T20762317. The house carries the 1737 date of its building on its front wall and the B&B rate ranges from £13 outside of summer and sharing bathroom facilities to £17 for en suite in Jul and Aug. **D** *Sheep Island View*, Main St, Ballintoy, T20769391. Has a terrific kitchen, includes one double at £20, can organize guided walks and has camping space. **D** *Whitepark Bay Hostel*, 6 miles west of Ballycastle on the A2, T20731745, F20732034. A top-notch YHANI hostel overlooking White Park Bay with 6-bed and 4-bed rooms, and 4 superb double rooms with TV and coffee-making facility, foreign exchange and a restaurant. Beds start at £10.50.

Eating

In Ballintoy village the *Carrick-a-rede* pub, T20762241, has pub food and a restaurant upstairs in the summer. Across the road the *Fullerton Arms*, T20769613, has a similar set-up, but the restaurant opens only between Wed and Sun in winter; daily in summer.

Perched on the rocks at Ballintoy, *Roark's Kitchen*, T20763632, is open daily between Jun and Aug from 1100 to 1900, and at weekends in Easter and Sep, for lovely light meals such as buttered mackerel or baked potato with filling for around £2.75 and lunches listed on a blackboard outside. The *National Trust tearoom* at Carrick-a-rede serves dismal fried food redeemed by some local breads.

Ballycastle

Colour map 2, grid A5

Ballycastle is a modestly vivacious little place with some history and a character reminiscent of the Republic. There are pubs with traditional music, fair restaurants and an infrastructure that recommends it both as a base for exploring the North Antrim coast and as a place to pause before or after seeing the Glens of Antrim on the east coast. Northern Ireland's only inhabited island (Rathlin Island) lies off the coast, Scotland is a short ferry ride away, and every year three festivals light up the place with song, dance and live music on a stage in the Diamond. The **tourist office** (7 Mary St, T20762024, open Mon-Fri, 0930-1700 – Jul-Aug until 1900 – Sat, 1000-1800 and Sun, 1400-1800) hands out the useful **Ballycastle Heritage Trail** leaflet that covers a variety of places of historical interest around town, including the little **Ballycastle Museum**. ■ *59 Castle St, T20762942, Jul-Aug, daily, noon-1800. Free.*

Sleeping
■ *on map*
Price codes:
see inside front cover

AL *Marine Hotel*, North St, T20762222. Self-catering options sleeping 2-6 people and has a pool. **B** *Beechwood*, 9 Beechwood Av, T20763631, stat@beechwoods.f9.co.uk Can be recommended for its quiet location and friendly welcome. The house has 2 double rooms sharing a bathroom, but best value has to be the 2 chalet-type rooms at the back with their own facilities including a fridge and sink. No avoiding the Ulster fry-up though. **B** *Ammiroy House*, 24 Quay Rd, T20762621, 2 rooms in a family house, is typical of the B&Bs along this road. **B** *Silversprings House*, 20 Silversprings, T20762080, is a distinguished-looking, 7-chimneyed house in a quiet cul-de-sac. **D** *Ballycastle Backpackers*, 4 North St, T20763612. A small hostel, but with 4 private rooms from £15. **D** *Castle Hostel*, 62 Quay Rd, T20769391. Has 30 beds including 2 private rooms for £17. The preferred hostel for some travellers.

Maguire's Strand Caravan Park, 32 Carrickmore Rd, off the A2 south of town, T20763294. *Silvercliffs Holiday Village*, 21 Clare Rd, T20762550. Popular campsite with an indoor pool, sauna and bar. *Watertop Open Farm*, 188 Cushendall Rd, is 6 miles southeast of town on the A2, T20762576. Charges £8.50 for each of its 5 pitches around a working farm.

No 10, facing the marina on North St, T20768110, serves modern Irish cuisine in generous proportions and with colourful presentation: about £25 for an meal featuring local seafood and occasional rarities such as char from Arctic waters off Iceland, plus lamb, duck and chicken. Reserve a window table for views looking across to the Mull of Kintyre (a mere 20 miles away), Fair Head and Rathlin Island. *Wysner's*, 16 Ann St, T20762372, has won awards for its meat-based dishes, though fish is also available. Steaks and surf 'n' turf are around £12 and a separate day menu downstairs in the café features bangers and champs (pork sausages and potato and shallots), pasta, and chicken dishes for around £5. Closed Sun. The *Glass Island Restaurant*, in the *Marine Hotel*, 1-3 North St, T2076222, has atypical hotel potato-based menu, is open daily until 2200, while the bar serves snacks.

 The Strand, 9 North St, T20762349, is the best place for inexpensive dishes of chicken, grills, pizza and pasta at around £6 and a choice of tempting ice-creams at £3.50. *Flash in the Pan*, Castle St, is an excellent, sit-in or take-out, traditional fish and chip outlet. There are 2 places next to Wysner's on Ann St competing for quick meals and coffee breaks: *Herald's Restaurant* at No 22 comes up with beef, potato and vegetables for £3.50 while *Donnelly's* at No 28 is a bread shop and an OK café. The *Antrim Arms*, 75 Castle St, serves pub food including lamb cutlets, steak and trout.

The Central Bar, Ann St, has a regular Wed night session of traditional music that goes al fresco in the summer with the occasional barbecue thrown in for good measure. For traditional Irish music, on a Thu night head for *McCarrolls Bar* on Ann St and save Fri for *The House of McDonnell*. In the same family for over 200 years, the House of McDonnell pub is grand for a quiet chat and a drink, and on a Sat night musicians are welcomed. The *Marine Hotel* has tame live music most nights in the summer.

Towards the end of **May** there is the 3-day *Northern Lights Festival* and in **mid-June** another 3 days are devoted to the Fleadh Amhrán Agus Rince. At the end of **August** the *Oul' Lammas Fair*, with a good claim to be Ireland's oldest traditional fair, is a very lively event. All the festivals see an explosion of live music in the pubs.

Eating
● *on map*
Price codes:
see inside front cover

If seeking out a local edible seaweed, dulse, go to the Fruit Shop in the Diamond. The shop also stocks yellowman, a chewy toffee eaten hereabouts

Entertainment

Festivals

Ballycastle

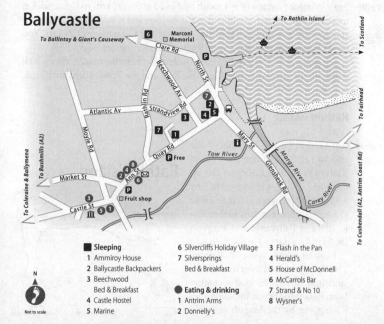

■ Sleeping
1 Ammiroy House
2 Ballycastle Backpackers
3 Beechwood
 Bed & Breakfast
4 Castle Hostel
5 Marine
6 Silvercliffs Holiday Village
7 Silversprings
 Bed & Breakfast

● Eating & drinking
1 Antrim Arms
2 Donnelly's
3 Flash in the Pan
4 Herald's
5 House of McDonnell
6 McCarrols Bar
7 Strand & No 10
8 Wysner's

To Rathlin Island
To Scotland
Marconi Memorial
To Ballintoy & Giant's Causeway
Clare Rd
North St
Beechwood Av
Strandview Rd
Rathlin Rd
Atlantic Av
Moyle Rd
Quay Rd
Market St
Ann St
Castle St
Fruit shop
Tow River
Mary St
Glenshesk Rd
Margy River
Carey River
To Fairhead
To Bushmills (A2)
To Coleraine & Ballymena
To Cushendall (A2, Antrim Coast Rd)
Free
N
Not to scale

County Antrim

☞ **"And her hands were bound behind her back"**

When Deirdre was born, a druid named her as a source of misfortune, but Conchobar had her brought up in secret with the intention of marrying her. It was not to be, for Deirdre knew in her heart that her lover would have black hair, a white body and red cheeks. She met such a man at Emain Macha (Navan Fort) and together with his two brothers they fled, pursued by the revengeful Conchobar, until they found refuge in Scotland and then on a remote island. Lured back with

a false message they landed at Ballycastle, but the brothers were murdered and Deirdre brought to Conchobar – "and her hands were bound behind her back" and later forced to marry one of his accomplices. At Emain Macha, on the day of her wedding, Deirdre commited suicide.

So runs a tale, first written down in the eighth century, that inspired Lady Gregory and through her Yeats and Synge and 20th-century writers a plenty.

Transport **Bus** *Ulsterbus* station, T20762365, Station Rd. Buses run to and from **Belfast** and **Coleraine**, Mon-Sat. See also page 544. *McGinn* T20763451. A private company running a Ballycastle to Belfast return bus. It departs from the Diamond at 1600 on Fri, 2000 on Sun, and from outside the *Europa Hotel* in Belfast at 1815 on Fri, 2145 on Sun. **Ferry** *The Argyll & Antrim Steam Packet Company* operates between Ballycastle and Campbeltown in Argyll, Scotland. **Taxis** *Connors*, T20763611; *Delargys*, T20762822; *Ronnies*, T20763221.

Directory **Banks** *First Trust*, *Northern Bank* and *Ulster Bank* are all in Ann St. Money can also be changed at the tourist office and the Marine Hotel. **Communications** Post **office**: 3 Ann St.

Walking around Ballycastle

The Ulster Way passes through Ballycastle but the route west of town is not recommended until Ballintoy is reached (see Walking the Causeway coast on page 546). While the route east is a tough hike of 20 miles (32 km) to Cushendall, a more manageable trek could end in Cushenden and would take in a glorious clifftop walk around Fair Head and the ascent of Caranmore (1,243 ft). You need *Ordnance Survey* maps 5 and 9 in the Discovery series.

For gentle strolls collect the *Forest Walks* leaflet from the tourist office which maps out the circular 2-mile Glentaisie Trail and the 3-mile Glenshank Trail, both waymarked.

Rathlin Island

Colour map 1, grid A5

Just 6 miles (9.6 km) from Ballycastle and 14 (22.5 km) from the Mull of Kintyre in Scotland, Rathlin has an inverted L-shape, 4 miles by 3 (6.5 by 4.8 km), and is never wider than a mile (1.6 km). Collect a map from the tourist office in Ballycastle and jump on the ferry for a day out in the fresh air.

Famous people come to Rathlin. The Vikings started their tour of Ireland here in 795CE. Half a century later, Robert the Bruce, in hiding after a whipping by the English at Perth,

Rathlin Island

East Lighthouse
West Lighthouse
The Manor House
Harbour
Mill Bay
Rathlin Sound
N
0 miles 1
0 km 1
To Ballycastle
South Lighthouse

was inspired by a spider to never give in, and left to fight the English again at Bannockburn. Sir Francis Drake commanded a ship sent here in 1575 to hunt down the family and friends of Sorley Boy MacDonnell (see box on page 555) and massacre them. Marconi, or at least his assistant, sent the world's first wireless message here from Ballycastle in 1891, and around a century later the entrepreneur Richard Branson came down in a balloon near here.

Walking and **bird-watching** are the main attractions of a visit, and there is a viewing platform at the West Lighthouse. In late spring and early summer the rocks are crowded with fulmars, guillemots, kittiwakes, Manx shearwaters, razorbills and puffins. ■ *Apr-Aug, T20763948.*

Activities on Rathlin

Diving trips can be arranged, **fishing** off the rocks is possible and boats can also be hired. Colonies of grey and common seals can be seen at Mill Bay, just south of the harbour and near the hostel and camping ground, and at Rue Point near the South Lighthouse. ■ *Diving: Tommy Cecil, T20763915. Boat hire: T20763922.*

A-B *The Manor House*, T20763964. A large Georgian house by the harbour, open all year and run by the National Trust as a B&B establishment. Good-value doubles but a single is expensive. **B** *Rathlin Guest House*, The Quay, T20763917. Open Apr-Sep. **D** *The Richard Branson Centre*, T20763915. Hostel with 26 beds, opens all year and charges £10 per person. No private rooms. Camping is free near the hostel. **D** *Soerneog View Hostel*, T20763954. Overlooks Mill Bay and is a short walk from the harbour. Open all year but only 6 beds, so book ahead in the summer.

Sleeping
*Price codes:
see inside front cover*

Dinner at the *Rathlin Guest House*, last orders at 1900, is £9.50, but needs booking in advance. *Chip-a-Hoy Restaurant*, at the harbour, opens in the summer between 1100 and 1800 for quick fish meals. *McCuaig's Bar* is nearby and serves breakfast, fish and chips, and champ and opens daily for food from 0900 until 2100. For a picnic on the island stock up with provisions at *Brady's* supermarket in Castle St or the *Co-Op* at the Diamond, Ballycastle.

Eating

Ferry *Caledonian MacBrayne*, T20769299, run the M.V. *Canna* on its 45-minute journey to Rathlin 4 times a day between Jun and Sep (0830, 1030, 1500 and 1700 and returning one hour later) and twice a day the rest of the year. Day return £7.80, bicycles £2, and best booked ahead in the summer.

Transport

Ballycastle to Cushendun

Unless you're in a hurry to be somewhere else, the inland route between Ballycastle and Cushendun on the A2 is best passed over for the sake of the coastal road via **Torr Head** and **Murlough Bay**. Other than walking parts of the Ulster Way, this route offers the best coastal scenery in Northern Ireland. At Murlough Bay there is a series of three car-parks with noticeboards detailing short walks in the area, and near the middle car-park a commemorative stone to British diplomat and Irish nationalist Roger Casement. After being hanged in London in 1916 for treason, his remains were finally returned in 1965 to this corner of Ireland where his family roots were.

Cushendun

The distinctive buildings of Cushendun were designed by the architect Clough Williams Ellis, who also designed Portmeirion in north Wales, where the cult

Colour map 1, grid A5

1960s television series *The Prisoner* was filmed. In 1912 Ronald and Maud MacNeil, later Lord and Lady Cushendun, commissioned William Ellis to design the Square with its dormer windows and slate roofs, and so pleased were they that more building followed in the same style. Most of Cushendun, the nearest port in Ireland to Britain, is now owned by the National Trust and it is a strange place, which manages to be attractive and alienating at the same time. There is a small **information office** in Main St, T21761506, and a leaflet describing three local walks of 2, 4 and 6 miles in length should be available.

Sleeping
Price codes:
see inside frotn cover

B *Cushendun Guesthouse*, Strandview Park, T21761266. Overlooking the harbour, only opens in Jul and Aug. B&B is £20 per person, sharing bathroom facilities, credit cards not accepted and 'room reservations at weekends for overseas visitors only'. Meals are served in the evening for around £10 and its *Ropeworks Bar* opens at 1700 each day. **B** *Villa Farmhouse*, 185 Torr Rd, T21761252. A more orthodox guesthouse with a reputation for good breakfasts and evening meals available if booked in advance. **C** *The Burns*, 116 Torr Rd. T21761285. Charges a flat £15 for person in each of its 2 rooms.

Camping The *Cushendun Caravan Park*, Glendun Rd, T21761254. Next to the safe beach, with 10 pitches for tents at £5 a night.

Eating

The *Cushendun Village Tea Room*, Main St, T21761281, looks the ideal place for a homely cup of tea and apple pie, but fails to live up to expectations. Sandwiches and toasties and grilled food with chips from £4-£8 are served and on Sat evenings an à la carte menu beckons. Just across the road, *McBride's* is a tiny pub that needs squeezing into, with hardly the elbow space needed to lift a pint to your mouth. Pub food is served daily in the summer.

Transport

For transport to and from Cushendun, see Cushendall below.

Cushendall

Colour map 1, grid A5

Cushendall is an engaging village, the name of which had been changed to Newtown Glens until a certain Francis Turnley turned up in the early 19th century, having made his fortune trading in China, bought the whole village, restored its original name and generally injected life and commerce into what was a very sleepy backwater. A predominately Catholic village, Cushendall was frequently visited by the Belfast poet John Hewitt (an annual summer school on Hewitt is held further down the coast at Garron Point) who was led to reflect on the religious divisions of Ulster:

> *This is our fate: 800 years' disaster*
> *crazily tangled as the Book of Kells;*
> *the dream's distortions and the land's division,*
> *the midnight raiders and the prison cells.*
> *Yet like Lir's children banished to the waters*
> *our hearts still listen for the landward bells.*

The village is gratifyingly free of tourists and there is not a great deal to see other than the Curfew Tower that Turnley had built in 1817 to house those who failed to share his ultra-industrious attitude to life. *McCollam's Bar* on Mill Street is definitely worth calling into, because the sessions of traditional music will give a fillip to any Friday night, and often a Saturday and a Tuesday in the summer as well. The second week in August, when the **Heart of the Glens Festival** arrives in Cushendall, sees all the pubs full to overflowing.

Take either Layde Road from the village past the hostel and a campsite or a cliff-top path from the north end of the beach to reach **Layde Old Church**, its miscellany of MacDonnells tombs and a church with a Michael Healy window, *The Light of the World*.

The **tourist office** is on Mill St, T21771180. It open in Jul-Aug, Mon-Sat, 1000-1300 and 1500-1930 but has varied, shorter hours rest of the year.

A *Thornlea Hotel*, 6 Coast Rd, T21771223, F21771362. The only hotel in town, has 13 rooms and charges up to £50 for a double. **A-B** *The Meadows*, 81 Coast Rd, T21772020. An award-winning B&B establishment on the main A2 road. **B** *Riverside*, 14 Mill St, T21771655. As central as you can get, next to the tourist office. **C** *The Burn*, 63 Ballymean Rd, T21771733. A mile outside of town on the B14 road. **D** *Cushendall Hostel*, Layde Rd, T21771344. YHANI hostel, one mile north of the village, with over 50 beds and some private rooms.

Sleeping
Price codes:
see inside front cover

Camping There are 2 caravan parks, which accept a small number of tent pitches: *Cushendall*, 62 Coast Rd, T21771699, £5; *Glenville*, 22 Layde Rd, T21771520, £3.

Harry's Restaurant, 10 Mill St, T21772022, with a bar menu from 1230 to 2130 of dishes such as chicken curry and prawn sandwich, and a more formal menu from 1800 featuring steak and fish dishes around £11. Sun lunch is £8.25. *The Half-Door*, 6 Bridge St, T21771300, opens in the evening for French-style cooking with similar prices to Harry's. For coffee breaks, salads and sandwiches, *Gillian's*, 6 Mill St, is a congenial place that opens daily until 1800. See below for other establishments in the area, at the Glenariff Forest Park.

Eating

Celtic Crafts, 3 Shore St, T21772019. Sells Celtic jewellery, Aran knitwear, Irish music CDs, instruments and even the odd hurling stick.

Shopping

Boat hire *Red Bay Boats*, Coast Rd, T21771331. **Fishing** licences and information from *O'Neills* shop next to the tourist office in Mill St. **Walking** Sun in summer at 1100 and 1400: enquire at the tourist office.

Sport

Bicycle Hire from *Ardclinis Activity Centre*, High St, T21771340. **Buses** Buses serve Cushendall and Cushendun from **Belfast** and **Ballymena**, Mon-Sat. No 162 travels daily between Cushendun and **Larne** via Cushendall and the 162A travels Mon-Fri between Cushendall and **Ballycastle** via Cushendun. See also the Antrim Coaster service on page 544.

Transport

The Glenariff River flows down to Waterfoot, south of Cushendall, and its glen is the most accessible of the famed Glens of Antrim, due mainly to the Forest Park and its waymarked trails. The Park's visitor centre is fairly useless. Consult the map on the board near the car-park for a brief explanation of the four available walks. The longest is a 5-mile Scenic Trail through forest and across the Inver River for views down the glen, and the most popular is a 3-mile Waterfall Trail. These walks can also be reached from a separate entrance at the back of the *Manor Lodge* restaurant and its free car-park, though someone will still be there to collect the £1.50 between June and August. The catwalk from the restaurant was originally built in the late 19th century to encourage day-trippers to use their Ballymena train to Parkmore station at the top of the glen.

The trails are rich in flowers: liverworts, mosses and ferns abound; in spring, bluebells and wild garlic and in summer woodruff, pink herb Robert and bugle. ■ *On the A43 Ballymena/Waterfoot road, T21758232. Daily from 1000. Car-park £3, pedestrian £1.50.*

Glenariff Forest Park

County Antrim

Eating There is a *Tea House*, T21758769, in the Forest Park serving quiche and salads, and the *Manor Lodge*, Glen Rd, T21758221, reached before the Park if travelling up from Cushendall, serves burgers, cod and chips, and salads for £6-£7 as well as grills and fish dishes from £11 to £16. There is also a bar and picnic tables.

Walking from Cushendall

Apart from walks in the Glenariff Forest Park (see above), the tourist office has a *Heart of the Glens Guide* that describes a variety of short walks from Cushendall and Cushendun into the glens. A section of the Ulster Way, from Cushendall or Waterfoot (also called Glenariff) to Carnlough is an exciting day's walk of around 11 miles (18 km). Although the Way signs peter out as you near Carnlough this will not present a problem if you have *Ordnance Survey* maps 9 and 5.

The *Moyle Way* is a 20-mile (32-km) route between Glenariff Forest Park (the starting point is opposite the Park entrance on the A43) and Ballycastle. The entire walk needs completing on one day and it no longer goes over Knocklayd, which was one of the highlights, but the tourist office in Cushendall sells a £2 leaflet covering the walk.

Carnlough and Glenarm

Colour map 1, grid A5

The splendid coast road that continues south to Carnlough was being completed when Thackeray reached this part of the country on his grand tour of 1842, and he was quick to perceive its importance: "one of the most noble and gallant works of art that is to be seen in any country … torn sheer through the rock here and there; and immense work of levelling, shovelling, picking, blasting, filling, is going on along the whole line". The local limestone, which gives Carnlough its characteristic colour, had already been blasted and picked for the coffers of the Marquis and Marchioness of Londonderry, and the fine stone bridge can still be seen that carried a rail line down to the harbour for export of the stone.

Carnlough

In Carnlough there is a **tourist office** of sorts in *McKillop's* shop on Harbour Road, T28885236, and you could ask here about the planned completion of a walk utilizing part of the track followed by the old railway line. Or just see for yourself by walking up Waterfall Street from the *Waterfall Inn* and along Private Road (which is not private in any sense), signposted to the waterfall, and then back to town following the route of the disused railway line.

Glenarm

There are also some walking possibilities around Glenarm, a couple of miles south of Carnlough on the other side of the bay, including a historical trail through the village itself, and the Layde Walk, which leads to a scenic viewing point and places for a picnic. Leaflets with maps are available from the irregularly opened local **tourist office** in the Community Hall, T28841087, or the Larne tourist office. If coming up from Belfast the picturesque village of Glenarm, with its attractive patterning in sections of pavement, lies at the foot of the first of the nine glens of Antrim and may be the first place that tempts you to linger. You might even like to find the time to do a little window-shopping (see 'Shopping', below).

Sleeping
Price codes:
see inside front cover

L-AL *Londonderry Arms Hotel*, Carnlough, T28885255, F28885263, ida@glensofantrim.com This ivy-clad building is the most comfortable and historic place for a night's lodging, but ask for one of the older-style bedrooms. The establishment has a real period feel and the package rate of around £88 per person for 2 nights' B&B and a

Sorley Boy and the MacDonnells

The MacDonnells were a branch of the Scottish MacDonalds who took over most of Antrim in the 16th century, a process completed by Sorley Boy MacDonnell who then had to deal with an early English attempt to colonize Ulster. His family were massacred on Rathlin Island by the English in 1575 but Sorely Boy fought back (see page 550) with grit. His son, Randy MacDonnell, accepted the English Crown in return for a grant of 300,000 acres and the earldom of Antrim. His great-great-grandson was the grandfather of Francis Anne Vane Tempest, Marchioness of Londonderry, who built a coaching inn that is now the Londonderry Arms at Carnlough.

dinner represents value for money. Packed lunches can be provided and suggested walk sheets are available. **B** *Bethany House*, Bay Rd, Carnlough, T28885667. Outside the village on the coast road overlooking the bay. **A** *Bridge Inn*, thebridge.inn@dnet.co.uk 2 Bridge St, Carnlough, T28885096. Has rooms sharing bathroom facilities for £17.50 per person and there is a popular pub below the bedrooms. **B** *Riverside House*, 13 Toberwine St, Glenarm, T28841474. In the centre of the village with its rear overlooking the river. **C** *Nine Glens*, 16 Toberwine St, Glenarm, T28841590. Is 200 yds from the harbour, private parking, open all year. **B** *Town Brae House*, Town Brae Rd, Glenarm, T28841043. A country house overlooking the village and with views of the Ayrshire coast, for those who want to get away from street pavements.

Eating The lunch menu at the *Londonderry Arms* in Carnlough has excellent choices such as Caesar-style salads or mussels for £3.50, pasta dishes for £5 or salmon for £7.50. High tea from 1700 to 1830 and formal dinner from 1900. There are 2 bars in Carnlough serving reliable pub food: the *Glencloy Inn* and the *Bridge Inn*, near each other on Bridge St and High St respectively. *The Gallery Coffee Shop*, 7 Toberwine St, Glenarm, is a small place with pine tables serving salads under £5 and roast beef and chips for £6. *The Schooner* bar on Castle St, Glenarm, serves pub grub from 1100 until 2300.

Shopping *Glenarm Pottery*, 26 Altmore St, T28841013. The workshop here uses traditional designs in sponge and sgraffito. *O'Kane's* antique shop, Toberwine T28841470. Opposite the *Gallery Coffee Shop*.

Directory **Tourist offices** *McKillop's Shop*, Carnlough, T28885236. *Community Hall*, Glenarm, T28841087. Opening hours irregular.

Glenarm to Larne

Travelling south, the sharply defined topography of the Antrim coast is coming to an end as one leaves Glenarm for the final stretch of road that continues to command the sea until Larne is reached. If you've just arrived off the ferry at Larne or travelled up from Belfast this is where the coastal scenery makes an immediate impact, but in either direction a place that might suggest a quick stop is **Ballygally**, mainly due to the eye-catching **AL** *Ballygally Castle Hotel*, T28583212. Sweeping sea views can be enjoyed from the bar while a remnant of the original 17th-century castle has bedrooms with modern pine furniture and a ghost room, which can be visited by non-residents. Bar food is around £6, a three-course dinner in the restaurant is £17.

County Antrim

Larne

Colour map 1, grid B6

Chances are you will only spend time in Larne if delayed by the ferry, but there are ways to while away time: the well organized **tourist office** has local information, including an Ulster American Heritage Trail, with maps describing plaques and graveyards associated with emigration and American forces stationed here in the Second World War. Narrow Gauge Rd. T28260088. Open Jul and Aug, Mon-Fri, 0900-1800, Sat, 0900-1700. Easter to Jun and Sep, Mon-Sat, 0900-1700. Oct-Easter, Mon-Fri, 0900-1700.

Carnfunnock Country park is a neat place for whiling away a sunny afternoon. Once the home of Lord and Lady Dixon it retains their walled garden, the old ice house and the family's private church. It has a caravan park, miniature railway, a wildlife garden and a maze. ■ *3.5 miles (5.6km) north of Larne on the coast road. Visitor centre, café, gift shop. Free.*

The **Carnegie Arts Centre** has old photographs and artefacts, and tells the story of the building of the Antrim coast road. ■ *2 Victoria Rd, T28279482. Tue-Sat 1400-1700. Free.*

The recent history of Larne has little to boast of: in 1974, to destroy the Sunningdale Agreement, masked UDA men closed the ferry, built a barricade of vehicles around the town and forced shops to close down.

Sleeping
Price codes: See inside front cover

AL *Highways Hotel*, Ballyloran, T28272272, F28275015. Just off the A8 road a mile outside Larne on the road to Belfast. **A** *Curran Court Hotel*, 84 Curran Rd, T28275505, F28260096. On the continuation of Main St and close to the ferry. **B** *Cairnview*, 13 Croft Heights, Ballygarry, T/F28583269. A B&B 4 miles north of Larne on the Antrim Coast Rd. 3 rooms at £18 per person. **B** *Manor Guest House*, 23 Olderfleet Rd, T28273305. B&B virtually next door to the ferry. **C** *Bellevue*, 35 Olderfleet Rd, T28270233. On the right, at the bottom of the road directly ahead when disembarking. No en-suite rooms.

Eating

The 2 hotels serve bar food and have restaurants and *Kiln*, out of town on the Old Glenarm Rd that runs north parallel to the coast road, T28260924, is a pub restaurant with a good local reputation. *Robert Brown's*, 21 Lower Cross St, comes recommended by locals. Café-style food is available at the ferry terminal, but *The Bailie*, 111 Main St, is a cheerful-looking pub serving inexpensive meals daily at lunchtime and from 1700 until 2000. There are a few other inexpensive places in Main St including *Carriages*, 105 Main St, and the *Golden Inn*, a Chinese place at 117 Main St. About a mile inland from Larne in the village of Cairncastle is *The Meeting House*, 120, Brustin Brae Rd, T583252 is a long-established pub which has good pub food, a restaurant serving fairly traditional food and traditional music on Sat and Wed evenings.

Sport

Diving *North Irish Lodge*, Islandmagee, T93382246. **Horse-riding** *Rainbow Equestrian Centre*, 24 Hollow Rd, Islandmagee. T93382929. *Islandmagee Riding Centre*, T28382108. **Leisure Centre** Tower Rd, T28260478, closes 2200 Mon-Fri and 1700 at weekend.

Transport

Buses Bus station on Circular Rd, T28272345. **Car hire** *Avis*, Terminal Building, Larne Harbour, T28260799. **Ferry** *P&O*, T0990-980777, operate 2 routes out of Larne: to Cairnryan in Scotland, with a 1-hour service on the *Superstar Express* and 2¼ hours on the *European Causeway*; and to Fleetwood in England. Larne Harbour, T28279221, is at the end of Olderfleet Rd. **Taxis** *AA*, T28277888. *Cas Cabs*, T28274983. **Train** Station, Circular Rd, T28260604.

Directory

Banks *Bank of Ireland* and *Northern Bank* in Main St along with building societies; *First Trust Bank*, Upper Main St; *Ulster Bank*, Upper Cross St. Exchange facility also at the tourist office. **Bird-watching and boat trips** Mr Galbarith, Islandmagee, T93382539. **Communications** Post office: Main St.

Islandmagee

Islandmagee can be reached on the B90 from Whitehead or by foot on a passenger ferry, T28273785/T28274085, between Larne and Ballylumford, that departs at 0730 and on the hour between 0800 and 1500 and then on the half hour until 1730.

Ins & outs
Colour map 1, grid B6

Little known outside the North of Ireland, Islandmagee is an island-like peninsula pointing north between Whitehead and Larne, with basalt cliffs facing Scotland but a more welcoming west side and a sandy and safe beach, Brown's Bay, on the north end, which receives a smattering of families on sunny summer days. Islandmagee, a teetotalling, conservative retreat where few foreign travellers venture, has its own little surprises. On the road between Mill Bay and Ballylumford, for instance, look out for the astonishing location of the **Ballylumford Dolmen**.

Sights

Talk of repairing **The Gobbins**, a clifftop walk on the east side, is still under repair and only a short part of it can be safely traversed. For information on walks and birdwatching call in to **Ford Farm Museum**, where the main attraction is butter-making and spinning demonstrations. ■ *Low Rd, T93353264. Mar-Oct, daily 1400-1800. £2.*

Half-way along on the west side, at Mill Bay facing Larne Lough, there is an oyster and mussel farm at the harbour, T93382246, where produce can be purchased, including lobster and crab.

See 'Sport' above for details of diving and other activities in the area.

The **A** *Millbay Inn*, 77 Millbay Rd, T93382436, has 4 rooms and is also the best place for food and the only place for a drink. It opens daily for lunch and, except on Sun, from 1900 for dinner. Traditional dishes such as champ and sausages, plus à la carte, under £15 for a meal. **B** *The Farm*, 69 Portmuck Rd, T93382252. Enjoys sea views and also has a self-catering cottage for rent, from £175 to £300 a week depending on the season. *Brown's Bay Caravan Park*, Brown's Bay, T70382497. Camping site run by the council, where a tent pitch is around £5.

Sleeping & eating

Carrickfergus and around

Passing the town on the A2 heading on along the north side of the Belfast Lough, it is impossible to miss Carrickfergus Castle, but don't be misled by its dramatic posture into thinking that the town itself is an exciting place. It is an unastonishing place that need hardly detain the visitor, especially if travelling north where more interesting destinations await. But if the weather is inclement there are sufficient diversions in and around Carrickfergus to pass a day. The **tourist office** is in the Heritage Plaza on Antrim St, T93366455. Open Apr-Sep, Mon-Sat, 1000-1800, Sun (Jul and Aug only) 1200-1800. Closes an hour earlier the rest of the year.

Colour map 1, grid B6

The castle is a formidable-looking Anglo-Norman edifice with a long history. A famous siege by Edward Bruce in 1315 was resisted for longer than it could otherwise have been with the help of the capture of some Scots, eight of whom provided an edible repast for the beleaguered forces. Sorley Boy MacDonnell ran amuck here in revenge for the massacre on Rathlin (see box on page 555), and there is plenty more to learn either in the castle or on the

Carrickfergus Castle

The good old days

"The inhabitants of all sexes and classes [of Islandmagee] are perhaps a more immoral race than is to be found in any other rural district in Antrim ... What makes their immorality the more disgusting is the openness and want of shame with which it is exhibited. The women whenever from home, or indeed whenever they can procure the means, drink raw spirits in such quantities as would astonish any but a native ... several have lost their reason, and many still remain as examples and warnings, in their paralysed bodies and shattered intellects, to those who are treading in their footsteps."

After Lord Dungannon broke up all 14 pubs on Islandmagee in the early 19th century a born-again temperance set in, the legacy of which can be seen today when you look for somewhere to have a drink on the peninsula. The same report also noted that Islandmagee had not "the slightest tinge of party or sectarian feeling."

Knight Ride, a monorail journey through history, situated in the tourist office complex ■ *Castle: T93351273. Apr-May and Sep, Mon-Sat 1000-1800, Sun 1400-1800; Jun-Aug, Mon-Sat 1000-1800, Sun 1200-1800; Oct-Mar, Mon-Sat 1000-1600, Sun 1400-1600. £2.70. Knight Ride: T93366455. Apr-Sep, Mon-Sat 1000-1800; Sun 1200-1800. Closes an hour earlier the rest of the year. £2.70. Joint ticket saves 10%.*

Carrickfergus Gasworks The industrial history here will make a welcome relief for anyone suffering from castle fatigue. The only Victorian coal-fired gasworks in Ireland, built in 1855 to light street lamps, they were still producing gas here in the early 1960s. ■ *T93351438. Jun-Aug, Sun 1400-1700. £1.50.*

The poet Louis MacNeice (1907-63) grew up in Carrickfergus, for his father was the rector of St Nicholas' church in the Market Place. The interior is not dull, there is a fine memorial to the Chichester family, and the adjoining cemetery is where the poet could "hear the voice of the minister tucking people into the ground". ■ *T93360061, mornings only.*

Andrew Jackson Centre The parents of the seventh US president emigrated from Carrickfergus in 1765, and a recreated dwelling of that period makes up the Andrew Jackson Centre and houses exhibitions on the president and the USA connection. Quite a dull place, which is enlivened a little by the adjoining **US Rangers' Centre** devoted to the First Battalion US Rangers who trained in Carrickfergus before leaving for Europe. ■ *Boneybefore. 2 miles north of Carrickfergus on the Larne Rd, T93366455. Apr-Oct, Mon-Fri, 1000-1300 and 1400-1800, Sat and Sun 1400-1800. £1.20.*

Sleeping & eating **L** *Dobbins Inn Hotel*, High St, T/F93351905. Ancient lineage but modern facilities in town-centre hotel. **C** *Langsgarden*, 72 Scotch Quarter, T/F93366369, overlooks Belfast Lough. Most rooms, at £16.50 per person, share bathroom facilities.

Meals throughout the day in comfortable, olde-worlde setting of *Dobbins Inn Hotel* or try trendy *The Central*, 13 High St, T93369729. *The Courtyard Coffee House*, 38 Scotch Quarter, is fine for lunch or afternoon tea, plus a take-away menu until closing time at 1645, Mon-Sat. Large portions for lunch at the *Northgate*, 59 North St, T93364136, and the *Tamarind*, 32 West St, T93355579, is OK for Indian food.

Inland Antrim

Inland Antrim has some pleasant countryside but it is of limited appeal to the traveller, especially when the scenic coast road beckons. But if you are travelling between Belfast and the north coast on the A26, the town of Ballymena makes for a far more diverting stop than nondescript Antrim town itself.

Ballymena and around

Presbyterian and ultra-loyal Ballymena was founded in the 17th century, for Lowland Scottish settlers, by William Adair from Kinhilt and developed into a thriving commercial town on the back of the linen industry from the middle of the 18th century onwards. Ballymena is where Loyalist leader the Reverend Ian Paisley comes from, and the actor Liam Neeson also grew up here. While there is not a lot to see in the town itself, Ballymena is a classic Protestant town and an essential part of the complex whole that makes up Northern Ireland. Adjoining the **tourist office** (Church St, T25638494 Mon-Fri, 0900-1700, Sat – Easter-Oct –1000-1600), there is a tiny **museum** filled with old photographs, radios and shaving mugs and every Wednesday between June and August a **town tour** takes place from the town hall. Contact the tourist office for confirmation of time and place. Try to find time for a short trip west of town to the Moravian church at Gracehill (see box next page).

Colour map 1, grid A5

The area's American connection is kept alive at Arthur Cottage, the ancestral home of long-forgotten 21st US president, Chester Alan Arthur. Worth a visit for the occasional summer evenings of song and storytelling or the afternoon craft demonstrations. ■ *Dreen, Cullybackey: from Cullybackey, northwest of Ballymena, take the B96 to Portglenone and it is signposted on the right, T25660300. May-Sep, Mon-Sat, 1030-1700 (1600 on Sat). Closed 12 Jul. £2. Craft demonstrations Jun-Aug, Tue, Fri and Sat at 1330.*

Arthur Cottage

To the east of town the A42 goes to the floral village of Broughshane, best visited in early summer or at the end of August when bulbs from the stock of the famous daffodil breeder Guy L Wilson can be purchased. From Broughshane the B94 to the distinctively contoured Slemish Mountain is signposted, and the way up the mountain is clearly marked from the car-park. People flock here on St Patrick's Day because of the mountain's association with the saint – he tended pigs here for six years as a young slave – but it is a quiet enough spot the rest of the year and outside of weekends the climb to the top and its views can be enjoyed in splendid isolation. The mountain is 1,437 ft (438 m) high but it is only a 700-ft (213-m) climb from the car-park.

Slemish Mountain

L *Galgorm Manor*, 136 Fenaghy Rd, Ballymena, T25881001, www.galgorm.com This 19th-century house was previously the home of a textile magnate, and can deliver comfort and recreation by way of river views, fishing rights, riding stables and clay pigeon shooting. **A** *Tullymore House*, 2 Carnlough Rd, Broughshane, T256861233, F256862238. Has a good reputation and a lovely setting. **B** *Ben Vista*, 79 Galgorm Rd, Ballymena, T2564609, michael.joyce@btinternet.com A large Victorian house conveniently close to the bus and train stations, charging £20 per person for B&B.

Sleeping
Price codes:
See inside
front cover

Good food in a classical-style restaurant at the *Galgorm Manor*, Fenaghy Rd, Ballymena, T25881001. Halibut with a vermouth sauce or duck with coriander pesto

Eating

County Antrim

Moravians in Antrim

The Moravian Church made a dramatic impact in Antrim with the arrival of the evangelist John Cennick in 1746. Of the 200 religious societies he established in Ireland most of them were in County Antrim, and Cennick has left a dramatic record of his encounters with traditional Protestantism and the numerous personality clashes he seemed to engender both within and outside of his church. The extent to which the establishment of a model church community at Gracehill furthered the

Moravian cause is debatable but there is no mistaking the evangelical zeal with which they pursued and applied their religious beliefs. Their dignified and unaffected village square, with the church open for services on a Sunday morning, and their gender-based cemetery with its flat tombstones are endearing and idiomatic expressions of their cult.

To reach Gracehill from Ballymena take the A2 west for less than two miles and look for a brown sign indicating the church down a road to the left.

might appear for lunch at £9.95, while dinner for £27.50 includes familiar dishes with a touch of class and an impressive wine list and, at weekends, live piano music. In Ballymena the *Fern Room*, 80 Church St, is a self-service restaurant inside *McKillens* department store and closes at 1700, but it is the best place for a quick meal and value for money: peppered meat balls with rice or chicken goulash are under £5. The *Thatch Inn*, 57 Main St, Broughshane, is the best place for pub food at lunchtime during the week while the *Pantry*, Jubilee Mews off Main St, opens until 1700 Mon-Sat and serves soup, stews and home-baked goodies. *Solomon Grundy's*, Tower Centre, is a long-established coffee shop which does soups, fresh bread and more substantial things with chicken. Child friendly.

Transport **Car hire** *Ballymena Car Hire*, 205 Cullybackey Rd, T25630077. **Taxis** *Regent Taxis*, 1 Hill St, T25644777.

Lisburn

Colour map 1, grid B5 Situated to the southwest of Belfast, and easily visited from the city by bus from the Europa Buscentre, the best reason for coming to Lisburn is the **Irish Linen Centre & Lisburn Museum**. The growing of flax and making of linen was a part of Irish farm life from earliest times but the plantations brought artisans from Britain, and before the end of the 17th century Ulster linen had acquired a particular renown. This did not conflict with any commercial interests in England and was allowed to develop unhindered. In 1698 a group of Huguenot weavers were paid to settle in Lisburn and their special skills were rapidly assimilated. By the end of the following century mechanization had been introduced into the bleaching process, and this set the stage for the development of Ireland's only major industry in the 19th century, with Belfast the world centre for linen manufacturing. Not until the 1920s and 30s did demand begin to drop and a terminal decline set in. The Centre and Museum tell the story and weaving workshops bring the craft to life. ■ *Market Sq, T92663377. Mon-Sat 0930-1700. Free admission to Museum; £2.75 for the Centre. Restaurant and linen and craft shop.*

Belfast

15

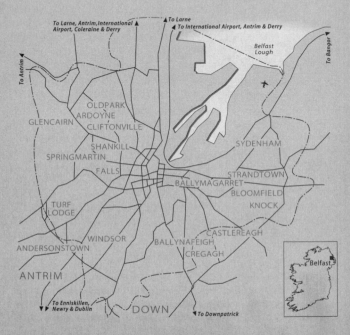

A name long synonymous with bombs and sectarianism, Belfast is today undergoing a miraculous renaissance. Big money is pouring in from governments and corporations, and restaurants and housing are mushrooming where derelict factories and burned-out buildings once reigned. It seems fairly certain that the people of Belfast's will to live a normal life outweighs the minority's need to cling to the hatreds of the past. The Falls Road, the Divis Flats, The Shankill, Andersonstown, the Ardoyne – these names still resound with visions of horror and mayhem, trembling schoolgirls and screaming housewives. A first-time visitor to Belfast sees the armoured cars, the gates that were once used to close down the city at night, the RUC posts and the grim murals, and their instinct is to move on – find somewhere nice to go. But this would be a mistake. This city has a life: its tourist infrastructure is sorted: hotels are bursting out of the pavement, restaurants have Michelin ratings and its pompous 19th-century architecture is a worthy monument to the men who built this city and a solid counterpoint to the flimsy steel and glass of the city's more modern developments.

Ins and outs

Getting there

Air Belfast is served by 2 airports : the Belfast International, T94484848, which handles most international flights, including flights from Heathrow, and Belfast City Airport, T90939093, which has a smaller number of flights, largely from regional airports in Britain. The international airport, at Aldergrove, is 19 miles (30 km) north of the city on the M2. From outside the airport, buses run to the Europa and Laganside bus stations every 30 mins, hourly on Sun. Taxis go from beside the bus stop and cost around £20. The city airport is 3 miles (5 km) northeast of the city. *Citybus* 21 runs from the airport to City Hall, or Sydenham Halt rail station is nearby and will connect with Central Station.

Boat Ferries arrive at several locations along the river. The *Seacat* ferries from Heysham and Troon and the Isle of Man (summer only) arrive at Donegall Quay, from where it is a 15-min walk to the city centre, unless you prefer to take a cab. From Ballast Quay, where the *Stena* ferry docks, the best option is again a cab, while an *Ulsterbus* connects Larne, 20 miles (30 km) north and where the *P&O* ferry from Cairnryan docks, with the Laganside bus station.

Bus Long-distance buses from the Republic or within Northern Ireland arrive at either Laganside bus station or the Europa bus station, both of which are very central.

Train Trains arrive at Central Station and a free bus service goes into the centre of town. Alternatively, it is possible get another train into Botanic Station for the university area.

Getting around

Bus A series of buses radiate out from the city centre in Donegall Sq, Upper Queen St, Wellington Pl and Castle St.

Taxi Taxi stands are outside the Europa bus station and in Donegall Sq, Smithfield market, and Bridge St. The Smithfield market cabs travel into Catholic west Belfast, taking several passengers at a time for about £1 per passenger, while the Bridge St cabs travel to Protestant west Belfast. Both groups of taxis do tourist tours of their territories for about £10 an hr and offer what may reliably be called partisan versions of Belfast's recent history. The Donegall Sq and Europa bus station taxis have a starting price of £1.50 and do not wait to load up with passengers first.

Car Car owners should note that while the severe parking restrictions of yore are more relaxed, there are still no parking areas around sensitive buildings such as RUC posts and the courthouse. There is no shortage of secure car parks and most streets have pay and display systems.

Tourist information The *Belfast Welcome Centre*, 47 Donegall Pl, T90246609, www.gotobelfast.com, has lots of useful, free information, a left luggage office and will book accommodation and travel for you. *Borde Faílte* is at 53 Castle St, T90327888, Mon-Fri 0900-1700, Sat 0900-1230, Mar to end-Sep only, and provides information for your onward journey to the Republic. There is a *Usit Now* office at the Fountain Centre, College St, BT1 6ET, T90324073, and at Queen's University Student Union Building, University Rd, BT7 1PE, T90241230.

★

Things to do in Belfast

- Take a tour of **City Hall** and try on the councillors' robes
- Visit the **Ulster Folk Park** and transport museum
- Have a drink in the **Crown Liquor Saloon**
- Walk through the **tropical ravine** in the Botanic Gardens
- Eat dinner at **Deane's** in *fin-de-siècle* splendour
- Take a **taxi tour** of West Belfast
- Wander around the footpaths of **Cave Hill**

Belfast

History

Belfast sits in a valley created by two rivers, the Lagan and the Farsett (now piped below the streets) which once necessitated a series of forts to guard their crossings. If you had wandered this way in the 12th century, you would have seen little more than a Norman castle, built in 1177. The land was under the control of the Gaelic lords, the O'Neills, until the Plantation (see page 645) began under James I, with a royal charter granted to Sir Arthur Chichester giving him the right to create a borough. By the middle of the 17th century a small town had blossomed. Carrickfergus, in Antrim, dominated trade in the area until Belfast's population rose to a critical mass with the immigration in the late 17th century of Huguenots fleeing persecution in France. They brought their traditional industry, linen production, and the burgeoning city now had a reason to expand. The Plantation continued with rope-making, shipping, and export of beef, corn and butter to Britain and France, making the city the fourth largest town in Ireland by the end of the century.

See also history of Northern Ireland on page 525

The 18th century saw a fourfold increase in population, and the further development of the shipbuilding and linen industries. Unlike other areas of Ulster, Belfast was inhabited by both Catholics and Protestants who lived harmoniously throughout the century, culminating in the formation in Belfast in 1791 of the United Irishmen, a cross-denominational nationalist organization. It was, of course, stamped out and many Protestant and Catholic men, who would be national heroes in other circumstances today, lost their lives.

The 18th century

The next half-century saw the development of sectarian differences in Belfast. From an initial apathy following the eradication of the United Irishmen, northern Protestants began to see the increasing militancy of the Catholics throughout Ireland as a threat. In the 1820s Protestant clubs were set up all over Ulster; their members made great parades, bore arms and formed bands to play anti-Catholic songs. After Catholic Emancipation in 1829 an Orange Order parade on 12 July was banned which led to riots all over the city.

Beginnings of sectarianism

As agricultural prices declined and the Industrial Revolution came to Belfast, thousands of the rural poor of both denominations flocked to the city to compete for scarce work. Catholic and Protestant no longer had a common interest; Catholic emancipation was restricted. Protestants now held all the power in the city, owned most of the industry and were increasingly reluctant to give up any power in the light of the increasing Irish Catholic militancy that threatened their power base. The Famine (see page 79) drove ever more people into the city where the inevitable fight for work and housing drove the two groups ever further apart.

In 1857 riots hit the streets of Belfast as huge Catholic and Protestant mobs met in open battle in the streets. This happened again in 1864, forcing the closure of factories. The Catholic minority suffered the worst of the attacks, the Catholic Pound district being sandwiched between Sandy Row and the Shankill Road. Reform of Parliament and changes in the property qualification to vote in 1867 gave Catholics more rights, but every move in favour of equality was met with an Orange, unionist reaction, with ever-increasing displays of affection for William of Orange each year on the 12 July. Further reforms, the disestablishment of the Church of Ireland and the introduction of the secret ballot, disturbed the control of the Protestants, but were met with the repeal of the act banning sectarian marches. Home Rule gained power in the rest of Ireland, but in Belfast it became the bogey that kept the riots coming each year on the glorious twelfth. The Home Rule Bill of 1886 polarized even liberal Protestants' feelings with Monster Meetings of Conservatives and Orangemen in Belfast opposed to the bill. Its eventual defeat was accompanied by the worst riots so far. Catholics drove Protestants out of their workplaces and were in their turn driven out of work and beaten by Protestant mobs; Catholic pubs were attacked and burned out. The police became a third party in the fighting, battling both Protestant and Catholic crowds: the police force was largely Catholic, commanded by Protestant officers. The riots continued out of the housing estates and factories and into the city centre, lasting from June to the end of September; between 31 and 50 people died. In the rest of Ulster the fighting was about landlords and land ownership but in Belfast it was purely sectarian – working people fighting among themselves for scarce resources and work.

Into the 20th century In 1891 Belfast officially outstripped Dublin in terms of population. Around 26% of its population was Catholic. It had an opera house and many grand commercial buildings. Besides shipbuilding and linen there was a flourishing engineering industry and this was Ireland's centre for building steam engines. In the early 20th century, the Gaelic Revival came to Belfast, and committed intellectuals on both sides of the sectarian divide found a common interest in Irish culture and tradition. But in 1911, the issue of Home Rule reared its head yet again, bringing to an end the period of relative peace. Unionists began to talk of taking power in Ulster, rather than accepting Home Rule for Ireland. The Ulster Volunteer Force was established in order to fight for independence and by 1912 there were 90,000 volunteers, and the old town hall in Belfast their headquarters.

The First World War brought a certain amount of prosperity to the region. In 1914 Harland and Wolff, the Belfast-based shipbuilders, were producing eight percent of the world output of ships. At first orders declined as workers were called up and materials became scarce but then the war orders came flooding in, and in 1918 Harland and Wolff launched 201,070 tons of merchant ships. Farmers knew a wealth previously unimagined as imports died away under U-boat attacks. The linen industry also boomed with orders for uniforms, tents and aeroplane fabric.

After 1918 hundreds of men inured to the horror of war returned to Belfast ready to take up the old quarrels. In the south, the Black and Tan war was a particularly bloody interlude, while in Belfast sectarian violence reached new heights. In 1920 Loyalist mobs drove all Catholics and socialists out of Harland and Wolff, Sirocco, Mackie's, McLaughlin and Harveys: all the big employers in Belfast. About 11,000 Catholic people lost their jobs in this way while Catholic houses and businesses were attacked and the convent of

St Matthew's Church in Belfast was burned down. Belfast Catholics, now a quarter of the population, fought back just as violently but were greatly out-numbered. The violence continued unabated for two years, the Catholics never regaining their jobs, which were given to Protestants. Because of the fear of the increasingly powerful IRA the Ulster Special Forces were created, made up entirely of Protestants: the B Specials in Belfast were part-time, uniformed and armed. Ironically, in 1921 the Protestants, who had fought for so long against it, got Home Rule while the 32 southern counties received dominion status.

In 1922 more riots and deaths occurred: 61 people were killed in March in Belfast alone. Outside the city the IRA was burning and looting, while inside the Catholic population suffered reprisals from Loyalists and B Specials alike: the Special Powers Act allowed suspects to be detained indefinitely without charge or trial. After the murder of an MP internment was introduced, as well as a curfew. In May 1922, 66 people died, two-thirds of them Catholic.

After the assassination of Michael Collins (see page 652) in that year, things calmed down a little with the southern government encouraging the IRA to join the mainstream Irish army. While the civil war and its aftermath raged in the south, those who might have caused disruption in the north were occu-pied and so peace broke out for a time in Belfast.

By the 1930s Belfast had settled to become an anti-Catholic, sectarian city with annual displays of Orange power attended by cabinet ministers who abused their southern Catholic neighbours, who, in retaliation, abused them. The economic war between Dublin and London polarized attitudes even more, and employers were encouraged by the Belfast government to employ Protestants who would be loyal to the state. In 1935 there were more riots as the Orange parades were first banned and then allowed. In 1937 the new con-stitution for the south set out a claim on the sovereignty of the north, as well as establishing the special position of the Catholic Church in the south; these claims made matters considerably worse.

The Second World War

Belfast had suffered during the Great Depression, but things began to boom again as war began to seem likely. An airport was built, and the industries that had benefited from the First World War came into their own again; Harland and Wolff received commissions to convert passenger ships for war use and two huge warships were built. In 1941, however, Belfast became a target for the Luftwaffe. The first waves of bombers missed the industrial targets, and hit instead the impoverished housing estates of the north city centre. Fires raged throughout the city, and fire engines from the south were sent up to help deal with them. Hundreds of people died and their corpses were laid out in the swimming baths and St George's Market. After this first night of bombing tens of thousands of people left the city. The second wave of attacks in May the same year saw Belfast become one huge conflagration across the harbour, with small firestorms breaking out in the industrial sites: half of the houses and most of the industry in the city were destroyed. The glow was visible 50 miles away. Mid-dle-class ladies living outside the city took in refugees, and were appalled at the condition of the slum children, whereas wealthier Belfast citizens retired to the hotels of Donegal for the duration of the war. Catholic churches opened their crypts to one and all as air raid shelters, and Protestant and Catholic stood shoulder to shoulder putting out the flames, uniting the two sides of the reli-gious divide. That, fortunately, was the last of the air raids over Belfast.

In 1942 American soldiers came to the city, completing a circle that began during the Famine years when thousands of Belfast Protestants left for the US.

The arrival of foreign troops on Irish soil sparked a protest from De Valera, and increased activity on the part of the IRA. After a gunfight in west Belfast six men were arrested and sentenced to death for the murder of an RUC man. Only one was executed but it brought back all the old antagonisms in the city. In 1943 an IRA man held up the audience of the Broadway cinema in the Falls Road and insisted that they take part in a commemoration for the dead of the Easter Rising. But suppression and arrest in both north and south ensured that by the end of the war the IRA was defunct.

To the present From 1945 to the mid-1960s the city experienced not so much sectarian harmony but at least a degree of peace. The modern trouble in the North began in the civil rights demonstrations in Derry but Belfast communities enthusiastically joined in (see page 656).

The present situation is one where an entire generation of people in their 20s want nothing to do with the old disputes; Belfast clubs resound to the enjoyment of young people who don't know or care what sect their dancing partners belong to, restaurant owners are glad of the custom from whomever walks into their place, the murals are fading away and only the desperately sad parts of the city still paint their kerbstones red, white and blue.

Sights

The chief tourist attraction in Belfast may strike you as a little tasteless: both the tourist association and local taxi drivers do tours of West Belfast, covering the major streets of the Troubles and their associated deaths. Tours of the city hall also tend to focus on the difficult times, while the city museum takes the opposite approach and denies that any trouble ever happened. Added to these, the zoo, the Botanic Gardens, a 19th-century castle and a new weir over the river take up no more than a couple of days' sightseeing, whereas there are nights and nights worth of eating out and dancing to be had if clubbing's your thing.

City centre

City Hall Dominating the centre of town in Donegall Sq is the massive City Hall, a
Currently the city pompous Victoriana testament to what money can buy. Completed in 1906,
council is split the Portland stone edifice, designed by Brumwell Thomas and covering 11
between Sinn acres, is topped by a copper dome 173 ft high. You can't wander around it at
Féin and Unionist will but there are guided tours from Monday to Saturday during the summer.
members, which Inside is an extravaganza of imported marble, stained glass dedicated to
must make work various moneymen and soldiers, and paintings of various mayors in their rega-
there noisy lia. Very few women feature in this place at all, except those who lead the guided tours. The tour takes in the council chamber, laid out in adversarial mode with tables in the middle for the press; the Great Hall, whose stained-glass windows were one of the few items to be protected from the German air raids during the Second World War; the banqueting hall; and robing rooms.

The grounds contain more testimony to the doings of men. Statues of Edward Harland, James Haslett, the Rt Hon Daniel Dixon, Lord Dufferin and RJ McMordie, several of the movers and shakers of the 19th century, all pay court to the quite lissom figure of Queen Victoria, flanked by figures representing spinning and shipbuilding and, as an afterthought, education. A cenotaph also stands in the grounds, as does a memorial to one of Belfast's biggest mistakes, the *Titanic*, which was built here.

The pediment over the main door depicts Hibernia, Minerva, Mercury, Industry, Labour, Liberty and Industry and some small boys.

For many years the city council was dominated by unionist politicians who were partly responsible for the failure of the 1985 Anglo-Irish agreement, in large part the same agreement that was made on Good Friday 1998. They refused to take part in council business while the Agreement was in place, effectively making the city unrunnable. A huge banner hung along the front of the building expressing their opposition to any dealings with the republic.

In 1988 an IRA bomb did what German air raids had failed to do, and destroyed the stained-glass windows of the Great Hall. ■ *Tours of City Hall: Jul-Sep, daily, 1030 and 1430; Oct-Jun, Wed only, 1430. Free.*

Donegall Square

There are a few other buildings around Donegall Square of some interest. At number 17 is the **Linen Hall Library**, which has been a lending library for over 200 years. Not much to look at from the outside, it has a vast collection of early Irish material and is used by research students studying the recent history of the Troubles. It is not a public library, although you can wander in and use the reading room and café on the first floor, and browse around the collection of prints that are on sale. The library was established in 1788 and its first librarian, Thomas Russell, was hanged in 1803 after an abortive Republican uprising. ■ *17 Donegall Sq. Open Mon-Fri, 0930-1730, Sat, 0930-1600. Free.*

A wander around the square reveals some more late Victorian bulwarks of respectability. The 1884-85 Robinson and Cleaver building stands out among the solidity: six storeys high with rounded corners rising to ornate turrets, its exterior is highly carved with cherubs, fruit and contemporary figures such as Victoria, Albert and, for some reason, George Washington. At the east side of the square is the Pearl Assurance building, originally called the Ocean building, erected between 1899 and 1902 in a Gothic revival style, with oddly shaped pinnacle towers creating a startling skyline. At the west of the Square is the Scottish Provident building (1897-99) covered in wild carvings of dolphins, sphinxes and lions as well as figures representing Belfast's industry.

Around the Albert Clocktower

Northwest of City Hall and close to the river is another cluster of late 19th-century constructions. Now restored and stabilized, for many years the Albert Clocktower leaned a little more with every year that passed and had to have several bits chopped off that looked as if they might bring the whole thing down. Beside it the troubled *AIB bank* was formerly the Northern Bank head office. Built in 1852 in Portland stone and granite, it makes a grandiose statement about the permanence of Protestant values, with giant Doric columns and a great carved frieze above the entrance. Along Waring Street, a block to the north of the clock tower, is the now unoccupied **Ulster Bank**, another magnificent temple to Mammon. Its architect won the commission in a competition where 67 other architects proposed designs. It is based on St Mark's Library in Venice, and has just about every architectural idiosyncrasy known at the time: Doric and Corinthian columns, allegorical sculptures, ornate railings and Victorian lamps.

Back down Victoria Street a little way, take time out to admire the façade of the **McCausland Hotel**, once two great warehouses whose fronts were preserved with their marble relief figures of the five continents and animals, and arcaded windows. Back at the Albert Tower the road sweeps round through some ugly modern road building past the **Custom House**, where once the

Belfast centre

Belfast

Sleeping

1 Europa *E2*
2 Hilton & Sonoma Restaurant *D5*
3 Linen House Hostal *B2*
4 McCausland *C4*
5 TENsq *E3*
6 Travelodge *E2*

Eating & drinking

1 Aero *E2*
2 Bank Gallery *E6*

3 Beaten Docket *E2*
4 Bewleys *C3*
5 Clements *D2*
6 Custom House *C4*
7 Deane's *E2*
8 Delaney's *C3*

Belfast

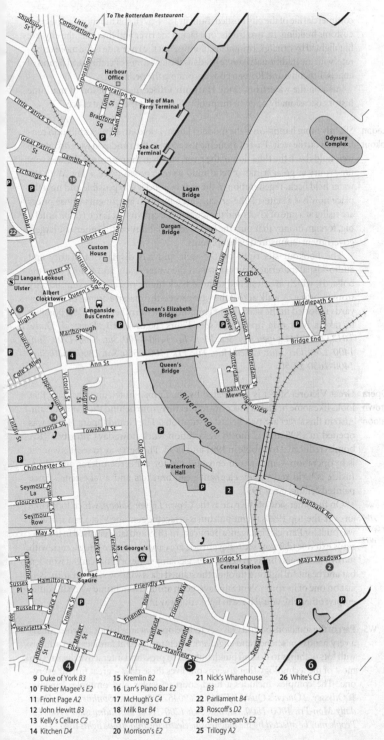

commercial life of the city bustled. Built in 1854-57, it still functions as the city's customs building. Its two fronts, one facing the river and the other the city, are highlighted by ornate Corinthian columns, but the river side is the more elaborate, with the traditional riverine heads as the keystones of arches, and figures of angels, Britannia and Roman gods decorating the pediment.

Also on the waterfront is the **Harbour Office**, its exhibition of maritime history occasionally open to the public. Enquire at the tourist office.

Lagan Lookout

Slightly more hands-on is the modern Lagan Lookout, a little exhibition centre built on the weir. Part of a scheme to renovate the rundown waterfront, the weir holds back the tidal flow of the river, which in the past made the area very unsavoury as great banks of fetid mud were exposed twice a day. With the water held back, regeneration of the area beyond it was possible and now the place now has a state-of-the-art concert hall, bijou apartments whose prices are rising at a rate of knots and the jewel in the crown that is the *Hilton* hotel – big, foreign money that puts the seal of respectability on the otherwise largely government- sponsored developments.

The Lookout sits right on the weir and has displays of history and audio-visual material. You can watch the water rising and falling over the bollards, which are designed to hold back high tides and prevent the city from flooding. A walk across the weir reveals the massive cranes of the shipyards reflected in the glass-walled buildings on the other bank. It is possible to take a boat ride upstream (see 'Tours' below). ■ *1, Donegall Quay, T01232-315444. Open Apr- Sep, Mon- Fri, 1000-1700, Sat, 1200-1700, Sun, 1400-1700; Oct-Mar, closed Mon, Tue-Fri, 1100-1530, Sat, 1300-1630, Sun, 1400-1630. £1.50.*

Grand Opera House & Crown Liquor Saloon

Great Victoria Street is dominated by the *Europa* hotel, an ugly place that looks like some brutalist piece of architecture from behind the Iron Curtain. Also in this street are two Belfast institutions. The Grand Opera House was opened in 1895 and is mostly restoration work nowadays after two IRA bombs reduced it to rubble in 1991 and 1993. The best way to see it is when it is in operation – and it is in constant use for concerts, operas and plays. Inside is lurid red velvet, elephant head brackets and a fake renaissance painted ceiling, circa 1991.

The pub was damaged by the bomb in the Opera House in 1993

On the other side of the road is the *Crown Liquor Saloon*, which looks like an over-the-top 1990s theme pub but is in fact the genuine Victorian article. It was built for Patrick Flanagan, a publican, in 1839 and later encased in the glorious exterior tiles you see today. Inside are carved wooden snugs, each with its own motto and brass match striker, gas lamps, the original carved wooden bar and beautiful lighting through the stained glass windows. If you are in Belfast on one of its somnolent Sundays, go in around lunchtime when it's quite empty; otherwise you'll have to fight your way in.

W5

Part of the squillion-pound Odyssey redevelopment area beside the river, this is a very hands-on science and engineering centre aimed at families and schools with lots of things to do and build, buttons to press and interactive displays on most of the technology that governs our lives these days – great fun for everyone. The complex includes a food court, cineplex and omniplex cinema. ■ *Odyssey, 2 Queen's Quay, BT39QQ, T90467700, www.w5online.co.uk Open daily Mon-Fri, 1000-1800, Sat and Sun 1200-1800. Last admission 1700. £5. People may be affected by the magnetism, electricity, and strobe lights used.*

West Belfast

West Belfast was a working-class area which developed around the linen industry – an area where sectarian violence created two entirely separate communities as far back as the late 19th century: the Catholic Falls and the Protestant Shankill. When the Troubles started in 1969, West Belfast, separated from the city centre by the Westlink motorway, became a battleground. The Falls Road, Crumlin Road, Divis Street, the Shankill are names that ring of riot, burning, assassination and mayhem. However, walk down any one of them today and you see streets that could be any suburb of Manchester or London – dull, suburban maisonettes, corner shops, kids on bikes, Victorian terraces. True, there are intermittent RUC posts looking like something from the Berlin Wall, the occasional armoured car with flaps at the sides to stop anyone rolling a petrol bomb underneath, and most places have rather more security devices than one would normally expect, but you have to look carefully to spot that there has been a sectarian war going on here for 25 years or more. The gable ends of houses tell the story in a series of badly drawn symbols – red hands, shamrock leaves, silhouettes of gunmen – a few which identify this struggle with those in other parts of the world.

A pleasant walk, if a stroll along some of the most battle hardened streets in Belfast to a cemetery where many of the Troubles' victims lie buried can be called pleasant, is along the now quiet suburban streets of the Falls to the **Milltown Cemetery**, where the Republican graves commemorate some of the many lives lost. The walk begins at the Smithfield market where, if you choose, you can negotiate with one of the cab-drivers for a personal tour of the area. Alternatively, head westwards along Divis Street towards Divis Tower, the last remaining building of the notorious **Divis Flats**. The roof was occupied for a time by a republican group, but is now part of an army post, along with the top two storeys (access by helicopter only). As you walk away from the city centre you can see the 'peace line' between the houses on your right, the iron wall built to keep apart the residents of the Falls and Shankill roads. What strikes home as you walk is the small size of the war zone – a few blocks east and west and only one block between the two warring groups. In Conway Street is **Conway Mill,** where you can take a tour of the old linen works and buy some crafts from the people who now use it. ■ *Tours are Tue and Thu, £3, T90326452, www.conwaymill.org* In Clonard Street is the **Church of the Holy Redeemer**, or Clonard Monastery, which has now entered the history books as the place where the initial, very secret, meetings leading to the 1994 IRA cease-fire took place. You will pass on the right the **Royal Victoria Hospital**, which dealt with many of the victims of the Troubles. Beyond the hospital at Number 216 Falls Rd, T90964188, look out for **An Culturlánn**, a cultural centre and **tourist information** point housed in an old Presbyterian church. It has a café and information on local events.

The **cemetery** itself is a quiet place, watched over by an army post opposite. In 1988 the war invaded the cemetery when a grenade was thrown at mourners at the funeral of Séan Savage, one of the IRA members killed in Gibraltar by the SAS. To find the Republican graves head south until the graves run out and then turn right along a tarmac path. Bobby Sands is buried here.

Beyond the cemetery the Falls Road continues into **Andersonstown**, another Republican estate where there are more murals. Beyond that is **Twinbrook**, where Bobby Sands lived, and where a gable end has been turned into a permanent memorial.

The Falls

The Shankill Road

A walk along the Shankill Road begins further north from the city centre. The murals are more in evidence here and are slightly more threatening: silhouettes of gunmen and slogans such as "We know who you are" adorn the walls. Typical symbols are the red hand of Ulster, maps of the six counties detached from the rest of the island, William of Orange on horseback, flags (usually the Union Jack and St George's cross but also the Scottish flag), and generally lots of red, white and blue posts, kerbstones, fences, and so on.

Trips along the Shankill can be arranged with the cab drivers at North Street. They should ask for about £10 for an hour. One possibility is to negotiate a trip out to **Fernhill House**, a museum that explores the history of the Shankill area. ■ *Glencairn Park. Open Mon-Sat, 1000-1600, Sun, 1000-1600. £2. Buses 39, 73, 63 travel along the Shankill Rd but not as far as Fernhill.*

South of the city centre

Ulster Museum & the Botanic Gardens

This is probably the least stressful place to visit in Belfast. Here you will find no mention of the Troubles; it is as if they never happened. The museum is laid out in a kind of walk around the interesting features of Ulster with some dinosaurs, an art collection and a bit of geology thrown in. The ground floor is occupied by some massive machinery connected with linen production and steam power. The size of it all is admirable. Huge boards set apart from the machines give a description of the process of linen manufacture, but it is difficult to connect the two. Heading onwards on this floor, you find a children's dinosaur exhibition. On the second floor are some interesting exhibits on early Ireland, this time much more hands on, with video clips, reconstructed huts and other bits and pieces. There is an interesting video regarding the making of flint tools which accompanies the Ballyclare hoard, a collection of used and blank flints that must once have been the stock-in-trade of a Neolithic flint maker. A display of Spanish artefacts, taken from the *Girona*, a sunken armada vessel excavated near the Giant's Causeway in 1968, gives a nice insight into life on the boats, and some odds and ends of ancient Egyptian and native American artefacts complete this level.

Level three is taken up with jewellery, glassware and a wildlife exhibition, while the top floor displays some of the museum's collection of art. ■ *Open Mon-Fri, 1000-1700, Sun, 1400-1700. Free. Exhibitions change regularly.*

The museum is in the grounds of the Botanic Gardens, rather a dull park, except for the two beautiful glasshouses. The gardens were begun in 1827, during the 19th-century craze for plant hunting. The 14 acres were open to the public for a fee, but those who bought shares in the enterprise were allowed in free. After 1841 the working classes were allowed in free on Saturdays. The gardens never really became self-supporting financially and were eventually sold to the Belfast City Corporation, which made them a public park in 1895.

The best section of the gardens is the reconstruction of a **tropical ravine**, begun in 1889 and extended in 1900 and again in 1902 to include the heated pond where you can see giant water lilies growing. It was renovated once more in 1980. Look out for pitcher plants, tree ferns, bananas, cinnamon trees, papyrus at the water's edge and a great mass of water hyacinth, an invasive weed all over the Far East.

The **Palm House**, completed in 1852, is more beautiful but less interesting inside being filled with plants that you can buy in department stores. The designer, Lanyon, used the new invention of curved glass to create the central elliptical dome with two wings. The building was renovated in 1975 when whole sections of glazing were replaced and a new heating system installed.

Stormont

Stormont, the site of the parliament of Northern Ireland, has become shorthand for the parliament itself. It was established as a result of the Government of Ireland Act of 1920 which devolved all domestic government except taxation to the Northern Ireland parliament at Stormont. When the civil rights campaign developed into open conflict with the Unionist-dominated government, and especially after the British army was called out in 1969, there was pressure on the government to cede its control over internal security. The refusal of Unionism to do this led to the dissolution of Stormont in March 1972. It remained in limbo until 29 November, 1999, when the impasse over the implementation of the Good Friday Agreement was overcome and a new power-sharing executive was formed ending direct rule from London (see page 658). Since that time the assembly has been suspended on several occasions, each in connection with the decommissioning of arms, but as of late 2001 a working settlement has been agreed and the assembly functions relatively smoothly.

■ *Open Apr-Sep, Mon-Fri, 1000-1700, Sat, Sun, bank holidays, 1400-1600; Oct-Mar, Mon-Fri, 1000-1600, closed 1300-1400. Free. Buses 69, 70, 71 from Donegall Sq east.*

North of the city

Cave Hill

The north of the city is defined by the high backdrop of mountains, which make up the country park of Cave Hill. Bought up by the city at various times from 1911, the park consists of about 750 acres of parkland, escarpments and woodland. It is grand wandering territory, criss-crossed with numerous footpaths, and is dotted with Bronze Age sites, including the caves themselves (which are man-made Iron Age mines). The best walk of all is to the top of the hill from where there are wonderful views of the city and lough, and even beyond them to the Scottish coast. ■ *Entrances to the country park are Belfast Castle, Belfast Zoo, Upper Cave Rd. Cave Hill Heritage Centre is in Belfast Castle.*

Belfast Castle

Set in the grounds of the country park is Belfast Castle, a Scottish baronial pile built in 1870 for the Marquis of Donegall. From a distance it looks imposing enough set against the mountains, but close up it is twee, with too many turrets and curlicues, rather in the style of Balmoral. It almost bankrupted the family, who fortunately married well and were able to complete it. It was given to the city in 1934 and refurbished in the 1970s at a cost of a couple of million pounds. It is run now as a series of businesses – a classy restaurant, a bistro, shop and pub all done up in Victorian street style – and is available for hire for weddings and functions. Inside is a small heritage centre with information about Cave Hill. ■ *Belfast Castle, Antrim Rd. T90776925. Open daily, 0900-1800. Free. If the heritage centre is closed, ask for the key at reception. Citybus 45, 46, 47, 48, 49, 50, 51 from Donegall Sq west.*

Belfast Zoo

The zoo is a pleasant day out for children of all ages, as long as you enjoy looking at captive animals. It is a vibrant place, and so it should be. It has had around £10 million invested into the creation of new enclosures and general renovation, meaning the animals are well kept and there are some unusual creatures. Some of Steve Bell's Falklands penguins live here, as do tapirs, spectacled bears and assorted monkeys. ■ *Open Apr-Sep, 1000-1800 daily; Oct-Mar 1000-1530. £4.80.*

East of Belfast

Ins & outs There are 2 routes east out of Belfast: the A20 goes past Stormont to Newtownards while the A2 passes the Ulster Folk & Transport Museum on its way to Bangor. Buses and trains travel to Bangor and there is the 15-mile (24 km) **North Down Coastal Path**, from Holywood to Groomsport, east of Bangor.

Stormont When Stormont was opened in 1932 it was accompanied by a triumphalist Protestant pageant, but now that the new, post-Good Friday, Assembly has finally been inaugurated here (see page 658), the political balance is a wee bit more level. Presumably, a public gallery will open in due course, but the grounds are always open and the shining neoclassical Parliament building stands at the end of a mile-long drive before a statue of Edward Carson. Edward Carson (1854-1935) was a Unionist leader who brought Ulster perilously close to civil war by using the threat of military action to scupper attempts at Irish independence in the years leading up to the establishment of Northern Ireland. ■ *Bus 16 or 17 from Donegall Sq in Belfast.*

Ulster Folk & Transport Museum This is justly praised as one of Ireland's best museums. Dozens of buildings have been transplanted here to form a vibrant recreation of life in Ulster around 1900, complete with staff in period costume. Both entertaining and educational, a visit to this outdoor folk park is highly recommended. A bridge leads across the road to the transport museum where the largest locomotive built in Ireland is just one of the myriad forms of transport represented. The *Titantic* exhibition pulls in the crowds but there is a lot more to see. ■ *Cultra, T90428428. Jul and Aug, Mon-Sat, 1030-1800, Sun, 1200-1800; Apr-Jun and Sep, Mon-Fri, 0930-1700, Sat, 1030-1800, Sun, 1200-1800; Oct-Mar, Mon-Fri, 0930-1600, Sat and Sun, 1230-1600. Last admission 1 hr before closing time. £4. Tea room. Trains and buses to Bangor stop at Cultra, 7 miles (11 km) east of Belfast.*

Essentials

Sleeping

In Dublin hotel prices go up in summer and at weekends; here the opposite happens. During the summer places close down for the marching season, and at weekends the city centre empties, a throwback to the old days of car bombs and assassinations. Hotels are popping up all over, but none has that genteel, laid-back quality of the best southern hotels. There are no great bargains in the city centre, but the hotels are classy enough. There are more modest places to the south of the city around the university, while B&Bs and hostels provide cheaper accommodation. The guesthouses and B&Bs tend to cost around £34-45 for a double room, the higher end having en-suite rooms in slightly bigger houses, the lower end being 1 or 2 rooms in someone's house with a shared bathroom. The most convenient of these are in the university area in the side streets between Malone and Lisburn Rds. Eglantine Av has several good value places.

Hotels
■ *on maps pages 570 & 578*
Price codes: see inside front cover

LL *TENsq*, 10 Donegall Sq east, T90241001, www.ten-sq.com Very classy boutique hotel in beautiful old bank buildings beside the City Hall. **LL** *Belfast Hilton*, 4, Lanyon Pl, BT1 3LP, T90277000, F90277277. Don't be put off by the dull reception and uniformed staff: if you can possibly afford it – stay here. It is a masterpiece of modernity in a sea of pompous Victoriana. Great views over the river, wonderful Hilton rooms, fluffy bathtowels, fitness centre and tiny pool, great *Sonoma* Restaurant with glass walls overlooking a hundred years of industry. Amazing discounts at weekends and does a good breakfast. **LL** *Europa Hotel*, Great Victoria St, BT2 7AP, T90327000, F90327800. The best you can say about his rather ugly eastern-European looking building is that it's central and comfortable. **LL** *McCausland Hotel*, 34-38 Victoria St, T90220200, F90220220, info@mccauslandhotel.com Made from gorgeously restored 19th-century warehouses, the best feature of this hotel is its façade and lobby. Rooms are relatively cramped, and a little disconcertingly unsoundproofed. Popular café bar and dining room. Good breakfasts. **LL** *Holiday Inn*, 22 Ormeau Av, BT2 8HS, T0870-4009005, F90626546. Very central, comfortable rooms, leisure centre, close to the Golden Mile. Ask for rooms on the Ormeau Av side to avoid the noise from the *Culpa* nightclub at weekends.

L *Duke's Hotel*, 65-67 University St, BT7 1HL, T90236666, F90237177. Well located at the end of the Golden Mile, interesting restaurant, big rooms, gym, good weekend rates. **L** *Stormont Hotel*, 587 Upper Newtownards Rd, BT4 3LP, T90658621, F90480240, Three miles out of the city, a business hotel with lots of facilities, including 2 restaurants, to make the holidaymaker happy too. **L** *Crescent Townhouse*, 13 Lower Cres, BT7 1NR, T90323349, F90320646. At the bottom of this price bracket, this is a small hotel with large, attractively appointed rooms. Set in the centre of the Golden Mile, its restaurant and bar are popular with office workers on their way home from work. The hotel itself is quiet, with the lobby upstairs, away from the activity of the bar and restaurant. **AL** *Wellington Park Hotel*, 21 Malone Rd, BT9 6RU, T90381111, F90665410, restaurant. Geared to business clientele, near to the Golden Mile, secure car parking.

AL *Benedicts of Belfast*, 7-21 Bradbury Pl, Shaftesbury Sq, BT7 1RQ, T90591999, F90591990, info@benedictshotel.co.uk Very new theme hotel with vaguely Gothic décor using reclaimed features from older buildings. Very central, big rooms, excellent value for money. Restaurant and breakfast to the sound of local music stations. Checking-in time 1400. **AL** *Ivanhoe Hotel*, 556 Saintfield Rd, BT8 8EU, T90812240, F90815516. Small, family-run hotel. Well appointed big rooms, comfortable bar that doubles as a bistro in the evenings, more formal restaurant for dinner. Bus or cab ride back into the city, in pleasant rural surroundings. Open for Sun lunch. **AL** *Madison's*, 59-63 Botanic Av, BT7 1JL, T90330040, F90328007. Restaurant. Very trendy, modern hotel, popular with local swingers. **A** *Holiday Inn Express*, 106 University St, BT7 1HP, T90311909, F90311910, express@holidayinn-ireland.com Excellent value, rate includes breakfast, close to the Golden Mile. Restaurant. **A** *Travelodge Belfast City*, 15, Brunswick St, T90333555, F90232999. The best value for the city centre, at £59.95 per room without breakfast. Newly renovated but slightly cramped rooms, this would suit non-breakfast-eaters. Also has restaurant.

A *Avenue House*, 23 Eglantine Av, T90665904, F90291810, stephen.kelly6@ ntlworld.com a Victorian style B&B with en-suite rooms, private parking. **A** *Ravenhill Guest House*, 690 Ravenhill Rd, BT6 0BZ, T90207444, F90282590, www.ravenhillguesthouse.com Pretty, child-friendly Victorian house in quiet location off the Ormeau Rd. Open fires, library, lots of maps and information.

B *Eglantine Guest House*, 21 Eglantine Av, T90667585, is inexpensive for a guesthouse. The same rates and facilities are available at **B** *Liserin Guest House*, 17 Eglantine Av, T90660769. **B** *Greenwood Guest House*, 25 Park Rd, BT7 2FW, T90202525, F90202530, www.greenwoodguesthouse.com Set beside parkland in a quiet side street off the Ormeau Rd this is a comfortable, family-run place. Good breakfasts.

Guesthouses & B&Bs

D *The Ark*, 18 University St, T90329626. Hostel comprising 2 Georgian town houses, 2 kitchens, double and single rooms. **D** *Arnie's Backpackers*, 63 Fitzwilliam St, BT9 6AX, T90242867. Dorm beds only, self-catering hostel in a small Victorian house just off the

Halls of residence & hostels

Belfast

South Belfast

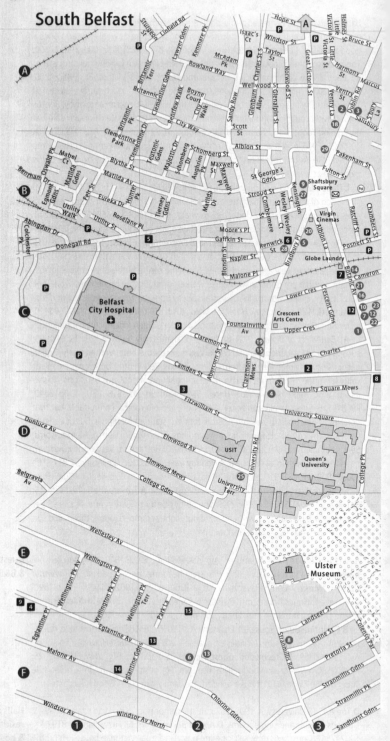

Belfast

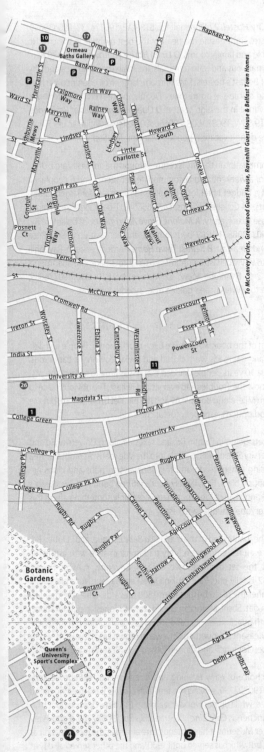

N

| 0 yards | 100 |
| 0 metres | 100 |

■ Sleeping

1 Academie Apartments *D4*
2 Ark *C3*
3 Arnie's Backpackers *D2*
4 Avenue House *E1*
5 Belfast City Hostel *B2*
6 Benedicts & Restaurant *B3*
7 Crescent Townhouse
  & Metro *C3*
8 Duke's *D3*
9 Eglantine Guest House *E1*
10 Holiday Inn *A4*
11 Holiday Inn Express *C5*
12 Madison's & Restaurant *C3*
13 Malone Grove
   Apartments *F2*
14 Malone View *F1*
15 Wellington Park *E2*

● Eating & drinking

1 Acapulco *C3*
2 Archana *A3*
3 Auntie Annie's *A3*
4 Beatrice Kennedy *D3*
5 Bishop's *B3*
6 Botanic Inn *F2*
7 Café Vincent's *C3*
8 Café Zinc *F3*
9 Cayenne *B2*
10 Clements *C3*
11 Culpa *A4*
12 Dragon City *C3*
13 Eglantine *F2*
14 Empire *C3*
15 Fitzy's *C3*
16 Julie's Kitchen *C3*
17 Katy Daly's & Limelight *A4*
18 La Belle Époque *A3*
19 La Salsa *C3*
20 Lavery's *B3*
21 Maggie May's *C3*
22 Maharajah *C3*
23 Moghul *C3*
24 Opus One *D3*
25 Parlour *D2*
26 Renshaw's *D3*
27 Revelations *B2*
28 Spuds *B3*
29 Square *B3*

golden mile. **D** *Belfast City Hostel*, 22 Donegall Rd, BT8 4AE, T90324733, F90439699. This is a very central hostel, right beside the heart of the best nightlife in the city. No self-catering, some double and family rooms. **D** *Linen House Youth Hostel*, 18-29 Kent St, BT1 2JA. Close to the main bus and train terminals, the main shopping area and City Hall, this is the largest of Belfast's hostels. Lots of room, large, well equipped kitchen, good security. Mixed and single-sex dormitories. Double rooms. Left luggage room, bike storage. Book in advance in the high season. **D** *Queen's Elms Halls of Residence*, 78 Malone Rd, Belfast, BT9 5BW, T90381608, F90666680, h.stewart@qub.ac.uk Single and twin rooms available during vacation periods, Mar-Apr, Jun-Sep.

Self-catering Most self-catering accommodation in the city is centred around the university area. Units can be hired for a week or a weekend and accommodate between 2 and 6 people. All work out at the range of a budget hotel for 6 people and much less for larger parties. **A** *L'Academie Apartments*, 14 College Gardens, T/F90666046. 1-bedroom flats in renovated Victorian house close to university. **A** *Malone Grove Apartments*, 70 Eglantine Av, BT9 6DY, T90388000, F90388088. 1- to 2-bedroom apartments near university. Price includes housekeeping and breakfast. **B** *Belfast Town Homes*, Ardenlee Green, Ravenhill Rd, BT6 0AB, T/F90806116 www.belfasttownhomes.co.uk 2-to 3-bedroom apartments in south Belfast. Sleep 2-6. **B** *Malone View*, 52 Malone Av, BT9 6ER, T90776889, cushmp@ntlworld Close to university and golden mile. 3-bedroom house.

Eating

Ten years ago this section of the book would have been much shorter. People just didn't go into town after dark; the roads were closed and it was downright dangerous. Some time during the last 10 years people decided that it was time to reclaim the city, and now you wouldn't know the Troubles had ever visited Belfast. The obvious place to look for food is the Golden Mile, along Botanic Av and the parallel University Rd, but the city centre has some good options, especially for lunch.

The Golden Mile
● *on maps*
Price codes:
see inside front cover

The Golden Mile really gets going in Dublin Rd, and takes off along University Rd and Botanic Av as far as University St, extending a little into the side roads. At night the area is full of punters discussing where to go and the doorways to pubs and clubs are blocked by the incongruously black-tied, largely good-natured bouncers. Restaurants vary with regard to price and style of food, but there is certainly something along this stretch of road to suit everyone's budget and tastes.

Expensive Starting at the 'haute' end of the market *La Belle Époque*, at 61 Dublin Rd, T90323244, comes very well recommended. Very traditional in style with authentic French food. Check out the set menu. Closed on Sun. *Cayenne*, 7 Ascot House, Shaftsbury Sq, T90331532, is telly-chef Paul Rankin's latest endeavour. Not a place for a romantic candlelight dinner the place bustles from 1800 onwards, while the menu is about as eclectic as it can get. Sushi, Moroccan spiced lamb, Indonesian peanut sauce, Italian penne, chicken with guacamole – just about every style of cuisine is mined here for its best and liveliest. Pleasant surroundings in a warm brown kind of way, service is just at the right pace. Open for lunch and dinner. Closed Sun. Reservations essential.

Mid-range Offering a choice of early evening and dinner menus is *Beatrice Kennedy's*, 44 University Rd, T90202290, serving modern Irish cuisine. Early evening menu is around £10 for 2 courses, while dinner works out around £18 plus. Open for lunch on Sun. Very popular with lunchers is *Café Zinc* , 12 Stranmillis Rd, T90682266, a good way out of town past the Ulster Museum. It has 2 menus, one aimed at the lunch market at around £10 for 2 courses but which is served until 1900, and the other served all day at around £20 for dinner. Lots of fish on the menu. Lastly, *Opus One*, 1 University St, T90590101 is a very fashionable, beautifully designed place – all wood and steel, goat's cheese and sun-dried things, dinner at £18 plus. Open Sun for good value set lunch. Very reasonable business lunches. Vegetarians have some good choices.

Cheap At around £15 or less for an evening meal there are lots of good choices to make all along the Golden Mile. At number 53 Dublin Rd is *Archana*, T90323719, winner of lots of awards for its Indian food. Downstairs for all those vegetarians fed up with choosing from the 2 options of most regular restaurants is a vegetarian restaurant called *Little India*. Very respectable vegetarian lunch thalis for around £3. Dinner upstairs at around £15. Open Sun evenings. At 89 Dublin Rd is *The Square 1*, where a set menu offers 3 courses at £11.50. Very fashionable place with some excellent lunch offers. Upstairs the à la carte is more expensive at around £25 plus. The style is modern Irish.

Along **Botanic Av** are some more pleasant places to eat. At 75 is *Acapulco* where you can eat inexpensive Mexican food daily. Just opposite are *Dragon City* at 82 and *The Maharajah* at 62, both serving western versions of their respective cuisines, but good places. Heading back into town, *Café Vincent* at 78 is open 7 days, does pasta dishes and is good for lunch. Next door in Cromwell St is another reliable Indian, *The Moghul*, while across the road at *Madison's* is an inexpensive and quite popular restaurant, open daily, serving modern Irish cuisine. On the corner of Botanic and Lower Cres is *Metro*, a very stylish place with an early evening menu (1800-1900) of 3 courses for £12.50, modern with Californian overtones.

Benedicts, 7-21 Bradbury Pl, BT7 1RQ, T90591999 has a heavily designed restaurant and a dizzying range of menus. Dinner in this Californian influenced but fairly traditional restaurant will be around £15. If you haven't tried wild boar, now's your chance. Several vegetarian options. Lunch around £8. Prices for main courses are determined by the time you choose to eat: at 1900 any main course is £7, at 2000 it's £8 and so on. Open Sun evenings. At number 32 is *Bishop's*, where you can get good fish and chips.

At number 23 **University Rd** is *La Salsa*, T90244588, for inexpensive Mexican. Try the all you can eat buffet for £9.95. Open Sun evenings. Close by is *Fitzy's*, with a large menu of sandwiches and more substantial pasta and steak choices. Vegetarian possibilities.

Fast food If you are after fast food or a snack the area abounds with them. Bradbury Pl probably has the largest range of big names, but in addition there are local places worth a look. *Spuds*, in Bradbury Pl, looks awful but has a good menu of filled potatoes, and other fast things. *Jenny's*, in Dublin Rd, is country kitchenish and has a range of sandwiches, quiche and lasagne till 1700, 6 days a week. *Revelations Internet Café*, Shaftesbury Sq, has, besides the World Wide Web, sandwiches and soup. In Botanic Av are *The Other Place*, *Ventnor's*, *Julie's Kitchen* and *Maggie May's*, all within sight of each other and offering sandwiches, and more substantial choices. At 66 Botanic Av is a branch of *Clements*, T90331827, with leather sofas, big cups and speciality coffees. You'll be temped to look around for Monica and Rachel. Nice sandwiches, wraps, bagels and extra brownie points for being open on Sun mornings. Close by and worthy of more brownie points is *Café Vincent's*, also doing snacks and designer coffees.

Pub lunches In the same area there are any number of pubs that do quite large lunch menus but which tend to focus on music and drink at night. In Bradbury Pl is *Lavery's*, which does pub food till about 1400, Mon-Sat. The *Botanic Inn* and the *Eglantine*, both in Malone Rd are student pubs but do pub food, the Botanic having the slightly better menu. *The Globe* in University Rd does lots of meal deals including some with free pints 1100-1800 except Sun, while the *Empire* in Botanic Av does pizzas and pasta from 1200-1400.

Belfast

The city centre

Expensive The place to be seen in the city centre is *Restaurant Michael Deane's*, 38 Howard St, T90560000. Upstairs is a restaurant where reservations well in advance are necessary as well as a well endowed charge card. Interestingly decorated with a kind of *fin de siècle* mood to the dining room, big silver lids on the dishes and little brushes for the crumbs between courses. Great for a special occasion. Best of all for the food and the views is the *Sonoma* restaurant in the *Hilton* hotel, which has a glorious curtain window out on to the river and the industry.

Mid-range Downstairs at *Deane's*, 38 Howard St, T90560000, is a brasserie which is enormously popular, focusing on modern Irish cooking where dinner will cost £15 plus. Way over in Hill St is an excellent place, *Nick's Warehouse*, T90439690, serving thoughtful modern Irish cuisine in a vast old warehouse. Avoid weekends when it gets very busy and noisy. Lunch is very popular too. *Aero*, at 44 Bedford St, open for lunch and dinner Mon to Sat serves more modern Irish food in a stark but pleasant environment. *Flannigan's*, above the *Crown Liquor Saloon* at 19 Amelia St serves basic food till 2100, 7 days a week. Not much for the vegetarian to get excited about, but children accompanying an adult eat free on Sun. *Larry's Piano Bar*, 36, Bedford St, T90325061, has a set dinner menu 7 days a week, live piano music till 0130 and lots of pictures around the walls. The menu is substantial with the occasional nod toward California. beyond. Close to the Albert Tower in Queen's Sq is *McHugh's* T890247830, a renovated 18th-century pub with an Asian fusion restaurant and bar food. Worth a visit for the interior of the pub. Around the Waterfront Hall are several new places to try. *Bank Gallery restaurant* The Edge, May's Meadow, T90322000 has an excellent pre-theatre menu of some good standard dishes such as salmon with saffron mash, confit duck with champ and chili jam or rib eye steak at £13.95 for 3 courses. Lastly, worth visiting for its views alone is *The Waterfront Brasserie*, T90244966 in the Waterfront Hall, which does breakfasts and lunches, and dinner between 1800-1930 when there is a show on. Dinner will cost around £19. Book in advance.

Cheap At lunchtime the city centre abounds with reasonably priced places for a designer sandwich or something more substantial. Several of them are open late on Thu till about 2100 for the late-night shopping. In Donegall Arcade is a branch of *Bewleys*, which isn't quite as trendy as the one in Grafton St in Dublin but can still offer a little more than the traditional scones and tea. Nearby is *Delaney's*, attractively designed with a wide, inexpensive menu, open 6 days a week 0900-1700. At 12-14 Arthur St and 27-29 Fountain St are 2 branches of *Roscoff's* which are very popular, do big breakfast and lunch menus and are good for a long relaxed lunch till 1800 (2100 on Thu). In Donegall Sq West (and several other locations around the city centre) is a branch of *Clements*, good for lounging on the sofas, drinking coffee and munching sandwiches.

Pub lunches City centre pubs also do a roaring lunchtime trade. In Commercial Court, the *Duke of York* is very popular, serving slightly more than the usual pub grub. The *Morning Star* in Pottinger's Entry is very adventurous about its food, and has gourmet evenings once a month. Expect crocodile and ostrich among the more regular menu items. Serves lunch from 1130-2100. In another of the little entries of the city centre is *White's Tavern*, Winecellar Entry with a more traditional menu, but the food has an excellent reputation. Get there early. *The John Hewitt*, 51 Donegall St, T90233768, is a good place to check out, both for the pub food and for the traditional music and storytelling sessions. *Fibber Magee's* in Keylan's Pl also does good food. In Victoria Sq is the *Kitchen Bar*, which does good authentic Ulster food till 1500 most days and later on Thu. Nothing on Sun. Its reputation is for Paddy's pizzas, made with a soda bread base and excellent value for money. Right in the centre at Donegall Sq West is *Apartment*, T90509777, a cocktail bar with bar food, open daily till late.

Entertainment

There are very few pubs in the city that don't have music of some kind or a late-night club attached somewhere. If it's just a drink you're after, the most atmospheric is, of course, *The Crown* in Great Victoria St with its authentic decorations and cosy snugs, but you must get there early if you want a seat. In the same area is *The Beaten Docket* with very loud disco music and a young crowd, and *Robinsons'* with 4 floors of assorted ways of drinking and listening to music. A board outside announces what is on. In Ormeau Av is *Katy Daly's*, T90325942, and *Limelight*, which have something musical on most nights. *Katy Daly's* has live local singer-songwriters on Wed and Sat.

Pubs & music
For up to date listings of events consult the free The Big List newspaper, available from the tourist office, rail and bus stations and newsagents

Moving out of town along the **Golden Mile** is another cluster of places. *Morrison's* in Bedford St has music at weekends and a good atmosphere at other times. *Auntie Annie's* in Dublin Rd has local live singers on Wed and Thu. In Bradbury Pl is *Lavery's*, a regular pub with a disco upstairs but the odd habit of charging an entry fee to the pub on busy nights. The *Belfast Empire* (see below) has live music most nights with an entry charge of around £6. The 'Bot' and the 'Egg', as the *Botanic Inn* and *Eglantine Inn* in Malone Rd are affectionately known, are also very popular with a young crowd and have either live music or a disco at weekends. In Elmwood Av is *The Parlour*, a very young place with inexpensive food, fake gas lights and lots of music.

Back **in town** there are several well established pubs in the entries with good music nights. The *Morning Star* in Pottinger's Entry is quiet at night but has a beautiful interior, *White's Tavern* is in Winecellar Entry and has jazz on Thu, and traditional Irish music on Fri and Sat. The *Rotterdam Bar*, in Pilot St, T90746021, has traditional Irish music on Mon and jazz on Tue, while the *Milk Bar*, Tomb St, T90278876, will appeal to young people.

For good **Irish music** *Kelly's Cellars* at 30 Bank St is worth a look in. *The Kitchen* in Victoria Sq has live music sessions at weekends. *The Front Page* (see below) has traditional Irish music on Sun evenings.

For **other types of live music** there is *McHughes* in Queen's Sq with jazz on Thu and something on most other nights, *The Front Page* in Upper Donegall St with live music from Wed to Sun, *The Duke of York* in Commercial Court with live music at weekends, and *Shenanigan's* in Howard St with live music from Thu to Sun. Out on Saintfield Rd is the *Ivanhoe Hotel* where there is a good bar for bar food and regular live jazz.

Clubbers might like to try out the *Trilogy* night club in Frames Complex, 2-14 Little Donegall St. *Thompson's Garage*, 3 Patterson's Pl, Arthur St, is the big draw in town on Sat night. *The Limelight*, in Ormeau Av is another seriously dedicated club. Others are clubs above the trendy pubs in town, *Madison's*, *Kaos*, in *Renshaw's Hotel*, *The M Club* in *Manhattan's*, 23 Bradbury Pl. *The Milk Bar*, 10-14 Tomb St is seriously upmarket, attracts minor celebs, plays chart hits and soul and expects its customers to look smart. *Culpa* Bankmore Sq, has lots of activity till about 0300. Again, dress up.

Clubs

There are galleries exhibiting contemporary work by local artists. *The Fenderevsky Gallery* at the *The Crescent Arts Centre*, 2-4 University Rd, has a changing exhibition of local painters such as Barrie Hall and Felim Egan, while the *Ormeau Baths Gallery* in Ormeau Av presents work of artists from all over Europe. The *Old Museum Arts Centre* in College Sq North also has varying exhibitions of local artists in a converted Georgian house. Smaller galleries can be visited at *Arches Art Gallery* in Holywood Rd, *Cavehill Gallery* in Cavehill Rd, *Catalyst Arts* at 5 Exchange Pl and the *Eakin Gallery* in Lisburn Rd.

Art galleries

The Virgin Cinemas, T90243200 are at the end of Dublin Rd, at Shaftesbury Sq, *The Movie House*, T90755000, is in the Yorkgate Centre on York St and *The Curzon*, T90641373, is on Ormeau Rd. The city's arty cinema is *Queen's Film Theatre*, 7 University Sq Mews, T90244857. Good value.

Cinemas

Belfast

Music venues The *Ulster Hall*, T90323900, in Bedford St, hosts classical performances by the Ulster Orchestra as well as some rock concerts. The *Waterfront Hall*, T90334455, Lanyan Pl, Laganside, hosts a whole range of events from classical music to school parents' evenings, stand-up gigs by ageing comics, ballet, jazz, and big name pop stars. *King's Hall*, T90665225, at Balmoral stages the really big rock shows.

Theatres The *Empire*, T90328110, in Botanic Av puts on various shows, its chief draw being the Comedy Club on Tue nights: this gets very full, so get there early. It starts at 2100 and entrance is £4. The *Grand Opera House*, Great Victoria St, T90241919, is worth a visit just for the decorations, but it regularly has big-name shows transferred from Dublin or London's West End. The *Lyric Theatre*, off Ridgeway St, which is off Stranmillis Rd south of the city, T90381081, is the city's serious theatre. It regularly has important modern productions. There is a student standby scheme where remaining tickets will be sold off at reduced prices to students after 1930 on the night of the production. The *Old Museum Arts Centre*, T90233332, in College Sq North, has a small theatre where the avant garde can be found. Look out also for events in the *Sheridan Theatre* in the Odyssey Complex.

Festivals

Cathedral Quarter Arts festival, in early **May**, T90232403 www.cqaf.com 10 days of music theatre, comedy, circus art exhibitions and street events. *Belfast City Summer Festival*, T90320202, late **May-Jun** includes all kinds of events from local stuff to major concerts, including the Lord Mayor's Show. *Orange Marches*, basically the city shuts down for 2 weeks around the height of the marching season, the first 2 weeks in **Jul**. Restaurants close, people take their holidays, nightlife draws to a halt. If you want to watch the last stand of triumphalist Loyalism, this is your chance. *Ardoyne Fleadh*, T90751056, is 3 days of open-air concerts and community events in north Belfast, in early **Aug**. *Féile an Phobail*, T90313440, takes place during the first 2 weeks in **Aug** and includes street parties, concerts, Irish-language events and a carnival parade. Originally a Republican-inspired event, it is now huge and includes contributions from Unionists. *Belfast Festival at Queens*, T90667687 for information, T90665577 for bookings. An arts festival with 400-plus shows during 3 weeks around **Nov**, based around Queen's University. Belfast's answer to the Edinburgh Festival.

Gay and lesbian

The gay scene in Belfast changed a couple of years ago with the opening of *Kremlin*, T809700, 96 Donegall St, a vastly extravagant place with a huge statue of Lenin outside. It is the largest gay venue in Ireland and attracts people from all over the island. Other gay venues are *Queen's Bar*, 4 Queen's Arcade, *Custom House*, Skipper St and *The Parliament* on the corner of Dunbar Link and Gordon St. *GLYNI* (Gay Lesbian Youth Northern Ireland) meets every Mon at *Cara-friend*, Cathedral Buildings, 64 Donegall St, admin@glyni.org.uk *Cara-friend* has a gay helpline, T90322023, Mon-Wed 0730-2200, while *Belfast Lesbian Helpline* is T90238668, 0730-2200 Thu. The *Northern Ireland Gay Rights Association* meets on the first Thu of each month. Contact them at PO Box 44, Belfast BT1 1SH. The social group for lesbian and bisexual women meets at Cara-friend on the third Sun of each month.

Shopping

Belfast is a depressingly similar to every other United Kingdom shopping centre, with its pedestrianized streets, lookalike malls and big chains, but at least it is in the city centre and not out in some disused quarry or beside a motorway. The main shopping area is around Donegall Pl, Royal Av and the Fountain area. Parking is simple enough in the centre, with lots of well marked car parks, and many of the big stores open on Sun afternoons. Thu is late-night shopping in many stores. All shops are closed on Easter Day and on Sun and Mon when 12 Jul falls on a Sun. The **Castlecourt Shopping Centre** is right in the middle of the pedestrianized area and bursts with British names, including *Debenhams*. North of the centre is the **Yorkgate Centre** with more shops, and smaller, less prosperous malls lurk around town.

Antiques **Donegall Pass** is the best place for looking for curios and more expensive items. Shops include *Alexander the Grate* which has an antiques market on Sat, *Archives*, *Past and Present* and *Oakland Antiques*. Nearby, in Bedford St, is *Blue Cat Antiques*. Particular mementos of the area might be the many pottery representations of King Billy on his white horse.

Books *Bookfinder's Café*, 47 University Rd, is good for browsing through their vast selection of second-hand books and reading for a while in the café upstairs. *Familia Bookshop* is at 64 Wellington Pl and has books on Irish issues while *An Leathrá Póilí*, 513 Falls Rd, has books on Irish issues from a Republican perspective. It also has a café. *Ex Libris*, Unit 28, Victoria Centre has a large stock of second-hand material and sells graphic novels while antique books can be found at *Roma Ryan's*, 73 Dublin Rd, which has prints and rare books. Two private dealers are *Emerald Isle Books* 539 Antrim Rd, T90370798, F90777288, and *P&B Rowan*, Carleton House, 92 Malone Rd, T90666448. Appointments are necessary at both. The regular bookshops can be found in the city centre. *Waterstones* is at 8 Royal Av, *Dillons* at 42 Fountain St, *Eason's* at 16 Ann St.

Arts & Crafts *Craftworks*, Bedford House, Bedford St has beautiful handmade clothes and craft objects from all over Ireland.

Markets *St George's Market* in May St has existed for many years and has undergone major renovations recently. It is still a fruit and vegetable market, but also has stalls selling bric-à-brac, second-hand and new clothes, and on Fri has more than 200 stallholders. It is also home to a twice monthly Sat farmers' market. Behind Castlecourt Shopping Centre the *Smithfield Retail Market* sells new and second-hand furniture and clothes.

Sporting *Surf Mountain* at 12 Brunswick St specialises in surfing gear but also has an excellent col-
goods lection of camping gear. There is a branch of *Millets* in Cornmarket with its usual collection of sportswear and camping equipment, and a shop called *Beaten Track* in Arthur St.

Sports

Football There are regular matches at Seaview, off Shore Rd, home ground of the Crusaders; the Oval, Redcliffe Pde, in the Newtownards Rd, home ground of Glentoran; and Solitude, Cliftonville, the home ground of Cliftonville. International matches are held at Windsor park Donegall Av, the home of Linfield Park football club, T90244198. For details of matches check the weekend papers or ring the Irish Football League on T90244888. **Gaelic Football** Matches at weekends at Roger Casement Park, Andersonstown Rd. **Hurling** Weekends, Roger Casement Park. The hurling final is in early Jul. **Ice skating** *Ice Bowl*, 111 Old Dundonald Rd, T90482611. Olympic-sized rink. *Ice hockey* The Belfast Giants play at the Odyssey Arena, www.belfastgiants.co.uk **Leisure centres** *Shankill Leisure Centre*, 100 Shankill Rd, T90241434, includes 'Water Wonderland' a leisure pool. *Maysfield Leisure Centre*, East Bridge St, T90241633. *Olympia Leisure Centre*, Boucher Rd, T90233369. **Rugby** *Malone Rugby Club*, Malone Park, off Woodstock Rd. *Collegians*, Deramore Park, Malone Rd. For details try the Irish Rugby

Football Union at T90649141. **Tennis** *Belfast Tennis Arena*, Ormeau Embankment, T90458024. **Ten-pin bowling** *Superbowl*, Bedford St. *Ice Bowl*, 11 Old Dundonald Rd, 30 lanes, 5 miles out of city centre.

Organized tours

Bailey's Historical Pub Tour of Ireland, T92683665 May-Sep Thu 1900 and Sat 1600. £6 excluding drinks from Flanagan's (above the Crown). A 2-hr walk around some of the city's oldest pubs, hidden away in some of the entries and back streets. *Belfast Castle* free tour. 1 hr. Advance booking necessary, T90776925. *Belfast City Hall* (see page 568) has free tours of the building, T90270456. *Belfast Walking Tour*, T90246609, Apr-Oct, 1400 Sun only. From tourist information centre, North Street. Covers the old town; 1½ hrs from 1600-1835. *Citybus Tours*, T90458484, www.translink.co.uk Offers 2 scheduled tours of the city, one that takes in much of the city's recent history around the Falls and Shankill Roads and another that takes a tour of the more regular tourist attractions of the city. Both tours depart from Castle Pl. Check for details of tours. £6. Tickets can be booked in advance or bought on the bus. On Wed only there is also a tour which takes in the *Laganside development* and includes a trip along the river on *"The Joyce"*. The same company does a tourist shuttle bus called the *City Hopper* which departs hourly until 1600 and stops at 10 visitor destinations around the city.

Various organizations in West Belfast do tours most of which seem to need largish numbers and advance booking. You could try the following: *Black Mountain Walks* T90585753.£10 for 3 hrs. Walks around the hills to the west of Belfast. *The Bog Meadows* T90314772. Walks around this nature conservation area. Two weeks notice required, 10 people minimum. £3 per person. *Lower Falls Walking Tours*, T90964188, minimum number 5, £4 per person, book in advance, departs taxi rank Castle St. *West Belfast Taxi Tours*, T90590800, www.wbta@aol.ie, 1-4 people £17 per hr and £12 per hr thereafter. Very partisan, but why not?

Transport

Air

See the Getting there section of the Essentials chapter (page 30) for flight connections to Britain, Europe and the US

For most flights the exit point will be **Belfast International Airport**, T94484848, www.bial.co.uk An airport bus goes to the airport at half-hourly intervals from the *Europa* bus centre, passing through *Laganside* bus centre on its route. You can pick up the bus at either stop. Cost is around £4 for a single, T90333000, www.translink.co.uk, for times. A taxi to the airport will cost around £20. Some private minicabs are not metered, so you should agree a price before setting off. *easyJet*, T0870-6000000, www.easyjet.com, does flights to **Liverpool**, **Luton**, **Amsterdam**, **Glasgow**, and **Edinburgh**.

Ferries

From Belfast *NorseMerchant Ferries*, T0870 600 4321, travel to **Liverpool** (8-9 hrs) from the Victoria terminal on West Bank Rd. *Stena Line*, T0870-5707070, does 10 sailings a day to **Stranraer** (2 hrs 30 mins) from Corry Rd, while the *Seacat*, catamaran, T0870-5523523, www.seacat.co.uk leaves from Donegall Quay for **Troon** (2 hrs 30 mins), the **Isle of Man** (2 hrs 45 mins, seasonally, Apr-Sep) and **Heysham**, near Lancaster (4 hrs). From Larne *P&O European Ferries*, T0870-2424777, travels to **Cairnryan** in Scotland (1 hr).

Train

Except for the excellent Belfast to Dublin route, trains are an expensive option when moving on from Belfast. There are 3 train routes out of Belfast: one travels north and then west along the lovely coastline scenery to Derry, another west and then south through Portadown towards Dublin, and a third, smaller line, travels east to Bangor. Trains leave from 2 stations, Gt Victoria St, T90230671, and Belfast Central, T90899411. From Belfast Central trains go to **Larne**, **Derry**, **Bangor**, **Portadown**, **Newry** and **Dublin**, while Gt

Victoria St serves Portadown, **Lisburn**, **Bangor**, **Larne Harbour** and **Derry**. A free citylink bus serves Belfast Central from Donegall Sq. The Belfast to Dublin route is very fast and comfortable and costs £15 one way, stopping at Portadown, Newry, Lisburn and **Dundalk**. There are no left-luggage facilities at the stations.

Bus *Europa Bus Centre*, T90333000, in Glengall St, has services to **Enniskillen**, **Tyrone**, **Derry**, **Armagh**, **Downpatrick**, **Kilkeel**, **Newcastle**, **Newry**, **Limavady**, **Portadown** via Lurgan, **Dungannon**, **Bundoran**, **Ballycastle**, the **ferry terminals**, and destinations in the Republic, including **Achill**, **Sligo**, **Ballina**, **Westport**, **Galway**, **Athlone**, **Cork**, **Dublin**. The Laganside bus station has services to **Cookstown**, **Portrush**, **Ballymena**, **Antrim**, **Larne**, **Coleraine**, **Portstewart**, **Ballycastle** and **Carrickfergus**. There is also a service to several **mainland Britain cities** via **Stranraer**. There are no left-luggage facilities at either bus station. A private company, *O'Donnell Buses*, T00353-7548356, operates a daily service between **Donegal**, **Derry** and Belfast. A pre-bookable express bus service operates between the **City Airport** and **Derry** and **Coleraine**, T40328500.

Car hire There are Avis, Budget, Europcar Rental, Hertz and McCausland desks in the arrivals hall at Belfast International Airport and Budget and Avis desks at the City Airport. Desks are manned as incoming flights arrive. Rental is per day or per week. *Avis*, 69 Great Victoria St, T90240404, Belfast International Airport T94422333, City Airport, T90452017. *Budget*, 96-102 Gt Victoria St, T90230700, Belfast International Airport TT94423332, City Airport T90451111. *Dan Dooley*, 175 Airport Rd, Crumlin, Co Antrim, T94452522, 0800-282189. *Europcar*, Belfast International Airport T94423444, City Airport T90450904. *Hertz*, Belfast International Airport, T94422533.

Bike hire *McConvey Cycles*, 467 Ormeau Rd, T90491163, hires bikes for £7 per day with a deposit of £30.The tourist office has details of some possible cycle tours of the region.

Directory

Airlines *Aer Lingus* T08459-737747, *British Airways* T0845 6060747. *British Midland* Suite, 2, Fountain Centre. *Jersey European* T90457200. **Banks** *Bank of Ireland* T90234334, 54 Donegall Pl (linked with Barclays). *Northern Bank* T90245277, Donegall Sq West. *Ulster Bank* T90244112, 47 Donegall Pl (linked with Natwest). **Bureau de change**: *GPO* Castle Pl and Shaftesbury Sq. *Thomas Cooke*, T90883900, 11 Donegall Pl and at *Belfast International Airport*, T94422536, open till 2000. **Communications** *GPO*, Castle Pl and Shaftesbury Sq Mon-Fri 0900-1730, Sat 0900-2100. **Internet**: *Revelations Café* Bradbury Pl, T90320337, info@revelations.co.uk **Embassies and consulates** Denmark and Sweden: *G Heyn & Sons Ltd*, Head Line Buildings, 10 Victoria St, BT1 3GP, T90230581. **Greece, Norway, Portugal**: *M F Ewings, (Shipping) Ltd*, Hurst House, 15-19 Corporation Sq, BT1 3AJ, T90242242. **Italy**: 7 Richmond Park, BT9 5EP, T90668854. **USA**: Consulate General, Queen's House, 14 Queen St, BT1 6EQ. **Medical services** Accident and Emergency services are at *Belfast City Hospital*, Lisburn Rd, T90329241, *Mater Hospital*, Crumlin Rd, T90741211, *Royal Victoria Hospital*, Grosvenor Rd, T90240503 and *Ulster Hospital*, Dundonald, T90484511. **Laundry** *Globe Laundry*, 37 Botanic Av, 0800-2100 Mon-Fri, 0800-1800 Sat, 1200-1800 Sun. **Libraries** *Belfast Central Library*, Royal Av, Mon and Thu 0930-2000, Tue, Wed, Fri 0930-1730, Sat 0930-1300. **Places of worship** *St Peter's Roman Catholic Cathedral*, Derby St. *St Anne's Church of Ireland Cathedral*, Donegall St. *Ballynafeigh Methodist Church*, Ormeau Rd. *The Belfast Hebrew Congregation*, 5 Fortwilliam Gdns, T90775013. **Useful addresses** *AA*, 108-110 Gt Victoria St, T0990-989989, breakdowns T0800-887766. *RAC*, T0345-3311133, breakdowns T0800-828282.

Counties Down & Armagh

16

Counties Down & Armagh

*Counties Down and Armagh are like neighbours that haven't spoken to each other for years: they share a fence but don't acknowledge one another. It is a generalization but Down likes to think of itself as British, whereas Armagh displays its Irish identity, and while Armagh has suffered disproportionately through the troubles of the last 30 years, Down has cocooned itself within a certain degree of smugness. Travelling through the county is a series of surprises: reminders of ugly sectarianism in towns like Kilkeel or Newtownards in the morning and yet by afternoon standing in awe of the shifting shades of green and purple where, in the words of the familiar song, "the **Mountains of Mourne** sweep down to the sea".*

*Armagh has always been border country, forming with Monaghan and Louth the southern edge of the drumlin belt that formed Ulster as a place apart when the Ice Age retreated, leaving massive boulders in its wake. St Patrick still found his way here and Cromwell confiscated over a third of the county. **Armagh** is a beautiful place and even a fleeting visit will whet the appetite for a longer stay. The historic city of Armagh should not be missed while the secret delights in the south of the county are waiting to be discovered by a new generation of visitors.*

County Down

Bangor

Colour map 1, grid B6

The railway link from Belfast put Bangor on the map as a late-Victorian seaside resort. However, these days the marina has put paid to the beach, and while a lingering seaside feel is still faintly in the air, the town is basically a commuter-fuelled, overwhelmingly Protestant, suburb of Belfast. However, several places of interest in the area (see below) mean that you may find yourself here looking for a meal or even an overnight stay.

For the town's only official 'sight', cross the road from the train and bus station and walk down to the rear of the town hall and the **North Down Heritage Centre**, with its mixed collection that ranges from a fifth-century BCE set of swords, a ninth-century handbell, the *Jordan Room* with its engrossing set of Far Eastern *objets d'art* and an observation beehive in the summer. ■ *Castle Park Av, T91271200. Open Jul and Aug, Mon-Sat, 1030-1730, Sun 1400-1730; Sep-Jun, Tue-Sat, 1030-1630 and Sun, 1400-1630. Free. Café.*

The **tourist office** is in one of Bangor's few surviving buildings of historical note, the **Old Custom House and Tower**, in Quay St between the *Marine Court* and *Bangor Bay Inn* hotels. T91270069. It's open Jun-Sep, Mon-Fri, 0900-1700 (1900 in Jul and Aug), Sat, 1000-1230, 1330-1630, Sun, 1300-1700 (1200-1800 in Jul and Aug); Oct-May, Mon-Fri, 1000-1700, Sat, 1000-1230, 1330-1600.

Sleeping
Price codes:
see inside front cover

AL *Marine Court Hotel*, 18-20 Quay St, T91451100, F91451200. Has a gym, pool and comfortable rooms. Weekend rate includes dinner. **AL** *Bangor Bay Inn*, 10 Seacliff Rd, T91270696, F91271678. A small hotel in a former doctor's residence where American officers were billeted in the 1940s and with large rooms overlooking the sea. Cheaper at weekends. **A** *Cairn Bay Lodge*, 278 Seacliff Rd, T91467636, F91457728. A detached house that is a B&B. **B** *Number 10*, Seacliff Rd, T91461077, heathermbell@ compuserve.com More typical of the other B&Bs also found lined up in Seacliff Rd and facing the sea. **C** *Leaside*, 22 Southwell Rd. A B&B just behind the rail and bus station.

Eating

Shanks, 150 Crawfordsburn Rd, Bangor, T853313, is one of Ireland's best restaurants and don't be put off by knowing it's designed by Conran. The food is broadly European, using local produce with imaginative, contemporary touches and venison from the local Clandeboye Estate is a winter speciality. In summer, lobster salad niçoise is a typical creation from the kitchen of Robbie Millar. Open Tue-Fri for lunch, around £17, and Tue-Sat for dinner for around twice that amount. House wine starts at below £13. The dining room at the *Bangor Bay Inn* on Seacliff Rd is a cosy little restaurant offering a relaxing evening meal for £15 and a good-value bistro menu. The *Marine Court Hotel* has a restaurant, and a popular bistro open until 2200 (closed Sun). The *Castle Garden* restaurant at the North Down Heritage Centre, T91270371, is a peaceful place for a coffee or lunch (closed Mon). *Bokhara*, 2A King St, T91452439, just off Main St, is an Indian restaurant with specials for around £8, good, if you don't mind the lurid food colouring in some dishes – it's a friendly and welcoming place. *Café Brazilia*, facing the clock tower on the marina, T91272763, has outdoor tables and is *the* place to enjoy a decent cup of coffee and one of their dozen toasties, potato bakes or sandwiches; all around £3. *Wolsey's Pub*, in the High St, T91460495, next to a useful second-hand bookshop, does a 2-course lunch for £5.50, while for fast-food joints, carry up the road and round the corner into the *Flagstaff Centre*. Up the hill of High St, *Donegan's*, T91463928, is an old-style Irish pub and restaurant with a 2-course lunch for £5.25 and main dishes on the menu around £8.

Things to do in Counties Down and Armagh ★

- Take a walk in **Tollymore Forest Park**
- Have a drink and a chat in **MC Larkin** in south Armagh
- Go bird-watching around **Strangford Lough**
- Look out for 18th-century graffiti in the old gaol in **Down County Museum**
- See Gulliver tell his story at **St Patrick's Trian** in Armagh
- Watch the universe go by and admire the beautiful old **observatory buildings** in Armagh city
- Visit **Navan Fort** and imagine what it must have been like thousands of years ago

---

Jenny Watts, T91270401, next door, does food and has folk music on a Tue and jazz on Sun from 1300-1500.

Scuba diving *David Vincent*, T91464671, or *Norsemaid Sea Enterprises* T91812081. **Sport**

Bus T91271143 and **train** T91899400/91270141 stations are next to each other on **Transport** Abbey St and there are frequent services between Bangor and **Belfast**. **Car** *A1 Car Hire*, 34a Central Av, T91464447. There are some free parking spaces on The Marina opposite the *Marine Court* hotel.

Around Bangor

This is on the coast and makes a pleasant change from museums and the like. **Crawfordsburn** **Grey Point Fort**, with its restored gun site, is a popular destination and the Park **Country Park** Centre provides an excellent introduction to the park's flora and ecology, the chief delight of coming here. ■ *Helen's Bay, off the B20, T91853621. Park open to dusk. Gun site 1400-1700, Apr-Sep, closed Tue. Oct-Mar, Sun only. Free.*

When the First World War broke out, the parliamentary leaders of national- **Somme** ists and unionists, John Redmond and Edward Carson, urged their support- **Heritage** ers to enlist and many thousands did so. The 16th and the 10th Divisions were **Centre** Catholic and nationalist respectively, while the 36th Ulster was a new division, created by 30,000 UVF men volunteering virtually as one body. In total some 200,000 Irishmen saw active service, and around 30,000 paid with their lives. The Ulster 36th Division were at the battle of the Somme from the beginning, in July 1916, suffering 5,000 casualties in the first 48 hours; they were joined by the 16th Division in September of that year. The Centre also has a static wall display reflecting the 10th Division's participation in the Gallipoli campaign.

Guided tours through the various displays and a reconstructed trench take from 45 minutes to an hour and, while interesting, rarely manage to convey the visceral horror of the war. A static exhibition on the role of Irish women during the war is just as enlightening. A good selection of books, posters and educational material is available. ■ *233 Bangor Rd, Newtownlands. T91823202. Jul and Aug, Mon-Fri, 1000-1700, Sat and Sun, 1200-1700; Apr-Jun and Sep, Mon-Thu, 1000-1600, Sat and Sun, 1200-1600. Oct-Mar, Mon-Thu, 1000-1600. £3.75. Situated north of Newtownlands on the A21.*

On the other side of the A21 from the Somme Heritage Centre, the Ark Open **Ark Open Farm** Farm has over 80 rare species of pigs, goats and poultry. There is also a tea room and picnic sites. ■ *T92820445. Mon-Sat 1000-1800, Sun, 1400-1800. £2.90, children £1.70.*

Scrabo Country Park The park itself is dominated by Scrabo Tower (122 steps to the top) built in 1857 as a memorial to the third Marquis of Londonderry. However, come here not for the tower, but for the panoramic views of Strangford Lough (see box page 597) and walks in the surrounding country park. ■ *T91811491. Tower open Easter and Jun-Sep, 1100-1830, closed Fri. Free. Just over a mile southwest of Newtownlands and signposted from there.*

Newtownards An ugly place with union jacks in your face, but there is a **tourist office** with useful information on the Ards Peninsula. ■ *31 Regent St, T91826846. Jul and Aug, Mon-Sat, 0900-1730; Sep-Jun, Mon-Sat, 0930-1700.*

Ards Peninsula

For a flavour of Presbyterian life on the peninsula in the early 20th century, there is no better novel than 'December Bride", by Sam Hanna Bell (1951), later made into a film The Ards Peninsula is the narrow slot of land between Strangford Lough and the Irish Sea. Of the two roads that run down either side of it, the windier A2, trailing its way through legions of caravan parks, takes a lot longer than the A20, which also passes Grey Abbey and Mount Stewart along the way. Without your own transport, relying on scheduled bus services (see Portaferry below) could prove time-consuming, but *Ulsterbus* conduct various day tours – general, historic homes, gardens, heritage, and wildlife – starting in Newtownards. Contact *Ulsterbus*, T91812391, or the tourist office in Newtownards, T91826846.

Coastal Route As you head east from Bangor on the A2 you will come to the village of **Donaghadee** where ferries plied to and from Scotland until Larne took over the service in 1849. Daniel O'Connell left from here six years earlier, after a failed attempt to gain the support of Ulster for the repeal of sectarian laws barring Catholics from sitting in parliament. After having a cup of tea thrown at him by a woman he remarked to a fisherman, "You have very pretty girls here." "Yes," the man replied, "but none of them are Repealers". The only boat journey now possible is a day trip to the uninhabited **Copeland Islands** off the coast for bird-watching. ■ *The RSPB, T90491547, handle trips to one of the islands; the two others can be reached with Nelson's Boats, Donaghadee, T91883403.*

Continuing south, near caravan-infested Millisle, **Ballycopeland Windmill** is a late 18th-century tower mill in use until 1915 and still in working order. ■ *Apr-Sep, Tue-Sat, 1000-1900. £1. On B172, 1 mile west of Millisle.* **Portavogie**, further down the coast, is a fishing port of local renown and fresh catches can be purchased here. At **Cloughey** there is a sandy beach safe for swimming, and at Kearney a fine beach walk before the main road heads inland for Portaferry.

Sleeping B *Anathoth*, 9 Edgewater, T91884004, is typical of the many B&Bs around Donaghadee. *Ballyvester Caravan Park*, Millisle Rd, Donaghadee, T91472118, includes 5 tent sites at £4 each, while *Donaghadee Caravan Park*, Edgewater, T91882369, has 10 sites at £6 each.

Eating In Donaghadee, *Grace Neills Inn*, 33 High St, T91882553, is a good bet for food or try the
If you can, save your appetite for Portaferry *Copelands Hotel*, 50 Warren Rd, T91888189. In Millisle the *Woburn Arms*, Main St, T91861461, and other inexpensive places to grab a bite.

East Strangford Lough Route The chief attractions of travelling the A20 route, apart from access to the east side of Strangford Lough where there are parking spaces and points to observe bird life, are Mount Stewart House and Greyabbey.

The English class structure was nothing if not precise and at **Mount Stewart House** even the visiting ladies' maids could pull some clout, having meals with the housekeeper in a special room and waited on by a lowly footman. One large bedroom was divided into cubicles for their sleeping arrangements, supervised by the head housekeeper who "wore grey alpaca in the morning and black silk in the evening" according to a maid who went home to her own lady to boast of the lavish wealth. Mount Stewart was home to the powerful Marquess of Londonderry, who also owned large tracts of County Durham in England from where coal from family mines was shipped in by the boatload to Strangford Lough. Unfortunately, very little of the social history of this grand country house is conveyed during the sometimes oleaginous tour that becomes like an animated page from a Sotheby's catalogue as it relates the date of this, the value of that, the spot where Castlereagh penned a letter, and whether the eyes in one portrait show a family resemblance to some other aristocratic has-been.

The **gardens** are also hugely disappointing, but best in the early morning when peacocks stroll, hares and rabbits sport and serene swans glide by on the lake. There are some fine specimens of mature trees, and a leaflet map guides you through the various set pieces laid out by Lady Londonderry in the 1920s. It is enlivened by the occasional jazz band on Sundays between April and Sep. ■ *T42788387. House: May-Sep, 1300-1800, daily except Tue; daily over Easter; Apr and Oct, Sat and Sun, 1300-1800. Last tour 1700. Garden: Apr-Sep, daily 1100-1800; Mar, Sun only, 1400-1700; Oct, Sat and Sun, 1100-1800. House and gardens, £3.50. Garden only £3. Tearoom.*

If you've ever endured a ferry journey to Ireland in a winter storm you will believe the story that Affreca, wife-to-be of John de Courcy, made a vow on her voyage to build an abbey if she arrived safely. The result in 1193 was **Greyabbey**, one of the earliest Gothic churches in Ireland, peopled by Cistercian monks from Cumberland in England. The Gothic style has survived best in the superb west door, while inside there are stone figures, a Norman knight and a female figure taken to represent Affreca. The **herb garden** containing examples of medicinal plants that medieval monks nurtured is also very pleasing. ■ *East side of Greyabbey village, less than 2 miles south of Mount Stewart House on the A20, T90543033. Apr-Sep, Tue-Sat, 1000-1900; Sun 1400-1900. £2.*

Portaferry
Colour map 1, grid B6

Portaferry, the visitor-friendly village from where ferries ply their way across the lough to Strangford, is the most interesting place on the Ards Peninsula for an overnight rest. Once an important little port with a herring industry, the village saw some action in the 1798 uprising and might have been captured by the rebels but for the timely presence of a government ship that fired on them from the quay. A more peaceful pursuit is offered nowadays at *Exploris*, an aquarium that attracts families but is of interest to all. There is a seal sanctuary, and sting rays, starfish and sea urchins to stroke in the touch tank. ■ *Castle St, T42728062. Open Apr-Aug, Mon-Fri, 1000-1800, Sat, 1100-1800, Sun, 1300-1800. Sep-Feb, closes one hour earlier. £3.85.*

Collect a map of the village from the **tourist office** on Castle St, T42729882, (open Easter and Jun-Sep, 1000-1700, Sat 1100-1800, Sun 1300-1800) and walk up **Windmill Hill** for fine views. Or shop in *The Harlequin* with its two floors of familiar crafts and gifts. The *Fiddler's Green* pub facing The Square has music at night.

Sleeping
Price codes:
See inside front cover

AL *The Narrows*, Shore Rd, T42728148, reservations@narrows.co.uk Not cheap at £42.50 per person sharing in the high season but packages with dinner for 1-3 nights' stay are worth considering, for this is Portaferry's smartest accommodation, with a

County Down

sauna and views of the ferry drifting by through the windows of uncluttered bedrooms (no alternative to the fried breakfast in the morning, however). **B** *Lough Cowey Lodge*, 9 Lough Cowey Rd, T42728263. Just outside the village. **C** *Adairs*, 22 The Square, T42728412. In the centre of the village. **C** *Barholm*, 11 The Strand, T42729598. A detached house overlooking the lough with hostel beds and double rooms, from £11. B&B also available.

Eating *The Narrows* restaurant in Shore Rd serves fresh fish and meat dishes with all the telltale touches of the modern and trendy – Puy lentils, shiitake mushrooms, Parmesan shavings – in a plain, pine-furnished room looking out at the lough. Expect to pay about £25 for an evening meal, £7 for lunch. The best alternative for a meal is *The Cornstore*, Castle St, T42729779, with chowder for £4.50, open prawn sandwiches for £8.50 and main dishes a little less. *Portaferry Hotel*, The Strand, does a good lunch including a children's menu, plus a basic set evening dinner for less than £20. Not a puy lentil in sight.

Transport The *Ulsterbus* 205/6 *Goldline* service runs Mon-Fri from **Belfast** at 0900, via **Newtownards** and **Greyabbey**, arriving in Portaferry at 1014. For local services check with the tourist office. **Boat** Ferries depart from **Strangford**, T44881637, on the hour and half-hour, 0730-2230 weekdays, 0800-2300 Sat, and 0930-2230 Sun. From Portaferry, departures are at quarter past and quarter to the hour 0745-2245 weekdays, 0815-2315 Sat, and 0945-2245 Sun. Single/same-day return fare for passengers is 85p/£1.40, for cars £4.20/£6.80.

Directory **Banks** *Northern Bank* has a branch in The Square. **Communications** Post Office in The Square.

Western shore of Strangford Lough

Colour map 1, grid B6

Another way of getting to the Ards Peninsula is on the A22 road by the western shore of Strangford Lough, and there are a couple of diversions worth taking along the way. **Castle Espie**, run by the Wildfowl and Wetlands Trust, is home to a large collection of ducks, geese and swans, and provides access to bird-watching hides over the lough. ■ *Ballydrain Rd, Comber. T9187414. Open Mar-Oct, Mon-Sat, 1030-1700, Sun, 1130-1800. Shorter hours in winter. £3. Signposted, 3 miles south of Comber.*

Strangford Lough

Newtownards
Carrowdore
Mount Stewart
Greyabbe
Chapel Island
South Island
Lisbane
Mahee Island
Kircubbin
A22
Killinchy
Islandmore
Pawle Island
Island Taggart
B6
B7 — Killyleagh
Portaferry
A22
National Trust Wildlife Centre
Strangford
A25 Balltculter
A7 Saul Raholp
Downpatrick

N

0 miles 2
0 km 2

⌂ Birdwatching hide or site
◗ Main island nesting site
◆ Nature reserve
↝ Main winter feeding area
🦭 Seals

Strangford Lough

Strangford Lough would be a lake but for a narrow 5-mile (8-km) gap at the southern end between Portaferry and Strangford that closes to 500 metres, whipping up some treacherous tides that probably explain the Viking appellation Strangfjörthr (the strong fjord). The lough is rich in wildlife: be in the northern half in winter to watch wildfowl, waders, gulls and auks feeding off the soft mud and sands; in autumn up to 15,000 pale-bellied brent-geese fly in from Arctic

Canada for rest and recreation on their way south; common and grey seals cling to rocks close to the shore and the occasional killer whale slips through the narrows.

Now managed by the National Trust, based at Castle Ward near Strangford, T44881411, the Wildlife Centre has a wealth of ecological and wildlife information and displays and opens Jul and Aug, 1400-1800, daily except Thu; Apr, May-Jun and Sep, Sat and Sun 1400-1800.

County Down

A little further south the **Nendrum Monastic Site** makes up for its scattered and scant remains by an informative visitor centre and a pacific setting very appropriate for the site of a monastic settlement. Founded in 445 by St Mochaoi, a pupil of St Patrick, it was rediscovered in 1844. ■ *Mahee Island. Museum open Apr-Sep, Tue-Sat, 1000-1900, Sun, 1400-1900. Shorter hours in winter. 75p. Free access to site.*

Comber has a few places to eat, including pub food at the *Castle Inn* in Castle St, but the *Old Schoolhouse Restaurant*, T91870870, next to Castle Espie, maintains its reputation for serving the best dishes, especially seafood, in the area.

Near the bottom of the lough, **Killyleagh Castle** looks like a film set but is actually one of Ireland's oldest inhabited castles, going back to the 12th century but given its schmaltzy appearance by Victorians. In 1913, when unionists resolved to use "all means which may be found necessary" to scupper Home Rule, the newly founded Ulster Volunteer Force trained in the grounds here. **Open-air concerts** are hekd here in the summer, tickets available from the A *Dufferin Arms*, T44828229, in the village.

Downpatrick

This is a thriving, tolerant little town. It has several cracking sites to visit, and it is well worth an overnight stay to do so. If you can make your visit on St Patrick's Day, all the better: you will see genuine cross-cultural celebrations. The **tourist office** is at 53A Market St, T612233. It's open Sep-Jul, Mon-Fri, 0900-1700, Sat, 0930-1700; Jul and Aug, Mon-Sat, 0900-1900, Sun, 1400-1800.

Colour map 1, grid B6

In the 12th century, Down was the capital of Dál Fiatach; the real trouble started when the Norman John de Courcy turned up here in 1177 from Dublin with 22 horsemen and 300 foot soldiers. Down's Gaelic ruler, Rory MacDonleavy, was routed from the town; several major battles followed, with hand-to-hand fighting along the banks of the Quoile River, but the small Norman force held fast.

History

So Down became the first Norman foothold in Ulster. De Courcy gave the ancient site of Dún-da-lethglas, which had been an Augustinian Priory before the Norman takeover, to the Church, and renamed it Downpatrick. By the 13th century it was the second most important Norman settlement in Ulster, after Armagh, with defensive walls, and a Benedictine monastery.

Downpatrick gaol saw its share of executions during the 1798 rebellion, when the area was second only to Wexford in the strength of the rebels and the

Antique city

Greyabbey Antiques, Main Sreet, Greyabbey village is home to over a dozen antique shops; opening hours vary, with Wednesday, Friday and Saturday being good days to visit. The Irvine Gallery,

T42788744, has oils and watercolours as well as paintings on silk. Rara Avis, T42788300, stocks textiles, painted furniture, ethnic jewellery. The Antique Shop, T42738333, sells... antiques.

ferocity with which they fought. After this the town went into a decline, which in a way is lucky for visitors, who can see the 18th-century structure of the town almost unencumbered by modernity.

Sights A church stood on the site of what is now **Down Cathedral** long before de Courcy generously gave back a little of what he had taken in the 12th century. The site is associated with Patrick, who built his first church, and is reputed to have died, at Saul, a few miles to the north. Before de Courcy, there was an Augustinian settlement on the hill. Nothing remains of it, or of the building that replaced it, which was destroyed in the 14th century. In 1609 James I made Down a cathedral, despite the fact that it was a set of ruins and the bishop was enthroned here beneath a gaping roof. Rebuilding got underway in the 18th century. Inside, it's a cosy little place with 18th-century box pews labelled with the names of their owners on little brass plaques. The organ is built on to a pulpitum, which you walk through to enter the church. The two thrones that face each other across the nave are the bishop's throne and the judge's seat, dating back to a time when trials were held in the church. In the graveyard the remains of St Patrick, St Colmcille and St Brigid are said to be buried. The stone that supposedly marks the site was put there in 1900. In the grounds are several other antiquities, which have largely been removed to here from other places. ■ *The Mall, T614922. Open Mon-Sat, 1000-1700, Sun, 1400-1700. Free. Services at 1130 Sun, 0930 daily. Choral evensong third Sun of the month at 1530.*

In the town's gaol, is the really excellent **Down County Museum**. There are exhibitions on St Patrick, the history of County Down with lots of fascinating material on the 1798 rebellion, a changing series of exhibitions of art and artefacts, and the barely changed prison cells complete with 18th-century graffiti and some unrealistic models. Sensors along the passages set off recorded prison noises, which can be quite startling if you are not expecting them. ■ *The Mall, T615218. Jul-mid-Sep, Mon-Fri, 1000-1700, Sat and Sun, 1400-1700; mid-Sep-Jun, Tue-Fri, 1000-1700, Sat and Sun, 1400-1700, also St Patrick's Day, Easter Mon. 1100-1700. Free. Shop.*

The **Saint Patrick Centre** is a very interactive kind of place detailing the life of the saint and the early church in Ireland. Aimed more at local children perhaps than the tourist market, this is good for a wander round on a rainy day and will genuinely interest those of a historical bent. ■ *T44619000. Jun-Aug, Mon-Sat, 0930-1900, Sun, 1300-1800. Apr, May and Sep, Mon-Sat, 0930-1730, Sun, 1300-17.30, Oct-Mar, Mon-Sat, 1000-1700, Sun 1300-1700.*

If nothing else convinces you that you are in the United Kingdom and not the Republic of Ireland, the wacky **Downpatrick Railway Museum** will: only the British are this barmy. This museum is run entirely by volunteers and is populated by every crumbling railway carriage that farmers could take off their fields and dump here. One of the trains actually works, and you can take a short train ride to **King Magnus Halt** on a restored but creaky steam engine whose provenance will be lovingly described by the volunteer guides. You can also visit the worksheds where skeleton carriages are being worked on, the signal box (carried brick by brick from Ballyclare) and the station house itself (actually the old gasworks building, also shifted block by block). The volunteers have great plans for expanding the line and adding more carriages, and their enthusiasm alone is worth the visit. ■ *Market St, T615779. Trains run from Jul-mid-Sep, 1400-1700, Sat and Sun, only. Also St Patrick's Day, Easter Sun and Mon, Hallowe'en weekend, Dec weekends, 1400-1700. Workshop and Station House: Jun-Sep, Mon-Sat, 1100-1400.*

There are a good few other things to peer at in this city. The **Roman Catholic church**, 'St Patrick's', is quite an impressive building: much more modern than the cathedral, Gothic-looking, and set on another hill. It was built in the late 19th century and replaces an earlier church of around 1787. Most of what you see, though, is a modern extension added to hold the increasing congregations in this predominantly Catholic town. Stained glass and mosaic panels detail the life of St Patrick. ■ *Open daily. Services Tue, Wed, Fri 1930; Sun, 0800, 1000, 1200, 1700.*

In Mount Crescent is a pathway leading to the **Mound of Down**, the remains of de Courcy's fortifications. It is a motte and bailey fortification, said to be the finest example of such in Ulster, probably built around 1200. Within sight of the Mound, and reached from the Belfast road, is **Inch Abbey**, another de Courcy job. Built around 1180, it was a Cistercian monastery, and is on the site of a much older place, called Inis Cumhscraigh, which dates back to at least 800. In its 12th-century state, this was a church, with a cloister and several community buildings, including a bakehouse, whose oven was found nearby. There are a good few walls remaining, even though the abbey was burned in 1404, and completely suppressed by 1541. ■ *Open Apr-Sep, Tue-Sat 1000-1300, 1330-1900, Sun 1400-1900; Oct-Apr closes at 1600. 75p. Turn left off the Belfast Rd at the Abbey Lodge Hotel.*

At **Saul** (Sabhal Pádraic), 2 miles (3 km) northeast of town, is the reputed site **Around** of Patrick's first church in Ireland which was said to be in a barn given to him **Downpatrick** by the local lord. An Augustinian monastery was built here some time after 1130, but today the site is occupied by a Church of Ireland building, erected in the 1930s in the style of a medieval church. There are a few ancient relics in the graveyard, including two mortuary houses of unknown date, cross pillars and a medieval gravestone. Inside the church, the font is 13th-century. If you are feeling a bit under the weather, go to **Struel Wells**, 1½ miles (2 km) east of Downpatrick: here there are four ancient wells reputed to have the power to heal internal organs, eyes, and body and limbs. ■ *Ardglass Rd. Free.*

AL *Tyrella House*, 100 Clanmaghery Rd, T851422, www.hiddenireland.com/tyrella A **Sleeping** good choice for an out-of-town, country-house sort of stay, has its own beechwoods, *Price codes:* private beach and stables. Also has a self-catering cottage. **A** *Abbey Lodge*, 38 Belfast *see inside front cover* Rd, T614511. Outside of town. **A** *Denvir's Hotel*, 14-16 English St, T612012. An ancient building recently renovated to a Spartan prettiness. The dining room has the most enormous fireplace with the old hooks that were used for smoking meat still in place. Huge rooms, very central but quiet. The best place to stay in Downpatrick. **B** *Arolsen*, 47 Roughal Park, T612656 bryancoburn@compuserve.com Fairly central B&B. Evening meals by arrangement. **B** *Dunnleath House*, 33 St Patrick's Dv, T613221. B&B with 2 big triple rooms. **C** *Hillside*, 62 Scotch St, T613134. A B&B in a listed Georgian house with 3 double rooms, 1 en suite. Residents' lounge.

County Down

Local maps

A useful series of free leaflets with maps outlining short walks in the Kilclief/ Killyleagh/Downpatrick/Castlewellan and districts is available from most tourist

*offices. **Ordnance Survey** Map No 21 in the Discovery series is also very useful if staying in the Strangford Lough area.*

Eating   Your best bet is *Denvir's*, which is enormously popular with locals and visitors alike; nothing special, but good hearty food and very reasonable prices. *Harry Afrika's* inside *Supervalu* shopping centre does grills and the like, and opens on Sun too, while *The Pepper Pot* is a conventional meat-centred caff in St Patrick's Av (closed Sun). *The China Garden*, 16 English St, T613364, offers a touch of the Orient and 2 courses for £7.50.

Pubs & music   *Denvir's* has music at weekends, usually country-style folk music or something louder. The other pubs have music, occasionally live. *The Cabin* at the bottom of Church St is a bright airy bar with live music on Sat nights.

Festivals   The big event of the year is **17th March**, *St Patrick's Day*, which is extended into a week of cross-cultural activities that attracts large crowds.

Sport   **Bowling** *Ownebeg Bowling Club*, St Patrick's Drive, T613287. **Cricket** *Downpatrick Cricket Club*, Strangford Rd, T612829. **Golf** *Downpatrick Golf Course*, Saul Rd, T615497. **Horseriding** *Tullymurry Equestrian Centre*, 145 Ballyduggan Rd, T811880. **Sailing** *Quoile Yacht Club*, 21 Castle Island Rd, T612266.

Directory   **Banks** *First Trust*, 15 Market St, Mon-Fri, 0930-1630, cashpoint. *Northern Bank*, 58 Market St, Mon, 0930-1700, Tue-Fri, 1000-1530, Sat, 0930-1230, cashpoint. **Communications** Post Office: 65 Lower Market St, Mon-Fri, 0900-1530, Sat, 0900-1230. **Cultural centres** *Down Arts Centre*, Irish St, T615283. **Hospitals and medical services** *Down Hospital*, Irish St, T613311. **Library** 79 Market St, T612895, Mon, Tue, Thu, 1000-2000, Fri, 1000-1700, Sat, 1000-1300, 1400-1700. **Places of worship** *Down Cathedral*, English St (see page 598 for services). **Useful addresses and telephone numbers** Royal Ulster Constabulary: 8 Irish St, T615011.

Strangford to Newcastle

Strangford   If it wasn't for the ferry crossing to Portaferry, Strangford would be a place to
Colour map 1, grid B6   miss. **Strangford Castle**, one of the many tower houses you'll see dotted around Strangford Lough, dates from the late 16th century (key-keeper lives opposite at 39 Castle Street), but that's all there is to see. The *Cuan Bar & Restaurant*, serving meals like mussels with pasta for £8.20, has a good local reputation but nowhere else is recommended. Two local campsites are *Castle Ward Caravan Park*, just over a mile west of the village on the A25, T44881680, with tent pitches for £7.50.

Castle Ward   Outside the village of Strangford, on the Downpatrick Road, Castle Ward is a distinctly odd 18th-century manor house now managed by the National Trust but formerly the property of Bernard and Ann Ward. The couple eventually parted, but before they did, the divorce of their minds was reflected permanently in the design of their house. The front of Castle Ward is classical in style (his taste), while the rear is Gothic (her preference), and the dichotomy is also apparent in the interior. The extensive grounds include a tower house and landscaped gardens. ■ *T44881204. House: Jun-Aug, 1300-1800, daily except Thu; Apr, May, Sep, Oct, Sat and Sun, 1300-1800; Easter daily, 1300-1800. £2.60. Last guided tour 1700. Grounds, £3.50 for car. On A25, under 2 miles west of Strangford.*

Kilclief Castle

Another quick stop could be made here, a couple of miles south of Strangford on the A2, where another fortified tower house stands in good condition and the interior gives some idea of just how well provided they could be. ■ *Open Jul and Aug, Tue-Sat, 1000-1900, Sun, 1400-1900. 75p.*

Ardglass
Colour map 1, grid B6

If you've taken a fancy to comparing tower houses, there are no less than seven of them at Ardglass, 8 miles (13 km) south of Strangford, one of which is now in the grounds of a golf club. In its late 19th-century heyday Ardglass was a profitable little fishing port cashing in on seasonal shoals of herring and mackerel, which were salted and exported to the West Indies. It is still a good place to purchase fresh fish and there are a couple of restaurants worth visiting as well as the only visitable tower house, **Jordan's Castle**. ■ *Open Jul and Aug, Tue-Sat, 1000-1900, and Sun, 1400-1900. 75p.*

County Down

Eating *Aldo's*, T44841315, in Castle Place, next to the post office, opens Thu-Sun at 1700 for high tea and à la carte dishes. **B** *Burford Lodge*, Quay Street, T44841141, does evening meals for residents. **B** *The Cottage*, Castle Pl, T44841080, has rooms but no evening meals. There is a big café in the harbour offering things with chips, or for Sun lunch food try *The Moorings* opposite Jordan's Castle.

Killough

The A2 follows the coast around an inlet, through the village of Killough, and from the coastguard station just south of the village there is an enjoyable 4-mile (6.4-km) circular **coastal path** that follows the shore across stiles until reaching Point Road near St John's Point Lighthouse. Turn right on to Point Road to head back to the village.

Tyrella beach

The A2 between Killough and Clough passes this beach, ideal for families due to a shallow sands, warden service and amenities, but consequently busy on a fine summer's day. When it is quieter, enjoy the dune walks or a beach walk to the east for up to an hour. £2 to park a car.

Clough
Colour map 1, grid B6

Before reaching Newcastle the road passes Clough, at the junction with the A25 from Downpatrick, and its eponymous **motte castle** with free access and fine views from the top of the mound. The original occupant of the castle living in his fortification on top of this artificial mound needed a good view to espy hostile movements, and the Clough motte also had defensive wooden palisades around the perimeter.

Dundrum
Colour map 1, grid C6

This village is the last stop, with a particularly fine castle: "one of the strongyst holtes that ever I sawe in Ireland", reported a henchman for the Tudor monarchy in 1538. The Norman de Courcy first established a castle here known as Rath. When he fell out of favour with King John and the land passed to Hugh de Lacy, de Courcy found himself unsuccessfully besieging his own Dundrum Castle in 1205. Hugh de Lacy added a sturdy keep and later a gatehouse to the castle and what you see today is still a very impressive sight. There are picnic tables in the car park, but more appealing is one of the many grassy areas under the shade of trees inside the castle grounds. ■ *Apr-Sep, Tue-Sat, 1000-1900; Sun, 1400-1900. 75p.*

Around the Mourne Mountains

South Down, between Newcastle and Newry, has a schizophrenic quality. On the one hand there are the majestic Mourne Mountains imposing their granite beauty on the surrounding wilderness, while down on the coast there are unimpressive towns that range from the working town of Newcastle to the downright sectarian Kilkeel. Seen in terms of nature and nurture there is no question about who wins out in this part of the world.

Newcastle

Colour map 1, grid C5   The excellent **tourist office** (on Central Promenade on the way out of town on the A2 to Kilkeel, T43722222, open Mon-Sat, 1000-1700, Sun, 1400-1800) is a good place to collect information and pick up a colour town map that lists useful amenities such as banks and chemists. Once your business is done, however, there is little reason to linger in Newcastle.

Walking around Newcastle

Mapping and information   Newcastle, with its shops and amenities, suggests itself as a quartermastering base for walking in the Mourne Mountains, and the Mourne Countryside Centre, 91 Central Promenade, T43726493, has information and literature on suggested walks. Experienced walkers will want to ascend to Slieve Donard, using *Ordnance Survey* Map No 29 in the Discovery series, while a gentler introduction is provided by Donard Park to the south of Newcastle. From here the mountain can be climbed, or you can try a shorter walk by just following the path up the slopes for a hour or so.

For even shorter walks, take Bryansford Road out of Newcastle to **Tollymore Forest Park**, covering some 500 acres at the foot of the Mourne Mountains and with four way-marked trails. Once a private estate, the mansion house fell into disrepair after the Second World War and was demolished in the early 1950s. What remains is a stupendous avenue of cedar trees leading up to where the house stood which form's a magnificent entrance to the park. The most interesting short walk is the **Rivers Trail** that follows the Shimna River through swathes of violets in early summer before crossing by Parnell's Bridge and returning through forest on the other side. A longer 8-mile (13-km) trail heads into the forest and offers excellent views of the countryside and Mourne Mountains. ■ *T43722428. Daily, 1000-dusk. Car £3.80, pedestrian £2. Tea room.*

Further inland, the **Castlewellan Forest Park** is famous for its arboretum that dates back to 1740, but walking is restricted to a 3-mile trail around a lake with sculptures created from local materials. Enjoy tea in the Queen Anne-style courtyard or bring food to eat in the picnic and barbecue areas. ■ *Castlewellan. T43778664. Open daily 1000-dusk. Car £3.80, pedestrian £2.*

Sleeping
Price codes:
See inside front cover

AL *Enniskeen House Hotel*, 98 Bryansford Rd, T43722392. Has bedrooms with views and the benefit of being a mile out of town, giving it the edge on the other available **AL** hotels. **B** *Arundel Guest House*, 23 Bryansford Rd, T43722232. Nearer town, and offers a reasonably priced but very early evening meal for £7 at 1730. **C** *Golf Links House*, 109 Dundrum Rd, T43722054, golflinkshouse@hotmail.com Also good value for rooms and meals. The YHANI **D** *Newcastle Hostel*, 30 Downs Rd, 50 yards from the bus station, T43722133. Has over 40 beds and is open all year. There are loads of caravan parks around town but the only one accepting campers is *Tollymore Forest Park*, Tullybrannigan Rd, T43722428, on the B180, 3 miles from town and charging between £6.50-£10 a night.

The oak-panelled restaurant at *Enniskeen House* has a £15.50 dinner with home-style **Eating** dishes like stuffed pork and apple sauce, steak, and scampi. The *Buck's Head* restaurant further out of town at 77 Main St, Dundrum, T43751868, is regarded as the most upmarket place in the area, and serves oysters and ostrich, though thankfully not in the same dish. Expect to pay £20-£25. Back in Newcastle, *Mario's*, 65 South Promenade, T43723912, has a large à la carte menu featuring Italian-style dishes, a reasonably priced set dinner and a carvery Sunday lunch. Open for evening meals from 1830 to 2030. For a pub lunch in comfortable and congenial surroundings, try the olde-Irish *Quinns* down from the tourist office in the direction of town.

Bus Bus station: Railway St, T43722296. *Ulsterbus Goldline* 237 runs Mon-Sat **Transport** between **Kilkeel** and **Belfast** via Newcastle. The 240 is a daily service between **Downpatrick** and **Newry**, also via Newcastle, and connecting with the daily 200 Newry to **Dublin** service.

Banks and their cashpoint machines are situated along Main St. Money can also be **Directory** changed at the tourist office. **Bicycle hire** from *Wiki Wiki Wheels*, 10b Donard St, T43723973. **Golf** *Royal County Down Golf Club*, T43723314.

Annalong is a small fishing village, 8 miles (12 km) south of Newcastle, and **Annalong** worth considering for an overnight stay. The beach is too shingly to attract *Colour map 1, grid C5* hordes of visitors, and near the harbour the 1830 **Annalong Corn Mill** makes for a mildly interesting visit when a flour-making demonstration is taking place. There is an adjoining herb garden. ■ *T43768736. Feb-Nov, Tue-Sat, 1100-1700. £1.30. Guided tours. Café.*

Sleeping LL *Glassdrumman Lodge*, 85 Mill Rd, signposted off the main road at the Newcastle end of the village, T43768451, www.glassdrummanlodge.co.uk Has a trout lough in the garden. Luxury accommodation. **B** *The Sycamores*, 52 Majors Hill, T43768279. Old farmhouse building with parts dating back to the 18th century and views out to sea. **C** *Oldtown Lodge*, 46 Oldtown Rd, A couple of miles out of the village, T43768350, a non-smoking B&B house which would make a useful base for local hillwalking, but no meals available.

Eating A 5-course dinner at *Glassdrumman Lodge* is £32.50. Pub food is available at *The Halfway House* at the Newcastle end of the village and there is also *The Light-house Bar* in Bath St.

Kilkeel

The small fishing town of Kilkeel seems an unlikely setting for the ugly face of *Colour map 1, grid C5* sectarianism but there is no mistaking the in-your-face triumphalism of the wall murals and the intimidating fluttering of an Ulster Volunteer Force flag in the town centre. Come the marching season, the minority of Catholics living here are virtual prisoners in their own homes and it is definitely a place to avoid at weekends in the summer when there is often a march or parade of one kind or another and roads are blocked off to traffic.

The **Mourne Grange Craft Shop**, 169 Newry Rd, T41760103, is worth a visit with heaps of craft goods and a tea room. Kilkeel also has a **diving school**, *San Miguel*, T41765885, F41764760, at the harbour, running fishing trips as well as diving courses for novices. For a general introduction to the role of fishing in Kilkeel's history, the **Nautilus Centre** by the harbour has displays and exhibits and a shop selling fresh fish. ■ *Rooney Rd. T41765555.*

Easter-Sep, Mon-Sat 1000-2100, Sun 1200-1800. Same hours the rest of the year but closing at 1800. The **tourist office** is on Newcastle St, T41762525. Open Apr-Sep, Mon-Sat, 0900-1730 (shorter hours in winter). An excellent source of local information.

Sleeping
Price codes:
see inside front cover

B *Heath Hall*, 160 Moyadd Rd, T41762612. A friendly farmhouse B&B, about a mile out of town in the countryside. **B** *Mourne Abbey*, 16 Greencastle Rd, T41762426. Half a mile south of town, opens from Easter-Sep and an evening meal is £10.

Self-catering *Mountain View House*, 20 Head Rd, Moyadd, T41723120. Rural self-catering from £25-£35 per night or £170-£250 a week. *Mountains of Mourne Cottages*, Hannas Close, T41765999, www.travel-Ireland.com/hannas Restored traditional Irish cottages in a private clachan. Sleeps 2-6, 2 nights £105, 3 nights £130.

Eating

For one of the most substantial pub lunches in Ireland, try *Jacob Halls* in Greencastle St in the middle of town. There is also *Food for Thought*, at the Nautilus Centre.

The Silent Valley
Colour map 1, grid C5

A huge reservoir supplying Belfast from the valley of the River Kilkeel was completed in 1933 and its story is told in the Information Centre near the car park in the reservoir grounds. The most incredible aspect of the whole project was the building of the **Mourne Wall** around the catchment area – Ireland's Great Wall – up to 8 ft high, 22 miles long and connecting the summits of 15 mountains. Why it was built, apart from being a massive job creation scheme, is not entirely clear, but it took from 1904-1923 to complete. A 3-mile **walk** by the side of the reservoir is well worth it for the fine views. ■ *Easter-Sep, 1000-1830; Oct-Apr, 1000-1600. £3 per car. In May, Jun and Sep at weekends, and daily in Jul and Aug, a bus service operates between the car park and the top of Ben Crom. £1.20 return. Coffee shop and craft shop.*

Kilkeel to Newry

Colour map 1, grid C5

A detour southwest from Kilkeel leads to the tip of a promontory where **Greencastle Fort** is situated. It was built by the rapacious Hugh de Lacy to stand sentinel over Carlingford Lough and the views from the castle are a better reason for making the journey here than the remains themselves. ■ *Jul-Aug, Tue-Sat, 1000-1900, Sun, 1400-1900. 75p.*

The A2 road gradually creeps closer to the north coast of the lough, looking across to the Cooley Peninsula in Louth, and passing a signpost to the **Kilfeagham dolmen** with its 35-tonne capstone, a few miles out from Kilkeel.

Rostrevor

The village of Rostrevor has more charm than most of the coastal towns in south Down and nearby **Kilbroney Park** has plenty of open space, riverside walks and an energetic path up to the 40-tonne, pink granite, Cloughmore boulder stone from where there are scenic views across to the Republic, as well as tennis courts and picnic areas. ■ *T41738134. Open Jun-Aug, daily, 0900-2220. Shorter hours the rest of the year.*

Sleeping B *Fir Trees*, 16 Killowen Old Rd, T41738602. A bungalow B&B overlooking the lough. **Self-catering** *Lecale Cottages*, 125 Kilbroney Rd, Rostrevor, T41738727, www.rostrevorholidays.com Three self-catering, traditional-style cottages, overlooking the lough and costing £150-£250 a week. 2 nights in the high season £65.

The park is also home to *Kilbroney Caravan Park*, T41738134, with 40 tent pitches for around £6 per night.

Eating Rostrevor has a few decent places to eat, better than any in Warrenpoint. They include the *Southfork Restaurant* in Church St, T41738276, *Top of the Town* in the *Kilbroney* bar in Bridge St, T41738236, which does meals for £9.95 till midnight, and pub food at the *Cloughmor Inn*.

Festivals The last week in **Jul** is the setting for Rostrevor's *Fiddler's Green Festival*, a celebration of Irish culture with a ceilí band on an open-air stage, nightly folk sessions in the pubs and classes for traditional instruments such as the fiddle, flute and pipes. Enquiries to 5 Cherry Hill, Rostrevor, Co. Down, BT34 3BD. T/F41739819, f.d.green@fnmail.com

On the road between Rostrevor and Warrenpoint is the **Narrow Water Castle** where de Lacy built a fortress in the 13th century to guard access to the river up to Newry. Narrow Water Castle was where, in 1979, the Provisionals hid a bomb in a haystack and detonated it from the shore of the Cooley Peninsula when a platoon of the 2nd Parachute Regiment passed by. Survivors took refuge in the gateway to the castle where another bomb had been planted. A total of 18 soldiers died and an Englishman on holiday was accidentally shot dead by an army helicopter returning fire on the Cooley Peninsula. ■ *Castle: guided tours normally available in Jul and Aug, Tue-Fri 1100-1630, but check with the tourist office in Warrenpoint, T41752256.*

Warrenpoint

Warrenpoint is not as interesting a town as its picturesque appearance and location might suggest. The pubs cater to Irish holidaymakers in the summer and at the *Marine Tavern* opposite the marina all spirits cost £1, pints £1.50, and consequently the place is heaving at night with intoxicated revellers. Many of the pubs have live music but it's more likely to be in the Country and Western vein than traditional Irish.

The **Burren Heritage Centre** is a 2 miles west of town, but with nothing to show except some fading models of archaeological sites, it is hardly worth a visit except on a very wet afternoon. ■ *T41773378. Open Apr-Sep, Tue-Fri 1100-1700, Sun, 1400-1700. Shorter hours in winter and closed on Sun. £1.*

Not a lot of choice, but not a problem either, for Newry and Rostrevor are nearby. **B** *Ryan B&B*, 19 Milltown St, Burren, T41772506, opens all year. **B** *The Mournes*, 16 Seaview, T41772610, is on the sea front overlooking Carlingford Lough but may not be the quietest place at the height of summer. Some en-suite rooms.

Sleeping
*Price codes:
see inside front cover*

The food scene is also rather dismal, with standard fare available at *Bennett's*, Church St, T41752053, which stays open until 2200 at weekends in the summer. *The Whistledown Inn*, facing the sea in aptly named Seaview, T41752697, has a large menu of snacks and salads plus fish, meat and grills from £5 to £10. The *Boathouse Inn*, 3 Marine Parade, T41753743, www.boathouseinn.com, has a good restaurant, the *Vechia Roma* with an evening meal for about £15. There is live music in the *Shenanigans* café bar on some evenings. A room here costs about £60.

Eating

The *Maiden of the Mournes Festival* is a week-long festival at the beginning of **Aug**, established in 1990 along the lines of the Rose of Tralee festival.

Festivals

Adventure centre: *The East Coast Adventure Centre*,T41774006, covers windsurfing, canoeing, archery and other activities.

Sport

Boat A ferry, T41777370, to **Omeath** in the Cooley peninsula operates 1100-1800, Jun-Sep, for £2 return and is usually peopled by locals crossing into the Republic to play the lottery and take advantage of pub opening hours.

Transport

County Down

Directory **Banks** Located in The Square, Queen St and Charlotte St. **Taxis** *Ace Taxis*, T41752256; *Classic*, T41752888.

Newry

Colour map 1, grid C5

Newry has suffered from a bad press for years and guide books have tended to write the place off; don't believe a word of it. It's not postcard pretty, but it has history and attitude, and in the coming years could see quite a few changes as the importance of the border further diminishes.

The flourishing activity of the 18th century associated with the Newry canal petered out with the coming of the railways, and economic decline set in. At the time of partition in 1922, it was so widely accepted that the Boundary Commission would allocate the town to the Republic that two businessmen, one Catholic and one Protestant and living respectively in Newry and Warrenpoint, exchanged their houses so they could live in the state of their choice. It was not to be, but the legacy surfaced in 1969, with the Civil Rights Association calling for pressure to be taken off the Bogside, when Newry was quick to rise in revolt. Finally, 30 years later, the appearance of two new hotels and the expansive Buttercrane Shopping Centre point to a new and more equitable future for the town. The **tourist office** is in the town hall, T3068877. Open Jun-Sep, Mon-Fri, 0900-1700, Sat 1000-1600; Oct-May, Mon-Fri, same hours but closed 1300-1400.

Nowadays Newry is at peace, and while there are no special attractions it is an interesting place to wander around because the lack of developments over the last 30 years has helped preserve examples of industrial architecture that will soon no doubt succumb to the bulldozer.

Architectural attractions

Right next to the tourist office, where a town map can be collected or a town walking guide purchased, stands the magisterial **town hall**. It dates from 1893, built on a bridge near where the road from Armagh becomes Canal Street and meets Merchants Quay by the side of the canal. Tucked away behind it is a more interesting example of late-Victorian building, a five-storey brick-built structure with three arched doorways built in 1879. An even better example of Victorian industrial architecture can be admired by leaving the town hall and walking away from the town centre and across the junction with Canal Street to **Sand's Mill** in New Street: seven floors of red and yellow bricks, arcaded, and still in use since it first opened to business in 1873.

Newry Museum

The Newry Museum, next to the town hall, is a history-based museum with assorted exhibits and a restored early 18th-century room, using original panelling taken from a local house of that period. Not rivetingly interesting but fine for a rainy afternoon. ■ *Arts Centre, Bank Parade. T30266232. Mon-Fri 1030-1630. Free.*

Sleeping
Price codes:
see inside front cover

L *Canal Court Hotel*, Merchants Quay, T30251234, www.canalcourthotel.com Alex Ferguson stayed here and, while that might deter the anti-Man-U league, he knew, as usual, what he was doing and chose the best on offer. A new hotel with smart new rooms, leisure centre with pool and weekend packages. **AL-A** *Francis Court Hotel*, Francis St, T30266926, F30252706. Another new kid on the block with 16 rooms and a gritty exterior that blends well with the town's character. Good bar food in *O'Dowd's* bar in the hotel. **AL** *Mourne Country Hotel*, 52 Belfast Rd, T30267922, F30260896. A little way out of town at the roundabout on the Belfast Rd, with weekend and midweek deals. **B** *Millvale House*, 8 Millvale Rd, T30263789. B&B with 4 rooms, serves high tea

Newry Canal

The River Clanrye and the Newry Canal make an unusual sight, running cheek by jowl through the centre of town. Surveying work for it started in 1703, prompted by the notion of transporting newly discovered coal in east Tyrone from Lough Neagh and out to sea through Newry and *the Carlingford Lough. The canal's completion in 1741 was a remarkable achievement. It pre-dated the first canals in Lancashire, England, was built without machinery, and remained in operation for almost 200 years. The whole canal is now in public ownership.*

County Down

for £5, dinner for £7 and stays open all year. **C** *Carrow House*, 22 Newtown Rd, Belleeks, T30878182. This B&B is not in town, but a bed there is only £12.50. Numerous other B&Bs in and around town: enquire at the tourist office.

First choice should be *Brass Monkey*, 1 Sandy St, T30263176, serving seafood, steaks **Eating** and salads daily till 2200. Expect to pay between £12 and £20 for a meal. The *Old Mill Restaurant* at the Canal Court Hotel has a set dinner for £24 plus à la carte offering a wide choice of starters, meat and fish dishes; stay with the tried and tested dishes. Bar food is served all day and the carvery lunch is £6. *O'Dowd's* bar in the *Francis Court* hotel is very popular. There are a couple of inexpensive cafés on Hill St, as you walk into the town centre from the tourist office and *Deli Lites*, 12 Monaghan St, serves up better-than-average sandwiches.

Bus Bus station: T30263531, Edward St (off Monaghan St). The 238 express service runs **Transport** daily between **Belfast** and Newry and from Newry the bus goes on to **Warrenpoint**, **Rostrevor** and **Kilkeel**. The 240 service runs between **Downpatrick** and Newry, also daily. The daily Belfast to **Dublin** express bus also stops in Newry. **Train** Train station: T30269271, a local bus ride out of town. The **Belfast** to **Dublin** trains stop every day.

Banks On Hill St. **Directory**

The Brontë Homeland

The tourist board has made the best out of the least interesting part of Down by dubbing an area to the south of Banbridge, about half-way between Newry and Belfast, the 'Brontë Homeland', as it was here that Patrick Brontë, father of the famous literary family, lived and worked before moving to Haworth in Yorkshire. If travelling south to Banbridge from Belfast, the Georgian-style town of **Hillsborough** offers a touch of genteel elegance: break here for tea and cakes. Alternatively, push on for Banbridge and stop outside of town at the **Banbridge Gateway Tourist Information Centre**. There is a café serving lunches and light meals and the centre sells a useful little collection of eight route cards with directions and maps for suggested local walks (including a Brontë walk) averaging 5 miles each and using public paths. ■ *200 Newry Rd, T40623322. Open Jul and Aug, Mon-Sat, 0900-1900, Sun, 1400-1800; Sep-Jun, Mon-Sat, 1000-1700; Easter-Oct, Sun, 1400-1800*

The first stop on a Brontë tour should be the **Brontë Homeland Interpretative Centre** at Drumballyroney Church and School House near Rathfriland, 8 miles from Banbridge off the B10. Patrick Brontë and the novelist sisters' brother, Bramwell, taught and preached here. The importance of Ireland in gaining an understanding of Emily and her brother is not a tenuous one, as Terry Eagleton shows clearly in his book, *Heathcliff and the Great*

Hunger. A free leaflet with a map outlines a tour that takes in four other sites associated with the Brontës' father and provides a good a reason as any for threading one's way through a little-visited part of Down. ■ *Church Hill Rd, T40631152. Open Mar-Sep, Tue-Fri, 1100-1700, Sat and Sun, 1400-1800. £2.*

County Armagh

Armagh City

Colour map 1, grid B4

Once the religious and cultural heart of Ireland Armagh has slumbered fairly peacefully through the economic regeneration of the last few years and beyond. The result is that the city stands almost exactly as it was when it was first laid out with the mall in the centre of town and the courthouse and gaol facing one another across from it. The gaol is thankfully empty now but the courthouse still stands as a great bastion of power, now fortified with railings and security cameras just in case the Troubles force their way back in.

Ins and outs

Getting there Armagh is easily accessible by bus from Belast, Dublin, Galway and Enniskillen as well as local towns (see 'Transport' page 614). The nearest train station is at Portadown, T38351422, which connects with the Dublin to Belfast line.

Getting around Everything in this little city is packed into three parallel streets and their side roads, with a couple of sights outside the town yet easily accessible by bus or car. The **tourist office** is at 40 English St, T521800. It has a bureau de change, fax and B&B booking servics. Open Sep-Jun, Mon-Sat, 0900-1700, Sun 1400-1700; Jul, Aug, Mon-Sat 0900-1730, Sun 1300-1730.

History

In the ninth century Armagh was the largest and most important settlement in Ireland, but the place was settled long before that. A neolithic circular enclosure, filled with pot shards, was revealed by a bomb in Scotch Street in 1979, and, outside of town, the Navan hill fort was the capital of the kings of Ulster from around 600BCE. St Patrick established a church here in the fifth century and a large monastic community developed, supporting schools, poor houses, and a lay community. Armagh became a beacon of learning while the rest of Europe fell into the Dark Ages.

At the height of its power Armagh bore the brunt of the Viking raids of Ulster. The Annals of Ulster record three raids; in 832 and again in 840 and 852, this time by Vikings who had settled in Dublin and came overland. After 866 there was a respite from the attacks as the Viking threat in Ulster passed on to the southern provinces, until 921 when a fresh series of plunderings began. The next to set his sights on Armagh was Brian Boru, the 10-11th century High King of Munster, who came relatively peacefully, paid a tribute to the church of Armagh and declared it the primacy of Ireland.

For the next 300 years the city remained an important centre of learning, while all around the Irish clans fought first one another and then the Normans for supremacy in Ulster. In the middle of the 16th century the Reformation came to Armagh, more powerfully than in other parts of Ireland because of the city's position within the Roman Catholic Church. The monasteries were disbanded, church property confiscated and all forms of religion except Anglicanism were banned from the churches. Armagh ceased to be a city.

Armagh entered a new golden age in the 18th century with a massive wave of building projects that created most of the modern city. Archbishop Richard Robinson and his friend the architect Thomas Cooley built the Bishop's Palace, the Public Library, the Gaol and the Royal School. A second wave by Francis Johnson built the Courthouse, the Bank of Ireland (now part of St Patrick's Trian) and the Observatory.

In the late 19th century the efforts of the Land Leaguers to get a fairer deal for small tenant farmers were met with Protestant riots in the city, the first real example of sectarian differences in Armagh, and in the 20th century the Depression brought more of the same. Never the flashpoint for disturbance that Derry or Belfast were during the Troubles, Armagh nevertheless saw some unpleasant scenes, notably the night in November 1968 when a convoy of Protestant cars led by Ian Paisley was stopped and 220 weapons, including two revolvers, were seized. The Loyalists held Armagh city refusing to leave while a civil rights march approached the city. Fortunately the civil rights marchers were persuaded to divert, thus avoiding serious bloodshed. Riots followed the introduction of internment in August 1971 and as the IRA gathered strength and support Armagh saw its share of bombs.

These days peace reigns in the city – the gates that were once used to shut up the centre remain open at night, the courthouse has been rebuilt after its destruction and the Arts Centre is encouraging nightlife back to the city.

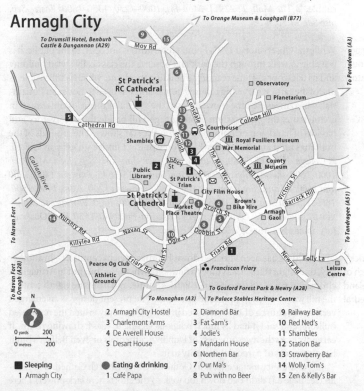

Armagh City

Sleeping
1 Armagh City

Eating & drinking
1 Café Papa

2 Armagh City Hostel	2 Diamond Bar	9 Railway Bar
3 Charlemont Arms	3 Fat Sam's	10 Red Ned's
4 De Averell House	4 Jodie's	11 Shambles
5 Desart House	5 Mandarin House	12 Station Bar
	6 Northern Bar	13 Strawberry Bar
	7 Our Ma's	14 Wolly Tom's
	8 Pub with no Beer	15 Zen & Kelly's Bar

County Armagh

Sights

St Patrick's Trian
Trading on the association of Swift with the town the best thing here is the story of Gulliver, told in one room by an extremely realistic giant, in others by a series of models in glass cases. There is also the story of Armagh, which is vaguely interesting but a bit too dependent on gadgetry, and the story of St Patrick. ■ *40, English St, T521801. Open Sep-Jul Mon-Sat1000-1730; Jul and Aug, additional opening Sun 1300-1800. £3.75. Café, shop.*

Armagh County Museum
Set in an old 1833 schoolhouse this is a pleasant hour's meander through the detritus of Armagh's past. Collected here are assorted bits and pieces – bog butter, leather shoes, an ox yoke discovered in the bogs, assorted carved stone heads found while renovations were taking place, old clothes, examples of the city's past as a lacemaking centre, Orange memorabilia, and an interesting display about the railway and its great disaster of 1889 when a day trip went horribly wrong and 89 people died. There is also a little display of stuffed animals and an art gallery, and downstairs an exhibition on the museum itself and its work. ■ *The Mall, T523070. Open Mon-Fri 1000-1700, Sat 1000-1300, 1400-1700. Closed bank holidays. Free.*

Royal Irish Fusiliers Museum
This is a vast collection of First World War medals, a dugout, uniforms, silver cups, banners and, more interestingly, an exhibit on the terrible damage done by the IRA bomb aimed at the nearby courthouse in 1993. The whole building more or less folded in on itself, but the museum was closed at the time and so there were no injuries. Most of the material on display was picked out of the rubble. ■ *The Mall, T522911. Mon-Fri, 1000-1230, 1330-1600; Easter-Sep, also Sat. £1.50.*

The Armagh Planetarium & Observatory
While the Observatory (1791, Francis Johnston) is not open to the public, it is possible to walk through the park and observe the classically styled building and its telescopes. At the rear of the building the dome, which is still visible, is one of the earliest surviving rotating domes and was used to house an Equatorial, which measured the movements of the stars. For those less interested in architecture, the Planetarium is on College Hill beside the observatory and has lots of hands-on exhibitions as well as the star shows. The grounds of the buildings hold an astropark, which you wouldn't notice unless you looked. ■ *College Hill, T523689. Planetarium open Jan-Jun, Sep, Dec, Mon-Fri, 1000-1600, shows daily at 1500, Sat and Sun, 1315-1645, shows at 1400, 1500 and 1600; Jul and Aug, Mon-Fri, 1000-1600, shows at 1200, 1300, 1400, 1500, 1600, Sat and Sun, 1315-1645, shows at 1400, 1500, 1600. Entrance to exhibition £1, shows £3.75. Observatory grounds Mon-Fri, 0930-1630. Free. Observatory dome open Apr-Sep, 0930-1430. Free.*

St Patrick's Church of Ireland Cathedral
This building has been knocked down 17 times in eight centuries – in another city, one might think it was time to find somewhere else, but not in Armagh. A church has stood on this site since Patrick's time, and from the eighth century the hill was covered in monastic buildings. The present design is an enlarged version of a church of 1268, restored in 1834. Thackeray visited the renovated building and said it had as much religious feeling to it as a drawing room. It certainly lacks the awesomeness of Dublin's cathedrals or even Belfast's but it has a cosy sort of parochial austerity to it.

Just as the Victorians' efforts to Gothicize Christ Church Cathedral in Dublin (see page 83) didn't go down too well, so the efforts here lack power. There are lots of accumulated bits and pieces around the church, the most fascinating of which is the brutal-looking Tandragee Man, an ancient granite idol, thus named because of the theory that he came from Tandragee in County Down. This and several other human figures in the church are thought to have been discovered when the church was renovated in the 19th century. Another of the figures shows a crudely carved man with rays radiating from his head, perhaps a sun god from pagan times or a representation of an early Irish man, who wore their hair in stiffened dreadlocks pulled back from their heads. There is also an amalgam of two high crosses, possibly 11th-century, thought to have been brought to the cathedral in 1441. Brian Boru is supposedly buried here; a slab on the exterior wall claims to be his burying place. ■ *Cathedral Close, T523142. Open Apr-Oct, daily 1000-1700; Nov-Mar 1000-1600. Conducted tours Jul and Aug, Mon-Sat, 1130 and 1430. Services Sun 1000, 1100, and 1430. Photographic permit £1 from verger or at the shop.*

Armagh Public Library

Close to the church in Cathedral Close is the public library (1771, Cooley), still very much in its original condition. You must ring to be let in. In the lobby is a series of displays about the *Book of Armagh*, currently in Dublin, while upstairs in the library itself is a pretty impressive collection of old books including an annotated copy of *Gulliver's Travels*, a 1611 Breeches Bible, a case of tiny books, a Roman missal from 1587 and a 13th-century Dutch missal. ■ *Cathedral Close, T523142. 0900-1700. Free.*

St Patrick's Roman Catholic Cathedral

Begun in 1840 in a neoclassical style, the design and building of this Cathedral were abandoned during the Famine. When work began again, it was in a different vein altogether. A third architect designed the interior of mosaic, fresco and stained glass, while the last person to have a hand in the design of this place was Liam McCormack in 1977-82. The result is, as many have pointed out, a little schizophrenic, but it certainly grips the imagination. The altar, like many other efforts of the 1970s, looks like it's used for pagan sacrifices rather than Catholic worship. ■ *Cathedral Rd, T37522802, services daily at 0900, 1030, 1200.*

Armagh Gaol

It's worth enquiring at the tourist office about Armagh Gaol, which, though it is not regularly open to the public, is well worth having a look at if you are lucky enough to be in town on one of the occasions when it is opened up. Destined to be a major tourist attraction in the next decade or so, it is presently crumbling badly but still stands as it was when it became notorious for its strip-searches of women political prisoners during the 1980s. Thomas Cooley is responsible for its design, and its façade is certainly beautiful enough. Inside are still the nets put up to catch suicides, the execution area (a nasty little corner of the building) and the burial places where the bodies of the truly bad were buried in quicklime. When this place was built there were no distinctions between types of criminal: debtors were incarcerated with murderers. Inside the yard was the treadwheel (no longer in existence) where, as a punishment for bad behaviour, prisoners were set to turn the wheel, stepping on to 8-inch-high steps and making 48 steps per minute. ■ *The Mall. For opening and entrance fee, enquire at the tourist office.*

The Palace Stables Heritage Centre

When Archbishop Robinson decided to make Armagh his headquarters in the 1760s, he couldn't be expected to live in any old shack and so this complex of buildings, restored in the late 1980s, is his personal statement of authority. The palace itself is now council offices, but a tour can be arranged to see the rooms and paintings. The chief tourist attraction here is the stables, which

County Armagh

have been converted into an exhibition about life in the late 18th century. Full of video clips, talking dummies and period bits and pieces, it's vaguely interesting, if you've nothing better to do. The other exhibits are more engaging: period rooms including a kitchen full of lovely old pots.

It's when you can see the mechanics of the big nob's house that this place really gets fascinating. In the ground is the ice house – filled in winter with packed snow and used to keep food fresh through the summer. Also there is the obligatory servants' tunnel, so that the good archbishop wouldn't have to watch the minions at work; a restored Victorian curvilinear conservatory; and the primate's chapel, an elegant personal church built in 1781 to a design by Francis Johnston. By the entrance gates are the remains of a 13th-century Franciscan friary founded in 1264. The grounds are full of things too, such as a sensory garden, walking trails and an ornamental garden. Extra marks to this place for being open on Sunday afternoons. ■ *Palace Demesne, Friary Rd, T529629. Sep-Mar, Mon-Sat, 1000-1700, Sun 1400-1700; Apr-Aug, Mon-Sat, 1000-1730, Sun 1000-1800. £3.50. Courtesy bus.*

Navan Fort An unremarkable-looking mound on a hilltop 2 miles (3.2 km) out of Armagh, this is Ireland's most significant ancient site. There is evidence of habitation here going back 7,000 years, but the most significant activity took place during the Bronze Age when the place was built and rebuilt about seven times, and finally, inexplicably, a huge wooden building was created, filled with limestone blocks and burned to the ground. In 1993 it acquired the obligatory heritage centre, which is quite attractively designed and does a pretty good job of explaining what is basically a big grassy mound at the moment. Excavations are planned for the future which may open up the site a little more. ■ *Killylea Rd, T525550. Access to the fort 24 hours and free. Courtesy bus in summer, or No 93 from the Mall. The centre should be open daily but check with the tourist office before setting out. Because of lack of funds it was closed in 2001 and may not reopen. Even if it is closed the site is well worth the trip.*

Essentials

Sleeping
■ *on map*
Price codes:
see inside front cover

You're not exactly spoilt for choice here – no major hotel chains, but there's a new hotel, a hostel and several B&Bs to choose from. **LL** *Armagh City Hotel* Friary Rd, T90385050, F90385055, www.mooneyhotelgroup.com This new kid on the block has everything you could wish for including leisure centre and pool, grounds where you can pretend to be lord of the manor, and a good restaurant. **A** *Charlemont Hotel*, 63-5 English St, T37522028, www.charlemontarmshotel.com Very central, good basic restaurant, newly renovated. **A** *Drumshill House*, 35 Moy Rd, T37522009. Out of town is this quite small, family-run establishment. Good for people with children – they have family rooms, pleasant gardens and an adventure playground. **A** *De Averell Guest House*, 3 Seven Houses, English St, T37511213, www.deaverell.com Nicely renovated Georgian house with pretty sitting room for guests. Has a respected restaurant and comfortable rooms. Very central. **C** *Desart Guest House*, The Desart, Desart Lane, off Cathedral Rd, T37522387. Actually classed as a B&B by the tourist board, this is small, with no en-suite rooms but good value. **B** *Ni Eoghain Lodge*, 32 Ennislare Rd, T525633. All rooms en suite, breakfast choices, cheap evening meals (a godsend on Armagh Sun nights), vegetarians catered for. **C-D** *Armagh City Hostel*, 39 Abbey St, T37511800, www.hini.org.uk YHANI hostel with dormitory accommodation and twin rooms, all en suite, cooking facilities and a restaurant. The place closes between 1100 and 1700 between Oct and Mar, which could be very inconvenient in miserable weather, but this is the best value for 2 people or a group of 4 sharing in town. Book well in advance.

Eating out in Armagh needs planning beforehand. Most places shut by 1730 and those that don't require a booking. *De Averell Guest House* (see above) serves a mixture of continental and local dishes and dinner, Wed-Sun until 2130, will cost around £15 per person. Open for lunches Mon-Sat. The *Drumshill Hotel*, on Moy Rd, serves steaks, salmon, chicken and lamb from 1700-2200, Mon-Sat, and a lunchtime carvery. The *Charlemont Arms*, has a fairly conventional potato based dinner menu for around £15, last orders are 2030. It's chief business is lunch, with a bigger menu but still along the same lines. The *Pub With No Beer*, 30 Thomas St, T37523586, opens Mon-Sat till 2130 and serves pub food – burgers, champ, salads, chicken pie etc. The *Zen*, a Chinese place above Kelly's bar deserves a medal for being open 7 nights till late and comes highly recommended by local people. Dinner for around £12. *Mandarin House*, 30 Scotch St, T3752228 deserves another, smaller one – open 6 days, closed Mon. Western and Chinese. *Café Papa*, 15 Thomas St, T37511205, does filled rolls, sandwiches and pastries at lunchtime but turns into a little bistro on Fri and Sat nights.

If it's just lunch you're after, there are a few more options. The best place in town is the *Pilgrim's Table*, 38, English St, T37521801, inside the St Patrick's Trian complex. It does homely kinds of dishes: filled potatoes, soups, hotpot and in pleasant surroundings. *Fat Sam's*, 7 English St, T37525559, is good for filled potato, a sandwich or pastry, Mon-Fri only. *Our Ma's Café*, 2 Lower English St, T511289, has an extensive menu of caff-type food and does a 3-course lunch for £3.50.

Most of the pubs do lunchtime pub grub. The best of them is a little out of town: the *Northern Bar*, 100 Railway St, T37527315, has a large menu ranging from sandwiches to a 3-course meal from 1230 to 1500 (1700 at weekends). The 3-course option will set you back around £7.50. Also open for Sun lunch. Vegetarian options. Other pubs to try for food are the *Station Bar*, T37523731, the *Strawberry Bar*, the *Diamond Bar*, T37523865, all in English St. *Calvert's Tavern*, 3 Scotch St, also serves bar lunches.

There is quite a lively nightlife among the pubs in Armagh. For traditional Irish music you could try the *Station Bar*, which has bands on Tue and Thu, or the *Railway Bar*, Mon. *Red Ned's* in Ogle St also has music at weekends. Other pubs have music at weekends, but it's likely to be tribute bands or a disco. The *Strawberry Bar* and the *Shambles Bar* have live music of some sort or another at weekends and *Wolly Tom's*, in Nursery Rd has live music Fri-Sun. Set-dancing classes are held on Mon at the *Pearse Og* club in Dalton Rd and visitors are welcome: £2, (T37511004, Pat Prunty). There are no classes during the summer months. The *Armagh Pipers Club* meets at the Dobbin St Community Centre on a monthly basis and visitors are welcome, T37511248, Eithne Vallely.

The £3.67 million *Market Place Theatre and Arts Centre*, (built thanks to lottery funding), T37521821, www.marketplacearmagh.com, is the city's major venue for theatre and concert performances. But besides visiting theatre and concerts it has a regular jazz night on the last Sat of each month and a stand-up comedy night on the last Thu of each month. Other centres used for theatre and other performances are *St Patrick's Parochial Hall*, The Orchard Leisure Centre in Folly Lane, T515920, and *St Patrick's Trian* (see page 610). In Market St, at the bottom of the Arts Centre, is *Armagh City Film House*, T511033. The Arts Centre has a display area for artwork.

In early **June** is the Armagh County *Fleadh Ceol*, a traditional music festival, including ceilis, street music and traditional music sessions in the pubs. *St Patrick's Day*, **17th March**, is celebrated with pub music, set dancing at the Palace Stables, a huge parade and a concert at St Patrick's Hall in Cathedral Rd.

Armagh Books, Barrack St, T37511988, Mon-Sat 0930-1730. With good coffee shop.

Eating
● on map
Price codes:
see inside front cover

County Armagh

Pubs & music

Entertainment

Festivals

Shopping

Tours & tour operators Armagh Tourist Information Centre, T37521800, organizes walking tours of the city at weekends Jun-Sep at 1100 (Sat only) and 1400. Tour lasts 2 hours and costs £4. Book in advance. They also produce an excellent leaflet which will take you around the Pilgrim's Trail, a waymarked walk around the city. Travel agents include: *Lunn Poly*, Scotch St, T37510786; *UlsterTravel*, English St, T37522919.

Transport **Bike** *Brown's Bikes*, 21 Scotch St, T37522782. **Bus** The bus station is at 14 Londsale Rd, T37522266. There are direct express buses to **Belfast** (14 or more a day, last bus leaves Armagh at 2050, fewer at weekends), **Dublin** (1 a day, 2 on Fri), **Cork** (1 a day, no Sun service), **Galway** (2 a day, 1 on Sun) and **Enniskillen** (1 a day, no Sun service), stopping at major towns along the route. Local buses connect with smaller towns in the area and a change at **Dungannon** brings connections to the **northern coast** and **Derry**. **Taxi** *Central Taxis*, T37526999; *City Taxis*, T37528852; *Shambles Taxis*, T37511170.

Directory **Banks** Around the junction of English St and College St. **Communications** Post Office: English St. **Genealogy** *Armagh Ancestry*, 40 English St, T37521802, F37510033. Mon-Fri, 1100-1600. **Hospitals** *Craigavon Area Hospital*, T38612014.

South Armagh – a tour

Colour map 1, grid C5 *Steeped in ancient culture, this is the most beautiful part of the county despite the assorted remnants of military paraphernalia that blight the green and grey hills. Even on a wet and doleful day the allure of Slieve Gullion is palpable and this tour starts in Newtownhamilton: reached to the south of Armagh city or the northwest of Dundalk on the A29, or from Newry by going due west on the A25. The tour finishes in Crossmaglen.*

Camlough From Newtownhamilton, take the A25 road east to Newry, and consider stopping in tricoloured Camlough for a drink or bar food in *Genie Mac's*, *Quinn's* or the *Village Inn*, in Main St, before passing on to Bessbrook, a purpose-built, time capsule of a mill town laid out in the 1840s by the Quaker Richardsons. This gem of a place, characterized by the generous use of local granite stone in its buildings, was known as 'the village without three Ps' because there were no pubs and thus no need for pawnshop or police station. Five soldiers were killed by a landmine near here at the height of the violence unleashed by the deaths of hunger strikers in May 1981.

Derrymore House On the Newry side of the A25, Derrymore House is a National Trust thatched 18th-century cottage where the Act of Union was drafted, and the picturesque park and woodlands that surround the cottage are always freely open. ■ *T30838361. May-Aug, Thu-Sat, 1400-1730; daily over Easter. £2.*

Killeavy churches Hop back to Camlough and turn left to take the road south passing a lake setting that can match Killarney's for sheer breathtaking beauty. Continue south to the Killeavy churches on the gentle slopes of Slieve Gullion, where St Monenna's nunnery lasted for a millennium after her death in the early sixth century. The western, 12th-century church is joined by a shared wall to a later 15th-century place of worship. St Monenna's likely burial place is marked by a large slab near the churchyard wall to the north and a holy well associated with her is a little way up the mountain to the west.

SOUTH ARMAGH **615**

Newtownhamilton

The genesis of Newtownhamilton can be traced back to an advertisement that appeared in the Belfast Newsletter *in 1747. A landlord, Alexander Hamilton, advertised some of his estate for leasing:*

"On each of the said farms there is plenty of good meadows and turf; a large river runs through the middle of said lands that never wants water sufficient to turn many mills … and a fall of 180 feet in less than two miles, and places where mill ponds may easily be made. By the great plenty of turf, water, bog, timber for building and meadows, the linen manufacture may be carried on, as cheap as in any part of Ireland."

On the other side of Killeavy village, on the B113, you will find the entrance to the Slieve Gullion Forest Park where an 8-mile (13-km) drive and a walking trail lead up to the summit. Weather permitting, there are unrivalled views of the random set of volcanic hills known as the Ring of Gullion. ■ *T30848084. Open Easter-Aug, 1000-dusk. £2.50 for a car. Visitor Centre, self catering apartments and coffee shop.*

Forest Park

A short detour to the east goes to **Jonesborough**, famous for its Sunday market which draws in a fair crowd. A couple of miles south of the village a path to the handsome **Kilnasaggart Stone** (*Cill na Sagart*, church of the priests) is signposted across fields. This eighth-century pillar is clearly and elegantly inscribed and marks an early Christian burial place. Jonesborough is also a good place to stop for a meal (see page 616).

Travel back to the B113 and continue south to tiny **Forkhill** where a perfect Guinness is served at *M C Larkin*, a lovely old-style pub on the right-hand side of the road. North of the village at Mullaghbawn (*An Mullach Ban*), the

Local entertainment

South Armagh

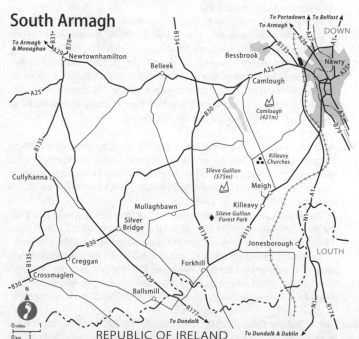

Tí Chulainn Cultural Centre has exhibitions and occasional live performances of traditional music, song and dance. Contact in advance to see what might be on. ■ *Mullach Ban.* *T30888828. tculainn@dial.pipex.com Jul and Aug, Mon-Sat, 1000-1730, Sun, 1300-1800. Rest of year, slightly shorter hours. Free.*

Crossmaglen & around

From Mullach Ban continue north to the junction with the B30 and turn left for Crossmaglen. In the 1880s over 150 young women were employed here in lace schools. Less than a century later the town's proximity to the border had made it infamous as the epicentre of militant republicanism; by the beginning of 1976 over 30 soldiers had been killed here, over half in the town square where a tourist office now stands as a refreshing sign of changing times. On the first and last Friday of every month a fair is held in the square. There's a **tourist office** at O'Fiaich House, T30868900. Mon-Fri, 0900-1700.

In the village of **Creggan**, 4 km northeast of Crossmaglen, the parish churchyard has interesting tombstones of local 18th-century Gaelic poets and other curiosities. Between Easter and September guided tours of the churchyard are available on Sunday afternoon; contact the rectory in Dundalk for details, T429371921, or pick up the useful leaflet on the churchyard from the tourist office in Crossmaglen.

Essentials

Sleeping
Price codes: see inside front cover

B *Murtaghs*, 13 North St, Crossmaglen, T30861378. A family-run bar and B&B place in the centre of town. Two double rooms, one with its own bathroom, and a single. **C** *Cnoc Mhuire*, 40, Annaghmare Rd, Crossmaglen, T30861896. Accommodation on a farm with hilltop views across to Slieve Gullion. **C** *Greenvale*, 141 Longfield Rd, Forkhill, T30888314. A farmhouse with views of Slieve Gullion. One double and one single, and horse-riding available on the farm.

Self-catering Self-catering in south Armagh would enable you really to get to know the area as well as making a useful base for visiting Dundalk and the Cooley Peninsula. *Slieve Gullion Courtyard*, Slieve Gullion Forest Park, 89 Dromintee Rd, T30848084. Apr-Sep £60- £75 per night midweek, Oct- Mar £50 - £60 per night midweek. *Benbree Self-Catering Cottage*, 67 Carrive Rd, Forkhill, T30888394. £175 a week for 3 bedrooms and good facilities. *Country Farm Cottage*, 139 Longfield Rd, Forkhill, T30888314. £110 a week and sleeps 5. *Mountain View*, 11 Cranny View, Mullach Ban, T30888410. £150 for the week, 2 bedrooms sleeping 5.

Eating

In Jonesborough the *Flurrybridge Inn*, T30848181, serves the best choice of food – European, Chinese and Indian – for miles around and opens in the evening Thu-Sun and at lunchtime on Sun, 1230-1530, for the open-air market. *Lima Country House*, 16 Drumalt Rd, Silverbridge, T30861944, serves evening meals between Mon and Sat, but telephone first.

The *Slieve Gullion Courtyard Restaurant*, 89 Dromintee Rd, Killeavey, T30848084, at the Slieve Gullion Forest Park, does meals on Sat and Sun from 1400 to 2200 with dishes from £5 to £15 and if you telephone ahead it is possible to book a meal during the week.

Crossmaglen has a few places to eat, including pub food in The Square at *Cartwheel*, Mon-Sat, in the evening. *Chums*, 46 The Square, does pub lunches as does Murtagh's (see 'Sleeping' above), while a couple of miles down the road the *Ashfield Golf Club*, Freeduff, Cullyhanna, T30868180, serves standard fare 1200-2100 (from 1400 on Mon).

Pubs & music

The *Tí Chulainn Cultural Centre*, Mullaghbawn, T30888828, has traditional music every second Sat, and on every second Tue there is a similar musical session at *The*

Welcome Inn, 35 Main St, Forkhill, T30888273. Also in Mullaghbawn, *O'Hanlon's Pub*, T30888759, is a favourite place for improvised eruptions of music whatever the day. Another place to look out traditional music is *Keenan's* in Crossmaglen.

Crossmaglen Horsefair, first Sat in **Sep**, enlivened by traditional music and dancing. On the Sunday 'The Big Race' takes place. *Singing Weekend* in Forkill and Mullach Bán on the first weekend of **Oct**. *South Armagh Community Festival* is a family event that takes place in **Jul**. *Lislea Drama Festival* in **Feb** and **Mar** sees plays and scripted folklore.   **Festivals**

Bicycle hire: *McCumiskey Cycles*, Dromintee, T30888593 **Horse-riding**: *Millbrook Equestrian Centre*, Bessbrook, T30838336. *Greenvale Trekking Centre*, Forkhill, T30888314. *Ring of Gullion Trekking Centre*, Mullaghbawn,T30889311.   **Sport**

Buses There is a bus service Mon-Sat between **Newry** and **Crossmaglen** via Camlough, T30263531. Other services run Mon-Sat between **Forkhill** and Newry and between **Bessbrook** and Newry. **Taxis** *Cross Cabs*, Crossmaglen, T30868550. *M.T. Taxis*, Crossmaglen, T30868300.   **Transport**

Banks The Square, Crossmaglen. **Communications** **Post office**: Newry St, Crossmaglen; 29 Main St, Forkhill; 2 Dromintee Rd, Killeavy.   **Directory**

North Armagh

A greater contrast with south Armagh is hard to find for in place of attractive countryside and progressive culture there is an unsightly industrial landscape and the backward sectarianism of Portadown.   *Colour map 1, grid B5*

The town of Portadown, where loyalist mobs rioted against the Anglo-Irish Agreement in 1985, is probably the least attractive place to visit in the whole of Ireland. At the time of writing, the Drumcree issue is still unresolved but if a settlement is found it may well involve a substantial injection of cash and resources into the beleagured Garvaghy Road area.   **Portadown**

To visit **Garvaghy Road** leave your vehicle in the Dunnes store car park or, closer still, the Wilson Street car park opposite the *Laser* electronics store. Garvaghy Road begins where the *Haldane Fisher & Ulster Carpet Mills Factory* sign can be seen and the Union Jacks soon give way to the tricolours of the Catholic enclave. To reach **Drumcree Church**, walk up the road for 1 mile and take the second turning on the right after the Mayfair Centre. Continue along this road for about a mile and it is on the left by the Y-junction.

There are also two National Trust houses in the area. The 17th-century **Ardress House** has a renowned neoclassical interior and a working farmyard outside. The tour takes you around beautifully furnished rooms filled with Adam fireplaces and family portraits. Outside is a fine park and children's playground. ■ *Ardress House: on B26, 7 miles (11.2 km) west of Portadown, T38851236. Easter and Jun-Aug, Wed-Mon, 1400-1800; Apr-May and Sep, Sat and Sun only, same hours. Guided tour. £2.70, farmyard only £2.40.*

Close by on Derrycaw Rd in Moy, is **The Argory** with what was a state-of-the-art gas lighting system in the early 19th century still illuminating some of the original furniture. All the paraphernalia of the 19th century nob is still there – carriages, the laundry, musical instruments and there are long walks in the 130 ha of gardens. ■ *The Argory: T38784753. Same hours as Ardress House. Tour £3. Car park £1.50.*

Drumcree and Garvaghy Road

The issue of whether the Orange Order has the right to march from Drumcree Church down Catholic Garvaghy Road on its route back to Portadown each July has become a major issue in the evolving politics of Ulster. David Trimble's rise to the leadership of the Unionist Party received vital support from diehard loyalists after he joined the march and championed their cause. In 1998, after the Parades Commission banned the march, the ensuing violence resulted in the death of three children in a Catholic house firebombed by loyalist extremists. The Orange Order is adamant about its right to march down the road, and the residents of Garvaghy Road are equally adamant that the days of triumphalist and provocative marches through Catholic areas are over. Since 1999 the stand-off has been relatively peaceful, but loyalists insist that they will maintain a presence outside Drumcree Church until their 'constitutional rights' are respected.

Loughall This is a pretty little village which nestles quietly in its surroundings and has a huge country park with lots of good walks and a lake where there is coarse fishing. Car park costs £2. It is also famous for being the place where the Orange Order was founded in 1795 after the battle of the Diamond between Catholic and Protestant militias.

The inn where the order was inaugurated is now the **Dan Winter Ancestral Home** and contains memorabilia from the Battle of the Diamond. ■ 9 *The Diamond, Derryloughan Rd, Loughall, T38851344. Mon-Sat, 1030-2030, Sun, 1400-2030. Voluntary donation. Call at the house next door for the key.*

In 1986 the Provisionals mounted an attack on the RUC station at Loughall but a tip-off led to an ambush by SAS soldiers, who fired 1,200 rounds killing eight of the Provisionals as well as an innocent civilian driving past in his car.

Loughall has some quality **antique shops** along its main street, including *Heritage Antiques*, T38891314, and *Meredith Antiques*, T38528739, and a noted restaurant, *The Famous Grouse*, T38891778, a couple of miles out on Ballyhagan Road.

Counties Tyrone & Fermanagh

17

Counties Tyrone & Fermanagh

Atlantic Ocean

Letterkenny

Derry

Lifford Strabane

To Coleraine

To Belfast

TYRONE

Donegal

Omagh

Cookstown

Lough Neagh

Ballyshannon

Dungannon

Lower Lough Erne

FERMANAGH

To Belfast

Manorhamilton

Enniskillen

Armagh

To Sligo

Upper Lough Erne

Monaghan

To Dublin

REPUBLIC OF IRELAND

To Cavan

*While the small county of Fermanagh has a modest and developing tourist infrastructure based around Lough Erne and the town of Enniskillen, Tyrone, which shares with Fermanagh a central role in defining Ulster both geographically and historically, tends not to feature highly in most travellers' itineraries. County Tyrone generally lacks the Bord Fáilte factor – the readily identifiable pre-packaged image – but of course this is precisely what makes it so appealing. For anyone contemplating a few days in an unhyped part of Ireland, taking in **country walks** in the **Sperrin Mountains** and **quiet villages** where nothing much happens and where the local population is thin on the ground, County Tyrone definitely fits the bill.*

*Fermanagh is defined by its central lake, **Lough Erne**, which is 50 miles (80 km) long. The lake is now joined to the River Shannon by the **Shannon to Erne Waterway**, making it the longest navigable inland waterway in Europe. The lakeland setting invites **water-based activities** and this undoubtedly is Fermanagh's main attraction, but in **Boa Island** and **Killadeas Churchyard**, the county also has cultural sites that rank among the most significant and intriguing to be found anywhere in Ireland.*

Private transport, car or bicycle, makes a big difference round here, and planning ahead for meals and accommodation is fairly vital outside of Enniskillen, Omagh and Cookstown but when that is done, the region is all yours.

County Tyrone

County Tyrone

History

History lies at the heart of Tyrone, for the Elizabethan conquest of this county, the most intractable part of an intractable province, sealed the fate of Gaelic Ireland. Surrounded by wood, bog and the Sperrin Mountains to the south, the O'Neills held out in their Tyrone homelands against the English in the second half of the 16th century. In 1562 Shane O'Neill came to London to parley with Elizabeth's government and the clash of cultures was evident to all: the doublets and hose and fancy ruffs of the English confronted the Gaelic entourage with their shoulder-length hair, cloaks and shirts of linen dyed yellow with urine. Shane only managed to buy some time and it was left to his nephew, Hugh O'Neill, to witness the final subjugation of Gaelic Ireland and the door left open for the plantations of the early 17th century.

In 1641 a rebellion started in Tyrone and spread across the country, and the same year the massacres of settlers by hungry and dispossessed Catholics – an event that still haunts the loyalist subconscious – was Cromwell's justification for his own massacres, "the righteous judgement of God", which reasserted foreign rule over Ireland. The killing and counter-killing continued intermittently over the following centuries, the most recent outrage being the horrific bombing that killed 29 people out shopping on a sunny Saturday afternoon in Omagh in August 1998.

Omagh

Colour map 1, grid B3   Church and State are represented in Omagh by the two overbearing monuments to the claims on people's lives in this part of the world: the Catholic church and the courthouse – an example of monstrous Victorian architecture, built in 1863 some 30 years before the church. They loom over the top half of the town, calling everyone to obedience to the Crown or God. The dissident republican group responsible (allegedly the Real IRA, although no one has actually been prosecuted) for the 1998 slaughter was probably intending to destroy the courthouse at the western end of the town's main street. The bomb went off, probably because they panicked and left it in the wrong place, at the east end of the street. A memorial garden for those who tragically lost their lives now marks the place where they died.

The **tourist office** is at 1 Market St, T82247831. It's open Jul-Aug, Mon-Fri, 0900-1730; Sep-Jun, Mon-Fri, 0900-1700; Easter-Sep additional Sat, 0900-1300, 1330-1730.

The Ulster American Folk Park   Emigration from Ireland has become so entwined with the Famine and with post-Famine history that it often comes as a surprise to learn that an exodus of impoverished Protestants began in the early 18th century from Ulster which alarmed the government, for "the humour has spread like a contagious distemper, and the people will hardly hear any body that tries to cure them of their madness". By the 1770s, some 10,000 were leaving annually and Benjamin Franklin estimated that one-third of Pennsylvania's population were Ulster Scots-Irish emigrants. The Ulster American Folk Park, which can claim that half of all US presidents to date are of Ulster descent, celebrates and records emigration to North America with a wealth of reconstructed buildings and

★

Things to do in Counties Tyrone and Fermanagh

- Visit the **Ulster American Folk Park** near Omagh
- Take a long walk in the **Sperrin mountains**
- Visit **Boa Island**, **Devenish Island** and **Killedeas Churchyard** north of Enniskillen
- Save the museums in and around **Castlederg** for a wet day
- Take a boat ride in **Lough Erne**

entire streets that make up one of Ireland's most successful museums. ■ *On A5, 3 miles north of Omagh, T82243292, www.folkpark.com Easter-Sep, Mon-Sat, 1100-1830, Sun, 1130-1900; Oct-Easter, Mon-Fri, 1030-1700. Last admission 90 mins before closing. £4. Café and shop.*

AL *Silverbirch*, 5 Gortin Rod, T82242520, www.silverbirchhotel.com Omagh's only hotel: one of those large modern places where the corridors are interchangeable and there are always big wedding parties at weekends. The rooms are comfortable and there is a popular restaurant. **A** *Hawthorn House*, 72 Old Mountfield Rd, T82252005. A way out of town off the Gortin Rd, but a comfortable guest house with an excellent restaurant. **B** *Ardmore*, 12 Tamlaght Rd, T82243381. Closest to town of the B&Bs, which are all around the outskirts. **C** *Bankhead*, 9 Lissan Rd, T82245592. Very reasonably priced, with 3 rooms, open all year. **D** *Omagh Independent Hostel*, Glenhordial, 9a Waterworks Rd, T82241973. Has rooms ranging in size from singles to dormitory and lots of room to relax. Free pickup from bus station.

Sleeping
Price codes: see inside front cover

Not being overly dependent on tourism, restaurants in Omagh tend to cater to shoppers or people out for a treat. The restaurant in the *Silverbirch* has an extensive menu, with dinner costing £15 or less, and lunchtime specials. *Hawthorn House* is the classiest place to eat – fresh local food, traditional Irish dishes, mixed with a welcome Californian touch – and usually needs booking in advance. Good lunches all week but Sun is particularly fine. Dinner £20 plus. In town, opposite the Catholic church at 29 George's St, T82250900 is *Grants*, a bistro-cum-pub open for lunch and dinner till 2200. It has lively dishes, which include chilli prawns, as well as more conventional food. Along the High St/Market St are lots of lunchtime places like *Bogan's Bar*, at 26 Market St, T82242183, and the *Shopper's Restaurant*, 38 High St, T82243545, which does things with chips and filled potatoes. The comfortable *Coach Inn*, Railway Terr, T82243330, is on the right just after the railway bridge on the road out to Enniskillen from the town centre. Bar food, including an excellent vegetarian salad, is served until 1800 when a separate dining area opens up with a menu of standard main courses between £8 and £12 and a small wine list.

Eating

The trendiest place is town is *Sally O'Brien's*, just behind the Town Hall on John St, with its wonderful window display. Open till past midnight, on the nights it has live music, you can catch Country and Western, blues and the occasional traditional session here. *The Inn at the Bridge*, which displays it allegiances in its Manchester United colours, has live music at weekends, mostly Irish Country and Western. On Castle St is *McElroy's* with lots of big copy bands. The *Silverbirch* has occasional live music but your best bet for traditional music is *Bogan's* on Market St. Check out also the *Dún Uladh Cultural Heritage Centre*, on the Carrickmore Rd, T82242777, which often has concerts, ballroom and Irish dancing sessions and traditional music.

Pubs & music

Bicycle *Conway Cycles*, 1 Old Market Pl, T82246195. **Car** *Tattyreagh Car Hire*, 110a Tattyreagh Rd, T82841731. **Taxi** *Glen Taxis*, T82246058. *P&I Taxis*, T82757200.

Transport

The Sperrins

Colour map 1, *The Sperrin Mountains, rolling areas of blanket bog with summits over 1,640 ft*
grid B3 & B4 *(500 m), stretch across north Tyrone from the border with Derry for some 35 miles*
(56 km) and encapsulate the appeal of this county: fresh air, uncluttered space,
country and hill walks from the casual to the demanding, archaeological sites and a
cultural history that is only now emerging from a long period of censorship. Omagh
is the nearest town of any size and with a fair choice of accommodation; though
Gortin is more convenient for the area, accommodation and places to eat are scarce.

The Sperrin This Heritage Centre provides introductory information on the ecology and
Heritage culture of the Sperrins, including the history of gold mining in the area and the
Centre chance to pan for some in a stream nearby. There is also a decent café.
■ *Glenelly Rd, Cranagh, Gortin, on B47, 9 miles (14.4 km) east of Plumbridge,*
T81648142. Open Easter-Oct, Mon-Sat, 1100-1800 (1130 on Sat), Sun,
1400-1900. £2, and 65p for pan hire.

The Ulster Recreating the history of human settlement in Ireland from the Stone Age to
History Park the plantations of the 17th century, this is quite a sophisticated display. The
guided tours are highly informative, and there is a restaurant and picnic area.
■ *Cullion, on B48, 7 miles (11.2 km) north of Omagh, T81648188. Open*
Apr-Sep, Mon-Sat 1030-1830, Sun 1130-1900; Oct-Mar, Mon-Fri 1030-1700.
Last admission 90 mins before closing. £3.25.

An Creagán This is another information centre, but with more activities, in the foothills of
Visitor Centre the Sperrins. The Centre is spearheading an attempt to resuscitate the culture of
the area, and details of local festivals dedicated to this purpose are available here.
There is a restaurant, a bar with live music at weekends, sessions of storytelling
and song throughout the year, self-catering cottages (see 'Sleeping' below), and
an 'interpretative exhibition' with an overview of the cultural, archaeological
and environmental landscape of the area. Bicycles can also be hired and there
are walking possibilities from the centre. ■ *Creggan, on the A505 half-way*
between Omagh and Cookstown, T80761112, www.an-creagan.com Apr-Sep,
daily 1100-1830; Oct-Mar, daily, 1100-1630. £2.

Walking in the Little is gleaned by just travelling through the Sperrins, but there are some
Sperrins waymarked trails and walking routes and one of the easiest to organize is a
 6-mile (10-km) section of the **Ulster Way** between Gortin and Glengawna.
Both places are on the B48 road along which Bus No 92 (Mon-Sat) travels
between Omagh and Gortin, so, with the help of a bus timetable, it is possible
to catch a bus to the start and/or from the end of the walk. The Way is marked
on *Ordnance Survey* map 13, although there is a small change from the map
just south of Gortin where it crosses the B48. Along the Way the route passes
the Ulster History Park (see above) and the **Gortin Glen Forest Park**, which
has its own waymarked trails and from here one could also walk 10 miles (16
km) of the Ulster Way as far as the Ulster American Folk Park (see above),
from where Bus No 97 travels to Omagh. Gortin Glen Forest Park also has a
vehicular drive through the forest and there is a café. ■ *On B48, 7 miles (11.2*
km) north of Omagh, T81648217. Daily 1000-dusk. £3 for car.

Short walks of between 6 and 10 miles (9.6-16 km) are also possible from
the An Creagán Visitor Centre, which provides walk sheets, and most of these
take in archaeological sites along the way.

The two highest points in the Sperrins, **Sawel Mountain** and **Dart Mountain**, can be climbed in one day and a good starting point is just to the east of Sperrin village on the B47 in the Glenelly valley. However, there have been problems with some landowners in the area and walking west of Dart Mountain is definitely not on. *Ordnance Survey* map No 13 is essential for this walk, and it might be worthwhile calling in at the Sperrin Heritage Centre (see above) to check your proposed route with them.

Essentials

B *Lenamore Lodge*, 19 Crickanboy Rd, Gortin, T/F8248460. Has 2 rooms, 1 with its own bathroom, for £30. **D** *Gortin Outdoor Centre*, Glenpark Rd, T82648083. A hostel with nearly 20 beds for £6 each, but only open Jul-Sep. **D** *Gortin Accommodation Suite and Activity Centre*, 62, main St, Gortin, T81648346, www.gortin.net is a complex of accommodation and activity centre which will suit most needs. It has a 40 bed hostel with family rooms for £7 per person sharing, as well as self catering houses which sleep 4.

Self-catering *An Clachan* self-catering cottages at Creggan are managed by the An Creagán Visitor Centre, T80761112, F80761116. Sleep from 2-6 people and cost from £60 for a 1-bedroom cottage over a weekend in the low season to £330 for a week in a 3-bedroomed cottage at high season. *Craignamaddy Barn*, 45 Gorticashel Rd, Gortin, T/F82647949, sutherland@btinternet.com Similar prices for a 2-bedroomed refurbished barn. *Gortin Glen Caravan and Camping Park*, Lisnaharney Rd, Lislap, T/F81648108. Plenty of tent pitches for £6 a night and is situated opposite the Gortin Glen Forest Park.

Sleeping *(margin label)*

The *An Creagán Restaurant*, at Creggan on the A505, T80761112, at the Visitor Centre is open daily for cheap lunches, and evening meals from £7, Thu-Sun. In Gortin the *Badoney Tavern*, 16 Main St, T81648157, serves pub meals in the evening from 1800 to 2100. The *Sperrin Heritage Centre*, east of Plumbridge on the B47, T81648142, serves very light meals until 1800 Mon-Sat and from 1400 to 1900 on a Sun. In Plumbridge *Pinkertons Café*, 25 Main St, T81648327, is open daily for steaks, curry and chicken meals.

Eating *(margin label)*

Sperrins Cycling Festival at the end of **May**. Contact 1 Lisnaharney Rd, Lislap, Omagh, BT79 7UE. T81647998/81247831. *Slieve Gullion Walking Festival* early **Jun**. Contact local tourist offices for details. *Sperrin Walking Weekend* mid-**Jun**. T71382204/883735. *Cookstown Walking Festival* late **Jun**. T96762205. *Three Peaks Challenge* mid-**Jul**. T91647998. *Sperrins Hillwalking Festival* early **Aug**, T79634570.

Festivals *Many festivals combine walking with evening entertainment & music* *(margin label)*

Sperrin Hillwalking, 2 Churchwell Lane, Magherafelt, County Tyrone, BT45 6AL, T79300050, F79300009, activities@sperrins.iol.ie Organizes walking packages: charges £130 for 2 days' walking plus accommodation, food and guide, £300 for a week.

Tour companies & travel agents *(margin label)*

Bicycle *An Creagán Visitor Centre*, T80761112. Bicycle hire, also cycling route information for 10- to 14-mile trips. *Gortin Glen Caravan and Camping Park*, Lisnaharney Rd, Lislap, T81648108. Bicycle hire.

Transport *(margin label)*

Castlederg and around

This is one of the least visited parts of Ireland and the Castlederg Visitor Centre is worth calling in at to learn something about the area and receive instructions on how to reach local archaeological sites. Such were the

Colour map 1, grid B3 *(margin label)*

County Tyrone *(vertical margin text)*

sectarian divisions of Castlederg, that the town used to have separate Protestant and Catholic Christmas trees erected annually, and one can wonder what the frontiersman Davy Crockett, whose family came from here, would have made of that. ■ *Visitor Centre: 26 Lower Strabane Rd, T81670795. Open Apr-Oct, Tue-Fri, 1100-1600, Sat, 1130-1600, Sun, 1400-1700. £1.20.*

Newtown-stewart There is a more idiosyncratic museum here in the **Gateway Centre and Museum** on the outskirts of town, an eccentric but diverting collection of the vernacular sort that major repositories of cultural relics never think are worth bothering about. It was all collected by one person: there is a lot relating to the two world wars but my favourite is the yoke specially designed for lifting hedgehogs. ■ *21 Moyle Rd, T81662414. Open Apr-Oct, Tue-Fri, 1100-1600, Sat, 1130-1600, Sun, 1400-1700. £1.20.*

If travelling the road between Newtownstewart and Strabane, **Sion Mills** is worth a look if only to peer in at the still-functioning linen factory that gave rise to this purpose-built mill village created by the Herdmans in 1835. It was praised by the myopic Halls in their 1843 tour of the country for giving work to 700 workers, mostly women, conveniently forgetting the 15-hour days and the horrific accidents that led Dickens to call the linen employers' union the Association for the Mangling of Operatives.

Strabane A beleaguered Catholic enclave that has seen its share of rioting during the last 30 years, Strabane has the rather sad distinction of being noted for the people that left the place. The novelist, Flann O'Brien, deserted at the age of 12 in 1923, and two centuries earlier John Dunlap, having learnt his trade as a printer, went off to America and printed the American Declaration of Independence. This, and other stories, can be found at the fairly uninspiring **Gray's Printer's Museum**. ■ *49 Main St, Strabane, T71884094. Open Tue-Sat, 1100-1700. Guided tours of the printing press Apr-Sep, 1400-1700. £1.80.*

Less significant was the emigration of one James Wilson in 1807, even though his grandfather managed to end up in the White House. Hence the **Wilson Ancestral Home**. ■ *Dergalt, 2 miles (3.2 km) from Strabane off the Plumbridge Rd, T71883735 for hours of opening. £1.*

Sleeping *Price codes: see inside front cover* **B** *Bide-A-Wee*, 181 Melmount Rd, Sion Mills, T81659571. Has an outdoor pool and tennis courts and a weekend package with meals is around £90 per person. **B** *Derg Arms*, 43 Main St, Castlederg, T81671644, F81670202. A pub in the centre of town. **C** *Ardmourne House*, 36 Congary Rd, Castlederg, T81670291. A modern house with kitchen facilities for guests, and pony trekking available.

Eating There are a few pubs in Castlederg serving pub grub, including *Castle Inn*, 48 Main St, T81671501, *Market Bar*, 59 Main St, T81671247, and the *Crescent Inn*, 1 Ferguson Cres, T81671161, which also has live music in the evening. In Newtownstewart, pubs with food include the *County Inn*, 43 Main St, T81662105, and the *Harry Avery Lounge*, 19 Dublin Rd, T81661431. If just passing through, the town is bypassed by the main road and inexpensive meals are available at *Aunt Jane's*, 21 Moyle Rd, right next to the Gateway Centre and Museum. In Strabane food is available every lunchtime except Sun at *Flann O'Brien*, 3 Derry Rd, T71884427, and the *Fir Trees Hotel*, Dublin Rd, T71382382, which serves meals such as duck in sweet and sour sauce, and grills.

Transport **Car hire** *McGillion*, 132 Melmount Rd, Sion Mills, T81658275.

Cookstown and around

The east of Tyrone is home to a scattered set of archaeological sites with Cookstown being the main town in the area.

Cookstown

Cookstown has had a troubled past ever since a Scottish landlord established a small town and market here in the 1620s. In the 1641 uprising the town was taken by the native Irish and burnt to the ground after its recapture by the army, and it lay derelict for a century until 1736. In that year the grandson of the original settler, inspired by the streets of Dublin and Edinburgh, laid out a new town with a main street stretching for well over a mile. During the Troubles in the 1970s, '80s and early '90s, a major army camp was established in the centre and driving into the town involved having a rifle pointed at your head until clearance was given.

There's a **tourist office** at the Burnavon, Burn Rd, T86769949, info@cookstown.gov.uk Open Sep-May Mon- Fri 0900-1700, Jun Mon-Sat 0900-1700, Jul and Aug, Mon-Sat 0900-1700, Sun 1400-1600.

Colour map 1, grid B4
For places to stay, see page 629

Beetling was a stage of linen production, consisting of pounding the fabric with wooden hammers, the 'beetles', until the weave was tightened and a smooth sheen gave the cloth its characteristic texture. Beetling started at this mill in the 1760s, and Wellbrook was the last mill still in operation when it finally closed down two centuries later. Working demonstrations are given in this National Trust property and exhibits explain the process. ■ *T86751735. Open Jul and Aug, Wed-Mon 1400-1800. Apr, May-Jun and Sep, Sat and Sun, 1400-1800. £2. 4 miles west of Cookstown off A505.*

Wellbrook Beetling Mill

Beaghmore Stone Circle is the most interesting of the ancient sites in the area and a more worthwhile journey than the flat and boring B73 road that leads to the largely illegible **Ardboe High Cross** on the shore of Lough Neagh. At Beaghmore, on the southern foothills of the Sperrins, archaeologists in 1945 discovered under the peat a strange series of stone circles and stone alignments as well as cairns. The run-of-the-mill stone circle is relatively easy to explain but the complex arrangement of stones at Beaghmore has so far eluded interpretation, especially the presence of many hundreds of small stones inside one of the seven circles. ■ *Free access. Between Cookstown and Gortin, signposted off A505.*

Beaghmore Stone Circle & Tullaghoge Fort

The enjoyment of a visit to Tullaghoge Fort will be in proportion to the degree of historical imagination brought to bear on the place, because all that remains today is a hillock, albeit with fine views. Between the 11th and 16th centuries the chieftain of the O'Neills was inaugurated here as ruler of Tyrone, an area which then extended beyond the present county confines, until Mountjoy arrived here in the wake of Kinsale and symbolically destroyed the ancient coronation stone seat. More to the point, he also burnt the corn in the fields, which led to cannibalism in the ensuing famine that brought O'Neill to his knees. ■ *Off B162 2½ miles (4 km) southeast of Cookstown.*

Dungannon and the Clogher Valley

Dungannon is a dreadfully dreary town, which sparked into life in 1968 when it became a focus of demonstration for the early civil rights movement in

Dungannon
Colour map 1, grid B4

County Tyrone

Northern Ireland. It was well known that Dungannon, like Derry, was gerry-mandered to produce a permanent Unionist council even though the population was split evenly between Catholics and Protestants, and the first civil rights march in August 1968 planned to end in Dungannon but was stopped by the RUC on the outskirts with dogs and 400 men. The only reason to pause here today is for a visit to the cross-community-inspired **Tyrone Crystal**, where guided tours of the factory workshop make it hard to resist purchasing something afterwards from the shop. ■ *T87725335. Open Mon-Fri 0930-1530, and also Sat between Apr and Oct. £2.*

Killymaddy Tourist Information, is on Ballygawley Rd, 7 miles (10 km) southwest of Dungannon, on the A4. T87767259. Open all year.

Benburb
Colour map 1, grid B4

To the south of Dungannon, the graceful village of Benburb, with a population under 300, has a quiet charm of its own, and a scenic riverside walk along the Blackwater in **Benburb Valley Park** has a rich and surprising bonus when the ruins of **Benburb Castle** are seen towering over the river. Shane O'Neill fortified the cliff-top location in the 16th century but it was a planter, Sir Richard Wingfield, who built the castle at the beginning of the following century and it was another 100 years before a house was actually built inside its walls. In 1646 an overwhelming victory by the Irish under Owen Roe O'Neill took place near here by the River Blackwater and resulted in the death of over 3,000 Scottish soldiers, an event which did a great deal to convince Cromwell of the need to thoroughly subdue the Irish once and for all. The Ulster historian Jonathan Barden (see page 679) has described this Battle of Benburb as "the greatest and most annihilating victory in arms the Irish ever won over the British." A model layout of the battle can be seen, just south of the village, in the **Benburb Valley Heritage Centre**. The centre is set in a 19th-century weaving factory and if you have missed the other places in Tyrone devoted to the history of the Ulster linen industry then this is a place to catch up on the subject, and enjoy a cup of tea in the tea room. ■ *Valley Park: 10 Main St, T37548170, 1000-dusk. Heritage Centre: Mill-town Rd. T37548170. Easter-Sep, 0900-1800. £2.*

Clogher Valley

The Blackwater River forms the Clogher Valley to the west of Benburb and the A4 travels west to Enniskillen. Along the way the **Grant Ancestral House** is yet another reminder of Ulster's connection with the US, this time through John Simpson, who was born here in 1738 and whose great-grandson distinguished himself in the American Civil War and became the 18th President, Ulysses Simpson Grant. The two rooms of Grant's small cottage have been restored in the style of the 19th century and there is also an outdoor display of Victorian farm equipment. ■ *Off A4, 13 miles (21 km) west of Dungannon, T85557133. Open Apr-Sep, Mon-Sat, 1200-1800, Sun 1400-1800. £1.50.*

The Carleton Trail

The novelist William Carleton (1794-1869) was born into a family of Irish-speaking peasants near Clogher, and his connection gives its name to this series of three walking and cycling routes, from 6-30 miles (10-48 km), that all start and finish in Clogher and follow minor roads and forest paths. Details and a map are available from the tourist office in Dungannon and the cottage where Carleton lived for a while before leaving for Dublin can be seen in **Clogher**, a village on the A4 half-way between Dungannon and Enniskillen. Food and accommodation is available here or a little further west at **Fivemiletown** (5 miles from Clogher) on the border with Fermanagh.

Essentials

Sleeping
Price codes:
see inside frotn cover

AL *Glenavon House Hotel*, 52 Drum Rd, Cookstown, T86764949, www.glenavonhotel.co.uk Has a pool and gym, and a double room is £80. **A** *Four Ways Hotel*, Main St, Fivemiletown, T89521260. This friendly place has 10 rooms, and weekend and 3-day packages. **AL** *Tullylagan Country House*, Tullylagan Rd, Cookstown, T86765100, F68761715. Quite good value and a decent restaurant. Check the special offers for B&B and dinner. **B** *Killycolp House*, 21 Killycolp Rd, Cookstown, T86763577. Does B&B for £20 per person in a Georgian house with original features that help make this friendly place a terrific night's lodging. **C** *River Furey House*, 24 Monaghan Rd, Clogher, T82548843. B&B at around £32 for a double room. Can also provide an inexpensive dinner. **C** *Sperrin View*, 37 Ballynagilly Rd, Cookstown, T86763990. Inexpensive, but the 2 rooms share bathroom facilities. **C** *Timpany Manor*, 53 Ballagh Rd, Clogher, T/F85521285. B&B charges around £32 for a double room.

Camping *Dungannon Park*, Moy Rd, T87727327. A caravan and camping park off the A29 less than 2 km from Dungannon, with 12 tent pitches at £6 each. *Killymaddy Tourist Amenity Centre*, 190 Ballygawley Rd, west of Dungannon on the A4, T87767259. Has a dozen tent pitches for £6 each. *Clogher Valley County Caravan Park*, Fardross Forest, T85548932. Signposted a mile or so west of Clogher on the A4 and accepts tents.

Eating

Benburb The *Cornmill Tea Room*, 89 Milltown Rd, T37549752, is in the Benburb Valley Heritage Centre and opens from 1000 to 1700, Tue-Sun, in the summer and Mon-Fri between Oct and Easter.

Clogher Pub food is available in *McSorley's Tavern*, 39 Main St, T85548673, and *Trident Inn*, 97 Main St, T85548924, while *Corrick House*, 20 Corrick Rd, T85548216, opens in the evening from 1730, Tue-Sun, for dinner under £20.

Cookstown *Otter Lodge*, 26 Dungannon Rd, T86765427, has a riverbank setting and, while the restaurant only opens Fri and Sat nights and Sun for lunch, the wine bar opens daily for lighter meals from 1200 to around 2200. The *Tullylagan Country House Restaurant* is a few miles south of town and serves an evening meal in a pleasant dining room for under £20 every night and lunch every day except Sat. Good value and tasty set lunches can be enjoyed in town at the *Courtyard*, 56 William St, T86765070, which closes at 1730 Mon-Sat and a couple of hours earlier on Wed. The *Royal Hotel*, serves food nightly till 2130.

Fivemiletown Pub food and meals available at the *Four Ways Hotel*.

Entertainment

Purpose-built arts centre hosts local and international productions, has a bar and restaurant. Check with the tourist office for what's on. The *Cookstown Leisure Centre*, T86763853, has a cafeteria, a swimming pool complex with slides and rides, sauna, 10 pin bowling, and multipurpose sports hall.

Transport

Bicycle *Clogher Valley County Caravan Park*, Fardross Forest, T85548932. Bike hire. **Buses** Bus station: Molesworth St, Cookstown, T86766440. Handles *Ulsterbus* services to **Belfast** and Dungannon. Scotch St, Dungannon, T87722251. Buses connect Dungannon with Cookstown every 30 mins or so during the day and there are also services between Dungannon and **Armagh**, **Monaghan** and **Dublin**.

Directory

Banks In James St and William St in Cookstown. **Communications** Post office: 49 James St, Cookstown. 20 Market Sq, Dungannon.

County Tyrone

County Fermanagh

History

Fermanagh's natural isolation is part and parcel of the county's stubborn resistance to early Norman intrusions in the 13th century, so imagine how prolonged and complex must have been the process of transition from the pagan world of the Celts to Christianity. This may help explain the exceptional nature of the ancient stone monuments found north of Enniskillen.

The Maguires came to rule Fermanagh from the early 14th century and before their land passed after two centuries to the O'Donnells, one of their bards praised the family to high heaven:

> Towards Ulster he [Brian Maguire] is the ocean's surface; towards Connacht a rampart of stone.
> Fermanagh of the fortunate ramparts is the Adam's paradise of Inisfáil.

After the defeat of Gaelic Ireland at Kinsale and the Flight of the Earls, Fermanagh eventually went the way of the rest of the island: planters took over Adam's paradise and built the castles still standing around Lough Erne. Enniskillen became a major military fortress and in the early 1920s the town and county were embroiled in conflict over Partition. The nationalist voice in this part of Ireland reached a climax in 1981 when the democratically elected Member of Parliament for Fermanagh and South Tyrone died in prison on a hunger strike.

Enniskillen

Colour map 1, grid B2 & 3

Another predominantly Catholic border town, Enniskillen doesn't have the old-world charm of Derry, but it's a lively enough place, with lots of development going on and a blossoming nightlife. The main reason to spend any time here, though, is as a base for exploring the area or taking off on a boat trip around Lough Erne. There's a **tourist office** on Wellington Rd, T66323110. Open Jul-Aug, Mon-Fri 0900-1900, Sat 1000-1800, Sun 1100-1800, Sep- Jun, Mon-Fri 0900-1730.

Enniskillen Castle

This is the chief tourist attraction of the town: a beautiful old building not used particularly effectively but worth a wander around. The castle has certainly seen some bloodshed over the years; the 16th century was probably its worst time: it changed hands from its original builders, the Maguires, to the O'Neill's (*not* by a negotiated sale), then later the same century the English took it off the O'Neills – poetic justice you might say. The only original 15th-century part of the building is the lower storey of the keep – now the regimental museum full of polished brass and pride. On the river side of the complex is the Watergate, a 17th-century addition with no gate in it. The heritage centre is housed in buildings from around the 18th century and holds assorted rural paraphernalia, two pretty naff videos about the area and changing exhibitions. ■ *Castle Barracks, T66325000. Open Mon, 1400-1700, Tue-Fri, 1000-1700, Sat and Sun, 1400-1700; Oct-Apr closed Sat and Sun; May and Jun closed Sun. £2.*

Buttermarket

The other place for a good wander around, this is now a craft village full of nice things to buy, especially the hand-painted furniture and copies of the White

The Hunger Strike

The origins of the hunger strike in Ireland are not clear and, while the suffragettes certainly offered an example to follow, the tactic has also been traced back to an early Irish tradition of fasting before an enemy in order to shame him for his misdeeds. Thomas Ashe was the first hunger striker to die, in 1917, protesting at conditions in Dublin's Mountjoy gaol and in 1920 Terence MacSwiney, the mayor of Cork, and two others died in London prisons. In Northern Ireland the tactic developed out of the *withdrawal of 'special category' status in 1976 which denied political status to republican prisoners. A 'dirty protest' campaign began, with prisoners refusing to clean out their cells, and in May 1981, a hunger strike began. The first hunger striker was Bobby Sands, the Member of Parliament for Tyrone and Fermanagh, but that cut little ice with Thatcher's government and he died in due course followed by 10 more men before the strike was called off in October 1981.*

Island stone figures, although you'd need a big rucksack to carry one of those away. ■ *Open Mon-Sat, 0930-1730. Coffee shop, craft workshops, gallery, craft shop, yoga studio.*

L *Manor House Country Hotel*, Killadeas, T68622200, www.manor-house-hotel.com A lovely old manor house 7 miles outside of town with fourposter beds, chandeliers and 19th-century charm combined with modern luxuries including pool, sauna etc. **L-AL** *Killyhevlin Hotel*, Dublin Rd, T66323481, F66324726. This is definitely the best place to stay in Enniskillen. Beside Lough Erne with truly stunning views (ask for a room at the back but be aware there's a £10 supplement for the view), lovely gardens to walk in and spacious rooms it's a little holiday all on its own. You can tie your boat up at the jetty or rent one of the self-catering bungalows for a week for £395 (less in the off-peak season). **AL** *Fort Lodge Hotel*, 72 Forthill St, T66323275, hotel@fortlodge.freeserve.co.uk A little way out of town, this hotel is beside Forthill park and done out in a kind of Baronial

Sleeping
■ *on map*
Price codes:
see inside
front cover

Enniskillen

To Airport, Castle Archdale & Kesh (B82)
To Irvinestown, Omagh & Londonderry (A32)

River Erne

Kestrel Waterbus

Brook Park

The Brook

Erne Hospital

Cherry Island

St Macartin's Cathedral

To Portora Royal School, Belleek, Ballyshannon & Donegal (A46)

Queen St
Library
Head St
Ann St
Darling St
Methodist
St Michael's RC
Buttermarket
Market
High St
Paget St
Down St
Queen Elizabeth Rd
Town Hall
War Memorial
E Bridge
FORTHILL
Coles Monument
Forthill St
Hollyhill Link Rd
Dunnes Stores
Belmore St

To Florence Court, Marble Arch Caves & Sligo (A4)

Fermanagh Lakeland Forum

Castle Island

Wellington Rd

Erneside Shopping Centre

River Erne

To Killyhevlin Hotel, Castle Coole (NT), Ardhowen Theatre, Armagh, Belfast & Dublin (A4)

Dublin Rd

To Tempo (B80)

Tempo Rd

To Golf Club

N

0 yards 200
0 metres 200

■ **Sleeping**
1 Belmore Court Motel
2 Fortlodge
3 Lakeland Canoe Centre
4 Railway

● **Eating & drinking**
1 Blake's of the Hollow
2 Bush
3 Crow's Nest
4 Franco's Pizzeria
5 Kamal Mahal

6 Mulligan's
7 Oscar's
8 Pat's Bar
9 Rebecca's
10 Saddler's
11 Scoff's

Hall style. It's a traditional pub with lunchtime carvery, comfortable bar and lots of travelling salesmen. Entertainment and special offers at weekends. **A** *Belmore Court Motel*, Tempo Rd, T66326633, F66326326. Self-catering rooms, prices based on room size, not the number of people staying, so this could work out at the very lowest end of this price bracket. Pleasant, modern rooms. Price goes down further if you stay 2 nights. **A** *Railway Hotel*, 34 Forthill St, T66322084, F66327480. Busy, small hotel, which has been here for 150 years. Music at weekends. **B** *Dromard House B&B*, Tamlaght, T66387250. 2 miles out of town in converted stable loft in farmhouse. Close to scenic walks. Good value. **B** *Mountview*, 61 Irvinestown Rd, T66323147, www.mountviewguests.com Pretty house and gardens close to town, snooker room, evening meal option. Will collect from town. **D** *Lakeland Canoe Centre*, Castle Island, T66324250. Very basic dormitory accommodation. Camping available. Free ferry service to island 0800-2400.

Eating
● *on map*
Price codes:
see inside
front cover

While there are any number of places open for lunch in town, breakfast and dinner can be a little more tricky. The *Killyhevlin* has a set evening meal, which is really quite good: 3 courses £15, 2 for £12. Ask for a window seat. The *Fort Lodge* has an à la carte menu 7 days. Last orders at both hotels are 2130. The *Railway Hotel* does bar food till 2130 in a fairly lively atmosphere. If you want classy food, there is *Oscar's* Belmore St, T66327037, open 7 days till 2300 with lots of recommendations to its name, some interesting items on the menu and attractive surroundings. Dinner will cost around £15 plus and there are vegetarian choices. *Saddlers* at 66 Belmore St, T66327432 does pub food and has an à la carte menu till 2245, 7 days, mostly seafood with several vegetarian choices. *Scoff's*, 17 Belmore St, T66342622, has a large evening menu with some nice things to eat on it in a mixture of traditional and modern. *Franco's Pizzeria*, Queen Elizabeth Rd, T66324424, is very popular, opens daily till 2200 and serves much more than pizza – shark and veal is also on the extensive menu. Beyond these your evening options are to eat early, try pub food or eat Chinese or Indian food. *Kamal Mahal's*, 1 Water St, T66325045, is open till midnight Wed-Mon and serves good Indian food in attractive surroundings. If you eat earlier the *Crow's Nest*, High St, T66325252, is a pub that has seriously gone into pub food with a huge menu of snacks and much more substantial dishes and serves food 6 days till 2100, 1430 Sun. *Mulligan's*, 33 Darling St, T66322059, is a very renovated sort of old pub with stained glass, tiled floors, cosy nooks and a bar-food menu, with 1 room dedicated to pub-style dining. It serves moderately interesting food 7 days till 2130. You might want to try the Irish stew with Bushmills. Lastly there's *Pat's Bar* in Townhall St, T66322040, doing grills and things with chips with main courses around £5-£7. Set lunch on Sun is £8.

At lunchtime there are so many places to choose from that it's difficult to know where to start. All the pubs already mentioned do pub food and in addition there is a string of good lunchtime stops along Townhall and East Bridge St all doing filled potatoes, chips and things, sandwiches and more substantial fare. You could also try *Rebecca's* in the Buttermarket, the *Bistro* in the shopping centre.

Pubs & music

There are some good pubs in Enniskillen. *Blake's of the Hollow* in Church St is very old and is divided up into little private rooms. At the back is a pool table and there is music on Thu. The *Crow's Nest* (see 'Eating' above) is a very trendy place at night and has a nightclub, *Thatch*, Wed, Fri, Sat and Sun as well as live music in the bars every night and weekend afternoons in summer. *The Bush* in Townhall St has regular traditional music sessions in summer. *The Railway Hotel* (see 'Sleeping' above) has live country music. Other pubs have occasional music sessions – check for notices. In addition to pubs and music there is the *Ardhowen Theatre*, Dublin Rd, T66325440, where there are performances of music and theatre and a good daytime café.

Sport

Boat hire *Erne Tours*, Round 'O' Jetty, Brook Park, Belleek Rd, T66322882. Hire the Kestrel to Devenish Island (1hr 45 mins), or self-drive boats with outboard per day. **Bowling** *Outdoor bowls*, Celtic Park Dublin Rd, May-Sep, 1200-1700, £2. **Fishing** *Erincurragh Cruising*, Blaney, T66641507. *Fermanagh Tourist Information Centre*, Wellington Rd, T66323110. *Home, Field and Stream*, 18 Church St, T66322114. **Leisure centre** *Lakeland Forum*, T66324121.

Transport

Air St Angelo Airport, Trory, T66325050. Four miles (6.4 km) north of Enniskillen, this airport handles charter flights in and out of Zürich (*Crossair*) and Jersey (*Brymon Airways*). It also offers pleasure flights of the area and a flight-training school. **Bicycle** *Lakeland Canoe Centre*, Castle Island, T66324250. Bike hire. **Bus** Bus station: Wellington Rd, T66322633, opposite the tourist office. It handles local buses to small villages in the area as well as regular services to **Belfast**, **Derry**, **Omagh**, **Dungannon**, **Cork**, **Sligo**, and the *Bus Éireann* **Dublin** to **Donegal** bus stops here. For the cross-border buses you can pay in either currency. **Car hire** *Lochside Garages*, Tempo Rd, T66324366. *Cyril Treacy*, 115 Sligo Rd, T66323610. **Taxis**, *Speedie Cabs*, T66327327. *Call-a-Cab*, T66324848. *County Cabs*, T66328888.

Directory

Banks *Bank of Ireland*, Townhall St. *First Trust*, East Bridge St. *Northern Bank*, Townhall St. *Ulster Bank*, Darling St. **Library** Halls Lane, T66322886. **Communications** Post office: East Bridge St.

Around Enniskillen

Castle Coole

Built in the late 18th century at massive expense by the first Earl of Belmore, who ruined himself in the process, this is said to be the finest neoclassical mansion in Ireland. It certainly cost enough and created lots of employment in the area for the many stonemasons, plasterers, carpenters and other craftsmen brought to the place to build it over two decades from 1789. Levelling the site took 18 months, while shipping the Portland stone for its exterior involved building a quay at Ballyshannon, chartering the brig *Martha*, and 10 miles of bullock carting. By 1791 there were 25 stone cutters, 26 masons, 10 stone sawyers, 17 carpenters and 83 labourers on the site, costing a total of £159.13s in wages for that year.

The house is a great day out, especially on a rainy day when its chilly interior matches its name perfectly. It is difficult to imagine the Belmore children having a good romp round this place. It was designed by James Wyatt, a contemporary of Gandon who designed many of the big houses of the Irish countryside. The main rooms are all pomp and austerity, the later 19th-century furniture adding a lumpiness to the fine lines of the 18th-century building, but that's what happens when Dad blows everything he has on the building and you have to wait a generation to put the furniture in. ■ *On A4, 1 mile (1.6 km) east of Enniskillen, T66322690. Open Jun-Aug, daily, 1300-1800; Apr, May and Sep, Sat and Sun and bank holidays 1300-1800; Easter, daily 1300-1800. £3. Guided tour only.*

Florence Court

What would the landed gentry of Northern Ireland do without the National Trust? They bought this pile in 1950 from the Coles, Earls of Enniskillen. The original building predates Castle Coole by 30 years; the wings are later additions by later generations of Coles. The place was damaged by fire in 1955 but has been partly restored. It is smaller and homelier, if such a word can be applied to these huge places, than Castle Coole. There is a walled garden and walks around the 200-year-old oakwoods. ■ *Southwest of Enniskillen on A4, then A32, 8 miles*

(13 km), T66348249. House: open Jun-Aug, daily 1300-1800, except Tue; Apr, May and Sep, Sat, Sun, bank holidays 1300-1800; Oct-Mar, closed. Last admission 1715. £3. Gardens: open Apr-Sep 1000-1900. Car £2. Tearoom.

Marble Arch Caves This is a very busy commercial enterprise and is best booked well in advance; you should be prepared for the 1-hour guided tour to be spent in a large company. The tour starts off with a boat trip underground and then on foot past stalactites and stalagmites and underground waterfalls. A good rainy day activity and great fun for children. ■ *Off A4, then A32, 12 miles (19.2 km) southwest of Enniskillen, T66348963. Mid-Mar-Sep, 1000-1600 (last tour). £6. Café, exhibition, shop.*

Around Lower Lough Erne

Colour map 1, grid B2 *A tour around Lower Lough Erne is a journey through cultural history from the prehistoric, Celtic, Iron Age, which began roughly around 500BCE, through the transition to Christianity a millennium later, and down the ensuing centuries to the Plantation of Ulster and the 1641 uprising. The journey is recorded through a series of remarkable stone monuments – pagan and semi-pagan deities, early Christian images, round towers and castles – relieved by a healthy small dose of 21st-century consumerism at the Belleek pottery works.*

The following circular route follows the A32 north of Enniskillen and proceeds along the east shore of Lower Lough Erne on the B82 to the village of Kesh and Boa Island. The A47 then goes along the northern shore to Belleek, where the A46 can be picked up for the return to Enniskillen back down the west side of the lough.

Devenish Island Sometimes it seems that round towers are two a penny in Ireland, but the one on Devenish Island (a 10-minute ferry ride from the mainland) is a particularly fine example. The doorway is the customary 10 ft (3 m) above ground level, and this common feature led to the conjecture that round towers were built as defensive structures. The old Irish name for the towers (*cloig theach*) means simply 'bell house' and the height of the doorway may have had more to do with preserving the physical integrity of the building, research having shown the foundations to be often quite shallow for a structure typically five storeys high. The mystery of the round towers is why builders chose to erect such tall structures beside typically small churches. Whatever the reason, they were built across Ireland between the late 10th and 13th centuries, and the example on Devenish can be partly dated to the 12th century because of the Romanesque sculptural decorations near its top.

Other sites and sights on the island are the ruins of the church and abbey, a High Cross, old gravestones, and a small museum. ■ *Open Apr-Sep, Tue-Sat 1000-1800, Sun 1400-1900. £2.25. Ferry departs at 1000,1300,1300,1700 from Trory Point, 4 miles (7 km) from Enniskillen and signposted off the A32.*

Killadeas Churchyard The establishment of Christianity in the northwest of Ireland is marked with a series of carved crosses and slabs thought by some to be associated with a particular outside impetus, perhaps from Scotland. Whatever the explanation, one of the most curious is the stone carving that lies in the graveyard of a church a few miles outside Enniskillen. One side of the rectangular slab bears the traditional image of a bishop with a bell and crozier, but the other side

Cruising through Ireland

With the restoration of the Ballinamore-Ballyconnell Canal in Leitrim, a 19th-century disaster which operated for nine years and was used in all that time by eight boats, a waterway route has opened up from Belleek at the far end of Lough Erne to the mouth of the River Shannon in Counties Kerry and Clare in the south, and to Dublin via the Grand Canal in the east. The route can encompass weeks of pottering about Lough Erne and the islands, side routes and jetties along its banks, or it can steam straight through to the Woodford River which is the start of the Shannon-Erne waterway. The river is navigable to Ballyconnell, where it joins the 62.5 km canal and lough stretches with their 34 stone bridges and 16 smart card-operated locks. From there the route passes by river, canal and lough to Leitrim, where it joins the Shannon. At Shannon Harbour the river links up with the Grand Canal, and it is possible to motor all the way to Dublin along the canal.

There are cruiser and canal boat hire companies all along the waterways. Many of them will arrange one-way hires, so that you do not have to return to your starting point, and all of them have fairly luxurious bases with restaurants, pools and other facilities. The following list covers the Shannon-Erne section, but boats from some of these operators can be taken on to the Grand Canal. Prices vary according to status and number of berths: on average a 4-6 berth cabin cruiser costs around £900 per week in the high season, around £700 in spring or autumn.

Carrick Craft, The Marina, Carrick-on-Shannon, Co. Leitrim, T07820236, F07821336, www.carrickcraft.com One way hires.

Emerald Star Line, The Marina, Carrick-on-Shannon, T07820234, info@emerald-star.com One way hire.

Belleek Charter Cruising, The Erne Gateway Marina, Belleek, Co. Fermanagh, T68658027, www.angelfire.com /co/belleekcruising

Manor House Marine, Lough Erne, Killadeas, Co. Fermanagh, T68628100, cruising@manormarine.com Huge marina with lots of resort facilities and up to 8-berth boats for hire.

Shannon-Erne Waterway Holidays, Blaney, Enniskillen, Co. Fermanagh, T6864, www.boatingireland.com One way hire. Will transfer your car to the next destination.

County Fermanagh

bears a startling image of a face that is anything but conventional and its positively pagan appearance contrasts dramatically with the ecclesiastical form. It looks as though the face was carved before the bishop, but both are impossible to date with any certainty. Showing clear signs of having been trimmed at probably a later date, the stone is thought to have been carved some time between 800 and 1000CE, a time when Christianity was still having to come to terms with pagan Ireland. ■ *To reach the churchyard take the B82 road along the eastern side of the lough and the church is on the left, a short way after the turn-off for the Manor House Country Hotel.*

Castle Archdale Country Park This park, containing a marina from which ferries depart, was a military base during the Second World War. There is a Centre with a tea room, nature trail, activities and an exhibition on the Battle of the Atlantic. ■ *Ten miles (16 km) from Enniskillen on the B82 Kesh Rd, T68621588. Open Jul and Aug, Tue-Sun, 1100-1900; Easter-Jun, Sun, 1200-1800.*

White Island The earliest references to a stone church in Ireland dates from CE788, and while the remains of the church on White Island are from the 12th century, there is archaeological evidence of an earlier wooden structure, which may well be contemporaneous with the curious stone figures built into the interior north wall.

They are thought to date from the 9th or 8th century, compelling evidence of White Island as one of Ireland's earliest Christian sites and lending support to one theory that the sculptured figures represent pilgrims and/or clerics. When you see the figures you may feel this is too prosaic an explanation, for there is something mysterious and even haunting about these large, grimacing faces, and presumably there was some iconographic significance to their belongings: bell, a staff, sword, shield, pouch, and small griffin-like animals. One of the figures is also a *sheela-na-gig*. ■ *The 15-minute ferry journey to White Island departs from Castle Archdale marina (in the Castle Archdale Country Park, see above) departing every hr on the hr for £3. T68621333. Jul and Aug, daily, 1100-1800; Apr, May and Jun, Sun, 1400-1800; Easter weekend, 1100-1800.*

Boa Island One of the two stone figures found on Boa Island at the northern tip of the lough is quite extraordinary. It is a **Janus idol** comprising two figures joined by their backs, with interwoven hair and sharing a belt; they have a stiff posture with arms crossed, bearded triangular faces and strange penetrating eyes that evoke Celtic magic in a very startling manner. It has been compared with the Tandragee Idol, now resting in Armagh Cathedral (see above), because of a supposedly shared sense of pagan inhumanity, but this could be disputed. The Tandragee figure is undoubtedly menacing, and if you come to Boa thinking of pagan gods as fearsome and a little barbaric then this Janus figure may seem similar in spirit; shake off these associations, however, and the face of the Boa idol can be read as genial and even a little mischievous. The mystery of interpretation is deepened when the context is taken into account: the idol is situated in an early Christian burial ground, as is the other two-sided figure in Killadeas Church, which also shows sign of being trimmed from a larger piece of stone. Virtually nothing is known about how the transition from paganism to Christianity was experienced in Ireland but these stone figures provide a fascinating and tantalizing glimpse of the interface between the two belief systems.

The other figure on Boa is known as the **Lustymore** or Lusty Man idol since it was brought here from nearby Lusty Beg Island. It is not as intriguing, and while the squatting posture has been likened to sheela-na-gig figures, this is mostly conjecture. ■ *Caldragh cemetery at the west end of Boa Island connected by a bridge and signposted off the A47.*

Castle Caldwell Within two decades of the defeat of the Irish at Kinsale even wild Fermanagh
Forest Park was ripe for plantations, and Castle Caldwell was one of the early castles built

on the shores of the lough. The crumbling ruins that stand today give little indication of how impressive it once looked, and when Arthur Young toured Ireland in 1776 the castle was already over 150 years old and enhanced by the natural beauty of the setting: "the promontories of thick wood, which shoot into Lough Earne, under the shade of a great ridge of mountains" led him to exclaim that "nothing can be more beautiful than the approach to Castle Caldwell". The grounds are now a wildlife reserve with shore walks and leaflets on trails can be picked up at the small centre during the summer. ■ *On A47, 4 miles (7 km) east of Belleek, T68631253. Free access 24 hours.*

Belleek A quiet little village on the shores of Lough Erne – looking a little bit like it has just emerged from the twilight zone, with burnt-out buildings, abandoned border crossings and huge observation posts badly disguised on the hillsides above – Belleek is home to the **Belleek Pottery Works**, T68658501. There is a good tour of the factory where you can see the parian china being made, a video about the history of the place and lots of display cabinets showing the

County Fermanagh

evolution of the style of the china. The pottery is highly burnished, hand-made and delicate: not much use for anything except admiring but it sells well, particularly the clover-leaf design. This is the best place to buy some if you want a piece. All seconds are smashed rather than allowed to lower the standard of the work. ■ *T68659300. Open Apr, Jun and Sep, Mon-Fri, 0900-1800, Sat, 1000-1800, Sun, 1400-1800; Oct, Mon-Fri, 0900-1730, Sat, 1000-1730, Sun, 1400-1800; Nov-Mar, Mon-Fri, 0900-1730; Jul and Aug, Mon-Fri, 0900-2000, Sat, 1000-1800, Sun, 1100-2000.*

Also in Belleek is the **Explore Erne** exhibition in the little tourist office, just outside the village. It has information on the waterway and its history. ■ *T68658866. Mar-Oct daily.*

Belleek picnic site The views over the lough are tremendous, and a car is needed to complete the 7-mile (11-kilometre) route through **Lough Navar Forest** to the viewpoint, but bring provisions for a picnic with a panorama. ■ *Open daily 1000-dusk. Car £2.50. Signposted off A46 between Belleek and Tully Castle.*

Tully Castle Built in the early 17th century for Sir John Hume, a Scottish planter, Tully Castle had a short life as a residence: in the 1641 uprising the Maguires laid siege to it. Hume surrendered upon a promise of being spared, but this proved of little worth to all the others who had fled here for safekeeping for they were slaughtered and the castle set alight. The castle and its formal garden have now been restored and there is a small visitor's centre, but if you only have time for one castle visit then consider instead a visit to the ruins of Monea Castle. ■ *Open Apr-Sep, Tue-Sat, 1000-1900, Sun, 1400-1900. £1.*

Monea Castle This castle was built around the same time as Tully and for another Scottish planter, Malcolm Hamilton, and although it has not been restored the ruins and the setting are more successful in evoking the past, and a Scottish past at that, than Tully. Four storeys high and with imposing towers there is little doubt that this castle was built with defence in mind. In 1641 it did fall for a short while to the insurgents but remained a home until well into the 18th century. The ruins slumber on. ■ *On B81 7 miles (11 km) northwest of Enniskillen. Free access 24 hours.*

Essentials

Sleeping
Price codes: see inside front cover

AL *Hotel Carlton*, 2 Main St, Belleek, T68658282. Modern hotel situated beside the lough with pleasant big rooms and friendly attention from staff. Nice grounds, good breakfasts but don't expect an early start. **AL** *The Courtyard*, Lusty Beg Island, T68632032, F68632033. Has its own car ferry from the pier on Boa Island, for transport to this private island with B&B single/doubles for £50/£70, restaurant and bar, indoor pool, sauna, tennis, cycling and canoeing. **A** *The Cedars*, 301 Killadeas Rd, Castle Archdale, T/F68621493. A smart country-house guesthouse with a bar and small restaurant area serving high tea and evening meals. **B** *The Fiddlestone*, 15-17 Main St, Belleek, T68658008. Traditional Irish pub with nice atmosphere and a bar close at hand. **D** *Castle Archdale Youth Hostel*, Castle Archdale Country Park, T/F68628118. Occupies a wing of an old courtyard complex with 2 main dormitories and 2 family rooms.

Camping *Blaney Caravan & Camping Park*, on the A46 at Blaney and adjacent to the service station, T68641634. Open all year but has only 10 pitches for tents, all at £8. *Castle Archdale Caravan Park*, T68621333. Charges £10 for one of its 50 tent pitches. *Lakeland Caravan Park*, Boa Island Rd, Drumrush, T68631578. Tent pitch £10. *Tir Navar Holiday Village*, Creamery St, Derrygonnelly, T68641673, has 10 pitches at £4, and for an extra charge it is possible to use the kitchen facilities that are on site. *Lough Melvin Holiday Centre*, Main St, Garrison, T68658142. Run by Fermanagh District Council and has plenty of tent pitches for £8.

Eating   **Belleek**   The *Hotel Carlton* has a restaurant and does pub food with lots of spicy options and a couple of vegetarian choices. The set menu is £18.95 and fairly traditional and the à la carte works out around £20 for 3 courses. The *Fiddlestone* and *McMorrow's* do bar food aimed at the passing tourists and there is a fast-food joint and the *Thatch Coffee Shop* does cakes and soup. Vegetarians could try the *Black Cat* which has several good vegetarian choices.

Kesh   *Lusty Beg Island Restaurant*, Lusty Beg Island, T68631342. Opens daily in the evening from 1830 to 2130 and there is also a tea room open from 0900 in the summer. *Drumrush Lodge*, Boa Island Rd, Kesh, T68631578, opens daily in the summer for affordable lunches and dinners. There are other eating possibilities along Main St in Kesh including pub food at the *May Fly* at No 14.

Sport   **Bicycle hire, Canoeing and Ponytrekking**   *Castle Archdale Country Park*, T68621588. **Watersports**   *Boa Island Activity Centre*, Tudor Farm, Boa Island Rd, T68631943. *Drumrush Watersports Centre*, Lakeland Caravan Park, Boa Island Rd, T68631943.

Transport   **Buses**   *Ulsterbus* No 194 Enniskillen to Pettigo via Irvinestown and Kesh, daily. Nos 59 and 59A **Enniskillen** to **Derrygonnelly** via **Monea** and **Blaney**, Mon-Sat. No 64 Enniskillen to **Belleek** via **Garrison**, Mon-Fri and Sun; on Thu travels on to **Bundoran**. No 261 **Belfast** to **Bundoran** via **Enniskillen** and **Belleek**, daily. No 99 **Enniskillen** to **Bundoran** via **Blaney** and **Belleek**, daily. T66322633.

Directory   **Craft courses** in painting, crafts, sculpture, pottery, cooking, spinning and weaving: *Ardress Craft Centre*, Ardress House, Kesh, T68631267, www.ardresshouse.co.uk   £25 a day including lunch or £60 full board.

Background

18

Background

History

The physical landscape was shaped millions of years ago when mountains formed in the wake of cooling lava, and a mere 200,000 years ago the famous valleys of Killarney were created by shifting blocks of ice. The post-glacial period brought a rise in sea level and these river valleys of the southwest flooded to form Dingle Bay, Bantry Bay and Killary Harbour. Around this time, too, the Aran Islands separated from the Burren and the wide Clew Bay flooded and its drumlins submerged, leaving their island crests. Between eight and ten thousand years ago, nomadic Mesolithic people from Europe came to the northwest fringes of the continent bearing flint instruments. By 5500 BCE, the east coast of Ireland had submerged and Ireland became an island.

Prehistory

Around 4000BCE people arrived with farming skills, and the first settled communities arose, as revealed in north Mayo at Céide Fields, giving rise, in the due course of centuries, to megalithic stone tombs which survive to this day. Court-tombs are probably the earliest, dating as far back as 3500BCE and characterized by an open space or court in front of the tomb, flanked by standing stones.

Passage-tombs are similar in that they are also covered by a stone mound but are more interesting to visit, not least because of the geometrical motifs inscribed on the stones, and the best places to see them are at Carrowkeel, Newgrange and Knowth. Equally dramatic are the portal-tombs or dolmens (from a Breton word meaning a 'stone table'), popularly known as Druids' altars, composed of three or more massive standing stones supporting one large capstone which can weigh up to 100 tons. They were built somewhere around 3000-2000BCE.

Newgrange, dating from around 2500BCE, stands as testimony to the astonishing engineering skills possessed by these people, and the National Museum in Dublin has dazzling displays of their achievements working with gold and silver and, later, bronze.

The Bronze Age, 2000-500BCE, gets its name from the main material used during a period which also made use of copper and gold, and a major site from this period is the stone circle at Lough Gur. Other stone circles belong to the ensuing Iron Age, built by a people who never developed an alphabet beyond the characters known as Ogham.

> Ice caps melted, sea levels rose and Ireland detached itself from Britain, but it took a longer time for the land joining Britain with Europe to be submerged. This is why snakes that had reached Britain on land could not travel further west to the island of Ireland, though the idea that St Patrick banished them is part of the Irish ABC

Background

The Celts

The Iron Age Celts are best viewed as a linguistic group, an offshoot of the Indo-European family, which emerged around 2000BCE and spread from Turkey in the east to Ireland in the west. From where exactly they came is open to interpretation and there is a theory that an Atlantic culture arrived in Ireland via the Mediterranean, through Spain and possibly north Africa. Berber jewellery and north African music and dance have a striking kinship with 'Celtic' art forms.

In the late 1990s Simon James, a scholar at the British Museum (see page 680), attacked the notion that the Celts as a uniform people ever existed, and he claimed that the idea they were somehow the first nation to emerge north of the Alps is a myth born of Celtomania. His debunking thesis is a useful corrective to the excessive claims of born-again Celtomaniacs, who would have us believe they are part of a long-repressed culture. Nevertheless, 'Celtic Ireland' remains a useful shorthand term for the pre-Christian period, and there are intriguing cultural overlaps between the Celts and those who followed them.

> "A land of fog and gloom ... Beyond it lies the Sea of Death, where Hell begins."
>
> Homer's 'Iliad' describes the far northwest of Europe

Much of what we know about pagan Celtic society in Ireland is due – ironically – to the earnest chronicling efforts of early Christian monks

The Celtic calendar was premised on the duality of dark and light – they counted nights rather than days – and great significance was attached to those pivotal moments when the two came together. Sunrise and sunset were such moments, while the two annual equinoxes – when day and night were momentarily balanced by the sun crossing the celestial equator – were profoundly magical in their import. The supernatural was most alive at these critical times and paganism was in awe of this cosmic balancing act.

The summer and winter solstices, when the sun is furthest away from the equator, were also powerful and dangerous moments in time. There were four great pagan festivals when Celts celebrated the turning points between the seasons. Most is known about Lughnasa, celebrated at the beginning of August and dedicated to the god Lug.

Monasticism

"The wind is fierce tonight Ploughing the wild white ocean; I need not dread fierce Vikings Crossing the Irish Sea."

Words of an anonymous monk scribbled in the margin of a 10th-century manuscript

The Romans never settled in Ireland, but men from Ireland served with Roman legions, and it was through the Romans that Christianity arrived on the island. The first bishop was appointed in 431 (the first bona fide date in Irish history), but it was the missionary Patrick who is now best associated with early Christian Ireland. Notwithstanding his iconic Irishness, Patrick first arrived as a captured slave from Britain and returned years later as a proselytizing missionary, establishing his main church in Armagh.

Christianity brought with it a world of learning and literacy as well as technological innovations like the mouldboard plough and the horizontal mill. Monastic organizations also allowed for organized farming, and the overall effect of these influences from 'across the water' was an increase in population which is associated with the 45,000 ring-forts that were built across Ireland during this era.

From the sixth to eighth centuries, when the rest of Europe was in the doldrums after the collapse of the Roman empire, Ireland's monasteries continued to burn the light of culture and learning. Irish monks travelled throughout Europe, rekindling some of the intellectual embers endangered by barbarism, and the survival of wonderful illuminated manuscripts provides eloquent testimony to their achievement.

Irish monasticism, associated above all with the great figure of Colum Cille, gave the Irish Church a unique idiom through its ability to fuse the sacred with the profane, recording pagan myths and soothing the revolutionary transition from a pagan world of magic and mysticism with a degree of sympathy that seems difficult to comprehend today. What explanation, other than a sensibility capable of being excited by paganism, accounts for Irish monks recording and preserving the pagan vernacular literature of their island? The stories and chronicles that they recorded are the primary source materials for the contemporary study of early Irish history, and it is thanks to them that we know the tales of Cuchulainn and the other Irish heroes and heroines.

Irish monasticism was also enriched by an ascetic Coptic strain, more akin to the eastern church than Rome, which incorporated a tradition of holy people seeking out secluded and remote hermitages – a *fuga mundi* or 'flight from the world' – which often became the seedbeds of monastic communities. This is the origin of Glendalough and the fastness of Skellig Michael – an 800-ft rock 8 miles off the remote Kerry coast – two holy sites which now attract tourist pilgrims in greater numbers than they ever did in their own austere times.

The Vikings

Norse Viking invaders first raided the monasteries of Ireland in the late 10th century, and in the following century Irish annals report sightings of vast fleets of ships appearing on the Boyne and the Liffey. The Danes came in their wake, and fierce fighting developed between the invaders and between them and the Irish.

Settlements and intermarriage with the Irish gave rise to coastal communities that would evolve into the towns of Dublin, Wexford, Waterford, Cork and Limerick. In 917 the king of Leinster was defeated by the Norse, commanded by Sitric, who went on to establish a strong kingdom in Dublin. Raiding parties by the Norse into the Irish interior is one plausible explanation for the building of defensive round towers near monasteries, for this is when many of them were built.

The Vikings kept paganism alive and healthy in Ireland until around the 11th century, a period which saw their defeat by the Irish under Brian Bóruma (Brian Boru) at the momentous battle of Clontarf in 1014. Brian Bóruma was killed at Clontarf and his body carried in state to Armagh, then the ecclesiastical capital of Ireland, the significance of this epic battle being recorded in both Irish annals and Icelandic sagas.

The coming of the Normans

After the death of Brian Bóruma, Ireland was torn apart by internecine dynastic wars that petered out when Rory O'Connor was accepted as king of all Ireland in the middle of the 12th century. Then in August 1167 one of his erstwhile rivals, Dermot MacMurrough, arrived home from exile, and with the help of Welsh soldiers set about reclaiming his kingdom. MacMurrough had earlier sought out the Norman King Henry II of England, and with promises of land had procured his support for an invasion of Ireland. The event proved to be traumatically momentous, for MacMurrough's support included the Earl of Pembroke, better known as Strongbow. When the Earl arrived in 1170, the stage was set for 800 years of foreign rule and conflict which still bedevils politics and peace in Northern Ireland. With the arrival of these French-speaking Normans, mostly from South Wales, Irish history would never be the same again.

Strongbow brought a professional army of 1000 men and their menacing longbows, and he first captured Waterford and then Dublin. Henry II, alarmed that this rich new conquest might slip from his personal grasp, began assembling his own fleet for an invasion. He landed in 1171 near Waterford with a fleet of 400 ships and as many as 4000 men. In the course of the 13th century the Normans began to build their great stone castles, and those at Kilkenny, Carrickfergus and Trim give some idea of the awe they must have instilled in the minds of the wood-building Gaels.

The Normans brought to Ireland the idea of the absolute ownership of land, as opposed to the Irish idea that land was only given in trust to individuals. Under Brehon Law, the ancient legal code of pre-Norman Ireland, woodlands were common land.

Conquered, not colonized

Henry II secured Waterford, Wexford and Dublin, and the Irish nobility submitted to his rule. Ireland had been conquered, and after a visit to Lismore the acquiescence of the Irish bishops was obtained, but the country was not yet colonized in any systematic way. Before leaving Ireland, Henry gave the central swathe of the country from the Shannon to the Boyne to the English family of Hugh de Lacy who, together with Strongbow, established a permanent English presence on the island. They soon intermarried with the Irish, and by the time Henry's son John, who became king in 1199, strengthened royal rule over Ireland, the first Anglo-Irish families had become established. A trickle of new English settlers came, lured by the promise of good land, and families like the Desmonds and the Butlers began to emerge as powerful Anglo-Irish political forces.

The mass of Irish peasants struggled and toiled as before, while their Irish lords brooded in the background ever ready to take advantage of internal power squabbles amongst the Anglo-Normans. English rule was confined to an area around

Dublin known as the Pale (hence the expression 'beyond the pale') while Gaelic custom and Brehon law – with communal property, secular marriage and divorce – operated for the majority of the population. The most powerful Norman-Irish families, known as the 'Old English', were the loyal Butlers and their earldom of Ormond, and the Fitzgeralds, whose earldoms of Kildare and Desmond became a thorn in the side of the English crown. Kilkenny became the political and cultural centre of medieval Anglo-Norman Ireland, and in 1366 a set of 36 clauses, the Statutes of Kilkenny, were passed as law in an attempt to preserve the English culture from the encroachments of Gaelic life. "Now many English of the said land, forsaking the English language, fashion, mode of riding, laws and usages, live and govern themselves according to the manners, fashion and language of the Irish enemies, and also have made divers marriages and alliances between themselves and the Irish." (The Statutes of Kilkenny.)

During the 16th century Henry VIII of England had trouble keeping some of these Anglo-Irish magnates under his control, and after his breach with Rome over his marriage to Anne Boleyn in 1533 this became a serious problem, because of the danger of European Catholic plots being hatched in Ireland. England became more serious about combating dissent in Ireland and suppressing Brehon law, but there were still five Anglo-Irish rebellions between 1568 and 1574. In 1580 Spanish and Italian Catholics landed at Smerwick in Kerry where, trapped by Lord Grey, 500 were slaughtered after they had surrendered. It was a sign of the times to come.

After the failure of rebellions by the Desmonds in 1569-73 and 1579-83, and consequent confiscations of land, the first plantations, planned in London, began in Munster. By 1592 there were over 3000 settlers, but some were killed after the Nine Years War broke out and their land was taken over by former owners. The colonists who were still around in 1598 fled to Irish towns and to England for safety. The colony was successfully re-established after 1601, spreading around Youghal, Kinsale and Baltimore and exporting wool and cattle. By 1641 there were over 20,000 settlers and the remnants of these families can still be traced in parts of West Cork.

"They looked like anatomies of death; they spake like ghosts crying out of their graves …. And if they found a plot of watercress or shamrocks, they flocked there as if to a feast."

Edmund Spenser, author of The Faerie Queen, describing the aftermath of the Desmond rebellion in Munster, where he was stationed

The end of Gaelic Ireland

The ruthless conquest of Ireland under Elizabeth I extended English control far beyond Dublin, but it met with strong resistance in Ulster, where the queen thought she had a willing ally in Hugh O'Neill. Instead, joining forces with Red Hugh O'Donnell, he rose in rebellion in what became known as the Nine Years War (1593-1603). Lacking artillery but employing successful guerrilla tactics, the rebels spread across Ireland, attempting unsuccessfully to enlist the support of the Anglo-Irish. Support came from the Spanish who landed a storm-weakened army at Kinsale in 1601, but they were trapped there. The English forces, who by now had been strengthened by the new military leadership of Lord Mountjoy, pursued a scorched earth policy as they pursued the rebels. At the same time the rebellion which had broken out in Munster was effectively met by Sir George Carew. The rebel leaders, O'Neill and O'Donnell, had no choice but to move their armies south in an attempt to join forces with the beleaguered Spanish. A tactical blunder by O'Neill handed victory to Mountjoy, the Spanish secured terms and sailed home, and the greatest challenge yet to English rule – one that would not be repeated until the War of Independence in the early 20th century – was over. It cost the English a massive £2 million but English control over Ireland was now complete.

An emotive and emblematic postscript to the end of Gaelic Ireland came in 1607 when the pardoned and humbled O'Neill left Ireland for ever, in the company of other chieftains. Known as the 'flight of the earls' it concluded with the death of Hugh O'Neill in Rome in 1616. It was the legacy of the flight of the earls and its aftermath that erupted on the streets of Derry and Belfast in 1968.

Background

Oliver Cromwell

Oliver Cromwell, with God on his side, meted out divine revenge for the 1641 rising to the "barbarous and bloodthirsty Irish". The massacre at Drogheda , where possibly 1,000 citizens were slaughtered, has ensured Cromwell's infamy as Ireland's most ruthless public enemy, though a remarkable book by Tom Reilly, published in 1999, paints a different picture (see page 152).

Cromwell went on to capture Cork, Kinsale and Bandon from the rebels, Catholicism was driven underground and his soldiers, as well as fresh waves of settlers, were rewarded with extensive grants of confiscated land.

Plantation and rebellion

The seeds of the present discord in Northern Ireland were laid within two weeks of Hugh O'Neill's departure, for this is how long it took to submit proposals for the plantation of the lands left behind in the flight of the earls. Ulster was surveyed, mapped and divided as thousands of Protestants took root, especially Scots in Down and Antrim, as both landlords and tenants. Such was the influx that by 1636 the government prohibited further emigration without licence from Scotland.

Settlers, known officially as undertakers, also moved into other parts of Ireland, and a radical and far-reaching change in the ownership of land took place. Nearly all of Gaelic Ireland was owned by about 2,000 Catholic gentry, but by 1660 they held only a little over 20%, and by the beginning of the 18th century the figure was below 15%.

Old English families grew alarmed at anti-Catholic measures and the threats to their property rights, and rebellion broke out in Ulster in 1641. Many of the leaders considered themselves loyal to the Crown, while others like Sir Phelim O'Neill were probably more keen to recover their lost land. The real revolutionaries were the native dispossessed Irish who rebelled against the injustice of plantation and the consequent shortage of land. The 1641 rising has gone down in loyalist mythology as a savage sectarian bloodletting, and violent outrages were indeed inflicted on Protestant settlers. Many were stripped naked in cruel mockery of having arrived in Ireland with nothing, and driven from their homes to perish in the winter cold. As many as 8,000 may have died, but propaganda multiplied this number out of all proportion and fuelled anti-Catholic hatred with lurid and exaggerated tales of torture and rape, and a premeditated plot to ethnically cleanse Ireland of Protestants. The rising was used as justification for the confiscation of two million acres of Irish land, while in England the rebellion became entwined with the emerging civil war as Charles I was accused of supporting the rebels. In 1649, after the execution of Charles, an army of 12,000 men landed in Ireland under Oliver Cromwell. When he left nine months later the ground was prepared for the final chapter in the colonization of Ireland, and the only refuge left for Catholics was across the Shannon in land-poor Connacht – thus the saying 'to hell or to Connacht'.

"You, unprovoked, put the English to the most unheard of and most barbarous massacre (without respect of sex or age) that ever the sun beheld."

From a broadsheet published by Cromwell in Cork in 1650, referring to events at Drogheda.

The Siege of Derry and the Battle of the Boyne

An estimated 150,000 emigrants arrived in Ireland in the 20 years after 1652, and it was the 17th century that saw large-scale deforestation as a direct result of the felling of trees for charcoal to sustain English industry. The second half of the century also witnessed a European power struggle that was to involve Ireland in a highly momentous manner. James II, who had been deposed from the English throne, landed in Kinsale in 1689 with French troops. The new king of England, William of Orange, was allied with Spain, the Dutch and the Pope, and together they were determined to oppose any increase in French power. "If Ireland should be lost,

Background

England will follow" was the fear in the English Houses of Parliament when they voted funds of over £1 million for another army to land in Ireland and oppose James. European politics became entwined with the Catholic and Protestant struggle in Ireland, and the stage was set for another dramatic confrontation.

The defeat of James was played out in two events that were to shape Ireland in fact and in myth: resistance of Derry to James' army, and the Battle of the Boyne, north of Dublin. The military commander in Derry, Robert Lundy, with the support of the Protestant bishop, was prepared to recognize James as the legitimate king before he arrived in Ireland, but many townspeople, alarmed at the thought of another 1641 massacre, thought otherwise. In December 1688 13 apprentice boys slammed the gates of Derry shut and Lundy, whose name and image is still reviled in loyalist wall art in Northern Ireland, was forced to flee the city in disguise. In April 1689 James laid siege to a defiant Derry – 'No surrender' was the clarion call – until, in July, a Williamite fleet managed to break through with supplies and save the city from starvation.

In May 1689, the last Irish parliament to include Catholics until 1922 took place in Dublin and in July William's army defeated James at the Battle of the Boyne, with cathedrals across Catholic Europe offering prayers in thanksgiving. King James fled the battlefield, earning for himself the epitaph *Séamus a chaca* (James the Shit), though Irish resistance lasted another year. The end truly came with Sarsfield surrendering at Limerick in October 1691 after securing an honourable peace and exile to France, where he died two years later fighting William of Orange: "Oh, that this were for Ireland" were his reported last words. Pockets of Irish soldiers fighting in Europe became known as the 'Wild Geese'; one became a general in the Russian army, another a governor of Spanish Louisiana.

The 18th century

The treaty negotiated at Limerick in 1691 promised religious tolerance, but this was reneged on with the passing of laws like one in 1695 that made it illegal for a Catholic to own a horse worth more than £5. By this time only about five percent of useful land in Ireland was owned by Catholics. The Protestant ruling class ruled the roost, Dublin flourished as their commercial and cultural capital, and the Protestant Ascendancy seemed too secure to ever feel threatened again. It was not to be.

The decade which began in 1790 is one of the most important in Irish history, not just for the tumultuous events of the 1798 uprising but also for the fact that it saw the birth of republicanism, unionism and Orangeism.

"Landlords of consequence have assured me that many of their cottiers would think themselves honoured by having their wives or daughters sent for to the bed of their masters, a mark of slavery that proves the oppression under which they live."

From Arthur Young's account of his travels around Ireland in 1776-78

The Irish Parliament can be traced back to medieval times, but it met very irregularly and even in the 18th century only once a year. Like its parent British institution, it was riddled with patronage and, quite apart from bizarre franchises that led to the election of MPs for 'rotten boroughs' where no one actually voted, only Protestants and Presbyterians were allowed to vote in elections. There were few Presbyterian MPs, mainly due to the property criteria for those eligible to vote, and in Ulster this led to Presbyterian interest in parliamentary reform. For most of the 18th century, the Parliament sitting in Dublin was completely subordinate to Westminster, but with the emergence of the Volunteers, and the pressure they were able to apply, there were constitutional changes in 1792 that came to be known under the term 'legislative independence'.

The Volunteers were a part-time military force originally created in 1778-79 for the purpose of protecting Ireland against a French invasion and generally maintaining law and order at a time when regular troops were needed to deal with the American Revolution. Predominantly based in Ulster and rising to 60,000 in number, the force consisted of urban, middle-class men, and as such emerged as a powerful expression of that class's aspirations for a greater say in the running of their country.

Background

Theobold Wolfe Tone

Wolfe Tone was born in 1763 into a Protestant middle-class family in Dublin. His father was a coachmaker and his mother the daughter of a sea captain. He more or less drifted into Dublin politics, and the height of his early political ambitions was a hoped-for seat in the Irish parliament. The French Revolution and Thomas Paine's Rights of Man helped radicalise his thinking and in 1791 he published An Argument on Behalf of the Catholics of Ireland. Calling for a united front of Catholics and Protestants, Tone's pamphlet was enormously popular and influential. In 1792 a further 10,000 copies were printed and Dublin Castle sent a copy to London to warn of this dangerous new polemic. By 1796 Tone was in France promoting a French invasion of Ireland, and
before the year was out he was sailing into Bantry Bay with over 14,000 French troops, only to be defeated by adverse weather that saw the remnants of the fleet returning to France in January 1797. In 1798 Tone was once again on board a French ship as part of a third invasion force (the second invasion had landed earlier in north Mayo). Bad weather again thwarted the expedition, but it was anyway too late to effect the outcome of the general uprising of 1798. Even the few ships that made it to Donegal were intercepted by the British. The ship Tone was on decided to make a fight of it, and Tone himself refused the offer of escaping on a French frigate. Tone was captured and sentenced to death, but took his own life before he could be hanged.

The 1792 reforms did not actually make the Irish Parliament autonomous, but they did help create a political climate which nurtured the idea that further constitutional change was both desirable and possible. There were demands for more regular sittings of Parliament, an extension of the Protestant electorate and other reforms, but they all came to nothing. English aristocratic rule, operating through Dublin Castle, remained firmly entrenched. The major reason for the failure of the post-1792 movement, led by Dublin radicals like James Napper Tandy (c.1737-1803) and the Belfast Presbyterian William Drennan (1754-1820), was the Catholic question. This revolved around the repeal of the Penal Laws, an issue that aroused deep-rooted fears amongst Protestants whose worst nightmares imagined a return to sectarian massacres and Catholic supremacy. They therefore argued for further political reforms, but these were clearly not to include equal rights for Catholics. Yet without the involvement of Catholics it was impossible for any reform movement to move up a gear and mount an effective challenge to British hegemony. As Wolfe Tone put it, it was foolish to plan "an edifice of freedom on a foundation of monopoly".

Wolfe Tone and 1798

Wolfe Tone changed everything by confronting the Catholic question and success-fully arguing that Catholics be brought into the political equation. Tone was by no means the first to propound the idea that Irish people should unite behind a non-denominational front, but he did crystallize the notion and made it common currency. Towards the end of 1791 he was invited to Belfast to help establish a new political association being formed there by Presbyterian radicals. It was Tone who suggested the name 'United Irishmen' for this new political club, and on his return to Dublin he quickly set up a branch there consisting of both Protestants and Catholics. Events moved quickly within the next couple of years: the Volunteers were out-lawed, and in 1794 the Dublin Society of United Irishmen was also outlawed. This pushed the movement underground, closer to outright republicanism and the con-templation of armed insurrection. When war broke out between Britain and France, Tone saw the opportunity to recruit some foreign help.

The first French invasion force was defeated by winter storms in 1796, but it gave the British a jolt – "England has not had such an escape since the Spanish Armada", declared Tone at the time – and the Irish such a fillip that within the next 18 months the United Irishmen claimed to have well over a quarter of a million members. The British authorities too were not idle, and developed counter-insurgency policies seriously weakened the effectiveness of the general insurrection that came in 1798. Many of the leaders were arrested, and the revolutionary movement suffered from a lack of co-ordination and the prevarications of the French in mounting another invasion fleet. Napoleon became more interested in a campaign in Egypt than in Europe's northern fringes, and his ships were in the Mediterranean when the uprising broke out.

The 1798 insurrection broke out across the country, starting in counties Dublin, Kildare and Meath in May, when mail coaches leaving the capital were stopped and set on fire. Government forces subdued the rebels, as they also did in eastern Ulster, but the uprising in County Wexford was more problematic. It cost around 30,000 lives, and was easily the most bloody event in Irish history since the 17th century.

Union and Daniel O'Connell

The events of 1798 convinced Britain that only the abolition of the Irish Parliament and a union of the English and Irish kingdoms could guarantee security. "Ireland is like a ship on fire, it must be extinguished or cut adrift", observed the British prime minister, Pitt, who set about securing the Act of Union which came into effect in 1801. The Catholic clergy was won over by a promise of Catholic emancipation that would allow Catholics to sit in the new parliament and hold other important positions, and existing members of the Irish Parliament were bought off with pensions and bribes.

The year 1803 marked the short-lived and abortive rebellion planned by 25-year-old Robert Emmet, who paid for his daring by being sentenced to be hanged, drawn and quartered. "Let no man write my epitaph . . . When my country takes her place among the nations of the earth, then, and not till then, let my epitaph be written. I have done." Emmet's last words from the dock in 1803.

The promised Catholic emancipation did not happen until a new leader arrived on the scene, Daniel O'Connell (1775-1847). The man who has given his name to countless streets in Irish towns was a prosperous middle-class radical of liberal instincts who captured the minds and hearts of ordinary Irish people. He created a political mass movement for Catholic emancipation through a Catholic Association with a membership of one penny a month. It was a revolutionary act and one that would reverberate through Europe, for never before had a popular reform movement been organized in this manner. Membership climbed to half a million, and with 100,000 Catholic 40-shilling freeholders with a vote the time was ripe for change. Public rallies were held throughout the country, and O'Connell stood as a candidate in a Clare by-election. He gained nearly 70% of the vote, and the British knew that a concession had to be made. Catholic emancipation became a reality in 1829, and a new mood of confidence spread like wildfire across Ireland.

Buoyed by success, O'Connell set about securing home rule – a repeal of the Act of Union and the return of an Irish Parliament. It was a far cry from Wolfe Tone's republicanism, and although it was meant to be achieved without physical force it had a very physical dimension. Giant public meetings, dubbed 'monster meetings' by *The Times*, attracted hundreds of thousands of people and, although he tried to keep within the law, legal grounds were found for him to be tried for sedition and he was sentenced to jail. Now aged 70, he was released after six months. A younger wing of the movement was now calling for more radical opposition to British rule.

Background

Nationalism and Famine

Thomas Davis (1814-45) split with O'Connell and articulated a new and more exciting idea by calling for a brake on Anglicization, a revival of the Irish language and a
"nationalism which may embrace Protestant, Catholic and Dissenter ... the Irishman
of a hundred generations and the stranger who is within our gate." Davis died suddenly of scarlet fever, but an Ulster Presbyterian, John Mitchel (1815-75), took the
movement further forward by agitating for an independent Irish republic. He was
sentenced to transportation for 14 years in 1848, and a small rebellion broke out the
same year but achieved little.

The failure of the 1848 rebellion was due not least to the awful Famine that was
traumatizing Ireland. A potato blight was first noticed in 1845 when the population
of Ireland was over 8 million and by 1851, when the Famine was over, the population had dropped to six and a half million; by 1901 the figure was four and a half million. Death through starvation and disease accounted for a million deaths, and
accelerated the process of emigration from Ireland as peasants desperately sought a
new and better life in North America and Australia. The Famine has been seen by
some historians as an act of genocide, with ships leaving some of the worse-affected
areas carrying profitable grain for export to Europe while peasants died for want of a
meal. Others point out that the prevailing philosophy of free trade made it impossible for people to think otherwise, and indeed for some the haemorrhaging of people
was seen as a positive economic gain.

Fenians and Home Rule

Irish tenants had no security of tenure on the land they rented, and if they could not
afford the rent most landlords had them evicted so that the land could be rented to
someone else. In 1850 a Tenant League was formed for land reform, but in 1858 an
organization of more consequence was formed, the Irish Republican Brotherhood
(IRB), more popularly known as the Fenians. In 1867 they mounted an abortive uprising: some of the participants were hanged, and a failed Fenian rescue of prisoners in
London led to an explosion which killed 30. For his part in this botched rescue a
Fenian was executed in the last public hanging in England.

Fenianism focussed the minds of English liberal politicians like Gladstone on the
problem of Ireland. In 1870 he introduced the first in what would become a series of
land reforms that the Tenant League had called for. At the same time a new Home Rule
movement arose in Ireland, its leader, Charles Stewart Parnell, taking up where Daniel
O'Connell had foundered. Parnell, a Protestant landlord with an American mother, was
quite prepared to use the threat of direct action alongside conventional political action,
and joined forces with the newly formed Land League. The Land League was founded
by the Fenian Michael Davitt in 1879 with Parnell as president, and together they led a
formidable campaign. Davitt used official statistics to show that fewer than 20,000 men
owned the whole of Ireland; in fact fewer than 2,000 owned 70% of the land, while 3
million tenants and labourers owned nothing. Radical mass action, which became
known as the Land War, demanded redistribution of land with compensation to landlords, and backed it up with a vigorous campaign that became famous for ostracizing
anyone who dared take over the land of an evicted tenant. One of the first to suffer was
a Captain Boycott – hence the new synonym for ostracism – and when Parnell was
imprisoned in 1881 he became even more of a hero, and a policy of withholding rents
altogether was put into action. He was released with a promise by Gladstone to introduce further, more far-reaching land reforms.

Even before the divorce issue destroyed Parnell (see box next page) he had started
to lose some of his political clout in Ireland when he failed to back campaigns for more

Background

👉 ## Parnell's downfall

After the 1885 general election, Parnell's Home Rule party wiped the board in southern Ireland and the following year Gladstone announced his conversion to the need for a dissolution of the union. Aged 76, he introduced the first Home Rule Bill to Parliament and then a bombshell came out of the sky in the form of one Captain O'Shea who, when filing for divorce on the grounds of his wife's adultery, named Parnell as the third party. It gave opponents of Home Rule a moral excuse for denouncing Parnell and when the Irish Catholic Church jumped up on the moral bandwagon, the Irish parliamentary party was split. Parnell married Katherine O'Shea in 1891 but died the following year, a broken and tired man.

vigorous action for land reform. His sister Anna never lost her drive in organizing the Ladies Land League, and struggled tirelessly across America for the cause, suffering disillusionment only when she realized that the Land League tended to benefit larger tenants and was not prepared to see through the need for a radical redistribution of land.

Gladstone's land reforms were carried even further by later Liberal and Conservative administrations which sought quite consciously to "kill Home Rule by kindness". The Ashbourne Act in 1885 allowed landlords to sell land to their tenants at fixed prices, and this was encouraged by the Wyndham Act of 1903 which saw landlords gaining a 12% payment, the Bonus, on top of the sale price. George Wyndham is said to have encountered an Irish peer in Monte Carlo brandishing his stack of chips and exclaiming to the Chief Secretary, "George! George! The Bonus." These reforms saw the end of the Protestant Ascendancy, because without the regular income from rents their economic base was terminally fractured. Leaking roofs went unrepaired, and as many of the 'big houses' entered the final chapters of their existence, so too did the memorable lifestyle of those who lived in them. To many observers, like Louis MacNeice, the end was long overdue: "In most cases these houses maintain no culture worth speaking of – nothing but absolute bravado, an insidious bonhomie, and a way with horses."

The land reforms introduced a whole new class of peasant proprietors, but the problem of Ireland – or rather, Ireland's problem with England – did not go away. A new struggle for national independence was under way.

Cultural revolution

"Damn Home Rule! What we're out for is the land. The land matters. All the rest is talk." This remark by a nationalist was recorded during the Land War, but the speaker was wrong, for all the rest was not just talk. In the closing decades of the 19th century, an emerging sense of national consciousness gave rise to a cultural revolution that allied itself with and radicalized the political movement in preparation for a break with Britain. The cultural renaissance started with events like the 1884 founding of the Gaelic Athletic Association (GAA) and its call for Irish sports to replace English ones.

In 1893 the Gaelic League was established in the wake of a seminal lecture by the Protestant Douglas Hyde on "The necessity of de-anglicising the Irish people." "We are daily importing from England ... her music, her dances and her manifold mannerisms, her games and her pastimes, to the utter discredit of our own grand national sports...as though we were ashamed of them," Hyde declared. In response there followed – in all senses of the word – a dramatic literary revolution that began with Anglo-Irish writers: Lady Gregory, WB Yeats and others founded the Irish Literary Theatre, later the Abbey Theatre, in 1898, and the following year Arthur Griffith started the *United Irishmen* newspaper. Griffith knew Yeats, but he also knew the

(Background)

socialist James Connolly, and out of such a matrix evolved the movement for complete separation from Britain and not just Home Rule. Sinn Féin ('Ourselves') was formed in 1907, and the idea of withdrawing elected Irish MPs from the British Parliament at Westminster began to take shape.

At this stage Irish MPs were still committed to Home Rule rather than complete independence, and when elections in 1910 left the nationalists holding the balance of power it seemed certain that the Liberal party would have no choice but to push through a Home Rule Bill. The ability of the House of Lords to veto legislation was limited by the Liberals to two years, and when Home Rule legislation was blocked by the House of Lords in 1912, it was only a matter of waiting. In September 1914 the bill became an act. By that time, however, events outside parliament's control were shaping Ireland's future.

Easter 1916

Armed opposition by Protestants to Home Rule in Ulster and the obvious willingness of groups in Ulster and Britain to subvert Home Rule quickly led to the formation of parallel nationalist forces. The Irish Volunteers were founded in 1913, and in March of the following year the Irish Citizen Army was re-formed from a nucleus force that had emerged in response to the lockout in a great Dublin strike of the year before. Militants like Hanna Sheehy Skeffington formed Cumann na mBan (Association of Women) to make sure women were not left out of the struggle. Erskine Childers, with his wife Molly and Mary Spring Rice, imported guns on his yacht *Asgard*, and soon Volunteers were marching openly on the streets of Dublin.

The outbreak of the First World War in August 1914 led to the suspension of the Home Rule Act, and when Redmond, the leader of the Irish MPs, declared support for the war and a willingness for nationalists to volunteer, this led to a decisive break with Sinn Féin. Redmond and the bulk of the Volunteers formed their own group and the radicals who were left, members of the IRB, began planning for an armed uprising in conjunction with James Connolly and the Irish Citizen Army.

On Easter Monday, 24 April 1916 strategic areas around Dublin were occupied, and an Irish Republic was declared from outside the occupied General Post Office on O'Connell Street.

While middle-class Dubliners were quick to condemn the rising as British troops moved in and the city centre became a war zone, the rebels gained some support in working-class areas. The insurgents surrendered on 29 April with the loss of around 64 republicans, 132 British troops and 250 civilians. Military trials and the shooting dead of 15 rebels, the first execution of rebels since Robert Emmet in 1803, led to a dramatic shift in public opinion and a surge in support for Sinn Féin. In July 1917 Eamon de Valera, the only commander of the rising to survive, won a by-election in Clare and became president of Sinn Féin. By the following year, after the death of Redmond, the Irish parliamentary party withdrew from Westminster and in the 1918 general election Sinn Féin swept the board. At the beginning of 1919, an alternative Irish government was formed in Dublin, with the minutes recorded in Irish and French, and the Republic, first declared in 1916, was ratified. In the same month the first shots were fired in what became known as the War of Independence.

Outside the GPO Patrick Pearse declared "the right of the people of Ireland to the ownership of Ireland and the unfettered control of Irish destinies to be sovereign and indefeasible" and called for the "allegiance of every Irishman and Irishwoman."

War of Independence

By January 1919 the Volunteers, who had shot dead two Royal Irish Constabulary men in Tipperary that month, were becoming known as the Irish Republican Army (IRA). Britain faced the problem that, much as they wanted to ignore the illegally constituted Irish government, it was fast becoming the de facto ruling body for the people of

Background

Ireland. Homeowners were paying tax, in the form of rates, to the new Dáil Éireann (Irish Parliament) and alternative Sinn Féin courts were operating across the country.

The ranks of the IRA were being filled by professional soldiers returning from the First World War, and Michael Collins emerged as the charismatic and intelligent director of organization for the new rebel army. Collins had taken part in the 1916 rising and was subsequently elected to the first Dáil for South Cork, becoming minister for finance, but he achieved popular and lasting fame as a guerrilla republican fighting the British. There were by now around 3,000 IRA men on active duty, and they forced the British into recruiting thousands of ex-servicemen to help the RIC defeat them. Known as the Black and Tans (a famous pack of hounds in Limerick) because they wore khaki and police caps and belts (there was no immediate supply of police uniforms available), they were responsible for retaliating against Collins' most daringly planned deed in 1920 when 10 government intelligence officers were assassinated one Sunday morning. The Black and Tans retaliated by executing three prisoners in jail, and driving lorries into Croke Park where a GAA game was taking place. They fired into the crowd, killing 14 and shooting a Tipperary player. The next month, December 1920, a large part of Cork City was burned in retaliation for a guerrilla attack that killed 18 Black and Tans at Kilmichael in County Cork.

Attempts by British intelligence to infiltrate the guerrilla republican movement failed because its officers could not understand the Irish accent; surveillance equipment, according to a secret report written in 1921 by the head of Dublin Castle (the headquarters of Britain's counter-insurgency group), failed because "microphones of English manufacture seem ill-adapted to the Irish brogue." The report made an observation that could easily have been made in Belfast in the 1970s or 80s: "It has been said that no European can fathom the mind of an Oriental, and it might equally be said that no Englishman can fully grasp the inner psychology of the Irish rebel character."

Partition and civil war

By May 1920, when the IRA were able to launch an attack on the Custom House in the heart of the capital, the British were ready to start talking. A truce was signed in July and peace talks scheduled in London. The perceived difficulty for the British in recognizing an Irish republic was the impact it might have in other parts of the Empire, especially India, so they bargained for an independent Ireland owing allegiance to King and Commonwealth. The Ulster problem was dealt with by the partition of Ireland, and the notion of a boundary commission that, the Irish delegates were told, would later recommend the transfer to Ireland of counties with a nationalist majority and thus render impractical the continued partition of Northern Ireland.

The sticking point was not partition but the required oath to the King and the British Commonwealth, the latter term being used here for the first time by Britain, and the denial of republican status to an independent Ireland. The delegates should have consulted with de Valera and others who were back in Dublin before signing any treaty, but Michael Collins, who was in London, knew that his guerrilla army was running out of ammunition; so, on the morning of 10 December, the treaty was signed in London pending ratification in the Dáil in Dublin.

The treaty was ratified but it was a close call – a majority of only seven secured its passage – and de Valera and his anti-Treaty supporters walked out of the Dáil in protest.

The split vote in the Treaty debate in the Dáil also led to a split in the IRA, and those opposed to the deal signed in London became known as the Irregulars. In April 1922 the Four Courts in Dublin were occupied by Irregulars, and following the assassination of a British army officer in London demands were made by Britain for action against the rebels. In June the Four Courts were shelled under orders from Collins, and a civil war began that divided families, occasioned terrible atrocities on

Ulster Says No

Background

The British Conservative Party's attitude to Ireland and the nature of present-day opposition to the Good Friday Agreement can be directly traced back to events in the early decades of the 20th century. Opposition to Home Rule in Ulster led to calls for retaining the union with Britain and Edward Carson, the lawyer who destroyed Oscar Wilde in court, emerged as the unionist leader. The Ulster Volunteer Force was formed in 1913, arms were imported from Germany, and calls for violent opposition to Home Rule became strident. There was no doubting the willingness of the 'law and order' Conservative Party led by Bonar Law to support such extra-parliamentary measures, and the façade of parliamentary politics was further weakened in 1914 when 58 British army officers stationed at the Curragh made it clear that they would refuse to take action against an armed uprising in Ulster. The Orange Order, resurrecting the 1641 rising and the Siege of Derry, was able to point to the Catholic Church's ruling that mixed marriages between Catholics and Protestants take place only in Catholic churches and that children of such marriages be brought up as Catholics. The fear that Home Rule meant Rome Rule was not paranoia; it was a fear fully justified in the light of the later Catholic-inspired legislation that characterized post-independence Ireland, but unionists acted as if the whole of Ulster was Protestant when they only constituted 56% of the population and held a majority in only four counties. This did not prevent Bonar Law from pledging active support for resistance to Home Rule: "We intend, with the help of the Almighty, to keep the pledge, and the keeping of it involves more than the making of speeches."

both sides, and led to a trauma in Irish politics that was felt well into the 1970s. It also killed far more people – over 800 government soldiers and around 5,000 anti-Treaty men – than the War of Independence, even though it lasted only a year.

Anti-revolution, 1920s-1950s

When the Irish finally took charge of their own country – or at least most of it – they inherited a sorry state of affairs. The British had confined industrial activity to the north, and the rural economy of the new state was stagnant after years of neglect. The political and social conservatism of the Catholic Church helped institutionalize a national malaise that was to last nearly half a century. In 1927 de Valera left Sinn Féin and founded a new party, Fianna Fáil ('Soldiers of Destiny'), which became the main opposition in the Dáil.

Disagreement with Britain over the payment of land annuities – de Valera refused to pay – led to Britain imposing high tariffs on Irish imports. Ireland retaliated in like manner, and life was hard for many. After the turmoil of revolutionary struggle and a bitter civil war, Ireland's leaders embarked on a social and political programme decidedly unrevolutionary in nature. In 1926 a Committee of Inquiry into Evil Literature led to the creation of a censorship board that kept most 20th-century classics out of the country. Freud, Sartre, Steinbeck, Salinger, Orwell, Gide, Mailer, Tennessee Williams, Dylan Thomas were all banned, not to mention every Irish writer then winning recognition elsewhere: Shaw, O'Casey, Joyce (for *Stephen Hero*, not *Ulysses*), Beckett, Behan, Kate O'Brien. Under successive de Valera governments the country went into a near-terminal state of moribund conservatism: Sean O'Casey summed up the malaise by declaring "We're standing on our knees now." The country closed in on itself, and the legacy of resentment at England saw Ireland refuse to take sides in World War II, withdraw from the Commonwealth and decline to join NATO.

Ireland remained officially neutral during the Second World War. Conscription was never extended to Northern Ireland. Yet 68,000 men enlisted from Southern Ireland, 52,900 from Northern Ireland. Southern Irishmen won eight Victoria Crosses, one went to a Belfast sailor

In 1937 de Valera produced a new constitution that enshrined church ideology: blasphemy was made a crime, divorce made impossible and, until the 1998 referendum allowed for their change, Articles 2 and 3 claimed the right to unite the whole of Ireland and oppose partition. In a radio broadcast in 1943 de Valera evoked a vision of Ireland as a rural paradise filled "with the contests of athletic youths and the laughter of comely maidens".

1960s – the awakening

In 1959 de Valera finally moved aside to become President of Ireland, a non-executive and largely ceremonial role, and his successor, Sean Lemass, started to breath new life into the country. The emigration rate halved as new jobs were created, and the ebullience of this era was enshrined in John F Kennedy's presidential visit in 1963. The great-grandson of an Irish emigrant, Kennedy's visit gave a much-needed boost to the national psyche. Three years later saw the 50th anniversary of the Easter Rising, and the event was marked by the blowing up of the 36m-high Nelson's Pillar in O'Connell Street in Dublin by unknown nationalists. The event, causing no injuries or damage to property, was received with glee, much humour being directed at the military experts who managed to damage surrounding properties while demolishing what remained of the statue's column. In 1962 the Republic's own television channel was established.

The Haughey era

Charles Haughey attracted a few nicknames during his long reign as Taoiseach between 1987 and 1992; while respected by many, his political machinations and dubious accumulation of wealth and privilege led to him also being labelled 'The Great National Bastard'. An acronym, GUBU ('Grotesque, Unprecedented, Bizarre and Unbelievable') was coined to define the era, based on Haughey's response to events surrounding a suspected serial killer staying in the apartment of the Attorney General and the latter's decision to go on holiday before discussing it with him.

GUBU sums up fairly well the life of a politician who in 1970 was on trial for gun running to the besieged nationalists in the north, before going on to manage successfully the economy by winning the confidence of both business and trade unions. He bought Inishvickillane, a small island off the Dingle Peninsula, and a mansion set in 200 acres of land, at the same time as owing a bank nearly IR£1 million. Largesse from important businessmen, most spectacularly IR£1 million from Ben Dunne (of Dunne's stores) which had not been declared to the income tax authorities, have been the subject of government tribunals, and there is no shortage of other scandals associated with Haughey's reign as Taoiseach. He finally came to political grief in 1992 over the phone tapping of journalists, but the Houdini of his age has still somehow managed to survive imprisonment over his financial shenanigans.

Contemporary Ireland

After Haughey's resignation in 1992 Albert Reynolds was elected Taoiseach of a Fianna Fáil-Progressive Democrat (PD) government, but this fell apart when Reynolds accused a PD of dishonest testimony to an inquiry into fraud in beef exports. It was a deliberate attempt to force an election and gain an outright majority for Fianna Fáil, but it failed miserably, and this a time a coalition government with Labour was formed. Another election followed in 1994 and a Fine Gael-Labour government took its turn until June 1997, when it was the turn of Fianna Fáil and the Progressive Democrats to rule under Bertie Ahern. This remains the ruling coalition of government, although in Ireland general elections and new governments are formed with what seems startling frequency.

Fianna Fáil and Fine Gael – Spot the Difference?

Sometimes, it seems, the historical difference between the two main political parties in Ireland is the only one worth mentioning. Fine Gael (pronounced 'Feen Gale') was formed in 1933 from an older pro-Treaty party whereas Fianna Fáil (pronounced 'Feena Foil') was founded by de Valera from the anti-Treaty faction of nationalists. Fianna Fáil still carries the mantle of republicanism, and because they were in power at the time of the 1998 negotiations over the North they were able to sell the Agreement to nationalists in the Republic in a way that Fine Gael could never have done. Apart from this ideological difference, it is difficult to tell the two apart. Fine Gael portrays itself as more middle class, gaining more support from farmers, professionals and business people than Fianna Fáil, which likes to present itself as the party of ordinary working people and small farmers. Their economic policies are basically the same, and what makes contemporary politics in Ireland so boring is the fact that the other main parties, the Progressive Democrats and Labour, offer few alternatives to the electorate. Coalition governments come and go, and the electorate seems not to care who really runs the country. A general election is set to take place in 2002 and, most likely, yet another coalition government will be cobbled together.

Background

Travelling through the countryside in the west of Ireland one is struck by what appears to be a cow-based economy. Indeed, over 70% of farm output comes from cattle and milk. In the eastern counties the land supports more cereals and giant fields of barley and beet thrive alongside the ubiquitous herd of black and white Fresian cows. What is surprising, however, is that less than 15% of the working population is engaged with the land. The prosperity that is so evident in contemporary Ireland is based on new light industries like electronics and computer components. Ireland's GDP now outstrips Britain's, and Eurokids flock to the capital for work and language learning. The 1916 rising is no longer celebrated, problems in the North are being argued over in constitutional non-violent terms, and Irish people at long last feel confident about themselves because, as more than one commentator has noted, Ireland may have lost the leprechaun but has most definitely found the pot of gold.

There are signs, however, that the pot of gold is too dependent on foreign investment for its own good. Towards the end of 2001, and continuing into 2002, a growing number of redundancies are occurring as foreign companies, especially American ones, close down factories and decamp with their fat profits intact. It remains to be seen if this is a temporary blip or a worrying indication of a future trend.

Northern Ireland

The origins of the Province

Northern Ireland came into existence with the Government of Ireland Act of 1920 and remained within the United Kingdom after the rest of the island achieved dominion status following the treaty of 1921. The story starts with the plantation of Ulster in the 17th century (see page 645), but the more pressing background to the partition of Ireland lay with the successful resistance of Ulster unionists in the 1911-14 period to the increasing likelihood of Home Rule for Ireland (see page 649). They originally wanted to be ruled directly from London, but grew to cherish their devolved parliament, where they enjoyed an overall majority of seats, once it became clear the British would let them get on with what was in effect a one-party state. In 1925 the boundary commission recommended no significant changes in the border between the Free State and Northern Ireland, and an issue that was not paramount in the causes or course of the civil war was left to fester.

From inequality to direct rule

From its inception in 1920 until the Good Friday Agreement of 1998, Northern Ireland was an artificial construct designed to secure unionist control. Three counties of Ulster – Cavan, Donegal and Monaghan – were excluded from its creation because their majority Catholic populations would have weakened the ability of unionists to control the state and form every government, until direct rule from Westminster was established in 1972. The Northern Ireland Parliament began life in Belfast City Hall in June 1921, moving to the grandiloquent, purpose-built building at Stormont, in the eastern suburbs of Belfast, in 1932. By this time, gerrymandering of the constituencies ensured unionist majorities and the Special Powers Act of 1922 gave the government the right to prohibit meetings or processions without cause. The 12th July, marking the defeat of Catholics at the Battle of the Boyne (see page 645), became a national holiday and Easter processions by Catholics were attacked. The Royal Ulster Constabulary (RUC) was formed in 1922 and its Catholic element rapidly declined from a peak of around 20% in 1923 to half that.

The civil and political strife that erupted in 1968, and which led four years later to direct rule, was the result of decades of misrule which saw Catholics became second-class citizens, discriminated against in housing and employment and their cultural identity as Irish people vigorously suppressed.

The Northern Ireland Civil Rights Movement, modelling itself on the movement for racial equality in the USA, was formed in 1967. The following year saw their marches attacked by loyalist gangs. In 1969 an Apprentice Boys' march notched up the level of violence. The event was an annual march, triumphantly celebrating the siege of 1689 (see page 645) that paraded through Catholic residential areas in Derry, but this time the march provoked rioting. The Protestant backlash saw Catholics fleeing as refugees across the border in trains that were stoned by mobs as they passed through Protestant areas. British troops were called in to restore order, the IRA re-emerged, direct rule was introduced and 30 years of bombing and bloodshed followed. Unionist control of the Stormont government between 1920 and 1972 allowed its permanent majority to vote down every nationalist proposal, bar one solitary measure – the 1930 Wild Birds Act.

It is easy to blame sectarian unionism for the inequalities and iniquities that led to the explosive events of the late 1960s and their aftermath, but it is equally clear that the sectarian Catholicism of the southern Ireland state gave Protestants in the North good reason to fear for their cultural survival in a united Ireland.

The British Army arrived in Northern Ireland in August 1969, intended as a short-term measure to deal with the escalating violence that was developing between Catholic street action and the loyalist backlash. At first, beleaguered Catholic residents welcomed the presence of troops but this soon changed as the army was seen to be not acting impartially. At this stage, the IRA was virtually non-existent but it quickly re-emerged as Catholic communities looked for support. The violence began to spiral upwards, with events like Bloody Sunday (see page 532) and the Provisional IRA soon eclipsing the less militant official wing of the movement. The Provisionals launched a campaign of terrorist warfare against the security forces and commercial targets, and the introduction of internment, imprisonment without trial, caused the violence to escalate even more. In 1970, 25 people died and by 1972 this number had reached 467 and all but 30 of these fatalities occurred after internment.

In March 1972, the British government suspended the Northern Ireland government at Stormont and direct rule was introduced. A new government post was created at Westminster, a secretary of state for Northern Ireland.

The collapse of politics

In 1973, the Sunningdale agreement was an attempt to find a political settlement. Although its power-sharing executive was established for a brief while, it was destroyed by the Ulster Workers Council, a loyalist grouping with paramilitary support. The inability or unwillingness – it depends on your point of view – of the British government to stand up to the Council heralded a new and bloodier chapter in the province's history.

What followed was an intense period of open warfare between the IRA and the security forces. The IRA campaign was extended to the British mainland, hoping to force the hand of the government into making a political deal. In 1974, a bomb in a pub in Birmingham killed 21 people and more pub bombings followed in Woolwich and Guildford. The Prevention of Terrorism Act was introduced to allow lengthy detention without trial and although people were found guilty and imprisoned for the Birmingham and Guildford bombings they were released after 15 years behind bars and admitted to be innocent (one died in prison).

Up until 1976, prisoners in Northern Ireland jails who were there by dint of their involvement in the ongoing conflict had a special status that gave them the right not to wear prison uniforms. Republican protests led to hunger strikes, and in1981 this led to the death of Bobby Sands (see box page 631), who by the time of his death had been elected Member of Parliament for Fermanagh and South Tyrone. Nine more hunger strikers died over the following months.

The road to peace

The mid-1980s saw a fresh start with the signing at Hillsborough in County Down of the Anglo-Irish Agreement. A chief architect was John Hume, leader of the moderate Catholic Social and Democratic and Labour Party, and the signatories were the British and Irish prime ministers. It was a significant step forward, recognizing the failure of attempts to bring peace to Northern Ireland by a purely internal settlement, and was motivated to some extent by alarm at the growing electoral success of Sinn Féin, the political wing of the IRA.

Even more significant was the Downing Street Declaration in 1993 which pointedly invited dialogue with Sinn Féin and the IRA. In August 1994 the IRA dramatically announced "a complete cessation of military operations", and loyalist paramilitary groups followed likewise. It seemed that everyone, including the gunmen, was tired of the endless violence, and Sinn Féin under Gerry Adams emerged with a new voice that recognized continual violence was not going to solve the problems. Unionism, also aware that some kind of compromise was necessary, would later elect David Trimble as a leader willing to negotiate with the traditional enemy.

Enter President Clinton, stage right, who now brought a powerful American influence to bear on the various talks and discussions that were going on in every camp. United States Senator George Mitchell headed an international commission that pushed matters forward with the enunciation of six ground rules for future discussions between the various parties. These included a commitment to peaceful means, but the astonishing progress that seemed to be in the making was shattered by a bomb at Canary Wharf in London, in 1996, announcing the end of the IRA ceasefire. The fragile alliance between moderate and diehard members of the IRA had come to an end over the perceived willingness of the British

Glossary of political terms

Alliance Party Formed in 1970, a non-sectarian mix of middle-class members of both communities, with seats in the Assembly but none at Westminster

Black and Tans British recruits, so-called from the colours of their uniform, recruited to combat republicans fighting for independence after 1918; infamous for their brutality

Civil War war that broke out in Ireland, after the signing of the 1921 Treaty, between those who accepted the Treaty and those who opposed it

Continuity IRA Also known as Irish Continuity Army Council, came to public notice in 1996 after claiming responsibility for a number of attacks.

Dáil Eireann the Irish parliament, often referred to as simply the Dáil (pronounced doil)

DUP The Democratic Unionist Party, led by Ian Paisley, vehemently anti-republican and opposed to the Good Friday Agreement

Fenian a member of the 19th-century Irish Republican Brotherhood

Fianna Fáil a political party (Soldiers of destiny), founded in 1927 by de Valera in terms of opposition to partition and while still perceived as some to be more republican than Fine Gael, it is every bit as right wing

Fine Gael a right-wing political party, with origins in the pro-Treaty group after 1922, barely distinguishable from Fianna Fáil

IRA Irish Republican Army. Between 1916 and 1921 the IRA was the army of the Provisional Government fighting the British and relatively dormant until trouble erupted in Northern Ireland at the end of the 1960s. Between 1970 and the still-existing ceasefire called in 1998 the IRA was actively engaged in a guerilla war against the British

Loyalist people in Northern Ireland, staunch Protestants mostly, who are strongly in favour of remaining part of Britain

LVF Loyalist Volunteer Force; Sectarian, paramilitary banned group

Nationalists people who wish to see an united Ireland

Orange Order Protestant society dedicated to preserving the memory of William's victory at the Battle of the Boyne. Founded in 1795 and formerly represented within the Ulster Unionist Party

government to bow to Unionist intransigence by insisting on the decommissioning of IRA weapons before talks could get under way.

The electoral defeat of Britain's Tory government in mid-1997, and its replacement by a Labour government not dependent on the Unionist votes at Westminster, heralded another fresh start. The IRA declared a restoration of their ceasefire and new talks got under way. Despite some outbreaks of violence at the end of 1997, including the assassination of Billy Wright, the leader of a loyalist paramilitary group, by a republican paramilitary group known as the Irish National Liberation Army (INLA), a breakthrough emerged and the Good Friday Agreement was signed in April 1998.

The Good Friday Agreement

The Good Friday Agreement provided for a new Assembly of 108 members and an executive of 12 from the various communities. The new Assembly would bring direct rule from Westminster to an end and return to a devolved government responsible for the affairs of Northern Ireland. The essential difference is that the new Assembly cannot be gerrymandered to ensure unionist control.

The Good Friday Agreement in 1998 reached as fine a political balance as could ever be achieved in Ireland and the terms of the agreement were resoundingly endorsed by referendums held both sides of the border: 71% in the North and 94% in the Republic voted yes to peace and a political settlement that accepted the need for compromise. Elections for the new assembly that would govern the

Progressive Democrats *a political party founded in 1985 by a group of Fianna Fáil politicians opposed to the rule of the then leader, Charles Haughey*

PUP *Progressive Unionist Party, the political wing of the UVF, and crucial to the success of the Good Friday Agreement. Led by David Ervine, a moderating force compared to the DUP.*

Real IRA *Formed in 1997 by dissident IRA members who opposed the peace process and the political leadership of Sinn Féin.*

Republicans *people committed to a united Ireland as a republic; sometimes used interchangeably with the term nationalist*

RUC *Royal Ulster Constabulary, Northern Ireland's armed police force, predominantly Protestant. Regarded by the Catholic community as sectarian; currently being reformed as a result of the post-Good Friday Agreement Patten report*

Sinn Fein *(Ourselves Alone): Nationalist organization founded in 1903 and nowadays a political party in Ireland, particularly strong in the North, where it represents the political wing of the IRA. Led by Gerry Adams.*

SDLP *Social Democratic and Labour Party, led by John Hume for many years, nationalist but not as republican as Sinn Fein.*

Treaty *the Treaty of 1921 that divided Ireland into the Republic and Northern Ireland*

Taoiseach *(pronounced 'tee-shock') the prime minister of the Republic*

UDA *Ulster Defence Association; Largest Protestant paramilitary organization, formed in 1971*

UDF *Ulster Defence Force, an illegal paramilitary Protestant organization*

UDP *Ulster Defence Regiment, political wing of the LVF*

UFF *Ulster Freedom Fighters; officially not existing, a Protestant paramilitary force used by the UDA to carry out attacks against republicans.*

UUP *Ulster Unionist Party, the largest and most important party opposed to republicanism, led by David Trimble.*

UVF *Ulster Volunteer Force, an illegal Protestant paramilitary force formed in 1966 and supported by several thousand hardliners.*

Background

six counties gave the Social and Democratic Party (SDLP), representing the moderate middle-class nationalist vote, 24 seats and 21.99% of the vote, the Ulster Unionist Party (UUP) 28 seats with 21.28% of the vote, the Democratic Unionist Party (DUP), hardline unionists opposed to the Good Friday Agreement, 18% and 20 seats, and Sinn Féin 18 seats with 17.65% of the vote.

Opposition to the Good Friday Agreement continued to threaten the chances of a lasting peace. The summer of 1998 saw the continuation of conflict over the Orange Order's traditional march through the Catholic Garvaghy Road area of Portadown (see box page 618). On the morning of July 12, a loyalist firebombing of a Catholic house in a mainly Protestant estate resulted in the death of three young children. Breakaway IRA dissidents formed the Real IRA and in August 1998 their bombing campaign led to horrific atrocity in Omagh, the worst in 30 years, a bomb which saw the slaughter of 29 people. Sinn Féin came off the fence with an unequivocal statement, followed by IRA visits to the homes of 60 members of the Real IRA within a 90-minute period making them an offer they could not refuse: on 7 September the Real IRA declared a total ceasefire.

Opposition to the Good Friday Agreement from hardline unionists continued to bedevil progress. As much as Trimble and his supporters wanted to move forward, there was sufficient unwillingness within his own party to bite the bullet of compromise, never mind the pressure from Ian Paisley to insist on IRA decommissioning as a pre-condition for any further movement.

Post-Good Friday

"We are committed to making conflict a thing of the past. There is a shared responsibility to removing the causes and to achieving an end to all conflict. Sinn Féin believe the violence we have seen [at Omagh] must be for all of us now a thing of the past, over, done with and gone."
Sinn Féin statement, 1 September 1998

The impasse over the implementation of the Good Friday Agreement was finally overcome in November 1999 when, after 300 hours of face-to-face talks between David Trimble and Gerry Adams, agreement was reached. In a remarkable switch of the language codes that characterise political talk in the six counties, Trimble spoke of the need to recognise different cultural traditions (acknowledging that both nationalists and republicans have rights) while Adams spoke of the need for de-commissioning (a possible end to the IRA).

On 29 November 1999 a new date entered the annals of Irish history when a coalition government was formed in Northern Ireland and direct rule from London was finally ended. The local government that had been dissolved in 1972 was replaced by one with David Trimble as First Minister but which for the first time included three Sinn Féin ministers, including as minister for education, Martin McGuinness, who could easily have been shot dead by security forces when he was the most wanted republican in Derry in the 1970s.

The future looks promising, especially after the decommissioning issue seemed to sort itself out in the course of 2001. Problems do remain, however. Diehard loyalists from Paisley's Democratic Unionist Party have taken their seats in the new Assembly with the sole purpose of trying to destroy it by whittling away at Protestant support for the present leader of the Ulster Unionist Party, David Trimble. The British government's decision to reform the overwhelmingly Protestant RUC, including a change of its name to the Police Service of Northern Ireland, has annoyed Unionists. Until the old Unionist order fully comes to terms with the new island of Ireland that is emerging, outbreaks of trouble are likely to continue. What can one say to the troubled Irish Protestant mind-set that believes that the victims of the Bloody Sunday were IRA men killed in previous gun battles whose bodies were recovered from a deep freeze?

Watch this space.

Culture

Art and architecture

Pre-Christian art & architecture

At Carrowmore in County Sligo, Swedish archaeologists have recently discovered the world's oldest building. The site (see page 481) has always been considered a Neolithic graveyard, built by people who had acquired the skills of farming and led fairly settled lives; then in summer 1999 a new site was discovered containing the cremated bones of about 50 people which carbon-dated to about 7,400 years ago, making its construction 700 years earlier than the oldest previously known free-standing building, a neolithic tomb near Poitiers in France. This indicates that in Ireland a mesolithic culture, a hunter-gatherer society, had all the skills required to erect substantial buildings.

Most of our knowledge of the architecture of early Ireland comes from funeral buildings. The earliest are the dolmens, tripod-like structures with upright megaliths supporting one or two massive capstones and covered by a cairn. Newgrange (see box on next page) represents the next stage of Irish art and architecture, adding the sophistication of corbelling for the roof and several chambers, many of them decorated with our earliest examples of Irish art – triple spirals, double spirals and lozenge patterns. The Bronze Age in Ireland has left us a legacy of quite stunning complex designs in gold torques, collars and pins, decorated bronze shields where the design

Newgrange

The monuments at Newgrange were constructed around 2500BCE, following a sweeping bend of the River Boyne and utilizing an area of some 12 sq km. There are three huge similarly sized hilltop mounds, Newgrange, Knowth and Dowth, with one tomb in the Newgrange cairn and two in each of the other two. A score of smaller passage tombs, known as satellite tombs, have been found and excavated in the area around the main monuments. Fragments of bones belonging to a few people, some cremated, were found by archaeologists working at Newgrange in the 1960s, but the site has been open for 300 years so this find is not conclusive.

Excavations at other passage tombs in Ireland have revealed evidence of mass burials, up to 24 people being buried together. The nearest equivalent groupings of megalithic tombs outside of Ireland are in Brittany and Orkney, and one theory is that the people who build these tombs at Newgrange came from Brittany, and before that the Iberian Peninsula. However, the art work of Newgrange has few parallels outside of Ireland, and it has been argued that the Boyne valley represents a unique Irish development.

The artwork inscribed on the stones at Newgrange are geometrical in design, and their non-representational nature suggests symbolic meanings. Whether they were conceived as ornamental in nature or whether they signify spiritual or magical ideas remains a mystery. In the case of some of the stones, like the huge entrance boulder, it is clear that the artist or artists regarded the whole stone as a canvas which was to be filled with an intricate and integrated pattern of spirals, concentric arcs and other designs that strove to utilize even the curving surface of the material. Tools – flint stones and wooden hammers – would have been fairly basic, and the carved motifs may be divided into curvilinear ones, like triple spirals, circles, arcs and serpent shapes, and rectilinear chevron zigzags, parallel lines, lozenge and triangular shapes. What is odd is that other types of megalithic tombs in Ireland show little evidence of any wish to inscribe patterns on stone in this way. Considering the unwieldy nature and the sheer size of these giant stones, the artwork that has survived represents one of the finest achievements of prehistoric art in Western Europe.

Background

is both functional and decorative. Like the weaponry, the architecture of this time reflected the need for defence with hill forts and promontory forts being simple stone boundaries which possibly had wooden structures inside.

The Iron age/early Christian period still saw defensive buildings in the raths and stone cashels, but usually no longer on high ground, and often with a souterrain for escape or hiding. Stonework had become decorative as well as functional, and we have several items in the Armagh cathedral and county museum reflecting this primitive but distinctly creative form, particularly the stone heads like the Tandragee Man with his brutalist appearance, and the figure with what seems rays emanating from its head. Other decorative effects are consistent with the La Tène style of decoration – swirling loops and whorls both on stonework and weapons.

This was a peaceful and productive time for Irish art and architecture before the Normans arrived, bringing their European sensibilities with them. Many people still lived in raths and crannógs, essentially settlements with an eye to defence, while church architecture was largely in the medium of wood, only a few stone buildings – such as the beehive huts of Skellig Michael or the ruins on Inismurray in County Sligo – still surviving. Where church buildings are of stone and have survived they are simple in design with arched doors, a simple nave added to the basic cell structure, and perhaps sculpture around the doors and windows. Some round towers such as the one

The early Christian period

at the monastery at Kells, County Meath, were built in the latter part of this period. The arts on the other hand were flourishing in the monasteries around the coast, demonstrated by the production of illuminated manuscripts such as the Book of Kells, the gold and metalwork of the beautiful Ardagh chalice in the National Museum, and the work of the stonemasons building the high crosses and tombs.

High crosses   Many of Ireland's Celtic crosses date back to this period before the Norman invasion. Sometimes as tall as 5m/15ft, they are carved from whatever stone was available, often sandstone or limestone which has not subsequently worn well. Their east side is often decorated in scenes from the Old Testament while the west side conveys stories from the New. Usually in the centre of the west face is the crucifixion surrounded by the typical carved and decorated ring of stone which may have stood for the cosmos, with Christ and his sacrifice at its centre. The stories chosen often illustrate a theme, and their purpose was practical – to teach and inspire the congregation. The base and side panels are covered in complex geometric designs like those in the illuminated manuscripts of the period, and when first erected they were probably painted so that the designs and stories stood out much more clearly. The best examples of high crosses from this period are at Glendalough, County Wicklow, Durrow and Clonmacnoise in County Offaly and Monasterboice in County Louth, a particularly beautiful example.

Round towers   The earliest of the Irish round towers are pre-Norman, although they continued to be built into the 12th century. They are the mediaeval equivalent of the muezzin's minaret, and once held a bell to call the monks in from the fields. Usually five storeys high, they have one window at each level, and their defensive nature is seen in the fact that the doorway is about 10 ft off the ground so that the steps could be drawn up to protect the church property in time of attack. Inside would have been a series of wooden storeys and steps.

Irish Romanesque   The Irish Romanesque style is most clearly seen in Cormac's Chapel at the Rock of Cashel in County Tipperary, and the 12th-century doorway to Clonfert Cathedral in County Galway. A typical arched doorway at Clonfert is surrounded by highly decorated columns which shelve inward in a style typical of this period, with ever more complicated swirls and patterns on the arches above the doorspace. The steeply arched pediment is again ornately carved with primitive human heads set in triangular recesses and surrounded by more ornate carvings.

Norman Gothic   The Normans brought European sophistication to the architecture of Ireland with complex gothic-style church buildings such as Christ Church Cathedral in Dublin and many monasteries, such as Sligo Abbey, which included a quadrangle with the church on the north side, the sacristy and meeting rooms on the east, refectory and dormitories on the south and storerooms on the west. Buildings were bigger and arches pointed, not for aesthetic reasons but because they were more efficient at loadbearing. Churches became larger with ornate triple-arched windows where the main characteristic of the Romanesque church had been a bulk of stone wall. Stained glass made an appearance, and later in the period the lancets between the windows become narrowed to thin stone pillars or mullions.

Secular architecture has been preserved in the form of castles, reflecting the period of warfare which filled the power vacuum after the death of Brian Boru. The first Normans built motte and bailey castles consisting of a huge mound of earth with a wooden tower on top and a semicircular fenced area at the bottom where the cattle were kept. Later, more settled Normans built square stone castles such as King John's Castle in Limerick, with towers at the corners.

Artistic expression in Norman times found its outlet in religious paraphernalia such as the shrines built to hold holy relics. Examples of these are in the Hunt Collection in Limerick and the National Gallery in Dublin.

This period was marked by the struggle between the Norman lords and the Gaelic chieftains, and as you might expect art and architecture was dominated by the need to build fortified houses and towns with protective walls around them. This is the age of the tower houses, a high square building capable of being defended but essentially a home. Artwork of the time is very practical – the misericords of St Mary's Cathedral in Limerick date back to this period, for example, and while they are beautifully carved with the figures of mythical animals they are also eminently useful pieces of church furniture.

The 15th & 16th centuries

The end of the 17th-century saw the first completely domestic and non-defensive Irish architecture. The castles and fortified houses of the Plantation years began to give way to grand mansions without any fortifications. An example of 17th-century architecture at its most creative is the 1680 Royal Hospital at Kilmainham, Dublin's oldest existing public building. Here style is as important as the purpose of the building, and great attention to detail has gone into both the exterior and interior of the building. The Georgian period saw a flowering of architecture in both public buildings and private houses in all of Ireland's cities, and in the countryside in the grand houses; a proud statement of ownership of the land on the part of the Protestant Ascendancy. Georgian architecture is modelled on the work of the 16th century architect Palladio, who left books of his designs for later architects to admire. Buildings are highly symmetrical with fake doors mirroring real doors so as to keep the symmetry. There is very little exterior ornamentation and much emphasis on proportion. The most famous and prolific of the Irish Georgian architects was Richard Castle, who designed much of Georgian Dublin as well as Powerscourt in County Wicklow.

The 17th & 18th centuries

The enormous creativity of the time was also expressing itself in the paintings of Nathaniel Hone and George Barret, and in the craft skills of the men such as Michael Stapleton, who created the plasterwork and woodcarvings of public buildings. In many cases the names of these artists are lost, but the men who made the intricate plasterwork of Newman House which still survives were called the Francini brothers. Georgian silverware is also very distinctive, as is cut glass.

With the Act of Union the great Georgian building spree came to an end, and apart from some public buildings architecture went into a decline. The Gothic Revival style emerged, characterized by architectural decoration such as flying buttresses, pointed arches and ribbed vaults. The middle years of the century saw a massive number of churches being built as Catholic emancipation gained momentum, but the Famine brought most building to a full stop. Railway station buildings in particular provided an outlet for the eclectic style of the time. Portrait painting was popular and sentimental, as were allegorical historical and biblical paintings such as those of Francis Danby. James Arthur O'Connor was another important painter of the time, concentrating on landscapes.

Victorian Ireland

After a brief Arts-and-Crafts-influenced Celtic Revival (Limerick Art Gallery contains some excellent examples) the modernist movement was the next big influence on Irish architecture, characterized by *Busáras* in Dublin and Dublin airport. Big blocks of concrete and glass followed, many of them borrowing ideas from ancient Irish structures – the public library in Bantry, for example, looks a little like a concrete dolmen if you squint sideways at it. In church architecture this pre-Celtic look has influenced the work of Liam McCormick in his additions to cathedrals such as the Catholic

The 20th century

Background

Cathedral in Armagh or the Church of St Aonghas at Burt, County Donegal. In the field of pure art Jack Yeats and Paul Henry are well known figures, focusing on ordinary events in the lives of their Irish subjects. In more modern times the most visually obvious aspect of art is in the many sculptures which decorate the cities and towns. With typical irreverence Dubliners have given these sometimes peculiar objects their own names, so Dublin now has 'the floozy in the jacuzzi', 'the hags with the bags' and 'the tart with the cart' among others.

Literature

See also 'Books' section, page 677
When it comes to Irish literature it is hard to know where to start. Take Irish playwrights, poets and novelists out of university English Literature syllabuses and there wouldn't be a lot left to teach. The Irish took the language that the English imposed on them and made their own inspired use of it, superimposing their own patterns and making it a musical language rather than one of shopkeepers and factory owners. But Irish literature flourished long before English ever drove out the native language, and is the oldest written literature in Europe.

Just as in ancient Greece, an oral tradition existed in pre-Christian Ireland for centuries before the monks arrived around the fifth century CE with their writing skills. It wasn't long before the monks began to write these epic stories down, and many of them have survived. The earliest of these is the Mythological Cycle which tells stories in prose of the Tuatha Dé Danaan, the deities of the pagan Irish. When the monks came to write down these stories the characters changed from deities (not allowed in Christianity with its single omnipotent god) to the heroes of the earlier culture. The main characters are Lug, the leader of the gods, the sea god Manannán and their families, and the chief story is that of their battle with the Formori, giants who first oppress them and then are defeated by them, calling up parallels with the Greek stories of the Olympians and Titans, and perhaps also reflecting an earlier struggle between belief systems.

The best known of the early Irish stories is the Ulster Cycle, a group of tales which features people called the Ulaid and the Connachta, the children of the gods, and the conflicts between them. The stories involve gods and heroes, magic and lots of fighting, death and blood, and feature Cú Chulain (or Cúchulainn) , the son of the god Lug, and Medb, a queen with magical powers associated with the goddess of sovereignty, often called Macha. The *Taín Bó Cuailnge*, (*The Book of the Dun Cow*), so called because part of it was written on vellum made from cowhide, contains many of these stories.

A third cycle of stories concerns the early rulers of Ireland, people such as Cormac McAirt, Conaire King of Tara, and others. They were composed between the ninth and twelfth centuries and deal with real figures from the sixth to eighth centuries. These stories would have been memorized by the *ollam*, professional story tellers and poets who would have brought them out on public occasions to recite.

The last cycle of stories is known as the Ossianic Cycle and deals with the exploits of Fionn mac Cumhaill and his sons and grandsons. The source of the stories is a 12th century text, featuring St Patrick, who meets Oisín, Fionn's son, and hears his stories and orders that they be written down. The cycle is seen as a reaction of the Gaels to the dominance of Cistercian monasticism in Ireland. Fionn and his band or Fianna are outlaws in the stories. Although the first written versions are medieval in origin, they are probably as old in oral tradition as the Ulster Cycle.

In the Middle Ages a tradition of bardic poets developed. These were a combination of praise-singers and *filí*, professional poets who memorized and told the stories of Celtic warriors and gods. Their function was to legitimize the chieftain who showed them patronage. As the centuries progressed the bards took up the political and social changes of the time, writing songs about the history of Ireland, the many

Wittgenstein's Dublin

The philosopher Wittgenstein visited Ireland on five occasions, spending almost two years there in total, appreciating the atmosphere of peace and the tranquillity of the landscape. His longest visit was in 1947, after he had given up his professorship in Cambridge. After staying first in a house in Redcross in County Wicklow and then in a remote location in Connemara, he returned to Dublin for the winter of 1948. He stayed at Ross's Hotel in Parkgate (now the Ashling) working on his final draft of what was posthumously published as Philosophical Investigations. Wittgenstein dabbled with the idea of settling in Dublin and becoming a psychiatrist and felt he could live in the city, though he had little time for Dublin's

Georgian architecture: "The people who built these houses had the good taste to know that they had nothing very important to say: and therefore they didn't attempt to express anything." Far more to his liking was Bewley's Café in Grafton Street where, after repeated visits, he was delighted to be recognized by a waitress who brought him his customary lunch of an omelette and coffee without being asked. Unlike Yeats, who reluctantly visited a pub on one occasion in his life, there is no record of Wittgenstein ever ordering a pint of Guinness in a bar. He did enjoy walking in Phoenix Park though, and in the Botanic Gardens he used to sit and think in one of the heated greenhouses and make jottings in his notebook.

battles fought, and the gradual decline of Gaelic Ireland in the face of Anglo-Irish control. By the 19th century the bardic tradition was almost extinct; some of the poems had been translated and printed but many were lost. Gaelic as a language was fast disappearing from Ireland. The Gaelic Revival in the late 19th century stirred things up a little, but the old style of epic writing had finished and the Irish-language poets of the 20th century wrote in a modern vernacular idiom about things that were real to them. In modern times there is a large output of writing in Irish, but a very small reading public.

As Gaelic went into terminal decline Anglo-Irish writing, as if to rub salt in the wounds of the conquered, flourished. The 17th century saw the terrible wit of Jonathan Swift (1667-1745), the son of an Englishman, born in Dublin and educated in Ireland. Deeply committed to Anglicanism, opposed to religious toleration or equality, he nonetheless used his writing to accuse the government in England of misgovernment and short-sightedness in relation to Ireland. A contemporary of Swift was William Congreve, genetically English but educated in Kilkenny and Dublin, and a lawyer at the Middle Temple in Dublin. He wrote comedies of manners and is considered one of the English Restoration dramatists. George Farquhar (1677-1707), another contemporary of Swift's, was the son of an Anglican clergyman from Derry, and may well have lived through some of the siege of that city. His stage comedies featured some of the first sympathetic stage Irishmen who, unlike those of previous writers, had a higher moral sense than the Englishmen they dealt with, and often, like Roebuck in Love and a Bottle, were the hero of the play. From Clonmel, County Tipperary, the son of an Englishman and Irishwoman, Laurence Sterne (1713-68) is famous for his novel Tristram Shandy. The novel is innovative and stands in the Anglo-Irish tradition despite his only half-Irishness. It self-consciously refers to Swift, and its influence can be seen in the work of James Joyce. Sheridan (1751-1816), Wilde (1854-1900) and Shaw (1856-1950) are more widely-read authors, all in the Anglo-Irish tradition but all living their adult lives in London.

An innovative novelist of the early 19th century is Maria Edgeworth (1767-1849) whose novels are among the earliest to be set in a specific region of the country; she inspired Sir Walter Scott in his writings. Much of the work of her middle years is heavy and moralistic, influenced by her father who actually wrote the worst of the sermonizing contained within them, but *Castle Rackrent*, *Belinda* and *Ormonde* are good reads and provide great insight into the Irish landlord classes of the 19th century. In her later years she spent much time trying to alleviate the sufferings of the people on her estate during the Famine.

Later writers from the same class are Edith Somerville (1858-1949) and Violet Martin (1862-1915), who wrote as Somerville and Ross. They examine the foolishness and pathos of the declining years of the big houses and their occupants. After Martin's death Somerville wrote several more successful novels, which she continued to publish under the joint names in the belief that she had an understanding with her partner which went beyond death.

At the end of the 19th century the Irish literary revival began with writing both in Irish and English. William Butler Yeats (1856-1939) was a member of the movement. The son of Irish Church of Ireland parents, he grew up in England and Ireland. He read translations of the Irish myths and became determined to revive the cultural heritage of Ireland, and his early poetry reflects that determination. In 1894 he met and made close friends with Lady Gregory, and the two planned the Irish Literary Theatre, to be realized as the Abbey Theatre in Dublin. His poetry is full of a sense of the mystical nature of the Irish countryside and sadness for the loss of the Celtic culture. In his last years he became disillusioned with Irish politics and took to spiritualism.

James Joyce (1882-1941) died just two years after Yeats, but was a very different kettle of fish. He scoffed at the mysticism of the Gaelic Revival, but his work is in many ways more recognizably Irish than anything Yeats wrote. He was the son of a Catholic chancer, who put his money into this and that and lost all of it. Extremely intelligent, Joyce was educated free of charge by the Jesuits, but then turned his back on his religion and Ireland and never lived there again. His works – *Dubliners*, a series of short stories; *A Portrait of the Artist as a young Man*; *Ulysses*; and *Finnegan's Wake* – make great reading for anyone interested in the workings of the Irish mind, and since the Irish state started to acknowledged his existence – some time after his death – he has gained the recognition in his own country that he deserves. You used to be able to see him artificially smiling at you from the now-defunct 10 pound note, or you can join the hundreds of people who celebrate his novel *Ulysses* on June 16th every year in Dublin.

A good friend of Joyce was Samuel Beckett (1909-89), Nobel Prize winner and author of the play *Waiting for Godot*. Beckett's biography reads like an adventure story – stalked by Joyce's daughter Lucia, stabbed by a pimp in the backstreets of Paris, a member of the Resistance during the war, betrayed but escaped to Free France, holder of the Croix de Guerre. His works are painfully funny though full of suffering, and he was notorious for refusing permission for his material to be produced for fear that it wouldn't be done exactly right. His shortest play is *Breath*, which lasts about a minute. He too despised the Celtic Revival, and in his novel *Murphy* the protagonist attempts to kill himself by repeatedly headbutting the buttocks of the statue of Cú Chulain in the GPO in O'Connell Street, which was erected in memory of those who died in the Easter Rising.

Kate O'Brien (1897-1974) was born in Limerick, the daughter of a horse dealer who made lots of money and then lost it. Her novels are about the complexities of being female and living up to the demands of the church. Several of them were, as you might expect, banned in Ireland. Her most famous novel is *The Ante-Room*. Although she lived most of her adult life in England, her novels are centred very much in the Irish middle classes.

Brendan Behan (1923-64) is another writer whose life story would fit neatly into one of his plays. Born into a working-class Dublin family, he was arrested and imprisoned in Britain at the age of 16 for taking part in an IRA bombing campaign. He

Field Day

At a time when no one wanted to know about Ireland and its culture, a relatively unknown writer, Brian Friel, and a very unknown actor, Stephen Rea, formed a theatre group called the Field Day Theatre company in Derry. They attracted the cooperation of other writers and people in the arts – Tom Paulin, Seamus Deane (a poet who later became the director of Field Day), David Hammond the film maker, and Seamus Heaney. Situated on the border of the two states, with the benefit of two cultural traditions, Catholic and Protestant, Field Day offered writers and audiences a 'Fifth Province', a place where it was safe to look at what Ireland was without breaking cultural taboos. One of its first successes was Friel's Translations, which was performed in the Guildhall in Derry and then went on tour around Ireland with Stephen Rea and Liam Neeson in its cast, playing in school halls to audiences of farmers who recognized its cultural significance. Throughout the 1980s Field Day grew in reputation, putting on productions by Friel, Tom Kilroy, Stewart Parker and Terry Eagleton, and producing pamphlets on all aspects of Irish culture, culminating in 1991 in the Field Day Anthology of Irish Writing, *which sadly left out most women writers. Coming under a barrage of revisionist and feminist criticism, Field Day closed down in 1992 but reformed in 1994.*

Background

spent three years in English borstals, where he began to practise his craft of writing. Back in Ireland he was arrested again for the attempted murder of a detective, and spent five more years in prison in Ireland. While in prison he wrote poetry in Irish and his autobiographical novel *Borstal Boy*. He died of drink at the height of his popularity. His best works are *The Quare Fellow* and *The Hostage*, both plays.

Like Behan, Sean O'Casey (1880-1964) was working-class, but this time born into a Protestant family. Like Behan he did manual work to make ends meet and in his early years was a great joiner... He 'joined' both the fledgling IRA and the Orange Order, but it was James Larkin's trade union which finally claimed his allegiance. His first play, *Shadow of a Gunman*, was produced by the Abbey Theatre in 1923, and was followed by *Juno and the Paycock* and *The Plough and the Stars*. His plays are written in the Dublin vernacular, and shocked and horrified middle-class Irish audiences with their language and honesty. Like other writers of his generation he was disgusted by the new Irish government and moved permanently to England.

In modern times the names come thick and fast. Christy Brown, Roddy Doyle, JP Donleavy, Liam O'Flaherty, John McGahern, John Banville, Mary Lavin, Edna O'Brien, Frank McCourt, Iris Murdoch, Clare Boylan, Molly Keane, Maeve Binchy are all highly successful and revered novelists.

Playwrights include Brian Friel, whose brilliant play Translations changed the way that people looked at Irish history, John B Keane whose play *The Field* is an essential read for anyone who wants to understand the Irish attitude to the land, Hugh Leonard, Tom Mackintyre and Martin Mc Donagh. Sebastian Barry, a novelist, short story writer and playwright, has had considerable critical success in London and New York with his plays *The Steward of Christendom* and *Our Lady of Sligo*, which are concerned with the sense of Irish identity and fitting in.

In poetry there is the Nobel Prize winner Seamus Heaney (1939-) from County Derry, Louis MacNeice (1907-1963) whose poetry, like Heaney's, is influenced by his Northern Ireland childhood, Patrick Kavanagh whose poetry reflects the harsh lives of a farming community in the North and Tom Paulin (1949-) from Belfast, whose poetry is full of the state of mind created by the political situation in the North. Other poets who write about Ireland include Thomas Kinsella, John Montague, Eavan Boland and Brendan Kennelly.

Cinema

See page 172 for more information on Irish cinema

Ireland has always provided an excellent source of actors and locations for movies, although the recent cash injections of the the last decade haven't always been available. In recent years both Dublin and Belfast have rarely had a day without a film crew blocking the streets, and in little pubs all over Ireland you can see black and white stills of the locals dressed up as mariners, Scottish warriors and 19th-century peasants amongst other things. In the 1950s the village of Cong came to the screens of the world in the movie *The Quiet Man* directed by John Ford, and has never really recovered. Then *Ryan's Daughter* was filmed on the Dingle Peninsula in 1970, and you can now take guided tours of the spots where Robert Mitchum nearly drowned and the set was built for the village, although most of it blew down in 1997. The next big star movie made with chiefly American actors was *Far and Away* in1991, a Cruise and Kidman vehicle which left everyone wincing at the Irish accents and which actually used some of the backstreets of Dublin to represent Boston. These were all movies with an Irish theme, but Ireland has provided some other strange locations. *Moby Dick* was filmed by John Huston around Youghal in County Cork in 1956, while *Educating Rita*, a movie about an English Open University student and her tutor, was filmed in Trinity College. In 1994 a piece of Irish mountainside became Scotland for a few weeks while Mel Gibson filmed *Braveheart*, and lots of Irish students as well as the territorial army filled in the crowd scenes. If you look very carefully you might see some of the same faces in *Saving Private Ryan* directed by Stephen Spielberg. The biggest surprise hit movie made in Ireland has to be *The Commitments*, directed by Alan Parker in 1990, filmed with an entirely Irish cast around north Dublin and displaying the grim reality of north Dublin life as opposed to the quaint beauty of the Irish countryside in the earlier big movies. It, and the previous year's *My Left Foot*, the story of a paralysed young boy's life directed by Jim Sheridan, set a high standard and created interest in the real Ireland which has spawned several good films since. In 1990 Jim Sheridan made *The Field*, from the play by John B Keane, about the desperate fight for one small field in western Ireland. Filmed around Leenane in County Galway, it is harsh and unsentimental in its portrayal of rural Ireland. The 1992 movie *The Crying Game* directed by Neil Jordan tells the bleak story of an IRA man who strikes up a relationship with the lover of the man he helped to kill. Jim Sheridan took up the theme of the Troubles in 1993 to make *In the Name of the Father* with Daniel Day-Lewis and Emma Thompson about the injustice meted out to the Conolly family, better known as the Guildford Four, in the early 1970s. In 1995 *Nothing Personal* took up the theme of the North again, this time looking at the chaos created in the lives of bystanders caught up in the Troubles and the terrible waste of young lives which the last 25 years has brought about. Michael Collins was a big blockbuster in 1996, which set the whole of Ireland arguing about the treatment of de Valera and displayed Julia Roberts' feeble efforts at an Irish accent. By this time the Troubles had become a moneyspinner, and 1996 also saw the release of *Some Mother's Son*, another innocent person caught up in the troubles as her son takes part in the hunger strike which killed Bobby Sands. Helen Mirren does an excellent job as the respectable mother. By this time the North and the IRA were almost a cliché: witness Harrison Ford inadvertently twice getting caught up in the Troubles, once with Brad Pitt doing the worst Irish accent ever recorded in *The Devil's Own* (1996).

To get back to intelligent movie-making, the best movie to come out of Ireland in 1998 was *The General*, directed by John Boorman, about a comical Dublin thug who gets caught up with the UVF and suffers the consequences. In the same year the first Irish road movie was released, *I Went Down* directed by Paddy Breathnach, a funny story about innocents mixed up with gangsters and refreshingly free of hooded gunmen.

Neil Jordan stands out in particular as an excellent Irish film-maker. Before he got big money and made *Michael Collins* his films included *Angel* (1982), set in Northern Ireland long before it became chic, *Mona Lisa*, *The Crying Game*, *The Company of Wolves*, and his most recent movie, set in small town Ireland, *The Butcher Boy*.

Music

The earliest form that Irish music is known to have taken is in the songs sung by the bards to the music of the metal-stringed harp. None of it was written down until the 17th century, and the earliest music to survive is the work of the harpist Turlough O'Carolan. Later collections date back to the Belfast harp festival of 1792. These were Gaelic and Scottish jigs and reels which took on an Irish character. In the 18th century the Irish traditional music that we recognize emerged. The harp, the instrument of the bards, was in decline, and the playing of reels and hornpipes on fiddle, flute and uillean pipes emerged. Each county had its own style of music, and some of the distinctions can still be heard. Early in the century the flute was introduced via Dublin.

The most commonly available printed source of music was the ballad sheets which emerged after every national event, telling the story in song; these sheets were bought and copied, thus making their way around the country. Murders, rebellions, hangings – the news travelled via the songsheets. Some of these songs outlived their immediate interest and survived; other disappeared. Dance masters travelled around the country, staying in each village for a few weeks and teaching the latest dances and tunes to the locals. They were eagerly awaited and received a royal welcome when they arrived. If two masters met on their journey the village would have a contest between them. This powerful social custom attracted even the Ascendancy class, busy listening to Handel in Dublin, and traditional music concerts took place in the houses of the rich.

In the 19th century traditional music continued as an unschooled family event, celebrated at wakes and weddings and at the crossroads at holiday periods. Songs were traditional ones or made up for the moment, about friends and relatives or events in history. Instruments were the tin whistle, the fiddle and the bodhrán, a quite modern instrument made of goatskin stretched over a frame and played with the hand or both ends of a wooden stick. Less common but much older are the uilleann pipes, a complicated version of the bagpipes with a much more complex range of sounds. You'll be lucky to see anyone play this instrument in Ireland – it takes a good few years to master.

The Famine almost destroyed Irish music altogether as those who practised it died or emigrated. The music that survived did so because the emigrants in America, Australia, London, Liverpool and Glasgow kept their culture alive and, thankfully, had the sense to record the tunes, far away from the music's origins. In the USA piping clubs emerged and Irish performers joined the Variety Club circuits, adapting their music to American tastes. The Taylor Brothers, an emigrant family from Drogheda, developed the uillean pipes, bringing them to concert pitch and making them more suitable for performance. Then in 1890 the Gaelic League regenerated interest in music in Ireland itself, inventing the *ceili*, a showcase for Irish music and dancing. Traditional music went into a bit of a decline in the middle years of this century with the advent of radio, but it emerged again in the 1960s, first with Seán O Riada and traditional band Ceoltóirí Chualann, but it was The Chieftains who took the combination of traditional instruments and orchestral arrangements of Irish music all over the world.

There are several branches of the traditional music scene. One is the rebel song, sung late at night in bars in Donegal and made almost respectable by bands such as the Wolfe Tones. Another is the Dublin-based bawdy strain, epitomized by the

Step we gaily on we go

*For some of the best traditional music currently being produced in Ireland, check out Ossian Publications (www.ossian.ie). They produce **John Feeley Celtic Classics**, excellent recordings of traditional songs on the classical guitar, and **Hammy Hamilton, Séamus Creagh, Con Ó Drisceoil It's No Secret**, great songs by three musicians who came to the fore in the famous Phoenix Bar on Union Quay in Cork city in the 1970s.*

***Van Morrison & The Chieftains Irish Heartbeat**, is a delightful collection of classics like Carrickfergus, Star of the County Down and Marie's Wedding. **John McCormack Popular Songs and Irish Ballads**, produced by EMI, is a collection worth listening to, as is **Joyce's Parlour Music**, by Magini Enterprises, and on sale at the James Joyce Ciultural Centre in Dublin.*

*   **Robert Gogan 130 Great Irish Ballads**, from Music Ireland, 61 Grosvenor Square, Rathmines, Dublin 6, is an invaluable collection of words and music scores which comes complete with a CD.*

Dubliners and their song *Seven Drunken Nights*, the last two of which were too bawdy to record. The most inward-looking and sentimental is the ballad, often involving dead wives and abandoned homes, sung by Daniel O'Donnell and a host of clones and closely linked to the American country music scene. In pubs all around the country what you are most likely to hear is a mixture of Irish dance tunes, Fonn Mall or slow airs and rebel songs. If you are lucky you might come across *sean nós*, a strange nasal unaccompanied singing in Irish which takes a great deal of effort both to sing and to listen to. To the untrained ear it sounds like a monotone but the trick is to listen for the subtle nuances of the song.

As traditional music has lost its sweater-and-corduroys image it has changed and fused with other musical traditions as new generations of talented players have taken it up. Christy Moore is probably Ireland's favourite traditional musician. He has been in the business since the early days of the 1960s and early on formed the band Planxty with Liam O'Flynn, Donal Lunny and Andy Irvine. Planxty mixed traditional music with acoustic guitar folk music and ballads, but above all it was their skill with instruments which marked them out. All of them have moved on to other careers, Moore forming the band Moving Hearts which fused his traditional style with his own compositions, jazz and rock music. Many of Moore's songs have political overtones and comment on the Troubles and Irish politics. Since 1998 he has retired to West Cork. Other musicians who have influenced the traditional music scene are Moore's brother, Luka Bloom, and Paul Brady, both of whom have played with Moore in different bands.

Most dynamic of all were the band Pogue Mahone (Irish for Kiss my Arse), Londoners led by the musical icon Shane McGowan. They were a wild mix of punk, rebel song, traditional ballad and just plain rock music. McGowan and the Pogues split over McGowan's chaotic lifestyle, and he now plays with a new band The Popes. If you listen to nothing else in Ireland, listen to some of McGowan's songs, some of the finest music to emerge from the rock music scene in the last decade.

Another icon of the Irish music scene is Van Morrison, who came to the fore via a very different route. In the 1960s he led the band Them with pop hits in Britain. He spent many years in the USA and made his mark with albums such as *Astral Weeks* and *Moondance*. As a solo singer he has recorded with The Chieftains and has figured prominently in the efforts to reach peace in the North, where his home town is Belfast.

There are many other names to mention in a description of the vibrant Irish music scene. You can't go far in Dublin without tripping over U2, who own the Clarence Hotel and the Kitchen nightclub, two of the coolest places to be seen in. Clannad belong to the traditional music scene and have been around for what seems like a very long time. Rory Gallagher, who died in 1996, achieved world fame with his

The bent note and the twisted word

Our understanding of pre-Christian attitudes to music depends on surviving Gaelic myths which suggest that the songs and music of the bards were much more than a bit of light entertainment while they feasted. Rhyme and music formed a powerful magical weapon in the war against one's enemies as a story from Lébor Gabadla, the Book of Invasions tells. Daghda, one of the three leaders of the Tuatha de Danaan, the triumvirate of deities of pagan Ireland, has the power of music and one day slips into his enemies' camp to rescue a friend. He uses music to put three spells on the enemies, making them weep with sad music, dance with happy music and finally fall asleep to soothing music, allowing the captive to escape. Another story, of Oengus son of Daghda, tells how he and his lover Caer Iborméith, in the form of swans, make such beautiful music as they fly together that all who hear it fall asleep.

Much later, in early Christian Ireland the bards were highly valued intellectuals who could make or break a reputation with their poetry and the idea of the power of rhyme and music lingered a long time in Irish culture. In the 1959 play by John B Keane, Sive, a travelling tinker poses real threats to the local people with his chanted curses.

music in the 60s and 70s, selling 30 million records and touring all over the world first with his band Taste and then pursuing a solo career. There are also the Boomtown Rats and Bob Geldof, who have produced some good pop music. The early 90s witnessed Sinead O'Connor's tempestuous appearance on the world music scene, while other women such as Mary Black, Dolores Keane and Maura O'Connell have had quieter but equally successful careers. Sharon Shannon is based firmly in the traditional music scene and plays vigorous accordion and fiddle music. A big name in the pre-teen market is Irish boy band Boyzone. Also very successful in the pop charts in 1998 were the four sisters of The Corrs, who have broken all kinds of sales records with their albums *Talk on Corners* and *Forgiven, not Forgotten*.

Irish sports

In Ireland you will encounter all the regular sports, and Irish people tune in to the Sky Sports stations just like the rest of Europe, but Ireland also has some sports which are purely Irish in origin, even if that origin wasn't too long ago. The Gaelic Athletic Association was established in 1884, around the time of the Gaelic Revival, and established rules for games which had more or less existed before but had never been organized. Gaelic football is the Irish version of the game played in America and is a cross between English rugby and English football. There are 15 players and the round ball is played with both the hands and feet. Goals, as in football, and scores, as in rugby, are possible, with one goal equal to three scores. It is a very physical, fast game with few rules about physical contact.

More popular is hurling, a kind of hockey which is played on the same pitch as Gaelic. It is a very old game. Brehon Law, the law which operated in pre-Christian Ireland, allowed for compensation for the families of those injured in hurling matches, and tradition says that the battle of Moytura, fought in 200BCE, began as a hurling match. Between the 14th and 17th centuries hurling was banned three times. Nowadays it's a little less rough than the days when whole clans became professional hurling players and fought for the various clan chiefs. As in Gaelic there are 15 players to a team, and the object is to get the soft ball between the opponent's goal posts. The stick is wide at one end, and good players can carry the ball for several paces balanced on the stick. It is recognized as one of the fastest team sports in the world. Both games are just as popular as regular football,

Francis O'Neill

Born near Bantry, County Cork, in 1849, the youngest of seven children, Francis O'Neill was a typical child of his time, speaking both Irish and English, attending the school in Bantry, and learning by ear to play the wooden flute. He was good at remembering the tunes – an advantage since no one he knew was literate in musical notation. He spent his first adult years on board ships and was shipwrecked on Baker Island, a little atoll 1,650 miles southwest of Honolulu, for some time before a passing American ship rescued him. Landing in San Francisco he settled in America and eventually became chief of police in

Chicago, arresting the anarchist Emma Goldman in 1901. His hobby remained traditional Irish music, and with the help of a musically literate fellow officer he began collecting and transcribing Irish tunes from the many Irish immigrants he encountered. Between 1903 and 1924 he published nine volumes of Irish tunes which would otherwise have been lost. While the collections became essential material for traditional musicians, his work as a collector and biographer of American Irish musicians was never recognized in Ireland, until in 1999 he got a hotel named after him in Smithfield, Dublin.

and each year the whole country bedecks itself with its county's colours as the two sets of teams play towards the All Ireland finals at Croke Park in September.

Lifestyle

When the city authorities tried to prevent an Ann Summers sex shop opening in O'Connell Street in Dublin, a 10,000-strong petition was part of the campaign directed against the attempted ban

The last 10 years have seen such changes that make it almost difficult to believe that the Ireland of the past ever existed. Ireland was an amazing little country, stuck out on the very western edge of Europe, poor, underdeveloped, underpopulated and with a history that just wouldn't go away and let it move on. Dominated by the Catholic Church physically, politically and emotionally, it was seriously in danger of becoming a banana republic, taking handouts from the EU, sending its brightest and best off to other countries to find work, forever in the shadow of its bullying big brother, Britain. It seemed unable to move decisively into the future.

Take women for example. Half the population, well educated, women have contributed to every aspect of Irish life from politics and war to science, medicine, art and literature. But try naming 10 famous Irish women. At the turn of the century Irish women were pretty much the social equals of their sisters in Britain – no vote, none in parliament, none at universities, no doctors. Irish suffragettes fought and suffered for their demands just as British ones did. Under the Free State Irish women got the vote, stood for the Dáil, attended universities, practised medicine, did very nearly everything that Irish men did. But within 20 years most of that had disappeared – under the Irish constitution and the laws passed in the 1930s women had no access to contraception, no right to terminate a pregnancy under any circumstances whatsoever, no right to divorce, no right to own the family home or take authority over the children, no senior civil service jobs, no place in industrial management and certainly no equality of pay. It was as if Irish women voluntarily gave up all the rights and freedoms they had won in the early years of the century. And, weirdly, this continued more or less well into the 1980s. The first women sat on juries in the 1970s, the first condoms became available outside a prescription from a chemist shop in 1993, it was EU laws that forced equal pay and opportunities into Irish law (if not into practice). Finally, in the late 1990s, contraception and abortion advice became available in Ireland, and a referendum narrowly put divorce in a very limited number of cases on to the statute books.

Dancing

Dancing has always been a tricky thing in Ireland. Traditionally Irish people have always loved to dance, and in the days before the radio and TV a good night out would have been spent at the crossroads where there was enough space and where people knew to meet each other, dancing set dances – a little bit like a hoedown with someone calling out the moves as partners moved about in fixed patterns of jigs and reels to the tune of a tin whistle, violin or accordion. In the 40s and 50s, when dance halls opened up, it offered the possibility of all kinds of shenanigans between unmarried men and women, and the church frowned heavily on it with the parish priest often turning up late at night to check on the souls of the young.

Then there is Irish dancing, the name given to the peculiar rigid dancing performed mostly by young girls in heavily embroidered dresses. All over Ireland – and England too – there are competitions for these dances with little girls competing for medals which they collect and sew on to a harp-shaped frame. Rooted in the dancing of sailors on shipboard (hornpipe) and probably a hangover from the military past, this quite frigid kind of dancing with the arms held firmly at the sides somehow produced Riverdance, the modern version with very short skirts and bare-chested leading men stamping about the stage. Unlike traditional music which is green and cool, Riverdance, which was a breath of fresh air when it first hit the stage, must surely now have a limited lifespan.

In the last decade Ireland has undergone seismic changes that no one would have believed possible. The Catholic Church has lost its place in politics forever, with terrible stories emerging about child abuse by priests and nuns (and covered up by the church), the treatment of unmarried mothers in the Magdalen laundries (laundry workshops run by nuns), the scandal – hilarious though it was – of Bishop Eamon Casey and his teenage son. There have been corruption charges against once invulnerable men; the Good Friday Agreement saw the end to Ireland's claim to sovereignty over the North; the 1995 divorce laws brought about after a very narrow referendum finally liberated thousands of people from dead marriages; and most amazingly of all the emergence of high-wattage economic growth which has led to Ireland becoming dubbed 'The Celtic Tiger'.

For two centuries Irish people had to leave their homes in order to prosper or even survive. There are millions of Irish-descended people living in Britain, something like 43 million Americans claim Irish descent, and the diaspora spreads to Australia and beyond. When American visas became hard to get in the 80s, the Irish government set up emigration agencies to arrange for young people to go to Europe for work. Suddenly the reverse is true, and not only are Irish people returning home to take up work but for the first time since the Plantation English people are emigrating to Ireland in large numbers. Europeans have been settling in Ireland for the past 30 years, but it was always the oddballs who discovered the real Ireland and gave up money, possessions and city life to live as blow-ins and hippies in little cottages in the west of Ireland, setting up hostels, potteries, small engineering businesses or cafés, or just signing on for unemployment benefit each week. But in the last few years companies like Microsoft and Dell, Fruit of the Loom and others have taken advantage of government subsidies and moved into the cities, providing employment and spending power that never existed before on such a scale. A few miles west of Dublin, in Leixlip, County Kildare, Intel has set up a $2.5billion plant employing 4,000 people, the biggest building project in the history of Ireland. FÁS, the employment agency, had 10,000 unfilled skilled vacancies in 1999. Forty-four thousand people moved to Ireland in 1998 to take up work, 21,000 of them from

Britain. Dublin, Limerick, Galway, Belfast even, have become young vibrant, cosmopolitan places where there are opportunities, a great social life, lots of beautiful countryside, and lots to spend your euros on, whether it be an extremely expensive apartment (Dublin prices now match London's), beautifully designed Irish clothes or a theme café bar serving post-modern bacon and cabbage.

If Dublin belongs to the young and mobile, the west still belongs to the culchies. In the villages of the west of Ireland scant attention is paid to *Microsoft* or *Intel*, although mobile phones have their uses when you're bringing the cows in. In Dublin not locking your front door is asking for trouble – in the west anyone with a door locked too often has something to hide. In Dublin the man walking towards you is a potential danger – in the west he's someone to chat to for a few minutes. No one locks up their car or even bothers parking it properly, pub closing time depends on how close the police are, while shops, banks and any other useful place you could visit in your lunch hour are firmly closed so that everyone can enjoy their lunch.

The Ireland that you visit in the 21st century is not the Ireland of the 1980s. It has undergone changes that the leaders of the 1916 Rebellion, de Valera, Michael Collins or even Gay Byrne, the radical TV chat show host of the 60s, could not have imagined or even wanted. It has moved into the 21st century with skill and panache, but whether Ireland's wealth of culture will survive the culture of wealth remains to be seen.

Land and environment

Geography

Ireland is an old country. Its oldest rock, near Rosslare in County Wexford, is 2,400 million years old. Geologists suggest that 4,000 million years ago Ireland was two separate halves, one attached to early America and one to early Europe. When the two continents collided Ireland was squashed together and raised above sea level; huge rivers appeared which dumped red sand into the south, making the old red sandstone of the Cork and Kerry peninsulas. Three hundred and seventy five million years ago, Ireland found itself under a shallow warm sea where millions of tiny sea creatures lived and died, their remains forming great limestone swathes filled with fossil remains. On top of the limestone, shale and clay collected and supported primeval trees which in their turn decayed to form coal. Then, 300 million years ago, the European and African tectonic plates collided, and the old red sandstone with its covering of limestone and shale burst upwards and sideways to make the mountains of West Cork and Kerry, the Ballyhouras, the Galtees, the mountains of Limerick, and finally the Clare hills. If you compare these today you will see how the Kerry mountains took the worst of the upheaval, folding alarmingly into almost vertical sandstone sheets, while the Clare hills are almost flat, demonstrating how the power of the movement declined.

The next big burst of activity occurred 65 million years ago as the American and European continents drifted apart, creating the Atlantic Ocean. The west of Ireland sank as its support fell away, while to the north and east great lava flows and molten rock poured upwards creating the Giant's Causeway, the Mourne Mountains, and Doon Hill in Connemara. About 35 million years ago a depression formed in the middle of Ireland, creating a central low lying plain drained by the Shannon and surrounded by mountains. The basic structure of the country was now in place, only requiring erosion by rivers, glaciers and icesheets, and a few late tectonic shifts. These relatively recent landforms include the Wicklow hills, Lough Hyne in West Cork, thousands of drumlins and many U-shaped glacier-carved valleys.

Forests

A thousand years ago Ireland was covered in dense broadleaved forests with cleared patches on the tops of hills. Its main arteries were the rivers and coasts. Communities depended utterly on woodland products and, before the Normans arrived, the Danes in Dublin exported wood to treeless Iceland and elsewhere. As various waves of invaders encroached on the land, roads were built for their armies and the forests were cleared for settlements, to fuel mineworkings or to build English ships, so that today almost none of the aboriginal forests of Ireland remain. The best examples are in the southwest, at Muckross in Killarney, Glengarriff and Knockomagh Woods near Skibbereen, West Cork, and Shillelagh in south Wicklow. Visiting these places, especially in autumn, is one of the delights of the southwest of Ireland. Despite Ireland's limited range of plants the woods are pollution free, and you can see this in the enormous range of lichens that cover the trees. Holly, ferns, honeysuckle, wood sorrel, anemones, bluebells and celandines flourish in the spring before the trees grow leaves to shade out the light. By contrast, if you look into the understorey of the fast-profit conifer plantations which now seem to cover so much of the upland areas of Ireland, very little thrives at all.

Raised bogs

Thanks to hundreds of years of decline and neglect, much of rural Ireland is today a paradise of undamaged environments, worked on in the past only by farmers using small-scale technology. As a result, ecological niches such as raised peat bogs which were lost years ago in other countries are still thriving here. When the ice retreated from Ireland 9,000 years ago, it left great dammed lakes which gradually filled with water plants. As they decayed and formed a subsoil, a habitat was created for plants such as reeds and sedges which could tolerate partly wet conditions. The decay process continued until the debris rose above the water level and became fenland. Meanwhile, in the middle of the bog, oxygen depletion was taking place and plants which could tolerate low levels of oxygen moved in, notably sphagnum moss. This plant can capture and store rainwater, and needs very little else as nutrient. It quickly builds great domes which stand above the water level and hold large quantities of water, raising the water table as they do so. Other plants are starved out and the sphagnum takes over the area. Over thousands of years these plants flourished, creating ever higher mounds as the plants underneath died and formed a new base.

The bogs of Ireland are most abundant along the west coast and almost non-existent in the east. They are an important habitat for thousands of plant and animal species, and in addition have covered and protected thousands of years of human habitation, so that any little museum in Ireland will contain artefacts found in the bogs, ranging from fossilized bog butter to jewellery, from weapons to whole bodies which have hardly deteriorated at all. Roadways, villages, field systems have all emerged from the bogs as they have been excavated. But there lies the problem. The bog is an intact entity, its structure holding the water which keeps it growing and surviving. If the bog is cut, even by a hand tool, the water drains away and the bog dies, becoming dry enough to support first heathers and then other moorland plants and trees. With the wholesale peat cutting taking place in modern times in the biggest bogs in Ireland, the entire bog habitat, even those parts protected by the government, is ultimately doomed.

The fields

The Irish landscape, even nowadays, is a network of small fields bounded by stone ditches or hedgerows of whitethorn and blackthorn. The east of the country is largely fertile arable land, growing vegetables and sugar beet, while the north has small orchards and the west is given over to bog, cattle, sheep and grass. Most farms once had both pasture land and cultivated fields for oats and rye, but in modern times this is rare. Animal feed is bought in, there are few horses to grow oats for, and barley is produced on a large scale or not at all. Many of the fields systems you see are ancient, having been marked out long before any recorded history took place. Traditionally field boundaries were made of earth and stone ditches, each year's cleared sods of grass being added to the ditch along with anything else the plough turned up. The ditches were planted with hawthorn slips, and over the years the seeds of oak, ash, elder, wild rose and honeysuckle were brought by birds and small creatures. The hedgerows have become highways for animal life, providing home and food for hundreds of species of animals. In the west of Ireland fuchsia, an introduced plant, has become the dominant hedgerow plant – not a good choice for the native bees which cannot feed on the narrow flowers. Rhododendron has become another useful plant, providing windbreak all year round, though its invasive nature threatens the few remaining oakwoods.

The seashore

A planned golf course at Doonbeg, County Clare, was put on hold in December 1999 after it was found to be the habitat of the rare narrow-mouth whorl snail (Vertigo angustior)

Ireland has more than 2000 miles of coastline, the eastern coasts being more heavily populated and sheltered. The major ports of Waterford, Wexford, Dublin and Belfast, being heavily industrialized, have taken over much of the coastal habitat, but the west and southern coasts are exposed and have high cliffs and so provide an unspoiled habitat for plant and animal life. From the cliffs all over the west coast seals, dolphins and migrant birds can be spotted, while in the mouth of the Shannon colonies of dolphins thrive. Although golf courses are breeding like rabbits all over the west, there are still some undamaged sand dunes which make up a complex ecosystem of their own. The marram grasses bind the dunes together and provide a solid base for other plants such as sea holly, heartsease, sea sandwort, burnet rose and the rare ladies tresses orchid to find a niche. These plants are a food source and shelter for snails, sand hoppers, and butterflies, which in their turn provide a food source for birds such as skylarks and meadow pipits. Many of Ireland's dune systems have revealed evidence of neolithic culture, shell middens and cooking places, and even traces of iron smelting. In the shallow seas in front of the dunes systems wading birds feed, and the summer sees migrants from northern climates which come to the west of Ireland to breed. High cliffs and the offshore islands provide a breeding ground for other sea birds. Here too there is evidence of early cultures in the many promontory forts and other antiquities.

Flora and fauna

After the end of the last Ice Age both Ireland and Britain were connected to Europe by land bridges, and plants and animals from the mainland quickly recolonized both soon-to-be islands. But Ireland was cut off sooner by the rising sea levels and consequently has a much smaller range of both plants (around 70% of Britain's species) and animals (65% of Britain's insect species, for example), even in today's polluted times. There are no snakes in Ireland, only two amphibians as compared with Britain's six, 354 bird species compared with Britain's 456, and so on. Not that you'd notice when walking around the countryside in Ireland where plants that survive in tiny niches in Britain peek out of every hedgerow. The plants and animals that Ireland is home to are less endangered here than in most of the rest of Europe. Interestingly, Ireland has 15 native species that are missing in the British flora and fauna. If you imagine a post-ice-age land link from Europe to Britain and then to Ireland you have to ask how the plants could have hopped over Britain, missing it completely and landing in Ireland The theory is that at some point a land link existed between Ireland and southern Europe, and that these plant and animal species travelled to Ireland this way, bypassing Britain. Three heathers, St Daboc's heath, Mediterranean heath and Mackay's heath, are found in tiny colonies in Connemara and Donegal and southern France, while the greater butterwort, an insectivorous plant, is found only in the southwest of Ireland. The strawberry tree is found only in the southwest of Ireland, Brittany and the Mediterranean, and the spotted slug is again restricted to the southwest of Ireland.

Fauna is a little less easy to spot – you're more likely to see a dolphin than a stoat, for example. Neither are they as safe in the Irish environment as you would think. Woodpeckers disappeared when the last of the primeval forests were cut down, the very common corncrake almost disappeared because improved artificial fertilizers have made two harvests of grass possible each year. The birds, which nested in the long grass, had no time to rear their young before the first grass was cut – consequently very few young Irish people have heard the call which was so familiar to their parents. With the commercial cutting of the peat bogs, hundreds of species could disappear. In contrast minks, not a native species, are a common roadkill. They were introduced in farms, from which they of course escaped, and have found a niche in the woodlands and hedgerows. In 1999 the varroa mite, which infests bee colonies and eventually destroys them, was found in County Sligo, so it is merely a matter of time before the wild bee population in Ireland is wiped out. That would change the entire face of the Irish countryside, since so many of its wild flowers depend on pollination by bees.

Books

All books are paperback unless stated as hardback (HB).

Art, architecture & gardens

Judith Hill *Irish Public Sculpture*, Four Courts Press, 1998 (HB); the stories and history behind the best of the many sculptures found across Ireland. **Sean Rothery** *The Buildings of Ireland* Lilliput Press, 1997; delicate ink drawings accompany each of the 194 buildings selected by the author as fine examples of buildings dotted around towns and dating from early Christian times to the 20th century. **Jeremy Williams** *Architecture in Ireland 1837-1921* Irish Academic Press, 1994 (HB); comprehensive gazetteer detailing the architecture of post-Georgian Ireland county by county and building by building; opinionated and knowledgeable.

Autobiography

Gerry Adams *Falls Memories*, Brandon, 1993; nostalgic and humorous memories of growing up in the Falls Road. **Tom Barry** *Guerilla Days in Ireland*, and **Dan Breen** *My Fight for Irish Freedom*, both published by Anvil Books, are the best two accounts of the nationalist war in the 1920s. **Aidan Higgins** *Donkey's Years* Minerva, 1995; the perfect companion piece to Frank McCourt's (see below) grim humour, set in the same period of time but a different part of the country, Kildare, and a profoundly different social class, the young Higgins having a privileged upbringing – materially, at least. But McCourt and Higgins have a lot in common as their memories remorselessly expose a terribly pained Irish childhood. **Patrick Kavanagh** *The Green Fool*, Penguin, 2001; first published in 1938, a poet's account of a rural childhood suffused with patriarchy. **Frank McCourt** *Angela's Ashes* Flamingo, 1997; although the winner of the 1997 Pulitzer Prize for Non-Fiction, this book merges with the novel form to tell the bittersweet memoir of the writer growing up in New York and Ireland in the 1930s and '40s. **Bobby Sands** *Bobby Sands Writings from Prison*, Mercier, 1998; secretly written and smuggled out from Long Kesh, a painful account of a man's attempt to preserve in prose and poetry his sense of identity.

Culture

Helen Brennan *The Story of Irish Dance*, Brandon, 1999; from medieval times to contemporary set dancing; far too sympathetic to *Riverdance* but a useful study nonetheless. **Terry Eagleton** *The Truth About The Irish*, New Island Books, 1999; a laugh a minute, literally, in this alphabet of Irish mores. Worth reading for the entry on B&Bs alone. **Dorothy Harrison Therman Margaret Johnson** *The Irish Heritage Cookbook*, Wolfhound Press, 1999; onion and Murphy's stout soup followed by chicken with cabbage and bacon, plus another 200 recipes of traditional and not-so-traditional meals. *Stories from Tory Island*, Town House & Country House, 1989; transcriptions of conversations with the Antrim islanders; foreword by Derek Hill. **Pat Levy** *Culture Shock! Ireland*, Graphic Arts Center Publishing, 2000; full of insights (well, we would say that wouldn't we?) into the lifestyle and mentality of contemporary Ireland. **Fintan O'Toole** *The Lie of the Land*, Verso, 1997; journalistic essays covering the decline of the Catholic Church, emigration, the Haughey era and other aspects of Irish life in the 90s. **J M Synge** *The Aran Islands*, Oxford; the 1907 travelogue sparkles with the writer's affection for the place, though tales told around turf fires about children taken by the fairies are now ancient history. **Fintan Vallely** *Companion to Irish Traditional Music*, Cork University Press, 1998, (HB); accompanied by a CD, a good reference for the enthusiast. **Fintan Vallely & Charlie Piggott** *Blooming Meadows*, Town House & Country House, 1998; the musical lives of over a score of musicians like Brendan Begley, Mary Begin, Paddy Keenan, Ann Mulqueen, and Sharon Shannon. Strictly for lovers of traditional Irish music, **John Waters** *An Intelligent Person's Guide to Modern Ireland*, Bloomsbury, 2001; a book that goes against the grain by questioning the worth of Ireland's leap into modernity.

Literature

The individual books listed here make up a very partial and subjective selection of mostly modern writers

General Elizabeth Healy *Literary Tour of Ireland*, Wolfhound, 2001; a hefty paperback but well worth packing if you want the literary background to different towns and areas of Ireland. **P J Kavanagh** *Voices in Ireland*, John Murray, London, 1994; this traveller's literary companion is an excellent paperback, divided into geographical regions, to stuff into your luggage. **Declan Kiberd** *Inventing Ireland: The Literature of the Modern Nation*, Cape, 1995; Wilde, Yeats, Joyce and Beckett – by way of lesser known writers like Sommerville and Ross, Elizabeth Bowen and others. Refreshing and stimulating look at the colonial and post-colonial writers of Ireland. **John Montague** *Company*, Duckworth, 2001; masterly account of literary life in Dublin in the 1950s. **Robert Nicholson** *The Ulysses Guide*, Methuen, 1988; the best practical *Ulysses* guide, it follows the 18 episodes on their original locations accompanied by clear maps, detailed directions and summaries of each episode. Suitable for the newcomer or the seasoned Joycean. **Ulick O'Connor** *Celtic Dawn*, Town House & Country House, 1985; a portrait of the Irish literary renaissance, told with warm affection. **David Pearce** *Irish Writing in the Twentieth Century*, Cork University Press, 2001; some 1,300 pages containing over 400 superb pieces of writing, including letters, diaries, songs, and essays as well as poems, plays, short stories and extracts from novels. **Robert Welch**, editor, *The Oxford Companion to Irish Literature*, Oxford, 1996; perfect general purpose reference guide to Ireland's literary heritage.

Novels & plays John Banin *The Nowlans*, Appletree, 1992 (HB); first published in 1826, this powerful novel confronts the strains of clerical celibacy. **Patricia Craig**, editor, *The Belfast Anthology*, Blackstaff, 1999, (HB); where else would Gerry Adams, Graham Greene, Philip Larkin and Van Morrison rub shoulders? Material from the 17th century to the present: memoirs, poetry, fiction, travel writing, history and letters. **Seamus Deane** *Reading in the Dark*, Vintage, 1997; set in Derry in the 1950s and 60s and reaching into a personal and political heart of darkness. **Micky Donnelly** *Doubletime*, Blackstaff, 2001; contemporary fiction by a Belfast writer. **James Joyce** *Ulysses*, Vintage, first published 1922; the first couple of chapters put most would-be readers off ever finishing the novel. Persevere, make use of a recorded reading (see CDs above) and listen to the voices of Dublin that have never been so astonishingly recreated in written form before or since. *Finnegans Wake* is another kettle of fish but recorded readings will open a window on this extraordinary work. **John B Keane**

Three Plays, Mercier Press, 1990; text of *Sive, the Field* and *Big Maggie* by the Kerry playwright who is finally being recognized. **Francis Ledwidge** *Selected Poems*, New Island Books, 2001; born in 1887, a worker and trade unionist who died in Flanders in 1917; the introduction to this collection by Seamus Heaney helps explain why he should be better known. **Charles Lever** *Lord Kilgoblin*, Appletree, 1992 (HB); first published in 1872, a gripping tale of Irish politics in the age of imperial misrule. **Patrick MacGill** *Children of the Dead End* and *The Rat-Pack*, New Island Books, 2001; two books, originally published in 1914 and 1915, that tell you more about the colonial Ireland than many a history book. **John McGahern** *Amongst Women*, Faber, 1990; perhaps the most resonant of McGahern's works, blending the personal and the political in a masterful and disturbing way. **John Montague** *Collected Poems*, Gallery Books, 1998; born in New York in 1929 but brought up in County Tyrone, this book is worth its price just for the poet's beautiful lyrics. **Richard Murphy** *Collected Poems*, Gallery Books, 2000; Anglo-Irish poet from Mayo who explores the past with a rare sensibility and a deep sense of history. **Éilís Ní Dhuibhne** *The Dancers Dancing*, Blackstaff Press, 1999; a group of girls attending a summer school in county Donegal provide a setting for this exploration of sex, politics, and Irishness. **Flann O'Brien** *The Third Policeman*, Grafton; written in 1940, this brilliantly subversive and enormously comic novel deconstructs the deadening conventionality of Irish life under deValera. **Brian O'Doherty** *The Deposition of Father McGreevy*, Arcadia; second novel by US-based Irish author which led to a Kerry councillor calling for a "Muslim-style fatwa" on the author because of the depiction of Kerry farmers having sex with sheep. **Sean O'Reilly** *Curfew and Other Stories*, Faber & Faber; Derry-born author's collection of eight, bleakly lyrical stories. Look out for his first novel, about to be published, *Love and Sleep*, **Somerville and Ross** *The Real Charlotte*, Quartet Books, 1977; the female cousins' most accomplished work, a haunting microcosm of the Anglo-Irish world. **Bairbre Tóibín** *The Rising*, New Island Books, 2001; a terrific first novel, both a love story and a dramatisation of events leading up to and including the 1916 Rising.

Patricia Boyle Haberstroh, editor, *Women Creating Women: Contemporary Irish Women Poets*, Attic Press, Cork, 1996; studies of the finest women poets writing in Ireland today: Eavan Boland, Eiléan Ní Chuilleanáin, Medbh McGuckian and Nuala Ní Dhomhnaill. **Seamus Heaney** *North*, Faber, 1975; Heaney's most controversial set of poems as he sets about confronting brute facts regarding colonialism and the social divisions of his country. His mythologizing instinct comes face to face with violence and the poetry reaches new heights. **Seamus Heaney** *Opened Ground*, Faber, 1998; to date, this is the closest Heaney comes to presenting his *oeuvre*, containing selections from *Wintering Out* (1972), *Stations* and *North* (1975), *Field Work* (1979), *Station Island* (1983), *The Haw Lantern* (1987), *Seeing Things* (1990) and *The Spirit Level* (1996). Enough here to last a lifetime. **John Montague** *Collected Poems*, Gallery Books, 1998; not so well known as Heaney but a major Irish poet, born in New York and reared on a farm in county Tyrone. **Richard Murphy** *Collected Poems*, Gallery Books, 2000; Fine poetry that illuminates Irish history and the Anglo-Irish identity.

General **Jonathan Barden** *A History of Ulster*, Belfast, 1992; easily the best history of the northern province, even-handed throughout and in a style that makes it a pleasure to read. Find a place for it in your luggage. **S J Connolly**, editor *The Oxford Companion to Irish History*, Oxford, 1998; comprehensive and indispensable reference guide for Irish history. **Sean Duffy**, editor, *Atlas of Irish History* Gill & Macmillan, 1997; a visual and highly satisfying summary of the sweep of Irish history and politics up to modern times. **R F Foster** *The Irish Story*, Allen Lane 2001 (HB); how the Irish construct their history and in doing so risk turning their country into a historical

Poetry

History

Background

theme park. **James Lydon** *The Making of Ireland*, Routledge, 1998; one of the best general histories of the country from ancient times onwards. *The Irish Story* Allen Lane, 2001 (HB); examines how key moments in Irish history have been transformed into narratives. An excellent introduction to one strand of current thinking on Irish history. *The Penguin Atlas of British & Irish History* Penguin, 2001; a multi-faceted approach to the entangled histories of the two countries, with maps galore. **John O'Beirne Ranelagh** *A Short History of Ireland*, Cambridge, 1983; updated to 1998, a useful one-volume account of Irish history. **ATQ Stewart** *The Shape of Irish History*, Blackstaff Press, 2001 (HB); not for the newcomer to Irish history, a series of canny reflections on Irish history through the centuries. **Charles Townshend** *Ireland: The 20th Century*, Arnold, 1998; detailed but readable account of modern Ireland from the origins of Sinn Féin onwards. **Margaret Ward**, editor, *In Their Own Voice: Women and Irish Nationalism*, Attic Press, 1995; anthology of women's accounts of the struggle for Irish independence.

Pre-history Peter Harbison *Pre-Christian Ireland*, Thames & Hudson, 1998; comprehensive and readable synthesis of early Ireland and its archaeology. **Simon James** *The Atlantic Celts*, British Museum Press, 1999; controversial but convincing thesis, delivering a big blow to New Age Celtists, that the false idea of an insular Celtic identity was engendered by the rise of nationalism in the 18th century. **Simon James** *Exploring the World of the Celts*, Thames & Hudson, 1993, (HB); well illustrated survey of Celtic history and culture. **Michael J O'Kelly** *Early Ireland*, Cambridge University Press, 1989; covering much the same ground as Harbison's book but with a more scholarly tone. **Clint Twist** *Atlas of the Celts*, George Philip Limited, 2001; less an atlas and more of a very visual general history of the Celts, their culture and impact.

Specialist Tom Barry *Guerilla Days in Ireland*, Anvil 1981; first published in 1949, a participant's extraordinary account of the war against the British in west Cork. I treasure the childhood memory of seeing an elderly but fit-looking man boarding a bus in Bantry and chatting to the driver and my grandfather pointing out that this was Tom Barry. **Dan Breen** *My Fight For Irish Freedom*, Anvil 1981; first published in 1924, the story of the guerilla war in Tipperary by a man who the wanted posters described as having as looking 'rather like a blacksmith coming from walk'. **Dáire and Nocholas Furlong**, editor, *The Women of 1798*, Four Courts Press, 1998; Long overdue account of the role of women in the tumultous events of 1798. **Maud Gonne McBride** *A Servant of the Queen*, Colin Smythe Ltd, 2000; the woman who told WB Yeats where to get off, matrimonially speaking, because fighting the British was a more urgent task. **Michael Hughes** *Ireland Divided: The Roots of the Modern Irish Problem*, University of Wales, 1994; useful introduction to the events leading to the partition of Ireland. **Thomas Keneally** *The Great Shame*, Chatto & Windus, 1998; the author of *Schindler's Ark* turns his masterly narrative art on to the story of Irish emigration. **Anne Marreco** *The Rebel Countess*, Phoenix Press 1967; good biography of the rebel Anglo-Irish countess who played her part in the 1916 Rising. **Susan McKay** *Northern Protestants*, Blackstaff Press 2000; a journalist offers an uncompromising, in-depth examination of her own people; prepare to be shocked. **Tom Reilly** *Cromwell An Honourable Enemy*, Brandon, 1999; who said Cromwell was the scourge of the Irish? A daring reassessment of the most reviled figure in Irish history. **Peter Somerville-Large** *The Coast of West Cork*, Appletree 1991; a worthwhile companion if travelling at length in west Cork between Clonakility and Ardgroom; full of history, impressions and anecdotes. **Peter Taylor** *Provos*, Bloomsbury, 1997; the most informative and balanced account of the IRA to be published. **Margaret Ward** *Hanna Sheehy Skeffington: A Life*, Attic Press, 1997; valuable biography of the feminist socialist who became an important figure in Sinn Féin at the turn of the century.

Terrence Dooley *The Decline of the Big House in Ireland*, Wolfhound 2001 (HB); using primary material, the author provides an in-depth social history of Irish landed families between 1860 and 1960. *Mary Carberry's West Cork Journals, 1898-1901*, Lilliput Press, 1998, (HB); encounters with local life and customs and the writer's winning indifference to the grander aspects of an Anglo-Irish Ascendancy makes this a fascinating read. *Seventy Years Young* Lilliput Press, 1991; Anglo-Irish memoirs of Elizabeth, Countess of Fingall, who married at the age of 17 into the Ascendancy and ended up working for the United Irishwomen. **Peter Somerville-Large** *The Irish Country House*, Sinclair-Stevenson, 1995 (HB); well illustrated and lively social history of the Ascendancy class in Ireland **David Thomson** *Woodbrook*, Vintage, 1991; a memoir of Anglo-Irish life in Sligo in the 1930s and a moving love-story. Lyrical and hauntingly sad.

The Anglo-Irish

A Beginner's Guide to Ireland's Seashore, Sherkin Island Marine Station, 1999; pocket-sized guide, in colour, for beginners of all ages. **David Cabot** *Ireland*, HarperCollins, 1999 (HB); expensive (£35) but comprehensive and well nigh indispensable account of the natural history of Ireland, focusing on the diverse habitats and with over 200 illustrations. **Robert Lloyd Praeger** *The Way That I Went*, Collins Press, 1998; one of Ireland's greatest naturalists (1865-1953) and of all his works, (*The Botanist in Ireland* (1934), *Natural History of Ireland* (1950), *Irish Landscape* (1953) and others), this topographical classic is his most memorable. **Frank Mitchell** and **Michael Ryan** *Treading the Irish Landscape*, Town House 2001; the shaping of Ireland from the beginning of time, the impact of monasteries, castles, war and modern agriculture. **M&S Murphy** *Ireland's Bird Life*, Sherkin Island Marine Station, 1994; large colour photographs to help the non-expert birdwatcher. **Charles Nelson** *Wild Plants of the Burren and the Aran Islands*, The Collins Press 1999; useful little, all-colour field guide for nature walks in the places it covers. **John Wilson Foster** *Nature in Ireland*, Lilliput Press, 1997; over 600 pages covering definitive histories of botany, geology, ornithology, woodlands and bogs of Ireland and adding up to a powerful reference source on how Irish nature has been studied.

Ecology & natural history

Background

Sandra Bardwell, Pat Levy and Gareth McCormack *Walking in Ireland*, Lonely Planet, 1999; practical guide to walks across the length and breadth of Ireland. **Kevin Corcoran** *West of Ireland Walks/West Cork Walks/Kerry Walks*, O'Brien Press, Dublin; superb little books with maps and ecological anecdotes of the politically correct kind along the way. **Paddy Dillon** *Exploring the South of Ireland*, Ward Lock, 1998; over 35 walks with route maps and relief diagrams. *The Ulster Way*, O'Brien Press, 1999; the complete Ulster Way written by a noted author of many walking guides. **Michael Fewer** *The Way-Marked Trails of Ireland*, Gill & Macmillan, 1996; a reliable guide to the best way-marked trails in the Republic, with maps and practical information on where to stay and eat. **David Herman** *Ireland and Great Walks Ireland*, Brockhampton Press, 1995 and 1999; two useful and practical walking guides. **J B Malone** *The Complete Wicklow Way*, O'Brien Press, 1999; an updated edition of a guide to this long-distance walk. Paddy Dillon **David Marshall** *Best Walks in Ireland*, Constable, London, 1996; five in the North and 15 in the Republic, graded in difficulty from an easy day's stroll to an ambitious and demanding climb up a mountain. Good maps, clear instructions and anecdotes along the way.

Walking guides

Simon Marsden and Duncan McLaren *In Ruins*, Little, Brown and Company, 1997. (HB); evocative photographs and informative text. **Mathias Oppersdorff** *People of the Road*, Syracuse University Press, 1997; a set of photographs of Travellers taken between the 1960s and the 90s, capturing just how at odds with contemporary Ireland they remain. **Jonathan Pitcher** and **Valerie Hall** *Flora Hibernica*, The Collins

Colour illustrated books

Press, 2001 (HB); colour-illustrated account of all the main vegetation types found in Ireland, from woodland, bogs and grasslands to sea shore. *The Most Beautiful Villages in Ireland*, Thames and Hudson, 2000 (HB); this is a book for the coffee table, or a gift for someone you want to persuade to make a trip to Ireland: a multitude of photographs that evoke many different aspects of Irish life and culture. **Alex Ritsema** *Discover the Islands of Ireland*, The Collins Press, 1999; not a walking guide as such but given that walking will be your main means of getting around on the islands this book has a wealth of information. **Peter Somerville-Large and Jason Hawkes** *Ireland From the Air*, Weidenfeld & Nicholson, London, (HB); arresting aerial images of the country with intelligent text. **Iain Zaczek** *Ancient Ireland*, Collins & Brown, 1998, (HB); the text is so-so but the photographs by David Lyons capture the other-worldly appeal of an island that tangibly evokes an ancient past.

Cookery **Darina Allen Ballymaloe** *Cookery Course*, Kyle Cathie Ltd, 2001 (HB); a doorstep of a book with over 1,000 recipes from the famous Ballymaloe Cookery School in Ireland and Footprint readers can purchase it without paying any hefty postage charges if they call T020-76927221 or from the publisher at 122 Arlington Rd, London NW1 7HP, quoting ref Foot1. **Margaret M Johnson** *The Irish Heritage Cookbook*, Wolfhound 1998; surprise your guests with black pudding and bacon salad, boxty, Irish stew, Irish whiskey cake, and lots more. **Molly O'Neill** *A Feast of Irish Cooking*, Colin Smythe Ltd, 2000; an inexpensive book of Irish recipes.

Journals *Film Ireland* FilmBase, Irish Film Centre, 6 Eustace Street, Dublin 2. F01-6796717, www.iftn.ie Film reviews, interviews, research articles. *History Ireland* P.O. Box 695, Dublin 8. F01-4533234, historyireland@connect.ie A refreshing range of articles from the obvious to the marginal. *Irish Studies Review* Carfax Publishing, PO Box 25, Abingdon, Oxfordshire, OX14 3UE. F01235-401550. A scholarly but broad-based journal covering history and the arts.

CDs *The Croppy Boy*, Ger Busher Gold Sun Records, Camelot, Coolcotts Lane, Wexford, Ireland, 1998. Music and drama rendering a stirring narrative of the 1798 insurgence in County Wexford; an engaging alternative to the hefty tomes that academics have devoted to the subject. *The Croppy's Complaint* Craft Recordings, 11 Merton Av, South Circular Road, Dublin 8. Music and song covering the 1798 rebellion. *Fellowship of Freedom* National Library of Ireland, Dublin; the context, causes and campaigns of the United Irishmen and their uprising. *Finnegans Wake*, read by Jim Norton with Marcella Riordan, Naxos Audio Books; 4 CDs or 4 cassettes include a booklet containing the abridged spoken text. The only way to make a start with this notoriously difficult but highly musical work. Naxos Audio also have readings of all the short stories from Joyce's *Dubliners* and other Irish classics, like Sterne's *Tristram Shandy*, are available as well. **Elizabeth Bowen** *The Last September*, (Audio Books, Bath, BA2 3AX). Bowen's Anglo-Irish comedy of manners set in the troublesome 1920s. Recorded on cassettes but CD versions can't be far away. Other Irish classics, including Brian Moore and Edna O'Brien, are also available through the same company; check their website at www. chivers.co.uk *The National Gallery of Ireland* National Gallery of Ireland, Dublin; one hundred of the best paintings, easy to install and use. *Ulysses*, read by Jim Norton with Marcella Riordan, Naxos Audio Books; these four CDs or four cassettes (and still abridged) should help you realise what all the acclaim is about.

Footnotes

19

Footnotes

Glossary

An Óige (literally 'the youth') Irish youth hostel association

Bailey enclosure beside a castle

Bally a town; hence the hundreds of places beginning with the prefix

Barbican defensive building at a gate or entrance to a castle

Bartizan defensive turret overhanging a wall

Bawn walled enclosure, part of a tower-house or castle

Beag & béal Irish for small

Bodhrán hand-held, goatskin drum (pronounced *boor-run*)

Boreen small lane

Bog decomposed vegetable matter, peat, used as a fuel

Bord Fáilte Irish Tourist Board

Bronze Age approximately between 2000 BC and 500 BC; between the Stone Age and Iron Age

Caher a fort build of stone without cement or concrete

Cairn a mound of stones

Capstone a massive stone, weighing as much as 100 tons, covering a megalithic tomb

Ceilí session of traditional Irish music and dancing

Celt Iron Age culture arriving in Ireland around 300 BC

Chancel east end of a church where the altar stands

Chevaux-de-frise projecting sharp stones placed in the ground outside an Iron Age fort to deter an enemy

Claddagh ring traditional ring from Connaught characterized by a crowned heart between two hands

Clochán beehive-shaped, stone-built hut from early Christian times

Cloister covered square-shaped passage accessing monastery

Corbel a projecting stone; and the name of a building technique where stones are built out, one above the other, forming a kind of vault

Court-tomb earliest kind of megalithic burial site

Craic common expression for a good time (pronounced *crack*)

Crannog ancient lake dwelling

Culchies Irish expression for country people, rarely used affectionately

Currach/curragh a small boat covered with a waterproof material, originally stretched hides and later tarred canvas

Demense landed property of country house or castle (pronounced *domain*)

Diamond town square, most common in Northern Ireland

Dolmen megalithic tomb consisting of a flat stone laid on upright ones

Dubh Irish for black

Dúchas Government department responsible for various historical sites in the Republic

Dun/Doo Irish for a fort

Éire Irish for Ireland

Fir Irish for men

Fulacht fiadh ancient method of outdoor cooking, using heated stones to bring water to the boil

Gaeltacht an Irish-speaking district

Garda policeman (plural: gardaí and pronounced *gar-dee*)

Inis Irish for island

Iron Age from around 500 BC to the arrival of Christianity

Jarvey driver of the traditional jaunting cars, most commonly found in Killarney

Kill/cill Irish for chapel or church

Lough a lake

Footnotes

Machicolation projecting wall parapet with openings at the bottom to hurl down stones at the enemy

Martello Tower round, squat tower built in coastal locations for protection against an expected French invasion by sea

Megalithic literally 'big stones', used to describe Stone Age burial tombs using large stones

Mná Irish for women

Motte round mound with flat top, used as a fortification by the Normans

Mullion a vertical bar dividing the lights in a window, hence the architectural term mullioned

Neolithic late Stone Age, 4000-2000 BC

North shorthand for Northern Ireland

NTIB Northern Ireland Tourist Board

Ogham a form of writing from around the 4th-9th centuries, inscribed on standing-stones

Oriel window a bay window that projects from its wall

Palladian architectural style of 17th and 18th centuries, characterized by symmetrical planning and classical forms; favourite style of many of the grander Anglo-Irish country houses

Passage grave Megalithic tomb consisting of a corridor of stones leading to a burial chamber

Piscina perforated stone basin for carrying away the water used in rinsing chalices

Plantation term referring to the settlement of the English and Scottish, beginning in the late 16th century in southwest Cork and in the early 17th century in Ulster

Poteen/poitín illicitly distilled spirit, made from potatoes or molasses, and still available in parts of Ireland (pronounced *putcheen*)

Ráth Irish for ring fort; ancient dwelling place surrounded by a rampart

Republic shorthand for the 26 counties of the Republic of Ireland

Romanesque 12th-century style of architecture characterized by rounded archs

Round Tower tall, circular, stone-built towers built from 9th century onwards and usually associated with monasteries

Sheila-na-gig a carved medieval female figure with exaggerated genitalia, most commonly found on exterior stonework. Thought to be an off-beat symbol from Romanesque and Gothic iconography representing the sin of lust, though Gaelic culture came to regard them as protective

Souterrain an underground passage in a ringfort (archaeological)

Strand commonly used term for a beach

TD elected members of the Dáil (*Teachta Dala*)

Tinkers politically incorrect term for travellers

Trá Irish for beach

Tricolour the green, white and orange flag of Ireland

Turf brick-sized blocks of peat used as fuel

Vernacular used as an architectural term to describe a building style that is traditionally associated with an area or a non-wealthy class

YHANI Youth Hostel Association of Northern Ireland

See the **Background** section for a glossary of political terms.

Place-names, townlands and translations

A townland, a division of land which defies its name by very often being non-urban, can vary in size from 1 acre to 7,000 acres. Their origins can sometimes be traced back to plantation divisions and old clan divisions while the etymologies of many of the 60,000 townlands in Ireland suggest ancient Gaelic origins rooted in a reverence for natural features. In Brian Friel's seminal play *Translations* (1980) the compulsory translation of Gaelic place-names into English by soldiers working on the Ordnance Survey becomes a powerful cultural metaphor for the invasion and expropriation of Ireland by the English.

The following glossary offers some help in recovering the original meaning behind the evocative names of places and townlands across Ireland. They are nearly all Gaelic in origin, although some reveal the impact of Christianity, like kill/cill from the Latin *cella*.

agh, augh, achadh	field	fóin	small cove
aglish	church	géar	sharp
ah, atha, áth	ford, crossing	glas, gleann	valley, green
aill, anna, canna	cliff	inbhear (inver)	river mouth
árd, ar	marshland	inis	island
as, ess, eas	high ground	kill, cill	church
aw, ow, atha	waterfall	kin	headland
bal, bel, béal	river	knock, cnoc	hill
bal, bally, baile	town	leac	flat rock
bán	white	léith	grey
beann (ben)	peak	lis, lios	fort
bearna	gap	lough, loch	lake
beg, beag	small	mainistir	monastery
binn	peak	moy, magh	lake
buí	yellow	maol	bare hillock
bun	bottom, base	mona, móna	bog, turf
caher, cahir	rock	mór	big
caol	narrow	oileán	island
carraig	rock	owen	river
cashel, caisel, caisleán	castle	poll	hole, hollow
céibh	quay	rath	ring-fort
cloich, cloch	stone	rinn, reen	headland, point
cnoc	rocky hill	rón	seal
cuainín	small harbour	ross	wood
derg, dearg	red	sceilig (skellig)	rock
doire	oakwood	sidh	a hill of the fairies
doo, dubh	black	slieve, sliabh	mountain
dumhaig	of the sandy shore	staca	pinnacle/stack (of rock)
dúna	of the fort	tir	country
dun, dún	fort	tubber, tobar	well
dysert	hermitage	trá, tráigh	beach
fada	long		

Map index

Index

Footnotes

Footnotes

Join the celebrations

WATERFORD
Museum of TREASURES
at the Granary

Winner of :

Irish Museum of the Year 1999

*Irish American Cultural Institute
- Heritage Award 2000*

*Adult & Children's Sound Guide available
Various language sound guides available*

Merchants Quay Waterford

Open 7 days

June July August	9.30am - 9.00pm
April, May & September	9.30am - 6.00pm
October - March	10.00am - 5.00pm

T:051-30 4500 **F:**051-30 4501

E:mail@waterfordtreasures.com www.waterfordtreasures.com

Waterford Corporation

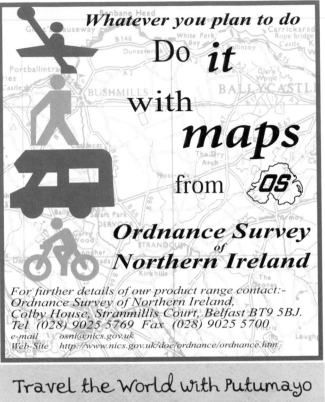
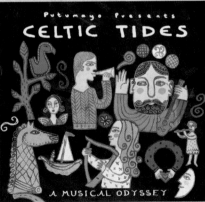

Ireland

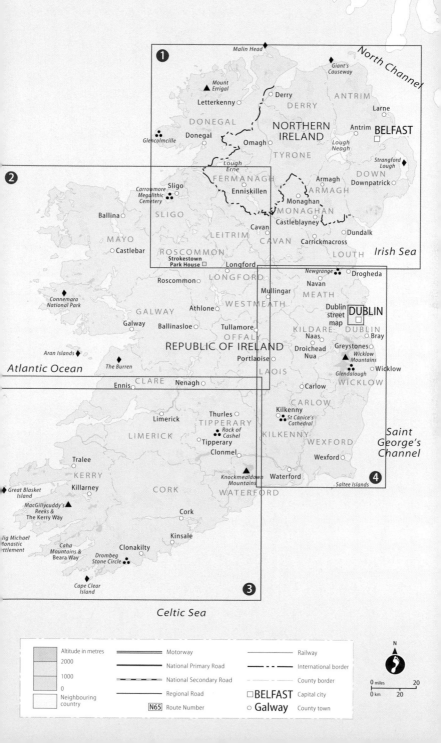

❶ Malin Head ◆

North Channel

Giant's Causeway ◆

▲ Mount Errigal

Letterkenny ○

Derry ○

ANTRIM

DERRY

Larne ○

Antrim ○

BELFAST □

DONEGAL

Donegal ○

Omagh ○

NORTHERN IRELAND

TYRONE

Lough Neagh

Glencolmcille ▲

Lough Erne

FERMANAGH

Enniskillen ○

Armagh ○

ARMAGH

DOWN

Downpatrick ○

Strangford Lough ◆

❷

Carrowmore Megalithic Cemetery ▲

Sligo ○

Monaghan ○

MONAGHAN

Castleblayney ○

Ballina ○

SLIGO

LEITRIM

Cavan ○

CAVAN

Dundalk ○

Castlebar ○

MAYO

ROSCOMMON

Carrickmacross ○

LOUTH

Irish Sea

Strokestown Park House □

Longford ○

Roscommon ○

LONGFORD

Newgrange ◆

Drogheda ○

Navan ○

MEATH

Connemara National Park ◆

GALWAY

Athlone ○

Mullingar ○

WESTMEATH

Galway ○

Ballinasloe ○

Tullamore ○

Dublin street map

DUBLIN □

KILDARE

DUBLIN

Bray ○

OFFALY

REPUBLIC OF IRELAND

Naas ○

Greystones ○

Aran Islands ◆

Portlaoise ○

Droichead Nua

▲ Wicklow Mountains

Atlantic Ocean

The Burren ◆

LAOIS

Glendalough ▲

Wicklow ○

CLARE

Nenagh ○

WICKLOW

Ennis ○

CARLOW

Limerick ○

Thurles ○

TIPPERARY

Rock of Cashel ▲

Kilkenny ○

St Canice's Cathedral ▲

LIMERICK

Tipperary ○

KILKENNY

WEXFORD

Tralee ○

Clonmel ○

Carlow ○

Saint George's Channel

KERRY

Great Blasket Island ◆

Killarney ○

CORK

Knockmealdown Mountains ▲

Waterford ○

Wexford ○

MacGillycuddy's Reeks & The Kerry Way ▲

WATERFORD

Saltee Islands

❹

ig Michael onastic ttlement ◆

Cork ○

Caha Mountains & Beara Way

Kinsale ○

Clonakilty ○

Drombeg Stone Circle ▲

❸

Cape Clear Island

Celtic Sea

Altitude in metres		Motorway	Railway
2000		National Primary Road	International border
1000		National Secondary Road	County border
0		Regional Road	**BELFAST** Capital city
Neighbouring country		N65 Route Number	○ **Galway** County town

N

0 miles 20

0 km 20

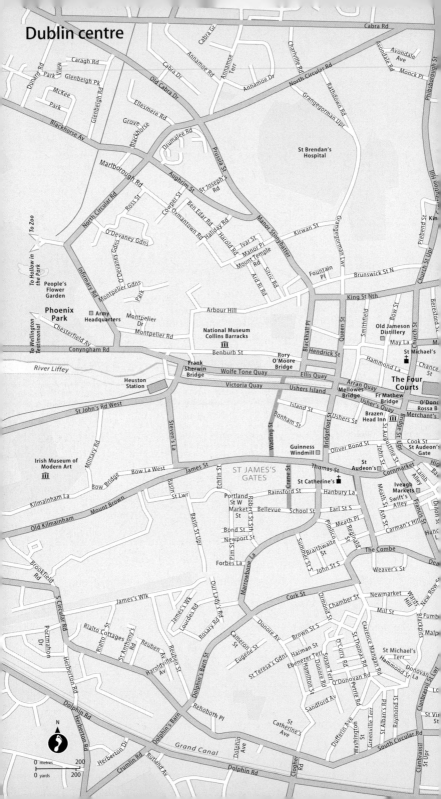

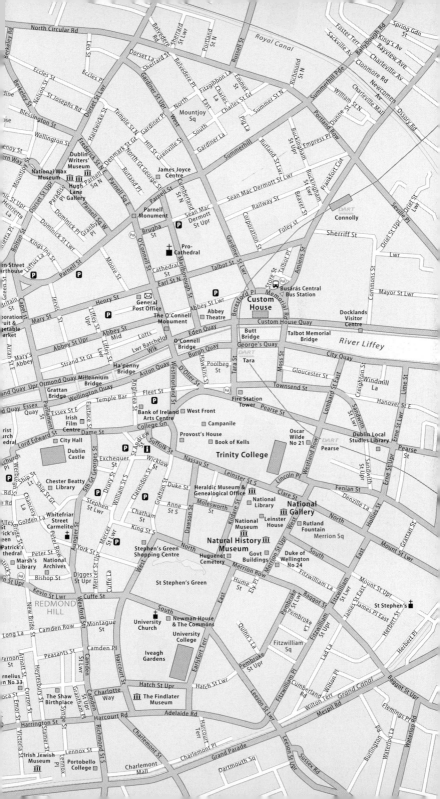

Map 1

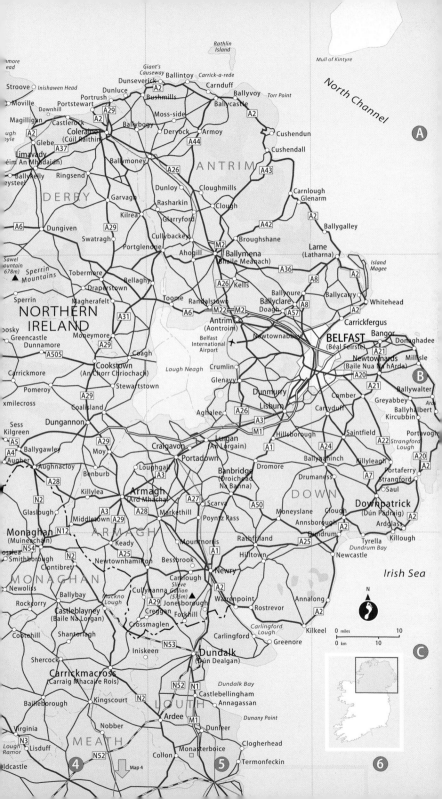

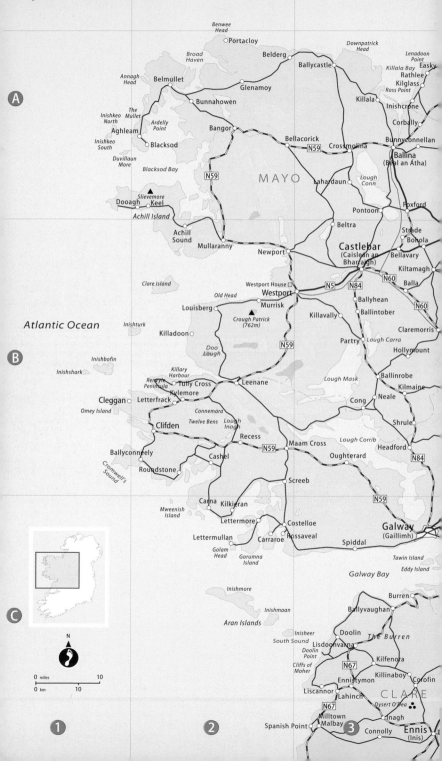

Map 2

Map 3

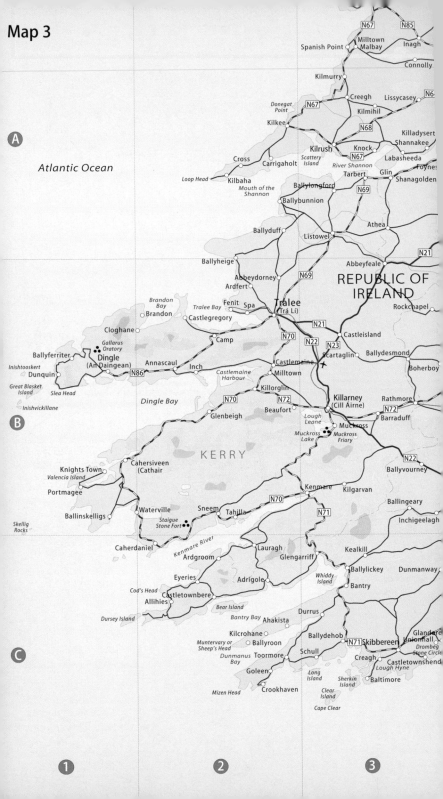

Spanish Point
Milltown Malbay
Inagh
N67
N85
Connolly
Kilmurry
Creegh
Lissycasey
N6
Donegat Point
N67
Kilmihil
Kilkee
N68
Killadysert
Shannakee
Kilrush
Knock
Cross
Carrigaholt
Scattery Island
River Shannon
Labasheeda
Foynes
Loop Head
Kilbaha
Tarbert
Glin
Shanagolden
Mouth of the Shannon
Ballylongford
N69
Athea
Ballybunnion
Ballyduff
Listowel
Ballyheige
Abbeyfeale
N21
Abbeydorney
N69
REPUBLIC OF IRELAND
Ardfert
Fenit
Spa
Tralee
(Trá Li)
Rockchapel
Brandon Bay
Tralee Bay
Brandon
Castlegregory
Cloghane
N70
Castleisland
Ballydesmond
Camp
N21
N22
Scartaglin
Gallarus Oratory
N23
Dingle
(An Daingean)
Annascaul
Inch
Castlemaine
Boherboy
Ballyferriter
N86
Milltown
Inishtooskert
Dunquin
Castlemaine Harbour
Killorglin
Killarney
(Cill Áirne)
Rathmore
Great Blasket Island
Slea Head
N70
N72
Barraduff
N72
Inishvickillane
Dingle Bay
Beaufort
Lough Leane
Glenbeigh
Muckross
KERRY
Muckross Lake
Muckross Friary
N22
Cahersiveen
(Cathair
Ballyvourney
Knights Town
Valencia Island
Kenmare
Kilgarvan
Portmagee
Ballingeary
N70
Waterville
Sneem
Tahilla
N71
Inchigeelagh
Ballinskelligs
Staigue Stone Fort
Skellig Rocks
Kealkill
Caherdaniel
Kenmare River
Lauragh
Ardgroom
Glengarriff
Ballylickey
Dunmanway
Eyeries
Adrigole
Whiddy Island
Bantry
Cod's Head
Castletownbere
Allihies
Bear Island
Durrus
Dursey Island
Bantry Bay
Ahakista
Glandore
Kilcrohane
Unionhall
Muntervary or Sheep's Head
Ballyroon
Ballydehob
N71
Skibbereen
Drombeg Stone Circle
Dunmanus Bay
Toormore
Schull
Creagh
Castletownshend
Goleen
Long Island
Lough Hyne
Baltimore
Mizen Head
Crookhaven
Clear Island
Sherkin Island
Cape Clear

1
2
3

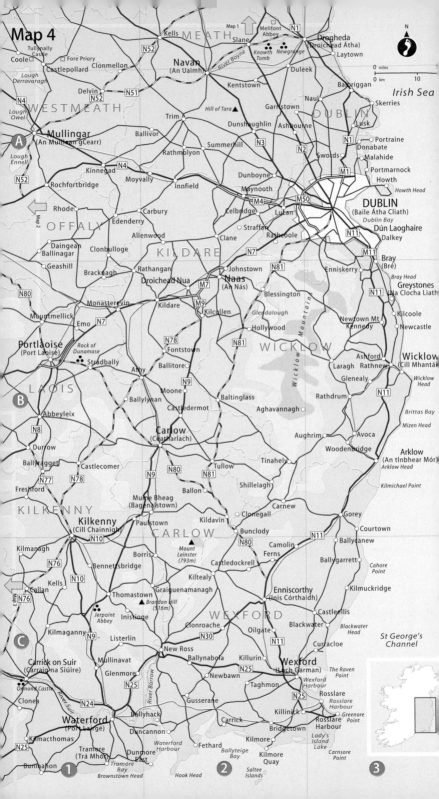

Acknowledgements

Seán Sheehan and Pat Levy would like to thank John Lahiffe at Bord Fáilte and Mo Durkan at the Northern Ireland Tourist Board for the help and consideration they have given to the Footprint Ireland Handbook. Special thanks to everyone at Footprint who has worked so hard to get this second edition out on time.

Many other people have helped in the writing of the second edition and our apologies to those whose names we have forgotten to add to the following list: Vincent Lynch and Gerrie Pitt in Dublin; Richard Hennessy in Kilkenny; Blathnaid Begley in Dingle; Dr Jane Edge in Bristol; Fionnula Keely at Bus Éireann; Marian McLaughlin at Dúchas; A G W Butler in London.

Staff at Bord Fáilte and the Northern Ireland Tourist Board have been wonderfully helpful and we would like to personally thank the following member of staff: Dympna Thompson in Waterford; Amanda Boyle in Donegal; Blathnaid Begley in Dingle; Brid O'Gorman in Ennis; Mary Lyons in Kilkee; Carmel Ryan in Killaloe; Siobhán in Waterville; Noreen Gannon on Achill; Aisling Joyce on Inishmore; Kerrie Ross at Down District Council; Denise Campbell in Cookstown; Alieen Laverty in Portrush; Philip McShane in Strabane and Maria Diamond in Ballymena.

About the authors

Pat Levy visited West Cork one Easter when she was 19 and the memory of the spring flowers and heather on the hills has continued to draw her back like a narcotic. Author of *Culture Shock! Ireland* and co-author of a walking guide to the island, Pat is now hooked for life and she looks forward to the time when she can tend to her garden in the west of Ireland full time.

Seán Sheehan was brought up in London but every summer holiday was spent in Ireland. After adult years of travelling and living in southeast Asia, Seán now has his home in the west of Ireland.

Sean and Pat are also the authors of the *Footprint Dublin Handbook*.